W9-AQV-833

NON-CIRCULATING

ROBERT ALTHANN S.J.

ELENCHUS OF BIBLICA

1998

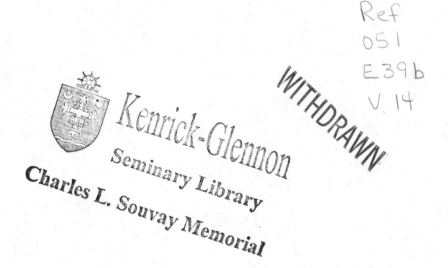

Kenrick-Glennon
Seminary Library
Charles L. Souvay Memorial

WITHDRAWN

Ref
051
E39b
V. 14

EDITRICE PONTIFICIO ISTITUTO BIBLICO
ROMA 2002

© 2002 E.P.I.B. – Roma

ISBN: 88-7653-618-3

EDITRICE PONTIFICIO ISTITUTO BIBLICO
Piazza della Pilotta, 35 - 00187 Roma, Italia

Urbes editionis — **Cities of publication**

AA	Ann Arbor	Lv(N)	Leuven (L-Neuve)
Amst	Amsterdam	M/Mi	Madrid/Milano
B	Berlin	Mkn	Maryknoll/
Ba/BA	Basel/Buenos Aires	Mp	Minneapolis
Barc	Barcelona	Mü/Müns('r)	München/Münster
Bo/Bru	Bologna/Brussel	N	Napoli
C	Cambridge, England	ND	NotreDame IN
CasM	Casale Monferrato	Neuk	Neukirchen/Verlag
Ch	Chicago	NHv	New Haven
CinB	Cinisello Balsamo	Nv	Nashville
CM	Cambridge, Mass.	NY	New York
ColMn	Collegeville MN	Ox	Oxford
Da:Wiss	Darmstadt, WissBuchg	P/Pd	Paris/Paderborn
DG	Downers Grove	Ph	Philadelphia
Dü	Düsseldorf	R/Rg	Roma/Regensburg
E	Edinburgh	S	Salamanca
ENJ	EnglewoodCliffs NJ	Sdr	Santander
F	Firenze	SF	San Francisco
Fra	Frankfurt/M	Shf	Sheffield
FrB/FrS	Freiburg-Br/Schweiz	Sto	Stockholm
Gö	Göttingen	Stu	Stuttgart
GR	Grand Rapids MI	T/TA	Torino/Tel Aviv
Gü	Gütersloh	Tü	Tübingen
Ha	Hamburg	U/W	Uppsala/Wien
Heid	Heidelberg	WL	Winona Lake IN
Hmw	Harmondsworth	Wmr	Warminster
J	Jerusalem	Wsb	Wiesbaden
K	København	Wsh	Washington D.C.
L/Lei	London/Leiden	Wsz	Warszawa
LA	Los Angeles	Wu	Wuppertal
Lp	Leipzig	Wü	Würzburg
LVL	Louisville KY	Z	Zürich

Punctuation: To separate a subtitle from its title, we use a COLON (:). The *semicolon* (;) serves to separate items that in other respects belong together. Hence, at the end of an entry a *semicolon* indicates a link with the following entry. This link may consist in the two entries having the same author or in the case of multiauthor works having the same book title; the author will be mentioned in the first entry of such a group, the common book title in the last entry, that is the one which concludes with a fullstop [period] (.).
Abbreviations: These follow S.M. Schwertner, **IATG**[2] (De Gruyter; Berlin 1992) as far as possible. A list of other abbreviations appears below.
Price of books: This is sometimes rounded off ($10 for $9.95).

4

Index systematicus — Contents

The present volume contains all the 1998 material of the Elenchus. Thanks are due to the Catholic Biblical Association of America for subsidising the cost of publication and to the staff of the Editrice Pontificio Istituto Biblico which assures the publication of the Elenchus. I should also like to thank Fr. Jean-Noël Aletti, S.J. for his patience and readiness to help in matters electronic, while Fr. Robert North, S.J. continues to send data which is gratefully received. Last but not least I thank the graduate students who have given generously of their time.

The materials for this volume were gathered from the libraries of the Pontifical Biblical Institute, the Pontifical Gregorian University and the University of Innsbruck. I thank the staff of these libraries for their unfailing courtesy and helpfulness. The Department of Biblical Studies at the University of Innsbruck continues to provide valuable assistance in supplying abundant bibliographical information and has become an indispensable element in the preparation of the Elenchus. The enterprise of the Elenchus is increasingly a cooperative one and it is hoped to extend this cooperation with the Department. We are meanwhile continuing to supply book reviews which may be accessed through BILDI on the internet (http://bildi.uibk.ac.at).

Acronyms: Periodica—Series (small).
8 fig.=ISSN; *10 fig.*=ISBN.

A: in Arabic.
AcBib: Acta Pontificii Instituti Biblici; R.
ACPQ: American Catholic Philosophical Quarterly; Wsh.
ACCS: Ancient Christian Commentary on Scripture; DG.
ACPQ: American Catholic Philosophical Quarterly; Wsh.
Acta Patristica et Byzantina; Pretoria.
Acta Theologica; Bloemfontein.
ActBib: Actualidad Bibliográfica; Barc.
Ad Gentes; Bo.
AETSC: Annales de l'Ecole Théologique Saint-Cyprien; Yaoundé, Cameroun.
AfR: Archiv für Religionsgeschichte; Stu.
AHIg: Anuario de historia de la iglesia; Pamplona.
AJPS: Asian Journal of Pentecostal Studies;
AJSR: Association for Jewish Studies Review; Waltham, MA.
Ä&L: Ägypten und Levante; Wien.
Alei Etzion; Alon Shvut.
Al-Mushir [**Urdu**]; Rawalpindi.
Alpha Omega; R.
Alternativas; Managua.
AltOrF: Altorientalische Forschungen; B.
AnáMnesis; México.
AncB: Anchor Bible; NY.
Ancient Philosophy; Pittsburgh.
ANESt [<Abr-n]: Ancient Near Eastern Studies; Melbourne.
Anime e corpi; Brezzo di Bedero, Va.
Annali Chieresi; Chieri.
Annals of Theology [**P.**]; Krákow.
AnnTh: Annales Theologici; R.
AnScR: Annali di Scienze Religiose; Mi.
Antologia Vieusseux; F.

Archaeology in the Biblical World; Shafter, CA.
ARET: Archivi reali di Ebla, testi; R.
ARGU: Arbeiten zur Religion und Geschichte des Urchristentums; Fra.
ARJ: The Annual of Rabbinic Judaism; Lei.
ASJ: Acta Sumerologica; Kyoto, Japan.
ATT: Archivo teologico torinese; Leumann (Torino).
AtT: Atualidade teológica; Rio de Janeiro.
Atualizaçâo; Belo Horizonte.
AulOr: Aula Orientalis (S: Supplement); Barc.
Auriensia; Ourense, Spain.
BAIAS: Bulletin of the Anglo-Israel Archaeological Society; L.
Barnabiti Studi; R.
Bazmavep; Venise.
BBR: Bulletin for Biblical Research; WL.
BCSMS: Bulletin of the Canadian Society for Mesopotamian Studies; Toronto.
BEgS: Bulletin of the Egyptological Seminar; NY.
Beit Mikra; J.
Bib(L): Bíblica; Lisboa.
BiblInterp (BiblInterp): Biblical Interpretation; Lei.
Biblioteca EstB: Biblioteca de Estudios Bíblicos; S.
BnS: La bibbia nella storia; Bo.
Bobolanum [**P.**]; Wsz.
Bogoslovni Vestnik [S.]; Ljubljana.
BolT: Boletín teológico; BA.
BoSm: Bogoslovska Smotra; Zagreb.
BRT: The Baptist Review of Theology / La revue baptiste de théologie; Gormely, Ontario.
BSÉG: Bulletin de la Société d'Égyptologie; Genève.
BSLP: Bulletin de la Société de Linguistique de Paris; P.
BuBbgB: Bulletin de bibliographie biblique; Lausanne.
Bulletin of Ecumenical Theology; Enugu, Nigeria.

Bulletin of Judaeo-Greek Studies; C.

Bulletin of Research of Christian Culture; Okayama, Japan.

BurH: Buried History; Melbourne.

BWM: Bibelwissenschaftliche Monographien; Gießen.

CAH: Cambridge Ancient History²; C.

Cahiers de l'Atelier; P.

Cahiers Ratisbonne; J.

CahPhRel: Cahiers de l'Ecole des Sciences philosophiques et religieuses; Bru.

CAL.N: Comprehensive Aramaic Lexicon, Newsletter; Cincinatti.

CamArchJ: Cambridge Archaeological Journal; C.

Carmel(V); Venasque.

Carmel(T); Toulouse.

Carthaginensia; Murcia.

Catalyst; Goroka, Papua New Guinea.

Catechisti parrocchiali; R.

Cathedra; Bogotá.

Cathedra [H.]; J.

Centro pro unione, Bulletin; R.

Chemins de Dialogue; Marseille.

Choisir; Genève.

Chongshin Review; Seoul.

Christian Thought; Seoul.

Chronology and Catastrophism Workshop; Luton.

Cias; Buenos Aires.

C: in Chinese.

CLEC: Common Life in the Early Church;

CLehre: Die Christenlehre; B.

CMAO: Contributi e Materiali di Archeologia Orientale; R.

Colloquium; Brisbane.

Comunidades; S.

ConAss: Convivium Assisiense; Assisi.

Confer; M.

Contacts; Courbevoie.

Contagion; Rocky Mount.

Convergência; São Paulo.

CoSe: Consacrazione e Servizio; R.

CredOg: Credereoggi; Padova.

CritRR: Critical Review of Books in Religion; Atlanta.

Crkva u Svijetu; Split.

Croire aujourd'hui; P.

Crux: Vancouver.

CTrB: Cahiers de traduction biblique; Pierrefitte, France.

CuesT: Cuestiones Teológicas; Medellin.

Cuestion Social, La; Mexico.

Cultura e libri; R.

CurResB: Currents in Research: Biblical Studies; Shf.

Daphnis; Amst.

ᴰ: Director dissertationis.

Diadokhē [ΔIAΔOXH]. Revista de Estudios de Filosofía Platónica y Cristiana; BA.

Didascalia; Rosario, ARG.

Direction; Fresno, CA.

DiscEg: Discussions in Egyptology; Oxf.

DissA: Dissertation Abstracts International; AA/L. -A [= US etc.]: 0419-4209 [C = Europe. 0307-6075].

DosP: Les Dossiers de la Bible; P.

DQ: Documenta Q; Leuven.

DSBP: Dizionario di spiritualità biblico-patristica; R.

DSD: Dead Sea Discoveries; Lei.

ᴱ: Editor, Herausgeber, a cura di.

Ecclesia orans; R.

Eccl(R): Ecclesia; R.

EfMex: Efemérides Mexicana; Tlalpan.

EgArch: Egyptian Archaeology; L.

ETJ: Ephrem's Theological Journal; Satna, India.

Emmanuel; St. Meinrads, IN.

Encounters; Markfield, U.K.

ERSY: Erasmus of Rotterdam Society Yearbook; Lexington.

EscrVedat: Escritos del Vedat; Valencia.

Esprit; P.

EThF: Ephemerides Theologicae Fluminenses; Rijeka.

Ethics & Medicine; Carlisle.

ETSI Journal; Igbaja, Nigeria.

EurJT: European Journal of Theology; Carlisle.
Evangel; E.
Evangelizzare; Bo.
EvV: Evangelio y Vida; León.
Exchange; Lei.
Faith & Mission; Wake Forest, NC.
Feminist Theology; Shf.
F: Festschrift.
FgNT: Filologia Neotestamentaria; Córdoba.
Filosofia oggi; Genova.
Firmana; Fermo.
Florensia; S. Giovanni in Fiore (CS).
FolTh: Folia theologica; Budapest.
Forum. Sonoma, CA.
Forum Religion; Stu.
Franciscanum; Bogotá.
Freiburger Universitätsblätter; FrB.
Fundamentum; Basel.
Furrow; Maynooth.
Gema; Yogyakarta.
Georgica; Konstanz.
G: in Greek.
Gnosis; SF.
Graphè; Lille.
H: in Hebrew.
Hagiographica; F.
Hamdard Islamicus; Karachi.
HBO: Hallesche Beiträge zur Orientwissenschaft; Halle.
Hekima Review; Nairobi.
Henoch; T.
History of European Ideas; Oxf.
HIL: Das Heilige Land; Köln.
Holy Land; J.
Horeb; Pozzo di Gotto (ME).
Horizons; Villanova, PA.
HorWi: Horizonty Wiary; Kraków.
Ho Theológos; Palermo.
Humanistica e teologia; Porto.
IAJS: Index of Articles on Jewish Studies; J.
Ichthys ΙΧΘΥΣ; Aarhus.
ICMR: Islam and Christian-Muslim Relations; Birmingham.
Igreja e Missão; Valadares, Cucujaes.

IHR: International History Review; Burnaby, Canada.
IJCT: International Journal of the Classical Tradition; New Brunswick, NJ.
Image; Seattle.
INTAMS.R: INTAMS [International Academy for Marital Spirituality] review; Sint-Genesius-Rode, Belgium.
Inter Fratres; Fabriano (AN).
Interpretation(F). Journal of Political Philosophy; Flushing.
Iran; L.
Isidorianum; Sevilla.
IslChr: Islamochristiana; R.
ITBT: Interpretatie; Zoetermeer.
ITE: Informationes Theologiae Europae; Fra.
Iter; Caracas.
Itin(M): Itinerarium; Messina.
JAAT: Journal of Asian and Asian American Theology; Claremont, Calif.
JAB: Journal for the Aramaic Bible; Shf.
JAGNES: Journal of the Association of Graduates in Near Eastern Studies; Berkeley, CA.
Jahrbuch Politische Theologie; Mü.
Japan Mission Journal; Tokyo.
JBTSA: Journal of Black Theology in South Africa; Atteridgeville.
JEarlyC: Journal of Early Christian Studies; Baltimore.
Jeevadhara; Alleppey, Kerala.
JEGTFF: Jahrbuch der Europäischen Gesellschaft für theologische Forschung von Frauen; Mainz.
JHiC: Journal of Higher Criticism; Montclair, NJ.
Jian Dao; Hong Kong.
J: in Japanese.
JISt: Journal of Interdisciplinary Studies; Pasadena, CA.
JJTP: Journal of Jewish Thought & Philosophy; Ba.
JKTh: Jahrbuch für kontextuelle Theologien; Fra.
JNSL: Journal of Northwest Semitic Languages; Stellenbosch.

Jota; Lv.
Journal of Ancient History; Moscow.
Journal of Constructive Theology; Durban.
Journal of Institutional and Theoretical Economics; Tü.
Journal of Medieval History; Amst.
Journal of Psychology and Judaism; NY.
Journal of Social History; Fairfax, VA.
JPentec: Journal of Pentecostal Theology; Shf (**S**: Supplement).
JPersp: Jerusalem Perspective; J.
JProgJud: Journal of Progressive Judaism; Shf.
JPURS: Jnanadeepa, Pune Journal of Religious Studies; Pune.
JRadRef: Journal from the Radical Reformation; Morrow, GA.
JRTR: Jahrbuch für Religionswissenschaft und Theologie der Religionen; FrB.
JSem: Journal for Semitics; Pretoria.
JSQ: Jewish Studies Quarterly; Tü.
JSSEA: Journal of the Society for the Study of Egyptian Antiquities; Toronto.
JTrTL: Journal of Translation and Textlinguistics; Dallas.
Jud.: Judaism; NY.
Kairos(G); Guatemala.
KaKe: Katorikku-Kenkyu [**J.**]; Tokyo.
Kerux; Escondido, CA.
K: in Korean.
Kwansei-Gakuin-Daigaku; Japan.
Labeo; N.
Landas. Journal of Loyola School of Theology; Manila.
Laós; Catania.
Literary and linguistic computing; Oxf.
Living Light; Wsh.
LSDC: La Sapienza della Croce; R.
Luther-Bulletin; Amst.
Luther Digest; Crestwood, Miss.
M: Memorial.

MAI: Masters Abstracts International; AA: 0898-9095.
MastJ: Master's Seminary Journal; Sun Valley, CA.
Mayéutica; Marcilla (Navarra).
MEAH: Miscellánea de Estudios Árabes y Hebraicos (**MEAH.A**: Árabe-Islam. **MEAH.H**: Hebreo); Granada.
MESA.B: Middle East Studies Association Bulletin; Muncie, IN.
MethT: Method and Theory in the Study of Religion; Toronto.
Mid-Stream; Indianapolis.
Miles Immaculatae; R.
MillSt: Milltown Studies; Dublin.
Missionalia; Menlo Park, South Africa.
MissTod: Mission Today; Shillong, India.
Mitteilungen für Anthropologie und Religionsgeschichte; Saarbrücken.
Mondo della Bibbia, Il; T.
Moralia; M.
MST Review; Manila.
NABU: Nouvelles Assyriologiques Brèves et Utilitaires; P.
NAC: New American Commentary; Nv.
NAOTS: Newsletter on African Old Testament Scholarship; Stavanger [0808-2413].
Naval Research Logistics; NY.
NEA(BA): Near Eastern Archaeology [BA]; Boston.
Nemalah; K.
Neukirchener Theologische Zeitschrift; Neuk.
NewTR: New Theology Review; Ch.
NHMS: Nag Hammadi and Manichaean Studies; Lei.
NIBC: New International Biblical Commentary; Peabody.
Nicolaus; Bari.
NIntB: The New Interpreter's Bible; Nv.
NotesTrans: Notes on Translation; Dallas.
NTGu: New Testament Guides; Shf.
Nuova Europa, La; Seriate (Bg).
Nuova Umanità; R.

Nuova Areopago, Il; Forlì.
Obnovljeni Život; Zagreb.
Ḥokhma; Lausanne.
Omnis Terra; R.
OrBibChr: Orbis biblicus et christianus; Glückstadt.
OrExp: Orient-Express, Notes et Nouvelles d'Archéologie Orientale; P.
Orient; Tokyo.
Orientamenti pastorali; Bo.
Orientamenti pedagogici; R.
P: in Polish.
Pacifica. Australian Theological Studies; Melbourne.
Paginas; Lima.
PaiC.: Paideia Cristiana; Rosario, ARG.
Paléorient; P.
Palestjinskji Sbornik [**R.**]; Moskva.
Parabola; NY.
Passaggi; Terni.
Pensiero politico, Il; F.
Phase; Barc.
Philosophiques; Montréal.
Physis; F.
PoeT: Poetics Today; Durham, NC.
PoST: Poznańskie studia teologiczne; Poznán (83-86360-18-6).
PredOT: Prediking van het Oude Testament; Baarn.
Presbyteri; Trento.
Presbyterion; St. Louis.
PresPast: Presenza Pastorale, R.
Prism; St. Paul, MN.
ProcGLM: Proceedings of the Eastern Great Lakes and Midwest Bible Societies; Buffalo.
Pro dialogo; Città del Vaticano.
ProEc: Pro ecclesia; Northfield, MN.
Prooftexts; Baltimore.
Proverbium; Burlington, VT.
Proyección; Granada.
ProySal: Proyecto Centro Salesiano de Estudios; BA.
Prudentia [.S]; Auckland, NZ.
Przegląd Tomistyczny; Wsz.
PzB: Protokolle zur Bibel; Klosterneuburg.

Qol; México.
Quaderni di azione sociale; R.
Quaderni di scienze religiose; Loreto.
Qumran Chronicle; Kraków.
QVC: Qüestions de Vida Cristiana; Barc.
R: in Russian.
R: *recensio*, book-review.
Ragion Pratica; Genova.
RANL: Rendiconti dell'Accademia Nazionale dei Lincei; R.
RASM: Revue africaine des sciences de la mission; Kinshasa.
RBBras: Revista Bíblica Brasileira; Fortaleza.
RCI: Rivista del clero italiano; R.
Reason and the Faith, The; Kwangju.
Recollectio; R.
Reformation, The; Oxf (Tyndale Soc.).
Religion; L.
Religious Research; Wsh.
RelT: Religion and Theology; Pretoria.
RenSt: Renaissance Studies; Oxf.
ResB: Reseña Bíblica; Estella.
RevCT: Revista de cultura teológica; São Paulo.
Revista católica; Santiago de Chile.
Revue d'éthique et de théologie morale; P.
RBLit: Review of Biblical Literature; Atlanta. [New 1999]
RF(CR): Revista de filosofia: San José, Costa Rica.»**RGRW**: Religions in the Graeco-Roman World; Lei.
Ribla: Revista de interpretação biblica latino-americana; Petrópolis.
RICAO: Revue de l'Institut Catholique de l'Afrique de l'Ouest; Abidjan.
Ricerche teologiche; Bo.
Rivista di archeologia; R.
Rivista di scienze religiose; R.
Roczniki Teologiczne; Lublin
Romania; P.

RRT: Reviews in Religion and Theology; L.
R&T: Religion and theology = Religie en teologie; Pretoria.
RTLu: Rivista Teologica di Lugano; Lugano.
S: Slovenian.
SAAA: Studies on the Apocryphal Acts of the Apostles; Kampen.
SAA Bulletin: State Archives of Assyria Bulletin; Padova.
SAAS: State Archives of Assyria, Studies; Helsinki.
Saeculum Christianum; Wsz.
San Juan de la Cruz; Sevilla.
SaThZ: Salzburger Theologische Zeitschrift; Salzburg.
SBL.SCSt: Society of Biblical Literature, Septuagint and Cognate Studies; Atlanta.
Science and Christian Belief; Carlisle.
Scriptura; Stellenbosch.
Scrittura e civiltà; F.
SdT: Studi di Teologia; R.
SEAP: Studi di Egittologia e di Antichità Puniche; Pisa.
Search; Dublin.
Sedes Sapientiae; Chéméré-le-Roi.
Segni e comprensione; Lecce.
SeK: Skrif en Kerk; Pretoria.
Semeia; Atlanta.
Seminarios; M.
Semiotica; Amst.
Sen.: Sendros; Costa Rica.
Servitium; CasM.
SetRel: Sette e Religioni; Bo.
Sevartham; Ranchi.
Sève; P.
Sewanee Theological Review; Sewanee, TN.
Shofar; West Lafayette, IN.
SIDIC: Service International de Documentation Judéo-Chrétienne; R.
Sinhak Jonmang; Kwangju, S. Korea.
Società, La; Verona.
Soleriana; Montevideo.
Soundings; Nv.
Sources; FrS.
Spiritual Life; Wsh.

Spiritus; P.
SPJMS: South Pacific Journal of Mission Studies; North Turramurra NSW.
SRATK: Studia nad Rodzina, Akademia Teologii Katolickiej; Wsz, 1429-2416.
Stauros. Bolletino trimestrale sulla teologia della Croce; Pescara.
Storia della storiografia; Mi.
»**StEL**: Studi epigrafici e linguistici; Verona.
St Mark's Review; Canberra.
StSp(K): Studies in Spirituality; Kampen.
Studi emigrazione; R.
Studia Textus Novi Testamenti; Osaka.
Studies in World Christianity; E.
Studi Fatti Ricerche; Mi.
Stulos. Theological Journal; Bandung, Indonesia.
StWC: Studies in World Christianity; E.
SUBB: Studia Universitatis Babeş-Bolyai; Cluj-Napoca, Romania.
Synaxis; Catania.
Tanima; Kochi, Kerala.
TCNN: Theological College of Northern Nigeria; Bukuru.
Teocomunicaçâo; Porto Alegre, Brasil.
Teologia Iusi; Caracas.
Ter Herkenning; 's-Gravenhage.
Tertium Millennium; R.
TGr.T Tesi Gregoriana, Serie Teologia; R.
TEuph: Transeuphratène; P.
Themelios; L.
Theoforum; Ottawa.
Theologica & Historica; Cagliari.
Theologika; Lima.
Théologiques; Montréal.
Theologischer; Siegburg.
Theology for Our Times; Bangalore.
Theotokos; R.
ThirdM: Third Millennium: Pune, India.
T&K: Texte und Kontexte; Stu.
TMA: The Merton Annual; Shf.

TrinJ: Trinity Journal; Deerfield, IL.
TTE: The Theological Educator; New Orleans.
[T]: Translator.
Tychique; Lyon.
Umat Baru; Yogyakarta, Indonesia.
Una Voce-Korrespondenz; Köln.
Viator; Turnhout.
Vie Chrétienne; P.
Vie, La: des communautés religieuses; Montréal.
Vita Sociale; F.
Vivarium; Catanzaro.
VivH: Vivens Homo; F.
VO: Vicino Oriente; R.
Volto dei volti, Il; R.
VTW: Voices from the Third World; Bangalore.
Vox latina; Saarbrücken.
Vox Patrum; Lublin.
VoxScr: Vox Scripturae; São Paulo.

WaW: Word and World; St. Paul, Minn.
Way, The; L.
WBC: Word Biblical Commentary; Waco.
West African Journal of Ecclesial Studies; Ibadan, Nigeria.
WUB: Welt und Umwelt der Bibel; Stu.
YESW: Yearbook of the European Society of Women in Theological Research; Lv.
Yonsei Journal of Theology; Seoul.
ZAC: Zeitschrift für antikes Christentum; B.
ZAR: Zeitschrift für altorientalische und biblische Rechtsgeschichte; Wsb.
ZME: Zeitschrift für medizinische Ethik; Salzburg.
ZNT: Zeitschrift für Neues Testament; Tü.

I. Bibliographica

A1 Opera collecta .1 **Festschriften**, memorials

1 ABAIEV, Vassilij Ivanovitch: Studia Iranica et Alanica: Festschrift for Prof... Abaev on the occasion of his 95th birthday. Serie Orientale Roma 82: R 1998, Istituto Italiano per l'Africa e l'Oriente 540 pp. Bibl.
2 ALBERIGO, Giuseppe: Cristianesimo nella storia. [E]**Melloni, Alberto; Menozzi, Daniele; Ruggieri, Giuseppe; Toschi, Massimo**: 1996, ⇒12,1; 13,2. [R]CDios 211 (1998) 656-658 (*Gutiérrez, J.*).
3 ALONSO SCHÖKEL, Luis: Saberes y sabores. [E]**Martín Rodríguez, Guillermo**: Bilbao 1998, Mensajero 270 pp. Homenaje a Luis Alonso Schökel [StLeg 41,313s—Flórez, Gonzalo].
4 ÇAMBEL, Halet: Light on top of the black hill: studies presented to Halet Çambel. [E]**Arsebük, Güven; Mellink, Machteld J.; Schirmer, Wulf**: Istanbul 1998, Ege Yayinlari xv; 844 pp. 975-807-020-7. Bibl.
5 ANDERSON, George Wishart: Understanding poets and prophets. [E]**Auld, A. Graeme**: JSOT.S 152: 1993, ⇒9,6. [R]BZ 42 (1998) 107-109 (*Scharbert, Josef*).
6 ASHTON, John: Understanding, studying and reading: New Testament essays in honour of John Ashton. [E]**Rowland, Christopher; Fletcher-Louis, Crispin H.T.**: JSNT.S 153: Shf 1998, JSOT 267 pp. £37.50/$62. 1-85075-828-X.
7 ÅKERSTRÖM-HOUGEN, Gunilla: Kairos: Studies in art history and literature in honour of professor Gunilla Åkerström-Hougen. [E]**Åström, Paul; Piltz, Elisabeth**: Studies in Mediterranean Archaeology and Literature, PockBaret-book 147: Jonsered 1998, Åströms 188 pp. 91-7081-1806.

Literature, PockBaret-book 147: Jonsered 1998, Åströms 188 pp. 91-7081-1806.

8 BARRELET, Marie-Thérèse: Florilegium marianum III: recueil d'études à la mémoire de Marie-Thérèse Barrelet. ^E**Charpin, Dominique: Durand, Jean-Marie**: P 1998, SEPOA 317 pp.

9 BERGMAN, Jan: "Being religious and living through the eyes": studies in religious iconography and iconology: in honour of... on the occasion of his 65th Birthday. ^E**Schalk, Peter**: AUUHR 14: U 1998, U Univ. Library 423 pp. 91-554-4199-8. collab. *Stausberg, Michael*; Bibl.

10 BETZ, Hans Dieter: Ancient and modern perspectives on the bible and culture: essays in honor of Hans Dieter Betz. ^E**Collins, Adela Yarbro**: Scholars Press Homage series 22: Atlanta, GA 1998, Scholars xv; 452 pp. $60. 0-7885-0521-1. Bibl.

11 BETZ, Otto; VAN DER WOUDE, Adam Simon: Qumran-Messianism: studies on the messianic expectations in the Dead Sea scrolls. ^E**Charlesworth, James H.; Lichtenberger, Hermann; Oegmema, Gerbern S.**: Tü 1998, Mohr 237 pp. 3-16146968-2.

12 BORGER, Rykle: Festschrift für Rykle Borger zu seinem 65. Geburtstag: tikip santakki mala basmu.... ^E**Maul, Stefan M.**: Cuneiform Monographs 10: Groningen 1998, STYX xvii; 377 pp. 90-5693-010-9. Bibl.

13 BOYLE, Leonard E.: Itineraria culturae medievalis: mélanges offerts au Père L.E. Boyle à l'occasion de son 75e anniversaire. ^E**Hamesse, Jacqueline**: Textes et Études du Moyen Age 10: Lv(N) 1998, Fédération Internationale des Instituts d'Études Médiévales. 3 vols.

14 BREKELMANS, C.H.: Deuteronomy and Deuteronomic literature. ^E**Vervenne, M.; Lust, J.**: BEThL 133: 1997, ⇒13,17. ^RJThS 49 (1998) 705-707 (*Nicholson, E.W.*); JNSL 24/1 (1998) 244-247 (*Stipp, Hermann-Josef*).

15 BRIEND, Jacques: Mélanges Jacques Briend. ^E**Elayi, J.; Sapin, J.**: TEuph 14-16: [Paris] 1998, Gabalda 3 Vols. 2-85021-. Bibl.

16 BRUEGGEMANN, Walter: God in the fray: a tribute to Walter Brueggemann. ^E**Linafelt, Tod; Beal, Timothy K.**: Mp 1998, Fortress xv; 350 pp. 0-8006-3090-4.

17 BSTEH, Andreas: 'Geglaubt habe ich, deshalb habe ich geredet'. ^E**Khoury, Adel Theodor; Vanoni, Gottfried**: Religionswissenschaftliche Studien 47: Wü 1998, Echter 587 pp. DM88 3-429-02071-9; 3-89375-169-6. Festschrift... zum 65. Geburtstag.

18 BURL, Aubrey: Prehistoric ritual and religion: essays in honour of Aubrey Burl. ^E**Gibson, Alex; Simpson, Derek**: Gloucester 1998, Sutton xiii; 242 pp. 0-7509-1598-6. Bibl.

ÇAMBEL, Halet: Light on top of the black hill. 1998 ⇒4.

19 CARGAS, Harry James: Peace, in deed: essays in honor of Harry James Cargas. ^E**Garber, Zev; Libowitz, Richard**: SFSHJ 162: Atlanta 1998, Scholars xi; 253 pp. 0-7885-8497-5.

20 CLAUSEN, Wendell Vernon: Style and tradition: studies in honor of Wendell Clausen. ^E**Knox, Peter; Foss, Clive**: Beiträge zur Altertumskunde 92: Stu 1998, Teubner xii; 325 pp. 3-519-07641-1.

21 COTSEN, Lloyd: Urkesh and the Hurrians: studies in honor of Lloyd Cotsen. ^E**Kelly-Buccellati, Marilyn; Buccellati, Giorgio**: Bibliotheca Mesopotamica 26; Urkesh/Mozan Studies 3: Malibu 1998, Undena 200 pp. 0-89003-502-2.

22 COUROYER, B.: Études égyptologiques et bibliques. ^E**Sigrist, Marcel**: CRB 36: 1997, ⇒13,21. ^RRivBib 46 (1998) 223-224 (*Balzaretti, Claudio*); BiOr 55 (1998) 730-732 (*Broze, Michèle*).

23 DOTHAN, Trude: Mediterranean peoples in transition: thirteenth to early tenth centuries B.C.E. [E]**Gitin, Sy; Mazar, Amihai; Stern, Ephraim**: J 1998, Israel Exploration Soc. xix; 481 pp. 965-221-036-6. [R]NEA(BA) 61 (1998) 261-262 (*Leonard, Albert*).

24 EMERTON, John A.: Wisdom in ancient Israel. [E]**Day, John; Gordon, Robert P.; Williamson, G.M.**: 1995, ⇒11/1,9... 13,3134. [R]VT 48 (1998) 266-270 (*Dell, Katharine J.*).

25 FERGUSON, Everett: The early church in its context: essays in honor of... [E]**Malherbe, Abraham J.; Norris, Frederick W.; Thompson, James W.**: NT.S 90: Lei 1998, Brill xviii; 362 pp. 90-04-10832-7.

26 FRANKFORT, Henri: Studi in memoria di Henri Frankfort (1897-1954): presentati dalla Scuola Romana di Archeologia Orientale. [E]**Matthiae, Paolo**: Contributi e materiali di archeologia orientale 7: R 1998, Università "La Sapienza" 590 pp.

27 FREEDMAN, David Noel: Fortunate the eyes that see. [E]**Beck, Astrid B.; Bartelt, Andrew H.; Raabe, Paul R.; Franke, Chris A**: 1995, ⇒11/1,10; 13,24. [R]JSSt 43 (1998) 137-141 (*Gillingham, Sue*).

28 FRERICHS, Ernest S.: Hesed ve-Emet: studies in honor of Ernest S. Frerichs. [E]**Magness, Jodi; Titin, Seymour**: BJSt 320: Atlanta 1998, Scholars xiv; 440 pp. $35. 0-7885-0509-2 [RB 106,313].

29 GIORDANO, Card. Michele : Sicut flumen pax tua. [E]**Ascione, Antonio; Gioia, Mario**: 1997, ⇒13,30. [R]CivCatt 149/3 (1998) 94-95 (*Vanzan, P.*).

30 GOLDENBERG, Gideon: Gideon Goldenberg Festschrift. [E]**Bar Asher, M.** Massorot 9-11: 1997, ⇒13,31. [R]JJS 49 (1998) 371-373 (*Morgenstern, Matthew*); Leš. 61 (1998) 213-215 [H] (*Mishor, Mordechay*).

31 GORDON, Cyrus Herzl: Boundaries of the ancient Near Eastern world: a tribute to Cyrus H. Gordon. [E]**Lubetski, Meir; Gottlieb, Claire; Keller, Sharon**: JSOT.S 273: Shf 1998, Academic 576 pp. £55/$90 1-85075-871-9. Bibl.

32 GOTTLIEB, Gunther: Contra qui ferat arma deos?: vier Augsburger Vorträge zur Religionsgeschichte der römischen Kaiserzeit. 1997, ⇒13,32. [R]RQ 93 (1998) 140-141 (*Klein, Richard*).

33 GROSSMANN, Peter: Themelia: Spätantike und koptologische Studien Peter Grossmann zum 65. Geburtstag. [E]**Krause, Martin; Schaten, Sofia**: Sprachen und Kulturen des Christlichen Orients 3: Wsb 1998, Reichert 348 pp. 3-89500-063-9.

34 GUNDLACH, Rolf: Wege öffnen. [E]**Schade-Busch, Mechtild**: ÄAT 35: Wsb 1996, Harrassowitz xvi; 393 pp. 3-447-03789-9. 26 pl. 83 fig. [ArOr 68,288ss—Bareš, Ladislav].

35 HAHN, Ferdinand: Die Verwurzelung des Christentums im Judentum [E]**Breytenbach, Cilliers**: 1996, ⇒12,34; 13,36. [R]ThR 63 (1998) 362-365 (*Wehnert, Jürgen*).

36 HALTON, Thomas Patrick: Nova & vetera: patristic studies in honor of Thomas Patrick Halton. [E]**Petruccione, John**: Wsh 1998, Catholic Univ. of America Pr. xxxv; (2) 277 pp. 0-8132-0900-5.

37 HAMILTON, Bernard: The Crusades and their sources: essays presented to Bernard Hamilton. Brookfield 1998, Ashgate xix; 297 pp. $77 [CHR 86,660s—Gervers, Michael].

38 HARL, Marguerite: KATA TOUS O': selon les Septante. [E]**Dorival, Gilles; Munnich, Olivier**. 1995, 11/1,13; 13,38. [R]RTL 29/1 (1998) 88-90 (*Auwers, J.-M.*).

39 HAYIM, Tadmor: Ah, Assyria: studies in Assyrian history and ancient Near Eastern historiography. ^ECogan, Mordechai; Eph'al, Israel: Scripta Hierosolymitana 33: J 1991, Magnes 347 pp. 0-685-53241-0 ^RBiOr 55 (1998) 465-468 (*Kwasman, T.*).

40 HELLER, Jan: Landgabe: Festschrift für Jan Heller zum 70. Geburtstag ^EPrudký, Martin: Praha 1995, ISE 302 pp. 80-85241-93-5. ^RDBAT 29 (1998) 298-300 (*Diebner, B.J.*).

41 HERIBAN, Jozef: Dummodo Christus annuntietur: studi in onore di prof. Jozef Heriban. ^EStrus, Andrzej; Blatnicky, Rudolf: BSRel 146: R 1998, LAS 541 pp. 88-213-0401-9. Bibl.

42 HOFFMANN, Paul: Von Jesus zum Christus: christologische Studien: Festgabe für Paul Hoffmann zum 65. Geburtstag. ^EHoppe, Rudolf; Busse, Ulrich: BZNW 93: B 1998, de Gruyter xii; 640 pp. DM268. 3-11-015546-X;

43 Wenn drei das Gleiche sagen—Studien zu den ersten drei Evangelien: mit einer Werkstattübersetzung des Q-Textes. ^EBrandenburger, Stefan H.; Hieke, Thomas: Theologie 14: Müns 1998, Lit ix; 258 pp. DM49.80. 3-8258-3673-8.

44 HOFIUS, Otfried: Jesus Christus als die Mitte der Schrift. ^ELandmesser, Christof; Eckstein, Hans-Joachim; Lichtenberger, Hermann. BZNW 86: 1997, ⇒13,41. ^RThPQ 146 (1998) 421-422 (*Niemand, Christoph*).

45 HOOKER, Morna Dorothy: Early Christian thought in its Jewish context. ^EBarclay, John M.G.; Sweet, John P.: 1996, ⇒12,43. ^RHeyJ 39 (1998) 331-332 (*Creagh-Fuller, T.*).

46 JEPPESEN, Knud: Alle ader ånder skal lovprise Herren!: det Gamle Testamente i tempel, synagoge og kirke [Let everybody that breathes praise the Lord! The Old Testament in the temple, the synagogue, and the church]. Frederiksberg 1998, 304 pp. [SJOT 13,155s—Jones, Ray Carlton].

47 JUDGE, Edwin: Ancient history in a modern university. ^EHillard, T.W., al., GR 1998, Eerdmans 2 vols. Proceedings... Macquarie University, July 1993 to mark 25 years of the teaching... and the retirement...

48 KAMPHAUS, Franz: 'Den Armen eine frohe Botschaft'. ^EHainz, Josef; Jüngling, Hans-Winfried; Sebott, Reinhold. 1997, ⇒13,46. ^RThRv 94 (1998) 625-627 (*Wieh, Hermann*).

49 KERTELGE, Karl: Ekklesiologie des NT. ^EKampling, Rainer; Söding, Thomas: 1996, ⇒12,48; 13,47. ^RCDios 111/1 (1998) 326-328 (*Gutiérrez, J.*); CivCatt 149/3 (1998) 271-282 (*Marucci, Corrado*).

50 KLAES, Norbert: Begegnung von Religionen und Kulturen. ^ELüddeckens, Dorothea: Dettelbach 1998, Röll. 3-927522-60-0.

51 KLAWEK, Aleksy: Mogilany 1995: papers on the Dead Sea Scrolls offered in memory of Aleksy Klawek. ^EKapera, Zdzislaw J.: Qumranica Mogilanensia 15: Kráków 1998, Enigma. Zl80. 83-86110-29-5 [ThLZ 124,1223—Meiser, Martin].

52 KLEIN, Günter: Paulus, Apostel Jesu Christi: Festschrift für Günter Klein zum 70. Geburtstag. ^ETrowitzsch, Michael: Tü 1998, Mohr ix; 366 pp. DM198. 3-16-146557-1.

53 KLIJN, A.F.J.: Text and testimony: essays on New Testament and Apocryphal literature. 1988, ⇒4,85. ^RThR 63 (1998) 365-367 (*Wehnert, Jürgen*).

54 KNIERIM, Rolf: Problems in biblical theology. ^ESun, Henry T.C.; Eades, Keith L. 1997, ⇒13,48. ^ROTEs 11/1 (1998) 202-206 (*Lombaard, C.J.S.*); JThS 49 (1998) 167-169 (*Coggins, Richard*).

55 KOESTER, Helmut: The future of early christianity. EPearson, Birger A. 1991, ⇒8,104. RThR 63 (1998) 367-370 (Wehnert, Jürgen).

56 KOLLESCH, Jutta: Text and tradition: studies in ancient medicine and its transmission. EFischer, K.-D.; Nickel, D.; Potter, P.: Studies in Ancient Medicine 18: Lei 1998, Brill xii; 340 pp. 90-04-11052-6.

57 KROTKOFF, Georg: Humanism, culture, and language in the Near East EAfsaruddin, Asma; Zahniser, A.H. Mathias 1997, ⇒13,49. RBiOr 55 (1998) 906-909 (Anghelescu, Nadia).

58 KÜNG, Hans: Hans Küng: breaking through. Häring, Hermann. L 1998, SCM xv; 377 pp. 0-334-02739-X.

59 LANCEL, Serge: Curiosité historique et intérêts philologiques: hommage à Serge Lancel. EColombat, B.; Mattei, P.: Recherches & travaux 54: Grenoble 1998, Univ. Stendhal 264 pp. [REAug 44,349].

60 LAPLANCHE, François: Entrer en matière: les prologues. EDubois, Jean-Daniel; Roussel, Bernard: Patrimoines, Religions du Livre: P 1998, Cerf 523 pp. FF350 [VS 153,768—Rousse-Lacordaire, Jérôme].

61 LÉGASSE, Simon: L'Evangile exploré. EMarchadour, Alain: LeDiv 166: 1996, ⇒12,51; 13,54. RRevBib 60 (1998) 62-63 (Levoratti, A.J.).

62 LINDNER, Manfred: Nach Petra und ins Königreich der Nabatäer: Notizen von Reisegefährten: für Manfred Lindner zum 80. Geburtstag EHübner, Ulrich; Knauf, Ernst Axel; Wenning, Robert: BBB 118: [Bodenheim] 1998, Philo xvi; 131 pp. 3-8257-0102-6. Bibl.

63 LIVSHITS, Vladimir: Studies in honor of Vladimir A. Livshits. EAltman Bromberg, Carol; Skjaervø, Prods O.: Bulletin of the Asia Institute 10: WL 1998, Eisenbrauns viii; 292. Bibl.

64 LOHFINK, Norbert: Der Psalter in Judentum und Christentum: Norbert Lohfink zum 70. Geburtstag. EZenger, Erich: Herders Biblische Studien 18: FrB 1998, Herder ix; 420 pp. 3-451-26664-4.

65 LORETZ, Oswald: "Und Mose schrieb dieses Lied auf": Studien zum Alten Testament und zum Alten Orient. Festschrift für Oswald Loretz zur Vollendung seines 70. Lebensjahres... EDietrich, Manfried; Kottsieper, Ingo: AOAT 250: Müns 1998, Ugarit-Verlag xviii; 955 pp. 3-927120-60-X; collab. Schaudig, Hanspeter; Bibl.

66 LÖNING, Karl: Fremde Zeichen: neutestamentliche Texte in der Konfrontation der Kulturen. ELeinhäupl-Wilke, Andreas; Lücking, Stefan: Theologie 15: Müns 1998, Lit 174 pp. 3-8258-3674-6.

67 MACK, Burton L.: Reimagining christian origins. ECastelli, Elizabeth A.; Taussig, Hal: 1996, ⇒12,54. RThR 63 (1998) 370-373 (Wehnert, Jürgen).

68 MACKENDRICK, Paul Lachlan: Qui miscuit utile dulci: Festschrift essays for Paul Lachlan MacKendrick. ESchmeling, Gareth; Mikalson, Jon D.; Brenk, Frederick E.: Wauconda, Illinois 1998, Bolchazy-Carducci xvi; 400 pp. 0-86516-406-1. 1 port.; bibl..

69 MALAMAT, Avraham: Eretz-Israel 24: Avraham Malamat Volume. 1993, ⇒9,91. RJSSt 43 (1998) 366-368 (Cathcart, Kevin J.).

70 MANGO, Cyril: Aetos: studies in honor of Cyril Mango presented to him on April 14, 1998. ESevcenko, Ihor; Hutter, Irmgard: Stu 1998, Teubner xx; 379 pp. 3-519-07440-0. Bibl.

71 MARGAIN, Jean: Études sémitiques et samaritaines. EFrey, Albert; Schattner-Rieser, Ursula: Histoire du texte biblique 4: Lausanne 1998, Zèbre 292 pp. 2-9700088-6-6. Bibl.

72 MARQUARDT, Friedrich-Wilhelm: Knospen und Früchtchen: ein studentischer Geburtstagsstrauß für... EBecker, Thorsten: B 1998, Wissenschaftlicherverlag. 3-932089-15-4.

73 MARSHALL, I. Howard: Jesus of Nazareth: Lord and Christ. ᴱ**Green, Joel B.; Turner, Max**: 1994, ⇒11/2,121; 12,55. ᴿRB 105 (1998) 105-108 (*Prendergast, Terrence*).

74 MARTINI, Card. Carlo Maria: La rivelazione attestata: la bibbia fra testo e teologia:... in onore del card. Carlo Maria Martini arcivescovo di Milano per... 70. compleanno. ᴱ**Angelini, Giuseppe**: Quodlibet 7: Mi 1998, Glossa xxiii; 356 pp. 88-7105-083-5. Bibl.;

75 La parola di Dio cresceva (At 12,24): scritti in onore di Carlo Maria Martini nel suo 70° compleanno. ᴱ**Fabris, Rinaldo**: RivBib.S 33: Bo 1998, EDB 597 pp. 88-10-30221-4. 1 port.; Bibl.

76 MARXSEN, Willi: Jesu Rede von Gott und ihre Nachgeschichte im frühen Christentum. ᴱ**Koch, Dietrich-A.**: 1989, ⇒5,131. ᴿThR 63 (1998) 373-377 (*Wehnert, Jürgen*).

77 MASON, Rex: After the exile. ᴱ**Barton, John; Reimer, David J.**: 1996, ⇒12,57. ᴿCBQ 60 (1998) 179-180 (*McKenzie, Steven L.*).

78 MCNAMARA, Martin: Targumic and cognate studies. ᴱ**Cathcart, Kevin J.; Maher, Michael J.** : JSOT.S 230: 1996, ⇒12,58. ᴿJSSt 43 (1998) 383-384 (*Lund, Jerome A.*); CBQ 60 (1998) 598-599 (*Brady, Christian M.M.*).

79 MERK, Otto: Wissenschaftsgeschichte und Exegese: gesammelte Aufsätze zum 65. Geburtstag. ᴱ**Gebauer, Roland; Karrer, Martin; Meiser, Martin**: BZNW 95: B 1998, de Gruyter viii; 467 pp. DM238. 3-11-016191-5.

80 METZGER, Bruce M.: The text of the New Testament in contemporary research. ᴱ**Ehrman, Bart D.; Holmes, Michael W.**: 1995, ⇒11/2,126; 12,59. ᴿJThS 49 (1998) 298-299 (*Delobel, Joël*).

81 MEURER, Siegfried: Die neue Gute Nachricht Bibel: Siegfried Meurer zum Abschied gewidmet. ᴱ**Jahr, Hannelore**: Bibel im Gespräch 5: Stu 1998, Deutsche Bibelgesellschaft 154 pp. 3-438-06226-7.

82 MEYER, Paul W.: Faith and history. ᴱ**Carroll, John T.**, *al.*, 1990, ⇒6,123*a; 7,1026. ᴿThR 63 (1998) 377-380 (*Wehnert, Jürgen*).

83 MORAG, Shelomo: Studies in Hebrew and Jewish languages. 1996, ⇒12,66. ᴿREJ 157/1-2 (1998) 225-234 (*Aslanov, Cyril*).

84 MURPHY, Roland E.: Wisdom, you are my sister. ᴱ**Barré, Michael L.**: CBQ.MS 29: 1997, ⇒13,69. ᴿLASBF 48 (1998) 577-586 (*Niccacci, Alviero*).

85 NARKISS, Bezalel: The real and ideal Jerusalem in Jewish, Christian and Islamic art: studies in honor of... his seventieth birthday. ᴱ**Kühnel, Bianca**: Jewish Art 23-24: J 1998, The Hebrew University of Jerusalem xxxviii; 689 pp. 965-391-007-8. Bibl.

86 NESTORI, Aldo: Domum tuam dilexi: miscellanea in onore di Aldo Nestori. SAC 53: Città del Vaticano 1998, Pontificio Istituto di Archeologia Cristiana xi; 862 pp. 88-85991-20-3.

87 OLSHAUSEN, Eckart.: Alte Geschichte: Wege—Einsichten—Horizonte:... zum 60. Geburtstag. ᴱ**Fellmeth, Ulrich; Sonnabend, Holger**: Spudasmata 69: Hildesheim 1998, Olms viii; 224 pp. 3-487-10725-2. Bibl.

88 PESTMAN, P.W.: The two faces of Graeco-Roman Egypt: Greek and Demotic and Greek-Demotic texts and studies presented to P.W. Pestman. ᴱ**Verhoogt, A.M.F.W.; Vleeming, S.P.**: PLB 30: Lei 1998, Brill xi; 193 pp. $115.50. 90-04-11226-X. 9 pl.

89 PEYRON, Amedeo Angelo Maria: Giornata di studio in onore di Amedeo Peyron. Torino 1996. ᴱ**Curto, Silvio**: F 1998, Istituto Papirologico G. Vitellio viii; 143 pp.

90 POKORNÝ, Petr: EPITOAUTO: studies in honour of Petr Pokorný on his sixty-fifth birthday. ᴱMrázek, Jiří, *al.*,: Praha 1998, Mlÿn 330 pp. 80-902296-0-3.

91 PORADA, Edith: Edith Porada memorial volume. ᴱOwen, David; Gernot, Wilhelm: 1995, ⇒11,2,151; 13,11799. ᴿJAOS 118 (1998) 588 (*Lion, Brigitte*).

92 POSCHARSKY, Peter: Vom Orient bis an den Rhein: Begegnungen mit der christlichen Archäologie. ᴱLange, Ulrike; Sörries, Reiner: 1997, ⇒13,73. ᴿDBAT 29 (1998) 317-319 (*Diebner, B.J.*).

93 PRAWER, Joshua: Sacred space: shrine, city, land. ᴱKedar, Benjamin Z.; Werblowsky, Raphael Juda Zwi: J 1998, The Israel Academy of Sciences and Humanities 348 pp. 0-333-66129-X. Proceedings of the international conference in memory of Joshua Prawer.

94 QUAEGEBEUR, Jan: Egyptian religion the last thousand years: studies dedicated to the memory of Jan Quaegebeur. ᴱClarysse, Willy; Schoors, Antoon; Willems, Harco: OLA 84-85: Leuven 1998, Peeters 2 vols. 90-429-0669-3.

95 QUATTORDIO MORESCHINi, Adriana: Do-ra-qe pe-re: Studi in memoria di... ᴱAgostiniani, Luciano, *al.*: Pisa 1998, Istituti Editoriali e Poligrafici Internazionali xiv; 394 pp. 88-8174-105-1.

96 RAINEY, Anson F.: Past links: studies in the languages and cultures of the ancient Near East. ᴱShlomo, Izre'el; Singer, Itamar; Zadok, Ran: IOS 18: WL 1998, Eisenbrauns 459 pp. 1-57506-035-3.

97 RÖMER, Willem H. Philibert: Dubsar anta-men: Studien zur Altorientalistik: Festschrift für... zur Vollendung seines 70. Lebensjahres. ᴱDietrich, Manfried; Loretz, Oswald: AOAT 253: Müns 1998, Ugarit-Verlag xviii; 512 pp. 3-927120-63-4. collab. *Balke, Thomas E.* Bibl.

98 RUIZ DE LA PEÑA, Juan Luis: Coram Deo. ᴱGonzález de Cardedal, Olegario; Fernández Sangrador, Jorge Juan: BSal.E 189: 1997, ⇒13,76. ᴿATG 61 (1998) 307-309 (*Olivares, E.*).

99 RUPPERT, Lothar: Ich bewirke das Heil und erschaffe das Unheil (Jesaja 45,7): Studien zur Botschaft der Propheten: Festschrift für ... zum 65. Geburtstag. ᴱDiedrich, Friedrich; Willmes, Bernd: FzB 88: Wü 1998, Echter 567 pp. DM56. 3-429-02013-1. Bibl.

100 SAARISALO, Aapeli: From the ancient sites of Israel: essays on archaeology, history and theology in memory of Aapeli Saarisalo (1896-1986). ᴱEskola, T.; Junkkaala, E.: Institia.S: Helsinki 1998, Theological Institute of Finland 197 pp. 952-9857-07-1 [IEJ 49,158].

101 SCHRAGE, Wolfgang: Ja und nein: christliche Theologie im Angesicht Israels: Festschrift zum 70. Geburtstag ... ᴱWengst, Klaus; Sass, Gerhard: Neuk 1998, Neuk 368 pp. 3-7887-1707-6. Zusammenarbeit mit *Katja Kriener; Rainer Stuhlmann*; Bibl.

102 SIERRA, Sergio Josef: Hebraica: miscellanea di studi... per il suo 75° compleanno. ᴱIsrael, Felice; Rabello, Alfredo M.; Somekh, Alberto M.: T 1998, Istituto di Studi Ebraici. 606 pp. Bibl.

103 SLOYAN, Gerard Stephen: Open Catholicism. ᴱEfroymson, David Patrick; Raines, John C.: 1997, ⇒13,88. ᴿWorship 72 (1998) 565-569 (*Joncas, Jan Michael*).

104 SNYDER, Graydon F.: Common Life in the early church: essays honoring Graydon F. Snyder. ᴱHills, Julian Victor, *al.*: Harrisburg, Pennsylvania 1998, Trinity xxx; 449 pp. $30. 1-56338-254-7. Bibl.

105 SOARES-PRABHU, George: The dharma of Jesus. ᴱD'Sa, Francis X.: 1997, ⇒13,89. ᴿJPJRS 1/1 (1998) 165-168 (*Padinjarekuttu, Isaac*).

106 SPEEL, Charles: Festschrift in honor of Charles Speel. ᴱSienkewicz, **Thomas J.; Betts, James E.**: Monmouth, Ill. 1996, Monmouth College xvi; 434 pp. [NThAR 2000,15].

107 SPEYER, Wolfgang: Chartulae: Festschrift für Wolfgang Speyer. ᴱ**Dassmann, Ernst; Thraede, Klaus; Engemann, Josef**: JAC.E 28: Müns 1998, Aschendorff xiv; 310 pp. 3-402-08112-1.

108 SPYCKET, Agnès: Collectanea orientalia. 1996, ⇒12,83; 13,90. ᴿBiOr 55 (1998) 519-560 (*Potts, D.T.*).

109 STADELMANN, Rainer: Stationen: Beiträge zur Kulturgeschichte Ägyptens. ᴱ**Guksch, Heike; Polz, Daniel**: Mainz 1998, Von Zabern xvii; 499 pp. 3-8053-2526-6. Bibl.

110 STARR, Richard Francis Strong: Richard F.S. Starr Memorial Volume. ᴱ**Owen, David I.; Wilhelm, Gernot**: 1996, ⇒12,85. ᴿJAOS 118 (1998) 588-589 (*Lion, Brigitte*).

111 STEGEMANN, Hartmut: Antikes Judentum und frühes Christentum: Festschrift für Hartmut Stegemann zum 65. Geburtstag. ᴱ**Kollmann, Bernd; Steudel, Annette; Reinbold, Wolfgang**: BZNW 97: B 1998, De Gruyter ix; 528 pp. 3-11-016199-0. Bibl.

112 STEINMETZ, David C.: Biblical interpretation in the era of the Reformation. ᴱ**Muller, Richard A.; Thompson, John L.**: 1996, ⇒12,86. ᴿSCJ 29/1 (1998) 151-154 (*McKim, Donald K.*); Faith & Mission 15/2 (1998) 107-108 (*Köstenberger, Andreas J.*).

113 STEK, John H.: Reading and hearing the word: from text to sermon, essays in honor of John H. Stek. ᴱ**Leder, Arie C.**: GR 1998, Calvin Theological Seminary 260 pp. $15 [CTJ 34,451—Walters, Stanley D.].

114 STUHLMACHER, Peter: Evangelium, Schriftauslegung, Kirche. ᴱ**Ådna, J.; Hafemann, S.J.; Hofius, O.**: 1997, ⇒13,92. ᴿOrdKor 39 (1998) 491-492 (*Giesen, Heinz*); ThR 63 (1998) 380-383 (*Wehnert, Jürgen*).

115 SUMMERS, Ray: Chronos, kairos, Christos II: chronological, nativity, and religious studies in memory of Ray Summers. ᴱ**Vardaman, E. Jerry**: Macon 1998, Mercer Univ. Press xvi; 320 pp. 0-86554-582-0.

116 SWEET, John Philip McMurdo: A vision for the church. ᴱ**Bockmuehl, Markus N.A.; Thompson, Michael B.**: 1997, ⇒13,93. ᴿThR 63 (1998) 476-477 (*Lohse, Eduard*).

117 SZARZYNSKA, Krystyna: Written on clay and stone: ancient Near Eastern studies presented... on the occasion of her 80th birthday. ᴱ**Braun, Jan**, *al.*: Wsz 1998, Agade 112 pp. 83-87111-07-4. Bibl.

118 THÉODORIDÈS, Aristide: Individu, société et spiritualité dans l'Égypte pharaonique et copte. ᴱ**Cannuyer, Christian; Kruchten, Jean-Marie**: 1993, ⇒9,151. ᴿCÉg 73 (1998) 67-69 (*Menu, Bernadette*).

119 TUCKER, Gene Milton: Prophets and paradigms. ᴱ**Reid, Stephen Breck**: JSOT.S 229: 1996, ⇒12,95. ᴿCBQ 60 (1998) 401-403 (*Dempsey, Carol J.*).

120 TYSON, Joseph B.: Literary studies in Luke-Acts: essays in honor of ... ᴱ**Thompson, Richard P.; Phillips, Thomas E.**: Macon, GA 1998, Mercer University Press xviii; 372 pp. $25 0-86554-563-4. Bibl.

121 VAN DER WOUDE, Adam Simon: Perspectives in the study of the Old Testament and early Judaism: a symposium in honour of... on the occasion of his 70th birthday. ᴱ**García Martínez, Florentino; Noort, Edward**: VT.S 73: Lei 1998, Brill xi; 284 pp. 90-04-11322-3.

122 VENETZ, Hermann-Josef: Auferstehung hat einen Namen: biblische Anstöße zum Christsein heute: Festschrift für... ᴱ**Bieberstein, Sabine; Kosch, Daniel**: Luzern 1998, Exodus ix; 310 pp. 3-905577-25-9.

123 WARD, William A.: Ancient Egyptian and Mediterranean studies: in memory of William A. Ward. ^E**Lesko, Leonard H.**: Providence, RI 1998, Brown Univ. xx; 271 pp. 0-9662685-0-4.
124 WETTER, Kard. Friedrich: Für Euch Bischof—mit Euch Christ. ^E**Weitlauff, Manfred; Neuner, Peter**: St. Ottilien 1998, Eos 984 pp. FS89. 3-88096-292-8.
125 WILL, Ernest: Hommages à Ernest Will. Syria 75: P 1998, IFAPO 345 pp. 2-912738-05-9 [NThAR 2000,274].
126 WRIGHT, David F.: Interpreting the bible: historical and theological studies in honour of David F. Wright. ^E**Lane, Anthony N.S.**: Leicester 1998, Apollos viii; 308 pp. 0-85111-455-5. Bibl.
127 YOUNG, Dwight W.: "Go to the land I will show you". ^E**Coleson, Joseph; Matthews, Victor H.**: 1996, ⇒12,107; 13,107. ^RJAOS 118 (1998) 603-604 (*Oller, Gary H.*).

A1.2 Miscellanea *unius* auctoris

128 **Abulafia, Anna Sapir** CStS 621: Aldershot 1998, Variorum xvi; 310 pp. $90. 0-86078-661-7.
129 **Andreau, Jean** Saggi di storia antica 12: R 1997, Bretschneider xxi; 432 pp.
130 **Bammel, Ernst** Judaica et Paulina: Kleine Schriften II. WUNT 91: 1997, ⇒13,109. ^RThLZ 123 (1998) 969-971 (*Siegert, Folker*).
131 **Barrett, Charles K.** Jesus and the word: and other essays. 1995, ⇒11/2,229; 13,110. ^RSJTh 51 (1998) 386-387 (*Stenschke, Christoph*).
132 **Bauckham, Richard J.** The fate of the dead: studies on the Jewish and christian apocalypses. NT.S 93: Lei 1998, Brill xvi; 425 pp. 90-04-11203-0.
133 **Beckwith, Roger T.** Calendar and chronology. AGJU 33: 1996, ⇒12,112; 13,112. ^RNT 40 (1998) 407-411 (*Collins, Nina L.*); ThLZ 123 (1998) 237-238 (*Strobel, August*); JThS 49 (1998) 291-293 (*Goulder, Michael*).
134 **Betz, Hans Dieter** Gesammelte Aufsätze, 4: Antike und Christentum. Tü 1998, Mohr vii; 309 pp. DM168. 3-16-147008-7.
135 **Betz, Otto** Aufsätze zur biblischen Theologie, 2: Jesus: der Herr der Kirche. WUNT 52: 1990, ⇒6,200. ^RThR 63 (1998) 383-385 (*Wehnert, Jürgen*).
136 **Blau, Joshua** Topics in Hebrew and Semitic linguistics. J 1998, Magnes 372 pp. 965-493-006-4.
137 **Blau, Yehoshua** עיונים בבלשנות עברית [Studies in Hebrew linguistics]. 1996, ⇒12,7623. ^RLeš. 61 (1998) 217-231 [H] (*Birnbaum, Gabriel*).
138 **Bonora, Antonioþä; Priotto, Michelangelo** Libri sapienziali e altri scritti. LOGOS. Corso di Studi Biblici 4: 1997, ⇒13,115. ^RItin. 6/10 (1998) 304-305 (*Costa, Giuseppe*).
139 **Brandenburger, Egon** Studien zur Geschichte und Theologie des Urchristentums. SBAB 15: 1993, ⇒9,187. ^RThR 63 (1998) 385-387 (*Wehnert, Jürgen*).
140 **Burchard, Christoph** Studien zur Theologie, Sprache und Umwelt des Neuen Testaments. ^E*Sänger, Dieter*: WUNT 107: Tü 1998, Mohr viii; 442 pp. DM178. 3-16-146997-6.
141 **Cazelles, Henri** Études d'histoire religieuse et de philologie biblique. 1996, ⇒12,120; 13,118. ^RJThS 49 (1998) 720-724 (*Davies, P.R.*).

142 **Clines, David J.A.** On the way to the postmodern: Old Testament essays, 1967-1998. JSOT.S 292-293: Shf 1998, Academic 2 vols. 1-85075-901-4 (v.1); -83-9 (v.2). Bibl.

143 **Cranfield, C.E.B.** On Romans and other New Testament essays. E 1998, Clark ix; 191 pp. $44. 0-567-08624-0.

144 **Das, Somen** Bible studies, sermons, prayers and reflections. Delhi 1998, ISPCK 124 pp. Rs65.

145 **Debenedetti, Giacomo** Profeti. ᴱ*Citton, Giuliana*: Mi 1998, Mondadori xxvi; 209 pp. 88-04-44698-6. Cinque conferenze del 1924; saggio introduttivo di *Cesare Segre*.

146 **Dillon, John M.** The great tradition: further studies in the development of Platonism and early christianity. CStS 599: Aldershot, Hampshire 1998, Variorum xii; 332 pp. 0-86078-671-4.

147 **Dinkler, Erich** Im Zeichen des Kreuzes: Aufsätze. BZNW 61: 1992, ⇒8,236a. ᴿThR 63 (1998) 387-389 (*Wehnert, Jürgen*).

148 **Dunn, James D.G.** The Christ and the Spirit: 1. christology; 2. pneumatology. E 1998, Clark xix; 462; xvi; 382 pp. £20. 0-567-08631-3; -2-1.

149 **Elm, Kaspar** Umbilicus mundi: Beiträge zur Geschichte Jerusalems, der Kreuzzüge, des Kapitels vom Heiligen Grab in Jerusalem und der Ritterorden. Instrumenta canonissarum regularium Sancti Sepulcri 7: Brugge 1998, Sint-Kruis iv; 566 pp.

150 **Fitzmyer, Joseph A.** To advance the gospel: New Testament studies. Biblical Resource: GR ²1998, Eerdmans xvii; 421 pp. £24; $35. 0-8028-4425-1.

151 **Frankemölle, Hubert** Jüdische Wurzeln christlicher Theologie: Studien zum biblischen Kontext neutestamentlicher Texte. BBB 116: [Bodenheim] 1998, Philo 466 pp. DM68. 3-8257-0096-8.

152 **Freedman, David N.** Divine commitment and human obligation, 2: Poetry and orthography. 1997, ⇒13,124. ᴿCBQ 60 (1998) 188-189 (*Murphy, Roland E.*);

153 Divine commitment and human obligation, 1-2: ᴱ*Huddlestun, John R.*: 1997, ⇒13,124. ᴿJQR 88 (1998) 259-261 (*Friedman, Richard Elliot*); LASBF 48 (1998) 588-589 (*Niccacci, Alviero*).

154 **Gasparro, Giulia S.** ORIGENE e la tradizione origeniana in Occidente. BSRel 142: R 1998, Las 426 pp. L55.000 [Ben. 46,515—Cocchini, Francesca].

155 **Gilbert, Maurice** Il a parlé par les prophètes: thèmes et figures bibliques. Le livre et le rouleau 2: Bru 1998, Lessius 404 pp. FB1.120. 2-87299-070-4. ᴿPOC 48 (1998) 437-439 (*Merceron, R.*).

156 **Goldenberg, Gideon** Studies in Semitic linguistics. J 1998, Magnes xi; 664 pp.

157 **Grabbe, Lester L.** Sacerdoti, profeti, indovini, sapienti nell'antico Israele. CinB 1998, San Paolo 350 pp.

158 **Hahn, Ferdinand** Exegetische Beiträge zum ökumenischen Gespräch. 1986, ⇒2,167; 3,231. ᴿThR 63 (1998) 389-391 (*Wehnert, Jürgen*).

159 **Hengel, Martin** Studies in early christology. 1995, ⇒11/2,268(!); 12,127. ᴿPacifica 11/1 (1998) 89-90 (*Painter, John*); HeyJ 39 (1998) 75-76 (*Turner, Geoffrey*);

160 Judaica et Hellenistica: Kleine Schriften I. WUNT 90: 1996, ⇒12,128; 13,134. ᴿSal. 60 (1998) 767-768 (*Vicent, R.*).

161 **Hermisson, Hans-Jürgen** Studien zu Prophetie und Weisheit: gesammelte Aufsätze. ᴱ*Barthel, Jörg; Jauss, Hannelore; Koenen, Klaus*. FAT 23: Tü 1998, Mohr viii; 333 pp. DM168. 3-16-146966-6.

162 **Holwerda, David E.** De Schrift opent een vergezicht: gebundele bij-dragen tot de exegese van het Niuwe Testament. Kampen 1998, Voor-hoeve 633 pp. 90-297-1617-7.

163 **Hurd, John Coolidge** The earlier letters of Paul—and other studies. Studies in the religion and history of early christianity 8: Fra 1998, Lang 212 pp. 3-631-33941-0 [NThAR 1999,224].

164 **Jay, Pierre** JÉRÔME lecteur de l'écriture. CEv.S 104: P 1998, Cerf 75 pp. FF40. 0222-9706.

165 **Jenni, Ernst** Studien zur Sprachwelt des Alten Testaments. 1997, ⇒13,138. ^RAnton. 73 (1998) 743-744 (*Nobile, Marco*); ATG 61 (1998) 402-405 (*Torres, A.*).

166 **Kaiser, Otto** Gottes und der Menschen Weisheit: gesammelte Aufsätze. BZAW 261: B 1998, De Gruyter viii; 320 pp. 3-11-016087-0.

167 **Kallai, Zecharia** Biblical historiography and historical geography: col-lection of studies. BEAT 44: Fra 1998, Lang 284 pp. 3-631-32395-6.

168 **Klagsbald, Victor** A l'ombre de Dieu: dix essais sur la symbolique dans l'art juif. 1997, ⇒13,141. ^RJQR 88 (1998) 356-357 (*Shatzmiller, Joseph*).

169 **Klopfenstein, Martin A.** Leben aus dem Wort: Beiträge zum Alten Testament. BEAT 40: 1996, ⇒12,132. ^ROLZ 93 (1998) 497-498 (*Kellenberger, Edgar*).

170 ^E**Lemaire, André** Le monde de la Bible. Folio/Histoire: P 1998, Gal-limard 714 pp. 2-07-040365-3. Bibl.

171 **Lohfink, Gerhard** Studien zum Neuen Testament. SBAB 5: 1989, ⇒5,300. ^RThR 63 (1998) 392-394 (*Wehnert, Jürgen*);

172 Studien zu Kohelet. SBAB 26: Stu 1998, Katholisches Bibelwerk 300 pp. DM79. 3-460-06261-4.

173 **Malamat, Abraham** Mari and the Bible. Studies in the history and culture of the ancient Near East 12: Lei 1998, Brill viii; 270 pp. ƒ136; $80. 90-04-10863-7.

174 **Mendels, Doron** Identity, religion and historiography: studies in Hellenistic history. JSPE.S 24: Shf 1998, Academic 480 pp. 1-85075-682-1.

175 **Merklein, Helmut M.** Studien zu Jesus und Paulus. WUNT 43: 1987, ⇒3,257. ^RThR 63 (1998) 394-396 (*Wehnert, Jürgen*);

176 Studien zu Jesus und Paulus II. WUNT 105: Tü 1998, Mohr xiv; 455 pp. 3-16-146863-5.

177 ^E**Mikasa, H.I.H. Prince Takahito** Essays on ancient Anatolia in the second millennium B.C.. Bulletin of the Middle Eastern Culture Center in Japan 10: Wsb 1998, Harrassowitz vii; 307 pp. [AfO 46-47,424ss—Gerber, Christoph].

178 ^E**Moreno García, Abdón** Tras la huella de los humanistas extremeños: manuscritos inéditos de Benito ARIAS MONTANO y PEDRO de Valencia. 1996, ⇒12,140. ^REstB 56 (1998) 431-432 (*García-Moreno, A.*).

179 **Mostert, Walter** Glaube und Hermeneutik: gesammelte Aufsätze ^E*Bühler, Pierre; Ebeling, Gerhard, al.*: Tü 1998, Mohr vi; 287 pp. DM148. 3-16-146967-4. [ThRv 95,490—Wenz, Gunther].

180 **Moule, C.F.D.** Forgiveness and reconciliation: biblical and theological essays. L 1998, SPCK xi; 244 pp. £25. 0-281-05139-9 [JThS 50,740ss—Grayston, K.].

181 **Neusner, Jacob** Jewish law from Moses to the Mishnah: the Hiram College lectures on religion for 1999 and other papers. SFSHJ 187: Atlanta, GA 1998, Scholars xiii; 186 pp. 0-7885-0495-9.

182 **Niederwimmer, Kurt** Quaestiones theologicae: gesammelte Aufsätze. [E]*Pratscher, Wilhelm; Öhler, Markus*: BZNW 90: B 1998, de Gruyter viii; 323 pp. 3-11-015711-X.

183 **Pate, C. Marvin** Four views on the book of Revelation. GR 1998, Zondervan 252 pp. 0-310-21080-1.

184 **Paulsen, Henning** Zur Literatur und Geschichte des frühen Christentums: gesammelte Aufsätze. [E]*Eisen, Ute E.*: WUNT 99: 1997, ⇒13,153. [R]OrdKor 39 (1998) 493-494 (*Giesen, Heinz*).

185 *Petry, Ronald D.* A summary of two bible studies by Graydon SNYDER. Echoes from the local tradition (1998) 55-58 [Exod 3,1-17: Acts 21,16-22,22].

186 **Pope, Marvin H.** Probative pontificating in Ugaritic and biblical literature: collected essays. [E]*Smith, Mark S.*: 1994, ⇒10,216. [R]JAOS 118 (1998) 568-569 (*Greenstein, Edward L.*).

187 **Ratzinger, Kard. Josef** Die Vielfalt der Religionen und der eine Bund. Hagen 1998, Urfeld 131 pp. DM29.80. 3-932857-20-8. [R]ZKTh 120 (1998) 462-465 (*Kreiml, Josef*).

188 **Ricoeur, Paul; Lacoque, André** La couleur des idées: P 1998, Seuil 456 pp. FF160. 2-02-031677-3. [R]Esprit 10 (1998) 223-227 (*Breton, Stanislas*).

189 **Riedinger, Rudolf** Kleine Schriften zu den Konzilsakten des 7. Jahrhunderts. IP 34: Steenbrugis 1998, Abbatia S. Petri xxiv; 346 pp. 2-503-50735-2. Bibl.

190 **Roloff, Jürgen** Exegetische Verantwortung in der Kirche: Aufsätze. 1990, ⇒6,289. [R]ThR 63 (1998) 396-398 (*Wehnert, Jürgen*).

191 **Rothstein, Arnold M.** Re-thinking biblical story and myth: critical essays on biblical interpretation: selected lectures at the Theodor Herzl Institute, 1986-1995. Lanham 1998, University Press of America x; 93 pp. 0-7618-1166-4.

192 **Rubinstein, Eliezer** Syntax and semantics: studies in Biblical Hebrew and Modern Hebrew. [E]*Borokovsky, Esther; Trummer, Penina*: TA 1998, Tel Aviv Univ. xiv; 287; 59* pp. Pref. *A. Dotan*; 32 art. Hebr.; 4 art. Eng. [REJ 159,513ss—Schattner-Rieser, U.].

193 **Ruckman, Peter S.** Theological studies. Pensacola, FL 1998, Bible Believers 752-1433 pp. [NThAR 1999,178].

194 **Saebø, Magne** On the way to canon: creative tradition history in the Old Testament. JSOT.S 191: Shf 1998, Academic 401 pp. £35. 1-85075-927-8.

195 **Schmidt, Ludwig** Gesammelte Aufsätze zum Pentateuch. BZAW 263: B 1998, De Gruyter viii; 286 pp. DM168. 3-11-016123-0. [R]ThLZ 123 (1998) 1203-1205 (*Levin, Christoph*).

196 **Schneider, Alfons Maria** Reticulum: ausgewählte Aufsätze und Katalog seiner Sammlungen. [E]*Seeliger, Hans Reinhard*: JAC.E 25: Müns 1998, Aschendorff x; 358 pp. 3-402-08109-1.

197 **Schürmann, Heinz** Im Knechtdienst Christi: zur weltpriesterlichen Existenz. Pd 1998, Bonifatius 419 pp. DM78. 3-89710-051-7;

198 Wort Gottes und Schriftauslegung: gesammelte Beiträge zur theologischen Mitte der Exegese. [E]*Backhaus, Knut*: Pd 1998, Schöningh 342 pp. 3-506-75236-3.

199 **Schweitzer, Albert** Straßburger Vorlesungen. [E]*Gräßer, Erich; Zürcher, Johann*: Werke aus dem Nachlaß 2: Mü 1998, Beck 759 pp. DM138. 3-406-41171-1 [ThR 64,477s—Zager, Werner].

200 **Seitz, Christopher R.** Word without end: the Old Testament as abiding theological witness. GR 1998, Eerdmans xi; 355 pp. $28. 0-8028-4322-0. [R]CBQ 60 (1998) 545-546 (*Murphy, Roland E.*); HBT 20 (1998) 162-163 (*Noble, Paul R.*).

201 **Seybold, Klaus** Studien zur Psalmenauslegung. Stu 1998, Kohlhammer 319 pp. 3-17-015576-8.

202 **Smend, Rudolf** Bibel, Theologie, Universität. KVR 1582: 1997, ⇒13,162. [R]ThLZ 123 (1998) 243 (*Reventlow, Henning Graf*).

203 **Thiede, Carsten Peter** Rekindling the word: in search of gospel truth. 1995, ⇒11/2,336; 13,164. [R]TJT 14/1 (1998) 106-107 (*Racine, Jean-François*).

204 **Trilling, Wolfgang** Studien zur Jesusüberlieferung. SBAB 1: 1988, ⇒4,275. [R]ThR 63 (1998) 398-399 (*Wehnert, Jürgen*).

205 **Walter, Nikolaus** Praeparatio Evangelica: Studien zur Umwelt, Exegese und Hermeneutik des Neuen Testaments. [E]*Kraus, Wolfgang; Wilk, Florian*: WUNT 98: 1997, ⇒13,167. [R]ThLZ 123 (1998) 390-392 (*Lohse, Eduard*); ThR 63 (1998) 399-402 (*Wehnert, Jürgen*).

206 **Westermann, Claus** Das mündliche Wort: Erkundungen im Alten Testament. AzTh 82: 1996, ⇒12,157. [R]BThZ 15 (1998) 279-280 (*Klemm, Peter*).

207 **Will, Édouard** Historica graeca-hellenistica: choix d'écrits 1953-1993. P 1998, De Boccard xi; 893 pp. [RH 301,881—Bertrand, Jean-Marie].

A1.3 *Plurium compilationes* biblicae

208 [E]**Alkier, Stefan; Brucker, Ralph** Exegese und Methodendiskussion. TANZ 23: Tü 1998, Francke xix; 302 pp. DM98. 3-7720-1874-2.

209 [E]**Amphoux, Christian-Bernard; Margain, Jean** Les premières traditions de la Bible. 1996, ⇒12,159. [R]RThPh 130 (1998) 345-346 (*Rose, Martin*); CBQ 60 (1998) 390-391 (*Laberge, Léo*).

210 **Anzulewicz, P.**, *al.*, Gesù servo: di Dio e degli uomini. "Cristologia" 6: R 1998, Herder 277 pp.

211 [E]**Armstrong, Donald** The truth about Jesus. GR 1998, Eerdmans viii; 160 pp. 1-85075-932-4.

212 **Barbaglio, Giuseppe**, *al.*, "La violenza". PSV 37: Bo 1998, EDB 321 pp.

213 [E]**Bauckham, Richard J.** The gospels for all christians: rethinking the gospel audiences. E 1998, Clark vi; 220 pp. $22. 0-567-08597-X [R]DBM 17 (1998) 120-122 (*Karavidopoulos, J.*).

214 [E]**Baudoz, Jean-François; Bourgeois, Henri** 20 ans de publications françaises sur Jésus. CJJC 75: P 1998, Desclée 157 pp. 2-7189-0946-3 [NThAR 2000,155].

215 [E]**Beal, Timothy Kandler; Gunn, David M.** Reading Bibles, writing bodies: identity and the Book. 1997, ⇒13,172. [R]RBBras 15 (1998) 448-449.

216 Biblische Hermeneutik. JBTh 12: Neuk 1998, Neuk viii; 424 pp. 3-7887-1642-8.

217 [ET]**Blowers, Paul M.** The Bible in Greek Christian antiquity. The Bible through the ages, 1: 1997, ⇒13,177. [R]JEarlyC 6 (1998) 694-696 (*Gorday, Peter J.*); SVTQ 42 (1998) 410-412 (*Behr, John*).

218 [E]**Brenner, Athalya** Genesis. The Feminist Companion to the Bible (Second series), 1: Shf 1998, Academic 276 pp. £17/$28. 1-85075-838-7. Bibl.

219 EBrenner, Athalya; Fontaine, Carole R. A feminist companion to reading the Bible: approaches, methods and strategies. 1997, ⇒13,180. RRBBras 15 (1998) 447-448;

220 Wisdom and Psalms. The Feminist Companion to the Bible (Second series), 2: Shf 1998, Academic 332 pp. 1-85075-917-0. Bibl.

221 EBuzzetti, Carlo; Ghidelli, C. La traduzione della Bibbia nella chiesa italiana, il Nuovo Testamento:. CinB 1998, San Paolo 208 pp. L28.100. 88-215-3792-7. Pres. G. Ravasi. Conferenza Episcopale Italiana. RRCI 79 (1998) 703-708.

222 ECasciaro, José María, al., Esperanza del hombre y revelación bíblica. 1996, ⇒12,173. XIV Simposio Internacional de Teología de la Universidad de Navarra. RCarthaginensia 14 (1998) 217-219 (Sanz Valdivieso, R.); CDios 211 (1998) 645-647 (Gutiérrez, J.).

223 EClines, David J.A.; Moore, Stephen D. Auguries: the jubilee volume of the Sheffield department of biblical studies. JSOT.S 269: Shf 1998, Academic 332 pp. 1-85075-911-1.

224 ECunningham, Mary B.; Allen, Pauline Preacher and audience: studies in early christian and Byzantine homiletics. A new history of the sermon 1: Lei 1998, Brill ix; 370 pp. 90-0410681-2.

225 EDavid, Robert Faut-il attendre le messie?: études sur le messianisme. Montréal 1998, Médiaspaul 238 pp. [RThPh 131,346—Macchi, Jean-Daniel].

226 EDavies, Philip R. The prophets. BiSe 42: 1996, ⇒12,174. RCBQ 60 (1998) 600-601 (Dearman, J. Andrew).

227 EDay, John T.; Lund, Eric; O'Donnell, Anne M. Word, church, and state: Tyndale Quincentenary essays. Wsh 1998, Catholic Univ. of America Pr. xxiv; 343 pp. 0-8132-0902-1.

228 EDonfried, Karl P.; Richardson, Peter Judaism and christianity in first-century Rome. GR 1998, Eerdmans xiv; 329 pp. $24. 0-8028-4265-8. Contributions from SNTS congresses 1992-1994.

229 EDuhaime, Jean; Mainville, Odette Entendre la voix du Dieu vivant. 1994, ⇒10,255*. REeT 29 (1998) 255-256 (Faucher, Alain).

230 EEdelman, Diana Vikander The triumph of Elohim: from Yahwisms to Judaisms 1995, ⇒11/1,79. RBiOr 55 (1998) 867-870 (Haak, Robert D.).

231 En busca del rostro de Jesús. M 1998, Palabra 167 pp. [RelCult 45,418—Martín López, Juan Carlos].

232 EEndres, J.C., al., Chronicles and its synoptic parallels in Samuel, Kings, and related biblical texts. ColMn 1998, Liturgical xxiv; 356 pp. $40. 0-814-65930-6 [Pacifica 12,85s—Campbell, Antony].

233 EEsler, Philip Modelling early christianity: social-scientific studies of the New Testament in its context. 1995, ⇒11/2,363; 13,190. RJThS 49 (1998) 281-284 (Oakes, Peter).

234 EEvans, Craig A.; Sanders, James A. The function of scripture in early Jewish and christian tradition. JSNT.S 154; Studies in scripture in early Judaism and Christianity 6: Shf 1998, JSOT 350 pp. £55/$85. 1-85075-830-1.

235 Cipriani, Settimio, al., La fede nella bibbia. DSBP 21. R 1998, Borla 271 pp. L37.000. 88-263-1213-3.

236 EFeigenson, Emily H. Beginning the journey: toward a women's commentary on Torah. NY 1998, Women of Reform Judaism xv; 169 pp. [NThAR 2000,310].

237 ^E**Fitzgerald, John T.** Friendship, flattery, and frankness of speech: studies on friendship in the New Testament world. NT.S 82: 1996, ⇒12,180. ^RJHS 118 (1998) 223-224 (*Powell, J.G.F.*).

238 ^E**Flesher, Paul V.M.** Targum Studies, II. Targum and Peshitta SF-SHJ 165: Atlanta 1998, Scholars 272 pp. $60. 0-7885-0447-9.

239 ^E**Frankenölle, Hubert** Der ungekündigte Bund? Antworten des Neuen Testaments. QD 172: FrB 1998, Herder 276 pp. 3-451-02172-2.

240 ^E**Frankowskiego, J.; Mędali, S.** Dzieje apostolskie—listy św. Pawła. Wprowadzenie w myśl i wezwanie ksiąg biblijnych 9: Wsz 1998, ATK 608 pp. ^RSTV 36/2 (1998) 180-182 (*Czajkowski, Michał*).

241 ^E**García Martínez, Florentino; Luttikhuizen, Gerard P.** Interpretations of the Flood. Themes in Biblical Narratives 1: Lei 1998, Brill xi; 202 pp.

242 ^E**Haase, Wolfgang** ANRW 2.26/3: 1996, ⇒12,183. ^RAnCl 67 (1998) 363-365 (*Wankenne, Jules*);

243 ANRW 2.34/3: 1997, ⇒13,202. ^RAnCl 67 (1998) 338-339 (*Raepsaet-Charlier, Marie-Thérèse*).

244 ^E**Jenner, K.D.; Wiegers, G.A.** Heilig boek en religieus gezag: ontstaan en functioneren van canonieke tradities. Leidse Studiën van de Godsdienst 2: Kampen 1998, Kok 319 pp. *f*50 [GThT 98,137].

245 ^E**Jones, L. Gregory; Buckley, James J.** Theology and scriptural imagination. Directions in modern theology. Oxf 1998, Blackwell 138 pp. 0-631-21075-X.

246 ^E**Keck, Leander E.** NIntB. 1 General and Old Testament articles: Genesis, Exodus, Leviticus 1994, ⇒10,1575... 13,207. ^RIThQ 63/2 (1998) 206-207 (*McConvery, Brendan*).

247 ^E**Keck, Leander E.; Petersen, David L.; Long, Thomas G.** NIntB. 8 General articles on the New Testament, the gospel of Matthew, the gospel of Mark 1995, ⇒11/1,92. ^RIThQ 63 (1998) 91-92 (*Drennan, Martin*).

248 ^E**Kee, Howard Clark; Borowsky, Irvin J.** Removing the Anti-Judaism from the New Testament. Ph 1996, American Interfaith Institute 180 pp. $20. 1-881060-01-X. ^RJSNT 69 (1998) 123-124 (*Roo, Jacqueline C.R. de*).

249 ^E**Kitzberger, Ingrid R.** The personal voice in biblical interpretation. NY 1998, Routledge 218 pp. $26 [BiTod 38,319—Bergant, Dianne].

250 ^E**Lacocque, André; Ricoeur, Paul** Thinking biblically: exegetical and hermeneutical studies. ^T*Pellauer, David*. Ch 1997, University of Chicago Press xix; 441 pp. $30. 0-226-71337-7. Bibl. [NThAR 1998,301].

251 **Boccaccini, Gabriele, al.,** L'eucaristia nella bibbia. DSBP 19. R 1998, Borla 158 pp. L37.000. 88-263-1210-9.

252 ^E**Longenecker, Richard N.** Life in the face of death: the resurrection message of the New Testament. McMaster New Testament Studies: GR 1998, Eerdmans x; 314 pp. $22. 0-8028-4474-X.

253 ^E**Marguerat, Daniel; Norelli, Enrico; Poffet, Jean-Michel** Jésus de Nazareth: nouvelles approches d'une énigme. MoBi 38: Genève 1998, Labor et F 612 pp. FS52. ^RÉtudes 389 (1998) 394-395 (*Gibert, Pierre*).

254 ^E**Marrocu, Giuseppe** L'obbedienza e la disobbedienza nella bibbia. Studio biblico teologico aquilano 17: 1997, ⇒13,216. ^RInter Fratres 48 (1998) 259-260 (*Martignani, Luigi*).

255 ^E**Mathys, Hans-Peter** Ebenbild Gottes—Herrscher über die Welt: Studien zu Würde und Auftrag des Menschen. BThSt 33: Neuk 1998, Neuk viii; 180 pp. 3-7887-1663-0.

256 ^E**Matthews, Victor Harold; Levinson, Bernard Malcolm; Frymer-Kensky, Tikva Simone** Gender and law in the Hebrew bible and the ancient Near East. JSOT.S 262: Shf 1998, Academic 251 pp. £35. 1-85075-886-7.

257 ^E**McKenzie, Steven L.; Graham, M. Patrick** The Hebrew Bible today: an introduction to critical issues. LVL 1998, Westminster xiv; 240 pp. $24. 0-664-25652-X.

258 ^E**Mébarki, Farah** Le Coran et la Bible. 1998, 90 pp. 0154-9049.

259 ^E**Minkoff, Harvey** Approaches to the bible: the best of *Bible Review*: composition, transmission, and language 1994, ⇒10,256*a. ^RBS 155 (1998) 489-491 (*Taylor, Richard A.*).

260 ^E**Pippin, Tina; Aichele, George** Violence, utopia, and the kingdom of God: fantasy and ideology in the bible. L 1998, Routledge xiv; 157 pp. 0-415-15667-X.

261 ^E**Prior, Michael** Western scholarship and the history of Palestine. L 1998, Melisende xvi; 111 pp. £9. 1-901-76402-8 [Month 32,414—Watson, John].

262 ^E**Reventlow, Henning Graf; Farmer, William R.** Biblical studies and the shifting of paradigms 1850-1914. JSOT.S 192: 1995, ⇒11/2,383... 13,224. ^RJThS 49 (1998) 305-309 (*O'Neill, J.C.*).

263 ^E**Rutgers, Leonard Victor**, *al.*, The use of sacred books in the ancient world. Contributions to Biblical Exegesis and Theology 22: Lv 1998, Peeters 316 pp. 90-429-0696-0.

264 ^E**Schäfer, Peter; Cohen, Mark R.** Toward the millennium: messianic expectations from the Bible to Waco. SHR 77: Lei 1998, Brill vi; 446 pp. $147. 90-04-11037-2.

265 ^E**Schneider, Theodor; Pannenberg, Wolfhart** Verbindliches Zeugnis III: Schriftverständnis und Schriftgebrauch. DiKi 10: FrB 1998, Herder 446 pp. FS 65. 3-451-26673-3.

266 ^E**Schoors, Antoon** Qohelet in the context of wisdom. BEThL 136: Lv 1998, Peeters xi; 528 pp. FB2.400. 90-429-0589-1. Colloque International 1995 Lv.

267 ^E**Segovia, Fernando F.; Tolbert, Mary Ann** Teaching the bible: the discourses and politics of biblical pedagogy. Mkn 1998, Orbis xi; 372 pp. $28. 1-57075-202-8 [ThD 46,291—Heiser, W. Charles].

268 ^E**Siebert-Hommes, Jopie** De vrouw van de nacht en andere verhalen uit de bijbel. Zoetermeer 1998, Meinema 154 pp. ƒ25. 90211-3701-1 [Phoe. 45,89—Folmer, M.L.].

269 **Thomas, Robert L.; Farnell, F. David** The Jesus crisis: the inroads of historical criticism into evangelical scholarship. GR 1998, Kregel 416 pp. $17. 0-8254-3811-X.

270 ^E**Toit, C.W. du** Images of Jesus. Pretoria 1997, Research Institute for Theology and Religion, UNISA 237 pp. $16/£10.

271 ^E**Tuckett, Christopher M.** The scriptures in the gospels. BEThL 131: 1997, ⇒13,234. ^RRSR 86 (1998) 429-431 (*Guillet, Jacques*); JThS 49 (1998) 759-764 (*North, Wendy Sproston*).

272 ^E**Ubbiali, Sergio** Il sacrificio: evento e rito. Contributi 15: Padova 1998, Messagero 492 pp. L50.000. 88-250-0721-3 [EO 16,137-138—Flores Arcas, Juan Javier].

273 ^E**Uro, Risto** Thomas at the crossroads: essays on the Gospel of Thomas. Studies of the New Testament and its world: E 1998, Clark xvii; 222 pp. £24. 0-567-08607-0.

274 ^E**Van Inwagen, Peter** The possibility of resurrection and other essays in christian apologetics. Boulder, CO 1998, Westview 200 pp. 0-8133-2732-6.

275 ^E**Van Liere, Lucien M.**, *al.*, Vragen om moeilijkheden: over het geschil tussen verzoening en bevrijding. Gorinchem 1998, Narratio 87 pp. f15. 90-5263-993-0. ^RInterpretatie 6/8 (1998) 31 (*Wilhelm, Han*).

276 ^E**Van Loopik, M.** Tweespalt en verbondenheid: joden en christenen in historisch perspectief: joodse reacties op christelijke theologie. Sleutelteksten in godsdienst en theologie 23: Zoetermeer 1998, Meinema 202 pp. f35. 90-211-6123-0 [GThT 98,137].

277 ^E**Van Segbroeck, Frans** De woorden die Jezus ons gegeven heeft. Lv 1998, Vlaamse Bijbelstichting 216 pp. f14.75. 90-334-4042-3 [ITBT 7/5,31—Roukema, Riemer].

278 ^E**Washington, Harold C.; Graham, Susan Lochrie; Thimmes, Pamela L.** Escaping Eden: new feminist perspectives on the bible. BiSe 65: Shf 1998, Academic 292 pp. 1-85075-980-4.

279 ^E**Wilkins, Michael J.; Moreland, J.P.** Jesus under fire: modern scholarship reinvents the historical Jesus. 1995, ⇒11/2,390... 13,4253. ^RFaith & Mission 15/2 (1998) 93-95 (*McDonald, Larry S.*).

280 ^E**Willhite, Keith; Gibson, Scott M.** The big idea of biblical preaching. GR 1998, Baker 181 pp.

A1.4 *Plurium compilationes* theologicae

281 **AA.VV** Understanding and discussion: approaches to Muslim-Christian dialogue. Collab. *Kolvenbach, Peter-Hans*; *Pittau, Giuseppe*, *al.* Inculturation 20: R 1998, E.P.U.G. viii; 71 pp. 88-7652-779-6.

282 ^E**Arcella, Luciano; Pisi, Paola; Scagno, Roberto** Confronto con Mircea ELIADE: archetipi mitici e identità storica. Di fronte e attraverso 482: Mi 1998, Jaca x; 463 pp. 88-16-40482-5.

283 ^E**Assmann, Jan; Janowski, Bernd; Welker, Michael** Gerechtigkeit: Richten und Retten in der abendländischen Tradition und ihren altorientalischen Ursprüngen. Kulte, Kulturen: Mü 1998, Fink 246 pp. 3-7705-3227-9. Ill.

284 ^E**Ayres, Lewis; Jones, Gareth** Christian origins: theology, rhetoric and community. L 1998, Routledge 219 pp. £15. 0-415-10750-4. ^RNBl 79 (1998) 458 (*Kerr, Fergus*).

285 ^E**Barclay, John M.G.; Sweet, John** Early christian thought in its Jewish context. 1996, ⇒12,43. ^RJThS 49 (1998) 799-802 (*Lieu, Judith*).

286 ^E**Baumgarten, Albert I.; Assmann, Jan; Stroumsa, Guy G.** Self, soul and body in religious experience. SHR 78: Lei 1998, Brill vi; 444 (2) pp. 90-04-10943-9.

287 ^E**Berchman, Robert M.** Mediators of the divine: horizons of prophecy, divination, dreams and theurgy in Mediterranean antiquity. SFSHJ 163: Atlanta, GA 1998, Scholars (6) 267 pp. 0-7885-0442-8.

288 ^E**Blazquez Martinez, José Maria; González Blanco, Antonino; González Fernández, Rafael** La tradición en la antigüedad tardía. Antigüedad y cristianismo 14: Murcia 1998, Univ. de Murcia 737 pp.

289 ^E**Brunner-Traut, Emma** Die Stifter der großen Religionen: Echnaton, Zarathustra, Mose, Jesus, Mani, Muhammad, Buddha, Konfuzius, Lao tze. Herder-Taschenbuch 4669: FrB ³1998, Herder 222 pp. 3-451-04669-5.

290 ^E**Bsteh, Andreas** Christentum in der Begegnung. Christlicher Glaube in der Begegnung mit dem Hinduismus. Studien zur Religionstheologie 4: Mödling 1998, St. Gabriel.

291 ^E**Confoy, Maryanne; Lee, Dorothy A.; Nowotny, Joan** Freedom and entrapment: women thinking theology. Blackburn, Australia 1998, DoveCollins xiv; 264 pp. $A25. 1-86371-555-X. ^RVJTR 62 (1998) 952-953 (*Lesser, R.H.*).

292 ^E**Crüsemann, Frank** Ich glaube an den Gott Israels: Fragen und Antworten zu einem Thema, das im christlichen Glaubensbekenntnis fehlt. Kaiser-Taschenbücher 168: Gü 1998, Kaiser 158 pp. 3-579-05168-7. collab. *Obst, Gabriele* [NThAR 1999,43].

293 ^E**Di Berardino, Angelo; Studer, Basil** History of Theology 1: the patristic period. 1997, ⇒13,241. ^RBTB 28 (1998) 86-88 (*Sloyan, Gerard S.*).

294 ^E**D'Onofrio, Giulio** History of theology III: the Renaissance. ColMn 1998, Liturgical ix; 649 pp. $100. [BTB 28,167s—Sloyan, Gerard S.].

295 ^E**Donohue, John J.; Troll, Christian W.** Faith, power, and violence: Muslims and Christians in a plural society, past and present. OCA 258: R 1998, Pont. Ist. Orientale 315 pp. 88-7210-322-3.

296 La fine del tempo. Quaderni teologici. Seminario di Brescia 8: [Brescia] 1998, Morcelliana 378 pp. 88-372-1690-4.

297 ^E**Gasparro, G. Sfameni** Destino e salvezza: tra culti pagani e gnosi cristiana. Cosenza 1998, Giordano 264 pp. 88-86919-05-0 [SMSR 64,373—Lancelotti, Maria Grazia].

298 ^E**Goodison, Lucy; Morris, Christine** Ancient goddesses: the myths and the evidence. L 1998, British Museum Press 224 pp. 0-7141-1761-7 [Kernos 12,301—Pirenne-Delforge, Vinciane].

299 ^E**Groß, Walter** Frauenordination: Stand der Diskussion in der katholischen Kirche. 1996, ⇒12,216. ^RRTL 29/1 (1998) 84-87 (*Dermience, Alice*).

300 ^E**Guerriero, Elio** L'uomo davanti a Dio: la preghiera nelle religioni e nella tradizione cristiana. CinB 1998, San Paolo 242 pp. 88-215-3781-1.

301 ^E**Hartlieb, Elisabeth; Methuen, Charlotte** Sources and resources of feminist theologies. JEGTFF 5: 1997, ⇒13,246. ^RJEGTFF (1998) 224-234 (*Heidemanns, Katja*).

302 ^E**Hayes, Michael A.; Porter, Wendy; Tombs, David** Religion and sexuality. Studies in Theology and Sexuality 2; Roehampton Institute London Papers 4: Shf 1998, Academic 438 pp. 1-85075-947-2.

303 ^E**Houtman, Alberdina; Poorthuis, Marcel; Schwartz, Joshua** Sanctity of time and space in tradition and modernity. Jewish and Christian Perspectives 1: Lei 1998, Brill xii; 390 pp. 90-04-11233-2.

304 ^E**Kanzian, Christian** Gott finden in allen Dingen: Theologie und Spiritualität. Theologische trends 7: Thaur 1998, Thaur 248 pp. DM34.80. 3-85400-076-6.

305 ^E**Klöckener, Martin; Richter, Klemens** Wie weit trägt das gemeinsame Priestertum?: liturgischer Leitungsdienst zwischen Ordination und Beauftragung. QD 171: FrB 1998, Herder 284 pp. 3-451-02171-4.

306 ^E**Kofsky, Arieh; Stroumsa, Guy G.** Sharing the sacred: religious contacts and conflicts in the Holy Land first-fifteenth centuries CE. J 1998, Yad Izhak Ben-Zvi x; 285 pp. 965-217-150-6.

307 ^E**Kunnumpuram, Kurien; D'Lima, Errol; Parappally, Jacob** The church in India: in search of a new identity. 1997, ⇒13,250. ^RJPJRS 1/1 (1998) 168-169 (*Pandikattu, Kuruvilla*).

308 ^E**Moraglia, Francesco** Dio Padre misericordioso. Genova 1998, Marietti 388 pp [StMor 37,496s—Tremblay, Réal].

309 ^E**Neusner, Jacob** Judaism in late antiquity, 2: Historical syntheses. HO 1/17: 1995, ⇒11/2,376... 13,9009. ^RRSR 86 (1998) 595-599 (*Beaude, Pierre-Marie*).

310 ^E**Sarnataro, Ciro** La terra e il seme: inculturazione ed ermeneutica della fede. Pref. *Russo, Adolfo*. BTNap 19: N 1998, D'Auria 302 pp. L38.000. 88-7092-145-X.

311 ^E**Schwager, Raymund** Relativierung der Wahrheit?: kontextuelle Christologie auf dem Prüfstand. QD 170: FrB 1998, Herder 248 pp. 3-451-02170-6.

312 ^E**Stern, David** Hellenism and Hebraism reconsidered: the poetics of cultural influence and exchange, 1-2. Poetics Today 19 (1998) 1-176, 179-330. 0333-5372.

313 ^E**Taricone, Fiorenza** Maschio e femmina li creò: l'immagine femminile nelle religioni e nelle scritture. Donne e terzo millennio 1: Negarine di S. Pietro in Cariano (Verona) 1998, Il Segno dei Gabrielli xiv; 202 pp. 88-86043-53-8.

314 ^E**Taylor, Mark C.** Critical terms for religious studies. Ch 1998, Univ. of Chicago Press v; 423 pp. $55. 0-226-79157-2 [Numen 48,117—Stuckrad, Kocku von].

315 ^E**Wagner, Harald** Mit Gott streiten: neue Zugänge zum Theodizee-Problem. QD 169: FrB 1998, Herder 155 pp. 3-451-02169-2.

A1.5 Plurium compilationes philologicae vel archaeologicae

316 **Arslan, E.A.**, *al.*, La 'parola' delle immagini e delle forme di scrittura: modi e techniche della comunicazione nel mondo antico. Messine 1998, Di.Sc.A.M. 313 pp. 88-8268-001-0 [REA 102,531s—Lamagna, Mario].

317 Artistas y artesanos en la antiguedad clasica. Cuadernos emeritenses 8: Mérida 1994, Musée national d'art romain 214 pp. Ill. ^RRAr (1998/2) 425-426 (*Bourgeois, Ariane*).

318 ^E**Bartlett, John R.** Archaeology and biblical interpretation. 1997, ⇒13,268. ^RNEA(BA) 61 (1998) 180-181 (*Dessel, J.P.*).

319 ^E**Bartl, Karin; Bernbeck, Reinhard; Heinz, Marlies** Zwischen Euphrat und Indus: aktuelle Forschungsprobleme in der vorderasiatischen Archäologie. 1995, ⇒13,267. ^RZA 88 (1998) 149-151 (*Edzard, D.O.*).

320 ^E**Borgen, Peder Johan; Robbins, Vernon Kay; Gowler, David B.** Recruitment, conquest, and conflict: strategies in Judaism, early christianity, and the Greco-Roman world. Emory Studies in Early Christianity 6: Atlanta, GA 1998, Scholars (8) 356 pp. 0-7885-0526-2.

321 ^E**Bournazel, Eric; Poly, Jean-Pierre** Les féodalités. Histoire générale des systèmes politiques: P 1998, PUF viii; 808 pp. 2-13-049334-3. Bibl.

322   ᴱBranigan, Keith Cemetery and society in the Aegean Bronze Age. Sheffield Studies in Aegean Archaeology 1: Shf 1998, Academic 173 pp. 1-85075-822-0.

323   ᴱCalci, Carmelo Roma oltre le mura: lineamenti storico topografici del territorio della V circoscrizione. R 1998, Associazione culturale Roma oltre le mura 238 pp.

324   ᴱCalderone, Salvatore Mediterraneo antico: economie, società, culture. Mediterraneo antico 1.1: Pisa 1998, Istituti editoriali e poligrafici internazionali 361 pp.

325   ᴱCharlesworth, James H.; Weaver, Walter P. The Dead Sea scrolls and the christian faith: in celebration of the jubilee year of the discovery of Qumran Cave I. Faith and Scholarship Colloquies: Harrisburg 1998, Trinity xviii; 76 pp. $12. 1-56338-232-6.

326   ᴱCoogan, Michael David The Oxford history of the biblical world. NY 1998, OUP xii; 643 pp. $50. 0-19-508707-0. Bibl.

327   ᴱCryer, Frederick H.; Thompson, Thomas L. Qumran between the Old and New Testaments. JSOT.S 290: Copenhagen International Seminar 6: Shf 1998, Academic 398 pp. £55. 1-85075-905-7.

328   ᴱDalley, Stephanie The legacy of Mesopotamia. Oxf 1998, OUP xviii; 227 pp. 0-19-814946-8. ᴿBiOr 55 (1998) 804-806 (Stol, M.).

329   ᴱDavis, Jack L. Sandy Pylos: an archaeological history from Nestor to Navarino. Austin 1998, University of Texas Press xliii; 342 pp. $25. 0-292-71595-1. 135 fig. [AJA 103,707s—Haggis, Donald C.].

330   ᴱEdwards, Douglas R.; McCollough, C. Thomas Archaeology and the Galilee: texts and contexts in the Graeco-Roman and Byzantine periods. SFSHJ 143: 1997, ⇒13,275. ᴿJJS 49 (1998) 360-362 (Schwartz, Joshua).

331   ᴱEggert, Manfred K.H.; Veit, Ulrich Theorie in der Archäologie: zur englischsprachigen Diskussion. Tübinger Archäologische Taschenbücher 1: Müns 1998, Waxmann 400 pp. DM38. 3-89325-594-X [ThLZ 124,1203—Conrad, Diethelm].

332   ᴱElwell, Walter A.; Yarbrough, Robert W. Readings from the first-century world: primary sources for New Testament study. Encountering biblical studies: GR 1998, Baker 223 pp. 0-8010-2157-X. Bibl. [NThAR 2000,281].

333   ᴱEvans, Craig A.; Flint, Peter W. Eschatology, messianism, and the Dead Sea Scrolls. SDSSRL: 1997, ⇒13,276. ᴿRTR 57 (1998) 151-152 (Davies, John A.); CBQ 60 (1998) 601-602 (Harrington, Daniel J.); BiOr 55 (1998) 888-890 (Van der Kooij, A.); RStT 17/1 (1998) 113-115 (Schuller, Eileen M.).

334   ᴱFlint, Peter W.; VanderKam, James C. The Dead Sea scrolls after fifty years: a comprehensive assessment. Lei 1998, Brill 2 vols. 90-04-10858-0. collab. Alvarez, Andrea E.

335   ᴱGasche, Hermann; Tanret, Michel Changing watercourses in Babylonia: towards a reconstruction of the ancient environment in Lower Mesopotamia, 1. Mesopotamian History and Environment 2; Memoirs 5: Ghent 1998, Univ. of Ghent x; 245 pp. FS92. 1-885923-13-9. Ill. [Mes. 34-35,236s—Cellerino, A.].

336   ᴱGonzález Blanco, Antonino; Matilla Séiquer, Gonzalo Romanización y cristianismo en la Siria Mesopotàmica. Antigüedad y cristianismo 15: [Murcia] 1998, Univ. de Murcia 654 pp.

337   ᴱGoodman, M. Jews in a Graeco-Roman world. Oxf 1998, Clarendon ix; 293 pp. £40. 0-19-815078-4 [ClR 50,131s—Lieu, Judith M.].

338 ^E**Gyselen, Rika** Parfums d'Orient. Bures-sur-Yvette 1998, Groupe pour l'étude de la civilisation du Moyen-Orient 212 pp.

339 ^E**Heuser, Manfred; Klimkeit, Hans-J.** Studies in Manichaean literature and art. NHMS 46: Lei 1998, Brill xi; 331 pp. 90-04-10716-9.

340 The Indo-European languages. Routledge language family descriptions: L 1998, Routledge xxiii; 526 pp. 0-415-06449-X.

341 JAC 41. Müns 1998, Aschendorffsche 280 pp. DM104. 3-402-08132-6. 11 pl. ^RJThS 51 (2000) 319-321 (*Chadwick, Henry*).

342 ^E**Joshel, Sandra R.; Murnaghan, Sheila** Women and slaves in Greco-Roman culture: differential equations. L 1998, Routledge xii; 287 pp. 0-415-16229-7. Bibl.

343 ^E**Kaye, Alan S.; Daniels, Peter T.** Phonologies of Asia and Africa: (including the Caucasus). WL 1997, Eisenbrauns 2 vols. $119.50. 1-57506-019-1. Technical Advisor *Peter T. Daniels*.

344 ^E**Koloski-Ostrow, Ann Olga; Lyons, Claire L.** Naked truths: women, sexuality and gender in classical art and archaeology. 1997, ⇒13,288. ^RAJA 102 (1998) 620-621 (*Talalay, Lauren E.*).

345 ^E**Krings, Véronique** La civilisation phénicienne et punique: manuel de recherche. HbOr I, 20: Lei 1995, ⇒11/2,726. Brill xx; 923 pp. ^RArOr 66 (1998) 389-391 (*Segert, Stanislav*).

346 ^E**Lana, Italo; Maltese, Enrico V.** Storia della civiltà letteraria greca e latina. v.1, Dalle origini al IV secolo a.C.; v.2, dall'ellenismo all'età di Traiano; v.3, dall'età degli Antonini alla fine del mondo antico. T 1998, UTET 3 vols. 88-02-05293-X.

347 ^E**Lapin, Hayim** Religious and ethnic communities in later Roman Palestine. Studies and texts in Jewish history and culture 5: Bethesda, MD 1998, University Press of Maryland xi; 298 pp. 1-883053-31-5.

348 ^E**Mathews, Roger** Ancient Anatolia: fifty years' work by the British Institute of Archaeology at Ankara. L 1998, Brit. Inst. of Archaeology at Ankara xx; 378 pp. $54. 147 fig.; 56 col. pl. [BASOR 319,87s—Kuniholm, Peter Ian].

349 ^E**Meskell, Lynn** Archaeology under fire: nationalism, politics and heritage in the eastern Mediterranean and Middle East. L 1998, Routledge x; 251 pp. 0-4151-16470-2.

350 ^E**Mikasa, Prince Takahito** Essays on ancient Anatolia and Syria in the second and third millennium B.C.. 1996, ⇒12,233. ^ROLZ 93 (1998) 648-650 (*Prechel, Doris*).

351 ^E**Molyneaux, Brian Leigh** The cultural life of images: visual representation in archaeology. 1997, ⇒13,292. ^RAJA 102 (1998) 619-620 (*Davis, Whitney*).

352 ^E**Montserrat, Dominic** Changing bodies, changing meanings: studies on the human body in antiquity. L 1998, Routledge xvi; 234 pp. 0-415-13584-2.

353 ^E**Muecke, Frances** Sidere mens eadem mutato. Prudentia.S: Auckland 1998, University of Auckland vi; 136 pp. NZ$15. 0110-487X. The Todd Memorial Lectures, the University of Sydney.

354 ^E**Muraoka, T.** Semantics of ancient Hebrew. Abr-n.S 6: Lv(N) 1998, Peeters xix; 151 pp. 90-429-0592-1 [NThAR 1998,334].

355 ^E**Neils, Jenifer** Worshipping Athena: panathenaia and Parthenon. 1996, ⇒12,235. ^RAJA 102 (1998) 203-204 (*Osborne, Robin*).

356 ^E**Peiser, Benny J.; Palmer, Trebor; Bailey, Mark E.** Natural catastrophes during Bronze Age civilisations: archaeological, geological, astronomical and cultural perspectives. BArR int. ser. 728: Oxf 1998, Archaeopress (3) 252 pp. 0-86054-916-X.

357 ^E**Rowlandson, Jane** Women and society in Greek and Roman Egypt: a sourcebook. C 1998, CUP xxi; 406 pp. $A45. 0-5215-8815-4 [Prudentia 31,163ss—McKechnie, Paul].

358 ^E**Schmeling, Gareth** The novel in the ancient world. Mn.S 159: 1996, ⇒12,238. ^RTJT 14/1 (1998) 100-102 (*Ascough, Richard S.*); CIR 48 (1998) 339-340 (*Swain, Simon*); JRS 88 (1998) 184-185 (*Pollmann, Karla*).

359 ^E**Shafer, Byron E.** Temples of ancient Egypt. L 1998, Tauris xii; 335 pp. £25. 1-86064-329-9. 112 pl. & fig. ^RAntiquity 72 (1998) 712-713 (*Thomas, Susanna*).

360 ^E**Shanks, Hershel** Los manuscritos del Mar Muerto: el principal descubirmiento contemporánco sobre el judaísmo, el cristianismo y la biblia. Paidós origines 5: Barc 1998, Paidós 398 pp. [EfMex 17,274ss—Zesati Estrada, Carlos].

361 ^E**Shirun-Grumach, Irene** Jerusalem studies in egyptology. ÄAT 40: Wsb 1998, Harrassowitz ix; 406 pp. 3-447-04085-8.

362 ^E**Silberman, Neil Asher; Small, David B.** The archaeology of Israel: constructing the past, interpreting the present. JSOT.S 237: 1997, ⇒13,9790. ^RAntiquity 72 (1998) 951-953 (*Whitelam, Keith*).

363 ^E**Sordi, Marta** Responsabilità, perdono e vendetta nel mondo antico. Contributi dell'Istituto di storia antica 24: Mi 1998, Vita e P viii; 301 pp. 88-343-0081-5.

364 ^E**Taylor, R.E.; Aitken, Martin J.** Chronometric dating in archaeology. Advances in Archaeological and Museum Science 2: NY 1997, Plenum xix; 395 pp. $95. 0-306-45715-6. 105 fig.; 17 tables. ^RAJA 102 (1998) 822-823 (*Manning, Sturt W.*).

365 ^E**Tsohatzidis, Savas L.** Foundations of speech act theory: philosophical and linguistic perspectives. L 1998, Routledge viii; 500 pp. 0-415-09524-7. Bibl.

366 ^E**Virgilio, Biagio** Studi ellenistici IV-VII. Pisa 1993-1994, Giardiri ^RAt. 86 (1998) 584-588 (inc. VIII) (*Asheri, David*);

367 Studi ellenistici VIII. 1996, ⇒12,246. ^RAt. 86 (1998) 584-587 (*Asheri, David*).

368 ^E**Wright, Rita P.** Gender and archaeology. 1996, ⇒12,249. ^RAJA 102 (1998) 181-182 (*Meskell, Lynn*).

A2.1 Acta *congressuum* biblica

369 ^E**Ahituv, Shmuel; Oren, Eliezer D.** The origin of early Israel—current debate: biblical, historical, and archaeological perspectives. Beer-Sheva 12: [Beer-Sheva] 1998, Ben-Gurion University viii; 176 pp. Irene Levi-Sala Seminar, 1997.

370 ^E**Ausín, Santiago** De la ruina a la afirmación: el entorno del reino de Israel en el siglo VIII a.C. 1997, ⇒13,314. ^RScrTh 30 (1998) 983-985 (*Aranda, Gonzalo*).

371 ^E**Beaude, Pierre-Marie** La bible en littérature. 1997, ⇒13,315. Actes du colloque international de Metz ^RRTL 29 (1998) 237-240 (*Bogaert, Pierre-Maurice*). Revue des Sciences Humaines 252 (1998) 213-214 (*Ducrey, Anne*).

372 ^E**Benyik, György** Példabeszédek: Szegedi Biblikus Konferencia Szeged, 1997. szeptember 1-4. Szeged 1998, [JATEPress] 227 pp.

373 ^EBorg, Marcus Jesus at 2000. Boulder 1998, Westview x; 175 pp. Symposium, Oregon State University, Feb. 8-10, 1996 [CThMi 27,133—Derr, Amandus J.].

374 ^EBorgen, Peder; Giversen, Søren The New Testament and Hellenistic Judaism. 1997 <1995>, ⇒13,318. ^RRTR 57 (1998) 91 (*Ovey, Michael J.*); RSR 86 (1998) 606-607 (*Beaude, Pierre-Marie*).

375 ^EBortone, Giuseppe Angeli e demoni nella Bibbia. Studio Biblico Teologico Aquilano 18: L'Aquila 1998, ISSRA xxvii; 303 pp. XVIII Corso Biblico.

376 ^ECampos Santiago, Jesús Actas de las IX Jornadas Bíblicas 1996. Zamora 1998, Dip. de Zamora 222 pp. 84-87066-27-5. Asociación Bíblica Española.

377 ^EColafemmina, Cesare Dagli dei a Dio: parole sacre e parole profetiche sulle sponde del Mediterraneo. 1997, ⇒13,322. Atti del Convegno Internazionale di Studi promosso dall'Associazione "Biblia" Bari, 13-15 settembre 1991. ^RRdT 39 (1998) 789-790 (*Infante, Renzo*); Nicolaus 25 (1998) 433-434 (*Curci, Gionatan*).

378 ^EDay, John King and messiah in Israel and the ancient Near East: proceedings of the Oxford Old Testament Seminar. JSOT.S 270: Shf 1998, Academic 528 pp. $85. 1-85075-946-41.

379 ^EEmerton, John A. Congress volume: Paris 1992. VT.S 61: 1995, ⇒11/1,135... 13,324. ^RRivBib 46 (1998) 224-228 (*Minissale, Antonino*).

380 ^EExum, J. Cheryl; Moore, Stephen D. Biblical studies / cultural studies: the third Sheffield Colloquium. JSOT.S 266; Gender, Culture, Theory 7: Shf 1998, Academic 506 pp. 1-85075-965-0.

381 ^EFabris, Rinaldo, *al.*, Bibbia, popoli e lingue. Religione: CasM 1998, Piemme 159 pp. 88-384-4566-4. Convegno internazionale (1998: Udine); Prolusione del Card. *Paul Poupard*;

382 Il confronto tra le diverse culture nella bibbia da Esdra a Paolo. RStB 10,1/2: Bo 1998, EDB 389 pp. XXXIV Settimana Biblica Nazionale, Roma 9-13 sett. 1996.

383 ^EGargano, Innocenzo L'eredità di Abrahamo: 'in te saranno benedetti tutti i popoli della terra' (Gen 12,3). Koinonia: Verucchio (RN) 1998, Pazzini 112 pp. L.22.000. 88-85124-55-0. Atti del XVIII Colloquio ebraico-cristiano di Camaldoli (4-8 dic. 1997) [ConAss 1 n.s.,441ss—Caponera, Annarita].

384 ^EHead, Peter M. Proclaiming the resurrection: papers from the first Oak Hill College Annual School of Theology. L 1998, Paternoster xiv; 130 pp. 0-85364-824-7. Bibl.

385 ^EHengel, Martin; Heckel, U. Paulus und das antike Judentum. WUNT 58: 1992, ⇒8,165*. ^RStPat 45 (1998) 254-258 (*Moda, Aldo*).

386 International Colloquium Bible and Computer 5, 1997, Aix-en-Provence: actes du Cinquième Colloque International Bible et Informatique: traduction et transmission, Aix-en-Provence, 1-4 Septembre 1997. Travaux de linguistique quantitative 65: P 1998, Champion 408 pp. 2-85203-940-0. Association Internationale Bible et Informatique.

387 ^EKieffer, René J.J.; Bergman, Jan La main de Dieu: die Hand Gottes. WUNT 94: 1997, ⇒13,328. ^RRTL 29/1 (1998) 90-91 (*Wénin, A.*); ThLZ 123 (1998) 1192-1194 (*Weippert, Helga*).

388 ^EKrašovec, Jože The interpretation of the bible: the international symposium in Slovenia. JSOT.S 289: Shf 1998, Academic 1909 pp. 1-85075-969-3;

389 Interpretation of the bible: international symposium on the interpretation of the bible on the occasion of the publication of the new Slovenian translation of the bible 17-20 September 1996 Ljubljana, Slovenia. [T]*Davis, Margaret, al.*, [Ljubljana] 1998, [Slovenska akademija znanosti in umetnosti] 1909 pp. £95/$150. 961-6242-22-9.

390 [E]**Leonardi, Lino** La bibbia in Italiano tra Medioevo et Rinascimento. F 1998, Galluzzo x; 442 pp. 88-87027-38-2. Atti del Convegno internazionale F, 8-9 nov. 1996.

391 [E]**Longenecker, Richard N.** The road from Damascus: the impact of Paul's conversion on his life, thought, and ministry. 1997, ⇒13,330 [R]ScrB 28 (1998) 53-54 (*Campbell, W.S.*).

392 [E]**Marchadour, Alain** Procès de Jésus, procès des juifs?: éclairage biblique et historique. LeDiv: P 1998, Cerf 214 pp. FF140. 2-204-05821-1. Contributions du colloque 'Procès de Jésus, procès des juifs', Toulouse, 1996.

393 [E]**Marin, Marcello; Girardi, Mario** Retorica ed esegesi biblica: il rilievo dei contenuti attraverso le forme. QVetChr 24: 1996, ⇒12,259. Atti del II seminario di antichità cristiane, Bari 1991. [R]Asp. 45 (1998) 292-293 (*Longobardo, Luigi*).

394 [E]**Moor, Johannes C. de** Intertextuality in Ugarit and Israel: papers read at the tenth joint meeting of the Society for Old Testament Study and het Oudtestamentisch Werkgezelschap in Nederland en België; Oxford, 1997. OTS 40: Lei 1998, Brill xi; 213 pp. 90-04-11154-9.

395 [E]**Padovese, Luigi** Atti del V Simposio di Tarso su S. Paolo Apostolo [1997]. Turchia: la Chiesa e la sua storia 12; Simposio di Tarso su S. Paolo Apostolo 5: R 1998, Pont. Ateneo Antoniano 404 pp.

396 [E]**Philonenko, Marc** Le trône de Dieu. WUNT 69: 1993, ⇒9,404. [R]Ist. 43 (1998) 343-345 (*Dupuy, B.*).

397 [E]**Porter, Stanley E.; Olbricht, Thomas H.** Rhetoric, scripture and theology: essays from the 1994 Pretoria Conference. JSNT.S 131: 1996, ⇒12,268. [R]CBQ 60 (1998) 399-401 (*Jaquette, James L.*).

398 [E]**Revell, Ernest John** Proceedings of the Twelfth International Congress of the International Organization for Masoretic Studies. SBL Masoretic Studies 8: 1996, ⇒12,270. [R]CBQ 60 (1998) 403-404 (*Greenspahn, Frederick E.*).

399 [E]**Salvesen, Alison** ORIGEN's Hexapla and fragments: papers presented at the Rich Seminar on the Hexapla, Oxford Centre for Hebrew and Jewish Studies, August 1994. TSAJ 58: Tü 1998, Mohr xvi; 500 pp. DM228. 3-16-146575-X.

400 [E]**Schlosser, Jacques** Paul de Tarse: congrès de L'ACFEB (Strasbourg, 1995). LeDiv 165: 1996, ⇒12,273. [R]NRTh 120 (1998) 632-634 (*Luciani, D.*); RevBib 60 (1998) 55-57 (*Levoratti, A.J.*).

401 [E]**Schunck, Klaus-Dietrich; Augustin, Matthias** "Lasset uns Brücken bauen...": collected communications to the XVth Congress of the International Organization for the Study of the Old Testament, Cambridge 1995. BEAT 42: Fra 1998, Lang 319 pp. 3-631-31014-5; 0-8204-3229-6.

402 Society of Biblical Literature 1998 Seminar Papers: I-II: 134th annual meeting November 21-24, 1998 Orlando, Florida. SBL.SPS 37: Atlanta, Georgia 1998, Scholars ix; 1012 pp. 0-7885-0489-4.

403 [E]**Stefani, Piero** La festa e la bibbia: atti del convegno internazionale "Voce di gioia e voce di giubilo: la festa e la Bibbia" Firenze, Palazzo Vecchio, 21-22 ottobre 1995. [Brescia] 1998, Morcelliana 100 pp. 88-372-1695-5. Bibl.; Associazione Laica di Cultura Biblica.

404 ^E**Trublet, Jacques** La sagesse biblique. LeDiv 160: 1995, ⇒11/1,117; 12,275. Actes du 15e Congrès de l'ACFEB (1993) ^RBZ 42 (1998) 125-126 (*Ebner, Martin*).

405 Uses of the bible. Month 31 (1998) 463-514. Catholic Theological Association Conference.

406 ^E**Valentini, Alberto**, *al.*, Luca—alcuni percorsi: la preghiera, lo Spirito Santo, la misericordia, i paradossi della passione, fatti e parole nei racconti pasquali. Sussidi biblici 62: Reggio Emilia 1998, San Lorenzo ii; 137 pp. 88-8071-080-X. Atti de "Le giornate del vangelo" a cura del CAB diocesi di Carpi.

407 ^E**Van der Kooij, Arie; Van der Toorn, Karel** Canonization and decanonization: papers presented to the international conference of the Leiden Institute for the Study of religions (LISOR), held at Leiden 9-10 January 1997. SHR 82: Lei 1998, Brill xxiii; 515 pp. 90-04-11246-4. Annotated bibliography compiled by *J.A.M. Snoeck*.

A2.3 Acta congressuum theologica

408 ^E**Allen, Pauline; Canning, Raymond; Cross, Lawrence** Prayer and spirituality in the early church. Everton Park, Queensland 1998, Centre for Early Christian Studies, Austral. Cath. Univ. xv; 409 pp. $40. 0-646-36055-8. Conf. Melbourne, 1996 [JEH 51,120s—Wickham, L.R.].

409 ^E**Bellelli, Gloria M.; Bianchi, Ugo** Orientalia Sacra Urbis Romae. 1997, ⇒13,345. ^RAnCl 67 (1998) 407-409 (*Turcan, Robert*).

410 ^E**Biebuyck, Benjamin; Dirven, René; Ries, John** Faith and fiction: interdisciplinary studies on the interplay between metaphor and religion: a selection... from 25th LAUD-Symposium, Mercator Univ. of Duisburg on "Metaphor and Religion". Duisburg Papers on Research in Language and Culture 37: Fra 1998, Lang 253 pp. 3-631-33760-4.

411 ^E**Duraisingh, Christopher** Called to one hope: the gospel in diverse cultures. Geneva 1998, WCC Publications xiv; 234 pp. £11.90/$18.90. Conf. world mission and evangelism, Salvador de Bahia, Brazil, 1996.

412 ^E**Finan, Thomas; Twomey, Vincent** Studies in patristic christology. Dublin 1998, Four Courts ix; 245 pp. £35. 1-85182-354-9. Proc. 3rd Maynooth Patristic Conf., Oct. 1996 [RB 106,147—Langlamet, F.].

413 ^E**Frogneux, Nathalie; Mies, Françoise** Emmanuel LÉVINAS et l'histoire. Facultés universitaires Notre-Dame de la Paix, "Philosophie" 5: P 1998, Cerf 409 pp. 2-87037-259-0. Actes du colloque international des facultés univ. Notre-Dames de la Paix (20-21-22 mai 1997).

414 ^E**Jones, Siân; Pearce, Sarah** Jewish local patriotism and self-identification in the Graeco-Roman period. JSPE.S 31: Shf 1998, Academic 156 pp. £31.50. 1-85075-832-8. Conference, Southampton.

415 ^E**Lavenant, René** Symposium Syriacum VII: Uppsala Univ. Aug. 1996. OCA 256: R 1998, Pont. Ist. Orientale 748 pp. 88-7210-319-3.

416 ^E**Mactoux, Marie-Madeleine; Geny, Evelyne** Discours religieux dans l'Antiquité. Besançon 1995, Besançon Univ. 322 pp. 2-251-60578-9. Actes du Colloque de Besançon 1995. ^RAnCl 67 (1998) 397-399 (*Pirenne-Delforge, Vinciane*).

417 ^E**Martini, Carlo Maria** El seguimiento de Cristo. 1997, ⇒13,354 ^RRevAg 41 (1998) 857-860 (*Sánchez-Gey Venegas, Juana*).

418 ^E**Meyer, Marvin; Mirecki, Paul** Ancient magic and ritual power. 1995, ⇒11/2,472. ^RBASPap 35 (1998) 223-227 (*Bohak, Gideon*).

419 ^E**Naro, Massimo** Martirio e vita cristiana: prospettive teologiche attuali: atti del sem. di studio... San Cataldo, 1996. Studi del Centro "A. Cammarata" 24: Caltanissetta 1997, Sciascia 306 pp. 88-8241-001-3.
420 ^E**Perrone, Lorenzo** Discorsi di verità: paganesimo, giudaismo e cristianesimo a confronto nel *Contro Celso* di ORIGENE. SEAug 61: R 1998, "Augustinianum" 281 pp. L50.000. 88-7961-036-8. Atti, II Convegno, Gruppo Italiano di Ricerca su "Origene e la Tradizione Alessandrina". ^RLASBF 48 (1998) 613-614 (*Paczkowski, Mieczysław Celestyn*).
421 ^E**Pouderon, Bernard; Doré, Joseph** Les apologistes chrétiens et la culture grecque. ThH 105: P 1998, Beauchesne xiii; 490 pp. 2-7010-1358-5.
422 ^E**Van den Broeck, Roelof; Hanegraaff, Wouter J.** Gnosis and hermeticism from antiquity to modern times. SUNY Series in Western Esoteric Traditions: NY 1998, SUNY Press x; 402 pp. 0-7914-3612-8.
423 ^E**Vanhoye, Albert** Il primato del successore di Pietro: atti del simposio teologico Roma, dic. 1996. Atti e Documenti 7: Città del Vaticano 1998, LEV 509 pp. 88-209-2489-7. Congr. per la Dottrina della Fede.

A2.5 *Acta* philologica *et* historica

424 ^E**Briquel-Chatonnet, Françoise** Mosaïque de langues, mosaïque culturelle: le bilinguisme dans le Proche-Orient Ancien. 1996, ⇒12,284. ^RBiOr 55 (1998) 79-81 (*Izre'el, Shlomo*); BSLP 93 (1998) 316-319 (*Kessler-Mesguich, Sophie*).
425 ^E**Bühler, Pierre; Karakash, Clairette** Quand interpréter c'est changer. 1995, ⇒11/2,673. ^RRThPh 130 (1998) 65-73 (*Rigo, Bernard*).
426 ^E**Cassio, A.C.; Poccetti, P.** Forme di religiosità e tradizioni sapienzali in Magna Grecia. 1994, ⇒11/2,676. Atti del convegno, Napoli 14-15 dicembre 1993. ^RCIR 48 (1998) 343-345 (*Lomas, Kathryn*).
427 ^E**Cavallo, Guglielmo** Congresso Internazionale di Papirologia: scrivere libri e documenti nel mondo antico: mostra di papiri della Biblioteca Medicea Laurenziana, Firenze, 25 agosto - 25 settembre 1998. Papyrologica Florentina 30: F 1998, Ministero per i Beni Culturali xv; 255 pp. L250.000. collab. *Bagnall, Roger S.*; 159 pl.
428 ^E**Chirassi, Ileana; Seppilli, Tullio** Sibille e linguaggi oracolari: mito, storia, tradizione. Coll. del Dipart. di Scienze Archeologiche 3: Pisa 1998, Univ. degli Studi di Macerata 822 pp. 88-8147-125-6. Atti del convegno internazionale di studi Macerata-Norcia sett. 1994 [Kernos 13,304ss—Suárez de la Torre, Emilio].
429 Les enjeux de la traduction: l'expérience des missions chrétiennes: Actes des sessions 1995 et 1996 de l'AFOM et du CREDIC. 1997, ⇒13,360. ^RMémoire Spiritaine 7 (1998) 155-56 (*Buis, Pierre*).
430 ^E**Geller, M.J.; Maehler, H.; Lewis, A.W.D.** Legal documents of the Hellenistic world. 1995, ⇒11/2,681. ^RBSOAS 61 (1998) 125-126 (*Rupprecht, Hans-A.*); JAOS 118 (1998) 450-451 (*Bagnall, Roger S.*).
431 ^E**Hansen, Mogens Herman** Polis and city-state an ancient concept and its modern equivalent. Det Kongelige Danske Videnskabernes Selskab. Historisk-filosofiske Meddelelser 76; Acts of the Copenhagen Polis Centre 5: K 1998, Munksgaard 217 pp. 87-7304-293-5. Bibl.; Royal Danish Academy of Sciences and Letters. Symposium 1998.
432 ^E**Kullmann, Wolfgang; Althoff, Jochen; Asper, Markus** Gattungen wissenschaftlicher Literatur in der Antike. Scriptoralia 95, A 22: Tü

1998, Narr 452 pp. DM158. 3-8233-5405-1. Symposium Fr/B, 1996 [AnCl 69,418s—Bodson, Liliane].

433 ᴱLévy, Carlos PHILON d'Alexandrie et le langage de la philosophie: actes du coll. internat., Centre d'études sur la philosophie hellénistique et romaine de l'Univ. de Paris XII—Val de Marne (Créteil, Fontenay, Paris, oct. 1995). Turnhout 1998, Brepols 559 pp. 2-503-50564-3 [EThL 76,473ss—Verheyden, J.].

434 ᴱLiscia Bemporad, Dora; Zatelli, Ida La cultura ebraica all'epoca di LORENZO il Magnifico: celebrazioni del V centenario della morte di Lorenzo il Magnifico. Accad. Toscana di Scienze e Lettere "La Colombaria", Studi 170: F 1998, Olschki xiii; 166 pp. 88-222-4682-9. Convegno di studio Firenze, 29 novembre 1992.

435 ᴱMaul, Stefan M., al., Entretiens sur l'antiquité classique: la biographie antique. EnAC 44: Genève 1998, Hardt viii; 290 pp. 8 exposés, discussions; Vandoeuvres 1997; introd. de Widu Wolfgang Ehlers.

436 ᴱMelaerts, Henri Le culte du souverain dans l'Égypte ptolémaïque au IIIe siècle avant notre ère: actes du coll. internat., Bru mai 1995. Studia hellenistica 34: Lv 1998, Peeters viii; (2) 108 pp. 90-429-0002-4.

437 ᴱMuraoka, Takamitsu; Elwolde, J.F. The Hebrew of the Dead Sea Scrolls and Ben Sira. StTDJ 26: 1997, ⇒13,369. Proc... symposium, Leiden Univ. Dec. 1995. ᴿJSJ 29 (1998) 344-346 (Morla, Victor).

438 ᴱNielsen, I.; Nielsen, H. Sigismund Meals in a social context: aspects of the communal meal in the Hellenistic and Roman world. Aarhus Studies in Mediterranean Antiquity 1: Aarhus 1998, Aarhus U.P. 245 pp. 56 fig. [REG 112,749—Hinard, François].

439 ᴱOvadiah, Asher Hellenic and Jewish arts: interaction, tradition and renewal. Pref. Dinstein, Y. Howard Gilman International Conferences 1: TA 1998, RAMOT; TA Univ. 965-274-255-4.

440 ᴱStanton, Graham N.; Stroumsa, Guy G. Tolerance and intolerance in early Judaism and Christianity. C 1998, CUP xiv; 370 pp. £40/$65. 0-521-59037-X. Symposium, Jerusalem; Bibl.

441 ᴱStone, Michael E.; Chazon, Esther G. Biblical perspectives: early use and interpretation of the bible in light of the Dead Sea scrolls: proc., 1st international symposium, Orion Center for the study of the Dead Sea scrolls and associated literature, 12-14 May, 1996. StTDJ 28: Lei 1998, Brill viii; 291 pp. ƒ160; $94.50. 90-04-10939-0.

442 ᴱUglione, Renato L'uomo antico e la natura: atti del convegno nazionale di studi, T 1997. T 1998, Celid 375 pp. L40.000. 88-7661-353-6 [AnCl 69,420s—Bodson, Liliane].

443 ᴱWorthington, I. Voice into text: orality and literacy in ancient Greece. Mn.S 153: Lei 1996, Brill x; 232 pp. £49. 90-0410-431-3. Conference Univ. of Tasmania [JHS 120,183s—Thomas, Rosalind].

A2.7 Acta orientalistica

444 ᴱBartl, Karin; Hauser, Stefan R. Continuity and change in northern Mesopotamia from the Hellenistic to the early Islamic period. 1996, ⇒12,296. Proc. coll. B April, 1994; fig. 8 tav. ᴿBSOAS 61 (1998) 327 (Bivar, A.D.H.); Mes. 33 (1998) 338-344 (Lippolis, C.).

445 ᴱBriquel-Chatonnet, Françoise; Lozachmeur, Hélène Proche-Orient ancien: temps vécu, temps pensé: actes de la Table-Ronde du 15 nov. 1997, organisée par l'URA 1062 "Études Sémitiques". Antiquités sémitiques 3: P 1998, Maisonneuve 239 pp. FF260. 2-7200-1114-2.

446 ^E**Cannuyer, C.; Ries, J.; Van Tongerloo, A.** Travel in the oriental civilizations. Acta Orientalia Belgica 11: Ath 1998, Société belge d'études orientales xv; 290 pp. [BiOr 57,395—Geus, C.J.H. de].

447 ^E**Dabrowa, Edward** Ancient Iran and the Mediterranean world: proc. of an internat. conf. in honor of Prof. József WOLSKI, Jagiellonian Univ., Cracow, Sept. 1996. Electrum 2: Krakow 1998, Jagiellonian Univ. Pr. 236 pp. 83-233-1140-4.

448 ^E**Parpola, Simo; Whiting, Robert M.** Assyria 1995: proc., 10th anniv. symp. of the Neo-Assyrian Text Corpus Project: Helsinki, Sept. 7-11, 1995. 1997, ⇒13,376. ^RMes. 33 (1998) 362-363 (*Fiorina, P.*).

449 ^E**Preißler, Holger; Stein, Heidi** Annäherung an das Fremde: XXVI. Deutscher Orientalistentag vom 25. bis 29. 9. 1995 in Leipzig. ZDMG.S 11: Stu 1998, Steiner ix; 638 pp. 3-515-07327-2. Vorträge.

450 ^E**Prosecky, Jiri** Intellectual life of the ancient Near East: papers presented at the 43rd Rencontre Assyriologique Internationale, Prague, July 1-5, 1996. Prague 1998, Oriental Institute 482 pp. 80-85425-30-0.

451 ^E**Rassart-Debergh, M.** Études Coptes V. CBCo 10: P 1998, Peeters x; 200 pp. 2-87723-408-8. Sixième journée d'études Limoges 18-20 juin 1993; Septième journée d'études Neuchâtel 18-20 mai 1995.

452 Rencontre Assyriologique Internationale 34, 1987, Istanbul. 6.-10.7.1987, Istanbul. Türk Tarih Kurumu yayinlari 3: Ankara 1998, Türk Tarih Kurumu xiii; 729; 213 pp. 975-16-0666-7.

453 ^E**Richter, Siegfried G.** Congresso Internazionale di Studi "Manicheismo e Oriente Cristiano": die Herakleides-Psalmen. The Manichaean Coptic Papyri in the Chester Beatty Library, Psalm Book 2/2; Corpus Fontium Manichaeorum, Coptica, 1, Liber Psalmorum 2/2: [Turnhout] 1998, Brepols (6); 124 pp. 2-503-50806-5.

454 ^E**Sims-Williams, Nicholas** European conference of Iranian studies. Beiträge zur Iranistik 17: Wsb 1998, Reichert 179 pp. 3-89500-070-1. Proc. 3rd European Conf. of Iranian Studies held in Cambridge, 11th to 15th September 1995; 17 pl.; Part.1, Old and Middle Iranian studies.

455 ^E**Staehelin, Elisabeth; Jaeger, Bertrand** Ägypten-Bilder: Akten des "Symposions zur Ägypten-Rezeption" Augst bei Basel, 1993. OBO 150: 1997, ⇒13,378. ^RBiOr 55 (1998) 727-730 (*Raven, Maarten J.*).

456 ^E**Veenhof, Klaas R.** Houses and households in ancient Mesopotamia. 1996, ⇒12,299. 40e Rencontre Assyriologique Internationale, Leiden, July 5-8, 1993 ^RMes. 33 (1998) 359-362 (*Fiorina, P.*).

A2.9 *Acta* archaeologica

457 ^E**Arcelin, Patrice; Tuffreau-Libre, Marie** La quantification des céramiques: conditions et protocole. Glux-en-Glenne 1998, Centre archéologique européen du Mont Beuvray 157 pp. FF98. 2-909668-18-5. 129 fig. [Antiquity 73,940—James, N.].

458 ^E**Argoud, Gilbert; Guillaumin, Jean-Yves** Sciences exactes et sciences appliquées à Alexandrie: actes du Colloque International de Saint-Étienne (6-8 juin 1996). Centre Jean-Palerne, Mémoires 16: Saint-Étienne 1998, Université de Saint-Étienne 434 pp. FF210. 2-86272-120-4 [Latomus 59,168ss—Callataÿ, Godefroid de].

459 ^E**Bakhouche, Béatrice; Moreau, Alain; Turpin, Jean-Claude** Les astres: actes du colloque de Montpellier 1995. Séminaire d'études des

mentalités antiques: Montpellier 1996, Univ. Valéry 320 + 296 pp.
FF125 + 125. 2-905397-96-9. 78 fig. [AnCl 69,423s—Deman, Albert].

460 ᴱBakirtzis, Charalambos; Koester, Helmut Philippi at the time of
Paul and after his death. Harrisburg 1998, Trinity xv; 87 pp. $16. 1-
56338-263-6 [ThD 46,285—Heiser, W. Charles].

461 ᴱBalmuth, Miriam S.; Tykot, Robert H. Sardinian and Aegean chronology: proceedings of the international colloquium 'Sardinian stratigraphy and Mediterranean chronology'. Studies in Sardinian Archaeology 5: Oxf 1998, Oxbow 403 pp. $75. 1-900188-82-1. 166 fig., 24 ta-
bles; Tufts Univ., 17-19.3.1995 [AJA 104,131—Knapp, A.B].

462 ᴱBats, M.; d'Agostino, B. Euboica: l'Eubea et la presenza euboica in
calcidica e in occidente. Centre Jean Bérard 16; AION Archivio Storico Antico 12: N 1998, Bérard 2-903189-56-0. Atti del conv. internaz.
di Napoli, 13-16.11.1996; [AJA 104,134—Papadopoulos, J.K.].

463 ᴱBietak, Manfred Haus und Palast im alten Ägypten—House and palace in ancient Egypt: symposium in Cairo, April 8-11, 1992. 1996,
⇒12,301. ᴿAJA 102 (1998) 828-830 (Weinstein, James M.).

464 ᴱBonacasa, Nicola, al., L'Egitto in Italia, dall'antichità al medioevo:
atti del III Congr. Internaz. Italo-Egiziano, Roma, CNR—Pompei, 13-
19 Nov. 1995. Monografie scientifiche, scienze umane e sociali: R
1998, Consiglio Nazionale delle Ricerche xv; 811 pp. 88-8080-013-2.

465 ᴱBorrell, Agustí; Fuente, Alfonso de la; Puig, Armand La Bíblia i el
Mediterrani: actes del Congrès de Barcelona 18-22 setembre de 1995.
1997, ⇒13,385. ᴿEThL 74 (1998) 443-444 (Verheyden, J.); RivBib 46
(1998) 345-347 (Priotto, Michelangelo); EE 73 (1998) 668-669
(Estévez López, Elisa); RET 58 (1998) 123-124 (Fernández, Barrado).

466 ᴱBrodsky, Harold Land and community: geography in Jewish studies.
Introd. Mitchell, Robert D. Studies and texts in Jewish history and culture 3: College Park 1998, Univ. Pr. of Maryland x; 418 pp. 1-88305-
330-7. Papers... at an International Conference on Geography in Jewish
Studies, Univ. of Maryland, 19-20 March, 1995; [NThAR 1998,362].

467 ᴱCharlesworth, James H. Caves of enlightenment: proc. of the ASOR
Dead Sea Scrolls Jubilee Symposium (1947-1997). North Richland
Hills 1998, BIBAL xviii; 139 pp. $15. 0-94-103768-1 [RB 106,475].

468 ᴱChristian, David; Benjamin, Craig Worlds of the silk roads: ancient
and modern: proc. from 2nd Conf. of the Australian Soc. for Inner
Asian Studies ((A.S.I.A.S) Macquarie Univ., Sept. 21-22, 1996. Silk
Road Studies 2: Turnhout 1998, Brepols v; 306 pp. 2-503-50651-8.

469 ᴱClarke, Graeme Identities in the eastern Mediterranean in antiquity.
Collab. Harrison, Derek. Mediterranean Archaeology 11: [Sydney]
1998, [Meditarch] (8) 294 pp. Proceedings of a conference held at the
Humanities Research Centre in Canberra 10-12 November, 1997.

470 ᴱColinart, Sylvie; Menu, Michel La couleur dans la peinture et
l'émaillage de l'Égypte ancienne. Bari 1998, Edipuglia 205 pp. 88-
7228-201-2. Actes de la Table Ronde, Ravello, 20-22 mars 1997.

471 ᴱCooper, Jerrold S.; Schwartz, Glenn M. The study of the ancient
Near East in the 21st century: Albright Centenn. Conf. 1996, ⇒12,303.
ᴿBSOAS 61 (1998) 127-128 (Crawford, Harriet); CBQ 60 (1998)
181-182 (Parker, Simon B.); ArOr 66 (1998) 73-75 (Segert, Stanislav).

472 ᴱCottam, S.; Dungworth, D.; Scott, S.; Taylor, J. TRAC 94: proc. of
the 4th annual theoretical Roman archaeology conf. Oxf 1994, Oxbow
150 pp. £10. 0-946897-81-6. ᴿCIR 48 (1998) 555-556 (Keay, Simon).

473 ^E**Dassmann, Ernst; Engemann, Josef** Akten des XII. Internationalen Kongresses für christliche Archäologie. SAC 52; JAC 20/1-2: 1995, ⇒12,304. ^RJEH 49 (1998) 506-508 (*Frend, W.H.C.*).

474 ^E**Durand, Jean-Marie** Mari, Ébla et les hourrites, 1. Amurru 1: 1996, ⇒12,306; 13,389. ^RJAOS 118 (1998) 287-289 (*Biggs, Robert D.*); AulOr 16 (1998) 300-302 (*Márquez Rowe, I.*).

475 ^E**Eyre, Christopher** Proceedings of the Seventh International Congress of Egyptologists Cambridge, 3-9 September 1995. OLA 82: Lv 1998, Peeters xii; 1245 pp. 90-429-0014-8.

476 ^E**Fortin, Michel; Aurenche, Olivier** Espace naturel, espace habité: en Syrie du Nord (10e-2e millénaires av. J-C.); natural space, inhabited space: in northern Syria (10th-2nd millennium B.C.). Bulletin 33; Travaux de la Maison de l'Orient 28: Québec 1998, Canadian Society for Mesopotamian Studies 304 pp. 2-903264-56-2; 0844-3416; 0766-0510. Actes du colloque, Univ. Laval (Québec) du 5 au 7 mai 1997.

477 ^E**Gitin, Seymour** Recent excavations in Israel: a view to the west. 1995, ⇒13,393. ^RBiOr 55 (1998) 265-267 (*Van der Steen, Eveline*); JNES 57 (1998) 143-144 (*Joffe, Alexander H.*);

478 ^E**Gitin, Sy; Mazar, Amihai; Stern, Ephraim** Mediterranean peoples in transition: 13th to early tenth centuries B.C.E.. J 1998, Israel Exploration Society 504 pp. [BAR 24/3,60—Meyers, Eric].

479 ^E**Gundlach, Rolf; Rochholz, Matthias** Feste im Tempel: 4. Ägyptologische Tempeltagung Köln, 10.-12. Oktober 1996. ÄAT 33.2: Wsb 1998, Harrassowitz 183 pp. 3-447-04067-x. Bibl.

480 ^E**Hamma, Kenneth** Alexander and Alexandrianism: symposium Getty Museum and Getty Center for the History of Art... April 22-25, 1993. 1996, ⇒12,311. ^RAJA 102 (1998) 453-454 (*Venit, Marjorie Susan*).

481 ^E**Haring, B.; Maaijer, R. de** Landless and hungry?: access to land in early and traditional societies: proc... seminar, Lei, 20-21 June, 1996. Lei 1998, Research School CNWS vii; (2) 198 pp. 90-5789-008-9.

482 ^E**Hägg, R.** Ancient Greek cult practice from the archaeological evidence: proc... 4th internat. sem. on ancient Greek cult. Acta Instituti Atheniensis Regni Sueciae 15: Sto 1998, Swedish Inst. at Athens 249 pp. 91-7916-036-0. 22-24.10.1993 [REG 113,684—Lefevre-Novaro, D.].

483 ^E**Kaper, Olaf E.** Life on the fringe: living in the southern Egyptian deserts during the Roman and early-Byzantine periods. Research School CNWS 71: Lei 1998, CNWS x; 315 pp. ƒ55. 90-5789-015-1. Proc. colloquium... 25th anniv. Netherlands Institute for Archaeology and Arabic Studies in Cairo 9-12 December 1996.

484 ^E**Karageorghis, Vassos; Stampolidis, Nikolaos** Eastern Mediterranean: Cyprus-Dodecanese-Crete 16th-6th cent. B.C.: proc. International Symposium Eastern Mediterranean. Athens 1998, Univ. of Crete 313 pp. 960-85468-7-7. Nicosia Rethymnon 13-16 May 1997.

485 ^E**Larsson Lovén, Lena; Strömberg, Agneta** Aspects of women in antiquity: proc. 1st Nordic Symposium on women's lives in antiquity, Göteborg 12-15.6.1997. Studies in Mediterr. Archaeol. and Literature, Pocket-book 153: Jonsered 1998, Aströms 191 pp. 91-7081-188-1.

486 ^E**Mendoni, L.G.; Mazarakis Ainian, A.** Kea-Kytnos: history and archaeology. Meletémata 27: Athens 1998, Research Centre for Greek and Roman Antiquity 766 pp. 960-7905-01-6. Proc. international symposium Kea-Kytnos, 22-25 June 1994; 646 fig./phot. [RB 103,478].

487 ^E**Palagia, Olga; Coulson, William D.E.** Regional schools in Hellenistic sculpture. Oxbow Monograph 90: Oxf 1998, Oxbow ix; 291

pp. $98. 1-900188-45-7. Proc. Internat. Conf., American School of Classical Studies at Athens, March 15-17, 1996.

488 ᴱPiltz, Elisabeth Byzantium and Islam in Scandinavia. Studies in Mediterranean archaeology 126: Jonsered 1998, Aström 139 pp. Acts of a Symposium at Uppsala University June 15-16 1996.

489 ᴱSalvini, Mirjo Un trentennio di ricerche storiche nei paesi del Mediterraneo e del Vicino Oriente. Roma 1998, Cons. Naz. delle Ricerche 110 pp. Relazione sull'attività dell'ISMEA-CNR 1968-1998; 16 pl.

490 ᴱSiegert, Folker; Kalms, Jürgen U. Internationales Josephus-Kolloquium Münster 1997: Vorträge aus dem Institutum Judaicum Delitzschianum. Münsteraner Judaistische Studien 2: Müns 1998, LIT 226 pp. DM39.80. 3-8258-3687-8.

491 ᴱSwiny, Stuart; Hohlfelder, Robert L.; Swiny, Helena Wylde Res Maritimae: Cyprus and the eastern Mediterranean from prehistory to late antiquity: proc. 2nd Internat. Symposium "Cities on the Sea" Nicosia, Cyprus, October 18-22, 1994. ASOR Archaeological Reports 4; Cyprus American Archaeological Research Institute. Monograph Series 1: Atlanta 1998, Scholars viii; 372 pp. $75. 0-7885-0393-6.

492 ᴱWestenholz, Joan M. Good Capital cities: urban planning and spiritual dimensions. Bible Lands Museum J Publ. 2: J 1998, Bible Lands Museum 232 pp. Proc. of the Symposium, May 27-29, 1996, J.

493 ᴱWiesehöfer, Josef Das Partherreich und seine Zeugnisse: the Arsacid Empire: sources and documentation: Beiträge des Internationalen Colloquiums, Eutin (27.-30. Juni 1996). Historia, Einzelschriften 122: Stu 1998, Steiner 570 pp. 3-515-07331-0.

A3.1 *Opera consultationis*—**Reference works** *plurium* infra

494 **LThK³**: Lexikon für Theologie und Kirche 7: Maximilian-Pazzi. FrB 1998, Herder 14 pp; 1540 col. 3-451-22007-5.

495 **RAC**: Reallexikon für Antike und Christentum, 1: Itinerarium-Juden; Juden (Forts.)-Jünger. Stu 1998, Hiersemann 1-160; 161-320 Sp.

496 **RGG⁴**: Religion in Geschichte und Gegenwart: Handwörterbuch für Theologie und Religionswissenschaft, 1 A-B. ᴱBetz, Hans Dieter. Tü 1998, Mohr liv; 1936 pp. DM398.

497 **RLA**: Reallexikon der Assyriologie, 9: Nab-Nanše. ᴱEdzard, D.O.: B 1998, De Gruyter 1-160 pp. Lief. 1/2.

498 **TDOT**: Theological dictionary of the Old Testament, 8: lākad̠-mōr ᴱBotterweck, G. Johannes, al., ᵀStott, Douglas W. 1997, ⇒13,416. ᴿIgreja e Missão 50 (1998) 272-273 (*Couto, A.*).

499 **TDOT**: Theological Dictionary of the Old Testament, 9 mārad-nāqâ ᴱBotterweck, G. Johannes, al., ᵀGreen, David E.. GR 1998, Eerdmans xxvi; 563 pp. $48; £30. 0-8028-2333-5.

500 **ThWAT** 10/5-7: Register/Literaturnachträge. ᴱFabry, Heinz-Josef, al., Stu 1998, Kohlhammer 257-448 pp. DM185. 3-17-015617-9.

501 **TRE** 29: Religionspsychologie-Samaritaner. ᴱKrause, Gerhard; Müller, Gerhard: B 1998, De Gruyter 798 pp. 3-11-016127-3/-013898-4.

502 **TRE**: Literaturangaben. ᴱMüller, Gerhard; Krause, Gerhard: B 1998, De Gruyter 3-11-002218-4. Teilw. mit Gesamttitel: De-Gruyter-Studienbuch; Register zu Band 1-27 erstellt von *Claus-Jürgen Thornton*, 504 pp, 3-11-016088-9.

A3.3 *Opera consultationis* **biblica** *non excerpta infra*—**not subindexed**

503 ^E**Alexander, Pat** Kleines Lexikon zur Bibel. RBtaschenbuch 726: Wu
³1998, Brockhaus 336 pp. 3-417-20726-6.

504 ^E**Balz, Horst; Schneider, Gerhard** Dizionario esegetico del Nuovo
Testamento, 1 1995, ⇒11/2,776; 13,421. ^RRTL 29/1 (1998) 92
(*Focant, C.*); CDios 211 (1998) 647-648 (*Gutiérrez, J.*);

505 Dizionario esegetico del Nuovo Testamento, 2 Kegchreai-ōphelimos.
Brescia 1998, Paideia 2046 col.; 22 pp. 88-394-0522-4 [RB 106,473].

506 ^E**Browning, W.R.F.** Diccionario de la biblia: guía básica sobre los
temas personajes y lugares bíblicos. Barc 1998, Paidós 495 pp.

507 ^E**Collins, John Joseph** The encyclopedia of apocalypticism, 1: The origins of apocalypticism in Judaism and Christianity, 2: apocalypticism
in western history and culture, 3: apocalypticism in the modern period
and the contemporary age. NY 1998, Continuum. 0-8264-1087-1.

508 ^E**Gérard, André Marie** Diccionario de la Biblia. 1996, ⇒12,347
^RCarthaginensia 14 (1998) 213-214 (*Tamayo Acosta, J.J.*).

509 ^E**Gispen, W.H.; Oosterhoff, B.J.; Ridderbos, H.N.** Bijbelse encyclo-
pedie. Kampen ²1998, Kok 755 pp. ƒ80. 90-242-0906-4 [KeTh
50,95—Spijkerboer, A.A.].

510 ^E**Görg, Manfred; Lang, Bernhard** Neues Bibel-Lexikon. Qudschu-
Satan. Solothurn 1998, Benziger DM39.80. 3-545-23063-5.

511 ^E**Hallbäck, Geert; Jensen, Hans Jürgen Lundager** Gads Bibel Lek-
sikon. K ²1998, Gads 2 vols; xv; 453; 469 pp. ^RNTT 99 (1998) 261-
262 (*Seim, Turid Karlsen*).

512 ^E**Kee, Howard Clark** The Cambridge companion to the bible. 1997,
⇒13,429. ^RRBBras 15 (1998) 445-446; HeyJ 39 (1998) 70-71
(*Corley, Jeremy*); ScrB 28 (1998) 43-44 (*Guest, P. Deryn*).

513 **Langley, Myrtle** Das kleine Bibel-Handbuch. Stu 1998, Kath. Bibelwerk 128 pp. 3-460-30464-2.

514 The life and times historical reference bible [KJV]. Milton Keynes
1997, Nelson xviii; 1709 pp. £25. 0-7852-0371-0 [Evangel
18,91—Baxter, Tony].

515 ^E**Luther, Ralf** Neutestamentliches Wörterbuch: eine Einführung in
Sprache und Sinn der urchristlichen Schriften. Metzingen 1998, Franz
297 pp. 3-7722-0269-1 [NThAR 1999,5].

516 ^E**Martin, R.P.; Davids, P.H.** Dictionary of the later New Testament
and its developments. Leicester 1998, IVP 1320 pp. 0-85111-751-1
[Evangel 17,101—Head, Peter M.].

517 ^E**McKim, Donald K.** Historical handbook of major biblical interpreters. DG 1998, IVP xxiii; 643 pp. $30. 0-8308-1452-3.

518 ^E**Metzger, Bruce M.; Coogan, Michael D.** Oxford Companion to the
Bible. 1993, ⇒9,844... 11/2,1113. ^RFrS 55 (1998) 347-349
(*O'Connor, Charles J.*); JAOS 118 (1998) 140-141 (*Cooper, Alan*).

519 **Mistrorigo, Antonio** Guida alfabetica alla bibbia. 1995, ⇒12,354
^RTS(I) sett-ott (1998) 27 (*Cavallaro, Ivano*).

520 ^E**Rienecker, Fritz; Maier, Gerhard** Lexikon zur Bibel [revised]. Wu
1998, Brockhaus viii; 1792 col. (22) pp. 3-417-24678-4.

521 ^E**Ryken, Leland; Wilhoit, James C.; Longman, Tremper III** Dictionary of biblical imagery. DG 1998, InterVarsity xxi; 1058 pp. $34.
0-8308-1451-5.

522 ^E**Selman, Martin J.; Manser, Martín H.** The Macmillan dictionary
of the Bible. Cons. ed. *Travis, Stephen H.* L 1998, Macmillan xx; 210
pp. 0-333-64805-6.

523 [E]**Van der Toorn, Karel; Becking, Bob; Van der Horst, Pieter W.**
Dictionary of deities and demons in the bible. 1995, ⇒11/2,800...
13,435. [R]JAOS 118 (1998) 79-80 (*Sasson, Jack M.*).
524 [E]**Witherup, Ronald D.** The bible companion: a handbook for beginners. NY 1998, Crossroad 264 pp. $10. 0-8245-1746-6.

A3.5 *Opera consultationis* theologica *non excerpta infra*

525 [E]**Cancik, Hubert; Gladigow, Burkhard; Kohl, Karl-Heinz** Handbuch religionswissenschaftlicher Grundbegriffe: Bd. IV: Kultbild-Rolle. Stu 1998, Kohlhammer 476 pp. 3-17-009556-0.
526 [E]**Döpp, Siegmar; Geerlings, Wilhelm** Lexikon der antiken christlichen Literatur. FrB 1998, Herder xvi; 652 pp. DM128. 3-451-23786-5. collab. *Bruns, Peter; Röwekamp, Georg; Skeb, Matthias.*
527 [E]**Esquerda Bifet, Juan** Diccionario de la evangelización. M 1998, BAC 804 pp. [R]Cart. 14 (1998) 474-475 (*Martínez Fresneda, F.*); [R]Ter. 49 (1998) 723-726 (*Pasquetto, Virgilio*).
528 [E]**Hillerbrand, Hans J.** The Oxford encyclopedia of the Reformation. 1996, ⇒12,362. [R]Reformation 3 (1998) 370-373 (*Collinson, Patrick*).
529 [E]**Mathon, G.; Baudry, G.-H.** Catholicisme: Tintoret-Travail; Travail-Union; Union-Vaudelin. P 1997, Letouzey 1-256; 257-512; 513-768 col. Fasc. 69-71.
530 [E]**Pacomio, Luciano; Occhipinti, Giuseppe** Lexicon: dizionario dei teologi. CasM 1998, Piemme 1421 pp. 88-384-3175-2.
531 [E]**Prokurat, Michael; Golitzin, Alexander; Peterson, Michael D.** Historical dictionary of the Orthodox Church. 1996, ⇒12,369. [R]JRH 22 (1998) 225-6 (*Doumanis, Nicholas*).
532 [E]**Reynal, Gérard** Dictionnaire des théologiens et de la théologie chrétienne. P 1998, Bayard 510 pp. FF230. 2-227-35528-X.
533 [E]**Sodi, Manlio; Triacca, Achille M.** Dizionario di omiletica. Pres. *Piovanelli, Card. Silvano*; pref. *Zavoli, Sergio.* Leumann (T) 1998, Elle Di Ci xix; 1708 pp. 88-01-01424-4.

A3.6 *Opera consultationis* generalia

534 [E]**Bearman, P.J.** The encyclopaedia of Islam, new ed./Encyclopédie de l'Islam, Nouvelle éd.: Index of subjects / Index des matières to Volumes/des Tomes I-IX and to the Suppl., Fasc./et du Suppl., Livraisons 1-6. Lei 1998, Brill vii; 297 pp. 90-04-11080-1 [vid. ⇒536, 543].
535 [E]**Becker, Udo** Lexikon der Symbole. Herder 4698: FrB 1998, Herder 352 pp. DM158. 3-451-04698-9.
536 [E]**Bianquis, Th.,** *al.,* Encyclopédie de l'Islam, Nouv. éd., 10: Ṭā'-Ṭā-hirides; Ṭāhirides-Tanẓīmāt; Tanẓīmāt-al-Ṭāsa. Lei 1998, Brill 3-112; 113-224; 225-336 pp. Livr. 163-164; 165-166; 167-168 [vid. ⇒534, 543].
537 [E]**De Grummond, Nancy Thomson** An encyclopedia of the history of classical archaeology. 1996, 2 vols. [R]AJA 104 (2000) 127-128 (*Shipley, Graham*).
538 [E]**Gilman, Sander L.; Zipes, Jack** The Yale companion to Jewish writing and thought in German culture, 1096-1996. 1997, ⇒13,450 [R]JJS 49 (1998) 390-392 (*Albanis, Elisabeth*).

539 ^E**Lurquin, G.** Elsevier's dictionary of Greek and Latin word constituents: Greek and Latin affixes, words and roots used in English, French, German, Dutch, Italian and Spanish. Amst 1998, Elsevier (8) 1192 pp. 0-444-82890-7.

540 ^E**Mey, Jacob L.** Concise encyclopedia of pragmatics. Amst 1998, Elsevier xxviii; 1200 pp. 0-08-04992-0. Consulting editor *R.E. Asher.*

541 ^E**Schoeps, Julius H.** Neues Lexikon des Judentums. Gü 1998, Bertelsmann 896 pp. 3-577-10604-2. Überarb. Neuausg.

542 ^E**Ueding, Gert** Historisches Wörterbuch der Rhetorik, 4: Hu-K. Tü 1998, Niemeyer vi: 790 pp. DM248. 3-484-68104-7.

543 ^E**Van Donzel, E.J.** The Encyclopaedia of Islam, new edition / Encyclopédie de l'Islam, nouvelle édition: index of proper names / index des noms propres to volumes / des tomes I-IX and to the supplement, fascicules/ et du supplément, livraisons 1-6. Lei 1998, Brill (8) 440 pp. 90-04-11082-8 [vid. ⇒534, 536].

544 ^E**Vauchez, André** Dictionnaire encyclopédique du Moyen Âge. 1997, ⇒13,454. ^RAnBoll 116 (1998) 430-432 (*Godding, Robert*).

545 ^E**Vernus, Pascal; Yoyotte, Jean** Dictionnaire des Pharaons. P 1998, Noêsis 226 pp. 2-911606-08-6.

A4.0 Bibliographiae, computers biblicae

546 *Alicki, Wiesław* Internet dla biblisty [Internet pro exegetis]. RBL 51 (1998) 50-57. **P.**

547 *Bader, Winfried* The encoding and interchange format of the text encoding initiative: a format for transmission and communication. Bible et informatique. 1998, ⇒386. Abstract, 389.

548 *Barbaglia, Silvio* Studi biblici e informatica. RStB 10/1-2 (1998) 329-389.

549 Biblica: index generalis vol. 51-75: 1970-1994. R 1997, E.P.I.B. 139 pp. L22.000. 0006-0887.

550 **Brown, Roy B.** Accordance software for biblical studies. Oak Tree Software 1998, Altamonte Springs, FL. Version 3.5; CD-Rom with manual by *Helene Brown.*

551 Bulletin de bibliographie biblique. ^E**Kaestli, Jean Daniel.** Lausanne 1998, Institut des sciences bibliques de l'Université de Lausanne. 3 issues a year.

552 **Clarysse, Willy** Leuven data-base of ancient books (LDAB). Lv 1998. Collab. *France, Jacques, al,* CD-ROM.

553 Early Church Fathers: book collection on CD-ROM. 1997. ^RChH 67 (1998) 558-559 (*O'Donnell, James J.*).

554 Elenchus bibliographicus 1998. EThL 74. ^ELust, J.; Verheyden, J., *al.* Lv 1998, Peeters 724* pp.

555 Era uma vez... 1. O menino Jesus, 1997; 2. a aldeia da música, 1998. 1997-1998, ⇒13,464. ^RBib(L) 7/7 (1998) 180-182 (*Morgado, Lopes*).

556 *Farthing, Geoffrey P.* "Community of error" may or may not mean community of origin: using probability theory to judge relationships accurately. Bible et informatique. 1998, ⇒386. 391-405.

557 *Gabrion, Hervé* Du texte à la lettre, ou de la contribution de l'analyse quantitative à l'art de se pencher sur un faux problème pour deboucher sur une vraie question. Bible et informatique. 1998, ⇒386. 71-80 [ססמך].

558 *Goodacre, Mark* Recent books in...New Testament studies. RRT (1998/1) 71-76.
559 *Guillet, Jacques* Bulletin d'exégèse du Nouveau Testament: évangiles synoptiques et Actes des Apôtres. RSR 86 (1998) 419-446.
560 ᴱHupper, William G. An index to English periodical literature on the Old Testament and ancient Near Eastern studies, 7. ATLA bibliography: Lanham 1998, Scarecrow [SJOT 13,158].
561 IZBG 45: ᴱLang, Bernhard. Dü 1998-1999, Patmos xv; 298 pp.
562 ᴱMaggioni, Bruno La sacra scrittura: documenti ufficiali della chiesa cattolica. Pisa 1996, Cassiopea Ipertesto in CD-ROM. ᴿItin. 6/10 (1998) 327-328 (*Cravotta, Giovanni*).
563 ᴱMills, Watson E. Index to periodical literature on Christ and the gospels. NTTS 27: Lei 1998, Brill xxix; 959 pp. 90-04-10098-9.
564 ᴱNeirynck, Frans; Verheyden, J.; Corstjens, R. The gospel of Matthew and the sayings source Q: a cumulative bibliography 1950-1995. BEThL 140: Lv 1998, Univ. Press 2 vols. FB3.800. 90-6186-933-1.
565 NTAb 42: ᴱHarrington, Daniel J. CM 1998, Weston Jesuit School of Theology 676 pp.
566 NThAR: Tü 1998, Universitätsbibliothek, Theologische Abt. Monthly.
567 OTA 21: ᴱBegg, Christopher T. Wsh 1998, Catholic Biblical Association 614 pp.
568 *Poon, Ronnie S.* A general survey on biblical/theological software. Jian Dao 91 (1998) 229-230. C.
569 ᴱSchwantes, Milton Bibliografia bíblica latino-americana, 8. Petrópolis 1998, Vozes 545 pp [PerTeol 30,472].
570 The Society for Old Testament Study: book list. ᴱGrabbe, Lester L.: JSOT 79 (1998) 1-226.
571 ᴱSussman, Ayala: ESI 18 (1998). 183 + 117 pp. 200+ articles listed in Hebrew + English trans.
572 ThD 45: Book survey. ᴱHeiser, W. Charles. Duluth, MN 1998, Theology Digest. 4 times a year.
573 *Van Gent, Anton; Fahner, Chris* Decoware and translation. Bible et informatique. 1998, ⇒386. 339-342.
574 *Wojciechowski, Micha* Metodologia studiów biblijnych: podstawowe wiadomości bibliograficzne [Zur Methodologie des Bibelstudiums: die bibliographischen Grundangaben]. STV 36/2 (1998) 99-111.
575 ZAW 110: Zeitschriften und Bücherschau. ᴱ*Waschke, Ernst-Joachim; Köckert, Matthias*. B 1998, De Gruyter. 82-158; 259-324; 433-483.
576 ZID: Tü 1998, Universitätsbibliothek, Theologische Abt. Monthly.
577 ZNW 89: ᴱWolter, Michael. B 1998, De Gruyter. 136-143; 289-294.

A4.3 *Bibliographiae diversae*

578 ᴱAnestidou, A.S. <ed> Index to Theol(A):A (1923) - Ξ (1989). Athens 1998. G.
579 ᴱAstigarraga, Juan Luis bis: Bibliographia anni 1997. Ter. 32 (2000) 524 pp.
580 ᴱ*Balconi, Carla, al.*, Bibliografia metodica degli studi di egittologia e di papirologia. Aeg. 78 (1998) 231-325.
581 ᴱBeinlich-Seeber, Christine Bibliographie Altägypten; 1822-1946. ÄA 61: Wsb 1998, Harrassowitz 3 vols. 3-447-03682-6. Teil I: Alphabetisches Verzeichnis A-I; Teil II: Alphabetisches Verzeichnis J-Z; Teil III: Indices.

582 *Betz, Dorothea* , *al.*, Dokumentation neuer Texte. ZAH 11 (1998) 109-124.
583 Bibliografía teológica comentada del área iberoamericana, 1996, no. 24. BA 1998, ISEDET 534 pp [CuMon 34,461—Maciel, M.A.].
584 *Bräker, Antje, al.*, Lexikalisches und grammatisches Material. ZAH 11 (1998) 210-224.
585 *Chappaz, Jean-Luc; Poggia, Sandra* Ressources égyptologiques informatisées 4. BSÉG 22 (1998) 107-136.
586 *Cohen, Nili; Rubeli-Guthauser, Nico* Bibliographie aller ins Deutsche übersetzten Werke der hebräischen Literatur: bis Sommer 1997. Jud. 54 (1998) 77-94.
587 *Domhardt, Yvonne* Auswahlbibliographie von Werken mit jüdisch-judaistischer Thematik, die seit Sommer 1997 bis Redaktionsschluss 1998 in Schweizer Verlagen erschienen sind bzw. durch Inhalt oder Verfasser/in die Schweiz betreffen. Bulletin der Schweizerischen Gesellschaft für Judaistische Forschung 7 (1998) 17-27.
588 *Ego, Beate; Kamlah, Jens; Lange, Armin* Dokumentation neuer Texte. ZAH 11 (1998) 225-232.
589 *Mazza, F.; Ribichini, S.* Bibliografia 26 (1.I.1997-31.XII.1997). RSFen 26 (1998) 247-268.
590 ᴱ**Rothschild, Jean-Pierre; Duval, Frédéric** Bibliographie annuelle du Moyen-Âge tardif: auteurs et textes latins, 8. P 1998, Brepols x; 627 pp. 2-503-50629-1.
591 ᴱ**Rublack, Hans-Christoph** Literaturbericht. ARG.L 27 (1998). 214 pp.
592 ᴱ**Soucek, Vladimír; Siegelová, Jana** Systematische Bibliographie der Hethitologie 1915-1995. HO 1 A: Anc. Near East 38: Lei 1998, Brill 3 vols. $290. 90-04-11205-7. ᴿMes. 33 (1998) 375 (*Lombardi, A.*).
593 ᴱ*Van Wijmen, Leo* Bibliographia carmelitana annualis 1998. Carmelus 46 (2000) 233-448.
594 *Wollmann, Ninette-Eileen* Bibliographie zur kirchlichen Zeitgeschichte. KZG 11 (1998) 411-530. Collab. *Lüder, Andreas.*

II. Introductio

B1.1 *Introductio tota vel VT*—Whole Bible or OT

595 **Ackermann, Sonja** Christliche Apologetik und heidnische Philosophie im Streit um das Alte Testament. SBB 36: 1997, ⇒13,494. ᴿBZ 42 (1998) 299-300 (*Lang, Bernhard*).
596 **Akenson, Donald Harman** Surpassing wonder: the invention of the bible and the talmuds. NY 1998, Harcourt, Brace xi; 658 pp. $40. 0-15-100418-8.
597 **Ardusso, Franco** Perché la bibbia è la parola di Dio: canone—ispirazione—ermeneutica—metodi di lettura. Cultura e fede—dogmatica 17: CinB 1998, San Paolo 112 pp. 88-215-3884-2.
598 **Bandstra, Barry L.** Reading the Old Testament: an introduction to the Hebrew Bible. 1995, ⇒11/2,1080. ᴿOTEs 11/1 (1998) 195-6 (*Spangenberg, Izak J.J.*).
599 **Barberá, Carlos,** *al.*, Ver, oír, gustar y tocar a Dios. 1996, ⇒12,416. ᴿSan Juan de la Cruz 21 (1998) 131-132 (*Nicolás, Flori de*).

600 **Benetti, Santos** La bibbia tematica: Antico Testamento. 1996, ⇒12,418; 13,503. ^RRTL 29 (1998) 373-375 (*Wénin, A.*); CivCatt 149/2 (1998) 192-194 (*Scaiola, D.*).

601 **Bensoussan, David** La bible prise au berceau, 1: période de gestation: le contexte culturel de la bible; 2: naissance: d'Abraham à Moïse; 3: —volution: saisir la bible. Montréal 1998, du Lys xxviii; 390 + xxvi; 311 + xxvii; 297 pp. 2-922505-01-4; -2-2; -3-0 [NThAR 2000,184].

602 *Della Rocca* Identità e alterità nel pensiero ebraico. Hum(B) 53 (1998) 653-658.

603 **Devijver, J.** Vingerafdrukken van God: bijbelverhalen eigentijds herlezen. Averbode 1998, Altiora 117 pp.

604 ^E**Fabris, R.** Introduzione generale alla Bibbia. Logos 1: 1994, ⇒10,722... 13,520. ^RCarthaginensia 14 (1998) 216-217 (*Sanz Valdivieso, R.*).

605 **Gillingham, Susan E.** One bible, many voices: different approaches to biblical studies. L 1998, SPCK xx; 280 pp. £16. 0-281-04886-X.

606 **Gomes, Peter J.** The good book. 1996, ⇒12,442. ^RBiRe 14/1 (1998) 10, 12 (*Holbert, John C.*).

607 **Hauer, Christian E.; Young, William A.** An introduction to the bible: a journey into three worlds. Upper Saddle River 1998, Prentice Hall 404 pp. $33.40.

608 *Hoet, Hendrik* Lezers inleiden in de bijbel. ITBT 6/1 (1998) 11-12.

609 **Kaiser, Otto** Grundriß der Einleitung in die kanonischen und deuterokanonischen Schriften des Alten Testaments. Die poetischen und weisheitlichen Werke. 1994, ⇒10,735... 13,536. ^RJBL 117 (1998) 111-112 (*Morgan, Donn F.*).

610 **Kissling, Paul J.** Reliable characters in the primary history: profiles of Moses, Joshua, Elijah and Elisha. JSOT.S 224: 1996, ⇒12,451; 13,538. ^RBBR 8 (1998) 239-240 (*Hess, Richard S.*); JBL 117 (1998) 114-116 (*Gladson, Jerry A.*).

611 **Kugel, James L.** Traditions of the bible: a guide to the bible as it was at the start of the common era. CM 1998, Harvard Univ. Press xx; 1055 pp. $75. 0-674-79151-7.

612 **Maeijer, Floor** Beeldige teksten; een bijbels ABC van symbolen. 1997, ⇒13,542. ^RInterpretatie 6/3 (1998) 33 (*Sondorp, Otto*).

613 **Maldamé, Jean-Michel** Un livre inspiré, la bible: le livre où Dieu se dit. Initiations: P 1998, Cerf 142 pp. FF80. 2-204-06023-2.

614 **Mason, Rex** Propaganda and subversion in the Old Testament. 1997, ⇒13,548. ^RRRT (1998/1) 57-59 (*Moberly, Walter*).

615 **Miquel, Pierre; Egron, Agnès; Picard, Paula** Les mots-clés de la Bible: révélation à Israël. Classiques Bibliques: P 1996, Beauchesne 347 pp. ^RLTP 54/1 (1998) 205-206 (*Guindon, Henri-M.*).

616 **Monforte, Josemaría** Conhecer a bíblia: iniciação à sagrada escritura. Lisboa 1998, Diel 236 pp. 972-8040-29-6.

617 **Moyise, Steve** Introduction to biblical studies. Cassell Biblical Studies: Herndon, Virginia 1998, Cassell 113 pp. $16. 0-304-70091-6.

618 *Pathrapankal, Joseph* Little traditions in the bible and their significance for the biblical religion. JDh 23 (1998) 39-56.

619 **Salibi, Kamal** The bible came from Arabia. 1996, ⇒12,471. ^RThRev 19 (1998) 134-159 (*Gangloff, Frédéric*).

620 *Seidl, Th.* Neues vom Alten Testament: Ergebnisse und Konsequenzen der jüngsten Forschung. ThG 41 (1998) 82-91.

621 **Simms, George Otto** Exploring the bible. 1996, ⇒12,475. ^RMilltown Studies 42 (1998) 166-167 (*Byrne, Patrick*).

622 **Stendebach, Franz J.** Introduzione all'Antico Testamento. GdT 251: Queriniana 1996, Brescia 424 pp. L55.000. [R]RdT 39 (1998) 136-138 (*Bretón, Santiago*).

623 **Struppe, Ursula; Kirchschläger, Walter** Einführung in das Alte und Neue Testament. Stu 1998, Kath. Bibelwerk 133 + 152 pp. 3-460-33035-X.

624 **Tábet, Michelangelo** Introduzione generale alla Bibbia. Abside 13: CinB 1998, San Paolo 416 pp. 88-215-3570-3.

625 Vademecum per il lettore della Bibbia. 1996, ⇒12,420. [R]FilTeo 12 (1998) 436-437 (*Cammarota, Gian Paolo*).

626 **VanBuren, Paul M.** According to the scriptures: the origins of the gospel and of the church's Old Testament. GR 1998, Eerdmans ix; 147 pp. $16. 0-8028-4535-5.

627 **Vaux, Roland de** Ancient Israel: its life and institutions. 1997 <1961>, ⇒13,561. [R]OTEs 11/1 (1998) 198-9 (*Hamman, Trevor*).

628 **Weber, Hans-Ruedi** Biblia: o livro que me lê: manual para estudos bíblicos. São Leopoldo 1998, Sinodal 91 pp. 85-233-0514-9.

629 **White, Ellen Gould (Harmon)** Patriarchi e profeti. Impruneta—FI 1998 <1915>, ADV 671 pp. 88-7659-084-6.

630 **Zenger, Erich** Einleitung in das Alte Testament. Studienbücher Theologie I 1: 1995, ⇒11/2,1147... 13,564. [R]ThPh 73 (1998) 90-95 (*Lohfink, Norbert*);

631 *al*., Einleitung in das Alte Testament. KStTh 1,1: Stu ³1998, Kohlhammer 548 pp. 3-17-015622-5;

632 Il primo Testamento: la Bibbia ebraica e i cristiani. 1997, ⇒13,567 [R]CrSt 19 (1998) 367-370 (*Cova, Gian Domenico*); Asp. 45 (1998) 587-595 (*Ascione, Antonio*); RdT 39 (1998) 451-454 (*Franco, Ettore*).

B1.2 'Invitations' to Bible or OT

633 **Bottigheimer, Ruth B.** The bible for children: from the age of Gutenberg to the present. 1996, ⇒12,495. [R]ChH 67/1 (1998) 209-210 (*Jodock, Darrell*).

634 **Brown, Schuyler** Text and psyche: experiencing scripture today. NY 1998, Continuum 141 pp. $19. 0-8264-1111-8.

635 **Brueggemann, Walter** The bible and postmodern imagination: texts under negotiation. 1993, ⇒9,867... 12,497 [RF]Wright D. (1998) 181-204 (Hart, Trevor A.).

636 **Buzzetti, Carlo** Bibbia per noi: leggere, attualizzare, comunicare. Guide per la prassi ecclesiale 18: Brescia 1997, Queriniana 156 pp. L16.000.

637 **Cahill, Thomas** The gifts of the Jews: how a tribe of desert nomads changed the way everyone thinks and feels. The hinges of history 2: NY 1998, Doubleday xii; 291 pp. $23.50. 0-3854-8248-5. [R]CrossCur 48 (1998) 568-569 (*Schiff, Shelley*).

638 **Davis, Kenneth C.** Don't know much about the bible. NY 1998, Eagle Brook 533 pp. $25. 0-688-14884-0.

639 **Di Berardino, Pedro Paulo** A 'lectio divina'. Espiritualidade: São Paulo 1998, Paulus 132 pp. 85-349-1092-8.

640 **Ferlo, Roger** Opening the Bible. 1997, ⇒13,586. [R]AThR 80/1 (1998) 140-144 (*Hawkins, Peter S.*).

641 *Gallagher, Michael Paul* The bible and post-christian culture. Month 31 (1998) 463-467.
642 **Getty-Sullivan, Mary Ann** God speaks to us in dreams and visions. ColMn 1998, Liturgical 63 pp. $18.
643 **Gilles-Sabaoun, Élisabeth** Mi primera biblia. M 1998, SM 93 pp. 84-348-6159-3.
644 *Kaiser, Otto* Die Bedeutung des Alten Testaments für Heiden, die manchmal auch Christen sind. Gesammelte Aufsätze. BZAW 261: 1998 <1994>, 282-290.
645 *Lambert, Pierre* Ouvrir la bible?: Dieu nous parle dans le Christ. VS 726 (1998) 53-54.
646 **McIlwain, Trevor** Auf festen Grund gebaut: in 50 Lektionen durch die Bibel. Neuhausen 1998, Hänssler DM60. [R]em 14 (1998) 152-153 (*Müller, Klaus W.*).
647 **Rogerson, John William** Beginning Old Testament study. L [2]1998 <1983>, SPCK xii; 164 pp. £10. 0-281-05103-8. [R]RRT (1998/4) 17-19 (*O'Kane, Martin*).
648 **Shoemaker, H. Stephen** GodStories: new narratives from sacred texts. Valley Forge 1998, Judson xxvi; 322 pp. $16. 0-8170-1265-6.
649 [E]**Tabuyo Ortega, María** La Biblia: contada a todas las gentes. M 1998, Anaya 414 pp. 84-207-8291-2. [R]SalTer 86 (1998) 765-767 (*Tabuyo, María*).
650 **Van Pelt, Bara; Fluiter, Anja A. de** Om te beginnen: bijbel voor jonge kinderen. Hilversum 1998, NZV 248 pp. ƒ44.50. 90-6986-203-4. [R]Interpretatie 6/7 (1998) 32-33 (*Huyzer, Richart*).
651 [E]**Zenger, Erich** Lebendige Welt der Bibel: Entdeckungsreise in das Alte Testament. 1997, ⇒13,565. [R]BiLi 71 (1998) 372-373 (*Stiglmayr, Arnold*).

B1.3 *Pedagogia biblica*—Bible-teaching techniques

652 *Ambichl, Katharina* Schüler als Dolmetscher der Heiligen Schrift?! CPB 111 (1998) 16-17.
653 *Armellada, Bernardino de* En pocas palabras: creo en la vida. EvV 40/2 (1998) 51-53.
654 *Bee-Schroedter, Heike* Neue Literatur zur Bibel für Kinder und Jugendliche. Diak. 29 (1998) 354-358.
655 *Birkner, Ralf* Bibelschule am Niederrhein. Lebendige Katechese 20 (1998) 58-60.
656 Een boodschap aan mensen: handboek voor kerkelijke communicatie. Gorinchem 1998, Narratio 376 pp. ƒ47.50. 90-5263-905-1. [R]ITBT 6/8 (1998) 34 (*Schelling, Piet*).
657 **Bortolini, José** La biblia: preguntas con respuesta: 160 cuestiones acerca de la escritura. Dabar 12: M 1998, San Pablo 342 pp. 84-285-2111-5.
658 *Büchner, Frauke* "Wenn du weißt, was du tust, bist du gesegnet!"—Schabbatfeiern im christlichen Religionsunterricht? EvErz 50 (1998) 354-386.
659 *Bühler, Clemens* Sasbacher Bibelschule am Geistlichen Zentrum Sasbach. Lebendige Katechese 20 (1998) 53-55.
660 **Chatelion Counet, P.** Over God zwijgen: postmodern bijbellesen. Wendingpublicatie: Zoetermeer 1998, Meinema 271 pp. ƒ40.

661 ^E**Ciccarese, Maria Pia** La letteratura cristiana antica nell'università italiana: il dibattito e l'insegnamento. Letture patristiche 5: F 1998, Nardini 279 pp. 88-10-42040-3.

662 *Dillmann, Rainer* Handlungsorientierte Bibelauslegung. Lebendige Katechese 20 (1998) 64-67.

663 *Dugandzic, Ivan* (Ne)zainteresiranost mladezi za Bibliju. BoSm 68 (1998) 33-46. **Croatian**.

664 **Eschenweck, Martina** 'Was wir hörten und erfuhren': Freisinger Bibelintensiv-Kurs: religionspädagogische Reflexionen über einen Entwurf von Bibelarbeit mit Erwachsenen. Diss. München 1996-1997; ^D*Schulz, E.* [ThRv 94,xv].

665 *Frauscher, Georg* "Biblische Phantasiereisen". CPB 111 (1998) 103-105.

666 *Gollinger, Hildegard* Wenn Kinder die Bibel nur noch im Religionsunterricht kennlernen—was wissen sie dann?. Lebendige Katechese 20 (1998) 40-44.

667 *Hecht, Anneliese* Methoden der Bibelarbeit. Lebendige Katechese 20 (1998) 34-40.

668 ^E**Hess, Richard S.; Wenham, Gordon H.** Make the Old Testament live: from curriculum to classroom. GR 1998, Eerdmans x; 218 pp. [ScrB 29,96ss—Norton, Gerard J.].

669 *Hirschi, Hans* Auferstehung als religionspädagogische Herausforderung. ^FVenetz, H. 1998, ⇒122. 101-107.

670 *Huscava, Ewald* Bibeltext—Imagination—Predigtereignis. Lebendige Katechese 20 (1998) 60-63.

671 **Johannsen, Friedrich** Alttestamentliches Arbeitsbuch für Religionspädagogen. UB 468: Stu 1998, Kohlhammer 311 pp. 3-17-015260-2 [NThAR 1999,3].

672 *Koerrenz, Ralf* Das hebräische Paradigma der Pädagogik. EvErz 50 (1998) 331-342.

673 *Mazzola, Rudolf* "Bibel-Teilen" Lebendige Katechese 20 (1998) 46-49.

674 **Melchert, Charles F.** Wise teaching: biblical wisdom and educational ministry. Harrisburg, Pennsylvania 1998, Trinity xi; 323 pp. 1-56338-139-7.

675 **Mora, Cesar** Nuevas formas de leer la biblia: animación bíblica de la pastoral en cinco fichas. México 1998, Paulinas 160 pp. [EfMex 17,419—Serraima Cirici, Enrique].

676 ^E**Most, Glenn W.** Editing Texts; Texte edieren. Aporemata 2: Gö 1998, Vandenhoeck & R xvi; 268 pp. 3-525-25901-8.

677 *Neubrand, Maria* Die Bibel entdecken: Lernen in der Bibelschule in Istanbul. Lebendige Katechese 20 (1998) 56-57.

678 **Oberthür, Rainer** Kinder fragen nach Leid und Gott: lernen mit der Bibel im Religionsunterricht: ein Praxisbuch. Mü 1998, Kösel 214 pp. DM34. Coll. *Mayer, A.* [Orientamenti pedagogici 46,954—Bissoli, C.].

679 *Pompey, Heinrich* Mit der Bibel die christliche Inspiration der caritativen Sozialarbeit entdecken. Lebendige Katechese 20 (1998) 71-78.

680 **Rechenmacher-Grünfelder**, Dorothea Weggeschichten des Alten Testaments: symboldidaktische Lernprozesse in der Bibelarbeit mit Erwachsenen und in der Schule. Diss. Wien; 1996-1997; ^D*Langer, W.* [ThRv 94,xix].

681 **Richards, Lawrence O.; Bredfeldt, Gary J.** Creative bible teaching. Ch ²1998, Moody 342 pp. 0-8024-1644-6. Bibl. [NThAR 2000,183].

682 *Ritter, Hermann* Bibel-teilen beim Freiburger Diözesanforum 1991/92. Lebendige Katechese 20 (1998) 49-52.

683 *Rottenwöhrer, Gerhard* Lernen—der Zugang zum Evangelium. MThZ 49 (1998) 33-37.
684 [E]**Segovia, Fernando F.; Tolbert, Mary Ann** Teaching the bible: the discourses and politics of biblical pedagogy. Mkn 1998, Orbis xi; 372 pp. $28. 1-57075-202-8 [ThD 46,291—Heiser, W. Charles].
685 *Seibold, Jorge R.* La Sagrada Escritura en la evangelización del Brasil: en los centenarios del Beato JOSÉ de Anchieta (1534-1597) y del P. Antonio VIEIRA (1608-1697). Strom. 54 (1998) 187-238.
686 *Seitz, Christopher* The changing face of Old Testament studies. Word without end. 1998 [1992], ⇒200. 75-82.
687 *Steiner, Josef* Was wollen wir mit der Bibel in der Gemeindekatechese. Lebendige Katechese 20 (1998) 44-46.
688 *Torres Millan, Fernando* Aprender la palabra: una aproximación pedagógica a la lectura comunitaria de la biblia. Alternativas 5 (1998) 11-12.
689 **Welzen, H.** 'Maak mijn ogen nieuw': (Ps 119,18). Teksten ten dienste van het leiden en spelen van bibliodrama 2: Zeist 1997, Pastoraal Centrum Utrecht 84 pp. 90-75416-02-4 [NThAR 2000,309].
690 *Wieland, Wolfgang* Kommentierter Überblick über Arbeitshilfen für die Bibelarbeit. Lebendige Katechese 20 (1998) 81-87.
691 **Zbigniew, Marek** Biblia w katechetycznej posłudze słowa. Wsz 1998, Salezjańskie 229 pp. **P.**

B2.1 Hermeneutica

692 *Agurides, Sabbas C.* The orthodox church and contemporary biblical research. DBM 17 (1998) 109-128.
693 **Alonso Schökel, Luis; Bravo Aragón, José María** A manual of hermeneutics. BiSe 54: Shf 1998, Academic 181 pp. 1-85075-850-6.
694 *Bach, Alice* On the road between Birmingham and Jerusalem. Semeia 82 (1998) 297-305.
695 *Bailey, Randall C.* The danger of ignoring one's own cultural bias in interpreting the text. The postcolonial bible. [E]**Sugirtharajah, R.S.** The Bible and Postcolonialism 1: Shf 1998, Academic 204 pp. £13. 1-85075-898-0. 66-90.
696 [E]**Baldermann, I.,** *al.,* Biblische Hermeneutik. Jahrbuch für biblische Theologie 12: Neuk 1998, Neuk viii; 419 pp. DM78. 3-7887-1642-8.
697 *Bardski, Krzystof* Patrystyczna interpretacja Pisma Świętego a współczesna biblistyka [Patristic interpretation of Scripture and modern biblical studies. Methodological suggestions]. WST 10 (1998) 117-123.
698 *Bartholomew, Craig* Reading the Old Testament in postmodern times. TynB 49 (1998) 91-114.
699 [E]**Barton, John** The Cambridge companion to biblical interpretation. Cambridge companion to religion: C 1998, CUP xv; 338 pp. £37.50/14. 0-521-48144-9.
700 *Bendel-Maidl, Lydia* Denken—Lesen—Beten: Interpretation—Teilnehmen des Menschen an der Kunst Gottes. ThGl 88 (1998) 78-94.
701 *Bennahmias, Richard* Postmodernité pragmatisme et théologie chrétienne évangélique. RHPhR 78 (1998) 57-77.
702 Berg, Horst Klaus "Laßt viele Funken sprühen ...!": über die Notwendigkeit und Chancen einer mehrdimensionalen Schriftauslegung. Lebendige Katechese 20 (1998) 1-6.

703 *Betz, Hans Dieter* Antiquity and christianity. JBL 117 (1998) 3-22.
704 Biblische Hermeneutik. JBTh 12: Neuk 1998, Neuk viii; 424 pp. 3-7887-1642-8.
705 *Black, C. Clifton* Serving the food of full-grown adults. Interp. 52 (1998) 341-353.
706 *Black, Fiona C.* Lost prophecies!: scholars amazed!: Weekly World News and the bible. Semeia 82 (1998) 127-149.
707 *Bockmuehl, Markus* 'To be or not to be': the possible futures of New Testament scholarship. SJTh 51 (1998) 271-306.
708 *Boer, Roland* King Solomon meets Annie Sprinkle. Semeia 82 (1998) 151-182;
709 Remembering Babylon: postcolonialism and Australian biblical studies. The postcolonial bible ⇒695. 24-48;
710 Western Marxism and the interpretation of the Hebrew Bible. JSOT 78 (1998) 3-21.
711 *Borgonovo, Gianantonio* Tôrah, testimonianza e scrittura: per un'ermeneutica teologica del testo biblico. ᶠMartini C., Rivelazione. 283-318.
712 *Botha, J.E.* Reading ancient texts more comprehensively: assessing a new methodology. Scriptura 64 (1998) 51-63.
713 *Botha, J. Eugene* A South African response to the postmodern bible—a time to break down or a time to build up?. Neotest. 32 (1998) 1-36.
714 *Brakke, David* Cultural Studies: ein neues Paradigma us-amerikanischer Exegese. ZNT 2 (1998) 69-77.
715 *Brett, Mark G.* Biblical studies and theology: negotiating the intersections. Biblical Interpretation 6 (1998) 131-141.
716 *Broadbent, Ralph* Ideology, culture, and British New Testament studies: the challenge of cultural studies. Semeia 82 (1998) 33-61.
717 *Brunini, Marcello* Cristo parola: riferimenti teologici e spirituali della 'lectio divina'. RCI 79 (1998) 745-763.
718 *Burgess, John P.* Scripture as sacramental word: rediscovering scripture's compelling power. Interp. 52 (1998) 380-391.
719 **Burgess, John P.** Why scripture matters: reading the bible in a time of church conflict. LVL 1998, Westminster xviii; 186 pp. $20. 0-664-25708-9.
720 **Buzzetti, Carlo** 4 x 1 um único trecho bíblico e vários "fazeres": guia prático de hermenêutica e pastoral bíblica. Estudos Bíblicos: [São Paulo] 1998, Paulinas 300 pp. 85-7311-951-9.
721 **Callow, Kathleen** Man and message: a guide to meaning-based text analysis. Lanham 1998, University Press of America xvi; 383 pp. 0-7618-1127-3.
722 **Carpenter, Joel A.** Revive us again: the reawakening of American fundamentalism. 1997, ⇒13,659. ᴿTS 59 (1998) 339-341 (*Fackre, Gabriel*).
723 **Casey, Michael W.** The battle over hermeneutics in the STONE-CAMPBELL movement, 1800-1870. Studies in American religion 67: Lewiston 1998, Mellen xii; 302 pp. $100.
724 *Chmiel, Jerzy* The visual interpretation of the bible: an outline. FolOr 34 (1998) 31-34.
725 *Chopineau, Jacques* Les mots et la parole: simples questions aux exégètes qui sont aussi des théologiens. Analecta Bruxellensia 3 (1998) 7-20.
726 Clines, David J.A. Methods in Old Testament study <1982>;

727 Possibilities and priorities of biblical interpretation in an international perspective <1993>;

728 Beyond synchronic/diachronic <1995>;

729 Varieties of indeterminacy <1995>. OT essays, 1. JSOT.S 292: 1998 ⇒142. 23-45/46-67/68-87/126-137;

730 The postmodern adventure in biblical studies. Auguries. JSOT.S 269: 1998 ⇒225. 276-291;

731 The pyramid and the net: the postmodern adventure in biblical studies. OT essays, 1. JSOT.S 292: 1998 ⇒142. 138-157.

732 *Croatto, J. Severino* Las nuevas hermenéuticas de la lectura bíblica: una mirada exegética: un ejercicio de hermenéutica bíblica sobre el bautismo. Alternativas 5 (1998) 15-36.

733 *Culpepper, R. Alan* Mapping the textures of New Testament criticism: a response to socio-rhetorical criticism. JSNT 70 (1998) 71-77.

734 *Daniélou, Jean* Herméneutique judéo-chrétienne. Bulletin des amis du Cardinal Daniélou (1998) <1963> 38-45.

735 **Davies, Philip R.** Whose bible is it anyway?. JSOT.S 204: 1995, ⇒13,672. ᴿJBL 117 (1998) 116-117 (*Patrick, Dale*).

736 *Dean, Margaret E.* Textured criticism. JSNT 70 (1998) 79-91.

737 *Del Agua, Agustín* Interpretación del Nuevo Testamento y métodos. EE 73 (1998) 3-42.

738 *Delorme, Jean* Orientations of a literary semiotics questioned by the bible. Semeia 81 (1998) 27-61.

739 *Di Sante, Carmine* L'inculturazione nella bibbia: riflessione teologica. RdT 39 (1998) 191-206.

740 **Dohmen, Christoph** Die Bibel und ihre Auslegung. Mü 1998, Beck 114 pp. DM14.80. 3-406-43299-9.

741 **Dohmen, Christoph; Stemberger, Günter** Hermeneutik der jüdischen Bibel und des Alten Testaments. KStTh 1, no. 2: 1996, ⇒12,604; 13,677. ᴿThLZ 123/4 (1998) 363-364 (*Ebach, Jürgen*).

742 *Donaldson, Laura E.* Are we all multiculturalists now?: biblical reading as cultural contact. Semeia 82 (1998) 79-97.

743 *Dowsett, Andrew C.* Cuts. Semeia 82 (1998) 247-280.

744 **Eden, Kathy** Hermeneutics and the rhetorical tradition: chapters in the ancient legacy and its humanist reception. 1997, ⇒13,679. ᴿRhetorica 16 (1998) 230-231 (*Miller, Richard A.*); SCJ 29 (1998) 1225-1227 (*Pender, Stephen*).

745 **Ewert, David** Verstehst du, was du liest?: Grundzüge einer biblischen Hermeneutik. Bornheim 1998, Puls 159 pp. 3-933398-03-7.

746 *Fabris, Rinaldo* Introduzione alla XXXIV settimana biblica: bibbia e cultura: storia dell'ermeneutica. RstB 10/1-2 (1998) 5-23.

747 **Fiedrowicz, Michael** Principes de l'interprétation de l'écriture dans l'église ancienne. Traditio christiana 10: Bern 1998, Lang xli; 203 pp. 3-906760-72-3.

748 *Fornberg, Tord* Kirishitan—ett ofrivilligt experiment i religiös inkulturering. SEÅ 63 (1998) 273-280.

749 ᴱ**Fowl, Stephen E.** The theological interpretation of scripture: classic and contemporary readings. 1997, ⇒13,244. ᴿJR 78 (1998) 447-449 (*Thiselton, Anthony C.*);

750 Engaging scripture: a model for theological interpretation. Challenges in contemporary theology: Oxf 1998, Blackwell vii; 219 pp. £50/£16. 0-631-20863-1/4-X.

751 *Fraade, Steven D.* Scripture, Targum, and Talmud as instruction: a complex textual story from the Sifra. [F]FRERICHS, E. BJSt 320: 1998 ⇒28. 109-122.

752 *Franco, Francesco* La verità metaforica: una prospettiva su Paul RICOEUR. StPat 45 (1998) 69-88.

753 *Fuente, Alfonso de la* Interpretación de la biblia y signos de los tiempos. RET 58 (1998) 105-116.

754 **Gadamer, Hans-Georg** La philosophie herméneutique. Epimethée: P 1996, PUF 264 pp. €30,18. 2-13-04-7344-X. [R]RTL 29 (1998) 367-369 *(Brito, Emilio)*.

755 *Gallazzi, Sandro* Nuevas hermenéuticas, nuevas sujetos, nuevas utopías. Alternativas 5 (1998) 37-59.

756 *Gilbert, Maurice* L'herméneutique biblique de LÉON XIII (1893) à PIE XII (1943). Il a parlé par les prophètes. 1998 <1994>, ⇒155. 29-53.

757 *Glancy, Jennifer A.* Text appeal: visual pleasure and biblical studies. Semeia 82 (1998) 63-78.

758 **Goldingay, John** Models for interpretation of Scripture. 1995, ⇒11/2,1298; 13,692. [R]EvQ 70 (1998) 88-90 *(Lucas, Ernest C.)*.

759 *Göllner, Reinhard* Was heißt existentielle Bibelauslegung?. Lebendige Katechese 20 (1998) 6-11.

760 [E]**Green, Joel B.** Hearing the New Testament: strategies for interpretation. 1995, ⇒11/2,372; 13,694. [R]EvQ 70 (1998) 84-85 *(Oakes, Peter)*.

761 *Griffiths, Richard* Mrs. Thatcher's bible. Semeia 82 (1998) 99-125.

762 *Grogan, Geoffrey* Is the bible hermeneutically self-sufficient? [F]WRIGHT D., 1998 ⇒126. 205-221.

763 *Harden Weaver, Rebecca* Access to scripture: experiencing the text. Interp. 52 (1998) 367-379.

764 *Hegele, Günter* Theologische Ansätze und andere Perspektiven für das Verständnis der Bibel in Stichworten. Evangelische Aspekte 8 (1998) 20-21.

765 [E]**Hempelmann, Heinzpeter** Grundfragen der Schriftauslegung: ein Arbeitsbuch. TVGMS 311; Bibelwissenschaftliche Monographie 2: Wu 1998, Brockhaus 153 pp. 3-417-29311-1.

766 *Hoeres, Walter* Das verratene Licht—unsere irregeleiteten Hermes-Jünger. Theologisches 28 (1998) 333-338.

767 **Hoffer, Victoria Kornbluth** A few bad men: their contribution to understanding the processes of biblical interpretation. [D]Yale 1998, 509 pp.

768 *Holter, Knut* It's not only a question of money!: African Old Testament scholarship between the myths and meanings of the South and the money and methods of the North. OTEs 11 (1998) 240-254.

769 *Horsley, Richard A.* Submerged biblical histories and imperial biblical studies. The postcolonial bible. 1998, ⇒695. 152-173.

770 *Jastrzembski, Volker* Das Alte Testament nach dem Holocaust: hermeneutische Überlegungen im Anschluß an eine Studienwoche [F]MARQUARDT, F.-W.. 1998 ⇒72. 173-180.

771 *Jecker, Urs* "Zerstört mir mit Eurem Gott nicht meine Sprache!": ein Plädoyer für bewußteres theologisches Reden. [F]VENETZ, H.. 1998 ⇒122. 257-264.

772 *Jensen, Robin M.* Giving texts vision and images voice: the promise and problems of interdisciplinary scholarship. [F]SNYDER, G.. 1998 ⇒104. 344-356.

773 *Johnson, Luke Timothy* Imagining the world scripture imagines. MoTh 14 (1998) 165-180.

774 **Johnston, Michael** Engaging the word. New Church's Teaching 3: CM 1998, Cowley xii; 181 pp. $12. 1-56101-146-0.

775 *Kahl, Werner* Falls Du verstehst, was ich meine: Paradigmenwechsel in der Exegese als Ausdruck und Voraussetzung einer ökumenischen Lektüre- und Lebensgemeischaft. Jahrbuch für kontextuelle Theologien 98 (1998) 155-166.

776 *Kalluveettil, Pul* Hermeneutics of liturgical traditions—biblical foundations. Tanima 7 (1998) 126-143.

777 *Karabidopulos, Ioannes D.* New directions in biblical hermeneutics. DBM 17 (1998) 48-62.

778 *Kärkkäinen, Veli-Matti* 'Reading in the Spirit in which it was written': Pentecostal bible reading in dialogue with catholic interpretation. OiC 34 (1998) 337-359.

779 *Klimek, Piotr* Izraelski sposób myślenia a lektura Pisma Świętego [The Hebrews' thinking mode and the reading of Holy Scripture]. WST 10 (1998) 109-116.

780 *Klopper, Frances* Oor 'n hermeneutiek van religieuse simbole. OTEs 11 (1998) 462-476.

781 **Konrad, Werner** Schreiben, Lesen—Reden, Hören: Hermeneutik im Spannungsfeld von Exegese und Homiletik. Diss. Regensburg 1996-1997, ᴰ*Schmuttermayr, G.* [ThRv 94,xviii].

782 *Krämer, Michael* Der Sinn der Heiligen Schrift und der mühsame Weg der Bibelwissenschaft, ihn historisch-kritisch zu erfassen. ꜰHERIBAN J.. 1998 ⇒41. 149-180.

783 *Kriener, Tobias* Gott einen Raum frei halten: Bemerkungen zur Aktualität des reformatorischen Grundsatzes sola scriptura. ꜰSCHRAGE, W.. 1998 ⇒101. 25-32.

784 *Kwok, Pui-lan* On color-coding Jesus: an interview with Kwok Pui-lan. The postcolonial bible. 1998 ⇒695. 176-188.

785 *Levine, Michael* God speak. RelSt 34 (1998) 1-16.

786 ᴱ**Lundin, Roger** Disciplining hermeneutics: interpretation in christian perspective. 1997, ⇒13,214. ᴿJSNT 71 (1998) 127-128 (*Pearson, Brook W.R.*).

787 *Luz, Ulrich* Kann die Bibel heute noch Grundlage für die Kirche sein?: über die Aufgabe der Exegese in einer religiös-pluralistischen Gesellschaft. NTS 44 (1998) 317-339.

788 *Marcos, Isabel* Le trajet de pèlerinage au couvent de Sao José de Ribamar. SémBib 90 (1998) 43-62.

789 *Martin, François* Lecture et traduction de la bible: la référence au texte original. SémBib 89 (1998) 3-18.

790 *Merlos A., Francisco* La palabra humana de cara a la Palabra de Dios. Qol 18 (1998) 13-20.

791 *Milano, Andrea* Teologia cristiana e ragione ermeneutica. StPat 45 (1998) 769-793.

792 *Moore, Steven D.* Between Birmingham and Jerusalem: cultural studies and biblical studies. Semeia 82 (1998) 1-32.

793 **Mostert, Walter** Glaube und Hermeneutik: gesammelte Aufsätze ᴱ**Bühler, Pierre; Ebeling, Gerhard**: Tü 1998, Mohr vi; 287 pp. DM148. 3-16-146967-4 [ThRv 95,490—Wenz, Gunther].

794 *Mukai, Takafumi* God is hidden behind the text: a proposal for biblical interpretation. Kwansei-Gakuin-Daigaku 3 (1998) 1-14.

795 *Murphy, Roland E.* The christian and the Old Testament. BiTod 36 (1998) 41-46.

796 *Müller, Hans-Peter* Albert SCHWEITZER und Rudolf BULTMANN: theologische Paradigmen unter der Herausforderung durch den Säkularismus. Glauben, Denken und Hoffen: alttestamentliche Botschaften in den Auseinandersetzungen unserer Zeit. **Müller, Hans-Peter**: Altes Testament und Moderne 1: Müns 1998, Lit 319 pp. 3-8258-3331-3. 263-285.

797 *Myers, Ched* Neither authoritarian nor diffident: conversing about biblical differences. Uniting Church studies 4 (1998) 17-29.

798 *Navia Velasco, Carmiña* Propuestas para una hermenéutica urabana. Alternativas 5 (1998) 203-211.

799 ᵀ**Neri, Umberto** FLACIO ILLIRICO: comprendere le scritture. Epifania della parola 10; Testi ermeneutici 5: Bo 1998, Dehoniane 80 pp. L18.000. 88-10-40233-2.

800 *Niederwimmer, Kurt* Unmittelbarkeit und Vermittlung als hermeneutisches Problem <1971>;

801 Interpretation als Vermittlung. Gesammelte Aufsätze. BZNW 90: 1998 <1994> ⇒182. 44-59/234-242.

802 **Oeming, Manfred** Biblische Hermeneutik: eine Einführung. Da 1998, Primus viii; 212 pp. DM39.80. 3-89678-316-5.

803 *Orecchia, Carlo* Univocità e polisemia del testo biblico nella storia dell'interpretazione. ᶠMARTINI C., Rivelazione. 1998 ⇒74. 99-131.

804 *Panier, Louis* From biblical text to literary enunciation and its subject. Semeia 81 (1998) 63-75.

805 **Patte, Daniel** Ethics of biblical interpretation. 1995, ⇒11/2,1331; 13,744. ᴿHeyJ 39 (1998) 329-330 (*McNamara, Martin*).

806 *Patte, Daniel* Critical biblical studies from a semiotics perspective. Semeia 81 (1998) 3-26;

807 The guarded personal voice of a male European-American biblical scholar. The personal voice. 1998, ⇒250. 12-24.

808 *Penicaud, Anne* Les amis inconnus: propositions pour une lecture. SémBib 89 (1998) 19-37.

809 *Pesce, Mauro* The ecumenical interpretation of the Old Testament and the historical meaning of the bible. ASEs 15 (1998) 327-355.

810 **Polk, Timothy H**. The biblical KIERKEGAARD: reading by the rule of faith. 1997, ⇒13,747. ᴿTS 59 (1998) 337-338 (*Khan, Abrahim H.*).

811 *Poucouta, Paulin* Engelbert MVENG: une lecture africaine de la bible. NRTh 120 (1998) 32-45.

812 *Punt, Jeremy* 'My kingdom for a method': methodological preoccupation in areas of South African New Testament scholarship. Neotest. 32 (1998) 135-160.

813 *Rendtorff, Rolf* What we miss by taking the bible apart. BiRe 14/1 (1998) 42-44.

814 *Reyes Archila, Francisco* Leer la biblia con los ojos de los niños: pequeños esbozos de un desafío. Alternativas 5 (1998) 213-230.

815 *Richard, Pablo* Un nuevo espacio y un nuevo sujeto para interpretar la palabra de Dios. Alternativas 5 (1998) 131-154.

816 *Riches, John* Text, church and world: in search of a theological hermeneutic. Biblical Interpretation 6 (1998) 205-234.

817 **Ricoeur, Paul; Lacoque, André** Penser la bible. La couleur des idées: P 1998, Seuil 456 pp. FF160. 2-02-031677-3. ᴿEsprit 10 (1998) 223-227 (*Breton, Stanislas*).

818 *Rizzi, Armido* Per un'ontologia biblica della libertà. FilTeo 12 (1998) 7-20.

819 *Rizzi, Giovanni* Le scritture tra metodi storico-critici moderni e principi ermeneutici fondamentali nel Guidaismo e nel Christianesimo. I. parte. RivBib 46 (1998) 179-222.

820 *Robbins, Vernon K.* Socio-rhetorical hermeneutics and commentary. FPOKORNÝ, P. 1998 ⇒90. 284-297.

821 **Rojtman, Betty** Black fire on white fire: an essay on Jewish hermeneutics, from midrash to kabbalah. Contraversions 10: Berkeley 1998, University of California Press xii; (2) 194 pp. 0-520-20320-8.

822 *Rose, Renate* Response from the Philippines to some of the Semeia articles. Semeia 81 (1998) 177-186.

823 *Sao, Calvin C.* Speech act theory and biblical studies. Jian Dao 10 (1998) 23-41.

824 *Schalk, Peter* Twisted cross: the religious nationalism of the German christians. StTh 52 (1998) 69-79.

825 *Scharbert, Josef* Altes Testament oder Erstes Testament?. FWETTER F. 1998 ⇒124. 3-10.

826 *Schmidt, Ingrid; Ruppel, Helmut* Selig, wer liest: zu einem neuen Lesen des sogenannten Alten Testamentes. EvErz 50 (1998) 343-354.

827 *Schulze, L.F.* Hoe post-modern is postmodernisme?: enkele gedagtes. Acta Theologica 18 (1998) 10-28.

828 *Schweizer, Eduard* Was geschieht, wenn wir ein so altes Dokument wie das Neue Testament lesen?. FPOKORNÝ, P. 1998, ⇒90. 314-320.

829 *Segalla, Giuseppe* Ermeneutica biblica: alla ricerca di chiavi per l'interpretazione della Sacra Scrittura. StPat 45 (1998) 627-654.

830 *Segovia, Fernando F.* Biblical criticism and postcolonial studies: toward a postcolonial optic. The postcolonial bible. 1998 ⇒695. 49-65.

831 My personal voice: the making of a postcolonial critic. The personal voice. 1998 ⇒250. 25-37.

832 *Seitz, Christopher* `And without God in the world': a hermeneutic of estrangement overcome. Word without end. 1998 ⇒200. 41-50.

833 *Smidt, J.C. de* Fundamentalism—a historical survey. Scriptura 64 (1998) 37-49.

834 *Sorrentino, Domenico* Esperienza spirituale e intelligenza della fede in 'Dei verbum' 8: sul senso di 'intima spiritualium rerum quam esperiuntur intelligentia'. La terra e il seme. BTNap 19: 1998 ⇒310. 153-174.

835 *Söding, Thomas* 'Mitte der Schrift'—'Einheit der Schrift': grundsätzliche Erwägungen zur Schrifthermeneutik. Verbindliches Zeugnis III. 1998 ⇒265. 43-82.

836 *Spaller, Christina* Strukturale Überlegungen zu biblisch-exegetischem Arbeiten. PzB 7 (1998) 1-16.

837 Le statut de la Bible et ses implications: la nature de la bible; l'interprétation biblique; la mise en pratique de la foi biblique—les trois déclarations de Chicago 1978, 1982, 1986. RRef 49 (1998) 3-61.

838 *Stroumsa, Guy G.* The christian hermeneutical revolution and its double helix. Use of sacred books. 1998 ⇒263. 9-28.

839 **Sugirtharajah, Rasiah S.** Asian biblical hermeneutics and postcolonialism: contesting the interpretations. The Bible and Liberation: Mkn 1998, Orbis xii; 148 pp. $20. 1-57075-205-2.

840 *Sugirtharajah, R.S.* Biblical studies after the Empire: from a colonial to a postcolonial mode of interpretation;

841 A postcolonial exploration of collusion and construction in biblical interpretation. The postcolonial bible. 1998 ⇒695. 12-22/91-116.

842 **Tate, W. Randolph** Biblical interpretation: an integrated approach. 1997 <1991> ⇒13,778. REeT(O) 29 (1998) 384-385 (*Vogels, Walter*).

843 *Thompson, Mark D.* Reformation perspectives on scripture: the written word of God. RTR 57 (1998) 105-120.
844 **Torrance, Thomas F.** Divine Meaning: studies in patristic hermeneutics. 1995, ⇒11/2,1355; 13,779. [R]SVTQ 42/1 (1998) 104-108 (*Behr, John*). JThS 49 (1998) 358-361 (*Widdicombe, Peter*).
845 *Urrea Carrillo, Mauricio* El trasfondo filosófico de la hermenéutica. Qol 16 (1998) 63-74.
846 *Van Deventer, H.J.M.* Oor paaie, sirkels en waarhede: 'n bydrae met betrekking tot die huidige hermeneutiese gesprek. Acta Theologica 18 (1998) 77-95.
847 **Vanhoozer, Kevin** Is there a meaning in this text?: the bible, the reader, and the morality of literary knowledge. GR 1998, Zondervan 496 pp. $30. 0-310-21156-5.
848 *Vanoni, Gottfried* 'Justice and peace embrace' (Ps 85:11): stimuli towards an SVD focus taken from the Old Testament. VSVD 39 (1998) 145-157.
849 *Van Spanje, T.E.* Contextualization: hermeneutical remarks. BJRL 80 (1998) 197-217.
850 **Voelz, J.W.** What does this mean?: principles of biblical interpretation in the post-modern world. 1995 ⇒11/2,1357. [R]AJTh 12 (1998) 449-452 (*Muthuraj, J.G.*).
851 **Washburn, Del** The original code in the bible: using science and mathematics to reveal God's fingerprints. Lanham 1998, Madison viii; 242 pp. 1-56833-115-0.
852 **Watson, Francis** Text, church and world: biblical interpretation in theological perspective. 1994 ⇒13,790. [R]AtK 131 (1998) 327-329 (*Pawlowski, Zdzislaw*); Pro Ecclesia 7 (1998) 365-367 (*Vanhoozer, Kevin J.*); JThS 49 (1998) 500-504 (*Ford, David F.*).
853 *Watson, Francis* A response to John RICHES. Biblical Interpretation 6 (1998) 235-242.
854 *Wessels, J.P.H.* Implications of a postmodernist reading of the Old Testament for textual meaning. OTEs 11 (1998) 600-614.
855 *West, Gerald* Biblical scholars inventing ancient Israel and 'ordinary readers' of the Bible re-inventing biblical studies. OTEs 11 (1998) 629-644.
856 *Wilken, Robert Louis* In defense of allegory. MoTh 14 (1998) 196-212.
857 *Williams, D.H.* The search for sola scriptura in the early church. Interp. 52 (1998) 354-366.
858 *Wolterstorff, Nicholas* Reply to LEVINE. RelSt 34 (1998) 17-23.
859 **Yeo, Khiok-Khng** What has Jerusalem to do with Beijing?: biblical interpretation from a Chinese perspective. Harrisburg, Pennsylvania 1998, Trinity x; 325 pp. $25. 1-56338-229-6.

B2.4 *Analysis* **narrationis** *biblicae*

860 *Chew, Kathryn* Focalization in XENOPHON of Ephesos' Ephesiaka. Ancient fiction. 1998, [E]**Hock, R.F.** ⇒B4.5. 47-59.
861 *Clines, David J.A.* X, X Ben Y, *Ben* Y: personal names in Hebrew narrative style. OT essays, 1. JSOT.S 292 1998 <1972>, ⇒142. 240-262.
862 *Day, Linda* Power, otherness, and gender in the biblical short stories. HBT 20 (1998) 109-127.
863 *Dieterman, Julia I.* Participant reference in isthmus mixe narrative discourse. JOTT 10 (1998) 47-79.

864 *Edwards, Douglas R.* Pleasurable reading or symbols of power?: religious themes and social context in Chariton. Ancient fiction. 1998, ^E**Hock, R.F.** ⇒B4.5. 31-46.

865 **Goldfajn, Tal** Word order and time in Biblical Hebrew narrative. Oxford Theological Monographs Oxf 1998, Clarendon xvi; 169 pp. $65. 0-19-826953-6.

866 **Grottanelli, Cristiano** Sette storie bibliche. StBi 119: 1998, Paideia 315 pp. L48.000. 88-394-0564-X.

867 **Heller, Roy Leslie** Narrative structure and discourse constellations: an analysis of clause function in Biblical Hebrew prose. ^DYale 1998, 581 pp.

868 *Hock, Ronald F.* Why New Testament scholars should read ancient novels. Ancient fiction. 1998, ^E**Hock, R.F.** ⇒B4.5. 121-138.

869 *Kahl, Werner* Strukturale Erzähltheorie am Beispiel des religionsgeschichtlichen Vergleichs neutestamentlicher und rabbinischer Versionen einer Story. Exegese und Methodendiskussion. TANZ 23: 1998 ⇒208. 155-176.

870 *Konstan, David* The invention of fiction. Ancient fiction. 1998, ^E**Hock, R.F.** ⇒B4.5. 3-17.

871 *Köstenberger, Andreas J.* Aesthetic theology—blessing or curse?: an assessment of narrative theology. Faith & Mission 15 (1998) 27-44.

872 *Kruger, Paul A.* "Nonverbal communication" in the Hebrew Bible: a few comments. JNSL 24 (1998) 141-164.

873 **Loughlin, Gerard** Telling God's story: Bible, Church and narrative theology. 1996, ^REvQ 70 (1998) 90-92 (*Johnson, Richard*): HeyJ 39 (1998) 98-99 (*McDonald, Patricia M.*): JR 78 (1998) 285-287 (*Placher, William*).

874 **Marais, Jacobus** Representation in Old Testament narrative texts. Biblical Interpretation 36 Lei 1998, Brill ix; 194 pp. 90-04-11234-0.

875 **Marguerat, Daniel; Bourquin, Yvan** Pour lire les récits bibliques: initiation à l'analyse narrative. P 1998, Cerf 242 pp. FF150;

876 La bible se raconte: initiation à l'analyse narrative. Pour lire les récits bibliques P 1998, Cerf 241 pp. FF150. 2-204-06114-X.

877 **Minette de Tillesse, Caetano** O Deus pelas costas: teologia narrativa da Bíblia. 1995 ⇒11/2,1386; 12,691. ^REstB 56 (1998) 424-426 (*Rubio, L.*);

878 RBB 12: Théologie narrative de la Bible. 1995 ⇒11/2,1387; 13,822 ^RDBAT 29 (1998) 295-297 (*Diebner, B.J.*).

879 *Pervo, Richard I.* A nihilist fabula: introducing the Life of Aesop. Ancient fiction. 1998, ^E**Hock, R.F.** ⇒B4.5. 77-120.

880 *Polak, Frank H.* תמורות ותקופות בלשון הסיפורת במקרא [Development and periodization of biblical prose narrative II]. Beit Mikra 153 (1998) 142-160.

881 **Prickett, Stephen** Origins of narrative: the romantic appropriation of the bible. 1996, ⇒12,696; 13,824. ^RBTB 28 (1998) 35-37 (*Malina, Bruce J.*): JR 78 (1998) 329-331 (*Dally, John*).

882 *Regt, Lénart J. de* Clause connections and the interruption of direct speech in Hebrew. Bible et informatique. 1998, ⇒386. 81-93.

883 **Reinhartz, Adele** "Why ask my name?": anonymity and identity in biblical narrative. NY 1998, OUP xii; 226 pp. $40. 0-19-509970-2.

884 **Revell, Ernest John** The designation of the individual: expressive usage in biblical narrative. 1996, ⇒12,469; 13,826. ^RJBL 117 (1998) 521-523 (*Meier, Samuel*).

885 *Salvatore, Emilio* Analisi narrativa: un nuovo approccio alla bibbia?. RdT 39 (1998) 387-409.
886 *Schmeling, Gareth* The spectrum of narrative: authority of the author. Ancient fiction. 1998, [E]**Hock, R.F.** ⇒B4.5. 19-29.
887 *Shea, Chris* Setting the stage for romances: XENOPHON of Ephesus and the Ecphrasis. Ancient fiction. 1998, [E]**Hock, R.F.** ⇒B4.5. 61-76.
888 *Talstra, Eep* From the "eclipse" to the "art" of biblical narrative: reflections on methods of biblical exegesis. [F]VAN DER WOUDE, A. VT.S 73: 1998, ⇒121. 1-41.
889 *Thomas, Christine M.* Stories without texts and without authors: the problem of fluidity in ancient novelistic texts and early christian literature. Ancient fiction. 1998, [E]**Hock, R.F.** ⇒B4.5. 273-291.
890 *Tolmie, D.F.* The analysis of events in biblical narratives. Acta Theologica 18 (1998) 50-76.
891 **Watts, James W.** Psalm and story: inset hymns in Hebrew narrative. JSOT.S 139: 1992, ⇒8,1228... 13,830. [R]VT 48/1 (1998) 134-135 (*Satterthwaite, P.E.*).
892 **Westermann, Claus** Erzählungen in den Schriften des Alten Testaments. Stu 1998, Calwer. Vor- und Nachwort von *Dieter Vetter*. [R]BThZ 15 (1998) 280-282 (*Klemm, Peter*).

B3.1 *Interpretatio ecclesiastica* **Bible and Church**

893 **Alcalá, Manuel** Sínodos, concilios, iglesias. BAC 14: M 1998, BAC 141 pp. 84-7914-352-5.
894 *Bertalot, Valdo* La bibbia in Italia dopo la 'Dei Verbum': il clima cattolico secondo lo sguardo di un valdese italiano. La traduzione. 1998, ⇒222. 91-98.
895 **Burigana, Riccardo** La bibbia nel concilio: la redazione della costituzione 'Dei verbum' del Vaticano II. TRSR 21: Bo 1998, Mulino 514 pp. L65.000. 88-15-06586-5.
896 **Campbell, Dwight P.** A primer on divine revelation. Princeton, NJ 1998, Scepter 74 pp.
897 [E]**Chiarinelli, Lorenzo** La bibbia nel magistero dei vescovi italiani. Bibbia, proposte e metodi 11: Leumann (Torino) 1998, Elle Di Ci 103 pp. 88-01-01062-1.
898 *Combrink, H. J. Bernard* The rhetoric of the church in the transition from the old to the new South Africa: socio-rhetorical criticism and ecclesiastical rhetoric. Neotest. 32 (1998) 289-307.
899 *Davies, Gordon F.* The parish, the bible and everything else: scripture and our common quest to make sense. NBl 79 (1998) 275-280.
900 *De Rosa, Gabriele* Alcune riflessioni sui 'tribunali della coscienza' e sulla 'Bibbia al rogo'. RSSR 53 (1998) 221-237.
901 *Duffy, Kevin* Exegetes and theologians. IThQ 63 (1998) 219-231.
902 **Flórez García, Gonzalo** Evangelio e iglesia. BAC Popular 138: M 1998, BAC 211 pp. 84-7914-364-9.
903 **Fragnito, Gigliola** La bibbia al rogo: la censura ecclesiastica e i volgarizzamenti della scrittura (1471-1605). 1996, ⇒12,716. [R]CFr 68 (1998) 345-347 (*Cargnoni, Costanzo*); JEH 49 (1998) 728-729 (*Higman, Francis*); CrSt 19 (1998) 686-688 (*Gilmont, Jean-François*); RSLR 34 (1998) 645-651 (*Erba, Achille*).
904 *Frajese, Vittorio* Riforma e antiriforma nella storia dei volgarizzamenti biblici. StStor 39 (1998) 23-40.

905 *Fuchs, Ottmar* Päpstliche Bibelkommission versöhnt zwischen Freiheit und Verbindlichkeit. BiLi 71 (1998) 55-60.

906 ^E**Ghiberti, Giuseppe; Mosetto, Francesco** L'interpretazione della bibbia nella chiesa. Percorsi e traguardi biblici: Leumann (T) 1998, Elle Di Ci 387 pp. 88-01-00658-8.

907 *Häring, Hermann* De schriften, 'ziel van de theologie': pleidooi voor een herontdekking van de bijbel. TTh 38 (1998) 280-300.

908 The interpretation of the bible in the church. 1993, ⇒9,1095. MD+SU»RMonth 31 (1998) 486-494 (*Robinson, Bernard P.*).

909 *Jossa, Giorgio* Ricera storica e interpretazione teologica: riflessioni sul documento della Pontificia Commissione Biblica "L'interpretazione della Bibbia nella chiesa". ^FMARTINI, C. RivBib.S 33: 1998, ⇒75. 47-55.

910 **Latourelle, René** Comment Dieu se révèle au monde: lecture commentée de la constitution de Vatican II sur la parole de Dieu. Montréal 1998, Fides 100 pp. $13. 2-7621-2016-0. ^RScEs 50 (1998) 387-388 (*Hamel, Édouard*).

911 *Murphy, Roland E.* What is catholic about catholic biblical scholarship?—revisited. BTB 28 (1998) 112-119.;

912 Zur "Aktualisierung" der Bibel. BiLi 71 (1998) 264-268.

913 **O'Collins, Gerald; Kendall, Daniel** The bible for theology: ten principles for the theological use of scripture. 1997, ⇒13,859. ^RHBT 20 (1998) 158-159 (*McKim, Donald K.*); ZKTh 120 (1998) 332-333 (*Neufeld, Karl H.*).

914 **Pelikan, Jaroslav** The reformation of the bible: the bible of the Reformation. 1996, ⇒12,730; 13,861. ^RAUSS 36 (1998) 150-152 (*Strand, Kenneth A.*).

915 *Poffet, Jean-Michel* Les chrétiens et la bible: les anciens et les modernes. Histoire du christianisme: P 1998, Cerf 150 pp. FF120. 2-204-05842-4.

916 *Roloff, Jürgen* Die Autorität der Kirche und die Interpretation der Bibel. DBM 17 (1998) 91-108.

917 *Rüterswörden, Udo* Anmerkungen eines Protestanten. BiLi 71 (1998) 154-159.

918 **Scholl, Norbert** Frohbotschaft statt Drohbotschaft: die biblischen Grundlagen des Kirchenvolks-Begehrens. Graz 1997, Styria 254 pp. AUS198/DM27. 3-222-12491-4. ^RZKTh 120 (1998) 244-245 (*Guggenberger, Wilhelm*).

919 **Schulz, Hans-Joachim** Bekenntnis statt Dogma: Kriterien der Vebindlichkeit kirchlicher Lehre. QD 163: FrB 1996, Herder 421 pp. AUS526. 3-451-02163-3. ^RZKTh 120 (1998) 75-84 [Antwort 184-197] (*Weß, Paul*).

920 *Segalla, Giuseppe* Church authority and bible interpretation. DBM 17 (1998) 69-90.

921 *Utzschneider, Helmut* Exegese als ökumenische Chance: Überlegungen eines lutherischen Alttestamentlers zum Dokument der Päpstlichen Bibelkommission. BiLi 71 (1998) 61-65.

922 Vatican archives: an inventory and guide to historical documents of the Holy See. NY 1998, OUP xl; 588 pp. 0-19-509552-9.

923 *Vignolo, Roberto* Metodi, ermeneutica, statuto del testo biblico: riflessioni a partire da "L'interpretazione della bibbia nella chiesa" (1993). ^FMARTINI C., Rivelazione. 1998, ⇒74. 29-97.

924 *Zehner, Joachim* Schriftauslegung und Lehramt: Zusammenfassung der neueren ökumenischen Diskussion: Perspektiven aus evangelischer Sicht. ThLZ 123 (1998) 943-954.

B3.2 *Homiletica*—The Bible in preaching

925 **Achtemeier, Elizabeth** Preaching hard texts of the Old Testament. Peabody, MA 1998, Hendrickson 192 pp.;
926 Preaching from the Minor Prophets: texts and sermon suggestions. GR 1998, Eerdmans xii; 143 pp. 0-8028-4370-0.
927 *Allen, Pauline* The sixth-century Greek homily: a re-assessment. Preacher and audience. 1998, ⇒226. 201-225.
928 **Allen, Ronald J.** Interpreting the gospel: an introduction to preaching. St. Louis 1998, Chalice xiv; 306 pp. $25. 0-8272-1619-X.
929 **Arntz, Klaus** Angesprochen: Predigten zu biblischen Themen. Kevelaer 1998, Butzon & B 141 pp. DM24.80.
930 *Borden, Paul* Is there really one big idea in that story?. Big idea. 1998, ⇒280. 67-80.
931 **Campbell, Charles L.** Preaching Jesus: new directions for homiletics in Hans FREI's postliberal theology. 1997, ⇒13,880. ᴿWorship 72 (1998) 464-465 (*Hilkert, Mary Catherine*).
932 **Carroll, John T.; Carroll, James R.** Preaching the hard sayings of Jesus. 1997, ⇒13,882. ᴿAThR 80/1 (1998) 93, 95 (*McDaniel, Judith M.*); EeT 29 (1998) 259-260 (*Michaud, Jean-Paul*).
933 **Davis, Ellen F.** Imagination shaped: Old Testament preaching in the Anglican tradition. 1995, ⇒11/2,1538. ᴿPro Ecclesia 7/1 (1998) 120-122 (*Jacobsen, David Schnasa*).
934 **Farris, Stephen** Preaching that matters: the bible and our lives. LVL 1998, Westminster John Knox 170 pp. $17. 0-664-25759-3.
935 *Farris, Stephen* Repartir boiteux, mais assuré d'une bénédiction: exégèse et prédication à la fin du deuxième millénaire. Hokhma 69 (1998) 41-55.
936 *Ferreiro, Alberto* Vincent FERRER's Beati Petri Apostoli: canonical and apocryphal sources in popular vernacular preaching. HThR 91 (1998) 41-57.
937 *Gibson, Scott M.* Philosophy versus method: big idea preaching's adaptability. Big idea. 1998, ⇒280. 163-172.
938 *Höslinger, Norbert* Predigt: biblisches Defizit?. BiLi 71 (1998) 159-160.
939 **Larsen, David L.** The company of the preachers: a history of biblical preaching from the Old Testament to the modern era. GR 1998, Kregel 894 pp. $35. 0-8254-3128-X.
940 *Litfin, Duane* New Testament challenges to big idea preaching. Big idea. 1998, ⇒280. 53-66.
941 **Martin, George** God's word. Huntington 1998, Our Sunday Visitor 199 pp. $9.
942 *Mattingly, Terry* Preaching the big idea to cultures and subcultures: exegeting the culture. Big idea. 1998, ⇒280. 81-94.
943 *Meredith, Anthony* The three Cappadocians on beneficence: a key to their audiences. Preacher and audience. 1998, ⇒226. 89-104.
944 **Miskotte, Kornelis** Heiko Das Wagnis der Predigt. AzTh 87: Stu 1998, Calwer xvii; 132 pp. 3-7668-3547-5.

945 *Moule, C.F.D.* Preaching the atonement. Forgiveness. 1998 [1983], ⇒180. 19-29.
946 *Munitiz, Joseph* ANASTASIOS of Sinai: speaking and writing to the people of God. Preacher and audience. 1998, ⇒226. 227-245.
947 **Norrington, David C.** To preach or not to preach: the church's urgent question. Carlisle 1996, Paternoster £12. ᴿIBSt 20 (1998) 127-130 (*Campbell, Denis*).
948 *Olivar, Alexander* Reflections on problems raised by early christian preaching. Preacher and audience. 1998, ⇒226. 21-32.
949 *Reed, John W.* Visualizing the big idea: stories that support rather than steal. Big idea. 1998, ⇒280. 147-162.
950 *Shelley, Bruce L.* The big idea and biblical theology's grand theme. Big idea. 1998, ⇒280. 95-107.
951 ᴱᵀ**Sheridan, J. Mark** RUFUS (Sotep, Episcopus): homilies on the gospels of Matthew and Luke: introduction, text, translation, commentary. Corpus dei manoscritti copti letterari: R 1998, CIM 360 pp. 88-85354-05-X.
952 *Smolík, Josef* Die Erneuerung der biblischen Predigt als Beitrag zum Ökumenismus. AnzSS 107 (1998) 424-428.
953 *Stowell, Joseph M.* Preaching for a change. Big idea. 1998, 125-145.
954 *Sunukjian, Donald R.* Sticking to the plot: the developmental flaw of the big idea sermon. Big idea. 1998, ⇒280. 111-124.
955 **Treiber, Martin** Die alttestamentliche Predigt Friedrich SCHLEIER-MACHERs. Diss. Heidelberg 1996-1997; ᴰEisinger, W. [ThRv 94,xiv].
956 *Waltke, Bruce* Old Testament interpretation issues for big idea preaching: problematic sources, poetics, and preaching the Old Testament: an exposition of Proverbs 26:1-12. Big idea. 1998, ⇒280. 41-52.
957 *Wenig, Scott A.* Biblical preaching that adapts and contextualizes. Big idea. 1998, ⇒280. 25-38.
958 ᴱ**Whitby, Mary** The propaganda of power: the role of panegyric in late antiquity. Mn.S 183: Lei 1998, Brill xi; 378 pp. $117.50. 90-04-10571-9.
959 *Willhite, Keith* A bullet versus buckshot: what makes the big idea work?. Big idea. 1998, ⇒280. 13-23.
960 *Willson, Patrick J.; Gaventa, Beverly Roberts* Preaching as the re-reading of scripture. Interp. 52 (1998) 392-404.

B3.3 Inerrantia, inspiratio

961 *Behr-Sigel, Elisabeth* La bible, la tradition, les sacraments, source de l'autorité dans l'église. Contacts 50 (1998) 204-214.
962 **Countryman, Louis William** Biblical authority or biblical tyranny?: scripture and the christian pilgrimage. Harrisburg, Pa. 1998, Trinity xi; 125 pp. 1-56101-088-X/338-085-4.
963 *Étienne, Jacques* Les droits de l'homme sont-ils d'inspiration individualiste?. RTL 29 (1998) 297-306.
964 *Franco, Ettore* "Il vento soffia dove vuole" (Gv 3,8): quel "fare" dello Spirito detto "ispirazione". RdT 39 (1998) 349-366.
965 **Fretheim, Terence E.; Froehlich, Karlfried** The bible as word of God in a post-modern age. Mp 1998, Fortress viii; 135 pp. $15. 0-8006-3094-7.
966 **Goldingay, John** Models for scripture. 1994, ⇒11/2,1599... 13,911. ᴿEvQ 70 (1998) 85-88 (*Lucas, Ernest C.*).

967 **Haarmann, Harald** Religion und Autorität: der Weg des Gottes ohne Konkurrenz. Hildesheim 1998, Olms 252 pp. 3-487-10507-1.
968 **Hendrix, Scott H.** Tradition and authority in the Reformation. CStS: 1996, ⇒12,772. ᴿChH 67/1 (1998) 148-149 (*Pragman, James H.*).
969 **Kline, Meredith G.** The structure of biblical authority. Eugene, OR 1997, Wipf & S 218 pp. 1-579-10069-4. ᴿApoll. 71 (1998) 778-781 (*Molino, Stefano*).
970 *Larkin, William J.* Approaches to and images of biblical authority for the postmodern mind. BBR 8 (1998) 129-138.
971 **Martin, François** Pour une théologie de la lettre: l'inspiration des Écritures. CFi 196: 1996, ⇒12,778; 13,917. ᴿRTL 29 (1998) 371-372 (*Focant, C.*).
972 **Murphy, Patrick E.** Contemporary evangelical theories of biblical inspiration in light of 2 Timothy 3:16a and 2 Peter 1:20-21. ᴰMontréal 1998, 384 pp.
973 *Neumann, Burkhard* Sola Scriptura: das reformatorische Schriftprinzip und seine Anfrage an die katholische Theologie. Cath(M) 52 (1998) 277-296.
974 ᴱ**Neusner, Jacob** Sacred texts and authority. The Pilgrim Library of world religions: Cleveland, OH 1998, Pilgrim xviii; 163 pp. 0-8298-1249-0.
975 *Plantinga, Alvin* Two (or more) kinds of scripture scholarship. MoTh 14 (1998) 243-278.
976 *Seitz, Christopher* Biblical authority in the late twentieth century: the Baltimore Declaration, scripture—reason—tradition, and the canonical approach. Word without end. 1998 [1993], ⇒200. 83-101.
977 **Tábet, Miguel Angel** Teologia della bibbia: studi su ispirazione ed ermeneutica biblica. Studi di teologia 7: R 1998, Armando 267 pp. L35.000. 88-7144-838-3.
978 *Vardaman, James W.* Oliver CROMWELL and the liberty of conscience. ᴹSUMMERS R. 1998, ⇒115. 211-218.
979 *Vaz, Armindo dos Santos* Repensar a teología de inspiração da bíblia. Did(L) 28 (1998) 59-91.
980 *Vogels, Walter* L'autorité de la bible ou l'autorité que le lecteur donne à la bible. EeT(O) 29/2 (1998) 179-197.

B3.4 **Traditio**

981 **Alcáin, José Antonio** La tradición. Teología 29: Bilbao 1998, Universidad de Deusto 767 pp. 84-748-5543-8.
982 **Backus, Irena Dorota** Das Prinzip "sola scriptura" und die Kirchenväter in den Disputationen von Baden (1526) und Bern (1528). 1997, ⇒13,933. ᴿCTJ 33 (1998) 486-487 (*Payton, James R.*).
983 ᴱ**Cremascoli, Giuseppe; Leonardi, Claudio** La Bibbia nel Medioevo. 1996, ⇒12,787; 13,934. ᴿAevum 72 (1998) 610-2 (*Barbieri, Edoardo*); EThL 74 (1998) 456-457 (*Verheyden, J.*).
984 *Jaffee, Martin S.* Oral culture in scriptural religion: some exploratory studies. RStR 24 (1998) 223-230.
985 **Navarro Lecanda, A.M.** 'Evangelii traditio': tradición como evangelización a la luz de Dei Verbum I-II. 1997, ⇒13,940. ᴿDid(L) 28 (1998) 222-223 (*Teixeira, João António Pinheiro*).
986 *Ragazzi, Cesare* Nuovo Testamento e Torà orale. Sette e religioni 8 (1998) 42-84.

987 **Veloso, Francisco J.** Reflexões: tradição e escritura. Lisboa 1995, Astoria 239 pp. [R]Did(L) 28/1 (1998) 235-37 (*Carreira das Neves, Joaquim*).

B3.5 Canon

988 **Abraham, William J.** Canon and criterion in christian theology: from the Fathers to feminism. Oxf 1998, Clarendon 508 pp. £60. 0-19-826939-0.
989 *Adriaanse, H.J.* Canonicity and the problem of the golden mean;
990 *Al-Azmeh, A.* The Muslim canon from late antiquity to the era of modernism. Canonization. SHR 82: 1998, ⇒407. 313-330/191-228.
991 **Barton, John** The spirit and the letter: studies in the biblical canon. 1997, ⇒13,942. [R]JThS 49 (1998) 162-167 (*Noble, Paul R.*);
992 Holy writings, sacred text: the canon in early christianity. LVL 1998, Westminster xiii; 210 pp. $18. 0-664-25778-X.
993 *Baum, Armin Daniel* PAPIAS, der Vorzug der Viva Vox und die Evangelienschriften. NTS 44 (1998) 144-151.
994 *Ben Zvi, Ehud* Looking at the primary (hi)story and the prophetic books as literary/theological units within the frame of the early second temple: some considerations. SJOT 12 (1998) 26-43.
995 *Boeve, L.* Tradition, (de)canonization, and the challenge of plurality. Canonization. SHR 82: 1998, ⇒407. 371-380.
996 **Chapman, Stephen Brian** The Law and the Prophets: a study in Old Testament canon formation. [D]Yale 1998, 541 pp.
997 *Christensen, Duane* The lost books of the bible. BiRe 14/5 (1998) 24-31.
998 *Clivaz, Claire* La troisième quête du Jésus historique et le canon: le défi de la réception communautaire: un essai de relecture historique. Jésus de Nazareth. 1998, ⇒253. 541-558.
999 *Cornille, C.* Canon formation in new religious movements: the case of the Japanese new religions. Canonization. SHR 82: 1998, ⇒407. 279-291.
1000 **Cross, Frank Moore** From epic to canon: history and literature in Ancient Israel. Baltimore 1998, Johns Hopkins University xv; 262 pp. 0-8018-5982-4.
1001 **Davies, Philip R.** Scribes and schools: the canonization of the Hebrew scriptures. Library of Ancient Israel: LVL 1998, Westminster xi; 219 pp. $24. 0-664-22077-0.
1002 *DeClaissé-Walford, Nancy L.* The dromedary saga: the formation of the canon of the Old Testament. RExp 95 (1998) 493-511.
1003 *Diebner, Bernd Jørg* "Deuterokanonisches" im Kanon des Neuen Testaments;
1004 Ekklesiologische Aspekte einer Kanon-Hermeneutik der Hebräischen Bibel (TNK). DBAT 29 (1998) 217-234/15-32.
1005 *Dolce, L.* Buddhist hermeneutics in medieval Japan: canonical texts, scholastic tradition, and sectarian polemics. Canonization. SHR 82: 1998, ⇒407. 229-243.
1006 *Farmer, William R.* Further reflections on the fourfold gospel canon. [F]FERGUSON, E. NT.S 90: 1998, ⇒25. 107-113.
1007 *Goody, J.* Canonization in oral and literate cultures;
1008 *Hettema, Th.L.* The canon: authority and fascination. Canonization. SHR 82: 1998, ⇒407. 3-16/391-398.

1009 ^E**Jenner, K.D.; Wiegers, G.A.** Heilig boek en religieus gezag: ontstaan en functioneren van canonieke tradities. Leidse Studiën van de
Godsdienst 2: Kampen 1998, Kok 319 pp. ƒ50.

1010 *Lang, B.* The "writings": a Hellenistic literary canon in the Hebrew
Bible;

1011 *Legendre, P.* La totémisation de la société: remarques sur les
montages canoniques et la question du sujet;

1012 *Lust, J.L.* Quotation formulae and canon in Qumran. Canonization.
SHR 82: 1998, ⇒407. 41-65/425-433/67-77.

1013 *McDonald, L.M.* The formation of the christian biblical canon. ²1995
⇒11/2,1650... 13,960. ^REstB 56 (1998) 111-117 (*Aranda, G.*).

1014 **Metzger, Bruce M.** The canon of the New Testament: its origin, development, and significance. Oxf 1997 <1987>, OUP 326 pp.
^RBAEO 34 (1998) 437-438 (*Monferrer Sala, Juan Pedro*).

1015 **Miller, John W.** The origins of the bible: rethinking canon history.
1994, ⇒10,1088... 12,812. ^RScrTh 30 (1998) 691-693 (*Aranda
Pérez, G.*).

1016 *Nobile, Marco* Genesi della torà nel periodo di formazione del
giudaismo del secondo tempio: alcune note. V Simposio di Tarso.
1998, ⇒395, 5-13.

1017 *Oegema, Gerbern S.* Kanon und Apokalyptik: die Rolle der
Apokalyptik im Kanonisierungsprozeß der christlichen Bibel. Interpretation of the Bible. JSOT.S 289: 1998, ⇒388. 277-295.

1018 **Ohme, Heinz** Kanon ekklesiastikos: die Bedeutung des altkirchlichen Kanonbegriffs. AKG 67: B 1998, De Gruyter xvii; 666 pp.
DM298. 3-11-015189-8.

1019 *Ritschl, D.* Bemerkungen zur Koagulation von 'Stories' und zum
Phänomen der Kanonisierung. Canonization. SHR 82: 1998, ⇒407.
381-390.

1020 *Sanders, James A.* "Spinning" the bible: how Judaism and
christianity shape the canon differently. BiRe 14/3 (1998) 22-29, 44-
45.

1021 *Sæbo, Magne* From 'unifying reflections' to the canon: aspects of the
traditio-historical final stages in the development of the Old Testament. On the way to canon. 1998 <1988>, ⇒194. 285-307.

1022 *Scalabrini, Patrizio Rota* Testo ed intertesto: confronto con la "lettura canonica" di CHILDS e SANDERS. ^FMARTINI C., Rivelazione.
1998, ⇒74. 161-195.

1023 *Schaper, J.* The rabbinic canon and the Old Testament of the early
church: a social-historical view. Canonization. SHR 82: 1998, ⇒407.
93-106.

1024 *Schenk, Wolfgang* Die Jesus-Rezeption des MARKION als theologisches Problem. ^FHOFFMANN, P., Von Jesus. BZNW 93: 1998, ⇒43.
507-528.

1025 *Sheeley, Steven M.* From "scripture" to "canon": the development of
the New Testament canon. RExp 95 (1998) 513-522.

1026 *Smith, J.Z.* Canons, catalogues and classics;

1027 *Snoek, J.A.M.* Canonization and decanonization: an annotated
bibliography;

1028 *Stausberg, M.* The invention of a canon: the case of Zoroastrianism.
Canonization. SHR 82: 1998, ⇒407. 295-311/435-506/257-277.

1029 *Sundberg, Albert C.* 'The Old Testament of the early church'
revisited. ^FSPEEL C. 1996, ⇒106. 88-110 [ZID 2000,18].

1030 *Swanson, P.L.* Apocryphal texts in Chinese Buddhism: T'ien-t'ai Chih-i's use of apocryphal scriptures. Canonization. SHR 82: 1998, ⇒407. 245-255.

1031 *Ter Borg, M.B.* Canon and social control. Canonization. SHR 82: 1998, ⇒407. 411-423.

1032 *Thériault, Jean-Yves* Approche sémiotique du canon biblique. EeT(O) 29 (1998) 163-178.

1033 *Tolbert, Mary Ann* Reading the Bible with authority: feminist interrogation of the canon. Escaping Eden. BiSe 65: 1998, ⇒278. 141-162.

1034 *Tomson, P.J.* The New Testament canon as the embodiment of evolving christian attitudes towards the Jews. Canonization. SHR 82: 1998, ⇒407. 107-131.

1035 **Trebolle Barrera, Julio** La bíblia judía y la bíblia cristiana. 1993, ⇒9,851... 12,825. ᴿRB 105 (1998) 137-139 (*Loza, J.*);

1036 The Jewish bible and the christian bible: an introduction to the history of the bible. GR 1998, Eerdmans 573 pp. 0-8028-4473-1.

1037 **Trobisch, David** Die Endredaktion des Neuen Testaments: eine Untersuchung zur Entstehung der christlichen Bibel. NTOA 31: 1996, ⇒12,826; 13,980. ᴿThZ 54 (1998) 180-183 (*Klinghardt, Mathias*); CBQ 60 (1998) 591-592 (*Turro, James C.*).

1038 *Van de Beek, A.* Being convinced: on the foundations of the christian canon;

1039 *Van der Kooij, Arie* The canonization of ancient books kept in the temple of Jerusalem;

1040 Introduction to canonization and decanonization;

1041 *Van Leeuwen, Th.M.* Texts, canon, and revelation in Paul RICOEUR's hermeneutics. Canonization. SHR 82: 1998, ⇒407. 331-349/17-40/XV-XXIII/399-409.

1042 *Veltri, Giuseppe* Tradent und traditum im antiken Judentum: zur 'Kanonformel' לא תספו ולא תגרעו. Hallesche Beiträge zur Orientwissenschaft 25 (1998) 196-221.

1043 *Venter, P.M.* Wat beteken "kanon" vandag?. HTS 54 (1998) 505-528.

1044 *Vos, H.M.* The canon as a straitjacket;

1045 *Zevit, Z.* The second-third century canonization of the Hebrew Bible and its influence on christian canonizing;

1046 *Zsengellér, J.* Canon and the Samaritans. Canonization. SHR 82: 1998, ⇒407. 351-370/133-160/161-171.

B4.1 *Interpretatio humanistica* **The Bible—man; health, toil, age**

1047 **Alonso Schökel, Luis** I nomi dell'amore: simboli matrimoniali nella bibbia. 1997 ⇒13,987. ᴿCivCatt 149/1 (1998) 526-527 (*Scaiola, D.*).

1048 **Bendor, Sôn̂î'a** The social structure of ancient Israel: the institution of the family (Beit 'Ab) from the settlement to the end of the monarchy. Jerusalem Biblical Studies 7: 1996, ⇒12,827; 13,991. ᴿThLZ 123 (1998) 347-350 (*Crüsemann, Frank*); BiOr 55 (1998) 238-240 (*Geus, C.H.J. de*); CBQ 60 (1998) 516-517 (*Benjamin, Don C.*).

1049 *Blocher, Henri* La guérison, aperçus bibliques et dogmatiques. Ḥokhma 67 (1998) 45-61.

1050 *Briend, Jacques; Quesnel, Michel* Le mariage: droit et coutumes. MoBi 115 (1998) 77-79.

1051 *Dearman, J. Andrew* The family in the Old Testament. Interp. 52 (1998) 117-129.

1052 *Graham, Larry Kent* Pastoral care of diverse families. Interp. 52 (1998) 161-177.

1053 *Guzman, Efren de* 'Out of Egypt I have called my son': a scriptural input and reflection on doing refugee work. People on the move 76 (1998) 21-27.

1054 *Harris, Rivkah* Representations of the elderly in ancient Mesopotamian literature. ^MWARD W. 1998, ⇒123. 121-128.

1055 **Jacques, André** Droits de l'homme et évangile. Questions ouvertes: P 1998, L'Atelier 152 pp. ^RSpiritus 39 (1998) 331-332 (*Aurenche, Guy*).

1056 *Knohl, Israel* In the face of death: mortality and religious life in the bible, in rabbinic literature and in the Pauline letters. Self, soul and body. SHR 78: 1998, ⇒286. 86-95.

1057 *Larchet, Jean-Claude* La maladie, la souffrance et la mort dans leurs rapports avec le péché ancestral. Conc(F) 278 (1998) 69-78.

1058 *Levi, Abramo* Gusto, odorato, tatto: la *bibbia* è fatta anche di questi sensi. Servitium 120 (1998) 14-24.

1059 **Myers, Dan A.** Golden rules for parenting: a child psychiatrist discovers the bible. Mahwah 1998, Paulist v; 162 pp. $11. 0-80913-7771.

1060 **Perdue, Leo G.** Families in ancient Israel. 1997, ⇒13,219. ^RCBQ 60 (1998) 602-603 (*Washington, Harold C.*).

1061 **Prior, Michael Patrick** The Bible and colonialism: a moral critique. BiSe 48: 1997, ⇒13,1006. ^RDoLi 48 (1998) 125-126 (*McCaughey, Terence*); HeyJ 39 (1998) 434-436 (*Carroll, Robert P.*); ScrB 28 (1998) 41-43 (*Whitelam, Keith W.*).

1062 *Purvis, Sally B.* A question of families. Interp. 52 (1998) 145-160.

1063 *Rubinkiewicz, Ryszard* Praca a oczekiwanie na lepsze jutro [Labour and expecting a better tomorrow]. RTCAT 45 (1998) 101-109. **P.**

1064 **Schroer, Silvia; Staubli, Thomas** Die Körpersymbolik der Bibel. Da 1998, Primus 272 pp. DM49.80. 3-89678-081-6. ^REK (1998) 551 (*Braun, Christina von*).

1065 *Souzenelle, Annick de* Toccare e ascoltare: il simbolismo della mano e dell'orecchio, Servitium 120 (1998) 25-41.

1066 ^E**Stol, Marten; Vleeming, Sven P.** The care of the elderly in the ancient Near East. Studies in the history and culture of the ancient Near East 14: Lei 1998, Brill 280 pp. $71,25. 90-04-10896-3.

1067 **Thomas, John Christopher** The devil, disease and deliverance: origins of illness in New Testament thought. JPentec.S 13: Shf 1998, Academic 360 pp. $22. 1-85075-869-7.

1068 *Trublet, J.* Bible et drogue. RSR 86 (1998) 201-220.

1069 **Van der Toorn, Karel** Family religion in Babylonia, Syria, and Israel: continuity and change in the forms of religious life. 1996, ⇒12,849; 13,1015. ^RBiOr 55 (1998) 225-230 (*Caquot, André*); RB 105 (1998) 615-617 (*Tarragon, J.-M. de*).

1070 **Wells, Louise** The Greek language of healing from Homer to New Testament times. BZNW 83: B 1998, de Gruyter xviii; 489 pp. DM208. 3-11-015389-0.

B4.2 *Femina, familia*; **Woman in the Bible** [⇒B4.1; H8,8s]

1071 **Ackerman, Susan** Warrior, dancer, seductress, queen: women in Judges and Biblical Israel. AncB Reference Library: NY 1998, Doubleday xv; 352 pp. 0-385-48424-0.
1072 **Ames, Frank Ritchel** Women and war in the Hebrew Bible. ᴰIliff 1998, 262 pp.
1073 **Armstrong, Carole** Women of the Bible with paintings from the great art musuems of the world. Blackburn 1998, HarperCollinsReligious 45 pp. AUS$27. 1-86371-725-0.
1074 **Aschkenasy, Nehama** Woman at the window: biblical tales of oppression and escape. Detroit, MICH 1998, Wayne State University Press 181 pp. $40/19. 0-8143-2626-9.
1075 **Bar-Ilan, Meir** Some Jewish women in antiquity. BJSt 317: Atlanta 1998, Scholars xiv; 165 pp. 0-7885-0496-7.
1076 ᴱ**Baskin, Judith R.** Jewish women in historical perspective. Detroit 1998, Wayne State University Press 384 pp. 0-8143-2713-3.
1077 **Bosetti, Elena** Donne nel popolo di Dio: 16 proposte per incontri biblici. Bibbia, proposte e metodi 10: Leumann (T) 1998, Elle Di Ci 160 pp. 88-01-00962-3.
1078 *Crüsemann, Frank* Eva—die erste Frau und ihre "Schuld": ein Beitrag zu einer kanonisch-sozialgeschichtlichen Lektüre der Urgeschichte. BiKi 53 (1998) 2-10.
1079 *Dillmann, Rainer* Verstoßen—doch auch geachtet: die Hagar-Überlieferung und ihre Vergegenwärtigung im Christentum. rhs 41 (1998) 383-397 [Gal 4,21-31].
1080 *Dumoulin, Pierre* La force de la femme dans l'Ancien Testament. Com(F) 23 (1998) 37-45.
1081 **Exum, J. Cheryl** Plotted, shot and painted: cultural representations of biblical women. JSOT.S 215: 1996, ⇒12,864; 13,1033. ᴿVT 48 (1998) 123-124 (*Dell, Katharine J.*).
1082 **Fletcher, Elizabeth** Women in the bible: a historical approach. 1997, ⇒13,3228. ᴿPacifica 11/2 (1998) 239-240 (*Macdonald, Marie*); ACR 75/2 (1998) 244-245 (*Kiley, Bernadette*).
1083 *Frymer-Kensky, Tikva* Virginity in the Bible. Gender and law. JSOT.S 262: 1998, ⇒256. 79-96.
1084 *Giles, Terry* Of heroines and stories. BiTod 36 (1998) 240-245.
1085 *Gössmann, Elisabeth* Eva—Gottes Meisterwerk: Wirkungsgeschichte der Eva-Traditionen in Mittelalter und Früher Neuzeit. BiKi 53 (1998) 21-26.
1086 *Gradwohl, Roland* "Jeder, der keine Frau hat, ist kein Mensch": Eva in der Tradition des Judentums. BiKi 53 (1998) 35-38.
1087 ᴱᵀ**Kenney, Theresa M.** Mulieres homines non esse: "Women are not human": an anonymous treatise and responses. NY 1998, Herder and H x; 174 pp. 0-8245-1775-X.
1088 *Kramer, Phyllis Silverman* Biblical women that come in pairs: the use of female pairs as a literary device in the Hebrew Bible. Genesis. 1998, ⇒219. 218-232.
1089 *Krausen, Halima* Das Paradies liegt zu Füßen der Mütter: Eva aus islamischer Sicht. BiKi 53 (1998) 39-40.
1090 **Méroz, Christianne** Trois femmes d'espérance: Miryam, Anne, Houlda. Poliez-le-Grand 1998, Moulin 80 pp.
1091 *Mullins, Patrick* The public, secular roles of women in biblical times. MillSt 43 (1998) 79-111.

1092   **Murphy, Cullen** The word according to Eve: women and the bible in ancient times and our own. Boston 1998, Houghton Mifflin xiii; (2) 302 pp. 0-395-70113-9.

1093   *Müllner, Ilse* Klagend lauter werden: Frauenstimmen im Alten Testament. BiLi 71 (1998) 304-314.

1094   *Niditch, Susan* Portrayals of women in the Hebrew Bible. Jewish women. 1998, ⇒1076. 25-45.

1095   **Pitzen, Marianne; Monheim, Marga; Franke, Julitta** Isebel: die Gegenspielerin des Propheten Elia. Szenarien aus Geschichte und Kunst: Bonn 1998, FrauenMuseum 135 pp. 3-928239-36-8.

1096   *Reuter, Eleonore* Drei Eva-Bücher. BiKi 53 (1998) 41-43.

1097   **Schulte, Hannelis** Dennoch gingen sie aufrecht: Frauengestalten im Alten Testament. Neuk 1995, Neuk 160 pp. FS27.50. 3-7887-1516-2. ^RDBAT 29 (1998) 285-286 (*Diebner, B.J.*).

1098   *Schüngel-Straumann, Helen* "Von einer Frau nahm die Sünde ihren Anfang, ihretwegen müssen wir alle sterben" (Sir 25,24): zur Wirkungs- und Rezeptionsgeschichte der ersten drei Kapitel der Genesis in biblischer Zeit. BiKi 53 (1998) 11-20.

1099   *Sharp, Donald B.* On the motherhood of Sarah: a Yahwistic theological comment. IBSt 20 (1998) 2-14.

1100   ^E**Siebert-Hommes, Jopie** De vrouw van de nacht en andere verhalen uit de bijbel. Zoetermeer 1998, Meinema 154 pp. *f*25. 90211-37011.

1101   *Smith, Carol* 'Queenship' in Israel?: the cases of Bathsheba, Jezebel and Athaliah. King and Messiah. JSOT.S 270: 1998 ⇒378. 142-162.

1102   *Spanier, Ktziah* The northern Israelite queen mother in the Judaean court: Athalia and Abi. ^FGORDON C. JSOT.S 273: 1998 ⇒31. 136-149.

B4.4 Influxus biblicus in litteraturam profanam, *generalia*

1103   Acheson, Susan 'Conceived at the grave's edge': the esoteric eschatology of H.D.'s trilogy. Literature & Theology 12 (1998) 187-204.

1104   **Alonso Schökel, Luis; Zurro Rodriguez, Eduardo** "Mis fuentes están en ti": estudios bíblicos de literatura española. Serie I. Estudios 67: M 1998, Univ. Pont. Comillas 335 pp. 84-8970829-0.

1105   ^E**Beaude, Pierre-Marie** La bible en littérature. 1997, ⇒13,315 ^RRTL 29 (1998) 237-240 (*Bogaert, Pierre-Maurice*); Revue des Sciences Humaines 252 (1998) 213-214 (*Ducrey, Anne*).

1106   **Bennett, Jim; Mandelbrote, Scott** The garden, the ark, the tower, the temple: biblical metaphors of knowlege in early modern Europe. Oxf 1998, Museum of the History of Science v; 199 pp. 0903374093.

1107   **Carro Celada, José Antonio** Jesucristo en la literatura española e hispanoamericana del siglo XX. M 1998, B.A.C. 142 pp. 84-7914-338-X.

1108   *Desjardins, Michel* Retrofitting Gnosticism: Philip K. DICK and christian origins. Violence. ⇒260. 1998, 122-133.

1109   *Dischner, Gisela* Transzendierung ins Diesseits: Christus als Gestalt der Freiheit im "Großinquisitor" von F.M. DOSTOJEWSKIJ. Edith-Stein-Jahrbuch 4 (1998) 283-296.

1110   *Doty, Gene* Blasphemy and the recovery of the sacred;

1111   *Doty, William G.* Imagining the future-possible. Violence. 1998, ⇒260. 92-103/104-121.

1112 *Emmerson, Richard K.* Apocalyptic themes and imagery in medieval and renaisance literature. Encyclopedia of apocalypticism II. 1998, ⇒507. 402-441.

1113 **Fernández Marcos, Natalio; Fernández Tejero, Emilia** Biblia y humanismo: textos, talantes y controversias del siglo XVI español. 1997, ⇒13,1075. [R]CDios 211 (1998) 661-662 (*Gutiérrez, J.*); RevAg 41 (1998) 825-826 (*Lazcano, Rafael*).

1114 **Fontaine, Jacques** Letteratura tardoantica: figure e percorsi. Letteratura cristiana antica 5: Brescia 1998, Morcelliana 252 pp. 88-372-1674-2.

1115 *Gillmayr-Bucher, Susanne* Biblical words transmitted by lyric poetry. Bible et informatique. 1998, ⇒386. 357-368.

1116 **González de Cardedal, Olegario** Cuatro poetas desde la otra ladera: UNAMUNO, JEAN PAUL, MACHADO, Oscar WILDE: prolegómenos para una cristología. 1996, ⇒12,907; 13,1079. [R]RET 58 (1998) 67-86 (*Álvarez Gómez, Mariano*).

1117 *Haas, Alois M.* Otherwordly[!] journeys in the Middle Ages. Encyclopedia of apocalypticism II. 1998, ⇒507. 442-466.

1118 [E]**Hock, Ronald F.; Chance, J. Bradley; Perkins, Judith** Ancient fiction and early christian narrative. SBL Symposium 6: Atlanta, GA 1998, Scholars ix; 317 pp. $50. 0-7885-0431-2.

1119 *Howard, Douglas L.* Mrs Dalloway: Virginia WOOLF's redemptive cycle. Literature & Theology 12 (1998) 149-158.

1120 **Hyland, Susan E.** Special birth narratives: an analysis of the scriptural narratives as compared with their contemporary literature. [D]Fuller 1998, 353 pp.

1121 **Jeffrey, David L.** People of the book: christian identity and literary culture. 1996, ⇒12,911. [R]RRT (1998/1) 46-48 (*Breadon, John*); Sal. 60 (1998) 346-348 (*Abbà, G.*).

1122 *King, Pamela M.* Calendar and text: Christ's ministry in the York plays and the liturgy. MAe 67 (1998) 30-59.

1123 [E]**Knauer, Bettina** Das Buch und die Bücher: Beiträge zum Verhältnis von Bibel, Religion und Literatur. Wü 1997, Königshausen & N 189 pp.

1124 *Kurz, Paul Konrad* Höre, Gott!: psalmistische Rede in der zeitgenössischen Literatur. US 53 (1998) 340-352.

1125 *Maltz, M.A.H.* The dynamics of intertextuality: the *Akedah* and other biblical allusions in Henry ABRAMOVITCH's *Psalm of the jealous God* and Matti MEGGED's *The Akedah*. JSem 8 (1996) 79-95.

1126 **Massie, Allan** Koning David: een roman. Baarn 1998, Callenbach 256 pp. *f*35. 90-266-0677-X.

1127 *Müllner, Ilse* Blickwechsel: Batseba und David in Romanen des 20. Jahrhunderts. Biblical Interpretation 6 (1998) 348-366.

1128 [E]**Nobel, Pierre** Poème anglo-normand sur l'Ancien Testament: édition et commentaire I: étude, notes, glossaire; II: texte et variantes. 1996, ⇒12,915. [R]CCMéd 41 (1998) 82-84 (*Short, Ian*).

1129 **Nytrová, Olga; Balabán, Milan** Ohlasy Starého Zákona v české literatuře 19. a 20 století [Echoes of the Old Testament in the Czech literature of the XIXth and XXth century]. 1997, ⇒13,1090. [R]CV 40/1 (1998) 73-74 (*Pokorný, Petr*).

1130 *Oesch, Josef M.* Biblische Prophetie in der deutschsprachigen Lyrik des 20. Jahrhunderts. Gott finden. 1998, ⇒304. 136-152.

1131 **Rutledge, Fleming** The Bible and the New York Times. GR 1998, Eerdmans xv; 228 pp. 0-8028-3778-6.

1132 *Sykes, John D.* The bible, western literature, and transformed readers: a review essay. PRSt 25 (1998) 279-286.

1133 *Thraede, Klaus* Buchgrenzen bei JUVENCUS. ^FSPEYER, W.. JAC.E 28: 1998, ⇒107. 285-294.

B4.5 *Exegesis litteraria*—The Bible itself as literature

1134 **Caird, George Bradford** The language and imagery of the Bible. 1996, ⇒12,423. ^RRExp 95 (1998) 450 (*Pelletier, Samuel R.*).

1135 *Cesarini, Remo* La bibbia: un grande testo letterario. Testimonianze 41 (1998) 11-21.

1136 *Clines, David J.A.* Story and poem: the Old Testament as literature and as scripture. OT essays, 1. JSOT.S 292: 1998 <1980>, ⇒142. 225-239.

1137 *Dawson, John David* Figural reading and the fashioning of christian identity in BOYARIN, AUERBACH and FREI. MoTh 14 (1998) 181-196.

1138 **Deidenbach, Hans** Begegnung und Heilung: Psychologie und Pädagogik in biblischen Geschichten. Fischer-Taschenbücher 13421: Fra 1998, Fischer 198 pp. 3-596-13421-8.

1139 **Dormeyer, Detlev** The New Testament among the writings of antiquity. BiSe 55: Shf 1998, Academic 324 pp. 1-85075-860-3.

1140 *Exum, J. Cheryl* Beyond the biblical horizon: the bible and the arts. Biblical Interpretation 6 (1998) 259-265.

1141 **Geller, Stephen A.** Sacred enigmas: literary religion in the Hebrew Bible. 1996, ⇒13,9535. ^RJQR 89 (1998) 171-174 (*Amit, Yairah*); Numen 45 (1998) 97-98 (*Lang, Bernhard*).

1142 **Gibson, J.C.L.** Language and imagery in the Old Testament. L 1998, SPCK ix; 166 p. ^RRRT (1998/4) 19-20 (*O'Kane, Martin*).

1143 *Gnilka, Joachim* Zur Sprache der Bibel. ^FWETTER F. 1998, ⇒124. 53-64.

1144 ^E**Hölscher, Andreas; Kampling, Rainer** Religiöse Sprache und ihre Bilder: von der Bibel bis zur modernen Lyrik. Schriften der Diözesanakademie 14: B 1998, Morus 283 pp. 3-87554-327-0.

1145 **Kirsch, Jonathan** The harlot by the side of the road: forbidden tales of the bible. 1997, ⇒13,1054. ^RBiRe 14/3 (1998) 10, 12 (*Crawford, Sidnie White*). [Gen 19,30-38; 34; 38; Exod 2,22].

1146 *Lemmer, Richard* Movement from allegory to methaphor or from metaphor to allegory?: 'discovering' religious truth. Neotest. 32 (1998) 95-114.

1147 **Matt, Peter von** Fils dévoyés, filles fourvoyées: les désastres familiaux dans la littérature. P 1998, Maison des sciences de l'homme 445 pp. FF190. 2-7351-0762-0.

1148 *Moor, Johannes C. de* Seventy!. ^FLORETZ O. AOAT 250: 1998, ⇒65. 199-203.

1149 **Niditch, Susan** Oral world and written word: ancient Israelite literature. 1996, ⇒12,896. ^RJThS 49 (1998) 699-705 (*Millard, Alan*); JAOS 118 (1998) 436-437 (*Van Seters, John*); JBL 117 (1998) 717-718 (*Culley, Robert C.*).

1150 *Poorthuis, Marcel* Bomen spreken: communicatie tussen mensen en bomen. Interpretatie 6/1 (1998) 19-22.

1151 *Pöttner, Martin* Sprachwissenschaft und neutestamentliche Exegese. ThLZ 123 (1998) 929-942.

1152 *Pyper, Hugh S.* The selfish text: the bible and memetics;
1153 *Schwartz, Regina M.* Teaching the bible 'as' literature 'in' culture. Biblical studies. JSOT.S 266: 1998, ⇒380. 70-90/190-202.
1154 **Weisman, Ze'ev** Political satire in the Bible. SBL.Semeia Studies 32: Atlanta, GA 1998, Scholars xii; 175 pp. $20. 0-7885-0380-4. [R]JQR 89 (1998) 180-181 (*Brettler, Marc Zvi*).
1155 *Welten, Peter* Babylon und Berlin: Geschichte und Wirkungsgeschichte eines biblischen Motivs. BThZ 15 (1998) 234-251.
1156 **Wills, Lawrence M.** The Jewish novel in the ancient world. 1995, ⇒11/2,6801...13,1073. [R]RStR 24 (1998) 335-336 (*Humphreys, W. Lee*).

B4.6 *Singuli auctores*—Bible influence on individual authors

1157 [E]**Bellenger, Yvonne** Le théâtre biblique de Jean DE LA TAILLE. Unichamp 72: P 1998, Champion 259 pp. FF98. 2-85203-925-7.
1158 **Besserman, Lawrence L.** CHAUCER's biblical poetics. Norman, OK 1998, Univ. of Oklahoma Press 352 pp. $40/18. 0-8061-3067-9/8-7.
1159 [E]**Boriaud, Jean-Yves** Saul le furieux: Jean de la TAILLE. P 1998, Ellipses 108 pp. FF60. 2-7298-5878-4.
1160 *Bortone, Giuseppe* Introduzione: angelo biblico in DANTE ed angelo secolarizzato in RILKE. Angeli e demoni. 1998, ⇒375. xi-xxvii.
1161 [E]**Charpentier, Françoise** Les tragédies de Jean de la TAILLE. Cahiers textuel 18: P 1998, Univ. Diderot 119 pp. FF90. 0766-4451.
1162 **Cooke, Paul D.** HOBBES and christianity: reassessing the bible in Leviathan. Lanham, MD 1996, Rowman & L 282 pp.
1163 *Edwards, J.A. Craig* 'Creative reverence': a womanist hermeneutics of imagination in Maude Irwin OWENS's 'Bathesda of sinners run'. Escaping Eden. BiSe 65: 1998, ⇒278. 233-243.
1164 **Frades Gaspar, Eduardo** El uso de la Biblia en los escritos de Fray Bartolomé de LAS CASAS. 1997, ⇒13,1109. [R]Studium 38 (1998) 363-364 (*Martínez, Felicísimo*).
1165 [E]**Fragonard, Marie-Madeleine** Par ta colère nous commes consumés: Jean de la TAILLE, auteur tragique. Références 14: Orléans 1998, Paradigme 236 pp. FF130. 2-87878-194-2.
1166 **Hasel, Frank** Scripture in the theologies of W. PANNENBERG and D.G. BLOESCH. EHS.T 555: 1996, ⇒12,917. [R]AUSS 36 (1998) 127-128 (*Norman, Bruce*).
1167 **Kuschel, Karl-Josef** Im Spiegel der Dichter: Mensch, Gott und Jesus in der Literatur des 20. Jahrhunderts. 1997, ⇒13,1113. [R]ThLZ 123 (1998) 1238-1239 (*Pöhlmann, Horst Georg*); PerTeol 30 (1998) 449-452 (*Soethe, Paulo Astor*); ThGl 88 (1998) 131-132 (*Garhammer, Erich*).
1168 *Kuschel, Karl-Josef* La pesadilla del fin de la humanidad: estudio sobre la idea del apocalipsis en la obra de Günter GRASS. Conc(E) 277 (1998) 519-529.
1169 *Müller, Hans-Peter* Rückzug Gottes ins Namenlose: zu einem Gedicht Paul CELANs. Glauben, Denken und Hoffen. 1998, ⇒796. 311-319.
1170 [ET]**Rey, André-Louis** Centons homériques (Homerocentra). SC 437: P 1998, Cerf 545 pp. 2-204-05998-6.

1171 **Rigo, Paola** Memoria classica e memoria biblica in DANTE. Saggi di lettere italiane 48: F 1994, Olschki 184 pp. L36.000. 88-222-4267-X. [R]CrSt 19 (1998) 684-685 (*Giombi, Samuele*).

1172 *Tschuggnall, Peter* "Dieses: Stirb und werde!": literarische Spiegelungen biblischer Zitate bei Max FRISCH und Heinrich BÖLL. Gott finden. 1998, ⇒304. 218-227 [Gen 1; Dt 5].

B4.7 *Interpretatio* psychiatrica

1173 **Drewermann, Eugen** La palabra de salvación y sanación: la fuerza liberadora de la fe. 1996, ⇒12,926. [R]Carthaginensia 14 (1998) 246-247 (*Tamayo Acosta, J.J.*).

1174 *Jaschke, Helmut* Psychologie und Schriftauslegung. Lebendige Katechese 20 (1998) 18-25.

1175 **Lüdemann, Gerd** The unholy in holy scripture: the dark side of the Bible. 1997, ⇒13,1142. [R]BTB 28 (1998) 38-39 (*Bossman, David*).

B5 Methodus exegeticus [⇒F2.1]

1176 *Adam, A.K.M.* Deconstruction and exegesis. Escaping Eden. BiSe 65: 1998, ⇒278. 99-110.

1177 *Alkier, Stefan; Brucker, Ralph* Einleitung: Neutestamentliche Exegesen interdisziplinär—ein Plädoyer. Exegese und Methodendiskussion. TANZ 23: ⇒208. 1998, IX-XIX.

1178 *Barton, John* What is a book?: modern exegesis and the literary conventions of ancient Israel. Intertextuality. OTS 40: 1998 ⇒394. 1-14.

1179 **Barton, John** Reading the Old Testament: method in biblical study. 1996, ⇒12,493. [R]ThLZ 123 (1998) 843-845 (*Bauer, Uwe F.W.*).

1180 *Bauckham, Richard J.* Response to Philip ESLER. SJTh 51 (1998) 249-253.

1181 **Berger, Klaus** As formas literárias do Novo Testamento. Bíblica Loyola 23: São Paulo 1998, Loyola 366 pp. 85-15-01672-9.

1182 *Bertuletti, Angelo* Esegesi biblica e teologia sistematica. [F]MARTINI C., Rivelazione. 1998 ⇒74. 133-157.

1183 *Blount, Brian K.* If you get MY meaning: introducing cultural exegesis. Exegese und Methodendiskussion. TANZ 23: 1998 ⇒208. 77-97.

1184 *Collins, Adela Yarbro* Literary history and cultural history. [F]BETZ, H. 1998 ⇒10. 155-159.

1185 *Craffert, Pieter F.* From apartheid readings to ordinary readings of the bible: has the ethics of interpretation changed?. Scriptura 64 (1998) 65-79.

1186 **Deist, Ferdinand** Ervaring, rede en metode in skrifuitleg: 'n wetenskaps-historiese ondersoek na skrifuitleg in die Ned Geref Kerk 1840-1990. 1994 ⇒13,1158. [R]OTEs 11 (1998) 645-646 (*Lombaard, C.J.S.*).

1187 *Dunn, James D.* Scholarly methods in the interpretation of the gopels. DBM 17 (1998) 47-68.

1188 *Esler, Philip F.* Community and gospel in early christianity: a response to Richard BAUCKHAM's Gospels for all christians. SJTh 51 (1998) 235-248.

1189 *Farkasfalvy, Denis* A heritage in search of heirs: the future of ancient christian exegesis. Com(US) 25 (1998) 505-519.
1190 *Fiedler, Peter* Wie Juden mit ihrer Bibel umgehen. Lebendige Katechese 20 (1998) 25-30.
1191 *Frades, Eduardo* Exégesis y teología. Iter 9 (1998) 32-86.
1192 *Frickenschmidt, Dirk* Evangelium als antike Biographie. ZNT 2 (1998) 29-39.
1193 *Gilbert, Maurice* Exégèse intégrale. Il a parlé par les prophètes. 1998 <1992> ⇒155. 55-68.
1194 *Goldingay, John* The ongoing story of biblical interpretation. ChM 112 (1998) 6-16.
1195 **Gosse, Bernard** Structuration des grands ensembles bibliques et intertextualité à l'époque perse: de la rédaction sacerdotale du livre d'Isaïe à la contestation de la Sagesse. BZAW 246: 1997, ⇒13,1163. ᴿETR 73 (1998) 115-116 (*Römer, Thomas*).
1196 *Gräßer, Erich* Evangelisch-katholische Exegese?: eine Standortbestimmung. ZThK 95 (1998) 185-196.
1197 **Harris, Harriet A.** Fundamentalism and evangelicals. Oxford Theological Monographs: Oxf 1998, Clarendon viii; 384 pp. £48. 0-19-826960-9.
1198 **Hirshman, Marc G.** A rivalry of genius: Jewish and christian biblical interpretation in late antiquity. 1996, ⇒12,956; 13,1171. ᴿJEarlyC 6 (1998) 316-317 (*Homan, Philip A.*).
1199 *Hurd, John C.* Certain uncertain certainties in New Testament studies. Earlier letters of Paul... ARGU 8: 1998 <1979> ⇒163. 109-116.
1200 **Johnstone, Christopher Lyle** Theory, text, context: issues in Greek rhetoric and oratory. 1996 ⇒12,957. ᴿRhetorica 16 (1998) 227-230 (*Pullman, George*).
1201 **Jonker, Louis Cloete** Exclusivity and variety: perspectives on multidimensional exegesis. Contributions to Biblical Exegesis and Theology 19: 1996, ⇒12,958. ᴿOTEs 11/1 (1998) 199-202 (*Lombaard, C.J.S.*); ThLZ 123 (1998) 847-848 (*Söding, Thomas*).
1202 *Klauck, Hans J.* Die katholische neutestamentliche Exegese zwischen Vatikanum I und Vatikanum II. ᶠWETTER F. 1998 ⇒124. 85-119.
1203 *Larsson, Gerhard* More quantitative Old Testament research?. ZAW 110 (1998) 570-580.
1204 **Levenson, Jon D.** The Hebrew Bible, the Old Testament, and historical criticism: Jews and Christians in biblical studies. 1993 ⇒9,1480... 12,963. ᴿJAOS 118 (1998) 141-142 (*Cooper, Alan*).
1205 **Linnemann, Eta** Bibelkritik auf dem Prüfstand: wie wissenschaftlich ist die 'wissenschaftliche Theologie'?. Nürnberg 1998, VTR 184 pp. 3-933372-19-4.
1206 **Lohfink, Gerhard** Ahora entiendo la biblia: crítica de las formas. Dabar 11: M 1997, San Pablo 253 pp. 84-285-2050-X.
1207 *Merklein, Helmut* Integrative Bibelauslegung?: methodische und hermeneutische Aspekte. Studien zu Jesus und Paulus II. WUNT 105: 1998 <1989> ⇒176. 114-122.
1208 **Ochs, Peter Peirce,** Pragmatism and the logic of scripture. C 1998, CUP x; 361 pp. £40. ·
1209 *Ohler, Annemarie* Exegese des Alten Testamentes—ein Rundblick. Lebendige Katechese 20 (1998) 11-17.
1210 *Rizzi, Giovanni* Modelli giudaici e giudeo-cristiani per un'inculturazione della fede. ED 51 (1998) 29-65.

1211 *Sampathkumar, Antoni Raj* Une lecture indienne des évangiles. Spiritus 39 (1998) 321-330.

1212 **Savage, James C.** Psychotherapy and exegesis: a study of parallel processes. ^DUnion Institute 1998, 297 pp.

1213 *Sæbo, Magne* Traditio-historical perspectives in the Old Testament: introductory remarks. On the way to canon. 1998 ⇒194. 21-33.

1214 *Schürmann, Heinz* Thesen zur kirchlichen Schriftauslegung <1982>;

1215 Anamnese als kirchlicher Basisvorgang: eine theologische Besinnnung <1988>;

1216 Bibelwissenschaft unter dem Wort Gottes: eine selbstkritische Besinnung <1989>;

1217 Die neuzeitliche Bibelwissenschaft als theologische Disciplin: ein interdisziplinärer Gesprächsbeitrag <1989>. Gesammelte Beiträge. 1998 ⇒197. 44-46/55-61/3-43/47-54.

1218 *Simian-Yofre, Horacio* Esegesi contemporanea. Dizionario di omiletica. 1998 ⇒533. 482-485.

1219 *Smidt, J.C. de* Reading ancient texts more comprehensively: assessing a new methodology. Scriptura 64 (1998) 51-63.

1220 **Söding, Thomas** Wege der Schriftauslegung: Methodenbuch zum Neuen Testament. FrB 1998, Herder 350 pp. DM39.80. 3-451-26545-1.

1221 **Steck, Odil Hannes** Old Testament exegesis: a guide to the methodology. SBL Resources for Biblical Study 39: Atlanta, GA 1998, Scholars xxiv; 202 pp. $20. 0-7885-0465-7.

1222 *Taylor, Nicolas H.* Cognitive dissonance and early christianity: a theory and its application reconsidered. R & T 5 (1998) 138-153.

1223 **Thiede, Carsten Peter** Bibelcode und Bibelworte: die Suche nach verschlüsselten Botschaften in der Heiligen Schrift. Gießen 1998, Brunnen 127 pp. DM22.80. 3-7655-1158-7.

1224 **Thomas, Robert L.; Farnell, F. David** The Jesus crisis: the inroads of historical criticism into evangelical scholarship. GR 1998, Kregel 416 pp. $17. 0-8254-3811-X.

1225 *Trigo, Pedro* Teología y exégesis. Iter 9 (1998) 7-30.

1226 **Van Bruggen, Jakob** Wie lesen wir die Bibel?: eine Einführung in die Schriftauslegung. Neuhausen-Stu 1998, Hänssler 217 pp. 3-7751-2955-3.

1227 *Van Wyk (jr), W.C.* Resepsieteorie en die studie van die Ou Testament in Suid-Afrika [Reception theory and the study of the Old Testament in South Africa]. JSem 9 (1997) 166-178.

1228 *Winninge, Mikael* Bibelanvändningen i ett brev om bibelanvändningen. SEÅ 63 (1998) 281-293.

1229 **Young, Frances Margaret** Biblical exegesis and the formation of christian culture. 1997 ⇒13,1219. ^RJEH 49 (1998) 331-332 (*Markus, R.A.*); SVTQ 42 (1998) 405-410 (*Behr, John*); RStT 17/1 (1998) 109-111 (*Eckert, Lowell*); JThS 49 (1998) 353-358 (*Dawson, David*).

III. Critica Textus, Versiones

D1   Textual criticism

1230   Bericht der Hermann Kunst-Stiftung zur Förderung der neutestamentlichen Textforschung für die Jahre 1995 bis 1998. Müns 1998, 86 pp.

1231   **Blount, Brian K.** Cultural interpretation: reorienting New Testament
criticism. 1995, ⇒11/2,1268. [R]JR 78 (1998) 105-107 (*Brown,
Michael J.*).

1232   *Dines, Jennifer* M. JEROME and the Hexapla: the witness of the commentary on Amos. Origen's Hexapla. TSAJ 58: 1998 ⇒399. 421-
436.

1233   **Parker, David C.** The living text of the gospels. 1997 ⇒13,1273.
[R]BiTr 49 (1998) 154-155 (*Ellingworth, Paul*); Theol. 101 (1998)
141-142 (*Harvey, A.E.*).

1234   *Pisano, Stephen* Traductions anciennes de la bible. Dictionnaire critique de théologie. 1998, [E]Lacoste, J.-Y. ⇒D8. 1155-1157.

1235   [E]**Sharpe III, John Lawrence; Van Kampen, Kimberly** The Bible
as book: the manuscript tradition. L 1998, British Library xi; 260 pp.
£40. 0-7123-4522-1.

1236   *Teshima, Isaiah* Textual criticism and early biblical interpretation.
Interpretation of the Bible. JSOT.S 289: 1998 ⇒388. 165-179.

D2.1   *Biblica hebraica*   Hebrew text

1237   *Adair, J.R.* Light from below: canonical and theological implications
of textual criticism. OTEs 11 (1998) 9-23.

1238   *Chiesa, Bruno* Lectio melior potior. Henoch 20 (1998) 305-327;
Richard SIMON e i principii della critica del testo ⇒1281.

1239   *Contini, Riccardo* I testi letterari aramaico-egiziani e l'Antico
Testamento. RstB 10/1-2 (1998) 81-104.

1240   *Flint, Peter W.* Columns I and II of the Hexapla: the evidence of the
Milan Palimpsest (Rahlfs 1098). Origen's Hexapla. TSAJ 58: 1998
⇒399. 125-132.

1241   [E]**Freedman, David Noel; Beck, Astrid B.; Sanders, James A.** The
Leningrad Codex: the facsimile edition. GR 1998, Eerdmans li; 1016
pp. 0-8028-3786-7.

1242   *Hendel, Ronald S.* Restoration project: the Hebrew Bible. BiRe 14/4
(1998) 23, 55.

1243   *Himmelfarb, Lea* The exegetical role of the *paseq*. Sef. 58 (1998)
243-260.

1244   *Jenkins, R.G.* The first column of the Hexapla: the evidence of the
Milan Codex (Rahlfs 1098) and the Cairo Genizah Fragment (Rahlfs
2005). Origen's Hexapla. TSAJ 58: 1998 ⇒399. 88-102.

1245   **Kelley, Page H.; Mynatt, Daniel S.; Crawford, Timothy G.** The
Masorah of Biblia Hebraica Stuttgartensia: introduction and annotated glossary. GR 1998, Eerdmans xiv; 241 pp. $26. 0-8028-4363-8.

1246   *Norton, Gerard J.* Observations on the first two columns of the
Hexapla. Origen's Hexapla. TSAJ 58: 1998 ⇒399. 103-124.

1247   *Olley, John W.* Texts have paragraphs too—a plea for inclusion in
critical editions. Textus 19 (1998) 111-125.

1248 *Penkower, Jordan S.* The chapter divisions in the 1525 Rabbinic Bible. VT 48 (1998) 350-374.
1249 **Perani, Mauro** Gli ebrei a Castel Goffredo: con uno studio sulla Bibbia Soncino di Brescia del 1494. F 1998, La giuntina 190 pp. 88-8057-081-1.
1250 *Person, Raymond F.* The ancient Israelite scribe as performer. JBL 117 (1998) 601-609.
1251 *Sanders, James A.* The Judaean Desert scrolls and the history of the text of the Hebrew Bible. Caves of enlightenment. 1998 ⇒467. 1-17.
1252 *Sánchez Salor, Eustaquio* Colaboradores de MONTANO en la Biblia Políglota. RevAg 41 (1998) 929-972.
1253 *Sæbo, Magne* From pluriformity to uniformity: the emergence of the Massoretic Text. On the way to canon. 1998 <1978> ⇒194. 36-46.
1254 *Sirat, C.; Biezunski, G.* Typologie des Sifré-Tora: élaboration de la base de données. Bible et informatique. 1998 ⇒386. 131-135.
1255 *Tov, Emanuel* Paratextual elements in the masoretic manuscripts of the bible compared with the Qumran evidence. ᶠSTEGEMANN, H. BZNW 97: 1998, ⇒111. 73-83;
1256 Sense divisions in the Qumran texts, the Masoretic text, and ancient translations of the Bible. Interpretation of the Bible. JSOT.S 289: 1998, ⇒388. 121-146;
1257 The significance of the texts from the Judean desert for the history of the text of the Hebrew Bible: a new synthesis. Qumran between OT and NT. JSOT.S 290: 1998 ⇒327. 277-309;
1258 Textual criticism of the Hebrew Bible 1947-1997. ᶠVAN DER WOUDE, A.. VT.S 73: 1998 ⇒121. 61-81.
1259 **Weil, Daniel Meir** The Masoretic chant of the Hebrew bible. 1996 ⇒12,1012. ᴿAJSR 23 (1998) 112-116 (*Levin, Saul*).

D2.2 **Targum**

1260 *Bissoli, Giovanni* I testi della centralizzazione del culto secondo il targum. SBFLA 48 (1998) 267-271.
1261 *Chilton, Bruce* Prophecy in the Targumim. Mediators of the divine. SFSHJ 163: 1998 ⇒287. 185-201.
1262 *Cook, Joan E.* Hannah's later songs: a study in comparative methods of interpretation. The function of scripture. 1998 ⇒236. 241-261 [1 Sam 2,1-10]..
1263 *Golomb, David M.* Methodological considerations in pentateuchal targumic research. JSPE 18 (1998) 3-25.
1264 *Klein, Michael* The Aramaic Targumim: translation and interpretation. Interpretation of the Bible. JSOT.S 289: 1998 ⇒388. 317-331.
1265 *Maher, Michael* God as judge in the targums. JSJ 29 (1998) 49-62.
1266 *Menn, Esther M.* Sanctification of the (divine) name: *Targum Neofiti*'s 'translation' of Genesis 38.25-26. The function of scripture. 1998 ⇒236. 206-240.
1267 *Pérez Fernández, Miguel* Il targum. Letteratura giudaica. 1998 ᴱ**Aranda Pérez, G.** ⇒K1.1. 467-492.
1268 *Ribera-Florit, Josep* Tendencias doctrinales del Targum de Ezequiel. ᶠMARGAIN, J. 1998 ⇒71. 259-268.
1269 *Rofé, Alexander* Biblical antecedents of the Targumic solution of metaphors (Ps 89:41-42,; Ezek 22:25-28; Gen 49:8-9, 14-15). Interpretation of the Bible. JSOT.S 289: 1998 ⇒388. 333-340.

1270 *Shepherd, David* Before BOMBERG: the case of the Targum of Job in the Rabbinic bible and the Solger Codex (MS Nürnberg). Bib. 79 (1998) 360-380.
1271 *Smelik, Willem F.* Translation and commentary in one: the interplay of pluses and substitutions in the Targum of the Prophets. JSJ 29 (1998) 245-260.
1272 **Sysling, Harry** Tehiyyat Ha-Metim: the resurrection of the dead in the Palestinian targums of the Pentateuch... classical rabbinic litera-ture. TSAJ 57: 1996 ⇒12,1306. [R]Sal. 60 (1998) 353-354 (*Vicent, R.*); ThLZ 123 (1998) 55-56 (*Van der Ploeg, J.P.M.*).
1273 *Tassin, Claude* Des versions bibliques anciennes à leurs artisans: Targum, Septante et Nouveau Testament. EstB 56 (1998) 315-334.

D3.1 *Textus graecus*—Greek NT

1274 *Aland, Barbara* 100 Jahre neutestamentliche Textforschung (1898-1998). Bericht der Hermann Kunst-Stiftung. 1998 ⇒1230. 22-41;
1275 Der Text des griechischen Neuen Testaments: ein Beispiel von inter-konfessioneller und internationaler Zusammenarbeit. Bericht der Hermann Kunst-Stiftung. 1998, ⇒1230. 53-60.
1276 [E]**Aland, Kurt; Rosenbaum, Hans-Udo** 2/1 Kirchenväter-Papyri: Teil 1: Beschreibungen: Repertorium der griechischen christlichen Papyri. PTS 42: 1995 ⇒⇒11/2,g053... 13,1253. [R]JThS 49 (1998) 812-818 (*Obbink, Dirk*).
1277 **Aland, Kurt** Kurzgefasste Liste der griechischen Handschriften des Neuen Testaments. ANTT 1: 1994 <1963> ⇒10,1414; 13,1252 [R]ThRv 94 (1998) 507-508 (*Elliott, J.K.*);
1278 [E]**Ammassari, Antonio** Bezae Codex Cantabrigiensis. 1996, ⇒12,1025. [R]RivBib 46 (1998) 238-240 (*Cavalletti, Sofia*).
1279 Die Arbeiten des Instituts und der Hermann Kunst-Stiftung 1995-1998. Bericht der Hermann Kunst-Stiftung. 1998 ⇒1230. 8-21.
1280 *Brandt, Pierre-Yves* Manuscrits grecs utilisés par ERASME pour son édition du Novum Instrumentum de 1516. ThZ 54 (1998) 120-124.
1281 *Chiesa, Bruno* Richard SIMON e i principii della critica del testo. Henoch 20 (1998) 339-348.
1282 **Clarke, Kent D.** Textual optimism: a critique of the United Bible Societies' Greek New Testament. JSNT.S 138: 1997, ⇒13,1255 [R]NT 40 (1998) 382-384 (*Ellingworth, Paul*); RBBras 15 (1998) 436-437; JThS 49 (1998) 293-297 (*Elliott, J.K.*).
1283 *Ellis, E.E.* New directions in the history of early christianity. [F]JUDGE E. 1998 ⇒47. 71-92.
1284 **Metzger, Bruce M.** Il testo del Nuovo Testamento. 1996, ⇒12,1047. [R]RivBib 46 (1998) 489-492 (*Passoni Dell'Acqua, Anna*).
1285 **Mullen, Roderic L.** The NT text of CYRIL of Jerusalem. SBL The NT in the Greek Fathers 7: 1997 ⇒13,1268. [R]NT 40 (1998) 384-386 (*Elliott, J.K.*).
1286 NESTLE-ALAND: 100 Jahre Novum Testamentum Graece 1898-1998. Stu 1998, Deutsche Bibelgesellschaft xxxii; 94*; 818 pp. 3-438-05108-7.
1287 Nuovo Testamento: greco-italiano. R 1996, Società Biblica Brit-tanica & Forestiera 51* + 850 pp. L80.000. 88-237-2068-0. [R]NT 40 (1998) 204-205 (*Elliott, J.K.*).

1288 *Omanson, Roger L.* A critical appraisal of the apparatus criticus. BiTr 49 (1998) 301-323;

1289 Punctuation in the New Testament: if only Paul had used the Chicago manual of style. BiRe 14/6 (1998) 40-43.

1290 ^E**Parker, D.C.; Amphoux, C.-B.** Codex Bezae. NTTS 22: 1996 ⇒12,265; 13,1271. ^RJThS 49 (1998) 300-302 (*Delobel, Joël*).

1291 *Puech, Émile; Mébarki, Farah* Markus und Matthäus: Irrwege und falsche Datierungen?. WUB 10 (1998) 44-45.

1292 *Quispel, Gilles* MARCION and the text of the New Testament. VigChr 52 (1998) 349-360.

1293 *Ramelli, Ilaria L.E.* I vangeli nel "Bezae Codex Cantabrigiensis". RSCI 52 (1998) 171-178.

1294 *Vocke, Harald* Kein Ende für die Textkritik der Evangelien: Qumran hat die modische Geringschätzung der Konjektur widerlegt. IKaZ 27 (1998) 283-288.

1295 *Welte, Michael* Über die Herkunft einiger Lesarten in den Katholischen Briefen. Bericht der Hermann Kunst-Stiftung. 1998 ⇒1230. 61-71.

D3.2 *Versiones graecae*—VT, Septuaginta etc.

1296 *Cimosa, Mario* La traduzione dei LXX usata dal NT: un esempio di intertestualità (Ab 2,4 citato in Rm 1,17; Gal 3,11 e Eb 10,38). ^FHE-RIBAN J.. 1998 ⇒41. 31-43;

1297 Translating the Old Testament. Interpretation of the Bible. JSOT.S 289: 1998 ⇒388. 1341-1357.

1298 *Cook, Johann* Greek philosophy and the Septuagint. JNSL 24/1 (1998) 177-191.

1299 *Cox, Claude* Traveling with Aquila, Symmachus, and Theodotion in Armenia. Origen's Hexapla. TSAJ 58: 1998 ⇒399. 302-316.

1300 **Cox, Claude E.** Aquila, Symmachus and Theodotion in Armenia. SBL.SCSt 42: 1996, ⇒12,984. ^RCBQ 60 (1998) 112-113 (*Mathews, Edward G.*).

1301 **Fernández Marcos, Natalio** Introducción a las versiones griegas de la Biblia. TECC 64: M 1998, CSIC 416 pp.

1302 *Fernández Marcos, Natalio* The textual context of the Hexapla: Lucianic texts and Vetus Latina. Origen's Hexapla. TSAJ 58: 1998 ⇒399. 408-420.

1303 *Greenspoon, Leonard J.* A preliminary publication of Max Leopold MARGOLIS's *Andreas Masius*, together with his discussion of Hexapla-Tetrapla. Origen's Hexapla. TSAJ 58: 1998 ⇒399. 39-69.

1304 ^E**Hengel, Martin; Schwemer, Anna Maria** Die Septuaginta zwischen Judentum und Christentum. WUNT 72: 1994 ⇒10,323a. ^RCBQ 60 (1998) 185-186 (*Wright, Benjamin G.*).

1305 *Jenkins, R.G.* Hexaplaric marginalia and the Hexapla-Tetrapla question. Origen's Hexapla. TSAJ 58: 1998 ⇒399. 73-87.

1306 *Kaimakis, Dimitris* Problems of translation in the text of the Old Testament. DBM 17 (1998) 37-47.

1307 *McLay, Tim* καιγε and Septuagint research. Textus 19 (1998) 127-139.

1308 **Muraoka, Takamitsu** Hebrew/Aramaic index to the Septuagint: keyed to the Hatch-Redpath concordance. GR 1998, Baker 160 pp. $20. 0-8010-2145-6.

1309 **Müller, Mogens** The first bible of the church: a plea for the Septuagint. JSOT.S 206: 1996 ⇒⇒12,1075; 13,1297. RThLZ 123 (1998) 239-242 (*Hübner, Hans*); RB 105 (1998) 426-430 (*Gourgues, Michel*).

1310 *Passoni Dell'Acqua, Anna* Notazioni cromatiche dall'Egitto greco-romano: la versione dei LXX e i papiri. Aeg. 78 (1998) 77-115.

1311 *Pummer, Reinhard* The Greek bible and the Samaritans. REJ 157 (1998) 269-358.

1312 *Scanlin, Harold P.* A new edition of ORIGEN's Hexapla: how it might be done. Origen's Hexapla. TSAJ 58: 1998 ⇒399. 439-449.

1313 *Schaper, Joachim* The origin and purpose of the fifth column of the Hexapla. Origen's Hexapla. TSAJ 58: 1998 ⇒399. 3-15.

1314 Simotas, Panagiotis N. Ἑρμηνευτικὴ ἔρευνα εἰς τὸ κείμενον τῆς Παλαιᾶς Διαθήκης ἐπὶ τῇ βάσει ἀρχαίων ἑλληνικῶν μεταφράσεων [Hermeneutical research in the text of the Old Testament on the basis of ancient Greek translations]. Theol(A) 69 (1998) 32-40, 214-243, 417-444, 609-659.

1315 *Szpek, Heidi M.* On the influence of Septuagint on the Peshitta. CBQ 60 (1998) 251-266.

1316 *Ulrich, Eugene* The relevance of the Dead Sea scrolls for Hexaplaric studies. Origen's Hexapla. TSAJ 58: 1998 ⇒399. 401-407.

1317 *Van der Kooij, Arie* Perspectives on the study of the Septuagint: who are the translators?. FVAN DER WOUDE, A. VT.S 73: 1998 ⇒121. 214-229.

1318 *Wasserstein, David J.* The Ptolemy and the hare: dating an old story about the translation of the Septuagint. SCI 17 (1998) 77-86.

1319 *Zipor, M.* Some considerations concerning column b' in the CATSS. Bible et informatique. 1998 ⇒386. 193-194.

D4 Versiones orientales

1320 **Avishur, Yitzhak** The oldest translation of the Early Prophets into Judaeo-Arabic. 1995 ⇒13,1308. RTarb. 67/2 (1998) ix-x (*Ben-Shammai, Haggai*); JQR 89 (1998) 236-238 (*Polliack, Meira*);

1321 יְשַׁעְיָהוּ וְיִרְמְיָהוּ כְּתַב יָד בּוֹדְלֵיָנָה עִם מָבוֹא וְהֶעָרוֹת [Isaiah and Jeremiah according to a manuscript of the Bodleian (Ms. Hunt 206)]. תַּרְגּוּם קָדוּם לִנְבִיאִים אַחֲרוֹנִים בַּעֲרָבִית-יְהוּדִית בָּבְלִית וְסוּרִית [A medieval translation of the latter prophets into Babylonian and Syrian Judaeo-Arabic]. J 1998, Magnes 241 pp. **H.**

1322 *Bacot, Şeÿna* Un évangéliaire copte-arabe illustré du début du XIXe siècle. Études Coptes V. 1998 ⇒451. 93-106.

1323 *Bar-Asher, Moshe* התגוּן בסורית ארץ-ישראלית [The Syropalestinian version of the bible]. Leš. 61 (1998) 131-143.

1324 *Brock, Sebastian P.* The Peshitta Old Testament: between Judaism and Christianity. CrSt 19 (1998) 483-502;

1325 Translating the New Testament into Syriac (classical and modern). Interpretation of the Bible. JSOT.S 289: 1998 ⇒388. 371-385.

1326 EDirksen, Piet B.; Van der Kooij, Arie The Peshitta as a translation. MPIL 8: 1995 ⇒11/1,76; 13,1315. RVT 48 (1998) 122-123 (*Williams, P.J.*).

1327 *Feder, Frank* Die systematische Numerierung der Handschriften des Alten Testamentes zur Edition der koptisch-sahidischen Septuaginta. HBO 26 (1998) 33-36.

1328   The Good News of Our Lord Jesus Christ: according to the four evangelists (Pshitto of Mardin). Istanbul 1998, Ohan Matbaacilik iv; 345 pp.

1329   *Gordon, Robert P.* The Syriac Old Testament: provenance, perspective and translation technique. Interpretation of the Bible. JSOT.S 289: 1998 ⇒388. 355-370.

1330   *Grierson, Roderick* 'Without note or a comment': British Library Or. 11360 and the text of the Peshitta New Testament. OrChr 82 (1998) 88-98.

1331   *Henne, Philippe* Le Christ dans le "Diatessaron". Graphè 7 (1998) 19-30.

1332   *Juckel, Andreas K.* Towards a critical edition of the Harklean Gospels. ParOr 23 (1998) 209-215.

1333   **Kiraz, George Anton** Comparative edition of the Syriac gospels. NTTS 21/1-4: 1996 ⇒12,1090; 13,1318. ᴿJSSt 43 (1998) 185-186 (*McCarthy, Carmel*).

1334   *Lenzi, Giovanni* L'antica versione siriaca dei vangeli dopo centocinquant'anni di ricerca. AnScR 3 (1998) 263-278.

1335   **Luisier, Philippe** Les citations vétéro-testamentaires dans les versions coptes des évangiles: recueil et analyse critique. COr 22: Genève 1998, Cramer 276 pp.

1336   *Salvesen, Alison* JACOB of Edessa and the text of scripture. Use of sacred books. 1998 ⇒263. 235-245.

1337   ᴱ**Schüssler, Karlheinz** Das sahidische Alte und Neue Testament: sa 1-20: Lfg. 1. Biblia coptica: die koptischen Bibeltexte. 1995 ⇒11/2,2621. ᴿBASPap 35 (1998) 229-233 (*Clackson, Sarah*);

1338   Das sahidische Alte und Neue Testament, 1/3: sa 49-92. Biblia Copta: Wsb 1998, Harrassowitz vii; 118 pp. DM88. 3-447-04097-1.

1339   *Sokoloff, Michael; Müller-Kessler, Christa* -המקרא הארמי הנוצרי הארץ-ישראלי: למאמרו של משה בר-אשר, |התבֹ|ך מסורית ארץ-ישראלית| [כרך זה, עמ' [143-131 [The Christian Palestinian Aramaic version of the Old Testament (Response to M. Bar-Asher, Leš. 61,131-143)]. Leš. 61 (1998) 253-257.

1340   *Van Esbroeck, Michel* Les versions orientales de la bible: une orientation bibliographique. Interpretation of the Bible. JSOT.S 289: 1998 ⇒388. 399-509.

D5 Versiones latinae

1341   Aus der Geschichte der lateinischen Bibel. BVLI 42 (1998) 39-40.

1342   La bibbia di Borso d'Este: commentario al codice. Modena 1997, Panini 611 pp; 2 vol.

1343   Biblische Handschriften: Verzeichnis und Sigel. BVLI 42 (1998) 22.

1344   ᴱ**Bouhot, Jean-Paul; Genest, Jean-François** La bibliothèque de l'abbaye de Clairvaux du XIIᵉ au XVIIIᵉ s., 2: les manuscrits conservés, 1: manuscrits bibliques, patristiques et théologiques. Documents... 33/2: P 1997, CNRS 766 pp.

1345   *Buble, Nikola* L'evangeliario di Traù (Trogir). RiCi 15 (1998) 211-215.

1346   *Fragnito, Gigliola* Il ritorno al latino, ovvero la fine dei volgarizzamenti. La bibbia in italiano. 1998 ⇒390. 395-407.

1347 ᴱ**Frede, Hermann Josef** Vetus Latina-Fragmente zum Alten Testament: die pelagianische Epistula ad quandam matronam Christianam. AGLB 28: 1996 ⇒12,1099. ᴿJBL 117 (1998) 548-549 *(Harvey, Paul B.)*.

1348 *Gameson, Richard* La bible de Saint-Vaast d'Arras et un manuscrit anglo-saxon de BOÈCE. Scr. 52 (1998) 316-321.

1349 *Gönna, Sigrid von der* Ein goldenes Evangelienbuch aus dem alten Mainzer Domschatz: zur Geschichte des 'Mainzer Evangeliars' (Hofbibliothek Aschaffenburg, Ms. 13) c. 1260-1303. AMRhKG 50 (1998) 131-153.

1350 *Lobrichon, Guy* Pour l'étude de la tradition et du texte de la Vulgate latine en Italie (XIIIᵉ siècle). La bibbia in italiano. 1998 ⇒390. 23-33.

1351 Nova Vulgata: bibliorum sacrorum editio. Città del Vaticano 1998, Libreria Editrice Vaticana 1854 pp. 88-209-2163-4.

1352 *Passoni Dell'Acqua, Anna* La bibbia nella chiesa antica in Italia: le versioni latine. La traduzione. 1998 ⇒222. 15-25.

1353 *Rouse, Richard H.; Rouse, Mary* Wandering scribes and traveling artists: RAULINUS of Fremington and his Bolognese bible. ᶠBOYLE L. 1998 ⇒13., 32-67.

1354 **Vernet, André; Bouhot, Jean-Paul; Genest, Jean-François** La bibliothèque de l'abbaye de Clairvaux du XIIᵉ au XVIIIᵉ siècle, 2: les manuscrits conservés, 1: manuscrits bibliques, patristiques et théologiques. P 1997, CNRS 768 pp.

1355 Vetus Latina: Arbeitsbericht der Stiftung, 42. Vetus Latina. Bericht des Instituts 31: FrB 1998, Herder 47 pp.

D6 Versiones modernae .1 *romanicae*, romance

1356 **Alonso Schökel, Luis** Nuevo Testamento. Biblia del peregrino. Bilbao 1998, Mensajero 381 pp. 84-271-2158-X.

1357 ᴱ**Alves, Herculano** Nova Bíblia dos Capuchinhos: versao dos textos originais. Lisboa 1998, Difusora Bíblica 2143 pp. 972-652-155-6 ᴿBib(L) 7/7 (1998) 178-180.

1358 *Argemi, Aureli* Bibbia e minoranze etnico-linguistiche: esperienza catalana. Bibbia, popoli e lingue. 1998 ⇒381. 129-144.

1359 *Asperti, Stefano* I vangeli in volgare italiano. La bibbia in italiano. 1998 ⇒390. 119-144.

1360 **Babut, Jean-Marc** Lire la Bible en traduction. LiBi 113: 1997, ⇒13,1339. ᴿCahiers de Traduction Biblique 30 (1998) 21 *(Schneider, Théo)*.

1361 *Bajard, J.; Poswick, R.-F.* Un regard critique et autonome sur une traduction: l'Heuriciel CIB-Microbile de la Concordance de la TOB. Bible et informatique. 1998 ⇒386. 221-240.

1362 *Barbieri, Edoardo* La bibbia nel medioevo in Italia: prassi di traduzione fino al Concilio di Trento. La traduzione. 1998 ⇒222. 26-35.

1363 *Barbieri, Edoardo* Panorama delle traduzioni bibliche in volgare prima del concilio di Trento. FolTh 9 (1998) 89-110.

1364 ᴱ**Beretta, Piergiorgio** Nuovo Testamento: Greco—Latino—Italiano. CinB 1998, San Paolo 15*(2); 2173 pp. L140.000. 88-215-3402-2.

1365 Bibbia Emmaus: nuovissima versione dai testi originali. CinB 1998, San Paolo xiii; (2) 2477 pp. 88-215-3220-8.

1366 La biblia cultural. M 1998, Propaganda Popular Católica 1840 pp.
84-288-1469-4.

1367 *Bissoli, Cesare* Bibbia, catechesi e pastorale: la revisione e
l'apostolato biblico. La traduzione. 1998 ⇒222. 186-193.

1368 *Brunel-Lobrichon, Geneviève* Les traductions de la bible en ancien
occitan. La bibbia in italiano. 1998 ⇒390. 247-254.

1369 *Buzzetti, Carlo* La bibbia in lingua italiana: le principali traduzioni
nel XX secolo;

1370 Un episodio condizionato: le condizioni del tradurre. La traduzione.
1998 ⇒222. 106-118/194-208;

1371 Traduzioni della Bibbia: un corso-base tra i corsi di teologia?: tra
esperienza e riflessione ermeneutico-pastorale: domande e proposte.
^FMARTINI, C. RivBib.S 33: 1998 ⇒75. 33-46.

1372 ^EBuzzetti, Carlo; Ghidelli, C. La traduzione della Bibbia nella
chiesa italiana, il Nuovo Testamento. CinB 1998, San Paolo 208 pp.
L28.100. 88-215-3792-7. ^RRCI 79 (1998) 703-708.

1373 *Buzzetti, Carlo; Ghidelli, Carlo* La traduzione della bibbia nella
chiesa cattolica: i documenti. La traduzione. 1998 ⇒222. 41-88.

1374 **Calabrese, Vincenzo** La traduzione in lingua volgare della Scrittura
nel pensiero di Mons. Giovanni Gaetano BOTTARI (1689-1775): Il
Cod. Ms. Cors. 1878 e altri inediti: un episodio emblematico del
"giansenismo" italiano. Studi religiosi 12: [Salerno] 1998, Elea 222
pp. 88-85269-79-6.

1375 *Corgnali, Duilio* Bibbia [friulana] per un popolo. Bibbia, popoli e
lingue. 1998 ⇒381. 145-157 [⇒1440].

1376 *Costa, Eugenio* Come hanno lavorato i revisori: il contexto e il
metodo. La traduzione. 1998 ⇒222. 127-138.

1377 ^TCuccu, Romanu M. Is evangélius de Gesu Cristu: passàus dàe su
Grégu antìgu in sardu campidanésu. (Cagliari] 1997, n.p. (6) xiii; 259
pp.

1378 *Danieli, Giuseppe* La revisione del Nuovo Testamento: motivazioni,
modalità, realizzazione;

1379 La bibbia in Italia nel XX secolo: la Pia Società San Girolamo;

1380 *D'Antonio, Ezio* La traduzione della bibbia CEI del 1971: motivi e
vicende di una iniziativa postconciliare. La traduzione. 1998 ⇒222.
121-126/36-40/99-105.

1381 *Delcorno, Carlo* Produzione e circolazione dei volgarizzamenti
religiosi tra medioevo e rinascimento;

1382 *Garavaglia, Gianpaolo* I lezionari in volgare italiano fra XIV e XVI
secolo: spunti per una ricerca. La bibbia in italiano. 1998 ⇒390. 3-
22/365-392;

1383 L'Italia e le traduzioni della Bibbia tra cinque e settecento: un caso di
mancata circolazione delle idee. BSSV 181 (1998) 141-158.

1384 *Ghidelli, Carlo* I risultati raggiunti: qualche esempio. La traduzione.
1998 ⇒222. 139-154.

1385 ^ETGuest, Gerald B. Bible moralisée: Codex Vindobonenis 2554,
Vienna, Österreichische Nationalbibliothek. Manuscripts in Minia-
ture 2: L 1995, Harvey M 144 pp. ^RCCMéd 41 (1998) 394-395
(Stirnemann, Patricia).

1386 *Morreale, Margherita* Alcune considerazioni sulla bibbia in volgare
con un aggiornamento del saggio 'Vernacular bible, Spain'
('Cambridge History of the Bible'). La bibbia in italiano. 1998
⇒390. 255-287.

1387 ^EO'Callaghan, José Nuevo Testamento griego-español. BAC 574: 1997, ⇒⇒13,1348. ^REM 66 (1998) 399-400 (*Martínez de Tejada Garaizábal, Jorge*).

1388 *Peri, Vittorio* Bibbia e minoranze etnico-linguistiche: esperienza friulana. Bibbia, popoli e lingue. 1998 ⇒381. 105-120.

1389 *Pollidori, Valentina* La glossa come tecnica di traduzione: diffusione e tipologia nei volgarizzamenti italiani della bibbia. La bibbia in italiano. 1998 ⇒390. 93-118.

1390 *Provera, Laura* Attenzione al linguaggio: attenzione ai referenti femminili della bibbia in lingua italiana. La traduzione. 1998 ⇒222. 164-174.

1391 **Puig i Tàrrech, Armand** La Bíblia a Catalunya, València i les Illes fins al Segle XV: Lliçó inaugural CURS 1997/98. Tarragona 1998, Institut Superior de Ciències Religioses Sant Fructuós Arquebisbat de Tarragona 112 pp.

1392 *Ranon, Angelo* La bibbia nelle scuole di teologia: la revisione della bibbia per gli studenti di teologia. La traduzione. 1998 ⇒222. 181-185.

1393 ^E**Rossano, P.** Tradurre la bibbia per il popolo di Dio: Morcelliana 1925-1985. Brescia 1986, Morcelliana 128 pp. L14.000. 88-372-1274-7. ^RRivLi 85 (1998) 765-766 (*Venturi, Gianfranco*).

1394 La Sacra Bibbia: Nuovo Testamento. 1997, ⇒13,1343. ^RRivLi 85 (1998) 685-687 (*Venturi, Gianfranco*).

1395 *Sneddon, Clive R.* Pour l'édition critique de la bible française du XIIIe siècle. La bibbia in italiano. 1998 ⇒390. 229-246.

1396 ^E**Ubieta Lopez, José Angel** Biblia de Jerusalén. Bilbao 1998, Desclée de B xviii; 1895 pp. 84-330-1304-1. ^RComunidades 26 (1998) 208-214 (*Rodríguez, Eliseo*).

1397 ^E**Vaux, Roland de** La Bible de Jérusalem. P 1998, Cerf 2195 pp. 0-8028-4473-1.

1398 *Villani, Giulio* La bibbia e la lingua italiana: problemi di lessico e di struttura. La traduzione. 1998 ⇒222. 155-163.

D6.2 *Versiones anglicae*—English Bible Translations

1399 *Bandstra, Barry L.* Translating Torah: a review essay. CScR 27 (1998) 353-358.

1400 **Beam, Kathryn, L.; Gagos, Traianos** The evolution of the English Bible: from papyri to King James. AA 1997, Univ. of Michigan Press $60. 0-472-99249-X.

1401 *Daniell, David* 'Gold, silver, ivory, apes and peacocks'. Word, Church, and State. 1998, ⇒229. 5-25.

1402 *Greenspoon, Leonard Jay* Traditional text, contemporary contexts: English-language scriptures for Jews and the history of Bible translating. Interpretation of the Bible. JSOT.S 289: 1998 ⇒388. 565-575.

1403 ^E**Hoyt, Thomas L.** The New Testament and Psalms: an inclusive version. 1995, ⇒11/2,2684; 13,1366. ^RCBQ 60 (1998) 571-573 (*Jensen, Joseph*).

1404 **Kohlenberger III, John R.; Swanson, James A.** The Hebrew-English concordance to the Old Testament: with the New International Version. GR 1998, Zondervan xvi; 2192 pp. 0-310-20839-4.

1405 New Testament for women: New International Version. Bangkok 1997, International Bible Society 544 pp.

88   Elenchus of Biblica 14, 1998   [III. Critica Textus, Versiones

1406   *Nielson, Jon; Skousen, Royal* How much of the King James Bible is William TYNDALE's?: an estimation based on sampling. Reformation 3 (1998) 49-74.
1407   ᴱ**Radmacher, Earl D.** The Nelson study bible: New King James version. Nv 1997, Nelson xxx; 2222 +195 + 12 pp. $30. ᴿBS 155 (1998) 109 (*Witmer, John A.*).
1408   **Remley, Paul G.** Old English biblical verse: studies in Genesis, Exodus and Daniel. CSASE 16: 1996 ⇒12,1139; 13,1367. ᴿJR 78 (1998) 609-610 (*Kim, Susan M.*).
1409   **Sampson, Emily Clyde Walter** Her works shall praise her: the biblical translation of Julia Evelina SMITH. ᴰClaremont 1998, 228 pp.
1410   ᴱ**Scherman, Nosson** Tanach: the Torah, Prophets, Writings: the twenty-four books of the bible newly translated and annotated. Artscroll: [Brooklyn, NY] 1998, Mesorah xxviii; 2079 pp. 0-89906-269-5/70-9/71-7/72-5.
1411   **Sheeley, Steven M.; Nash, Robert N.** The Bible in English translation: an essential guide. 1997, ⇒13,1369. ᴿRRT 1998/2, 80 (*Wollaston, Isabel*); New Theology Review 11/3 (1998) 84-85 (*Di Lella, Alexander A.*).
1412   *Zwink, Eberhard* Confusion about TYNDALE: the Stuttgart copy of the 1526 New Testament in English. Reformation 3 (1998) 29-48.

D6.3 *Versiones germanicae*—Deutsche Bibelübersetzungen

1413   **Alexander, Pat** Meine allererste Bibel. FrB 1998, Herder 480 pp ᴿDiak. 29 (1998) 355-356 (*Bee-Schroedter, Heike*).
1414   Die Bibel des 20. Jahrhunderts: Altes und Neues Testament: Gesamtausgabe in der Einheitsübersetzung. Augsburg 1998, Pattloch 1288 pp. ÖS1080. 3-629-01077-6.
1415   *Boendermaker, J.P.* ROSENZWEIGs visie op LUTHERs vertaalwerk [Rosenzweig's appreciation of Luther's Bible translation]. Luther Digest 6 (1998) 5-7.
1416   ᵀᴱ**Brand, Maria** Stille Zeit Bibel: Elberfelder Bibel revidierte Fassung mit Texten zur persönlichen Andacht. Wu 1998, Brockhaus xii; 1620 pp. 3-417-25879-0.
1417   ᵀ**Buber, Martin; Rosenzweig, Franz** Die hebräische Bibel: das Alte Testament. ᴱ*Schneider, Lambert.* Gerlingen 1997 <1961>, Bleicher. ᴿFrRu NF 5 (1998) 127-128 (*Licharz, Werner*).
1418   Die Chagall-Bibel: Einheitsübersetzung der Heiligen Schrift. Stu 1998, Kath. Bibelwerk 895 pp. 3-460-31955-0/68-2.
1419   *Ellingworth, Paul* Die Gute Nachricht Bibel in internationaler Sicht. ᶠMEURER, S.. 1998, ⇒81. 93-108.
1420   **Frech, Stephan Veit** Magnificat und Benedictus deutsch: Martin LUTHERs bibelhumanistische Übersetzung in der Rezeption des ERASMUS von Rotterdam. Zürcher Germanistische Studien 44: Bern 1995, Lang 320 pp. FS67. 3-906755-38-X. ᴿLuJ 65 (1998) 183-184 (*Beyer, Michael*).
1421   *Haubeck, Wilfrid* Neue kommunikative deutsche Bibelübersetzungen: Gute Nachricht Bibel, Hoffnung für alle und Neue Genfer Übersetzung: ein Vergleich am Beispiel von Matthäus 5-7 und Römer 3-5;
1422   *Haug, Hellmut* Die Gute Nachricht Bibel: Geschichte—Prinzipien—Beispiele. ᶠMEURER, S. 1998 ⇒81. 76-92/20-47.

1423 **Himmighöfer, Traudel** Die Zürcher Bibel bis zum Tode Zwinglis (1531). VIEG 154: 1995 ⇒11/2,2705; 13,1377. ᴿZwing. 25 (1998) 190-198 (*Sonderegger, Stefan*).

1424 *Höslinger, Norbert; Lange, Joachim* Die Gute Nachricht als interkonfessionelle Übersetzung: aus katholischer Sicht;

1425 *Jahr, Hannelore* Vorwort. ᶠMEURER, S.. 1998 ⇒81. 111-114/11-17.

1426 ᴱ**Jens, Walter** Die vier Evangelien: Matthäus, Markus, Lukas, Johannes. Stu 1998, Radius 479 pp. 3-87173-145-5.

1427 ᴱ**Joerg, Urs; Hoffmann, David Marc** Die Bibel in der Schweiz: Ursprung und Geschichte. 1997 ⇒13,1378. ᴿCFr 68 (1998) 347-349 (*Maranesi, Pietro*).

1428 *Klaiber, Walter* Die "alte" und die "neue" Gute Nachricht: ein Vergleich anhand des Römer- und Galaterbriefs. ᶠMEURER, S. 1998 ⇒81. 48-61.

1429 **Köder, Sieger** Eine Tübinger Bibel in Bildern. Stu 1998, Kath. Bildungswerk 122 pp. DM98. 3-460-30653-X.

1430 **Köster, Uwe** Studien zu den katholischen deutschen Bibelübersetzungen im 16., 17. und 18. Jahrhundert. 1995 ⇒11/2,2706; 13,138. ᴿJEH 49 (1998) 563-564 (*Price, David*).

1431 *Moser, Dietz-Rüdiger* Bibbia, società e letteratura in Germania. Bibbia, popoli e lingue. 1998 ⇒381. 79-101.

1432 *Runge, Ekkehard* Nicht verboten und nicht erwünscht: Bibel und Bibelübersetzungen in der ehemaligen DDR. ᶠMEURER, S. 1998 ⇒81. 115-136.

1433 ᴱ**Schäfer, Heinz** Biblische Redensarten und Sprichwörter: 3000 Fundstellen aus der Lutherbibel. Stu 1998, Dt. Bibelges. 563 pp. 3-438-06212-7.

1434 ᴱ**Splett, Jochen** Das Bremer Evangelistar. QFSKG 110: 1996 ⇒12,1153. ᴿMAe 67/1 (1998) 169-70 (*Wulf, Christine*).

1435 *Wegener, Hildburg* "... und macht die Menschen zu meinen Jüngern und Jüngerinnen": die Revision der Gute Nachricht Bibel in gemäßigt "frauengerechter Sprache". ᶠMEURER, S. 1998 ⇒81. 62-73.

1436 Wenzelsbibel: Kommentarband 1, 2. ᴱ**Krieger, Michaela**: Codices Selecti 70: Graz 1998, Akad. Dr.- und Verl.-Anst. 250 + 96 pp. 3-201-01708-6.

1437 *Wiesemann, Ursula* Die Gute Nachricht als Hilfe bei der Übersetzungsarbeit. ᶠMEURER, S. 1998 ⇒81. 137-146.

1438 **Winter, Julie M.** Luther bible research in the context of volkish nationalism in the twentieth century. Literatur and the sciences of man 19: NY 1998, Lang (10), 144 pp. 0-8204-3879-0.

1439 *Zenger, Erich* Neues Licht auf alte Weisheit: was die Gute Nachricht Bibel an Verständnishilfen über die traditionellen Bibelübersetzungen hinaus bringt. ᶠMEURER, S. 1998 ⇒81. 147-152.

D6.4 **Versiones slavoniae** *et variae*

1440 *Beline, Antoni* The Friulan Bible: the fulfilment of a wish and a right of the Friulan people (1997) [⇒1375; 1388];

1441 *Benyik, György* Ein Beitrag zur Geschichte der ungarischen Bibelübersetzungen. Interpretation of the Bible. JSOT.S 289: 1998 ⇒388. 1315-1326/1243-1276;

1442 Hungarian bible translations. FolTh 9 (1998) 213-244.

1443 La bibbia nella lingua vietnamita. Thành Pho Ho Chí Minh 1998,
      Nhà Xuat Ban 2443 pp.
1444 Biblija 1499 goda i Biblija v sinodal'nom perevode, 9: Priloždnija
      naučnoe opisanie. Moskva 1998, Izdat. Otd. Moskovskogo Patriar-
      chata 511 pp. 5-87389-014-5. **R**.
1445 *Birdsall, J.* Neville Georgian translations of the Bible. Interpretation
      of the Bible;
1446 *Blau, Joshua* SAADYA Gaon's Pentateuch translation and the
      stabilization of mediaeval Judaeo-Arabic culture;
1447 *Cooper, Henry R.* The origins of the church Slavonic version of the
      Bible: an alternative hypothesis. Interpretation of the Bible. JSOT.S
      289: 1998 ⇒388. 387-391/393-398/959-974.
1448 De noordnederlandse historiebijbel. Middeleeuwse studies en bron-
      nen 56: Hilversum 1998, Verloren 845 pp. 90-6550-027-8.
1449 *Delicostopoulos, Athan* Major Greek translations of the Bible. Inter-
      pretation of the Bible. JSOT.S 289: 1998 ⇒388. 297-316.
1450 **den Hollander, A.A.** De nederlandse bijbelvertalingen 1522-1545
      [Dutch translations of the Bible 1522-1545]. BBN 33: 1997
      ⇒13,1388. ᴿSCJ 29 (1998) 562-565 (*Hakkenberg, Michael*).
1451 *Dimitrov, I.* Bulgarische Übersetzungen des Neuen Testaments in den
      letzten zwei Jahrhunderten. ᶠPOKORNÝ, P. 1998 ⇒90. 88-95.
1452 *Hannick, Christian* Die Rekonstruktion der altslavischen Evangelien
      bei Josef VAJS und ihre vermeintlichen griechischen Vorlagen. Inter-
      pretation of the Bible. JSOT.S 289: 1998 ⇒388. 943-958.
1453 **Himbaza, Innocent** Transmettre la bible: critique exégétique de la
      traduction de l'Ancien Testament: le cas du Rwanda. ᴰFrS 1998;
      ᴰ*Schenker, Adrian*. 409 pp.
1454 *Hrovat, Jasna; Smolik, Marijan; Zadnikar, Anica* Bibliography of
      Slovenian translations of biblical texts. Interpretation of the Bible.
      JSOT.S 289: 1998 ⇒388. 1075-1107.
1455 **Kamčatnov, Aleksandr M.** Istorija i germenevtika slavjanskoj
      Biblii. Moskva 1998, Nauka 220 pp. 5-02-011674-2. **R**.
1456 *Knezović, Katica* Zagrebačka Biblija (1968-1998) I: nastanak
      Zagrebačka Biblije [The Zagreb Bible (1968-1998) I: the origins of
      the Zagreb Bible]. Obnovljeni Život 53 (1998) 107-130. **Croatian**.
1457 *Krašovec, Jože* Bibbia e minoranze etnico-linguistiche: esperienza
      slovena. Bibbia, popoli e lingue. 1998 ⇒381. 121-127 [Gen 11,1-9];
1458 Slovenian translations of the Bible. Interpretation of the Bible.
      JSOT.S 289: 1998 ⇒388. 1039-1074.
1459 ᵀ**Mercieca, G.; Cauchi, Nikol; Sant, Karm** Il-Bibbja: Il-Kotba
      Mqaddsa migjuba bil-Malti mill-ilsna originali l-Lhudi u l-Grieg
      mill- Ghaqda Biblika Maltija.... Malta 1996, Ghaqda Biblika Maltija
      pag. varia. 99909-973-0-6.
1460 *Metzger, Bruce M.* The first translation of the New Testament into
      Pennsylvania Dutch (1994);
1461 *Moszyński, Leszek* Zwei slavische Renaissancepsalterübersetzungen
      aus dem Hebräischen: die slovenische von Primož Trubar 1566 und
      die polnische von Szymon Budny 1572 (Ähnlichkeiten und
      Unterschiede ihrer Übersetzungsmethoden);
1462 *Nazor, Anica* The Bible in Croato-Glagolitic liturgical books;
1463 *Pečirková, Jaroslava* Czech translations of the Bible;
1464 *Peklaj, Marijan* Set expressions in the Pentateuch: a challenge for the
      new Slovenian translation of the bible. Interpretation of the Bible.

JSOT.S 289: 1998 ⇒388. 1305-1313/985-1003/1031-1037/1167-1200/1109-1115.

1465 ᵀ**Popowski, Remigiusz; Wojciechowski, Michal** Grecko-Polski, Nowy Testament: Wydanie interlinearne z Kodami gramatycznymi. Prymasowska Seria Biblijna: Wsz 1997, Oficyna Wydawnicza "Vocatio" xlvi; 1236 pp. 83-85435-18-2. **P.**

1466 *Rebić, Adalbert* Die Übersetzung der Bibel ins Kroatische: eine kurze Übersicht;

1467 *Salowski, Martin G.* Bibelübersetzungen ins Lausitzer Sorbische;

1468 *Sæbo, Magne* Die neue norwegische Bibelübersetzung—Probleme und Erfahrungen;

1469 *Übersicht über nordische Bibelübersetzungen: in Auswahl;*

1470 *Stojčevska-Antić, Vera* La Bible en Macédoine;

1471 *Stolyarov, Alexander* Translation of the Bible into Tungus-Manchu languages;

1472 *Thomson, Francis J.* The Slavonic translation of the Old Testament. Interpretation of the Bible. JSOT.S 289: 1998 ⇒388. 1131-1145/1235-1242/1285-1295/1277-1283/1147-1165/1297-1303/605-920.

1473 **Vries, A. de** Het kleine verschil: man/vrouw-stereotypen in enkele moderne Nederlandse vertalingen van het Oude Testament. Kamper Studies: Kampen 1998, Kok 182 pp. *f*45.

1474 ᴱ**Welzen, P.H.M.** Exegeten aan het werk: vertalen en interpreteren van de bijbel. 's Hertogenbosch 1998, Katholieke Bijbelstichting 236 pp. 90-6173-848-2.

1475 **Wendland, Ernst R.** Buku loyera: an introduction to the new Chichewa bible translation. Kachere monograph 6: Blantyre 1998, CLAIM 224 pp. 99908-16-08-5.

1476 *Wodecki, Bernard* Polish translations of the Bible. Interpretation of the Bible. JSOT.S 289: 1998 ⇒388. 1201-1233.

1477 *Yorke, Gosnell L.O.R.* Translating the Old Testament in Africa: an Afrocentric approach. NAOTS 4 (1998) 10-13.

D7 *Problema vertentis*—Bible translation techniques

1478 *Andersen, F.I.; Forbes A.D.* Approximate graph-matching as an enabler of example-based translation. Bible et informatique. 1998 ⇒386. 285-314.

1479 **Askani, Hans-Christoph** Das Problem der Übersetzung dargestellt an Franz ROSENZWEIG: die Methoden und Prinzipien der Rosenzweigschen und BUBER-Rosenzweigschen Übersetzungen. HUTh 35: 1997, ⇒13,1403. ᴿFZPhTh 45 (1998) 595-598 (*Schenker, Adrian*); ETR 73 (1998) 148-150 (*Askani, Hans-Christoph*).

1480 *Briend, Jacques* La traduction biblique. RICP 65 (1998) 117-122.

1481 *Brunn, Dave* The 'pure' vernacular: are we producing a translation that is understandable today?. BiTr 49 (1998) 425-430.

1482 **Carson, D.A.** The inclusive language debate: a plea for realism. GR 1998, Baker 221 pp. 0-8010-5835-X.

1483 *Dax, Françoise de* Les différents modes d'approche du lexique en traduction. RICP 65 (1998) 159-164.

1484 *Doré, Joseph* Pour la traduction. RICP 65 (1998) 181-186.

1485 *Dupont-Roc, Roselyne* La parole de Dieu en d'autres langues. RICP (1998) 189-212.

1486 *Ellingworth, Paul* Translating the language of leadership;
1487 *Haydon, Les* Making the most of resources for translation projects. BiTr 49 (1998) 126-138/445-448.
1488 *Hengel, Martin* Apostolische Ehen und Familien. Interpretation of the Bible. JSOT.S 289: 1998 ⇒388. 257-276.
1489 **Kassühlke, Rudolf** Eine Bibel—viele Übersetzungen: ein Überblick mit Hilfen zur Beurteilung. Haan 1998, Brockhaus 159 pp. 3-417-20560-3.
1490 *Koffi, Ettien N.* La traduction de la conjonction 'mais': des défis inattendus. Cahiers de Traduction Biblique 30 (1998) 3-9.
1491 *Ladmiral, Jean-René* Théorie de la traduction: la question du littéralisme. RICP (1998) 137-157.
1492 *Mankowski, Paul* The necessary failure of inclusive-language translations: a linguistic elucidation. Thom. 62 (1998) 445-468.
1493 *Mitchell, William* The involvement of women in bible translation: hope versus reality. BiTr 49 (1998) 437-441.
1494 *Mojola, Aloo Osotsi* Interaction between exegete and translator: a translator's view. NAOTS 4 (1998) 2-4.
1495 *Muntingh, L.M.* 'n Ondersoek na die plek en inhoud van ekwivalensie binne die moderne vertaalwetenskap met besondere verwysing na die Nuwe Afrikaanse Bybelvertaling. OTEs 11 (1998) 499-521.
1496 *Nida, Eugene A.* A challenge for translators. ^FPOKORNÝ, P. 1998 ⇒90. 264-270;
1497 The contribution of linguistics and computers to bible translating. Bible et informatique. 1998 ⇒386. 27-37.
1498 *Noss, Philip A.* Methods of bible translation: an ecumenical approach. RASM 8 (1998) 74-95;
1499 Scripture translation in Afica: the state of the art. JNSL 24/2 (1998) 63-76.
1500 *Nwachukwu, Fortunatus* Inculturation and the translation of biblical personal names: the example of a Nigerian language. Bulletin of Ecumenical Theology 10 (1998) 93-113.
1501 *Ofulue, Yetunde* Translating exclamations. BiTr 49 (1998) 201-207.
1502 *Parker, Simon B.* Pushing the limits: issues in Jewish bible translation. ^FFRERICHS, E. BJSt 320: 1998 ⇒28. 73-80.
1503 *Pippin, Tina* Translation happens: a feminist perspective on translation theories. Escaping Eden. BiSe 65: 1998 ⇒278. 163-176.
1504 *Poeder, Jeen* Connotation and the marking of meanings in bible translation. Bible et informatique. 1998 ⇒386. 315-337.
1505 *Polliack, Meira* Medieval Karaite methods of translating biblical narrative into Arabic. VT 48 (1998) 375-398.
1506 *Ponsart, Brigitte* L'environnement du traducteur. RICP 65 (1998) 165-174.
1507 *Schneider, Théo* Containers and contents: a case of functional equivalence. BiTr 49 (1998) 215-225.
1508 *Seitz, Christopher* Reader competence and the offense of biblical language: the limitations of so-called inclusive language. Word without end. 1998 [1993] ⇒200. 292-299.
1509 **Strauss, Mark L.** Distorting scripture?: the challenge of bible translation & gender accuracy. DG 1998, InterVarsity 240 pp. 0-8308-1940-1.
1510 *Surkova, Elena* The theological, philosophical and linguistic background of CONSTANTINE the philosopher's concept of translation. Interpretation of the Bible. JSOT.S 289: 1998 ⇒388. 975-984.

1511 *Van der Merwe, Christo H.J.* The Centre for Bible Translation in Africa. NAOTS 4 (1998) 4-6.
1512 *Vander Stichele, Caroline* 'Hoort dan, gij vrouwen, het woord des Heren'. Interpretatie 6/7 (1998) 12-13.
1513 **Venuti, Lawrence** The translator's invisibility: a history of translation. 1995.⇒12,1217. [R]BiTr 49 (1998) 148-152 (*Wilt, Timothy*).
1514 *Vries, Anneke de* Beyond inclusive language: gender stereotypes in translations of the Old Testament;
1515 *Vries, Lourens de* Body part tally counting and bible translation in Papua New Guinea and Irian Jaya. BiTr 49 (1998) 103-116/409-414.

D8 *Concordantiae, lexica specialia*—Specialized dictionaries, synopses

1516 [E]**Balz, Horst; Schneider, Gerhard** Diccionario exegético del Nuevo Testamento, 2: λ-ω. Biblioteca de Estudios Bíblicos 91: S 1998, Sígueme 2214 col.; 50 pp. [R]EstTrin 32/1-2 (1998) 222-224 (*Vázquez Allegue, Jaime*).
1517 **Bosch Navarro, Juan** Diccionario de ecumenismo. Estella 1998, Verbo Divino 450 pp. [R]TE 42 (1998) 284-285 (*Esponera Cerdán, A.*).
1518 [E]**Cross, Frank Leslie; Livingstone, Elizabeth A.** The Oxford dictionary of the christian church. [3]1997, ⇒13,1437. [R]ChH 67/1 (1998) 211-212 (*Wainwright, Geoffrey*); AUSS 36 (1998) 143-145 (*Strand, Kenneth A.*); IThQ 63 (1998) 401-403 (*Henry, Martin*); MAe 67/1 (1998) 112-13 (*Pugin, Graham*).
1519 **Dawson, Warren R.; Uphill, Eric P.** Who was who in Egyptology. [3]1995, ⇒11/2,b498. [R]BiOr 55 (1998) 81-86 (*Cannuyer, Cristian*).
1520 Dictionnaire du Judaïsme. Encyclopaedia Universalis: P 1998, Albin M 893 pp. 2-226-09618-3.
1521 Grande enciclopedia illustrata della bibbia. [E]**Prato, Gian Luigi**. CasM 1997, Piemme 3 vols. [R]CivCatt 149/3 (1998) 99-100 (*Simone, M.*).
1522 **Hatch, Edwin; Redpath, Henry Adeney** A concordance to the Septuagint: and the other Greek versions of the Old Testament (including the apocryphal books). "Introductory Essay" by *Robert A. Kraft* and *Emanuel Tov*; "Hebrew/Aramaic Index to the Septuagint" by *Takamitsu Muraoka* GR [2]1998, Baker xxviii; 1497 (2) 368 pp. $125. 0-8010-2141-3.
1523 [E]**Lacoste, Jean-Yves** Dictionnaire critique de théologie. P 1998, PUF 1298 pp. FF5828. 2-13-048825-0. [R]PerTeol 30 (1998) 285-291 (*Taborda, Francisco*); CM(F) 43 (1998) 343-346 (*Daix, Georges*).
1524 **Mills, Watson E.** Lutterworth dictionary of the Bible. C 1998, Lutterworth xxx; 994 pp. £20. 0-7188-2974-3.
1525 **Pickering, D.** Bibel Quiz: Fragen und Antworten. 1997 ⇒13,1445. [R]Diak. 29 (1998) 356-357 (*Bee-Schroedter, Heike*).
1526 *Poppi, Angelico* Sinossi recenti dei vangeli in greco: rilievi e proposte. [F]MARTINI, C.. RivBib.S 33: 1998 ⇒75. 117-136.
1527 *Samir, Samir H.* Concordances et synopses du Nouveau Testament Syriaque. ParOr 23 (1998) 233-239.
1528 **Sáenz-Badillos, Ángel; Targarona Borrás, Judit** Diccionario de autores judíos (Sefarad. siglos X-XV). Córdoba 1998, El Almendro 227 pp.

1529 **Sierra Bravo, Restituto** Diccionario social de los Padres de la Iglesia. 1997 ⇒13,445. ᴿTE 42 (1998) 281-283 (*Ramón, Lucía*).
1530 **Solomon, Norman** Historical dictionary of Judaism. Historical dictionaries of religions, philosophies, and movements 19: Lanham 1998, Scarecrow viii; 521 pp. 0-8108-3497-9.
1531 **Thoumieu, Marc** Dizionario d'iconografia romanica. 1997 ⇒13,1450. ᴿCivCatt 149/1 (1998) 416-418 (*Sale, G.*).
1532 *Van Wieringen, Archibald L.H.M.* Form and function: some hermeneutic remarks on semantics and analogies: an answer to Prof. SCHWEIZER. BN 95 (1998) 30-32.
1533 **Vidal Manzanares, César** Dizionario di Gesù e dei vangeli. Città del Vaticano 1998, Libreria Editrice Vaticana 371 pp. L35.000. 88-209-2518-4.

IV. Exegesis generalis VT vel cum NT

D9 Commentaries on the whole Bible or OT

1534 ᴱ**Brown, Raymond E.; Fitzmyer, Joseph A.; Murphy, Roland E.** Nuovo grande commentario biblico. 1997, ⇒13,1454. ᴿRdT 39 (1998) 135-136 (*Cattaneo, Enrico*); CivCatt 149/3 (1998) 546-547 (*Scaiola, D.*).
1535 ᴱ**Farmer, William R.** The international bible commentary: a catholic and ecumenical commentary for the twenty-first century. ColMn 1998, Liturgical lii; 1918 pp. £80. 0-8146-12454-5.
1536 ᴱ**Guthrie, Donald; Motyer, J. Alec** Kommentar zur Bibel: AT und NT in einem Band. RBtaschenbuch 727: Wu 1998, Brockhaus xvi; 996 + 630 pp. 3-417-20727-4.
1537 ᴱ**Keck, Leander E.** NIntB 4: the first book of Maccabees, the second book of Maccabees, introduction to Hebrew poetry, the book of Job, the book of Psalms. 1996 ⇒12,1229. ᴿCBQ 60 (1998) 336-337 (*Boadt, Lawrence*);
1538 NIntB 2: Numbers, Deuteronomy, introduction to narrative literature, Joshua, Judges Ruth, 1&2 Samuel. Nv 1998, Abingdon xviii; 1388 pp. £45.
1539 **Newsom, Carol A.** 2 Da Ester ai Deuterocanonici. La bibbia delle donne: un commento. T 1998, Claudiana 304 pp. L36.000.
1540 **Trapp, John** A commentary on the OT and NT. 1997 <1856-1868> 5 vols, ⇒13,1457. ᴿCTJ 33 (1998) 484-485 (*Muller, Richard A.*).
1541 *Zinkuratire, Victor* The African Bible Project. NAOTS 4 (1998) 7-9.

V. Libri historici VT

E1.1 Pentateuchus, Torah *Textus, commentarii*

1542 **Artus, Olivier; Noël, Damien** Les livres de la loi: Exode, Lévitique, Nombres, Deutéronome: commentaire pastoral. Commentaires: P 1998, Bayard xii; 214 pp. 2-227-36612-5.

1543 *Blau, Joshua* לתורה רס‏|ג תרגום של הי‏|א המאה מתחילת מזרחי־יד בכתב עיונים
[Saadya Gaon's pentateuch translation in light of an early-eleventh-century Egyptian manuscript]. Leš. 61 (1998) 111-130.

1544 ᴱ**Borbone, Pier G.** <ed> The Pentateuch. The Old Testament in Syriac: pt. 5. Concordance, 1. 1997, ⇒13,1459. ᴿCBQ 60 (1998) 539-540 (*Di Lella, Alexander A.*).

1545 ᴱ**Cesarano, Nino** A Bibbia. Nola 1998, Arte Globo 316 pp. 88-8264-117-1.

1546 **Glessmer, Uwe** Einleitung in die Targume zum Pentateuch. TSAJ 48: 1995, ⇒11/1,155. ᴿJAOS 118 (1998) 279-280 (*Chilton, Bruce*).

1547 *Halivni, David Weiss* Revelation, textual criticism, and divine writ. Jdm 47 (1998) 193-213.

1548 **Houtman, Cees** Der Pentateuch. 1994 ⇒10,1584... 12,1267. ᴿBZ 42 (1998) 109-110 (*Lohfink, Norbert*).

1549 *Joosten, Jan* Greek and Latin words in the Peshitta pentateuch: first soundings. Symposium Syriacum VII. 1998 ⇒415. 37-47.

1550 **Nodet, Étienne** Le pentateuque. La Bible de Josèphe. 1996 ⇒12,1250. ᴿRTL 29 (1998) 540-541 (*Auwers, J.-M.*); JSJ 29 (1998) 110-113 (*Fernández Marcos, N.*).

1551 Pentateuco: traducción y notas. Sagrada biblia. 1997 ⇒13,14*67* ᴿEstTrin 32 (1998) 438-440 (*Vázquez Allegue, Jaime*).

1552 *Polak, Frank H.* Classifying the minuses of the Septuagint on the pentateuch. Bible et informatique. 1998 ⇒386. 241-260.

1553 **Polliak, Meira** The Karaite tradition of Arabic bible translation: a linguistic and exegetical study of Karaite translations of the pentateuch from the tenth and eleventh centuries C.E. EJM 17: Lei 1997, Brill xx; 338 pp. ᴿTarb. 67/3 (1998) x (*Blau, Joshua*).

1554 *Salvesen, Alison* Symmachus readings in the Pentateuch. Origen's Hexapla. TSAJ 58: 1998 ⇒399. 177-198.

1555 *Tal, Abraham* The Hebrew Pentateuch in the eyes of the Samaritan translator. Interpretation of the Bible. JSOT.S 289: 1998 ⇒388. 341-354.

1556 *Tov, Emanuel* Rewritten bible compositions and biblical manuscripts, with special attention to the Samaritan Pentateuch. DSD 5 (1998) 334-354.

1557 **Walton, John H.; Matthews, Victor H.** The IVP bible commentary: Genesis-Deuteronomy. DG 1997, InterVarsity. ᴿAsbTJ 53 (1998) 85-88 (*Fleming, Daniel*).

E1.2 *Pentateuchus* Introductio: Fontes JEDP

1558 *Artus, Olivier* Le pentateuque. CEv 106 (1998) 4-60.

1559 *Ausloos, Hans* The need for a "controlling framework" in determining the relationship between Genesis-Numbers and the so-called Deuteronomistic literature. JNSL 24/2 (1998) 77-89.

1560 *Bauks, Michaela* Une "complexité plus simple": nouveau modèle pour l'exégèse du pentateuque?: à propos d'un livre récent. ETR 73 (1998) 231-238.

1561 **Blenkinsopp, Joseph** Il pentateuco. BiBi(B) 21: 1996 ⇒12,1258. ᴿGr. 79 (1998) 385-388 (*Prato, Gian Luigi*).

1562   **Bloom, Harold; Rosenberg, David** El libro de J. Barc 1995, Inter-
       zona 337 pp. [T]*Mínguez, Néstor; Cohen, Marcelo; Castelli, Nora.*
       [R]BAEO 34 (1998) 430-433 (*Monferrer Sala, Juan Pedro*).

1563   *Brandscheidt, Renate* Noach und Abraham: Urgeschichte und
       Heilsgeschichte im Werk des Jahwisten. TThZ 107 (1998) 1-24.

1564   *Dohmen, Christoph* Wenn die Argumente ausgehen ... Anmerkungen
       zur Krisenstimmung in der Pentateuchforschung. BiKi 53 (1998)
       113-117.

1565   *Duhaime, Jean* Le pentateuque: débats et recherches. ScEs 50 (1998)
       235-239.

1566   *Fanuli, Antonio* Il pentateucho secondo J. BLENKINSOPP. RdT 39
       (1998) 905-921.

1567   *Frankel, David* Two priestly conceptions of guidance in the wilder-
       ness. JSOT 81 (1998) 31-37.

1568   **Fretheim, Terence E.** The pentateuch. 1996 ⇒12,1263. [R]LTP 54
       (1998) 622-624 (*Faucher, Alain*).

1569   **Friedman, Richard Elliott** The hidden book in the bible [J]. [San
       Francisco] 1998, HarperSanFrancisco xii; 402 pp. 0-06-063003-5.

1570   **García Santos, Amador-Angel** El pentateuco: historia y sentido.
       Horizonte Dos Mil - Textos y monografias 12: S 1998, San Esteban
       292 pp. 84-89761-70-1. [R]Comunidades 26 (1998) 215-216
       (*Rodríguez, Eliseo*).

1571   **Gorman, Frank H.** The ideology of ritual... in the priestly theology.
       JSOT.S 91: 1990 ⇒6,2059... 9,1760. [R]ThR 63 (1998) 260-261
       (*Schmidt, Ludwig*).

1572   *Hossfeld, Frank-Lothar* Die Tora oder der Pentateuch-Anfang und
       Basis des Alten und Ersten Testaments. BiKi 53 (1998) 106-112.

1573   *Knauf, Ernst Axel* Audiatur et altera pars: zur Logik der Pentateuch-
       Redaktion. BiKi 53 (1998) 118-126.

1574   *Knipping, Burkhard R.* Redaktionen: unverzichtbar, aber in
       Urkunden- bzw. Quellentheorie nicht angemessen berücksichtigt. BN
       95 (1998) 45-70.

1575   **Kopciowski, Elia** Invito alla lettura della Torà. Schulim Vogelmann:
       F 1998, Giuntina 277 pp. 88-8057-056-0.

1576   **Krapf, Thomas M.** Die Priesterschrift und die vorexilische Zeit:
       Yehezkiel KAUFMANNs vernachlässigter Beitrag zur Geschichte der
       biblischen Religion. OBO 119: 1992 ⇒8,1971... 12,1272. [R]VT 48
       (1998) 279-281 (*Emerton, John A.E.*).

1577   **Kugel, James L.** The Bible as it was. 1997 ⇒13,1477. [R]CrossCur 48
       (1998) 566-568 (*Rast, Walter E.*).

1578   **Lemche, Niels Peter** Prelude to Israel's past: background and begin-
       nings of Israelite history and identity. Peabody 1998, Henrickson 247
       pp. $25.

1579   **Linden, Nico ter** Es wird erzählt...: von der Schöpfung bis zum
       Gelobten Land. [T]*Häring, Stefan.* Gü 1998, Gü'er 319 pp. 3-579-
       02221-0.

1580   *Loader, J.A.* The redactional manifestation of pentateuchal theology.
       OTEs 11 (1998) 487-498.

1581   **Lohfink, Norbert** Theology of the pentateuch: themes of the priestly
       narrative and Deuteronomy. 1994 ⇒10,201. [R]MSR 55/1 (1998) 90-
       91 (*Breuvart, Jean-Marie*).

1582   [E]**Mills, Watson Early; Wilson, Richard Francis** Pentateuch/Torah.
       Mercer Commentary on the Bible 1: [Macon, GA] 1998, Mercer
       University Press lviii; 226 pp. 0-86554-506-5.

1583 **Mullen, E.T.** Ethnic myths and pentateuchal foundations. 1997 ⇒13,1482. [R]IBSt 20 (1998) 46-48 (*Alexander, T.D.*).

1584 **Nicholson, Ernest Wilson** The pentateuch in the twentieth century: the legacy of Julius WELLHAUSEN. Oxf 1998, Clarendon ix; 294 pp. $75. 0-19-826958-7.

1585 *Sacchi, Paolo* The pentateuch, the deuteronomist and SPINOZA. Henoch 20 (1998) 291-303.

1586 *Sæbo, Magne* Priestly theology and priestly code: the character of the priestly layer in the Pentateuch. On the way to canon. 1998 <1981> ⇒194. 144-161.

1587 *Schmidt, Ludwig* Väterverheißungen und Pentateuchfrage. Gesammelte Aufsätze zum Pentateuch <1992>;

1588 Israel ein Segen für die Völker? (Das Ziel des jahwistischen Werkes-—eine Auseinandersetzung mit H.W. Wolff) <1973/74>;

1589 Überlegungen zum Jahwisten <1977>;

1590 Weisheit und Geschichte beim Elohisten <1996>. Gesammelte Aufsätze zum Pentateuch. BZAW 263: 1998 ⇒195. 110-136/1-17/18-37/150-166.

1591 **Ska, Jean Louis** Introduzione alla lettura del pentateuco: chiavi per l'interpretazione dei primi cinque libri della bibbia.. Collana biblica: R 1998, Dehoniane 315 pp. L32.000. 88-396-0751-X.

1592 **Whybray, R. Norman** Introduction to the Pentateuch. 1995 ⇒11/1,171... 13,1490. [R]JSSt 43 (1998) 151-152 (*Davies, Eryl W.*); VJTR 62 (1998) 441-442 (*Raj, M.I.*);

1593 El Pentateuco: estudio metodológico. 1995 ⇒11/1,172. [R]San Juan de la Cruz 21 (1998) 154-155 (*Contreras, Francisco*).

1594 **Wynn-Williams, Damian J.** The state of the Pentateuch: a comparison of the approaches of M. NOTH and E. BLUM. BZAW 249: 1997 ⇒13,1491. [R]OLZ 93 (1998) 659-660 (*Oßwald, Eva*); BiOr 55 (1998) 862-865 (*Davies, Philip R.*); JBL 117 (1998) 721-723 (*Carr, David M.*).

E1.3 *Pentateuchus,* themata

1595 **Abella, Josef** Pentateuco: perché l'uomo viva. Lettura pastorale della Bibbia. Parola-Missione 1: Bo 1998, EDB 428 pp. L43.000. 88-10-20141-8.

1596 *Bloom, Maureen* The legacy of 'sacred' and 'profane' in ancient Israel: interpretations of DURKHEIM's classifications. Jewish Studies Quarterly 5 (1998) 103-123.

1597 **Den Dulk, Maarten** Vijf kansen: een theologie die begint bij Mozes. Zoetermeer 1998, Meinema 240 pp. f37.50. 90-211-3709-7. [R]Interpretatie 6/4 (1998) 31-32 (*Westra, Gerben*).

1598 *Derby, Josiah* The wilderness experience. JBQ 26 (1998) 193-197.

1599 **Laffey, Alice** The pentateuch: a liberation-critical reading. A Liberation-critical reading of the Old Testament: Mp 1998, Fortress 216 pp. $21. 0-8006-2872-1.

1600 **Meirovich, Harvey Warren** The vindication of Judaism: the polemics of the HERTZ pentateuch. Moreshet 14: NY 1998, Jewish Theol. Sem. of America xvi; 304 pp. 0-87334-073-6.

1601 **Pola, Thomas** Die ursprüngliche Priesterschrift: Beobachtungen zur Literarkritik und Traditionsgeschichte von P[g]. WMANT 70: 1995 ⇒11/1,185. [R]LASBF 48 (1998) 569-573 (*Cortese, Enzo*).

1602 Rösel, Martin Theo-logie der griechischen Bibel: zur Wiedergabe der
      Gottesaussagen im LXX-Pentateuch. VT 48 (1998) 49-62.
1603 Sperling, S. David The original Torah: the political intent of the
      Bible's writers. Reappraisals in Jewish social and intellectual history:
      NY 1998, University Press xiv; 185 pp. $40. 0-8147-8094-6.
1604 Van Seters, John The Pentateuch (Genesis, Exodus, Leviticus, Num-
      bers, Deuteronomy). Hebrew Bible today. 1998 ⇒257. 3-49.
1605 ᴱZenger, Erich Die Tora als Kanon für Juden und Christen. 1996
      ⇒12,1308. ᴿBiLi 71 (1998) 369-372 (Oeming, Manfred); ThLZ 123
      (1998) 41-46 (Berlejung, Angelika); FrRu NF 5 (1998) 142-143
      (Oberforcher, Robert).

E1.4 Genesis; textus, commentarii

1606 Arnold, Bill T. Encountering the book of Genesis. Encountering
      biblical studies: GR 1998, Baker 234 pp. $25. 0-8010-2177-4.
1607 Asendorf, Ulrich Lectura in biblia: LUTHERs Genesisvorlesungen
      (1535-1545). FSÖTh 87: Gö 1998, Vandenhoeck & R 528 pp.
      DM178. 3-525562-94-2.
1608 Bianchi, Enzo Adam, où es-tu?: traité de théologie spirituelle:
      Genèse 1-11. Epiphanie-tradition monastique-initiation: P 1998, Cerf
      353 pp. FF199.
1609 ᴱBraner, Baruch; Freiman, Eli חרלב|ג עם ביאור תורה חומשי חמישה
      Rabbinic pentateuch with commentary on the torah by R. Levi ben
      GERSHON (Gersonides) I: בראשית. J 1993, Maaliyot 606 pp. ᴿREJ
      157/1-2 (1998) 234-236 (Touati, Charles).
1610 ᴱBrenner, Athalya Genesis. The Feminist Companion to the Bible
      (2nd series) 1: Shf 1998, Academic 276 pp. £17/$28. 1-85075-838-7.
1611 ᴱDavies, Philip R.; Clines, David J.A. The world of Genesis: per-
      sons, places, perspectives. JSOT.S 257: Shf 1998, Academic 179 pp.
      1-85075-875-1.
1612 ᵀᴱÉgron, Sr. Agnès Genèse. Les écritures, océan de mystères. Foi
      vivante: P 1998, Cerf 251 pp. FF55. 2-204-05990-0.
1613 ᴱFeyerick, Ada Genesis: world of myths and patriarchs. 1996
      ⇒12,1317. ᴿAeg. 78 (1998) 212-213 (Passoni Dell'Acqua, Anna).
1614 The first book of Moses, called Genesis: Authorised King James Ver-
      sion. Pocket Canons: E 1998 Canongate xiv; 126 pp. 0-86241-789-9.
1615 Gunkel, Hermann אַגָּדוֹת בְּרֵאשִׁית: מָבוֹ לְסֵפֶר בְּרֵאשִׁית: סְרָפוּת הַמִּקְרָה [The
      legends of Genesis]. 16 סִפְרִיַת הָאֶנְצִקְלוֹפֶדְיָה הַמִּקְרָאִת: J 1998, Mosad
      Beyaliq 13 + 192 pp. 965-342-692-3.
1616 ᵀHamman, A.-G. L'homme icône de Dieu: la Genèse relue par
      l'église des Pères. CPF 70-71: P 1998, Migne 319 pp.
1617 Hargreaves, John A guide to Genesis. SPCK Internat. Study Guide
      3: Reading, UK 1998, SPCK xiii; 175 pp. $13. 0-281-05155-0.
1618 Hendel, Ronald S. The text of Genesis 1-11: textual studies and
      critical edition. NY 1998, OUP xv; 168 pp. $30. 0-19-511961-4.
1619 Mathews, Kenneth A. Genesis 1-11:26. NAC 1A: 1996 ⇒12,1327;
      13,1516. ᴿAUSS 36 (1998) 145-146 (Miller, James E.); RevBib 60
      (1998) 123-125 (Croatto, J. Severino).
1620 ᵀᴱMposik, Charles Fragment d'un commentaire sur la Genèse. Les
      dix paroles: P 1998, Verdier 114 pp. FF95. 2-86432-292-7.
1621 ᵀRavasi, Gianfranco La Genesi: capitoli 1-11. Archivi di arte antica:
      T 1998, Allemandi 207 pp. 88-422-0809-4.

1622 **Reyburn, William D.; Fry, Euan McG.** A handbook on Genesis. UBS Handbook: NY 1998, UBS x; 1149 pp. 0-8267-0100-0.
1623 **Ruiz de Galarreta, José Enrique** El libro del Génesis: Para gente normal. La Biblia para gente normal: Bilbao 1998, Mensajero 202 pp. PTA1.380. 84-271-2148-2.
1624 **Soggin, J. Alberto** Das Buch Genesis: Kommentar. 1997 ⇒13,1530. ᴿBib. 79 (1998) 563-565 (*Ska, Jean Louis*).

E1.5 *Genesis*, topics

1625 *Alter, Robert* Reading Genesis. Jdm 47 (1998) 475-479.
1626 *Borgonovo, Gianantonio* Giustizia punitiva e misericordia in Gen 1-11. PSV 37 (1998) 53-68.
1627 **Brayford, Susan Ann** The taming and shaming of Sarah in the Septuagint of Genesis. ᴰIliff 1998, 297 pp.
1628 *Carr, David* βιβλος γενεσεως revisited: a synchronic analysis of patterns in Genesis as part of the Torah. ZAW 110 (1998) 159-172, 327-347;
1629 Intratextuality and intertextuality—joining transmission history and interpretation history in the study of Genesis. Bibel und Midrasch ᴱ**Bodendorfer, G.** FAT 22: 1998 ⇒K6.5. 97-112;
1630 **Carr, David McClain** Reading the fractures of Genesis: historical and literary approaches. 1996 ⇒12,1345; 13,1537. ᴿBib. 79 (1998) 120-124 (*Ska, Jean Louis*); CBQ 60 (1998) 322-323 (*Hendel, Ronald S.*); BiOr 55 (1998) 858-862 (*Otto, Eckart*); JBL 117 (1998) 120-121 (*Fretheim, Terence E.*).
1631 **Fischer, Irmtraud** Die Erzeltern Israels: feministisch-theologische Studien zu Genesis 12-26. BZAW 222: 1994 ⇒10,2027... 12,1613. ᴿEstB 56 (1998) 118-122 (*Arambarri, J.*).
1632 **Gilboa, Ruth** Intercourses in the book of Genesis: mythic motifs in creator-created relationships. Lewes 1998, Book Guild xx; 306 pp. 1-85776-2320.
1633 ᵀ**Hayward, C.T.R.** JEROME's *Hebrew questions on Genesis*. 1995 ⇒11/1,225... 13,1545. ᴿHeyJ 39 (1998) 76-77 (*McNamara, Martin*).
1634 **Kochanek, Piotr** La géographie sacrée du centre dans les strates pré- et postexiliques de la Genèse. ᴰLv(N) 1998, ᴰ*Bogaert, P.-M.*, 418 pp.
1635 **Maalouf, Tony Tamer** Ishmael in biblical history. ᴰDallas 1998, 297 pp.
1636 *Millard, Matthias* Anfang und Schluß der Genesis in klassischen jüdischen Kommentaren—Überlegungen zur Genesis als erstem Buch der Tora. Bibel und Midrasch. ᴱ**Bodendorfer, G.** FAT 22: 1998 ⇒K6.5. 167-190.
1637 **Rosenblatt, Naomi H.** Wrestling with angels: what Genesis teaches us about our spiritual identity: sexuality and personal relationships. 1997 <1995> ⇒13,1558. ᴿSynaxis 16/1 (1998) 318-321 (*Minissale, Antonino*).
1638 **Rota Scalabrini, Patrizio** Un Dio per amico: leggere e pregare il libro di Genesi. Vivere da protagonisti: Mi 1998, Paoline 152 pp. 88-315-1602-7.
1639 ᴱ**Weber, Dorothea** AUGUSTINUS: de Genesi contra Manichaeos. CSEL 91: W 1998, Verl. der ÖAK 196 pp. 3-7001-2713-8. ᴿAug. 38 (1998) 497-501 (*Bengt, Alexanderson*).

1640 **Witte, Markus** Die biblische Urgeschichte: Redaktions- und
theologiegeschichtliche Beobachtungen zu Genesis 1,1-11,26.
BZAW 265: B 1998, De Gruyter xii; 388 pp. 3-11-016209-1.

E1.6 **Creatio,** *Genesis 1s*

1641 [E]**Amand de Mendieta, Emmanuel; Rudberg, Stig Y.** BASILIUS
Caesariensis: Homilien zum Hexaemeron: homiliae in Hexaemeron.
GCS N.F. 2: 1997 ⇒13,1565. [R]JEarlyC 6 (1998) 323-324 (*Harrison,
Nonna Verna*).

1642 *Barr, James* Adam: single man, or all humanity?. [F]FRERICHS, E. BJSt
320: 1998 ⇒28. 3-12;

1643 Ein Mann oder die Menschen?: zur Anthropologie von Genesis 1.
Ebenbild Gottes. BThSt 33: 1998 ⇒255. 75-93;

1644 Was everything that God created really good?: a question in the first
verse of the Bible. [F]BRUEGGEMANN, W. 1998 ⇒16. 55-65.

1645 *Bauks, Michaela* Le rôle de l'Esprit Saint dans la création: quelques
considérations à partir de l'histoire de la réception de Gn 1,2. LV.F
53 (1998) 21-33.

1646 *Beaudry, Marcel; Nodet, Étienne* Le Tigre et l'Euphrate en Benjamin. Bib. 79 (1998) 97-102 [Gen 2,14].

1647 *Ben-Ḥayyim, Zeʾev* הצעה כנגדו עזר" [עזר כנגדו: a proposal]. Leš. 61
(1998) 45-50 [Gen 2,18.20].

1648 *Blumenthal, David R.* Many voices, one voice. Jdm 47 (1998) 465-
474 [Gen 1,1-2,3].

1649 *Büsing, Gerhard* Adam und die Tiere—Beobachtungen zum Verständnis der erzählten Namengebung in Gen 2,19f. Bibel und
Midrasch. [E]**Bodendorfer, G.** FAT 22: 1998 ⇒K6.5. 191-208 [Gen
2,19-20].

1650 *Croatto, José Severíno* On the semiotic reading of Genesis 1-3: a
response from Argentina. Semeia 81 (1998) 187-210.

1651 *Égasse, Corinne* Le sabbat, premier cadeau de Dieu. UnChr 129
(1998) 39-42.

1652 **Fergusson, David** The cosmos and the creator. L 1998, SPCK 110
pp. £10. [R]SJTh 51 (1998) 507-508 (*Torrance, Thomas F.*).

1653 *Futato, Mark D.* Because it had rained: a study of Gen 2:5-7 with
implications for Gen 2:4-25 and Gen 1:1-2:3. WThJ 60 (1998) 1-21.

1654 **Gandara, Alejandro** Las primeras palabras de la creación.
Argumentos 212: Barc 1998, Anagrama 280 pp. 84-339-0562-7.

1655 *Gilbert, Maurice* Une seule chair (Gn 2,34). Il a parlé par les
prophètes. 1998 <1978> ⇒155. 83-98.

1656 *Görg, Manfred* Das Übersetzungsproblem in Gen 2,1. BN 95 (1998)
5-11.

1657 *Gradwohl, Roland* "Wer einen einzigen Menschen (am Leben) erhält,
erhält eine volle Welt": des Menschen Gottebenbildlichkeit in der
jüdischen Lehre. Ebenbild Gottes. BThSt 33: 1998 ⇒255. 107-122.

1658 *Gregersen, Niels Henrik* The idea of creation and the theory of
autopoietic processes. Zygon 33 (1998) 333-367.

1659 *Hurwitz, M.S.* The language of 'creatio ex nihilo'. Hellenic and
Jewish arts. 1998 ⇒439. 41-50.

1660 *Jeppesen, Knud* What was created in the beginning?. "Lasset uns
Brücken bauen...". BEAT 42: 1998 ⇒401. 59-65.

1661 *Klopfenstein, Martin A.* "Und siehe, es war sehr gut!" (Genesis 1,31): worin besteht die Güte der Schöpfung nach dem ersten Kapitel der hebräischen Bibel?. Ebenbild Gottes. BThSt 33: 1998 ⇒255. 56-74.

1662 *Lacocque, André* Cracks in the wall. Thinking biblically. 1998 ⇒251. 3-29.

1663 **Löning, Karl; Zenger, Erich** Als Anfang schuf Gott: biblische Schöpfungstheologien. 1997 ⇒13,1590. [R]BiLi 71 (1998) 373-374 (*Roloff, Jürgen*); ThRv 94 (1998) 502-505 (*Meier, Claudia*).

1664 **Maranesi, Pietro** Verbum inspiratum, chiave ermeneutica dell'Hexaëmeron di San BONAVENTURA. BSC 51: 1996 ⇒12,1390; 13,1592. [R]Laur. 39 (1998) 538-540 (*Van Asseldonk, Optatus*).

1665 **Martínez de Pisón, Ramón** Création et liberté: essai d'anthropologie chrétienne. 1997 ⇒13,1594. [R]SR 27 (1998) 97-99 (*Perron, Louis*).

1666 *Mercier, Philippe* En guise d'éditorial: souviens-toi du sabbat pour le sanctifier. UnChr 129 (1998) 2-5.

1667 *Moor, Johannes C. de* The duality in God and man: Gen. 1:26-27 as P's interpretation of the Yahwistic creation account. Intertextuality. OTS 40: 1998 ⇒394. 112-125.

1668 *Norin, Stig* Boskapsdjur, kräldjur och vilda djur: reflektioner över Gen 1:24-25. SEÅ 63 (1998) 19-30.

1669 **Nothomb, Paul** Les récits bibliques de la création. Vers la seconde alliance: P [2]1998, Différence 217 pp. FF120. 2-7291-1205-7.

1670 **Rebic, Adalberto** Stvaranje svijeta i covjeka: egzegeza i biblijska teologija Post 1-3 s uvodom u Petoknjizje. Svezak 33: Zagreb 1996, Krscanska Sadasnjost 175 pp. 953-151-117-9. **Croatian.**

1671 *Ricoeur, Paul* Penser la création. Penser la bible. 1998 ⇒188. 57-102;

1672 Thinking creation. Thinking biblically. 1998 ⇒251. 31-67.

1673 *Sanz Giménez-Rico, Enrique* ¿Qué significa 'creador del cielo y de la tierra'?. SalTer 87 (1998) 375-386.

1674 **Seebaß, Horst** Urgeschichte (1,1-11,26). Genesis, 1. 1996 ⇒12,1408. [R]BZ 42 (1998) 300-303 (*Ruppert, Lothar*); Protest. 53 (1998) 26-29 (*Soggin, J.A.*).

1675 *Stefani, Piero* FRANCESCO, la lode, il creato e gli animali. Hum(B) 53 (1998) 665-671.

1676 *Tschirch, Reinmar* Die Schöpfungserzählungen in Kinderbibeln: eine kritische theologische Analyse neuerer Kinderbibelausgaben. BiKi 53 (1998) 140-144.

1677 *Uehlinger, Christoph* Nicht nur Knochenfrau: zu einem wenig beachteten Aspekt der zweiten Schöpfungserzählung. BiKi 53 (1998) 31-34.

1678 *Van Wolde, Ellen* The creation of coherence. Semeia 81 (1998) 159-174.

1679 *Vermeylen, J.* Tradition et rédaction en Genèse 1. Transeuphratène 16 (1998) 127-147.

1680 *Weippert, Manfred* Tier und Mensch in einer menschenarmen Welt: zum sog. dominium terrae in Genesis 1. Ebenbild Gottes. BThSt 33: 1998 ⇒255. 35-55.

E1.7 *Genesis 1s*: **Bible and myth** [⇒M3.8]

1681   **Aláez, Octavio** Mitos y biblia a la luz de la ciencia. Libros Hiperión 170: M 1998, Hiperión 173 pp. 84-7517-559-7.

1682   **Barksdale, Ethelbert Courtland** Enchanted paths and magic words: the quantum mind and time travel in science and in literary myth. Ars Interpretandi/The art of interpretation 8: NY 1998, Lang xxi; 394 pp. 0-8204-3850-2.

1683   *Clines, David J.A.* Humanity as the image of God. OT essays, 2. JSOT.S 293: 1998 <1968> ⇒142. 447-497 [Gen 1,26].

1684   *Frymer-Kensky, Tikva* Creation myths breed violence. BiRe 14/3 (1998) 17, 47.

1685   ᴱ**Hörner, Volker; Leiner, Martin** Die Wirklichkeit des Mythos: eine theologische Spurensuche. Gü 1998, Kaiser 104 pp. 3-579-00396-8.

1686   **Jaspers, Karl; Bultmann, Rudolf** Il problema della demitizzazione. 1995 ⇒11/2,k488. ᴿFilTeo 12/1 (1998) 191-2 (*Pezza, Lucia*).

1687   *Kaiser, Otto* Der Mensch, Gottes Ebenbild und Statthalter auf Erden. Gesammelte Aufsätze. BZAW 261: 1998 <1991> ⇒166. 43-55.

1688   *Lambert, Wilfred G.* Technical terminology for creation in the ancient Near East. Intellectual life. 1998 ⇒450. 189-193.

1689   *Lardinois, André* How the days fit the works in HESIOD's *Works and days*. AJP 119 (1998) 319-336.

1690   *Müller, Hans-Peter* Rechtfertigung des Mythos in bibeltheologischer und hermeneutischer Hinsicht. Christlicher Glaube in der Begegnung mit dem Hinduismus. 1998 ⇒290. 63-77.

1691   *Ouro, Roberto* The earth of Genesis 1:2: abiotic or chaotic? (part 1). AUSS 36 (1998) 259-276.

1692   **Page, Hugh R.** The myth of cosmic rebellion: a study of its reflexes in Ugaritic and biblical literature. VT.S 65: 1996 ⇒12,1448. ᴿCBQ 60 (1998) 541-542 (*Walls, Neal H.*).

1693   ᴱ**Patton, Laurie L.; Doniger, Wendy** Myth and method. 1996 ⇒12,222. ᴿJR 78 (1998) 482-484 (*Alles, Gregory D.*).

1694   *Piepke, Joachim G.* Mythos und Offenbarung: Gen 1-3 im Kontext der universalen Schöpfungsmythen. Anthr. 93 (1998) 507-519.

1695   *Simkins, Ronald A.* Gender construction in the Yahwist creation myth. Genesis. 1998 ⇒219. 32-52.

1696   **Yvanoff, Xavier** Mythes sur l'origine de l'homme. P 1998, Errance 539 pp. 2-87772-151-5.

E1.8 *Gen 1s, Jos 10,13...*: **The Bible, the Church and science**

1697   **Arnould, Jacques** La théologie après DARWIN: éléments pour une théologie de la création dans une perspective évolutionniste. Théologies: P 1998, Cerf 302 pp. 2-204-05848-3.

1698   **Beauchamp, André** Devant la création: regards de science, regards de foi. 1997 ⇒13,1637. ᴿSR 27 (1998) 96-97 (*Simard, Noël*).

1699   **Cazeaux, Jacques** Le refus de la guerre sainte: Josué, Juges et Ruth. LeDiv 174: P 1998, Cerf 250 pp. FF145. 2-204-06022-4.

1700   Creation and evolution: proceedings of the ITEST Workshop October, 1997. St. Louis, MO 1998, ITEST Faith/Science Press (4) iv; 263 pp. 1-885583-06-0.

1701 *Dziedzic, Andrzej La création* d'Agrippa d'Aubigné comme un lieu de l'inscription de la connaissance: l'analyse de l'intertexte biblique et scientifique. Aevum 72 (1998) 759-776.

1702 **Guth, Alan H.** The inflationary universe: the quest for a new theory of cosmic origins. Reading, Mass. 1998, Perseus xv (2); 358 pp. 0-201-14942-7.

1703 *Harrison, Peter* The Bible, Protestantism, and the rise of natural science. C 1998, CUP xi; 313 pp. £40. 0-521-59196-1.

1704 **Hoyle, Fred** L'origine dell'universo e l'origine della religione. Mi 1998, Mondadori 100 pp. L9.000.

1705 **Matthews, Clifford N.; Varghese, Roy A.** Cosmic beginnings. 1995 ⇒11/2,615. RZygon 33/1 (1998) 161-164 (*Padgett, Alan G.*).

1706 *Murphy, George L.* The theology of the cross and God's work in the world. Zygon 33 (1998) 221-231.

1707 ERae, **Murray** Science and theology. 1994 ⇒10,389*; 11/2,2392 RZygon 33 (1998) 296-299 (*Peterson, Gregory R.*).

1708 **Ratzsch, Del** The battle of beginnings. 1996 ⇒12,1482. RAUSS 36 (1998) 152-155 (*Jensen, Karen G.*).

1709 **Ross, Hugh** The Genesis question: scientific advances and the accuracy of Genesis. Colorado Springs 1998, NavPress 235 pp. 1-57683-111-6.

1710 **Roth, Ariel A.** Origins: linking science and scripture. Hagerstown, MD 1998, Review and Herald 384 pp. $30.

1711 **Whedbee, J. William** The Bible and the cosmic vision. C 1998, CUP xii; 315 pp. $60. 0-521-49507-5.

1712 **Worthing, Mark William** God, creation, and contemporary physics. 1996 ⇒12,1488. RZygon 33 (1998) 303-306 (*Carlson, Richard F.*).

E1.9 *Peccatum originale*, **the sin of Eden**, *Genesis 2-3*

1713 *Baldacci, Osvaldo* Immaginate località geografiche del paradiso terrestre. RANL 9 (1998) 607-611.

1713* *Balducci, C.* Il diavolo oggi. Angeli e demoni. 1998 ⇒375. 273-297.

1714 **Berger, Klaus** Wozu ist der Teufel da?. Stu 1998, Quell 240 pp. 3-7918-1956-9.

1715 *Bolewski, Jącek* Teolog o kreacjach Ewy [Le théologien devant les créations d'Ève]. PrzPow 115 (1998) 89-98.

1716 *Calderini, Simonetta* Woman, 'sin' and 'lust': the fall of Adam and Eve according to classical and modern Muslim exegesis. Religion & sexuality. 1998 ⇒302. 49-63.

1717 **Cerbelaud, Dominique** Le diable. 1997 ⇒13,1670. RRThom 98 (1998) 327-329 (*Bonino, Serge-Thomas*).

1718 **Claret, Bernd J.** 'Geheimnis des Bösen': ... Teufel. 1997 ⇒13,1672. RAlpha Omega 1 (1998) 504-505 (*Furlong, Jude*).

1719 **Conklin, Edward** Getting back into the garden of Eden. Lanham 1998, University Press of America viii; 154 pp. 0-7618-1140-0.

1720 *De Carlo, G.* Il demonio artefice della caduta e il peccato dell'uomo: il tentatore da Gen 3 a Sap 2,24;

1721 *Deiana, G.* L'evoluzione della figura del demonio nell'Antico Testamento. Angeli e demoni. 1998, ⇒375. 1-36/117-142.

1722 **Dohmen, Christoph** Schöpfung und Tod: die Entfaltung theologischer und anthropologischer Konzeptionen in Gen 2/3. SBB 35: 1996 ⇒12,1505. RThZ 54 (1998) 268-269 (*Weber, Beat*).

1723   *Ernst, Michael* Adam: zur Relecture eines alttestamentlichen Motivs in neutestamentlichen Texten. PzB 7 (1998) 43-52 [1 Tim 2,13-14].

1724   ^E**Fleischer, Dirk** Otto Justus Basilius HESSE: Versuch einer biblischen Dämonologie, oder Untersuchung der Lehre der heiligen Schrift vom Teufel und seiner Macht. Wissen und Kritik 15: Waltrop 1998 <1776>, Spenner lxxxviii; [56] 356 pp. 3-933688-07-8.

1725   *Galeotti, Gary* Satan's identity reconsidered. Faith & Mission 15 (1998) 72-86 [Deut 6,4-9].

1726   *Garbowski, Christopher* Czy Adam mógł być kobietą?: pytanie do biblisty [Adam aurait-il pu être femme?: interrogation à un bibliste]. PrzPow 115 (1998) 85-88.

1727   **Heller, Karin** E coppia li creò. R 1998, Borla 182 pp. L20.000.

1728   *Höhne-Sparborth, José* El engaño de la serpiente: una lectura de Gn 2-3 partiendo de experiencias corporales conflictivas. Alternativas 5 (1998) 169-184.

1729   *Korsak, Mary Phil* A fresh look at the Garden of Eden. Semeia 81 (1998) 131-144.

1730   *Kübel, Paul* Ein Wortspiel in Genesis 3 und sein Hintergrund: die "kluge" Schlange und die "nackten" Menschen. BN 93 (1998) 11-22 [Gen 3,1].

1731   *Lacocque, André* Lézardes dans le mur: Genèse 2-3. Penser la bible. 1998 ⇒188. 19-55.

1732   **Lavatori, Renzo** Satana un caso serio: studio di demonologia cristiana. 1996 ⇒12,1525. ^RScC 126 (1998) 690-694 (*Croce, Vittorio*).

1733   *Lavaud, Claudie* Pour être responsable, faut-il être libre?: petite catéchèse sur Genèse 2-3. Com(F) 23 (1998) 74-79.

1734   **Leisch-Kiesl, Monika** Eva als andere. 1992 ⇒10,14321. ^RBiKi 53/1 (1998) 42-43 (*Reuter, Eleonore*).

1735   **Loh, Johannes** Paradies im Widerspiel der Mächte: Mythenlogik—eine Herausforderung für die Theologie. BEAT 43: Fra 1998 Lang 338 pp. 3-631-32173-2.

1736   *Martin-Grunenwald, Michèle* La promesse et le face à face avec Dieu. LV(L) 239 (1998) 33-51.

1737   **Minois, Georges** Le diable. Que sais-je? 3423: P 1998, PUF 126 pp. 2-13-049562-1.

1738   *Moreau, Luc* Le paradis, notre espérance. LV(L) 239 (1998) 63-79.

1739   *Nardoni, Enrique* Género literario y teología de Génesis 2-3. RevBib 60 (1998) 65-90.

1740   *Narrowe, Morton H.* Another look at the tree of good and evil. JBQ 26 (1998) 184-188.

1741   *Neusner, Jacob* Systematizing Eden. Jewish law. 1998 ⇒181. 21-41.

1742   **Nielsen, Kirsten** Satan—the Prodigal Son?: a family problem in the bible. Shf 1998, Academic 198 pp. £15. ^RRRT (1998/4) 98-99 (*Meggitt, Justin*).

1743   **Pagels, Elaine** L'origine de Satan. 1997 ⇒13,1697. ^RChoisir (juin 1998) 38 (*Hug, Joseh*).

1744   **Panier, Louis** Le péché originel: naissance de l'homme sauvé. Théologies: 1996 ⇒12,1538; 13,1698. ^RSémBib 91 (1998) 58-63 (*Fortin, Anne*).

1745   *Rabkin, Eric S.* Eat and grow strong: the super-natural power of forbidden fruit. Violence. 1998 ⇒260. 8-23.

1746   *Ricca, Paolo* Il peccato originale. Hum(B) 53 (1998) 659-664.

1747 *Rottzoll, Dirk U.* Die Schöpfungs- und Fallerzählung in Gen 2f, Teil 2: die Schöpfungserzählung. ZAW 110 (1998) 1-15.
1748 *Rüterswörden, Udo* Erwägungen zur alttestamentlichen Paradiesvorstellung. ThLZ 123 (1998) 1153-1161.
1749 *Savasta, Carmelo* Gen 3,1-19 (V). BeO 40 (1998) 3-18.
1750 *Schenker, Adrian* Le monde à venir dans l'Ancien Testament. LV(L) (1998) 25-31.
1751 **Schüngel-Straumann, Helen** Die Frau am Anfang—Eva und die Folgen. 1997 ⇒13,1707. [R]BiKi 53/1 (1998) 41-42 (*Reuter, Eleonore*).
1752 *Schüngel-Straumann, Helen* 'From a woman sin had its beginning, and because of her we all die' (Sir 25:24). ThD 45 (1998) 203-212.
1753 **Schwager, Raymund** Erbsünde und Heilsdrama: im Kontext von E-volution, Gentechnologie und Apokalyptik. 1997 ⇒13,1708. [R]FZPhTh 45 (1998) 610-613 (*Hallensleben, Barbara*).
1754 *Sharon, Diane M.* The doom of paradise: literary patterns in accounts of paradise and mortality in the Hebrew Bible and the ancient Near East. Genesis. 1998 ⇒219. 53-80.
1755 *Stadelmann, Luís* The Garden of Eden. Month 31 (1998) 442-443.
1756 **Van der Hoeven, T.H.** Het imago van Satan: een cultuur-theologisch onderzoek naar een duivels tegenbeeld. Kampen 1998, Kok 393 pp. ƒ69.50. 90-242-9427-4.
1757 **Vaz, Armindo dos Santos** A visão das origens em Gen 2,4b-3,24 como coerência temática e unidade literária. 1996 ⇒12,1557. [R]Did(L) 28/1 (1998) 237-41 (*Ramos, José Augusto*); Bib(L) 7/7 (1998) 163-165 (*Alves, Herculano*).
1758 *Vogels, Walter* "Like one of us, knowing tôb and ra`" (Gen 3:22). Semeia 81 (1998) 145-157.
1759 *Youngblood, Ronald F.* Fallen star: the evolution of Lucifer. BiRe 14/6 (1998) 22-31, 47.

E2.1 **Cain and Abel**; *gigantes, longaevi; Genesis 4s*

1760 *Bailey, Nicholas A.* "What's wrong with my word order?": topic, focus, information flow, and other pragmatic aspects of some biblical genealogies. JOTT 10 (1998) 1-29.
1761 *Ballabio, Fabio* 'Dov'è tuo fratello?' (Gen 4,1-16): una lettura a fronte del pluralismo religioso. Studi Fatti Ricerche 83 (1998) 11-12.
1762 *Baumgart, Norbert* Clemens Gen 5,29—ein Brückenvers in der Urgeschichte und zugleich ein Erzählerkommentar. BN 92 (1998) 21-37.
1763 *Calloud, Jean* Caïn et Abel: l'homme et son frère-II. SémBib 92 (1998) 3-34.
1764 *Cerbelaud, Dominique* Premières relectures juives et chrétiennes du texte biblique. CEv.S 105 (1998) 5-38.
1765 **Cerbelaud, Dominique; Dahan, Gilbert** Caïn et Abel: Genèse 4. CEv.S 105: P 1998, Cerf 107 pp. FF50. 0222-9706.
1766 *Clines, David J.A.* The significance of the 'Sons of God' episode (Genesis 6.1-4) in the context of the 'Primeval History' (Genesis 1-11). OT essays, 1. JSOT.S 292: 1998 <1979> ⇒142. 337-350.
1767 *Dahan, Gilbert* Exégèse chrétienne et exégèse juive dans l'Occident médiéval. CEv.S 105 (1998) 59-76.

1768 *Desclais, Jean-Louis* Qâbîl et Hâbîl: réflexions musulmanes sur le premier fratricide. CEv.S 105 (1998) 53-58.

1769 *Elwolde, John* Human and divine sexuality: the *Zohar* on Genesis 5.2. Religion & sexuality. 1998 ⇒302. 64-84.

1770 *Fraade, Steven D.* Enosh and his generation revisited. Biblical figures. ᴱ**Stone, M.** 1998 ⇒K1.1. 59-86 [Gen 4,26; Sir 44; 49; Rom 10,12].

1771 **Freeman, Travis Richard** The chronological value of Genesis 5 and 11 in light of recent biblical investigation. ᴰSouthwestern Baptist Theol. Sem. 1998, 209 pp.

1772 *Heinzerling, Rüdiger* "Einweihung" durch Henoch?: die Bedeutung der Altersangaben in Genesis 5. ZAW 110 (1998) 581-589.

1773 *Lenchak, Timothy A.* Puzzling passages: Genesis 6:4. BiTod 36 (1998) 54.

1774 *Malamat, Abraham* King lists of the Old Babylonian period and biblical genealogies. Mari and the bible. 1998 [1968] ⇒173. 219-235.

1775 *Paterson, Linda* Marcabru et le lignage de Caïn: *Bel m'es cant son li frug madur* (PC 293.13). CCMéd 41 (1998) 241-255.

1776 *Pelletier, Anne-Marie* Caïn et Abel dans la littérature du XIXᵉ siècle. CEv.S 105 (1998) 88-101.

1777 *Pippin, Tina* They might be giants: Genesis 6:1-4 and women's encouner with the supernatural. Violence. 1998 ⇒260. 47-59.

1778 *Roussel, Bernard* Martin LUTHER, lecteur de Gn 4,1-16: le juste et l'hypocrite. CEv.S 105 (1998) 77-85.

1779 *Schmitt, Armin* Übersetzung als Interpretation: die Henochüberlieferung der Septuaginta (Gen 5,21-24) im Licht der hellenistischen Epoche. Interpretation of the Bible. JSOT.S 289: 1998 ⇒388. 181-200.

1780 *Scopello, Madeleine* Les interprétations gnostiques. CEv.S 105 (1998) 39-52 [Gen 4].

1781 *Turner, John D.* The Gnostic Seth. Biblical figures. ᴱ**Stone, M.** 1998 ⇒K1.1. 33-58 [Gen 4,25; 5,3].

1782 *Wiesel, Elie* Cain & Abel: "He who kills, kills his brother". BiRe 14/1 (1998) 20-21.

E2.2 *Diluvium*, **the Flood**; Gilgameš (Atraḫasis); **Genesis 6...**

1783 *Benjamins, H.S.* Noah, the ark, and the Flood in early christian theology: the ship of the church in the making;

1784 *Bremmer, Jan N.* Near Eastern and native traditions in APOLLODORUS' account of the Flood. Interpretations. 1998 ⇒242. 134-149/39-55.

1785 *Clines, David J.A.* The theology of the Flood narrative. OT essays, 2. JSOT.S 293: 1998 <1973> ⇒142. 508-523.

1786 *Dimant, Devorah* Noah in early Jewish literature. Biblical figures ᴱ**Stone, M.** 1998 ⇒K1.1. 123-150.

1787 *Fontana, Raniero* Noachismo: un'indagine preliminare. Cahiers Ratisbonne 3 (1997) 80-116;

1788 La figura di Noë secondo i rabbini. Cahiers Ratisbonne 5 (1998) 58-110.

1789 *Fouts, David M.* Peleg in Gen 10:25. JETS 41 (1998) 17-21.

1790 *García Martínez, Florentino* Interpretations of the Flood in the Dead Sea scrolls. Interpretations. 1998 ⇒242. 86-108.

1791   *George, A.R.* The day the earth divided: a geological aetiology in the Babylonian Gilgameš epic. Rencontre Ass. 34. 1998 ⇒452. 179-183.

1792   *Greenstein, Edward L.* The retelling of the flood story in the Gilgamesh epic. [F]FRERICHS, E.. BJSt 320: 1998 ⇒28. 197-204.

1793   **Harland, Peter J.** The value of human life: a study of the story of the flood (Genesis 6-9). VT.S 64: 1996 ⇒12,1587. [R]CBQ 60 (1998) 113-115 *(Carr, David)*; ThLZ 123 (1998) 40-41 *(Witte, Markus)*.

1794   *Harland, P.J.* Vertical or horizontal: the sin of Babel. VT 48 (1998) 515-533.

1795   *Hilhorst, A.* The Noah story: was it known to the Greeks?. Interpretations. 1998 ⇒242. 56-65.

1796   *Holloway, Steven W.* The shape of Utnapishtim's ark: a rejoinder. ZAW 110 (1998) 617-626.

1797   *Kochanek, Piotr* Les strates rédactionnelles de la table des nations et l'inversion de la loi de primogéniture. EThL 74 (1998) 273-299.

1798   *Landy, Francis* Flood and fludd. Biblical studies. JSOT.S 266: 1998 ⇒380. 117-158.

1799   *Luttikhuizen, Gerard P.* Biblical narrative in Gnostic revision: the story of Noah and the Flood in classic Gnostic mythology. Interpretations. 1998 ⇒242. 109-123.

1800   *Mařik, Tomáš* Bemerkungen zur formalen und inhaltlichen Interpretation des 'Gilgameš und Akka'. ArOr 66 (1998) 265-269.

1801   *Noort, Ed* The stories of the great flood: notes on Gen 6:5-9:17 in its context of the ancient Near East. Interpretations. 1998 ⇒242. 1-38.

1802   [E]**Parpola, Simo** The standard Babylonian epic of Gilgamesh. 1997 ⇒13,1749. [R]Mes. 33 (1998) 371-373 *(D'Agostino, F.)*.

1803   *Parpola, Simo* The esoteric meaning of the name of Gilgamesh. Intellectual life. 1998 ⇒450. 315-329.

1804   *Penicaud, Anne* L'histoire de Noé (livre de la Genèse, VI,5 à IX,28). SémBib 91 (1998) 33-52.

1805   *Robertson, O.P.* Current critical questions concerning the "curse of Ham" (Gen. 9:20-27). JETS 41 (1998) 177-188.

1806   *Rösel, Martin* Die Chronologie der Flut in Gen 7-8: keine neuen textkritischen Lösungen. ZAW 110 (1998) 590-593.

1807   *Rubin, Milka* The language of creation or the primordial language: a case of cultural polemics in antiquity. JJS 49 (1998) 306-333.

1808   *Schrader, Lutz* Kommentierende Redaktion im Noah—Sintflut-Komplex der Genesis. ZAW 110 (1998) 489-502.

1809   *Seidl, Ursula* Das Flut-Ungeheuer abūbu. ZA 88 (1998) 100-113.

1810   [T]**Silva Castillo, Jorge** Gilgamesh, o la angustia por la muerte (poema bibilonio). 1995 ⇒13,1749. [R]JNES 57 (1998) 148-150 *(Rubio P., J. Gonzalo)*.

1811   *Ska, Jean Louis* La benedizione di Babele. Bibbia, popoli e lingue. 1998 ⇒381. 47-62.

1812   *Van Bekkum, Wout J.* The lesson of the Flood: מַבּוּל in rabbinic tradition;

1813   *Vandermeersch, Patrick* Where will the water stick?: considerations of a psychoanalyst about the stories of the Flood;

1814   *Van Ruiten, J.T.A.G.M.* The interpretation of the Flood story in the book of Jubilees;

1815   *Vermij, Rienk* The Flood and the scientific revolution: Thomas BURNET's system of natural providence. Interpretations. 1998 ⇒242. 124-133/167-193/66-85/150-166.

1816   **Villa, Nereo** Il sacro simbolo dell'arcobaleno: numerologia biblica sulla reincarnazione. Biblioteca universale 12: [Casalgrande (Reggio Emilia)] 1998, SeaR 146 pp.

1817   *Wilcke, Claus* Zu "Gilgameš und Akka": Überlegungen zur Zeit von Entstehung und Niederschrift, wie auch zum Text des Epos mit einem Exkurs über Überlieferung von "Šulgi A" und von "Lugalbanda II". [F]RÖMER, W. AOAT 253: 1998 ⇒97. 457-485.

E2.3 Patriarchae, Abraham; *Genesis 12s*

1818   *Aries, Wolf D.* Ahmed Konflikt der Gedächtnisse: der abrahamische Dialog aus muslimischer Sicht. JRTR 6 (1998) 40-53.

1819   *Bertalot, Renzo* Abramo nel Nouvo Testamento. Studi ecumenici 16 (1998) 213-221.

1820   *Borgman, Paul* Abraham and Sarah: literary text and the rhetorics of reflection. The function of scripture. 1998 ⇒236. 45-77.

1821   **Bruckner, James Kevin** A literary and theological analysis of implied law in the Abrahamic narrative: implied oughts as a case study. [D]Luther Sem. 1998, 333 pp. [Gen 17,15; 18,12-15; 21,1-6].

1822   *Delaney, Carol* Abraham and the seeds of patriarchy. Genesis. 1998 ⇒219. 129-149.

1823   **Delaney, Carol Lowery** Abraham on trial: the social legacy of biblical myth. Princeton, NJ 1998, Princeton University Press xv; 333 pp. $30. 0-691-05985-3.

1824   *Di Porto, Bruno* Abramo lo straniero: padre di una nazione e padre dei credenti. FilTeo 12 (1998) 255-265.

1825   *Fischer, Irmtraud* Genesis 12-50: die Ursprungsgeschichte Israels als Frauengeschichte. Kompendium Feministische Bibelauslegung. [E]**Schottroff, L.**: 1998 ⇒H8.9. 12-25.

1826   *Frost, Naomi* Four bible studies in the life of Abraham. Evangel 16 (1998) 66-69.

1827   *Gellman, Jerome* The figure of Abraham in Hasidic literature. HThR 91 (1998) 279-300.

1828   **Habel, Norman C.** The land is mine: six biblical land ideologies. 1995 ⇒11/1,393... 13,1762. [R]TJT 14/1 (1998) 94-96 (*Anderson, Marvin L.*).

1829   **Janson, Aad G.** De Abrahamcyclus in de Genesiscommentaar van Efrem de Syriër. [D]Leiden. 1998, 270 pp.

1830   *Kofsky, Aryeh* Mamre: a case of a regional cult?. Sharing the sacred. 1998 ⇒306. 19-30 [Gen 13,18].

1831   **Kuschel, Karl-Josef** Abraham: sign of hope for Jews, christians and muslims. 1995 ⇒11/2,4245... 13,1765. [R]Pro Ecclesia 7/1 (1998) 116-118 (*LaHurd, Carol Schersten*);

1832   La controversia su Abramo: ciò che divide—e ciò che unisce ebrei, cristiani e musulmani. 1996 ⇒12,9082; 13,1766. [R]RdT 39 (1998) 790-791 (*Poggi, Vincenzo*); CivCatt 149/4 (1998) 42-52 (*Vanzan, Piersandro*).

1833   **Lafon, Guy** Abrão: a invenção da fé. Bauru 1998, EDUSC 238 pp.

1834   *MacKinlay, Judith* Reading with choices and controls: Genesis 12. Feminist Theology 17 (1998) 75-87.

1835   **Massignon, Louis** Les trois prières d'Abraham. 1997 ⇒13,1769. [R]Ibla 61/1 (1998) 102-104 (*Mayaud, Charles*); OCP 64/1 (1998)

222-223 (*Poggi, V.*); VS 726 (1998) 174-176 (*Jomier, Jacques*); IslChr 24 (1998) 247-249 (*Rocalve, Pierre*).

1836 *Mitri, Tarik* Dialogue au sujet d'Abraham et à notre sujet en son nom. IslChr 24 (1998) 1-11. Å.

1837 *Miyake, Lynn* Abraham's journey: a model for contemplative christians. Spiritual Life 44 (1998) 141-147.

1838 **Moberly, R.W.L.** Genesis 12-50. OTGu: 1992 ⇒8,2340. [R]VJTR 62 (1998) 442-444 (*Raj, M.I.*).

1839 **Naumann, Thomas Ismael**: Ismael: theologische und erzählanalytische Studien zu einem biblischen Konzept der Selbstwahrnehmung Israels im Kreis der Völker aus der Nachkommenschaft Abrahams. Diss.-Habil. Bern 1996-1997, [D]*Dietrich, W.*

1840 *Nickelsburg, George W.E.* Abraham the convert: a Jewish tradition and its use by the apostle Paul. Biblical figures. [E]**Stone, M.** 1998 ⇒K1.1. 151-175 [Gen 15,6; 11,20-12,5; Gal 3,6-4,11].

1841 **Pagolu, Augustine** The religion of the patriarchs. JSOT.S 277: Shf 1998, Academic 290 pp. 1-85075-935-9.

1842 *Petit, Madeleine; Krumeich, Kirsten* Juda (Patriarch). RAC 146. 1998 ⇒495. 38-63.

1843 *Phillips, Elaine A.* Incredulity, faith, and textual purposes: postbiblical responses to the laughter of Abraham and Sarah. The function of scripture. 1998 ⇒236. 22-33.

1848 *Soggin, J. Alberto* I patriarchi biblici come nomadi. [F]SIERRA J. 1998 ⇒102. 517-519.

1849 *Van Oord, Jos* Jakob in levende lijve. Interpretatie 6/3 (1998) 7-9.

1850 **Vogels, Walter** Abrahán y sy leyenda: Génesis 12,-25,11. 1997 ⇒13,1781. [R]Igreja e Missão 50 (1998) 400-402 (*Couto, A.*);

1851 Abraham et sa légende: Genèse 12,1-25,11. LiBi 110: 1996 ⇒12, 1635; 13,1782. [R]Igreja e Missão 50 (1998) 273-275 (*Couto, A.*).

1852 *Wénin, André* Abram et Saraï en Égypte (Gn 12,10-20) ou la place de Saraï dans l'élection. RTL 29 (1998) 433-456.

E2.4 **Melchisedech, Sodoma**; *Genesis 14...19*

1853 *Barzilai, Gabriel* לפרשנותה של התיבה 'אז'—במקרא על פי חיבור פולמוסי מהמאה ה-19 [The fate of the wicked of Sodom and Gomorrah in an ancient interpretation from Qumran (4Q252 Col 3)]. BetM 154-155 (1998) 323-331.

1854 *Berger, Paul R.* Die älteste historische Nachricht über Anatolien in der Bibel. Rencontre Assyr. 34. 1998 ⇒452. 495-497.

1855 *Brenner, Rachel F.* Rereading the story of Sodom and Gomorrah in the aftermath of the Holocaust. [F]CARGAS H.. 1998 ⇒19. 71-81.

1856 Discovered: Sodom and Gomorrah!. Nv 1992, Wyatt Archaeological Research. Video 45 min. [R]BArR 24/5 (1998) 60, 62 (*Gierlowski-Kordesch, Elizabeth*).

1857 *Els, Pieter J.J.S.* Old Testament perspectives on interfaith dialogue: the significance of the Abram-Melchizedek episode of Genesis 14. Studies in Interreligious Dialogue 8 (1998) 191-207.

1858 *Newman, Judith H.* Lot in Sodom: the post-mortem of a city and the afterlife of a biblical text. Function of scripture. 1998 ⇒236. 34-44.

1859 *Pearson, Birger A.* Melchizedek in early Judaism, christianity, and Gnosticism. Biblical figures. [E]**Stone, M.** 1998 ⇒K1.1. 176-202 [Gen 14,18-20; Ps 110,4; Heb 5-7].

E2.5 **The Covenant** (alliance, Bund): *Foedus, Genesis 15...*

1860 *Alp, Sedat* Zur Datierung des Ulmitešup-Vertrags. AltOrF 25 (1998) 54-60.

1861 **Blaschke, Andreas** Beschneidung: Zeugnisse der Bibel und verwandter Texte. TANZ 28: Tü 1998, Francke xii; 568 pp. 3-7720-2820-9.

1862 **Briend, J.; Lebrun, R.; Puech, E.** Tratados e juramentos no Antigo Oriente Próximo. Documentos do Mundo da Bíblia 12: São Paulo 1998, Paulus 138 pp. 85-349-1020-0.

1863 **Edel, Elmar** Der Vertrag zwischen Ramses II. von Ägypten und Hattusili III. von Hatti. WVDOG 95: 1997 ⇒13,1790. ᴿOLZ 93 (1998) 627-629 (*Kitchen, Kenneth A.*).

1864 **Elazar, Daniel J.** Covenant and civil society: the constitutional matrix of modern democracy. The covenant tradition in politics 4. New Brunswick 1998, Transaction x; 404 pp. 1-56000-311-1;

1865 Covenant and commonwealth: from christian separation through the Protestant Reformation. The covenant tradition in politics 2. 1996 ⇒12,1646. ᴿRP 60/1 (1998) 168-171 (*Gross, George M.*).

1866 Covenant polity in biblical Israel: biblical foundations and Jewish expressions. The covenant tradition in politics I. 1995 ⇒11/1,422 ᴿRP 60/1 (1998) 168-170 (*Gross, George M.*).

1867 *Gosse, Bernard* Exode 3,7 et la dépendance de l'alliance du Sinaï par rapport à l'alliance avec les Patriarches dans la rédaction du Pentateuch. ScEs 50 (1998) 45-55;

1868 L'Alliance avec Abraham et les relectures de l'histoire d'Israël en Ne 9, Ps 105-106, 135-136 et 1 Ch 16. TEuph 15 (1998) 123-135.

1869 *Jankowski, Gerhard* Dieses Land: die Verheißung des Landes in den Evangelien und den apostolischen Schriften. TeKo 21 (1998) 51-58.

1870 *Laato, Antti* The royal covenant ideology in Judah. "Lasset uns Brücken bauen...". BEAT 42: 1998 ⇒401. 93-100.

1871 *Lehmann, Klaus P.* Die Gerechten erben das Land, und ewig wohnen sie drauf (Ps 37,29): Anmerkungen zum alttestamentlichen Dreiecksverhältnis zwischen JHWH, dem Volk Israel und beider Land. TeKo 21 (1998) 15-39.

1872 *Malamat, Abraham* A note on the ritual of treaty making in Mari and the bible. Mari and the bible. 1998 [1995] ⇒173. 168-171.

1873 **Rendtorff, Rolf** The covenant formulary: an exegetical and theological investigation. OT Studies: E 1998, Clark xiv; 105 pp. £18. 0-567-08605-4;

1874 Die "Bundesformel". SBS 160: 1995 ⇒11/1,425... 13,1797. ᴿZAR 4 (1998) 296-303 (*Otto, Eckart*); ITS 35 (1998) 202-207 (*Ceresko, Anthony R.*).

1875 *Rizzi, Armido* Dio e l'uomo nello specchio dell'alleanza. RCI 79 (1998) 485-496.

1876 *Streck, Michael P.* Die Flüche im Sukzessionsvertrag Asarhaddons. ZAR 4 (1998) 165-191.

1877 *Mourlon Beernaert, Pierre* La bible dans les étoiles... LV.F 53 (1998) 387-402 [Gen 15,5].

1878 *Oeming, Manfred* Der Glaube Abrahams: zur Rezeptionsgeschichte von Gen 15.6 in der Zeit des zweiten Tempels. ZAW 110 (1998) 16-33.

1879 *Dozeman, Thomas B.* The wilderness and salvation history in the Hagar story. JBL 117 (1998) 23-43 [Gen 16].

1880 *Diebner, Bernd Jørg* Gen 17 als Mitte eines Päsach-Zyklus der Torah. DBAT 29 (1998) 33-55;

1881 Gen 17 als Mitte eines Päsach-Zyklus der Torah. CV 40 (1998) 101-125.

1882 *Papagiannopoulos, John C.* Ἡ περιτομὴ τῶν ἀρχαίων Ἰσραηλιτῶν ὑπὸ κοινωνιολογικὴν ἔποψιν [Ancient Israelite circumcision from a social view-point]. Theol(A) 69 (1998) 445-453 [Gen 17].

1883 *Moore, James F.* Going down to Sodom: re-thinking the tradition in dialogue. [F]CARGAS H. 1998 ⇒19. 99-117 [Gen 18; Mt 10].

1884 **Pettinger, Michael Francis** Sodom: the judgment of the pentapolis in the Christian West to the year 1000. Washington 1998, 402 pp [Gen 18-19].

1885 Bechtel, Lyn M. Boundary issues in Genesis 19.1-38. Escaping Eden. BiSe 65: 1998 ⇒278. 22-40;

1886 A feminist reading of Genesis 19.1-11. Genesis 1998 ⇒219. 108-128.

1887 *Clackson, Sarah* An unedited Coptic leaf of *Genesis* in Cambridge University Library (P.Camb.UL Or. 1699 II i) (Plates 19-20). BAS-Pap 35 (1998) 135-143.

1888 *Roth-Rotem, Joseph* האכספוזיציה בסיפור גירוש ישמעאל [The exposition of the banishment of Ishma'el story (Genesis 21:9-21)]. Beit Mikra 153 (1998) 113-125. **H.**

1889 *Gruber, Mayer I.* Genesis 21.12: a new reading of an ambiguous text. Genesis. 1998 ⇒219. 172-179.

E2.6 The 'Aqedâ, Isaac, Genesis 22...

1890 *Diebner, Bernd Jørg* Noch einmal zu Gen 22,2: 'rṣ hmrjh;

1891 ...dass Abraham nur einmal 'im Lande' war und ansonsten zumeist in Idumäa lebte. DBAT 29 (1998) 58-72/73-91.

1892 *Feldman, Yael S.* Isaac or Oedipus?: Jewish tradition and the Israeli Aqedah. Biblical studies. JSOT.S 266: 1998 ⇒380. 159-189.

1893 *Kalimi, Isaac* Zion or Gerizim?: the association of Abraham and the Aqeda with Zion / Gerizim in Jewish and Samaritan sources. [F]GORDON, C. JSOT.S 273: 1998 ⇒31. 442-457.

1894 **Kundert, Lukas** Die Opferung, Bindung Isaaks: 1. Gen 22,1-19 im Alten Testament, im Frühjudentum und im Neuen Testament. WMANT 78: Neuk 1998, Neuk xi; 334 pp. 3-7887-1668-1.

1895 *Levenson, Jon D.* Abusing Abraham: traditions, religious histories, and modern misinterpretations. Jdm 47 (1998) 259-277.

1896 *Loewenthal, Elena* La 'Aqedah: alcune considerazioni. [F]SIERRA J. 1998 ⇒102. 311-314.

1897 *Neef, Heinz-Dieter* "Abraham! Abraham!" Gen 22,1-19 als theologische Erzählung. JNSL 24/2 (1998) 45-62.

1898 **Neef, Heinz-Dieter** Die Prüfung Abrahams: eine exegetisch-theologische Studie zu Gen 22,1-19. AzTh 90: Stu 1998, Calwer 102 pp. 3-7668-3612-9.

1899 *Schult, Hermann* Eine Glosse zu "Moriya". DBAT 29 (1998) 56-57.

1900 **Vaccaro, Jody Lyn** Early Jewish and christian interpretations of the character of Isaac in Genesis 22. [D]ND 1998, 359 pp.

1901   *Van Rhijn, Aat; Meulink-Korf, Hanneke* De binding van Jitschak
       (Genesis 22:1-19). Interpretatie 6/4 (1998) 4-7.

1902   *Gillmayr-Bucher, Susanne* Von welcher sozialen Wirklichkeit erzählt
       Genesis 24?. PzB 7 (1998) 17-27.

E2.7 **Jacob** and Esau: ladder dream; *Jacob, somnium, Gen 25...*

1903   *Schmidt, Ludwig* Die Darstellung Isaaks in Genesis 26,1-33 und ihr
       Verhältnis zu den Parallelen in den Abrahamerzählungen. Gesam-
       melte Aufsätze zum Pentateuch. BZAW 263: 1998 ⇒195. 167-223.
1904   *Propp, William H.C.* Pulling the goat hair over Isaac's eyes. BiRe
       14/5 (1998) 20 [Gen 27].
1905   *Schmidt, Ludwig* Jakob erschleicht sich den väterlichen Segen:
       Literarkritik und Redaktion von Genesis 27,1-45. Gesammelte
       Aufsätze zum Pentateuch. BZAW 263: 1998 <1988> ⇒195. 85-109.
1906   *Wiesel, Elie* Esau. BiRe 14/2 (1998) 26-27.
1907   **Isaacs, Ronald H.** Ascending Jacob's ladder: Jewish views of
       angels, demons, and evil spirits. Northvale, NJ 1998, Aronson xii;
       157 pp. 0-7657-5965-9.
1908   *Van Seters, John* Divine encounter at Bethel (Gen 28,10-22) in
       recent literary-critical study of Genesis. ZAW 110 (1998) 503-513.
1909   **Heck, Christian** L'échelle céleste dans l'art du moyen âge. 1997
       ⇒13,1825. [R]CCMéd 41 (1998) 75-76 (*Cahn, Walter*); RHPhR 78
       (1998) 365-366 (*Prigent, P.*) [Gen 28,10-22].
1910   *Schmidt, Ludwig* El und die Landverheißung in Bet-El (Die Erzäh-
       lung von Jakob in Bet-El: Gen 28,11-22). Gesammelte Aufsätze zum
       Pentateuch. BZAW 263: 1998 <1994> ⇒195. 137-149.
1911   *Mutius, Hans-Georg* Eine völlig verkannte Nominalform im Kontext
       von Genesis 29,4?. BN 94 (1998) 15-21.

E2.8 **Jacob's wrestling; the Angels;** *Gen 31-36 & 38*

1912   *Heltzer, M.* New light from Emar on Genesis 31: the theft of the
       Teraphim. [F]LORETZ O. AOAT 250: 1998 ⇒65. 357-362.
1913   *Lapsley, J.E.* The voice of Rachel: resistance and polyphony in
       Genesis 31.14-35. Genesis. 1998 ⇒219. 233-248.
1914   *Herr, Bertram* Die reine Rahel: eine Anmerkung zu Gen 31,35. ZAW
       110 (1998) 238-239.

1915   **Anelli, Giuseppe** Angeli e demoni: dati e riflessioni per una "nuova
       evangelizzazione". Sussidi biblici 59: [Reggio Emilia] 1998, San
       Lorenzo (4) ix; 48 pp. 88-8071-074-5.
1916   *Balducci, C.* Il diavolo oggi. Angeli e demoni. 1998 ⇒375. 273-297.
1917   *Cimosa, M.* Gli angeli e i demoni nella letteratura apocalittica inter-
       testamentaria. Angeli e demoni. 1998 ⇒375. 37-78.
1918   *Del Zotto, C.M.* L'angelo custode nella tradizione biblica e
       paleocristiana. Angeli e demoni. 1998 ⇒375. 195-231.
1919   *Diebner, Bernd Jørg* Zur Einführung 'Israels' in die Torah (Gen
       32,29). DBAT 29 (1998) 92-95.

1920 **Dörfel, Donata** Engel in der apokalyptischen Literatur und ihre theologische Relevanz: am Beispiel von Ezechiel, Sacharja, Daniel und Erstem Henoch. Theologische Studien: Aachen 1998, Shaker 291 pp. 3-8265-2681-3.

1921 **Gieschen, Charles A.** Angelomorphic christology: antecedents and early evidence. AGJU 42: Lei 1998, Brill xvi; 403 pp. ƒ185/$109. 90-04-10840-8.

1922 **Keck, David** Angels and angelology in the Middle Ages. NY 1998, OUP 260 pp. $45.

1923 *Lavatori, R.* Gli angeli hanno ancora motivo di resistere?. Angeli e demoni. 1998 ⇒375. 233-271.

1924 *McKenna, Megan* Angeli: se non ci fossero bisognerebbe inventarli. 1997 ⇒13,1845. ᴿAnime e Corpi 36 (1998) 524-525.

1925 *Miles, Jack* Jacob's wrestling match: was it an angel or Esau?. BiRe 14/5 (1998) 22-23 [Gen 32].

1926 *Novoa M., Carlos J.* Dios con nosotros: los ángeles. ThX 48 (1998) 239-250.

1927 **Panteghini, Giacomo** Angeli e demoni: il ritorno dell'invisibile. 1997 ⇒13,1850. ᴿPerTeol 30 (1998) 296-298 (*Ruiz de Gopegui, Juan A.*).

1928 *Reijnen, Anne Marie* Un ange qui passe...et ne cesse revenir: la figure de l'ange dans les écritures, la tradition et la théologie. LV.F 53 (1998) 446-456.

1929 *Schmidt, Ludwig* Der Kampf Jakobs am Jabbok (Gen. 32,23-33). Gesammelte Aufsätze zum Pentateuch. BZAW 263: 1998 <1977/78> ⇒195. 38-56.

1930 *Wielenga, Bastiaan* Experiences with a biblical story. The postcolonial bible. 1998 ⇒695. 189-198 [Gen 32-33].

1932 *Lensink, Henk* De profetie van Genesis 34. ITBT 6/8 (1998) 25-26.

1933 *Scholz, Susanne* Through whose eyes?: a 'right' reading of Genesis 34. Genesis. 1998 ⇒219. 150-171;

1934 Was it really rape in Genesis 34?: biblical scholarship as a reflection of cultural assumptions. Escaping Eden. BiSe 65: 1998 ⇒278. 182-198.

1936 *Jonge, Marinus de; Tromp, Johannes* Jacob's son Levi in the Old Testament pseudepigrapha and related literature. Biblical figures. ᴱStone, M. 1998 ⇒K1.1. 203-236 [Gen 35,23; 46,11; Ps 106,30-31; Wis 18,20-25].

1937 **Hoekveld-Meijer, Gerda** Esau: salvation in disguise: Genesis 36. 1996 ⇒12,1706. ᴿDBAT 29 (1998) 264-266 (*Diebner, B.J.*); CBQ 60 (1998) 116-117 (*Nagel, Elizabeth M.*).

E2.9 **Joseph**; Jacob's blessings; *Genesis 37; 39-50*

1938 *Ages, Arnold* Dreamer, schemer, slave and prince: understanding Joseph's dreams. BiRe 14(2 (1998) 46-53.

1939 *Berlyn, P.J.* His brothers' keeper. JBQ 26 (1998) 73-83.

1940 *Brenner, Athalya; Van Henten, Jan Willem* Madame Potiphar through a culture trip, or, which side are you on?. Biblical studies. JSOT.S 266: 1998 ⇒380. 203-219.

1941   **Goldman, Shalom** The wiles of women/the wiles of men: Joseph and
       Potiphar's wife in ancient Near Eastern, Jewish and Islamic folklore.
       1995 ⇒11/1,503. ᴿAJSR 23 (1998) 124-126 (*Greenspahn, Frederick
       E.*); JR 78 (1998) 326-327 (*Menn, Esther M.*).
1942   *Hollander, Harm W.* The portrayal of Joseph in Hellenistic Jewish
       and early christian literature. Biblical figures. ᴱ**Stone, M.** 1998
       ⇒K1.1. 237-263.
1943   *Lacocque, André* An ancestral narrative: the Joseph story. Thinking
       biblically. 1998 ⇒251. 365-397.
1944   **Martindale, Gary Carl** 'And Joseph wept': stylistics of affect in
       Genesis 37-50. ᴰBaylor 1998, 243 pp.
1945   *Schweizer, Harald* Der Computer und Übersetzungen unterschiedlich
       starker Wörtlichkeit: Erfahrungen mit dem Text der Josefsgeschichte.
       Bible et informatique. 1998 ⇒386. 95-112;
1946   Nachträge zur Interpretation der Josefsgeschichte. ThZ 54 (1998)
       300-324.
1947   *Soller, Moshe* Why no message from Joseph to his father?;
1948   *Steinberg, Jonathan A.* Joseph and revolutionary Egypt. JBQ 26
       (1998) 158-167/101-106.
1949   **Westermann, Claus** Joseph: studies of the Joseph stories in Genesis.
       E 1996, Clark xi; 112 pp. $12. 0-567-08516-3. ᴿBiOr 55 (1998) 865-
       867 (*Hettema, T.L.*).

1950   *Harris, J.S. Randolph* Genesis 44:18-34. Interp. 52 (1998) 178-181.
1951   *Loader, Jimmy A.* God have or has?: unclarity and insight. JNSL 24/1
       (1998) 129-140 [Gen 45,5].
1952   *Deurloo, Karel Adriaan* Der Text der Versklavung Ägyptens im
       Kontext des Josef-Zyklus (Gen 47,13-26). TeKo 21 (1998) 41-49.
1953   **Dias, Mário Lopes** As bênçãos de Jacob—leitura messiânica de Gn
       49. Viseu 1998, Universidade Católica Portuguesa 326 pp. ᴿBib(L)
       7/7 (1998) 155-156 (*Alves, Herculano*).
1954   *Schmitt, Hans-Christoph* Eschatologische Stammesgeschichte im
       Pentateuch: zum Judaspruch von Gen 49,8-12. ᶠSTEGEMANN, H.,
       BZNW 97: 1998 ⇒111. 1-11.
1955   *Szwarc, Urszula* Ten który 'przyjdzie': analiza porownawcza tekstów
       Rdz 49,8-12 Oraz Pwt 33,7 [The one who 'will come': a comparative
       analysis of the texts Gn 49,8-12 and Deut 33,7]. Roczniki Teolo-
       giczne 45 (1998) 5-16.
1956   *Sæbo, Magne* Divine names and epithets in Genesis 49.24b-25a:
       methodological and traditio-historical remarks. On the way to canon.
       1998 <1993> ⇒194. 58-77.

E3.1   **Exodus event and theme;** *textus, commentarii*

1957   *Ahituv, Shmuel* The Exodus—survey of the theories of the last fifty
       years. Jerusalem studies. ÄAT 40: 1998 ⇒361. 127-132.
1958   **Alonso Schökel, Luis** Salvezza e liberazione: l'Esodo. 1996
       ⇒12,1763. ᴿCivCatt 149/1 (1998) 418-420 (*Scaiola, D.*).
1959   **Ashby, Godfrey** Go out and meet God: a commentary on the book of
       Exodus. International Theological Commentary: GR 1998, Eerdmans
       xiv; 146 pp. $16. 0-8028-4332-8. ᴿRExp 95 (1998) 449 (*Biddle,
       Mark E.*).

1960 **Auzou, Georges** Dalla servitù al servizio: il libro dell'Esodo. Lettura pastorale della Bibbia 25: 1997 ⇒13,1890. ^RAsp. 45 (1998) 289-290 (*Castello, Gaetano*).

1961 *Avery-Peck, Alan J.* The Exodus in Jewish faith: the problem of God's intervention in history. ARJ 1 (1998) 3-22.

1962 **Brown, Jeff R.** Der Exodus: eine exegetische und hermeneutische Untersuchung des Auszugs Israels aus Ägypten durch das Rote Meer. ^T*Baumgartner, Jakob; Mayer, Thomas*: Nürnberg 1998, VTR 134 pp. 3-933372-17-8.

1963 *Chacko, Mani* Crisis and hope in the Exodus story. BiBh 24 (1998) 223-252.

1964 *Couto, António* O êxodo e a aliança: história e teologia [The exodus and the covenant: history and theology]. HumTeo 19 (1998) 251-277.

1965 *Domínguez, Jorge* Éxodo: acontecimiento y relato: aportes a la ética social cristiana. Voces 12 (1998) 9-23.

1966 **Dozeman, Thomas B.** God at war: power in the Exodus tradition. 1996 ⇒12,1769. ^RCBQ 60 (1998) 327-329 (*Owens, J. Edward*); JQR 89 (1998) 239-240 (*Sarna, Nahum M.*).

1967 **Ellis, Carl F.** Free at last?: the gospel in the African-American experience. 1996 ⇒12,1770. ^RAUSS 36 (1998) 122-124 (*Mulzac, Kenneth D.*).

1968 *Görg, Manfred* Der sogenannte Exodus zwischen Erinnerung und Polemik. Jerusalem studies. ÄAT 40: 1998 ⇒361. 159-172.

1969 *Hoffman, Yair* The Exodus—tradition and reality: the status of the Exodus tradition in ancient Israel. Jerusalem studies. ÄAT 40: 1998 ⇒361. 193-202.

1970 **Hoffmeier, James K.** Israel in Egypt. 1997 ⇒13,1912. ^RAsbTJ 53 (1998) 88-90 (*Arnold, Bill T.*).

1971 **Jacob, Benno** The second book of the bible: Exodus. 1992 ⇒8,2468... 10,2143. ^REstB 56 (1998) 122-123 (*García Santos, A.*).

1972 *Homan, Michael M.* A tensile etymology for Aaron: 'aharon > 'ahalon. BN 95 (1998) 21-22.

1973 **Johnstone, William** Chronicles and Exodus: an analogy and its application. JSOT.S 275: Shf 1998, Academic 331 pp. £46/$75. 1-85075-881-6.

1974 *Kallai, Zecharia* The Exodus: a historiographical approach. Jerusalem studies. ÄAT 40: 1998 ⇒361. 203-205.

1975 *Malamat, Abraham* Let my people go and go and go and go: Egyptian records support a centuries-long exodus. BArR 24 (1998) 62-66, 85.

1976 **Marti, Kurt** Alleati di Dio. Meditazioni bibliche: T 1998, Claudiana 95 pp. 88-7016-284-2.

1977 *Mazzinghi, Luca* 'Il Signore passerà per colpire l'Egitto': la violenza di Dio nel racconto dell'Esodo. PSV 37 (1998) 69-82.

1978 **Newsome, James D.** Exodus. Interpretation Bible studies: LVL 1998, Geneva vii; 134 pp. $7. 0-664-50020-X.

1979 ^T**Paul, Rudolf** D Befreiong: s zwoete Buach vom Mose. Tü 1998, Silberburg 175 pp. 3-87407-281-9.

1980 *Pompey, Heinrich* Exodus—Existenz. LS 49 (1998) 113-118.

1981 **Qui Nieto, Jesus** The exodus in the first Fathers of the Church ^DNavarra, Spain 1998, 416 pp.

1982   The second book of Moses, called Exodus: Authorised King James
       Version. Pocket Canons: E 1998, Canongate xvi; 109 pp. 0-86241-
       790-2.
1983   **Smith, Mark S.** The pilgrimage pattern in Exodus. JSOT.S 239:
       1997 ⇒13,1929. ^RCBQ 60 (1998) 546-547 (*Laberge, Léo*).
1984   *Tiffany, Frederick C.* Facing the wilderness/encountering chaos. QR
       18 (1998) 55-69.
1985   **Utzschneider, Helmut** Gottes langer Atem: die Exoduserzählung
       (Ex 1-14) in ästhetischer und historischer Sicht. SBS 166: 1996
       ⇒12,1793. ^RThZ 54 (1998) 270-271 (*Weber, Beat*).
1986   **Valdès, Zoé** El libro del Éxodo. Barc 1998, Bolsillo 122 pp.
1987   ^E**Vervenne, Marc** Studies in the book of Exodus. BEThL 126: 1996
       ⇒12,1794; 13,1888. ^RLouvSt 23 (1998) 280-282 (*Eynikel, Erik*);
       ZKTh 120 (1998) 424-426 (*Frevel, Christian*).
1988   *Wiesel, Elie* Aaron: the teflon kid. BiRe 14/4 (1998) 26-27.
1989   *Zeeb, Frank* Israels Auszug aus Ägypten: Theologie des Alten Testa-
       ments und/oder Religionsgeschichte Israels: die Tradition vom
       Exodus in einigen neueren theologischen Entwürfen. ^FLORETZ O.
       AOAT 250: 1998 ⇒65. 897-925.

E3.2 **Moyses**—Pharaoh, Goshen—*Exodus 1...*

1990   **Assmann, Jan** Moses the Egyptian. 1997 ⇒13,1935. ^RBAR 24/2
       (1998) 68 (*Hendel, Ronald*); ChH 67 (1998) 842-844 (*Boyarin,
       Daniel*); JR 78 (1998) 656-658 (*Stroumsa, Guy G.*); RHR 215 (1998)
       509-511 (*Le Brun, Jacques*); BiOr 55 (1998) 758-764 (*Tobin, Vin-
       cent A.*);
1991   Moses der Ägypter: Entzifferung einer Gedächtnisspur. Mü 1998,
       Hanser 349 pp. DM49.80. 3-446-19302-2.
1992   **Bernstein, Richard J.** FREUD and the legacy of Moses. Cambridge
       Studies in Religion and Critical Thought 4: C 1998, CUP xii; 151 pp.
       0-521-63877-1.
1993   *Bidaut, Bernard* La figure de Moïse dans le troisième évangile.
       LV(L) 49/2 (1998) 37-51.
1994   *Breytenbach, A.P.* Moses versus die Messias: `n Samaritaanse
       tradisie. SeK 19 (1998) 534-543.
1995   **Chouraqui, André** Moisés. 1997 ⇒13,1948. ^RNatGrac 45 (1998)
       403-404 (*Rivera, Enrique*).
1996   **Didier-Weill, Alain** Invocations Dionysos, Moïse, saint Paul et
       FREUD. P 1998, Calmann-Lévy 198 pp. ^RÉtudes 389 (1998) 390-392
       (*Julien, Philippe*).
1997   ^E**Duquoc, Christian** Moïse, le prophète de Dieu. LV(L) 49/2 (1998)
       3-69.
1998   *Frankemölle, Hubert* Mose in Deutungen des Neuen Testaments.
       Jüdische Wurzeln. BBB 116: 1998 <1994> ⇒151. 91-107.
1999   *Guillaud, Michel* Musa, l'interlocuteur de Dieu. LV(L) 49/2 (1998)
       63-69.
2000   *Jagersma, H.* 'Mozes neemt het op voor zijn broeders' Exodus 2:11-
       15a. Interpretatie 6/4 (1998) 12-13.
2001   **Kirsch, Jonathan** Moses: a life. NY 1998, Ballantine 432 pp. $27.
       0-345-41269-9.
2002   *Lee, Nancy C.* Genocide's lament: Moses, Pharaoh's daughter, and the
       former Yugoslavia. ^FBRUEGGEMANN, W.. 1998 ⇒16. 66-82.

2003 *Luchetta, Claude* Moïse et le talmud. LV(L) 49/2 (1998) 53-61.
2004 *Magonet, Jonathan* RASHI on Exodus I:1-14. Bibel und Midrasch ^E**Bodendorfer, G.** FAT 22: 1998 ⇒K6.5. 209-227.
2005 *Manns, Frédéric* The grave of Moses in Jewish literature. Mount Nebo. ^E**Piccirillo, M.** SBF.CMa 27: 1998 ⇒T4.8. 65-69.
2006 **Meier, Levi** Moses, the prince, the prophet: his life, legend & message for our lives. Woodstock, VT 1998, Jewish Lights x; 198 pp. $24. 1-58023-013-X.
2007 **Nohrnberg, James** Like unto Moses: the constituting of an interruption. 1995 ⇒11/1,576...13,1970. ^RVT 48 (1998) 130-132 (*Lipton, Diana*).
2008 *Olinger, Danny* Moses—in Egypt and Midian: Exodus 2:11-25. Kerux 13 (1998) 16-22.
2009 **Palmer, David Bruce** Text and concept in Exodus 1:1-2:25: a case study in exegetical method. ^DClaremont 1998, 342 pp.
2010 *Römer, Thomas* Moïse entre théologie et histoire. LV(L) 49/2 (1998) 7-16.
2011 *Siebert-Hommes, Jopie* Let the daughters live!: the literary architecture of Exodus 1-2 as a key for interpretation. Biblical interpretation 37: Lei 1998, Brill xii; 145 pp. 90-04-10778-9.
2012 **Stein, Hannes** Moses und die Offenbarung der Demokratie. B 1998, Rohwolt 222 pp. DM36.
2013 **Vogels, Walter** Moïse aux multiples visages: de l'Exode au Deutéronome. LiBi 114: P 1998, Cerf 300 pp. 2-204-05969-2.
2014 *Watts, James W.* The legal characterization of Moses in the rhetoric of the Pentateuch. JBL 117 (1998) 415-426.

E3.3 **Nomen divinum, Tetragrammaton;** *Exodus 3,14...***Plagues**

2015 *Arana, Andrés Ibáñez* 'ehyeh 'ašer 'ehyeh (Ex 3,14a). ScrVict 45 (1998) 5-49.
2016 **Bindella, Francesco** Il fondamento del Nome, fondazione di pneumatologia: esposizione sintetica. Praesidium Assisiense 4: Assisi 1998, Porziuncola 76 pp. 88-270-0372-X.
2017 **Brichto, Herbert C.** The names of God: poetic readings in biblical beginnings. NY 1998, OUP xvii; 462 pp. $65. 0-19-510965-1.
2018 *Cohen, Herbert* From monolatry to monotheism. JBQ 26 (1998) 124-126.
2019 *Diebner, Bernd Jørg* "... und sie berührte...": zur 'Mitte' von Ex 4,24-26. DBAT 29 (1998) 96-98.
2020 **Faivre, Daniel** L'idée de Dieu chez les hébreux nomades. 1996 ⇒12,1829. ^RETR 73 (1998) 608-609 (*Nocquet, Dany*).
2021 *Gilbert, Maurice* Le Saint d'Israël. Il a parlé par les prophètes. 1998 ⇒155. 191-204.
2022 **Gnuse, Robert Karl** No other gods: emergent monotheism in Israel. JSOT.S 241: 1997 ⇒13,1990. ^RBZ 42 (1998) 292-295 (*Albertz, Rainer*); BTB 28 (1998) 123 (*Craghan, John F.*).
2023 *Jomier, Jacques* Les 99 beaux noms divins. VS 726 (1998) 147-154.
2024 *Koch, Klaus* Jahwäs Übersiedlung vom Wüstenberg nach Kanaan: zur Herkunft von Israels Gottesverständnis. ^FLORETZ O. AOAT 250: 1998 ⇒65. 437-474.
2025 *Lacocque, André* La révélation des révélations: Exode 3,14. Penser la bible. 1998 ⇒188. 305-334;

2026 The revelation of revelations. Thinking biblically. 1998 ⇒251. 307-329.

2027 *López Pego, Álvaro* Sobre el origen de los teónimos Yah y Yahweh. EstB 56 (1998) 5-39.

2028 *Lutzky, Harriet* Shadday as a goddess epithet. VT 48 (1998) 15-36.

2029 **Moor, Johannes Cornelis de** The rise of Yahwism: the roots of Israelite monotheism. BEThL 91: 1997 ⇒13,1997. [R]Or. 67 (1998) 556-557 (*Gianto, Agustinus*).

2030 **Noak, Oswald** Jahwe und Elohim 26 41: die mathematische Entfaltung dieser Namen durch den Codex Sinaiticus der Evangelien und der Apostelgeschichte. Pritzwalk 1998, Koch 60 pp. 3-00-004060-9.

2031 *Phillips, Anthony; Phillips, Lucy* The origin of 'I am' in Exodus 3.14. JSOT 78 (1998) 81-84.

2032 *Pollack, Stuart* The speech defect of Moses (Ex. 4:10). JBQ 26 (1998) 121-123.

2033 *Rao, Naveen* Doctrine of God in Exodus 6:2-9: challenge of a hermeneutical task in a religiously pluralistic community. BiBh 24 (1998) 3-16.

2034 *Rechenmacher, Hans* Jahwe allein!: namenkundliche Überlegungen zur Monotheismusdebatte. [F]WETTER F. 1998 ⇒124. 37-52.

2035 *Rey, Bernard* Moïse et la révélation du Nom. LV(L) 49/2 (1998) 83-91.

2036 *Ricoeur, Paul* De l'interprétation à la traduction. Penser la bible. 1998 ⇒188. 335-371 [Exod 3,14];

2037 From interpretation to translation. Thinking biblically. 1998 ⇒251. 332-361 [Exod 3,14].

2038 *Sæbo, Magne* God's name in Exodus 3.13-15: an expression of revelation or of veiling?. On the way to canon. 1998 <1981> ⇒194. 78-92.

2039 **Scarpelli, Giacomo** Il Dio solo: le misteriose origini del monoteismo. Mi 1998, Mondadori 222 pp. L29.000.

2040 *Schmidt, Ludwig* Diachrone und synchrone Exegese am Beispiel von Exodus 3-4. Gesammelte Aufsätze zum Pentateuch. BZAW 263: 1998 ⇒195. 224-250.

2041 **Scriba, Albrecht** Die Geschichte des Motivkomplexes Theophanie. FRLANT 167: 1995 ⇒11/1,598... 13,2003. [R]Bib. 79 (1998) 131-132 (*Fossum, Jarl*).

2042 *Seitz, Christopher* The call of Moses and the `revelation' of the divine name: source-critical logic and its legacy;

2043 The divine name in christian scripture. Word without end. 1998 ⇒200. 229-247/251-262.

2044 *Soskice, Janet Martin* The gift of the name: Moses and the burning bush. Gr. 79 (1998) 231-246.

2045 *Wiesel, Elie* Jethro. BiRe 14/3 (1998) 20-21.

2046 *Deloche, Pascale* Moïse face au Pharaon et face à son peuple: le thème de l'endurcissement. LV(L) 49/2 (1998) 17-36.

2047 *Himbaza, Innocent* La troisième et la quatrième plaies d'Égypte. BN 94 (1998) 68-78 [Exod 8,12-28].

2048 *Lemmelijn, Bénédicte* As many texts as plagues: a preliminary report of the main results of the textcritical evaluation of Exod 7:14-11:10. JNSL 24/2 (1998) 111-125.

2049 *Liss, Hanna* Die Funktion der "Verstockung" Pharaos in der Erzählung vom Auszug aus Ägypten (Ex 7-14). BN 93 (1998) 56-76.

E3.4 Pascha, sanguis, sacrificium: **Passover, blood, sacrifice**, *Ex 11...*

2050 **Chiodi, Silvia Maria** Offerte "funebri" nella Lagas presargonica. 1997 ⇒13,2026. [R]UF 30 (1998) 912-917 *(Balke, Thomas E.)*.

2051 *Edelman, Diana Vikander* The creation of Exodus 14-15. Jerusalem studies in Egyptology. ÄAT 40: 1998 ⇒361. 137-158.

2052 *Ekenberg, Anders* Judisk och kristen påsk: ett gåtfullt samband. SEÅ 63 (1998) 261-272.

2053 **Goodhart, Sandor** Sacrificing commentary: reading the end of literature. 1996 ⇒12,1873. [R]JR 78 (1998) 496-498 *(Britt, Brian)*.

2054 *Gosse, Bernard* Exodus 19.18 in the biblical redaction. "Lasset uns Brücken bauen...". BEAT 42: 1998 ⇒401. 41-43 [Isa 4,5].

2055 **Grappe, Christian; Marx, Alfred** Le sacrifice: vocation et subversion du sacrifice dans les deux Testaments. EssBib 29: Genève 1998, Labor et Fides 91 pp. FS27. 2-8309-0880-5.

2056 *Heinsohn, Gunnar* The catastrophic emergence of civilization: the coming of blood sacrifice in the Bronze Age. Natural catastrophes. 1998 ⇒356. 172-186.

2057 *Janicki, Jan Józef* Pascha—centrum roku liturgicznego Starego i Nowego Ludu Bożego [Pascha—centrum anni liturgici Veteris ac Novi Populi Dei]. RBL 51 (1998) 101-114.

2058 **Kvarme, Ole Kristian** Åtte dager i Jerusalem: en bok om Jesu påske, om jødisk og kristen påskefeiring. 1996 ⇒12,1876. [R]TTK 69 (1998) 236-237 *(Kullerud, Ole Fredrik)*.

2059 *Leene, Hendrik* Offer en plaatsvervanging in het Oude Testament. GThT 98 (1998) 157-167.

2060 *Lim Teng Kok, Johnson* Parallel scripts, paradigm shifts. BZ 42 (1998) 81-90 [Exod 17; Num 20].

2061 *Ribichini, Sergio* La proibizione del sacrificio umano cartaginese [F]LORETZ O. AOAT 250: 1998 ⇒65. 655-668.

2062 **Sassmann, Christiane Karin** Die Opferbereitschaft Israels. EHS.T 529: 1995 ⇒12,7146; 13,2045. [R]JQR 89 (1998) 175-176 *(Blum, Erhard)*.

2063 **Schart, Aaron** Mose und Israel im Konflikt: eine redaktionsgeschichtliche Studie zu den Wüstenerzählungen. OBO 98: 1990 ⇒6,2647... 9,2327. [R]ThR 63 (1998) 254-257 *(Schmidt, Ludwig)*.

2064 **Schuil, A.** Amalek: onderzoek naar oorsprong en ontwikkeling van Amaleks rol in het Oude Testament. 1997 ⇒13,2047. [R]Interpretatie 6/4 (1998) 25-26 *(Rooze, Egbert)* [Exod 17,8-16].

2065 [E]**Shire, Michael** Die Pessach Haggada. Mü 1998, Knesebeck 66 pp. [E]**Ubbiali, Sergio** Il sacrificio 1998 ⇒272.

2066 *Vervenne, Marc* Metaphors for destruction in Exodus 15. JNSL 24/2 (1998) 179-194.

2067 *Vikander Edelman, Diana* The creation of Exodus 14-15. Jerusalem studies. ÄAT 40: 1998 ⇒361. 137-158.

2068 **Wong, Fook-Kong** Manna revisited: a study of the mythological and interpretative contexts of manna. [D]Harvard 1998, 228 pp [Exod 16].

E3.5 **Decalogus**, *Ex 20=Dt 5; Ex 21ss;* **Ancient Near East Law**

2069 **Oswald, Wolfgang** Israel am Gottesberg: eine Untersuchung zur Literargeschichte der vorderen Sinaiperikope Ex 19-24 und deren historischem Hintergrund. OBO 159: FrS 1998, Univ.-Verl. vii; 286 pp. FS89. 3-7278-1161-7. ᴿBib. 79 (1998) 568-573 (*Utzschneider, Helmut*); RBBras 15 (1998) 476-477.

2070 *Bast, Robert J.* From two kingdoms to two tables: the ten commandments and the christian magistrate. ARG 89 (1998) 79-95.

2071 *Freund, Richard A.* The decalogue in early Judaism and christianity. The function of scripture. 1998 ⇒236. 124-141.

2072 *Hauerwas, Stanley* The truth about God: the decalogue as condition for truthful speech. NZSTh 40 (1998) 17-39.

2073 *Lang, Bernhard* The Decalogue in the light of a newly published palaeo-Hebrew inscription (Hebrew ostracon Moussaïeff No. 1). JSOT 77 (1998) 21-25.

2074 *Lee, Jeong Woo (James)* Introduction to the Ten Commandments: Exodus 20:1-3; Luke 12:48. Kerux 13 (1998) 23-34.

2075 **Schmidt, Werner H.** I dieci comandamenti e l'etica veterotestamentaria. CSB 114: 1996 ⇒12,1930. ᴿRivBib 46 (1998) 237-238 (*Bretón, Santiago*); Sal. 60 (1998) 777-778 (*Vicent, R.*).

2076 *Wengert, Timothy* 'Fear and love' in the ten commandments. Luther Digest 6 (1998) 66-70.

2077 *Bayer, Oswald* "Ich bin der Herr, dein Gott ...": das erste Gebot in seiner Bedeutung für die Grundlegung der Ethik ["I am the Lord, your God...': the first commandment in its foundational ethical implications]. Luther Digest 6 (1998) 42-44.

2078 ᴱ**Dietrich, Walter; Klopfenstein, Martin A.** Ein Gott allein? JHWH-Verehrung und biblischer Monotheismus im Kontext der israelitischen und altorientalischen Religionsgeschichte. OBO 139: 1994 ⇒10,467*... 13,2062. ᴿOLZ 93 (1998) 467-494 (*Timm, Stefan*).

2079 *Chalier, Catherine* L'image dans le judaïsme: l'invisible en proximité. NRTh 120 (1998) 590-604.

2080 *Koorevaar, H.* Who or what may not be made?: the structure and meaning of Exodus 20:23. JSem 8 (1996) 223-255.

2081 *Levi Della Torre, Stefano* 'Non ti farai alcuna immagine'. RasIsr 64 (1998) 1-28.

2082 *Lewis, Theodore J.* Divine images and aniconism in ancient Israel. JAOS 118 (1998) 36-53.

2083 **Mettinger, Tryggve N.D.** No graven image?: Israelite aniconism in its ancient Near Eastern context. CB.OT 42: 1995 ⇒11/1,672... 13,2069. ᴿJThS 49 (1998) 182-183 (*Curtis, A.H.W.*).

2084 *Oelmüller, Willi* Die Macht der Bilder und die Grenzen von Bildverboten: das biblische Bilderverbot philosophisch betrachtet. Orien. 62 (1998) 163-167.

2085 ᴱ**Rainer, Michael J.; Janßen, Hans-Gerd** Jahrbuch Politische Theologie, 2: Bilderverbot. 1997. ᴿJBTh 13 (1998) 301-305 (*Höhn, Hans-Joachim*).

2086 *Schroer, Silvia* Du sollst dir kein Bildnis machen oder: welche Bilder verbietet das Bilderverbot?. Religiöse Sprache. 1998 ⇒1144. 101-113.

2087 ᴱ**Van der Toorn, Karel** The image and the book: iconic cults, aniconism, and the rise of book religion in Israel and the ancient Near East. 1997 ⇒13,2073. ᴿDBAT 29 (1998) 293-294 (*Diebner, B.J.*);

AuOr 16 (1998) 141-142 (*Olmo Lete, G. del*); VT 48 (1998) 575-577 (*Emerton, J.A.*).

2088 *Weinrich, Michael* Die Profanisierung der Bilder: zur Bild-problematik zwischen Kult und Kunst in der reformatorischen Theologie. Religiöse Sprache. 1998 ⇒1144. 151-174.

2089 *Lenzen, Verena* Die Heiligung des göttlichen Namens. LS 49 (1998) 55-59.

2090 *Katzoff, Ranon; Schreiber, Bertram M.* Week and Sabbath in Judaean Desert documents. SCI 17 (1998) 102-114.

2091 *Körting, Corinna; Spieckermann, Hermann* Sabbat I: Altes Testament. TRE 29. 1998 ⇒501. 518-521.

2092 *Gilbert, Maurice* Honore ton père et ta mère. Il a parlé par les prophètes. 1998 <1989> ⇒155. 135-143.

2093 *Lacocque, André* 'Tu ne commettras pas de meurtre': Exode 20,13. Penser la bible. 1998 ⇒188. 103-155;

2094 Thou shalt not kill. Thinking biblically. 1998 ⇒251. 71-109.

2095 *Ricoeur, Paul* Une obéissance aimante. Penser la bible. 1998 ⇒188. 157-189;

2096 Thou shalt not kill': a loving obedience. Thinking biblically. 1998 ⇒251. 111-138.

2097 **Houtman, Cornelis** Das Bundesbuch: ein Kommentar. DMOA 24: 1997 ⇒13,2081. [R]Bib. 79 (1998) 414-417 (*Otto, Eckart*).

2098 *Pressler, Carolyn* Wives and daughters, bond and free: views of women in the slave laws of Exodus 21.2-11. Gender and law. JSOT.S 262: 1998 ⇒256. 147-172.

2099 *Schenker, Adrian* Die Analyse der Intentionalität im Bundesbuch (Ex 21-23). JNSL 24/2 (1998) 1-12;

2100 The biblical legislation on the release of slaves: the road from Exodus to Leviticus. JSOT 78 (1998) 23-41;

2101 Der Boden und seine Produktivität im Sabbat- und Jubeljahr: das dominium terrae in Ex 23,10f und Lev 5,2-12. Ebenbild Gottes. BThSt 33: 1998 ⇒255. 94-106.

2102 *Sparks, Kent* A comparative study of the biblical נבלה laws. ZAW 110 (1998) 594-600 [{Ex 22,30; Lev 17,15; 22,08; Dt 14,21].

2103 *Van Seters, John* The law on child sacrifice in Exod 22,28b-29. EThL 74 (1998) 364-372.

2104 **Bovati, Pietro** Re-establishing justice: legal terms, concepts and procedures in the Hebrew Bible. JSOT.S 105: 1994 ⇒10,2276; 11/1,696. [R]ThZ 54 (1998) 166 (*Weber, Beat*).

2105 **Burnette-Bletsch, Rhonda Jean** My bone and my flesh: the agrarian family in biblical law. [D]Duke 1998, 389 pp.

2106 **Crüsemann, Frank** The torah: theology and social history of Old Testament law. 1996 ⇒12,1989. [R]AUSS 36 (1998) 119-122 (*Henry, Eric L.*).

2107 *Domergue, Marcel* Du bon usage de la loi. Croire aujourd'hui 56 (1998) 6-9;

2108 La loi du père. Croire aujourd'hui 61 (1998) 6-9.

2109 **Drosnin, Michael** The Bible code. 1997 ⇒13,2091. [R]AtK 130 (1998) 306-308 (*Borucki, Janusz*).

2110 [E]**Focant, C.** La loi dans l'un et l'autre Testament. LeDiv 168: 1997 ⇒13,195. [R]LV(L) 49/1 (1998) 107-109 (*Genuyt, F.*); ScEs 50 (1998) 380-381 (*Vogels, Walter*).

2111 *Frymer-Kensky, Tikva* Gender and law: an introduction. Gender and law. JSOT.S 262: 1998 ⇒256. 17-24.
2112 *Gilbert, Maurice* La loi du talion. Il a parlé par les prophètes. 1998 <1984> ⇒155. 145-155.
2113 *Hofmann, Frank M.* Weisung und Gesetz—Lust und Last: Tora und Gebot in der jüdischen und christlichen Tradition. RKZ 139 (1998) 13-16.
2114 *Matthews, Victor H.* Honor and shame in gender-related legal situations in the Hebrew Bible. Gender and law. JSOT.S 262: 1998 ⇒256. 97-112;
2115 The social context of law in the second temple period. BTB 28 (1998) 7-15.
2116 *Mercier, Philippe* La loi et la naissance des sujets: à partir d'une lecture de l'Exode. LV(L) 49/2 (1998) 71-81.
2117 *Otto, Eckart* Gerechtigkeit und Erbarmen im Recht des Alten Testaments und seiner christlichen Rezeption. Gerechtigkeit. 1998 ⇒283. 79-95.
2118 **Porten, Bezalel** The Elephantine papyri in English. DMOA 22: 1996 ⇒12,2009. ᴿJSSt 43 (1998) 183-184 (*Naveh, Joseph*).
2119 *Rumianek, Ryszard* Odwet w Starym Testamencie [La legge del taglione]. WST 10 (1998) 89-94.
2120 *Schiffman, Lawrence H.* The prohibition of judicial corruption in the Dead Sea scrolls, PHILO, JOSEPHUS and Talmudic law. BJSt 320: ᶠFRERICHS 1998 ⇒28. 155-178 [Ex 18,21; 23,6-8; Dt 16,19; 10,17-18].
2121 *Susaimanickam, J.* Judicial activism in the Old Testament. Jeevadhara 28 (1998) 38-45.

2122 *Aadhill, Abdulilllah* Der Prolog des Codex Hammurapi in einer Abschrift aus Sippar. Rencontre Assyr. 34. 1998 ⇒452. 717-729.
2123 ᴱ**Allam, Schafik** Grund und Boden in Altägypten. 1994 ⇒10,443; 12,295. ᴿZSSR.R 115 (1998) 462-471 (*Hengstl, Joachim*).
2124 **Alterman, Mark R.** Form and meaning in Exodus 20-23 in the light of its ancient Near Eastern literary context. ᴰMid-America Baptist Theol. Sem 1998, 198 pp.
2125 **Arnaoutoglou, Ilias** Ancient Greek laws: a sourcebook. L 1998, Routledge xxii; 164 pp. 0-415-14984-3/5-1.
2126 *Bouzon, Emanuel* Recht und Wissenschaft in der Redaktionsgeschichte der keilschriftlichen Rechtssammlungen. ᶠRÖMER, W. AOAT 253: 1998 ⇒97. 39-61.
2127 *Cornil, Pierre* Le traité de Suppiluliuma et Shattiwaza. RIDA 45 (1998) 13-30.
2128 *Haase, Richard* Eine Grenzstreitigkeit in der hethitischen Rechtssatzung. WO 29 (1998) 124-126.
2129 **Haase, Richard** Keilschriftrechtliches. Leonberg 1998, Haase viii; 59 pp.
2130 *Haase, Richard* Wasserrecht in den keilschriftlichen Rechtscorpora. AltOrF 25 (1998) 222-226.
2131 *Hallo, William W.* Sharecropping in the edict of Ammi-saduqa ᶠFRERICHS, E. BJSt 320: 1998 ⇒28. 205-216.
2132 **Hoffner, Harry A.** The laws of the Hittites: a critical edition. DMOA 23: 1997 ⇒13,2108. ᴿZAR 4 (1998) 287-290 (*Haase, Richard*).

2133 *Kaiser, Otto* Gott und Mensch als Gesetzgeber in Platons Nomoi
      ᶠSTEGEMANN, H. BZNW 97: 1998 ⇒111. 278-295.
2134 *Otto, Eckart* Neue Aspekte zum keilschriftlichen Prozeßrecht in
      Babylonien und Assyrien. ZAR 4 (1998) 263-283;
2135 Soziale Restitution und Vertragsrecht: *mīšaru(m), (an)durāru(m),
      kirenzi, parā tarnumar, šᵉmiṭṭᵃ und dᵉrôr* in Mesopotamien, Syrien, in
      der hebräischen Bibel und die Frage des Rechtstransfers im alten
      Orient. RA 92 (1998) 125-160.
2136 **Radner, K.** Die neuassyrischen Privatrechtsurkunden als Quelle für
      Mensch und Umwelt. SAAS 6: 1997 ⇒13,2115. ᴿMes. 33 (1998)
      373-374 (*D'Agostino, F.*).
2137 *Roth, Martha Tobi* Gender and law: a case study from ancient
      Mesopotamia. Gender and law. JSOT.S 262: 1998 ⇒256. 173-184.
2138 **Roth, Martha T.** Law collections from Mesopotamia and Asia
      Minor. 1995 ⇒11/1,716; 13,2116. ᴿZAR 4 (1998) 303-309 (*Streck,
      Michael P.*); JAOS 118 (1998) 29-35 (*Yaron, Reuven*).
2139 **Saporetti, Claudio** Antiche leggi: i "codici" del Vicino Oriente
      antico. Orizzonti della storia: Mi 1998, Rusconi 485 pp. 88-18-
      88057-8.
2140 *Zer-Kavod, Mordechai* The Code of Hammurabi and the laws of the
      torah. JBQ 26 (1998) 107-110.

E3.6 **Cultus,** *Exodus 24-40*

2141 *Alonso García, Rosa María* Ex 34,10-28: un estudio histórico-
      literario. EstB 56 (1998) 433-464.
2142 *Anbar, Moshé* Deux cérémonies d'alliance dans Ex 24 à la lumière
      des Archives royales de Mari. UF 30 (1998) 1-4.
2143 *Bar-On, Shimon* The festival calendars in Exodus xxiii 14-19 and
      xxxiv 18-26. VT 48 (1998) 161-195.
2144 *Bianchi, Enzo* La festa escatologica. Festa e bibbia. 1998 ⇒403.
      163-181.
2145 *Blenkinsopp, Joseph* The Judaean priesthood during the Neo-
      Babylonian and Achaemenid periods: a hypothetical reconstruction.
      CBQ 60 (1998) 25-43.
2146 *Caro, Luciano* La festa delle Capanne. Festa e bibbia. 1998 ⇒403.
      145-161.
2147 *Clines, David J.A.* Sacred space, holy places and suchlike. OT
      essays, 2. JSOT.S 293: 1998 <1993> ⇒142. 542-554;
2148 The evidence for an autumnal New Year in pre-exilic Israel
      reconsidered;
2149 New Year <1976>. OT essays, 1. JSOT.S 292: 1998 ⇒142. 371-
      394/426-435.
2150 *Cortese, Enzo* The priestly tent (Ex 25-31.35-40): literary criticism
      and the theology of P today. SBFLA 48 (1998) 9-30.
2151 *Dohmen, Christoph* "Nicht sieht mich der Mensch und lebt" (Ex
      33,20): Aspekte der Gottesschau im Alten Testament. JBTh 13
      (1998) 31-51.
2152 *Fleming, Daniel* The biblical tradition of anointing priests. JBL 117
      (1998) 401-414.
2153 ᴱ**Frankfurter, David T.M.** Pilgrimage and holy space in late antique
      Egypt. RGRW 134: Lei 1998, Brill xiv; 517 pp. 90-04-11127-1.

2154 *Gane, Roy E.* Schedules for deities: macrostructure of Israelite, Babylonian, and Hittite sancta purification days. AUSS 36 (1998) 231-244.

2155 *Groß, Walter* "Rezeption" in Ex 31,12-17 und Lev 26,39-45: sprachliche Form und theologisch-konzeptionelle Leistung. Der ungekündigte Bund?. QD 172: 1998 ⇒240. 44-63.

2156 **Howard, Kevin** The feasts of the Lord. Nv 1998, Nelson 224 pp. 0-7852-7518-5.

2157 *Japhet, Sara* Some biblical concepts of sacred place. ᴹPRAWER J. 1998 ⇒93. 55-72.

2158 *Kaiser, Otto* Kult und Kultkritik im Alten Testament. ᶠLORETZ O. AOAT 250: 1998 ⇒65. 401-426.

2159 **Kunin, Seth Daniel** God's place in the world: sacred space and sacred place in Judaism. Cassell religious studies: L 1998, Cassell vii; 163 pp. 0-304-33748-X.

2160 *Malamat, Abraham* The sacred sea. ᴹPRAWER J. 1998 ⇒93. 45-54;

2161 The sacred sea. Mari and the bible. 1998 ⇒173. 24-32.

2162 **Nurmela, Risto** The Levites: their emergence as a second-class priesthood. SFSHJ 193: Atlanta 1998, Scholars ix; 212 pp. $45. 0-7885-0518-1.

2163 *Olyan, Saul M.* What do shaving rites accomplish and what do they signal in biblical ritual contexts?. JBL 117 (1998) 611-622.

2164 *Pummer, Reinhard* Samaritan tabernacle drawings. Numen 45 (1998) 30-68.

2165 **Renaud, Bernard** L'alliance, un mystère de miséricorde: une lecture d'Exode 32-34. LeDiv 169: P 1998, Cerf 336 pp. FF175. 2-204-05739-8. ᴿRThPh 130 (1998) 343-345 (*Rose, Martin*).

2166 *Schwartz, Joshua* 'To stand—perhaps to sit': sitting and standing in the Azarah in the second temple period. Sanctity of time. 1998 ⇒303. 167-189.

2167 *Sed-Rajna, Gabrielle* Images of the tabernacle/temple in late antique and medieval art: the state of research. ᶠNARKISS, B. 1998 ⇒85. 42-53.

2168 **Ulfgard, Håkan** The story of Sukkot: the setting, shaping, and sequel of the biblical feast of Tabernacles. BGBE 34: Tü 1998, Mohr xii; 347 pp. DM168. 3-16-147017-6.

2169 **Vroman, Akiva Jaap** On God, space & time. New Brunswick, NJ 1998, Transaction xii; 251 pp. 1-56000-397-9.

E3.7 **Leviticus**; *Jubilee*

2170 **Budd, Philip J.** Leviticus. NCBC: 1996 ⇒12,2075; 13,2164. ᴿCBQ 60 (1998) 111-112 (*Williams, Tyler F.*); JSSt 43 (1998) 368-371 (*Khan, Geoffrey*); Anton. 73 (1998) 153-154 (*Nobile, Marco*); JBL 117 (1998) 121-123 (*Gorman, Frank H.*).

2171 **Gerstenberger, Erhard S.** Leviticus: a commentary. OTL: 1996 ⇒12,2086. ᴿJR 78 (1998) 606-607 (*Anderson, Gary A.*).

2172 **Gorman, Frank H.** Divine presence and community: a commentary on the book of Leviticus. International Theological Commentary: 1997 ⇒13,2169. ᴿRExp 95 (1998) 453 (*Biddle, Mark E.*).

2173 *Rogl, Christine; Schlor, Ingrid* Ein unediertes Blatt zum Leviticus/Numeri-Copdex sa 11. Enchoria 24 (1998) 78-89.

2174 Sæbo, Magne Observations on the text history of Leviticus and the value of some Cairo Genizah variants. On the way to canon. 1998 <1990> ⇒194. 47-55.

2175 Talmon, Shemaryahu Fragments of two Leviticus scrolls from Masada. Textus 19 (1998) 27-44.

2176 Wevers, John William Notes on the Greek text of Leviticus. SBL.SCS 44: 1997 ⇒13,2180. RBib. 79 (1998) 551-562 (Zipor, Moshe A.).

2177 Zipor, Moshe A. The Greek version of Leviticus. Bib. 79 (1998) 551-562.

2178 Averkamp-Peters, Britta Levitikus 15: Überlegungen zu Unreinheit und Geschlechterkonstruktion. FMARQUARDT, F.-W. 1998 ⇒72. 181-203.

2179 Azevedo, Joaquim Las implicaciones de חלה y רקיק con la expectación mesiánica neotestamentaria. Theologika 13 (1998) 193-208.

2180 Bellinger, W.H. Leviticus and ambiguity. PRSt 25 1998, 217-225.

2181 Bryan, David Cosmos, chaos and the kosher mentality. JSPE.S 12: 1995 ⇒11/2,3170; 13,2163. RJQR 89 (1998) 253-254 (VanderKam, James C.).

2182 Carmichael, Calum M. Law, legend and incest in the bible: Leviticus 18-20. 1997 ⇒13,2191. RZAR 4 (1998) 284-287 (Otto, Eckart); CrossCur 48 (1998) 570-571 (Streete, Gail Corrington).

2183 Deiana, Giovanni Il giorno dell'espiazione: il kippur nella tradizione biblica. RivBib.S 30: 1994 ⇒10,2338... 13,2187. RCBQ 60 (1998) 523-524 (Kolarcik, Michael).

2184 Duhaime, Jean Lois alimentaires et pureté corporelle dans le Lévitique: l'approche de Mary DOUGLAS et sa réception par Jacob MILGROM. Religiologiques 17 (1998) 19-35.

2185 Falcke, Heino Die heilsame Unterbrechung: Bibelstudie über Sabbat und Jobeljahr. Evangelische Aspekte 8 (1998) 57-62.

2186 Fauth, Wolfgang Auf den Spuren des biblischen 'Azazel (Lev 16): einige Residuen der Gestalt oder des Namens in jüdisch-aramäischen, griechischen, koptischen, äthiopischen, syrischen und mandäischen Texten. ZAW 110 (1998) 514-534.

2187 Feld, Gerburgis Levitikus: das ABC der Schöpfung. Kompendium Feministische Bibelauslegung. ESchottroff, L.: 1998 ⇒H8.9. 40-53.

2188 Gravrock, Mark P. Blood and seed: toward a reading of Leviticus 18 as Christian Scripture. DLuther Sem. 1998, 386 pp.

2189 Hayes, John H. Atonement in the book of Leviticus. Interp. 52 (1998) 5-15.

2190 Heller, Jan Der Name Asasel. CV 40 (1998) 126-130.

2191 Hildenbrand, Michael Dean Structure and theology in the Holiness Code. California, DBerkeley 1998, 339 pp.

2192 Joosten, J. The Numeruswechsel in the Holiness Code (Lev. XVII-XXVI). "Lasset uns Brücken bauen.". BEAT 42: 1998 ⇒401. 67-71.

2193 Joosten, Jan People and land in the holiness code: an exegetical study of the ideational framework of the law in Lev. 17-26. VT.S 67: 1996 ⇒12,2127. RThLZ 123 (1998) 129-132 (Otto, Eckart).

2194 Joosten, Jan Covenant theology in the holiness code. ZAR 4 (1998) 145-164.

2195 Klingbeil, Gerald A. A comparative study of the ritual of ordination as found in Leviticus 8 and Emar 369. Lewiston 1998, Mellen (10) xiv; 679 pp. $140. 0-7734-2241-2.

2196 *Maluf, Leonard* The Passover festival in the book of Leviticus. BiTod 36 (1998) 17-23.
2197 *Milgrom, Jacob* Booths according to Leviticus XXIII and Nehemiah VIII. "Lasset uns Brücken bauen...". BEAT 42: 1998 ⇒401. 81-85.
2198 **Moskala, Jiri** The laws of clean and unclean animals of Leviticus 11: their nature, theology, and rationale (an intertextual study ^DAndrews 1998, 484 pp.
2199 *Nash, Kathleen S.* The feast of Booths. BiTod 36 (1998) 29-35.
2200 *Neudecker, Reinhard* L'amore del prossimo: interpretazioni ebraiche su Levitico 19,18. Asp. 45 (1998) 483-502.
2201 *Oosting, Berthil* De wondere woorden van Leviticus. ITBT 6/1 (1998) 13-16.
2202 *Organ, Barbara* The sabbath in Leviticus. BiTod 36 (1998) 11-16.
2203 *Polan, Gregory J.* The rituals of Leviticus 16 and 23. BiTod 36 (1998) 5-10.
2204 ^E**Sawyer, John F.A.** Reading Leviticus: a conversation with Mary DOUGLAS. JSOT.S 227: 1996 ⇒12,203. ^RZAR 4 (1998) 310-315 (*Otto, Eckart*); CBQ 60 (1998) 604-605 (*Anderson, Gary A.*).
2205 *Vall, Gregory* The feast of Weeks. BiTod 36 (1998) 24-28.
2206 *Wegner, Judith Romney* "Coming before the Lord": *lipne JHWH* and the exclusion of women from the divine presence. ^FFRERICHS, E. BJSt 320: 1998 ⇒28. 81-91.
2207 *Zatelli, Ida* The origin of the biblical scapegoat ritual: the evidence of two Eblaite texts. VT 48 (1998) 254-263.

2208 *Bianchi, Francesco* Il giubileo nei testi ebraici canonici e post-canonici;
2209 Bottini, Laura Il giubileo in due autori arabo-cristiani. Le origini degli anni giubilari. 1998 ⇒2236. 75-137/221-239.
2210 *Cavedo, Romeo* Anno sabbatico e giubileo nell'Antico Testamento. RCI 79 (1998) 566-573.
2211 *Gallazzi, Sandro* Jubileo: ¡aquí y ahora!. Alternativas 5 (1998) 123-144.
2212 *Gottwald, Norman K.* The biblical jubilee: in whose interests?;
2213 *Jospe, Raphael* Sabbath, sabbatical and jubilee: Jewish ethical perspectives. The jubilee challenge. 1997 ⇒13,2178. 33-40/77-98.
2214 *Klenicki, Leon* Jewish understandings of sabbatical year and jubilee. The jubilee challenge. 1997 ⇒13,2178. 41-52.
2215 *Madaro, Paola* Il giubileo nell'interpretazione dei padri greci. Le origini degli anni giubilari. 1998 ⇒2236. 185-220.
2216 *Martini, Carlo Maria* I giubilei: segmenti di senso contro lo sfruttamento dell'uomo. Interviewer *De Carli, Giuseppe*: Com(I) 158 (1998) 78-81;
2217 Le vocabulaire du jubilé. Com(F) 23 (1998) 43-46.
2218 *Milgrom, Jacob* Leviticus 25 and some postulates of the jubilee;
2219 *Müller-Fahrenholz, Geiko* The jubilee: time ceilings for the growth of money?;
2220 *Nicole, Jacques* The jubilee: some christian understandings throughout history. The jubilee challenge. 1997 ⇒13,2178. 28-32/53-58/104-111.
2221 *Orsatti, Mauro* Anno giubilare o anno santo nella bibbia. Com(I) 160-161 (1998) 9-15.
2222 **Palacios Vasquez, Eddy Mauricio** The year of jubilee in biblical tradition. ^DNavarra, Spain 1998, 321 pp.

2223 **Pitta, Antonio** L'anno della liberazione: il giubileo e le sue istanze bibliche. CinB 1998, San Paolo 138 pp.
2224 *Pixley, Jorge V.* Bases bíblicas del jubileo. Alternativas 5 (1998) 113-122.
2225 *Raiser, Konrad* Utopia and responsibility. The jubilee challenge. 1997 ⇒13,2178. 15-27.
2226 *Ska, Jean Louis* Qualche osservazioni sui fondamenti biblici del giubileo. Firmana 18 (1998) 45-59.
2227 *Smyth, Geraldine* Sabbath and jubilee;
2228 *Solomon, Norman* Economics of the jubilee;
2229 *Spray, Paul* Five areas for jubilee today;
2230 *Ucko, Hans* The jubilee as a challenge;
2231 *Usog, Carmelita M.* Sound the trumpet for justice, liberty and freedom. The jubilee challenge. 1997 ⇒13,2178. 59-76/150-164/134-139/1-14/188-195.
2232 *Van Leeuwen, Th. Marius* The jubilee challenge. ER 50 (1998) 244-249.
2233 *Vischer, Lukas* The year of jubilee: a model for the churches?;
2234 *Widyatmadja, Josef P.* Partnership to eliminate the debt: a historical perspective. The jubilee challenge. 1997 ⇒13,2178. 140-149/179-187.
2235 *Zappella, Marco* Rilettura di un percorso. Le origini degli anni giubilari. 1998 ⇒2236. 241-272.
2236 [E]**Zappella, Marco** Le origini degli anni giubilari: dalle tavolette in cuneiforme dei Sumeri ai manoscritti arabi del Mille dopo Cristo. CasM 1998, Piemme 303 pp. L38.000. 88-384-4096-4.

E3.8 *Numeri*: **Numbers, Balaam**

2237 [E]**Basser, Herbert W.** Avraham BEN-DAWID: commentary to Sifre Numbers/Pseudo-Rabad. SFSHJ 198: Atlanta 1998, Scholars ii; 175; civ pp. 0-7885-0507-6.
2238 **Budd, Philip J.** Numbers. WBC 5: 1984 ⇒65,2252... 3,2512. [R]ThR 63 (1998) 242-244 (*Schmidt, Ludwig*).
2239 **Davies, Eryl W.** Numbers. NCeB: 1995 ⇒11/1,782... 13,2202 [R]ThR 63 (1998) 245-246 (*Schmidt, Ludwig*).
2240 **Levine, Baruch A.** Numbers 1-20. AncB 4A: 1993 ⇒9,2479... 13,2206. [R]ThR 63 (1998) 244-245 (*Schmidt, Ludwig*).
2241 **Licht, Jacob** פירוש על ספר במדבר [A commentary on the book of Numbers (XXII-XXXVI)]. 1995 ⇒11/1,787; 12,2145. [R]JSSt 43 (1998) 155-157 (*Nitzan, Bilhah*); AJSR 23 (1998) 109-110 (*Milgrom, Jacob*).
2242 **Milgrom, Jacob** Numbers. 1990 ⇒6,2768... 11/1,789. [R]ThR 63 (1998) 247-249 (*Schmidt, Ludwig*).
2243 **Seebaß, Horst** Num 10,11-15,41. Numeri 2. BKAT 4/2: 1993-1995 ⇒9,2485; 11/1,792. [R]ThR 63 (1998) 246-247 (*Schmidt, Ludwig*).
2244 **Wevers, John William** Notes on the Greek text of Numbers. SBL.SCS 46: Atlanta, GA 1998, Scholars xlviii; 653 pp. $55. 0-7885-0504-1.

2245 **Berlinerblau, Jacques** The vow and the 'popular religious groups' of ancient Israel. JSOT.S 210: 1996 ⇒12,2138. [R]JSSt 43 (1998) 148-151 (*Smith, Mark S.*); JBL 117 (1998) 517-519 (*Garber, Zev*).

2246   **Douglas, Mary** In the wilderness: the doctrine of defilement in the book of Numbers. JSOT.S 158: 1993 ⇒9,2477... 12,2142. ᴿThR 63 (1998) 253-254 (*Schmidt, Ludwig*).

2247   ᵀᴱ**Doutreleau, Louis** ORIGÈNE: homélies sur les Nombres, 1: Homélies I-X. SC 415: 1996 ⇒12,2143; 13,2204. ᴿJThS 49 (1998) 369-370 (*Lienhard, Joseph T.*).

2248   **Olson, Dennis T.** The death of the old and the birth of the new: the framework of the book of Numbers and the pentateuch. BJSt 72: 1985 ⇒2,1906*; 3,2515*. ᴿThR 63 (1998) 252-253 (*Schmidt, Ludwig*).

2249   *Phillips, Elaine A.* The singular prophet and ideals of Torah: Miriam, Aaron, and Moses in early rabbinic texts. The function of scripture. 1998 ⇒236. 78-88.

2250   *Seebaß, Horst* Zum Stand der Pentateuchforschung: das Buch Numeri. ᶠVAN DER WOUDE, A. VT.S 73: 1998 ⇒121. 109-121.

2251   *Spencer, John R.* פקד, the Levites, and Numbers 1-4. ZAW 110 (1998) 535-546.

2252   *Taggar-Cohen, Ada* Law and family in the book of Numbers: the Levites and the *tidennūtu* documents from Nuzi. VT 48 (1998) 74-94.

2253   *Humphreys, Colin J.* The number of people in the Exodus from Egypt: decoding mathematically the very large numbers in Numbers i and xxvi. VT 48 (1998) 196-213.

2254   *Keller, Sharon R.* An Egyptian analogue to the priestly blessing ᶠGORDON, C. JSOT.S 273: 1998 ⇒31. 338-345 [Num 6,24-26].

2255   **Lee, Won Woo** Punishment and forgiveness in Israel's migratory campaign: the macrostructure of Numbers 10:11-36:13. ᴰClaremont 1998, 346 pp.

2256   *Schmidt, Ludwig* Mose, die 70 Ältesten und die Propheten in Numeri 11 und 12. Gesammelte Aufsätze zum Pentateuch. BZAW 263: 1998 ⇒195. 251-279.

2257   *Barthel, Jörg* Die Last des Amtes oder: von rechter und falscher Klage: Numeri 11,4-34. ThFPr 24 (1998) 74-103.

2258   *Artus, O.* Nb 11,26-29: une critique prophétique préexilique du pouvoir politique et du culte?. Transeuphratène 14 (1998) 79-89.

2259   *Hymes, David C.* Numbers 12: of priests, prophets, or "none of the above". AJBI 24 (1998) 3-32.

2260   **Rabe, Norbert** Vom Gerücht zum Gericht: die Kundschafter-erzählung Num 13.14 als Neuansatz in der Pentateuchforschung. THLI 8: 1994 ⇒9,2494; 12,2152. ᴿThR 63 (1998) 259-260 (*Schmidt, Ludwig*) [Num 13-14].

2261   *Harris, Rachel T.* The ritual of the red heifer. JBQ 26 (1998) 198-200 [Num 19,1-22].

2262   *Seebaß, Horst* Wollte Mose ursprünglich nach Edom?: zu Num 20, 14-21. "Lasset uns Brücken bauen...". BEAT 42: 1998 ⇒401. 73-79.

2263   *Ulrich, Dean R.* The framing function of the narratives about Zelophehad's daughters. JETS 41 (1998) 529-538 [Num 27,1-11; 36].

2264   *Cathcart, Kevin J.* Numbers 24:17 in ancient translations and interpretations. Interpretation of the Bible. JSOT.S 289: 1998 ⇒388. 511-520.

2265   **Greene, John T.** Balaam and his interpreters. BJSt 244: 1992 ⇒8,2665... 10,2367. ᴿThR 63 (1998) 263-265 (*Schmidt, Ludwig*).

2266 *Malamat, Abraham `mm l'bādād yiškōn*: a diplomatic report from Mari and an oracle of Balaam. Mari and the bible. 1998 [1985] ⇒173. 216-218 [Num 23,9].

2267 **Meadows, Jack Irwin** An investigative study of RASHI's and MAIMONIDES' Messianic interpretations of the star prophecy in Numbers 24:14-19. ᴰTrinity 1998, 322 pp.

2268 **Moore, Michael S.** The Balaam traditions. SBL.DS 113: 1990 ⇒6,2790... 10,2373. ᴿThR 63 (1998) 265-266 (*Schmidt, Ludwig*).

2269 **Rouillard, Hedwige** La péricope de Balaam. EtB 4: 1985 ⇒1,2627...5,2557. ᴿThR 63 (1998) 262-263 (*Schmidt, Ludwig*).

2270 *Schmidt, Ludwig* Die alttestamentliche Bileamerzählung. Gesammelte Aufsätze z. Pentateuch. BZAW 263: 1998 <1979> ⇒195. 57-84.

E3.9 Liber Deuteronomii

2271 **Apicella, Alfredo** Il libro del Deuteronomio. Valenza 1998, "Il Messaggero Cristiano" 182 pp.

2272 **Braulik, Georg** Studien zum Buch Deuteronomium. SBAB 24: 1997 ⇒13,2240. ᴿThLZ 123 (1998) 962-964 (*Levin, Christoph*).

2273 ᵀ**Clarke, Ernest George** Targum Pseudo-Jonathan: Deuteronomy. The Aramaic Bible 5 B.: E 1998, Clark x; 122 pp. $65. 0567085767.

2274 ᵀ**Cortes, Enric; Martínez, Teresa** Commentario tannaitico al libro del Deuteronomio: Pisqa 1-160; Pisqa 161-357. 1989-1997 ⇒13,2230. ᴿRET 58 (1998) 255-256 (*Barrado, P.*).

2275 **Wright, Christopher J.H.** Deuteronomy. New International Biblical Commentary. Old Testament Series 4: 1996 ⇒12,2171. ᴿCBQ 60 (1998) 550-551 (*Morrow, William S.*).

2276 *Bayun, L.S.* Divination in ancient Near East: Hittite oracles. VDI 224 (1998) 30-36. **R**.

2277 **Blacketer, Raymond Andrew** L'école de Dieu: pedagogy and rhetoric in Calvin's interpretation of Deuteronomy. Diss. Calvin Theological Seminary 1998. ᴰ*Muller, R.*: ii; 399 pp. ᴿCTJ 33 (1998) 577-578.

2278 *Braulik, Georg* Durften auch Frauen in Israel opfern?: Beobachtungen zur Sinn- und Festgestalt des Opfers im Deuteronomium. LJ 48 (1998) 222-248.

2279 *Carrière, Jean-Marie* Le "pays" dans le Deutéronome: une notion construite. Transeuphratène 14 (1998) 113-132.

2280 **Dahmen, Ulrich** Leviten und Priester im Deuteronomium: literarkritische und redaktionsgeschichtliche Studien. BBB 110: 1996 ⇒12,2180. ᴿBib 79 (1998) 268-271 (*Nelson, Richard D.*).

2281 *Eisen, Arnold* Taking hold of Deuteronomy. Jdm 47 (1998) 321-328.

2282 *Engelmann, Angelika* Deuteronomium: Recht und Gerechtigkeit für Frauen im Gesetz. Kompendium Feministische Bibelauslegung. ᴱ**Schottroff, L.**: 1998 ⇒H8.9. 67-79.

2283 **Jeffers, Ann** Magic and divination in Ancient Palestine and Syria. 1996 ⇒12,2187. ᴿSJOT 12 (1998) 314-315 (*Jeppesen, Knud*); JAOS 118 (1998) 591-592 (*Cryer, Frederick H.*); RSFen 26 (1998) 243-246 (*Ribichini, Sergio*).

2284 *Lohfink, Norbert* Der Neue Bund im Buch Deuteronomium?. ZAR 4 (1998) 100-125.

2285 *McConville, J.G.* King and Messiah in Deuteronomy and the Deuteronomistic History. King and Messiah. JSOT.S 270: 1998 ⇒378. 271-295.

2286 *Mettinger, Tryggve N.D.* The name and the glory: the Zion-Sabaoth theology and its exilic successors. JNSL 24/1 (1998) 1-24.

2287 **Millar, J. Gary** Now choose life: theology and ethics in Deuteronomy. New Studies in Biblical Theology 6: [Leicester] 1998, Apollos 216 pp. $24. 0-85111-515-2.

2288 *Otto, Eckart* "Das Deuteronomium krönt die Arbeit der Propheten": Gesetz und Prophetie im Deuteronomium. ᶠRUPPERT, L. FzB 88: 1998 ⇒99. 277-309;

2289 False weights in the scales of biblical justice?: different views of women from patriarchal hierarchy to religious equality in the Book of Deuteronomy. Gender and law. JSOT.S 262: 1998 ⇒256. 128-146.

2290 ᴱ**Veijola, Timo** Das Deuteronomium und seine Querbeziehungen. SESJ 62: 1996 ⇒12,209; 13,2260. ᴿCBQ 60 (1998) 190-192 (*Miller, Patrick D.*).

2291 **Wilson, Ian** Out of the midst of the fire: divine presence in Deuteronomy. SBL.DS 151: 1995 ⇒11/1,866; 13,2263. ᴿJBL 117 (1998) 723-725 (*Morrow, William S.*).

2292 *Lohfink, Norbert* Geschichtstypologie in Deuteronomium 1-3. "Lasset uns Brücken bauen...". BEAT 42: 1998 ⇒401. 87-92.

2293 *O'Kennedy, D.F.* Prayer in Moab (Dt 3:23-29): the relationship between the recorded prayer and its historical geographical setting. OTEs 11 (1998) 288-305.

2294 *Draper, James T.* The ground of all truth: Deut. 6:4-9. Faith & Mission 15 (1998) 53-62.

2295 **Gerhardsson, Birger** The Shema in the New Testament: Deut 6:4-5 in significant passages. 1996 ⇒12,2213. ᴿBibl.Interp. 6 (1998) 446-448 (*Nanos, Mark D.*).

2296 **Loretz, Oswald** Des Gottes Einzigkeit:... zum 'Schma Jisrael'. 1997 ⇒13,2253. ᴿBib. 79 (1998) 283-288 (*Veijola, Timo*); ActBib 35 (1998) 172-173 (*Boada, J.*).

2297 *Pressler, Carolyn* The Shema': a Protestant feminist reading. Escaping Eden. BiSe 65: 1998 ⇒278. 41-52.

2298 *Hamilton, Jeffries M.* How read an abhorrent text: Deuteronomy 13 and the nature of authority. HBT 20 (1998) 12-32.

2299 **Morrow, William S.** Scribing the center: organization and redaction in Deuteronomy 14:1-17:13. SBL.MS 49: 1995 ⇒11/1,887... 13,2269. ᴿBiOr 55 (1998) 487-491 (*Otto, Eckart*); ABR 46 (1998) 86-87 (*O'Brien, Mark A.*).

2300 *Maier, Johann* Grundlage und Anwendung des Verbots der Rückkehr nach Ägypten. 1998, 225-244 [Dt 17,17; 28,68].

2301 *Washington, Harold C.* 'Lest he die in the battle and another man take her': violence and the construction of gender in the laws of Deuteronomy 20-22. Gender & law. JSOT.S 262: 1998 ⇒256. 185-213.

2302 *Rand, Herbert* The bird's nest *mitzvah*: a personal aggadic interpretation. JBQ 26 (1998) 127-128 [Dt 22,6-7].

2303 *Brewer, David I.* Deuteronomy 24:1-4 and the origin of the Jewish divorce certificate. JJS 49 (1998) 230-243.

2304 *Volgger, David* Dtn 24,1-4—ein Verbot von Wiederverheiratung?. BN 92 (1998) 85-96.

2305 *Warren, Andrew* Did Moses permit divorce?: modal "weqaṭal" as key to New Testament readings of Deuteronomy 24:1-4. TynB 49 (1998) 39-56.

2306 *Barker, Paul A.* The theology of Deuteronomy 27. TynB 49 (1998) 277-303.

2307 *Shemesh, Aharon; Werman, Cana* Hidden things and their revelation. RdQ 18 (1998) 409-427⸣[Dt 29,28].

2308 **Sanders, Paul** The provenance of Deuteronomy 32. OTS 37: 1996 ⇒12,2231; 13,2289. ᴿBiOr 55 (1998) 240-241 (*Begg, Christopher*); ThLZ 123 (1998) 132-134 (*Reventlow, Henning Graf*).

2309 *Segert, Stanislav* Song of Moses and Ugaritic poetry: some parallelistic observations. ᶠLORETZ O. AOAT 250: 1998 ⇒65. 701-711 [Dt 32].

2310 *Beyerle, Stefan* Evidence of a polymorphic text: towards the text-history of Deuteronomy 33. DSD 5 (1998) 215-232.

2311 **Beyerle, Stefan** Der Mosesegen im Deuteronomium... Dt 33. BZAW 250: 1997 ⇒13,2290. ᴿThLZ 123 (1998) 125-128 (*Zobel, Hans-Jürgen*).

2312 *Talmon, Shemaryahu* Fragments of a Deuteronomy scroll from Masada: Deuteronomy 33.17-34.6 (1043/A-D). ᶠGORDON, C. JSOT.S 273: 1998 ⇒31. 150-161.

2313 *Propp, William H.C.* Why Moses could not enter the promised land. BiRe 14/3 (1998) 36-40, 42-43 [Dt 34,6-7].

E4.1 *Origo Israelis in Canaan: Deuteronomista:* **Liber Josue**

2314 ᴱ**Ahituv, Shmuel; Oren, Eliezer D.** The origin of early Israel—current debate: biblical, historical, and archaeological perspectives. Beer-Sheva 12: Beer-Sheva 1998, Ben-Gurion Univ. viii; 176 pp.

2315 **Fritz, Volkmar O.** Die Entstehung Israels im 12. und 11. Jahrhundert v. Chr. 1996 ⇒12,2244; 13,2299. ᴿVT 48 (1998) 567-569 (*Emerton, J.A.*).

2316 **Hostetter, Edwin C.** Nations mightier and more numerous: the biblical view of Palestine's pre-Israelite peoples. BIBAL.DS 3: 1995 ⇒11/2,9217; 13,9756. ᴿCBQ 60 (1998) 117-118 (*Spencer, John R.*).

2317 **Isserlin, Benedikt S.** The Israelites. L 1998, Thames & H 304 pp. £28. 0-500-05082-1.

2318 **Jericke, Detlef** Die Landnahme im Negev: protoisraelitische Gruppen im Süden Palästinas: eine archäologische und exegetische Studie. ADPV 20: 1997 ⇒13,2302. ᴿRBBras 15 (1998) 458-460.

2319 **Lemche, Niels Peter** Die Vorgeschichte Israels. Biblische Enzyklopädie 1: 1996 ⇒12,2247; 13,2304. ᴿBib. 79 (1998) 573-575 (*Engel, Helmut*); VT 48 (1998) 573-575 (*Emerton, J.A.*).

2320 **McDermott, John J.** What are they saying about the formation of Israel?. Mahwah 1998, Paulist 113 pp. $11. 0-8091-3838-7.

2321 *Michniewicz, Wojciech* The Israel's origin theories. CoTh 68A (1998) 5-22.

2322 *Stager, Lawrence* Forging an identity: the emergence of ancient Israel. The Oxford history. 1998 ⇒326. 123-175.

2323 *Ash, Paul S.* Jeroboam I and the Deuteronomistic historian's ideology of the founder. CBQ 60 (1998) 16-24.

2324 *McKenzie, Steven L.* Mizpah of Benjamin and the date of the Deuteronomistic History. "Lasset uns Brücken bauen...". BEAT 42: 1998 ⇒401. 149-155.
2325 *Montero, Domingo* El imperio davídico-salomónico: la constitución del primitivo Israel. Evangelio y Vida 40 (1998) 149-151.
2326 ᴱ**Pury, Albert de; Römer, Thomas; Macchi, Jean-Daniel** Israël construit son histoire: l'historiographie deutéronomiste à la lumière des recherches récentes. MoBi 34: 1996 ⇒12,199; 13,2323. ᴿCoTh 68 (1998) 223-226 (*Chrostowski, Waldemar*); RBBras 15 (1998) 480-482; ETR 73 (1998) 114-115 (*Gutiérrez, Miguel*).
2327 *Stipp, Hermann-Josef* Die sechste und siebte Fürbitte des Tempel- weihegebets (1 Kön 8,44-51) in der Diskussion um das Deutero- nomistische Geschichtswerk. JNSL 24/1 (1998) 193-216.
2328 **Stone, Kenneth A.** Sex, honor and power in the deuteronomistic his- tory: a narratological and anthropological analysis. JSOT.S 234: 1996 ⇒12,2267. ᴿCBQ 60 (1998) 349-350 (*Yee, Gale A.*); JBL 117 (1998) 341-342 (*McKenzie, Steven L.*).

2329 *Auld, A.G.* Le texte hébreu et le texte grec de Josué: une comparaison à partir du chapitre 5. FV 97 (1998) 67-78.
2330 ᴱ**Briffard, Colette; Lanoir, Corinne** Josué. FV 97 (1998). 120 pp. FF65. 0015-5357.
2331 *Crown, A.D.* Was there a Samaritan book of Joshua?. ᶠJUDGE E. 1998 ⇒47. 15-22.
2332 *Klein, George L.* Joshua: an annotated bibliography. SWJT 41 (1998) 102-110.
2333 ᵀ**Moatti-Fine, Jacqueline** La Bible d'Alexandrie 6: Jésus (Josué). 1996 ⇒12,2279. ᴿSef. 58 (1998) 437-439 (*Fernández Marcos, N.*).
2334 **Nelson, Richard Donald** Joshua: a commentary. 1997 ⇒13,2333. ᴿBTB 28 (1998) 123-124 (*Gnuse, Robert Karl*);
2335 The historical books. Interpreting Biblical Texts: Nv 1998, Abingdon 190 pp. $19. 0-6870-0843-3.
2336 **Noort, Edward** Das Buch Josua: Forschungsgeschichte und Problemfelder. EdF 292: Da:Wiss 1998, vii; 343 pp. 3-534-02827-9.
2337 *Rosel, H.N.* ספרי נביאים ראשונים—הרכב, היווצרות והמסר [The books of the Former Prophets—their formation and their function]. BetM 154- 155 (1998) 245-255.
2338 *Sipilä, Seppo* Max Leopold MARGOLIS and the Origenic recension in Joshua. Origen's Hexapla. TSAJ 58: 1998 ⇒399. 16-38.
2339 ᴱ**Stiver, Dan R.** Joshua. RExp 95 (1998) 151-284.
2340 **Synowiec, Juliusz Stanislaw** Izrael opowiada swoje dzieje: Wprowadzenie do ksiag: Powtórzonego Prawa, Jozuego, Sedziów, Samuela i Królewskich. Kraków 1998, Wydawnictwo Oo. Fran- ciszkanów "Bratni Zew" 275 pp. 83-86991-13-5.

2341 **Auld, A. Graeme** Joshua retold: synoptic perspectives. Old Testa- ment Studies: E 1998, Clark x; 179 pp. £20. 0-567-08603-8.
2342 *Biddle, Mark E.* Literary structures in the book of Joshua. RExp 95 (1998) 189-201.
2343 *Browning, Daniel C.* "The hill country is not enough for us": recent archaeology and the book of Joshua. SWJT 41 (1998) 25-43.
2344 *Butler, Trent C.* The theology of Joshua. RExp 95 (1998) 203-225.
2345 *DeClaissé-Walford, Nancy L.* Covenant in the book of Joshua. RExp 95 (1998) 227-234.

2346 *Drinkard, Joel F.* The history and archaeology of the book of Joshua and the conquest/settlement period. RExp 95 (1998) 171-188.
2347 *Ehrlich, Carl Stephan* Josué dans le judaïsme. FV 97 (1998) 95-110.
2348 *Ellis, Robert R.* The theological boundaries of inclusion and exclusion in the book of Joshua. RExp 95 (1998) 235-250.
2349 *Faye, Jean-Pierre* De Josué conquérant à la cité de paix, un parcours libre sur la frontière. FV 97 (1998) 111-120.
2350 *Görg, Manfred* Die Anfänge der kritischen Datierung des Buches Josua. BN 94 (1998) 11-14.
2351 *Holloway, Jeph* The ethical dilemma of holy war. SWJT 41 (1998) 44-69.
2352 *Langston, Scott M.* Reading the book of Joshua. SWJT 41 (1998) 7-24.
2353 *Mendoza, González* Libro de Josué (11). EvV 40 (1998) 66-68.
2354 *Moatti-Fine, Jacqueline* Jéricho à la lumière des lectures anciennes. FV 97 (1998) 81-94.
2355 *Nardi, Carlo* Giosuè nel primo cristianesimo. RAMi 23 (1998) 147-159.
2356 *Nelson, Jimmie L.* Preaching from the book of Joshua. SWJT 41 (1998) 86-101.
2357 *Noort, Ed* 4QJosh[a] and the history of tradition in the book of Joshua. JNSL 24/2 (1998) 127-144 [Ex 24,4-7; Dt 27,5-7; Josh 8,30-35].
2358 *Prior, Michael* A land flowing with milk, honey and people. ScrB 28 (1998) 2-17.
2359 **Rowlett, Lori L.** Joshua and the rhetoric of violence: a new historicist analysis. JSOT.S 226: 1996 ⇒12,2292; 13,2348. [R]CBQ 60 (1998) 129-130 (*Williams, James G.*); JBL 117 (1998) 519-520 (*Hawk, L. Daniel*).
2360 *Römer, T.* Pentateuque, hexateuque et historiographie deutéronomiste: le problème du début et de la fin du livre de Josué. Transeuphratène 16 (1998) 71-86.
2361 *Römer, Thomas C.* Le livre de Josué: histoire d'une propagande, propagande d'une histoire. FV 97 (1998) 5-20.
2362 **Russotto, Mario** Giosuè: finalmente la terra!. La Bibbia nelle nostre mani 14: CinB 1998, San Paolo 70 pp. 88-215-3795-1.
2363 *Sipilä, Seppo* THEODORET of Cyrrhus and the book of Joshua— Theodoret's *Quaestiones* revisited. Textus 19 (1998) 157-170.
2364 *Taylor, Larry M.* Theological themes in the book of Joshua. SWJT 41 (1998) 70-85.
2365 *Wiesel, Elie* Joshua: silent at the tent door. BiRe 14/6 (1998) 20-21.

2366 *Howard, David M.* "Three days" in Joshua 1-3: resolving a chronological conundrum. JETS 41 (1998) 539-550.
2367 *Römer, Thomas Chr.* Josué, lecteur de la Torah (Jos 1,8). "Lasset uns Brücken bauen...". BEAT 42: 1998 ⇒401. 117-124.
2368 *Lanoir, Corinne* Rahab, traîtresse ou passeuse? (Josué 2 et 6). FV 97 (1998) 33-39.
2369 *Howard, David M.* Rahab's faith: an exposition of Joshua 2:1-14. RExp 95 (1998) 271-277;
2370 *Guillaume, Philippe* Une traversée qui n'en finit pas (Josué 3-4). FV 97 (1998) 21-32.
2371 *Adam, A.K.* Crossing over, pressing on. PSB 19 (1998) 236-241 [Josh 3,14-4,7].

2372 *Hertog, Cornelis G. den* Jos 5,4-6 in der griechischen Übersetzung. ZAW 110 (1998) 601-606.
2373 *Dieterlé, Christiane* Le monceau de pierres de Josué 7,26 ou: que faire du Dieu cruel?. FV 97 (1998) 41-54.
2374 *Briend, Jacques* Josué 10: une conquête en morceaux. FV 97 (1998) 55-65.
2375 *Latvus, Kari* From army campsite to partners in peace: the changing role of the Gibeonites in the redaction process of Josh. x 1-8; xi 19. "Lasset uns Brücken bauen...". BEAT 42: 1998 ⇒401. 111-115.
2376 *Hess, Richard S.* Rhetorical forms in Joshua 10:4. ᶠLORETZ O. AOAT 250: 1998 ⇒65. 363-367.
2377 *Ofer, Avi* עָרֵי הַמִּדְבָּר שֶׁבִּיהוּדָה הַמִּקְרָאִית [The desert towns of Judah]. Cathedra 90 (1998) 7-32 [Josh 15,61-62].
2378 *Kallai, Zecharia* The system of Levitic cities and cities of refuge: a historical-geographical study in biblical historiography. Biblical historiography. 1998 ⇒167. 23-62 [Josh 21].
2379 *Noort, Ed* Zu Stand und Perspektiven: der Glaube Israels zwischen Religionsgeschichte und Theologie: der Fall Josua 24. ᶠVAN DER WOUDE, A. VT.S 73: 1998 ⇒121. 82-108.
2380 *Bugg, Charles B.* Joshua 24:14-18—the choice. RExp 95 (1998) 279-284.

E4.2 *Liber Judicum*: **Richter, Judges**

2381 *Becker, Uwe* Richterbuch. TRE 29. 1998 ⇒501. 194-200.
2382 *Exum, J. Cheryl* Das Buch der Richter: verschlüsselte Botschaften für Frauen. Kompendium Feministische Bibelauslegung. ᴱ**Schottroff, L.**: 1998 ⇒H8.9. 90-103.
2383 *Guest, P. Deryn* Can Judges survive without sources?: challenging the consensus. JSOT 78 (1998) 43-61.
2384 *Hackett, Jo Ann* "There was no king in Israel": the era of the Judges. The Oxford history. 1998 ⇒326. 177-218.
2385 *Mayer, Désirée* Passages dans le livre des Juges. SémBib 92 (1998) 35-43.
2386 *Nel, Philip J.* From violence to anarchy: plot and character in Judges. "Lasset uns Brücken bauen...". BEAT 42: 1998 ⇒401. 125-133.
2387 **O'Connell, Robert H.** The rhetoric of the book of Judges. VT.S 63: 1996 ⇒12,2303; 13,2360. ᴿCBQ 60 (1998) 537-538 (*Exum, J. Cheryl*); JQR 88 (1998) 275-279 (*Amit, Yairah*); JThS 49 (1998) 172-176 (*Mayes, A.D.H.*).
2388 **Russotto, Mario** I Giudici: fedeltà nella prova. La Bibbia nelle nostre mani 17: CinB 1998, San Paolo 80 pp. 88-215-3829-X.
2389 **Smelik, Willem F.** The targum of Judges. OTS 36: 1995 ⇒11/1,983; 13,2361. ᴿCBQ 60 (1998) 347-348 (*Garber, Zev*); BiOr 55 (1998) 890-893 (*Gordon, R.P.*); JQR 89 (1998) 225-229 (*McNamara, Martin*); JBL 117 (1998) 174-175 (*Grossfeld, Bernard*).
2390 *Tollington, Janet E.* The book of Judges: the result of post-exilic exegesis?. Intertextuality. OTS 40: 1998 ⇒394. 186-196.

2391 *Guillaume, Philippe* An anti-Judean manifesto in Judges 1. BN 95 (1998) 12-17.
2392 *Álvarez Barredo, Miguel* Convergencias redaccionales sobre la conquista de la tierra prometida en Jue 1,1-2,5. Cart. 14 (1998) 1-42.

2393 *Alvarez Barredo, Miguel* Aspectos literarios y lectura teológico de Jue 2,6-3,6. Anton. 73 (1998) 219-239.
2394 *Jull, Tom A.* mqrh in Judges 3: a scatological reading. JSOT 81 (1998) 63-75.
2395 *Alvarez Barredo, Miguel* Los relatos sobre los primeros Jueces (Jue 3,7-4): enfoques literarios y teológicos. Anton. 73 (1998) 407-457.
2396 **Alejandrino, Miriam R.** Deborah and Barak: a literary, historical, and theological analysis of Judges 4 and 5. Diss. Extr. Gregoriana *DConroy, Charles*: R 1998, xiii; 102 pp.
2397 *Álvarez Barredo, Miguel* El cántico de Débora (Jue 5,1-31): perfiles literarios y teológicos. VyV 56 (1998) 327-370.
2398 **Becker-Spörl, Silvia** 'Und sang Debora·an jenem Tag': Untersuchungen zu Sprache und Intention des Deboraliedes (Ri 5). EHS.T 620: Fra 1998, Lang xi; 354 pp. 3-631-32943-1.
2399 *Miller, Geoffrey P.* A riposte form in the song of Deborah. Gender and law. JSOT.S 262: 1998 ⇒256. 113-127.
2400 *Craig, Kenneth M. Jr.* Bargaining in Tov (Judges 11,4-11): the many directions of so-called direct speech. Bib. 79 (1998) 76-85.
2401 *Fleishman, Joseph* עוולה בשפטית בתקופת השופטים ותיקונה [An undone evil in the book of Judges (the case of Jephthah)]. Beit Mikra 153 (1998) 129-141 [Judg 11].
2402 *Römer, Thomas C.* Why would the Deuteronomists tell about the sacrifice of Jephthah's daughter?. JSOT 77 (1998) 27-38 [Judg 11].
2403 **Bauer, Uwe F.** 'Warum nur übertretet ihr sein Geheiß?': eine synchrone Exegese der Anti-Erzählung von Richter 17-18. Diss-Habil. Neudendettelsau 1997. *DUtzschneider, H.*: BEAT 45: Fra 1998, Lang 463 pp. 3-631-32200-3.
2404 *Gillmayr-Bucher, Susanne* Eigentlich wollte ich nur das Weltall ein bisschen anritzen": Nelly SACHS' szenische Dichtung "Simson fällt durch Jahrtausende"—Relecture einer biblischen Erzählung. PzB 7 (1998) 95-121 [Judg 13-16].
2405 *Heltzer, Michael* Dishonest behavior of sons towards parents in ancient western Asia. AltOrF 25 (1998) 285-288 [Judg 17,1-4].
2406 *Bach, Alice* Rereading the body politic: women and violence in Judges 21. Biblical Interpretation 6 (1998) 1-19.

E4.3 **Liber Ruth,** '*V Rotuli*', the Five Scrolls

2407 *E***Bengtsson, Per Å.** Two Arabic versions of the book of Ruth: text edition and language studies. 1995 ⇒11/1,1025; 13,2387. *R*VT 48 (1998) 433-435 (*Polliack, Meira*); BSOAS 61 (1998) 128-129 (*Khan, Geoffrey*); JSSt 43 (1998) 197-202 (*Shehadeh, Haseeb*); Muséon 111 (1998) 458-462 (*Grand'Henry, J.*).
2408 *Bons, Eberhard* Die Septuaginta-Version des Buches Rut. BZ 42 (1998) 202-224.
2409 *Bregantini, Giancarlo* Da Mara a Noemi: la cooperazione: un itinerario di coraggio. Horeb 19 (1998) 11-19.
2410 **Bush, Frederic William** Ruth, Esther. WBC 9: 1996 ⇒12,2326; 13,2391. *R*BS 155 (1998) 493-494 (*Chisholm, Robert B.*).
2411 **Caso, Ángeles** Los libros de Ruth, Judit y Ester. Barc 1998, Bolsillo 126 pp.

2412   *Herr, Denise Dick* Men are from Judah, women are from Bethlehem: how a modern bestseller illuminates the book of Ruth. BiRe 14/4 (1998) 34-41, 54-55.

2413   *Masenya, Madipoane J.* Ngwetši (bride): the Naomi-Ruth story from an African-South African woman's perspective. JFSR 14 (1998) 81-90.

2414   *Meinhold, Arndt* Ruth (Buch). TRE 29. 1998 ⇒501. 508-511.

2415   **Mesters, Carlos; Storniolo, Ivo** Historias de Rut, Judit y Ester: introducción a tres libros del Antiguo Testamento. Dabar 7: M 1996, San Pablo 207 pp. 84-285-1903-X.

2416   *Moore, Michael S.* Ruth the Moabite and the blessing of foreigners. CBQ 60 (1998) 203-217.

2417   **Nielsen, Kirsten** Ruth: a commentary. 1997 ⇒13,2403. ᴿCBQ 60 (1998) 338-339 (*Moore, Michael S.*); Bib. 79 (1998) 417-419 (*Berlin, Adele*).

2418   *Ushedo, Benedict* Forensic narration in the book of Ruth. ScrB 28 (1998) 28-40.

2419   **Van Wolde, Ellen** Ruth and Naomi. 1997 ⇒13,2407. ᴿRRT (1998/1) 38-40 (*Gillingham, Susan*).

2420   **Vílchez Líndez, José** Rut y Ester. Nueva Biblia Española, Narraciones II: Estella 1998, Verbo Div. 418 pp. PTA4.500. 84-8169-231-X.

2421   ᴱ**Waard, Jan de** Librum Ruth. Biblia Hebraica Quinta, Fasc. extra seriem. Stu 1998, Dt. Bibelges. xxxix; 25 pp.

2422   **Wénin, André** Le livre de Ruth: une approche narrative. CEv 104: P 1998, Cerf 67 pp.

2423   *King, Greg A.* Ruth 2:1-13. Interp. 52 (1998) 182-184.

2424   *Wénin, André* La stratégie déjouée de Noémi en Rt 3. EstB 56 (1998) 179-199.

E4.4 1-2 Samuel

2425   *Garsiel, Moshe* משחקי מלים, צימודים ודרשות שם כתכסיס ריטורי-ספרותי בספר שמואל [Wordplays, puns and puns upon names as a literary and rhetorical device in the book of Samuel]. Beit Mikra 156 (1998) 1-14.

2426   **Gibert, Pierre** Os livros de Samuel e dos Reis—da lenda à história. Cadernos Bíblicos 60: Lisboa 1998, Difusora Bíblica 60 pp.

2427   **Jobling, David** 1 Samuel. Berit Olam: ColMn 1998, Liturgical 330 pp. $35. 0-8146-5047-3.

2428   **Saley, Richard J.** The Samuel manuscript of JACOB of Edessa: a study in its underlying textual traditions. MPIL 9: Lei 1998, Brill xii; 138 pp. 90-04-11214-6.

2429   **Salibi, Kamal S.** The historicity of biblical Israel: studies in 1 & 2 Samuel. L 1998, NABU xl; 288 pp. 1-897750-60-9.

2430   *Salvesen, Alison* An edition of JACOB of Edessa's version of I-II Samuel. Symposium Syriacum VII. 1998 ⇒415. 13-22.

2431   **Stoebe, Hans-Joachim** Das zweite Buch Samuelis. KAT 8/2: 1994 ⇒10,2545; 11/1,1053. ᴿThRv 94 (1998) 381-384 (*Schäfer-Lichtenberger, Christa*).

2432   ᴱ**Van Staalduine-Sulman , Eveline** A bilingual concordance to the targum of the prophets, 3, 5: Samuel. 1996 ⇒12,2362, 2364. ᴿCBQ 60 (1998) 549-550 (*Golomb, David M.*).

2433 *Beré, Paul* 1 Sam 3.3a: 'et la lampe de Dieu n'était pas encore éteinte'. Hekima Review 19 (1998) 49-57.

2434 *Orel, Vladimir* The great fall of Dagon. ZAW 110 (1998) 427-432 [1 Sam 5,2-4].

E4.5 *1 Sam 7...Initia potestatis regiae,* Origins of kingship

2435 **Crawford, Barry Craig** Saul among the prophets: the thematology of King Saul. ᴰCalifornia, Riverside 1998, 286 pp.

2436 *Dietrich, Manfried; Dietrich, Walter* Zwischen Gott und Volk: Einführung des Königtums und Auswahl des Königs nach mesopotamischer und israelitischer Anschauung. ᶠLORETZ O. AOAT 250: 1998 ⇒65. 215-264.

2437 **Goodblatt, David** The monarchic principle: studies in Jewish self-government in antiquity. TSAJ 38: 1994 ⇒10,2571(!); 12,2386. ᴿJQR 88 (1998) 317-324 (*Levine, Lee*).

2438 *Malamat, Abraham; Artzi, P.* The Great King: a pre-eminent royal title in cuneiform sources and `in' the bible. Mari and the bible. 1998 [1993] ⇒173. 192-215;

2439 Episodes involving Samuel and Saul and the prophetic texts from Mari. ᶠFRERICHS, E. BJSt 320: 1998 ⇒28. 225-229;

2440 Episodes involving Samuel and Saul and the prophetic texts from Mari. Mari and the bible. 1998 ⇒173. 102-105.

2441 *Meyers, Carol* Kinship and kingship: the early monarchy. The Oxford history. 1998 ⇒326. 221-271.

2442 *Rooke, Deborah W.* Kingship as priesthood: the relationship between the high priesthood and the monarchy;

2443 *Salvesen, Alison* The trappings of royalty in ancient Hebrew. King and Messiah. JSOT.S 270: 1998 ⇒378. 187-208/119-141.

2444 *Večko, Snežna* Začetki izraelskega kraljestva: zavrženje in izvolitev [Beginnings of Israelite kingdom: rejection and election]. Bogoslovni Vestnik 58 (1998) 267-280;

2445 Saul—the persecutor or the persecuted one?. Interpretation of the Bible. JSOT.S 289: 1998 ⇒388. 201-216.

2446 *Nihan, Christophe* L'injustice des fils de Samuel, au tournant d'une époque: quelques remarques sur la fonction de 1 Samuel 8,1-5 dans son contexte littéraire. BN 94 (1998) 26-32.

2447 *Dinkelaker, Veit* Die Tyrannis im biblischen Verfassungsdenken: eine motiv- und kulturgeschichtliche Untersuchung zu 1 Sam 8,10-18: Plato 'nacherzählt'?. DBAT 29 (1998) 99-138.

2448 *Couffignal, Robert* Le récit du règne de Saül (1 Samuel 9-31): étude de structures. ETR 73 (1998) 3-20.

2449 *Anbar, Moshé* La critique biblique à la lumière des archives royales de Mari III: 1 S 12,3. Bib. 79 (1998) 549-550.

2450 *Malamat, Abraham* Deity revokes kingship—towards intellectual reasoning in Mari and in the bible. Mari and the bible. 1998 ⇒173. 157-162 [1 Sam 15,28; 1 Kgs 11,11];

2451 Deity revokes kingship—towards intellectual reasoning in Mari and in the bible. Intellectual life. 1998 ⇒450. 231-235 [1 Sam 15,28; 1 Kgs 11,11].

E4.6 *1 Sam 16...2 Sam: Accessio Davidis.* **David's Rise**

2452 **Costacurta, Bruna** Con la citara y con la honda: la subida de David hacia el trono. Bilbao 1998, Desclée de B 255 pp.

2453 *Esler, Philip F.* The madness of Saul: a cultural reading of 1 Samuel 8-31. Biblical studies. JSOT.S 266: 1998 ⇒380. 220-262.

2454 **Nitsche, Stefan Ark** David gegen Goliath: die Geschichte der Geschichten einer Geschichte: zur fachübergreifenden Rezeption einer biblischen Story. AT und Moderne 4: Müns 1998, Lit 367 pp. DM48.80. 3-8258-3093-4 [1 Sam 17-18].

2455 *Couffignal, Robert* David et Goliath: un conte merveilleux: ètude littéraiere de 1 Samuel 17 et 18,1-30. BLE 99 (1998) 431-442.

2456 *Zehnder, Markus* Exegetische Beoachtungen zu den David-Jonathan-Geschichten. Bib. 79 (1998) 153-179 [1 Sam 18-20].

2457 *Edenburg, Cynthia* How (not) to murder a king: variations on a theme in 1 Sam 24; 26. SJOT 12 (1998) 64-85.

2458 *Nicol, George G.* David, Abigail and Bathsheba, Nabal and Uriah: transformations within a triangle. SJOT 12 (1998) 130-145 [1 Sam 25; 2 Sam 11].

2459 **Kleiner, Michael** Saul in En-Dor Wahrsagung oder Totenbeschwörung?: eine...Untersuchung zu 1 Sam 28. EThSt 66: 1995 ⇒11/1,1125; 13,2476. ᴿJThS 49 (1998) 176-178 (*Murray, D.F.*).

2460 *Cortesi, Alessandro* Davide: un progetto troppo umano. Coscienza 50 (1998) 47-48.

2461 *Daube, David* Absalom and the ideal king. VT 48 (1998) 315-325.

2462 **Hentschel, Georg** 2 Samuel. NEB: 1994 ⇒10,2540; 12,2441 ᴿRivBib 46 (1998) 350-352 (*Cardellini, Innocenzo*).

2463 **Keys, Gillian** The wages of sin: a reappraisal of the 'Succession Narrative'. JSOT.S 221: 1996 ⇒12,2442; 13,2480. ᴿBib. 79 (1998) 129-131 (*Long, Burke O.*); CBQ 60 (1998) 332-333 (*Hawk, L. Daniel*).

2464 **Jiménez Hernández, E.** David: un hombre según el corazón de Dios: según la escritura y el midrash. Baracaldo 1998, Grafite 326 pp.

2465 **Landay, Jerry M.** David: power, lust and betrayal in biblical times. Berkeley 1998, Seaston xiv; 169 pp. $19. 1-5697-5159-5.

2466 **Massie, Allan** Koning David: een roman. Baarn 1998, Callenbach 256 pp. *f*35. 90-266-0677-X.

2467 *Noort, Ed* Die Philister, David und Jerusalem. ᶠBORGER R. 1998 ⇒12. 199-213.

2468 *O'Kane, Martin* The biblical king David and his artistic and literary afterlives. Biblical Interpretation 6 (1998) 313-347.

2469 **Seiler, Stefan** Die Geschichte von der Thronfolge Davids (2 Sam 9-20; 1 Kön 1-2): Untersuchungen zur Literarkritik und Tendenz. BZAW 267: B 1998, De Gruyter xv; 364 pp. DM198. 3-11-0162342.

2470 *Zenger, Erich* David as musician and poet: plotted and painted. Biblical studies. JSOT.S 266: 1998 ⇒380. 263-298.

2471 **Orji, Chukwuemeka** And Yahweh delivered David wherever he went (2Sam 8,6b.14b): composition and redaction criticsm of 2Sam 1-8. ᴰGregoriana, Extr. ᴰ*Pisano, Stephen*: R 1998, E.P.U.G. 181 pp.

2472 *Van Zyl, A.H.* Jy was baie na aan my hart (2 Sam 1:26). SeK 19 (1998) 664-675.

2473 *Herbert, Edward D.; Gordon, Robert P.* A reading in 4QSamᵃ and the murder of Abner. Textus 19 (1998) 75-80 [2 Sam 2,24].

2474   *Olyan, Saul M.* "Anyone blind or lame shall not enter the house": on the interpretation of Second Samuel 5:8b. CBQ 60 (1998) 218-227.

2475   **Murray, Donald F.** Divine prerogative and royal pretension: pragmatics, poetics and polemics in a narrative sequence about David (2 Samuel 5.17-7.29). JSOT.S 264: Shf 1998, Academic 360 pp. £50/$85. 1-85075-930-8.

2476   *Robert, Philippe de* L'avenir d'un oracle: citations et relectures bibliques de 2 Samuel 7. ETR 73 (1998) 483-490.

2477   *Knoppers, Gary N.* David's relation to Moses: the contexts, content and conditions of the Davidic promises. King and Messiah. JSOT.S 270: 1998 ⇒378. 91-118 [2 Sam 7].

2478   *Malamat, Abraham* A Mari prophecy and Nathan's dynastic oracle. Mari and the bible. 1998 [1980] ⇒173. 106-121 [2 Sam 7,1-17].

2479   *Hentschel, Georg* War Natan der Wortführer der Jebusiter?. ^FRUPPERT L. FzB 88: 1998 ⇒99. 181-208 [2Sm 7,1-17; 12,1-15; 1Kgs 1].

2480   **Pyper, Hugh S.** David as reader: 2 Samuel 12:1-15 and the poetics of fatherhood. 1996 ⇒12,2450. ^RCBQ 60 (1998) 341-342 (*White, Hugh C.*).

2481   *Rudman, Dominic* Reliving the rape of Tamar: Absalom's revenge in 2 Samuel 13. OTEs 11 (1998) 326-339.

2482   **Müllner, Ilse** Gewalt im Hause Davids: die Erzählung von Tamar und Amnon (2 Sam 13,1-22). 1997 ⇒13,2495. ^RBZ 42 (1998) 303-304 (*Fischer, Irmtraud*).

2483   *Gray, Mark* Amnon: a chip off the old block?: rhetorical strategy in 2 Samuel 13.7-15: the rape of Tamar and the humiliation of the poor. JSOT 77 (1998) 39-54.

2484   *Oren, Natan* וַתְּכַל דָּוִד הַמֶּלֶךְ לָצֵאת אֶל־אַבְשָׁלוֹם ['And the soul of King David failed with longing for Abshalom')]. Beit Mikra 153 (1998) 126-128 [2 Sam 13,39].

2485   *Althann, R.* An unrecognised repetition at 2 Samuel 15,8. JSem 9 (1997) 179-184.

2486   *Na'aman, Nadav* Ittai the Gittite. BN 94 (1998) 22-25 [2 Sam 15,13-16,14].

2487   *Hopkins, Simon* II Sam. 17:28—beds, sofas, and Hebrew lexicography. SCI 17 (1998) 1-9.

2488   *Kruger, Paul A.* "Liminality" in 2 Samuel 19:1-9: a short note. JNSL 24/2 (1998) 195-199.

2489   *Gosse, Bernard* Subversion de la législation du pentateuque et symboliques respectives des lignées de David et de Saül dans les livres de Samuel et de Ruth. ZAW 110 (1998) 34-49 [Exod 21,12-17; Dt 24,19; 25,5-10; Ruth 2,7.15; 2 Sam 21,1-14].

2490   *Marx, Alfred* Note sur la traduction et la fonction de II Samuel 22,30 // Psaume 18,30. ZAW 110 (1998) 240-243.

2491   *Gnuse, Robert* Spilt water-tales of David: (2 Sam 23,13-17) and Alexander (Arrian, Anabasis of Alexander 6.26.1-3). SJOT 12 (1998) 233-248.

E4.7 *Libri Regum:* **Solomon, Temple: 1 Kings...**

2492   *Bietenhard, Sophia* Armee und Heerführer in den Königsbüchern. RB 105 (1998) 492-519.

2493 **Galil, Gershon** The chronology of the kings of Israel and Judah. 1996 ⇒12,2467. ᴿCBQ 60 (1998) 525-527 (*Launderville, Dale*); BASOR 318 (2000) 74-76 (*Vaughn, Andrew G.*); JThS 49 (1998) 178-181 (*Mitchell, T.C.*).

2494 **House, Paul R.** 1, 2 Kings. NAC 8: 1995 ⇒11/1,1152; 13,2508 ᴿAUSS 36 (1998) 134-135 (*Treiyer, H.R.*); CBTJ 14/1 (1998) 69-70 (*Mayes, Preston*).

2495 **Knoppers, Gary N.** Two nations under God: the Deuteronomistic History of Solomon and the dual monarchies. HSM 52-53: 1993-94 ⇒9,2807...13,2521. ᴿJNES 57 (1998) 141-143 (*Thompson, T.L.*).

2496 **Linville, James Richard** Israel in the book of Kings: the past as a project of social identity. JSOT.S 272: Shf 1998, Academic 331 pp. 1-85075-859-X.

2497 ᴱ**Martínez Borobio, Emiliano** Targum Jonatán de los Profetas Primeros en tradición Babilónica III: I-II Reyes. TECC 63: M 1998, Instituto de Filología, C.S.I.C. 414 pp. 84-00-07720-2.

2498 **McGovern, B. Richard** An analysis of the relationship between idolatry and divine retribution in the account of the northern kingdom. ᴰNew Orleans Baptist Theol. Sem. 1998, 256 pp.

2499 ᵀ**Vogüé, Adalbert de** GRÉGOIRE le Grand: commentaire sur le premier livre des Rois tome III (III,38-IV,78). SC 432: P 1998, Cerf 466 pp. FF254. 2-204-06080-1.

2500 **Walsh, Jerome T.** 1 Kings. 1996 ⇒12,2465; 13,2511. ᴿBiTr 49 (1998) 355-356 (*Omanson, Roger L.*); RBBras 15 (1998) 483-484; JBL 117 (1998) 123-124 (*Nelson, Richard D.*).

2501 *Bar, Shaul* A better image for Solomon. BiTod 36 (1998) 221-226 [2 Chr 1,1-13].

2502 *Noël, Damien* Le réalisme politique dans la Bible. Cahiers de l'Atelier 477 (1998) 43-50.

2503 **Sansoni, Umberto** Il nodo di Salomone: simbolo e archetipo d'alleanza. Mi 1998, Electa 247 pp. 88-435-6390-4.

2504 **Särkiö, Pekka** Exodus und Salomo: Erwägungen zur verdeckten Salomokritik anhand von Ex 1-2; 5; 14 und 32. SESJ 71: Helsinki 1998, Finnische Exegetische Ges. iii; 185 pp. 951-9217-26-6.

2505 *Särkiö, Pekka* Salomo/Salomoschriften I: Altes Testament. TRE 29. 1998 ⇒501. 724-727.

2506 **Wälchli, Stefan** Der weise König Salomo: eine Studie zu den Erzählungen von der Weisheit Salomos in ihrem alttestamentlichen und altorientalischen Kontext. BWANT 141: Stu 1999, Kohlhammer 263 pp. 3-17-014844-3. ᴿUF 30 (1998) 932-934 (*Dietrich, Manfried*).

2507 **Barker, Margaret** On earth as it is in heaven: temple symbolism in the New Testament. 1995 ⇒11/1,1186. ᴿSJTh 51 (1998) 381-382 (*Lang, Bernhard*).

2508 *Busse, Heribert* The temple of Jerusalem and its restitution by 'Abd al-Malik b. Marwan. ᶠNARKISS, B. 1998 ⇒85. 23-33.

2509 *Davies, John A.* The *Temple Scroll* and the missing temple of the New Testament. RTR 57 (1998) 70-79.

2510 *Hurowitz, Victor Avigdor* Ascending the mountain of the Lord: a glimpse into the Solomonic temple. Capital cities. 1998 ⇒492. 215-223.

2511   *Kazovsky, Lola* Kantor PIRANESI and VILLALPANDO: the concept of
       the temple in European architectural theory. ^FNARKISS, B. 1998
       ⇒85. 226-244.
2512   King Solomon's seal. Ariel 106 (1998) 15-24.
2513   *Krieger, Klaus-Stefan* Das reinigende Feuer: die Zerstörung des
       Zweiten Tempels in der Darstellung des JOSEPHUS. BiKi 53 (1998)
       73-78.
2514   *Mendels, Doron* The temple in the Hellenistic period and in Judaism.
       ^MPRAWER J. 1998 ⇒93. 73-83.
2515   *Naredi-Rainer, Paul von* Between VATABLE and VILLAPANDO:
       aspects of postmedieval reception of the temple in Christian art.
       ^FNARKISS, B. 1998 ⇒85. 218-225.
2516   **Pasesler, Kurt** Das Tempelwort Jesu: die Traditionen von Tempel-
       zerstörung und Tempelerneuerung im Neuen Testament. Diss.
       Erlangen-Nürnberg 1996-1997. ^D*Roloff, J.* [ThRv 94,x].
2517   *Pippal, Martina* Relations of time and space: the temple of Jerusalem
       as the Domus Ecclesiae in the Carolingian period. ^FNARKISS, B. 1998
       ⇒85. 67-78.
2518   **Schmidt, Francis** O pensamento do Templo: de Jerusalém a Qum-
       ran: identidade e laço social no judaísmo antigo. Bíblica Loyola 22:
       São Paulo 1998, Loyola 280 pp. 85-15-01537-4.
2519   *Shalev-Khalifa, N.* סיפורה של משלחת פארקר—בעקבות אוצרות המקדש
       שחפרה בעיר־דוד בשנים 1909 1911 [In search of the temple treasure—
       the story of the Parker expedition in the City of David, 1909-1911].
       Qad. 31 (1998) 126-133.
2520   *Smelik, Klass A.* De weerslag van de verwoesting van de eerste
       tempel. Analecta Bruxellensia 3 (1998) 79-87.
2521   *Soucek, Priscilla* The temple after Solomon: the role of Maryam Bint
       'Imran and her Miḥrab. ^FNARKISS, B. 1998 ⇒85. 34-41.
2522   *Tomson, Peter J.* De verwoesting van de tweede tempel in de joodse
       en de christelijke overlevering. Analecta Bruxellensia 3 (1998) 88-
       102.
2523   **Volgger, David** Verbindliche Tora am einzigen Tempel: zu Motiv
       und Ort der Komposition von 1.2 Kön. ATSAT 61: St. Ottilien 1998,
       EOS (6) vi; 418 pp. 3-88096-561-7.
2524   *Weber, Annette* Ark and curtain: monuments for a Jewish nation in
       exile. ^FNARKISS, B. 1998 ⇒85. 89-99.
2525   *Weiss, Daniel H.* Haec est domus Domini firmiter edificata: the
       image of the temple in crusader art. ^FNARKISS, B. 1998 ⇒85. 210-
       217.

2526   *Van Keulen, Percy S.F.* The background of 3 Kgdms 2:46c. JNSL
       24/2 (1998) 91-110.
2527   *Rendsburg, Gary A.* The guilty party in 1 Kings III 16-28. VT 48
       (1998) 534-541.
2528   *Wénin, André* Le roi, la femme et la sagesse: une lecture de 1 Rois
       3,16-18. RTL 29 (1998) 29-45.
2529   *Kallai, Zecharia* Solomon's districts reconsidered. Biblical
       historiography. 1998 [1987] ⇒167. 92-110 [1 Kgs 4,7-17].
2530   *Hollenback, George M.* The value of Pi and the circumference of the
       'Molten Sea' in 3 Kingdoms 7,10. Bib. 79 (1998) 409-412.
2531   *Byl, John* On the capacity of Solomon's molten sea. VT 48 (1998)
       309-314 [1 Kgs 7,23-26; 2 Chr 4,2-5].

2532 *Müller, Christoph G.* Deux notes de traduction. Cahiers de Traduction Biblique 30 (1998) 16-18 [1 Kgs 7,23-26; Ps 19,5].
2533 *Viberg, Åke* 'A mantle torn is a kingdom lost': the tradition history of
a deuteronomistic theme (I Kings xi 29-31). "Lasset uns Brücken
bauen...". BEAT 42: 1998 ⇒401. 135-140.
2534 **Talshir, Zipora** The alternative story of the division of the kingdom:
3 Kingdoms 12:24a-z. JBS 6: 1993 ⇒ [R]BiOr 55 (1998) 491-494
(*Van Keulen, Percy S.F.*).

E4.8 *1 Regum 17-22*: *Elias,* **Elijah**

2535 *Boulanger Limonchy, Carlos* El arrebato de Elías al cielo: 2 Re 2.
Teologia Iusi (1998) 43-63.
2536 *Höffken, Peter* Einige Aspekte des Textes "Elia am Horeb"—1
Könige 19. BZ 42 (1998) 71-80.
2537 *Jacobson, Howard* Elijah's sleeping Baal. Bib. 79 (1998) 413.
2538 *Marx, Alfred* Mais pourquoi donc Élie a-t-il tué les prophètes de Baal
(1 Rois 18,40)?. RHPhR 78 (1998) 15-32.
2539 *Mikołajczak, Mieczysław* Samoofiarowanie Eliasza (1 Krl 17,21)
[Elias orans semetipsum offert (1 Reg 17,21)]. RBL 51 (1998) 81-87.
2540 [ET]**Minotta, Dario Maria** Sant' AMBROGIO: De Nabuthae. Oxenford
99: F 1998, Atheneum 150 pp. 88-7255-153-6.
2541 Olley, John W. YHWH and his zealous prophet: the presentation of
Elijah in 1 and 2 Kings. JSOT 80 (1998) 25-51.
2542 **Öhler, Markus** Elia im Neuen Testament: Untersuchungen zur
Bedeutung des alttestamentlichen Propheten im frühen Christentum.
BZNW 88: 1997 ⇒13,2610. [R]BZ 42 (1998) 258-261 (*Mell, Ulrich*);
JJS 49 (1998) 354-355 (*Joynes, Christine E.*).
2543 *Pienaar, D.N.* Military aspects of 1 Kings 20. "Lasset uns Brücken
bauen...". BEAT 42: 1998 ⇒401. 141-158.
2544 **Poirot, Sr. Eliane** Les prophètes Elie et Elisée dans la littérature
chrétienne ancienne. Monastica: Turnhout 1998, Brepols 644 pp.
[R]NV 74/2 (1998) 104-105 (*Borel, Jean*); POC 48 (1998) 209-210
(*Attinger, D.*).
2545 *Schilling, Klaus* Eine Stimme verschwebenden Schweigens: ganzheit-
liche Bibelarbeit zu 1 Kön 19,8-13. LS 49 (1998) 374-379.
2546 *Schnepf, Eberhard* Genista raetam: de loco refectionis Heliae
profetae. DBAT 29 (1998) 187-188.
2547 *Simian-Yofre, Horacio* Elia profeta. Dizionario di omiletica. 1998
⇒533. 432-436.
2548 **White, Marsha C.** The Elijah legends and Jehu's coup. BJSt 311:
1997 ⇒13,2616. [R]JQR 88 (1998) 337-338 (*Marcus, David*).
2549 *Zapff, Burkard M.* "Da stand ein Prophet auf wie Feuer..." (Sir 48,1):
zur Redaktionsgeschichte und Theologie des Opferwettstreits auf
dem Karmel in 1 Kön 18,19-40. [F]RUPPERT, L. FzB 88: 1998 ⇒99.
527-551.

E4.9 **2 Reg 1**...*Elisaeus, Elisha*... Ezechias, Josias

2550 *Clines, David J.A.* Regnal year reckoning in the last years of the
kingdom of Judah. OT essays, 1. JSOT.S 292: 1998 <1972> ⇒142.
395-425.

2551 *Delamarter, Steve* The vilification of Jehoiakim (A.K.A. Eliakim and Joiakim) in early Judaism. The function of scripture. 1998 ⇒236. 190-204.

2552 **Fritz, Volkmar** Das zweite Buch der Könige. ZBK.AT 10/2: Z 1998, Theologischer 155 pp. 3-290-10993-3.

2553 *Koops, Robert* 'The oil tree' and 'dove's dung': translating flora in 1-2 Kings. BiTr 49 (1998) 207-215.

2554 **Neudorfer, Heinz-Werner** Das zweite Buch der Könige. Wu 1998, Brockhaus 340 pp. 3-417-25232-6.

2555 *O'Brien, Mark A.* The portrayal of prophets in 2 Kings 2. ABR 46 (1998) 1-16.

2556 *Satterthwaite, Philip E.* The Elisha narratives and the coherence of 2 Kings 2-8. TynB 49 (1998) 1-28.

2557 *Van Veldhuizen, Piet* 2 Koningen 2:1-18. Interpretatie 6/7 (1998) 14-16 [Rom 1,17].

2558 *Zipor, Moshe A.* The cannibal women and their judgment before the helpless king (2 Kings 6:24ff.). Abr-n. 35 (1998) 84-94.

2559 *Hens-Piazza, Gina* Forms of violence and the violence of forms: two cannibal mothers before a king (2 Kings 6:24-33). JFSR 14 (1998) 91-104.

2560 *Na'aman, Nadav* Jehu son of Omri: legitimizing a loyal vassal by his overlord. IEJ 48 (1998) 236-238 [2 Kgs 9-10];

2561 Royal inscriptions and the histories of Joash and Ahaz, kings of Judah. VT 48 (1998) 333-349 [2 Kgs 11; 12,5-17; 16,10-12; 22].

2562 *Smelik, Klaas A.D.* The representation of King Ahaz in 2 Kings 16 and 2 Chronicles 28. Intertextuality. OTS 40: 1998 ⇒394. 143-185.

2563 *Schipper, Bernd Ulrich* Wer war "So', König von Ägypten" (2 Kön 17,4)?. BN 92 (1998) 71-84.

2564 *Chrostowski, Waldemar* "Nic nie zostallo, jak tylko samo pokolenie Judy" (2 Krl 17,18b)—Czy naprawde?: Zagllada Samarii i Królestwa Izraela oraz jej skutki. CoTh 68 (1998) 5-22. P.

2565 **Van Keulen, Percy S.F.** Manasseh through the eyes of the deuteronomists: the Manasseh account (2 Kings 21:1-18) and the final chapters of the deuteronomistic history. 1995 ⇒11/1,1288... 13,2631. [R]JAOS 118 (1998) 439-440 (*McKenzie, Steven L.*).

2566 *Hoppe, Leslie J.* The death of Josiah and the meaning of Deuteronomy. SBFLA 48 (1998) 31-47 [2 Kgs 22-23].

2567 *Toloni, Giancarlo* Una strage di sacerdoti?: dalla storiografia alla storia in 2 Re 23,4b-5. EstB 56 (1998) 41-60.

2568 *Gerhards, Meik* Die Begnadigung Jojachins—Überlegungen zu 2.Kön.25,27-30 (mit einem Anhang zu den Nennungen Jojachins auf Zuteilungslisten aus Babylon). BN 94 (1998) 52-67.

E5.2 *Chronicorum libri*—The books of Chronicles

2569 *Abadie, Philippe* Quelle place occupe l'exode dans le livre des Chroniques?. Cahiers de l'Atelier 482 (1998) 90-100.

2570 **Dyck, Jonathan E.** The theocratic ideology of the Chronicler. Biblical interpretation 33: Lei 1998, Brill xi, 256 pp. ƒ90/$51.50. 90-04-11146-8.

2571   ^E**Endres, J.C.** Chronicles and its synoptic parallels in Samuel, Kings, and related biblical texts. ColMn 1998, Liturgical xxiv; 356 pp. $40. 0-814-65930-6.

2572   **Fernández Marcos, Natalio; Busto Saiz, José Ramón** El texto antioqueno de la Biblia griega, 3: 1-2 Crónicas. TEstCisn 60: 1996 ⇒12,2557. ^RSef. 58 (1998) 428-430 (*Cañas Reillo, J.M.*); JThS 49 (1998) 199-201 (*Brock, Sebastian*).

2573   ^E**Gordon, R.P.** The Old Testament in Syriac: according to the peshitta version, 4: Chronicles Fasc. 2. Lei 1998, Brill xlviii; 158 pp. 90-04-10960-9.

2574   **Johnstone, William** Chronicles and Exodus: an analogy and its application. JSOT.S 275: Shf 1998, Academic 331 pp. £46/$75. 1-85075-881-6.

2575   *Kalimi, Isaac* History of interpretation: the book of Chronicles in Jewish tradition from Daniel to SPINOZA. RB 105 (1998) 5-41;

2576   Könnte die aramäische Grabinschrift aus Ägypten als Indikation für die Datierung der Chronikbücher fungieren?. ZAW 110 (1998) 79-81.

2577   *Knoppers, Gary N.* Of kings, prophets, and priests. BiTod 36 (1998) 214-220.

2578   **Kuntzmann, Raymond** La fonction prophétique en 1-2 Chroniques: du ministère de la parole au service de l'institution communautaire ^FRUPPERT, L.. FzB 88: 1998 ⇒99. 245-258.

2579   **Peltonen, Kai** History debated: the historical reliability of Chronicles in pre-critical and critical research. SESJ 64: 1996 ⇒12,2567. ^RCBQ 60 (1998) 542-543 (*Schniedewind, William M.*); JBL 117 (1998) 728-731 (*Knoppers, Gary N.*).

2580   **Riley, William** Kings and cultus in Chronicles: worship and the reinterpretation of history. JSOT.S 160: 1993 ⇒9,2877... 12,2570 ^RIThQ 63 (1998) 96-97 (*McConvery, Brendan*).

2581   **Weinberg, Joel** Der Chronist in seiner Mitwelt. BZAW 239: 1996 ⇒12,2573. ^RBiOr 55 (1998) 245-247 (*Dirksen, P.B.*); CBQ 60 (1998) 134-135 (*Greifenhagen, F.V.*).

2582   *Wright, John W.* The founding father: the structure of the Chronicler's David narrative. JBL 117 (1998) 45-59.

2583   *Steiner, Richard C.* Bitte-Ya, daughter of Pharao (1 Chr 4,18), and Bint(i)-'Anat, daughter of Ramesses II. Bib. 79 (1998) 394-408.

2584   *Williams, P.J.* The LXX of 1 Chronicles 5:1-2 as an exposition of Genesis 48-49. TynB 49 (1998) 369-371.

2585   *Müller, Walter W.* Zum biblischen Personennamen Bimhal (1 Chr 7,33). BN 91 (1998) 12-15.

2586   *Dirksen, Piet B.* 1 Chronicles 9,26-33: its position in chapter 9. Bib. 79 (1998) 91-96.

2587   *Beentjes, Pancratius C.* Transformations of space and time: Nathan's oracle and David's prayer in 1 Chronicles 17. Sanctity of time. 1998 ⇒303. 27-44.

2588   *Kelly, Brian E.* David's disqualification in 1 Chronicles 22.8: a response to Piet B. DIRKSEN. JSOT 80 (1998) 53-61.

2589   *Toloni, Giancarlo* La funzione sintattica ed il significato di διαδεχομέμους in 1 Cr 26,18b. BeO 40 (1998) 99-109.

2590   *Dirksen, Peter B.* The composition of 1 Chronicles 26:20-32. JNSL 24/2 (1998) 145-155.

2591 *Klein, Ralph, W.* Prophets and prophecy in the books of Chronicles. BiTod 36 (1998) 227-232 [2 Chr 1,1-13].

2592 *Dempsey, Deirdre Ann* The ark and the temple in 1 and 2 Chronicles. BiTod 36 (1998) 233-239 [2 Chr 1,1-13].

2593 **Fries, Joachim** "Im Dienst am Hause des Herrn": literaturwissenschaftliche Untersuchungen zu 2 Chr 29-31: zur Hiskijatradition in Chronik. ATSAT 60: St. Ottilien 1998, EOS xv; 427 pp. 3-88096-560-9.

2594 *Halpern, Baruch* Why Manasseh is blamed for the Babylonian exile: the evolution of a biblical tradition. VT 48 (1998) 473-514 [2 Chr 33,12-19].

2595 *Van der Kooij, Arie* The death of Josiah according to 1 Esdras. Textus 19 (1998) 97-109 [2 Chr 35,20-25].

E5.4 *Esdrae libri*—Ezra, Nehemiah

2596 *Abadie, Philippe* Le livre d'Esdras: un midrash de l'Exode?. Transeuphratène 14 (1998) 19-31.

2597 **Becker, Joachim** Der Ich-Bericht des Nehemiabuches als chronistische Gestaltung. FzB 87: Wü 1998, Echter 121 pp. 3-429-02012-3.

2598 *Becking, Bob* Ezra on the move .... trends and perspectives on the character and his book. [F]VAN DER WOUDE, A. VT.S 73: 1998 ⇒121. 154-179.

2599 *Bergren, Theodore A.* Ezra and Nehemiah square off in the apocrypha and pseudepigrapha. Biblical figures. [E]**Stone, M.** 1998 ⇒K1.1. 340-365 [Sir 44-50; 2 Macc 1,10-2,18].

2600 **Brown, Raymond Edward** The message of Nehemiah: God's servant in a time of change. The Bible Speaks Today: [Nottingham] 1998, IVP 256 pp. 0-85111-580-2.

2601 *Clines, David J.A.* The force of the text: a response to Tamara C. ESKENAZI's 'Ezra-Nehemiah: from text to actuality'. OT essays, 1. JSOT.S 292: 1998 <1989> ⇒142. 351-367.

2602 *Garbini, Giovanni* La figura di Esdra nella letteratura e nella storia. RstB 10/1-2 (1998) 59-67.

2603 **Grabbe, Lester L.** Ezra-Nehemiah. OT readings: L 1998, Routledge x; 209 pp. £15. 0-415-14153-6.

2604 *Grabbe, Lester L.* Triumph of the pious or failure of the xenophobes?: the Ezra-Nehemiah reforms and their Nachgeschichte. Jewish local patriotism. JSPE.S 31: 1998 ⇒414. 50-65.

2605 *Marcus, David* Is the book of Nehemiah a translation from Aramaic?. [F]GORDON, C. JSOT.S 273: 1998 ⇒31. 103-110.

2606 **Schunck, Klaus-Dietrich** Nehemia. BKAT 23/2, Fasc. 1: Neuk 1998, Neuk 1-80 pp. 3-7887-1611-8.

2607 *Sérandour, Arnaud* A propos des calendriers des livres d'Esdras et de Néhémie. [F]MARGAIN, J. 1998 ⇒71. 281-289.

2608 *Steins, Georg* Das Esra-Nehemia-Buch (Teil 1): Annäherungen;
2609 (Teil 2/3): der wiedergewonnene Anfang;
2610 (Teil 4): Tora und Leben. BiLi 71 (1998) 33-37/260-263/360-363.

2611 **Van Wijk-Bos, Johanna W.H.** Ezra, Nehemiah, and Esther. Westminster Bible companion: LVL 1998, Westminster x; 147 pp. 0-664-25597-3.

2612 *Zadok, Ran* On the relibility of the genealogical and prosopo-graphical lists of the Israelites in the Old Testament. TelAv 25 (1998) 228-254.

2613 *Van Wyk, W.C.* The enemies in Ezra 1-6: interaction between text and reader. JSem 8 (1996) 34-48.

2614 *Fleishman, Joseph* An echo of optimism in Ezra 6:19-22. HUCA 69 (1998) 15-29.

2615 *Heltzer, Michael* The right of Ezra to demand obedience to "the laws of the king" from gentiles of the V satrapy (Ez. 7: 25-26). ZAR 4 (1998) 192-196.

2616 *Van Grol, Harm W.M.* Exegesis of the exile—exegesis of scripture?: Ezra 9:6-9. Intertextuality. OTS 40: 1998 ⇒394. 31-61.

2617 *Newman, Judith H.* Nehemiah 9 and the scripturalization of prayer in the second temple period. The function of scripture. 1998 ⇒236. 112-123.

2618 *Janzen, J. Gerald* Nehemiah ix and the Aqedah. "Lasset uns Brücken bauen...". BEAT 42: 1998 ⇒401. 311-314.

2619 *Clines, David J.A.* Nehemiah 10 as an example of early Jewish bibli-cal exegesis. OT essays, 1. JSOT.S 292: 1998 <1981> ⇒142. 88-94.

2620 *Andrews, Isolde* Being open to the vision: a study from Fourth Ezra. JLT 12 (1998) 231-241.

2621 *Nápole, Gabriel* Liber Ezrae Quartus: estudio de la obra, y traduc-ción a partir de la versión latina. EsVe 28 (1998) 7-193.

2622 *Pezzoli-Olgiati, Daria* Im Spannungsfeld zwischen Weltende und Offenbarung: apokalyptische Zeitmodelle. Zukunft unter Zeitdruck: auf den Spuren 'Apokalypse'. Z 1998, Theologischer. 11-32 [4 Esd.].

2623 *Schmid, Konrad* Esras Begegnung mit Zion: die Deutung der Zerstö-rung Jerusalems im 4. Esrabuch und das Problem des "bösen Her-zens". JSJ 29 (1998) 261-277.

2624 *Nuvolone, Flavio G.* Valeur ajoutée pour investissements bibliogra-phiques 'apocryphes' (*Visio Esdrae B*, 95-96). Nomen latinum: mé-langes offerts au prof. André SCHNEIDER. ᴱKnoepfler, Denis. Univ. de Neuchâtel, recueil de travaux...44: Genève 1997, Droz 181-190.

2625 **Bergren, Theodore A.** Sixth Ezra: the text and origin. NY 1998, OUP xiv; 282 pp. $50. 0-19-511201-6.

E5.5 Libri Tobiae, Judith, Esther

2626 ᴱ**Brenner, Athalya** A feminist companion to Esther, Judith and Susanna. Feminist Companion to the Bible 7: 1995 ⇒11/1,1343; 12,2601. ᴿRStR 24 (1998) 339-340 (*Humphreys, W. Lee*).
        Caso, Ángeles Los libros de Ruth, Judit y Ester ⇒2411.
        Mesters, C. Historias de Rut, Judit y Ester 1996 ⇒2415.

2627 Tobit. BVLI 42 (1998) 23-24.

2628 **Fregni, G.** Tobi e Sara: itinerario di fede per giovani sposi. Bo 1998, EDB 126 pp. L13.000.

2629 *Soll, Will* The family as scriptural and social construct in Tobit. The function of scripture. 1998 ⇒236. 166-175.

2630 *Bogaert, Pierre-Maurice* Judith. RAC 147. 1998 ⇒495. 245-258.
2631 Judith. BVLI 42 (1998) 24-25.
2632 *Gabriella del Signore* Giuditta e Achior: il futuro nelle mani dei deboli. Horeb 19 (1998) 36-42.
2633 ᴱ**Griffith, Mark** Judith. Exeter Medieval English Texts and Studies: Exeter 1997, Univ. of Exeter Press xiv; 223 pp. $19.
2634 *Piras, Antonio* Il testo di Giuditta 9,2-19 (9,2-14 LXX) in Lucifero di Cagliari. Theologica & Historica 7 (1998) 85-119.
2635 **Stocker, Margarita** Judith, sexual warrior: women and power in western culture. NHv 1998, Yale University Press 278 pp. £25. 0-300-07365-8.
2636 *Vílchez, José* Judit, prototipo de mujer. Proyección 45 (1998) 315-320.

2637 **Arzt, Silvia** 'Ich finde, daß sehr großer Mut dazugehört, in dieser Zeit einem Mann nicht zu gehorchen: noch dazu dem König': die geschlechtsspezifische Rezeption biblischer Erzählungen exemplifiziert an einer exegetischen, wirkungsgeschichtlichen, rezeptionsästhetischen und empirischen Untersuchung zur Erzählung vom Widerstand der Waschti in Ester 1. ᴰSalzburg 1996-1997, ᴰ*Bucher, A.* [ThRv 94,xviii].
2638 *Arzt, Silvia* Ist Widerstand von Frauen Kindern zumutbar?: Einblicke in die Wirkungsgeschichte von Ester 1 in Kinderbibeln. PzB 7 (1998) 122-126.
2639 *Bush, Frederic W.* The book of Esther: opus non gratum in the christian canon. BBR 8 (1998) 39-54.
    Bush, Frederic William Ruth, Esther 1996 ⇒2410.
2640 *Butting, Klara* Das Buch Ester: vom Widerstand gegen Antisemitismus und Sexismus. Kompendium Feministische Bibelauslegung ᴱ**Schottroff, L.**: 1998 ⇒H8.9. 169-179.
2641 *Clines, David J.A.* In quest of the historical Mordecai <1991>;
2642 Reading Esther from left to right: contemporary strategies for reading a biblical text <1990>. OT essays, 1. JSOT.S 292: 1998 ⇒142. 436-443/3-22.
2643 **Craig, Kenneth M.** Reading Esther. 1995 ⇒11/1,1366... 13,2705. ᴿRStR 24 (1998) 336-338 (*Humphreys, W. Lee*); JBL 117 (1998) 346-348 (*Day, Linda*).
2644 **Day, Linda** Three faces of a queen: characterization in... Esther. JSOT.S 186: 1995 11/1,1367; 13,2706. ᴿJAOS 118 (1998) 93-94 (*Berlin, Adele*); RStR 24 (1998) 338-339 (*Humphreys, W. Lee*).
2645 ᵀ**Ego, Beate** Targum Scheni zu Ester. TSAJ 54: 1996 ⇒⇒12,2618. ᴿSal. 60 (1998) 160-161 (*Vicent, R.*).
2646 *Friedman, Shamma* מחיקת המן [Erasing Haman]. Leš. 61 (1998) 259-263.
2647 **Grossfeld, Bernard** The targum Sheni to the book of Esther. 1994 ⇒10,2827; 12,2619. ᴿJSSt 43 (1998) 385-387 (*Beattie, D.R.G.*).
2648 *Humphreys, W. Lee* The story of Esther in its several forms: recent studies. RStR 24 (1998) 335-342.
2649 *Jobes, Karen H.* How an assassination changed the Greek text of Esther. ZAW 110 (1998) 75-78.
2650 **Jobes, Karen Hill** The Alpha-Text of Esther. SBL.DS 153: 1996 ⇒13,2712. ᴿJSSt 43 (1998) 172-175 (*Kahana, Hanna*).

2651 **Laniak, Timothy S.** Shame and honor in the book of Esther. SBL.DS 165: Atlanta, GA 1998, Scholars xiii; 205 pp. $35. 0-7885-0505-X.
2652 **Levenson, Jon D.** Esther. 1997 ⇒13,2714. ᴿRStR 24 (1998) 340-342 (*Humphreys, W. Lee*); CBQ 60 (1998) 534-535 (*Day, Linda*).
2653 **Steck, Odil Hannes; Kratz, Reinhard Gregor; Kottsieper, Ingo** Das Buch Baruch; der Brief des Jeremia; Zusätze zu Ester und Daniel. ATD. Apokryphen 5: Gö 1998, Vandenhoeck & R 328 pp. DM68. 3-525-51405-0. ᴿEstAg 33 (1998) 377-378 (*Mielgo, C.*).
   Vílchez Líndez, José Rut y Ester 1998 ⇒2420.
2654 *Wechsler, Michael G.* The Purim-Passover connection: a reflection of Jewish exegetical tradition in the Peshitta book of Esther. JBL 117 (1998) 321-327.

E5.8 *Machabaeorum libri,* 1-2[3-4] Maccabees

2655 *Bar-Kochva, Bezalel* תיאור קרב בית־זכריה: המצאה ספרותית או מציאות היסטורית? [The description of the battle of Beth Zacharia—literary fiction or historical fact?]. Cathedra 86 (1998) 7-22 [1 Macc 6,28-47].
2656 **Bartlett, John R.** 1 Maccabees. Guides to Apocrypha & Pseudepigrapha: Shf 1998, Academic 111 pp. 1-85075-763-1.
2657 *Boschi, Bernardo Gianluigi* I Maccabei: confronto e conflitto culturale. RstB 10/1-2 (1998) 105-127.
2658 *Brenk, Frederick E.* Jerusalem—Hierapolis: the revolt under Antiochos IV Epiphanes in the light of evidence for Hierapolis of Phrygia, Babylon, and other cities. Relighting the souls: studies in Plutarch, Greek literature, religion, and philosophy and in the New Testament background. Stu 1998, Steiner 420 pp. 3-515-07158-X. 354-393.
2659 *Carneiro Lopes, Paulo César* Literatura: Macabéa, Macabeus e as metáforas da resistência. Vozes 92 (1998) 121-136.
2660 *Rappaport, U.* A note on the use of the bible in 1 Maccabees. Biblical perspectives. StTDJ 28: 1998 ⇒441. 175-179.
2661 *Schwartz, Daniel R.* The other in 1 and 2 Maccabees. Tolerance. 1998 ⇒440. 30-37.
2662 *Volgger, David* 1 Makk 1: der Konflikt zwischen Hellenen und Juden—die makkabäische Reichspropaganda. Anton. 73 (1998) 459-481.

2663 *Gerber, Christine* Das zweite Makkabäerbuch: was die Geschichte lehrt. Kompendium Feministische Bibelauslegung. ᴱ**Schottroff, L.**: 1998 ⇒H8.9. 392-400.
2664 *Himmelfarb, Martha* Judaism and Hellenism in 2 Maccabees. Poetics Today 19 (1998) 19-40.
2665 *Mendels, Doron* A note on the tradition of Antiochus IV's death. Identity. JSPE.S 24: 1998 <1981> ⇒174. 352-356 [2 Macc 1,13-16; 9,5-27].
2666 *Schwartz, Daniel R.* On something biblical about 2 Maccabees. Biblical perspectives. StTDJ 28: 1998 ⇒441. 223-232.

2667 **DeSilva, David A.** 4 Maccabees. Guides to Apocrypha & Pseudepigrapha: Shf 1998, Academic 173 pp. £9/$15. 1-85075-896-4.

2668 *Moore, Stephen D.; Anderson, Janice Capel* Taking it like a man: masculinity in 4 Maccabees. JBL 117 (1998) 249-273.

VI. Libri didactici VT

E6.1 *Poesis metrica,* **Biblical** and Semitic **versification**

2669 **Cross, Frank M.; Freedman, David Noel** Studies in ancient Yahwistic poetry. 1997 ⇒13,2736. ROTEs 11 (1998) 196-7 [Afrikaans] (*Nel, P.J.*); LASBF 48 (1998) 586-588 (*Niccacci, Alviero*).

2670 **Fokkelman, Johannes Petrus** Major poems of the Hebrew Bible: at the interface of hermeneutics and structural analysis. SSN 37: [Assen] 1998, Van Gorcum vii; 206 pp. *f*140; $70. 90-232-3367-0.

2671 *Hobbs, Gerald* Connaissances bibliques, religion populaire: les premiers psaumes versifiés de la réforme à Strasbourg 1524-1527. RHPhR 78 (1998) 415-433.

2672 **Korpel, Marjo Christina Annette; Moor, Johannes C. de** The structure of classical Hebrew poetry: Isaiah 40-55. OTS 41: Lei 1998, Brill xi; 752 pp. $212. 90-04-11261-8.

2673 *Kuntz, J. Kenneth* Biblical Hebrew poetry in recent research, part I. CurResB 6 (1998) 31-64.

2674 *Sivan, Daniel; Yona, Shamir* Pivot words or expressions in Biblical Hebrew and in Ugaritic poetry. VT 48 (1998) 399-407.

2675 *Spreafico, Ambrogio* Nahum i 10 and Isaiah i 12-13: double-duty modifier. VT 48 (1998) 104-110.

2676 *Tropper, Josef* Sprachliche Archaismen im Parallelismus membrorum in der akkadischen und ugaritischen Epik. AulOr 16 (1998) 103-110.

2677 **Vance, Donald Richard** Toward a poetics of Biblical Hebrew poetry: the question of meter. DIliff 1998, 533 pp.

2678 *Van Rensburg, J.F.J.* A numerical characterization of poetical lines, statistical theory and Young Babylonian application. JSem 9 (1997) 39-47.

2679 *Wachter, Rudolf* 'Oral poetry' in ungewohntem Kontext: Hinweise auf mündliche Dichtungstechnik in den pompejanischen Wandinschriften. ZPE 121 (1998) 73-89.

2680 *Watson, W.G.E.* a poesía fenicia y púnica. AulOr 16 (1998) 281-283.

2681 *Young, Ian* The "archaic" poetry of the Pentateuch in the MT, Samaritan Pentateuch and 4QExodc. Abr-n. 35 (1998) 74-83.

E6.2 **Psalmi, textus**

2682 **Alonso Schökel, Luis** Salmi e cantici. 1996 ⇒12,2664. RCivCatt 149/1 (1998) 204-205 (*Scaiola, D.*).

2683 **Boese, Helmut** Psalmen 101-150. Anonymi Glosa Psalmorum ex traditione seniorum, 2. AGLB 25: 1994 ⇒10,2905. RPIBA 21 (1998) 114-118 (*McNamara, Martin*).

2684 *Chazelle, Celia* Archbishops Ebo and Hincmar of Reims and the Utrecht Psalter. Approaches to early-medieval art. ENees, **Lawrence**: CM 1998, The Medieval Academy of America. 97-119.

2685   **Cotter, Jim** Psalms for a pilgrim people. Harrisburg, PA 1998, Morehouse 352 pp.
2686   *Ferguson, Thomas S.* Africana Psalm collects and the "Psalter of Charlemagne": African or Carolingian?. RBen 108 (1998) 44-57.
2687   *Flint, Peter W.* The book of Psalms in the light of the Dead Sea Scrolls. VT 48 (1998) 453-472.
2688   *Gneuss, H.* A newly found fragment of an Anglo-Saxon psalter. Anglo-Saxon England 27 (1998) 273-287.
2689   *Lentes, Thomas* Text des Kanons und Heiliger Text: der Psalter im Mittelalter. ^FLOHFINK, N. 1998 ⇒64. 323-354.
2690   *McNamara, Martin* Some affiliations of the St Columba series of psalm headings: a preliminary study (part I). PIBA 21 (1998) 87-111.
2691   ^T**Rondoni, Davide** Poesia dell'uomo e di Dio: i salmi. I rombi 11: Genova 1998, Marietti xvii; 228 pp. 88-211-6305-9.
2692   ^T**Stadler, Alisa** Die Psalmen. Ill. von *Elke Staller*. Innsbruck 1998, Tyrolia 264 pp. ÖS348.

E6.3 Psalmi, introductio

2693   ^E**Alonso Schökel, Luis** Salmos y cánticos. Bilbao 1998, Mensajero 351 pp. 84-271-2183-0.
2694   *Clines, David J.A.* Psalm research since 1955: II, the literary genres. OT essays, 2. JSOT.S 293: 1998 <1969> ⇒142. 665-686.
2695   *Gilbert, Maurice* Les Psaumes. Il a parlé par les prophètes. 1998 ⇒155. 249-287.
2696   **Gunkel, Hermann** An introduction to the psalms: the genres of the religious lyric of Israel. Mercer Library of Biblical Studies: Macon, GA 1998, Mercer Univ. Pr. ix; 388 pp. $45. 0-86554-579-0.
2697   **Mello, A.** L'arpa a dieci corde: introduzione al Salterio. Spiritualità biblica: Magnano (Biella) 1998, Qiqajon 199 pp. L25.000. ^RLASBF 48 (1998) 573-575 (*Cortese, Enzo*).
2698   *Olędzka-Frybesowa, Aleksandra* Psalmy w ikonografii Wschodu i Zachodu [Les psaumes dans l'iconographie de l'Orient et de l'Occident]. PrzPow 115 (1998) 199-210.
2699   *Scaiola, Donatella* La lettura dei salmi: testi, tendenze, prospettive. RCI 79 (1998) 33-43.
2700   *Seybold, Klaus* Beiträge zur Psalmenforschung der 70er Jahre <1981>;
2701   Beiträge zur Psalmenforschung der jüngsten Zeit. Studien zur Psalmenauslegung <1996>. 1998 ⇒201. 9-26/46-74.
2702   *Stadelmann, Luís* Método exegético para intepretar os salmos. PerTeol 30 (1998) 421-430.
2703   **Tromp, Nico** Woorden die wegen wijzen: zin zoeken in de psalmen. Averbode 1998, Altiora 359 pp. 90-304-0935-5.
2704   **Wendland, E.** Analyzing the Psalms: with exercises for Bible students and translators. WL 1998, Eisenbrauns 235 pp. $18.
2705   **Whybray, R. Norman** Reading the psalms as a book. JSOT.S 222: 1996 ⇒12,2693; 13,2787. ^RStPat 45 (1998) 520-521 (*Lorenzin, Tiziano*); ThZ 54 (1998) 167-168 (*Weber, Beat*).
2707   **Zenger, Erich** Dein Angesicht suche ich: neue Psamenauslegungen. FrB 1998, Herder 184 pp. DM29.80. 3-451-26668-7.

E6.4 Psalmi, commentarii

2708 [TE]**Alobaidi, Joseph** Le commentaire des Psaumes par le qaraïte Salmon BEN YERUHAM: Psaumes 1-10. 1996 ⇒12,2695. [R]Henoch 20 (1998) 377-378 (*Chiesa, Bruno*).

2709 **Creach, Jerome Frederick Davis** Psalms. Interpretation Bible studies: LVL 1998, Geneva vii; 106 pp. $7. 0-664-50021-8.

2710 **Davidson, Robert** The vitality of worship: a commentary on the book of Psalms. GR 1998, Eerdmans ix; 484 pp. 0-8028-4246-1.

2711 **Fiedrowicz, Michael** Psalmus vox totius Christi: Studien zu AUGUSTINs 'Enarrationes in Psalmos'. 1997 ⇒13,2799. [R]Anuario de Historia de la Iglesia 7 (1998) 482-483 (*Ramos-Lissón, D.*); EstAg 33 (1998) 610-611 (*Luis, P. de*); ThPh 73 (1998) 275-277 (*Sieben, H.J.*).

2712 **Fisher, John (St.)** Exposition of the Seven Penitential Psalms. San Francisco 1998, Ignatius xxxvii; 284 pp. $15. 0-89870-622-X.

2713 **Girard, Marc** Les psaumes redécouverts: de la structure au sens. 1996 ⇒65,2642...13,2802. [R]BZ 42 (1998) 310-312 (*Zenger, Erich*); CBQ 60 (1998) 329-331 (*Culley, Robert C.*).

2714 **Goulder, Michael D.** Studies in the psalter, IV: the psalms of the return (Book V, Psalms 107-150). JSOT.S 258: Shf 1998, Academic 352 pp. $85. 1-85075-866-2.

2715 [T]**Gruber, Mayer Irvin** RASHI's commentary on Psalms 1-89 (Books I-III): with English translation, introduction and notes. SFSHJ 161: Atlanta, GA 1998, Scholars xiv, 448, 48, x pp. 0-7885-0435-5.

2716 **Harman, Allan** Commentary on the Psalms. Fearn 1998, Christian Focus 454 pp. £25.

2717 *Jamourlian, Serop* Un bref aperçu sur le 'Commentaire des Psaumes' de Nerses LAMBRONATZI. Bazmavep 156 (1998) 60-72.

2718 **Lifschitz, Daniel** É tempo di cantare: il grande salterio. Testi e commenti 9, 10: Bo 1998, EDB lxv; 185; ix; 395 pp. L27.000 + 39.000. 88-10-20595-2; -8-7.

2719 *Seybold, Klaus* Psalmenkommentare 1972-1994. Studien zur Psalmenauslegung. 1998 <1995> ⇒201. 27-45.

2720 *Taylor, David G.K.* The manuscript tradition of DANIEL of Ṣalaḥ's Psalm commentary. Symposium Syriacum VII. 1998 ⇒415. 49-59.

2721 Salmos 101-150. Santo AGOSTINHO: comentário aos salmos (Enarrationes in psalmos). Trad. pelas monjas Beneditinas do Mosteiro de Maria Mãe de Cristo. Patristica 9/3: São Paulo 1998, Paulus 1172 pp. [R]RBBras 15 (1998) 573-577 [3 vols ⇒13,2807].

E6.5 Psalmi, themata

2722 **Bader, Günter** Psalterium affectuum palaestra: Prolegomena zu einer Theologie des Psalters. HUTh 33: 1996 ⇒12,2719; 13,2813 [R]EL 112 (1998) 405-407 (*Raffa, Vincenzo*).

2723 *Bail, Ulrike* Die Psalmen: "Who is speaking may be all that matters". Kompendium Feministische Bibelauslegung. [E]**Schottroff, L.**: 1998 ⇒H8.9. 180-191.

2724 *Botha, P.J.* The 'Enthronement Psalms': a claim to the world-wide honour of Yahweh. OTEs 11 (1998) 24-39.

2725 **Cho, Yong Kyu** The Hallelujah Psalms in the context of the Hebrew Psalter. [D]Southern Baptist Theol. Sem. 1998, 242 pp.

2726 *Clines, David J.A.* The Psalms and the king. OT essays, 2. JSOT.S
293: 1998 <1975> ⇒142. 687-700.
2727 **Conti, Martino** Presente e futuro dell'uomo nei salmi sapienziali.
SPAA 34: R 1998, Pont. Athenaeum Antonianum 392 pp. L50.000.
88-7257-033-6.
2728 *Corrigan, K.* The 'Jewish satyr' in the 9th century Byzantine psalters.
Hellenic and Jewish arts. 1998 ⇒439. 351-368.
2729 **Corwin, Christopher Mark** The wisdom psalm classification problem. ᴰGraduate Theological Union 1998, 199 pp.
2730 **Creach, Jerome F.D.** Yahweh as refuge and the editing of the
Hebrew psalter. JSOT.S 217: 1996 ⇒12,2733. ᴿStPat 45/2 (1998)
521-522 (*Lorenzin, Tiziano*).
2731 *Creach, Jerome* The shape of book four of the Psalter and the shape
of Second Isaiah. JSOT 80 (1998) 63-76.
2732 **Emmendörffer, Michael** Der ferne Gott: eine Untersuchung der alttestamentlichen Volksklagelieder vor dem Hintergrund der
mesopotamischen Literatur. FAT 21: Tü 1998, Mohr x; 328 pp.
DM168. 3-16-146773-6.
2733 *Fujita, Neil S.* Sacred space in the Psalms. BiTod 36 (1998) 371-376.
2734 *Gerstenberger, Erhard S.* Christliche Psalmenlektüre?. ᶠSCHRAGE,
W. 1998 ⇒101. 43-54.
2735 *Gillingham, S.E.* The Messiah in the Psalms: a question of reception
history and the Psalter. King and Messiah. JSOT.S 270: 1998 ⇒378.
209-237.
2736 **Goulder, Michael D.** Studies in the Psalter, 3: the psalms of Asaph
and the pentateuch. JSOT.S 233: 1996 ⇒12,2746. ᴿThZ 54 (1998)
169-171 (*Weber, Beat*); JBL 117 (1998) 523-524 (*Schniedewind,
William M.*).
2737 **Grelot, Pierre** Le mystère du Christ dans les Psaumes. CJJC 74: P
1998, Desclée 292 pp. FF150. 2-7189-0944-7.
2738 *Grossberg, Daniel* The literary treatment of nature in Psalms
ᶠGORDON, C. JSOT.S 273: 1998 ⇒31. 69-87.
2739 *Hossfeld, Frank-Lothar* Das Prophetische in den Psalmen: zur Got-
tesrede der Asafpsalmen im Vergleich mit der des ersten und zweiten
Davidpsalters. ᶠRUPPERT, L. FzB 88: 1998 ⇒99. 223-243.
2740 *Hossfeld, Frank-Lothar* Die unterschiedlichen Profile der beiden
Davidsammlungen Ps 3-41 und Ps 51-72. ᶠLOHFINK, N. 1998 ⇒64.
59-73.
2741 *Hunter, J.H.* Theophany verses in the Hebrew psalms. OTEs 11
(1998) 255-270.
2742 *Irsigler, H.* Quest for justice as reconciliation of the poor and the
righteous in Psalms 37, 49 and 73. SeK 19 (1998) 584-604.
2743 *Janowski, Bernd* Die "Kleine Biblia": zur Bedeutung der Psalmen für
eine Theologie des Alten Testaments. ᶠLOHFINK, N. 1998 ⇒64. 381-
420.
2744 **Jinkins, Michael** In the house of the Lord: inhabiting the psalms of
lament. ColMn 1998, Liturgical x; 142 pp. $13. 0-8146-2494-4.
2745 *Lombaard, C.J.S.* Some remarks on the patriarchs in the Psalms.
OTEs 11 (1998) 59-70.
2746 *Löning, Karl* Die Funktion des Psalters im Neuen Testament. ᶠLOH-
FINK, N. 1998 ⇒64. 269-295.
2747 *Marlowe, W. Creighton* Music of missions: themes of outreach in the
psalms. Miss. 26 (1998) 445-456.

2748 *McNamara, Martin* Christology and the interpretation of the Psalms in the early Irish church. Studies in patristic christology. 1998 ⇒412. 196-233.

2749 *Millard, Matthias* Zum Problem des elohistischen Psalters: Überlegungen zum Gebrauch von יהוה und אלהים im Psalter. [F]LOHFINK, N. 1998 ⇒64. 75-100.

2750 *Miller, Patrick D.* The end of the Psalter: a response to Erich ZENGER. JSOT 80 (1998) 103-110.

2751 *Müller, Hans-Peter* Punische Weihinschriften und alttestamentliche Psalmen im religionsgeschichtlichen Zusammenhang. Or. 67 (1998) 477-496.

2752 *Nel, Philip J.* The theology of the Royal Psalms. OTEs 11 (1998) 71-92.

2753 **Pedersen, Kirsten Stofregen** Traditional Ethiopian exegesis of the book of Psalms. ÄthF 36: 1995 ⇒12,2762. [R]JSSt 43 (1998) 163-165 (*Ullendorff, Edward*).

2754 *Plantin, Henry* Psalmöverskrifternas omtolkning i Septuaginta-Psaltaren. SEÅ 63 (1998) 41-60.

2755 **Polster, Ronald B.** Evil and the biblical discourse of lament. [D]Toronto 1998, 221 pp.

2756 **Riede, Peter** Im Netz des Jägers: Bilder von Bedrängnis und Schutz in den Individualpsalmen des Alten Testaments. Diss. Münster 1998. [D]*Janowski, B.* vi; 420 pp [ThLZ 124,244].

2757 *Schaper, Joachim* Der Septuaginta-Psalter: Interpretation, Aktualisierung und liturgische Verwendung der biblischen Psalmen im hellenistischen Judentum. [F]LOHFINK, N. 1998 ⇒64. 165-183.

2758 **Schneider-Flume, Gunda** Glaubenserfahrung in den Psalmen: Leben in der Geschichte mit Gott. BTSP 15: Gö 1998, Vandenhoeck & R 172 pp. DM29.80. 3-525-61360-1.

2759 *Schroer, Silvia* 'Under the shadow of your wings': the metaphor of God's wings in the Psalms, Exodus 19.4, Deuteronomy 32.11 and Malachi 3.20, as seen through the perspectives of feminism and the history of religion. Wisdom and psalms. 1998 ⇒221. 264-282.

2760 *Schröer, Henning* Gott ist mein Psalm: Teilhabe und Freigabe: der christlich-jüdische Dialog in rezeptionsästhetischer Sicht am Beispiel der Psalmen. [F]SCHRAGE, W. 1998 ⇒101. 55-64.

2761 *Seybold, Klaus* Das 'wir' in den Asaph-Psalmen: spezifische Probleme einer Psalmgruppe <1994>;

2762 In der Angst noch Hoffnung: drei persönliche Zeugnisse aus den Psalmen. Studien zur Psalmenauslegung. 1998 ⇒201. 231-243/288-304.

2763 *Stemberger, Günter* Psalmen in Liturgie und Predigt der rabbinischen Zeit. [F]LOHFINK, N. 1998 ⇒64. 199-213.

2764 **Tanner, Beth LaNeel** Reading between the lines: the book of Psalms and intertextuality. [D]Princeton Theol. Sem. 1998, 239 pp.

2765 *Van Rooy, H.F.* The message of a number [of] psalms as interpreted in Syriac psalm headings. SeK 19 (1998) 653-663.

2766 *Vegas Montaner, Luis* Discoursive texts and perfect tense in Psalms. Bible et informatique. 1998 ⇒386. 137-160.

2767 *Zenger, Erich* Der Psalter als Buch: Beobachtungen zu seiner Entstehung, Komposition und Funktion. [F]LOHFINK, N. 1998 ⇒64. 1-57;

2768 The composition and theology of the fifth book of Psalms, Psalms 107-145. JSOT 80 (1998) 77-102.

E6.6 *Psalmi: oratio, liturgia*—Psalms as prayer

2769 **Alonso Schökel, Luis** O Espírito Santo e os Salmos: Salmos e exercícios. São Paulo 1998, Loyola 182 pp. 85-15-01755-X.

2770 *Brettler, Marc Zvi* Women and Psalms: toward an understanding of the role of women's prayer in the Israelite cult. Gender and law. JSOT.S 262: 1998 ⇒256. 25-56.

2771 **Chittister, Joan** The Psalms: new reflections on the psalms for every day of the year. NY 1998, Crossroad 142 pp. £9. 0-8245-1748-2.

2772 *Clines, David J.A.* Psalm research since 1955: I, the Psalms and the cult. OT essays, 2. JSOT.S 293: 1998 <1967> ⇒142. 639-664.

2773 **Dawn, Marva J.** I'm lonely, LORD—how long?: meditations on the Psalms. GR 1998, Eerdmans 240 pp. $15.

2774 **Dollen, Charles J.** Prayer book of the kings: the Psalms. NY 1998, Alba 280 pp. $17. 0-8189-0751-7.

2775 **Fenz, Augustinus Kurt** 'Mein ganzes Glück bist Du!' (Ps 16,2): Psalmenmeditationen—Schritte zur Vertiefung <German>. Lp 1998, Benno 296 pp. DM32. 3-7462-1267-7.

2776 *Garcia, Jaime* Prier les psaumes à l'école de saint AUGUSTIN. VieCon 70 (1998) 220-229.

2777 *Gerhards, Albert* Die Psalmen in der römischen Liturgie: eine Bestandsaufnahme des Psalmengebrauchs in Stundengebet und Meßfeier. ᶠLOHFINK, N. 1998 ⇒64. 355-379.

2778 *Gilbert, Maurice* Les liturgies pénitentielles dans l'Ancien Testament. Il a parlé par les prophètes. 1998 <1991> ⇒155. 289-305.

2779 **Guardini, Romano** Deutscher Psalter: theologische Gebete. ᴱ*Henrich, Franz.* Romano Guardini Werke: Mainz 1998, Matthias-Grünewald 344 pp. DM32. 3-7867-2128-9.

2780 Guttenberg, Adelheid von Aggressives Beten?: die Sprache der Psalmen heute. US 53 1998, 327-339.

2781 *Mager, Inge* Zur vergessenen Problematik des Psalmliedes im 16. und 17. Jahrhundert. JLH 37 (1998) 139-149.

2782 **Menichelli, Ernesto** I salmi: rileggere la storia nel clima della preghiera. Interpretare la Bibbia oggi 2; Leggere la Bibbia per mezzo della Bibbia 2: Brescia 1998, Queriniana 124 pp. L17.000. 88-399-2461-2.

2783 **Möller, Håkan** Den wallinska psalmen. 1997 ⇒13,2866. ᴿTTK 69 (1998) 235-236 (*Akslen, Laila*); KHÅ 98/1 (1998) 216-219 (*Wrede, Gösta*).

2784 *Murphy, Roland E.* The Hebrew psalmist and the christian today. BiTod 36 (1998) 103-109.

2785 *Nitsche, Stefan A.* Kein Grund zu klagen?: die Psalmenrezeption im Evangelischen Gesangbuch. BiLi 71 (1998) 336-347.

2786 *Ognibeni, Bruno* Se non fossi tuo: meditazioni e note su quindici salmi e una poesia di GREGORIO di Nazianzo. Già e non ancora 322: Mi 1998, Jaca 238 pp. L26.000. 88-16-30322-0 [Ps 8; 22; 23; 42; 43; 51; 90; 91; 119; 122; 126; 127; 130; 137; 139].

2787 *Ohler, Annemarie* Psalmen im Alltag. LS 49 (1998) 46-49.

2788 Prier avec les psaumes. D'après des notes transcrites de Sr Myriam. UnChr 132 (1998) 16-22.

2789 **Quillo, Ronald** The psalms, prayers of many moods. Mahwah 1998, Paulist 260 pp. $20.

2790 ^{ET}**Richter, Mario** Sieur de SPONDE: meditazioni sui salmi e poesie. ^T*Gemma, Manuela; Focardi, Paolo.* Biblioteca di letteratura: CinB 1998, San Paolo 498 pp. 88-215-3361-1 [Ps 14; 53; 48; 50; 62].
2791 *Rimaud, Didier* Les psaumes sont des outils de la prière. Interviewer *Feron, Martin.* Vie chrétienne 431 (1998) 26-28.
2792 *Spieckermann, Hermann* Psalmen und Psalter: Suchbewegungen des Forschens und Betens. ^FVAN DER WOUDE, A. VT.S 73: 1998 ⇒121. 137-153 [Ps 51].
2793 *Taft, Robert F.* The origins and development of the Byzantine communion psalmody II. Studi sull'Oriente Cristiano 2 (1998) 85-107.
2794 *Vos, C.J.A.* Die liturgie in die spieël van die Psalms. SeK 19 (1998) 686-704.
2795 **Wahl, Thomas Peter** The Lord's song in a foreign land: the Psalms as prayer. ColMn 1998, Liturgical 214 pp. $17.

E6.7 *Psalmi: versiculi*—**Psalms by number and verse**

2796 *Grzybek, Stanisław* Ludzkie drogi naszego życia w kontekście Psalmu 1 [De viis hominum in Ps 1]. RBL 51 (1998) 1-7.
2797 *Sixdenier, Guy-Dominique* Le Psaume 2 dans 4QFlorilegium et dans Jephet Ben Ali, In Psalmos: essai de comparaison de leurs exégèses et méthodes. ^FMARGAIN, J. 1998 ⇒71. 251-257.
2798 *Renaud, B.* La structure du Psaume 2. Transeuphratène 16 (1998) 57-70.
2799 *Clines, David J.A.* Universal dominion in Psalm 2. OT essays, 2. JSOT.S 293: 1998 ⇒142. 701-707.
2800 *Auffret, Pierre* Sur ton peuple ta bénédiction!: étude structurelle du Psaume 3. ScEs 50 (1998) 315-334.
2801 *Prinsloo, G.T.M.* Psalm 5: a theology of tension and reconciliation. SeK 19 (1998) 628-643.
2802 *Silva, A.A. da* Psalm 6: van wanhoop tot geloofsekerheid. SeK 19 (1998) 554-565.
2803 *Heil, Christoph* "πάντες ἐργάται ἀδικίας" revisited: the reception of Ps 6,9a LXX in Q and in Luke. ^FHOFFMANN, P. BZNW 93: 1998 ⇒43. 261-276 [Lk 13,27].
2804 **Peterson, Margaret Kim** Psalm 8: a theological and historical analysis of its interpretation. ^DDuke 1998, 305 pp.
2805 *Kaiser, Otto* Erwägungen zu Psalm 8. Gesammelte Aufsätze. BZAW 261: 1998 <1994> ⇒166. 56-70.
2806 **Urassa, Wenceslaus Mkeni** Psalm 8 and its christological reinterpretations in the New Testament context: an inter-contextual study in biblical hermeneutics. EHS.T 577: Fra 1998, Lang 281 pp. 3-631-30539-7.
2807 *Prinsloo, Gert T.M.* Man's word—God's word: a theology of antithesis in Psalm 12. ZAW 110 (1998) 390-402.
2808 *Coetzee, J.* Worstel met God: argumenteringstrategieë en hul socioretoriese funksie in Psalm 13. SeK 19 (1998) 544-553.
2809 **Aparicio Rodríguez, Ángel** Tú eres mi bien: análsis exegético y teológico del Sal. 16: aplicación a la vida religiosa. 1993 ⇒9,3100... 13,2879. ^RVyV 56 (1998) 505-507 (*Álvarez Barredo, Miguel*).
2810 *Seybold, Klaus* Der Weg des Lebens: eine Studie zu Psalm 16. Studien zur Psalmenauslegung. 1998 <1984> ⇒201. 75-84.

2811 *Clines, David* The tree of knowledge and the law of Yahweh (Psalm 19). OT essays, 2. JSOT.S 293: 1998 <1974> ⇒142. 708-715.
2812 *Prinsloo, G.T.M.* Psalm 20 and its Aramaic parallel: a reappraisal. JSem 9 (1997) 48-86.
2813 *Rose, André* La lecture chrétienne du psaume 21: Dieu mon Dieu, pourquoi m'as-tu abandonné?. Sedes Sapientiae 16 (1998) 16-32.
2814 *Koltun-Fromm, Naomi* Psalm 22's christological interpretive tradition in light of christian anti-Jewish polemic. JEarlyC 6 (1998) 37-57.
2815 *Lacocque, André* My God, my God, why have you forsaken me?. Thinking biblically. 1998 ⇒251. 187-232;
2816 'Mon Dieu, mon Dieu, pourquoi m'as-tu abandonné?': Psaume 22. Penser la bible. 1998 ⇒188. 247-278.
2817 *Hibbard, Angela M.* Psalm 22 and the paschal mystery. BiTod 36 (1998) 111-116.
2818 *Ricoeur, Paul* La plainte comme prière. Penser la bible. 1998 ⇒188. 279-304 [Ps 22];
2819 Lamentation as prayer. Thinking biblically. 1998 ⇒251. 211-232 [Ps 22].
2820 *Auffret, Pierre* Tu m'as répondu: étude structurelle du psaume 22. SJOT 12 (1998) 102-129.
2821 *Kaltner, John* Psalm 22:17b: second guessing "The old guess". JBL 117 (1998) 503-506.
2822 *Heller, Jan* Belebte Seele (Ps 22,30). CV 40 (1998) 131-136.
2823 *Seybold, Klaus* Psalm 29: Redaktion und Rezeption. Studien zur Psalmenauslegung. 1998 <1978> ⇒201. 85-111.
2824 *Bazak, Jacob* [תהלים כט] |אלימן בני ל-ה' הבו| [Psalm 29]. Beit Mikra 156 (1998) 70-82.
2825 *Hoffman, Yair* Psalm 29:7. Textus 19 (1998) 81-85.
2826 *Alonso Schökel, Luis* En la mano de Dios (Salmo 31). EstB 56 (1998) 405-415.
2827 **Gahler, Sabine** Gott der Schöpfung—Gott des Heils: Untersuchungen zum anthologischen Psalm 33. EHS.T 649: Fra 1998, Lang 202 pp. 3-631-33369-2.
2828 ᵀ**Crouzel, Henri; Brésard, Luc** ORIGÈNE: homélies sur les psaumes 36 à 38. SC 411: 1995, ᴿJThS 49 (1998) 829-830 (*Gould, Graham*).
2829 **Weidmann, Clemens** AUGUSTINUS und das Maximianistenkonzil von Cebarsussi: zur historischen und textgeschichtlichen Bedeutung von Enarratio in Psalmum 36, 2, 18-23. DÖAW.PH 655; VKCLK 16: W 1998, Verlag der ÖAK 70 pp. 3-7001-2705-7.
2830 *Kaiser, Otto* Psalm 39. Gesammelte Aufsätze. BZAW 261: 1998 <1995> ⇒166. 71-83.
2831 *Frigato, Monica* Quasi regina dominaris: l'interpretazione del salmo 44 nelle omelie ambrosiane sulla verginità. Consacrazione e Servizio 46 (1998) 62-66.
2832 *Human, D.J.* Psalm 44: 'Why do you hide your face, O God?!'. SeK 19 (1998) 566-583.
2833 **Grünbeck, Elisabeth** Christologische Schriftargumentation und Bildersprache: zum Konflikt zwischen Metapherninterpretation und dogmatischen Schriftbeweistraditionen in der patristischen Auslegung des 44. (45.) Psalms. SVigChr 26: 1994 ⇒10,3013... 13,2908. ᴿRSR 86 (1998) 243-244 (*Sesboüé, Bernard*).
2834 *Zapff, Burkard M.* "Eine feste Burg ist unser Gott"—Beobachtungen zu Ps 46. BN 95 (1998) 79-93.

2835 *Meding, Wichmann von* Eine feste Burg ist unser Gott: Martin
      LUTHERs christliche Auslegung des Psalms 46 [A mighty fortress is
      our God: Martin Luther's christian interpretation of Psalm 46].
      Luther Digest 6 (1998) 11-13.
2836 *Bohle, Gudrun* Zur Traditionsgeschichte von Psalm 51: prophetische
      Verkündigung und Kultausübung werden zum Gebet. FolTh 9 (1998)
      111-122.
2837 *González, Jesús* ¡Pero Dios es mi socorro!. EvV 40 (1998) 47-49.
2838 *Kselman, John S.; Barré, Michael L.* Psalm 55: problems and
      proposals. CBQ 60 (1998) 440-462.
2839 *Bail, Ulrike* 'O God, hear my prayer': Psalm 55 and violence against
      women. Wisdom and psalms. 1998 ⇒221. 242-263.
2840 *González, Jesús* Salmo 56 (55): "En Dios confío y no temo: ¿qué
      podrá hacerme el hombre?". Evangelio y Vida 40 (1998) 155-158.
2841 *Seybold, Klaus* Psalm LVIII: ein Lösungsversuch. Studien zur Psal-
      menauslegung. 1998 <1980> ⇒201. 112-124.
2842 *Primmer, Adolf* AUGUSTINUS und der Astrologe: zu Enarratio in Psal-
      mum 61. ^FSPEYER, W.. JAC.E 28: 1998 ⇒107. 253-262.
2843 *Seybold, Klaus* Asyl? Psalm 62—Zeugnis eines Verfolgten. Studien
      zur Psalmenauslegung. 1998 <1992> ⇒201. 125-129.
2844 *Meynet, Roland* Le Psaume 67: "Je ferai de toi la lumière des
      nations". NRTh 120 (1998) 3-17.
2845 *Tillmann, Norbert* 'Das Wasser bis zum Hals': Gestalt, Geschichte
      und Theologie des 69. Psalms. 1993 ⇒9,3135; 11/1,1627. ^RBZ 42
      (1998) 114-115 (*Willmes, Bernd*).
2846 *Sæbo, Magne* From empire to world rule: some remarks on Psalms
      72.8; 89.26; Zechariah 9.10b. On the way to canon. 1998 <1978>
      ⇒194. 122-130.
2847 *Ruprecht, Eberhard* Wer sind die "Könige der Inseln"?: zur
      Semantik von 'i. ZAW 110 (1998) 607-609.
2848 *Wendland, Ernst* Introit 'into the sanctuary of God' (Psalm 73:17):
      entering the theological 'heart' of the psalm at the centre of the
      Psalter. OTEs 11 (1998) 128-153.
2849 *Gosse, Bernard* Les Psaumes 75-76 en rapport à la rédaction du
      Psautier et à celle du livre d'Isaïe. BeO 40 (1998) 219-228.
2850 *Seybold, Klaus* Psalm 76. Studien zur Psalmenauslegung. 1998
      (1989) ⇒201. 130-146.
2851 *Van den Hoek, Annewies* 'I said, you are gods...': the significance of
      Psalm 82 for some early christian authors. Use of sacred books. 1998
      ⇒263. 203-219.
2852 *Barasch, Moshe* Die zwei Figuren der Gerechtigkeit. Gerechtigkeit.
      Kulte, Kulturen: 1998 ⇒283. 183-203.
2853 *Heim, Knut M.* The (God-)forsaken king of Psalm 89: a historical and
      intertextual enquiry. King and Messiah. JSOT.S 270: 1998 ⇒378.
      296-322.
2854 *Steymans, Hans Ulrich* Der (un-)glaubwürdige Bund von Psalm 89.
      ZAR 4 (1998) 126-144.
2855 *Urbrock, William J.* Psalm 90: Moses, mortality, and... the morning.
      CThMi 25 (1998) 26-29.
2856 *Seybold, Klaus* Zu den Zeitvorstellungen in Psalm 90. Studien zur
      Psalmenauslegung. 1998 ⇒201. 147-160.
2857 *Nachtergael, Georges* À propos d'un papyrus documentaire et d'un
      ostracon biblique d'Éléphantine. CÉg 73 (1998) 116-120.

2858 **Howard, David M.** The structure of Psalms 93-100. Biblical and Judaic Studies 5: 1997 ⇒13,2938. [R]RExp 95 (1998) 290-291 (*deClaissé-Walford, Nancy L.*); JBL 117 (1998) 725-726 (*Allen, Leslie C.*).

2859 *Rimaud, Didier* Psaume 94: le peuple qu'il conduit. Vie chrétienne 428 (1998) 21-24.

2860 *Auffret, Pierre* Qui se lèvera pour moi?: étude structurelle du Psaume 94. RivBib 46 (1998) 129-156.

2861 *Seidl, Theodor* Scheltwort als Befreiungsrede: eine Deutung der deuteronomistischen Paränese für Israel in Ps 95,7c-11. [F]KLINGER. 1998 ⇒2862. 107-120.

2862 [F]**KLINGER, Elmar** Das Volk Gottes—ein Ort der Befreiung: Festschrift für Elmar Klinger. [E]*Keul, Hildegund; Sander, Hans-Joachim*: Wü 1998, Echter.

2863 *Schiller, Johannes* Bemerkungen zur Analyse und Interpretation von Psalm 99. BN 91 (1998) 77-89 [Exod 34,7].

2864 *Weber, Beat* Psalm 100. BN 91 (1998) 90-97.

2865 *Jeremias, J.* Ps 100 als Auslegung von Ps 93-99. SeK 19 (1998) 605-615.

2866 *MacEwen, Alastair* "Make a joyful noise unto the Lord". Vox reformata 63 (1998) 67-73 [Ps 100,1].

2867 **Brunert, Gunild** Ps 102 im Kontext des vierten Psalmenbuches. SBS 30: 1996 ⇒12,2879; 13,2945. [R]ThZ 54 (1998) 83-84 (*Weber, Beat*).

2868 *O'Kennedy, D.F.* The relationship between justice and forgiveness in Psalm 103. Scriptura 65 (1998) 109-121.

2869 *Seybold, Klaus* Psalm 104 im Spiegel seiner Unterschrift. Studien zur Psalmenauslegung. 1998 <1984> ⇒201. 161-172.

2870 *Brüning, Christian* "Sendest du deinen Geist aus, so wird das Angesicht der Erde erneuert": Ps 104 und die Anfänge der Geisttheologie in der Heiligen Schrift. EuA 74 (1998) 121-138.

2871 *Tanner, Beth LaNeel* Hearing the cries unspoken: an intertextual-feminist reading of Psalm 109. Wisdom and psalms. 1998 ⇒221. 283-301.

2872 **Van der Velden, Frank** Psalm 109 und die Aussagen zur Feindschädigung in den Psalmen. SBB 37: 1997 ⇒13,2951. [R]Bib. 79 (1998) 576-579 (*Bons, Eberhard*).

2873 **Güntner, Diana** Das Gedenken mittels Psalmen im Neuen Testament: zum Psalmengebrauch der frühen Kirche am Modell des Psalms 110. Diss. [D]Häußling. Benediktbeuerer Studien 5: Mü 1998, Don Bosco 429 pp. 3-7698-1090-2.

2874 *Dore, J.* L'évocation de Melchisédech et le problème de l'origine du Psaume 110. Transeuphratène 15 (1998) 19-53.

2875 *Tournay, Raymond Jacques* Les relectures du psaume 110 (109) et l'allusion à Gédéon. RB 105 (1998) 321-331 [Judg 7,7; 8,28].

2876 *Brown, William P.* A royal performance: critical notes on Psalm 110:3aG-b. JBL 117 (1998) 93-96.

2877 *Auffret, Pierre* En mémoire éternelle sera le juste: étude structurelle du psaume cxii. VT 48 (1998) 2-14.

2878 *Bureau, Bruno* Exercices spirituels et exercice rhétorique dans les commentaires antiques et médiévaux du Ps 113,1-6. RTL 29 (1998) 46-67, 180-201.

2879 *Prinsloo, G.T.M.* Tremble before the Lord: myth and history in Psalm 114. OTEs 11 (1998) 306-325.

2880 *Ghidelli, Carlo* Lampada sui miei passi: commento al salmo 118. Spiritualità senza frontiere 21: M 1998, Paoline 142 pp. 88-315-1617-5.

2881 **Mark, Martin** Meine Stärke und mein Schutz ist der Herr: poetologisch-theologische Studie zu Psalm 118. FzB 92: Wü 1998, Echter 550 pp. 3-429-02144-8.

2882 **Berder, Michel** "La pierre rejetée par les bâtisseurs": psaume 118,22-23 et son emploi dans les traditions juives et dans le Nouveau Testament. EtB 31: 1996 ⇒12,2891; 13,2957. ᴿRB 105 (1998) 147-148 (*Taylor, Justin*); CBQ 60 (1998) 144-145 (*Evans, Craig A.*).

2883 *Becker, Joachim; Lippe, Werne* Zur Deutung von Ps 118,24. BN 94 (1998) 44-51.

2884 *Jędrzejewski, Sylwester* Prawo dawcą życia w świetle Ps 119 [La legge dattore di vita nella luce del Sal. 119]. Roczniki Teologiczne 45 (1998) 37-53. **P**.

2885 ᵀ**Riain, Ide Ni** Homilies of Saint AMBROSE on Psalm 118(119). Dublin 1998, Halcyon xvi; 328 pp. IR£15. 1-902232-04-6.

2886 *Eriksson, LarsOlov* Vägen i Psaltaren 119. SEÅ 63 (1998) 31-40.

2887 *Booij, Thijs* Psalm 119,89-91. Bib. 79 (1998) 539-541.

2888 *Seybold, Klaus* Die Redaktion der Wallfahrtspsalmen. Studien zur Psalmenauslegung. 1998 <1979> ⇒201. 208-230 [Ps 120-134].

2889 *Davies, Philip R.* Yahweh as minder. OTEs 11 (1998) 427-437 [Ps 121].

2890 **Willmes, Bernd** Jahwe—ein schlummernder Beschützer?: zur Exegese und zum theologischen Verständnis von Psalm 121. Biblisch-theologische Studien 35: Neuk 1998, Neuk viii; 96 pp. 3-7887-1665-7.

2891 *Ognibeni, Bruno* Sal 122,8: augurio di pace o intercessione di pace?. Lat. 64 (1998) 215-220.

2892 *Felten, Gustavo* Orando los salmos: salmo 122 (121). Revista Católica 2 (1998) 121-125.

2893 *Weiss, Meir* קבכ תהלים של עניינו :'שבטים עלי ששם [To which tribes would make pilgrimage]. Tarb. 67 (1998) 147-152.

2894 *Snyman, S.D.* Psalm 126: `n perspektief vanuit die hede na die verlede en die toekoms. SeK 19 (1998) 644-652.

2895 *Ararat, Nisan* לציון העליה מתקופת שיר—|המעלות שיר| [['A song of ascents': a poem from the period of the ascent to Zion]. Beit Mikra 156 (1998) 83-90.

2896 *Seybold, Klaus* Erfolgsrisiko: Predigt über Psalm 127,1. Studien zur Psalmenauslegung. 1998 (1994) ⇒201. 305-309.

2897 *Robinson, Bernard P.* Form and meaning in Psalm 131. Bib. 79 (1998) 180-197.

2898 *Botha, P.J.* To honour Yahweh in the face of adversity: a socio-critical analysis of Psalm 131. SeK 19 (1998) 525-533.

2899 *Viviers, H.* 'Jy is net 'n sandkorrel, maar só is alle mense`—nadenke oor Psalm 131. SeK 19 (1998) 676-685.

2900 *Snijders, L.A.* Het samenzitten der broeders. ITBT 6/1 (1998) 23-24 [Ps 133].

2901 *Noegel, Scott* The Aegean Ogygos of Boeotia and the biblical Og of Bashan: reflections of the same myth. ZAW 110 (1998) 411-426 [Dt 4,47; 29,7; Josh 2,10; 9,10; Neh 9,22; Ps 135; 136,20].

2902 *Felten, Gustavo* Orando los salmos: Salmo 138 (137): gracias, Señor. Revista Católica 98 (1998) 293-297.

2903 *Beuken, W.A.M.* De psalmist als Hizkia, zoon van David: een inter-
testuele lezing van Psalm 138 en Jesaja 36-38. SeK 19 (1998) 513-
524.
2904 *Seybold, Klaus* Psalm 141: ein neuer Anlauf. Studien zur Psalmenauslegung. 1998 <1993> ⇒201. 173-188.
2905 *Blumenthal, David* Psalm 145: a liturgical reading. ᶠFRERICHS, E.
BJSt 320: 1998 ⇒28. 13-35.
2906 *Auffret, Pierre* Qu'ils disent la gloire de ton règne!: étude structurelle
du psaume 145. ScEs 50 (1998) 57-78.
2907 **Sedlmeier, Franz** Jerusalem—Jahwes Bau: Untersuchungen zu
Komposition und Theologie von Psalm 147. FzB 79: 1996
⇒12,2914; 13,2982. ᴿCBQ 60 (1998) 131-132 (*Craghan, John F.*).
2908 *Risse, Siegfried* Exegese zwischen Tradition und empirischer
Erkenntnis: "Rabeneltern"—zur Auslegungsgeschichte von Psalm
147,9b und Ijob 38,41. PzB 7 (1998) 127-136.
2909 *Škulj, Edo* Musical instruments in Psalm 150. Interpretation of the
Bible. JSOT.S 289: 1998 ⇒388. 1117-1130.

2910 *Van Rooy, H.F.* A second version of the Syriac Psalm 151. OTEs 11
(1998) 567-581.
2911 *Amara, Dalia* Psalm 151 from Qumran and its relation to Psalm 151
LXX. Textus 19 (1998) 183-185.
2912 *Van Rooy, H.F.* The marginal notes to the Syriac apocryphal psalms
in manuscript 12t4. VT 48 (1998) 542-554 [Ps 151-154].

7.1 Job, *textus, commentarii*

2913 ᴱ**Boadt, Lawrence** The book of Job: why do the innocent suffer?.
Classic Bible: New York 1997, St. Martin's 120 pp. $13.
2914 The book of Job. RSV; preface by *Cynthia Ozick*. Vintage spiritual
classics: NY 1998, Vintage xxv; 109 pp. 0-3757-0022-6.
2915 The book of Job: Authorised King James Version. Pocket Canons: E
1998, Canongate xv; 80 pp. 0-86241-791-0.
2916 *Cornagliotti, Anna* La situazione stemmatica vetero-testamentaria: i
libri dell'Ecclesiastico e di Giobbe. La bibbia in italiano. 1998
⇒390. 201-225.
2917 *Fuchs, Gotthard* Hiob und seine Botschaften: neue Literatur. BiLi 71
(1998) 357-359.
2918 **Gentry, Peter John** The asterisked materials in the Greek Job. SCSt
38: 1995 ⇒11/1,1696; 12,2920. ᴿJSSt 43 (1998) 165-167 (*Stec,
David M.*); JAOS 118 (1998) 593-594 (*Tov, Emanuel*).
2919 *Gentry, Peter J.* The asterisked materials in the Greek Job and the
question of the καιγε recension. Textus 19 (1998) 141-156;
2920 The place of Theodotion-Job in the textual history of the Septuagint.
Origen's Hexapla. TSAJ 58: 1998 ⇒399. 199-230.
2921 **Radermakers, J.** Dieu, Job et la sagesse: lecture continue et texte.
Bru 1998, Lessius 360 pp. FB895. ᴿNRTh 120 (1998) 465-466
(*Wargnies, Ph.*).
2922 ᵀ**Scheindlin, Raymond P.** The book of Job. NY 1998, Norton 237
pp. $24. 0-393-04626-5.
2923 *Simian-Yofre, Horacio* Giobbe (libro di). Dizionario di omiletica.
1998 ⇒533. 628-631.

2924 **Verdegaal, C.M.L.** De statenbijbel en de rabbijnen: een oderzoek naar de betekenis van de rabbijnse traditie voor de vertaling van het boek Job. TFT Studies 28: 1998, Tilburg University Press 307 pp. ƒ78.50. 90-361-9808-9.

2925 **Whybray, Norman** Job. Readings: Shf 1998, JSOT 187 pp. £37.50/$57.50/£13/$19.50. 1-85075-839-5/-40-9.

2926 **Wolfers, David** Deep things out of darkness: the book of Job: essays and a new English translation. 1995 ⇒11/1,1703; 13,3001. [R]Pacifica 11/1 (1998) 78-80 (*Moss, Alan*).

E7.2 *Job: themata,* **Topics...** *Versiculi,* **Verse numbers**

2927 *Balentine, Samuel E.* "What are human beings, that you make so much of them?": divine disclosure from the whirlwind: "Look at Behemoth". [F]BRUEGGEMANN, W. 1998 ⇒16. 259-278.

2928 [E]**Becker, Hansjakob** Warum?—Hiob interdisziplinär diskutiert. Mainzer Universitätsgespräche Wintersemester 1997/98; Studium generale / Universität Mainz: Mainz 1998, 166 pp.

2929 *Becker, Hansjakob* Hiobsbotschaften—Hiobs Botschaften: ein Beitrag zum Verhältnis von Bibel, Liturgie und Pastoral. Entschluss 53 (1998) 22-25.

2930 *Berges, Ulrich* Ijob: Klage und Anklage als Weg der Befreiung?. BiLi 71 (1998) 321-326.

2931 *Bochet, Marc* Job, figure inspiratrice du théâtre de l'absurde. Graphè 17 (1998) 165-171;

2932 L'expressionnisme et le cri de Job. Études 388/1 (1998) 89-97.

2933 *Boorer, Suzanne* Job's hope: A reading of the book of Job from the perspective of hope. Colloquium 30 (1998) 101-122.

2934 *Borgonovo, Gianantonio* La notte e il suo sole: luce e tenebre nel libro di Giobbe: analisi simbolica. AnBib 135: 1995 ⇒11/1,1708; 13,3005. [R]Synaxis 16/1 (1998) 311-325 (*Sfienti, Carmela Corradini*).

2935 *Brinkman, Martien E.* Als ik Job niet had. GThT 98 (1998) 20-25.

2936 *Chapalain, Claude* Cheminer avec le libre de Job. SémBib 89 (1998) 51-56.

2937 **Cheney, Michael** Dust, wind and agony: character, speech and genre in Job. CB.OT 36: 1994 ⇒10,3090... 13,3010. [R]JBL 117 (1998) 343-344 (*Odell, Margaret S.*).

2938 *Clines, David J.A.* In search of the Indian Job <1983>;

2939 The arguments of Job's three friends <1982>;

2940 Those golden days: Job and the perils of nostalgia. OT essays, 2. JSOT.S 293: 1998, 770-791/719-734/792-800.

2941 Dailey, Thomas F. The repentant Job. 1994, [R]CBQ 60 (1998) 324-325 (*Vall, Gregory*).

2942 *Deselaers, Paul* Lebensbuch Ijob. Entschluss 53 (1998) 5-6.

2943 *Ebach, Jürgen* Der "Fall Hiob" und das "Hiobproblem". Warum?. 1998 ⇒2928. 7-34.

2944 *Gilbert, Maurice* Job et Jésus dans la tradition chrétienne. Il a parlé par les prophètes. 1998 ⇒155. 233-248.

2945 **Grimm, Markus** "Dies Leben ist der Tod": Vergänglichkeit in den Reden Ijobs—Entwurf einer Textsemantik. ATSAT 62: St. Ottilien 1998, EOS xii; 250 pp. 3-88096-562-5.

2946   *Gruber, Mayer I.* Human and divine wisdom in the book of Job
       ᶠGORDON, C. JSOT.S 273: 1998 ⇒31. 88-102.
2947   *Halter, Didier* Job et CALVIN: réflexions sur le livre de Job au travers
       des prédications de Calvin. FV 97 (1998) 25-37.
2948   *Hermisson, Hans-Jürgen* Notizen zu Hiob. Gesammelte Aufsätze.
       FAT 23: 1998 <1989> ⇒161. 286-299.
2949   **Hoffman, Yair** A blemished perfection: the book of Job in context.
       JSOT.S 213: 1996 ⇒12,2955; 13,3017. ᴿABR 46 (1998) 88-89
       (*Schindler, Audrey*); BBR 8 (1998) 242-244 (*Harbin, Michael A.*);
       JQR 88 (1998) 282-285 (*Berlin, Adele*); JBL 117 (1998) 344-346
       (*McLaughlin, John L.*).
2950   **Israel, Martin** The way of growth. 1997 ⇒13,3018. ᴿRRT (1998/1)
       55-56 (*Platten, Stephen*).
2951   *Jobsen, Aarnoud* Job op het leesrooster. Interpretatie 6/1 (1998) 4-6.
2952   *Jochum, Herbert* Hiob und die Shoah. Warum?. 1998 ⇒2928. 101-
       120.
2953   *Kammerer, Gabriele* 'Aus dem beschädigten Leben': das Exil als Er-
       fahrungshintergrund von Margarete SUSMANs Hiobdeutung—ent-
       deckt mit Theodor W. ADORNOs Hilfe. ᶠMARQUARDT, F.-W. 1998
       ⇒72. 37-49.
2954   **Kiš, A.Z.** Knijga o Jobu u hrvatskoglgolskoj književnosti. 1997
       ⇒13,3019. ᴿBogoslovni Vestnik 58/3 (1998) 370-373 (*Bizjak, Jurij*).
2955   *Klopfenstein, Martin ḥinnam* im Hiobbuch. "Lasset uns Brücken
       bauen...". BEAT 42: 1998 ⇒401. 287-290.
2956   **Küntzli, Arnold** Gotteskrise: Fragen zu Hiob: Lob des Agnostizis-
       mus. Rowohlts Enzyklopädie 55596: Reinbek bei Hamburg 1998,
       Rowohlt 350 pp. 3-499-55596-4.
2957   *Langenhorst, Georg* Zuviel "Warum" gefragt?: Hiob in der Literatur
       des 20. Jahrhunderts. Warum?. 1998 ⇒2928. 121-145.
2958   *Lawrie, Douglas G.* The dialectical grammar of Job and Qoheleth: a
       Burkean analysis. Scriptura 66 (1998) 217-234.
2959   *Lytle-Vieira, Jane E.* Job and the mystery of suffering. Spiritual Life
       44 (1998) 76-86.
2960   *Madanu, Francis* Hope in suffering: Job as a model (a study on an
       innocent sufferer). BiBh 24 (1998) 253-271.
2961   *Maier, Christl; Schroer, Silvia* What about Job?: questioning the
       book of 'the righteous sufferer'. Wisdom and psalms. 1998 ⇒221.
       175-204.
2962   **Nemo, Philippe** Job and the excess of evil. Postface by *Emmanuel
       Levinas*; postscript by *Michael Kigel*. Pittsburgh, PA 1998, Duquesne
       Univ. Pr. 255 pp. 0-8207-0285-4.
2963   *Niewiadomski, Józef* Das "Hiobproblem" in den Religionen: ein Ver-
       such im Kontext der Perspektive von René GIRARD. Warum?. 1998
       ⇒2928. 53-72.
2964   **Noegel, Scott B.** Janus parallelism in the book of Job. JSOT.S 223:
       1996 ⇒12,2966. ᴿJAOS 118 (1998) 602-603 (*Creason, Stuart*);
       CBQ 60 (1998) 127-128 (*O'Connor, Kathleen M.*); AJSR 23 (1998)
       110-112 (*Kaminsky, Joel S.*).
2965   *Oelmüller, Willi* Philosophische Fragen und Antworten zu Leiden
       und Katastrophen. Warum?. 1998 ⇒2928. 73-100.
2966   *Pesch, Wilhelm* Hiob: Trostbuch in der Begleitung Schwerkranker.
       Warum?. 1998 ⇒2928. 147-165.

2967 **Poma, Andrea** Avranno fine le parole vane?: una lettura del libro di Giobbe. Dimensioni dello spirito 35: CinB 1998, San Paolo 213 pp. 88-215-3527-4.

2968 *Ritter Müller, Petra* Gott antwortet Ijob: eine Auslegung. Entschluss 53 (1998) 12-13.

2969 *Rozik, E.* 'The book of Job': a dialogue between cultures. Hellenic and Jewish arts. 1998 ⇒439. 369-384.

2970 *Seybold, Klaus* Psalmen im Buch Hiob: eine Skizze. Studien zur Psalmenauslegung. 1998 <1996> ⇒201. 270-287.

2971 *Strauß, Hans* Die "Freunde" Hiobs—ein Kreis frommer Weiser im Hintergrund des Hiobbuches. BN 95 (1998) 71-78.

2972 *Tafferner, Andrea* Das Buch Ijob lesen. Entschluss 53 (1998) 8-9.

2973 *Terrien, Samuel* The iconography of Job through the centuries: artists as biblical interpreters. 1996 ⇒12,2984; 13,3037. [R]RHPhR 78 (1998) 333-335 (*Prigent, P.*); ThTo 55 (1998) 248-249 (*Dixon, John W.*).

2974 **Trutta-Szabo, Diane** Prince Ludwig of Anhalt's Book of Job: an example of Christian Hebraism during the Thirty Years' War. [D]Pittsburgh 1998, 315 pp.

2975 *Viljoen, Jaco* 'n psigologiese verstaan van die boek Job:'n beskouing van W Brueggemann se bydrae tot'n psigologiese verstaan van die boek Job, in die gesprek rondom psigologiese skriftverstaan. OTEs 11 (1998) 115-127.

2976 **Vogels, Walter** Job. LiBi 104: 1995 ⇒11/1,1755; 12,2987. [R]EstB 56 (1998) 284-285 (*Morla, V.*).

2977 *Wiesel, Elie* Job. [F]CARGAS H. 1998 ⇒19. 119-134.

2978 *Clines, David J.A.* False naivety in the prologue to Job. OT essays, 2. JSOT.S 293: 1998 <1985> ⇒142. 735-744 [Job 1-2].

2979 *Sasson, Victor* The literary and theological function of Job's wife in the book of Job. Bib. 79 (1998) 86-90 [Job 2,10].

2980 *Clines, David J.A.* Job 4.13: a Byronic suggestion <1980>;

2981 Verb modality and the interpretation of Job 4.20-21 <1980>. OT essays, 2. JSOT.S 293: 1998 ⇒142. 745-747/748-751.

2982 *Reifler, Erwin* Semantic parallelisms in Job 5. JBQ 26 (1998) 143-148.

2983 *Clines, David J.A.* Job 5.1-8: a new exegesis. OT essays, 2. JSOT.S 293: 1998 <1981> ⇒142. 752-761.

2984 **Egger-Wenzel, Renate** 'Von der Freiheit Gottes, anders zu sein': die zentrale Rolle der Kapitel 9 und 10 für das Ijobbuch. Diss. Benediktbeuern 1996/97: [D]Wahl. FzB 83: Wü 1998, Echter 321 pp. 3-429-01933-8.

2985 *Clines, David J.A.* Belief, desire and wish in Job 19,23-27: clues for the identity of Job's 'redeemer'. OT essays, 2. JSOT.S 293: 1998 <1988> ⇒142. 762-769.

2986 *Gosling, Frank A.* An unsafe investigation of Job 19:25. JNSL 24/2 (1998) 157-166.

2987 **Witte, Markus** Philologische Notizen zu Hiob 21-27. BZAW 234: 1995 ⇒11/1,1764... 13,3053. [R]OLZ 93 (1998) 188-190 (*Mommer, Peter*);

2988 Vom Leiden zur Lehre: der dritte Redegang (Hiob 21-27) und die Redaktionsgeschichte des Hiobbuches. BZAW 230: 1994 ⇒10,3134 ...13,3052. [R]BiOr 55 (1998) 879-881 (*Holman, Jan*).

2989 *Hermisson, Hans-Jürgen* Von Gottes und Hiobs Nutzen: zur Aus-
      legung von Hi 22. Gesammelte Aufsätze. FAT 23: 1998 <1996>
      ⇒161. 300-319.
2990 *Clines, David J.A.* Quarter days gone: Job 24 and the absence of
      God. ᶠBRUEGGEMANN, W. 1998 ⇒16. 242-258;
2991 Quarter days gone: Job 24 and the absence of God. OT Essays, 2.
      JSOT.S 293: 1998 ⇒142. 801-819.
2992 **Waters, Larry Joe** Elihu's view of suffering in Job 32-37. ᴰDallas
      1998, 316 pp.
2993 *Weinberg, J.* Was Elihu, the son of Barachel, the author of the book
      of Job?: a hypothesis. Transeuphratène 16 (1998) 149-166.
2994 **Hubble, Rosemary A.** Conversation on the dung heap: reflections on
      Job. ColMn 1998, Liturgical xi; 100 pp. 0-8146-2503-7 [Job 32-37].
2995 *Sacks, Robert D.* The book of Job: translation and commentary on
      chapters 32 through 38. Interpretation(F) 25 (1998) 293-329.
2996 *Althann, Robert* Syntax and meaning in Job 35,15. JNSL 24/1 (1998)
      71-74.
2997 *Illman, Karl-Johan* Did God answer Job?. "Lasset uns Brücken bau-
      en...". BEAT 42: 1998 ⇒401. 275-285 [Job 38-41].
2998 *Zaradijakiš, Antonija* Particularités des traductions de l'Ancien Tes-
      tament dans le glagolisme croate (Job 38-39). Interpretation of the
      Bible. JSOT.S 289: 1998 ⇒388. 1015-1029.
2999 *Wilcox, Karl G.* 'Who is this...?': a reading of Job 38.2. JSOT 78
      (1998) 85-95.

E7.3 *Canticum Canticorum,* **Song of Songs, Hohelied,** *textus, comm.*

3000 **Ben-Gersôn, Lewî** Commentary on Song of Songs. YJS 28: NHv
      1998, Yale Univ. Press xxxi; 161 pp. 0-300-07147-7.
3001 **Bergant, Dianne** Il Cantico dei Cantici. Guide spirituali all'Antico
      Testamento: R 1998, Città N 173 pp. 88-311-3745-X;
3002 Song of Songs: the love poetry of scripture. Hyde Park, NY 1998,
      New City 167 pp. $10.
3003 **Bloch, Ariel; Bloch, Chana** The Song of Songs. 1995 ⇒11/1,1781;
      12,3013. ᴿJSSt 43 (1998) 167-169 (*Landy, Francis*).
3004 ᴱ**Boadt, Lawrence** The Song of Solomon: love poetry of the spirit.
      Classic Bible: New York 1997, St. Martin's 64 pp. $11.
3005 ᵀ**Bonato, Vincenzo** GREGORIO di Nissa: omelie sul Cantico dei
      cantici. 1995 ⇒11/1,1782; 12,3014. ᴿCivCatt 149/3 (1998) 543-544
      (*Cremascoli, G.*).
3006 Canticum Canticorum. BVLI 42 (1998) 25-28.
3007 *Cuomo, Luisa Ferretti* Verso la metà del XV secolo, un umanista
      impara l'ebraico?: da un quadernetto di studio: la traduzione inter-
      lineare del Cantico dei Cantici. La bibbia in italiano. 1998 ⇒390.
      329-363.
3008 *Deselaers, Paul* Das Hohelied Salomos. GuL 71 (1998) 442-453.
3009 *Dirksen, Piet B.* The Peshitta text of Song of Songs. Textus 19
      (1998) 171-181.
3010 ᴱ**Guérard, Marie-Gabrielle** NIL d'Ancyre: commentaire sur le
      Cantique des Cantiques, 1. SC 403: 1994 ⇒10,3166... 13,3072.
      ᴿRSR 86 (1998) 224-225 (*Sesboüé, Bernard*).
3011 Das Hohelied Salomos. Dtv 12545: Mü 1998, Dt. Taschenbuch-Verl.
      124 pp. 3-423-12545-4.

3012 Hooglied: hebreeuwse tekst en Nederlandse vertaling. Haarlem; 's-Hertogenbosch 1998, Nederlands Bijbelgenootschap; Katholieke Bijbelstichting 48 pp. *f*20. 90-6126-074-4.

3013 ^T**Jay, Peter** The Song of Sòngs. Some Classics from Anvil: L 1998, Anvil 62 pp. 0-85646-286-1.

3014 ^T**Kellner, Menachem** Levi ben Gershom (GERSONIDES): commentary on Song of Songs. NHv 1998, Yale University Press xxxi; 161 pp. $30. 0-300-07147-7.

3015 ^{TE}**Kiecker, James George** The postilla of NICHOLAS of Lyra on the Song of Songs. Reformation Texts with Translation (1350-1650), Biblical Studies 3: Milwaukee 1998, Marquette $15. 0-87462-703-6. ^RThPQ 146 (1998) 422-423 (*Böhmisch, Franz*).

3016 **Luzzatto, Amos** Una lettura ebraica del Cantico dei Cantici. 1997 ⇒13,3074. ^RRasIsr 64/2 (1998) 153-154 (*Piperno, Umberto*).

3017 **Mathieu, Bernard** La poésie amoureuse de l'Égypte ancienne: recherches sur un genre littéraire au Nouvel Empire. 1996 ⇒13,3074. ^RBiOr 55 (1998) 397-400 (*Brunsch, Wolfgang*).

3018 ^E**Ohly, Friedrich** Das St. Trudperter Hohelied: eine Lehre der liebenden Gotteserkenntnis. Fra 1998, Deutscher Klassiker-Verlag 1402 pp. DM198.

3019 ^E**Pablo Maroto, Daniel; Rodríguez, José Vicente** Santa TERESA de Jesús: meditaciones sobre los Cantares: exclamaciones. 1997 <1994> ⇒13,3075. ^RSan Juan de la Cruz 21 (1998) 152-153 (*Maqueda Gil, Antonio*).

3020 *Ratsahavi, Yehudah* שיר השירים' לרב סעדיה [The targum of the 'Song of Songs' by R. Saʻdiyah]. BetM 154-155 (1998) 256-262.

3021 ^E**Rotelle, John E.** AEGIDIUS Romanus: commentary on the Song of Songs and other writings. Augustinian 10: Villanova, PA 1998, Augustinian 359 pp. 0-941491-96-X/-95-1.

3022 *Sæbo, Magne* On the canonicity of the Song of Songs. On the way to canon. 1998 <1996> ⇒194. 271-284.

3023 The Song of Solomon: Authorised King James Version. Pocket Canons: E 1998, Canongate xviii; 15 pp. 0-86241-793-7.

3024 *Treat, Jay Curry* AQUILA, FIELD, and the Song of Songs. Origen's Hexapla. TSAJ 58: 1998 ⇒399. 135-176.

3025 ^{TE}**Vregille, Bernard de; Neyrand, Louis** APPONIUS: commentaire sur le Cantique des Cantiques: tome II: livres IV-VIII. SC 421: 1997 ⇒13,3083. ^RScEs 50 (1998) 247-248 (*Barry, Catherine*);

3026 APPONIUS: commentaire sur le Cantique des cantiques, 3. Livres IX-XII; Edition bilingue latin-français. SC 422: P 1998, Cerf 342 pp. FF219. 2-204-05901-3 [BCLF 602,2261].

E7.4 **Canticum**, *themata, versiculi*

3027 *Albrektson, Bertil* Sjunga eller beskära?: om översättningsproblem i Höga visan. SEÅ 63 (1998) 61-68.

3028 **Andiñach, Pablo R.** Cantar de los cantares: el fuego y la ternura. 1997 ⇒13,3085. ^RRevBib 60 (1998) 222-224 (*Mendoza, Claudia*).

3029 *Black, Fiona C.; Exum, J. Cheryl* Semiotics in stained glass: Edward BURNE-JONES's Song of Songs. Biblical studies. JSOT.S 266: 1998 ⇒380. 315-342.

3030 *Borzumato, Francesca* Spunti di ricerca dall'Expositio in Canticum Canticorum di Pietro di Giovanni OLIVI. AFH 91 (1998) 551-570.

3031 *Brenner, Athalya* Das Hohelied: Polyphonie der Liebe. Kompendium Feministische Bibelauslegung. [E]**Schottroff, L.**: 1998 ⇒H8.9. 233-245.

3032 *Carr, D.M.* The Song of Songs as a microcosm of the canonization and decanonization process. Canonization. SHR 82: 1998 ⇒407. 173-189.

3033 **Di Lagopesole, Cristina** Omelia sul Cantico dei Cantici, Epitalamio. Manduria 1997, Lacaita 59 pp. [R]RiCi 15 (1998) 233-234 *(Bianchi, Sante)*.

3034 *Exum, J. Cheryl* Developing strategies of feminist criticism/developing strategies for commentating the Song of Songs. Auguries. JSOT.S 269: 1998 ⇒225. 206-249.

3035 *Fulton, Rachel* "Quae est ista quae ascendit sicut aurora consurgens?": the Song of Songs as the Historia for the office of the Assumption. MS 60 (1998) 55-122.

3036 *Hascher-Burger, Ulrike* Zwischen Apokalypse und Hohemlied: Brautmystik in Gesängen aus der Devotio Moderna. OGE 72 (1998) 246-261.

3037 *Holmyard, Harold R.* Solomon's perfect one. BS 155 (1998) 164-171.

3038 *Jacobs, Andrew S.* 'Solomon's salacious song': FOUCAULT's author function and the early christian interpretation of the *Canticum Canticorum*. Medieval Encounters 4 (1998) 1-23.

3039 **LaCocque, André C.** Romance, she wrote: a hermeneutical essay on Song of Songs. Harrisburg, Pennsylvania 1998, Trinity xvi; 240 pp. $19. 1-56338-233-4.

3040 *Lacocque, André* La Sulamite: le Cantique des Cantiques. Penser la bible. 1998 ⇒188. 373-410;

3041 The Shulamite. Thinking biblically. 1998 ⇒251. 235-263.

3042 [E]**Leclercq, J.** BERNARD de Clairvaux: sermons sur le Cantique, 1: 1-15. SC 414: 1996 ⇒12,3051. [R]RMab 9 (1998) 321-322 *(Bermon, Pascale)*.

3043 *Nissinen, Martti* Love lyrics of Nabû and Tašmetu: an Assyrian Song of Songs?. [F]LORETZ O. AOAT 250: 1998 ⇒65. 585-634.

3044 *Pelland, Gilles* Ex ipso sponso splendorem decoris accipiens.... Gr. 79 (1998) 113-127.

3045 *Ricoeur, Paul* La métaphore nuptiale. Penser la bible. 1998 ⇒188. 411-457;

3046 La métaphore nuptiale dans le *Cantique des Cantiques*. Esprit 242 (1998) 114-126;

3047 The nuptial metaphor. Thinking biblically. 1998 ⇒251. 266-303.

3048 *Rogerson, John W.* The use of the Song of Songs in J.S. BACH's church cantatas. Biblical studies. 1998 ⇒380. 343-351.

3049 *Schlageter, Johannes* Von göttlicher in menschlicher Liebe: Petrus Johannis OLIVI: Expositio in Canticum Canticorum. AFH 91 (1998) 517-532.

3050 [T]**Simonetti, Manlio** ORIGENES: il Cantico dei Cantici: in Canticum Canticorum homiliae II. Scrittori greci e latini: Mi 1998, Mondadori xl; 173 pp. 88-04-42287-4.

3051 *Stadler, Michael* Erlösende Erotik: ethische Aspekte im Hohenlied. Zeitschrift für Theologie und Gemeinde 3 (1998) 53-82.

3052 [T]**Verdeyen, Paul; Fassetta, Raffaele** BERNARD de Clairvaux: sermons sur le Cantique, 2: 16-32. SC 431: P 1998, Cerf 495 pp.

3053 *Walsh, Carey Ellen* A startling voice: woman's desire in the Song of Songs. BTB 28 (1998) 129-134.
3054 *Watson, Wilfred G.E.* Parallel word pairs in the Song of Songs FLORETZ O. AOAT 250: 1998 ⇒65. 785-808.

3055 *Holman, Jan* A fresh attempt at understanding the imagery of Canticles 3:6-11. "Lasset uns Brücken bauen...". BEAT 42: 1998 ⇒401. 303-309.
3056 *Müller, Hans-Peter* Eine Parallele zur Weingartenmetapher des Hohenliedes aus der frühgriechischen Lyrik. FLORETZ O. AOAT 250: 1998 ⇒65. 569-584.
3057 *Lenzi, Alan* The translation of Song of Songs 5,8. BiTr 49 (1998) 116-123.
3058 *Frolov, Serge* No return for Shulammite: reflections on Cant 7,1. ZAW 110 (1998) 256-258.

E7.5 *Libri sapientiales*—Wisdom literature

3059 **Bergant, Dianne** Israel's wisdom literature: a liberation-critical reading. 1997 ⇒13,3118. RNew Theology Review 11/3 (1998) 86-87 (*Cook, Joan E.*); CBQ 60 (1998) 519-521 (*Smith-Christopher, Daniel L.*).
3060 **Brown, William P.** Character in crisis: a fresh approach to the wisdom literature of the Old Testament. 1996 ⇒12,3058. RPro Ecclesia 7 (1998) 495-496 (*Davis, Ellen F.*).
3061 *Carrière, Jean-Marie* Petite introduction à la sagesse biblique. Cahiers de l'Atelier 481 (1998) 88-96.
3062 **Clifford, Richard J.** The Wisdom literature. Interpreting Biblical Texts: Nv 1998, Abingdon 181 pp. 0-687-00846-8.
3063 **Collins, John Joseph** Jewish wisdom in the Hellenistic age. 1997 ⇒13,3129. RRRT (1998/4) 31-33 (*Hempel, Charlotte*).
3064 **Crenshaw, James L.** Education in ancient Israel: across the deadening silence. AncB Reference Library: NY 1998, Doubleday 320 pp. $35;
3065 Old Testament wisdom: an introduction. LVL 1998, Westminster 255 pp. $20. 0-664-25462-4.
3066 *Dell, Katharine J.* The king in the wisdom literature. King and Messiah. JSOT.S 270: 1998 ⇒378. 163-186.
3067 *Dieleman, Jacco* Fear of women?: representations of women in demotic wisdom texts. SAÄK 25 (1998) 7-46.
3068 *George, A.R.; Al-Rawi, F.N.H.* Tablets from the Sippar library, 7: three wisdom texts. Iraq 60 (1998) 187-206.
3069 *Gilbert, Maurice* Maîtres de sagesse et sagesse de Dieu. Il a parlé par les prophètes. 1998 <1980> ⇒155. 307-331.
3070 *Hermisson, Hans-Jürgen* Zur Schöpfungstheologie der Weisheit. Gesammelte Aufsätze. FAT 23: 1998 <1978> ⇒161. 269-285.
3071 *Hilber, John W.* Old Testament wisdom and the integration debate in christian counseling. BS 155 (1998) 411-422.
3072 EJanowski, Bernd Weisheit außerhalb der kanonischen Weisheitsschriften. 1996 ⇒12,3071. RThLZ 123 (1998) 964-965 (*Kaiser, Otto*).

3073 *Kaiser, Otto* Einfache Sittlichkeit und theonome Ethik in der altestamentlichen Weisheit. Gesammelte Aufsätze. BZAW 261: 1998 <1997> ⇒166. 18-42.

3074 *Kitchen, Kenneth A.* Biblical instructional wisdom: the decisive voice of the ancient Near East. [F]GORDON, C. JSOT.S 273: 1998 ⇒31. 346-363.

3075 **Lalouette, Claire** Sagesse sémitique: de l'Égypte ancienne à l'Islam. P 1998, Albin M 272 pp. 2-226-09610-8.

3076 *Lesko, Leonard H.* The perception of women in Pharaonic Egyptian wisdom literature. [M]WARD W. 1998 ⇒123. 163-171.

3077 **McKinlay, Judith E.** Gendering wisdom the host: biblical invitations to eat and drink. JSOT.S 216: 1996 ⇒12,3076. [R]CBQ 60 (1998) 335-336 (*Burns, Camilla*).

3078 **Melchert, Charles F.** Wise teaching: biblical wisdom and educational ministry. Harrisburg, Pennsylvania 1998, Trinity xi; 323 pp. 1-56338-139-7.

3079 **Murphy, Roland E.** The tree of life: an exploration of biblical wisdom literature. 1996 ⇒12,3080. [R]Pacifica 11 (1998) 324-326 (*Moss, Alan*); ThLZ 123 (1998) 967-969 (*Kaiser, Otto*); LASBF 48 (1998) 575-577 (*Niccacci, Alviero*).

3080 *Murphy, Roland E.* Wisdom and creation. Wisdom and psalms. 1998 ⇒221. 32-42.

3081 *Nel, Philip J.* Juxtaposition and logic in the wisdom saying. JNSL 24/1 (1998) 115-127.

3082 *Niebuhr, Karl-Wilhelm* Weisheit als Thema biblischer Theologie. KuD 44 (1998) 40-60.

3083 *Noonan, Brian B.* Wisdom literature among the witchmongers. Wisdom and psalms. 1998 ⇒221. 169-174.

3084 *Saldarini, Anthony J.* Human wisdom is divine. BiRe 14/2 (1998) 18, 53.

3085 **Schroer, Silvia** Die Weisheit hat ihr Haus gebaut: Studien zur Gestalt der Sophia in den biblischen Schriften. 1996 ⇒12,149. [R]ThRv 94 (1998) 808-809 (*Sattler, Dorothea*).

3086 *Spieckermann, Hermann* Ludlul bel nemeqi und die Frage nach der Gerechtigkeit Gottes. [F]BORGER R. 1998 ⇒12. 329-341.

3087 **Urbach, Ephraïm E.** Les sages d'Israël: conceptions et croyances des maîtres du talmud. 1996 ⇒12,3094. [R]ETR 73 (1998) 271-272 (*Léonard, Jeanne Marie*); NRTh 120 (1998) 485-486 (*Luciani, D.*); RSR 86 (1998) 592-595 (*Beaude, Pierre-Marie*).

3088 *Webster, Jane S.* Sophia: engendering wisdom in Proverbs, Ben Sira and the Wisdom of Solomon. JSOT 78 (1998) 63-79.

3089 *Young, Ian M.* Israelite literacy: interpreting the evidence. VT 48 (1998) 239-253, 408-422.

E7.6 **Proverbiorum liber,** *themata, versiculi*

3090 *Bland, Dave* The formation of character in the book of Proverbs.
     · RestQ 40 (1998) 221-237.

3091 [E]**Boadt, Lawrence** Sayings of the wise: the legacy of King Solomon. Classic Bible: New York 1998, St. Martin's 107 pp. $12.

3092 **Bricker, Daniel P.** The innocent sufferer in the book of Proverbs [D]Fuller 1998, 319 pp.

3093 ^{ET}**Châtillon, Jean; Dumontier, Maurice; Grélois, Alexis** Galand de REIGNY: petit livre de Proverbes. SC 436: P 1998, Cerf 231 pp. 2-204-06082-8.

3094 *Cook, J.* How much Hellenism in the Hebrew Proverbs?. "Lasset uns Brücken bauen...". BEAT 42: 1998 ⇒401. 291-301;

3095 Septuagint Proverbs—and canonization. Canonization. SHR 82: 1998 ⇒407. 79-91;

3096 The Proverbs version of "The new English translation of the Septuagint" (NETS): some methodological considerations. Bible et informatique. 1998 ⇒386. 263-282.

3097 ^E**Isoz, C. Claire** Sanson de **Nantuil**: les Proverbes de Salemon, III: introduction, notes and glossary. Anglo-Norman Texts 50: L 1994, Anglo-Norman Text Society x; 188 pp. ^RCCMéd 41 (1998) 396-397 (*Merrilees, Brian*).

3098 *Likeng, Paul Bitjick* The use of animal imagery in Proverbs. BiTr 49 (1998) 225-232.

3099 *Loader, J.A.* Learning in the indicative. JSem 8 (1996) 21-33.

3100 *Murphy, Roland E.* A brief note on translating Proverbs. CBQ 60 (1998) 621-625.

3101 **Murphy, Roland Edmund** Proverbs. WBC 22: Nv 1998, Nelson lxxv; 306 pp. $33. 0-8499-0221-5.

3102 Proverbs: Authorised King James Version. Pocket Canons: E 1998, Canongate xvii; 92 pp. 0-86241-792-9.

3103 *Sæbo, Magne* From collections to book—a new approach to the history of tradition and redaction of the book of Proverbs. On the way to canon. 1998 <1986> ⇒194. 250-258.

3104 *Snell, Daniel C.* The relation between the Targum and the Peshiṭta of Proverbs. ZAW 110 (1998) 72-74.

3105 *Van Oorschot, Jürgen* Der Gerechte und die Frevler im Buch der Sprüche: ein Beitrag zu Theologie und Religionsgeschichte des frühen Judentums. BZ 42 (1998) 225-238.

3106 **Washington, Harold C.** Wealth and poverty in the instruction of Amenemope and the Hebrew Proverbs. SBL.DS 142: 1994 ⇒12, 3124; 13,3179. ^RJAOS 118 (1998) 282-284 (*Fox, Michael V.*).

3107 **Westermann, Claus** Il libro dei Proverbi. Spiritualità 76: [Brescia] 1998, Queriniana 141 pp. L20.000. 88-399-1376-9.

3108 **Whybray, R. Norman** The book of Proverbs: a survey of modern study. 1995 ⇒11/1,1904; 13,3161. ^RBiOr 55 (1998) 873-878 (*Cook, Johann*); JThS 49 (1998) 191-194 (*Heim, Knut*).

3109 *Zinelli, Fabio* 'Donde noi metreme lo primo in francescho': i proverbi tradotti dal francese ed il loro insermento nelle sillogi bibliche. La bibbia in italiano. 1998 ⇒390. 145-199.

3110 **Baumann, Gerlinde** Die Weisheitsgestalt in Proverbien 1-9. FAT 16: 1996 ⇒12,3130. ^RThLZ 123 (1998) 361-363 (*Krispenz, Jutta*); JThS 49 (1998) 195-196 (*Whybray, Norman*).

3111 **Harris, Scott L.** Proverbs 1-9: a study of inner-biblical interpretation. SBL.DS 150: 1995 ⇒11/1,1938; 13,3187. ^RCBQ 60 (1998) 528-530 (*Penchansky, David*).

3112 *Maier, Christl* Conflicting attractions: parental wisdom and the 'strange women' in Proverbs 1-9;

3113 *Baumann, Gerlinde* A figure with many facets: the literary and theological functions of personified wisdom in Proverbs 1-9. Wisdom and psalms. 1998 ⇒221. 92-108/44-78.

3114 *Cascante Gómez, Fernando A.* Between text and sermon: Proverbs 1:1-19. Interp. 52 (1998) 407-411.
3115 *Bascom, Robert* Can a woman be wise?: issues in the translation of wisdom pictured as a woman. BiTr 49 (1998) 442-445 [Prov 1,20-33; 8,1-9,6].
3116 *Bellis, Alice Ogden* The gender and motives of the wisdom teacher in Proverbs 7. Wisdom and psalms. 1998 ⇒221. 79-91.
3117 *Meinhold, Arndt* Das Wortspiel רזון-רצון in Prov 14,28-35. ZAW 110 (1998) 615-616.
3118 *Niccacci, Alviero* Proverbi 23,26-24,22. SBFLA 48 (1998) 49-103.
3119 *Mutius, Hans-Georg von* Eine bisher nicht beachtete hebräische Textvariante zu Proverbia 24,16 aus dem Babylonischen Talmud. BN 92 (1998) 16-20.
3120 *Fry, Euan; Reyburn, William* Translating an apparent contradiction: Proverbs 26.4-5. BiTr 49 (1998) 246-247.
3121 *Cathcart, Kevin J. Bᵉḥopnāw* in Proverbs xxx 4. VT 48 (1998) 264-265.

E7.7 *Ecclesiastes*—Qohelet; *textus, themata, versiculi*

3122 ᴱ**Chomarat, Jacques** Ecclesiastes (libri III-IV). Opera omnia Desiderii Erasmi Roterodami: ordinis quinti tomus quintus. Amst 1994, North-Holland 422 pp. ƒ450. ᴿGn. 70 (1998) 313-317 (*Nesselrath, Heinz-Günther*).
3123 Ecclesiastes or, the Preacher: Authorised King James Version. Pocket Canons: E 1998, Canongate xii; 26 pp. 0-86241-794-5.
3124 *Lavoie, Jean J.; Mehramooz, Minoo* Quelques remarques sur les manuscrits judéo-persans du Qohélet de la Bibliothèque National de France. Religiologiques 17 (1998) 195-215.
3125 **Longman, Tremper** The book of Ecclesiastes. NICOT: GR 1998, Eerdmans xvi; 306 pp. $35. 0-8028-2366-1. ᴿIgreja e Missão 50 (1998) 275-276 (*Couto, A.*); Kerux 13/3 (1998) 16-39 (*Kline, M.M.*).
3126 **Michel, Diethelm** Qohelet. EdF 258: 1988 ⇒4,3527... 6,3632 ᴿThRv 94 (1998) 364-365 (*Schwienhorst-Schönberger, Ludger*).
3127 *Salters, Robert B.* Observations on the Targum to Qoheleth. JNSL 24/2 (1998) 13-24.
3128 **Seow, Choon-Leong** Ecclesiastes. AncB 18C: 1997 ⇒13,3216. ᴿJR 78 (1998) 607-608 (*Burkes, Shannon*).
3129 ᴱ**Taradach, Madeleine; Ferrer, Joan** Un targum de Qohéleth: editio princeps du LMS. M-2 de Salamanca. MoBi 37: Genève 1998, Labor et F 165 pp. FF48. 2-8309-0876-7.
3130 ᵀ**Vinel, Françoise** GRÉGOIRE de Nysse: homélies sur l'Ecclésiaste. SC 416: 1996 ⇒12,3177; 13,3219. ᴿBib. 79/1 (1998) 143-144 (*Canévet, Mariette*).

3131 **Anderson, William H.U.** Qoheleth and its pessimistic theology: hermeneutical struggles in wisdom literature. Mellen 54: Lewiston 1997, Mellen xviii; 274 pp. ᴿBS 155 (1998) 119-120 (*Zuck, Roy B.*).
3132 *Anderson, William H.* The curse of work in Qoheleth: an exposé of Genesis 3:17-19 in Ecclesiastes. EvQ 70 (1998) 99-113;
3133 Philosophical considerations in a genre analysis of Qoheleth. VT 48 (1998) 289-300.

3134 **Backhaus, Franz Josef** "Es gibt nichts Besseres für den Menschen" [Koh 3, 22]: Studien zur Komposition und zur Weisheitskritik im Buch Kohelet. BBB 121: Bodenheim 1998, Philo (12) 330 pp. 3-8257-0122-0.

3135 *Backhaus, Franz Josef* Kohelet und die "Diatribe": hermeneutische und methodologische Überlegungen zu einem noch ausstehenden Stilvergleich. BZ 42 (1998) 248-256;

3136 **Backhaus, Franz Josef** Denn Zeit und Zufall trifft sie alle: zu Komposition...im Buch Qohelet. BBB 83: 1993 ⇒10,3285. [R]ThRv 94 (1998) 367-368 (*Schwienhorst-Schönberger, Ludger*).

3137 *Bakon, Shimon* Koheleth. JBQ 26 (1998) 168-176.

3138 *Bardski, Krzysztof* "Vanità delle vanità, tutto è vanità": il hebel dell'Ecclesiaste nell'interpretazione di GIROLAMO. CoTh 68A (1998) 39-81.

3139 **Bartholomew, Craig G.** Reading Ecclesiastes: Old Testament exegesis and hermeneutical theory. AnBib 139: R 1998, E.P.I.B. vii; 319 pp. €23,24. 88-7653-139-4.

3140 *Beal, Timothy K.* C(ha)osmopolis: Qohelet's last words. [F]BRUEGGEMANN W. 1998 ⇒16. 290-304.

    [E]**Boadt, Lawrence** Sayings of the wise. ⇒3091.

3141 *Carvalho, José Carlos* A suposta influência grega em Qohelet. Did(L) 28 (1998) 137-156.

3142 **Christianson, Eric S.** A time to tell: narrative strategies in Ecclesiastes. JSOT.S 280: Shf 1998, Academic 299 pp. £49/$82. 1-85075-982-0.

3143 *Christianson, Eric S.* Qohelet and the/his self among the deconstructed;

3144 *Cook, Johann* Aspects of the relationship between the Septuagint versions of Kohelet and Proverbs;

3145 *Crenshaw, James L.* Qoheleth's understanding of intellectual inquiry;

3146 *D'Alario, Vittoria* Liberté de Dieu ou destin?: un autre dilemme dans l'interprétation du Qohélet. Qohelet. BEThL 136: 1998 ⇒266. 425-433/481-492/205-224/457-463.

3147 **Fischer, Alexander Achilles** Skepsis oder Furcht Gottes?: Studien zur Komposition und Theologie des Buches Kohelet. BZAW 247: 1997 ⇒13,3228. [R]ThRv 94 (1998) 369-372 (*Schwienhorst-Schönberger, Ludger*); ThLZ 123 (1998) 38-40 (*Krüger, Thomas*).

3148 *Fox, Michael V.* The inner structure of Qohelet's thought. Qohelet. BEThL 136: 1998 ⇒266. 225-238.

3149 *Gatti, Roberto* 'La filosofia dolorosa' di LEOPARDI e Qohelet: 'vanitá' e 'infinito' nei due autori. Hum(B) 53 (1998) 332-346.

3150 *Gianto, Agustinus* Human destiny in Emar and Qohelet;

3151 *Gilbert, Maurice* Qohelet et Ben Sira. Qohelet. BEThL 136: 1998 ⇒266. 473-479/161-179.

3152 *Hirshman, Marc* פשט ודרש ירדו כרוכים: על כתב־יד 'חדש' של מדרש קהלת ופירושו של ר' יעקב אבן ג'יאני לקהלת [*Peshat* and *derash* side-by-side: a newly rediscovered manuscript of *Midrash Qohelet* and of R. Jacob ALGIANI's commentary on Qohelet]. Tarb. 67 (1998) 397-406.

3153 *Kaiser, Otto* Beiträge zur Kohelet-Forschung: eine Nachlese <1995>;

3154 Determination und Freiheit beim Kohelet / Prediger Salomo und in der Frühen Stoa <1989>;

3155 Die Botschaft des Buches Kohelet <1995>;

3156 Schicksal, Leid und Gott: ein Gespräch mit dem Kohelet, Prediger Salomo <1987>. Gesammelte Aufsätze. BZAW 261: 1998 ⇒166. 149-200/84-105/126-148/84-105.

3157 **Klein, Christian** Kohelet und die Weisheit Israels. BWANT 132: 1994 ⇒10,3292. ᴿThRv 94 (1998) 368-369 (*Schwienhorst-Schönberger, Ludger*); LuThK 22 (1998) 213-215 (*Salzmann, Jorg C.*).

3158 *Krüger, Thomas* Theologische Gegenwartsdeutung im Buch Kohelet. 1990 ⇒6,3627. ᴿThRv 94 (1998) 366-367 (*Schwienhorst-Schönberger, Ludger*).

3159 *Lange, Armin* In Diskussion mit dem Tempel: zur Auseinandersetzung zwischen Kohelet und weisheitlichen Kreisen am Jerusalemer Tempel. Qohelet. BEThL 136: 1998 ⇒266. 113-159.

3160 **Lavatori, Renzo; Sole, Luciano** Qohelet: l'uomo dal cuore libero. 1997 ⇒13,3236. ᴿED 51/1 (1998) 209-211 (*Bianchi, F.*).

3161 *Lohfink, Norbert melek, šallîṭ* und *mōšēl* bei Kohelet und die Abfassungszeit des Buches <1981>;

3162 Der Bibel skeptische Hintertür: Versuch, den Ort des Buchs Kohelet neu zu bestimmen. Studien zu Kohelet <1980>. SBAB 26: 1998 ⇒172. 71-82/11-30;

3163 Ist Kohelets הבל-Aussage erkenntnistheoretisch gemeint?. Qohelet. BEThL 136: 1998 ⇒266. 41-59;

3164 Kohelet übersetzen: Berichte aus einer Übersetzerwerkstatt;

3165 Zu הבל im Buch Kohelet. Studien zu Kohelet. SBAB 26: 1998 ⇒172. 259-290/215-258.

3166 **Lys, Daniel** Des contresens du bonheur ou l'implacable lucidité de Qohèlèth. Poliez-le-Grand 1998, Moulin 79 pp.

3167 *Michel, Diethelm* 'Unter der Sonne': zur Immanenz bei Qohelet. Qohelet. BEThL 136: 1998 ⇒266. 93-111.

3168 *Miller, Douglas B.* Qohelet's symbolic use of hbl. JBL 117 (1998) 437-454.

3169 *Papone, Paolo* Il Qohelet nel contesto della letteratura sapienziale: novità e apertura al confronto culturale. RstB 10/1-2 (1998) 199-216.

3170 *Paulson, Gail N.* The use of Qoheleth in BONHOEFFER's "Ethics". WaW 18 (1998) 307-313.

3171 *Perry, T. Anthony* Kohelet's minimalist theology;

3172 *Richter, Hans-Friedemann* Kohelet—Philosoph und Poet;

3173 *Rudman, Dominic* The anatomy of the wise man: wisdom, sorrow and joy in the book of Ecclesiastes. Qohelet. BEThL 136: 1998 ⇒266. 451-456/435-449/465-471.

3174 **Salvarani, Brunetto** C'era una volta un re...: Salomone che scrisse il Qohelet. Letteratura biblica 10: T 1998, Paoline 158 pp. 88-315-1673-6.

3175 *Schoors, Antoon* The word טוב in the book of Qoheleth. ᶠLORETZ O. AOAT 250: 1998 ⇒65. 685-700;

3176 Words typical of Qohelet. Qohelet. BEThL 136: 1998 ⇒266. 17-39.

3177 **Schwienhorst-Schönberger, Ludger** 'Nicht im Menschen gründet das Glück' (Koh 2,24): Kohelet im Spannungsfeld jüdischer Weisheit und hellenistischer Philosophiè. 1994 ⇒10,3302... 12,3182. ᴿBZ 42 (1998) 115-118 (*Kaiser, Otto*).

3178 *Schwienhorst-Schönberger, Ludger* Neues unter der Sonne: zehn Jahre Kohelet-Forschung (1987-1997). ThRv 94 (1998) 363-376.

3179 *Simian-Yofre, Horacio* Qohelet (libro di). Dizionario di omiletica. 1998 ⇒533. 1297-1300.

3180 *Spieckermann, Hermann* Suchen und Finden: Kohelets kritische Reflexionen. Bib. 79 (1998) 305-332.

3181 **Tse, Mary Wai-Yi** The concept of God in the book of Ecclesiastes. DWestminster Theological Seminary 1998, 264 pp.

3182 *Whybray, R.N.* Qoheleth as a theologian;

3183 *Wilson, Lindsay* Artful ambiguity in Ecclesiastes 1,1-11: a wisdom technique?. Qohelet. BEThL 136: 1998 ⇒266. 239-265/357-365.

3184 *Lohfink, Norbert* Koh 1,2 'alles ist Windhauch'—universale oder anthropologische Aussage?. Studien zu Kohelet. SBAB 26: 1998 <1989> ⇒172. 125-142.

3185 *Anderson, William H.U.* The poetic inclusio of Qoheleth in relation to 1,2 and 12,8. SJOT 12 (1998) 203-213.

3186 *Kamano, Naoto* Character and cosmology: rhetoric of Qoh 1,3-3,9. Qohelet. BEThL 136: 1998 ⇒266. 419-424.

3187 *Lohfink, Norbert* Die Wiederkehr des immer Gleichen: eine frühe Synthese zwischen griechischem und jüdischem Weltgefühl in Kohelet 1,4-11. Studien zu Kohelet. SBAB 26: 1998 <1983> ⇒172. 95-124.

3188 *Smelik, K.A.D.* A re-interpretation of Ecclesiastes 2,12b;

3189 *Byargeon, Rick W.* The significance of ambiguity in Ecclesiastes 2,24-26. Qohelet. BEThL 136: 1998 ⇒266. 385-389/367-372.

3190 *Fox, Michael V.* Time in Qohelet's "catalogue of times". JNSL 24/1 (1998) 25-39 [Qoh 3,1-9; 11,1-6].

3191 *Vonach, Andreas* Gottes Souveränität anerkennen: zum Verständnis der "Kanonformel" in Koh 3,14. Qohelet. BEThL 136: 1998 ⇒266. 391-397.

3192 *Piras, Antonio* A proposito di una citazione latina pregeronimiana di Qoh 3,15-16 in Lucifero di Cagliari, Ath. 1,35,19s. Studi in onore di Ottorino Pietro ALBERTI. EAtzeni, Francesco; Cabizzosu, Tonino: Cagliari 1998, Della Torre. 73-84.

3193 *Vonach, Andreas* Bibelauslegung als Wertvermittlung: religiös motivierte Gesellschaftskritik am Beispiel des Buches Kohelet. Gott finden. 1998 ⇒304. 228-241 [Qoh 3,16-20; 4,1-4].

3194 *Fischer, Alexander Achilles* Kohelet und die frühe Apokalyptik: eine Auslegung von Koh 3,16-21. Qohelet. BEThL 136: 1998 ⇒266. 339-356.

3195 *Lohfink, Norbert* Warum ist der Tor unfähig, böse zu handeln? (Koh 4,17). Studien zu Kohelet. SBAB 26: 1998 <1983> ⇒172. 83-94.

3196 *Hieke, Thomas* Wie hast Du's mit der Religion?: Sprechhandlungen und Wirkintentionen in Kohelet 4,17-5,6;

3197 *Spangenberg, I.J.J.* A century of wrestling with Qohelet: the research history of the book illustrated with a discussion of Qoh 4,17-5,6. Qohelet. BEThL 136: 1998 ⇒266. 319-338/61-91.

3198 *Lohfink, Norbert* Kohelet und die Banken: zur Übersetzung von Kohelet v 12-16 <1989>;

3199 *Lohfink, Norbert* Koh 5,17-19—Offenbarung durch Freude. Studien zu Kohelet <1990>. SBAB 26: 1998 ⇒172. 143-150/151-165.

3200 *Lavoie, Jean-Jacques* La philosophie comme réflexion sur la mort: étude de Qohélet 7,1-4. LTP 54 (1998) 91-107.

3201 *Schwienhorst-Schönberger, Ludger* Via media: Koh 7,15-18 und die griechisch-hellenistische Philosophie. Qohelet. BEThL 136: 1998 ⇒266. 181-203.

3202 *Lohfink, Norbert* War Kohelet ein Frauenfeind?: ein Versuch, die Logik und den Gegenstand von Koh. 7,23-8,1a herauszufinden. Studien zu Kohelet. SBAB 26: 1998 <1980> ⇒172. 31-69.

3203 *Fontaine, Carole R.* 'Many devices' (Qoheleth 7.23-8.1): Qoheleth, misogyny and the Malleus Maleficarum. Wisdom and psalms. 1998 ⇒221. 137-168.

3204 *Stolze, Jürgen* Kohelet und die Frauen: ein Versuch zu Gedankengang und Sinn von Kohelet 7,23-29. ThFPr 24 (1998) 51-63.

3205 *Christianson, Eric S.* Qoheleth the 'old boy' and Qoheleth the 'new man': misogynism, the womb and a paradox in Ecclesiastes. Wisdom and psalms. 1998 ⇒221. 109-136 [Qoh 7,25-29].

3206 *Pahk, Johan Y.S.* The significance of אשר in Qoh 7,26: 'more bitter than death is the woman, if she is a snare'. Qohelet. BEThL 136: 1998 ⇒266. 373-383.

3207 *Long, V. Philips* One man among a thousand, but not a woman among them: a note on the use of *maṣa* in Ecclesiastes vii 28. "Lasset uns Brücken bauen...". BEAT 42: 1998 ⇒401. 101-109.

3208 *Beentjes, Panc* 'Who is like the wise?': some notes on Qohelet 8,1-15. Qohelet. BEThL 136: 1998 ⇒266. 303-315.

3209 *Bianchi, Francesco* Qohelet 10,8-11 or the misfortunes of wisdom. BeO 40 (1998) 111-117.

3210 *Kruger, H.A.J.* Old age frailty versus cosmic deterioration?: a few remarks on the interpretation of Qohelet 11,7-12,8. Qohelet. BEThL 136: 1998 ⇒266. 399-411.

3211 *Lohfink, Norbert* Grenzen und Einbindung des Kohelet-Schlußgedichts <1994>;

3212 Freu dich, Jüngling—doch nicht, weil du jung bist: zum Formproblem im Schlußgedicht Kohelets (Koh 11,9-12,8) <1995>. Studien zu Kohelet. SBAB 26: 1998 ⇒172. 167-180/181-214.

3213 *Van der Wal, A.J.O.* Qohelet 12,1a: a relatively unique statement in Israel's wisdom tradition;

3214 *Auwers, J.-M.* Problèmes d'interprétation de l'épilogue de Qohèlèt. [Qoh 12,9-14]. Qohelet. BEThL 136: 1998 ⇒266. 413-418/267-282.

E7.8 *Liber Sapientiae*—Wisdom of Solomon

3215 *Cheon, Samuel* Anonymity in the Wisdom of Solomon. JSPE 18 (1998) 111-119.

3216 *Drijvers, Hendrik J.W.* Salomo/Salomoschriften III: Sapientia Salomonis, Psalmen Salomos und Oden Salomos. TRE 29. 1998 ⇒501. 730-732.

3217 **Engel, Helmut** Das Buch der Weisheit. Neuer Stuttgarter Kommentar: Altes Testament 16: Stu 1998, Kath. Bibelwerk 322 pp. DM56. 3-460-07161-3.

3218 *Mazzinghi, Luca* Il libro della Sapienza: elementi culturali. RstB 10/1-2 (1998) 179-197.

3219 **Mazzinghi, Luca** La Sapienza: tra Antico e Nuovo Testamento. La Bibbia nelle nostre mani 12: CinB 1998, San Paolo 64 pp. 88-215-3731-5.

3220 **Fabbri, Marco Valerio** Creazione e salvezza nel libro della Sapienza: esegesi di Sapienza 1,13-15. Studi di teologia 6: R 1998, Armando 334 pp. 88-7144-890-1.

3221 **Thallapalli, Amruthanadan Joseph** The book of Wisdom 6:22-
      10:21, an economium of wisdom, and its inculturation in the Indian
      wisdom tradition. R 1998, E.P.U.G. 145 pp. [JPURS 2/2,169-171—
      Menezes, Rui de].
3222 *Hübner, Hans* Existentiale Interpretation von Sap 7: zur Hermeneutik
      der Sapientia Salomonis. ᶠSTEGEMANN, H. BZNW 97: 1998 ⇒111.
      266-277.
3223 *Enns, Peter* A retelling of the Song at the Sea in Wisdom 10.20-21.
      The function of scripture. 1998 ⇒236. 142-165.
3224 *Poniży, Bogdan* Panteizm w Księdze Mądrości (13,1-9) na tle krytyki
      bałwochwalstwa w Biblii [Pantheism in the book of Wisdom (13,1-9)
      against the background of biblical criticism of idolatry]. PoST 8
      (1998) 27-60.
3225 **Mazzinghi, Luca** Notte di paura e di luce: esegesi di Sap 17,1-18,4.
      AnBib 134: 1995 ⇒11/1,2042... 13,3297. ᴿEstB 56 (1998) 285-286
      (*Morla, V.*).

E7.9 *Ecclesiasticus, Siracides;* **Wisdom of Jesus Sirach**

3226 ᴱ**Beentjes, Pancratius C.** The book of Ben Sira in modern research.
      BZAW 255: 1997 ⇒13,3298. ᴿSynaxis 16/1 (1998) 316-318
      (*Minissale, Antonino*); RBBras 15 (1998) 493-495;
3227 The book of Ben Sira in Hebrew. VT.S 68: 1997 ⇒13,3299. ᴿCBQ
      60 (1998) 107-108 (*Di Lella, Alexander A.*); BZ 42 (1998) 118-119
      (*Schreiner, Josef*).
3228 **Coggins, Richard J.** Sirach. Guides to Apocrypha &
      Pseudepigrapha: Shf 1998, Academic 111 pp. £9. 1-85075-7658.
3229 *Cornagliotti, Anna* La situazione stemmatica vetero-testamentaria: i
      libri dell'Ecclesiastico e di Giobbe. La bibbia in italiano. 1998
      ⇒390. 201-225.
3230 ᴱ**Egger-Wenzel, Renate; Krammer, Ingrid** Der Einzelne und seine
      Gemeinschaft bei Ben Sira. BZAW 270: B 1998, De Gruyter viii;
      320 pp. 3-11-016371-3.
3231 **Minissale, Antonino** La versione greca del Siracide: confronto con il
      testo ebraico alla luce dell'attività midrascica e del metodo
      targumico. AnBib 133: 1995 ⇒11/1,2043... 13,3310. ᴿCrSt 19/1
      (1998) 180-184 (*Niccacci, Alviero*); Gr. 79 (1998) 173-176 (*Prato,
      Gian Luigi*).
3232 ᴱ**Muraoka, Takamitsu; Elwolde, J.F.** The Hebrew of the Dead Sea
      Scrolls and Ben Sira. StTDJ 26: 1997 ⇒13,369. ᴿJSJ 29 (1998) 344-
      346 (*Morla, Victor*).
3233 ᴱ**Reiterer, Friedrich Vinzenz** Bibliographie zu Ben Sira. BZAW
      266: B 1998, de Gruyter x; 347 pp. DM198. 3-11-016136-2.
3234 **Schrader, Lutz** Verwandtschaft der Peschitta mit der (alt)lateini-
      schen Übersetzung im Sirachbuch?. BN.B 11: Mü 1998, Inst. für
      Bibl. Exegese 75 pp.
3235 Sirach (Ecclesiasticus). BVLI 42 (1998) 28-31.
3236 ᴱ**Thiele, Walter** Sirach (Ecclesiasticus), 7. Lief. Sir 16,21-19,28. VL
      11/2. FrB 1998, Herder 481-560 pp.

3237 *Calduch-Benages, Núria* Fear for the powerful or respect for
      authority?;

3238 *Corley, Jeremy* Friendship according to Ben Sira. Der Einzelne. BZAW 270: 1998 ⇒3230. 87-102/65-71.
3239 *Flusser, David* הנסתרת לה' אלהינו'[דב' כט],[כח, בן סירא והאיסיים ['The secret things belong unto the Lord our God': Ecclesiasticus and the Essenes]. Tarb. 67 (1998) 407-410.
3240 *Kaiser, Otto* Anknüpfung und Widerspruch: die Antwort der jüdischen Weisheit auf die Herausforderung durch den Hellenismus. Gesammelte Aufsätze. BZAW 261: 1998 <1995> ⇒166. 201-216;
3241 Die Rezeption der stoischen Providenz bei Ben Sira. JNSL 24/1 (1998) 41-54.
3242 *Kieweler, Hans-Volker* Benehmen bei Tisch. Der Einzelne. BZAW 270: 1998 ⇒3230. 191-215.
3243 **Krammer, Ingrid** Die Auswirkungen des Verhaltens zum Mitmenschen auf die Beziehung zu Gott im Buch Ben Sira. Diss. Salzburg 1996-1997; [D]*Reiterer, F.* [ThRv 94,xviii].
3244 *Minissale, Antonino* Ben Siras Selbstverständnis in Bezug auf Autoritäten der Gesellschaft. Der Einzelne. BZAW 270: 1998 ⇒3230. 103-115.
3245 *Morla Asensio, Víctor* Poverty and wealth: Ben Sira's view of possessions. Der Einzelne. BZAW 270: 1998 ⇒3230. 151-178.
3246 *Murphy, Roland E.* Sin, repentance, and forgiveness in Sirach. Der Einzelne. BZAW 270: 1998 ⇒3230. 261-270.
3247 *Prato, Gian L.* Sapienza e Torah in Ben Sira: meccanismi comparativi culturali e conseguenze ideologico-religiose. RstB 10 (1998) 129-151.
3248 [E]**Reiterer, Friedrich Vinzenz** Freundschaft bei Ben Sira. BZAW 244: 1996 ⇒12,3224. [R]Synaxis 16/1 (1998) 314-316 (*Minissale, Antonino*); OLZ 93 (1998) 501-504 (*Wischmeyer, Oda*); ThLZ 123 (1998) 245-247 (*Meiser, Martin*); BZ 42 (1998) 119-120 (*Schreiner, Josef*).
3249 *Schrader, Lutz* Beruf, Arbeit und Muße als Sinnerfüllung bei Jesus Sirach. Der Einzelne. BZAW 270: 1998 ⇒3230. 117-149.
3250 **Schrader, Lutz** Leiden und Gerechtigkeit: Studien zur Theologie und Textgeschichte des Sirachbuches. BET 27: 1994 ⇒13,3337 [R]JAOS 118 (1998) 77-79 (*Crenshaw, James L.*).
3251 *Söding, Thomas* Nächstenliebe bei Jesus Sirach: eine Notiz zur weisheitlichen Ethik. BZ 42 (1998) 239-247.
3252 *Wahl, Otto* Lebensfreude und Genuß bei Jesus Sirach. Der Einzelne. BZAW 270: 1998 ⇒3230. 271-284.
3253 *Walkenhorst, Karl Heinz* Weise werden und altern bei Ben Sira. Der Einzelne. BZAW 270: 1998 ⇒3230. 217-237.
3254 *Wright, Benjamin G.* The discourse of riches and poverty in the book of Ben Sira. SBL.SP part 2. SBL.SPS 37: 1998 ⇒402. 559-578.

3255 *Legrand, Thierry* Siracide (syriaque) 1,20c-z: "une addition syriaque et ses résonances esséniennes...". [F]MARGAIN, J.. 1998 ⇒71. 123-134.
3256 *Beentjes, Pancratius C.* "Sei den Waisen wie ein Vater und den Witwen wie ein Gatte": ein kleiner Kommentar zu Ben Sira 4,1-10. Der Einzelne. BZAW 270: 1998 ⇒3230. 51-64.
3257 *Witczyk, Henryk* Il testo ebraico di Sir 4,17-18 e i suoi paralleli. CoTh 68A (1998) 23-38.
3258 *Kaiser, Otto* Carpe diem und Memento mori bei Ben Sira. [F]RÖMER, W.. AOAT 253: 1998 ⇒97. 185-203 [Qoh 9,4-10: Sir 14,11-19; 9,11-12].

3259 *Egger-Wenzel, Renate* "Denn harte Knechtschaft und Schande ist es, wenn eine Frau ihren Mann ernährt" (Sir 25,22);

3260 *Gilbert, Maurice* Prêt, aumône et caution. Der Einzelne. BZAW 270: 1998, ⇒3230. 23-49/179-189 [Sir 26-29].

3261 *Kaiser, Otto* Was ein Freund nicht tun darf: eine Auslegung von Sir 27,16-21. Gesammelte Aufsätze. BZAW 261: 1998 <1995> ⇒166. 217-232.

3262 *Krammer, Ingrid* "Wer anderen eine Grube gräbt, fällt selbst hinein: Ben Sira als Tradent eines bekannten Sprichwortes. Der Einzelne. BZAW 270: 1998 ⇒3230. 239-260 [Ps 7; 9-10; 35; 57; Prov 26,20-28; Sir 27,25-29; Qoh 10,8-9].

3263 *Sauer, Georg* Der Ratgeber (Sir 37,7-15): Textgeschichte als Auslegungsgeschichte und Bedeutungswandel. Der Einzelne. BZAW 270: 1998 ⇒3230. 73-85.

3264 *McConvery, Brendan* Ben Sira's "Praise of the physician" (Sir 38:1-15) in the light of some Hippocratic writings. PIBA 21 (1998) 62-86.

3265 **Brown, Teresa Rash** Sinners, idol-worshippers and fools among the men of Hesed: Ben Sira's pedagogy in 'Praise of the Fathers' (Sir 44-50). ^DGraduate Theological Union 1998, 224 pp.

3266 *Asurmendi, Jesús* Ben Sira et les prophètes. Transeuphratène 14 (1998) 91-102 [Sir 47-49].

3267 *Toloni, Giancarlo* 'Fosti chiamato con il nome glorioso' (Sir 47,18aα): studio di un'immagine allusiva. Aevum 72 (1998) 3-15.

3268 **Hildesheim, Ralph** Bis daß ein Prophet aufstand wie Feuer: Untersuchungen zum Prophetenverständnis des Ben Sira in Sir 48,1-49,16. TThSt 58: 1996 ⇒12,3245; 13,3352. ^RCBQ 60 (1998) 530-531 (*Corley, Jeremy*).

VII. Libri prophetici VT

E8.1 Prophetismus

3269 **Abrego de Lacy, José Maria** I libri profetici. 1996 ⇒12,3247; 13,3355. ^RRivBib 46 (1998) 231-233 (*Marconcini, Benito*).

3270 **Blenkinsopp, Joseph** Storia della profezia in Israele. 1997 ⇒13,3362. ^RCivCatt 149/3 (1998) 322-324 (*Scaiola, D.*);

3271 Geschichte der Prophetie in Israel: von den Anfängen bis zum hellenistische Zeitalter. Stu 1998, Kohlhammer 296 pp. 3-17-011774-2.

3272 *Boer, Roland* Ezekiel's Axl, or anarchism and ecstasy. Violence. 1998 ⇒260. 24-46.

3273 ^E**Cagni, Luigi** Le profezie di Mari. TVOA 2/2: 1995 ⇒11/1,2096; 12,3260. ^RPaVi 43/2 (1998) 63 (*Rolla, Armando*).

3274 **Cavedo, Romeo** Profetas: historia y teología del profetismo en el Antiguo Testamento. Dabar 3: M 1996, San Pablo 270 pp. 84-285-1838-6.

3275 **Clements, Ronald E.** Old Testament prophecy: from oracles to canon. 1996 ⇒13,3373. ^RJBL 117 (1998) 129-130 (*Mewsome, James D.*).

3276 **Cook, Stephen L.** Prophecy & apocalypticism. 1995 ⇒13,3373 ^RJThS 49 (1998) 189-191 (*Grabbe, Lester L.*).

3277 **Darsey, James** The prophetic tradition and radical rhetoric in America. 1997 ⇒13,3379. ᴿThTo 55 (1998) 474-475 (*Brueggemann, Walter*).

3278 ᴱ**Davies, Philip R.** The prophets. BiSe 42: 1996 ⇒12,174. ᴿCBQ 60 (1998) 600-601 (*Dearman, J. Andrew*).

3279 *Debenedetti, Giacomo* Introduzione; le tre rivelazioni; valore etico del messaggio profetico;

3280 I rapporti d'Israele con la terra e l'evoluzione del divino; il profetismo collegiale: Samuele ed Elia... Amos pastore. Profeti. 1998 <1924> ⇒145. 5-27/31-59.

3281 **DeVries, Simon J.** From old revelation to new: a tradition-historical and redaction-critical study of temporal transactions in prophetic prediction. 1995 ⇒11/1,2109; 12,3270. ᴿJSSt 43 (1998) 157-160 (*Williamson, H.G.M.*).

3282 *Díaz Mateos, Manuel* 'No despreciar la profecía': Espíritu, profecía y vida religiosa. RTLi 32 (1998) 121-134.

3283 **Draï, Raphaël** La communication prophétique, 3: l'économie chabbatique. P 1998, Fayard 555 pp. FF198. 2-213-60099-6.

3284 **Eaton, John H.** Mysterious messengers: a course on Hebrew prophecy from Amos onwards. GR 1998, Eerdmans x; 214 pp. 0-8028-4495-2.

3285 *Franco B., José Luis* Los profetas y la ética social cristiana. Voces 12 (1998) 25-42.

3286 *Gilbert, Maurice* La disponibilité des prophètes <1979>;

3287 Vrais et faux prophètes <1974>. Il a parlé par les prophètes. 1998 ⇒155. 159-168/169-189.

3288 *Gitin, Seymour* The Philistines in the prophetic texts: an archaeological perspective. ᶠFRERICHS, E. BJSt 320: 1998 ⇒28. 273-290.

3289 **Gowan, Donald E.** Theology of the prophetic books: the death and resurrection of Israel. LVL 1998, Westminster xi; 250 pp. 0-664-25689-9.

3290 *Grabbe, Lester L.* Poets, scribes, or preachers?: the reality of prophecy in the second temple period. SBL.SP part 2. SBL.SPS 37: 1998 ⇒402. 524-545.

3291 *Grottanelli, Cristiano* Possessione e visione nella dinamica della parola rivelata. Sibille. 1998 ⇒428. 43-52.

3292 *Haak, Robert D.* The Philistines in the prophetic texts. ᶠFrerichs, E. BJSt 320: 1998 ⇒28. 37-51.

3293 *Harvey, Julien* Expérience de Dieu expérience prophétique. Cahiers de Spiritualité ignatienne 22 (1998) <1976> 211-216.

3294 **Ice, Thomas; Demy, Timothy** Prophecy watch. Eugene, OR 1998, Harvest 279 pp. $10.

3295 *Jacob, Edmond* La prière prophétique. FV 97 (1998) 1-14.

3296 *Karp, Andrew* Prophecy and divination in archaic Greek literature. Mediators of the divine. SFSHJ 163: 1998 ⇒287. 9-44.

3297 **Koenen, Klaus** Heil den Gerechten—Unheil den Sündern!: ein Beitrag zur Theologie der Prophetenbücher. BZAW 229: 1994 ⇒10,3361... 13,3401. ᴿBZ 42 (1998) 305-307 (*Willmes, Bernd*).

3298 **Laato, Antti J.** History and ideology in the OT prophetic literature. CB.OT 41: 1996 ⇒12,3282. ᴿCBQ 60 (1998) 121-123 (*Dearman, J. Andrew*); JBL 117 (1998) 125-126 (*McLaughlin, John L.*).

3299 **Lehnhart, Bernhard** Prophet und König im Nordreich Israel: Studien zur sogenannten vorklassischen Prophetie im Nordreich Israel anhand der Samuel-, Elija- und Elischa-Überlieferung. ᴰSt. Georgen 1996-1997: ᴰ*Lohfink, N.*

3300 *Loza Vera, J.* Una invitación a la conversión: la denuncia de los pecados del pueblo en el Antiguo Testamento. RevBib 60 (1998) 129-181.

3301 *Malamat, Abraham* Intuitive prophecy—a general survey. Mari and the bible <1992>;

3302 Prophetic revelations in Mari and the bible: complementary considerations <1966>;

3303 Parallels between the new prophecies from Mari and biblical prophecy <1989>;

3304 New light from Mari (*ARM* XXVI) on biblical prophecy <1991>;

3305 The secret council and prophetic involvement in Mari and Israel <1991>;

3306 A new prophetic message from Aleppo and its biblical counterparts <1993>. Mari and the bible. 1998 ⇒173. 59-82/83-101/122-127/128-133/134-141/151-156.

3307 *Margalit, Baruch* Ninth-century Israelite prophecy in the light of contemporary NWSemitic epigraphs. ᶠLᴏʀᴇᴛᴢ O. AOAT 250: 1998 ⇒65. 515-532.

3308 *Mathew, K.V.* Crisis and hope in Israel's exile. BiBh 24 (1998) 272-283.

3309 **Mosconi, Luis** Profetas da bíblia: para cristãos e cristãs rumo ao novo milênio. São Paulo 1998, Loyola 148 pp. 85-15-01798-9.

3310 *Nissinen, Martti* Prophecy against the king in Neo-Assyrian sources. "Lasset uns Brücken bauen...". BEAT 42: 1998 ⇒401. 157-170.

3311 **Nissinen, Martti** Reference to prophecy in neo-Assyrian sources. SAAS 7: [Helsinki] 1998, The Neo-Assyrian Text Corpus Project x; 194 pp. $35. 951-45-8079-6.

3312 **Paas, Stefan** Schepping en oordeel: een onderzoek naar scheppingsvoorstellingen bij enkele profeten uit de achste eeuw voor Christus. Diss. Utrecht 1998; Eng. sum.; Heerenveen 1998, Groen 395 pp. 90-5030-975-5 [NThAR 1999,253].

3313 *Priotto, Michelangelo* Il banchetto escatologico nelle profezie dell'Antico Testamento. L'eucaristia nella bibbia. DSBP 19: 1998 ⇒218. 15-47.

3314 **Ravasi, Gianfranco** I profeti. PaVi: Mi 1998, Áncora 295 pp. 88-7610-662-6.

3315 *Reimer, David J.* Political prophets?: political exegesis and prophetic theology. Intertextuality. OTS 40: 1998 ⇒394. 126-142.

3316 ᴱ**Rusconi, Roberto** The book of prophecies edited by Christopher Cᴏʟᴜᴍʙᴜs. Repertorium Columbianum 3: 1997 ⇒13,3419. ᴿSCJ 29 (1998) 922-924 (*Barnes, Robin B.*).

3317 *Schmidt, Werner H.* Einsicht als Ziel prophetischer Verkündigung ᶠRᴜᴘᴘᴇʀᴛ, L. FzB 88: 1998 ⇒99. 377-396.

3318 *Shaw, Gregory* Divination in the Neoplatonism of Iamblichus. Mediators of the divine. SFSHJ 163: 1998 ⇒287. 225-267.

3319 *Sherwood, Yvonne M.* Prophetic scatology: prophecy and the art of sensation. Semeia 82 (1998) 183-224.

3320 **Spreafico, Ambrogio** La voce di Dio: per capire i profeti. Studi biblici 33: Bo 1998, EDB 296 pp. L34.000. 88-10-40734-2.

3321 **Steck, Odil Hannes** Die Prophetenbücher und ihr theologisches Zeugnis. 1996 ⇒12,3309. ᴿThLZ 123 (1998) 370-371 (*Kessler,*

Rainer); Bib. 79 (1998) 271-275 (*Becker, Joachim*); Sal. 60 (1998) 352-353 (*Vicent, R.*).

3322   **Van Dam, Cornelis** The Urim and Thummim: a means of revelation in ancient Israel. 1997 ⇒13,3431. [R]JQR 88 (1998) 263-274 (*Hurowitz, Victor Avigdor*).

3323   *Van der Toorn, Karel* Old Babylonian prophecy between the oral and the written. JNSL 24/1 (1998) 55-70.

3324   **Vogels, W.** I profeti: saggio di teologia biblica. 1994 ⇒10,3374; 12,3310. [R]Inter Fratres 48 (1998) 257-258 (*Martignani, Luigi*).

3325   **Walvoord, John F.** End times: understanding today's world events in biblical prophecy. Swindoll Leadership library: Nv 1998, Word 243 pp. $25. 0-8499-1377-2.

3326   [F]**WATTS, John D.W.** Forming prophetic literature. JSOT.S 235: 1996 ⇒12,105. [R]CBQ 60 (1998) 406-407 (*Sweeney, Marvin A.*).

3327   **Wiesel, Elie** Célébration prophétique: portraits et légendes. P 1998, Seuil 315 pp. FF140. 2-02-033284-1.

E8.2 **Proto-Isaias,** *textus, commentarii*

3328   **Berges, Ulrich** Das Buch Jesaja: Komposition und Endgestalt. Herders biblische Studien 16: FrB 1998, Herder 591 pp. DM118. 3-451-26592-3.

3329   *Fischer, Irmtraud* Das Buch Jesaja: das Buch der weiblichen Metaphern. Kompendium Feministische Bibelauslegung. 1998 [E]**Schottroff, L.**: 1998 ⇒H8.9. 246-257.

3330   *Gosse, Bernard* La rédaction du livre d'Isaïe en rapport au livre d'Amos et au Psautier. Henoch 20 (1998) 259-270.

3331   [E]**Gryson, Roger** Esaias 1-39; 40,1-54,17. Die Reste der altlateinischen Bibel nach Petrus Sabatier 12: I, II Fasc. 1-7. 1987-1996 ⇒12,3322; 13,3443. [R]JBL 117 (1998) 549-551 (*Harvey, Paul B.*).

3332   **Laato, Antti** 'About Zion I will not be silent': the book of Isaiah as an ideological unity. CB.OT 44: Sto 1998, Almqvist & W 241 pp. 91-22-01811-5.

3333   [E]**Melugin, Roy F.; Sweeney, Marvin Alan** New visions of Isaiah. JSOT.S 214: 1996 ⇒12,3331. [R]CBQ 60 (1998) 189-190 (*Irwin, William H.*).

3334   *Morfino, Mauro Maria* Lo spirito Santo-'ruach qudsha/nebu'ah' nel Targum di Isaia. Theologica & Historica 7 (1998) 21-48.

3335   *Seitz, Christopher* Isaiah and the search for a new paradigm: authorship and inspiration;

3336   Isaiah and Lamentations: the suffering and afflicted Zion;

3337   Isaiah in parish bible study: the question of the place of the reader in biblical texts 194-212;

3338   Isaiah in New Testament, lectionary, pulpit. Word without end. 1998 ⇒200. 113-129/130-149/213-228.

3339   **Simian-Yofre, Horacio** Testi isaiani dell'Avvento: esegesi e liturgia. CSB 29: 1996 ⇒12,3341. [R]RivBib 46 (1998) 233-235 (*Marconcini, Benito*).

3340   **Sweeney, Marvin Alan** Isaiah 1-39: with an introduction to prophetic literature. FOTL 16: 1996 ⇒12,3346. [R]JSSt 43 (1998) 160-161 (*Clements, R.E.*); JAOS 118 (1998) 143 (*Soggin, J.A.*); Bijdr. 59 (1998) 338-339 (*Beuken, Willem A.M.*); CBQ 60 (1998) 351-352 (*Polan, Gregory J.*).

E8.3 **Isaias 1-39,** *themata, versiculi*

3341 **Becker, Uwe** Jesaja—von der Botschaft zum Buch. FRLANT 178: 1997 ⇒13,3463. [R]Bib. 79 (1998) 565-568 (*Clements, R.E.*).

3342 *Buchanan, George Wesley* Isaianic midrash and the Exodus. The function of scripture. 1998 ⇒236. 89-109.

3343 *Debenedetti, Giacomo* Isaia. Profeti. 1998 <1924> ⇒145. 87-110. ʼ

3344 **Fischer, Irmtraud** Tora für Israel—Tora für die Völker: das Konzept des Jesajabuches. SBS 164: 1995 ⇒11/1,2200; 12,3353. [R]ITS 35/1 (1998) 85-88 (*Ceresko, Anthony R.*); JBL 117 (1998) 126-129 (*Carr, David M.*).

3345 *Hermisson, Hans-Jürgen* Zukunftserwartung und Gegenwartskritik in der Verkündigung Jesajas <1973>;

3346 Der verborgene Gott im Buch Jesaja <1994>. Gesammelte Aufsätze. FAT 23: 1998 ⇒161. 81-104/105-116.

3347 **Parekh, Samson C.** The lexical and theological significance on the root kadash in the Book of Isaiah. [D]Dallas 1998, 292 pp.

3348 *Seijas de los Ríos, Guadalupe* Discoursive texts and perfect tense in Isaiah. Bible et informatique. 1998 ⇒386. 113-130.

3349 **Williamson, Hugh Godfrey Maturin** Variations on a theme: king, messiah and servant in the book of Isaiah. The Didsbury Lectures 1997: Carlisle 1998, Paternoster xiii; 241 pp. 0-85364-870-0.

3350 *Willis, John T.* Exclusivistic and inclusivistic aspects of the concept of "the people of God" in the book of Isaiah. RestQ 40 (1998) 3-12.

3351 *Goldingay, John* Isaiah i 1 and ii 1. VT 48 (1998) 326-332.

3352 *Irudaya, Raj* Celebration by a non-community?: socio-pastoral reflections on Isaiah 1:2-20. VJTR 62 (1998) 473-486.

3353 **Bartelt, Andrew H.** The book around Immanuel: style and structure in Isaiah 2-12. 1996 ⇒12,3362. [R]Bib. 79 (1998) 124-129 (*Sweeney, Marvin A.*).

3354 *Schwartz, Baruch J.* Torah from Zion: Isaiah's temple vision (Isaiah 2:1-4). Sanctity of time. 1998 ⇒303. 11-26.

3355 *Bartelmus, Rüdiger* Beobachtungen zur literarischen Struktur des sog. Weinbergslieds (Jes 5,1-7): Möglichkeiten und Grenzen der formgeschichtlichen Methode bei der Interpretation von Texten aus dem corpus propheticum. ZAW 110 (1998) 50-66.

3356 *Ogden, Graham* Translating Isaiah 5.1: what does the poet sing?. BiTr 49 (1998) 245-246.

3357 **Van Wieringen, Archibald L.H.M.** The implied reader in Isaiah 6-12. BiblInterp 34: Lei 1998, Brill xi; 300 pp. ƒ160. 90-04-11222-7.

3358 **Hartenstein, Friedhelm** Die Unzugänglichkeit Gottes im Heiligtum: Jesaja 6 und der Wohnort JHWHs in der Jerusalemer Kulttradition. WMANT 75: 1997 ⇒13,3501. [R]SEL 15 (1998) 121-122 (*Niehr, Herbert*).

3359 *Robinson, Geoffrey D.* The motif of deafness and blindness in Isaiah 6:9-10: a contextual, literary, and theological analysis. BBR 8 (1998) 167-186.

3360 *Irsigler, Hubert* Beobachtungen zur Rezeptionsgeschichte des "Immanuel" in Jesaja 7-11. [F]HOFFMANN, P., Von Jesus. BZNW 93: 1998 ⇒43. 3-23.

3361 *Sæbo, Magne* Form-historical perspectives on Isaiah 7.3-9. On the way to canon. 1998 <1960> ⇒194. 93-107.

3362 *Menzies, Glen W.* To what does faith lead?: the two-stranded textual tradition of Isaiah 7.9b. JSOT 80 (1998) 111-128.

3363 *Sæbo, Magne* Traditio-historical perspectives on Isaiah 8.9-10: an attempt to clarify an old crux interpretum. On the way to canon. 1998 <1964> ⇒194. 108-121.

3364 *Menken, Maarten J.J.* The textual form of the quotation from Isaiah 8:23-9:1 in Matthew 4:15-16. RB 105 (1998) 526-545.

3365 *Lust, Johan* Messianism in the Septuagint: Isaiah 8:23b-9:6 (9:1-7). Interpretation of the Bible. JSOT.S 289: 1998 ⇒388. 147-163.

3366 *Lepore, Luciano* Isaia 8,23b (9,1-6): ricostruzione letteraria e riletture teologiche. RivBib 46 (1998) 257-276.

3367 *Waschke, Ernst-Joachim* Die Stellung der Königstexte im Jesajabuch im Vergleich zu den Königspsalmen 2, 72 und 89. ZAW 110 (1998) 348-364 [Isa 9,1-6; 11,1-8; 32,1-5; 32,15-20; 55,1-5].

3368 **Shipp, R. Mark** Of dead kings and dirges: myth and meaning in Isaiah 14:4b-21. ᴰPrinceton Theol. Sem. 1998, 211 pp.

3369 *Weippert, Manfred* Ar und Kir in Jesaja 15,1: mit Erwägungen zur historischen Geographie Moabs. ZAW 110 (1998) 547-555.

3370 *Lubetski, Meir; Gottlieb, Claire* Isaiah 18: the Egyptian nexus ᶠGORDON, C. JSOT.S 273: 1998 ⇒31. 364-384.

3371 *Niccacci, Alviero* Isaiah xviii-xx from an Egyptological perspective. VT 48 (1998) 214-238.

3372 *Krašovec, Jože* Healing of Egypt through judgement and the creation of a universal chosen people (Isaiah 19:16-25). Jerusalem studies. ÄAT 40: 1998 ⇒361. 295-305.

3373 *Wodecki, Bernard* The heights of the religious universalism in Is XIX:16-25. "Lasset uns Brücken bauen...". BEAT 42: 1998 ⇒401. 171-191.

3374 *Israelit-Groll, Sarah* The Egyptian background to Isaiah 19.18. ᶠGORDON, C. JSOT.S 273: 1998 ⇒31. 300-303.

3375 **Van der Kooij, Arie** The oracle of Tyre: the Septuagint of Isaiah XXIII as version and vision. VT.S 71: Lei 1998, Brill ix; 214 pp. $81. 90-04-11152-2.

3376 *Polaski, Donald C.* Reflections on a Mosaic covenant: the eternal covenant (Isaiah 24,5) and intertextuality. JSOT 77 (1998) 55-73.

3377 *Niewiadomski, Józef* "... ein Festmahl für alle ...": biblisch-systematische Reminiszenz. ThPQ 146 (1998) 47-51 [Isa 25,6-8].

3378 *Van der Kooij, Arie* The teacher Messiah and worldwide peace: some comments on Symmachus' version of Isaiah 25:7-8. JNSL 24/1 (1998) 75-82.

3379 *Polaski, Donald C.* The politics of prayer: a new historicist reading of Isaiah 26. PRSt 25 (1998) 357-371.

3380 *Wahl, Otto* "Wir haben eine befestigte Stadt": zur Botschaft von Jes 26,1-6. ᶠRUPPERT, L. FzB 88: 1998 ⇒99. 459-481.

3381 *Day, John N.* God and Leviathan in Isaiah 27:1. BS 155 (1998) 423-436.

3382 *Beuken, Willem André Maria* Women and the spirit, the ox and the ass. EThL 74 (1998) 5-26 [Isa 28-32].

3383 *Deck, Scholastika* Kein Exodus bei Jesaja?. ᶠRUPPERT, L. FzB 88: 1998 ⇒99. 31-47 [Exod 14,28; 14,13-14; Isa 31,1-3; 30,15].

3384 *Williamson, H.G.M.* The messianic texts in Isaiah 1-39. King and Messiah. JSOT.S 270: 1998 ⇒378. 238-270 [Isa 32,1-5; 7,1-17; 8,23-9,6; 11,1-5].

3385 *Ballard, H.W.* Is Lilith fair?: an observation from Isaiah 34:14. RExp 95 (1998) 583-588.
3386 **Mbuwayesango, Dora Rudo** The defense of Zion and the House of David: Isaiah 36-39 in the context of Isaiah 1-39. ^DEmory 1998, 207 pp.
3387 *Höffken, Peter* Zur Eigenart von Jes 39 par. II Reg 20,12-19. ZAW 110 (1998) 244-249.

E8.4 Deutero-Isaias 40-52: *commentarii, themata, versiculi*

3388 **Barstad, Hans M.** The Babylonian captivity of the book of Isaiah: 'exilic' Judah and the provenance of Isaiah 40-55. 1997 ⇒13,3528. ^RThLZ 123 (1998) 1199-1200 (*Höffken, Peter*); BiOr 55 (1998) 870-873 (*Labahn, Antje*).
3389 *Boer, Roland* Deutero-Isaiah: historical materialism and biblical theology. Biblical Interpretation 6 (1998) 181-204.
3390 *Brettler, Marc Zvi* Incompatible metaphors for YHWH in Isaiah 40-66. JSOT 78 (1998) 97-120.
3391 *Coggins, Richard J.* Do we still need Deutero-Isaiah?. JSOT 81 (1998) 77-92.
3392 *Feuerstein, Rüdiger* Weshalb gibt es "Deuterojesaja"?. ^FRUPPERT, L. FzB 88: 1998 ⇒99. 93-134.
3393 *Gilbert, Maurice* Nouvelle création et expérience historique. Il a parlé par les prophètes. 1998 ⇒155. 215-230.
3394 ^E**Grabbe, Lester L.** Leading captivity captive: 'the exile' as history and ideology. JSOT.S 278: Shf 1998, Academic 161 pp. £35/$57.50. 1-85075-907-3.
3395 *Haag, Ernst* Israel und David als Zeugen Jahwes nach Deuterojesaja. ^FRUPPERT, L. FzB 88: 1998 ⇒99. 157-180.
3396 *Hermisson, Hans-Jürgen* Jakob und Zion, Schöpfung und Heil: zur Einheit der Theologie Deuterojesajas <1990>;
3397 Einheit und Komplexität Deuterojesajas: Probleme der Redaktionsgeschichte von 40-55 <1989>;
3398 Diskussionsworte bei Deuterojesaja: zur theologischen Argumentation des Propheten <1971>;
3399 Gottesknecht und Gottes Knechte: zur ältesten Deutung eines deuterojesajanischen Themas <1996>. Gesammelte Aufsätze. FAT 23: 1998 ⇒161. 117-131/132-157/158-173/241-266.
3400 **Höffken, Peter** Das Buch Jesaja: Kapitel 40-66. Neuer Stuttgarter Kommentar: AT 18: Stu 1998, Kath. Bibelwerk 282 pp. 3-460-07182-6.
3401 **Irsigler, Hubert** Ein Weg aus der Gewalt?: Gottesknecht kontra Kyros im Deuterojesajabuch. Beiträge zur Friedensethik 28: Stu 1998, Kohlhammer 40 pp. 3-17-015272-6.
3402 **Kim, Hyun Chul Paul** Salvation of Israel and the nations in Isaiah 40-55: a study of texts and concepts. ^DClaremont 1998, 383 pp.
3403 **Koole, Jan L.** Isaiah 3/2: Isaiah 49-55. HCOT: Lv 1998, Peeters xxv; 454 pp. 90-429-0679-0;
3404 Isaiah 40-48. Isaiah 3/1. HCOT: 1997 ⇒13,3538. ^RBiOr 55 (1998) 494-497 (*Höffken, Peter*); ThLZ 123 (1998) 850-852 (*Hermisson, Hans-Jürgen*).

3405 **Korpel, Marjo Christina A.; De Moor, Johannes C.** The structure of classical Hebrew poetry: Isaiah 40-55. OTS 41: Lei 1998, Brill xi; 752 pp. $212. 90-04-11261-8.

3406 *Korpel, M.C.A.; Moor, J.Ç. de; Sepmeijer, F.* Consistency with regard to tenses: Targum and Peshiṭta in two samples from Deutero-Isaiah. Bible et informatique. 1998 ⇒386. 195-220.

3407 **Lee, Stephen** Creation and redemption in Isaiah 40-55. Jian Dao dissertation, bible and Literature 2: Hong Kong 1995, Alliance bible Seminary xxii; 219 pp. 962-7997-12-9.

3408 **Małecki, Zdisław** Monoteizm w Księdze Deuteroizajasza. Kraków 1998, 289 pp [RBL 52,90—Poniży, Bogdan]. **P**.

3409 **Oswalt, John N.** The book of Isaiah: chapters 40-66. NIBC.OT: GR 1998, Eerdmans xviii; 755 pp. $48. 0-8028-2534-6. [R]BS 155 (1998) 494-496 (*Chisholm, Robert B.*).

3410 **Rosenbaum, Michael** Word-order variation in Isaiah 40-55: a functional perspective. SSN 36: 1997 ⇒13,3548. [R]BiOr 55 (1998) 484-485 (*Van Wieringen, Archibald L.H.M.*); JThS 49 (1998) 707-709 (*Williamson, H.G.M.*).

3411 *Schreiner, Josef* Zum Stellenwert von Menschenreden im prophetischen Gotteswort bei Jesaja 40-55. [F]RUPPERT, L. FzB 88: 1998 ⇒99. 431-458.

3412 *Seitz, Christopher* How is the prophet Isaiah present in the latter half of the book?: the logic of chapters 40-66 within the book of Isaiah. Word without end. 1998 <1996> ⇒200. 168-193.

3413 **Sommer, Benjamin D.** A prophet reads scripture: allusions in Isaiah 40-66. Palo Alto 1998, Stanford Univ. Press xiii; 355 pp. $49.50.

3414 *Carroll, Robert P.* Biblical ideolatry: Ideologiekritik, biblical studies and the problematics of ideology. JNSL 24/1 (1998) 101-114 [Isa 40-48].

3415 *Clines, David J.A.* The parallelism of greater precision: notes from Isaiah 40 for a theory of Hebrew poetry. OT essays, 1. JSOT.S 292: 1998 <1987> ⇒142. 314-336.

3416 *Görg, Manfred* Revision von Schöpfung und Geschichte: auf dem Wege zu einer Strukturbestimmung von Jes 40,1-8(11). [F]RUPPERT, L. FzB 88: 1998 ⇒99. 135-156.

3417 *Dick, Michael Brennan* Second Isaiah's parody on making a cult image:(Isaiah 40:18-20; 41:6-7) and the Babylonian *Mis Pî*. "Lasset uns Brücken bauen...". 1998 ⇒401. 193-202.

3418 **Farfán Navarro, Enrique** El desierto transformado. AnBib 130: 1992 ⇒7,3192... 12,3409. [R]EstB 56 (1998) 543-545 (*Ramis, F.*) [Isa 41,17-20].

3419 *Biger, Gideon; Liphschitz, Nili* ‫אשים‬ ‫שמן‬ ‫ועץ‬ ‫והדס‬ ‫שטה‬ ,‫ארז‬ ‫במדבר‬ ‫אתן‬ ['I will ‫במקתא‬ ‫השממה‬ ‫הפתחת‬ ‫נס‬ ‫על‬ — ‫יחדין‬ ‫ותאשור‬ ‫תדהר‬ ,‫ברוש‬ ‫בערבה‬ plant in the wilderness the *erez*, the *shittah*, the *hadas*, and *etz shemen*: I will set in the desert the *brosh*, *tidhar*, and *teashur* together': on the miracle of flourishing the wilderness in the Bible]. Beit Mikra 153 (1998) 161-174 [Isa 41,19].

3420 *Clements, Ronald E.* "Who is blind but my servant?" (Isaiah 42:19): how then shall we read Isaiah?. [F]BRUEGGEMANN, W. 1998 ⇒16. 143-156.

3421 *Tyrol, Anton* L'amore di YHWH verso gli esuli di Babilonia in Is 43,1-13: aspetti critici ed esegetici. FolTh 9 (1998) 123-161.

3422 *Goldingay, John* Isaiah 43,22-28. ZAW 110 (1998) 173-191.
3423 *Blau, Joshua* A misunderstood medieval translation of *śered* (Isaiah 44:13) and its impact on modern scholarship. Topics in Hebrew... linguistics. 1998 <1995> ⇒136. 283-289.
3424 *Finley, John* Isaiah 51:1-3—liberty's rock, freedom's quarry. RExp 95 (1998) 109-113.
3425 *Frankemölle, Hubert* Jesus als deuterojesajanischer Freudenbote?: zur Rezeption von Jes 52,7 und 61,1 im Neuen Testament, durch Jesus und in den Targumim. Jüdische Wurzeln. BBB 116: 1998 <1989> ⇒151. 131-160.

E8.5 *Isaiae 53ss, Carmina Servi YHWH:* Servant Songs

3426 *Albrecht, Ralf* Sühne und Stellvertretung in Jesaja 53. JETh 12 (1998) 7-24.
3427 [ET]**Alobaidi, Joseph** The messiah in Isaiah 53: the commentaries of Saadia GAON, Salmon ben YERUHAM and Yefet ben ELI on Is 52,13-53,12. La Bible dans l'histoire, textes et études 2: Bern 1998, Lang 211 pp. DM55. 0-8204-4201-1.
3428 *Bailey, Daniel P.* Concepts of Stellvertretung in the interpretation of Isaiah 53;
3429 The suffering servant: recent Tübingen scholarship on Isaiah 53. Jesus and the suffering servant. 1998 ⇒3430. 223-250/251-259.
3430 [E]**Bellinger, William H.; Farmer, William R.** Jesus and the suffering servant: Isaiah 53 and christian origins. Harrisburg 1998, Trinity 325 pp. $25. 1-56338-230-X.
3431 *Clements, R.E.* Isaiah 53 and the restoration of Israel;
3432 *Farmer, William R.* Reflections on Isaiah 53 and Christian origins. Jesus and the suffering servant. 1998 ⇒3430. 39-54/260-280.
3433 [E]**Gryson, Roger** Esaias, Fasc. 7-10: 53,3-65,23. VL 12/2. FrB 1996-1997, Herder 1281-1600 pp. 3-451-00127-6/8-4/9-2/30-6. [R]JThS 49 (1998) 201-203 (*Elliott, J.K.*);
3434 Esaias, pars 2, fasc. 8-11: Is 54,17-fin; conclusion: histoire du texte; correction et compléments; index des témoins; table des matières. VL 12. FrB 1996-1997, Herder 1361-1707 pp.
3435 *Hanson, Paul D.* The world of the servant of the Lord in Isaiah 40-55. Jesus and the suffering servant. 1998 ⇒3430. 9-22.
3436 *Hermisson, Hans-Jürgen* Das vierte Gottesknechtslied im deuterojesajanischen Kontext <1996>;
3437 Der Lohn des Knechts <1981>;
3438 Israel und der Gottesknecht bei Deuterojesaja <1982>. Gesammelte Aufsätze. FAT 23: 1998 ⇒161. 220-240/177-196/197-219.
3439 *Holc, Milan* I canti del Servio di JHWH nell'interpretazione del giudaismo precristiano. Gesù Servo. 1998 ⇒210. 7-28.
3440 *Hooker, Morna D.* Response to Mikeal PARSONS. Jesus and the suffering servant. 1998 ⇒3430. 120-124.
3441 [E]**Janowski, Bernd; Stuhlmacher, Peter** Der leidende Gottesknecht: Jesaja 53... mit einer Bibliographie zu Jes 53. FAT 14: 1996 ⇒12,3432; 13,3582. [R]JThS 49 (1998) 709-713 (*Schaper, Joachim*); OTEs 11 (1998) 357-360 [Afrikaans] (*Booy, G.M.*).
3442 *Korpel, M.C.A.* Antwort an Peter HÖFFKEN anlässlich der Symmetrie in Jesaja LV. VT 48 (1998) 97-98.

3443 **Lavilla Martín, M.A.** La imagen del Siervo en el pensamiento de san FRANCISCO de Asís, segùn sus escritos. 1995 ⇒12,343 RComunidades 26 (1998) 22-23 (*Anxo Pena, Miguel*).

3444 **Masini, Mario** Il Servo del Signore: lectio divina dei carmi del profeta Isaia. Mi 1998, Paoline 418 pp.

3445 *Melugin, Roy F.* On reading Isaiah 53 as Christian scripture. Jesus and the suffering servant. 1998 ⇒3430. 55-69.

3446 *Reichenbach, Bruce R.* "By his stripes we are healed". JETS 41 (1998) 551-560 [Isa 52,13-53,12].

3447 *Reventlow, Henning* Basic issues in the interpretation of Isaiah 53. Jesus and the suffering servant. 1998 ⇒3430. 23-38.

3448 *Sapp, David A.* The LXX, 1QIsa, and MT versions of Isaiah 53 and the christian doctrine of atonement. Jesus and the suffering servant. 1998 ⇒3430. 170-192.

3449 *Sæbo, Magne* From the individual to the collective: a pattern of inner-biblical interpretation. On the way to canon. 1998 <1989> ⇒194. 259-270.

3450 *Venier, Elio* Il 'Servus Jahwé' e il Santo Volto. Il Volto dei Volti 1 (1998) 12-19.

3451 *Volgger, David* Das 'Schuldopfer' Ascham in Jes 53,10 und die Interpretation des sogenannten vierten Gottesknechtliedes. Bib. 79 (1998) 473-498.

3452 *Wright, N.T.* The servant and Jesus: the relevance of the colloquy for the current quest for Jesus. Jesus and the suffering servant. 1998 ⇒3430. 281-297.

3453 *Zurli, Emanuela* Il quarto canto del Servo del Signore (Is 52,13-53,12). VM 52 (1998) 15-51.

E8.6 [Trito]Isaias 56-66

3454 *Croatto, J. Severino* La inclusion social den el programa del Tercer Isaias: exégesis de Isaías 56:1-8 y 66:18-24. RevBib 60 (1998) 91-110.

3455 *Diebner, Bernd Jørg* Mehrere Hände—ein Text: Jes 58 und die Grenzen der Literarkritik. DBAT 29 (1998) 139-156.

3456 *Halpern, Baruch* The new names of Isaiah 62:4: Jeremiah's reception in the restoration and the politics of "Third Isaiah". JBL 117 (1998) 623-643.

3457 **Kakule Vyakuno, Joseph Emmanuel** Question sociale et pratique religieuse à partir d'Is 58.: étude littéraire, théologique et historique. Toulouse 1998, Institut Catholique de Toulouse 2 vols.

3458 **Ruszowski, Leszek** Eine Untersuchung zum literarischen Wandel der Auffassung von 'Volk' und 'Gemeinde' in Jes. 56-66. Diss. Basel 1997-1998: DSeybold, K. [ThRv 94,iii].

E8.7 Jeremias

3459 **Boersma, Hans** Eating God's words; the life of Jeremiah: a study guide. Revelation: GR 1998, CRC 64 pp. 1-5612-380-7.

3460 EBogaert, Pierre-Maurice Le livre de Jérémie. BEThL 54: 1997 <1981> ⇒13,3612. RRivBib 46 (1998) 485-487 (*Prato, Gian Luigi*).

3461 **Brueggemann, Walter** A commentary on Jeremiah: exile and homecoming. GR 1998, Eerdmans xiv; 502 pp. £20. 0-8028-0280-X.

3462 ^E**Curtis, Adrian H.W.; Römer, Thomas** The book of Jeremiah and its reception: le livre de Jérémie et sa réception. BEThL 128: 1997 ⇒13,186. ^RBZ 42 (1998) 307-309 (*Fischer, Georg*); OLZ 93 (1998) 660-663 (*Thiel, W.*); JNSL 24/1 (1998) 241-244 (*Stipp, Hermann-Josef*).

3463 *Debenedetti, Giacomo* Geremia. Profeti. 1998 <1924> ⇒145. 113-137.

3464 **Keown, Gerald L.; Scalise, Pamela J.; Smothers, Thomas G.** Jeremiah 26-52. WBC 27: 1995 ⇒11/1,2310. ^RIThQ 63 (1998) 404 (*McConvery, Brendan*).

3465 *Marquis, Galen* The text-critical relevance of the Three in the book of Jeremiah: an examination of the critical apparatus of the Hebrew University Bible Project edition. Origen's Hexapla. TSAJ 58: 1998 ⇒399. 255-273.

3466 **McKane, William** Commentary on Jeremiah XXVI-LII. Jeremiah, 2. ICC: 1996 ⇒12,3455; 13,3622. ^RBZ 42 (1998) 309-310 (*Fischer, Georg*); JSSt 43 (1998) 371-373 (*Applegate, John*); AThR 80 (1998) 415-416 (*Viviano, Pauline A.*).

3467 **Mello, A.** Geremia: commento esegetico-spirituale. 1997 ⇒13,3623. ^RAsp. 45 (1998) 427-429 (*Casale, Cesare Marcheselli*).

3468 ^E**Rabin, C.; Talmon, S.; Tov, E.** The book of Jeremiah. The Hebrew University Bible Project: 1997 ⇒13,3624. ^RCBQ 60 (1998) 543-544 (*Althann, Robert*).

3469 ^E**Sepmeijer, Floris** A bilingual concordance to the targum of the prophets 12, 13, 14: Jeremiah 1, 2, 3: A (Aleph)-Z (Zajin); Ḥ (Chet)-S (Samek); ' (Ajin)-T (Taw). Lei 1998, Brill 322; 309; 363 pp. 90-04-11012-7; -3-5; -4-3. $131+131+131.

3470 **Stipp, Hermann-Josef** Deuterojeremianische Konkordanz. ATSAT 63: St. Ottilien 1998, EOS (6) 193 pp. 3-88096-563-3.

3471 **Thompson, Henry O.** The book of Jeremiah: an annotated bibliography. ATLA.BS 41: 1996 ⇒12,3457. ^RCBQ 60 (1998) 548-549 (*McConville, J.G.*).

3472 *Villapadierna, Carlos de* El profeta Jeremías. Evangelio y Vida 40 (1998) 38-40, 146-148.

3473 **Virgili, Rosanna** Geremia, l'incendio e la speranza: la figura e il messaggio del profeta. Quaderni di Camaldoli 13; Meditazioni 7: Bo 1998, EDB 123 pp. L14.000. 88-10-41113-7.

3474 *Anderson, Jeff S.* The metonymical curse as propaganda in the book of Jeremiah. BBR 8 (1998) 1-13.

3475 *Applegate, John* The fate of Zedekiah: redactional debate in the book of Jeremiah. VT 48 (1998) 137-160, 301-308 [Jer 24,1-10; 27,17; 21,1-10; 38,17-23; 25,4-7].

3476 *Bauer, Angela* Das Buch Jeremia: wenn kluge Klagefrauen und prophetische Pornographie den Weg ins Exil weisen. Kompendium Feministische Bibelauslegung. 1998 ^E**Schottroff, L.**: 1998 ⇒H8.9. 258-269;

3477 Jeremiah as female impersonator: roles of difference in gender perception and gender perceptivity. Escaping Eden. BiSe 65: 1998 ⇒278. 199-207.

3478 *Fuchs, Gisela* "Du bist mir zum Trugbach geworden": verwandte Motive in den Konfessionen Jeremias und den Klagen Hiobs (Zweiter Teil). BZ 42 (1998) 19-38.

3479 *Gosse, Bernard* The Masoretic redaction of Jeremiah: an explanation. JSOT 77 (1998) 75-80 [Jer 19,8-11; 36; 30-31; 50,13; 51,37].

3480 **Hadey, Jean** Le statut du temple dans le livre du prophète Jérémie. Diss. Strasbourg 1998: ᴰ*Heintz, J.-G.*, 343 pp [RTL 30,574].

3481 *Hermisson, Hans-Jürgen* Die 'Königsspruch'-Sammlung im Jeremia-buch—von der Anfangs- zur Endgestalt <1990>;

3482 Jahwes und Jeremias Rechtsstreit: zum Thema der Konfessionen Jeremias <1987>. Gesammelte Aufsätze. FAT 23: 1998 ⇒161. 37-58/5-36.

3483 *Huwyler, Beat* Text und Redaktion in den Völkersprüchen des Jeremiabuches. "Lasset uns Brücken bauen...". BEAT 42: 1998 ⇒401. 203-209.

3484 **Jantas, Anna** Idea pojednania z Bogiem w ksiedze proroka Jeremiasza [[L'idée de réconciliation avec Dieu dans le livre du prophète Jérémie]. Diss. Lublin 1998: ᴰ*Rubinkiewicz, R.*, 220 pp [RTL 30,574]. **P**.

3485 *Macchi, Jean-Daniel* Les doublets dans les oracles contre les nations du livre de Jérémie. "Lasset uns Brücken bauen...". BEAT 42: 1998 ⇒401. 211-222.

3486 *Snell, Daniel C.* Intellectual freedom in the ancient Near East. Intellectual life. 1998 ⇒450. 359-363.

3487 **Stipp, Hermann-Josef** Das masoretische und alexandrinische Sondergut des Jeremiabuches: textgeschichtlicher Rang, Eigenarten, Triebkräfte. OBO 136: 1994 ⇒10,3516... 13,3625. ᴿBZ 42 (1998) 121-122 (*Thiel, Winfried*).

3488 **Stulman, Louis** Order amid chaos: Jeremiah as symbolic tapestry. BiSe 57: Shf 1998, Academic 204 pp. $23.75. 1-85075-976-6.

3489 *Thiel, Winfried* Das Jeremiabuch als Literatur. VF 43 (1998) 76-84.

3490 *Wehrle, Josef* Jeremia—leidenschaftlicher und leidgeprüfter Künder des Jahwewortes. ᶠWETTER F. 1998 ⇒124. 11-36.

3491 *Olyan, Saul M.* "To uproot and to pull down, to build and to plant": Jer 1:10 and its earliest interpreters. ᶠFRERICHS, E.. BJSt 320: 1998 ⇒28. 63-72.

3492 *Roshwalb, Esther H.* Build-up and climax in Jeremiah's visions and laments. ᶠGORDON, C. JSOT.S 273: 1998 ⇒31. 111-135 [Jer 1,11-14; 15,10-21].

3493 **Ozment, Elaine Starr Wells** Metaphor in Jeremiah 2-6. ᴰSouthern Baptist Theol. Sem. 1998, 184 pp.

3494 *O'Connor, Kathleen M.* The tears of God and divine character in Jeremiah 2-9. ᶠBRUEGGEMANN, W. 1998 ⇒16. 172-185.

3495 *Herrmann, Siegfried* Jeremia 3—der Inhalt und seine Form ᶠRUPPERT, L. FzB 88: 1998 ⇒99. 209-221.

3496 *Maier, Christl* Die Klage der Tochter Zion: ein Beitrag zur Weiblich-keitsmetaphorik im Jeremiabuch. BThZ 15 (1998) 176-189 [Jer 4,19-21; 10,19-20].

3497 *Trimpe, Birgit* "Ich schaue auf die Erde und siehe, sie ist tohu-wabohu" (Jer 4,23): eine intertextuelle Auslegung von Jer 4,23-28 und Gen 1. BiKi 53 (1998) 135-139.

3498 *Rudman, Dominic* Creation and fall in Jeremiah x 12-16. VT 48 (1998) 63-73.

3499 *Wischnowsky, Marc* Jerusalems herrliche Herde (Jer 13,20): ein Beispiel für eine verborgene Bezugnahme im Jeremiabuch. ZAW 110 (1998) 610-614.

3500 *Smit, J.H.* War-related terminology and imagery in Jeremiah 15:10-21. OTEs 11 (1998) 105-114.

3501 *Clines, David J.A.* Form, occasion and redaction in Jeremiah 20 <1976>;

3502 'You tried to persuade me' and 'Violence! outrage!' in Jeremiah 20.7-8 <1978>. OT essays, 1. JSOT.S 292: 1998 ⇒142. 263-284/285-292.

3503 *Snyman, S.D.* A note on *pth* and *ykl* in Jeremiah XX 7-13. VT 48 (1998) 559-563.

3504 *Lenchak, Timothy A.* Puzzling passages: Jer 20:14. BiTod 36 (1998) 318-319.

3505 *Thelle, Rannfrid* דרש את־יהוה: the prophetic act of consulting Yhwh in Jeremiah 21,2 and 37,7. SJOT 12 (1998) 249-256.

13506 *Hermisson, Hans-Jürgen* Kriterien 'wahrer' und 'falscher' Prophetie im Alten Testament: zur Auslegung von Jeremia 23,16-22 und Jeremia 28,8-9. Gesammelte Aufsätze. FAT 23: 1998 <1995>, 59-76.

3507 **Yates, Gary Eugene** 'The people have not obeyed': a literary and rhetorical study of Jeremiah 26-45. ᴰDallas 1998, 307 pp.

3508 *Gilbert, Maurice* Jérémie écrit aux exilés. Il a parlé par les prophètes. 1998 <1979> ⇒155. 205-214 [29,4-23].

3509 *Gosse, Bernard* La menace qui vient du nord, les retournements d'oracles contre Babylone et Jérémie 30-31. EstB 56 (1998) 289-314.

3510 **Schmid, Konrad** Buchgestalten des Jeremiabuches: Untersuchungen zur Redaktions- und Rezeptionsgeschichte von Jer 30-33 im Kontext des Buches. 1996 ⇒12,3495; 13,3676. ᴿCBQ 60 (1998) 344-345 (*Biddle, Mark E.*).

3511 *Becking, Bob* The times they are a changing: an interpretation of Jeremiah 30,12-17. SJOT 12 (1998) 3-25.

3512 *Bergerhof, Kurt* Bibelarbeit über Jeremia 31,31-34. ᶠLORETZ O. AOAT 250: 1998 ⇒65. 101-108.

3513 **Marafioti, Domenico** Sant'AGOSTINO e la nuova alleanza: l'interpretazione agostiniana di Geremia 31,31-34 nell'ambito dell'esegesi patristica. Aloisiana 26: 1995 ⇒11/1,2371... 13,3679. ᴿCrSt 19 (1998) 663-667 (*Lettieri, Gaetano*).

3514 *Ferry, J.* "Je restaurerai Juda et Israël" (Jr 33,7.9.26): l'écriture de Jérémie 33. Transeuphratène 15 (1998) 69-82.

3515 *Jacot, Pierre-Alain* Une fidélité qui dévoile des infidélités: la leçon des Rékabites dans Jérémie 35. Hokhma 69 (1998) 14-26.

3516 *Migsch, Herbert* Wohnten die Rechabiter in Jerusalem in Häusern oder in Zelten?: die Verbformationen in Jer 35,8-11. Bib. 79 (1998) 242-257.

3517 *Wahl, Harald Martin* Die Entstehung der Schriftprophetie nach Jer 36. ZAW 110 (1998) 365-389.

3518 *Mrówczyński, Jarosław* Kerygmatyczny charakter symbolicznej czynności zatopienia zwoju w Eufracie (Jr 51,59-64) [Kerygmatic sense of symbolic actions in Jr 51,59-64]. WST 10 (1998) 95-108.

3519 *Fischer, Georg* Jeremia 52—ein Schlüssel zum Jeremiabuch. Bib. 79 (1998) 333-359.

E8.8 **Lamentationes**, *Threni*; **Baruch**

3520 **Droin, Jean-Marc** Le livre des Lamentations: une traduction et un commentaire. EssBib: 1995 ⇒11/1,2386; 13,3700. [R]LTP 54/1 (1998) 198-199 (*Faucher, Alain*).
3521 *Häusl, Maria* Die Klagelieder: Zions Stimme in der Not. Kompendium Feministische Bibelauslegung. 1998 [E]**Schottroff, L.**: 1998 ⇒H8.9. 270-277.
3522 *Linafelt, Tod* The impossibility of mourning: Lamentations after the Holocaust. [F]BRUEGGEMANN, W. 1998 ⇒16. 279-289.
3523 **Renkema, Johan** Lamentations. HCOT: Lv 1998, Peeters 641 pp. FB2.100. 90-429-0677-4.
3524 *Salters, R.B.* Searching for pattern in Lamentations. OTEs 11 (1998) 93-104.
3525 *Sæbø, Magne* Who is 'the man' in Lamentations 3.1?. On the way to canon. 1998 <1993> ⇒194. 131-142.

3526 **Kabasele Mukenge, André** L'unité littéraire du livre de Baruch. P 1998, Gabalda 504 pp. FF490. 2-85021-105-2.
3527 **Steck, Odil Hannes; Kratz, Reinhard Gregor; Kottsieper, Ingo** Das Buch Baruch; der Brief des Jeremia; Zusätze zu Ester und Daniel. ATD.Apokryphen 5: Gö 1998, Vandenhoeck & R 328 pp. DM68. 3-525-51405-0. [R]EstAg 33 (1998) 377-378 (*Mielgo, C.*).
3528 *Wright, Edward J.* Baruch: his evolution from scribe to apocalyptic seer. Biblical figures. [E]**Stone, M.** 1998 ⇒K1.1. 264-289.

3529 *Laato, Antti* The apocalypse of the Syriac Baruch and the date of the end. JSPE 18 (1998) 39-46.
3530 *Riaud, Jean* Quelques réflexions sur l'*Apocalypse grecque de Baruch* ou *III Baruch* à la lumière d'un ouvrage récent. Sem. 48 (1998) 89-99.

3531 *Heininger, Bernhard* Totenerweckung oder Weckruf (ParJer 7,12-20)?: gnostische Spurensuche in den Paralipomena Jeremiae. SNTU.A 23 (1998) 79-112.
3532 **Herzer, Jens** Die Paralipomena Jeremiae: Studien zu Tradition und Redaktion einer Haggada des frühen Judentums. TSAJ 43: 1994 ⇒10,3558b; 13,3706. [R]JQR 88 (1998) 291-294 (*Copeland, Kirsti*).
3533 **Schaller, Berndt** Paralipomena Jeremiou. JSHRZ I/8: Gü 1998, Gü'er 661-777 pp. DM108. 3-579-03919-9.

E8.9 **Ezekiel:** *textus, commentarii; themata, versiculi*

3534 **Block, Daniel I.** The book of Ezekiel: chapters 1-24. 1997 ⇒13,3709. [R]Anton. 73 (1998) 744-745 (*Nobile, Marco*); BS 155 (1998) 496-497 (*Merrill, Eugene H.*);
3535 The book of Ezekiel: chapters 25-48. NIC: GR 1998, Eerdmans xxiii; 826 pp. $50. 0-8028-2536-2.
3536 **Maier, Gerhard** Der Prophet Hesekiel: 1. Teil: Kapitel 1 bis 24. WStB: Wu 1998, Brockhaus 342 pp. 3-417-25235-0/-25335-7.
3537 **Pohlmann, Karl-Friedrich** Das Buch des Propheten Hesekiel (Ezechiel) Kapitel 1-19. ATD 22/1: 1996 ⇒12,3539; 13,3714. [R]JThS 49

(1998) 714-716 (*Clements, R.E.*); JBL 117 (1998) 524-526 (*Lang, Bernhard*).

3538 *Aslanoff, Cyril* Les gloses judéo-helléniques du commentaire de RE'UEL sur Ézéchiel. REJ 157 (1998) 7-45.
3539 *Brodsky, Harold* Ezekiel's map of restoration. Land and community. 1998 ⇒466. 17-29.
3540 *Callender, Dexter E.* The primal man in Ezekiel and the image of God. SBL.SP part 2. SBL.SPS 37: 1998 ⇒402. 606-625.
3541 *Fredericks, Daniel C.* Diglossia, revelation, and Ezekiel's inaugural rite. JETS 41 1998, 189-199.
3542 **Hutchens, Kenneth Dean** Although Yahweh was there: the land in the book of Ezekiel. ^DEmory 1998, 747 pp.
3543 *Joyce, Paul M.* King and Messiah in Ezekiel. King and Messiah. JSOT.S 270: 1998 ⇒378. 323-337.
3544 *Kasher, Rimon* שארית, תשובה וברית לבירורים שינויים בעמדותיו של הנביא יחזקאל מעמדה 'אופטימית' לעמדה 'פסימית' [Remnant, repentance, and covenant in the book of Ezekiel]. Beit Mikra 156 (1998) 15-34.
3545 **Kenney, Mark G.** The role of nature in the dirges and taunt songs in the book of Ezekiel. Diss. Pont. Univ. S. Thomae in Urbe. ^D*Agius, Joseph*: R 1998, xv; 333 pp.
3546 **Kessler, Stephan Ch.** GREGOR der Große als Exeget: eine theologische Interpretation der Ezechielhomilien. IThS 43: 1995 ⇒11/1,-2404. ^RBiLi 71 (1998) 279-281 (*Hieke, Thomas*).
3547 **Kim, Gun-Tai Luc** Le concept du droit et de la justice chez Ézéchiel, et sa nouveauté par rapport aux prophètes du VIIIe siècle. Diss. Institut catholique de Paris 1998: ^D*Asurmendi, Jesus*: 389 pp. ^RRICP 67 (1998) 239-242 (*Asurmendi, Jesus*).
3548 *Kutsko, John F.* Will the real ṣelem 'ĕlōhîm please stand up?: the image of God in the book of Ezekiel. SBL.SP part 1. SBL.SPS 37: 1998 ⇒402. 55-85.
3549 *Lacocque, André* From death to life. Thinking biblically. 1998 ⇒251. 141-164.
3550 *Malamat, Abraham* New Mari documents and prophecy in Ezekiel. Mari and the bible. 1998 <1997> ⇒173. 142-150 [Ezek 1,3; 37,19; 3,1].
3551 *Odell, Margaret S.* You are what you eat: Ezekiel and the scroll. JBL 117 (1998) 229-248.
3552 *Rooker, Mark F.* The use of the Old Testament in the book of Ezekiel. Faith & Mission 15 (1998) 45-52.
3553 *Rumianek, Ryszard* Pojęcie grzechu w księdze Ezechiela [La notion du péché dans le livre d'Ézéchiel]. Bobolanum 9 (1998) 339-353.
3554 *Schussman, Aviva* The prophet Ezekiel in Islamic literature: Jewish traces and Islamic adaptations. Biblical figures. 1998 ^EStone, M. 1998 ⇒K1.1. 316-339.
3555 ^E**Sozzi Manci, Maria Assunta** Le figlie di Abramo: donne, sessualità e religione. Percorsi dell'identità femminile nel Novecento 5: Mi 1998, Guerini 94 pp. 88-7802-867-3.
3556 *Willmes, Bernd* Hoffnung auf Rettung im Ezechielbuch. ^FRUPPERT, L.. FzB 88: 1998 ⇒99. 483-526.

3557 **Lieb, Michael** Children of Ezekiel: aliens, UFOs, the crisis of race, and the advent of the end time. Durham, NC 1998, Duke University x; 308 pp. $55/19 [Ezek 1].

3558 *Wright, Benjamin G.* Talking with God and losing his head: extra-biblical traditions about the prophet Ezekiel. Biblical figures. [E]**Stone, M.** 1998 ⇒K1.1. 290-315 [1,1-2; 24].
3559 *Odell, Margaret S.* The particle and the prophet: observations on Ezekiel ii 6. VT 48 (1998) 425-432.
3560 *Böckler, Annette* Ist Gott schuldig, wenn ein Gerechter stolpert?: zur Exegese von Ez. III 20. VT 48 (1998) 437-452.
3561 *Kasher, Rimon* (27-22 ,ג יח) פרשת הָאָלֶם בספר יחזקאל [Ezekiel's dumbness (Ez 3:22-27): a new approach]. BetM 156 (1998) 227-244.
3562 **Bodendorfer, Gerhard** Das Drama des Bundes: Ezechiel 16 in rabbinischer Perspektive. 1997 ⇒13,3729. [R]FrRu NF 5 (1998) 206-207 (*Vonach, Andreas*).
3563 *Dempsey, Carol J.* The 'whore' of Ezekiel 16: the impact and ramifications of gender-specific metaphors in light of biblical law and divine judgment. Gender and law. JSOT.S 262: 1998 ⇒256. 57-78.
3564 *Shields, Mary E.* Gender and violence in Ezekiel 23;
3565 *Odell, Margaret S.* Genre and persona in Ezekiel 24:15-24. SBL.SP part 2. SBL.SPS 37: 1998 ⇒402. 86-105/626-648.
3566 **Anaparambil, James Raphael** A prophet against imperial boasting and trade: Ezekiel 28,1-10.11-19. Diss. excerpt Pont. Univ. Urbaniana: [D]*Spreafico, Ambrogio.* R 1998, xiii; 76, xlvii pp.
3567 *Rumianek, Ryszard* 'Gog z krainy Magog' (Ez 38,2) [Gog aus dem Land Magog]. STV 36 (1998) 19-24.
3568 *Dell'Era, Antonio* La pecora smarrita. BeO 40 (1998) 229-233.
3569 *Lacocque, André* De la mort à la vie: Ézéchiel 37. Penser la bible. 1998 ⇒188. 191-222.
3570 *Ricoeur, Paul* Sentinel of imminence. Thinking biblically. 1998 ⇒251. 165-183;
3571 Sentinelle de l'imminence. Penser la bible. 1998 ⇒188. 223-245.
3572 *Kasher, Rimmon* Anthropomorphism, holiness and cult: a new look at Ezekiel 40-48. ZAW 110 (1998) 192-208.
3573 **Stevenson, Kalinda Rose** Vision of transformation: the territorial rhetoric of Ezekiel 40-48. SBL.DS 154: 1996 ⇒12,3585; 13,3726 [R]CBQ 60 (1998) 348-349 (*Brueggemann, Walter*); JQR 89 (1998) 209-212 (*Kasher, Rimon*).
3574 *Konkel, Michael* Das Datum der zweiten Tempelvision Ezechiels (Ez 40,1). BN 92 (1998) 55-70.

E9.1 Apocalyptica VT

3575 *Aranda Pérez, Gonzalo* El destierro de Babilonia y las raíces de la Apocalíptica. EstB 56 (1998) 335-355.
3576 *Barker, Margaret* Beyond the veil of the temple: the high priestly origins of the apocalypses. SJTh 51 (1998) 1-21.
3577 *Beyerle, Stefan* Die Wiederentdeckung der Apokalyptik in den Schriften Altisraels und des Frühjudentums. VF 43 (1998) 34-59.
3578 *Clifford, Richard J.* The roots of apocalypticism in Near Eastern myth. Encyclopedia of apocalypticism I. 1998 ⇒507. 3-38.
3579 *Collins, John J.* From prophecy to apocalypticism: the expectation of the end. Encyclopedia of apocalypticism I. 1998 ⇒507. 129-161.
3580 **Collins, John J.** Apocalypticism in the Dead Sea Scrolls. 1997 ⇒13,3751. [R]RRT (1998/1) 53-54 (*Hempel, Charlotte*);

3581 The apocalyptic imagination: an introduction to Jewish apocalyptic literature. Biblical Resource: GR 1998, Eerdmans xiii; 337 pp. $30. 0-8028-4371-9.

3582 *Cook, Johann* Hope for the earth" in the early Judaic era (Jewish apocalypticism)?. Scriptura 66 (1998) 235-243.

3583 *Fabry, Heinz-Josef* Die frühjüdische Apokalyptik als Reaktion auf Fremdherrschaft: zur Funktion von 4Q246. FStegemann, H.: BZNW 97: 1998 ⇒111. 84-98.

3584 *Gruenwald, Ithamar* A case study of scripture and culture: apocalypticism as cultural identity in past and present. FBetz, H. 1998 ⇒10. 252-280.

3585 **Hahn, Ferdinand** Frühjüdische und urchristliche Apokalyptik: eine Einführung. BThSt 36: Neuk 1998, Neuk xiii; 174 pp. 3-7887-16673.

3586 *Hultgård, Anders* Persian apocalypticism. Encyclopedia of apocalypticism I. 1998 ⇒507. 39-83.

3587 *Jędrzejewski, Sylwester* Apokaliptyka jako rodzaj literacki [De genere litterario apocalyptico]. RBL 51 (1998) 29-35.

3588 *Okure, Teresa* Del Génesis al Apocalipsis: la apocalíptica en perspectiva bíblica. Conc(E) 277 (1998) 533-542.

3589 *Quesnel, Michel* Il successo delle apocalissi. Mondo della bibbia 44 (1998) 19-21.

3590 **Sacchi, Paolo** Jewish apocalyptic and its history. JSPE.S 20: 1996 ⇒12,3602. RRdQ 18 (1998) 397-602 (*Martone, Corrado*).

3591 *Sæbo, Magne* Old Testament apocalyptic in its relation to prophecy and wisdom: the view of Gerhard von Rad reconsidered. On the way to canon. 1998 <1994> ⇒194. 232-247.

3592 *Smith, Jonathan Z.* Cross-cultural reflections on apocalypticism FBetz, H. 1998 ⇒10. 281-285.

E9.2 **Daniel**: *textus, commentarii: themata, versiculi*

3593 **Bauer, Dieter** Das Buch Daniel. Neuer Stuttgarter Kommentar, AT 22: 1996 ⇒12,3605. RCBQ 60 (1998) 319-320 (*Collins, John J.*).

3594 *McLay, Tim* It's a question of influence: the Theodotion and Old Greek texts of Daniel. Origen's Hexapla. TSAJ 58: 1998 ⇒399. 231-254.

3595 **McLay, Tim** The OG and Th versions of Daniel. SBL.SCSt 43: 1996 ⇒12,3621. RCBQ 60 (1998) 125-126 (*Cox, Claude E.*).

3596 **Meadowcroft, T.J.** Aramaic Daniel and Greek Daniel: a literary comparison. JSOT.S 198: 1995 ⇒11/1,2475; 13,3768. RTrin.Journal 19 (1998) 114-118 (*Collins, C. John*); JBL 117 (1998) 731-732 (*Taylor, Bernard A.*).

Steck, O., *al.*, Das Buch Baruch, Zusätze zu...Daniel ⇒2653.

3597 **Berrigan, Daniel** Daniel: under the siege of the divine. Farmington, PA 1998, Plough xi; 216 pp. $17.

3598 *Dalla Vecchia, Flavio* Annunciare la fine: il libro di Daniele. La fine del tempo. 1998 ⇒296. 17-34.

3599 **Getz, Gene A.** Daniel: standing firm for God. Men of character: Nv 1998, Broadman & H x; 195 pp. 0-8054-6172-8.

3600 **Koch, Klaus** Europa, Rom und der Kaiser vor dem Hintergrund von zwei Jahrtausenden Rezeption des Buches Daniel. 1997 ⇒13,3781.

^{R}ThLZ 123 (1998) 848-850 (*Haag, Ernst*); CBQ 60 (1998) 533-534 (*Redditt, Paul L.*).

3601   *Mendels, Doron* The five empires; a note on a propagandistic *topos*. Identity. JSPE.S 24: 1998 <1981> ⇒174. 314-323.

3602   *Tengström, Sven* Tre etapper i Danielsbokens litterära tillblivelse. SEÅ 63 (1998) 69-92.

3603   *Armistead, David* The images of Daniel 2 and 7: a literary approach. Stulos theological journal 6 (1998) 51-62.

3604   *Lensink, Henk* Drie mannen in het vuur. ITBT 6/3 (1998) 14-17 [Dan 3].

3605   *Mark, Martin* Der Lobgesang der drei jungen Männer. TThZ 107 (1998) 45-61 [Dan 3].

3606   *Vergani, Emidio* La fucina di verità: storia, escatologia e parenesi ecclesiale nell'esegesi su Dn 3 di EFREM il Siro. CrSt 19 (1998) 597-630.

3607   *Van Deventer, H.J.M.* We did not hear the bagpipe": a note on Daniel 3. OTEs 11 (1998) 340-349.

3608   *Collins, John J.* New light on the Book of Daniel from the Dead Sea scrolls. ^{F}VAN DER WOUDE, A. VT.S 73: 1998 ⇒121. 180-196.

3609   *Van der Toorn, Karel* In the lions' den: the Babylonian background of a biblical motif. CBQ 60 (1998) 626-640 [Dan 6].

3610   *Dulaey, Martine* Daniel dans la fosse aux lions: lectures de Dn 6 dans l'Église ancienne. RevSR 72 (1998) 38-50.

3611   *Avalos, Hector* Daniel 9:24-25 and Mesopotamian temple rededications. JBL 117 (1998) 507-511.

3612   *Redditt, Paul L.* Daniel 11 and the sociohistorical setting of the book of Daniel. CBQ 60 (1998) 463-474;

3613   Calculating the "times": Daniel 12:5-13. PRSt 25 (1998) 373-379.

3614   **Pennacchietti, Fabrizio A.** Susanna nel deserto: riflessi di un racconto biblico nella cultura arabo-islamica. T 1998, Zamorani 125 pp. 88-7158-066-4 [Dan 13].

3615   *Pennacchietti, Fabrizio A.* Lo sfondo mitologico e folclorico del racconto di 'Susanna e i vecchioni'. ^{F}SIERRA J. 1998 ⇒102. 409-423 [Dan 13].

3616   *Koenen, Klaus* Von der todesmutigen Susanna zum begabten Daniel: zur Überlieferungsgeschichte der Susanna-Erzählung. ThZ 54 (1998) 1-13 [Dan 13].

E9.3 *Prophetae Minores,* **Dōdekaprophetōn...Hosea, Joel**

3617   **Achtemeier, Elizabeth** Minor Prophets I. 1996 ⇒12,3647. ^{R}EeT 29 (1998) 257-259 (*Vogels, Walter*).

3618   **Birch, Bruce C.** Hosea, Joel, and Amos. 1997 ⇒13,3814. ^{R}CBQ 60 (1998) 521-522 (*Jones, Barry A.*).

3619   **Carbone, S.P.; Rizzi, G.** Abaquq, Abdia, Nahum, Sofonia: lettura ebraica greca aramaica. La parola et la sua tradizione: Bo 1998, EDB 496 pp.

3620   *Curtis, Byron G.* The daughter of Zion oracles and the appendices to Malachi: evidence on the latter redactors and redactions of the Book of the Twelve. SBL.SP part 2. SBL.SPS 37: 1998 ⇒402. 872-892.

3621   *Debenedetti, Giacomo* Amos; Osea. Profeti. 1998 <1924> ⇒145. 63-84.

3622 **Guenther, Allen R.** Hosea, Amos. Believers Church Bible Com-
      mentary: Waterloo, ON 1998, Herald 429 pp. $20.
3623 *House, Paul R.* The character of God in the Book of the Twelve.
      SBL.SP part 2. SBL.SPS 37: 1998 ⇒402. 831-849.
3624 **Jeremias, Jörg** Hosea und Amos: Studien zu den Anfängen des
      Dodekapropheton. FAT 13: 1996 ⇒12,3669; 13,3819. ᴿThLZ 123
      (1998) 364-370 (*Dietrich, Walter*); JThS 49 (1998) 183-187
      (*Macintosh, A.A.*).
3625 *Jeremias, Jörg* Neuere Tendenzen der Forschung an den Kleinen
      Propheten. ᶠVAN DER WOUDE, A. VT.S 73: 1998 ⇒121. 122-136.
3626 **Macintosh, Andrew Alexander** A critical and exegetical com-
      mentary on Hosea. ICC: 1997 ⇒13,3837. ᴿBib 79 (1998) 275-279
      (*Simian-Yofre, Horacio*); JThS 49 (1998) 716-719 (*Gelston, A.*);
      ThLZ 123 (1998) 966-967 (*Cathcart, Kevin J.*); CBQ 60 (1998) 535-
      537 (*Yee, Gale A.*).
3627 **McComiskey, Thomas Edward; Motyer, J. Alec; Stuart, Douglas**
      Zephaniah, Haggai, Zechariah, and Malachi. The Minor Prophets: an
      exegetical and expository commentary, 3. GR 1998, Baker xii; 897-
      1412 pp. $35. 0-8010-2055-7.
3628 **Prior, David** The message of Joel, Micah, Habakkuk: listening to the
      voice of God. The Bible Speaks Today: Leicester 1998, Inter-Varsity
      279 pp. 0-85111-586-1.
3629 *Rendtorff, Rolf* Alas for the day!: the "day of the Lord" in the book of
      the Twelve. ᶠBRUEGGEMANN, W. 1998 ⇒16. 186-197.
3630 *Schart, Aaron* Redactional models: comparisons, contrasts, agree-
      ments, disagreements. SBL.SP part 2. SBL.SPS 37: 1998 ⇒402.
      893-908.
3631 *Schart, Aaron* Zur Redaktionsgeschichte des Zwölfprophetenbuchs.
      VF 43 (1998) 13-33.
3632 ᴱ**Sgargi, Giorgio** Gioele, Amos, Abdia: versione ufficiale italiana
      confrontata con ebraico masoretico, greco dei Settanta, siriaco della
      Peshitta, latino della Vulgata; Targum Jonathan: commenti di autori
      latini (GIROLAMO); greci (CIRILLO Alessandrino); medioevali
      (RUPERTO di Deutz); riformatori (LUTERO e CALVINO); moderni
      (KELLER, AMSLER, WOLFF, BERNINI, LOSS). BIBLIA.AT 32-34: Bo
      1998, EDB lxxxviii; 283 pp. L62.000. 88-10-20592-8.

3633 *Bons, Eberhard* L'approche "métaphorologique" du livre d'Osée (1).
      RevSR 72 (1998) 133-155.
3634 **Eidevall, Göran** Grapes in the desert: metaphors, models, and
      themes in Hosea 4-14. CB.OT 43: 1996 ⇒12,3691; 13,3831. ᴿBib
      79 (1998) 421-424 (*Nissinen, Martti*).
3635 **Holt, Else Kragelund** Prophesying the past: the use of Israel's his-
      tory in the book of Hosea. JSOT.S 194: 1995 ⇒11/1,2513...
      13,3835. ᴿJAOS 118 (1998) 138-139 (*Hurowitz, Victor*).
3636 *Joosten, Jan* Exegesis in the Septuagint version of Hosea. Intertex-
      tuality. OTS 40: 1998 ⇒394. 62-85.
3637 *Lewis, Jack P.* Metaphors in Hosea. ᶠSPEEL C. 1996 ⇒106. 71-87.
3638 *Mendecki, Norbert* Postdeuteronomistische Redaktion des Buches
      Hosea?. "Lasset uns Brücken bauen...". BEAT 42: 1998 ⇒401. 223-
      244.
3639 **Schulz-Rauch, Martin** Hosea und Jeremia: zur Wirkungsgeschichte
      des Hoseabuches. Calwer Theologische Monographien, A, Bibelwis-

senschaft 16: Stu 1996, Calwer ix; 259 pp. DM68. 3-7668-3381-2
[R]JBL 117 (1998) 526-527 (*Begg, Christopher T.*).

3640 **Seifert, Brigitte** Metaphorisches Reden von Gott im Hoseabuch.
FRLANT 166: 1996 ⇒12,3675; 13,3842. [R]JBL 117 (1998) 527-529
(*Sweeney, Marvin A.*).

3641 *Silva Retamales, Santiago* Tradición del "Éxodo" en Oseas. EstB 56
(1998) 145-178.

3642 *Simian-Yofre, Horacio* Osea (libro di). Dizionario di omiletica. 1998
⇒533. 1053-1056;

3643 The Minor Prophets; Hosea; Baal. International bible commentary.
1998 ⇒1535. 1108-1123.

3644 **Trotter, James Marion** Reading Hosea in Achaemenid Yehud
[D]Emory 1998, 400 pp.

3645 *Weitzman, Michael* The reliability of retroversions of the Three from
the Syrohexapla: a pilot study in Hosea. Origen's Hexapla. TSAJ 58:
1998 ⇒399. 317-359.

3646 **Wendland, Ernst R.** The discourse analysis of Hebrew prophetic
literature: determining the larger textual units of Hosea and Joel.
Lewiston 1995, Mellen xiii; 381 pp. $100. 0-7734-2371-0. [R]BiTr 49
(1998) 152-154 (*Andersen, Francis I.*).

3647 *Schenker, Adrian* Kinder der Prostitution, Kinder ohne Familie und
ohne soziale Stellung: ein freundschaftliches Sed contra für Lothar
RUPPERT und eine These zu Hos 1. [F]RUPPERT, L. FzB 88: 1998 ⇒99.
355-369.

3648 *Gruber, Mayer I.* A re-evaluation of Hosea 1-2: philology informed
by life experience. The personal voice. 1998 ⇒250. 170-182.

3649 **Sherwood, Yvonne** The prostitute and the prophet: Hosea's marriage in literary-theoretical perspective. JSOT.S 212: 1996
⇒12,3683; 13,3845. [R]JBL 117 (1998) 348-350 (*Kissling, Paul J.*)
[Hos 1-3].

3650 **Törnkvist, Rut** The use and abuse of female sexual imagery in the
book of Hosea: a feminist critical approach to Hos 1-3. AUU Women
in Religion 7: U 1998, U Univ. 196 pp. 91-554-4135-1.

3651 **Wénin, André** Osée et Gomer, parabole de la fidélité de Dieu (Os 1-
3). Connaître la Bible 9: Bru 1998, Lumen Vitae 64 pp. FB220. 2-
87324-111-X.

3652 **Wacker, Marie-Theres** Figurationen des Weiblichen im Hoseabuch.
1996 ⇒12,3681. [R]INTAMS.R 4 (1998) 115-117 (*Opgen-Rhein, Hermann*) [Hos 1-3].

3653 *Scherer, Andreas* "Gehe wiederum hin!": zum Verhältnis von Hos. 3
zu Hos. 1. BN 95 (1998) 23-29.

3654 *Clines, David J.A.* Hosea 2: structure and interpretation. OT essays,
1. JSOT.S 292: 1998 <1979> ⇒142. 293-313.

3655 *Morag, Shelomo* עיון לשוני—דברי הפיוס :דברי הושע של הגדולה המטפורה [The
'great metaphor' of Hosea (2:4-17): the appeasement (2:16-17): some
linguistic notes]. Tarb. 68 (1998) 5-11.

3656 *Nutt, Aurica* "Die lebensfördernde Macht der Göttin und ihre
Vitalität" im Hintergrund von Hos 2?: ikonographische Untersuchungen. BN 91 (1998) 47-63.

3657 *Mölle, Herbert* Das Ende der Priester von Israel: Beobachtungen zur
Redaktion in Hos 4,1-10. [F]RUPPERT, L. FzB 88: 1998 ⇒99. 259-276.

3658 *Dochhorn, Jan* Auferstehung am dritten Tag?: eine problematische
Parallele zu Hos 6,2. ZAH 11 (1998) 200-204.

3659 *Irvine, Stuart A.* Enmity in the house of God (Hosea 9:7-9). JBL 117 (1998) 645-653.

3660 *Polliack, Meira* לדמותו של יעקב בהושע יֹב: גישות טיפולוגיות בפרשנות ימי הביניים ובמחקר החדש [Jacob's figure in Hosea 12—typological approaches in medieval Jewish exeegesis and in modern bible criticism]. BetM 154-155 (1998) 277-302.

3661 *Schmitt, Hans-Christoph* Der Kampf Jakobs mit Gott in Hos 12,3ff. und in Gen 32,23ff.: zum Verständnis der Verborgenheit Gottes im Hoseabuch und im Elohistischen Geschichtswerk;

3662 *Diedrich, Friedrich* "Bewahre Solidarität und Gerechtigkeit bei deinem Tun, und hoffe auf deinen Gott immerdar!" (Hosea 12,7): Überlegungen zur Ethik im Hoseabuch. [F]Ruppert, L. FzB 88: 1998 ⇒99. 397-430/61-91.

3663 **Lima, Maria de Lourdes Corrêa** Salvação entre juízo, conversão a graça: a perspectiva escatológica de Os 14,2-9 [Salvation within judgment: conversion and grace: the eschatological perspective in Hos 14,2-9]. TGr.T 35: R 1998, E.P.U.G. 356 pp. €18,7. 88-7652-780-X.

3664 *Oestreich, Bernhard* Metaphors and similes for Yahweh in Hosea 14:2-9 (1-8): a study of Hoseanic pictorial language. Friedensauer Schriftenreihe, A, Theologie 1: Fra 1998, Lang 278 pp. 3-631-33666-7.

3665 *Dennison, James T.* Enveloped by God: Hosea 14:4-8. Kerux 13 (1998) 35-41.

3666 *Gangloff, Frederic* "Je suis son 'Anat et son 'Ašerâh" (Os 14,9). EThL 74 (1998) 373-385.

3667 *Crenshaw, James L.* Joel's silence and interpreters' readiness to indict the innocent. "Lasset uns Brücken bauen...". BEAT 42: 1998 ⇒401. 255-259.

3668 **McQueen, Larry R.** Joel and the spirit: the cry of a prophetic hermeneutic. 1995 ⇒12,3699. [R]EvQ 70 (1998) 64-66-263-265 (*Hudson, D. Neil*).

3669 *Noguchi, Takako* A study of the verbs in Joel 2:4-9: the author's style or Aramaic influence?. Orient 33 (1998) 103-114.

3670 *Hymes, David C.* Notes on Joel 3:1-5. Asian journal of Pentecostal studies 1 (1998) 83-103.

E9.4 Amos

3671 **Bovati, Pietro; Meynet, Roland** Il libro del profeta Amos. 1995 ⇒11/1,2564; 12,3703. [R]RivBib 46 (1998) 106-109 (*Marconcini, Benito*);

3672 Le livre du prophète Amos. 1994 ⇒10,3690... 13,3858. [R]JThS 49 (1998) 187-189 (*Carroll, Robert P.*).

Guenther, Allen R. Hosea, Amos 1998 ⇒3622.

3673 **Jeremias, Jörg** Der Prophet Amos. ATD 24/2: 1995 ⇒11/1,2566... 13,3859. [R]ThLZ 123/4 (1998) 364-370 (*Dietrich, Walter*);

3674 The book of Amos: a commentary. OTL: Ph 1998, Westminster xix; 177 pp. $26. 0-664-22086-X. [R]RBBras 15 (1998) 491-492.

3675 *Melugin, Roy F.* Amos in recent research. CurResB 6 (1998) 65-101.

3676 **Pfeifer, Gerhard** Hebräische Wortkonkordanz zum Amosbuch. Fra 1998, Lang 86 pp. 3-631-31538-4.

3677 *Cotterell, Peter* A question of peak. BiTr 49 (1998) 139-148.

3678 *Ercolano, Giuseppe* Il libro di Amos specchio di una società. Asp. 45 (1998) 215-230.

3679 *Hermanson, Eric A.* Biblical Hebrew: conceptual metaphor categories in the book of Amos. OTEs 11 (1998) 438-451.

3680 **Jaruzelska, Izabela** Amos and the officialdom in the Kingdom of Israel: the socio-economic position of the officials in the light of the biblical, the epigraphic and archaeological evidence. Uniwersytet im. Adama Mickiewicza w Poznaniu. Seria socjologia 25: Poznan 1998, Wydawnictwo Naukowe 240 pp. 83-232-0910-3. P.

3681 *Jaruzelska, Izabela* Ursędnicy królewscy w VIII wieku przed Chr. W Księdze proroka Amaosa: szkic z biblijnej teorii społeczeństwa [Amos and the royal officials in the 8th century B.C.: an essay on the biblical theory of society]. PoST 8 (1998) 11-26. P.

3682 *Lescow, Theodor* Das vorexilische Amosbuch: Erwägungen zu seiner Kompositionsgeschichte. BN 93 (1998) 23-55.

3683 *Marrs, Rick R.* Amos and the power of proclamation. RestQ 40 (1998) 13-24.

3684 *Moltz, Howard* A literary interpretation of the book of Amos. Horizons 25 (1998) 58-71.

3685 **Oliver, Anthony** Creation and redemption in Amos: a multi-faceted approach with emphasis on the hymns. [D]Trinity 1998, 276 pp.

3686 *Rilett Wood, Joyce* Tragic and comic forms in Amos. Biblical Interpretation 6 (1998) 20-48.

3687 **Rottzoll, Dirk U.** Studien zur Redaktion und Komposition des Amosbuchs. BZAW 243: 1996 ⇒12,3716. [R]CBQ 60 (1998) 342-343 (*Petersen, David L.*).

3688 *Rösel, Hartmut N.* Kleine Studien zur Auslegung des Amosbuches. BZ 42 (1998) 2-18.

3689 **Schart, Aaron** Die Entstehung des Zwölfprophetenbuchs: Neubearbeitungen von Amos im Rahmen schriftenübergreifender Redaktionsprozesse. BZAW 260: B 1998, de Gruyter xi; 342 pp. DM178. 3-11-016078-1.

3690 *Bordreuil, Pierre* Amos 1:5: La Beqaʿ septentrionale de l'Eden au paradis. Syr. 75 (1998) 55-59.

3691 *Witaszek, Gabriel* Teologia sądu boga nad Izraelem (Am 2,6-16): analiza retoryczna [La teologia del giudizio divino su Israele (Am 2,6-16): l'analisi retorica]. Roczniki Teologiczne 45 (1998) 17-35.

3692 *Dijkstra, Meindert* Textual remarks on the hymn-fragment Amos 4: 13. "Lasset uns Brücken bauen...". BEAT 42: 1998 ⇒401. 245-253.

3693 *Noble, Paul R.* Amos and Amaziah in context: synchronic and diachronic approaches to Amos 7-8. CBQ 60 (1998) 423-439.

3694 *Hoffmeier, James K.* Once again the 'plumb line' vision of Amos 7.7-9: an interpretive clue from Egypt?. [F]GORDON, C. JSOT.S 273: 1998 ⇒31. 304-319.

E9.5 Jonas

3695 **Brotzman, Ellis R.; Martin, Raymond A.** Jonah: computer generated tools for the correlated Greek and Hebrew texts. Computer Bible 59a pt.1: Lewiston 1998, Mellen ix; 176 pp. 0-7734-4119-0.

3696 *Alexandru, Johannes* Ein Kapitel 'apokrypher' Kanon-Geschichte Jona betreffend. DBAT 29 (1998) 259-261.
3697 **Bolin, Thomas M.** Freedom beyond forgiveness: the book of Jonah re-examined. JSOT.S 236: 1997 ⇒13,3885. ᴿBib 79 (1998) 280-283 (*Eynikel, Erik*); JBL 117 (1998) 350-351 (*Galambush, Julie*).
3698 *Carroll, Robert P.* Jonah as a book of ritual responses. "Lasset uns Brücken bauen...". BEAT 42: 1998 ⇒401. 261-268.
3699 *Cortesi, Alessandro* Giona e la grande città. Coscienza 50 (1998) 46-48.
3700 *Diebner, Bernd Jørg* "Beim Aufgang der Morgenröte": Jona Purpur-wurm—stichig. DBAT 29 (1998) 157-167.
3701 *Erroux-Morfin, M.* L'Oxyrhynque et le monstre de Jonas. Études Coptes V. 1998 ⇒451. 7-14.
3702 *Houk, Cornelius B.* Linguistic patterns in Jonah. JSOT 77 (1998) 81-102.
3703 *Huber, Konrad* Zeichen des Jona" und "mehr als Jona": die Gestalt des Jona im Neuen Testament und ihr Beitrag zur bibeltheologischen Fragestellung. PzB 7 (1998) 77-94.
3704 *Jonker, Louis C.* Reading Jonah multidimensionally: a multidimensional reading strategy for biblical interpretation. Scriptura 64 (1998) 1-15.
3705 *Meves, Christa* Die zeitlose Wahrheit der Jona-Geschichte. Theologisches 28 (1998) 203-207.
3706 *Prieto Fernández, Francisco José* Jonás y la ruina de Israel: un estudio sobre el *In Ionam* de JERÓNIMO. Auriensia 1 (1998) 87-177.
3707 *Sherwood, Yvonne* Cross-currents in the book of Jonah: some Jewish and cultural midrashim on a traditional text. Biblical Interpretation 6 (1998) 49-79.
3708 *Steffen, Uwe* Pflanzenkunde und -symbolik zur Jona-Geschichte. DBAT 29 (1998) 179-186.
3709 *Trible, Phyllis* Divine incongruities in the book of Jonah. ᶠBRUEGGE-MANN, W. 1998 ⇒16. 198-208.
3710 *Wendland, Ernst R.* Recursion and variation in the 'prophecy' of Jonah: on the rhetorical impact of stylistic technique in Hebrew narrative discourse, wiht special reference to irony and enigma. AUSS 36 (1998) 81-110.

3711 *Smelik, Klaas A.D.* Das Unterscheidungsmerkmal: zur Funktion des Psalms im Buche Jona. DBAT 29 (1998) 168-178 [Jonah 2].
3712 *Donovan Turner, Mary* Between text and sermon: Jonah 3:10-4:11. Interp. 52 (1998) 411-414.

E9.6 *Micheas,* Micah

3713 **McKane, William** The book of Micah: introduction and commentary. E 1998, Clark xiv; 241 pp. £25. 0-567-08615-1.

3714 *Barker, Kenneth L.* A literary analysis of the book of Micah. BS 155 (1998) 437-448.
3715 *Biddle, Mark E.* "Israel" and "Jacob" in the Book of Micah: Micah in the context of the Twelve. SBL.SP part 2. SBL.SPS 37: 1998 ⇒402. 850-871.
3716 *Bietenhard, Sophia* Das Buch Micha: Ruf nach Gerechtigkeit— Hoffnung für alle. Kompendium Feministische Bibelauslegung. ᴱ**Schottroff, L.**: 1998 ⇒H8.9. 338-346.
3717 **Cha, Jun-Hee** Micha und Jeremia. BBB 107: 1996 ⇒12,3767; 13,3906. ᴿBiOr 55 (1998) 242-245 (*Wagenaar, Jan A.*).
3718 **Jacobs, Mignon R.** Conceptual coherence of the book of Micah ᴰClaremont 1998, 308 pp.
3719 **Metzner, Gabriele** Kompositionsgeschichte des Michabuches. EHS.T 635: Fra 1998, Lang 209 pp. 3-631-33459-1.
3720 *Runions, Erin* Zion is burning: "gender fuck" in Micah. Semeia 82 (1998) 225-246.

3721 *Ben Zvi, Ehud* Micah 1.2-16: observations and possible implications. JSOT 77 (1998) 103-120.
3722 **Wagenaar, Jan A.** Oordeel en heil: een onderzoek naar samenhang tussen de heils- en onheilsprofetieën in Micha 2-5. 1995 ⇒11/1, 2652; 13,3910. ᴿVT 48 (1998) 286-287 (*Williams, P.J.*).
3723 *Sedlmeier, Franz* Die Universalisierung der Heilshoffnung nach Micha 4,1-5. TThZ 107 (1998) 62-81.
3724 *Rodgers Jensen, Renée* Micah 4:1-5. Interp. 52 (1998) 417-420.

E9.7 *Abdias, Sophonias...* **Obadiah, Zephaniah, Nahum**

3725 **Ben Zvi, Ehud** A historical-critical study of the book of Obadiah. BZAW 242: 1996 ⇒13,3921. ᴿOLZ 93 (1998) 190-192 (*Schunck, Klaus-Dietrich*); CBQ 60 (1998) 518-519 (*Raabe, Paul R.*).
3726 *Nogalski, James D.* Obadiah 7: textual corruption or politically charged metaphor?. ZAW 110 (1998) 67-71.
3727 **Rossi, Luiz Alexandre Solano** Como ler o livro de Abdias. São Paulo 1998, Paulus 32 pp.

3728 *Bail, Ulrike* Das Buch Zefanja oder: das dreifache Jerusalem. Kompendium Feministische Bibelauslegung. ᴱ**Schottroff, L.**: 1998 ⇒H8.9. 359-365.
3729 **Ryou, Daniel Hojoon** Zephaniah's oracles against the nations: a synchronic and diachronic study of Zephaniah 2:1-3:8. Bibl.Interp. 13: 1995 ⇒11/1,2668; 13,3924. ᴿJSSt 43 (1998) 161-162 (*Mason, Rex*).
3730 **Weigl, Michael** Zefanja und das 'Israel der Armen': eine Untersuchung zur Theologie des Buches Zefanja. 1994 ⇒10,3763... 12,3799. ᴿBZ 42 (1998) 122-124 (*Kessler, Rainer*).
3731 *Weimar, Peter* Zef 1 und das Problem der Komposition der Zefanjaprophetie. ᶠLORETZ O. AOAT 250: 1998 ⇒65. 809-832.

3732 *Baumann, Gerlinde* Das Buch Nahum: der gerechte Gott als sexueller Gewalttäter. Kompendium Feministische Bibelauslegung. ᴱ**Schottroff, L.**: 1998 ⇒H8.9. 347-353.
3733 *Spronk, Klaas* Acrostics in the book of Nahum. ZAW 110 (1998) 209-222.

3734 Wendland, E.R. What's the 'good news'—check out 'the feet'!: prophetic rhetoric and the salvific centre of Nahum's 'vision'. OTEs 11
(1998) 154-181.
3735 *Wessels, Wilhelm J.* Nahum, an uneasy expression of Yahweh's
power. OTEs 11 (1998) 615-628.

E9.8 *Habacuc,* **Habakkuk**

3736 *Ábrego, José M.* Habacuc: el profeta en su puesto de guardia. RevBib
60 (1998) 111-116.
3737 *Bail, Ulrike* Das Buch Habakuk: ein politisches Nachtgebet.
Kompendium Feministische Bibelauslegung. [E]**Schottroff, L.**: 1998
⇒H8.9.354-358.
3738 *Brzegowy, Tadeusz* 'A sprawiedliwy żyć będzie dzięki swej wierze':
religijne przesłanie proroka Habakuka ['Iustus autem in fide sua
vivet': de missione religiosa Habacuc]. RBL 51 (1998) 7-17. P.
3739 **Cleaver-Bartholomew, David Gordon** An analysis of the Old
Greek version of Habakkuk. [D]Claremont 1998, 369 pp.
3740 **Haak, Robert D.** Habakkuk. VT.S 44: 1992 ⇒7,3483... 11/1,2683.
[R]JSSt 43 (1998) 373-375 (*Cathcart, Kevin J.*).

3741 *Fitzmyer, Joseph A.* Habakkuk 2:3-4 and the New Testament. To
advance the gospel. 1998 <1981> ⇒150. 236-246.
3742 *Seybold, Klaus* Habakuk 2,4 und sein Kontext. Studien zur Psalmenauslegung. 1998 <1992> ⇒201. 189-198.
3743 *Penna, Romano* Il giusto e la fede: Abacuc 2,4b e le sue antiche riletture giudaiche e cristiane. [F]MARTINI, C. SRivBib 33: 1998 ⇒75.
359-380.
3744 *Bodendorfer, Gerhard* "Der Gerechte wird aus dem Glauben leben"—Hab 2,4b und eine kanonisch-dialogische Bibeltheologie im
jüdisch-christlichen Gespräch. Bibel und Midrasch. [E]**Bodendorfer,
Gerhard**: FAT 22: 1998 ⇒K6.5. 13-41.

E9.9 *Aggaeus,* **Haggai**—*Zacharias,* **Zechariah**—*Malachias,* **Malachi**

3745 **Fijnvandraat, J.G.** Terugzien en vooruitkijken: bijbelstudies bij de
profetie van Haggaï. Vaassen 1998, Medema 128 pp. 90-6353-294-6.
3746 *Kessler, John* 't (le temps) en Aggée I 2-4: conflit théologique ou
"sagesse mondaine"?. VT 48 (1998) 555-559.
3747 **Walborn, Ronald Charles** Breaking the spirit of poverty: perspectives on wealth and poverty from the prophet Haggai. [D]Fuller 1998,
128 pp.

3748 *Amar, Ariella* The menorah of Zechariah's vision: olive trees and
grapevines. [F]NARKISS, B. 1998 ⇒85. 79-88.
3749 *Deissler, Alfons* Sach 12,10—die grosse crux interpretum. [F]RUPPERT,
L. FzB 88: 1998 ⇒99. 49-60.
3750 *Fox, Harry* The forelife of ideas and the afterlife of texts. RB 105
1998, 520-525 [Zech 14].
3751 **Kunz, Andreas** Ablehnung des Krieges: Untersuchungen zu Sacharja 9 und 10. Herders Biblische Studien 17; Herder's Biblical Studies
17: FrB 1998, Herder ix; 427 pp. 3-451-26665-2.

3752 *Lacocque, André* 'Et aspicient ad me quem confixerunt'. Thinking biblically. 1998 ⇒251. 401-441 [Zech 12,10].
3753 **Person, Raymond F.** Second Zechariah and the Deuteronomic School. JSOT.S 167: 1993 ⇒8,4097... 11/1,2709. [R]JNES 57 (1998) 48-50 (*Laubscher, F. du T.*).
3754 **Tai, Nicholas Ho Fai** Prophetie als Schriftauslegung in Sacharja 9-14: traditions- und kompositionsgeschichtliche Studien. CThM.BW 17: 1996 ⇒12,3844. [R]JBL 117 (1998) 351-353 (*Redditt, Paul L.*).
3755 **Tigchelaar, Eibert J.C.** Prophets of old and the day of the end: Zechariah, the Book of Watchers and apocalyptic. OTS 35: 1996 ⇒12, 3835; 13,3947. [R]ThLZ 123 (1998) 251-253 (*Bosshard-Nepustil, Erich*).
3756 *Verhelst, Stéphane* L'Apocalypse de Zacharie, Siméon et Jacques. RB 105 (1998) 81-104.
3757 *Willi-Plein, Ina* Sacharja/Sacharjabuch. TRE 29. 1998 ⇒501. 539-547.
3758 **Wolff, Hans Walter** Dodekapropheton, 7/1: Sacharja 1-8. BK 14.7/1: Neuk 1998, Neuk viii; 568 pp. 3-7887-1345-3.

3759 *Clark, David* A discourse approach to problems in Malachi 2.10-16. BiTr 49 (1998) 415-425.
3760 *Haag, Ernst* Gottes Bund mit Levi nach Maleachi 2: historische und theologische Aspekte des Priestertums im Alten Testament. TThZ 107 (1998) 25-44.
3761 **Hill, Andrew E.** Malachi: a new translation with introduction and commentary. AncB 25D: NY 1998, Doubleday xliii; 436 pp. $38. 0-385-46892-X.
3762 **Hugenberger, G.P.** Marriage as a covenant: a study of biblical law and ethics governing marriage, developed from the perspective of Malachi. VT.S 52: 1994 ⇒10,3795; 11/1,2713. [R]EvQ 70 (1998) 356-357 (*Wenham, G.J.*).
3763 *Mariottini, Claude F.* Malachi: a prophet for his time. JBQ 26 (1998) 149-157.
3764 *Petersen, David L.* Malachi: the form-critical task. "Lasset uns Brücken bauen...". BEAT 42: 1998 ⇒401. 269-274.

VIII. NT Exegesis generalis

F1.1 New Testament Introduction

3765 **Aguirre Monasterio, Rafael; Rodríguez Carmona, Antonio** Vangeli sinottici e Atti degli Apostoli. 1995 ⇒12,3856. [R]RivBib 46 (1998) 355-358 (*Fabris, Rinaldo*).
3766 *Alori, Angelico* Gesù va incontro a chi è in peccato. PalCl 77 (1998) 49-55.
3767 **Audet, Jean-Paul** Le projet évangélique de Jésus: sa mise en œuvre, son style, son sens et sa portée, despuis les commencements jusqu'à la fin de l'âge apostolique. Canton d'Orford, Québec 1998 <1969>, Sources 163 pp. 2-922395-00-6.
3768 **Battaglia, Oscar** Introduzione al Nuovo Testamento. Commenti e studi biblici: Assisi 1998, Cittadella 388 pp. 88-308-0635-8.

3769 **Bell, Albert A.** Exploring the New Testament world: an illustrated guide to the world of Jesus and the first christians. Nv 1998, Nelson 322 pp.

3770 **Boismard, Marie-Émile** À l'aube du christianisme: avant la naissance des dogmes. P 1998, Cerf 182 pp. FF95. 2-204-05977-3. [R]RB 105 (1998) 608-612 (*Mora, Vincent*).

3771 **Borgen, Peder** Early christianity and Hellenistic Judaism. 1996 ⇒12,116; 13,3959. [R]ThLZ 123 (1998) 377-378 (*Wehnert, Jürgen*).

3772 **Bovon, François** Révélations et écritures: Nouveau Testament et littérature apocryphe chrétienne: recueil d'articles. 1993 ⇒9,186 [R]RSR 86 (1998) 432-433 (*Guillet, Jacques*).

3773 **Branick, Vincent P.** Understanding the New Testament and its message: an introduction. NY 1998, Paulist iii; 412 pp. $20. 0-8091-3780-1.

3774 **Broer, Ingo** Einleitung in das Neue Testament: 1. die synoptischen Evangelien, die Apostelgeschichte und die johanneische Literatur. NEB.NT Ergänzungsband 2: Wü 1998, Echter 287 pp. DM48. 3-429-01990-7.

3775 **Brown, Raymond Edward** An introduction to the New Testament. 1997 ⇒13,3961. [R]Faith & Mission 15/2 (1998) 97-98 (*Köstenberger, Andreas J.*); Month 31 (1998) 516-517 (*King, Nicholas*); AnnTh 12 (1998) 533-536 (*Estrada, Bernardo*); TS 59 (1998) 509-511 (*Dillon, Richard J.*); ScrTh 30 (1998) 689-690 (*Silva, Á. de*).

3776 **Conzelmann, Hans** Arbeitsbuch zum Neuen Testament. UTB 52: Tü 1998, Mohr xix; 590 pp. 3-8252-0052-3.

3777 **Court, John M.** Reading the New Testament. NT Readings: 1997 ⇒13,3966. [R]Bibl.Interp. 6 (1998) 439-440 (*Bond, Helen K.*).

3778 **Cousin, Hugues; Lémonon, Jean-Pierre; Massonnet, Jean** Le monde où vivait Jésus. P 1998, Cerf 800 pp. FF350. 2-204-05686-3. [R]CEv 106 (1998) 65-66 (*Gruson, Ph.*).

3779 [E]**Dalla Vecchia, Flavio** Ridatare i vangeli?. 1997 ⇒13,4038. [R]StPat 45/1 (1998) 153-158 (*Leonardi, Giovanni*); Gr. 79 (1998) 389-390 (*Farahian, Edmond*).

3780 **Dorfmeyer, Detlev** The New Testament among the writings of antiquity. BiSe 55: Shf 1998, Academic 324 pp. £18; $28.50. 1-85075-860-3.

3781 [E]**Du Toit, A.B.** The New Testament milieu. Guide to the NT 2: Johannesburg 1998, Orion xxix; 531 pp. 0-7987-0695-3.

3782 **Elwell, Walter A.; Yarbrough, Robert W.** Encountering the New Testament: a historical and theological survey. GR 1998, Baker 448 pp. $45. 0-8010-2156-1.

3783 [E]**Evans, Craig A.; Porter, Stanley E.** New Testament backgrounds: a Sheffield reader. BiSe 43: 1997 ⇒13,3975. [R]ThLZ 123 (1998) 57-59 (*Schenk, Wolfgang*).

3784 [E]**Filoramo, Giovanni; Menozzi, Daniele** Storia del cristianesimo. 1997 ⇒13,3977. [R]Firmana 17 (1998) 143-146 (*Petruzzi, Paolo*).

3785 [E]**Flichy, Odile** Le milieu du Nouveau Testament: diversité du judaïsme et des communautés chrétiennes au premier siècle. P 1998, Médiasèvres 288 pp. 2-900-38845-7.

3786 **Garrison, Roman** The Graeco-Roman context of early christian literature. JSNT.S 137: 1997 ⇒13,3981. [R]Bibl.Interp. 6 (1998) 444-446 (*Meggitt, Justin*).

3787 **Guillaume, J.-M.** Jésus-Christ en son temps: dates, lieux, personnes dans le Nouveau Testament. Vivre la parole: 1997 ⇒13,398 RVieCon 70 (1998) 338-339 (*Luciani, Didier*).

3788 T**Guyot, Peter** Das frühe Christentum bis zum Ende der Verfolgungen: eine Dokumentation. E*Klein, Richard.* TzF 60, 62: 1996 ⇒12,3876. RLatomus 57 (1998) 939-941 (*Inglebert, H.*).

3789 **Jasiński, Tomasz** Über die Anfänge des Neuen Testaments = Bdelygma tēs erēmōseōs. Poznań 1998, Inst. Historii UAM 33 pp. 83-86650-32-X.

3790 **Johnson, Jerome R.** At the right time: dating the events of the New Testament. Havre de Grace, MD 1998, Bathkol 624 pp. $20. 0-9665749-0-7.

3791 **Josaitis, Norman F.; Lanning, Michael J.** New Testament: a course on Jesus and his disciples. Sadlier Faith and Witness: NY 1998, Sadlier 192 pp. $14.60.

3792 **Karris, Robert J.** A symphony of New Testament hymns: commentary on Philippians 2:5-11, Colossians 1:15-20, Ephesians 2:14-16, 1 Timothy 3:16, Titus 3:4-7, 1 Peter 3:18-22, and 2 Timothy 2:11-13. 1996 ⇒12,3883. RCBQ 60 (1998) 161-162 (*Danker, Frederick W.*).

3793 **Keener, Craig S.** Kommentar zum Umfeld des Neuen Testaments: historische, kulturelle und archäologische Hintergründe, 1-3. Neuhausen-Stu 1998, Hänssler 532 + 454 + 436 pp. 3-7751-2934-0.

3794 **Kelly, Joseph F.** The world of the early christians. 1997 ⇒13,3989. RAThR 80/1 (1998) 96-97 (*Vivian, Tim*); ChH 67 (1998) 351-353 (*Bobertz, Charles A.*).

3795 **Kirchschläger, Walter** Einführung in das Neue Testament. 1995 ⇒11/2,2149. RBogoslovni Vestnik 58/3 (1998) 365-368 (*Rozman, Francè*).

3796 E**Longenecker, Richard N.** Patterns of discipleship in the New Testament. 1996 ⇒12,188. RPacifica 11 (1998) 215-217 (*Trainor, Michael*); SR 27 (1998) 212-213 (*Marshall, John*); AsbTJ 53 (1998) 90-92 (*Green, Joel B.*); AUSS 36 (1998) 295-297 (*Melbourne, Bertram L.*).

3797 **Mack, Burton L.** Wie schreven het Nieuwe Testament werkelijk?: feiten, mythen en motieven. 1997 ⇒13,3994. RInterpretatie 6/8 (1998) 27-30 (*Mellink, Osger*).

3798 **Malina, Bruce J.** The social world of Jesus and the Gospels. 1996 ⇒12,3893; 13,3996. RJRH 22/2 (1998) 222-23 (*Lieu, Judith*); Bibl.Interp. 6 (1998) 451-452 (*Bash, Anthony*); JThS 49 (1998) 215-219 (*Meggitt, Justin J.*).

3799 *Manns, Frederick* Everyday life in the time of Jesus II. Holy Land 18 (1998) 171-180.

3800 **Matheus, Robert** Palestine in Jesus' time. Vadavathoor 1998, OIRSI 512 pp. 81-86063-43-9.

3801 **Mestre i Godes, Jesús** Els primers cristians: del divendres sant (any 30) al concili de Nicea (any 325). 1997 ⇒13,3999. RAnuario de Historia de la Iglesia 7 (1998) 483-484 (*Blasi, F.*).

3802 **Nicoletti, Sabatino** Le origini del cristianesimo nella Roma imperiale. Biblioteca '80, Saggi: F 1998, L'Autore Libri 105 pp. 88-8254-155-X.

3803 **Nodet, Étienne; Taylor, Justin** The origins of christianity: an exploration. Michael Glazier Book: ColMn 1998, Liturgical xix; 475 pp. $40.

3804 **Ogden, Daniel Kelly; Skinner, Andrew C.** New Testament apostles testify of Christ: a guide to Acts through Revelation. Salt Lake City 1998, Deseret vii; 424 pp. 1-573-45304-8.

3805 **Osman, Ahmed** Out of Egypt: the roots of christianity revealed. L 1998, Century xviii; 270 pp. 0-7126-7962-6.

3806 **Popkes, Wiard** Paränese und Neues Testament. SBS 168: 1996 ⇒12,3900; 13,4005. [R]ThGl 88 (1998) 116-117 (*Backhaus, Knut*).

3807 **Rhoads, David** The challenge of diversity. 1996 ⇒12,3904. [R]CBQ 60 (1998) 171-172 (*Branick, Vincent P.*); New Theology Review 11/4 (1998) 88-89 (*McDonald, Patricia M.*).

3808 **Rinaldi, Giancarlo** La bibbia dei pagani, 2: testi e documenti. La bibbia nella storia 20: Bo 1998, EDB 653 pp.

3809 **Schnelle, Udo** The history and theology of the New Testament writings. L 1998, SCM xv; 573 pp. 0-334-02730-6.

3810 **Sicre, José Luis** El cuadrante: introducción a los evangelios. 1996 ⇒12,4203. [R]EstB 56 (1998) 126-127 (*Barrado, P.*).

3811 **Stark, Rodney** The rise of christianity: a sociologist reconsiders history. 1996 ⇒12,3918; 13,4018. [R]JEarlyC 6 (1998) 162-184 (*Klutz, Todd E.*) and 185-226 (*Hopkins, Keith*) and 227-257 [Stark's response 260-267] (*Castelli, Elizabeth A.*); ASSR 43/4 (1998) 122-123 (*Dubois, Jean-Daniel*); JR 78 (1998) 616-617 (*Burns, J. Patout*); JThS 49 (1998) 328-335 (*Maier, Harry O.*);

3812 De eerste eeuwen: een sociologische visie op het ontstaan van het christendom. Baarn 1998, Ten Have 254 pp. *f*45. 90-259-4723-9.

3813 **Untergaßmair, Franz Georg** Handbuch der Einleitung: 1. Evangelien und Apostelgeschichte. Vechtaer Beiträge zur Theologie 4/1: Kevelaer 1998, Butzon & B 192 pp. DM26.80. 3-7666-0142-3.

3814 [TE]**Van der Horst, Pieter Willem** Bronnen voor de studie van de wereld van het vroege christendom: joodse en pagane teksten uit de periode van Alexander de Grote tot keizer Constantijn. 1997 ⇒13,4021. [R]KeTh 49/1 (1998) 72-73 (*Van der Woude, A.S.*).

3815 **Wright, N.T.** The New Testament and the people of God. 1992 ⇒8, 4209... 13,4022. [R]BS 155 (1998) 467-473 (*Ingolfsland, Dennis*).

F1.2 *Origo Evangeliorum,* the origin of the Gospels

3816 **Alexander, Loveday** Ancient book production and the circulation of the gospels. The gospels. 1998 ⇒213. 71-111.

3817 **Amphoux, Christian-Bernard** La parole qui devient évangile: l'évangile, ses rédacteurs, ses auteurs. 1990 ⇒9,4087. [R]Ist. 43 (1998) 433-434 (*Dupuy, B.*).

3818 *Barton, Stephen C.* Can we identify the gospel audiences?;

3819 *Bauckham, Richard* For whom were gospels written?;

3820 *Burridge, Richard A.* About people, by people, for people: gospel genre and audiences. The gospels. 1998 ⇒213. 173-194/9-48/113-145.

3821 **Gallo, Italo** Studi sulla biografia greca. Storie e testi 7: 1997 ⇒13, 4025. [R]Orph. 19-20 (1998-99) 464-471 (*Abbamonte, Giancarlo*).

3822 **Mucci, Ugo** Il vangelo: commentato dal professor CAFIERO. Sezione di narrativa: N 1998, Lettere italiane 85 pp. 88-7188-192-3.

3823 **Powell, Mark Alan** Fortress introduction to the four gospels. Mp 1998, Fortress vii; 184 pp. $16. 0-8006-3075-0.

3824 *Richter, Hans-Friedemann* Megfigyelések és mérlegelések az egangéliumok előtörténetével kapcsolatban [Beobachtungen und Erwägungen zur Entstehung der Evangelien]. Példabeszédek. 1998 ⇒372. 143-149.

3825 **Testa, Giuseppe** L'evangelo prima dei vangeli: dall'annuncio orale ai testi scritti. La Bibbia nelle nostre mani 16: CinB 1998, San Paolo 54 pp. 88-215-3822-2.

3826 *Thompson, Michael B.* The holy internet: communication between churches in the first christian generation. The gospels. 1998 ⇒213. 49-70.

3827 *Victor, Ulrich* Was ein Texthistoriker zur Entstehung der Evangelien sagen kann. Bib. 79 (1998) 499-514.

3828 *Watson, Francis* Toward a literal reading of the gospels. The gospels. 1998 ⇒213. 195-217.

3829 **Wills, Lawrence Mitchell** The quest of the historical gospel: Mark, John and the origins of the gospel genre. 1997 ⇒13,4032. ᴿRRT 1998/2, 45-6 (*Goulder, Michael*).

F1.3 **Historicitas,** *chronologia* **Evangeliorum**

3830 **Blomberg, Craig L.** Jesus and the gospels: an introduction and survey. 1997 ⇒13,4036. ᴿAUSS 36 (1998) 285-287 (*Blake, Garfield D.*); AsbTJ 53 (1998) 92-94 (*Snodgrass, Klyne*).

3831 **Ceruti-Cendrier, M.-Chr.** Les évangiles sont des reportages, n'en déplaise à certains. P 1997, Téqui 370 pp. FF59.

3832 *Heras, Guillermo* El Gólgota y el Sepulcro: los estudios realizados: ¿qué aportan a los datos evangélicos?. BiFe 24 (1998) 476-545.

3833 **Thiede, Carsten Peter** Ein Fisch für den römischen Kaiser: Juden, Griechen und Römer: die Welt des Jesus Christus. Da 1998, Luchterhand 389 pp. 3-630-87994-2.

F1.4 *Jesus historicus*—**The human Jesus**

3834 *Abrahamsen, Valerie* The Jesus myth according to Barbara Walker. JHiC 5 (1998) 188-202.

3835 *Aguirre Monasterio, R.* Estado actual de los estudios sobre el Jesús historico despues de BULTMANN. IX Jornadas Bíblicas. 1998 ⇒376. 55-85.

3836 **Allen, Charlotte** The human Christ: the search for the historical Jesus. NY 1998, Free xv; 383 pp. $26. 0-684-82725-5.

3837 **Allison, Dale C.** Jesus of Nazareth: millenarian prophet. Mp 1998, Fortress xii; 255 pp. $20. 0-8006-3144-7.

3838 **Antes, Peter** Jesus zur Einführung. Zur Einführung 169: Ha 1998, Junius 180 pp. 3-88506-969-5.

3839 *Arendse, Roger A.* The historical Jesus, eschatology and hope for the earth?. Scriptura 66 (1998) 245-268.

3840 ᴱ**Armstrong, Donald** The truth about Jesus. GR 1998, Eerdmans viii; 160 pp. 1-85075-932-4.

3841 ᴱ**Arnal, William E.; Desjardins, Michel** Whose historical Jesus?. SCJud 7: Waterloo, Ont. 1997, Wilfid Laurier Univ. Pr. 337 pp. $28. 0-88920-295-8. ᴿCBQ 60 (1998) 597-598 (*McKnight, Scot*).

3842 **Arnéra, Georges** Jésus, lecteur de l'Écriture. Scriptura: Genève 1998, L'Eau Vive 171 pp. 2-88035-029-8.
3843 **Balthasar, Hans Urs von** Czy Jezus nas zna?: czy my znamy Jezusa?. Kraków 1998, WAM·72 pp.
3844 *Barbaglio, Giuseppe* Le parole violente sulla bocca di Gesù. PSV 37 (1998) 117-129.
3845 **Barry, William A.** ¿Quién decís que soy yo?: encuentro com el Jesús histórico en la oración. ^T*Mier, Milagros Amado*. El Pozo de Siquem 94: Maliaño 1998, Sal Terrae 157 pp. 84-293-1261-7.
3846 **Becker, Jürgen** Jesus von Nazareth. 1996 ⇒12,3948; 13,4068. ^RThLZ 123 (1998) 388-389 (*Kieffer, René*); CV 40 (1998) 171-178 (*Stenschke, Christoph*); JBL 117 (1998) 360-361 (*Evans, Craig A.*);
3847 Jesus of Nazareth. B 1998, De Gruyter x; 386 pp. 3-11-015772-1.
3848 *Bellinger, William H.; Farmer, William R.* Introduction. Jesus and the suffering servant. 1998 ⇒3430. 1-7.
3849 *Berger, Klaus* Kriterien für echte Jesusworte?. ZNT 1 (1998) 52-58.
3850 **Berger, Klaus** Wer war Jesus wirklich?. 1995 ⇒12,3949. ^RDBAT 29 (1998) 305-307 (*Diebner, B.J.*).
3851 *Betz, Hans Dieter* Jesus and the Cynics: survey and analysis of a hypothesis. Gesammelte Aufsätze IV. 1998 <1994> ⇒134. 32-56.
3852 *Betz, Otto* Jesus and Isaiah 53. Jesus and the suffering servant. 1998 ⇒3430. 70-87.
3853 *Bénétreau, Samuel* Jésus ou Paul?: qui est le fondateur du christianisme?. RRef 49 (1998) 59-75.
3854 **Boismard, Marie-Émile** Jésus, un homme de Nazareth. 1996 ⇒12,4796; 13,4074. ^RRSR 86 (1998) 426-427 (*Guillet, Jacques*); POC 48 (1998) 207-209 (*Ternant, P.*).
3855 **Bolyki, János** Jesu Tischgemeinschaften. WUNT 2/96: Tü 1998, Mohr xi; 261 pp. DM98. 3-16-14809-0. ^RActBib 35 (1998) 168-169 (*Boada, J.*).
3856 ^E**Borg, Marcus** Jesus at 2000. 1996 ⇒12,3953. ^RRBBras 15 (1998) 511-512.
3857 **Borg, Marcus J.; Wright, Nicholas Thomas** The meaning of Jesus: two visions. SF 1998, HarperSF xi; 288 pp. $24. 0-06060-875-7.
3858 **Borg, Marcus J.** Conflict, holiness, and politics in the teachings of Jesus. Harrisburg, PA 1998, Trinity xxvi; 309 pp. 1-56338-227-X.
3859 *Borg, Marcus J.* Jesus and God;
3860 Jesus before and after easter: Jewish mystic and christian messiah;
3861 Seeing Jesus: sources, lenses, and method;
3862 Why was Jesus killed?. The meaning of Jesus. 1998 ⇒3857. 145-156/53-76/3-14/79-91.
3863 *Bouttier, Michel* Composantes d'une quête insoluble. Jésus de Nazareth. 1998 ⇒253. 529-539.
3864 **Boyd, Gregory A.** Cynic sage or son of God?. GR 1995, Baker 416 pp. $18. 0-8010-2118-9. ^RTrin.Journal 19 (1998) 110-114 (*Köstenberger, Andreas J.*).
3865 *Bruners, Wilhelm* Wie Jesus Menschen begegnet ist. LS 49 (1998) 99-107.
3866 *Cahill, Michael* An uncertain Jesus: theological and scholarly ambiguities. IThQ 63 (1998) 22-38.
3867 *Calero de los Ríos, Antonio Mª.* Jesús, el hijo de María. Isidorianum 7 (1998) 27-50.

3868 **Campbell, Steuart** The rise and fall of Jesus: the ultimate explanation for the origin of christianity. E 1996, Explicit 208 pp. 0-
9521512-1-9.
3869 *Cassell, David* Response to Scot McKnight's 'The hermeneutics of
confessing Jesus as Lord'. ExAu 14 (1998) 18-20.
3870 *Castelli, Ferdinando* Immagini de Gesù nella letteratura del
novecento. Firmana 18 (1998) 29-41.
3871 *Caulley, Thomas S.* "What's right with the Jesus seminar?". RestQ 40
(1998) 239-252.
3872 **Chilton, Bruce D.** Pure kingdom...the historical Jesus. 1996
⇒13,4087. ᴿJR 78 (1998) 425-427 *(Jackson-McCabe, Matt A.)*.
3873 **Conconi, Giorgio** When Jesus smiled. Staten Island, NY 1998, Alba
147 pp. $6.
3874 *Craig, William Lane* Rediscovering the historical Jesus: the presup-
positions and presumptions of the Jesus Seminar;
3875 Rediscovering the historical Jesus: the evidence for Jesus. Faith &
Mission 15 (1998) 3-15/16-26.
3876 **Crotty, Robert** The Jesus question: the historical search. 1996
⇒12,3967. ᴿPacifica 11/1 (1998) 90-92 *(Hamilton, Andrew)*.
3877 *Cuvillier, Elian* La question du Jésus historique dans l'exégèse fran-
cophone: aperçu historique et évaluation critique. Jésus de Nazareth.
1998 ⇒253. 59-88.
3878 *Davis, Stephen T.* 'This is truly the savior of the world': the theological significance of the earthly Jesus. ExAu 14 (1998) 97-103.
3879 *Demke, Christoph* Von der Vollmacht Jesu. ᶠPOKORNÝ, P. 1998
⇒90. 82-87.
3880 *De Préville, Agnès* Haben die ersten Christen Jesus auf Bildern
dargestellt?. WUB 10 (1998) 46-51.
3881 *Downing, F. Gerald* Deeper reflections on the Jewish cynic Jesus.
JBL 117 (1998) 97-104.
3882 **Dreyfus, François** Věděl Ježiš, že je Bůh?. Praha 1998, Krystal 127
pp. 80-85929-28-7.
3883 **Duquesne, Jacques** Jesús. 1996 ⇒12,3976. ᴿTE 42 (1998) 276-278
(Gelabert, Martín);
3884 Il vero Dio di Gesù. CasM 1998, Piemme 223 pp. L25.000.
3885 *Emanuel, Simcha* חשבון הלוח וחשבון הקץ: פולמוס יהודי-נוצרי בשנת 1100
[A Jewish-Christian debate—France, 1100]. Zion 63 (1998) 143-155.
3886 ᴱ**Engberg-Pedersen, Troels** Den historiske Jesus og hans betydning.
K 1998, Gyldendal 181 pp.
3887 Los enigmas del Gólgota: aproximación al Jesús histórico (III). *Var.
auct.* BiFe 24 (1998) 397-561.
3888 **Evans, C. Stephen** The historical Christ and the Jesus of faith: the
incarnational narrative as history. 1996 ⇒12,3979; 13,4102. ᴿACPQ
72 (1998) 465-468 *(Perkins, Robert L.)*; AThR 80 (1998) 627-629
(Moss, David); JBL 117 (1998) 168-170 *(Johnson, Luke Timothy)*.
3889 **Focant, Camille,** *al.*, Le Jésus de l'histoire. 1997 ⇒13,4119. ᴿRTL
29 (1998) 248-249 *(Dermience, Alice)*.
3890 **Forward, M.** Jesus: a short biography. Oxf 1998, Oneworld x; 182
pp. £9. 1-85168-172-8.
3891 *Freyne, Seán* In search of the real Jesus. Furrow 49 (1998) 527-538.
3892 *Funk, Robert Walter* Honest to Jesus: Jesus for a new millennium.
1996 ⇒12,3986; 13,4123. ᴿJBL 117 (1998) 740-742 *(Johnson, Luke
Timothy)*.

3893 **Funk, Robert Walter** The acts of Jesus: the search for the authentic deeds of Jesus. SF 1998, Harper SF xxiv; (2) 569 pp. 0-06-06978-9.

3894 *Fusco, Vittorio* La quête du Jésus historique: bilan et perspectives. Jésus de Nazareth. 1998 ⇒253. 25-57.

3895 *Fusco, Vittorio* La ricerca del Gesù storico: bilancio e prospettive ᶠMARTINI, C. RivBib.S 33: 1998 ⇒75. 487-519.

3896 **Girzone, Joseph F.** A portrait of Jesus. East Melbourne 1998, HarperCollins 179 pp. $17. 1-86371-754-4.

3897 *Gnilka, Joachim; Sánchez de Murillo, José* Jesus von Nazaret: ein Gespräch mit Joachim GNILKA. Edith-Stein-Jahrbuch 4 (1998) 63-80.

3898 *González de Cardedal, Olegario* Soledad y compañía de Jésus. Salm. 45 (1998) 55-103.

3899 *Grappe, Christian* Jésus: Messie prétendu ou Messie prétendant?: entre les catégories de messianité revendiquée et de messianité prétendue, la figure du Jésus historique envisagée à partir d'une comparaison avec celles d'autres personnages de son temps. Jésus de Nazareth. 1998 ⇒253. 269-291.

3900 **Green, Barbara** 'What profit for us?': remembering the story of Jesus. 1996 ⇒12,3993. ᴿCBQ 60 (1998) 527-528 (*Dempsey, Carol J.*).

3901 **Grelot, Pierre** Jésus de Nazareth, Christ et Seigneur: une lecture de l'évangile, 2. LeDiv 170: P 1998, Cerf 553 pp. 2-204-05710-X.

3902 **Grenier, Brian** Jesus, o mestre. São Paulo 1998, Paulus 131 pp. 85-349-1086-3.

3903 **Griffin, Albert Kirby** In his own words: the beliefs and teachings of Jesus. Commack, NY 1998, Troitsa x; 145 pp. 1-56072-448-X.

3904 *Guijarro Oporto, Santiago* Reino y familia en conflicto: una aportación al estudio del Jesús histórico. EstB 56 (1998) 507-541.

3905 *Gunton, Colin* Martin KÄHLER revisited: variations on Hebrews 4:15. ExAu 14 (1998) 21-30.

3906 **Hack, Christine** Leraar of verlosser?: verwarring over Jezus. Zoetermeer 1998, Boekencentrum 112 pp. ƒ21.50. 90-239-0468-0.

3907 *Haight, Roger* El impacto de la investigación del Jesús histórico sobre la cristología. SelTeol 37 (1998) 127-134.

3908 **Hall, David R.** The gospel framework: fiction or fact?: a critical evaluation of *Der Rahmen der Geschichte Jesu* by Karl Ludwig SCHMIDT. Carlisle 1998, Paternoster xi; 175 pp. 0-85364-799-2.

3909 *Heiligenthal, Roman* Echte Jesusworte?: eine Einführung zur Kontroverse Klaus BERGER versus Walter SCHMITHALS. ZNT 1 (1998) 48-49.

3910 **Heiligenthal, Roman** Der verfälschte Jesus: eine Kritik moderner Jesusbilder. 1997 ⇒13,4133. ᴿSTV 36 (1998) 187-193 (*Załęski, Jan*).

3911 *Heras, Guillermo* Recapitulación final [⇒3887];

3912 Temas introductorios: las personas, el tiempo y el lugar [Gólgota] [⇒3887]. BiFe 24 (1998) 548-561/397-402.

3913 **Heyer, Cees J. den** Der Mann aus Nazaret: Bilanz der Jesusforschung. Dü 1998, Patmos 253 pp. DM39.80. 3-491-7797-9.

3914 **Holloway, Gary** The unexpected Jesus: a surprising look at the Savior. Joplin, Mo. 1998, College 141 pp. 0-89900-817-8.

3915 *Hooker, Morna D.* Did the use of Isaiah 53 to interpret his mission begin with Jesus?. Jesus and the suffering servant. 1998 ⇒3430. 88-103.

3916 **Hooker, Morna Dorothy** The signs of a prophet: the prophetic actions of Jesus. 1997 ⇒13,4137. ᴿJThS 49 (1998) 734-736 (*Stanton, Graham N.*).

3917 *Hoppe, Rudolf* Jesusliteratur zwischen Einseitigkeit und Sensations-
       lust. WUB 10 (1998) 7-8.
3918 *Hubaut, Michel A.* Pour une histoire de Jésus. Graphè 7 (1998) 11-
       18.
3919 **Irudayam, Susai Michael** "Come and see": an introduction to the
       life of Jesus in Tamil. Chennai 1998, St. Paul's Bible Institute xv;
       116 pp.
3920 *Jacobs, Maretha* 'Historical Jesuses', their movements and the
       church. Neotest. 32 (1998) 405-423.
3921 ^E**Jeanrond, Verner; Theobald, Christoph** La redécouverte de
       Jésus: qui dites-vous que je suis?. Conc(F)269 (1997) ⇒13,4143
       ^RCoTh 68/1 (1998) 259-267 (*Horoszewicz, Michał*).
3922 **Jonge, Marinus de** God's final envoy: early christology and Jesus'
       own view of his mission. Studying the Historical Jesus: GR 1998,
       Eerdmans x; 166 pp. $18. 0-8028-4482-0.
3923 **Jossa, Giorgio** La verità dei vangeli: Gesù di Nazaret tra storia e
       fede. Argomenti 12: R 1998, Carocci 181 pp. 88-430-1194-4.
3924 *Keller, Marie Noël* Jesus the teacher. CThMi 25 (1998) 450-460.
3925 *Klusmann, Carl-Peter* Zur Vergesetzlichung der Botschaft Jesu
       ^FHOFFMANN, P., Von Jesus. BZNW 93: 1998 ⇒43. 615-619.
3926 *Kosch, Daniel* Jesusliteratur 1993-1997: eine Umschau. BiKi 53
       (1998) 213-219.
3927 *Krieger, Klaus-Stefan* Die Zeichenpropheten—eine Hilfe zum Ver-
       ständnis des Wirkens Jesu?. ^FHOFFMANN, P., Von Jesus. BZNW 93:
       1998 ⇒43. 175-188.
3928 *Kulisz, Józef; Mostowska Baliszewska, Aleksandra* Jésu de l'histoire
       et le Christ de la foi. CoTh 68A (1998) 89-114.
3929 **Laurentin, René** Vie authentique de Jésus-Christ: récit. 1996
       ⇒12,4013; 13,4159. ^RSt Juan de la Cruz 14 (1998) 276-278 (*Contre-
       ras Molina, Francisco*); Mar. 60 (1998) 723-725 (*Gharib, Georges*);
3930 Vida auténtica de Jesucristo, vol. 1: relato, vol. 2: fundamentos,
       pruebas y justificación. Bilbao 1998, Desclée de Brouwer 577 + 237
       pp. 84-330-1285-1.
3931 *Légasse, Simon* Notes et critiques. BLE 99 (1998) 443-454.
3932 **Létourneau, Pierre; Poirier, Paul-Hubert** Sur les traces de Jésus:
       parcours historique et biblique. [Montréal] 1998, Médiaspaul 181 pp.
       2-89420-155-9.
3933 *Loader, William R.* Mark 7:1-23 and the historical Jesus. Colloquium
       30 (1998) 123-151.
3934 **Loader, William** Jesus and the fundamentalism of his day. Mel-
       bourne 1998, Uniting Education 155 pp. $20. 0-80-2838-219.
3935 **Lüdemann, Gerd** Der große Betrug und was Jesus wirklich sagte
       und tat. Lüneburg 1998, zu Klampen 125 pp. 3-924245-70-3;
3936 The great deception: and what Jesus really said and did. L 1998,
       SCM xi; 114 pp. 0-334-02747-0.
3937 **Maass, Fritz** Der historische Jesus. 1996 ⇒12,4020. ^RDBAT 29
       (1998) 307-309 (*Diebner, B.J.*).
3938 **Magnani, Giovanni** Jesus: construtor e mestre: novas perspectivas
       sobre seu ambiente de vida. Aparecida 1998, Santuário 277 pp. 88-
       308-0599-8.
3939 *Marcheselli-Casale, Cesare* Gesù di Nazaret, messia di Israele?:
       verso un dialogo sempre più costruttivo tra cristiani ed ebrei. ^FMAR-
       TINI, C. RivBib.S 33: 1998 ⇒75. 521-539.

3940 *Marguerat, Daniel* Ein ungelöstes Rätsel;
3941 Jesus, Johannes und andere Propheten der Erneuerung. WUB 10 (1998) 3-6/31-34;
3942 Jésus le sage et Jésus le prophète;
3943 Les révisions qui nous attendent. Jésus de Nazareth. 1998 ⇒253. 293-317/561-565.
3944 **Martín Descalzo, José Luis** Gesù di Nazaret: vita e mistero. R 1998, Dehoniane 1424 pp. 88-396-0422-7.
3945 *März, Claus-Peter* Jesus nach dem Zeugnis der Evangelien. WUB 10 (1998) 9-12.
3946 *McDade, John* Jesus in recent research. Month 31 (1998) 495-505.
3947 *McGaughty, Lane C.* Words before deeds: why start with the sayings. Forum 1 n.s. (1998) 387-398.
3948 *McKnight, Scot* The hermeneutics of confessing Jesus as 'Lord'. ExAu 14 (1998) 3-17.
3949 **Meier, John P.** Un judío marginal: nueva visión del Jesús histórico, 2/1: Juan y Jesús: el reino de Dios. [T]*Fernández Martínez, Serafín.* Estella 1999, Verbo Divino 592 pp. 84-8169-230-1.
3950 *Meyer-Blank, Michael* Zwischen Exegese und Videoclip: Jesus Christus in der Bibeldidaktik. ZNT 1 (1998) 65-77.
3951 **Meyer, Marvin W.** The unknown sayings of Jesus. SF 1998, Harper SF xxvi; 182 pp. 0-06-065588-7.
3952 *Meyers, Eric M.* Jesus und seine galiläische Lebenswelt. ZNT 1 (1998) 27-39.
3953 *Mikhael, Mary* Jesus and women: confusing samples. ThRev 19 (1998) 29-43.
3954 *Moore, Stephen D.* Ugly thoughts: on the face and physique of the historical Jesus. Biblical studies. 1998 ⇒380. 376-399.
3955 **Morrice, William G.** Hidden sayings of Jesus: words attributed to Jesus outside the four gospels. 1997 ⇒13,4186. [R]CV 40 (1998) 186-189 (*Segert, Stanislav*); RTR 57 (1998) 154-155 (*Bolt, Peter*); RBBras 15 (1998) 521-522.
3956 *Moxnes, Halvor* The historical Jesus: from master narrative to cultural context. BTB 28 (1998) 135-149.
3957 **Munro, Winsome** Jesus, born of a slave: the social and economic origins of Jesus' message. SBEC 37: Lewiston, NY 1998, Mellen 705 pp. 0-7734-2440-7.
3958 *Müller, Peter* Neue Trends in der Jesusforschung. ZNT 1 (1998) 2-16.
3959 **Nautin, Pierre** L'évangile retrouvé: Jésus et l'évangile retrouvé. Christianisme antique 5: P 1998, Beauchesne 282 pp. FF144. 2-7010-1376-3.
3960 **Neumann, Johannes** Der galiläische Messias. 1986 ⇒3,3840. [R]DBAT 29 (1998) 310-312 (*Diebner, B.J.*).
3961 *Norelli, Enrico* La question des sources. Jésus de Nazareth. 1998 ⇒253. 567-572.
3962 **O'Neill, John** Who did Jesus think he was?. Bibl.Interp. 11: 1995 ⇒11/2,2174; 13,4193. [R]EstAg 33 (1998) 383-384 (*Cineira, D.A.*).
3963 **Owens, Virginia** Stem Looking for Jesus. LVL 1998, Westminster vi; 261 pp. $18.
3964 *Pagazzi, Giovanni Cesare* Fenomenologia dell'evento cristologico: la storia di Gesù e la verità di Dio. RdT 39 1998, 777-781.

3965   *Patterson, Stephen J.* The historical Jesus and the search for God. HTS 54 (1998) 476-504.

3966   **Patterson, Stephen J.** The God of Jesus: the historical Jesus and the search for meaning. Harrisburg, Pennsylvania 1998, Trinity xiii; 305 pp. $20. 1-56338-228-8.

3967   **Perrot, Charles** Jésus. Que sais-je?: P 1998, PUF 128 pp. FF49. 2-13-048699-1.

3968   *Pfüller, Wolfgang* Überlegungen zum Stellenwert der historischen Frage nach Jesus für die Christologie. ThZ 54 (1998) 325-344.

3969   **Phipps, William E.** The sexuality of Jesus. 1996 ⇒12,4040. ᴿBS 155 (1998) 144-145 (*Bailey, James L.*).

3970   *Pisarek, Stanislaw* Jesus—the evangelizer. ᶠPOKORNÝ, P. 1998 ⇒90. 271-283.

3971   **Pixner, Bargil** With Jesus in Jerusalem: his first and last days in Judea. 1996 ⇒12,4044. ᴿRB 105 (1998) 304-306 (*Murphy-O'Connor, J.*).

3972   *Poffet, Jean-Michel* Une stratégie de l'indirect. Jésus de Nazareth. 1998 ⇒253. 573-576.

3973   **Potin, Jean** Jesus: la storia vera: la cronaca, gli eventi, i protagonisti di un fatto realmente accaduto. Guida alla bibbia 17: Mi 1998, San Paolo 522 pp. 88-215-3631-9.

3974   **Powell, Mark Allan** Jesus as a figure in history: how modern historians view the Man from Galilee. LVL 1998, Westminster 238 pp. $22. 0-664-25703-8.

3975   *Pragasam, Arul* The quest for the historical Jesus in contemporary scholarship. VJTR 62 (1998) 251-269.

3976   *Quesnel, Michel* Literarische Quellen über das Leben Jesu. WUB 10 (1998) 15-19.

3977   *Rau, Eckhard* Jesu Auseinandersetzung mit Pharisäern über seine Zuwendung zu Sünderinnen und Sündern: Lk 15,11-32 und Lk 18,10-14a als Worte des historischen Jesus. ZNW 89 (1998) 5-29.

3978   **Renan, Ernest** Vita di Gesù. 1997 ⇒13,4204. ᴿParamita 17/1 (1998) 47-49 (*Ballabio, Eugenio*).

3979   *Robinson, James M.* Der wahre Jesus?: der historische Jesus im Spruchevangelium Q. ZNT 1 (1998) 17-26.

3980   **Rolland, Philippe** Jésus et les historiens. P 1998, De Paris 93 pp. FF59. 2-85162-015-0.

3981   **Roloff, Jürgen** Jesusforschung am Ausgang des 20. Jahrhunderts. Bayerische Akad. der Wissenschaften. Phil.-hist. Kl. Sitzungsberichte 1998,4: Mü 1998, Verlag der Bayerischen Akademie der Wissenschaft 57 pp. 3-7696-1601-4.

3982   *Miller, Robert J.* History is not optional: a response to the Real Jesus by Luke Timothy Johnson. BTB 28 (1998) 27-34.

3983   **Roose, Hanna** 'Das Zeugnis Jesu': seine Bedeutung für die Christologie, Eschatologie und Prophetie in der Offenbarung. Diss. Saarland 1996-1997 [ThRv 94,xviii].

3984   *Rosen, Klaus* Das Christentum in den heidnischen Quellen des 1. und 2. Jahrhunderts. WUB 10 (1998) 13-14.

3985   **Sanders, Ed P.** Sohn Gottes: eine historische Biographie Jesu. ᵀ*Enderwitz, Ulrich.* Stu 1996, Klett-Cotta 452 pp. 3-608-91721-7. ᴿZNT 1/1 (1998) 78-80 (*Busch, Peter*).

3986   *Sanders, Jack T.* The criterion of coherence and the randomness of charisma: poring through some aporias in the Jesus tradition. NTS 44 (1998) 1-25.

3987 **Savagnone, Giuseppe** Il Dio della differenza: indagine su Gesù. Leumann 1998, Elledici 221 pp. L18.000. 88-01-01128-8.

3988 *Scalabrin, Sandro* La verità storica di Cristo: alcuni recenti volumi in edizione italiana. RPLi 206 (1998) 67-72.

3989 **Scheele, Paul-Werner** Abba—Amen: Urworte Jesu Christi, Grundworte des Christen. Wü 1998, Echter 374 pp. 3-429-02021-2.

3990 *Schlette, Heinz Robert* Die Theologie der Religionen, der neue Relativismus und die Frage nach Jesus. FHOFFMANN, P., Von Jesus. BZNW 93: 1998 ⇒43. 621-630.

3991 *Schlosser, Jacques* Die Überlieferung der Worte und Taten. WUB 10 (1998) 39-42.

3992 *Schmidt, Daryl D.* Sane eschatology: Albert SCHWEITZER's profile of Jesus. Forum 1 n.s. (1998) 241-260.

3993 *Schmithals, Walter* Gibt es Kriterien für die Bestimmung echter Jesusworte?. ZNT 1 (1998) 59-64.

3994 **Schnackenburg, Rudolf** La persona di Gesù Cristo nei quattro vangeli. CTNT.S 4: 1995 ⇒11/2,2197; 12,4056. RCarthaginensia 14 (1998) 224-226 (*Álvarez Barredo, M.*); RivBib 46 (1998) 361-364 (*Fabris, Rinaldo*); ScrTh 30 (1998) 314-315 (*García-Moreno, A.*);

3995 Jesus Christus im Spiegel der vier Evangelien. Akzente: FrB 1998, Herder 357 pp. 3-451-26712-8;

3996 Amistad con Jesús. S 1998, Sígueme 106 pp. PTA990.

3997 *Schöttler, Heinz-Günther* Jesus im Bibliodrama. Lebendige Katechese 20 (1998) 148-151.

3998 *Schreurs, Nico* Hoe is er heil in Jezus?: nut en noodzaak van het onderzoek naar de historische Jezus. TTh 38 (1998) 169-188.

3999 *Schröter, Jens* Markus, Q und der historische Jesus: methodische und exegetische Erwägungen zu den Anfängen der Rezeption der Verkündigung Jesu. ZNW 89 (1998) 173-200.

4000 *Schürmann, Heinz* Jesu Basileia-Verkündigung und das christologische Kerygma als Mitte der Schrift. Gesammelte Beiträge. 1998 <1983> ⇒197. 234-239.

4001 *Scott, Bernard Brandon* Holmes on the case: E.P. SANDERS' profile of Jesus. Forum 1 n.s. (1998) 261-273.

4002 *Segalla, Giuseppe* Un Gesù storico incerto e frammentato: guadagno o perdita per la fede?. StPat 45 (1998) 3-19.

4003 *Seitz, Christopher* Of mortal appearance: the earthly Jesus and Isaiah as a type of christian scripture. ExAu 14 (1998) 31-41;

4004 In accordance with the scriptures': creed, scripture, and 'historical Jesus'. Word without end. 1998 ⇒200. 51-60.

4005 *Sesboüé, Bernard* La question du Jésus historique au regard de la foi. Jésus de Nazareth. 1998 ⇒253. 503-513.

4006 **Sesboüé, Bernard** Jésus-Christ à l'image des hommes: brève enquête sur les représentations de Jésus à travers l'histoire. 1997 ⇒13,4226. RScEs 50 (1998) 382-384 (*Dufort, Jean-Marc*).

4007 *Shuster, Marguerite* The use and misuse of the idea of the imitation of Christ. ExAu 14 (1998) 70-81.

4008 *Siegert, Folker* Einheit und Verschiedenheit im Judentum des ersten Jahrhunderts. WUB 10 (1998) 20-30.

4009 *Siegert, Folker* Jésus et Paul: une relation contestée. Jésus de Nazareth. 1998 ⇒253. 439-457.

4010 *Smith, Mahlon H.* Israel's prodigal son: reflections on reimaging Jesus. Forum 1 n.s. (1998) 431-466.

4011 **Spoto, Donald** The hidden Jesus: a new life. NY 1998, St. Martin's xxi; 312 pp. 0-3121-9282-7.
4012 **Stanton, Graham** Dichter bij Jezus?: nieuw licht op de evangeliën. 1997 ⇒13,4230. [R]ITBT 6/1 (1998) 34 (*Dubbink, Joep*);
4013 La verità del vangelo: dalle recenti scoperte nuova luce su Gesù e i vangeli. Guida alla Bibbia 19: CinB 1998, San Paolo 257 pp. 88-215-3759-5.
4014 **Strobel, Lee** The case for Christ. GR 1998, Zondervan 297 pp. $19.
4015 **Tan, Kim Huat** The Zion traditions and the aims of Jesus. MSSNTS 91: 1997 ⇒13,4235. [R]JThS 49 (1998) 212-214 (*Moule, C.F.D.*).
4016 *Taussig, Hal* Jesus in the company of sages: nothing hidden that won't be made known. Forum 1 n.s. (1998) 399-429.
4017 *Theissen, Gerd* Jésus et la crise sociale de son temps: aspects socio-historiques de la recherche du Jésus historique. Jésus de Nazareth. 1998 ⇒253. 125-155.
4018 **Theissen, Gerd; Merz, Annette** Der historische Jesus. 1996 ⇒12,4068; 13,4237. [R]EK (1998/3) 171-172 (*Feldmeier, Reinhard*); ThLZ 123/4 (1998) 387-388 (*Kieffer, René*); DBAT 29 (1998) 309-310 (*Diebner, B.J.*);
4019 The historical Jesus: a comprehensive guide. L 1998, SCM xxix; 642 pp. £25. 0-334-02696-2. [R]LouvSt 23 (1998) 373-374 (*Verheyden, Joseph*).
4020 **Theissen, Gerd; Winter, Dagmar** Die Kriterienfrage in der Jesus-forschung. NTOA 34: 1997 ⇒13,4238. [R]JThS 49 (1998) 736-739 (*Marsh, Clive*); ThRv 94 (1998) 509-510 (*Dautzenberg, Gerhard*).
4021 **Throckmorton, Burton H.** Jesus Christ: the message of the gospels, the hope of the church. LVL 1998, Westminster 145 pp. $13. 0-664-25735-6.
4022 *Tilliette, Xavier* Gesù non ha mai riso. Com(I) 157 (1998) 69-73.
4023 *Turner, Geoffrey* Still questing—looking for the historical Jesus. ScrB 28 (1998) 18-27.
4024 **Van Bruggen, Jakob** Christ on earth: the gospel narratives as history. GR 1998, Baker 320 pp. 0-8010-2186-3.
4025 *Vanhoye, Albert* La prière filiale de Jésus. Christus 178 (1998) 239-254.
4026 [E]**Van Segbroeck, Frans** De woorden die Jezus ons gegeven heeft. Lv 1998, Vlaamse Bijbelstichting 216 pp. ƒ14.75. 90-334-4042-3.
4027 *Veitch, James* Patrolling the right path: Tom Wright's figure of Jesus. Forum 1 n.s. (1998) 349-385.
4028 *Vicent Cernuda, Antonio* De la hostilidad Galilea a la conjura final contra Jesús. EstB 56 (1998) 465-490.
4029 *Vllauri, Emiliano* Volti di Gesù negli studi più recenti. Laur. 39 (1998) 293-337.
4030 *Ward, Graham* The gendered body of the Jewish Jesus. Religion & sexuality. 1998 ⇒302. 170-192.
4031 **Watson, Alan** Jesus: a profile. Athens 1998, University of Georgia Press xi; 180 pp. $35. 0-8203-1970-8.
4032 **Weaver, Walter P.** The historical Jesus in the twentieth century: 1900-1950. Harrisburg 1998, Trinity xii; 449 pp. $30.
4033 *Wolter, Michael* "Jesus Messias"?. WUB 10 (1998) 35-37.
4034 *Wright, N. Thomas* Jesus and the identity of God. ExAu 14 (1998) 42-56.

4035 **Wright, Nicholas Thomas** Jesus and the victory of God. 1996
⇒12,6939; 13,4255. ^RMoTh 14 (1998) 468-471 (*Thompson,
Marianne Meye*); ThTo 55/1 (1998) 104-106 (*Fitzmyer, Joseph A.*);
AUSS 36 (1998) 158-159 (*Maier, Paul L.*); JThS 49 (1998) 727-734
(*Dunn, James D.G.*); TS 59 (1998) 322-323 (*Brown, Schuyler*); CBQ
60 (1998) 592-594 (*Kealy, Sean P.*); BS 155 (1998) 467-473
(*Ingolfsland, Dennis*); JSNT 69 (1998) 95-103 (*Casey, Maurice*);
JSNT 69 (1998) 77-94 (*Marsh, Clive*).
4036 *Wright, N.T.* Knowing Jesus: faith and history;
4037 The mission and message of Jesus. The meaning of Jesus. 1998
⇒3857. 15-27/31-52;
4038 Theology, history and Jesus: a response to Maurice Casey and Clive
Marsh. JSNT 69 (1998) 105-112;
4039 Jesus and the quest. Truth about Jesus. 1998 ⇒211. 4-25.
4040 *Zeller, Dieter* Zwei neue Jesusbücher im Vergleich. ThQ 178 (1998)
52-60.
4041 *Zevini, Giorgio* Il Gesù della storia e il Cristo della fede: il valore
storico-critico dei vangeli. ^FHERIBAN J. 1998 ⇒41. 181-195.
4042 **Zuurmond, Rochus** Procurais o Jesus histórico?. Bíblica Loyola 24:
São Paulo 1998, Loyola 128 pp. 85-15-01819-5.

F1.5 *Jesus et Israel*—**Jesus the Jew**

4043 *Betz, Hans Dieter* WELLHAUSEN's dictum 'Jesus was not a christian,
but a Jew' in light of present scholarship. Gesammelte Aufsätze IV.
1998 <1991> ⇒134. 1-31.
4044 **Buzzard, Anthony F.** Our Father, who aren't in heaven: the forgotten christianity of Jesus, the Jew. Morrow 1995, Atlanta Bible College 277 pp. ^REvQ 69/2 (1997) 163-164 (*Brower, K.E.*).
4045 **Charlesworth, James Hamilton** Gesù nel giudaismo del suo tempo:
alla luce delle più recenti scoperte. ^E*Tomasetto, Domenico*. PBT 30:
T ²1998, Claudiana 302 pp. 88-7016-193-5;
4046 Gesù... scoperte. 1994 ⇒10,4038... 13,4262. ^RSal. 60 (1998) 569-
570 (*Amato, A.*).
4047 *Duvelot, Willem S.* De jood Jezus. ITBT 6/3 (1998) 18-19.
4048 Erich BLOCH: ein vergessener jüdischer Jesus-Forscher. Brief an
Clemens Thoma. FrRu 5 NF (1998) 36-38.
4049 *Harrington, Daniel J.* Retrieving the Jewishness of Jesus: recent
developments. New Theology Review 11/2 (1998) 5-19.
4050 *Heschel, Susannah* Abraham GEIGER and the Jewish Jesus. Chicago
Studies in the History of Judaism: Ch 1998, University of Chicago
Press xii; (2) 317 pp. 0-226-32958-5.
4051 *Hills, Julian V.* The Jewish genius: Jesus according to John MEIER.
Forum 1 n.s. (1998) 327-347.
4052 **Maccoby, Hyam** Jesus und der jüdische Freiheitskampf. ^E*Hoevels,
Fritz Eric*. Unerwünschte Bücher zur Kirchengeschichte 2: FrB 1996,
Ahriman xiii; 160 pp. 3-89484-501-5.
4053 **Meier, John P.** A marginal Jew: rethinking the historical Jesus, 1-2.
1994 ⇒10,4069...13,4273. ^RBS 155 (1998) 460-467 (*Ingolfsland,
Dennis*);
4054 Un judío marginal: nueva visión del Jesús histórico, 1: las raíces del
problema y de la persona. Estella 1998, Verbo Divino 472 pp.

4055 *Sanders, Ed Parish* La rupture de Jésus avec le judaïsme. Jésus de
      Nazareth. 1998 ⇒253. 209-222.

4056 **Spong, John Shelby** Liberating the gospels: reading the Bible with
      Jewish eyes. 1996 ⇒12,4104. ᴿTheol. 101 (1998) 143-144 (*Bur-
      ridge, Richard A.*).

4057 *Tatum, W. Barnes* Jesus the Jew: an analysis of Geza VERMES' tril-
      ogy. Forum 1 n.s. 1998, 275-289.

4058 **Vidal, Marie** Un juif nommé Jésus: une lecture de l'évangile à la
      lumière de la Torah. Spiritualités: 1996 ⇒12,4108; 13,4284.
      ᴿCahiers de l'Atelier 478 (1998) 99-100 (*Giacometti, Louis*).

4059 Un judío llamado Jesús. 1997 ⇒13,4285. ᴿScrTh 30 (1998) 695-697
      (*Hernández Urigüen, R.*).

4060 **Young, Brad H.** Jesus the Jewish theologian. 1995 ⇒11/2,2279...
      13,4288. ᴿTJT 14/1 (1998) 110-111 (*Derrenbacker, Robert*); IThQ
      63 (1998) 97-98 (*Drennan, Martin*).

F1.6 *Jesus in Ecclesia*—The Church Jesus

4061 *Amaladoss, Michael* 'Who do you say that I am?': speaking of Jesus
      in India today. EAPR 34 (1998) 211-224.

4062 *Echlin, Edward P.* Jesus and the star folk. NBl 79 (1998) 146-153.

4063 *Moule, C.F.D.* Jesus of Nazareth and the church's Lord. Forgiveness.
      1998 <1983> ⇒180. 81-94.

4064 *Pedrini, Arnaldo* Per una conoscenza più profonda del Cristo (ricerca
      ascetico-pastorale). PalCl 77 (1998) 57-68.

4065 *Pryce, Mark* On modelling relationships: Jesus, men and friendship.
      Way 38 (1998) 307-317.

4066 **Sachot, Maurice** L'invention du Christ: genèse d'une religion. 1997
      ⇒13,4315. ᴿRSR 86 (1998) 443-445 (*Guillet, Jacques*).

4067 **Shore, Paul** The *Vita Christi* of LUDOLPH of Saxony and its
      influence on the *Spiritual Exercises* of IGNATIUS of Loyola. Studies
      in the Spirituality of Jesuits 30/1: St. Louis 1998, Seminar on Jesuit
      Spirituality 35 pp.

F1.7 *Jesus 'anormalis'*: to atheists, psychoanalysts, romance...

4068 **Altizer, Thomas J.J.** The contemporary Jesus. 1997 ⇒13,4323.
      ᴿTheol. 101 (1998) 447-448 (*Hyman, Gavin*); JSNT 69 (1998) 116-
      117 (*Gibson, Arthur*).

4069 *Arumí i Blancafort, Eduard JesuCrist Superstar*: paradigma de la
      modernitat. QVC 192 (1998) 26-34.

4070 ᴱ**Atwan, Robert; Dardess, George; Rosenthal, Peggy** Divine
      inspiration: the life of Jesus in world poetry. Oxf 1998, OUP 580 pp.
      $35. ᴿCrossCur 48 (1998) 397-399 (*Keen, Suzanne*).

4071 *Bach, Bernard* La figure de Jésus dans le lyrisme de
      l'expressionnisme allemand. Graphè 17 (1998) 137-161.

4072 **Baugh, Lloyd** Imaging the divine: Jesus and Christ figures in films.
      1997 ⇒13,4326. ᴿAThR 80 (1998) 460-461 (*Phillips, Gene D.*); TS
      59 (1998) 346-347 (*Soukup, Paul A.*).

4073 **Bernard-Marie** Le cinquième évangile d'après les agrapha et quel-
      ques mystiques. P 1998, Renaissance 276 pp. FF109.

4074 **Borrmans, Maurice** Jésus et les musulmans d'aujourd'hui. CJJC 69: 1996, [R]Cahiers de l'Atelier 478 (1998) 100-101 (*Guillaud, Michel*); Ad Gentes 2/1 (1998) 97-98 (*Lagarde, Michel*).

4075 *Caparrós Lera, J.M. The last temptation of Christ* (1988): una recerca de la veritat?. QVC 192 (1998) 35-46.

4076 *Chattaway, Peter T.* Jesus in the movies. BiRe 14/1 (1998) 28-35, 45-46.

4077 *Davies, Philip R.* Life of Brian research. Biblical studies. JSOT.S 266: 1998 ⇒380. 400-414.

4078 **Delmaire, Jean-Marie; Zakka, Najib** Jésus dans la littérature arabe et hébraïque contemporaine. Racines et modèles: P 1998, PU du Septentrion 236 pp. FF150. 2-85939-550-4.

4079 **Dominian, Jack** One like us: a psychological interpretation of Jesus. L 1998, Darton, L & T xv; 237 pp. £11. 0-232-52210-3.

4080 *Gálik, Marián* GU CHENGs Roman *Ying'er* und die Bibel. China Heute 17 (1998) 66-73.

4081 **Hesse, Günter** Warum lachten die Juden über Jesus?: eine kollektive Reaktion und ihre psychiatrischen Aspekte. B 1998, Frieling 539 pp. 3-8280-0237-4.

4082 *Jossua, Jean-Pierre* Visages de Jésus dans la littérature française au 19e siècle. Jésus de Nazareth. 1998 ⇒253. 107-121.

4083 **Kaiser, Gerhard** Christus im Spiegel der Dichtung: exemplarische Interpretationen vom Barock bis hin zur Gegenwart. 1997 ⇒13, 4344. [R]RdT 39 (1998) 317-318 (*Steinmetz, Franz-Josef*).

4084 **Kindler, Helmut** Leg mich wie ein Siegel auf dein Herz: ein Indizien-Roman über die kinderreiche 'Heilige Familie' in Nazareth. 1997 ⇒13,4345. [R]EK (1998/4) 237-238 (*Huizing, Klaas*).

4085 *Kreppold, Guido* Jesus—tiefenpsychologisch. Lebendige Katechese 20 (1998) 103-111.

4086 *Kuschel, Karl-Josef* Jesus im Kontext der Dichter: große Jesus-Romane des 20. Jahrhunderts im interkulturellen Vergleich. Relativierung. 1998 ⇒311. 9-29.

4087 **Langenhorst, Georg** Jesus ging nach Hollywood: die Wiederentdeckung Jesu in Literatur und Film der Gegenwart. Dü 1998, Patmos 296 pp. DM39.80. 3-491-72386-6. [R]ComSoc 31 (1998) 354-357 (*Kampmann, Susanne*).

4088 **Mailer, Norman** Das Jesus-Evangelium. Mü 1998, Bertelsmann 224 pp. DM37. [R]EK (1998) 743 (*Huizing, Klaas*).

4089 *Marujo, António* Jesus Cristo e os melos de comunicação social. Igreja e Missão 50 (1998) 207-221.

4090 **Mauriac, François** Vita di Gesù. Genova 1998, Marietti 119 pp.

4091 *McKevitt, Daniel* Jesus in the cinema. Month 31 (1998) 248-249.

4092 **Melzer-Keller, Helga** Jesus und die Frauen: eine Verhältnisbestimmung nach der synoptischen Überlieferung. 1997 ⇒13,7841. [R]STV 36/2 (1998) 193-198 (*Załęski, Jan*).

4093 **Mien, Aleksander** Jesus, mestre de Nazaré. [T]*Silva, Irami B.* São Paulo 1998, Cidade Nova 312 pp.

4094 **Pelikan, Jaroslav Jan** The illustrated Jesus through the centuries. 1997 ⇒13,4352. [R]America 179/3 (1998) 27-28 (*Murray, Pius*).

4095 **Phipps, William E.** Muhammed and Jesus: a comparison of the prophets and their teachings. 1996 ⇒12,4142; 13,4354. [R]TS 59 (1998) 511-512 (*McAuliffe, Jane Dammen*).

4096   **Prigent, Pierre** Jésus au cinéma. 1997 ⇒13,4358. [R]RHPhR 78/1 (1998) 128 (*François, Ph.*).
4097   **Saramago, José** O evangelho segundo Jesus Cristo: romance. O campo da palavra: Lisboa 1998, Caminho 445 pp. 972-21-0524-8.
4098   **Schatten, Thomas** Jesus Christus: eine Nacherzählung des Evangeliums. Dü 1998, Schatten 141 pp. DM6. 3-9805688-4-9.
4099   *Schwab, Hans-Rüdiger* Der zeitgenössische Jesusroman: "Was er wirklich gemeint hat". WUB 10 (1998) 59-62.
4100   **Schwager, Raymund** Jesus of Nazareth: how he understood his life. [T]*Williams, James G.* NY 1998, Crossroad 187 pp. £13/$15.
4101   **Sorel, Andrés** Jesús, llamado el Cristo. 1997 ⇒13,4360. [R]EE 73 (1998) 513-514 (*Piñero, Antonio*).
4102   **Stolp, H.** Jezus van Nazareth: esoterisch bijbellesen. Deventer 1998, Ankh-Hermes 194 pp. *f*29.50.
4103   **Vallet, Odon** Jésus et Bouddha: destins croisés du christianisme et du bouddhisme. 1996 ⇒12,4145. [R]Pro Dialogo 97/1 (1998) 142 (*Give, Bernard de*); Cahiers de l'Atelier 478 (1998) 98-99 (*Bourgeois, Henri*).
4104   **Zwick, Reinhold** Evangelienrezeption im Jesusfilm: ein Beitrag zur intermedialen Wirkungsgeschichte des Neuen Testaments. STPS 25: Wü 1998, Echter 528 pp. DM64. [R]ComSoc 31 (1998) 347-350 (*Hasenberg, Peter*).

F2.1 *Exegesis creativa*—**innovative methods** [⇒B5]

4105   **Aichele, George** The postmodern Bible: the Bible and culture collective. 1995 ⇒11/2,1970. [R]CBQ 60 (1998) 137-139 (*Segovia, Fernando F.*).
4106   **Hens-Piazza, Gina** Of methods, monarchs, and meanings: a socio-rhetorical approach to exegesis. 1996 ⇒12,4155. [R]JBL 117 (1998) 515-517 (*Hobbs, T.R.*).
4107   **Lausberg, Heinrich** Handbook of literary rhetoric: a foundation for literary study. [E]*Orton, David E.; Anderson, R. Dean.* Lei 1998, Brill xxxi; 921 pp. 90-04-10705-3.
4108   **Meynet, Roland** Rhetorical analysis: an introduction to biblical rhetoric. JSOT.S 256: Shf 1998, Academic 386 pp. £55. 1-85075-870-0;
4109   Rhétorique sémitique: textes de la bible et de la tradition musulmane. Patrimoines: P 1998, Cerf 347 pp. FF185. 2-204-05951-X. [R]LASBF 48 (1998) 590-591 (*Cortese, Enzo*).
4110   **Onuki, Takashi** Sammelbericht als Kommunikation: Studien zur Erzählkunst der Evangelien. WMANT 73: 1997 ⇒13,4376. [R]BZ 42 (1998) 128-130 (*Dormeyer, Detlev*).
4111   **Robbins, Vernon K.** The tapestry of early Christian discourse: rhetoric, society, ideology. 1996 ⇒12,4166; 13,4377. [R]JSNT 70 (1998) 79-91 (*Dean, Margaret E.*); JSNT 70 (1998) 93-100 (*Newby, Gordon D.*); JSNT 70 (1998) 71-77 (*Culpepper, R. Alan*); JRH 22 (1998) 343-345 (*Ward, John*); CBQ 60 (1998) 381-383 (*Braun, Willi*); AUSS 36 (1998) 306-308 (*Dupertuis, Rubén*).
4112   **Weren, Wim** Vensters op Jezus: methoden in de uitleg van de evangeliën. Zoetermeer 1998, Meinema 215 pp. *f*40. 90-211-3710-0.

F2.2 *Unitas VT-NT:* The Unity of OT-NT and NT

4113 *Beauchamp, Paul* Un livre et deux communautés. Procès de Jésus. 1998 ⇒392. 15-27.

4114 *Bolin, Thomas M.* "A stranger and an alien among you" (Genesis 23: 4): the Old Testament in early Jewish and Christian self-identity. [F]SNYDER, G. 1998 ⇒104. 57-76.

4115 *De Benedetti, Paolo* La qualità teologica del Tanakh. [F]MARTINI C., Rivelazione. 1998 ⇒74. 275-281.

4116 *Giesen, Heinz* Schriftauslegung im Frühjudentum und im Neuen Testament. ThG 41 (1998) 213-223.

4117 *Kaiprampatt, George* Scripture in the hands of Jesus. VJTR 62 (1998) 857-872.

4118 **Liebers, Reinhold** 'Wie geschrieben steht': Studien zu einer besonderen Art frühchristlichen Schriftbezuges. 1993 ⇒9,4383... 12, 4180. [R]Bijdr. 59 (1998) 345-346 (*Vandenholen, Hans*).

4119 Mussies, Gerard Remarks on quotation formulas in gospels and Acts. Use of sacred books. 1998 ⇒263. 49-60.

4120 *Seitz, Christopher* The Old Testament as abiding theological witness: inscripting a theological curriculum <1997>;

4121 God as other, God as holy: election and disclosure in christian scripture;

4122 Old Testament or Hebrew Bible?: some theological considerations <1996>. Word without end. 1998 ⇒200. 3-12/13-27/61-74.

F2.5 *Commentarii*—Commentaries on the whole NT

4123 **Tuñi, Josep-Oriol; Alegre, Xavier** Scritti giovannei e lettere cattoliche. Introduzione allo studio della Bibbia 8: 1997 ⇒13,4407 [R]Anton. 73 (1998) 745-746 (*Nobile, Marco*).

4124 [E]**Vigini, Giuliano** Il Nuovo Testamento: vangeli e Atti degli Apostoli. Mi 1997, Paoline 593 pp. L25.000. [R]CivCatt 149/3 (1998) 329-331 (*Scaiola, D.*).

IX. Evangelia

F2.6 Evangelia Synoptica; *textus, synopses, commentarii*

4125 **Kudasiewicz, Joseph** The synoptic gospels today. 1996 ⇒12,4195; 13,4409. [R]ACR 75/1 (1998) 125-126 (*Beirne, Margaret*).

4126 **Linden, N.M.A. ter** Het verhaal gaat...2. Amst 1998, Balans 310 pp. *f*39.50. 90-5018-492-8. [R]ITBT 6/4 (1998) 33-4 (*Monshouwer, Dirk*).

4127 **Marconcini, Benito** Los sinópticos: formación, redacción, teología. M 1998, San Pablo 250 pp. PTA1.800. [R]Augustinus 43 (1998) 436-437 (*Pérez, Tomás*).

F2.7 *Problema synopticum:* **The Synoptic Problem**

4128 ^E**Brandenburger, Stefan H.; Hieke, Thomas** Wenn drei das Glei-
      che sagen—Studien zu den ersten drei Evangelien: mit einer Werk-
      stattübersetzung des Q-Textes. Theologie 14: Müns 1998, Lit ix; 258
      pp. 3-8258-3673-8.

4129 **Catchpole, David R.** The quest for Q. 1993 ⇒9,4407... 11/2,240.
      ^REvQ 70 (1998) 68-71 (*Meadors, Edward P.*).

4130 *Fahner, Chris* Old Testament translation features and the Synoptic
      problem. Bible et informatique. 1998 ⇒386. 167-192.

4131 *Farkasfalvy, Denis* The Papias fragments on Mark and Matthew and
      their relationship to Luke's prologue: an essay on the pre-history of
      the synoptic problem. ^FFERGUSON, E. NT.S 90: 1998 ⇒25. 92-106.

4132 *Farmer, William R.* The present state of the synoptic problem. ^FTY-
      SON J. 1998 ⇒120. 11-36.

4133 *Fitzmyer, Joseph A.* The priority of Mark and the 'Q' source in Luke.
      To advance the gospel. 1998 <1970> ⇒150. 3-40.

4134 **Fleddermann, Harry T.** Mark and Q: a study of the overlap texts.
      BEThL 122: 1995 ⇒11/1,2735... 13,4425. ^RRTL 29/1 (1998) 75-78
      (*Focant, Camille*).

4135 *Franklin, Eric* A passion narrative for Q?. ^FASHTON J. JSNT.S 153:
      1998 ⇒6. 30-47.

4136 *Fuchs, Albert* Die agreements der Einzugsperikope Mk 11,1-10 par
      Mt 21,1-9 par Lk 19,28-38. SNTU.A 23 (1998) 215-227.

4137 *Goodacre, Mark* Fatigue in the synoptics. NTS 44 (1998) 45-58.

4138 **Head, Peter M.** Christology and the synoptic problem: an argument
      for Markan priority. MSSNTS 94: 1997 ⇒13,4427. ^RJThS 49 (1998)
      739-741 (*Moule, C.F.D.*); Bib. 79 (1998) 425-429 (*Fleddermann,
      Harry T.*).

4139 ^E**Heil, Christoph** Q 12:8-12: Confessing or denying, speaking
      against the Holy Spirit, hearings before synagogues. DQ: 1997
      ⇒13,4428. ^REThL 74 (1998) 433-436 (*Neirynck, F.*).

4140 *Heil, Christoph* Das Spruchevangelium Q—Stand der Forschung.
      BiLi 71 (1998) 37-39.

4141 **Kim, Hyung-Dong** A study of Q: the kingdom of God and its rejec-
      tion as a hermeneutical key in Q. ^DDrew 1998, 282 pp.

4142 **Kirk, Alan** The composition of the sayings source: genre, synchrony,
      and wisdom redaction in Q. NT.S 91: Lei 1998, Brill xiii; 443 pp.
      *f*235/$138.50. 90-04-11085-2.

4143 *Kloppenberg, John S.* L'évangile 'Q' et le Jésus historique. Jésus de
      Nazareth. 1998 ⇒253. 225-268.

4144 *Luz, Ulrich* Matthäus und Q. ^FHOFFMANN, P., Von Jesus. BZNW 93:
      1998 ⇒43. 201-215.

4145 ^E**McNicol, Allan James** Beyond the Q impasse: Luke's use of Mat-
      thew. 1996 ⇒12,4227. ^RTJT 14/1 (1998) 83-88 (*Derrenbacker,
      Robert A.*); JBL 117 (1998) 363-365 (*Tuckett, Christopher*).

4146 *Merk, Otto* Die synoptische Redenquelle im Werk von Werner Georg
      KÜMMEL: eine Bestandsaufnahme. ^FHoffmann, P., Von Jesus.
      BZNW 93: 1998 ⇒43. 191-200.

4147 *Peabody, David B.* Luke's sequential use of the sayings of Jesus from
      Matthew's great discourses: a chapter in the source-critical analysis
      of Luke on the two-gospel (neo-Griesbach) hypothesis. ^FTYSON J.
      1998 ⇒120. 37-58.

4148 *Robinson, James M.* The Matthean trajectory from Q to Mark. FBETZ, H. 1998 ⇒10. 122-154;
4149 The sequence of Q: the lament over Jerusalem;
4150 *Schlosser, Jacques* Q 11,23 et la christologie. FHOFFMANN, P., Von Jesu. BZNW 93: 1998, ⇒43. 225-260/217-224.
4151 *Scholer, David M.* Q bibliography supplement IX: 1998. SBL.SP part 2. SBL.SPS 37: 1998 ⇒402. 1005-1012.
4152 *Siegert, Folker* Die Quelle Q, ein frühchristliches Dokument über Jesu. WUB 10 (1998) 43.
4153 EUro, Risto Symbols and strata: essays on the sayings gospel Q. SESJ 65: 1996 ⇒12,208; 13,4441. RCBQ 60 (1998) 605-607 (*Fleddermann, Harry T.*).
4154 *Vacherot, Jacques-Marie; Légasse, Simon* Le chercheur: mathématique et exégèse. BLE 99 (1998) 139-145.
4155 *Vassiliadis, Petros* Pauline theology, the origins of christianity and the challenge of Q: a personal journey. V Simposio di Tarso. 1998 ⇒395. 41-60.

F2.8 Synoptica: themata

4156 ECarruth, Shawn Q 12:49-59: children against parents—judging the time—settling out of court. Documenta Q: 1997 ⇒13,4447. RLouvSt 23 (1998) 286-287 (*Verheyden, Joseph*).
4157 ECarruth, Shawn; Robinson, James M.; Heil, Christopher Q 4:1-13,16: the temptations of Jesus—Nazara. Documenta Q: 1996 ⇒12,4248. RLouvSt 23 (1998) 283-286 (*Verheyden, Joseph*).
4158 *Court, John M.* The gospels as prophecy. FPOKORNÝ, P. 1998 ⇒90. 55-66.
4159 Ebner, Martin Jesus—ein Weisheitslehrer?: synoptische Weisheitslogien im Traditionsprozeß. Herders biblische Studien 15: FrB 1998, Herder xii; 483 pp. DM108. 3-451-26546-X.
4160 Guijarro Oporto, Santiago Fidelidades en conflicto—la ruptura con la familia por causa del discipulado y de la misión en la tradición sinóptica. Plenitudo temporis: estudios sobre los orígenes y la antigüedad cristiana 4: S 1998, Publ. Universidad Pontificia 473 pp. 84-7299-421-X. RBib(L) 7/7 (1998) 174-176 (*Alves, Herculano*).
4161 *Hagner, Donald A.* Gospel, kingdom, and resurrection in the synoptic gospels. Life in the face of death. 1998 ⇒252. 99-121.
4162 Horsley, Richard A. The kingdom of God and the renewal of Israel: synoptic gospels, Jesus movements, and apocalypticism. Encyclopedia of apocalypticism I. 1998 ⇒507. 303-344.
4163 *Liperi, Bastianina* La fede nei vangeli sinottici. La fede nella bibbia. DSBP 21: 1998 ⇒224. 83-114.
4164 Meiser, Martin Die Reaktion des Volkes auf Jesus: eine redaktionskritische Untersuchung zu den synoptischen Evangelien. BZNW 96: B 1998, De Gruyter xii; 437 pp. DM228. 3-11-016364-0.
4165 Merklein, Helmut Die Jesusgeschichte—synoptisch gelesen. SBS 156: 1994 ⇒10,4260... 12,4256. RThZ 54 (1998) 179-180 (*Rese, Martin*).
4166 *Moule, C.F.D.* The function of the synoptic gospels. Forgiveness. 1998 <1985> ⇒180. 179-189.

4167 *Nereparampil, Lucius* Good news to the poor: the synoptic view of evangelization. BiBh 24 (1998) 139-148.

4168 *Neves, Joaquim Carreira das* A 'catequese' como chave hermenêutica dos evangelhos sinópticos. Did(L) 28 (1998) 93-136.

4169 **Sánchez Mielgo, Gerardo** Claves para leer los evangelios sinópticos. Horizontes dos mil 9: S 1998, San Esteban 280 pp. Ptas2.300. 84-8260-043-5. [R]TE 42 (1998) 415-418 (*García Santos, Á.*); EsVe 28 (1998) 500-502.

4170 **Theissen, Gerd** Colorido local y contexto histórico en los evangelios: una contribución a la historia de la tradición sinóptica. Biblioteca de estudios bíblicos 195: 1997 ⇒13,4456. [R]EstTrin 32/1-2 (1998) 228-230 (*Aurrecoechea, José Luis*); RevAg 41 (1998) 1203-1205 (*Sabugal, Santos*); RET 58 (1998) 121-123 (*Fernández, Barrado*).

4171 **Tuckett, Christopher M.** Q and the history of early christianity: studies on Q. 1996 ⇒12,4260; 13,4457. [R]HeyJ 39 (1998) 73-74 (*McNamara, Martin*); JBL 117 (1998) 744-746 (*Patterson, Stephen J.*).

4172 *Vos, Johan S.* De plaatsvervangende zoendood van Jezus in de synoptische evangeliën: een bijdrage aan het debat over de verzoening. GThT 98 (1998) 147-157.

F3.1 **Matthaei evangelium:** *textus, commentarii*

4173 [E]**Ammassari, Antonio** Il vangelo di Matteo nella colonna latina del Bezae Codex Cantabrigiensis. 1996 ⇒12,4262. [R]RivBib 46 (1998) 238-240 (*Cavalletti, Sofia*).

4174 *Boismard, Marie-Émile* L'Ancien Testament grec dans l'Évangile de Matthieu: Septante ou Théodotion?. Interpretation of the Bible. JSOT.S 289: 1998 ⇒388. 245-256.

4175 **Bortolini, José** Círculos bíblicos sobre o evangelho de Mateus. São Paulo 1998, Paulus 54 pp.

4176 **Calloud, Jean; Genuyt, François** L'évangile de Matthieu, 3: lecture sémiotique des chapitres 21 à 28. Lyon 1998, Centre Thomas More ii; 124 pp. FF75. 2-905600-16-0.

4177 [T]**Castillo Bejarano, M.** JUVENCO: historia evangélica. Biblioteca Clásicos Griegos 249: M 1998, Gredos 236 pp.

4178 **Davies, W.D.; Allison, Dale C.** The gospel according to Saint Matthew, 3: Matthew XIX-XXVIII. ICC: 1997 ⇒13,4465. [R]BZ 42 (1998) 130-133 (*Klauck, Hans-Josef*).

4179 **Fausti, Silvano** Una comunità legge il vangelo di Matteo I. Lettura pastorale della Bibbia 29: Bo 1998, EDB 284 pp. L33.000. 88-10-20594-4.

4180 **France, R.T.** Matthew: evangelist & teacher. New Testament profiles: DG 1998 <1989>, Inter-Varsity 345 pp. $23. 0-8308-1511-2.

4181 *Frankemölle, Hubert* Das Matthäusevangelium als heilige Schrift und die heilige Schrift des früheren Bundes: von der Zwei-Quellen- zur Drei-Quellen-Theorie. Jüdische Wurzeln. BBB 116: 1998 <1993> ⇒151. 233-259.

4182 **Frankemölle, Hubert** Matthäus-Kommentar. 1994-1997, 2 vols. ⇒13,4467. [R]BiLi 71 (1998) 277-278 (*Söding, Thomas*); FrRu NF 5 (1998) 118-124 (*Renker, Alwin*).

4183 **Gamba, Giuseppe Giovanni** Mt 1,1-4,16: chi è Gesù Cristo. Vangelo di San Matteo: una proposta di letture, 1. BSRel 137: R 1998, LAS 326 pp. 88-213-0376-4.

4184 The gospel according to Matthew: Authorised King James Version. Pocket Canons: E 1998, Canongate xv; 78 pp. 0-86241-795-3.

4185 **Grasso, Santi** Il vangelo di Matteo. CBi: 1995 ⇒11/1,2815; 13,4468. [R]PaVi 43/2 (1998) 60-61 (*Rolla, Armando*).

4186 **Hagner, Donald A.** Matthew 14-28. WBC 33B: 1995 ⇒11/1,2819... 13,4470. [R]Trin.Journal 19 (1998) 126-129 (*Lamerson, Samuel*); IThQ 63 (1998) 405-406 (*McConvery, Brendan*).

4187 **Joosten, Jan** The Syriac language of the Peshitta and Old Syriac versions of Matthew. SStLL 22: 1996 ⇒12,4275. [R]Or. 67 (1998) 147-149 (*Morrison, Craig*); JSSt 43 (1998) 187-188 (*Gelston, A.*); BiOr 55 (1998) 898-901 (*Owens, R.J.*).

4188 **Leonardi, Giovanni** Vangelo secondo Matteo: traduzione strutturata, analisi letteraria e narrativa, messaggio e problemi introduttori. Sussidi biblici 63-64: Reggio Emilia 1998, San Lorenzo 264 pp. L25.000. 88-8071-082-6.

4189 *Léon-Dufour, Xavier* O evangelho segundo S. Mateus;

4190 O evangelho eclesiástico o evangelho segundo São Mateus. RCB 87-88 (1998) 21-45/47-61.

4191 **Long, Thomas G.** Matthew. 1997 ⇒13,4475. [R]IBSt 20 (1998) 132-134 (*Campbell, Dennis*).

4192 **McKenzie, Alyce M.** Matthew. Interpretation Bible studies: LVL 1998, Geneva vii; 112 pp. 0-664-50022-6.

4193 **Mello, Alberto** Evangelo secondo Matteo: commento midrashico e narrativo. 1995 ⇒11/1,2829; 13,4479. [R]Hum(B) 53 (1998) 1054-1055 (*Stefani, Piero*).

4194 **Mosconi, Luis** Evangelho de Jesus Cristo segundo Mateus: para cristãos e cristãs rumo ao novo milênio. São Paulo 1998, Loyola 134 pp. 85-15-01818-7.

4195 **Muñoz Iglesias, S.** Comentario al evvangelio según san Mateo. M 1998, Espiritualidad 396 pp. 84-7068-255-5.

4196 [E]**Olsson, Birger; Burskog, Samuel; Übelacker, Walter** Matteus och hans läsare—förr och nu: Matteussyumposiet i Lund den 27-28 sept 1996. Religio 48: Lund 1997, Teologiska Institutionen i Lund 114 pp.

4197 **Scholl, Norbert** Ein Bestseller entsteht: das Matthäus-Evangelium. Rg 1998, Pustet 158 pp. 3-7917-1618-2.

4198 [T]**Scognamiglio, Rosario** ORIGENES: commentarii in Matthaeum: commento al vangelo di Matteo/1: (libri X-XII). CTePa 145: R 1998, Città N 399 pp. 88-311-3145-1.

4199 **Senior, Donald** Matthew. Abingdon NT Commentaries: Nv 1998, Abingdon 358 pp. $25. 0-687-05766-3.

4200 **Thiede, Carsten Peter; D'Ancona, Matthew** The Jesus papyrus. 1997 ⇒13,4487. [R]ACR 75/1 (1998) 128-130 (*Doyle, B. Rod*); JRH 22/1 (1998) 104-50 (*Pickering, Stuart R.*).

4201 **Thiede, Carsten Peter** Jésus selon Matthieu: la nouvelle datation du papyrus Magdalen d'Oxford et l'origine des évangiles. 1996 ⇒12, 4287. [R]RB 105 (1998) 589-596 (*Grelot, Pierre*).

4202 **Weber, George P.; Miller, Robert L.** Breaking open the gospel of Matthew. Cincinnati, Ohio 1998, St. Anthony Messenger 137 pp. $10. 0-86716-320-8.

4203 **Wiefel, Wolfgang** Das Evangelium nach Matthäus. ThHK 1: B 1998, Evangelische Verlagsanstalt xxiv; 497 pp. DM64. 3-374-01639-1.

F3.2 **Themata** *de Matthaeo*

4204 **Bingham, Dwight Jeffrey** IRENAEUS' use of Matthew's gospel in 'Adversus Haereses'. Diss. Dallas Theol. Sem. 1995. ^D*Blaising, Craig A.* Traditio exegetica graeca 7: Lv 1998, Peeters xv; 357 pp. $75. 90-6831-964-7. ^RSalm. 45 (1998) 483-486 (*Trevijano, R.*).
4205 *Bowe, Barbara E.* The criteria for judgment in the gospel of Matthew. BiTod 36 (1998) 295-300.
4206 *Carter, Warren* Learning to live as faithful disciples. BiTod 36 (1998) 287-293;
4207 Jesus' "I have come" statements in Matthew's gospel. CBQ 60 (1998) 44-62;
4208 Toward an imperial-critical reading of Matthew's Gospel. SBL.SP part 1. SBL.SPS 37: 1998 ⇒402. 296-324.
4209 **Carter, Warren** Matthew: storyteller, interpreter, evangelist. 1996 ⇒12,4299. ^RCBQ 60 (1998) 149-151 (*Zilonka, Paul*).
4210 A comunidade de Mateus. RCB 87-88 (1998) 63-98.
4211 **Dautzenberg, Gerhard** Studien zur Theologie der Jesustradition. SBAB 19: 1995 ⇒11/2,247; 13,122. ^RThPh 73 (1998) 269-270 (*Beutler, J.*).
4212 *Davies, Margaret* Stereotyping the other: the 'Pharisees' in the gospel according to Matthew. Biblical studies. JSOT.S 266: 1998 ⇒380. 415-432.
4213 *Edin, Mary H.* Learning what righteousness means: Hosea 6:6 and the ethic of mercy in Matthew's gospel. WaW 18 (1998) 355-363.
4214 *Frankemölle, Hubert* Die matthäische Kirche als Gemeinschaft des Glaubens: Prolegomena zu einer bundestheologischen Ekklesiologie <1996>;
4215 Die Tora Gottes für Israel, die Jünger Jesu und die Völker nach dem Matthäusevangelium <1996>;
4216 Der 'ungekündigte Bund' im Matthäusevangelium?: oder: von der Unverbrüchlichkeit der Treue Gottes im Matthäusevangelium zu Israel und zu den Völkern. Jüdische Wurzeln. BBB 116: 1998 ⇒151. 365-405/261-293/329-363.
4217 *Frenschkowski, Marco* Traum und Traumdeutungen im Matthäusevangelium: einige Beobachtungen. JAC 41 (1998) 5-47.
4218 **Gielen, Marlis** Der Konflikt Jesu mit den religiösen und politischen Autoritäten seines Volkes im Spiegel der matthäischen Jesusgeschichte. BBB 115: Bodenheim 1998, Philo xvi; 500 pp. 3-8257-0095-X.
4219 *Gnadt, Martina S.* Das Evangelium nach Matthäus: judenchristliche Gemeinden im Widerstand gegen die Pax Romana. Kompendium Feministische Bibelauslegung. ^E**Schottroff, L.**: 1998 ⇒H8.9. 483-498.
4220 **Grasso, Santi** Conoscere Gesù per riconoscere se stessi: testi scelti del vangelo di Matteo. Davanti a te: Commento spirituale per la Lectio divina: R 1998, Dehoniane 207 pp. 88-396-0763-3.
4221 *Hagner, Donald A.* Law, righteousness, and discipleship in Matthew. WaW 18 (1998) 364-371.

4222 *Hare, Douglas R.* Current trends in Matthean scholarship. WaW 18 (1998) 405-410.
4223 **Harrington, Wilfred John** Matthew: sage theologian: the Jesus of Matthew. Dublin 1998, Columba 116 pp. £9. 1-85607-245-2.
4224 *Hartin, Patrick J.* Disciples as authorities within Matthew's Christian-Jewish community. Neotest. 32 (1998) 389-404.
4225 *Hertig, Paul* The multi-ethnic journeys of Jesus in Matthew: margin-center dynamics. Miss. 26 (1998) 23-35.
4226 **Hertig, Paul** Matthew's narrative use of Galilee in the multicultural and missiological journeys of Jesus. Mellen 46: Lewiston, NY 1998, Mellen x; 189 pp. $90. 0-7734-2444-X.
4227 *Hultgren, Arland J.* Mission and ministry in Matthew. WaW 18 (1998) 341-347.
4228 A igreja de Mateus. RCB 87-88 (1998) 99-133.
4229 *Kampen, John* Communal discipline in the social world of the Matthean community. [F]SNYDER, G. 1998 ⇒104. 158-174.
4230 *Kingsbury, Jack Dean* The significance of the earthly Jesus in the gospel of Matthew. ExAu 14 (1998) 59-65.
4231 **Kingsbury, Jack Dean** Matteo: un racconto. BiBi(B) 23: [Brescia] 1998, Queriniana 213 pp. L32.000. 88-399-2023-4.
4232 *Kowalczyk, Andrzej* The genre of the gospel of Matthew. FolOr 34 (1998) 45-52.
4233 *Krentz, Edgar* Identity formation: Matthew as resource and guide. WaW 18 (1998) 411-417.
4234 *Kvalbein, Hans* Hat Matthäus die Juden aufgegeben?: Bemerkungen zu Ulrich LUZ' Matthäus-Deutung. ThBeitr 29 (1998) 301-314.
4235 *Leske, Adrian M.* Isaiah and Matthew: the prophetic influence in the first gospel: a report on current research. Jesus and the suffering servant. 1998 ⇒3430. 152-169.
4236 *Luomanen, Petri* Corpus mixtum—an appropriate description of Matthew's community?. JBL 117 (1998) 469-480.
4237 **Luomanen, Petri** Entering the kingdom of heaven: a study on the structure of Matthew's view of salvation. WUNT 2/101: Tü 1998, Mohr xiii; 343 pp. DM118. 3-16-146940-2.
4238 *Luz, Ulrich* Zum Problem der Übersetzung der matthäischen "Anti-judaismen". [F]POKORNÝ, P. 1998 ⇒90. 246-256.
4239 **Luz, Ulrich** The theology of the gospel of Matthew. 1995 ⇒11/1, 2874... 13,4522. [R]RB 105 (1998) 620-623 (*Viviano, B.T.*).
4240 **Mazzinghi, Luca; Tarocchi, Stefano** Matteo il vangelo del regno dei cieli: guida per una lettura in comune. Bo 1998, EDB 95 pp. 88-10-90435-4.
4241 **Mazzocchi, L.; Forzani, J.; Tallarico, A.** Il vangelo secondo Matteo e lo Zen: meditazioni della domenica. Bo 1995, EDB [R]Il Regno 43 (1998) 670-680 (*Favaro, Gaetano*).
4242 *McIver, Robert K.* The place of the Matthean community in the stream of early christian history. [F]JUDGE E. 1998 ⇒47. 110-120.
4243 *Meagher, P.M.* The theology of Matthew, I. VJTR 62 (1998) 930-937.
4244 **Neyrey, Jerome H.** Honor and shame in the gospel of Matthew. LVL 1998, Westminster 287 pp. $30.
4245 *Pauw, D.A.* Die invloed van emosies op gebeure in die Matteus-Evangelie. Acta Theologica 18 (1998) 72-107.

4246 *Pikaza, Xabier* Mesías judío, Cristo universal (Mt 1-4): la figura de Jesús ante el tercer milenio. EstTrin 32 (1998) 283-356.

4247 *Powell, Mark A.* Matthew as pastor: the presence of God. WaW 18 (1998) 348-354.

4248 **Schackl-Raber, Ursula** Aufgespürte Frauenarbeit in Männerberichten: explizite und implizite Frauenarbeit im Matthäusevangelium auf dem Hintergrund einer sozialgeschichtlich-feministischen Analyse. Diss. Salzburg 1996-1997, [D]*Beilner, W.* [ThRv 94,xviii].

4249 **Scheuermann, Georg** Gemeinde im Umbruch: eine sozialgeschichtliche Studie zum Matthäusevangelium. FzB 77: 1996 ⇒12,4339; 13,4528. [R]RivBib 46 (1998) 248-250 (*Barbaglio, Giuseppe*).

4250 *Segalla, Giuseppe* La tradizione di Gesù e la rivelazione di Dio ad Israele in Matteo. [F]MARTINI C., Rivelazione. 1998 ⇒74. 197-234.

4251 *Senior, Donald* Matthew's gospel as ethical guide. BiTod 36 (1998) 273-279.

4252 **Sim, David C.** Apocalyptic eschatology in the gospel of Matthew. MSSNTS 88: 1996 ⇒12,4344. [R]EvQ 70 (1998) 265-268 (*Wilson, Alistair*); TJT 14/1 (1998) 102-103 (*Kloppenborg, John S.*); CBQ 60 (1998) 174-175 (*Weber, Kathleen*); JThS 49 (1998) 225-229 (*Nolland, J.L.*); JBL 117 (1998) 534-536 (*Powell, Mark Allan*);

4253 The gospel of Matthew and christian Judaism: the history and social setting of the Matthean community. Studies of the NT and its world: E 1998, Clark xvi; 347 pp. £27.50. 0-567-08641-0.

4254 *Stegner, William Richard* Leadership and governance in the Matthean community. [F]SNYDER, G. 1998 ⇒104. 147-157.

4255 *Tellan, Sergio* I fondamenti teologici della correzione fraterna in Matteo. Laur. 39 (1998) 339-411.

4256 *Varickasseril, J.* Jesus' confrontational style: a paradigm for mission in the third millennium. IMR 20 (1998) 21-33.

4257 *Vledder, Evert-Jan* Barmhartigheid en geen offerande!. ITBT 6/8 (1998) 4-6.

4258 *Wainwright, Elaine M.* Tradition makers / tradition shapers: women of the Matthean tradition. WaW 18 (1998) 380-388.

4259 **Wainwright, Elaine Mary** Shall we look for another?: a feminist rereading of the Matthean Jesus. The Bible & Liberation: Mkn 1998, Orbis Books xii; 178 pp. $18. 1-57075-184-6.

F3.3 *Mt 1s (Lc 1s⇒F7.5) Infantia Jesu*—**Infancy Gospels**

4260 *Bee-Schroedter, Heike* Auf Weihnachten vorbereiten. Lebendige Katechese 20 (1998) 152-154.

4261 *Borg, Marcus J.* The meaning of the birth stories. The meaning of Jesus. 1998 ⇒3857. 179-186.

4262 *Boynton, Susan* Performative exegesis in the Fleury *Interfectio puerorum*. Viator 29 (1998) 39-64.

4263 *Cabra, Piergiordano* La santa famiglia modello di vita. RVS 52 (1998) 147-164.

4264 *Cranfield, C.E.B.* Some reflections on the subject of the virgin birth. On Romans. 1998 <1988> ⇒143. 151-165.

4265 **Dohmen, Christoph** Von Weihnachten keine Spur?: adventliche Entdeckungen im Alten Testament. FrB 1998, Herder 144 pp. DM26.80. 3-451-26683-0.

4266 *Fitzmyer, Joseph A.* The virginal conception of Jesus in the New Testament. To advance the gospel. 1998 <1973> ⇒150. 41-78.
4267 *Giordani, G.* La figura degli angeli nei vangeli dell'infanzia'. Angeli e demoni. 1998 ⇒375. 143-167.
4268 *Hendricks, William L.* The infancy narratives as texts of terror, verbal and visual. ᴹSUMMERS, R. 1998 ⇒115. 243-256.
4269 **Herrmann, Dieter B.** Der Stern von Bethlehem: die Wissenschaft auf den Spuren des Weihnachtssterns. B 1998, Paetec 96 pp. 3-895167-695-8.
4270 *Hoffmeister-Höfener, Thomas* Von der Suche nach Gottes Ort in der Geschichte: Erzähltopik und Textpragmatik in Mt 1-2. ᶠLÖNING, K. 1998 ⇒66. 11-24.
4271 *Kasiłowsky, Piotr* L'évangile de l'enfance de Jésus (Mt 1-2). PrzPow 917 (1998) 9-22. **P**.
4272 *Kelly, Joseph F.* The early Irish interpretation of the Infancy Narratives. ᶠHALTON T. 1998, 40-49.
4273 *Kokkinos, Nikos* The relative chronology of the nativity in TERTULLIAN. ᴹSUMMERS, R. 1998 ⇒115. 119-131.
4274 **Lorber, Jacob** La infancia de Jesús. Sevilla 1998, Muñoz Moga 468 pp. 84-8010-064-8.
4275 **Lüdemann, Gerd** Virgin birth?: the real story of Mary and her son Jesus. L 1998, SCM xvii; 157 pp. £13. 0-334-02724-1. ᴿRBBras 15 (1998) 581-582
4276 **Mayordomo-Marín, Moisés** Den Anfang hören: leserorientierte Evangelienexegese am Beispiel von Matthäus 1-2. FRLANT 180: Gö 1998, Vandenhoeck & R 448 pp. DM98. 3-525-53864-2.
4277 **Mittmann-Richert, Ulrike** Magnifikat und Benediktus: die ältesten Zeugnisse der judenchristlichen Tradition von der Geburt des Messias. WUNT 2/90: Tü 1996, Mohr viii; 303 pp. 3-16-146590-3. ᴿBZ 42 (1998) 137-140 (*Kauf, Thomas*).
4278 *Muñoz Iglesias, Salvador* Lo histórico en los evangelios de la infancia. EstMar 64 (1998) 3-36.
4279 **Poot, Henk** Jozef: een messiaanse geschiedenis. n.p. 1998, Novapres 313 pp. ƒ44.90. 90-6318-165-5.
4280 **Roll, Susan** Toward the origins of Christmas. Liturgia Condenda 5: 1995 ⇒13,4563. ᴿBijdr. 59 (1998) 471-472 (*Rouwhorst, G.*).
4281 *Scarola, Jack V.* A chronology of the nativity era. ᴹSUMMERS, R. 1998 ⇒115. 61-84.
4282 **Stramare, Tarcisio** Vangelo dei misteri della vita nascosta di Gesù. Bornato in Franciacorta, BS 1998, Sardini 320 pp.
4283 *Van Aarde, Andries G.* Jesus' father: the quest for the historical Joseph. HTS 54 (1998) 315-333.
4284 *Voicu, Sever J.* Verso il testo primitivo dei Παιδικα του Κυριου Ιησου "Racconti dell'infanzia del Signore Gesù". Apocrypha 9 (1998) 7-95.
4285 *Wright, N.T.* Born of a virgin?. The meaning of Jesus. 1998 ⇒3857. 171-178.

4286 *Forte, Bruno* Dialogare con l''altro': riflessioni a partire dall' 'Historia salutis' e dal rapporto chiesa-Israele. La terra e il seme. BTNap 19: 1998 ⇒310. 103-116 [Mt 1,1-17].
4287 *Légasse, Simon* Joseph pouvait-il répudier Marie "en secret"?: note sur Matthieu 1,19. BLE 99 (1998) 369-372.

4288   *Neuner, Joseph* Immanuel, God with us (Is 7:14, Mt 1:23). VJTR 62 (1998) 562-566.
4289   *Keller, Hans-Ulrich* Der Stern der Weisen: astronomische Informationen. KatBl 123 (1998) 380-381.
4290   *Raimbault, Christophe* Une analyse structurelle de l'adoration des mages en Mt 2,1-12. EstB 56 (1998) 221-235.
4291   *Nolland, John* The sources for Matthew 2:1-12. CBQ 60 (1998) 283-300.
4292   **Trexler, Richard C.** The journey of the Magi: meanings in history of a christian story. 1997, [R]Annales 53 (1998) 1286-1288 (*Dénouée, Claire*).
4293   *Stramare, Tarcisio* Matteo 2,1-12: Gesù adorato dai Magi a Betlemme (v. 6) e tu, Betlemme, terra di Giuda. BeO 40 (1998) 119-125.
4294   *Maier, Paul L.* Herod and the infants of Bethlehem. [M]SUMMERS, R. 1998 ⇒115. 169-189.

F3.4   *Mt 3...Baptismus Jesus,* **Beginnings of the Public Life**

4295   *Chilton, Bruce D.* Yoḥanan the purifier and his immersion. TJT 14 (1998) 197-212.
4296   *Frankemölle, Hubert* Johannes der Täufer und Jesus im Matthäusevangelium: Jesus als Nachfolger der Täufers. Jüdische Wurzeln. BBB 116: 1998 <1996> ⇒151. 109-130.
4297   **Gibson, Jeffrey B.** The temptations of Jesus in early Christianity. JSNT.S 112: 1995 ⇒11/1,2963... 13,4611. [R]TJT 14/1 (1998) 93-94 (*Shantz, Colleen*) [Mk 1,9-13; 8,1-13].
4298   *Kabazzi-Kisirinya, S.* Was Jesus tempted by the devil?—hard facts from the scriptures. African Christian Studies 14 (1998) 67-85.
4299   *Kasiłowski, Piotr* Kuszenie Jezusa [La tentation de Jésus]. PrzPow 115 (1998) 265-283. P.
4300   *McDonnell, Kilian* Quaestio disputata: IRENAEUS on the baptism of Jesus: a rejoinder to Daniel A. Smith. TS 59 (1998) 317-321.
4301   **Taylor, Joan E.** The Immerser: John the Baptist within Second Temple Judaism. 1997 ⇒13,4601. [R]Theol. 101 (1998) 144-145 (*Houlden, Leslie*).
4302   **Yamasaki, Gary** John the Baptist in life and death: audience-oriented criticism of Matthew's narrative. JSNT.S 167: Shf 1998, Academic 176 pp. 1-85075-916-2.

4303   **McDonnell, Kilian** The baptism of Jesus in the Jordan: the trinitarian and cosmic order of salvation. 1996 ⇒12,4404. [R]JEarlyC 6 (1998) 321-322 (*O'Keefe, John J.*); Worship 72 (1998) 371-373 (*Wilken, Robert Louis*) [Mt 3,13-17].
4304   *Strijdom, Johan* A historical Jesus hallucinating during his initial spirit-possession experience: a response to Stevan Davies' interpretation of Jesus' baptism by John. HTS 54 (1998) 588-602 [Mt 3,13-17; Mk 1,9-11].
4305   **Puthenpurackal, Chacko** Meaning and function of Matthew 4,23-5,2 and 9,35-10,5a. Diss. extr. Pont. Univ. Urbaniana 1998; [D]*Grilli, Massimo*: R 1998, x; 122 pp [NThAR 2000,153].

F3.5 **Mt 5...Sermon on the Mount** [...plain, Lk 6,17]

4306 *Betz, Hans Dieter* The portrait of Jesus in the Sermon on the Mount. CThMi 25 (1998) 165-175.
4307 **Betz, Hans Dieter** The sermon on the mount. 1995 ⇒11/1,2966; 12,4418. ᴿJR 78 (1998) 100-102 (*Boring, M. Eugene*); JThS 49 (1998) 219-225 (*Catchpole, David*); JBL 117 (1998) 136-138 (*Allison, Dale C.*).
4308 *Burchard, Christoph* Versuch, das Thema der Bergpredigt zu finden. Studien zur Theologie. 1998 ⇒140. 27-50.
4309 **Dumais, Marcel** Le sermon sur la montagne: état de la recherche: interprétation. 1995 ⇒11/1,2972... 13,4619. ᴿRivBib 46 (1998) 244-247 (*Borghi, Ernesto*); RB 105 (1998) 597-603 (*Gourgues, Michel*).
4310 *Dumais, Marcel* The Sermon on the Mount: an unattainable way of life?. ChiSt 37 (1998) 316-326.
4311 ᴱ**Feldmeier, Reinhard** "Salz der Erde": Zugänge zur Bergpredigt. BTSP 14: Gö 1998, Vandenhoeck & R 265 pp. 3-525-61358-X.
4312 *Feldmeier, Reinhard* Verpflichtende Gnade: die Bergpredigt im Kontext des ersten Evangeliums. "Salz der Erde". 1998 ⇒4311. 15-107.
4313 *Gábriš, Karol* Conseguenze significative dell'analogia tra legge-vangelo e preoccupazione-sollecitudine. ᶠHᴇʀɪʙᴀɴ J. 1998 ⇒41. 247-258.
4314 *Gómez, Enrique* Aɢᴜsᴛíɴ lee a Mateo: descubrimiento de la gratuidad en la propuesta mateana. Augustinus 43 (1998) 229-280.
4315 *Harrington, Daniel J.* The Sermon on the Mount: what is it?. BiTod 36 (1998) 280-286.
4316 *Hendel, Ronald S.* The law in the gospel. BiRe 14/2 (1998) 20, 52.
4317 *Johner, Michel* L'éthique de Jésus: à propos du Sermon sur la montagne. RRef 49 (1998) 27-43.
4318 *Kunstmann, Joachim* Die Bergpredigt in Sekundarstufe I und II. "Salz der Erde". 1998 ⇒4311. 234-264.
4319 *Lang, Walter* Die Eigenart der Ethik Jesu. Der Fels 29 (1998) 204-207 [Mt 5; 22,37-40].
4320 **Machinek, Marian** Die Auslegung der Bergpredigt bei L.N. Tᴏʟsᴛᴏᴊ im Kontext seines ethisch-religiösen Systems. Moraltheologische Studien: Systematische Abt. 25: St. Ottilien 1998, EOS 348 pp.
4321 *Machinek, Marian* Kazanie na Górze: profetyczna prowokacja czy program życiowy? [De Sermone in Monte: provocatio prophetica an vitae ratio?]. RBL 51 (1998) 87-101.
4322 **Neri, Umberto** Il Discorso della montagna: catechesi biblica su Mt. 5-7. Le àncore: Mi 1998, Àncora 142 pp. 88-7610-649-9.
4323 *Oberforcher, Robert* Vom Dekalog zur Bergpredigt: Grundzüge und Aktualität der biblischen Ethik. Jetzt 3 (1998) 6-11 [Gal 5,1].
4324 *O'Donovan, Oliver* Gerechtigkeit und Urteil. NZSTh 40 (1998) 1-16.
4325 *Oppel, Katharina* Die Bergpredigt: eine spirituelle Hausordnung für die matthäische Gemeinde. Jetzt 3 (1998) 26-32.
4326 *Ostermayer, Vera* Die Bergpredigt—(k)ein Thema für Kinder in der Grundschule?. "Salz der Erde". 1998 ⇒4311. 216-233.
4327 **Patte, Daniel** Discipleship according to the Sermon on the Mount: four legitimate readings, four plausible views of discipleship, and their relative values. 1996 ⇒12,4427. ᴿJBL 117 (1998) 361-363 (*Carter, Warren*).

4328 *Pokorny, Peter* Die Bergpredigt / Feldrede als supra-ethisches System. ^FSCHRAGE, W. 1998 ⇒101. 183-193 [Lk 6].
4329 *Ritter, Werner H.* Von der bildenden Kraft der Bergpredigt. "Salz der Erde". 1998 ⇒4311. 173-215.
4330 *Rochais, Gérard* Le sermon sur la montagne. ScEs 50 (1998) 241-245.
4331 *Schoberth, Ingrid* "Habt acht auf eure Frömmigkeit"—Bergpredigt auf dem Weg. "Salz der Erde". 1998 ⇒4311. 141-172.
4332 *Schoberth, Wolfgang* Die bessere Gerechtigkeit und die realistischere Politik: ein Versuch zur politischen Ethik. "Salz der Erde". 1998 ⇒4311. 108-140.
4333 *Troadec, H.* Os discursos do mestre. RCB 87-88 (1998) 135-160.
4334 *Wick, Peter* Volkspredigt contra Gemeinderegel?: Matthäus 5-7 im Vergleich zu Matthäus 18. KuI 13 (1998) 138-153.

4335 *Reid, Barbara* Puzzling passages: Matt 5:13-14. BiTod 36 (1998) 256-257.
4336 *Wong, Eric* Two interpretations of law in Matthew. Jian Dao 10 (1998) 1-21 [5,17-20; 7,12]. C.
4337 *Sim, David C.* Are the least included in the kingdom of heaven?: the meaning of Matthew 5:19. HTS 54 (1998) 573-587.
4338 *Frankemölle, Hubert* Die sogenannten Antithesen des Matthäus (Mt 5,21ff): hebt Matthäus für Christus das 'Alte' Testament auf?: von der Macht der Vorurteile. Jüdische Wurzeln. BBB 116: 1998 <1994> ⇒151. 295-328.
4339 *Kim, Sook Y.* Las antítesis en Mateo 5 y la actitud de Jesús hacia la ley. Theologika 13 (1998) 209-228.
4340 *Zawadzki, Ryszard* Antytetzy Kazania na Górze (Mt 5,21-48) we wspóllczesnej egzegezie. CoTh 68 (1998) 23-68.
4341 *Cuvillier, Élian* Chronique matthéenne 4: "vous avez entendu qu'il a été dit..." (Mt 5/27a). ETR 73 (1998) 239-256.
4342 *Badiolo Saenz de Ugarte, José Antonio* El amor a los enemigos: Mt 5,43-48. ScrVict 46 (1998) 5-59.
4343 *Wick, Peter* Der historische Ort von Mt 6. 1-18. RB 105 (1998) 332-358.
4344 *Giesen, Heinz* Eigentum im Urteil Jesu und der Jesustradition. IKaZ 27 (1998) 1-14 [Mt 6,24].
4345 *Robinson, James M.; Heil, Christoph* Zeugnisse eines schriftlichen, griechischen vorkanonischen Textes: Mt 6,28b x1*, P.Oxy. 655 I,1-17 (EvTh 36) und Q 12,27. ZNW 89 (1998) 30-44.
4346 *Schober, Theodor* Vom Hausbau 1. Du bist eingeladen. ^EJepsen, M. 1998 ⇒F4.3. 51-52 [Mt 7,24-27].

F3.6 **Mt 5,3-11** (Lc 6,20-22) **Beatitudines**

4347 **Aparicio, A.** Las Bienaventuranzas evangélicas en la vida consagrada: un nuevo pueblo en éxodo. Debarim: M 1998, Claretianas 340 pp.
4348 Aspectos doutrinais. RCB 87-88 (1998) 173-182.
4349 *Dormeyer, Detlev* Beatitudes and mysteries. ^FBETZ, H. 1998 ⇒10. 345-357.
4350 **Gerardi, Renzo** Alla sequela di Gesù: etica delle beatitudini, doni dello Spirito, virtù. CETO 30: Bo 1998, EDB 161 pp. 88-10-404807.

4351 *Gourgues, Michel* Sur l'articulation des béatitudes matthéennes (Mt 5.3-12): une proposition. NTS 44 (1998) 340-356.

4352 *Hellholm, David* Beatitudes and their illocutionary functions. ^FBETZ, H. 1998 ⇒10. 286-344.

4353 *Ilan, Tal* The provocative approach once again: a response to Adiel Schremer. HThR 91 (1998) 203-204.

4354 **Martini, Carlo Maria** Le beatitudini. Mi 1998, In dialogo 84 pp. 88-8123-098-4.

4355 *Pereira, Ney Brasil* Notas para um estudo sobre as bem-aventuranças. RCB 87-88 (1998) 161-172.

4356 **Pinckaers, Servais** The pursuit of happiness—God's way: living the beatitudes. Staten Island, NY 1998, Alba 204 pp. $6.

4357 *Smith, Robert H.* "Blessed are the poor in (Holy) Spirit"?. WaW 18 (1998) 389-396.

4358 **Testaferri, Francesco** La nuova legge del regno: riflessioni sulle beatitudini (Mt 5,3-10). CinB 1998, San Paolo 92 pp. 88-215-3758-7.

4359 *Tremblay, Julie* St. John CHRYSOSTOM and the beatitudes. Nicolaus 25 (1998) 199-217.

4360 **Cereti, Giovanni** Divorzio, nuove nozze e penitenza nella chiesa primitiva. Studi ricerche 26: Bo 1998, Dehoniane 438 pp.

4361 *Fitzmyer, Joseph A.* The Matthean divorce texts and some new Palestinian evidence. To advance the gospel. 1998 <1976> ⇒150. 79-111.

4362 **Kleinschmidt, Frank** Ehefragen im Neuen Testament: Ehe, Ehelosigkeit, Ehescheidung, Verheiratung Verwitweter und Geschiedener im Neuen Testament. Diss. Göttingen 1997. ARGU 7: Fra 1998, Lang 302 pp. DM89. 3-631-33001-4.

4363 *Paperon, Bernard* Le divorce dans la tradition hébraïque: les sources talmudiques. RDC 48 (1998) 7-33.

4364 **Scarponi, Carlos Alberto** Paternidad-maternidad de los divorciados vueltos a casar a la luz del evangelio. Convivir, I—Matrimonio cristiano: BA 1998, Paulinas 64 pp.

4365 *Schremer, Adiel* Divorce in Papyrus Şe'elim 13 once again: a reply to Tal Ilan. HThR 91 (1998) 193-202.

F3.7 *Mt 6,9-13 (Lc 11,2-4)* **Oratio Jesu**, Pater Noster, **Lord's Prayer**

4366 *Arand, Charles P.* The battle cry of faith: the catechisms' exposition of the Lord's Prayer. Luther Digest 6 (1998) 32-7.

4367 *Baudler, Georg* "Gib uns heute das Zionsbrot": Überlegungen zur Brotbitte des Vaterunsers (Mt 6,11). KatBl 123 (1998) 220-229.

4368 **Benini, T.** Orar el Padrenuestro. Sdr 1998, Sal Terrae 214 pp.

4369 *Bianca Maria* Il Padre nostro secondo s. MASSIMO, palestinese. PalCl 77 (1998) 897-902.

4370 **Bondi, Roberta C.** A place to pray: reflections on the Lord's Prayer. Nv 1998, Abingdon 144 pp. $17. 0-687-02574-5.

4371 *Bourguet, Daniel* Approches du Notre Père. UnChr 132 (1998) 4-15.

4372 *Burchard, Christoph* Zu Matthäus 8,5-13. Studien zur Theologie. WUNT 107: 1998 <1993> ⇒140. 65-76.

4373 *Byargeon, Rick W.* Echoes of wisdom in the Lord's prayer (Matt 6:9-13). JETS 41 (1998) 353-365.

4374 *Caro C., Cristián* 'Padre nuestro'. Revista Católica 2 (1998) 103-108.

4375 *Casado, Abelardo Lobato* Pregare il *Padre nostro*: la catechesi di San TOMMASO d'Aquino. RTLu 3 (1998) 667-683.

4376 **Di Sante, Carmine** El Padre Nuestro: la experiencia de Dios en la tradición judeo-cristiana. S 1998, Trinitario 245 pp.

4377 *Genuyt, François* Le Notre-Père selon Saint Matthieu. LV(L) 240 (1998) 27-37.

4378 *Gielen, Marlis* "Und führe uns nicht in Versuchung": die 6. Vaterunser Bitte—eine Anfechtung für das biblische Gottesbild?. ZNW 89 (1998) 201-216.

4379 *Grasmück, Ernst Ludwig* Aspekte zur Auslegung des Vaterunsers in der Zeit der Alten Kirche. ᶠHOFFMANN, P., Von Jesus. BZNW 93: 1998 ⇒43. 485-505.

4380 *Kubski, Grzegorz* Egzegetyczne procedury Augusta Cieszkowskiego w 'Ojcze nasz' [Biblical text in August Ciezkowski's 'Our Father']. PoST 8 (1998) 61-78.

4381 **La Potterie, Ignace de** La Preghiera di Gesù. Seoul 1998, St Pauls 207 pp. 89-8015-152-7. **Korean.**

4382 **Maggioni, Bruno** Padre nostro. Sestante 7: Mi 1998 <1995>, Vita e Pensiero 140 pp. ᴿRCI 79 (1998) 857-859 (*Bagni, Arcangelo*).

4383 ᴱ**Moreno García, Abdón; Nocon, Arkadiusz** Un comentario inédito a Mt 6,9-13 de PEDRO de Valencia (1555-1620): ad orationem dominicam illam *Pater noster, qui es in coelis* symbola. RET 58 (1998) 87-104.

4384 *Moule, C.F.D.* An unsolved problem in the temptation-clause in the Lord's prayer. Forgiveness. 1998 <1974> ⇒180. 190-204.

4385 **Muro, Nos** La oración del Padrenuestro, según san AGUSTÍN. M 1998, San Pablo 120 pp.

4386 **Nieto, Evaristo Martín** El Padre Nuestro: la oración de la utopía. Dabar 2: M 1996, San Pablo 243 pp. 84-285-1810-6.

4387 *Ornelas de Carvalho, José* Ousamos dizer 'Pai Nosso'. Bib(L) 7 (1998) 99-135.

4388 *Perugini, Antonella* Quando pregate dite: Padre nostro. Presenza Pastorale 68 (1998) 321-326.

4389 *Philonenko, Marc* La sixième demande du "Notre Père" et le livre des Jubilés. RHPhR 78 (1998) 27-37 [Mt 6,13].

4390 *Pichler, J. Hannes* Von der Einheit aller Überlieferung: ein dialogischer Diskurs anhand des Vaterunsers über die Letzten Dinge im Lichte des 'großen Bogens der Tradition'. ᶠBSTEH, A. 1998 ⇒17. 375-393.

4391 **Rovira Belloso, Josep M.** El torno al Padrenuestro. M 1998, Narcea 109 pp.

4392 **Sante, Carmine de** El Padre Nuestro: la experiencia de Dios en la tradición judeo-cristina. S 1998, Secretariado Trinitario 241 pp.

4393 *Singles, Donna* Jésus en prière. LV(L) 240 (1998) 41-52.

4394 *Tournay, Raymond Jacques* "Ne nous laisse pas entrer en tentation". NRTh 120 (1998) 440-443.

4395 **Wilson, Alistair I.** The disciples' prayer: a fresh look at a familiar text. RTR 57 (1998) 136-150.

4396 *Martin, Francis* St. Matthew's spiritual understanding of the healing of the centurion's boy. Com(US) 25 (1998) 160-177 [Mt 8,5-13].

4397 *Bockmuehl, Markus* 'Let the dead bury their dead' (Matt. 8:22/Luke 9:60): Jesus and the Halakhah. JThS 49 (1998) 553-581.

F4.1 *Mt 9-12; Miracula Jesu*—The Gospel miracles

4398 **Bee-Schroedter, Heike** Neutestamentliche Wundergeschichten im Spiegel vergangener und gegenwärtiger Rezeptionen: historisch-exegetische und empirisch-entwicklungspsychologische Studien. SBB 39: Stu 1998, Kath. Bibelwerk xii; 482 pp. DM89. 3-460-00391-X.
4399 **Berger, Klaus** Darf man an Wunder glauben?. 1996 ⇒12,4487; 13,4694. [R]AtK 130 (1998) 142-144 (*Anderwald, Andrzej*).
4400 **Houston, John** Reported miracles: a critique of HUME. 1994 ⇒10,4465... 12,4493. [R]ThPh 73 (1998) 615-617 (*Wiertz, O.*).
4401 *Kahl, Werner* Überlegungen zu einer interkulturellen Verständigung über neutestamentliche Wunder. ZMR 82 (1998) 98-106.
4402 **Kollmann, Bernd** Jesus und die Christen als Wundertäter: Studien zu Magie, Medizin und Schmanismus in Antike und Christentum. FRLANT 170: 1996 ⇒12,4498; 13,4705. [R]EstAg 33 (1998) 382-383 (*Cineira, D.A.*); ThLZ 123 (1998) 151-153 (*Böcher, Otto*); JBL 117 (1998) 533-534 (*Martin, Dale B.*).
4403 **Koskenniemi, Erkki** APOLLONIOS von Tyana in der neutestamentlichen Exegese. WUNT 2/61: 1994 ⇒10,4470; 11/2,2078. [R]JR 78 (1998) 428-431 (*Collins, Adela Yarbro*).
4404 *Koskenniemi, Erkki* APOLLONIUS of Tyana: a typical θεῖος ἀνήρ?. JBL 117 (1998) 455-467.
4405 **Leone, Salvino** La medicina di fronte ai miracoli. 1997 ⇒13,4707. [R]Asp. 45 (1998) 436-438 (*Scognamiglio, Edoardo*).
4406 *Merz, Annette* Jesus als Wundertäter: Konturen, Perspektiven, Deutungen. ZNT 1 (1998) 40-47.
4407 *Monshouwer, Dirk* Verstaanbaar en doorzichtig. Interpretatie 6/4 (1998) 20-22.
4408 **Mullin, Robert Bruce** Miracles and the modern religious imagination. 1996 ⇒12,4500. [R]ThTo 54 (1998) 545-6, 548 (*Moorhead, James H.*); HR 38 (1998) 92-93 (*Greeley, Andrew*).
4409 *Pérez-Soba Díez del Corral, José Maria* Comprender las curaciones de Jesús: reflexiones desde el análisis fenomenológico de las religiones tradicionales. RET 58 (1998) 35-66.
4410 **Quevedo, Oscar G.** Os milagres e a ciência. São Paulo 1998, Loyola 786 pp. 85-15-01704-0.
4411 *Starowieyski, Marek* Materiały do poznania legendy i kultu apostołów (3): teksty o świętym Andrzeju Apostole [Materiaux pour connaitre la légende et le culte des Apôtres]. WST 10 (1998) 125-152.
4412 **Trummer, Peter** Dass meine Augen sich öffnen: kleine biblische Erkenntnislehre am Beispiel der Blindenheilungen Jesu. Kohlhammer/Theologie: Stu 1998, Kohlhammer 223 pp. DM39.80. 3-17-015279-3. [R]PzB 7 (1998) 148-149 (*Schwarz, Roland*).
4413 **Trunk, Dieter** Der messianische Heiler: eine redaktions- und religionsgeschichtliche Studie zu den Exorzismen im Matthäusevangelium. Herders Biblische Studien 3: 1994 ⇒10,4487... 13,4713. [R]BZ 42 (1998) 133-135 (*Kirchschläger, Walter*).

4414 *Agurides, Sabbas C.* The mission of the twelve Apostles within a per-
      secuted church (Matthew 10,1-42). DBM 17 (1998) 5-36. **G.**
4415 *Park, Eung Chun* The mission discourse in Matthew's interpretation.
      WUNT 2/81: 1995 ⇒11/2,3072; 13,4716. [R]CBQ 60 (1998) 582-583
      (Wainwright, Elaine M.) [Mt 10,1-42].
4416 **Bedouelle, Guy** Thomas l'Apôtre. 1997 ⇒13,4722. [R]NV 73/2
      (1998) 104-6 *(Morerod, Charles).*
4417 **Filhò, Cônego Pedro Terra** Sao Judas Tadeu e seu tempo. Rio de
      Janeiro 1998, Thex.Ed. 135 pp. 85-85575-32-8.
4418 *Kvalbein, Hans* The wonders of the end-time: metaphoric language in
      4Q521 and the interpretation of Matthew 11.5 par. JSPE 18 (1998)
      87-110.
4419 *Hasselhorn, Johannes* Von den spielenden Kindern 1. Du bist
      eingeladen. 1998 ⇒4434. 55-56.
4420 *Menken, Maarten J.J.* The quotation from Isaiah 42:1-4 in Matthew
      12:18-21: its relation with the Matthean context. Bijdr. 59 (1998)
      251-266.
4421 *Derrett, J. Duncan M.* Every "idle" word that men speak (Mt 12,36).
      EstB 56 (1998) 261-265.
4422 **Markwart, Herzog** 'Descensus ad inferos': eine religionsphilosophi-
      sche Untersuchung der Motive und Interpretationen mit besonderer
      Berücksichtigung der monographischen Literatur seit dem 16. Jahr-
      hundert. FTS 53: Fra 1997, Knecht 510 pp. DM92. 3-7820-0759-X
      [Mt 12,40].
4423 *Stottele, Christoph* Von der Rückkehr der bösen Geister 1. Du bist
      eingeladen. 1998 ⇒4434. 59-60 [Mt 12,43-45].

F4.3 Mt 13... *Parabolae Jesu*—The Parables

4424 *Bailey, Mark L.* Guidelines for interpreting Jesus' parables. BS 155
      (1998) 29-38.
4425 *Begley, John J.* The parables of Jesus and the Ignatian exercises. RfR
      57 (1998) 472-483.
4426 **Blomberg, Craig L.** Die Gleichnisse Jesu: ihre Interpretation in
      Theorie und Praxis. TVG 248: Wu 1998, Brockhaus 312 pp. 3-417-
      29428-2.
4427 **Donahue, John R.** El evangelio como parábola. 1997 ⇒13,4741.
      [R]RF 237 (1998) 217-218 *(Vallarino, Jesús M.ª).*
4428 **Etchells, Ruth** A reading of the parables of Jesus. L 1998, Darton, L
      & T 198 pp. £10. 0-232-52189-1.
4429 **Fernández Ramos, Felipe** El reino en parábolas. 1996 ⇒12,4525.
      [R]EstB 56 (1998) 557-559 *(González Fraile, A.).*
4430 *Gnilka, Joachim* Jézus személye és a példabeszédek [Jesu Reden in
      Gleichnissen]. Példabeszédek. 1998 ⇒372. 21-30. **Hungarian.**
4431 **Grasso, Santi** "Lectio Divina" delle parabole di Gesù. Leggere le
      Scritture 5: Padova 1998, Messaggero 188 pp. 88-250-0689-6.
4432 *Hasselhorn, Johannes* Die Gleichnisse bei Matthäus, Markus und
      Lukas. Du bist eingeladen. 1998 ⇒4434. 13-14.
4433 *Hoppe, Rudolf* Példabeszéd és befogaddás (Nagy vascora/királyi
      menyegző példázata Jézus igehirdetésében és az evangéliumi
      hagyományban) [Jesu Gleichnisse und ihre Wirkungsgeschichte].
      Példabeszédek. 1998 ⇒372. 45-54. **Hungarian.**

4434 ^E**Jepsen, Maria** Du bist eingeladen: alle Gleichnisse Jesu vom Reich Gottes. Stu 1998, Kreuz 160 pp. 3-7831-1657-0.

4435 **Jones, Ivor Harold** The Matthean parables: a literary and historical commentary. NT.S 80: 1995 ⇒11/1,3105; 13,4747. ^RThLZ 123 (1998) 253-254 (*Wrege, Hans-Theo*).

4436 *Kähler, Christoph* Egyszerűség és komplexitás kérdése a peldabeszédekben (Interpretációs modellek a liberális teológiától a modern kommunikációs elméletekig) [Schlichtheit und Komplexität der Gleichnisse Jesu]. Példabeszédek. 1998 ⇒372. 55-67. **Hungarian.**

4437 **Kähler, Christoph** Jesu Gleichnisse als Poesie und Therapie: Versuch eines integrativen Zugangs zum kommunikativen Aspekt von den Gleichnissen Jesu. WUNT 2/78: 1995 ⇒11/1,3106... 13,4749 ^RBogoslovni Vestnik 58/3 (1998) 353-354 (*Mlinar, Anton*).

4438 *Liong, Hok* Parable as allegory revisited: a general remark. Stulos theological journal 6 (1998) 51-62.

4439 *Lohse, Eduard* Vorwort. Du bist eingeladen. 1998 ⇒4434. 11-12;

4440 Zum Verständnis der Gleichnisse Jesu. Du bist eingeladen. 1998 ⇒4434. 146-154.

4441 **Marguerat, Daniel** As parábolas. Cadernos Bíblicos 61: Lisboa 1998, Difusora Bíblica 76 pp.

4442 **Meurer, Hermann-Josef** Die Gleichnisse Jesu als Metaphern: Paul Ricoeurs Hermeneutik der Gleichniserzählung Jesu im Horizont des Symbols "Gottesherrschaft/Reich Gottes". BBB 111: 1997 ⇒13,4756. ^RBZ 42 (1998) 257-258 (*Weiser, Alfons*).

4443 **Moynahan, Michael E.** Once upon a mystery. Mahwah 1998, Paulist v; 198 pp. $15.

4444 *Poorthuis, Marcel* Het schokeffect va de parabel. Interpretatie 6/7 (1998) 9-11.

4445 **Ramos, Felipe Fernández** El reino en parábolas. 1996 ⇒12,4536; 13,4759. ^RRivBib 46 (1998) 358-361 (*Estrada, Bernardo*).

4446 *Reinstorf, Dieter; Van Aarde, Andries G.* Jesus' kingdom parables as metaphorical stories: a challenge to a conventional worldview. HTS 54 (1998) 603-622.

4447 *Rocha e Melo, Luís* O sentido espiritual das parábolas. Brot. 146 (1998) 467-479.

4448 **Sapp, David Wayne** An analysis of the criteria used by the Jesus Seminar to establish the authenticity of the parables of Jesus. ^DMid-America Baptist Theol. Sem. 1998, 194 pp.

4449 *Schmithals, Walter* Példabeszédek a szinoptikus evangéliumokban [Die Gleichnisreden in den Synoptischen Evangelien]. Példabeszédek. 1998 ⇒372. 151-173. **Hungarian.**

4450 *Wierzbicka, Anna* The meaning of Jesus' parables: a semantic approach to the gospels. Faith and fiction. 1998 ⇒410. 17-55.

4451 **Young, Bradford H.** The parables: Jewish tradition and christian interpretation. [Peabody, MASS] 1998, Hendrickson xv; 332 pp. $25. 1-56563-244-3.

4452 *Burchard, Christoph* Senfkorn, Sauerteig, Schatz und Perle in Matthäus 13. Studien zur Theologie. WUNT 107: 1998 <1988> ⇒140. 77-107.

4453 *Bailey, Mark L.* The parable of the sower and the soils. BS 155 (1998) 172-188 [Mt 13].

4454 *Schober, Theodor* Vom Sämann 3. Du bist eingeladen. 1998 ⇒4434. 20-22 [Mt 13].
4455 *Bailey, Mark L.* The parable of the tares. BS 155 (1998) 266-279 [Mt 13,24-30].
4456 *Schober, Theodor* Vom Unkraut unter dem Weizen. Du bist eingeladen. 1998 ⇒4434. 87-89 [Mt 13].
4457 *Bailey, Mark L.* The parable of the mustard seed. BS 155 (1998) 449-459 [Mt 13,31-32].
4458 *Menken, Maarten J.J.* Isaiah and the 'hidden things': the quotation from Psalm 78:2 in Matthew 13:35. Use of sacred books. 1998 ⇒263. 61-77.
4459 *Greim, Horst* Vom Schatz und von der Perle. Du bist eingeladen. 1998 ⇒4434. 90-91 [Mt 13,44-46].
4460 *Knoll, Günter* Vom Fischnetz. Du bist eingeladen. 1998 ⇒4434. 92-93 [Mt 13,47-50].
4461 *Stramare, Tarcisio* San Giuseppe e la redenzione del lavoro. Com(I) 159 (1998) 25-31 [Mt 13,55].
4462 **Pesch, Rudolf** Leben für alle: das Wunder der Brotvermehrung. Fra 1998, Knecht 158 pp. 3-7820-0789-1 [Mt 14,13-21//].
4463 *Dettwiler, Andreas* La conception mathéene de la foi: à l'exemple de Matthieu 14/22-33). ETR 73 (1998) 333-347.
4464 *Pilch, John J.* Walking on the sea. BiTod 36 (1998) 117-123 [Mt 14,22-33].
4465 **Baudoz, Jean-François** Les miettes de la table: étude synoptique et socio-religieuse de Mt 15,21-28 et de Mc 7,24-30. EtB 27: 1995 ⇒11/1,3123; 12,4552. [R]RSR 86 (1998) 428-429 (*Guillet, Jacques*).
4466 *Holmberg, Bengt* Debatten Jesus inte vann. SEÅ 63 (1998) 167-176 [Mt 15,21-28; Mk 7,24-30].

F4.5 Mt 16...*Primatus promissus*—The promise to Peter

4467 **Grappe, Christian** Images de Pierre aux deux premiers siècles. EHPR 75: 1995 ⇒13,4786. [R]StPat 45 (1998) 528-529 (*Corsato, Celestino*).
4468 *Hünermann, Peter* Ministerio y evangelio: la forma del servicio de Pedro al final del segundo milenio. SelTeol 37 (1998) 91-97.
4469 *Kereszty, Roch* A catholic response to W. PANNENBERG regarding the Petrine ministry of the Bishop of Rome;
4470 *Pannenberg, Wolfhart* A Lutheran's reflections on the Petrine ministry of the Bishop of Rome. Com(US) 25 (1998) 619-629/604-618.
4471 *Pesch, Rudolf* Was an Petrus sichtbar war, ist in den Primat eingegangen. Il primato. 1998 ⇒423. 22-111.
4472 **Schatz, Klaus** Papal primacy: from its origins to the present. 1996 ⇒12,4566; 13,4793. [R]ChH 67/1 (1998) 215-216 (*Kosztolnyik, Z.J.*); Gr. 79 (1998) 586-588 (*Chappin, Marcel*); HeyJ 39 (1998) 82 (*Tanner, Norman*).

4473 *Viviano, Benedict* Thomas Peter as Jesus' mouth: Matthew 16:13-20 in the light of Exodus 4:10-17 and other models. SBL.SP part 1. SBL.SPS 37: 1998 ⇒402. 226-252.
4474 *Diebner, Bernd Jørg* "Glückselig bist du, Simon, Sohn des Jona" (Mt 16,17): Anmerkungen zum 'Vaternamen' des Apostel-Fürsten. DBAT 29 (1998) 207-216.

4475 *Luke, K.* The bars of Sheol. BiBh 24 (1998) 114-128 [Mt 16,18].
4476 **Moses, A.D.A.** Matthew's transfiguration story and Jewish-Christian controversy. JSNT.S 122: 1996 ⇒13,4799. ᴿRB 105 (1998) 618-620 (*Viviano, B.T.*) [Mt 17,01-09].
4477 *Ramshaw, Elaine J.* Power and forgiveness in Matthew 18. WaW 18 (1998) 397-404.
4478 *Kozhynava, Ala* On a biblical quotation in an old Slavic text. Interpretation of the Bible. JSOT.S 289: 1998 ⇒389. 1005-1014 [Mt 18,11].
4479 *Holtz, Traugott* Das Gleichnis vom verlorenen Schaf (Mt 18,12-14 / Lk 15,3-7)—die Vollmacht Jesu. ᶠPOKORNÝ, P. 1998 ⇒90. 163-175;
4480 As elveszett bárányról vett példabeszéd (Mt 18,12-14/Lk 15,3-7): Jézus teljhatalma [Das Gleichnis vom Verlorenen Schaf (Mt 18,12-14/ Lk 15,3-7): die Vollmacht Jesu]. Példabeszédek. 1998 ⇒372. 31-43.
4481 *Schober, Theodor* Vom verlorenen Schaf 1. Du bist eingeladen. 1998 ⇒4434. 63-64 [Mt 18,12-14].
4482 *Duling, Dennis C.* Matthew 18:15-17: conflict, confrontation, and conflict resolution in a "fictive kin" association. SBL.SP part 1. SBL.SPS 37: 1998 ⇒402. 253-295.
4483 *Grasso, Santi* La parabola del re buono e del servo spietato (Mt 18,21-35): analisi narratologica. RivBib 46 (1998) 19-41.
4484 *Ritt, Hubert* Vom unbarmherzigen Gläubiger. Du bist eingeladen. 1998 ⇒4434. 94-96.
4485 *Hoffmann, Paul* Herrscher in oder Richter über Israel?: Mt 19,28/Lk 22,28-30 in der synoptischen Überlieferung. ᶠSCHRAGE, W. 1998 ⇒101. 253-264.

F4.8 **Mt 20...***Regnum eschatologicum*—**Kingdom eschatology**

4486 *Allison, Dale C.* The eschatology of Jesus. Encyclopedia of apocalypticism I. 1998 ⇒507. 267-302.
4487 **Fuellenbach, John** The kingdom of God: the message of Jesus today. 1995 ⇒11/1,3160... 13,4812. ᴿIThQ 63 (1998) 98-99 (*McConvery, Brendan*).
4488 *Kvalbein, Hans* The kingdom of God in the ethics of Jesus. CV 40 (1998) 197-227.
4489 *Merklein, Helmut* Die Reich-Gottes-Verkündigung Jesu. Studien zu Jesus und Paulus II. WUNT 105: 1998 <1988> ⇒176. 125-153.
4490 *Wright, N.T.* The future of Jesus. The meaning of Jesus. 1998 ⇒3857. 197-204.

4491 *Kissling, Christian* Der Weinbergbesitzer und die Gerechtigkeit ᶠVENETZ, H. 1998 ⇒122. 157-165 [Mt 20,1-15].
4492 *Schröder, Richard* Die Arbeiter im Weinberg: Bibelarbeit über Mt. 20,1-16, gehalten auf dem Kirchentag in Leipzig 1997. ZdZ 52 (1998) 69-71.
4493 *Lachenmann, Hanna* Von den Arbeitern im Weinberg. Du bist eingeladen. 1998 ⇒4434. 97-99 [Mt 20,1-16].
4494 *Tatum, W.B.* Jesus' so-called triumphal entry: on making an ass of the Romans. FORUM 1 (1998) 129-143 [Mt 21,1-9//].
4495 *Moulton, Mark* Jesus' goal for temple and tree: a thematic revisit of Matt 21:12-22. JETS 41 (1998) 561-572.

4496 *Gourges, Michel* Una parábola, tres lecturas: los hijos de reacciones opuestas (Mt 21:28-32). AnáMnesis 8 (1998) 5-22.
4497 *Odin, Karl-Alfred* Von den ungleichen Söhnen. Du bist eingeladen. 1998 ⇒4434. 100-101 [Mt 21,28-32].
4498 *Merklein, Helmut* Von mörderischen Weingärtnern 2. Du bist eingeladen. 1998 ⇒4434. 35-37 [Mt 21,33-46]. .
4499 *Sudo, Ichiro* Ethnizität und Heil-Exegese von Mt 21,43. AJBI 24 (1998) 33-65.
4500 *Hoppe, Rudolf* Das Gastmahlgleichnis Jesu (Mt 22,1-10/Lk 14,16-24) und seine vorevangelische Traditionsgeschichte. ᶠHOFFMANN, P., Von Jesus. BZNW 93: 1998 ⇒43. 277-293.
4501 *Odin, Karl Alfred* Vom großen Abendmahl 1. Du bist eingeladen. 1998 ⇒4434. 67-69 [Mt 22,1-14].
4502 *Burchard, Christoph* Das doppelte Liebesgebot in der frühen christlichen Überlieferung. Studien zur Theologie. WUNT 107: 1998 <1970> ⇒140. 3-26 [Mt 22,34-40].
4503 **Meisinger, Hubert** Liebesgebot und Altruismusforschung: ein exegetischer Beitrag zum Dialog zwischen Theologie und Naturwissenschaft. NTOA 33: 1996 ⇒12,4601. ᴿThR 63 (1998) 227-228 (*Lohse, Eduard*) [Mt 22,35-40].
4504 *Becker, Hans-Jürgen* Die Zerstörung Jerusalems bei Matthäus und den Rabbinen. NTS 44 (1998) 59-73 [Mt 23].
4505 *Marguerat, Daniel* Quand Jésus fait le procès des juifs: Matthieu 23 et l'antijudaïsme. Procès de Jésus. 1998 ⇒392. 101-125.
4506 *Luz, Ulrich* Wehe euch, ihr Schriftgelehrten und Pharisäer, Heuchler!: Ja und Nein zu einem schwierigen Text. ᶠSCHRAGE, W. 1998 ⇒101. 265-276.
4507 *Genuyt, François* Matthieu 23. SémBib 89 & 92 (1998) 39-49 & 45-55.
4508 *Galot, J.* O discurso escatológico (Mt 24). RCB 87-88 (1998) 183-189.
4509 **McNicol, Allan J.** Jesus' directions for the future: a source and redaction-history study of the use and eschatological traditions in Paul and the synoptic accounts of Jesus' last eschatological discourse. 1996 ⇒12,4606. ᴿJThS 49 (1998) 749-751 (*Tuckett, C.M.*); CBQ 60 (1998) 580-582 (*Maloney, Elliott C.*).
4510 **Dlungwana, Mlungisi Pius** Jesus' parousia in the context of the crucifixion: an exegetical analysis of Matthew 24:1-26:2 using the semiotic method. ᴰOttowa 1998, 242 pp.
4511 *Bannach, Klaus* Vom Feigenbaum 2 [Mt 24,32-36];
4512 *Schober, Theodor* Vom wachsamen Hausherrn 1 [Mt 24,42-44];
4513 *Deichmann, Christa* Vom treuen und vom bösen Knecht 1 [Mt 24,45-51];
4514 *Ziegler, Hans* Von den wartenden Frauen [Mt 25,1-13]. Du bist eingeladen. 1998 ⇒4434. 43-44/73-74/77-78/102-103.
4515 *Peres, Imre* A tíz szűz példázata (Mt 25,1-13). Példabeszédek. 1998 ᶠ372. 105-117. **Hungarian.**
4516 *Leduc, Francis* La parabole des dix vierges commentée par Jean CHRYSOSTOME. POC 48 (1998) 63-72.
4517 *Krusche, Werner* Vom anvertrauten Gut 1 [Mt 25,14-30];
4518 Vom Weltgericht [Mt 25,31-46]. Du bist eingeladen. 1998, 81-83/104-106.
4519 *Heil, John Paul* The double meaning of the narrative of universal judgement in Matthew 25.31-46. JSNT 69 (1998) 3-14.

4520 *Abma, Henk* De zeven werken van barmhartigheid. Interpretatie 6/3 (1998) 4-6 [Mt 25,31-46].
4521 *Cranfield, C.E.B.* Who are Christ's brothers (Matthew 25.40)?. On Romans. 1998 <1994> ⇒143. 125-135.
4522 *Guerra Gomez, Manuel* ¿Pneûma, un elemento pneumatológico (Espíritu Santo) o antropológico (el alma/espíritu del hombre)?: Jn 19,30; Math 25,50, et par., en los escritos cristianos de los primeros siglos y en los no cristianos. Burg. 39 (1998) 31-78.

F5.1 *Redemptio*, Mt 26, *Ultima coena;* **The Eucharist** [⇒H7.4]

4523 *Cimosa, Mario* Dal banchetto pasquale alla cena eucaristica. L'eucaristia nella bibbia. DSBP 19: 1998 ⇒218. 48-71.
4524 **Espinel Marcos, J.L.** La eucaristía del Nuevo Testamento. 1997 ⇒13,4865. ᴿComunidades 26 (1998) 33-35 (*Vázquez, Xaime*); Cart. 14 (1998) 470 (*Martínez Fresneda, F.*); PhilipSac 33 (1998) 563-564 (*Mina, Macario Ofilada*).
4525 **Gerlach, Karl** The antenicene Pascha: a rhetorical history. Liturgia condenda 7: Lv 1998, Peeters xix; 434 pp. FB1570. 90-429-0570-0.
4526 *Koenig, John* Jesus and the eucharist. Truth about Jesus. 1998 ⇒211. 101-119.
4527 **Mazza, Enrico** La celebrazione eucaristica: genesi del rito e sviluppo dell'interpretazione. Liturgia 11: CinB 1996, Paoline 420 pp. 88-215-3269-0.
4528 **McNeil, Brian** The Master is here: biblical reflections on eucharistic adoration. 1997 ⇒13,4891. ᴿMilltown Studies 42 (1998) 176-178 (*Moloney, Raymond*).
4529 **Metzger, M.** Le repas du Seigneur. Strasbourg 1997, Signe 204 pp.
4530 **O'Loughlin, Frank** The eucharist: doing what Jesus said. 1997 ⇒13,4899. ᴿPacifica 11/1 (1998) 94-96 (*Hamilton, Andrew*).
4531 *Panimolle, Salvatore A.* La cena del Signore, fonte e vertice della vita cristiana. L'eucaristia nella bibbia. DSBP 19: 1998 ⇒218. 7-14.
4532 **Stewart-Sykes, Alistair** The Lamb's high feast: Melito, Peri Pascha and the Quartodeciman Paschal Liturgy at Sardis. SVigChr 42: Lei 1998, Brill xiii; 229 pp. 90-04-11236-7.
4533 *Tragan, Pius-Ramon* La cena del Signore negli scritti sinottici e paolini. L'eucaristia nella bibbia. DSBP 19: 1998 ⇒218. 82-129.

4534 *Bielecki, Tomasz* Some research problems concerning Caiaphas. FolOr 34 (1998) 65-70 [Mt 26,3].
4535 **Thiede, Carsten Peter; Ancona, Matthew d'** Eyewitness to Jesus: amazing new manuscript evidence about the origin of the Gospels. 1996 ⇒12,4647; 13,4919. ᴿJRH 22/1 (1998) 104-05 (*Pickering, Stuart R.*) [Mt 26,6-7].
4536 *Hofius, Otfried* "Für euch gegeben zur Vergebung der Sünden": vom Sinn des Heiligen Abendmahls. ZThK 95 (1998) 313-337 [Mt 26,26-28//].

F5.3 **Mt 26,30...**//*Passio Christi;* **Passion narrative**

4537 *Alegre Santamaría, X.* Los responsables de la muerte de Jesús. IX Jornadas Bíblicas. 1998 ⇒376. 109-141.

4538 *Barth, Gerhard* Il significato della morte di Gesù Cristo: l'interpretazione del Nuovo Testamento. PBT 38: 1995 ⇒11/1,3212. [R]RStRel 12 (1998) 507-508 (*Lorusso, Giacomo*).

4539 *Battaglia, Vincenzo* La passione di Cristo nei commenti al Cantico dei Cantici. La Sapienza della Croce 13 (1998) 323-336.

4540 *Beaude, Pierre-Marie* Jésus le roi des juifs: citations, énoncés et énonciation. Procès de Jésus. 1998 ⇒392. 35-51.

4541 **Berger, Klaus** Wozu ist Jesus am Kreuz gestorben?. Stu 1998, Quell 232 pp. DM29.80. 3-7918-1955-0.

4542 *Bergèse, Daniel* De Gethsémané à Golgotha: le procès de Jésus, approche historique. RRef 49 (1998) 9-26.

4543 *Bock, Darrell L.* Crucifixion, Qumran, and the Jewish interrogation of Jesus. [F]Tyson J. 1998 ⇒120. 3-10.

4544 **Bond, Helen Katharine** Pontius Pilate in history and interpretation. MSSNTS 100: C 1998, CUP xxvi; 249 pp. £37.50. 0-521-63114-9.

4545 *Bösen, Willibald* Warum musste Jesus "wirklich" sterben?. KatBl 123 (1998) 76-81.

4546 [E]**Carroll, John T.; Green, Joel B.** The death of Jesus in early Christianity. 1995 ⇒11/1,3216. [R]OCP 64/1 (1998) 199-200 (*Podskalsky, G.*); EstB 56 (1998) 127-130 (*Urbán, A.*).

4547 *Cohen, Monique-Lise* Paix et vérité: le procès de Jésus à la lumière d'un midrash. Procès de Jésus. 1998 ⇒392. 193-201.

4548 **Cohn, Chaim** Der Prozeß und Tod Jesu aus jüdischer Sicht. 1997 ⇒13,4931. [R]EK (1998/4) 235-236 (*Osten-Sacken, Peter von der*).

4549 **Dauzat, Pierre-Emmanuel** Le suicide du Christ: une théologie. Perspectives critiques: P 1998, PUF 229 pp. FF136. 2-13-049444-7.

4550 **Derbes, Anne** Picturing the Passion in late medieval Italy. 1996 ⇒12,4661. [R]SCJ 29/1 (1998) 107-109 (*Smith, Rachel Hostetter*); JRH 22 (1998) 345-346 (*Parnham, David*).

4551 *Di Porto, Bruno; Dianich, Severino* Il messia sconfitto: l'enigma della morte di Gesù. RdT 39 (1998) 763-772.

4552 **Egger, Peter** "Crucifixus sub Pontio Pilato": das "Crimen" Jesu von Nazareth im Spannungsfeld römischer und jüdischer Verwaltungs- und Rechtsstrukturen NTA 32: 1997 ⇒13,4933. [R]BZ 42 (1998) 264-267 (*Horn, Friedrich W.*); ThR 63 (1998) 351-352 (*Lohse, Eduard*).

4553 *Fitzmyer, Joseph A.* Crucifixion in ancient Palestine, Qumran literature, and the New Testament. To advance the gospel. 1998 <1978> ⇒150. 125-146.

4554 *Genest, Olivette* From historical-critical exegesis to Greimassian semiotics: a christological issue, the meaning of Jesus's death. Semeia 81 (1998) 95-112.

4555 *Gibson, Aleksey* The image of Judas in the work of M.A. Voloshin. The Russian Review 57 (1998) 264-278.

4556 **Gilliéron, Bernard** Il a été crucifié: regards multiples du Nouveau Testament sur la mort de Jésus. Poliez-le-Grand 1998, Moulin 79 pp. FF58.

4557 *Giorgini, Fabiano* Il volto di Gesù nel Getsemani. Il Volto dei Volti 1 (1998) 72-77.

4558 **Gooch, Paul W.** Reflections on Jesus and Socrates: word and silence. 1997 ⇒13,4936. [R]SR 27 (1998) 323-324 (*Kroeker, Travis*).

4559 **Hermosilla Molina, Antonio** La pasión de Cristo vista por un médico. 1997 ⇒13,4938. [R]Isidorianum 7 (1998) 299-301 (*Calero, Antonio M[a].*).

4560 **Holtz, Gudrun** Der Herrscher und der Weise im Gespräch: Studien zu Form, Funktion und Situation der neutestamentlichen Verhörgespräche und der Gespräche zwischen jüdischen Weisen und Fremdherrschern. ANTZ 6: 1996 ⇒12,4671. [R]ThLZ 123 (1998) 854-856 (*Müller, Ulrich*).

4561 **Kiehl, Erich H.** The passion of our Lord. Eugene, Or. 1998, Wipf & Stock 224 pp.

4562 **Klassen, William** Judas: betrayer or friend of Jesus?. 1996 ⇒12,4675; 13,4941. [R]RB 105 (1998) 151-152 (*Murphy-O'Connor, J.*); EvQ 70 (1998) 273-275 (*Oakes, Peter*); JR 78 (1998) 104-105 (*Paffenroth, Kim*); JBL 117 (1998) 134-136 (*Brown, Raymond E.*).

4563 **Krimphove, Dieter** 'Wir haben ein Gesetz...!': rechtliche Anmerkungen zum Strafverfahren gegen Jesus. Ius vivens B: Rechtsgeschichtliche Abhandlungen 5: Müns 1997, LIT ix; 248 pp. 3-8258-2706-2.

4564 *Kurth, Christina* Der Prozeß Jesu aus der Perspektive jüdischer Forscher: Überlegungen zum Vorwurf der Schuld der Juden am Tod Jesu. KuI 13 (1998) 46-58.

4565 *Lavas, George P.* The rock of Calvary: uncovering Christ's crucifixion site. [F]NARKISS, B. 1998 ⇒85. 147-150.

4566 *Légasse, Simon* Le procès de Jésus: exégèse et histoire. Procès de Jésus. 1998 ⇒392. 31-34.

4567 *Lémonon, Jean-Pierre* Les causes de la mort de Jésus. Jésus de Nazareth. 1998 ⇒253. 349-369.

4568 **Maggioni, Bruno** Los relatos de la Pasión en los cuatro evangelios. 1997 ⇒13,4947. [R]EfMex 16 (1998) 229-235 (*Cárdenas Pallares, José*).

4569 *Magne, Jean* Jésus devant Pilate. RB 105 (1998) 42-69.

4570 *Mangatt, George* Jesus' prayer. BiBh 24 (1998) 27-36.

4571 [E]**Marchadour, Alain** Procès de Jésus, procès des juifs?: éclairage biblique et historique. LeDiv: P 1998, Cerf 214 pp. FF140. 2-204-05821-1.

4572 **Marcus, Joel** Jesus and the Holocaust: reflections on suffering and hope. 1997 ⇒13,4948. [R]ThTo 55/1 (1998) 98-100 (*Linafelt, Tod*).

4573 *Merklein, Helmut* Wie hat Jesus seinen Tod verstanden?. Studien zu Jesus und Paulus II. WUNT 105: 1998 <1996> ⇒176. 174-189.

4574 *Moule, C.F.D.* The gravamen against Jesus. Forgiveness. 1998 [1987] ⇒180. 95-115.

4575 **Pinckaers, Servais Th.** Un grand chant d'amour, la Passion selon saint Matthieu. 1997 ⇒13,4953. [R]Sedes Sapientiae 16/1 (1998) 69-72 (*Bazelaire, Thomas-M. de*).

4576 *Poupard, Paul* La passion et la culture. Cultures et Foi 6 (1998) 88-96.

4577 **Ross, Ellen M.** The grief of God: images of the suffering Jesus in late medieval England. NY 1997, OUP xiii, 200 pp. £42. 0-19-510451-X. [R]ChH 67/1 (1998) 138-140 (*Byrne, Joseph P.*).

4578 *Roy, Louis* The passion of Jesus: a test case for providence. NBl 79 (1998) 512-523.

4579 *Schmidt, Daryl D.* The Septuagintal influence in shaping the passion narratives: with special attention to Matthew. FORUM 1 (1998) 95-118.

4580   *Senior, Donald* The gospel of Matthew and the passion of Jesus: theological and pastoral perspectives. WaW 18 (1998) 372-379.
4581   **Sloyan, Gerard S.** The crucifixion of Jesus: history, myth, faith. 1995 ⇒11/1,3244... 13,4957. [R]Horizons 25 (1998) 95-112 [with resp. by author] (*Mayeski, Marie Anne; Cunningham, Lawrence S.; Miles, Margaret R.; Slusser, Michael; Van Beeck, Frans Jozef*).
4582   *Stegemann, Wolfgang* Der Prozeß Jesu: Gründe für die Entlastung der Juden vom Tötungsvorwurf. Diak. 29 (1998) 121-126;
4583   Gab es eine jüdische Beteiligung an der Kreuzigung Jesu?. KuI 13 (1998) 3-24.
4584   *Suhl, Alfred* Beobachtungen zu den Passionsgeschichten der synoptischen Evangelien. [F]HOFFMANN, P., Von Jesus. BZNW 93: 1998 ⇒43. 321-377.
4585   *Terbuyken, Peri; Kremer, Christian Josef* Judas Iskariot. RAC 146. 1998 ⇒495. 142-160.
4586   **Treanor, Oliver** This is my beloved Son: aspects of the Passion. 1997 ⇒13,4961. [R]IThQ 63 (1998) 412-413 (*Madden, Nicholas*).
4587   *Trilling, W.* Paixão e ressurreição em Mateus. RCB 87-88 (1998) 191-211.
4588   **Watson, Alan** The trial of Jesus. 1995 ⇒11/1,3249. [R]BiRe 14/1 · (1998) 14, 47 (*Saldarini, Anthony J.*).
4589   *Wells, Paul* Que s'est-il passé à la croix?. RRef 49 (1998) 45-58.
4590   *Wright, N.T.* The crux of faith. The meaning of Jesus. 1998 ⇒3857. 93-107.
4591   *Zibawi, Mahmoud* La passion du Christ: du signe à l'icône. Contacts 50 (1998) 33-50.

4592   *Meynet, Roland* Procès de Jésus, procès de tous les hommes: Mt 26,57-27,26 et Mc 14,53-15,20. Procès de Jésus. 1998 ⇒392. 75-99.
4593   *Van Aarde, Andries G.* Matthew 27:45-53 and the turning of the tide in Israel's history. BTB 28 (1998) 16-26.

F5.6 Mt 28//: Resurrectio

4594   **Andrews, Richard; Schellenberger, Paul** The tomb of God: the body of Jesus and the solution to a 2000-year-old mystery. 1996 ⇒12,4721. [R]EeT 29 (1998) 260-262 (*Coyle, J. Kevin*).
4595   **Biddle, Martin** Das Grab Christi: neutestamentliche Quellen—historische und archäologische Forschungen—überraschende Erkenntnisse. [T]*Pitt-Killet, Heike.* Biblische Archäologie und Zeitgeschichte 5: Gießen 1998, Brunnen 192 pp. 3-7655-9804-6.
4596   *Boismard, Marie-Émile* ¿Es necesario aún hablar de 'resurrección'?: los datos bíblicos. 1996 ⇒12,4728. [R]San Juan de la Cruz 21 (1998) 132-133 (*Monteagudo, Ángel*).
4597   *Borg, Marcus J.* The truth of Easter. The meaning of Jesus. 1998 ⇒3857. 129-142.
4598   **Brambilla, Franco Giulio** Il Crocifisso risorto: risurrezione di Gesù e fede dei discepoli. BTCon 99: Brescia 1998, Queriniana 325 pp. L42.000. 88-399-0399-2.
4599   *Brantschen, Johannes B.* Wir erwarten die Auferstehung der Toten und das Leben der kommenden Welt. [F]VENETZ, H. 1998 ⇒122. 93-100.

4600 **Bravo Lazcano, Carlos** El fundamento de la fe de Pascua. Santafé de Bogotá 1998, Facultad de Teología, Universidad Javeriana 152 pp. ^RThX 48 (1998) 254-256 (*Neira F., Germán*).

4601 *Butterworth, Mike* Old Testament antecedents to Jesus' resurrection. Proclaiming the resurrection. 1998 ⇒384. 1-28.

4602 *Bühler, Pierre* Jésus, la résurrection et la théologie: la pertinence théologique de la question du Jésus historique. Jésus de Nazareth. 1998 ⇒253. 515-528.

4603 *Cranfield, C.E.B.* The resurrection of Jesus Christ. On Romans. 1998 <1989-90> ⇒143. 137-150.

4604 *Dalferth, Ingolf U.* Volles Grab, leerer Glaube?: zum Streit um die Auferweckung des Gekreuzigten. ZThK 95 (1998) 379-409.

4605 ^E**Davis, Stephen T.; Kendall, Daniel: O'Collins, Gerald** The resurrection: an interdisciplinary symposium on the resurrection of Jesus. 1997 ⇒13,4975. ^RJThS 49 (1998) 907-909 (*Nineham, Dennis*); Gr. 79 (1998) 169-172 (*O'Collins, Gerald*); HeyJ 39 (1998) 333-335 (*Winter, Michael M.*).

4606 **Essen, Georg** Historische Vernunft und Auferweckung Jesu. TSTP 9: 1995 ⇒11/1,3269... 13,4979. ^RThLZ 123 (1998) 90-93 (*Merk, Otto*).

4607 *Etzold, Eckhard* Ist der Osterglaube ein Produkt der Verkündigung Jesu?: zur Frage nach dem Charakter der Auferstehungsvisionen. PTh 87 (1998) 68-72.

4608 **Federici, Tommaso** Resuscitò Cristo!: commento alle letture bibliche della divina liturgia bizantina. Quad. di Oriente Cristiano 8: 1996 ⇒12,4733; 13,4980. ^RCivCatt 149/4 (1998) 452-453 (*Capizzi, C.*).

4609 *Fitzmyer, Joseph A.* The resurrection of Jesus Christ according to the New Testament. To advance the gospel. 1998 <1987> ⇒150. 369-381.

4610 **Fraijó, Manuel; Alegre, Xavier; Tornos, Andrés** La fe cristiana en la resurrección. Cuadernos Fe y Secularidad 41/42: M 1998, Fe y S 77 pp. ^RMCom 56 (1998) 531-532 (*Revuelta González, M.*).

4611 *Frankemölle, Hubert* Auferweckung Jesu—(nur) ein Zeichen apokalyptischer Endzeit?: ein Zwischenruf. *(a)* Jüdische Wurzeln. BBB 116: 1998 ⇒151. 209-232;

4612 *(b)* ^FHoffmann, P., Von Jesus. BZNW 93: 1998 ⇒43. 45-69.

4613 *Goldsworthy, Graeme L.* "With flesh and bones": a biblical theology of the bodily resurrection of Christ. RTR 57 (1998) 121-135.

4614 *Greshake, Gisbert* Auferstehung im Tod: ein "parteiischer" Rückblick auf eine theologische Diskussion. ThPh 73 (1998) 538-557.

4615 *Gubler, Marie-Louise* Resurrection: the first fruits of those who have fallen asleep. ThD 45 (1998) 117-122.

4616 *Heinze, Rudi* The resurrection of Jesus in English Puritan thought. Proclaiming the resurrection. 1998 ⇒384. 81-106.

4617 *Heller, Dagmar* La date de Pâques: un facteur de division entre les églises. UnChr 129 (1998) 23-33.

4618 *Jung, Rainer* Lauter Visionen. Streit um die Auferstehung. 1998 ⇒4626. 122-125.

4619 **Kessler, William Thomas** Peter as the first witness of the risen Lord: an historical and theological investigation. Diss. Gregoriana 1995. TGr.T 37: R 1998, E.P.U.G. 240 pp. €12.39. 88-7652-785-0.

4620 *Koester, Helmut* The memory of Jesus' death and the worship of the risen Lord. HThR 91 (1998) 335-350.

4621 *Kosch, Daniel* Auferstehung mitten am Tage. ^FVENETZ, H. 1998
⇒122. 47-57.
4622 *Kremer, Jacob* Tod und Errettung aus dem Tod: Überlegungen zur
bildhaften Sprache der Bibel. ^FPOKORNÝ, P. 1998 ⇒90. 234-245.
4623 *Küchler, Max* "Was sucht ihr den Lebenden bei den Toten?": Gedanken zur Neugierde an einem leeren Grab voller Verheißung. ^FVenetz,
H. 1998 ⇒122. 69-81.
4624 *Longenecker, Richard N.* Introduction. Life in the face of death. 1998
⇒252. 1-18.
4625 **Lorenzen, Thorwald** Resurrection and discipleship: interpretive
models, biblical reflections, theological consequences. 1995
⇒11/1,3278; 12,3889. ^RITS 35 (1998) 199-202 (*Legrand, L.*).
4626 ^E**Lüdemann, Gerd; Wischnath, Rolf** Streit um die Auferstehung:
der Disput in Fürstenwalde: eine Dokumentation. B 1998, Wichern
125 pp. DM24. 3-88981-109-4. ^REK (1998/11) 684 (*Demke, Christoph*).
4627 *Lüdemann, Gerd* Notfalls auch gegen Gott;
4628 Warum die Kirche lügen muß. Streit um die Auferstehung. 1998
⇒4626. 21-22/15-20.
4629 *Manzi, Franco* La risurrezione di Gesù Cristo secondo Matteo nel
contesto giudaico e anticotestamentario. RivBib 46 (1998) 277-315.
4630 **März, Claus-Peter** Hoffnung auf Leben: die biblische Botschaft von
der Auferstehung. Begegnung mit der Bibel: 1995 ⇒11/1,3288;
12,4746. ^RCoTh 68/1 (1998) 245-251 (*Załeski, Jan*).
4631 **McKenzie, Leon** Pagan resurrection myths and the resurrection of
Jesus: a christian perspective. 1997 ⇒13,4988. ^RCTJ 33 (1998) 544-
546 (*Hoezee, Scott*).
4632 *Mettinger, Tryggve N.D.* The "dying and rising God": a survey of
research from FRAZER to the present day. SEÅ 63 (1998) 111-123.
4633 **Müller, Ulrich B.** Die Entstehung des Glaubens an die Auferstehung
Jesu: historische Aspekte und Bedingungen. SBS 172: Stu 1998,
Kath. Bibelwerk 85 pp. 3-460-04721-6.
4634 **Osborne, Kenan B.** The resurrection of Jesus: new considerations
for its theological interpretation. 1997 ⇒13,4990. ^RHPR 98/10
(1998) 71-73 (*Reilly, Matthew V.*).
4635 *Phillips, Peter* Seeing with eyes of faith: SCHILLEBEECKX and the
resurrection of Jesus. NBl 79 (1998) 241-250.
4636 **Pikaza, Xabier** Camino de Pascua: misterios de gloria. 1996
⇒12,4750. ^RThX 48/1 (1998) 136-137 (*Navarro S., Rosana Elena*).
4637 *Pilch, John J.* Appearances of the risen Jesus in cultural context:
experiences of alternate reality. BTB 28 (1998) 52-60.
4638 *Quiring, Andreas W.* Das Grab Jesu: leer oder voll?. Streit um die
Auferstehung. 1998 ⇒4626. 117-121.
4639 *Reinmuth, Eckart* Historik und Exegese—zum Streit um die Auferstehung Jesu nach der Moderne. Exegese und Methodendiskussion.
TANZ 23: 1998 ⇒208. 1-20.
4640 *Röder, Hans-Jürgen* Frappierende Nähe zur vulgärmarxistischen Kir-
chenkritik. Streit um die Auferstehung. 1998 ⇒4626. 114-116.
4641 **Russell, Jeffrey Burton** A history of heaven: the singing silence.
1997 ⇒13,4996. ^RCHR 84 (1998) 699-700 (*Emmerson, Richard K.*).
4642 ^E**Russo, Giovanni** Gesù Cristo morto e risorto per noi consegna lo
Spirito: meditazione teologica sul mistero pasquale. Leumann (T)
1998, Elle Di Ci 303 pp. L37.000. 88-01-00996-8. ^RActBib 35
(1998) 163-165 (*O'Callaghan, Josep*).

4643 *Selvatico, Pietro* Die Auferweckung Jesu—ein Mirakel?;
4644 *Strobel, Regula* An jenem Tag wurde in Jerusalem ein Auferstande-
ner gekreuzigt: aufständische Gedanken zu Auferstehung aus feministischer Perspektive. [F]VENETZ, H. 1998 ⇒122. 83-92/29-36.
4645 *Swoboda, Antoni* Próba racjnalnego uzasadnienia zmartwychwstania
według ATENAGORASA z Aten [Essai de justification rationelle de la
résurrection selon Atenagoras d'Athènes]. AtK 131 (1998) 269-275.
4646 *Vahrenhorst, Martin* "Se non è vero, è ben trovato": die Frauen und
das leere Grab. ZNW 89 (1998) 282-288.
4647 Verso una data comune per la Pasqua. Consiglio Mondiale delle Chiese; Consiglio delle Chiese del Medio Oriente—Aleppo, 5-10 marzo
1997. [T]*Compagnoni, Giordano Monzio.* RPLi 206 (1998) 72-85.
4648 *Weder, Hans* Das weltliche Rätsel und das göttliche Geheimnis der
Auferweckung Jesu. PTh 87 (1998) 73-85.
4649 *Winch, Peter* LESSING und die Auferstehung. DZPh 46 (1998) 731-
751.
4650 *Wischnath, Rolf* Aus Ruinen auferstanden;
4651 Schäume oder Wirklichkeit. Streit um die Auferstehung. 1998
⇒4626. 23-30/31-34.
4652 *Wright, N.T.* The transforming reality of the bodily resurrection. The
meaning of Jesus. 1998 ⇒3857. 111-127.
4653 *Zeller, Dieter* Hellenistische Vorgaben für den Glauben an die Auferstehung Jesu?. [F]HOFFMANN, P., Von Jesus. BZNW 93: 1998 ⇒43.
71-91.

4654 *Reeves, Keith H.* They worshipped him, and they doubted: Matthew
28.17. BiTr 49 (1998) 344-349.
4655 **Friesen, Abraham** ERASMUS, the Anabaptists, and the Great Commission. GR 1998, Eerdmans xi; 196 pp. $18. 0-8028-4448-0 [Mt
28,19-20].
4656 *Ras, J.M.* Matteus 28:19-20: enkele tekskritiese en eksegetiese op-
merkings aan die hand van Nestle-Aland se 27e uitgawe van die
Griekse Nuwe Testament. HTS 54 (1998) 810-831.

F6.1 Evangelium Marci—*Textus, commentarii*

4657 [E]**Aland, Kurt** Text und Textwert der griechischen Handschriften des
Neuen Testaments: 4. die synoptischen Evangelien: 1. das
Markusevangelium, T. 1. Handschriftenliste und vergleichende Bes-
chreibung; T. 2. Resultate der Kollation und Hauptliste. ANTT 21: B
1998, De Gruyter viii; 692; 684 pp. 3-11-016169-9; -170-2.
4658 [E]**Ammassari, Antonio** Il vangelo di Marco nella colonna latina del
Bezae Codex Cantabrigiensis. 1996 ⇒12,4765. [R]RivBib 46 (1998)
238-240 (*Cavalletti, Sofia*).
4659 **Armellini, F.; Usubelli, A.** Lo seguirono lungo la via: il vangelo secondo Marco. Bo 1998, EDB 246 pp. L22.000.
4660 **Bodrato, Aldo** Il vangelo delle meraviglie: commento... Marco.
1996 ⇒12,4767. [R]Ter. 49 (1998) 722-723 (*Pasquetto, Virgilio*).
4661 **Cahill, Michael** The first commentary on Mark: an annotated translation. Oxf 1998, OUP 154 pp. £33.50. 0-19-511601-1. [R]PIBA 21
(1998) 118-120 (*McNamara, Martin*).
4662 [E]**Cahill, Michael** Expositio evangelii secundum Marcum. CChr.SL
82: 1997 ⇒13,5007. [R]RBen 108 (1998) 390-391 (*Bogaert, P.-M.*).

4663   **Cole, R. Alan** Il vangelo secondo Marco: introduzione e commentario. Commentari al Nuovo Testamento: R 1998, GBU 440 pp.
4664   **Eckey, Wilfried** Das Markusevangelium: Orientierung am Weg Jesu:
ein Kommentar. Neuk 1998, Neuk xii; 456 pp. FS62. 3-7887-1703-3.
4665   The gospel according to Mark: Authorised King James Version.
Pocket Canons: E 1998, Canongate xii; 50 pp. 0-86241-796-1.
4666   **Hare, Douglas R.A.** Mark. 1996 ⇒12,4773; 13,5015. ᴿHBT 20
(1998) 164-165 (*Allison, Dale C.*).
4667   **Lamarche, Paul** Évangile de Marc: commentaire. EtB 33: 1996
⇒12,4778; 13,5019. ᴿRSR 86 (1998) 420-422 (*Guillet, Jacques*).
4668   **Lentzen-Deis, Fritzleo** Comentario al evangelio de Marcos: modelo
de nueva evangelización. Evangelio y cultura 1: Estella (Navarra)
1998, Verbo Divino 491 pp. 84-8169-249-2;
4669   Das Markus-Evangelium: ein Kommentar für die Praxis. Stu 1998,
Kath. Bibelwerk xii; 363 pp. 3-460-33121-6.
4670   **Légasse, Simon** L'évangile de Marc. LeDiv.Commentaires 5: 1997
⇒13,5020. ᴿBib 79 (1998) 289-293 (*Gundry, Robert H.*); RSR 86
(1998) 422-423 (*Guillet, Jacques*).
4671   **Mateos, Juan; Camacho, Fernando** El evangelio de Marcos: análisis lingüístico y comentario exegético I. 1993 ⇒9,4912; 11/1,3318.
ᴿEstB 56 (1998) 546-547 (*Ródenas, A.*).
4672   **Mateos, Juan; Camacho, Fernando** Marcos: texto e comentário.
ᵀ*Vidigal, José Raimundo*. Comentários Bíblicos: São Paulo 1998,
Paulus 395 pp. 85-349-1111-8.
4673   ᴱ**Oden, Thomas C.; Hall, Christopher Alan** Mark. ACCS.NT 2:
DG 1998, InterVarsity xxxv; 281 pp. 0-8308-1487-6.
4674   **Pikaza Ibarrondo, Xabier** Il vangelo di Marco. 1996 ⇒12,4783.
ᴿCivCatt 149/2 (1998) 97-98 (*Scaiola, D.*).
4675   ᴱ**Rodríguez Carmona, Antonio** El evangelio de Marcos. ResB 17
(1998) 1-68.
4676   **Van Iersel, Bas M.F.** Mark: a reader-response commentary. JSNT.S
164: Shf 1998, Academic 556 pp. £55. 1-85075-829-8.
4677   *Vazquez Allegue, Xaime* 7Q5 ¿el manuscrito más antiguo de
Marcos?. Comp. 42 (1998) 7-16 [Mk 6,52-53].
4678   **Vickers, Paul V.** Person to person: the gospel of Mark. West Chester, Pa. 1998, Swedenborg xxiii; 287 pp. 0-87785-380-0.

F6.2 *Evangelium Marci,* **Themata**

4679   **Aichele, George** Jesus framed: biblical limits. 1996 ⇒12,4792;
13,5029. ᴿJRH 22 (1998) 337-339 (*Poetker, Katrina*); CBQ 60
(1998) 353-354 (*Kloppenborg, John S.*).
4680   *Aichele, George* Jesus' violence. Violence. 1998 ⇒260. 72-91.
4681   **Bain, Bruce Alan** Literary surface structures in Mark: identifying
christology as the purpose of the gospel. ᴰFuller 1998, 240 pp.
4682   *Bauckham, Richard* John for readers of Mark. The gospels. 1998
⇒213. 147-171.
4683   *Bedenbender, Andreas* Echos, Spiegelbilder, Rätseltexte: Beobachtungen zur Komposition des Markusevangeliums (3. Teil). TeKo 21
(1998) 1-136.
4684   **Blackburn, Barry** Theios Aner and the Markan miracle traditions.
WUNT 40: 1992 ⇒7,4284... 9,4920. ᴿStPat 45/1 (1998) 199-201
(*Moda, Aldo*).

4685 **Blount, Brian K.** God preach! Mark's kingdom message and the black church today. Bible and Liberation: Mkn 1998, Orbis xiii; 290 pp. $25. 1-57075-171-4.

4686 *Bolt, Peter G.* "...With a view to the forgiveness of sins": Jesus and forgiveness in Mark's gospel. RTR 57 (1998) 53-69.

4687 *Buetubela, Balembo* Point de vue de l'évangile de Marc sur les Juifs. RAT 22 (1998) 5-19.

4688 **Casey, Maurice** Aramaic sources of Mark's gospel. MSSNTS 102: C 1998, CUP x; 278 pp. $60. 0-521-63314-1.

4689 *Conrady, Jürgen; Vouga, François* Zur Interpretation der Erzählungen von Exorzismen im Markusevangelium: ein Werkstattbericht aus einem interdisziplinären Dialog zwischen einem Arzt und einem Theologen. Exegese und Methodendiskussion. TANZ 23: 1998 ⇒ 208. 257-270.

4690 *Contreras Molina, Francisco* El secreto mesiánico. ResB 17 (1998) 41-49.

4691 *Danove, Paul L.* The narrative rhetoric of Mark's ambiguous characterization of the disciples. JSNT 70 (1998) 21-38.

4692 *Dautzenberg, Gerhard* Markus und das Gesetz: Überlegungen zur gleichnamigen Untersuchung von Heikki Sariola. BZ 42 (1998) 91-95.

4693 *Díaz Rodelas, Juan Miguel* Los milagros de Jesús en el evangelio de Marcos. ResB 17 (1998) 21-32.

4694 **Doyle, Stephen C.** A retreat with Mark: embracing discipleship. Cincinnati 1998, St Anthony Messenger Press 96 pp. $9. 0-86716-324-0.

4695 *Duquoc, Christian* Le silence de Jésus et le secret messianique. VS 727 (1998) 211-218.

4696 **Dwyer, Timothy** The motif of wonder in the gospel of Mark. JSNT.S 128: 1996 ⇒12,4804; 13,5047. ᴿCV 40 (1998) 178-180 (*Pokorný, Petr*); BBR 8 (1998) 246-247 (*Trites, Allison A.*).

4697 *Eisen, Ute E.* Das Markusevangelium erzählt: literary criticism und Evangelienauslegung. Exegese und Methodendiskussion. TANZ 23: 1998 ⇒208. 135-153.

4698 *Fander, Monika* Das Evangelium nach Markus: Frauen als wahre Nachfolgerinnen Jesu. Kompendium Feministische Bibelauslegung. ᴱSchottroff, L.: 1998 ⇒H8.9. 499-512.

4699 **Francis, Leslie J.** Personality type and scripture: exploring Mark's gospel. 1997 ⇒13,5053. ᴿRRT (1998/1) 23-26 (*Atkins, Peter*).

4700 *Hanson, James* The disciples in Mark's gospel: beyond the pastoral/polemical debate. HBT 20 (1998) 128-155.

4701 **Harder, Lydia Neufeld** Obedience, suspicion and the gospel of Mark: a Mennonite-feminist exploration of biblical authority. Studies in women & religion 5; Études sur les femmes et la religion 5: Waterloo, Ontario 1998, Laurier Univ. Pr. xii; 168 pp. 0-88920-305-9.

4702 **Hauser, Michael** Die Herrschaft Gottes im Markusevangelium. EHS.T 647: Fra 1998, Lang v; 175 pp. 3-631-33903-8.

4703 *Hedrick, Charles W.* Conceiving the narrative: colors in Achilles TATIUS and the gospel of Mark. Ancient fiction. 1998 ⇒1118. 177-197.

4704 *Hurd, John C.* Isaiah's curse according to Mark. Earlier letters of Paul. ARGU 8: 1998 <1973> ⇒163. 85-96.

4705 *Joynes, Christine E.* A question of identity: 'Who do people say that I am?': Elijah, John the Baptist and Jesus in Mark's gospel. ᶠASHTON J. JSNT.S 153: 1998 ⇒6. 15-29.

4706 *Kasiłowski, Piotr* Modlitwa w ewangelii św. Marka [La prière   dans l'évangile selon saint Marc]. Bobolanum 9 (1998) 319-337.

4707 *Kertelge, Karl* Jézus messiási küldetése Márk által közvetített példabeszédeinek fényében [Jeus im Lichte seiner Gleichnisse nach dem Markus-Evangelium]. Példabeszédek. 1998 ⇒372. 73-77. **Hungarian.**

4708 **Kmiecik, Ulrich** Der Menschensohn im Markusevangelium. FzB 81: 1997 ⇒13,5066. ᴿSTV 36/2 (1998) 182-187 (*Załęski, Jan*); ATG 61 (1998) 295 (*Rodríguez Carmona, A.*).

4709 *Leal Salazar, Gabriel* Conocer a Jesús. ResB 17 (1998) 50-61.

4710 *MacDonald, Dennis R.* Secrecy and recognitions in the Odyssey and Mark: where WREDE went wrong. Ancient fiction. 1998 ⇒1118. 139-153.

4711 *Manns, Frédéric* Le milieu sémitique de l'évangile de Marc. SBFLA 48 (1998) 125-142.

4712 **Martini, Carlo M.** La llamada de Jesús: orar con el evangelio de Marcos. M 1998, Narcea 105 pp.

4713 **Mazzocchi, L.; Forzani, J.** Il vangelo secondo Marco e lo Zen. 1996 ⇒12,4830. ᴿIl Regno 43 (1998) 677-680 (*Favaro, Gaetano*).

4714 *Neyrey, Jerome H.* Questions, Chreiai, and challenges to honor: the interface of rhetoric and culture in Mark's gospel. CBQ 60 (1998) 657-681.

4715 *Niederwimmer, Kurt* Johannes Markus und die Frage nach dem Verfasser des zweiten Evangeliums. Gesammelte Aufsätze. BZNW 90: 1998 <1967> ⇒182. 31-43.

4716 **Parker, Neil Ronald** The Marcan portrayal of the 'Jewish' unbeliever as a function of the Marcan references to the Jewish Bible: the hermeneutical basis of a theological construct. ᴰEmmanuel Col. of Victoria U. in U. of Toronto 1998, 501 pp.

4717 **Perini, Giovanni** Le domande di Gesù nel vangelo di Marco: approccio pragmatico: ricorrenze, uso e funzioni. ᴰPont. Univ. Lateranensis. Dissertatio, Romana 22: Mi 1998, Glossa ix; 149 pp. L24. 000. 88-7105-090-8.

4718 *Pérez Herrero, Francisco* El plan de Marcos. ResB 17 (1998) 13-20.

4719 **Pikaza, Xabier** Pan, casa, palabra: la iglesia en Marcos. Biblioteca EstB 94: S 1998, Sígueme 446 pp. 84-301-1322-3. ᴿCart. 14 (1998) 444-445 (*García Domene, J.C.*); PhilipSac 33 (1998) 554-556 (*Mina, Macario Ofilada*).

4720 *Rodríguez Carmona, Antonio* Marcos, una cristología correctiva. ResB 17 (1998) 5-12.

4721 *Ruiz Pérez, Maria Dolores* El feminismo secreto de Marcos. Com(E) 31 (1998) 3-23.

4722 **Schildgen, Brenda Deen** Power and prejudice: the reception of the gospel of Mark. Detroit 1998, Wayne State Univ. Press 201 pp. $35. 0-8143-2785-0;

4723 Crisis and continuity: time in the gospel of Mark. JSNT.S 159: Shf 1998, JSOT 176 pp. 1-85075-851-4.

4724 **Shiner, Whitney Taylor** Follow me!: disciples in Markan rhetoric. SBL.DS 145: 1995 ⇒12,4847. ᴿJBL 117 (1998) 636-538 (*Marcus, Joel*).

4725 *Shiner, Whitney* Creating plot in episodic narratives: the Life of Aesop and the gospel of Mark. Ancient fiction. 1998 ⇒1118. 155-176.

4726   ^E**Söding, Thomas** Der Evangelist als Theologe: Studien zum Markusevangelium. SBS 163: 1995 ⇒11/1,3402. ^RThRv 94 (1998) 513-
514 (*Theobald, Michael*).   ✦

4727   *Standaert, Benoît* L'initiation comme rite et son importance pour la
compréhension de l'évangile de Marc. PosLuth 46 (1998) 369-378.

4728   *Sugawara, Yuji* The minor characters in Mark's gospel: their roles
and functions. AJBI 24 (1998) 66-82.

4729   *Theißen, Gerd* Evangelienschreibung und Gemeindeleitung: prag-
matische Motive bei der Abfassung des Markusevangeliums. ^FSTEGE-
MANN, H. BZNW 97: 1998 ⇒111. 389-414.

4730   *Wallis, Ethel E.* Mark's goal-oriented plot structure. JOTT 10 (1998)
30-46.

4731   *Watts, Rikki E.* Isaiah's new exodus and Mark. WUNT 2/88: 1997
⇒13,5106. ^RRBBras 15 (1998) 524-525.

4732   *Weigandt, Peter* Die Parabeln Jesu aus der Sicht des Evangelisten
Markus. Példabeszédek. 1998 ⇒372. 195-216. **Hungarian.**

4733   **Zager, Werner** Gottesherrschaft und Endgericht in der Verkündigung Jesu: eine Untersuchung zur markinischen Jesusüberlieferung
einschliesslich der Q-Parallelen. BZNW 82: 1996 ⇒12,4859; 13,
5109. ^RCBQ 60 (1998) 388-389 (*Derrenbacker, Robert A.*); Bib. 79
(1998) 429-432 (*Kloppenborg, John S.*); BZ 42 (1998) 135-136
(*Reiser, Marius*); JBL 117 (1998) 538-539 (*Carroll, John T.*).

F6.3 Evangelii Marci versiculi

4734   **Klauck, Hans-Josef** Vorspiel im Himmel?: Erzähltechnik und
Theologie im Markusprolog. BThSt 32: 1997 ⇒13,5119. ^RThRv 94
(1998) 512-513 (*Dormeyer, Detlev*); ThPQ 146 (1998) 307-309
(*Niemand, Christoph*).

4735   *Moyise, Steve* Is Mark's opening quotation the key to his use of Scripture?. IBSt 20 (1998) 146-158 [Mk 1,2-3].

4736   *Ernst, Josef* Wo Johannes taufte. ^FSTEGEMANN, H. BZNW 97: 1998
⇒111. 350-363 [Mk 1,9].

4737   **Garrett, Susan R.** The temptations of Jesus in Mark's gospel. GR
1998, Eerdmans x; 212 pp. $20. 0-8028-4259-3. ^RLASBF 48 (1998)
592-594 (*Chrupcała, Lesław Daniel*) [Mk 1,12-13].

4738   *Füssel, Kuno* Auch mit Dämonen läßt sich reden, man muß es nur
können: eine Auslegung von Mk 1,21-28. ^FVENETZ, H. 1998 ⇒122.
147-156.

4739   *Cebulj, Christian* Warum fasten Deine Jünger nicht?: zur Fastenfrage
in Mk 2,18-22. Entschluss 53 (1998) 24.

4740   *Gamba, Giuseppe Giovanni* I giorni dello sposo: struttura letteraria e
significato funzionale di Marco 2,18-22. Ricerche teologiche 9
(1998) 245-282.

4741   *Kahl, Werner* Ist es erlaubt, am Sabbat Leben zu retten oder zu töten?
(Marc. 3:4): Lebensbewahrung am Sabbat im Kontext der Schriften
vom Toten Meer und der Mischna. NT 40 (1998) 313-335.

4742   *Reid, Barbara* Puzzling passages: Mark 3,28-29. BiTod 36 (1998)
124-125.

4743   *Engelen, Jan C.M.* Het koning-zijn van God: Marcus 4. ITBT 6/4
(1998) 27-30.

4744 *Müller, Peter* Megértés az olvasá folyamatában: Példabeszéd Márk
      4-ben [Verstehen im Prozess des Lesens: die Gleichnisse in Markus
      4]. Példabeszédek. 1998 ⇒372. 89-103. **Hungarian.**

4745 **Mell, Ulrich** Die Zeit der Gottesherrschaft: zur Allegorie und zum
      Gleichnis von Markus 4,1-9. BWANT 144: Stu 1998, Kohlhammer
      163 pp. DM59.80. 2-17-015896-1.

4746 *Dienst, Karl* Vom Sämann 1. Du bist eingeladen. 1998 ⇒4434. 16-
      17 [Mk 4,1-9].

4747 *Muñoz León, Domingo* Parábolas ¿para que no entiendan?. ResB 17
      (1998) 33-40 [Isa 6,9-10; Mk 4,11-12].

4748 *Dienst, Karl* Vom Sämann 2. Du bist eingeladen. 1998 ⇒4434. 18-
      19 [Mk 4,13-20].

4749 *Geist, Heinz* Vom Wachsen der Saat. Du bist eingeladen. 1998
      ⇒4434. 47-48.

4750 *Boscolo, Gastone* La parabola del granello di senape. StPat 45
      (1998) 669-697 [Mk 4,30-31].

4751 *Möhring, Marianne* Vom Senfkorn und vom Sauerteig 1. Du bist
      eingeladen. 1998 ⇒4434. 26-27 [Mk 4,30-34].

4752 *Kotansky, Roy D.* Jesus and Heracles in Cádiz (TA GADEIRA):
      death, myth, and monsters at the "straits of Gibraltar" (Mark 4:35-
      5:43). ᶠBETZ, H. 1998 ⇒10. 160-229.

4753 *Sand, Anne* "Versteht ihr noch nicht?": das Unverständnis der Jünger
      in den Boot- und Broterzählungen in Mk 4,35-8,21. ᶠLÖNING, K.
      1998 ⇒66. 41-56.

4754 *Merklein, Helmut* Die Heilung des Besessenen von Gerasa (Mk 5,1-
      20): ein Fallbeispiel für die tiefenpsychologische Deutung E.
      DREWERMANNs und die historisch-kritische Exegese. Studien zu
      Jesus und Paulus II. WUNT 105: 1998 <1992> ⇒176. 190-210.

4755 *Johnson, Earl S.* Mark 5:1-20: the other side. IBSt 20 (1998) 50-74.

4756 *Zwick, Reinhold* Filmwissenschaft und Exegese: auf den Spuren des
      impliziten Betrachters der 'Auferstehung' des Besessenen von Gerasa
      (Mk 5,1-20). Exegese und Methodendiskussion. TANZ 23: 1998
      ⇒208. 177-210.

4757 *Delorme, Jean* John the Baptist's head—the word perverted: a read-
      ing of a narrative (Mark 6:14-29). Semeia 81 (1998) 115-129.

4758 *Dormeyer, Detlev* Der grausame Prophetentod des Täufers und die
      weiteren Umstände (Mk 6,17-29). ᶠPOKORNÝ, P. 1998 ⇒90. 96-106.

4759 *Vernet, J.M.* Si riafferma il papiro 7Q5 come Mc 6,52-53?. RivBib
      46 (1998) 43-60.

4760 *Theißen, Gerd* Das Reinheitslogion Mk 7,15 und die Trennung von
      Juden und Christen. ᶠSCHRAGE, W. 1998 ⇒101. 235-251.

4761 *Sacchi, Alessandro* "Lascia prima che si sazino i figli ..." (Mc 7,27a):
      Gesù e i gentili nel vangelo di Marco. ᶠMARTINI, C. RivBib.S 33:
      1998 ⇒75. 137-154.

4762 **Carvalho, José** Ornelas de Caminho de morte, destino de vida—o
      projecto do Filho do Homem e dos seus discípulos à luz de Mc 8,27-
      9,1. Diss. Univ. Católica Portuguesa 1998; ᴰ*Lentzen Deis, Fritzleo;
      Beutler, Johannes*. Lisboa 1998, Didaskália 482 pp. ᴿBib(L) 7/7
      (1998) 161-162 (*Alves, Herculano*).

4763 **Moeser, Marion Carol** The anecdote in the cultural worlds of the
      first gospel: a study of brief stories in the Demonax, the Mishnah,
      and Mark 8:27-10:45. ND 1998, 350 pp.

4764 *Ebner, Martin* Neue Töne in einer neuen Form (II): narrative Annäherung an das Markusevangelium: das Herzstück des Evangeliums (Mk 8,27-10,52). BiLi 71 (1998) 137-144.

4765 *Frankemölle, Hubert* Jüdische Messiaserwartung und christlicher Messiasglaube: hermeneutische Anmerkungen im Kontext des Petrusbekenntnisses Mk 8,29. Jüdische Wurzeln. BBB 116: 1998 <1978> ⇒151. 161-175.

4766 *Basser, Herbert W.* The Jewish roots of the transfiguration. BiRe 14/3 (1998) 30-35 [Mk 9,2-8].

4767 *Cárdenas Pallares, José* Futuro de Jesus: futuro de sus discípulos (Mc 9:2-8,9-13). EfMex 16 (1998) 325-345.

4768 *Grillo, Margherita* La fede di un papà. TS(I) sett.-ott. (1998) 22-26 [Mk 9,24].

4769 **Drewermann, Eugen** Psicoanálisis y teología moral II: caminos y rodeos del amor. 1996 ⇒12,4918. ᴿCarthaginensia 14 (1998) 249-251 (*Tamayo Acosta, J.J.*) [Mk 10,1-12].

4770 *Gándara, Daniel Landgrave* Jesús y los pobres en Mc 10,21: reflexiones exegetico-teologicas. EfMex 16 (1998) 5-32.

4771 *Oberweis, Michael* Das Martyrium der Zebedaiden in Mk 10.35-40 (Mt 20.20-3) und Offb 11.3-13. NTS 44 (1998) 74-92.

4772 *Watts, Rikki E.* Jesus' death, Isaiah 53, and Mark 10:45: a crux revisited. Jesus and the suffering servant. 1998 ⇒3430. 125-151.

4773 *Frings, Christian* Jesus der Arzt der Kranken. Camillianum 9 (1998) 69-75.

4774 *Kiley, Mark* Marcan ark typology and the debate over Jesus' trip(s) to Jerusalem. ᴹSummers, R. 1998 ⇒115. 203-210.

4775 *Vidović, Marinko* Isus proklinje smokvu ili ...?. BoSm 68 (1998) 347-361.

4776 *Cárdenas Pallares, José* Un orden que se acaba (Mc 11:12-25). EfMex 16 (1998) 157-177.

4777 *Betz, Hans Dieter* Jesus and the purity of the temple (Mark 11:15-18): a comparative religion approach. Gesammelte Aufsätze IV. 1998 <1997> ⇒10. 57-77.

4778 *Derrett, J.D.* Questioning Jesus's authority (Mark 11:27-33). DR 116 (1998) 257-270.

4779 *Marcus, Joel* The intertextual polemic of the Markan vineyard parable. Tolerance. 1998 ⇒440. 211-227 [Mk 12,1-9].

4780 *Moor, Johannes C. de* The targumic background of Mark 12:1-12: the parable of the wicked tenants. JSJ 29 (1998) 63-80.

4781 *Dard, Pierre* La pierre rejeteé et devenue pierre d'angle: analyse intertextuelle à partir de Mc 12,1-12. SémBib 90 (1998) 3-42.

4782 *Weren, Wim J.C.* The use of Isaiah 5,1-7 in the parable of the tenants (Mark 12,1-12; Matthew 21,33-46). Bib. 79 (1998) 1-26.

4783 *Baur, Wolfgang* Von mörderischen Weingärtnern 1. Du bist eingeladen. 1998 ⇒4434. 32-34 [Mk 12,1-12].

4784 *Snodgrass, Klyne R.* Recent research on the parable of the wicked tenants: an assessment. BBR 8 (1998) 187-215 [Mk 12,1-12].

4785 *Schwank, Benedikt* Példabeszéd a szőlőskertről és a s a szőlőtőről szóló beszéd (Mk 12,1-12 par és Jn 15,1-17 a 4Q500 frag. 1 jelzésű töredék fényében) [Weinberggleichnis (Mk 12,1-12 parr) und Weinstockrede (Joh 15,1-17) im Licht von 4Q500 Fragment 1]. Példabeszédek. 1998 ⇒372. 175-184. **Hungarian.**

4786 **Saginala, Paul** Prakash The great commandment and entering into the kingdom of God: a biblical-theological study of Mk 12:38-34. Diss. excerpt Pont. Univ. Urbaniana. R 1998, Pont. Univ. Urbaniana viii; 97 pp.

4787 *Aguirre, Rafael* El primer mandamiento como principio de libertad y de crítica cultural. SalTer 86 (1998) 629-641.

4788 *DiCicco, Mario* What can one give in exchange for one's life?: a narrative-critical study of the widow and her offering, Mark 12:41-44. CThMi 25 (1998) 441-449.

4789 *Montagnini, Felice* Fine del mondo?... fine di un mondo?... il discorso escatologico in Mc 13. La fine del tempo. 1998 ⇒296. 35-57.

4790 *Müller, Peter* Zeitvorstellungen in Markus 13. NT 40 (1998) 209-230.

4791 **Dyer, Keith D.** The prophecy on the mount: Mark 13 and the gathering of the new community. Diss. Melbourne College of Divinity 1991. International Theological Studies 2: Bern 1998, Lang 338 pp. £31. 3-906759-71-7.

4792 *Kraft, Sigisbert* Vom Feigenbaum 1. Du bist eingeladen. 1998 ⇒4434. 41-42 [Mk 13,24-32].

4793 *Schlatter, Theo* Vom Senfkorn und vom Sauerteig 2. Du bist eingeladen. 1998 ⇒4434. 28-29 [Mk 13,31-35].

4794 *Kraft, Sigisbert* Vom Türhüter. Du bist eingeladen. 1998 ⇒4434. 49-50 [Mk 13,33-37].

4795 *Broer, Ingo* Auslegung der Heiligen Schrift zwischen historischer Kritik und Tiefenpsychologie: zu Mk 14,32-42. [F]HOFFMANN, P., Von Jesus. BZNW 93: 1998 ⇒43. 379-404.

4796 *Burchard, Christoph* Markus 15,34. Studien zur Theologie. WUNT 107: 1998 <1983> ⇒140. 108-118.

F6.8 **Passio secundum Marcum, 14,1...[⇒F5.3]**

4797 *Collins, Adela Yarbro* Finding meaning in the death of Jesus. JR 78 (1998) 175-196.

4798 *Sabin, Marie* Women transformed: the ending of Mark is the beginning of wisdom. CrossCur 48 (1998) 149-168.

4799 *Malzoni, Cláudio V.* Da cabeça aos pés: a unção de Jesus em Betânia, em Mc 14,3-9 e nos textos afins na tradição evangélica. PerTeol 30 (1998) 95-106.

4800 **Teixeira, Cézar** A importância de mesa de refeiçao no anúncio da traiçao: Mc 14,17-21. Diss. excerpt. R 1998, Pont. Univ. S. Thoma 233 pp.

4801 *Van Cangh, Jean-Marie* Evolution in the tradition of the last supper (Mk 14,22-26 and par.). [F]STEGEMANN, H. BZNW 97: 1998 ⇒111. 364-388.

4802 *Murphy-O'Connor, Jerome* What really happened at Gethsemane?. BiRe 14/2 (1998) 1998, 28-39, 52 [Mk 14,26-42].

4803 *Chamard-Bois, Pierre* L'heure du Fils de l'homme: Marc 14,32-42. SémBib 91 (1998) 53-57.

4804 *Leonardi, Giovanni* Paura e angoscia di Gesù al Getsemani (Mc 14,33b). StPat 45 (1998) 385-399.

4805 *Winter, S.C.* The arrest of Jesus: Mrk 14:43-52 (par.) and John 18:2-12. FORUM 1 (1998) 145-162.

4806 *Haren, Michael J.* The naked young man: a historian's hypothesis on Mark 14,51-52. Bib. 79 (1998) 525-531.

4807 *Chilton, Bruce D.* The so-called trial before the Sanhedrin: Mark 14:53-72. FORUM 1 (1998) 163-180.

4808 **Borrell, Augustí** The good news of Peter's denial: a narrative and rhetorical reading of Mark 14:54.66-72. International Studies in Formative Christianity and Judaism 7: Atlanta 1998, Scholars xiv; 250 pp. $60. 0-7885-0449-5. ᴿTer. 49 (1998) 719-722 (*Pasquetto, Virgilio*).

4809 **Bock, Darrell L.** Blasphemy and exaltation in Judaism and the final examination of Jesus: a philological-historical study of the key Jewish themes impacting Mark 14:61-64. WUNT 2/106: Tü 1998, Mohr xiv; 285 pp. DM98. 3-16-147052-4.

4810 *Chamard-Bois, Pierre* La libération de Pierre: Marc 14,66-72. SémBib 92 (1998) 56-59.

4811 *Hagedorn, Anselm C.; Neyrey, Jerome H.* 'It was out of envy that they handed Jesus over' (Mark 15.10): the anatomy of envy and the gospel of Mark. JSNT 69 (1998) 15-56.

4812 *Schwemer, Anna M.* Jesu letzte Worte am Kreuz (Mk 15,34; Lk 23,46; Joh 19,28ff). ThBeitr 29 (1998) 5-29.

4813 *Kim, Tae Hun* The anarthrous υἱός Θεοῦ in Mark 15,39 and the Roman imperial cult. Bib. 79 (1998) 221-241.

4814 *Strübind, Kim* Der Gott der Lebenden: Osterpredigt über Mk 16,1-8. Zeitschrift für Theologie und Gemeinde 3 (1998) 346-351.

4815 *Merklein, Helmut* Mk 16,1-8 als Epilog des Markusevangeliums. Studien zu Jesus und Paulus II. WUNT 105: 1998 <1993> ⇒176. 211-240.

4816 *Frankemölle, Hubert* Hat Gott Jesus im Tode verlassen?: zur Theodizee-Problematik im Markusevangelium: Anmerkungen zu Mk 16,1-8 im Kontext. Jüdische Wurzeln. BBB 116: 1998 <1996> ⇒151. 177-207.

4817 *Izquierdo, Antonio* MC 16,8c: ¿un final sorprendente?. Alpha Omega 1 (1998) 417-442.

X. Opus Lucanum

F7.1 *Opus Lucanum*—Luke-Acts

4818 **Aletti, Jean-Noël** Il racconto come teologia: studio narrativo del terzo vangelo e del libro degli Atti degli Apostoli. 1996 ⇒12,4982. ᴿAsp. 45 (1998) 595-597 (*Lucariello, Donato*): CivCatt 149/2 (1998) 314-316 (*Scaiola, D.*).

4819 **Allen, Oscar Wesley, Jr.** The death of Herod: the narrative and theological function of retribution in Luke-Acts. 1997 ⇒13,5215. ᴿCBQ 60 (1998) 355-356 (*Pervo, Richard I.*); Bib. 79 (1998) 432-436 (*Böhlemann, Peter*).

4820 **Arlandson, James Malcolm** Women, class, and society in early christianity: models from Luke-Acts. 1997 ⇒13,5216. ᴿRRT (1998/1) 44-46 (*Need, Stephen W.*).

4821 *Ayuch, Daniel Alberto* Die lukanische Johannesepisode (Lk 3,1-22) und das Jesajabuch: Weisheit und Prophetie im lukanischen Geschichtswerk. [F]LÖNING, K. 1998 ⇒66. 57-68.

4822 *Borghi, Ernesto* La responsabilità della gioia: prospettive lucane per la vita di ogni essere umano. RTLu 3 (1998) 509-521.

4823 **Brawley, Robert Lawson** Text to text pours forth speech: voices of Scripture in Luke-Acts. ISBL: 1995 ⇒11/1,3563; 13,5221. [R]EstB 56 (1998) 549-550 (*Ródenas, A.*).

4824 *Brawley, Robert L.* The God of promises and the Jews in Luke-Acts. [F]TYSON J. 1998 ⇒120. 279-296;

4825 Offspring and parent: a Lucan prolegomena to ethics. SBL.SP part 2. SBL.SPS 37: 1998 ⇒402. 807-830.

4826 *Chrupcała, Lesław D.* Gesù Cristo, la salvezza e il regno di Dio: per una discussione sull'unità tematica dell'opera lucana. SBFLA 48 (1998) 143-178.

4827 *Fitzmyer, Joseph A.* Jesus in the early church through the eyes of Luke-Acts <1987>;

4828 The use of the Old Testament in Luke-Acts <1992>. To advance the gospel. 1998 ⇒150. 249-264/295-313.

4829 **Fletcher-Louis, Crispin H.T.** Luke-Acts: angels, christology and soteriology. WUNT 2/94: 1997 ⇒13,5226. [R]BS 155 (1998) 245-246 (*Bock, Darrell L.*).

4830 **Gallagher, Robert Lloyd** Luke, the Holy Spirit and mission: an integrative analysis of selected Protestant 'writings' in theology, mission and Lukan studies. [D]Fuller 1998, 344 pp.

4831 *Ghidelli, Carlo* "Evangelizzare" nell'opera lucana. [F]MARTINI, C. Riv Bib.S 33: 1998 ⇒75. 311-320.

4832 **Gourgues, Michel** Les deux livres de Luc: clés de lecture du troisième évangile et des Actes. Connaître la Bible 7/8: Bru 1998, Lumen Vitae 111 pp. FB350.

4833 **Hoet, Hendrik** De adem van het echte leven, over de Geest. Halewijn 1998, Antwerpen 86 pp. 90-73503-09-4.

4834 **Kim, Kyoung-Jin** Stewardship and almsgiving in Luke's theology. JSNT.S 155: Shf 1998, Academic 318 pp. £50/$85. 1-85075-834-4.

4835 *Kruijf, Theo de* The name christians: a label or a challenge?. Bijdr. 59 (1998) 3-19.

4836 **Lane, Thomas Joseph** Luke and the gentile Mission: gospel anticipates Acts. EHS.T 571: 1996 ⇒12,5006; 13,5235. [R]Miss. 26 (1998) 365-366 (*Hertig, Paul*); VSVD 39 (1998) 308-310 (*Müller, Karl*).

4837 *Larsson, Edvin* Till debatten om lukasskrifternas enhet och Apostlagärningarnas genre. SEÅ 63 (1998) 189-200.

4838 **Löning, Karl** Das Geschichtswerk des Lukas, 1: Israels Hoffnung und Gottes Geheimnisse. UB 455: 1997 ⇒13,5236. [R]BZ 42 (1998) 267-269 (*Müller, Christoph*); BiLi 71 (1998) 76-77 (*Hieke, Thomas*).

4839 *MacNicol, Allan J.* Rebuilding the house of David: the function of the Benedictus in Luke-Acts. RestQ 40 (1998) 25-38 [Lk 1,68-79].

4840 *Manicardi, Ermenegildo* L'esperienza dello Spirito Santo nel vangelo secondo Luca e in Atti. Luca—alcuni percorsi. 1998 ⇒406. 39-65.

4841 *Manjaly, T.* Spirit and mission (Lk-Acts). IMR 20 (1998) 86-94.

4842 **Marshall, I. Howard** Luke: historian & theologian. New Testament profiles: DG 1998 <1970, 1979>, Inter-Varsity 252 pp. $20. 0-8308-1513-9.

4843 *Merk, Otto* Das Reich Gottes in den lukanischen Schriften. ^FMERK O.
      BZNW 95: 1998 <1975> ⇒79. 272-291.
4844 **Muir, Steven C.** Healing, initiation and community in Luke-Acts: a
      comparative analysis. ^DOttawa 1998, 343 pp.
4845 **O'Toole, Robert** L'unità della teologia di Luca. 1994 ⇒10,4900;
      12,5011. ^RRivBib 46 (1998) 109-113 (*Grasso, Santi*).
4846 *Parsons, Mikeal C.* The place of Jerusalem on the Lukan landscape:
      an exercise in symbolic cartography. ^FTYSON J. 1998 ⇒120. 155-
      171.
4847 *Peterson, David* Resurrection apologetics and the theology of Luke-
      Acts. Proclaiming the resurrection. 1998 ⇒384. 29-57.
4848 **Phillips, Thomas E.** Reading issues of wealth and poverty in the
      Third Gospel and Acts. ^DSouthern Methodist 1998, 520 pp.
4849 **Pokorny, Petr** Theologie der lukanischen Schriften. FRLANT 174:
      Gö 1998, Vandenhoeck & R 225 pp. DM48. 3-525-53861-8/-57-X.
      ^RLASBF 48 (1998) 595-601 (*Chrupcała, Lesław Daniel*).
4850 **Price, Robert M.** The widow traditions in Luke-Acts: a feminist-
      critical scrutiny. SBL.DS 155: 1997 ⇒13,5244. ^RBibl.Interp. 6
      (1998) 453-455 (*Signore, Francesca*).
4851 **Reinmuth, Eckart** PSEUDO-PHILO und Lukas: Studien zum Liber
      Antiquitatum Biblicarum. WUNT 2/74: 1994 ⇒10,4907... 13,5247.
      ^RJQR 88 (1998) 325-327 (*Levison, John R.*).
4852 *Sanders, Jack T.* Can anything bad come out of Nazareth, or did
      Luke think that history moved in a line or in a circle?. ^FTYSON J.
      1998 ⇒120. 297-312.
4853 *Sieg, Franciszek* The kingdom of God in Luke's gospel and Acts as
      compared with the reign of God and the Lamb in the Revelation of
      John. FolOr 34 (1998) 53-57.
4854 *Squires, J.T.* Fate and free will in Hellenistic histories and Luke-Acts.
      ^FJUDGE E. 1998 ⇒47. 131-137.
4855 *Talbert, Charles H.; Stepp, Perry L.* Succession in Mediterranean an-
      tiquity: part 1: the Lukan milieu; part 2: Luke-Acts. SBL.SP part 1.
      SBL.SPS 37: 1998 ⇒402. 148-168; 169-179.
4856 *Thomas, André; Van Aarde, Andries G.* Samaria as belangeruimte in
      Lukas-Handelinge. HTS 54 (1998) 760-788.
4857 *Tremolada, Pierantonio* La teologia di Luca (1986-1996). ScC 126
      (1998) 59-108.
4858 **Turner, Max** Power from on high: the spirit in Israel's restoration
      and witness in Luke-Acts. JPentec.S 9: 1996 ⇒12,5026; 13,5254.
      ^RStudies in World Christianity 4/1 (1998) 142-143 (*Badcock, Gary
      D.*); CBQ 60 (1998) 177-178 (*Montague, George T.*).
      ^FTYSON, J. Literary studies in Luke-Acts 1998 ⇒120.
4859 *Valentini, Aberto* La preghiera nell'opera di Luca. Luca—alcuni per-
      corsi. 1998 ⇒406. 1-18.
4860 **Watt, Jonathan M.** Code-switching in Luke and Acts. 1997 ⇒13,
      5256. ^RBiTr 49 (1998) 349-352 (*Noss, Philip A.*).

F7.3 Evangelium Lucae—*Textus, commentarii*

4861 ^E**Ammassari, Antonio** Il vangelo di Luca nella colonna latina del
      Bezae Codex Cantabrigiensis. 1996 ⇒12,5028. ^RRivBib 46 (1998)
      238-240 (*Cavalletti, Sofia*).

4862 **Bock, Darrell L.** Luke, 2: 9:51-24:53. 1996 ⇒13,5259. ᴿAsbTJ 53 (1998) 94-96 (*Green, Joel B.*); JBL 117 (1998) 138-140 (*Matthews, Christopher R.*).

4863 **Boismard, Marie-Émile** En quête du Proto-Luc. EtB 37: 1997 ⇒13,5260. ᴿRB 105 (1998) 272-278 (*Taylor, Justin*); ThLZ 123 (1998) 983-985 (*Wiefel, Wolfgang*).

4864 **Bovon, François** L'évangile selon saint Luc: 1,1-9,50; 9,51-14,35. 1991-1996 ⇒7,4439... 13,5262. ᴿNRTh 120 (1998) 107-109 (*Rader-makers, J.*);

4865 L'évangile selon saint Luc (9,51-14,35). Commentaire du Nouveau Testament 3B: 1996 ⇒12,5032; 13,5262. ᴿRSR 86 (1998) 423-425 (*Guillet, Jacques*); CBQ 60 (1998) 360-361 (*Kurz, William S.*).

4866 **Ernst, Josef** Das Evangelium nach Lukas. RNT: 1993 ⇒10,4925; 13,5265. ᴿAnton. 73 (1998) 158-159 (*Nobile, Marco*).

4867 **Girard, Marc** De Luc à Théophile: un évangile fait sur mesure pour notre temps. Parole d'acqualité 8: P 1998, Médiaspaul 356 pp. 2-89420-113-3.

4868 **González Caballero, A.** El evangelio de San Lucas en caló: texto bilingüe. Córdoba 1998, El Almend 208 pp. 84-8005-037-3.

4869 The gospel according to Luke: Authorised King James Version. Pocket Canons: E 1998, Canongate xiii; 81 pp. 0-86241-797-X.

4870 **Goulder, Michael D.** Luke, a new paradigm. JSNT.S 20: 1989 ⇒5,5066... 8,5309. ᴿETR 73 (1998) 263-264 (*Corsani, Bruno*).

4871 **Graumann, Thomas** Christus interpres: die Einheit von Auslegung und Verkündigung in der Lukaserklärung des AMBROSIUS von Mailand. PTS 41: 1994 ⇒10,4943; 12,5057. ᴿCrSt 19 (1998) 653-655 (*Gori, Franco*); JThS 49 (1998) 392-394 (*Lenox-Conyngham, Andrew*).

4872 **Green, Joel B.** The gospel of Luke. NICNT: 1997 ⇒13,5269. ᴿRRT (1998/2) 46-8 (*Goodacre, Mark*); LASBF 48 (1998) 595-597 (*Chrupcala, Lesław Daniel*); Bib. 79 (1998) 579-582 (*Talbert, Charles H.*).

4873 **Hendrickx, Herman** The third gospel for the third world, 1: preface and infancy narrative (Luke 1:1-2:52). 1996 ⇒12,5035. ᴿJBL 117 (1998) 748-750 (*Legrand, Lucien*);

4874 The third gospel for the third world, 2B: ministry in Galilee. ColMn 1998, Liturgical vii; 329 pp. $20. 0-8146-5872-5.

4875 **Infante, Lorenzo** Sulle strade della gioia: con il vangelo secondo Luca. Vivere da protagonisti 10: Mi ²1998, Paoline 195 pp. 88-315-1506-3.

4876 *Meagher, P.M.* The gospel of Luke. VJTR 62 (1998) 339-348.

4877 **Meynet, Roland** L'évangile selon saint Luc: analyse rhétorique. 1988 ⇒4,5126...6,5349. ᴿETR 73 (1998) 259-260 (*Corsani, Bruno*);

4878 Czytaliście św. Łukasza?: Przewodnik, który prowadzi do Spotkania. Kraków 1998, WAM 262 pp. **P.**

4879 **Schürmann, Heinz** Il vangelo di Luca, 2/1: 9,51-11,54. ᵀGatti, Vincenzo. Comm. Teol. del NT III/2.1: Brescia 1998, Paideia 515 pp. L98.000. 88-394-0560-7.

4880 *Terra, João E. Martins* O caminho de Lucas. RCB 85-86 (1998) 5-40.

F7.4 *Lucae themata*—Luke's Gospel, topics

4881 **Ayuch, Daniel Alberto** Sozialgerechtes Handeln als Ausdruck einer eschatologischen Vision: zum Zusammenhang von Offenbarungswissen und Sozialethik in den lukanischen Schlüsselreden. MThA 54: Altenberge 1998, Oros xii; 230 pp. 3-89375-166-1.

4882 *Bedenbender, Andreas* Geschlechtertausch und Geschlechtsverlust (Lk 24,10 und Pred 7,27): zur Funktion der Attribute "männlich" und "weiblich" im Lukasevangelium und im Prediger Salomo. TeKo 21 (1998) 17-34.

4883 *Bellinzoni, Arthur J.* The gospel of Luke in the second century CE ᶠTYSON J. 1998 ⇒120. 59-76.

4884 *Bidaut, Bernard* La figure de Moïse dans le troisième évangile. LV(L) 49 (1998) 37-51.

4885 **Bieberstein, Sabine** Verschwiegene Jüngerinnen—vergessene Zeuginnen: gebrochene Konzepte im Lukasevangelium. NTOA 38: Gö 1998, Vandenhoeck & R xii; 314 pp. DM113. 3-525-53938-X.

4886 *Borghi, Ernesto* La responsabilità della gioia: prospettive lucane per la vita di ogni essere umano. RTLu 3 (1998) 509-521.

4887 *Bosetti, Maria Elena* Luca evangelista della misericordia. Luca—alcuni percorsi. 1998 ⇒406. 67-83.

4888 **Buckwalter, H. Douglas** The character and purpose of Luke's christology. MSSNTS 89: 1996 ⇒12,5409; 13,5286. ᴿEvQ 70 (1998) 268-270 (*Stenschke, Christoph W.*); JThS 49 (1998) 743-746 (*Franklin, E.*).

4889 **Chrupcała, Lesław** Il regno opera della Trinità nel vangelo di Luca. Foreword *Forte, Bruno*. ASBF 45: J 1998, Franciscan Printing Press 276 pp. $25.

4890 **Conzelmann, Hans** Il centro del tempo: la teologia di Luca. 1996 ⇒12,5052. ᴿCivCatt 149/2 (1998) 622-623 (*Scaiola, D.*).

4891 *Crawford, Timothy G.* Taking the promised land, leaving the promised land: Luke's use of Joshua for a christian foundation story. RExp 95 (1998) 251-261.

4892 **Darr, John A.** Herod the Fox: audience criticism and Lukan characterization. JSNT.S 163: Shf 1998, Academic 241 pp. £37.50. 1-85075-883-2.

4893 **Doble, Peter** The paradox of salvation: Luke's theology of the cross. MSSNTS 87: 1996 ⇒12,5054. ᴿEvQ 70 (1998) 71-72 (*Agan, C.J.*); BL 117 (1998) 140-142 (*Green, Joel B.*).

4894 *Farina, Marcella* Lasciarsi aprire il cuore: un umanesimo nella coniugazione di femminile e maschile. Theotokos 63 (1998) 85-101.

4895 *Giurisato, G.* Come Luca struttura il viaggio e le altre parti del suo vangelo: una composizione paradigmatica: 12,13-34.35-48; 16,1-18.19-31. RivBib 46 (1998) 419-484.

4896 ᴱGómez-Acebo, Isabel; Navarro Puerto, Mercedes; Pikaza Ibarrondo, Xabier Relectura de Lucas. En clave de mujer...: [Bilbao] 1998, Desclée de Brouwer 238 pp. 84-330-1282-7.

4897 **Gray, Tim** Mission of the Messiah. Steubenville, OH 1998, Emmaus Road 149 pp. $16.

4898 **Harrington, Wilfred John** Luke: gracious theologian: the Jesus of Luke. Black Rock 1997, Columba 119 pp. 1-85607-206-1.

4899 *Hughes, Tomaz* A refundação da vida religiosa à luz de Lucas. Convergência 33 (1998) 615-620.

4900   *Kemdirim, Protus O.* The Lucan and African traditional attitude to the poor: implications for the African church. West African Journal of Ecclesial Studies 4 (1998) 68-79.

4901   **Knight, Jonathan** Luke's gospel. NT Readings: L 1998, Routledge viii; 232 pp. £15. [R]RRT (1998/4) 101-102 (*Goodacre, Mark*).

4902   **Kügler, Joachim** Pharao und Christus?: religionsgeschichtliche Untersuchung zur Frage einer Verbindung zwischen altägyptischer Königstheologie und neutestamentlicher: Christologie im Lukasevangelium. BBB 113: 1997 ⇒13,5304. [R]BZ 42 (1998) 269-270 (*Radl, Walter*) [Acts 13,32-33].

4903   [T]**Lienhard, Joseph** ORIGEN: homilies on Luke. FaCh 94: 1996 ⇒12,5060; 13,5306. [R]EvQ 70 (1998) 279-281 (*Bostock, Gerald*).

4904   **Martini, Carlo Maria** El itinerario del discípulo: a la luz del evangelio de Lucas. 1997 ⇒13,5308. [R]Seminarios 44 (1998) 505-506 (*Morata, Alonso*).

4905   **Mazzocchi, L.; Forzani, J.** Il vangelo secondo Luca e lo Zen. 1997 ⇒13,5309. [R]Il Regno 43 (1998) 677-680 (*Favaro, Gaetano*).

4906   **Meynet, Roland** La preghiera nel vangelo di Luca. CivCatt 149/3 1998, 379-392.

4907   *Nickelsburg, George W.E.* Revisiting the rich and the poor in 1 Enoch 92-105 and the gospel according to Luke. SBL.SP part 2. SBL.SPS 37: 1998 ⇒402. 579-605.

4908   *Okorie, A.M.* The function of the parables in the narrative of Luke. RevBib 60 (1998) 183-193.

4909   **Paoli, A.** La raíz del hombre: meditaciones sobre el evangelio de Lucas. San Lorenzo del Escorial 1998, Escurialenses 300 pp.

4910   *Phillips, Thomas E.* Subtlety as a literary technique in Luke's characterization of Jews and Judaism. [F]TYSON J. 1998 ⇒120. 313-326.

4911   **Reid, Barbara E.** Choosing the better part?: women in the gospel of Luke. 1996 ⇒12,5070. [R]CBQ 60 (1998) 170-171 (*Thompson, Mary R.*); JBL 117 (1998) 539-541 (*Karris, Robert J.*).

4912   **Seland, Torrey** Establishment violence in PHILO and Luke: a study of non-conformity to the Torah and Jewish vigilante reactions. Bibl.Interp. 15: 1995 ⇒11/1,3649... 13,5319. [R]JQR 88 (1998) 372-374 (*Winston, David*).

4913   *Soubigou, Louis* A utilização litúrgica e pastoral da vida pública de Jesus segundo Lucas (para o terceiro ano: ano C). RCB 85-86 (1998) 151-158.

4914   *Tannehill, Robert C.* Freedom and responsibility in scripture interpretation, with application to Luke. [F]TYSON J. 1998 ⇒120. 265-278.

4915   **Tucker, Jeffrey T.** Example stories: perspectives on four parables in the gospel of Luke. JSNT.S 162: Shf 1998, Academic 444 pp. £55. 1-85075-897-2.

4916   *Walker, William O.* Acts and the Pauline corpus revisited: Peter's speech at the Jerusalem Conference. [F]TYSON J. 1998 ⇒120. 77-86.

4917   **Wasserberg, Günter** Aus Israels Mitte—Heil für die Welt: eine narrativ-exegetische Studie zur Theologie des Lukas. BZNW 92: B 1998, de Gruyter xviii; 418 pp. 3-11-015864-7.

4918   *Weinrich, Michael* Das Geheimnis der Kirche nach dem Evangelisten Lukas: Bibelarbeit vor der Hauptversammlung des Reformierten Bundes in Emden am 12. Juni 1998. RKZ 139 (1998) 281-286.

4919   *Wolter, Michael* Die Juden und die Obrigkeit bei Lukas. [F]SCHRAGE, W. 1998 ⇒101. 277-290.

4920 *Wright, N.T.* Upstaging the emperor. BiRe 14/1 (1998) 17, 47.

F7.5 *Infantia, cantica*—**Magnificat, Benedictus: Luc. 1-3**

4921 **Adams, James Wallis** An analysis of the historicity of the Jesus birth narrative in Luke and its place in the christology of the Third Gospel. DMid-America Baptist Theol. Sem 1998, 199 pp.

4922 *Berliet, Gérard* Zacharie et Syméon face à l'action de l'Esprit. Vie Chrétienne 435 (1998) 2-7.

4923 **Boismard, Marie-Émile** L'évangile de l'enfance (Luc 1-2) selon le Proto-Luc. EtB 35: 1997 ⇒13,5334. RThLZ 123 (1998) 380-381 (*Wiefel, Wolfgang*); ScEs 50 (1998) 377-380 (*D'Aragon, Jean-Louis*).

4924 *Cocchini, Francesca* Penetriamo le parole di Maria (II). Monastica 39 (1998) 15-29.

4925 *Cywinski, Eugênio* Historicidade do evangelho da infância segundo São Lucas. RCB 85-86 (1998) 95-104.

4926 *Flecha, José-Román* Zacarías, o el camino de la paz. EvV 40 (1998) 62-64.

4927 **Janssen, Claudia** Elisabet und Hanna: zwei widerständige alte Frauen in neutestamentlicher Zeit: eine sozialgeschichtliche Untersuchung. Mainz 1998, Grünewald 246 pp. 3-7867-2071-1.

4928 *Klein, Hans* Die Legitimation der Täufer- und der Jesusbewegung nach den Kindheitsgeschichten des Lukas. FPOKORNY, P. 1998 ⇒90. 208-217.

4929 *Kozar, Joseph Vlcek* Reading the opening chapter of Luke from a feminist perspective. Escaping Eden. BiSe 65: 1998 ⇒278. 53-68.

4930 *Laurini, Heládio C.* Esquema exegético-litúrgico de Lc 1-2. RCB 85-86 (1998) 127-144.

4931 *Shuler, Philip L.* The rhetorical character of Luke 1-2. FTYSON J. 1998 ⇒120. 173-189.

4932 *Terra, João E. Martins* A Ave-Maria a luz do Antigo Testamento;
4933 Análise do texto bíblico da Ave-Maria;
4934 Exegese do texto bíblico da Ave-Maria;
4935 O evangelho da infância (Lc 1-2) à luz do AT. RCB 85-86 (1998) 81-86/61-66/67-80/41-59.

4936 *Valentini, Alberto* I cantici del vangelo dell'infanzia. Luca—alcuni percorsi. 1998 ⇒406. 19-38.

4937 *Wolter, Michael* Wann wurde Maria schwanger?: eine vernachlässigte Frage und ihre Bedeutung für das Verständnis der lukanischen Vorgeschichte (Lk 1-2). FHOFFMANN, P., Von Jesus. BZNW 93: 1998 ⇒43. 405-422.

4938 *Lombardi, Michela* Convenzioni storiografiche, moduli retorici greco-ellenistici e tradizione giudaico-cristiana nel prologo del vangelo di Luca. Orph. 19-20 (1998-1999) 326-362.

4939 *Schürmann, Heinz* Evangelienschrift und kirchliche Unterweisung; die repräsentative Funktion der Schrift nach Lk 1,1-4. Gesammelte Beiträge. 1998 <1962> ⇒197. 91-118.

4940 **Muñoz Nieto, Jesús María** Tiempo de anuncio: estudio de Lc 1,5-2,52. 1994 ⇒10,4970... 12,5084. 323 pp. REstB 56 (1998) 282-284 (*González Fraile, A.*).

4941 *Gnuse, Robert* The temple theophanies of Jaddus, Hyrcanus, and Zechariah. Bib. 79 (1998) 457-472 [Lk 1,5-23].
4942 *Zbik, Francisco* 'O Espírito Santo descerá sobre ti e a virtude do Altíssimo te cobrirá com a sua sombra' (Lc 1,35). RCB 85-86 (1998) 105-112.

4943 *Gherardini, Brunero* Maria nel commento di LUTERO al 'Magnificat'. RivLi 85 (1998) 315-325.
4944 ᴱ**Valentini, Alberto** Il canto della Figlia di Sion (Lc 1,46-55). Theotokos 5,2: R 1998, Monfortane 391-784.
4945 *Terra, João E. Martins* O Magnificat. RCB 85-86 (1998) 87-93.
4946 *Zbik, Francisco* 'Magnificat': o hino da rainha do mundo. RCB 85-86 (1998) 113-121.
4947 *Largo Domínguez, Pablo* El Magnificat: una reflexión libre en clave eclesial. EphMar 48 (1998) 365-374.
4948 *Aparicio Rodríguez, Ángel* El 'Magnificat' desde la humillación. EphMar 48 (1998) 335-363.
4949 *Schreiner, Josef* Magnificat: Gebet aus Gottes Wort. ThGl 88 (1998) 13-25.
4950 *Palumbieri, S.* Un 'Magnificat' per il terzo millennio: dimensione antropologica del cantico. Mi 1998, Paoline 201 pp.
4951 **Oliveira, Lourival Gonçalves de** Magnificat (o louvor de Maria). Petrópolis 1998, Vozes 79 pp.

4952 *Mussies, Gerard* The date of Jesus' birth in Jewish and Samaritan sources. JSJ 29 (1998) 416-437 [Lk 2,1-5].
4953 *Winandy, Jacques* Du Kataluma à la crèche. NTS 44 (1998) 618-622 [Lk 2,7].
4954 *Derrett, J. Duncan M.* ἀνθρώποι εὐδοκίας (Lk 2:14b). FgNT 11 (1998) 101-106.
4955 *Koet, Bart J.* Holy place and Hannah's prayer: a comparison of LAB 50-51 and Luke 2:22-39 à propos 1 Samuel 1-2. Sanctity of time. 1998 ⇒303. 45-72.

4956 *Carfagna, Antonella* Lectio divina di Lc 2,34-35 sullo sfondo della Presentazione al tempio;
4957 *Evenou, Jean* Il vangelo della Presentazione del Signore nelle liturgie diocesane francesi (XVII-XIX sec.);
4958 *Rossé, Gérard* Approcci esegetici al testo della presentazione (Lc 2,22-40). Theotokos 63 (1998) 141-165/167-181/17-30.
4959 *LaGrand, James* Luke's portrait of Simeon (Luke 2:25-35): aged saint or hesitant terrorist?. ᶠSNYDER, G. 1998 ⇒104. 175-185.
4960 *Ruspi, Walther* Catechesi su Lc 2,34-35. Theotokos 63 (1998) 121-140.
4961 *Serra, Aristide* La profezia di Simeone (Lc 2,34-35) nella tradizione greco-latina dei secoli II-XIV: contenuti e proposte. Mar. 60 (1998) 239-384.
4962 *Pierini, Franco* Antiche riletture patristiche di Lc 2,34-35;
4963 *Curtoni, Mariarosa Filzi* Maria di fronte alle parole di Simeone: lettura psicologica [Lk 2,34-35]. Theotokos 63 (1998) 31-38/103-119.
4964 *Levebvre, Philippe* Anne de la tribu d'Asher: le bonheur d'une femme (Lc 2,36-38). SémBib 91 (1998) 3-32.

4965   *Chakoian, Karen* Luke 2:41-52. Interp. 52 (1998) 185-190.
4966   *Kirk, Alan* Upbraiding wisdom: John's speech and the beginning of Q
       (Q 3:7-9, 16-17). NT 40 (1998) 1-16.
4967   *Stricher, Joseph* Avec la puissance de l'Esprit [Lk 3,23-4,15]. Vie
       Chrétienne 430 (1998) 22-26.

F7.6 Evangelium Lucae 4,1...

4968   *Mattam, Zacharias* The temptations of Christ (Lk 4:1-13). FHERIBAN
       J. 1998 ⇒41. 197-212.
4969   *Aldebert, Heiner* Bibliodrama religionspädagogisch: mit einer 11.
       Klasse dem Teufel in der Wüste (Lk. 4,1-13) standhalten. EvErz 50
       (1998) 214-234.
4970   *Stricher, Joseph* Dans la synagogue de Nazareth. Vie chrétienne 431
       (1998) 2-5 [Lk 4,14-22].
4971   *Kerstiens, Ferdinand* Das Kapital bedienen ...?: zu Apg 4,32-35 und
       Lk 4,16-23. Diak. 29 (1998) 64-66.
4972   *Magnante, Antonio* Jésus, missionnaire et évangélisateur. Omnis
       Terra 37 (1998) 155-159 [Lk 4,16-30].
4973   *Sloan, Robert B.* The favorable year of the lord: an abbreviation and
       addenda. MSummers, R. 1998 ⇒115. 265-279 [Lk 4,18-19].
4974   *Vardaman, E. Jerry* Progress in the study of the sabbatical/jubilee
       cycle since Sloan. MSummers, R. 1998 ⇒115. 281-312 [Lk 4,18-19].
4975   *Breytenbach, A.P.B.* 'Seun van Josef' uit 'n Noord-Israelitiese per-
       spektief. OTEs 11 (1998) 415-426 [Lk 4,22].
4976   *Ashton, Mark* Luke 4:31-44: the voice of authority. Evangel 16
       (1998) 70-73.
4977   *Batten, Alicia* Patience breeds wisdom: Q 6:40 in context. CBQ 60
       (1998) 641-656.
4978   *Lohse, Eduard* Vom Hausbau 2. Du bist eingeladen. 1998 ⇒4434.
       53-54 [Lk 6,47-49].
4979   *Dupont, Jacques* A ressurreição do moço de Naim (Lc 7,11-16).
       RCB 85-86 (1998) 145-149.
4980   *Grün, Anselm* Die Heilung des Muttersohnes. LS 49 (1998) 76-77
       [Lk 7,11-17].
4981   *Mantels, Helga* Von den spielenden Kindern 2. Du bist eingeladen.
       1998 ⇒4434. 57-58 [Lk 7,31-35].
4982   *Hornsby, Teresa J.* Why is she crying?: a feminist interpretation of
       Luke 7.36-50. Escaping Eden. BiSe 65: 1998 ⇒278. 91-103.
4983   *Kilgallen, John J.* Forgiveness of sins (Luke 7:36-50). NT 40 (1998)
       105-116.
4984   *Hahne, Barbara* Vom Umgang mit Schulden. Du bist eingeladen.
       1998 ⇒4434. 107-109 [Lk 7,36-50].
4985   *Applegate, Judith K.* 'And she wet his feet with her tears': a feminist
       interpretation of Luke 7.36-50. Escaping Eden. BiSe 65: 1998 ⇒278.
       69-90.
4986   *Ritt, Hubert* Vom Sämann 4. Du bist eingeladen. 1998 ⇒4434. 23-25
       [Lk 8,4-15].
4987   *Schürmann, Heinz* Lukanische Reflexionen über die Wortverkündi-
       gung in Lk 8,4-21. Gesammelte Beiträge. 1998 <1967> ⇒197. 119-
       135.

4988 *Miller, Robert J.* Source criticism and the limits of certainty: the Lukan transfiguration story as a test case. EThL 74 (1998) 127-144 [Lk 9,28-36].

F7.7 *Iter hierosolymitanum—Lc 9,51...*—**Jerusalem journey**

4989 *Eluvathingal, Frederick* Jesus' travel narrative according to Luke—part II. BiBh 24 (1998) 103-113.
4990 **Moessner, David P.** Lord of the banquet: the literary and theological significance of the Lukan travel narrative. Harrisburg, Pennsylvania 1998, Trinity xxxvi; 372 pp. 1-56338-242-3.
4991 ᶠ**Zuurmond, Rochus** YHWH—Kyrios—antitheism or: the power of the word. ᴱ*Deurloo, Karel A.; Diebner, Bernd Jörg.* DBAT.B 14: 1996 ⇒12,109. ᴿDBAT 29 (1998) 300-301 (*Diebner, B.J.*).

4992 *Plessis, Isak J. du* The church before the church—focussing on Luke 10:1-24. Neotest. 32 (1998) 343-366.
4993 *González Buelta, Benjamin* 'No llevéis alforjas para el camino'. Sal Ter 86 (1998) 711-719 [Lk 10,4].
4994 *Orth, Gerhart* Vom barmherzigen Samariter. Du bist eingeladen. 1998 ⇒4434. 110-112 [Lk 10,25-37].
4995 *Soriano Arias, Fernando* Parabola del buen neosamaritano (Lc 10,25-37). Alternativas 5 (1998) 267-268.
4996 *Saldarini, Anthony J.* Feeling love and doing love. BiRe 14/6 (1998) 16, 47 [Lk 10,27].
4997 *Reid, Barbara E.* Puzzling passages: Luke 10:29-37. BiTod 36 (1998) 387-388.
4998 *Vesco, Jean-Luc* Le samaritain qui s'est fait prochain. VS 728 (1998) 391-399 [Lk 10,29-37].
4999 *Gourgues, Michel* The priest, the Levite, and the Samaritan revisited: a critical note on Luke 10:31-35. JBL 117 (1998) 709-713.
5000 *Snijders, Bert* Een zuster zit bij de broeders. ITBT 6/3 (1998) 22-24 [Lk 10,38-42].
5001 *Rakoczy, Susan* Martha and Mary: sorting out the dilemma. Studies in Spirituality 8 (1998) 58-80 [Lk 10,38-42].
5002 *Ellis, E.E.; Ockinga, B.G.* The tradition history of the Mary-Martha pericope in Luke (10:38-42). ᶠJUDGE E. 1998 ⇒47. 93-97.
5003 *Collins, John N.* Did Luke intend a disservice to women in the Martha and Mary story?. BTB 28 (1998) 104-111.
5004 *Barbi, Augusto* Marta e Maria di fronte al Signore (Lc 10,38-42). Com(I) 159 (1998) 13-24.
5005 *Ellis, Pamela* The better part. Month 31 (1998) 58-61 [Lk 10,38-42].

5006 *Robbins, Vernon K.* From enthymeme to theology in Luke 11:1-13. ᶠTYSON J. (1998) 191-214.
5007 *Mantels, Helga* Vom bittenden Freund. Du bist eingeladen. 1998 ⇒4434. 113-114 [Lk 11,5-8].
5008 *Van der Horst, Pieter* "The finger of God": miscellaneous notes on Luke 11:20 and its Umwelt. Id., Hellenism—Judaism—Christianity. 1998 ⇒Q6.5. 171-183.
5009 *Müller, Beda* Von der Rückkehr der bösen Geister 2. Du bist eingeladen. 1998 ⇒4434. 61-62 [Lk 11,24-26].

5010 *Mendham, P.M.* 'The yeast of the pharisees': rethinking a christian prejudice. ^FJUDGE E. 1998 ⇒47. 34-42 [Lk 12,1].

5011 *Hoffmann, Paul* Der Menschensohn in Lukas 12.8. NTS 44 (1998) 357-379.

5012 *Nuber, Anette* Vom törichten Reichen. Du bist eingeladen. 1998 ⇒4434. 115-116 [Lk 12,13-21].

5013 *Hasselhorn, Johannes* Vom wachsamen Hausherrn 2. Du bist eingeladen. 1998 ⇒4434. 75-76 [Lk 12,39-40].

5014 *Fletcher-Louis, Crispin H.T.* The gospel thief saying (Luke 12.39-40 and Matthew 24.43-44) reconsidered. ^FASHTON J. JSNT.S 153: 1998 ⇒6. 48-68.

5015 *Thoma, Clemens* Der treue und verlässliche Verwalter (Lk 12,42-44) im rabbinischen Zusammenhang. ^FVENETZ, H. 1998 ⇒122. 137-140.

5016 *Hillenbrand, Karl* Vom treuen und vom bösen Knecht 2. Du bist eingeladen. 1998 ⇒4434. 79-80 [Lk 12,42-48].

5017 *Gamba, Giuseppe Giovanni* Il detto di Gesù sul fuoco (Lc 12,49) e la persecuzione dei cristiani del 64 d.Cr. Sal. 60 (1998) 683-709.

5018 *Hirschler, Horst* Vom unfruchtbaren Feigenbaum. Du bist eingeladen. 1998 ⇒4434. 117-118 [Lk 13,6-9].

5019 *Bieberstein, Sabine* Aufrechte Frauen und das Reich Gottes: zum literarischen Zusammenhang von Lk 13,10-21. ^FVENETZ, H. 1998 ⇒122. 37-46.

5020 *Hirschler, Horst* Vom Senfkorn und vom Sauerteig 3. Du bist eingeladen. 1998 ⇒4434. 30-31 [Lk 13,18-21].

5021 *Falcke, Heino* Von der engen und von der verschlossenen Tür. Du bist eingeladen. 1998 ⇒4434. 119-121 [Lk 13,22-30].

5022 *Braun, Willi* Feasting and social rhetoric in Luke 14. 1995 ⇒11/1, 3741... 13,5441. ^RJThS 49 (1998) 229-233 (*Esler, Philip F.*).

5023 *Lemke-Seppälä, Marjatta* Vom rechten Platz. Du bist eingeladen. 1998 ⇒4434. 122-123 [Lk 14,7-11].

5024 *Hasselhorn, Johannes* Von den rechten Gästen. Du bist eingeladen. 1998 ⇒4434. 124-125 [Lk 14,12-14].

5025 *Krusche, Werner* Vom großen Abendmahl 2. Du bist eingeladen. 1998 ⇒4434. 70-72 [Lk 14,15-24].

5026 *Snodgrass, Klyne* Common life with Jesus: the parable of the banquet in Luke 14:16-24. ^FSNYDER, G. 1998 ⇒104. 186-201.

5027 *Krusche, Werner* Vom rechten Planen. Du bist eingeladen. 1998 ⇒4434. 126-128 [Lk 14,25-35].

5028 *Singer, Christophe* La difficulté d'être disciple: Luc 14/25-35. ETR 73 (1998) 21-36.

5029 *Martini, Carlo Maria* Il padre d'Israele. Studi Fatti Ricerche 83 (1998) 6-7. <Lettera pastorale 1998-1999, pp. 29-32 [Lk 15].

5030 **Basset, Lytta** La joie imprenable: pour une théologie de la prodigalité. 1996 ⇒12,5141. ^RRHPhR 78/1 (1998) 112-113 (*Pfrimmer, T.*) [Lk 15].

5031 *Münch-Labacher, Gudrun* Gleichnisauslegung in den Lukas-Homilien des CYRILL von Alexandrien—die Homilien zur Gleichnistrilogie in Lk 15. ThQ 178 (1998) 287-293.

5032 **Barreiro, Álvaro** A parábola do pai misericordioso. São Paulo 1998, Loyola 143 pp. 85-15-01844-6. ^RPerTeol 30 (1998) 461-462 (*Konings, Johan*) [Lk 15].

264   Elenchus of Biblica 14, 1998   [X. Opus Lucanum

5033 *Foerster, Jean-Luc-Marie* 'Un homme avait deux fils' (Luc 15): libres variations sur un chemin de mort et de résurrection. VS 726 (1998) 15-26.
5034 *Krusche, Werner* Vom verlorenen Schaf 2. Du bist eingeladen. 1998 ⇒4434. 65-66 [Lk 15,1-7]. ˙
5035 *Neuner, J.* Listen to the Spirit: "a man had two sons" (Lk 15:1f: 11-32). VJTR 62 (1998) 506-509.
5036 *Brutschek, Jutta* Von der suchenden Frau. Du bist eingeladen. 1998 ⇒4434. 129-130.
5037 *Pindel, Roman* Obraz ojca w przypowieści o synu marnotrawnym (Łk 15,11-32) [Das Bild des Vaters im Gleichnis vom verlorenen Sohn (Lk 15,11-32)]. ACra 30-31 (1998-1999) 261-273. **P**.
5038 *Brambilla, Franco Giulio* Ritornare al Padre: la difficile riconciliazione: commento a Lc 15,11-32. RCI 79 (1998) 726-744.
5039 *Serra, Aristide* La fuga e il ritorno del figlio prodigo (Lc 15,11-32): parabola del peccato e della conversione d'Israele?. ᶠMARTINI, C. RivBib.S 33: 1998 ⇒75. 233-250.
5040 *Krusche, Werner* Vom liebenden Vater. Du bist eingeladen. 1998 ⇒4434. 131-133 [Lk 15,11-32].
5041 *Alviti, Pietro* Un padre e due figli: rileggendo la parabola. Presenza Pastorale 68 (1998) 315-319 [Lk 15,11-32].
5042 *Brown, Colin* The parable of the rebellious son(s). SJTh 51 (1998) 391-405 [Lk 15,11-32].
5043 **Nouwen, Henri J.M.** The return of the Prodigal Son: a story of homecoming. Mumbai 1998, St Paul 143 pp. Rs50. 81-7109-363-9.
5044 *O'Meara, Robert* "Luring the crocus through the snow": the parable of the man who had two sons (Luke 15:11-32). ABR 46 (1998) 17-35.
5045 *Beilner, Wolfgang* Jézus példabeszédei: interpretációs megközelítések Lk 15,11-32 tükrében [Wege zur Auslegung der Gleichnisse Jesu anhand von Lk 15,11-32];
5046 *Rau, Eckhard* Jézus vitája a farizeusokkal a bűnösök megszólítása miatt (Lk 15,11-32 és Lk 18,10-14a) mint a történeti Jézus szavai [Jesu Auseinandersetzung mit Pharisäern über seine Zuwendung zu Sünderinnen und Sündern Lk 15,11-32 und 18,10-14a als Worte des historischen Jesus]. Példabeszédek. 1998 ⇒372. 7-19/119-142. **Hungarian.**

5047 *Schober, Theodor* Vom unehrlichen Verwalter. Du bist eingeladen. 1998 ⇒4434. 134-136 [Lk 16,1-9].
5048 *Gagnon, Robert A.J.* A second look at two Lukan parables: reflections on the unjust steward and the good Samaritan. HBT 20 (1998) 1-11 [Lk 16,01-09; 10,29-37].
5049 *Burchard, Christoph* Zu Lukas 16,16. Studien zur Theologie. WUNT 107: 1998 <1984> ⇒140. 119-125.
5050 *Bauckham, Richard* The rich man and Lazarus: the parable and the parallels. Fate of the dead. NT.S 93: 1998 <1991> ⇒132. 97-118.
5051 *Merklein, Helmut* Vom reichen Mann und armen Lazarus. Du bist eingeladen. 1998 ⇒4434. 137-139 [Lk 16,19-31].

5052 *Wehr, Lothar* Die Rettung der "Kleinen": der Auftrag der Jüngergemeinde nach Lk 17,1-10. ᶠWETTER F. 1998 ⇒124. 65-83.
5053 *Kindt-Siegwalt, Irmgard* Vom unnützen Sklaven. Du bist eingeladen. 1998 ⇒4434. 140-141 [Lk 17,7-10].

5054 *Schenker, Adrian* Sind wir unnütze oder nichtsnutzige oder unbeholfene, hilflose Knechte?: die Bedeutung von ἀχρεῖος in Luk 17,10. ᶠVENETZ, H.. 1998 ⇒122. 141-146.
5055 *Neirynck, Frans* Saving/losing one's life: Luke 17,33 (Q?) and Mark 8,35. ᶠHOFFMANN, P., Von Jesus. BZNW 93: 1998 ⇒43. 295-318.

5056 *Weidauer, Ruth* Vom trägen Richter und der Witwe. Du bist eingeladen. 1998 ⇒4434. 142-143 [Lk 18,1-8].
5057 *Kilgallen, John J.* The importance of the redactor in Luke 18,9-14. Bib. 79 (1998) 69-75.
5058 *Weidauer, Ruth* Vom Pharisäer und Zöllner. Du bist eingeladen. 1998 ⇒4434. 144-145 [Lk 18,9-14].
5059 *Keresztes, Pál* Példabeszéd a farizeusról és a vámosról (Lk 18,9-14). Példabeszédek. 1998 ⇒372. 69-71. **Hungarian.**
5060 *Kostka, Ulrike* Der Patient 'Mensch' im Spiegel biblischer Texte: das biblische Paradigma 'Krankheit und Heilung' am Beispiel der Heilung des Blinden bei Jericho (Lk 18,35-43). ᶠLÖNING, K. 1998 ⇒66. 69-82.
5061 *Mattam, Zacharias* The cure of the blind man of Jericho (Lk 18,35-43): a kerygmatic, patristic and theological study. BiBh 24 (1998) 17-26.

5062 *Bauer, Uwe F.W.* Der wilde Feigenbaum von Jericho (Lk 19,4[1-10]). DBAT 29 (1998) 189-198.
5063 *Busse, Ulrich* Dechiffrierung eines lukanischen Schlüsseltextes (Lk 19,11-27). ᶠHOFFMANN, P., Von Jesus. BZNW 93: 1998 ⇒43. 423-441.
5064 *Hasselhorn, Jost* Vom anvertrauten Gut 2. Du bist eingeladen. 1998 ⇒4434. 84-86 [Lk 19,11-27].
5065 *Rossé, Gerard* La parabola delle mine (Lc 19,11-28). PSV 37 (1998) 131-142.
5066 *Freckmann, Klaus* Von mörderischen Weingärtnern 3 [Lk 20,9-18];
5067 *Lutz, Berthold* Vom Feigenbaum 3 [Lk 21,29-33]. Du bist eingeladen. 1998 ⇒4434. 38-40/45-46.

F7.8 **Passio—***Lc 22...*

5068 **Matson, Mark Alan** In dialogue with another gospel?: the influence of the Fourth Gospel on the passion narrative of the Gospel of Luke. ᴰDuke 1998, 490 pp.

5069 *Manzi, Franco* I paradossi della passione secondo Luca (Lc 22-23). Luca—alcuni percorsi. 1998 ⇒406. 85-113.
5070 *Busey, Robert S.* Luke 22:7-23. Interp. 52 (1998) 70-73.
5071 **Tremolada, Pierantonio** "E fu annoverato fra iniqui": prospettive di lettura della Passione secondo Luca alla luce di Lc 22,37 (Is 53,12d). AnBib 137: 1997 ⇒13,5485. ᴿCivCatt 149/3 (1998) 205-207 (*Scaiola, D.*).
5072 *Tremolada, Pierantonio* Prospettive di lettura della Passione secondo Luca alla luce di Lc 22,37 (Is 53,12d). RstB 10/1-2 (1998) 317-327.
5073 **Harrington, Jay M.** The Lukan passion narrative: the Markan material in Lk 22,54-23,25. ᴰLeuven 1998, ᴰ*Neirynck, F.* v; 660 pp.

5074 *Schlosser, Jacques* La comparution de Jésus devant Pilate d'après Lc 23,1-25. Procès de Jésus. 1998 ⇒392. 53-73.
5075 *Ehman, John W.* Luke 23:1-49. Interp. 52 (1998) 74-76.
5076 *Hoover, Roy W.* Selected special Lukan material in the passion narrative: Luke 23:33-43,47b-49. FORUM 1 (1998) 119-127.
5077 *Manicardi, Ermenegildo* L'ultima parola di Gesù secondo Luca e il racconto della morte di Stefano in Atti. ᶠMARTINI, C. RivBib.S 33: 1998 ⇒75. 251-270 [Lk 23,46; Acts 7,58-8,01].
5078 *Barbi, Augusto* Il motivo dominante dei racconti pasquali (Lc 24): i fatti e la parola. Luca—alcuni percorsi. 1998 ⇒406. 115-136.
5079 *Magnante, Antonio* La misión como testimonio: Lucas 24. Omnis Terra 30 (1998) 326-330.
5080 *Grappe, Christian* Au croisement des lectures et aux origines du repas communautaire: le récit des pèlerins d'Emmaüs: Luc 24/13-35. ETR 73 (1998) 491-501.

F8.1 *Actus Apostolorum*, **Acts**—*text, commentary, topics*

5081 ᴱ**Ammassari, Antonio** Gli Atti del Cristo risorto: note di commento sulla struttura letteraria e le lezioni degli 'Atti degli Apostoli' nella colonna latina del 'Bezae Codex Cantabrigiensis'. Città del Vaticano 1998, Libreria Editrice Vaticana 117 pp.
5082 **Barrett, Charles Kingsley** A critical and exegetical commentary on the Acts of the Apostles, 2: introduction and commentary on Acts XV-XXVIII. ICC: E 1998, Clark cxx; 695-1272 pp. £40. 0-567-08542-2.
5083 ᴱ**Bauckham, Richard** The book of Acts in its Palestinian setting. 1995 ⇒11/1,3784... 13,5500. ᴿHeyJ 39 (1998) 74-75 (*McNamara, Martin*).
5084 **Bruce, Frederick Fyvie** Hechos de los Apóstoles: introducción, comentario y notas. BA 1998, Nueva Creación 596 pp. 0-8028-0949-9.
5085 **Fernando, Ajith** Acts. NIV application commentary: GR 1998, Zondervan 656 pp. 0-310-49410-9.
5086 **Fitzmyer, Joseph A.** The Acts of the Apostles: a new translation with introduction and commentary. AncB 31: NY 1998, Doubleday xxxiv; 830 pp. $45. 0-385-49020-8.
5087 **Jervell, Jacob Stephan** Die Apostelgeschichte. KEK 3: Gö 1998, Vandenhoeck & R 635 pp. DM198. 3-525-51627-4.
5088 **Leonardi, Giovanni** Atti degli Apostoli. Sussidi biblici 61: Reggio Emilia 1998, San Lorenzo 210 pp. L23.000 + 20.000. 88-8071-0788.
5089 **Maggioni, Bruno; Bagni, Arcangelo** Atti degli Apostoli. Vicenza 1998, Istituto San Gaetano 351 pp. L18.000. 88-86833-27-X.
5090 **Nielsen, Jan T.** Handelingen I: een praktische bijbelverklaring. Tekst & Toelichting: Kampen 1998, Kok 175 pp. ƒ35. 90-242-9351-0.
5091 *Rius-Camps, Josep* Las variantes de la recensión occidental de los Hechos de los apostoles (X) (Hch 4,32-5,16). FgNT 11 (1998) 107-122.
5092 **Rossé, Gérard** Atti degli Apostoli: commento esegetico e teologico. R 1998, Città N 893 pp. L110.000. 88-311-3622-4.
5093 ᴱ**Swanson, Reuben J.** New Testament Greek manuscripts: variant readings arranged in horizontal lines against Codex Vaticanus: the Acts of the Apostles. Shf 1998, Academic xxvii; 513 pp. $40. 0-86585-055-0.

5094 **Talbert, Charles H.** Reading Acts: a literary and theological commentary on the Acts of the Apostles. 1997 ⇒13,5541. ^{R}JR 78 (1998) 669-670 (*Mount, Christopher*).

5095 **Taylor, Justin** Les Actes des deux apôtres, 6: commentaire historique (Act. 18,23-28,31). EtB 30: 1996 ⇒12,5215; 13,5543. ^{R}CBQ 60 (1998) 383-385 (*Rogers, Patrick*).

5096 **Walaskay, Paul W.** Acts. Westminster Bible Companion: LVL 1998, Westminster xii; 250 pp. $20. 0-664-25261-3.

5097 **Witherington III, Ben** The Acts of the Apostles: a socio-rhetorical commentary. GR 1998, Eerdmans xlviii; 875 pp. $50. 0-8028-4501-0. ^{R}AsbTJ 53 (1998) 96-97 (*Marshall, I. Howard*).

5098 *Alexander, Loveday* Fact, fiction and the genre of Acts. NTS 44 (1998) 380-399;

5099 Marathon or Jericho?: reading Acts in dialogue with biblical and Greek historiography. Auguries. JSOT.S 269: 1998 ⇒225. 92-125.

5100 *Barbieri, Edoardo* Domenico CAVALCA volgarizzatore degli 'Actus Apostolorum'. La bibbia in italiano. 1998 ⇒390. 291-328.

5101 *Barr, George K.* Significant scale changes in the gospels and Acts. IBSt 20 (1998) 75-91.

5102 *Bendemann, Reinhard von* Paulus und Israel in der Apostelgeschichte des Lukas. ^{F}SCHRAGE, W. 1998 ⇒101. 291-303.

5103 *Betori, Giuseppe* Confermare le chiese con la parola dell'esortazione: ἐπιστηρίζειν nel libro degli Atti. ^{F}MARTINI, C. RivBib.S 33: 1998 ⇒75. 345-356.

5104 *Biguzzi, G.* Angeli e demoni negli Atti degli Apostoli. Angeli e demoni. 1998 ⇒375. 169-193.

5105 *Bizetti, Paolo; Mangoni, Beatrice Durante* Le comunità cristiane nel libro degli Atti. PaVi 43 (1998) 47-48.

5106 *Black, C. Clifton* John Mark in the Acts of the Apostles. ^{F}TYSON J. 1998 ⇒120. 101-120.

5107 *Blanco Pacheco, Severiano* María y el Espíritu en los Hechos de los Apóstoles. EphMar 48 (1998) 223-230.

5108 *Bolyki, János* The theological tendency of the Bezaean text of the book of Acts. ^{F}POKORNÝ, P. 1998 ⇒90. 23-32.

5109 **Bossuyt, Philippe** L'Esprit en Actes: lire les Actes des Apôtres. Le livre et rouleau 3: Bru 1998, Lessius 174 pp. 2-87299-072-0.

5110 **Bossuyt, Philippe; Radermakers, Jean** Témoins de la parole de la grâce: Actes des Apôtres 1, Texte, 2: lecture continue. IET 16: 1995 ⇒11/1,3786; 12,5183. ^{R}Gr. 79 (1998) 571-573 (*Farahian, Edmond*).

5111 *Bottino, Adriana* La testimonianza nel libro degli Atti. ^{F}MARTINI, C. RivBib.S 33: 1998 ⇒75. 321-343.

5112 *Casalegno, Alberto* 'O Espírito disse a Filipe"—reflexões sobre o Espírito nos Atos dos Apóstolos a partir de 8,26-40. PerTeol 30 (1998) 37-56.

5113 *Chance, J. Bradley* Divine prognostications and the movement of story: an intertextual exploration of XENOPHON's Ephesian Tale and the Acts of the Apostles. Ancient fiction. 1998 ⇒1118. 219-234.

5114 *Couto, António* O Espirito Santo protagonista da missão nos Actos. Igreja e Missão 50 (1998) 373-392.

5115 *Delobel, J.* The "Apostolic Decree" in recent research on the "Western" text of Acts. ^{F}POKORNÝ, P. 1998 ⇒90. 67-81.

5116   *Dunn, James D.G.* κύριος in Acts. The Christ and the Spirit, 1: christology. 1998 ⇒148. 241-253.
5117   *Ferrari, Pier Luigi* Gesù interprete delle scritture negli Atti degli Apostoli. PaVi 43 (1998) 42-46.
5118   *Fitzmyer, Joseph A.* The designations of christians in Acts and their significance. To advance the gospel. 1998 <1989> ⇒150. 314-331.
5119   *Gebauer, Roland* Mission und Zeugnis: zum Verhältnis von missionarischer Wirksamkeit und Zeugenschaft in der Apostelgeschichte. NT 40 (1998) 54-72.
5120   *Green, Joel B.* "Witnesses of his resurrection": resurrection, salvation, discipleship, and mission in the Acts of the Apostles. Life in the face of death. 1998 ⇒252. 227-246.
5121   **Hillier, Richard** ARATOR on the Acts of the Apostles. 1993 ⇒9, 5292: 10,5067. [R]Spec. 73 (1998) 535-537 (*D'Angelo, Mary Rose*).
5122   **Jervell, Jacob Stephan** The theology of the Acts of the Apostles. 1996 ⇒12,5193. [R]EvQ 70 (1998) 75-77 (*Marshall, I. Howard*); JBL 117 (1998) 147-149 (*Tannehill, Robert C.*).
5123   **Klauck, Hans-Josef** Magie und Heidentum in der Apostelgeschichte des Lukas. SBS 167: 1996 ⇒12,5194. [R]NT 40 (1998) 395-396 (*Stenschke, Christoph*); ThGl 88 (1998) 115-116 (*Backhaus, Knut*).
5124   **Lentz, John Clayton** Le portrait de Paul selon Luc dans les Actes des Apôtres. LeDiv 172: P 1998, Cerf 261 pp. FF180. 2-204-058440.
5125   *Marguerat, Daniel* Voyages et voyageurs dans le livre des Actes et la culture gréco-romaine. RHPhR 78 (1998) 33-59.
5126   [E]**Marshall, I. Howard; Peterson, David** Witness to the gospel: the theology of Acts. GR 1998, Eerdmans xvi; 610 pp. $45. 0-8028-4435-9.
5127   *Moule, C.F.D.* The christology of Acts. Forgiveness. 1998 [1966] ⇒180. 51-80.
5128   **Nodet, Etienne; Taylor, Justin** Essai sur les origines du christianisme. 1997 ⇒13,5527. [R]RSR 86 (1998) 437-440 (*Guillet, Jacques*).
5129   *O'Loughlin, Thomas* Maps and Acts: a problem in carthography and exegesis. PIBA 21 (1998) 33-61.
5130   [E]**Orsatti, Mauro** Atti degli Apostoli 2: la chiesa alla prova. PaVi 43 (1998) 1-46.
5131   *Panimolle, Salvatore A.* La fede negli Atti degli apostoli. La fede nella bibbia. DSBP 21: 1998 ⇒224. 164-207.
5132   **Pao, David Wei Chun** Acts and the Isaianic new exodus. [D]Harvard 1998, 338 pp.
5133   *Paulson, Steve* Theological exegesis: lessons from Acts for the Easter season. Pro Ecclesia 7 (1998) 91-103.
5134   *Plümacher, Eckhard* τερατεια: Fiktion und Wunder in der hellenistisch-römischen Geschichtsschreibung und in der Apostelgeschichte. ZNW 89 (1998) 66-90.
5135   *Read-Heimerdinger, Jenny* Barnabas in Acts: a study of his role in the text of Codex Bezae. JSNT 72 (1998) 23-66.
5136   **Reimer, Ivoni Richter** Women in the Acts of the Apostles: a feminist liberation perspective. 1995 ⇒11/1,3816; 13,5535. [R]New Theology Review 11/1 (1998) 110-111 (*Reid, Barbara E.*).
5137   *Reinbold, Wolfgang* Die "Hellenisten": kritische Anmerkungen zu einem Fachbegriff der neutestamentlichen Wissenschaft. BZ 42 (1998) 96-102.
5138   *Richard, Pablo* El espíritu Santo y la misión en los orígenes de la iglesia según los Hechos de los Apóstoles. MisEx(M) 163 (1998) 5-17.

5139   *Rossé, Gérard* Le sezioni-noi degli Atti. [F]MARTINI, C. RivBib.S 33: 1998 ⇒75. 295-309.
5140   *Talbert, Charles H.* Conversion in the Acts of the Apostles: ancient auditors' perceptions. [F]TYSON J. 1998 ⇒120. 141-153.
5141   *Verhoef, Eduard Syzygos* in Phil 4:3 and the author of the "we-sections" in Acts. JHiC 5 (1998) 209-219.
5142   **Vouga, François** Les premiers pas du christianisme. MoBi 35: 1997 ⇒13,5545. [R]RSR 86 (1998) 440-441 (*Guillet, Jacques*); ETR 73 (1998) 618-619 (*Cuvillier, Élian*).
5143   **Wendel, Ulrich** Gemeinde in Kraft: das Gemeindeverständnis in den Summarien der Apostelgeschichte. Neuk. Theol. Diss. und Habilitationen 20: Neuk 1998, Neuk xiii; 303 pp. DM98. 3-7887-1669-X.
5144   [E]**Witherington III, Ben** History, literature and society in... Acts. 1996 ⇒12,5223. [R]CBQ 60 (1998) 409-410 (*O'Toole, Robert F.*).
5145   **Woodall, David L.** Israel in the book of Acts: the foundation of Lukan ecclesiology. [D]Trinity 1998, 415 pp.

F8.3 *Ecclesia primaeva Actuum:* Die Urgemeinde

5146   *Annen, Franz* Die Volksversammlung Gottes. [F]VENETZ, H. 1998 ⇒122. 179-193.
5147   *Horn, Friedrich Wilhelm* Die Gütergemeinschaft der Urgemeinde. EvTh 58 (1998) 370-383.
5148   *Kirchschläger, Walter* "Unfehlbarkeit" als ekklesiologische Dimension in den urchristlichen Gemeinden: eine Anfrage. [F]VENETZ, H. 1998 ⇒122. 195-204.
5149   *Lanne, Emmanuel* Unité et eucharistie, don de l'Esprit. Irén. 71 (1998) 42-61.
5150   *Lindemann, Andreas* The beginnings of christian life in Jerusalem according to the summaries in the Acts of the Apostles (Acts 2:42-47; 4:32-37; 5:12-16). [F]SNYDER, G. 1998 ⇒104. 202-218.
5151   **Manns, Frederic** L'Israele di Dio: sinagoga e chiesa alle origini cristiane. CSB 32: Bo 1998, EDB 374 pp. L55.000;
5152   L'Israël de Dieu: essais sur le christianisme primitif. ASBF 42: 1996 ⇒12,5230; 13,5551. [R]EstB 56 (1998) 141-143 (*Huarte, J.*).
5153   *O'Neill, J.C.* New Testament monasteries. [F]SNYDER, G. 1998 ⇒104. 118-132.
5154   **Padovese, Luigi** Il problema della politica nelle prime comunità cristiane. CasM 1998, Piemme 272 pp. 88-384-2786-0.
5155   *Reumann, John* One Lord, one faith, one god, but many house churches. [F]SNYDER, G. 1998 ⇒104. 106-117.
5156   **Riesner, Rainer** Essener und Urgemeinde in Jerusalem: neue Funde und Quellen. Studien zur biblischen Archäologie und Zeitgeschichte 6: Wu 1998, Brockhaus xi; 215 pp. 3-7655-9806-2.
5157   *Schmidt, Daryl D.* The Jesus tradition in the common life of early christian communities. [F]SNYDER, G. 1998 ⇒104. 135-146.
5158   *Stemberger, Günter* Judenchristen. RAC 147. 1998 ⇒495. 228-245.
5159   **Trocmé, Étienne** L'enfance du christianisme. 1997 ⇒13,5552. [R]FV 97/2 (1998) 83-88 (*Bouttier, Michel*); RSR 86 (1998) 436-437 (*Guillet, Jacques*).

F8.5 **Ascensio, Pentecostes; ministerium Petri**—*Act 1...*

5160 **Atra, Brian Joseph** An examination of the speeches of Peter in Acts: implications for the authorship and thought of First Peter. DMid-America Baptist Theol. Sem. 1998, 242 pp.
5161 *Dion, Marie-Paul* L'Ascension: l'énigmatique présence et la montée mystique. EeT(O) 29 (1998) 63-90.
5162 *Fitzmyer, Joseph A.* The Ascension of Christ and Pentecost. To advance the gospel. 1998 <1984> ⇒150. 265-294.
5163 *George, K.M.* Sunday, Pentecost and the jubilee tradition: a patristic perspective. The jubilee challenge. 1997 ⇒13,2178. 99-103.
5164 **Katurnarich, Sergio M.** Il ritorno di Pietro a Gerusalemme. L'alingua 147: Mi 1998, Spirali 183 pp. 88-7770-517-5.
5165 **Matson, David L.** Household conversion narratives in Acts: pattern and interpretation. JSNT.S 123: 1996 ⇒12,5238; 13,5555. RCBQ 60 (1998) 165-167 (*Balch, David L.*).
5166 *Stander, Hendrik F.* Fourth- and fifth-century homilists on the ascension of Christ. FFERGUSON, E. NT.S 90: 1998 ⇒25. 268-286.
5167 EStricher, **Joseph** L'Esprit de Pentecôte. DosB 71 (1998) 2-26 [Acts 2].
5168 *Van Meenen, Bernard* Un Esprit inaugural: don de l'Esprit et commencement de la vie chrétienne selon quelques textes du Nouveau Testament. QuLi 79 (1998) 202-213.

5169 *Thompson, Richard P.* Believers and religious leaders in Jerusalem: contrasting portraits of Jews in Acts 1-7. FTYSON J. 1998 ⇒120. 327-344.
5170 *Carrión, M.* Volviendo a 'Los Hechos': introducción (1,1-11). EvV 40 (1998) 69-71.
5171 *Crystal, David* Why did the crowd think St Peter was drunk?: an exercise in applied sociolingistics. NBl 79 (1998) 72-76 [Acts 2].
5172 *Rakocy, Waldemar* Mowa Piotra w dniu Pięćdziesiątnicy: model pierwotnego kerygmatu [Peter's speech at Pentecost: a model of the primary kerygma]. RTCAT 45 (1998) 111-122 [Acts 2,14-41]. P.
5173 *Wendel, Ulrich* Bibelarbeit zu Apg 2,42-47. JETh 12 (1998) 101-113.
5174 *Grasso, Santi* Il secondo discorso di Pietro (At 3,1-26);
5175 *Barbi, Augusto* L'inizio della persecuzione a Gerusalemme (At 4,1-31). PaVi 43 (1998) 12-16/4-11.
5176 *Sandnes, Karl Olav* Beyond 'love language': a critical examination of Krister STENDAHL's exegesis of Acts 4:12. StTh 52 (1998) 43-56.
5177 *Kilgallen, John J.* Your servant Jesus whom you anointed (Acts 4,27). RB 105 (1998) 185-201 [Acts 10,38; Ps 2,1-2; Lk 4,18].
5178 *Infante, Renzo* Anania e Saffira (At 5,1-11). PaVi 43 (1998) 17-21.
5179 *Heller, Karin* L'intervento di Gamaliele (At 5,17-42). PaVi 43 (1998) 22-26.
5180 *Darr, John A.* Irenic or ironic?: another look at Gamaliel before the Sanhedrin (Acts 5:33-42). FTYSON J. 1998 ⇒120. 121-139.
5181 *Seland, Torrey* Once more—the Hellenists, Hebrew, and Stephen: conflicts and conflict-management in Acts 6-7. Recruitment. 1998 ⇒320. 169-207.
5182 *Orsatti, Mauro* La istituzione dei sette: un metodo ecclesiale per affrontare e superare i problemi (At 6,1-7). PaVi 43 (1998) 27-33.

5183 *Finsterbusch, Karin* Christologie als Blasphemie: das Hauptthema der Stephanusperikope in lukanischer Perspektive. BN 92 (1998) 38-54 [Acts 6,8-8,3].

5184 *Neudorfer, Heinz-Werner* Bemerkungen zur Theologie der Stefanusrede. JETh 12 (1998) 37-75 [Acts 7].

5185 *Ghidelli, Carlo* Il discorso di Stefano e la sua morte (At 7). PaVi 43 (1998) 34-41.

5186 *Parsons, Mikeal C.* Isaiah 53 in Acts 8: a reply to Professor Morna HOOKER. Jesus and the suffering servant. 1998 ⇒3430. 104-119.

5187 *Squires, John T.* The function of Acts 8.4-12.25. NTS 44 (1998) 608-617.

5188 **Heintz, Florent** Simon "le Magicien": Actes 8, 5-25 et l'accusation de magie contre les prophètes thaumaturges dans l'antiquité. CRB 39: 1997 ⇒13,5573. ᴿMSR 55/2 (1998) 105-109 (*Hatem, Jad*).

5189 *Unseth, Peter* Semantic shift on a geographical term. BiTr 49 (1998) 323-331 [Acts 8,27: Αιείοψ].

5190 **Stachow, Mary Ann** 'Do you understand what you are reading?' (Acts 8:30): a historical-critical reexamination of the pericope of Philip and the Ethiopian (Acts 8:26-40). ᴰCatholic U. of America 1998, 379 pp.

5191 *Barbi, Augusto* I tre racconti di conversione/chiamata di Paolo (At 9; 22; 26): una analisi narrativa. ᶠMARTINI C., Rivelazione. 1998 ⇒74. 235-271.

5192 *Townsend, John T.* Acts 9:1-29 and early church tradition. ᶠTYSON J. 1998 ⇒120. 87-98.

5193 *Lim, Yeu C.* Acts 10: a gentile model for Pentecostal experience. Asian journal of Pentecostal studies 1 (1998) 62-72.

5194 **Handy, David Allan** The Gentile pentecost: a literary study of the story of Peter and Cornelius (Acts 10:1-11:18). ᴰUnion Theol. Sem. in Virginia 1998, 131 pp.

5195 *Doglio, Claudio* "Pneumatikôs" (Ap 11,8): lettura biblica nello Spirito. ᶠMARTINI, C. RivBib.S 33: 1998 ⇒75. 77-86.

5196 **Steitz, Walter Richard** The significance of Acts 12:1-24 as a narrative transition within the Book of Acts. ᴰDallas 1998, 290 pp.

5197 *Papadopoulos, Nectarios* Κριτική παρατήρηση στὸ Πράχ. 12,25 [A critical observation about Acts 12,25]. Theol(A) 69 (1998) 504-512.

F8.7 Act 13...*Itinera Pauli;* Paul's Journeys

5198 **Breytenbach, Cilliers** Paulus und Barnabas in der Provinz Galatien: Studien zu Apostelgeschichte 13f.; 16,6; 18,23 und den Adressaten des Galaterbriefes. AGJU 38: 1996 ⇒12,5270. ᴿThRv 94 (1998) 385-387 (*Borse, Udo*); CBQ 60 (1998) 557-558 (*Green, Joel B.*).

5199 **Dauer, Anton** Paulus und die christliche Gemeinde im syrischen Antiochia: kritische Bestandsaufnahme der modernen Forschung mit einigen weiterführenden Überlegungen. BBB 106: Weinheim 1996, Beltz Athenäum 299 pp. 3-89547-106-2.

5200 **Faber, Gustav** Auf den Spuren des Paulus: eine Reise durch den Mittelmeerraum. Herder-Bücherei 4099; Herder-Spektrum: FrB 1998, Herder 319 pp. 3-451-04099-9.

15201 *Günther, Matthias* Die gescheiterte Mission: niemand weiß so recht etwas über das paulinische Werk in Ephesus zu sagen. LM N.F. 1 (1998) 32-34.

5202   **Johnson, Luke Timothy** Scripture & discernment: decision making
       in the church. 1996 ⇒12,5284. ^RCrossCur 48 (1998) 268-270
       (*Thompson, William M.*).
5203   *Mendels, Doron* Pagan or Jewish?: the presentation of Paul's mission
       in the book of Acts. Identity. JSPE.S 24: 1998 <1996> ⇒174. 394-
       419.
5204   **Mosser, David Neil** The persuasive power of Lucan rhetoric: an exe-
       getical study of two Pauline speeches and the implications for con-
       temporary preaching. ^DTexas, Austin 1998, 271 pp.
5205   *Murray, George W.* Paul's corporate evangelism in the book of Acts.
       BS 155 (1998) 189-200.
5206   **Schreiber, Stefan** Paulus als Wundertäter: redaktionsgeschichtliche
       Untersuchungen zur Apostelgeschichte und den authentischen Pau-
       lusbriefen. BZNW 79: 1996 ⇒12,5278; 13,5582. ^RThPQ 146 (1998)
       81-82 (*Niemand, Christoph*); JBL 117 (1998) 149-151 (*Achtemeier,
       Paul J.*).
5207   **Thorton, C.J.** Der Zeuge...Lukas als Historiker der Paulusreisen.
       WUNT 56: 1992 ⇒7,4711... 12,5282. ^RStPat 45/1 (1998) 202-203
       (*Moda, Aldo*).

5208   **Lin, Bonaventura** Wundertaten und Mission: dramatische Episoden
       in Apg 13-14. EHS.T 623: Fra 1998, Lang xvii; 327 pp. 3-631-
       33180-0.
5209   **Cagnasso, Franco; Pezzini, Domenico** Pieni di gioia e di Spirito
       Santo: Atti 13-14: la missione di Paolo e Barnaba. Strumenti di
       animazione missionaria: Bo 1998, EMI 111 pp. 88-307-0820-8.
5210   *Destro, Adriana; Pesce, Mauro* I discorsi di Paolo in Atti 13 e 14:
       mise en histoire e memoria sociale. V Simposio di Tarso. 1998 ⇒
       395. 163-181.
5211   *Taylor, Justin* St. Paul's missionfield: the world of Acts 13-28. PIBA
       21 (1998) 9-24.
5212   *Spencer, F. Scott* Paul's Odyssey in Acts: status struggles and island
       adventures. BTB 28 (1998) 150-159.
5213   *Collin, M.* Ac 13, 16-38: un commentaire messianique de Gn 15.
       Transeuphratène 14 (1998) 153-165 [2 Sam 7,6-16; Ps 88,20-21].
5214   **Pichler, Josef** Paulusrezeption in der Apostelgeschichte: Untersu-
       chungen zur Rede im pisidischen Antiochien. IThS 50: 1997
       ⇒13,5587. ^RThPQ 146 (1998) 309-310 (*Niemand, Christoph*);
       ZKTh 120 (1998) 215-216 (*Hasitschka, Martin*) [Acts 13,16-52].
5215   **Hilary, Mbachu** Inculturation theology of the Jerusalem Council in
       Acts 15: an inspiration for the Igbo church today. EHS.T 520: 1995
       ⇒11/1,3911; 12,5286. ^RAHC 29/2 (1998) 501-503 (*Bürkle, Horst*).
5216   **Wehnert, Jürgen** Die Reinheit des "christlichen Gottesvolkes" aus
       Juden und Heiden: Studien zum historischen und theologischen Hin-
       tergrund des sogenannten Aposteldekrets. FRLANT 173: 1997
       ⇒13,5595. ^RThLZ 123 (1998) 859-860 (*Horn, Friedrich W.*);
       OrdKor 39 (1998) 494-495 (*Giesen, Heinz*) [Acts 15].
5217   *Ascough, Richard S.* Civic pride at Philippi: the text-critical problem
       of Acts 16.12. NTS 44 (1998) 93-103.
5218   *Hagene, Sylvia* Fremde Götter und neue Lehren: Apg 17,16-
       34—kein Propädeutikum für gebildete Heiden. ^FLÖNING, K. 1998
       ⇒66. 99-114.

5219 *Isizoh, Chidi D.* A reading of the Areopagus speech (Acts 17,22-31) from the African traditional religious perspective. African Christian Studies 14 (1998) 1-25.

5220 *Fitzmyer, Joseph A.* 'A certain Sceva, a Jew, a chief priest' (Acts 19:14). To advance the gospel. 1998 <1991> ⇒150. 332-338.

5221 *Iovino, Paolo* Il discorso di Paolo a Mileto (At 20,17-38): redazione, struttura, interpretazione. ᶠMARTINI, C. RivBib.S 33: 1998 ⇒75. 271-293.

5222 *Schürmann, Heinz* Das Testament des Paulus für die Kirche Apg 20,18-35 <1962>. Im Knechtsdienst Christi: zur weltpriesterlichen Existenz. ᴱ*Scholtissek, Klaus.* Pd 1998, Bonifatius 419 pp. 3-89710-051-7. 104-144.

5223 *Neusner, Jacob* Vow-taking, the Nazirites and the law: does James's advice to Paul accord with the halakhah?. Jewish law. 1998 ⇒181. 137-157 [Acts 21,23-24].

5224 *Lücking, Stefan* "Die vielen Buchstaben treiben dich in den Wahnsinn" (Apg 26,24): neutestamentliche Reflexionen über Schriftlichkeit und Schriftkultur. ᶠLÖNING, K. 1998 ⇒66. 115-130.

5225 *Lehnert, Volker* Absage an Israel oder offener Schluß?: Apg 28,25-28 als paradoxe Intervention. ThBeitr 29 (1998) 315-323.

XI. Johannes

G1.1 *Corpus johanneum:* John and his community

5226 *Beutler, Johannes* Gesetz und Gebot in Evangelium und Briefen des Johannes. ᶠPOKORNÝ, P. 1998 ⇒90. 9-22.

5227 **Beutler, Johannes** Studien zu den johanneischen Schriften. SBAB 25: Stu 1998, Katholisches Bibelwerk 336 pp. DM79. 3-460-062517.

5228 **Boismard, Marie-Émile** Le martyre de Jean l'apôtre. CRB 35: 1996 ⇒12,5308. ᴿRivBib 46 (1998) 116-119 (*Rigato, Maria-Luisa*).

5229 **Culpepper, R. Alan** The gospel and the letters of John. Interpreting Biblical Texts: Nv 1998, Abingdon 327 pp. $20. 0-687-00851-4.

5230 **Dreyfus, Paul** Saint Jean: un grand reporter sur les traces de l'évangéliste. P 1998, Bayard 334 pp. 2-227-350-15-6.

5231 **Feuillet, André** Les promesses de l'Esprit Saint en saint Jean: leur importance et la lumière projetée sur elles par les autres écrits du Nouveau Testament. P 1998, Téqui 127 pp. FF58. 2-7403-0537-0.

5232 **García-Moreno, Antonio** Juan, el hijo del trueno. Pamplona 1998, Eunate 166 pp. 84-7768-094-9.

5233 **Hengel, Martin** La questione giovannea. StBi 120: Brescia 1998, Paideia 339 pp. 88-394-0567-4.

5234 *Hills, Julian V.* "Sin is lawlessness" (1 John 3:4): social definition in the Johannine community. ᶠSNYDER, G. 1998 ⇒104. 286-299.

5235 Johannes entdecken: Lese- und Arbeitsbuch zum Johannesevangelium. Bibel im Jahr: 1998: Stu 1998, Kath. Bibelwerk 142 pp. DM 14.80. 3-460-19993-8.

5236 *Klauck, Hans-Josef* Die Liebe ist konkret—oder Grenzen des Liebesgebots. BiKi 53 (1998) 176-182.

5237 *Marrow, Stanley B.* Johannine ecclesiology. ChiSt 37 (1998) 27-36.

5238 *Misiurek, Jerzy* Św. Jan apostoł ewangelista—pierwszy mistyk chrześcijański [St. John the apostle—the first christian mystic]. Roczniki Teologiczne 45 (1998) 19-29. P.
5239 *Morgen, Michèle* Bulletin d'exégèse du Nouveau Testament: la littérature johannique. RSR 86 (1998) 291-320.
5240 *Niederwimmer, Kurt* Zur Eschatologie im Corpus Johanneum. Gesammelte Aufsätze. BZNW 90: 1998 <1997> ⇒182. 290-300.
5241 *O'Grady, John F.* The beloved disciple, his community and the church. ChiSt 37 (1998) 16-26.
5242 *Panimolle, Salvatore* La fede e l'incredulità negli scritti giovannei. La fede nella bibbia. DSBP 21: 1998 ⇒224. 217-251.
5243 *Pasquetto, Virgilio* Il lessico antropologico del vangelo e delle lettere di Giovanni. Ter. 49 (1998) 115-163;
5244 Pneumatologia e antropologia nel vangelo e nelle lettere di Giovanni. MF 98 (1998) 497-558.
5245 **Pongutá H., Silvestre** El evangelio según San Juan: cartas de San Juan: una presentación. 1994 ⇒10,5253. ^RPerTeol 30/1 (1998) 114-115 (*Konings, Johan*).
5246 *Pretorius, Niek* Redemption of the earth or from the earth?: the gospel of John and the Johannine Epistles. Scriptura 66 (1998) 269-278.
5247 *Reinhartz, Adele* The Johannine community and its Jewish neighbors: a reappraisal. "What is John?", 2. 1998 ⇒5254. 111-138.
5248 *Rezza, Dario* Un Dio che è Padre: Dio Padre nel vangelo di Giovanni e nell'Apocalisse. PalCl 77 (1998) 865-884.
5249 **Rinke, Johannes** Kerygma und Autopsie: der christologische Disput als Spiegel johanneischer Gemeindegeschichte. 1997 ⇒13,5621. ^RBZ 42 (1998) 142-145 (*Theobald, Michael*).
5250 **Rossé, Gérard** Christsein in Gemeinschaft: bibeltheologische Reflexionen zu den johanneischen Schriften. Theologie und Glaube: Mü 1998, Neue Stadt 143 pp. 3-87996-367-3.
5251 **Ruyter, Benjamin W.J. de** De gemeente van de evangelist Johannes: haar polemiek en haar geschiedenis. Delft 1998, Eburon xii; 203 pp. 90-5166-630-X.
5252 **Schmid, Martin** Brunnen des Himmels: Johannes-Paraphrasen. Stu 1998, Radius 117 pp. 3-87173-171-4.
5253 **Schwankl, Otto** Licht und Finsternis. 1995 ⇒11/1,4096; 12,5324. ^RBZ 42 (1998) 140-142 (*Theobald, Michael*).
5254 ^E**Segovia, Fernando F.** 'What is John?', 2: literary and social readings of the fourth gospel. SBL.Symposium series 7: Atlanta, GA 1998, Scholars xii; 361 pp. $30. 0-7885-0491-6.
5255 **Smalley, Stephen S.** John: evangelist and interpreter. DG 1998 <1978>, InterVarsity xviii; 340 pp. $20. 0-8308-1514-7.
5256 **Vidal, Senén** Los escritos originales de la comunidad del discípulo 'amigo' de Jesús: el evangelio y las cartas de Juan. Biblioteca de Est. Bíbl. 93: 1997 ⇒13,5630. ^RRevAg 41 (1998) 830-832 (*Sabugal, Santos*); EfMex 16 (1998) 270-271 (*Carillo Alday, Salvador*).

G1.2 **Evangelium Johannis:** *textus, commentarii*

5257 ^E**Ammassari, Antonio** Il vangelo di Giovanni nella colonna latina del Bezae Codex Cantabrigiensis. 1996 ⇒12,5329. ^RRivBib 46 (1998) 238-240 (*Cavalletti, Sofia*).

5258 **Arminjon, Blaise** Queremos ver a Jesús: descubrir su rostro en el e-vangelio de Juan: 1, la vida pública (Juan, cap. 1-11); 2, pasión y resurrección. Enséñanos a orar 11-12: Mensajero 1998, Bilbao 153; 169 pp. 84-271-2159/60-1.

5259 ᴱ**Elliott, W.J.; Parker, David C.** The New Testament in Greek, 4: the gospel according to St. John, 1: the papyri. NTTS 20: 1995 ⇒11/1,3965; 13,5635. ᴿRSR 86 (1998) 304-305 (*Morgen, Michèle*); JThS 49 (1998) 286-289 (*Birdsall, J. Neville*).

5260 **Espinel Marcos, José Luis** Evangelio según San Juan: introducción, traducción y comentario. Horizonte Dos Mil—Textos y monografias 11: S 1998, San Esteban 286 pp. Pta2.400. 84-89761-70-1.

5261 **Fallon, Michael B.** The gospel according to Saint John: an intro-ductory commentary. [Kensington, NSW Australia] 1998, Chevalier 386 pp. 0-86940-264-1.

5262 ᴱ**Feld, Helmut** In evangelium secundum Johannem commentarius. Pars prior. Ioannis Calvini opera exegetica, 11/1. 1997 ⇒13,5636. ᴿSCJ 29 (1998) 846-848 (*Pitkin, Barbara*); RSLR 34 (1998) 677-678 (*Bettoni, Anna*).

5263 **García Moreno, Antonio** El evangelio según San Juan: introducción y exegesis. 1996 ⇒12,5337; 13,5637. ᴿEstB 56 (1998) 550-553 (*Rodríguez-Ruiz, M.*).

5264 **Gárrett B., Ricardo** Comentario al evangelio de Juan. Terrassa (Barc) 1998, Clie 256 pp. 84-8267-028-X.

5265 The gospel according to John: Authorised King James Version. Pocket Canons: E 1998, Canongate xvi; 61 pp. 0-86241-798-8.

5266 **Hofrichter, Peter Leander** Modell und Vorlage der Synoptiker: das vorredaktionelle 'Johannesevangelium'. 1997 ⇒13,5641. ᴿATG 61 (1998) 293-294 (*Contreras Molina, F.*).

5267 **Keil, Günther** Das Johannesevangelium: ein philosophischer und theologischer Kommentar. 1997 ⇒13,5643. ᴿBiLi 71 (1998) 74-75 (*Woschitz, Karl Matthäus*).

5268 **Lenzi, Giovanni** Il vangelo di Giovanni: secondo l'antica versione siriaca. Sussidi biblici 60: Reggio Emilia 1998, San Lorenzo (4) xxxv; 100 pp. 88-8071-075-3.

5269 **Léon-Dufour, Xavier** Lecture de l'évangile selon Jean I-IV. 1990-1996 ⇒6,5650... 13,5646. ᴿNRTh 120 (1998) 289-290 (*Raderma-kers, J.*);

5270 Leitura do evangelho segundo João (IV: capítulos 18-21). Bíblica Loyola 16: São Paulo 1998, Loyola 262 pp. 85-15-01649-4. ᴿPerTe-ol 30 (1998) 446-448 (*Konings, Johan*).

5271 **Malina, Bruce J.; Rohrbaugh, Richard L.** Social-science commen-tary on the gospel of John. Mp 1998, Fortress x; 326 pp. $19. 0-8006-2992-2.

5272 **Moloney, Francis J.** Signs and shadows: reading John 5-12. 1996 ⇒12,5346; 13,5648. ᴿPacifica 11/1 (1998) 80-82 (*Lieu, Judith*); CBQ 60 (1998) 167-169 (*Black, C. Clifton*); JBL 117 (1998) 142-144 (*Koester, Craig R.*);

5273 The gospel of John. Sacra Pagina 4: ColMn 1998, Liturgical xxii; 594 pp. $35. 0-8146-5806-7.

5274 *Neirynck, F.* John and the synoptics in recent commentaries. EThL 74 (1998) 386-397.

5275 **Rao, O.M.** St John's gospel: a commentary. Delhi 1998, ISPCK xvi; 418 pp. Rs120. 81-7214-432-6.

5276 **Ridderbos, Herman N.** The gospel according to John: a theological
commentary. 1997 ⇒13,5652. [R]RTR 57 (1998) 94-95 (*Ovey, Michael J.*); Trin.Journal 19 (1998) 122-126 (*Köstenberger, Andreas J.*).
5277 **Sanford, John A.** Das Johannesevangelium: eine tiefenpsychologi-
sche Auslegung, 2: Kapitel 7-21. Mü 1998, Claudius 222 pp. 3-532-
62218-1.
5278 **Schenke, Ludger** Johannes: Kommentar. Dü 1998, Patmos 443 pp.
DM68.
5279 **Schnelle, Udo** Das Evangelium nach Johannes. ThHK 4: Lp 1998,
Evangelische Verlagsanstalt xxvi; 321 pp. DM54. 3-374-01673-1.
5280 **Wilckens, Ulrich** Das Evangelium nach Johannes. NTD 4: Gö 1998,
Vandenhoeck & R viii; 353 pp. DM64. 3-525-51379-8.
5281 **Witherington III, Ben** John's wisdom: a commentary on the fourth
gospel. 1996 ⇒12,5354; 13,5656. [R]Pro Ecclesia 7/1 (1998) 118-119
(*Cory, Catherine*); EvQ 70 (1998) 72-74 (*Mathewson, David*).

G1.3 **Introductio** *in Evangelium Johannis*

5282 [E]**Ashton, John** The interpretation of John. 1997 ⇒13,5658. [R]ScrB
28 (1998) 48-49 (*Goodacre, Mark*).
5283 **Brown, Raymond E.** The gospel according to John—an overview.
ChiSt 37 1998, 5-15.
5284 **García-Moreno, Antonio** Introducción al misterio: evangelio de San
Juan. 1997 ⇒13,5663. [R]Mar. 60 (1998) 645-648 (*Masini, Mario*).
5285 **González, Justo L.** Tres meses en la escuela de Juan: estudios sobre
el evangelio de Juan. Nv 1998, Abingdon vii; 168 pp. 0-687-022088.
5286 **López Fernández, Enrique** El mundo joánico: introducción al cuarto evangelio. Oviedo 1998, Lib. del Arzobispado 450 pp. PTA2.000.
5287 **Nordsieck, Reinhard** Johannes: zur Frage nach Verfasser und Entstehung des vierten Evangeliums: ein neuer Versuch. Neuk 1998,
Neuk 143 pp. DM39.80.
5288 *Osiek, Carolyn* John, a gospel for our time. BiTod 36 (1998) 72-78.
5289 *Reinhartz, Adele* On travel, translation, and ethnography: Johannine
scholarship at the turn of the century. "What is John?", 2. 1998
⇒5254. 249-256.
5290 *Rohrbaugh, Richard L.* The gospel of John in the twenty-first
century. "What is John?", 2. 1998 ⇒5254. 257-263.
5291 Scholtissek, Klaus Johannine studies: a survey of recent research with
special regard to German contributions. CurResB 6 (1998) 227-259.
5292 **Schulz, Hans-Joachim** Wie entstand das Johannesevangelium?:
neue Erkenntnisse zur Motivgeschichte, Verfasserschaft und
Datierung. SWKA 31: W 1998, Wiener Kath. Akad. 28 pp.
5293 [F]**Smith, D. Moody** Exploring the gospel of John. 1996 ⇒12,82;
13,5756. [R]RSR 86 (1998) 316-318 (*Morgen, Michèle*); NT 40 (1998)
389-392 (*Menken, Maarten J.J.*); CBQ 60 (1998) 392-393 (*Boer,
Martinus C. de*).
5294 **Thiering, Barbara** The book that Jesus wrote: John's gospel. Sydney 1998, Doubleday x; 323 pp. 0-86824-712-X.

G1.4 *Themata de evangelio Johannis*—**John's Gospel, topics**

5295 **Anderson, Paul N.** The christology of the fourth gospel: its unity and disunity in the light of John 6. 1996 ⇒12,5375; 13,5671. [R]CDios 111 (1998) 330-331 (*Gutiérrez, J.*); AThR 80 (1998) 272-273 (*Sowers, Sidney G.*); RSR 86 (1998) 296-299 (*Morgen, Michèle*); CBQ 60 (1998) 139-140 (*Carroll, John T.*); JThS 49 (1998) 751-758 (*Borgen, Peder*); Pacifica 11 (1998) 335-338 (*Moloney, Francis J.*); JR 78 (1998) 613-614 (*Snyder, Graydon F.*); JBL 117 (1998) 144-145 (*Painter, John*).

5296 *Arkadas, Demetrios* The liturgical character of eschatology according to the gospel of John. DBM 17 (1998) 63-74.

5297 **Ball, David Mark** 'I Am' in John's gospel: literary function, background and theological implications. JSNT.S 124: 1996 ⇒12,5376; 13,5674. [R]EvQ 70 (1998) 271-273 (*Hingle, N.N.*); Bibl.Interp. 6 (1998) 437-438 (*Gates-Brown, Tricia*).

5298 *Báez, Silvio José* El evangelio de San Juan en los escritos de TERESA de Lisieux. Ter. 49 (1998) 51-72.

5299 *Becker, Jürgen* Das Geist- und Gemeindeverständnis des vierten E-vangelisten. ZNW 89 (1998) 217-234.

5300 **Berger, Klaus** Im Anfang war Johannes: Datierung und Theologie des Evangeliums. 1997 ⇒13,5681. [R]BZ 42 (1998) 271-272 (*Reim, Günter*); ThLZ 123 (1998) 980-983 (*Broer, Ingo*); BiLi 71 (1998) 377-379 (*Beilner, Wolfgang*); Biblos 47 (1998) 318-319 (*Förster, Hans*).

5301 [T]**Berrouard, M.-F.** Saint AUGUSTIN: homélies sur l'évangile de saint Jean LXXX-CIII. BAug 9 sér. 74 B: P 1998, Institut d'Études Augustiniennes 531 pp.

5302 *Beutler, Johannes* Die Stunde Jesu im Johannesevangelium. Studien. SBAB 25: 1998 ⇒5227. 317-322.

5303 *Blanchard, Yves-Maries* Né d'un vouloir de chair?: la conception virginale au regard du quatrième évangile. EtMar (1998) 25-34.

5304 **Boismard, Marie-Émile** Moses or Jesus: an essay in Johannine christology. 1993 ⇒9,5500. [R]Neotest. 32 (1998) 242-243 (*Van der Merwe, D.G.*).

5305 *Boismard, Marie-Émile* Le disciple que Jésus aimait d'après Jn 21,1 ss et 1,35 ss. RB 105 (1998) 76-80.

5306 *Brant, Jo-Ann A.* Divine birth and apparent parents: the plot of the fourth gospel. Ancient fiction. 1998 ⇒1118. 199-217.

5307 *Capper, Brian J.* 'With the oldest monks ...': light from Essene history on the career of the beloved disciple?. JThS 49 (1998) 1-55.

5308 **Caron, Gérald** Qui sont les 'juifs' de l'évangile de Jean?. RFTP 35: 1997 ⇒13,5685. [R]SR 27 (1998) 81-82 (*Guillemette, Yves*); CBQ 60 (1998) 560-561 (*Quitslund, Sonya A.*).

5309 *Catchpole, David* The beloved disciple and Nathanael. [F]ASHTON J. JSNT.S 153: 1998 ⇒6. 69-92.

5310 *Collins, Raymond F.* Characters proclaim the good news. ChiSt 37 (1998) 47-57.

5311 *Co, Maria Anicia* Reading and sense-experiencing the gospel of John. The personal voice. 1998 ⇒250. 86-96.

5312 **Countryman, L. William** The mystical way in the fourth gospel: crossing over into God. Valley Forge, Pa. 1995, Trinity ix; 164 pp. 1-56338-103-6.

5313 *Devillers, Luc* La lettre de Soumaïos et les Ioudaioi johanniques. RB 105 (1998) 556-581.

5314 *Diefenbach, Manfred* Ökumenische Probleme infolge johanneischer Auslegung: eine wirkungs- und rezeptionsgeschichtliche Betrachtung des johanneischen Petrusbildes. Cath(M) 52 (1998) 44-66.

5315 **Dorsey, Bea Mary** Wisdom in the gospels of Thomas and John ᴰMarquette 1998, 176 pp.

5316 *Dube, Musa W.* Savior of the world but not of this world: a post-colonial reading of spatial construction in John. The postcolonial bible. 1998 ⇒695. 118-135.

5317 *Du Rand, Jan A.* Reading the fourth gospel like a literary symphony. "What is John?", 2. 1998 ⇒5254. 5-18.

5318 **DuToit, David S.** Theios anthropos: zur Verwendung von θεῖος ἄνθρωπος und sinnverwandten Ausdrücken in der Literatur der Kaiserzeit. WUNT 2/91: 1997 ⇒13,5694. ᴿThRv 94 (1998) 505-506 (*Ebner, Martin*); JAC 41 (1998) 223-224 (*Rosen, Klaus*).

5319 *Dvorak, James D.* The relationship between John and the synoptic gospels. JETS 41 (1998) 201-238.

5320 **Ensor, P.W.** Jesus and his 'works': the Johannine sayings in historical perspective. WUNT 2/85: 1996 ⇒12,5403; 13,5695. ᴿNT 40 (1998) 392-395 (*Menken, Maarten J.J.*).

5321 *Estrada, Bernardo* La missione dello "Spirito di verità" nel vangelo di Giovanni. Annales theologici 12 (1998) 375-405.

5322 **Farmer, Craig S.** The gospel of John in the sixteenth century: the Johannine exegesis of Wolfgang MUSCULUS. 1997 ⇒13,5662. ᴿChH 67/1 (1998) 149-151 (*Wengert, Timothy J.*); SCJ 29/1 (1998) 243-245 (*Ford, James Thomas*).

5323 **Fehribach, Adeline** The women in the life of the bridegroom: a feminist historical-literary analysis and interpretation of the female characters in the fourth gospel. ColMn 1998, Glazier vii; 222 pp. $20.

5324 **Ferraro, Giuseppe** Il Paraclito, Cristo, il Padre nel quarto vangelo. 1996 ⇒12,5408; 13,5700. ᴿCBQ 60 (1998) 563-564 (*Forestell, J. Terence*);

5325 Lo Spirito Santo nei commentari al quarto vangelo di BRUNO di Segni, RUPERTO di Deutz, BONAVENTURA e ALBERTO Magno. Letture bibliche (Vaticano) 11: Città del Vaticano 1998, Vaticana 222 pp. L30.000. 88-209-2633-4.

5326 *Ferraro, Giuseppe* Lo Spirito Santo nel commento di ECKHART al quarto vangelo. Ang. 75 (1998) 47-128.

5327 **Ferreira, Johan** Johannine ecclesiology. JSNT.S 160: Shf 1998, JSOT 246 pp. £46/$75. 1-85075-887-5.

5328 *Findeis, Hans Jürgen* Indische Rezeption des Johannesevangeliums in interkultureller Perspektive. ᶠKLAES, N. 1998 ⇒50. 203-229.

5329 **Frey, Jörg** Die johanneische Eschatologie I: ihre Probleme im Spiegel der Forschung seit REIMARUS. WUNT 96: 1997 ⇒13,5702. ᴿBZ 42 (1998) 275-278 (*Rinke, Johannes*); RSR 86 (1998) 309-312 (*Morgen, Michèle*); ThRv 94 (1998) 515-517 (*Scholtissek, Klaus*); OrdKor 39 (1998) 365-366 (*Giesen, Heinz*); DBM 17 (1998) 102-108 (*Karakolis, Chr.*); TThZ 107 (1998) 323-324 (*Reiser, Marius*);

5330 Die johanneische Eschatologie, II: das johanneische Zeitverständnis. WUNT 110: Tü 1998, Mohr xv; 369 pp. DM178. 3-16-146845-7.

5331 **Frühwald-König, Johannes** Tempel und Kult: ein Beitrag zur Christologie des Johannesevangeliums. ᴰRg 1996-1997, ᴰ*Schmut-*

termayr, G. BU 27: Rg 1998, Pustet 278 pp. DM48. 3-7917-1581-X [Jn 2,13-22; 4,1-26; 5,1-18; 7].

5332 *Fuente, Alfonso de la* Trasfondo cultural del cuarto evangelio: sobre el ocaso del dilema judaísmo/gnosticismo. EstB 56 (1998) 491-506.

5333 **García Moreno, Antonio** El cuarto evangelio: aspectos teológicos. Cienpuertas, ciencaminos' 2: 1996 ⇒12,5411; 13,5704. REstB 56 (1998) 553-555 (*Rodríguez-Ruiz, M.*).

5334 **Grelot, Pierre** Les juifs dans l'évangile selon Jean. CRB 34: 1995 ⇒11/1,4044... 13,5707. RRSR 86 (1998) 305-306 (*Morgen, Michèle*); CBQ 60 (1998) 154-155 (*Bauer, David R.*); EstB 56 (1998) 556-557 (*Rodríguez-Ruiz, M.*).

5335 *Habermann, Ruth* Das Evangelium nach Johannes: Orte der Frauen. Kompendium Feministische Bibelauslegung. 1998 ESchottroff, L.: 1998 ⇒H8.9. 527-541.

5336 **Hammes, Axel** Der Ruf ins Leben: eine theologisch-hermeneutische Untersuchung zur Eschatologie des Johannesvangeliums mit einem Ausblick auf ihre Wirkungsgeschichte. BBB 112: 1997 ⇒13,5708 RBZ 42 (1998) 272-275 (*Frey, Jörg*).

5337 **Hergenröder, Clemens** Wir schauten seine Herrlichkeit: das johanneische Sprechen vom Sehen im Horizont von Selbsterschliessung Jesu und Antwort des Menschen. FzB 80: 1996 ⇒12,5419; 13,5709. REstAg 33 (1998) 381-382 (*Cineira, D.A.*); ThLZ 123 (1998) 987-989 (*Beutler, Johannes*); ThRv 94 (1998) 65-68 (*Scholtissek, Klaus*).

5338 *Hill, Charles E.* What Papias said about John (and Luke): a 'new' Papian fragment. JThS 49 (1998) 582-629.

5339 *Howard-Brook, Wes* Reading for/about our lives: politics, poetics, and personhood in the fourth gospel. "What is John?", 2. 1998 ⇒5254. 213-230.

5340 *Jerumanis, Pascal-Marie* Réaliser la communion avec Dieu: croire, vivre et demeurer dans l'évangile selon S. Jean. EtB 32: 1996 ⇒12,5423; 13,5713. RCDios 211 (1998) 650-651 (*Gutiérrez, J.*); CBQ 60 (1998) 368-370 (*Spatafora, Andrea*); Gr. 79 (1998) 177-178 (*Ferraro, Giuseppe*); RThom 98 (1998) 166-168 (*Antoniotti, Louise-Marie*); JThS 49 (1998) 239-241 (*Edwards, Ruth B.*).

5341 **Jones, Larry Paul** The symbol of water in the gospel of John. JSNT. S 145: 1997 ⇒13,5714. RBibl.Interp. 6 (1998) 448-450 (*Gates-Brown, Tricia*).

5342 **Kanagaraj, Jey J.** 'Mysticism' in the gospel of John: an inquiry into its background. JSNT.S 158: Shf 1998, JSOT 356 pp. 1-85075-8654.

5343 *Kieffer, René* L'image royale de Jésus dans l'évangile de Jean FBERGMAN J. 1998 ⇒9. 241-250.

5344 *Kinzer, Mark* Temple christology in the gospel of John. SBL.SP part 1. SBL.SPS 37: 1998 ⇒402. 447-464.

5345 *Kitzberger, Ingrid Rosa* "How can this be?" (John 3:9): a feminist-theological re-reading of the gospel of John. "What is John?", 2. 1998 ⇒5254. 19-41.

5346 *Köstenberger, Andreas J.* Jesus as rabbi in the fourth gospel. BBR 8 (1998) 97-128.

5347 **Köstenberger, Andreas J.** The missions of Jesus and the disciples according to the fourth gospel: with implications for the fourth gospel's purpose and the mission of the contemporary church. GR 1998, Eerdmans xvi; 271 pp. $30. 0-8028-4255-0. RRRT (1998/4) 13-17 (*Need, Stephen W.*).

5348   *Kuthirakkattel, Scaria* Johannine perspective of sacraments. BiBh 24 (1998) 149-171.
5349   *L'Éplattenier, Charles* 'Les juifs' dans le quatrième évangile. Procès de Jésus. 1998 ⇒392. 127-131.
5350   *Lieu, Judith M.* The mother of the son in the fourth gospel. JBL 117 (1998) 61-77.
5351   *Lincoln, Andrew T.* "I am the resurrection and the life": the resurrection message of the fourth gospel. Life in the face of death. 1998 ⇒252. 122-144.
5352   *Lombard, Herman A.* Orthodoxy and other-wordliness of the church: Johannine perspectives on christianity in a new South Africa. Neotest. 32 (1998) 497-508.
5353   **Lorenzini, Ezio** Il vangelo sandwich: inserimenti redazionali in cinque brani di Giovanni. Lyceum, saggi e ricerche 15: Cesena 1998, "Il Ponte Vecchio" 173 pp. L20.000. 88-8312-012-4.
5354   *Manns, Frédéric* Elements de christologie johannique. BeO 40 (1998) 169-192.
5355   **Martignani, Luigi** "Il mio giorno": indagine esegetico-teologica sull'uso del termine ἡμέρα nel quarto vangelo. ᴰGregoriana; ᴰ*Caba, José.* AnGr 275: R 1998, E.P.U.G. 444 pp. €24.78. 88-7652-803-2.
5356   *Martin, Troy W.* Assessing the Johannine epithet "the mother of Jesus". CBQ 60 (1998) 63-73.
5357   *Merklein, Helmut* Gott und Welt: eine exemplarische Interpretation von Joh 2,23-3,21; 12,20-36 zur theologischen Bestimmung des johanneischen Dualismus. Studien zu Jesus und Paulus II. WUNT 105: 1998 <1996> ⇒175. 263-281.
5358   *Meye Thompson, Marianne* After virtual reality: reading the gospel of John at the turn of the century. "What is John?", 2. 1998 ⇒5254. 231-238.
5359   *Moloney, Francis J.* An adventure with Nicodemus. The personal voice. 1998 ⇒250. 97-110.
5360   *Moloney, Francis J.* God so loved the world: the Jesus of John's gospel. ACR 75 (1998) 195-205.
5361   *Moore, Stephen D.* Some ugly thoughts on the fourth gospel at the threshold of the third millennium. "What is John?", 2. 1998 ⇒5254. 239-247.
5362   *Morujao, Geraldo* La relazione fra rivelare (ἐξηγεισθαι) Dio e glorificare (δοξάζειν) il Padre, nel contesto di parola e gloria del IV vangelo. Annales theologici 12 (1998) 169-179.
5363   *Muñoz León, Domingo* Cristo y María en el evangelio de San Juan: Caná y el Calvario. EstMar 64 (1998) 37-63.
5364   *Neuenschwander, Bernhard* Mystik im Johannesevangelium: eine hermeneutische Untersuchung aufgrund der Auseinandersetzung mit Zen-Meister Hisamatsu Shin'ichi. Bibl.Interp. 31: Lei 1998, Brill xii; 369 pp. $126.50. 90-04-11035-6.
5365   *Neyrey, Jerome H.* The sociology of secrecy and the fourth gospel. "What is John?", 2. 1998 ⇒5254. 79-109.
5366   **Nimmo, Victoria J.** 'Where are you from?' (John 19:9): Johannine characterization and the significance of origin. ᴰCh 1998, 420 pp.
5367   **Obermann, Andreas** Die christologische Erfüllung der Schrift im Johannesevangelium: eine Untersuchung zur johanneischen Hermeneutik anhand der Schriftzitate. WUNT 2/83: 1996 ⇒12,5453; 13,5742. ᴿPacifica 11/1 (1998) 83-85 (*Moloney, Francis J.*); StPat

45 (1998) 523-524 (*Segalla, Giuseppe*); RSR 86 (1998) 313-314 (*Morgen, Michèle*); CBQ 60 (1998) 375-377 (*Moloney, Francis J.*); JThS 49 (1998) 237-239 (*Williams, Catrin H.*).

5368 O'Day, Gail R. The word become flesh: story and theology in the gospel of John. "What is John?", 2. 1998 ⇒5254. 67-76.

5369 *Ohhara, Mami* The realization of 'life' in John's gospel. KaKe 67 (1998) 125-166. J.

5370 **Oñate Ojeda, Juan Angel** El Paráclito y notas exegéticas sobre la Santísima Trinidad en San Juan. Valentina 44: Valencia 1998, Facultad de Teología San Vicente Ferrer 90 pp. 84-95269-03-1.

5371 **Orchard, Helen C.** Courting betrayal: Jesus as victim in the gospel of John. JSNT.S 161; Gender, Culture, Theory 5: Shf 1998, Academic 293 pp. £50. 1-85075-892-1.

5372 **Østenstad, Gunnar H.** Patterns of redemption in the fourth gospel: an experiment in structural analysis. SBEC 38: Lewiston 1998, Mellen xxx; 370 pp. $110. 0-7734-8396-9.

5373 *Panimolle, Salvatore A.* L'eucaristia nel quarto vangelo. L'eucaristia nella bibbia. DSBP 19: 1998 ⇒218. 130-155.

5374 *Pazdan, Mary Margaret* Jesus, disciples, and Jewish feasts in John. BiTod 36 (1998) 79-85.

5375 **Philippe, Marie-Dominique** Wherever he goes: Rev. 14:4: a retreat on the gospel of John. Laredo, Tex. 1998, Congregation of Saint John 349 pp. 0-567-08729-8.

5376 *Piñero, A.* Interaction of Judaism and Hellenism in the gospel of John. Hellenic and Jewish arts. 1998 ⇒439. 93-122.

5377 **Rahner, Johanna** "Er aber sprach vom Tempel seines Leibes": Jesus von Nazaret als Ort der Offenbarung Gottes im vierten Evangelium. DFrB 1997; DOberlinner, L. BBB 117: Bodenheim 1998, Philo ix; 381 pp. DM98. 3-8257-00976.

5378 **Reilly, John** Praying John. 1997 ⇒13,5749. RACR 75/2 (1998) 238-239 (*Ridley, Francis*).

5379 *Rensberger, David* Sectarianism and theological interpretation in John. "What is John?", 2. 1998 ⇒5254. 139-156.

5380 *Rodríguez-Ruiz, Miguel* Estructura del evangelio de San Juan desde el punto de vista cristológico y eclesiológico. EstB 56 (1998) 74-96.

5381 **Rossé, Gerard** The spirituality of communion. NY 1998, NY City Press 124 pp. $10.

5382 *Rudolph, Kurt* Zum Streit um Johannes gnosticus. FSTEGEMANN, H. BZNW 97: 1998 ⇒111. 415-427.

5383 *Ryen, Jon O.* Kirkeforståelsen i Johannesevangeliet. TTK 69 (1998) 97-115.

5384 **Sadananda, Daniel Rathnakara** The Johannine exegesis of God: an exploration into the Johannine understanding of God. Diss. Bethel 1996-1997; DLindemann, A.

5385 *Saldarini, Anthony J.* Passover in the gospel of John. BiTod 36 (1998) 86-91.

5386 **Santos, Bento Silva** Teologia do evangelho de São João. Aparecida, SP 1993, Santuário 421 pp. RREB 58 (1998) 991-993 (*Voigt, Simão*).

5387 *Schenke, Ludger* Christologie als Theologie: Versuch über das Johannesevangelium. FHOFFMANN, P., Von Jesus. BZNW 93: 1998 ⇒43. 445-465.

5388 **Schneiders, Sandra M.** 'Because of the woman's testimony ...': reexamining the issue of authorship in the fourth gospel. NTS 44 (1998) 513-535.

5389 *Schnelle, Udo* Johannes als Geisttheologe. NT 40 (1998) 17-31.
5390 *Scholtissek, Klaus* Ironie und Rollenwechsel im Johannesevangelium. ZNW 89 (1998) 235-255.
5391 *Schottroff, Luise* Sexuality in John's gospel. ThD 45 (1998) 103-107.
5392 *Segalla, Giuseppe* Ritualità cristologica ed esperienza spirituale nel vangelo secondo Giovanni. Teol(Br) 23 (1998) 330-362.
5393 ᴱ**Segovia, Fernando F.** What is John?', 1: readers and readings of the fourth gospel. 1996 ⇒12,5470. ᴿCBQ 60 (1998) 404-406 (*Wahlde, Urban C. von*).
5394 *Segovia, Fernando F.* Reading readers reading John: an exercise in intercultural criticism. "What is John?", 2. 1998 ⇒5254. 281-322.
5395 *Senior, Donald* The eloquent meaning of Jesus' death in the gospel of John. ChiSt 37 (1998) 37-46.
5396 *Sevrin, Jean-Marie* La fin et le temps dans l'évangile selon Jean. Revue d'éthique et de théologie morale.S 207 (1998) 101-124.
5397 **Simoens, Yves** Selon Jean, 1: une traduction; 2-3: une interprétation. 1997 ⇒13,5755. ᴿCDios 111/1 (1998) 328-330 (*Gutiérrez, J.*); StPat 45 (1998) 274-276 (*Segalla, Giuseppe*); NRTh 120 (1998) 290-292 (*Radermakers, J.*); RSR 86 (1998) 294-295 (*Morgen, Michèle*).
5398 **Smith, Dwight Moody** La teologia del vangelo di Giovanni. ᵀ*Campanini, Saverio*. Letture bibliche 15: Brescia 1998, Paideia 235 pp. L35.000. 88-394-0562-3.
5399 *Staley, Jeffrey L.* The politics of place and the place of politics in the gospel of John. "What is John?", 2". 1998 ⇒5254. 265-277;
5400 Fathers and sons: fragments from an autobiographical midrash on John's gospel. The personal voice. 1998 ⇒250. 65-85.
5401 **Staley, Jeffrey L.** Reading with a passion: rhetoric, autobiography, and the American West in the gospel of John. 1995 ⇒11/1,4100; 13,5761. ᴿTJT 14/1 (1998) 104-105 (*Braun, Willi*); JBL 117 (1998) 366-367 (*Moore, Stephen D.*).
5402 *Syreeni, Kari* Den sublimerade kroppen: Jesu kroppslighet som symbol i Johannesevangeliet. SEÅ 63 (1998) 201-215.
5403 *Thompson, Marianne M.* Reflections on worship in the gospel of John. PSB 19 (1998) 259-278.
5404 *Tolmie, D. Francois* The characterization of God in the fourth gospel. JSNT 69 (1998) 57-75.
5405 **Tovey, Derek** Narrative art and act in the fourth gospel. JSNT.S 151: 1997 ⇒13,5762. ᴿPacifica 11 (1998) 333-335 (*Moloney, Francis*).
5406 *Tuñí, Josep Oriol* Teología judía y cristología joánica. RLAT 15 (1998) 139-162.
5407 *Van den Heever, Gerhard* Finding data in unexpected places (or: from text linguistics to socio-rhetoric): a socio-rhetorical reading of John's gospel. SBL.SP part 2. SBL.SPS 37: 1998 ⇒402. 649-676.
5408 *Van der Watt, Jan Gabriël* The dynamics of metaphor in the gospel of John. SNTU.A 23 (1998) 29-78.
5409 **Van Tilborg, Sjef** Reading John in Ephesus. NT.S 83: 1996 ⇒12, 5488; 13,5766. ᴿBib. 79 (1998) 134-137 (*Segalla, Giuseppe*); JSNT 70 (1998) 117 (*Pearson, Brook*); JThS 49 (1998) 265-273 (*Horsley, G.H.R.*); JBL 117 (1998) 541-542 (*Rensberger, David*).
5410 *Wainwright, Elaine* Jesus Sophia. BiTod 36 (1998) 92-97.
5411 **Westermann, Claus** The gospel of John: in the light of the Old Testament. [Peabody, MASS] 1998, Hendrickson 106 pp. $10. 1-56563-237-0.

5412 *Winandy, Jacques* Le disciple que Jésus aimait: pour une vision élargie du problème. RB 105 (1998) 70-75.
5413 **Zangenberg, Jürgen** Frühes Christentum in Samarien: topographische und traditionsgeschichtliche Studien zu den Samarientexten im Johannesevangelium. TANZ 27: Tü 1998, Francke xiv; 291 pp. 3-7720-1878-5.
5414 *Zevini, Giorgio* I giudei e il quarto vangelo. PSV 37 (1998) 143-161.
5415 *Zumstein, Jean* La rèfèrence au Jésus terrestre dans l'évangile selon Jean. Jésus de Nazareth. 1998 ⇒253. 459-474.

G1.5 Johannis Prologus 1,1...

5416 *Böhm, Thomas* Bemerkungen zu den syrischen Übersetzungen des Johannesprologs. ZNW 89 (1998) 45-65.
5417 **Cholin, M.** Le prologue et la dynamique de l'évangile de Jean. 1995 ⇒11/1,4118; 12,5499. [R]RB 105 (1998) 278-281 (*Devillers, Luc*).
5418 *Gellermann, Hermann* Hebräische Bibel und Johannesprolog (Joh. 1,1-14). [F]MARQUARDT, F.-W. 1998 ⇒72. 205-232.
5419 *Hofstra, Johan D.* The sources used by ISHO'DAD of Merw in his commentary on St. John, chapter I. Symposium Syriacum VII. 1998 ⇒415. 23-35.
5420 **Jasper, Alison** The shining garment of the text: gendered readings of John's Prologue. JSNT.S 165: Shf 1998, Academic 266 pp. £40/$65/£15/$20. 1-85075-893-X.
5421 *Merklein, Helmut* Geschöpf und Kind: zur Theologie der hymnischen Vorlage des Johannesprologs. Studien zu Jesus und Paulus II. WUNT 105: 1998 <1996> ⇒175. 241-261.
5422 *Segalla, Giuseppe* Il prologo di Giovanni (1,1-18) nell'orizzonte culturale dei suoi primi lettori. RstB 10/1-2 (1998) 251-278.
5423 *Viviano, Benedict T.* Bemerkungen zur Struktur des Johannesprologs. [F]VENETZ, H. 1998 ⇒122. 167-175;
5424 The structure of the prologue of John (1:1-18): a note. RB 105 (1998) 176-184.

5425 *Alexeev, Anatoly A.* John 1:1-5 in Russian: a survey of translating problems. [F]POKORNÝ, P. 1998 ⇒90. 5-8.
5426 *Niederwimmer, Kurt* Et Verbum caro factum est: eine Meditation zu Johannes 1,14. Gesammelte Aufsätze. BZNW 90: 1998 <1990> ⇒182. 196-206.
5427 *Görg, Manfred* Fleischwerdung des Logos: auslegungs- und religionsgeschichtliche Anmerkungen zu Joh 1,14a. [F]HOFFMANN, P., Von Jesus. BZNW 93: 1998 ⇒43. 467-482.
5428 *Fernando, G. Charles A.* John 1:17 as window to the realities of law and love in the fourth gospel. BiBh 24 (1998) 172-191.
5429 *Pagazzi, Giovanni Cesare* "Unico Dio generato" (Gv 1,18): idee per una cristologia del "Figlio". Teol(Br) 23 (1998) 66-99.
5430 *Busse, Ulrich* Das Eröffnungszeugnis Joh 1,19-34—Erzählstrategie und -ziel. [F]Pokorny, P. 1998 ⇒90. 33-41.
5431 *Byron, Brian Francis* Bethany across the Jordan or simply across the Jordan. ABR 46 (1998) 36-54 [Jn 1,28].
5432 *Renju, Peter M.* The lamb of God (John 1.29,36). BiTr 49 (1998) 232-239.

5433   *Ernst, Josef* "Kommt und seht!" (Joh 1,39). AnzSS 107 (1998) 291.
5434   a) *Schreiber, Stefan* Die Jüngerberufungsszene Joh 1,43-51 als literarische Einheit. SNTU.A 23 (1998) 5-28.
b) *Fenske, Wolfgang* Unter dem Feigenbaum sah ich dich (Joh 1,48):
die Bedeutung der Nathanaelperikope für die Gesamtrezeption des
Johannesevangeliums. ThZ 54 (1998) 210-227.

5435   *Monshouwer, Dirk* Dreifältig 'Kana': von 'Kana in Galiläa' zum 'Zion'
in Judäa. DBAT 29 (1998) 199-206.
5436   *Schnider, Franz* Das frühe Christentum angesichts der Dionysischen
Mysterien: religionswissenschaftliche Überlegungen zu Joh 2,1-11.
^FKLAES, N. 1998 ⇒50. 119-133.
5437   *Kuthirakkattel, Scaria* The beginning of the symbols: the meaning
and function of Jn 2:1-11. BiBh 24 (1998) 79-102.
5438   *Little, Edmund* Echoes of the Old Testament: in the wine of Cana in
Galilee (John 2:1-11) and the multiplication of the loaves and fish
(John 6:1-15): towards an appreciation. CRB 41: P 1998, Gabalda ix;
210 pp. FF240. 2-85021-110-9.
5439   *Cocchini, Francesca* Penetriamo le parole di Maria (III). Monastica
39 (1998) 4-18 [Jn 2,3-5].
5440   *Kreitzer, Larry J.* The temple incident of John 2.13-25: a preview of
what is to come. ^FASHTON J. JSNT.S 153: 1998 ⇒6. 93-101.

G1.6 Jn 3ss... Nicodemus, Samaritana

5441   **Schmidl, Martin** Jesus und Nikodemus: Gespräch zur johanneischen
Christologie: Joh 3 in schichtenspezifischer Sicht. BU 28: Rg 1998,
Pustet (10) ix; 490 pp. DM68. 3-7917-1625-5.
5442   *Zaleski, Philip* The night journey of Nicodemus. Parabola 23 (1998)
61-68.

5443   *Outtier, Bernard* La sainte Samaritaine chez les Arméniens. ^FMAR-
GAIN, J. 1998 ⇒71. 203-212.
5444   *Zimmermann, Mirjam; Zimmermann, Ruben* Brautwerbung in Samarien?: von der moralischen zur metaphorischen Interpretation von Joh
4. ZNT 2 (1998) 40-51.
5445   *Schottroff, Luise* The Samaritan woman and the notion of sexuality in
the fourth gospel. "What is John?", 2. 1998 ⇒5254. 157-181.
5446   *Xavier, A. Aloysius* The Samaritan woman and Martha of Bethany: a
comparative study of John 4 and 11. ITS 35 (1998) 291-299.
5447   *Kitzberger, Ingrid Rosa* Border crossing and meeting Jesus at the
well: an autobiographical re-reading of the Samaritan woman's story
in John 4:1-44. The personal voice. 1998 ⇒250. 111-127.
5448   ^E**Bori, Pier C.** In spirito e verità: letture di Giovanni 4,23-24. 1996
⇒12,5539; 13,5814. ^RCivCatt 149/2 (1998) 91-92 (*Scaiola, D.*).
5449   *Van Belle, Gilbert* The faith of the Galileans: the parenthesis in Jn
4,44. EThL 74 (1998) 27-44.

5450   *Rigato, Maria Luisa* L'infermo trentottenne presso "la Riserva" Betsaida (Gv 5,1-6.14) nell'immaginario cultuale giovanneo. ^FMARTINI,
C. RivBib.S 33: 1998 ⇒75. 171-194.

5451 *Labahn, Michael* Eine Spurensuche anhand von Joh 5.1-18: Bemerkungen zu Wachstum und Wandel der Heilung eines Lahmen. NTS
44 (1998) 159-179.
5452 *McGrath, James F.* A rebellious son?: Hugo Odeberg and the interpretation of John 5.18. NTS 44 (1998) 470-473.

G1.7 Panis Vitae—*Jn 6*...

5453 *Yeago, David S.* The bread of life: patristic christology and evangelical soteriology in Martin LUTHER's sermons on John 6. Luther Digest
6 (1998) 26-9.
5454 *Kügler, Joachim* Der König als Brotspender: religionsgeschichtliche
Überlegungen zu JosAs 4,7; 25,5 und Joh 6,15. ZNW 89 (1998) 118-
124.
5455 **Madden, Patrick J.** Jesus' walking on the sea: an investigation of
the origin of the narrative account. BZNW 81: 1997 ⇒13,58 2 3
ᴿEThL 74 (1998) 436-438 (*Neirynck, F.*); ThLZ 123 (1998) 60-61
(*Schille, Gottfried*); JBL 117 (1998) 746-748 (*Meadors, Edward*) [Jn
6,16-21//; 21,1-14].

5456 **Camarero Maria, Lorenzo** Revelaciones solemnes de Jesús: derás
cristológico en Jn 7-8 (fiesta de las tendas). 1997 ⇒13,5841. ᴿRSR
86 (1998) 300 (*Morgen, Michèle*); ATG 61 (1998) 288-291
(*Contreras Molina, Francisco*); ScrTh 30 (1998) 322-323 (*García-
Moreno, A.*).
5457 **Boismard, Marie-Émile** Critique textuelle ou critique littéraire?:
Jean 7,1-51. CRB 40: P 1998, Gabalda 110 pp. FF150. 285021-1079.
5458 *Caragounis, Chrys C.* Jesus, his brothers and the journey to the feast
(John 7:8-10). SEÅ 63 (1998) 177-187.
5459 **Werbylo, Walter M.** An integration of the patristic exegesis and the
modern exegesis of John 7:37-39. Excerpt Diss. Gregoriana; ᴰ*Gargano, Guido.* R 1998, 95 pp.
5460 *Marcus, Joel* Rivers of living water from Jesus' belly (John 7:38).
JBL 117 (1998) 328-330.
5461 *Lenzi, Giovanni* Il contributo della Vetus Syra alla esegesi di Gv
7,37-38. CrSt 19 (1998) 503-518.

5462 **Aus, Roger David** 'Caught in the act', walking on the sea, and the
release of Barabbas revisited. SFSHJ 157: Atlanta, GA 1998, Scholars xii; 184 pp. $50. 0-7885-0407-X [Jn 7,53-8,11; Mk 6,42-52;
15,6-15].
5463 **Toensing, Holly Joan** The politics of insertion: the pericope of the
adulterous woman and its textual history. ᴰVanderbilt 1998, 241 pp
[Jn 7,53-8,11].
5464 *Orsatti, Mauro* Verità e amore, oggi sposi: appunti su Gv 8,1-11.
RTLu 3 (1998) 707-713.
5465 *Eggen, Wiel* Jn 8:1-11, a finger writing down the history: on dialogue
beyond canonicity. Exchange 27 (1998) 98-120.
5466 *Pertini, Miguel Ángel* La genialidad gramatical de Jn 8,25. EstB 56
(1998) 371-404.

5467 *Derrett, J.D.* "Dost thou teach us?". DR 116 (1998) 183-194 [Jn 9].

5468 *Cook, Guillermo* Seeing, judging and acting: evangelism in Jesus'
       way: a biblical study on chapter 9 of the gospel of John. IRM 87
       (1998) 388-396.
5469 *Marconi, Gilberto* La vista del cieco: struttura di Gv 9,1-41. Gr. 79
       (1998) 625-643.
5470 *Leinhäupl-Wilke, Andreas* Die Karriere des Blindgeborenen als Test-
       fall johanneischer Identität: textpragmatische Erwägungen zu Joh
       9,1-41. ᶠLÖNING, K. 1998 ⇒66. 83-98.
5471 *Panimolle, Salvatore A.* Il buon pastore nel vangelo di Giovanni
       ᶠMARTINI, C. RivBib.S 33: 1998 ⇒75. 215-229 [Jn 10].
5472 *Chennattu, Rekha* The Good Shepherd (Jn 10): a political perspec-
       tive. JPJRS 1 (1998) 93-105.
5473 *Gemünden, Petra von* Palmensymbolik in Joh 12,13. ZDPV 114
       (1998) 39-70.
5474 *Regopulos, Georgios C.* Jesus and the Greeks: the exegetical
       approach of John 12,20-26. DBM 17 (1998) 81-101. **G.**
5475 **Adeso, Patrick** Universal salvation in John 12:32. Excerpt Diss.
       Gregoriana; ᴰ*Caba, José.* R 1998, 95 pp.
5476 **Scannell, Timothy Joseph** Fulfillment of Johannine signs: a study of
       John 12:37-50. ᴰFordham 1998, 185 pp.

G1.8 Jn 13... Sermo sacerdotalis et Passio

5477 **Boer, Martinus C. de** Johannine perspectives on the death of Jesus.
       Contributions to Biblical Exegesis and Theology 17: 1996
       ⇒12,5583; 13,5864. ᴿRSR 86 (1998) 306-309 (*Morgen, Michèle*);
       CBQ 60 (1998) 151-152 (*Sloyan, Gerard S.*).
5478 **Dettwiler, Andreas** Die Gegenwart des Erhöhten: eine exegetische
       Studie zu den johanneischen Abschiedsreden (Joh 13,31 - 16,33)
       unter besonderer Berücksichtigung ihres Relecture-Charakters.
       FRLANT 169: 1995 ⇒11/1,4240... 13,5877. ᴿRSR 86 (1998) 302-
       304 (*Morgen, Michèle*); JBL 117 (1998) 146-147 (*Kysar, Robert*).
5479 **Dietzfelbinger, Christian** Der Abschied des Kommenden: eine Aus-
       legung der johanneischen Abschiedsreden. WUNT 2/95: 1997 ⇒13,
       5866. ᴿBiLi 71 (1998) 78-79 (*Scholtissek, Klaus*); OrdKor 39 (1998)
       367-368 (*Giesen, Heinz*); ThRv 94 (1998) 514-515 (*März, Claus-
       Peter*).
5480 *Fortna, Robert T.* A pre-Johannine passion narrative as historical
       source: reconstructed text and critique. FORUM 1 (1998) 71-94.
5481 **Hoegen-Rohls, Christina** Der nachösterliche Johannes: die Ab-
       schiedsreden als hermeneutischer Schlüssel zum vierten Evangelium.
       WUNT 2/84: 1996 ⇒12,5588; 13,5878. ᴿRSR 86 (1998) 301-302
       (*Morgen, Michèle*); CBQ 60 (1998) 157-158 (*Neufeld, Dietmar*).
5482 *Jasper, Alison* Reading for pleasure/reading for pain: feminist reflec-
       tions on the Passion narrative in John's gospel. Religion & sexuality.
       1998 ⇒302. 203-213.
5483 *Kobayashi, Hiroko* What did John the Evangelist see in Jesus on the
       cross?: using as a key 'hypsothenai=to be lifted up'. KaKe 67 (1998)
       97-123. **J.**
5484 **Léon-Dufour, Xavier** Lectura del evangelio de Juan, 4: 18-21. ᵀ*Or-
       tiz García, Alfonso.* Biblioteca de estudios bíblicos 96: S 1998,
       Sígueme 295 pp. 84-301-1324-X. ᴿComunidades 26 (1998) 217-218
       (*González, Rafael*);

5485 Lecture de l'évangile selon Jean, 4: l'heure de la glorification. Parole de Dieu 34: 1996 ⇒12,5591; 13,5868. [R]RSR 86 (1998) 293-294 (*Morgen, Michèle*); ScrTh 30 (1998) 320-322 (*García-Moreno, A.*).

5486 *Meggitt, Justin J.* Artemidorus and the Johannine crucifixion. JHiC 5 (1998) 203-208.

5487 **Moloney, Francis J.** Glory not dishonor: reading John 13-21. Mp 1998, Fortress xvii; 217 pp. 0-8006-3140-4.

5488 *Moloney, Francis J.* The function of John 13-17 within the Johannine narrative. "What is John?", 2. 1998 ⇒5254. 43-66.

5489 *Ramos, Felipe F.* Proverbios sobre al Paráclito. Evangelio y Vida 40 (1998) 44-46, 152-154.

5490 **Tolmie, D.F.** Jesus' farewell to the disciples: John 13:1-17:26 in narratological perspective. Bibl.Interp. 12: 1995 ⇒11/1,4235; 13,5872. [R]EstAg 33 (1998) 380-381 (*Cineira, D.A.*).

5491 *Buckley, Jorunn Jacobsen* Presenting the poison in the gospel of John. Violence. 1998 ⇒260. 60-71 [Jn 13].

5492 **Martini, Carlo Maria** Du, Herr, willst uns die Füße waschen?: Meditationsgedanken zum Evangelium der Fußwaschung. Mü [2]1998, Neue Stadt 79 pp. DM19,80. 3-87996-378-9 [Jn 13,1-20].

5493 *Young, David* Is servanthood enough?. Echoes from the local tradition (1998) 35-38 [Jn 13,1-20].

5494 *Kieffer, René* L'arrière-fond juif du lavement des pieds. RB 105 (1998) 546-555 [Jn 13,1-20];

5495 Fottvagningens tolkning mot dess judiska bakgrund. SEÅ 63 1998, 217-223 [Jn 13,1-20].

5496 *Osculati, Roberto* 'Chi ha visto me ha visto il Padre' (Gv 14,9): Gesù e la rivelazione di Dio. Laós 5 (1998) 3-10.

5497 *Moloney, Francis J.* The Johannine Paraclete and Jesus. [F]HERIBAN J. 1998 ⇒41. 213-228 [Jn 14,16].

5498 *Greiner, Albert* Trois pierres précieuses en Jean 14,23-29. PosLuth 46 (1998) 379-381.

5499 *Keaty, Anthony W.* THOMAS's authority for identifying charity as friendship: Aristotle or John 15?. Thom. 62 (1998) 581-601.

5500 *Schwank, Benedikt* Bildbetrachtung: "Ich bin der wahre Weinstock" (Joh 15,1). EuA 74 (1998) 241-243.

5501 *Zani, Lorenzo* 'Mi darete testimonianza' (Gv 15,27): lo Spirito è testimone di Gesù e ne continua la missione. Presbyteri 32 (1998) 379-386.

5502 *Segovia, Fernando F.* Inclusion and exclusion in John 17: an intercultural reading. "What is John?", 2. 1998 ⇒5254. 183-210.

5503 *Irons, Lee* 'Christus Agonistes': the betrayal and arrest of the I AM: John 18:1-14. Kerux 13 (1998) 3-15.

5504 *De Maria, Antonio* Il mio regno non è di questo mondo: breve analisi del commento patristico a Gv 18,36. Laós 5 (1998) 11-18.

5505 *Schürmann, Heinz* Jesu letzte Weisung: Joh 19,26-27a. Gesammelte Beiträge. 1998 <1969> ⇒197. 272-292.

5506 *Guerra Gomez, Manuel* ¿Pneûma, un elemento pneumatológico (Espíritu Santo) o antropológico (el alma/espíritu del hombre)?: Jn 19,30; Math 25,50, et par., en los escritos cristianos de los primeros siglos y en los no cristianos. Burg. 39 (1998) 31-78.

5507 *Gnidovec, Franc* Kristusovo vstajenje v Janezovem evangeliju [Christ's resurrection in the gospel according to John]. Bogoslovni Vestnik 58 (1998) 491-503. **Slovenian.**
5508 *Theobald, Michael* Der johanneische Osterglaube und die Grenzen seiner narrativen Vermittlung (Joh 20). ᶠHOFFMANN, P., Von Jesus. BZNW 93: 1998 ⇒43. 93-123.
5509 *Durken, Daniel* Empty tombs. BiTod 36 (1998) 98-102.
5510 *Lee, Dorothy A.* Turning from death to life: a biblical reflection on Mary Magdalene (John 20:1-18). ER 50 (1998) 112-120.
5511 *Ebner, Martin* Wer liebt mehr?: die liebende Jüngerin und der geliebte Jünger nach Joh 20,1-18. BZ 42 (1998) 39-55.
5512 *Grassi, Joseph A.* The wounds of Jesus: exegesis, biblical piety, and liturgy. Worship 72 (1998) 141-147 [Jn 20,19-29].
5513 *Derrett, J. Duncan M.* Why did Jesus blow on the disciples? (John 20,22). BeO 40 (1998) 235-246.
5514 **Bonney, William L.** Why the risen Jesus appeared to Thomas: an analysis of John 20:24-29 in the context of a synchronic reading of the gospel. ᴰFordham 1998, 299 pp.
5515 *Van Belle, Gilbert* The meaning of σημεῖα in Jn 20,30-31. EThL 74 (1998) 300-325.
5516 *Manns, Frédéric* Jean 21: contribution à l'ecclésiologie du quatrième évangile. ᶠMARTINI, C. RivBib.S 33: 1998 ⇒75. 195-213.
5517 *Brooke, George J.* 4Q252 and the 153 fish of John 21:11. ᶠSTEGE-MANN, H. BZNW 97: 1998 ⇒111. 253-265.
5518 *Berliet, Gérard* Pierre et l'expérience de la rédemption: l'apparition de Jésus ressuscité au bord du lac: Jn 21, 15-22. Vie Chrétienne 430 (1998) 2-5.

G2.1 Epistulae Johannis

5519 **Barnes, Peter** Knowing where we stand: the message of John's epistles. Darlington 1998, Evangelical 160 pp. £5. 0-85234-414-7.
5520 **Calvin, Jean** 1,2,& 3 John. The Crossway Classic Commentaries: Wheaton, IL 1998, Crossway Books vii; 9-128 pp. 0-89107-993-9.
5521 **Stott, John Robert Walmsley** Les épîtres de Jean. Commentaire évangélique de la bible 20: Vaux-sur-Seine 1998, Edifac 221 pp. 2-904407-22-7.
5522 **Vannini, Francesco** 1, 2, 3 Giovanni. Brescia 1998, Queriniana 148 pp. L19.000. 88-399-1590-7.

5523 *Arens, Eduardo* Das Wort des Lebens: eine kontextuelle Lektüre des ersten Johannesbriefes aus Lateinamerika. BiKi 53 (1998) 205-208.
5524 *Beutler, Johannes* Der erste Johannesbrief als Zeugnis der johanneischen Schule. BiKi 53 (1998) 170-175.
5525 *Borbury, William* Antichrist among Jews and Gentiles. Jews in a Graeco-Roman world. 1998 ⇒337. 113-133.
5526 *Cavalcoli, Giovanni* L'Anticristo di NIETZSCHE e l'Anticristo della bibbia. SacDo 43 (1998) 77-134.
5527 *Dalbesio, Anselmo* Il messaggio teologico della prima lettera di Giovanni. Laur. 39 (1998) 15-292.
5528 **Giurisato, Giorgio** Struttura e teologia della prima lettera di Giovanni: analisi letteraria e retorica, contenuto teologico. Diss. Gregoriana

1997; ^D*Vanni, Ugo.* AnBib 138: R 1998, E.P.I.B. (4) 720 pp. €50,61. 88-7653-138-6.

5529 *Griffith, Terry* A non-polemical reading of 1 John: sin, christology and the limits of Johannine christianity. TynB 49 (1998) 253-276.

5530 **Lavatori, Renzo; Sole, Luciano** Gesù Cristo venuto nella carne: il criterio dell'identità cristiana secondo la Prima Lettera di Giovanni. Lettura pastorale della Bibbia, Bibbia e spiritualità 5: Bo 1998, EDB 176 pp. L20.000. 88-10-20150-7.

5531 **Mills, Donald William** The concept of sinlessness in 1 John in relation to Johannine eschatology. ^DWestminster Theol. Sem. 1998, 438 pp.

5532 *Richards, W. Larry* An analysis of ALAND's Teststellen in 1 John. NTS 44 (1998) 26-44.

5533 *Rusconi, Roberto* Antichrist and antichrists. Encyclopedia of apocalypticism II. 1998 ⇒507. 287-325.

5534 *Theobald, Michael* Der Streit um Jesus als Testfall des Glaubens: Christologie im ersten Johannesbrief. BiKi 53 (1998) 183-189.

5535 *Thoams, John Christopher* The literary structure of 1 John. NT 40 (1998) 369-381.

5536 *Umoh, Camillus* Die Lektüre des ersten Johannesbriefes im afrikanischen Kontext. BiKi 53 (1998) 200-204.

5537 *Van der Watt, Jan Gabriel* My reading of 1 John in Africa. The personal voice. 1998 ⇒250. 142-155.

5538 ^{ET}**Verde, Armando F.; Giaconi, Elettra** SAVONAROLA: sermones in primam divi Ioannis epistolam secondo l'autografo. Savonarola e la Toscana, Atti e documenti 3: F 1998, SISMEL xxxii; 312 pp. 88-87027-09-9.

5539 *Weidemann, Hans-Ulrich* "Das habe ich euch geschrieben ...": neuere deutschsprachige Kommentare zum ersten Johannesbrief. BiKi 53 (1998) 209-212.

5540 *Wright, Rosemary Muir* Satán y el Anticristo, ¿símbolos necesarios?. Conc(E) 274 (1998) 81-91 [Conc(I) 34/1,85-97; Conc(GB) 1998/1,56-64; Conc(F) 274,71-80; Conc(D) 34/1,48-55; Conc(P) 274,70-80].

5541 **Wu, Daniel Tao-Chung** An analysis of the structure of 1 John using discourse analysis. ^DSouthern Bapist Theol. Sem. 1998, 208 pp.

5542 *Gubler, Marie-Louise* "Wer sagt, er sei im Licht, aber seinen Bruder haßt, ist noch in der Finsternis ..." (1 Joh 2,9). Diak. 29 (1998) 222-228.

5543 **Heid, Stefan** Chiliasmus und Antichrist-Mythos: eine frühchristliche Kontroverse um das Heilige Land. Studien zur alten Kirchengeschichte 6: 1993 ⇒9,5674... 13,5919. ^ROLZ 93 (1998) 193-195 (*Bull, Klaus-Michael*) [1 Jn 2,18].

5544 *Porsch, Felix* "... daß sie alle nicht zu uns gehörten" (1 Joh 2,19): der Umgang mit Dissidenten im 1 Joh. BiKi 53 (1998) 190-194.

5545 *De Waal Dryden, J.* The sense of σπέρμα in 1 John 3:9: in light of lexical evidence. FgNT 11 (1998) 85-100.

5546 *Ortkemper, Franz-Josef* "Gott ist größer als unser Herz ..." (1 Joh 3,18-20). BiKi 53 (1998) 197-199.

5547 *Mitchell, Margaret M.* "Diotrephes does not receive us": the lexicographical and social context of 3 John 9-10. JBL 117 (1998) 299-320.

G2.3 *Apocalypsis Johannis*—**Revelation: text, commentaries**

5548 Apocalypsis. BVLI 42 (1998) 36-39.
5549 **Aune, David E.** Revelation 17-22. WBC 52C: Waco, Tex. 1998, Word Books xlvi; 906-1354 pp. $35. 0-8499-1545-7;
5550 Revelation: 1-5. WBC 52A: 1997, [R]Bib. 79 (1998) 582-585 (*Biguzzi, Giancarlo*);
5551 Revelation 6-16. WBC 52B: Dallas, Tex. 1998, Word Books xlv; 378-903 pp. $30. 0-8499-0251-7.
5552 **Barr, David L.** Tales of the end: a narrative commentary on the book of Revelation. The storytellers Bible 1: Santa Rosa, Calif. 1998, Polebridge xii; 228 pp.
5553 **Burr, David** OLIVI's peaceable kingdom: a reading of the Apocalypse Commentary. 1993 ⇒9,5682. [R]CrSt 19/1 (1998) 197-201 (*Schmolinsky, Sabine*).
5554 [TE]**Dulaey, Martine** VICTORIN de Poetovio: sur l'Apocalypse: (suivi de) fragment chronologique (et de) la construction du monde. SC 423: 1997 ⇒13,5929. [R]JThS 49 (1998) 834-839 (*Hill, Charles E.*).
5555 **Giesen, Heinz** Die Offenbarung des Johannes. RNT: 1997 ⇒13, 5935. [R]OrdKor 39 (1998) 240-241 (*Porsch, Felix*); ThG 41 (1998) 150-151 (*Böcher, Otto*); ThPh 73 (1998) 578-580 (*Baumert, N.*).
5556 **Harrington, Daniel** Revelation. Hyde Park, NY 1998, New City 166 pp. $10.
5557 **Heer, Jos de** De Apocalyps van Johannes: hemelse ontmanteling van aardse machten. Zoetermeer 1998, Meinema 297 pp. *f*39.90. 90-211-3707-0. [R]Interpretatie 6/8 (1998) 7-8 (*Hoet, Hendrik*).
5558 *Leonardi, Lino* Versioni e revisioni dell'Apocalisse in volgare: obiettivi e metodi di una ricerca. La bibbia in italiano. 1998 ⇒390. 37-92.
5559 **Meldau, Volker** Die Wende aller Zeiten: eine Auslegung der Offenbarung die Johannes aus katholisch-apostolischer Sicht. Marburg 1998, Tectum 370 pp. 3-8288-9022-9.
5560 **Mounce, Robert H.** The book of Revelation. The New International Commentary on the NT: GR 1998, Eerdmans xxxvi; 439 pp. $44. 0-8028-2537-0. [R]RExp 95 (1998) 455 (*Pelletier, Samuel R.*).
5561 **Murphy, Frederick James** Fallen is Babylon: the revelation to John. The New Testament in context: Harrisburg, Pennsylvania 1998, Trinity xx; 472 pp. $30. 1-56338-152-4.
5562 **Niewenhuis, Jan** Het laatste woord: Openbaring van Johannes voor de gemeente van nu. Kampen 1998, Kok. [R]ITBT 6/8 (1998) 7-8 (*Hoet, Hendrik*).
5563 **Prigent, Pierre** L'Apocalypse. LiBi 117: P 1998, Cerf 290 pp. 2-204-05815-7.
5564 *Rapisarda, Grazia* Per una storia dell'esegesi irlandese: incerti auctoris *Commentarius in Apocalypsin.* Orph. 19-20 (1998-99) 378-394.
5565 Revelation: Authorised King James Version. Pocket Canons: E 1998, Canongate xiv; 50 pp. 0-86241-800-3.
5566 **Richard, Pablo** Apokalypse. 1996 ⇒11/1,4332; 13,5952. [R]Conc(D) 34 (1998) 469-470 (*Reck, Norbert*).
5567 **Talbert, Charles H.** The Apocalypse: a reading of the Revelation of John. 1994 ⇒10,5484... 12,5680. [R]Pro Ecclesia 7 (1998) 367-368 (*Landry, David T.*).
5568 **Thompson, Leonard L.** Revelation. Abingdon New Testament Commentaries: Nv 1998, Abingdon 207 pp. $22. 0-687-05679-9.

5569   **Pate, C. Marvin** Four views on the book of Revelation. GR 1998, Zondervan 252 pp. 0-310-21080-1.
5570   *Pate, C. Marvin* Introduction to Revelation. Four views. 1998 ⇒5569. 9-34.

G2.4 *Apocalypsis, themata*—Revelation, topics

5571   *Akerboom, T.H.M.* 'Er zullen grote tekenen zijn': een verkenning van LUTHERs verstaan van de Apocalyps in de context van zijn tijd. Luther-Bulletin 7 (1998) 62-75.
5572   *Armogathe, Jean-Robert* Interpretations of the Revelation of John: 1500-1800. Encyclopedia of apocalypticism II. 1998 ⇒507. 185-203.
5573   *Backus, Irena* The church fathers and the canonicity of the Apocalypse in the sixteenth century: ERASMUS, Frans TITELMANS, and Theodore BEZA. SCJ 29 (1998) 651-665.
5574   *Banazac, Gregory A.; Ceja, Luis* Reyes La esperanza en el desierto mesianico: los padres de la iglesia latinoamericana y el libro del Apocalipsis. EfMex 16 (1998) 199-207.
5575   **Beale, Gregory K.** John's use of the Old Testament in Revelation. JSNT.S 166: Shf 1998, Academic 443 pp. £55/$85. 1-85075-894-8.
5576   **Bedriñán, Claudio** La dimensión socio-politica del mensaje teológico del Apocalipsis. TGr.T 11: 1996 ⇒12,5692; 13,5963. [R]CDios 111/1 (1998) 334-336 (*Gutiérrez, J.*); EstB 56 (1998) 417-423 (*Urbán, A.*).
5577   *Bertazzoli, Raffaella* L'Apocalisse nell'iconografia bizantina e orientale. Mondo della bibbia 44 (1998) 24-27.
5578   *Biguzzi, Giancarlo* Ephesus, its Artemision, its temple to the Flavian emperors, and idolatry in Revelation. NT 40 (1998) 276-290;
5579   I testi violenti e scomodi dell'Apocalisse. PSV 1998, 177-197;
5580   John on Patmos and the "persecution" in the Apocalypse. EstB 56 1(1998) 201-220.
5581   *Boyer, Frédéric* Enigmi per imparare a leggere. Mondo della bibbia 44 (1998) 15-16.
5582   *Böcher, Otto* Die Bildwelt der Apokalypse des Johannes. JBTh 13 (1998) 77-105.
5583   **Böcher, Otto** Die Johannesapokalypse. EdF 41: Da:Wiss 1998, xvii; 191 pp. 3-534-04905-5.
5584   **Burdon, Christopher** The Apocalypse in England: revelation unravelling, 1700-1834. 1997 ⇒13,5967. [R]Theol. 101 (1998) 220-221 (*Newport, Kenneth*).
5585   **Butler, Brett Jack** Irony in the Book of Revelation. [D]Southern Baptist Theol. Sem. 1998, 210 pp.
5586   **Calaway, Bernie L.** Revealing the revelation: a guide to the literature of the Apocalypse. SF 1998, International Scholars viii; (2) 632 pp. 1-57309-155-3.
5587   *Carrez, Maurice* Io, Giovanni,...mi trovavo nell'isola chiamata Patmos... Mondo della bibbia 44 (1998) 5-10.
5588   *Charlesworth, James H.* How Barisat bellowed: folklore, humor, and iconography in the Jewish apocalypses and the Apocalypse of John. Dead Sea Scrolls & Christian Origins Library 3: North Richland Hills, TX 1998, BIBAL xiii; 60 pp. $9. 0-941037-64-9.

5589 **Christie, Yves** L'Apocalypse de Jean: sens et développements de ses visions synthétiques. 1996 ⇒12,5704; 13,5971. ^RHZ 266/2 (1998) 474-475 *(Tewes, Ludger)*.
5590 *Collins, Adela Yarbro* The book of Revelation. Encyclopedia of apocalypticism I. 1998 ⇒507. 384-414;
5591 Source criticism of the book of Revelation. BR 43 (1998) 50-53.
5592 **Collins, C.** Authority figures: metaphors of mastery from the *Iliad* to the *Apocalypse*. 1996 ⇒12,5705. ^RClR 48/1 (1998) 204 *(Goldhill, Simon)*.
5593 ^E**Collins, John Joseph; Emmerson, Richard K.; Herzman, Ronald B.** The apocalyptic imagination in medieval literature. 1992 ⇒8,m30. ^REHR 113 (1998) 146-147 *(Murray, Alexander)*.
5594 **Corsani, Bruno** L'Apocalisse e l'apocalittica del Nuovo Testamento. 1997 ⇒13,5927. ^RCDios 211 (1998) 652 *(Gutiérrez, J.)*.
5595 ^E**Dianich, Severino** Sempre apocalisse: un testo biblico e le sue risonanze storiche. Saggi Piemme: CasM 1998, Piemme 205 pp. 88-384-3094-2.
5596 **Donegani, Isabelle** "A cause de la parole de Dieu et du témoignage de Jésus...": le témoignage comme parole de sens et d'espérance dans l'Apocalypse de Jean. EtB 36: 1997 ⇒13,5977. ^RThLZ 123 (1998) 852-854 *(Rissi, Mathias)*.
5597 **Enebral Casares, A.M.** El Apocalipsis, ayer y hoy. La Laguna 1998, Benchomo 299 pp;
5598 Apocalipsis: historia de unas bodas. La Laguna 1998, Benchomo 303 pp.
5599 **Fekkes III, Jan** Isaiah and prophetic traditions in the book of Revelation. JSNT.S 93: 1994, ^REvQ 70 (1998) 156-159 *(Beale, Greg K.)*.
5600 **Fiorenza, Elisabeth Schüssler** The book of Revelation: justice and judgment. Mp 1998, Fortress xii; 243 pp. $21.
5601 *Ford, Josephine M.* The christological function of the hymns in the Apocalypse of John. AUSS 36 (1998) 207-229.
5602 *Gentry, Kenneth L.* A Preterist view of Revelation. Four views. 1998 ⇒5569. 35-92.
5603 **Gradl, Veronica** Gedanken zur geheimen Offenbarung des Johannes, Teil 1: Prat: zur Psychodynamik der Menschlichkeit. Innsbruck 1998, Gradl 312 pp. 3-9500929-2-7.
5604 *Hamstra, Sam* An idealist view of Revelation. Four views. 1998 ⇒5569. 93-131.
5605 *Hasitschka, Martin* Anbetung des Drachen oder Huldigung vor dem Lamm: Horrorvisionen und Hoffnungsbilder in der Apokalypse des Johannes (Offb). Entschluss 53 (1998) 8-10.
5606 *Heer, Jos de* De Apocalyps is hard nodig. ITBT 6/7 (1998) 20-23.
5607 **Heinze, André** Johannesapokalypse und johanneische Schriften: geschichtliche und traditionsgeschichtliche Untersuchungen. BWANT 142: Stu 1998, Kohlhammer 400 pp. DM89. 3-17-015404-4.
5608 **Horn, Stephen Norwood** The author's use of hymns as summaries of the theology of the Book of Revelation. ^DNew Orleans Baptist Theol. Sem. 1998, 169 pp.
5609 *Johns, Loren L.* The Lamb in the rhetorical program of the Apocalypse of John. SBL.SP part 2. SBL.SPS 37: 1998 ⇒402. 762-784.
5610 **Johns, Loren L.** The origins and rhetorical force of the lamb christology of the Apocalypse of John. ^DPrinceton Theol. Sem. 1998, 282 pp.

5611 *Keller, Catherine* La fascinación del Apocalipsis y del mal escatológico. Conc(E) 274 (1998) 93-104 [Conc(I) 34/1,98-111; Conc(GB)
1998/1,65-73; Conc(F) 274,81-91; Conc(D) 34/1,56-65; Conc(P)
274,81-91].

5612 **Keller, Catherine** Apocalypse now and then: a feminist approach to
the end of the world. 1996 ⇒12,5715; 13,5987. [R]CrossCur 48 (1998)
257-261 (*Burton-Christie, Douglas*).

5613 **Kerner, Jürgen** Die Ethik der Johannesapokalypse im Vergleich mit
der des 4. Esra: ein Beitrag zum Verhältnis von Apokalyptik und
Ethik. BZNW 94: B 1998, De Gruyter xi; 316 pp. DM288/188. 3-11-
016152-4.

5614 *Khiok-khng, Yeo* What has Jerusalem to do with Beijing?: the book
of Revelation and Chinese christians. SBL.SP part 2. SBL.SPS 37:
1998 ⇒402. 991-1004.

5615 **Kraybill, J. Nelson** Imperial cult and commerce in John's Apoca-
lypse. JSNT.S 132: 1996 ⇒12,5719. [R]CBQ 60 (1998) 162-163
(*Thompson, Leonard L.*); JBL 117 (1998) 373-375 (*Wilson, J.
Christian*).

5616 *Kuschel, Karl-Josef* Der Alptraum vom Ende der Menschheit: Auseinandersetzung mit der Apokalypse im Werk von Günter GRASS.
Conc(D) 34 (1998) 361-369.

5617 *Lee, Michelle V.* A call to martyrdom: function as method and message in Revelation. NT 40 (1998) 164-194.

5618 **MacKenzie, Robert K.** The author of the Apocalypse: a review of
the prevailing hypothesis of Jewish-Christian authorship. 1997
⇒13,5990. [R]JBL 117 (1998) 756-758 (*Farmer, Ronald L.*).

5619 **Malina, Bruce J.** On the genre and message of Revelation: star
visions and sky journeys. 1995 ⇒11/1,4386... 13,5991. [R]HeyJ 39
(1998) 437-438 (*Sylwanowicz, Michael*).

5620 **Marshall, John William** Parables of the war: reading the Apocalypse within Judaism and during the Judaean War. [D]Princeton Univ.
1998, 521 pp.

5621 **Mazzeo, Michele** Dio padre e signore: nel libro dell'Apocalisse.
Cammini nello Spirito 14: Mi 1998, Paoline 390 pp. 88-315-1613-2;

5622 Lo Spirito parla alla chiesa, nel libro dell'Apocalisse. Cammini nello
spirito 10: Mi 1998, Paoline 360 pp. L23.000. 88-315-1514-4.

5623 *Mentré, Mireille* L'Apocalisse nella pittura mozarabica. Mondo della
bibbia 44 (1998) 32-35;

5624 L'Apocalisse nell'arte medioevale. Mondo della bibbia 44 (1998) 28-
31.

5625 **Mìrete Pina, Angel** 666: Apocalipsis I a XIII: una profecía
cumplida. Ensayos 117: M 1998, Encuentro 373 pp. 84-7490-472-2.

5626 *Moore, Stephen D.* Revolting Revelations. The personal voice. 1998
⇒250. 183-200.

5627 *Morandini, Simone* I cieli nuovi e la terra nuova: il futturo del cosmo,
tra riecerca scientifica e teologia. Studi ecumenici 16 (1998) 367-
386.

5628 **Munger, Marcia Alice** The rhetoric and function of angels in the
book of Revelation. [D]Trinity 1998, 336 pp.

5629 *Munoa, Philip B.* Christianizing Jewish apocalypticism: D.E. AUNE's
proposal for understanding Revelation. BR 43 (1998) 54-60.

5630 **Naden, Roy C.** The lamb among the beasts. 1996 ⇒12,5730.
[R]AUSS 36 (1998) 148-149 (*Matak, Dragutin*).

5631 *Noguez A., Armando* Resistir a la bestia: el mansaje ético social del Apocalipsis. Voces 12 (1998) 93-131.
5632 *Orsatti, Mauro* La speranza nell'Apocalisse: note su una virtù difficile e trascurata. RTLu 3 (1998) 27-52;
5633 Il tempo nell'Apocalisse: abbraccio di eternità. La fine del tempo. 1998 ⇒296. 59-88.
5634 *Pate, C. Marvin* Conclusion. Four views. 1998 ⇒5569. 231-232;
5635 A progressive dispensationalist view of Revelation. Four views. 1998 ⇒5569. 133-175.
5636 **Paulien, Jon** The book of Revelation and the Old Testament. BR 43 (1998) 61-69.
5637 **Peterson, Eugene H.** Laatste woorden: de Openbaring van Johannes en de biddende verbeelding. Gorinchem 1998, Ekklesia 253 pp. f29.90. 90-755-6906-8.
5638 **Pezzoli-Olgiati, Daria** Täuschung und Klarheit: zur Wechselwirkung zwischen Vision und Geschichte in der Johannesoffenbarung. FRLANT 175: 1997 ⇒13,5996. ᴿThLZ 123 (1998) 857-859 (*Bücher, Otto*).
5639 *Poucouta, Paulin* Inventer la terre: l'Apocalypse aujourd'hui. LV.F 53 (1998) 403-414.
5640 *Prévost, Jean-Pierre* La suggestione della fine dei tempi. Mondo della bibbia 44 (1998) 13-14.
5641 *Price, Robert M.* Saint John's apothecary: différance, textuality, and the advent of meaning. Biblical Interpretation 6 (1998) 105-112.
5642 **Resseguie, James L.** Revelation unsealed: a narrative critical approach to John's Apocalypse. Biblical interpretation 32: Lei 1998, Brill ix; 233 pp. f143. 90-04-11129-8.
5643 *Rezza, Dario* L'immaginario simbolico dell'Apocalisse. PalCl 77 (1998) 625-638.
5644 *Riemer, Ulrike* Das Tier auf dem Kaiserthron?: eine Untersuchung zur Offenbarung des Johannes als historischer Quelle. Beiträge zur Altertumskunde 114: Stu 1998, Teubner x; 200 pp. 3-519-07663-2.
5645 *Rossing, Barbara* River of life in God's new Jerusalem: an ecological vision for earth's future. CThMi 25 (1998) 487-499.
5646 **Royalty, Robert M.** The streets of heaven: the ideology of wealth in the Apocalypse of John. Macon, GA 1998, Mercer Univ. Pr. viii; 292 pp. $28. 0-86554-609-6.
5647 ᴱ**Rusconi, Roberto** Storia e figure de l'apocalisse fra '500 e '600. Opere di Gioacchino da Fiore: testi e strumenti 7: 1996 ⇒12,5747. ᴿCFr 68 (1998) 357-359 (*Bérubé, Camille*).
5648 **Simojoki, Anssi** Apocalypse interpreted: the types of interpretation of the Book of Revelation in Finland, 1944-1995, from the Second World War to the post-Cold War world. Abo Akademi, Finland 1998, 220 pp.
5649 *Slater, Thomas B.* On the social setting of the Revelation to John. NTS 44 (1998) 232-256.
5650 *Smith, Robert H.* 'Worthy is the lamb' and other songs of Revelation. CThMi 25 (1998) 500-506.
5651 *Stanley, John E.* Two futures—Jürgen MOLTMANN's eschatology and Revelation's apocalyptic. AsbTJ 53 (1998) 37-48.
5652 *Stefani, Piero* L'Apocalisse nella storia. Asp. 45 (1998) 583-586.
5653 ᴱ**Strecker, Georg; Schnelle, Udo** Texte zur Briefliteratur und zur Johannesapokalypse. Neuer Wettstein: Texte zum Neuen Testament

aus Griechentum und Hellenismus, Teilbd. 1/2. 1996 ⇒12,5754.
[R]ZKTh 120 (1998) 218-220 (*Oberforcher, Robert*).

5654 **Stuckenbruck, Loren T.** Angel veneration and christology: a study
in early Judaism and in the christology of the Apocalypse of John.
WUNT 2/70: 1995 ⇒11/1,4422... 13,6014. [R]BZ 42 (1998) 148-150
(*Löhr, Hermut*).

5655 *Sys, Jacques* "Et c'est une femme": retour sur l'Apocalypse. Graphè 7
(1998) 173-184.

5656 *Taeger, Jens-W.* Begründetes Schweigen: Paulus und paulinische
Tradition in der Johannesapokalypse. [F]KLEIN, G. 1998 ⇒52. 187-
204.

5657 *Thomas, Robert L.* A classical dispensationalist view of Revelation.
Four views. 1998 ⇒5569. 177-229.

5658 *Trites, Allison A.* Witness and the resurrection in the Apocalypse of
John. Life in the face of death. 1998 ⇒252. 270-288.

5659 *Ulfgard, Håkan* El apocalipsis hoy: reconocer su originalidad, respe-
tar su mensaje permanente. Conc(E) 277 (1998) 543-552 [Conc(I)
34,572-583; Conc(D) 34,378-386; Conc(F) 277,47-56; Conc(P) 277,
38-47; Conc(GB) 1998/4,31-39].

5660 **VanderKam, James C.; Adler, William** The Jewish apocalyptic
heritage in early christianity. CRI 3/4: 1996 ⇒12,5757. [R]Prudentia
30/1 (1998) 71-73 (*McKechnie, Paul*); VigChr 52 (1998) 217-220
(*Tromp, J.*); Sal. 60 (1998) 572-573 (*Vicent, R.*).

5661 *Van Henten, Jan Willem* Anti-judaïsme in de Openbaring van Johannes?. Interpretatie 6/4 (1998) 14-17.

5662 *Vanni, Ugo* La fede nell'Apocalisse. La fede nella bibbia. DSBP 21:
1998 ⇒224. 252-271;

5663 Linguaggio, simboli ed esperienza mistica nel libro dell'Apocalisse.
Gr. 79 (1998) 5-28, 473-501.

5664 *Voorwinde, Stephen* Worship—the key to the book of Revelation?.
Vox reformata 63 (1998) 3-35.

G2.5 *Apocalypsis*, **Revelation 1,1...**

5665 **Rissi, Mathias** Die Hure Babylon und die Verführung der Heiligen:
eine Studie zur Apokalypse des Johannes. BWANT 136: 1995 ⇒
11/1,4464... 13,6045. [R]NT 40 (1998) 400-402 (*Schnabel, E.J.*).

5666 *Biguzzi, G.* 'All'angelo della chiesa di ..., scrivi!' (Ap 2,1 ecc.).
Angeli e demoni. 1998 ⇒375. 79-116.

5667 **Poucouta, Paulin** Lettres aux églises d'Afrique: Apocalypse 1-3.
1997 ⇒13,6024. [R]AETSC 3 (1998) 209-210 (*Chiappo, Michele*).

5668 **Biguzzi, Giancarlo** I settenari nella struttura dell'Apocalisse: analisi,
storia della ricerca, interpretazione. SRivBib 31: 1996 ⇒12,5694;
13,5965. [R]CDios 211 (1998) 653-654 (*Gutiérrez, J.*); RivBib 46
(1998) 369-373 (*Doglio, Claudio*); CBQ 60 (1998) 358-359
(*Winkler, Jude*); Anton. 73 (1998) 369-371 (*Alvarez Barredo,
Miguel*); Gr. 79 (1998) 179-180 (*Marconi, Gilberto*); CivCatt 149/2
(1998) 413-414 (*Scaiola, D.*) [Rev 1-3].

5669 *Sikora, Ryszard Adam* '[...] Odstąpiłeś od twej pierwotnej miłosci'
(Ap 2,4) ['(...) You neglected your first love' (Rev 2,4)]. Roczniki
Teologiczne 45 (1998) 167-179. **P**.

5670 *Wong, Daniel K.K.* The tree of life in Revelation 2:7. BS 155 (1998) 211-226.

5671 *Bredin, Mark R.J.* The synagogue of Satan accusation in Revelation 2:9. BTB 28 (1998) 160-164.

5672 *Wong, Daniel K.K.* The hidden manna and the white stone in Revelation 2:17. BS 155 (1998) 346-354.

5673 *Afzal, Cameron* Wheels of time: merkavah exegesis in Revelation 4. SBL.SP part 1. SBL.SPS 37: 1998 ⇒402. 465-482.

5674 *Giblin, Charles Homer* From and before the throne: Revelation 4:5-6a integrating the imagery of Revelation 4-16. CBQ 60 (1998) 500-513.

5675 *Grelot, Pierre* L'imagerie des quatre vivants symboliques. FMARGAIN, J. 1998 ⇒71. 241-250.

5676 *Wannenmacher, Eva Julia* De septem sigillis: Exegese zwischen Tradition und Innovation. Florensia 12 (1998) 7-18.

5677 *Hofius, Otfried* 'Αρνίον—Widder oder Lamm?: Erwägungen zur Bedeutung des Wortes in der Johannesapokalypse. ZNW 89 (1998) 272-281.

5678 *Lambrecht, Jan* The opening of the seals (Rev 6,1-8,6). Bib. 79 (1998) 198-220.

5679 *Bachmann, Michael* Noch ein Blick auf den ersten apokalyptischen Reiter (von Apk 6.1-2). NTS 44 (1998) 257-278.

5680 *Wick, Peter* There was silence in heaven (Revelation 8:1): an annotation to Israel Knohl's "Between voice and silence". JBL 117 (1998) 512-514.

5681 *Farkaš, Pavol* Il simbolo della 'donna' di *Ap* 12 e la sua interpretazione. FHERIBAN J. 1998 ⇒41. 229-246.

5682 *Alkier, Stefan* Hinrichtungen und Befreiungen: Wahn—Vision—Wirklichkeit in Apg 12: Skizzen eines semiotischen Lektüreverfahrens und seiner theoretischen Grundlagen. Exegese und Methodendiskussion. TANZ 23: 1998 ⇒208. 111-133.

5683 *Díez Merino, Luis* La mujer y el varón destinado a gobernar (¿Apocalipsis 12 un midrás de Génesis 3,15?). EstMar 64 (1998) 111-156.

5684 **Busch, Peter** Der gefallene Drache: Mythenexegese am Beispiel von Apokalypse 12. TANZ 19: 1996 ⇒12,5772; 13,6039. RCBQ 60 (1998) 148-149 (*Morton, Russell*).

5685 **Ulland, Harald** Die Vision als Radikalisierung der Wirklichkeit in der Apokalypse des Johannes: das Verhältnis der sieben Sendschreiben zu Apokalypse 12-13. TANZ 21: 1997 ⇒13,6035. RBZ 42 (1998) 150-152 (*Giesen, Heinz*).

5686 *Wiegard, Jesaja Michael* Lebensfristen oder Lebensmut?: "... eine Zeit und zwei Zeiten und eine halbe Zeit ..." (Apk 12,14). FLÖNING, K. 1998 ⇒66. 159-174.

5687 *López, Javier* La figura de la bestia entre historia y profecía: investigación teológico-bíblica de Apocalipsis 13,1-18. TGr.T 39: R 1998, E.P.U.G. 303 pp. €17,55. 88-7652-791-5.

5688 *deSilva, David A.* The persuasive strategy of the Apocalypse: a socio-rhetorical investigation of Revelation 14:6-13. SBL.SP part 2. SBL.SPS 37: 1998 ⇒402. 785-806.

5689 *Miller, Kevin E.* The nuptial eschatology of Revelation 19-22. CBQ 60 (1998) 301-318.

5690 *Malina, Bruce J.* How a cosmic lamb marries: the image of the wedding of the lamb (Rev 19:7 ff.). BTB 28 (1998) 75-83.

5691   *Müller, Ulrich B.* "Das Wort Gottes": der Name des Reiters auf weißem Pferd (Apk 19,13). [F]STEGEMANN, H. BZNW 97: 1998 ⇒ 111. 474-487.

G2.7 Millenniarismus, *Apc 20...*

5692   *Baumgarten, Albert I.* The pursuit of the millennium in early Judaism. Tolerance. 1998 ⇒440. 38-60.
5693   *Berruto, Anna Maria* Millenarismo e montanismo. ASEs 15 (1998) 85-100.
5694   *Brasher, Brenda E.* From revelation to the X-Files: an autopsy of millennialism in American popular culture. Semeia 82 (1998) 281-295.
5695   *Castagno, Adele Monaci* ORIGENE e DIONIGI di Alessandria sulle promesse: continuità e differenze. ASEs 15 (1998) 101-123.
5696   **Contreras Molina, Francisco** La nueva Jerusalén: esperanza de la iglesia. Biblioteca EstB 101: S 1998, Sígueme 284 pp. 84-301-1350-9. [R]SalTer 86 (1998) 929-930 (*Pulido, Jesús*).
5697   *Curti, Carmelo* GIROLAMO e il millenarismo di VITTORINO de Petovio. ASEs 15 (1998) 191-203.
5698   **Fuster, Sebastián** Milenarismos: el cristianismo en la encrucijada del año 2000. 1997 ⇒13,6056. [R]TE 42 (1998) 125-127 (*Bosch, Juan*).
5699   *Gianotto, Claudio* Il millenarismo giudaico. ASEs 15 (1998) 21-51.
5700   *Guinot, Jean-Noël* THÉODORET e le millénarisme d'APOLLINAIRE. ASEs 15 (1998) 153-180.
5701   *Hadfield, Andrew* Late Elizabethan Protestantism, colonalism, and the fear of the Apocalypse. Reformation 3 (1998) 303-322.
5702   *Lerner, Robert E.* Millennialism. Encyclopedia of apocalypticism II. 1998 ⇒507. 326-360.
5703   *Mara, Maria Grazia* AGOSTINO e il millenarismo. ASEs 15 (1998) 217-230.
5704   Il millenarismo cristiano e i suoi fondamenti scritturistici. ASEs 15 (1998) 3-273.
5705   **O'Leary, Stephen D.** Arguing the Apocalypse: a theory of millennial rhetoric. 1994 ⇒10,5562... 13,6060. [R]HR 38 (1998) 93-95 (*Ziolkowski, Eric J.*).
5706   *Pani, Giancarlo* Il millenarismo: PAPIA, GIUSTINO e IRENEO. ASEs 15 (1998) .
5707   *Pose, Eugenio Romero Ratio e gratia* en TICONIO;
5708   *Prinzivalli, Emanuela* Il millenarismo in oriente da METODIO ad APOLLINARE;
5709   *Savigni, Raffaele* Il tema del millennio in alcuni acommentari altomedievali latini. ASEs 15 (1998) 53-84/201-215/125-151/231-273.
5710   *Simonetti, Manlio* Il millenarismo cristiano dal I al V secolo. ASEs 15 (1998) 7-20.
5711   *Singles, Donna* L'homme aux prises avec la gloire. LV(L) 239 (1998) 53-62.
5712   **Soares, Sebastião Armando Gameleira** O fim do mundo. Estudos bíblicos 59: Petrópolis 1998, Vozes 77 pp.
5713   *Van Bragt, Jan* Apocalyptic thought in christianity and Buddhism. Japanese Mission Journal 52 (1998) 161-170.

5714 *Williams, Stephen* Evangelicals and eschatology: a contentious case. ^FWright D. 1998 ⇒126. 291-308.

5715 *Bauckham, Richard* Resurrection as giving back the dead. Fate of the dead. NT.S 93: 1998 <1993> ⇒132. 269-289 [Rev 20,13].

5716 *Vetrali, Tecle* Gerusalemme, dimora di Dio (Ap 21,1-7);

5717 *Giraldo, Roberto* Ecco, io faccio nuove tutte le cose" (Ap 21,5): la novità nell'esperienza e nella vita delle chiese;

5718 *Sartori, Luigi* "Io sono il principio e la fine" (Ap 21,6);

5719 *Bertalot, Renzo* L'acqua della vita: "a chi ha sete io darò gratuitamente l'acqua della vita" (Ap 21,6). Studi ecumenici 16 (1998) 281-300/321-339/341-353/315-319.

XII. Paulus

G3.1 Pauli biographia

5720 **Anderson, R. Dean** Ancient rhetorical theory and Paul. Contributions to Biblical Exegesis and Theology 18: 1996 ⇒12,5797; 13,6068. ^RCBQ 60 (1998) 356-358 (*Mitchell, Margaret M.*).

5721 *Álvarez, D.* Pablo "un ciudadano romano". EstAg 33 (1998) 455-486.

5722 **Barbaglio, Giuseppe** Pablo de Tarso y los origenes cristianos. Biblioteca de estudios bíblicos 65: S 1997, Sígueme 391 pp. 8430110895.

5723 **Bartolomé, Juan José** Pablo de Tarso: una introduccíon a la vida y a la obra de un apóstol de Cristo. 1997 ⇒13,6070. ^RRTLi 32 (1998) 215-216 (*Chávarry, Francisco Javier*).

5724 **Bornkamm, Günther** Paulo: vida e obra. ^T*Brod, Bertilo.* Petrópolis 1992, Vozes 287 pp. ^RRBBras 14 (1997) 413-415.

5725 **Buscemi, Alfio Marcello** Paolo: vita, opera e messaggio. ASBF 43: 1996 ⇒12,5804; 13,6073. ^RCDios 111 (1998) 333-34 (*Gutiérrez, J.*).

5726 *Chilton, Bruce* The mystery of Paul. BiRe 14/1 (1998) 36-41, 46-47.

5727 **Comblin, Joseph** Pablo, apóstol de Jesucristo. Dabar 1: M 1996, San Pablo 177 pp. 84-285-1748-7.

5728 **Didier-Weill, Alain** Invocations Dionysos, Moïse, saint Paul et Freud. P 1998, Calmann-Lévy 198 pp. ^RÉtudes 389 (1998) 390-392 (*Julien, Philippe*).

5729 **Gnilka, Joachim** Pablo de Tarso: apóstol y testigo. Barc 1998, Herder 319 pp. Pta3.600. 84-254-2012-1. ^RRevista Católica 98 (1998) 354-356 (*Ferrada Moreira, Andrés*);

5730 Paolo di Tarso: apostolo e testimone. CTNT.S 6: Brescia 1998, Paideia 427 pp. L66.000. 88-394-0558-5.

5731 **Hengel, Martin; Schwemer, Anna Maria** Paul between Damascus and Antioch. 1997 ⇒13,6080. ^RLouvSt 23 (1998) 288-290 (*Koperski, Veronica*); Faith & Mission 15/2 (1998) 91-92 (*Köstenberger, Andreas J.*); JThS 49 (1998) 242-245 (*Barrett, C.K.*); JBL 117 (1998) 752-754 (*Donaldson, Terence L.*);

5732 Paulus zwischen Damaskus und Antiochien: die unbekannten Jahre des Apostels. WUNT 108: Tü 1998, Mohr xxii; 543 pp. DM198. 3-16-146749-3.

5733 **Heyer, Cornelius J. den** Paulus: man van twee werelden. Zoetermeer 1998, Meinema 323 pp. 90-211-3706-2.

5734 **Meggitt, Justin J.** Paul, poverty and survival. E 1998, Clark xiv; 268 pp. £24. 0-567-08604-6.
5735 *Miranda, Americo* La chiamata di Paolo nella comunità cristiana nelle tre narrazioni degli Atti dell'episodio di Damasco (At 9,1-19a; 22,3-21; 26,9-23). RivBib 46 (1998) 61-88.
5736 **Murphy-O'Connor, Jerome** Paul: a critical life. 1996 ⇒12,5811; 13,6084. ᴿJThS 49 (1998) 245-248 (*North, J. Lionel*).
5737 *O'Brien Wicker, Kathleen* Conversion and culture: a comparative study of the conversions of Paul and two twentieth-century African christians. ᶠBETZ, H. 1998 ⇒10. 358-391.
5738 *Penna, Romano* Casi di violenza nella biografia di Paolo. PSV 37 (1998) 163-176.
5739 **Poffet, Jean-Michel** Paul de Tarse. Regards: Montrouge 1998, Nouvelle Cité 159 pp. ᴿNV 73/2 (1998) 106-108 (*Morerod, Charles*).
5740 **Riesner, Rainer** Paul's early period: chronology, mission strategy, and theology. GR 1998, Eerdmans xvi; 535 pp. $50. 0-8028-4166-X. ᵀ*Stott, Doug.* ᴿCart. 14 (1998) 445-447 (*Sanz Valdivieso, R.*); LASBF 48 (1998) 604-609 (*Buscemi, Alfio Marcello*).
5741 *Roetzel, Calvin J.* Paul as organic intellectual: the shaper of apocalyptic myths. ᶠSNYDER, G. 1998 ⇒104. 221-243.
5742 **Roetzel, Calvin J.** Paul: the man and the myth. Studies on personalities of the New Testament: Columbia, SC 1998, Univ. of South Carolina Press xii; 269 pp. $35. 1-57003-264-5.
5743 **Sanders, Ed Parish** San Paolo. 1997 ⇒13,6089. ᴿHum(B) 53 (1998) 1056-1057 (*Capelli, Piero*).
5744 *Schwemer, Anna Maria* Paulus in Antiochien. BZ 42 (1998) 161-180.
5745 **Wallace, Richard; Williams, Wynne** The three worlds of Paul of Tarsus. L 1998, Routledge xiii; 239 pp. 0-415-13591-5.
5746 **Wansink, Craig S.** Chained in Christ: the experience and rhetoric of Paul's imprisonments. JSNT.S 130: 1996 ⇒12,5822; 13,6093. ᴿCBQ 60 (1998) 387-388 (*Fitzgerald, John T.*).

G3.2 Corpus paulinum; *generalia, technica epistularis*

5747 *Alexander, Loveday* "Better to marry than to burn": St. Paul and the Greek novel. Ancient fiction. 1998 ⇒1118. 235-256.
5748 *Ardovino, Adriano* HEIDEGGER interprete di Paolo: l'esperienza effettiva della vita e il senso della temporalità in quanto tale. AnScR 3 (1998) 305-335.
5749 **Ballarini, L.** Paolo e il dialogo Chiesa-Israele. CSB 31: 1997 ⇒13,6099. ᴿRivBib 46 (1998) 503-505 (*Cova, Gian Domenico*).
5750 **Baumert, Norbert** Woman and man in Paul: overcoming a misunderstanding. 1996 ⇒12,5828; 13,6101. ᴿCBQ 60 (1998) 142-144 (*Getty, Mary Ann*).
5751 *Dassmann, Ernst* Aspekte frühchristlicher Paulusverehrung. ᶠSPEYER, W. JAC.E 28: 1998 ⇒107. 87-103.
5752 **Downing, F. Gerald** Cynics, Paul and the Pauline churches: Cynics and christian Origins II. L 1998, Routledge xi; 369 pp. $65. 0-415-17159-8.
5753 *Fürst, Alfons* Pseudepigraphie und Apostolizität im apokryphen Briefwechsel zwischen Seneca und Paulus. JAC 41 (1998) 77-117.

5754 **Güting, Eberhard W.; Mealand, David L.** Asyndeton in Paul: a text-critical and statistical enquiry into Pauline style. SBEC 39: Lewiston, NY 1998, Mellen xiv; 205 pp. $90. 0-7734-8369-1.

5755 *Hartman, D.* Epistolary conventions and social change in Paul's letters. ᶠJUDGE E. 1998 ⇒47. 195-204.

5756 **Harvey, John D.** Listening to the text: oral patterning in Paul's Letters. ETS Studies 1: GR 1998, Baker xviii; 357 pp. $25. 0-8010-2200-2.

5757 **Heil, Johannes** Kompilation oder Konstruktion?: die Juden in den Pauluskommentaren des 9. Jahrhunderts. Forschungen zur Geschichte der Juden: A, Abh. 6: Hannover 1998, Hahn xiv; 492 pp. 3-7752-5615-6.

5758 *Hester, James D.* Speaker, audience and situations: a modified interactional model. Neotest. 32 (1998) 75-94.

5759 *Holloway, Paul A.* Paul's pointed prose: the Sententia in Roman rhetoric and Paul. NT 40 (1998) 32-53.

5760 *Hurd, John C.* Pauline chronology and Pauline theology <1967>;
5761 The sequence of Paul's letters <1967>;
5762 'The Jesus whom Paul preaches' (Acts 19:13) <1984>. Earlier letters of Paul. ARGU 8: 1998 ⇒163. 9-30/31-45/163-181.

5763 **Hübner, Hans** Vetus Testamentum in Novo, 2: Corpus Paulinum. 1997 ⇒13,6107. ᴿJThS 49 (1998) 765-766 (*Ellis, E. Earle*); NT 40 (1998) 101-102 (*Elliott, J.K.*).

5764 **Klauck, Hans-Josef** Die antike Briefliteratur und das Neue Testament: ein Lehr- und Arbeitsbuch. UTB 2022: Pd 1998, Schöningh 367 pp. DM39.80. 3-506-99496-4.

5765 **Lim, Timothy H.** Holy Scripture in the Qumran commentaries and Pauline letters. 1997 ⇒13,6333. ᴿDSD 5 (1998) 246-248 (*Murphy-O'Connor, Jerome*); JThS 49 (1998) 781-784 (*Stanley, Christopher*).

5766 *Lips, Hermann von* Der Gedanke des Vorbilds im Neuen Testament. EvTh 58 (1998) 295-309.

5767 *Llewelyn, S.R.* Directions for the delivery of letters and the epistles of St Paul. ᶠJUDGE E. 1998 ⇒47. 184-194.

5768 **Lütgehetmann, Walter** Paulus für Einsteiger. Kontur 139: Pd 1998, Bonifatius 287 pp. DM29.80.

5769 **Meißner, Stefan** Die Heimholung des Ketzers: Studien zur jüdischen Auseinandersetzung mit Paulus. WUNT 2/87: 1996 ⇒12,5844; 13,6114. ᴿJBL 117 (1998) 750-752 (*Westerholm, Stephen*).

5770 *Mitchell, Margaret M.* 'A variable and many-sorted man': John CHRYSOSTOM's treatment of Pauline inconsistency. JEarlyC 6 (1998) 93-111.

5771 **Müller, Markus** Vom Schluss zum Ganzen: zur Bedeutung des paulinischen Briefkorpusabschlusses. FRLANT 172: 1996 ⇒11/1,4525; 12,5847. ᴿOrdKor 39 (1998) 369-370 (*Giesen, Heinz*); ThLZ 123 (1998) 856-857 (*Becker, Jürgen*); ThRv 94 (1998) 519-520 (*Scholtissek, Klaus*); JThS 49 (1998) 263-264 (*Ellingworth, Paul*).

5772 *Müller, Markus* Der sogenannte 'schriftstellerische Plural'—neu betrachtet: zur Frage der Mitarbeiter als Mitverfasser der Paulusbriefe. BZ 42 (1998) 181-201.

5773 **Noormann, Rolf** IRENÄUS als Paulus Interpret. WUNT 2/66: 1994 ⇒10,5721... 13,6118. ᴿThRv 94 (1998) 390-391 (*Viciano, Albert*).

5774 ᴱ**Padovese, Luigi** Atti del IV Simposio di Tarso su S. Paolo Apostolo [1995]. 1996 ⇒12,263; 13,6120. ᴿCDios 111/1 (1998) 331-332 (*Gutiérrez, J.*); Sal. 60 (1998) 568-569 (*Ptak, Miroslaw*).

5775 **Perriman, Andrew** Speaking of women: interpreting Paul. Leicester 1998, Apollos 237 pp. 0-85111-458-X.

5776 *Pickering, S.R.* The dating of the Chester Beatty-Michigan codex of the Pauline epistles. ^FJUDGE E. 1998 ⇒47. 216-227.

5777 **Potvin, Jacinthe** Trajectoire de la vision paulinienne sur les femmes: ambivalence ou cohérence?. ^DOttawa 1998, 264 pp.

5778 *Penna, Romano* Aperture universalistiche in Paolo e nella cultura del suo tempo. RstB 10/1-2 (1998) 279-315.

5779 **Raj, Joseph Jaswant** Grace in the Saiva Siddhāntam and in St. Paul: a contribution in inter-faith cross-cultural understanding. Madras 1989, South Indian Salesian Society xxix; 743 pp. ^RITS 35/1 (1998) 74-84 (*DeSmet, Richard V.*).

5780 *Richards, E. Randolph* The codex and the early collection of Paul's letters. BBR 8 (1998) 151-166.

5781 **Roetzel, Calvin J.** The letters of Paul: conversations in context. LVL 1998, Westminster xii; 241 pp. $20. 0-664-25782-8.

5782 **Sánchez Bosch, Jordi** Escritos paulinos. Introducción al estudio de la Biblia 7: Estella 1998, Verbo Divino 525 pp. 84-7151-908-9.

5783 **Spencer, Aída Besançon** Paul's literary style: a stylistic and historical comparison of II Corinthians 11:16-12:13, Romans 8:9-39, and Philippians 3:2-4:13. Lanham 1998, University Press of America x; 256 pp. 0-7618-1264-4.

5784 **Weima, Jeffrey A.D.** Neglected endings: the significance of the Pauline letter closings. JSNT.S 101: 1994 ⇒10,5617... 12,5864. ^RSR 27 (1998) 80-81 (*Donaldson, Terence L.*).

5785 **Wilk, Florian** Die Bedeutung des Jesajabuches für Paulus. FRLANT 179: Gö 1998, Vandenhoeck & R vi; 461 pp. DM128. 3-525-538634.

G3.3 Pauli theologia

5786 *Bachl, Gottfried* Dank an Paulus: Abschiedsvorlesung von der Theologischen Fakultät Salzburg. SaThZ 2 (1998) 106-118.

5787 *Barbaglio, Giuseppe* Lo Spirito di Dio in San Paolo. MF 98 (1998) 475-496.

5788 **Barcley, William Bayless** 'Christ in you': a study in Paul's theology and ethics. ^DBoston Univ. 1998, 221 pp.

5789 *Basevi, Claudio* Lo Spirito Santo negli scritti paolini. StCatt 42 (1998) 621-624.

5790 **Beck, Timothy D.** The spirit of the New Age: the eschatological dimensions of the work of the Holy Spirit in the writings of Paul the Apostle and Juergen MOLTMANN. ^DSouthern Methodist 1998, 277 pp.

5791 *Boer, M.C. de* Paul and apocalyptic eschatology. Encyclopedia of apocalypticism I. 1998 ⇒507. 345-383.

5792 *Buscemi, Marcello* Lo Spirito Santo in S. Paolo. Consacrazione e Servizio 46 (1998) 9-23.

5793 **Christiansen, Ellen Juhl** The covenant in Judaism and Paul: a study of ritual boundaries as identity markers. AGJU 27: 1995 ⇒11/1, 4556. ^RCBQ 60 (1998) 361-363 (*Chesnutt, Randall D.*).

5794 *Cipriani, Settimio* La fede nell'epistolario paolino. La fede nella bibbia. DSBP 21: 1998 ⇒224. 115-141.

5795 *Cousar, Charles B.* Paul and the death of Jesus. Interp. 52 (1998) 38-52.

5796 *Cranfield, C.E.B.* On the πίστις χριστοῦ question. On Romans. 1998
⇒143. 81-97.

5797 **DeKlavon, David Raymond** The Holy Spirit as a means of confir-
mation in the letters of Paul. ᴰSouthern Baptist Theol. Sem. 1998,
328 pp.

5798 **Díaz-Rodelas, Juan Miguel** Pablo y la ley: la novedad de Rom 7,7-
8,4 en el conjunto de la reflexión paulina sobre la ley. EMISJ 28:
1994 ⇒10,5803...13,6143. ᴿScrTh 30 (1998) 985-986 (*Basevi,
Claudio*).

5799 **Dognin, Paul-Dominique** Paul, théologien de la confiance en Dieu.
Connaître la Bible 10: Bru 1998, Lumen Vitae 64 pp. 2-87324-1136.

5800 **Dunn, James D.G.** The theology of Paul the apostle. GR 1998,
Eerdmans xxxvi; 808 pp. $45. 0-8028-3844-8. ᴿNBl 79 (1998) 459-
460 (*Marley, Euan*); ETR 73 (1998) 615-616 (*Cuvillier, Élian*);
Theol. 101 (1998) 458-459 (*Morgan, Robert*); RB 105 (1998) 582-
589 (*Murphy-O'Connor, Jerome*); Neotest. 32 (1998) 246-247
(*Taylor, N.H.*); Bib. 79 (1998) 436-438 (*Légasse, S.*); JSNT 72
(1998) 91-111 (*Campbell, Douglas A.*) & 67-90 (*Matlock, R. Barry*)
& 113-120 (*Dunn, James D.G.*).

5801 *Eckert, Jost* Gottes Bundesstiftungen und der Neue Bund bei Paulus.
Der ungekündigte Bund?. QD 172: 1998 ⇒240. 135-156.

5802 **Erlemann, Kurt** Alt und neu bei Paulus und im Hebräerbrief: frühchristliche Standortbestimmung im Vergleich. ThZ 54 (1998) 345-
367.

5803 **Eskola, Timo** Theodicy and predestination in Pauline soteriology.
WUNT 2/100: Tü 1998, Siebeck xv; 353 pp. DM128. 3-16-1468945.

5804 **Fee, Gordon D.** Paul, the Spirit and the people of God. 1996
⇒12,5881. ᴿRExp 95 (1998) 460 (*McGraw, Larry; Niang, Aliou*);
AsbTJ 53 (1998) 98-99 (*Sumney, Jerry L.*).

5805 *Fitzmyer, Joseph A.* Reconciliation in Pauline theology <1975>;
5806 The gospel in the theology of Paul <1979>. To advance the gospel.
1998 ⇒150. 162-185/149-161.

5807 *Gaffin, Richard B.* "Life-giving spirit": probing the center of Paul's
pneumatology. JETS 41 (1998) 573-589.

5808 *Gager, John G.* Paul's contradictions: can they be resolved?. BiRe
14/6 (1998) 32-39.

5809 **Giglioli, Alberto** L'uomo o il creato? Κρίσις in S. Paolo. 1994
⇒13,6148. ᴿAsp. 45 (1998) 290-291 (*Di Palma, Gaetano*).

5810 *Gonsalves, Francis* Paul and IGNATIUS: servants of the Spirit. VJTR
62 (1998) 449-460.

5811 *Hahn, Ferdinand* Die Interpretatio Christiana des Alten Testaments
bei Paulus. ᶠSCHRAGE, W. 1998 ⇒101. 65-75.

5812 *Hansen, G. Walter* Resurrection and the christian life in Paul's letters. Life in the face of death. 1998 ⇒252. 203-224.

5813 *Hays, Richard B.* 'Who has believed our message?': Paul's reading
of Isaiah. SBL.SP part 2. SBL.SPS 37: 1998 ⇒402. 205-225.

5814 **Hotze, Gerhard** Paradoxien bei Paulus: Untersuchungen zu einer e-
lementaren Denkform in seiner Theologie. NTA 33: 1997 ⇒13,6156.
ᴿTThZ 107 (1998) 326-327 (*Reiser, Marius*).

5815 *Jankowski, Augustyn* Dwie Świątynie Ducha Świętego według
Listów Pawłowych [Duo templa Spiritus Sancti secundum epistulas
Paulinas]. RBL 51 (1998) 17-29.

5816 *Kanagaraj, Jey J.* Ecological concern in Paul's theology. EvQ 70
(1998) 291-309.

5817 **Kraus, Wolfgang** Das Volk Gottes: zur Grundelegung der Ekklesiologie bei Paulus. WUNT 2/85: 1996 ⇒12,5893; 13,6160. [R]ÖR 47/1 (1998) 154-155 (*März, Claus-Peter*); ThR 63 (1998) 450-451 (*Gestrich, Christof*); JBL 117 (1998) 368-369 (*Donaldson, Terence L.*).

5818 *Lee, Han S.* A fresh look at Paul's theology of the Law. Chongshin theological journal 3 (1998) 84-114.

5819 *Lessing, Eckhard* "Der Vorsprung der Sünde vor dem Gesetz": systematische Erwägungen zum paulinischen Sündenverständnis unter besonderer Berücksichtigung von Rm 5 12ff und Rm 7. [F]KLEIN, G. 1998 ⇒52. 285-295.

5820 *Légasse, Simon* Ministère apostolique et travail profane selon Paul. Laur. 39 (1998) 473-483.

5821 **Limbeck, M.** Mit Paulus Christ sein. 1989 ⇒6,6033; 8,6086. [R]Bogoslovni Vestnik 58/3 (1998) 368-370 (*Rozman, Francè*).

5822 *Litwak, Kenneth D.* Echoes of scripture?: a critical survey of recent works on Paul's use of the Old Testament. CurResB 6 (1998) 260-288.

5823 **Macky, Peter W.** St. Paul's cosmic war myth: a military version of the gospel. Westminster College library of biblical symbolism 2: NY 1998, Lang xiv; 309 pp. $53.95.

5824 **Matand Bulembat, Jean-Bosco** Noyau et enjeux de l'eschatologie paulinienne: de l'apocalyptique juive et de l'eschatologie hellénistique dans quelques argumentations de l'apôtre Paul: études rhétorico-exégétique de 1 Co 15,35-58; 2 Co 5,1-10 et Rm 8,18-30. BZNW 84: 1997 ⇒13,6170. [R]ThRv 94 (1998) 520-522 (*Dautzenberg, Gerhard*).

5825 *Matlock, R. Barry* A future for Paul?. Auguries. JSOT.S 269: 1998 ⇒225. 144-183.

5826 *Mauser, Ulrich* One God and trinitarian language in the letters of Paul. HBT 20 (1998) 99-108.

5827 **McLean, Bradley Hudson** The cursed Christ: Mediterranean expulsion rituals and Pauline soteriology. JSNT.S 126: 1996 ⇒12,5899; 13,6171. [R]JBL 117 (1998) 158-160 (*Sumney, Jerry L.*).

5828 *Merk, Otto* Nachahmung Christi: zu ethischen Perspektiven in der paulinischen Theologie. [F]MERK O. BZNW 95: 1998 <1989> ⇒79. 302-336.

5829 *Merklein, Helmut* Der Theologe als Prophet: zur Funktion prophetischen Redens im theologischen Diskurs des Paulus <1992>;

5830 Der (neue) Bund als Thema der paulinischen Theologie <1996>;

5831 Paulus und die Sünde. Studien zu Jesus und Paulus II <1996>. WUNT 105: 1998 ⇒176. 377-404/357-376/316-356.

5832 **Minguet Mico, José** El Espíritu Santo según San Pablo. 1997 ⇒13,6173. [R]AnVal 24 (1998) 253-255 (*Arnau-García, Ramón*).

5833 *Misztal, Wojciech* Stary porządek niewoli grzechu i śmierci: czlowiek przed przyjściem Chrystusa [Die alte Ordnung der Sklaverei der Sünde und des Todes: der Mensch vor dem Kommen Christi]. STV 36 (1998) 25-42. P.

5834 **Musuyu Faliyala, Joseph** La kaine ktisis en St. Paul: (Gal 6,15 et 2 Co 5,17). Diss. extr. Pont. Univ. Urbaniana. R 1998, xxxix; 53 pp.

5835 *Niederwimmer, Kurt* Paulus und die analogia entis. Gesammelte Aufsätze. BZNW 90: 1998 <1996> ⇒182. 280-289.

5836 *Pelser, G.M.M.* Once more the body of Christ in Paul. Neotest. 32 (1998) 525-545.

5837 *Pitta, Antonio* Così "inesperto nell'arte retorica"? (cf. 2Cor 11,6): retorica e messaggio paolino. [F]MARTINI, C. RivBib.S 33: 1998 ⇒75. 411-435.

5838 **Pitta, Antonio** Il paradosso della Croce: saggi di teologia paolina. Piemme religione: CasM 1998, Piemme 478 pp. 88-384-4038-7.

5839 *Sass, Gerhard* Der alte und der neue Bund bei Paulus;

5840 *Schenk, Wolfgang* 'Kreuzestheologie' bei Paulus: zu den 'cultural codes' von σταυρός, σκόλοψ, ξύλον. [F]SCHRAGE, W. 1998 ⇒101. 223-234/93-109.

5841 **Schweitzer, Albert** The mysticism of Paul the Apostle. Baltimore, MD 1998, Johns Hopkins Univ. xxvii; 411 pp. 0-8018-6098-9.

5842 **Söding, Thomas** Das Wort vom Kreuz: Studien zur paulinischen Theologie. WUNT 93: 1997 ⇒13,6185. [R]OrdKor 39 (1998) 370-371 (*Giesen, Heinz*).

5843 **Stevens, Judith A.** Paul's construction of soma and selfhood: a feminist critique. [D]Union Theol. Sem. 1998, 276 pp.

5844 *Tiedemann, Holger* Paulinische Soma—Pathologia sexualis—FOU-CAULTS genealogische Geschichtsschreibung und neutestamentliche Exegese. Exegese und Methodendiskussion. TANZ 23: 1998 ⇒208. 57-76.

5845 **Westerholm, Stephen** Preface to the study of Paul. 1997 ⇒13,6189. [R]SR 27 (1998) 211-212 (*Longenecker, Richard N.*).

5846 *Widła, Bogusław* Ludzie Apokalipsy [Die Menschen der Apokalypse]. STV 36 (1998) 43-49.

5847 *Wilk, Florian* Die Wege Gottes: Rechtfertigung und Schrift bei Paulus. LM N.F. 1 (1998) 34-37.

5848 **Williams, Demetrius K.** The terminology of the cross and the rhetoric of Paul. SBL.SP part 2. SBL.SPS 37: 1998 ⇒402. 677-699.

5849 *Wright, N.T.* The new inheritance according to Paul. BiRe 14/3 (1998) 16, 47.

5850 **Wright, T.** Paulus van Tarsus: een kennismaking met zijn theologie. Zoetermeer 1998, Boekencentrum 196 pp.

5851 **Young, Brad H.** Paul the Jewish theologian: a pharisee among christians. 1997 ⇒13,6192. [R]RevBib 60 (1998) 219-221 (*Levoratti, A.J.*); HBT 20 (1998) 166-167 (*Thielman, Frank*).

5852 **Yu, Seung Won** Paul's pneumatic epistemology: its significance in his letters. [D]Duke 1998, 335 pp.

G3.4 *Pauli stylus et modus operandi*—Paul's image

5853 *Barton, Stephen C.* Paul and the limits of tolerance. Tolerance. 1998 ⇒440. 121-134.

5854 *Dunn, James D.G.* Paul: apostate or apostle of Israel?. ZNW 89 (1998) 256-271.

5855 **Glad, Clarence E.** Paul and Philodemus: adaptability in Epicurean and early Christian psychagogy. NT.S 81: 1995, ⇒13,6196. [R]EstAg 33 (1998) 424-425 (*Antolín, J.*); CBQ 60 (1998) 366-367 (*Vaage, Leif E.*) [Rom 14,1-15,14; 8-10].

5856 *Guillet, Jacques* Paul apôtre: ce n'est plus moi, c'est Christ qui vit en moi. Croire aujourd'hui 61 (1998) 30-31.

5857 *Heininger, Bernhard* Einmal Tarsus und zurück (Apg 9,30; 11,25-26): Paulus als Lehrer nach der Apostelgeschichte. MThZ 49 (1998) 125-143.

5858   **Lentz, John Clayton** Le portrait de Paul selon Luc dans les Actes des Apôtres. [T]*Chabot, Nicole de; Trimaille, Michel.* LeDiv 172: P 1998, Cerf 261 pp. FF180. 2-204-05844-0. Bibl.

5859   **Malina, Bruce J.; Neyrey, Jerome H.** Portraits of Paul. 1996, ⇒12,5940; 13,6199. [R]BTB 28 (1998) 84-85 (*de Vos, Craig S.*); JR 78 (1998) 611-613 (*Mitchell, Margaret M.*); JSNT 69 (1998) 117-119 (*Pearson, Brook*).

5860   *Merk, Otto* Erwägungen zum Paulusbild in der deutschen Aufklärung: Paulusforschung bei Johann Salomo SEMLER und in seinem Umkreis. [F]MERK O. BZNW 95: 1998 <1992> ⇒79. 71-97.

5861   *Moore, Stephen D.* Que(e)rying Paul: preliminary questions. Auguries. JSOT.S 269: 1998 ⇒225. 250-274.

5862   **Palmer, Gesine** Ein Freispruch für Paulus: John TOLANDs Theorie des Judenchristentums. Mit einer Neuausgabe von Tolands 'Nazarenus' von *Claus-Michael Palmer.* ANTZ 7: 1996 ⇒12,5943. [R]ThLZ 123 (1998) 153-155 (*Martin, Friedrich*); FrRu 5 NF (1998) 57-59 (*Gubler, Marie-Louise*).

5863   *Sázava, Zdeněk* Der Apostel Paulus—in zwei Fassungen?. [F]HERIBAN J. 1998 ⇒41. 23-30.

5864   *Thurén, Lauri* Was Paul sincere?: questioning the apostle's ethos. Scriptura 65 (1998) 109-121.

5865   **Wright, Nicholas T.** What Saint Paul really said. 1997 ⇒13,6205. [R]Faith & Mission 15/2 (1998) 87-88 (*Köstenberger, Andreas J.*).

G3.5 **Apostolus Gentium** [⇒G4.6, Israel et Lex/Jews & Law]

5866   **Adinolfi, Marco** Da Antiochia a Roma: con Paolo nel mondo greco-romano. 1996 ⇒12,5948. [R]RivBib 46 (1998) 250-251 (*Laconi, Mauro*).

5867   *Bartolomé, Juan José* 'Soy lo que soy por gracia de Dios' (1 Cor 15,10): la experiencia de la salvación como clave para la lectura de Pablo. [F]HERIBAN J. 1998 ⇒41. 85-104.

5868   **Becker, Jürgen** Paulus: der Apostel der Völker. UTB 2014: Tü [2]1998, Mohr ix; 524 pp. 3-8252-2014-1.

5869   *Beimdieke, Hildegund* Missionary methods—St. Paul's or ours. em 14/2 (1998) 47-50.

5870   *Betz, Hans Dieter* Paul between Judaism and Hellenism: creating a space for christianity. Gesammelte Aufsätze IV. 1998 ⇒134. 244-266.

5871   *Botha, Pieter J.J.* Paul and gossip: a social mechanism in early christian communities. Neotest. 32 (1998) 267-288.

5872   [E]**Dunn, James D.G.** Paul and the Mosaic law. WUNT 89: 1996 ⇒12,176; 13,6215. [R]Sal. 60 (1998) 351-352 (*Vicent, R.*).

5873   **Ellis, E.** Earle Pauline theology: ministry and society. 1997 <1989> ⇒13,6216. [R]RExp 95 (1998) 452 (*McGraw, Larry; Niang, Aliou*).

5874   **Goulder, Michael** A tale of two missions. 1994 ⇒10,5108a... 13,5550. [R]NT 40 (1998) 295-298 (*Elliott, J.K.*).

5875   *Malherbe, Abraham J.* Conversion to Paul's gospel. [F]FERGUSON, E. 1998 ⇒25. 230-244.

5876   **O'Brien, P.T.** Gospel and mission in the writings of Paul: an exegetical and theological analysis. 1995 ⇒11/1,4622; 13,6222.

[R]Missionalia 26/1 (1998) 136-138 (*Botha, Pieter J.J.*); EvQ 70 (1998) 83-84 (*Oakes, Peter*).

5877 *Penna, Romano* Aperture universalistiche in Paolo e nella cultura del suo tempo. RstB 10/1-2 (1998) 279-315.

5878 **Rossi De Gasperis, Francesco** Paolo di Tarso evangelo di Gesù: messia crocefisso, fatto Signore glorioso mediante la risurrezione dai morti (At 2,36; Rm 1,1-4). Betel brevi saggi spirituali 7: R 1998, Lipa 115 pp. 88-86517-45-9.

5879 *Segal, Alan F.* Paul and the beginning of christian conversion. Recruitment. 1998 ⇒320. 79-111.

5880 *Zirker, Hans* Paulus als »apóstolos«, Mohammed als 'rasûl'—der Gesandte in Bibel und Koran. [F]BSTEH, A. 1998 ⇒17. 550-573.

G3.6 *Pauli fundamentum* philosophicum [G4.3] *et* morale

5881 *Brouwer, Rinse Reeling* De nuances van Paulus. Interpretatie 6/8 (1998) 14-16.

5882 **Finsterbusch, Karin** Die Thora als Lebensweisung für Heidenchristen: Studien zur Bedeutung der Thora für die paulinische Ethik. StUNT 20: 1996 ⇒12,5964; 13,6226. [R]JThS 49 (1998) 784-787 (*Bockmuehl, M.*); JBL 117 (1998) 151-152 (*Westerholm, Stephen*).

5883 **Given, Mark Douglas** A sophistic Paul: ambiguity, cunning, and deception in Greece and Rome. [D]North Carolina 1998, 265 pp.

5884 **Jeong-Ae Lee, Veronica** Human weakness in Paul: a study of the spiritual thought of St. Paul in his letters for the renewal of christian life. R 1998, iii; 306 pp. Diss. Pont. Univ. S. Thomae.

5885 *Kloppenborg, John S.* Status und Wohltätigkeit bei Paulus und Jakobus. [F]HOFFMANN, P., Von Jesus. BZNW 93: 1998 ⇒43. 127-154.

5886 *Muñoz García, Ángel* La argumentación de Pablo de Tarso: conceptos 'racionalistas' de su predicación. AnáMnesis 15 (1998) 19-38.

      Perrot, Charles La conscience selon saint Paul 1998 ⇒9265.

5887 [E]**Rosner, Brian S.** Understanding Paul's ethics: twentieth century approaches. 1995, ⇒11/1,110... 13,6231. [R]EvQ 70 (1998) 80-82 (*Oakes, Peter*).

5888 *Stachowiak, Lech R.* The ethics of the Qumran community and Pauline ethics. [T]*Pasicki, Adam.* Qumran Chronicle 8/1-2 (1998) 63-82.

5889 *Tiedemann, Holger* Das Gesetz in den Gliedern—Paulus und das sexuelle Begehren. ZNT 2 (1998) 18-28.

G3.7 *Pauli* communitates *et* spiritualitas

5890 **Ascough, Richard S.** What are they saying about the formation of Pauline churches?. Mahwah 1998, Paulist viii; 133 pp. $10. 0-8091-3768-2 [BiTod 36,263—Senior, Donald].

5891 *Clarke, Andrew D.* Be imitators of me": Paul's model of leadership. TynB 49 (1998) 329-360.

5892 *Craffert, Pieter F.* The Pauline household communities: their nature as social entities. Neotest. 32 (1998) 309-341.

5893 **Gehring, Roger W.** Hausgemeinde und Mission: von Jesus bis Paulus. [D]Tübingen 1998, 390 pp. [NThAR 1999,74].

5894 *Guillet, Jacques* Paul apôtre: amis et compagnons. Croire aujourd'hui 59 (1998) 34-35;

5895 Paul apôtre: le converti. Croire aujourd'hui 57 (1998) 30-31;
5896 Paul apôtre: Paul et ses communautés. Croire aujourd'hui 60 (1998) 32-33.
5897 **Kittredge, Cynthia Briggs** Community and authority: the rhetoric of obedience in the Pauline tradition. HThS 45: Harrisburg 1998, Trinity xviii; 186 pp. 1-56338-262-8.
5898 *Malan, F.S.* Church singing according to the Pauline epistles. Neotest. 32 (1998) 509-524.
5899 **Maloney, George** The mystery of Christ in you: the mystical vision of Saint Paul. NY 1998, Alba xvii; 136 pp. $9. 0-8189-0802-5 [PIBA 21,122—Magennis, Feidhlimidh T.].
5900 **Maness, Stephen Lee** The Pauline congregations, Paul, and his co-workers: determinative trajectories for the ministries of Paul's partners in the gospel. ᴰSouthwestern Baptist Theol. Sem. 1998, 176 pp.
5901 *Marshall, P.J.* The enigmatic apostle: Paul and social change: did Paul seek to transform Graeco-Roman society?. ᶠJUDGE E. 1998 ⇒47. 153-174.
5902 **Meier, Hans-Christoph** Mystik bei Paulus: zur Phänomenologie religiöser Erfahrung im Neuen Testament. TANZ 26: Tü 1998, Francke x; 342 pp. DM86. 3-7720-1877-7.
5903 *Oster, Richard E.* "Congregations of the gentiles" (Rom 16:4): a culture-based ecclesiology in the letters of Paul. RestQ 40/1 (1998) 39-52.
5904 **Pinckaers, Servais Théodore** Życie duchowe chrześcijanina według św. Pawła i św. Tomasza z Akwinu [La vita spirituale del cristiano secondo San Paolo e San Tommaso d'Aquino]. 1998, Pallottinum 336 pp [CoTh 69,208ss—Weron, Eugeniusz]. P.
5905 *Schürmann, Heinz* Christus als Lebensraum und als Lebensform: Grundlegung einer theologischen Ständelehre bei Paulus. Im Knechtsdienst Christi. 1998 <1980> ⇒198. 145-160.
5906 *Söding, Thomas* Kooperation in den paulinischen Gemeinden: eine neutestamentliche Perspektive. BiLi 71 (1998) 108-116.
5907 **Weise, Edda** Paulus—Apostel Jesu Christi—Lehrer seiner Gemeinden. ᴰTü 1998-1999; ᴰ*Stuhlmacher, P.* vi; 372 pp [ThLZ 124,1182].

G3.8 *Pauli receptio,* history of research

5908 **Beker, J. Christiaan** Heirs of Paul. 1991, ⇒7,5102... 11/1,4680 ᴿPacifica 11/2 (1998) 213-2115 (*Kruse, Colin*).
      Litwak, K. Echoes... recent works on Paul's use of the OT 1998 ⇒5822.
5909 *Matlock, R. Barry* Almost cultural studies?: reflections on the 'new perspective' on Paul. Biblical studies. JSOT.S 266: 1998 ⇒380. 433-459.
5910 *Riches, John K.* Readings of AUGUSTINE on Paul: their impact on critical studies of Paul. SBL.SPS 37. 1998 ⇒402. 943-967.

G3.9 *Themata particularia de Paulo,* details

5911 **Alves, Manuel Isidro** Sagrado e santidade: simbolismo da linguagem cultual em S. Paulo. Fundamenta 16: 1996 ⇒12,6008. ᴿDid(L) 28 (1998) 217-221 (*Oliveira, Anacleto de*).

5912   **Bash, Anthony** Ambassadors for Christ: an exploration of ambassadorial language in the New Testament. WUNT 2/92: 1997, ⇒13, 6261 [R]JThS 49 (1998) 278-281 (*North, J. Lionel*).
5913   *Derickson, Gary W.* The cessation of healing miracles in Paul's ministry. BS 155 (1998) 299-315.
5914   *Gamba, Giuseppe Giovanni* Il carteggio tra SENECA e San Paolo: il 'problema' della sua autenticità. Sal. 60 (1998) 209-250.
5915   **Graffam-Minkus, Melanie** Der soziale Status des Apostel Paulus: eine sozial-anthropologische Untersuchung. [D]Augustana 1996-1997; [D]*Stegemann, W.* [ThRv 94,xviii].
5916   *Linss, Wilhlem C.* The hidden humor of St. Paul. CThMi 25 (1998) 195-199.
5917   *Pitta, Antonio* La funzione soteriologica d'Isacco nell'epistolario paolino. V Simposio di Tarso. 1998 ⇒395. 137-161.
5918   *Saunders, Ross* Attatlus, Paul and *Paideia*: the contribution of *I. Eph.202* to Pauline studies. [F]JUDGE E. 1998 ⇒47. 175-183.
5919   *Taylor, Stephen S.* Paul and the Persian sage: some observations on APHRAHAT's use of the Pauline corpus. The function of scripture. 1998 ⇒236. 312-331.
5920   **Winter, Bruce W.** PHILO and Paul among the sophists. MSSNTS 96: 1997 ⇒13,6273. [R]JThS 49 (1998) 788-789 (*Downing, F. Gerald*); TrinJ 19 (1998) 246-249 (*Schreiner, Thomas R.*).

G4.1 **Ad Romanos** *Textus, commentarii*

5921   *Aletti, Jean-Noël* Romans. International bible commentary. 1998 ⇒1535. 1553-1600.
5922   *Balz, Horst* Römerbrief. TRE 29. 1998 ⇒501. 291-311.
5923   [E]**Bammel, Caroline P. Hammond** Der Römerbriefkommentar des ORIGINES: kritische Ausgabe der Übersetzung RUFINs: Buch 7-10. Aus dem Nachlass hrsg. von *H.J. Frede* und *H. Stanjek*. AGLB 34: FrB 1998, Herder 357 pp. 3-451-21945-X [NThAR 1998,336].
5924   **Barth, Karl** Carta a los Romanos. Introd. *Gesteira, Manuel*; [T]*Martínez de la Pera, Abelardo* BAC 583: M 1998, BAC 611 pp. Ptas4.038. 84-7914-348-7. [R]Cart. 14 (1998) 456-457 (*Martínez Fresneda, F.*); Com(E) 31 (1998) 177-178 (*Burgos, M. de*).
5925   [E]**Bray, Gerald Lewis** Romans. Ancient Christian Commentary on Scripture, NT 6: DG 1998, InterVarsity xxvii; 404 pp. 0-8308-14914.
5926   **Byrne, Brendan** Romans. Sacra Pagina 6: 1996 ⇒12,6031; 13,6278. [R]Pacifica 11/1 (1998) 85-88 (*Moloney, Francis J.*); CBQ 60 (1998) 558-560 (*Nanos, Mark D.*); RBBras 15 (1998) 547-549.
5927   **Cranfield, C.E.B.** La lettera di Paolo ai Romani: cap. 1-8. [T]*Tomasetto, D.; Corsani, B.* Parola per l'uomo d'oggi 11: T 1998, Claudiana 254 pp. L36.000.
5928   *Epistula ad Romanos.* BVLI 42 (1998) 31-33.
5929   **Jankowski, Gerhard** Die große Hoffnung: Paulus an die Römer: eine Auslegung. Reihe im Lehrhaus 5: B 1998, Alektor 335 pp. 3-88425-069-8 [NThAR 2000,154].
5930   **Johnson, Luke Timothy** Reading Romans: a literary and theological commentary. 1997 ⇒13,6284. [R]RB 105 (1998) 627-628 (*Murphy-O'Connor, J.*).

5931 [E]**Martel, Gérard de** Expositiones Pauli Epistolarum ad Romanos, Galathas et Ephesios e codice Sancti Michaelis in periculo Maris. CChr.CM 151: 1995 ⇒12,6006. Avranches, Bibl. mun. 79. [R]EThL 74 (1998) 458-459 (*Verheyden, J.*).

5932 **Moo, Douglas J.** The epistle to the Romans. NIC: 1996 [[2]1998] ⇒12,6043; 13,6285. [R]Pacifica 11 (1998) 211-213 (*Byrne, Brendan*); JThS 49 (1998) 766-772 (*Longenecker, Bruce W.*); CBQ 60 (1998) 371-373 (*Fitzmyer, Joseph A.*); BS 155 (1998) 247-248 (*Hoehner, Harold W.*).

5933 **Mounce, Robert H.** Romans. NAC 27: 1995 ⇒11/1,4718; 13,6287. [R]AUSS 36 (1998) 300-301 (*Badenas, Roberto*).

5934 **Peterson, Erik** Der Brief an die Römer. [E]*Nichtweiss, Barbara.* Ausgewählte Schriften 6: 1997 ⇒13,6289. [R]LM (1998/11) 45-46 (*Lohse, Eduard*); ActBib 35 (1998) 173-174 (*Boada, J.*); ThGl 88 (1998) 251-252 (*Fuchs, Gotthard*).

5935 **Pitta, Antonio** Lettere ai Galati e ai Romani: il vangelo della salvezza. La Bibbia nelle nostre mani 11: CinB 1998, San Paolo 56 pp. 88-215-3721-8.

5936 **Pohl, Adolf** Der Brief des Paulus an die Römer. WStB Ergänzungsfolge: Wu 1998, Brockhaus 324 pp. 3-417-25026-9. Bibl.

5937 [T]**Scarampi, Lella** TEODORETO di Cirro: commentario alla lettera ai Romani. Cultura cristiana antica: testi: R 1998, Borla 230 pp. Introd., note di *Francesca Cocchini.* [R]Aug. 38 (1998) 508-509 (*Grossi, Vittorino*).

5938 **Schlatter, Adolf** Romans: the righteousness of God. [T]*Schatzmann, S.S.* 1995 <1935> ⇒11/1,4724; 13,6291. [R]IThQ 63 (1998) 93-94 (*McConvery, Brendan*).

5939 **Schmidt-Lauber, Gabriele** LUTHERs Vorlesung über den Römerbrief 1515/16. 1994 ⇒10,5740; 11/1,4725. [R]ZKG 109 (1998) 128-130 (*Zschoch, Hellmut*).

5940 **Schreiner, Thomas R.** Romans. Baker Exegetical Commentary on the NT: GR 1998, Baker xxi; 919 pp. $40. 0-8010-2149-9. Bibl.

5941 **Stuhlmacher, Peter** Der Brief an die Römer. NTD 6: Gö [15]1998, Vandenhoeck & R 237 pp. 3-525-51372-0 [NThAR 1999,46].

5942 **Zeller, Dieter** La lettera ai Romani. Il Nuovo Testamento commentato: [Brescia] 1998, Morcelliana 451 pp. 88-372-1671-8. Bibl.

G4.2 *Ad Romanos: themata,* topics

5943 *Anderson, Gary Alan* The status of the torah in the pre-Sinaitic period: St. Paul's epistle to the Romans. Biblical perspectives. StTDJ 28: 1998 ⇒441. 1-23.

5944 *Bray, Gerald* Attitudes towards Jews in patristic commentaries on Romans. [F]WRIGHT D. 1998 ⇒126. 29-46.

5945 *Campbell, William S.* Favouritism and egalitarianism: irreconcilable emphases in Romans?. SBL.SPS 37: 1998 ⇒402. 12-32.

5946 **Cosgrove, Charles H.** Elusive Israel: the puzzle of election in Romans. 1997 ⇒13,6296. [R]BiRe 14/2 (1998) 14, 16 (*Saldarini, Anthony*).

5947 *Cranfield, C.E.B.* 'The works of the law' in the epistle to the Romans <1991>;

5948   Sanctification as freedom: Paul's teaching on sanctification: with spe-
       cial reference to the epistle to the Romans <1994-95>.
5949   Some comments on Professor J.D.G. DUNN's *Christology in the mak-
       ing*: with special reference to the evidence of the epistle to the Ro-
       mans <1987>;
5950   Preaching on Romans <1987-88>;
5951   Giving a dog a bad name: a note on H. RÄISÄNEN's *Paul and the law*
       <1990>;
5952   Has the Old Testament law a place in the christian life?: a response to
       Professor WESTERHOLM <1993>. On Romans. 1998 ⇒143. 1-14/33-
       49/51-68/69-80/99-107/109-124.
5953   *Dunn, James D.G.* Whatever happened to "Works of the Law"?
       [F]POKORNÝ, P. 1998 ⇒90. 107-120.
5954   **Enderlein, Steven Eugene** The Gospel is not shameful: the argu-
       mentative structure of Romans in the light of classical rhetoric. [D]Mar-
       quette 1998, 360 pp.
5955   *Fitzmyer, Joseph A.* Paul and the law. To advance the gospel. 1998
       <1967> ⇒150. 186-201.
5956   **Graham, Marilyn Grace** On reincarnation: the gospel according to
       Paul: an interpretive matrix explaining Romans. Miami 1998, Quest
       293 pp. 0-9665824-0-3. Bibl.
5957   *Jewett, Robert* The God of peace in Romans: reflections on crucial
       Lutheran texts. CThMi 25 (1998) 186-194 [5,1; 15,33; 16,20].
5958   *Kalin, Everett R.* Rereading Romans: ethnic issues (or, 'how can I
       find a gracious community?'). CThMi 25 (1998) 461-472.
5959   **Klein, Wilhelm** Gottes Wort im Römerbrief: Vorträge im Kolleg
       1958-1961. [E]*Rauch, Albert*. Rg 1998, Ostkirchliches Institut 520 pp.
       DM40. Sonderheft des 107. Jahrgangs Katalog. Correspondenzblatt
       für die ehemaligen Alumnen des Collegium Germanico-Hungaricum
       zu Rom. [R]ThGl 88 (1998) 412-416 (*Hallensleben, Barbara*).
5960   *Longacre, Robert E.; Wallis, Wilber B.* Soteriology and eschatology
       in Romans. JETS 41 (1998) 367-382.
5961   *Manzi, Franco* Dall'ira del Dio giusto alla misericordia del Dio
       paziente: interpretazione esegetica ed ermeneutica di alcune categorie
       giuridiche in Rm 1,16-17 e 1,18-3,20. ScC 126 (1998) 551-634.
5962   **Morgan, Robert** Romans. 1995 ⇒13,6286. [R]Religion 28/1 (1998)
       91-92 (*Roberts, Richard H.*).
5963   **Nanos, Mark D.** The mystery of Romans: the Jewish context of
       Paul's letter. 1996 ⇒12,6062; 13,6310. [R]JQR 89 (1998) 222-224
       (*Levine, Amy-Jill*).
5964   **Quanbeck, Philip Arden, II** Parrhesia and community in Romans.
       [D]Luther Sem. 1998, 281 pp.
5965   **Quesnel, Michel** Les chrétiens et la loi juive: une lecture de l'épître
       aux Romains. LiBi 116: P 1998, Cerf 124 pp. FF85. 2-204-05831-9
       [RB 105,628s—Murphy-O'Connor, J.].
5966   **Schaeffer, Francis A.** The finished work of Christ: the truth of
       Romans 1-8. Wheaton, Ill. 1998, Crossway xi; 239 pp [NThAR
       2000,154].
5967   *Schille, Gottfried* Dialogische Elemente im Römerbrief. SNTU.A 23
       (1998) 153-191.
5968   *Schreiner, Thomas R.* Reading Romans theologically: a review arti-
       cle. JETS 41 (1998) 641-650.
5969   *Seifrid, Mark A.* Natural revelation and the purpose of the law in
       Romans. TynB 49 (1998) 115-129.

5970 *Starnitzke, Dierk* Die Bedeutung des Individulitätskonzeptes für das Verständnis des Römerbriefes: Individualitätstheorie und Exegese. Exegese und Methodendiskussion. TANZ 23: 1998 ⇒208. 33-56.

5971 *Wagner, J. Ross* The heralds of Isaiah and the mission of Paul: an investigation of Paul's use of Isaiah 51-55 in Romans. Jesus and the suffering servant. 1998 ⇒3430. 193-222.

G4.3 *Naturalis cognitio Dei*, Rom 1-4

5972 *Theißen, Gerd* Auferstehungsbotschaft und Zeitgeschichte: über einige politische Anspielungen im ersten Kapitel des Römerbriefs. [F]VE-NETZ, H. 1998 ⇒122. 59-68.

5973 *Rogers, Eugene F.* The narrative of natural law in AQUINAS's commentary on Romans 1. TS 59 (1998) 254-276.

5974 *Lohse, Eduard* Das Präskript des Römerbriefes als theologisches Programm. [F]KLEIN, G. 1998 ⇒52. 65-78 [1,1-17].

5975 *Beintker, Michael* Die Souveränität des Evangeliums: einige Erwägungen im Anschluß an Römer 1,16. [F]KLEIN, G. 1998 ⇒52. 259-272.

5976 *Velunta, Revelation Enriquez* ἐκ πίστεως εἰς πίστιν and the Filipinos' sense of indebtedness. SBL.SPS 37: 1998 ⇒402. 33-54 [1,16-17].

5977 *Gijsbertsen, Bart* In het evangelie of in mensen?. ITBT 6/7 (1998) 7-8 [1,17].

5978 **Bell, Richard H.** No one seeks for God: an exegetical and theological study of Romans 1.18-3.20. WUNT 106: Tü 1998, Mohr xxiv; 359 pp. DM158. 3-16-146864-3. Bibl.

5979 *Baker, Bruce A.* Romans 1:18-21 and presuppositional apologetics. BS 155 (1998) 280-298.

5980 *Soto Bruna, María Jesús* Conocimiento e iluminación en la primera generación franciscana: a propósito de Rom 1,20. ScrTh 30 (1998) 881-889 [1,20].

5981 *Balch, David L.* Romans 1:24-27, science, and homosexuality. CThMi 25 (1998) 433-440.

5982 **Berkley, Timothy Wayne** From a broken covenant to circumcision of the heart: Pauline intertextual exegesis in Romans 2:17-29. [D]Marquette 1998, 250 pp.

5983 *Barclay, John M.G.* Paul and PHILO on circumcision: Romans 2.25-9 in social and cultural context. NTS 44 (1998) 536-556.

5984 *Burnett, Gary W.* Individual and collective aspects of Pauline soteriology in Romans 3. IBSt 20 (1998) 159-188.

5985 **Baaij, Pieter K.** De God antwoordende mens: exegetische studie van Romeinen 3:21-8:39. Heerenveen 1998, Groen 761 pp. *f*79. 90-5030-968-2.

5986 *Pulcinelli, Giuseppe* "È stata manifestata la giustizia di Dio": l'interpretazione di Rm 3,21-22 e la sua funzione nel contesto. Lat. 64 (1998) 7-47.

5987 *Wengst, Klaus* 'Gerechtigkeit Gottes' für die Völker: ein Versuch, Röm 3,21-31 anders zu lesen. [F]SCHRAGE, W. 1998 ⇒101. 139-151.

5988 *Burchard, Christoph* Glaubensgerechtigkeit als Weisung der Tora bei Paulus. Studien NT. WUNT 107: 1998 <1997> ⇒140. 241-262 [Rom 3,27-31; Gal 3,10-12].

5989 **Neubrand, Maria** Abraham—Vater von Juden und Nichtjuden: eine exegetische Studie zu Röm 4. FzB 85: Wü 1998, Echter xiii; 329 pp. DM48. 3-429-01978-8 [BZ 44,151—Eckert, Jost].

G4.4 *Redemptio cosmica*: **Rom 5-8**

5990 *Gräßer, Erich* Der ruhmlose Abraham (Röm 4,2): Nachdenkliches zu Gesetz und Sünde bei Paulus. [F]KLEIN, G. 1998 ⇒52. 3-22.

5991 **Reid, Marty L.** Augustinian and Pauline rhetoric in Romans five. 1996 ⇒12,6085; 13,6333. [R]JEarlyC 6 (1998) 679-680 (*Pang-White, Ann A.*).

5992 *Bobrinskoy, Boris* The Adamic heritage according to Fr. John MEYENDORFF. SVTQ 42/1 (1998) 33-44 [5,12].

5993 *Artola, Antonio María* La madre del mesías en Rom 5,12. EstMar 64 (1998) 65-110.

5994 *Fitzmyer, Joseph A.* The consecutive meaning of ἐφ' ᾧ in Romans 5:12. To advance the gospel. 1998 <1993> ⇒150. 349-368.

5995 *Cranfield, C.E.B.* A note on Romans 5.20-21. On Romans. 1998 ⇒143.

5996 *Petersen, Anders Klostergaard* Shedding new light on Paul's understanding of baptism: a ritual-theoretical approach to Romans 6. StTh 52 (1998) 3-28.

5997 *Pelser, Gert M.M.* Could the 'formulas' dying and rising with Christ be expressions of Pauline mysticism?. Neotest. 32 (1998) 115-134 [6,1-11].

5998 *Cranfield, C.E.B.* Romans 6.1-14 revisited. On Romans. 1998 <1994-95> ⇒143. 23-31.

5999 *Burchard, Christoph* Römer 7,2-3 im Kontext. [F]STEGEMANN, H. BZNW 97: 1998 ⇒111. 443-456.

6000 *Édart, Jean-Baptiste* De la nécessité d'un sauveur: rhétorique et théologie de Rm 7, 7-25. RB 105 (1998) 359-396.

6001 *Burke, Trevor J.* Adoption and the Spirit in Romans 8. EvQ 70 (1998) 311-324.

6002 *Dillon, Richard J.* The spirit as taskmaster and troublemaker in Romans 8. CBQ 60 (1998) 682-702.

6003 *Brodeur, Scott* La dimensione escatologica della morale cristiana in Romani 8. StMor 36 (1998) 393-419 [sum. res. 418].

6004 *Smith, Geoffrey* The function of "likewise" (hosautos) in Romans 8:26. TynB 49 (1998) 29-38.

G4.6 *Israel et Lex*; **The Law and the Jews,** *Rom 9-11*

6005 *Aletti, Jean-Noël* Israël et sa loi selon Saint Paul: une image caricaturale?. Études (April 1998) 499-511.

6006 **Aletti, Jean-Noël** Israël et la loi dans la lettre aux Romains. LeDiv 173: P 1998, Cerf 320 pp. FF185. 2-204-05964-1. Bibl. [R]MoBi 115 (1998) 68 [interview] (*Préville, Agnès*).

6007 *Bekken, Per Jarle* Election, obedience, and eschatology: Deuteronomy 30:2-14 in Romans 9-11 and the writings of Philo. Recruitment. 1998 ⇒320. 315-331.

6008 *Boers, Hendrikus* Judaism and the church in Paul's thought. Neotest. 32 (1998) 249-266.

6009 *Frankemölle, Hubert* Juden und Christen nach Paulus: Israel als Volk Gottes und das Selbstverständnis der christlichen Kirche. Jüdische Wurzeln. BBB 116: 1998 <1984> ⇒151. 73-90.

6010   **Gignac, Alain** Juifs et chrétiens à l'École de Paul de Tarse: enjeux
       identitaires et éthiques d'une lecture de Romains 9-11. ^DMontréal
       1997; ^D*Mainville, O.* Sciences bibliques 9: Montréal 1997, Médias-
       paul 342 pp [NThAR 2000,312].
6011   **Kruse, Colin G.** Paul, the law and justification. 1996 ⇒12,6112;
       13,6358. ^RRTR 57 (1998) 152-153 (*Thompson, Mark D.*).
6012   **Lodge, John G.** Romans 9-11: a reader-response analysis. 1996
       ⇒12,6113. ^RCBQ 60 (1998) 573-574 (*Hensell, Eugene*); JBL 117
       (1998) 369-371 (*Stanley, Christopher D.*).
6013   *Perrot, Charles* La situation religieuse d'Israël selon Paul: Rm 9-11.
       Procès de Jésus. 1998 ⇒392. 133-151.
6014   **Stowers, Stanley K.** A rereading of Romans: justice, Jews and
       gentiles. 1994 ⇒10,5812; 12,6119. ^RLTP 54/1 (1998) 181-192
       (*Gignac, Alain*).
6015   *Wasserberg, Guenter* Romans 9-11 and Jewish-Christian dialogue:
       prospects and provisos. SBL.SPS 37: 1998 ⇒402. 1-11.

6016   *Burchard, Christoph* Römer 9,25 ἐν τῷ Ὡσηὲ. Studien NT. WUNT
       107: 1998 <1984> ⇒140. 229.
6017   **Lloyd-Jones, D. Martyn** Romans: an exposition of chapter 10—sav-
       ing faith. E 1997, Banner of Truth 416 pp. £17. 0-85151-734-4.
6018   *Brown, Michael Joseph* Faith, knowledge, and the law; or maybe the
       Jews will be saved: CLEMENT of Alexandria's reading of Roman's 10-
       11 in Stromateis 2. SBL.SPS 37: 1998 ⇒402. 921-942.
6019   *Haacker, Klaus* "Ende des Gesetzes" und kein Ende?: zur Diskussion
       über τέλος νόμου in Röm 10,4. ^FSCHRAGE, W. 1998 ⇒101. 127-138.
6020   **Amen, Alicia Maglaya** A history of interpretation of τέλος νόμου in
       Romans 10:4. ^DSouthern Baptist Theol. Sem. 1998, 208 pp.
6021   *Grech, Prosper* Il retroscena di Rom 10,5-13 e il discorso ad Antio-
       chia. V Simposio di Tarso. 1998 ⇒395. 105-114.
6022   *Mrożek, Andrzej* Profeta Elia in Rm 11,2-4: alcune considerazioni
       sulla citazione. ^FHERIBAN J. 1998 ⇒41. 45-55.
6023   **Harding, Mark** The salvation of Israel and the logic of Romans
       11:11-36. ABR 46 (1998) 55-69.
6024   **Parr, Charles James** The catechetical implications of the image of
       the olive tree in Romans 11:17-24 for the Jewish-Christian dialogue.
       ^DCatholic U. of America 1998, 431 pp.
6025   *Fernández Eyzaguirre, Samuel* Israel y las naciones: interpretación
       origeniana de Rom 11,25-26. TyV 39 (1998) 212-221.
6026   **Keller, Winfrid**—Israels Heil: Röm 11,25-27—die
       These von 'Sonderweg' in der Diskussion. SBB 40: Stu 1998, Kath.
       Bibelwerk xvii; 329 pp. 3-460-00401-0.
6027   *Mußner, Franz* Gottes "Bund" mit Israel nach Röm 11,27. Der
       ungekündigte Bund?. QD 172: 1998 ⇒240. 157-170.
6028   *López de las Heras, L.* Santo TOMÁS, exégeta: su comentario de Rom
       11,33-36. Studium 38 (1998) 197-219.

G4.8 Rom 12...

6029   **Borghi, Ernesto** Il senso della vita: leggere Romani 12-13 oggi.
       Cammini nello spirito 11: Mi 1998, Paoline 289 pp. 88-315-1573-X.
       ^DFribourg 1996 [NThAR 1999,4].

6030 *Gaston, Lloyd* Faith in Romans 12 in the light of the common life of the Roman church. ᶠSNYDER, G. 1998 ⇒104. 258-264.

6031 *Reichert, Angelika* Gottes universaler Heilswille und der kommunikative Gottesdienst: exegetische Anmerkungen zu Röm 12,1-2. ᶠKLEIN, G. 1998 ⇒52. 79-95.

6032 *Mazzeo, Michele* Il discernimento della volontà di Dio in Rm 12,1-2: un itinerario dinamico. V Simposio di Tarso. 1998 ⇒395. 115-135.

6033 *Strübind, Andrea* Versöhnte Gemeinschaft: Bibelarbeit über Röm 12,3-8. Zeitschrift für Theologie und Gemeinde 3 (1998) 333-345.

6034 *Sensing, Timothy R.* From exegesis to sermon in Romans 12:9-21. RestQ 40/3 (1998) 171-187.

6035 *Yinger, Kent L.* Romans 12:14-21 and nonretaliation in second temple Judaism: addressing persecution within the community. CBQ 60 (1998) 74-96.

6036 *Pokorný, Petr* Römer 12,14-21 und die Aufforderung zur Feindesliebe (Q 6,27 Par.) und zum Gewaltverzicht (Q 6,29f. Par. und Mt 5,39A). ᶠHERIBAN J. 1998 ⇒41. 105-112.

6037 *Klassen, William* Pursue peace: a concrete ethical mandate (Romans 12:18-21). ᶠSCHRAGE, W. 1998 ⇒101. 195-207.

6038 *Voelz, James W.* A self-conscious reader-response interpretation of Romans 13:1-7. The personal voice. 1998 ⇒250. 156-169.

6039 *Merklein, Helmut* Sinn und Zweck von Röm 13,1-7: zur semantischen und pragmatischen Struktur eines umstrittenen Textes. Studien zu Jesus und Paulus II. WUNT 105: 1998 <1989> ⇒175. 405-437.

6040 *Burchard, Christoph* Die Summe der Gebote (Röm 13,7-10): das ganze Gesetz (Gal 5,13-15) und das Christusgesetz (Gal 6,2; Röm 15,1-6; 1 Kor 9,21). Studien NT. WUNT 107: 1998 <1993> ⇒140. 151-183.

6041 *Jewett, Robert* Are there allusions to the love feast in Romans 13:8-10?. ᶠSNYDER, G. 1998 ⇒104. 265-278.

6042 *Miller, Susan F.* Romans 14:1-15:7—unity in the essentials, opinions in the non-essentials, charity in everything. RExp 95 (1998) 103-108.

6043 *Mongillo, Dalmazio* La sollecitudine per i 'deboli nella fede': prospettive dalla lectura ad Romanos cc.14-15,13 di TOMMASO d'Aquino. V Simposio di Tarso. 1998 ⇒395. 281-299.

6044 *Merz, Annette* "Was dem Frieden dient": zum Umgang mit unlösbaren Konflikten in der Gemeinde: sozialgeschichtliche Bibelauslegung zu Römer 14,7-23. JK 59 (1998) 368-373.

6045 *Lewis, Jack P.* "The Kingdom of God ... is righteousness, peace, and joy in the Holy Spirit" (Rom 14:17): a survey of interpretation. RestQ 40/1 (1998) 53-68.

6046 *Dunne, Thomas* Towards an explanation of a crux interpretum: Romans 15,19. DBM 17/1 (1998) 75-80.

6047 *Barr, George K.* Romans 16 and the tent makers. IBSt 20 (1998) 98-113.

6048 *Omanson, Roger L.* Who's who in Romans 16: identifying men and women among the people Paul sent greetings to. BiTr 49 (1998) 430-436.

6049 *Hungs, Franz J.* Ich wünsche nur, daß ihr verständig bleibt" (Röm 16,19): Erwägungen zu einem gewandelten Verständnis von Askese. OrdKor 39 (1998) 445-452.

6050 *Hellholm, David* The "revelation-schema" and its adaptation in the Coptic gnostic Apocalypse of Peter. SEÅ 63 (1998) 233-248 [16,25-27].

G5.1 Epistulae ad Corinthios I (vel I-II), *textus, commentarii*

6051 [E]**Bieringer, Reimund** The Corinthian correspondence. BEThL 125: 1996 ⇒12,6143; 13,6389. [R]JThS 49 (1998) 248-253 (*Horrell, David*).

6052 The epistles of Paul the apostle to the Corinthians: Authorised King James Version. Pocket Canons: E 1998, Canongate xii; 52 pp. 0-86241-799-6 [NThAR 2000,124].

6053 Epistula ad Corinthios. BVLI 42 (1998) 33-36.

6054 [E]**Frede, Hermann Josef; Stanjek, Herbert** Sedulii Scotti collectaneum in apostolum II: in epistolas ad Corinthios usque ad Hebraeos. AGLB 32: 1997 ⇒13,6392. [R]PIBA 21 (1998) 112-114 (*McNamara, Martin*).

6055 **Witherington III, Ben** Conflict and community in Corinth: a sociorhetorical commentary on 1 and 2 Corinthians. 1995 ⇒11/1,4839... 13,6403. [R]CThMi 25 (1998) 222 (*Krentz, Edgar*).

6056 [T]**Barbaglio, Giuseppe** La prima lettera ai Corinzi. Scritti delle origini cristiane 7: 1995 ⇒11/1,4829... 13,6388. [R]Gr. 79 (1998) 573-574 (*Marconi, Gilberto*).

6057 **Calvin, John** The first epistle to the Corinthians. 1996 ⇒12,6144 [R]EvQ 70 (1998) 275-276 (*Rosner, Brian S.*).

6058 **Hannah, Darrel D.** The text of I Corinthians in the writings of ORIGEN. SBL.The NT in the Greek Fathers 4: 1997 ⇒13,6394. [R]NT 40 (1998) 386-388 (*Elliott, J.K.*); JThS 49 (1998) 830-833 (*Kovacs, Judith L.*).

6059 **Horsley, Richard A.** 1 Corinthians. Abingdon New Testament Commentaries: Nv 1998, Abingdon 240 pp. $21. 0-687-05838-4.

6060 **Kremer, Jacob** Der erste Brief an die Korinther. 1997 ⇒13,6399. [R]OrdKor 39/2 (1998) 239-240 (*Giesen, Heinz*).

6061 **Murphy-O'Connor, Jerome** 1 Corinthians. 1997 ⇒13,6401. [R]ScrB 28 (1998) 50-51 (*Stafford, Barbara*).

6062 **Sacchi, Alessandro** Una comunità si interroga: prima lettera di Paolo ai Corinzi. Cammini nello Spirito 12: Mi 1998, Paoline 368 pp. L26. 000. 88-315-1606-X. Bibl.

6063 **Strabeli, Mauro** Primeira carta aos Coríntios: explicação e atualização. Carta dos Apóstolos 2: São Paulo 1998, Paulus 191 pp. 85-349-1145-2 [PerTeol 30,321].

6064 **Wolff, Christian** Der erste Brief des Paulus an die Korinther. ThHK 7: 1996 ⇒12,6156. [R]ThLZ 123 (1998) 392-394 (*Aejmelaeus, Lars*); ThRv 94 (1998) 387-388 (*Eckert, Jost*).

G5.2 *1 & 1-2 ad Corinthios*—themata, topics

6065 *Bowe, Barbara E.* The rhetoric of love in Corinth: from Paul to CLEMENT of Rome. [F]SNYDER, G. 1998 ⇒104. 244-257.

6066   **Dickerson, Patrick Lynn** Apollos in Acts and First Corinthians
       ^DVirginia 1998, 328 pp.
6067   *Ellingworth, Paul* ἡ ἐκκλησία αἱ ἐκκλησίαι in the Pauline corpus
       with special reference to 1 Corinthians 11.2-16 and 14.33b-35. ^FPO-
       KORNÝ, P. 1998 ⇒90. 121-129.
6068   **Eriksson, Anders** Traditions as rhetorical proof: Pauline argumenta-
       tion in I Corinthians. CB.NT 29: Sto 1998, Almqvist & W xiv; 352
       pp. £20.60. 91-22-01775-5. ^DLund. ^RRRT (1998/4) 105-106
       (*Goulder, Michael*).
6069   *Furnish, Victor Paul* Paul and the Corinthians: the letters, the chal-
       lenges of ministry, the gospel. Interp. 52 (1998) 229-245.
6070   *Glancy, Jennifer A.* Obstacles to slaves' participation in the Corinthi-
       an church. JBL 117 (1998) 481-501.
6071   *Goulder, Michael D.* The unity of the Corinthian correspondence.
       JHiC 5/2 (1998) 220-237.
6072   *Guillet, Jacques* Paul apôtre: Corinthe: un peuple nombreux, une
       communauté fragile. Croire aujourd'hui 62 (1998) 30-31.
6073   **Herrera Sánchez, César** La comunidad, proyecto de Pablo en Co-
       rinto. Santafé de Bogotà 1998, "La Palabra" 326 (5) pp.
6074   *Hollander, Harm W.* The meaning of the term "law" (νόμος) in 1
       Corinthians. NT 40 (1998) 117-135.
6075   **Horrell, David G.** The social ethos of the Corinthian correspond-
       ence: interests and ideology from 1 Corinthians to 1 Clement. 1996
       ⇒12,6167. ^RPacifica 11 (1998) 221-223 (*Dawes, Gregory W.*); ABR
       46 (1998) 93-94 (*Watson, Nigel M.*); CBQ 60 (1998) 566-568
       (*Bowe, Barbara E.*); JThS 49 (1998) 253-260 (*Esler, Philip F.*).
6076   **Hunt, Allen Rhea** The inspired body: Paul, the Corinthians, and
       divine inspiration. 1996 ⇒12,6168; 13,6413. ^RCBQ 60 (1998) 367-
       368 (*McDonald, Patricia M.*).
6077   *Hurd, John C.* Good news and the integrity of 1 Corinthians. Earlier
       letters of Paul. ARGU 8: 1998 <1994> ⇒163. 183-206.
6078   *Jones, Nicholas F.* The organization of Corinth again. ZPE 120
       (1998) 49-56.
6079   *Koch, Dietrich-Alex* "Seid unanstößig für Juden und für Griechen
       und für die Gemeinde Gottes" (1 Kor 10,32): christliche Identität im
       μάκελλον in Korinth und bei Privateinladungen. ^FKLEIN, G. 1998
       ⇒52. 35-54.
6080   **Martin, Dale B.** The Corinthian body. 1995 ⇒11/1,4849... 13,6416.
       ^RPro Ecclesia 7 (1998) 368-369 (*Fowl, Stephen*).
6081   **Martini, Carlo Maria** L'utopia alla prova di una comunità: medita-
       zioni sulla prima lettera ai Corinti. CasM 1998, Piemme 160 pp. 88-
       384-4557-5..
6082   *Newton, Derek* Deity and diet: the dilemma of sacrificial food at
       Corinth. ^DSheffield; ^D*Alexander, Loveday.* JSNT.S 169: Shf 1998,
       Academic 434 pp. £55/$85. 1-85075-932-4. Bibl.
6083   *Niederwimmer, Kurt* Erkennen und lieben: Gedanken zum Verhältnis
       von Gnosis und Agape im ersten Korintherbrief. Gesammelte
       Aufsätze. BZNW 90: 1998 <1965> ⇒182. 1-30.
6084   *Peterlin, Davorin* The Corinthian church between Paul's and
       Clement's time. AsbTJ 53/2 (1998) 49-57.
6085   **Ramsaran, Rollin A.** Liberating words: Paul's use of rhetorical max-
       ims in 1 Corinthians 1-10. 1996 ⇒12,6177. ^RCBQ 60 (1998) 583-
       584 (*Marrow, Stanley B.*).

6086   *Schottroff, Luise* A feminist hermeneutic of 1 Corinthians. Escaping Eden. BiSe 65: 1998 ⇒278. 208-215.

6087   *Silva, David A. de* "Let the one who claims honor establish that claim in the Lord": honor discourse in the Corinthian correspondence. BTB 28 (1998) 61-74.

6088   **Stott, Teresa Lynn** Symbolic healing and the body at Corinth: an anthropological analysis of Paul's rhetoric. ᴰVanderbilt 1998, 405 pp.

G5.3 **1 Cor 1-7**: *sapientia crucis... abusus matrimonii*

6089   *Merklein, Helmut* Impliziert das Bekenntnis zum Gekreuzigten ein Nein zum Judentum?: zur Interpretation der oppositionellen Semantik von 1 Kor 1,18-25. ᶠSCHRAGE, W. 1998 ⇒101. 111-126;

6090   Das paulinische Paradox des Kreuzes. Studien zu Jesus und Paulus II. WUNT 105: 1998 <1997> ⇒175. 285-302 [1,18-25].

6091   *Hanges, James C.* 1 Corinthians 4:6 and the possibility of written bylaws in the Corinthian church. JBL 117 (1998) 275-298.

6092   *Tyler, Ronald L.* First Corinthians 4:6 and Hellenistic pedagogy. CBQ 60 (1998) 97-103.

6093   *Wagner, J. Ross* 'Not beyond the things which are written': a call to boast only in the Lord (1 Cor 4.6). NTS 44 (1998) 279-287 [1,31].

6094   *Jüngel, Eberhard* Narren um Christi willen: Predigt über 1Kor 4,8-10. ᶠKLEIN, G. 1998 ⇒52. 323-330.

6095   *Spencer, William David* La signification du mot 'puissance' dans l'enseignement de Paul (1 Co 4,9-20). Hokhma 69 (1998) 27-40.

6096   *Olkland, Jorunn* Om Kristi ene, rene kropp og relevansen av 1 Korinterbrev 5 i kirketukt-diskusjoner. Ung teologi 31/1 (1998) 19-31.

6097   *De Vos, Craig Steven* Stepmothers, concubines and the case of πορνεία in 1 Corinthians 5. NTS 44 (1998) 104-114.

6098   *Shillington, V. George* Atonement texture in 1 Corinthians 5.5. JSNT 71 (1998) 29-50.

6099   *Winter, Bruce W.* Homosexual terminology in 1 Corinthians 6:9: the Roman context and the Greek loan-word. ᶠWRIGHT D. 1998 ⇒126. 275-290.

6100   *Rosner, Brian S.* Temple prostitution in 1 Corinthians 6:12-20. NT 40 (1998) 336-351.

6101   *Baldanza, Giuseppe* La metafora sponsale in 1 Cor 6,12-20: riflessi sull'ecclesiologia. Sal. 60 (1998) 619-637.

6102   *Foulkes, Irene* Cuando un texto bíblico se dirige a varones, ¿qué sentido puede tener para una mujer? 1 Co 6,12-20. Alternativas 5/11-12 (1998) 155-168 [ThIK 21/1,71].

6103   *Baldanza, Giuseppe* L'uso della metafora sponsale in 1Cor 6,12-20: riflessi sull'ecclesiologia. RivBib 46 (1998) 317-340.

6104   *Niederwimmer, Kurt* Zur Analyse der asketischen Motivation in 1. Kor. 7. Gesammelte Aufsätze. BZNW 90: 1998 <1974> ⇒182. 60-69.

6105   *Harnisch, Wolfgang* Christusbindung oder Weltbezug?: sachkritische Erwägungen zur paulinischen Argumentation in 1Kor 7. ᶠSTEGEMANN, H. BZNW 97: 1998 ⇒111. 457-473.

6106 **Dudrey, Russell Paul** The social and legal setting of 1 Corinthians 7:17-35: de facto slave marriages in the church at Corinth. ᴰMinnesota 1998, 542 pp.
6107 *Winter, Bruce W.* Puberty or passion?: the referent of "hyperakmos" in 1 Corinthians 7:36. TynB 49 (1998) 71-89.

G5.4 *Idolothyta... Eucharistia:* **1 Cor 8-11**

6108 *Hurtado, L.W.* The origin of the Nomina Sacra: a proposal. JBL 117 (1998) 655-673.
6109 *Oropeza, B.J.* Laying to rest the midrash: Paul's message on meat sacrificed to idols in light of the Deuteronomic tradition. Bib. 79 (1998) 57-68 [8,1-11,1; Dt 32].
6110 *Sibinga, Joost Smit* The composition of 1 Cor. 9 and its context. NT 40 (1998) 136-163.
6111 *Khiok-khng, Yeo* Differentiation and mutuality of male-female relations in 1 Corinthians 11:2-16. BR 43 (1998) 7-21.
6112 **Blattenberger, David E.** Rethinking 1 Corinthians 11:2-16 through archaeological and moral-rhetorical analysis. SBEC 36: 1997 ⇒13,6475.ᴿTrinJ 19 (1998) 253-255 (*Clarke, Andrew D.*).
6113 *Fitzmyer, Joseph A.* κεφαλή in 1 Corinthians 11:3. To advance the gospel. 1998 <1993> ⇒150. 341-348.
6114 *Das, A.A.* 1 Corinthians 11:17-34 revisited. CTQ 62 (1998) 187-208.
6115 *Hahn, Ferdinand* Das Herrenmahl bei Paulus. ᶠKLEIN, G. 1998 ⇒52. 23-33 [11,23-26].
6116 *Merendino, Rosario Pius* Questo è il mio corpo: (lo offro) per voi!: 1Cor 11,24. ᶠMARTINI, C. RivBib.S 33: 1998 ⇒75. 381-390.

G5.5 **1 Cor 12s... Glossolalia, charismata**

6117 **Bonneau, Guy** Prophétisme et institution dans le christianisme primitif. Sciences bibliques, Études 4: P 1998, Médiaspaul 232 pp. 2-89420-108-7. Bibl.
6118 **Ebner, Ferdinand** La parola e le realtà spirituali: frammenti pneumatologici. ᴱ*Zucal, Silvano.* Classici del pensiero 9: CinB 1998, San Paolo 399 pp. 88-215-3820-6. Bibl.
6119 *Fabbro, Franco* Prospettive d'interpretazione della glossolalia Paolina sotto il profilo della neurolinguistica. RivBib 46 (1998) 157-178.
6120 *Filoramo, Giovanni* Riflessioni in margine al profetismo cristiano primitivo. RSLR 34/1 (1998) 95-107.
6121 **Forbes, Christopher** Prophecy and inspired speech in early christianity and its Hellenistic environment. 1997 ⇒13,6485. ᴿBibl.Interp. 6 (1998) 442-444 (*Lee, Min-Kyu*); NT 40 (1998) 402-405 (*Schnabel, E.J.*); EvQ 70 (1998) 78-80 (*Thiselton, Anthony C.*).
6122 **Gillespie, Thomas W.** The first theologians: a study in early Christian prophecy. 1994 ⇒10,5918...13,6488. ᴿThTo 54/4 (1998) 537-538 (*Cousar, Charles B.*); TJT 14/1 (1998) 96-98 (*Knowles, Michael P.*).
6123 *Hvidt, Niels* Christian Prophecy and revelation: a theological survey on the problem of christian prophecy. StTh 52 (1998) 147-161.
6124 **Martini, Carlo Maria** Uomini e donne dello spirito: meditazioni sui doni dello Spirito Santo. Religione: CasM 1998, Piemme 174 pp. 88-384-3036-5.

6125 *Schnabel, Eckhard J.* Urchristliche Glossolalie: Thesen. JETh 12 (1998) 77-99.

6126 *Schürmann, Heinz* Die geistlichen Gnadengaben in den paulinischen Gemeinden. Im Knechtsdienst Christi. 1998 <1966> ⇒198. 20-57.

6127 Turner, Max Tongues: an experience for all in the Pauline churches?. Asian Journal of Pentecostal Studies 1 (1998) 231-253 [12-14].

6128 *Walker, William O.* Is First Corinthians 13 a non-Pauline interpolation?. CBQ 60 (1998) 484-499.

6129 *Yorke, Gosnell L.O.R.* 1 Corinthians 13:1 revisited: some Afroliturgical and missiological implications. Missionalia 26 (1998) 378-391 Sum. 378.

6130 *Kreisel-Liebermann, Hanna* "Ich will euch einen köstlicheren Weg zeigen": 1. Korinther 13,1-13. JK 59/1 (1998) 32-35.

6131 *Adinolfi, Marco* 1 Cor 13,4-7 e le diatribe di EPITTETO. V Simposio di Tarso. 1998 ⇒395. 15-28.

6132 *Schrage, Wolfgang* Was bleibt und was fällt: zur Eschatologie in 1Kor 13,8-13. ᶠKLEIN, G. 1998 ⇒52. 97-107.

6133 *Eriksson, Anders* "Women tongue speakers, be silent": a reconstruction through Paul's rhetoric. BiblInterp 6 (1998) 80-104 [14,33-36].

6134 *Payne, Philip B.* MS. 88 as evidence for a text without 1 Cor 14.34-5. NTS 44 (1998) 152-158.

6135 *Porter, Wendy J.* λαλέω: a word about women, music and sensuality in the church. Religion & sexuality. 1998 ⇒302. 101-124 [14,34-35].

G5.6 **Resurrectio;** *1 Cor 15...*[⇒F5.6]

6136 *Alborghetti, Patrizio* Karl BARTH e la risurrezione dei morti. RTLu 3 (1998) 71-112. Sum., Zsfs., som. 111s.

6137 *Baumert, Norbert* "Mit Christus sterben und auferstehen": Paulus zu Gegenwart und Zukunft der Auferstehung. Entschluss 53/6 (1998) 21-23.

6138 **Bynum, Caroline Walker** The resurrection of the body in western christianity. LHR 15: 1995 ⇒11/1,4940... 13,6506. ᴿCHR 84 (1998) 521-523 (*Pelikan, Jaroslav*).

6139 *Harris, Murray J.* Resurrection and immortality in the Pauline corpus. Life in the face of death. 1998 ⇒252. 147-170 .

6140 *Head, Peter* Jesus' resurrection in Pauline thought. Proclaiming the resurrection. 1998 ⇒384. 58-80.

6141 *Longenecker, Richard N.* Is there development in Paul's resurrection thought?. Life in the face of death. 1998 ⇒252. 171-202.

6142 *Meyer, Charles R.* Resurrection. ChiSt 37/1 (1998) 87-99.

6143 *Segal, Alan F.* Paul's thinking about resurrection in its Jewish context. NTS 44 (1998) 400-419.

6144 *Walter, Nikolaus* Leibliche Auferstehung?:zur Frage der Hellenisierung der Auferweckungshoffnung bei Paulus. ᶠKLEIN, G. 1998 ⇒52. 109-127.

6145 **Wong, John Bryant** A theology of the resurrected body in light of scripture, christian anthropology, christian ethics, philosophical reflection, and current scientific knowledge. ᴰFuller 1998, 374 pp.

6146 *Lindemann, Andreas* Paulus als Zeuge der Auferstehung Jesu Christi.
^FKLEIN, G. 1998 ⇒52. 55-64 [1 Cor 15].

6147 *Diederen, Andreas* "So verkünden wir, und so habt ihr geglaubt": zur
pragmatischen Funktion von 1 Kor 15,1-11. ^FLÖNING, K. 1998 ⇒66.
143-157.

6148 *Taylor, Justin* Why did Paul persecute the church?. Tolerance. 1998
⇒440. 99-120 [1 Cor 15,9-10; Gal 1,13-14; Phil 3,5-6; 1 Tim 1,12-
13.

6149 **Lewis, Scott Martin** "So that God may be all in all": the apocalyptic
message of 1 Corinthians 15,12-34. ^DGregoriana 1995, ^D*Aletti, Jean-
Noël*. TGr.T 42: R 1998, E.P.U.G. 248 pp. €14,46. 88-7652-794-X.
Bibl.

6150 *Fredrickson, David E.* God, Christ, and all things in 1 Corinthians
15:28. WaW 18 (1998) 254-263.

6151 *Burchard, Christoph* 1 Korinther 15,39-41. Studien NT. WUNT 107:
1998 <1984> ⇒140. 203-228.

6152 **Brodeur, Scott** The Holy Spirit's agency in the resurrection of the
dead: an exegetico-theological study of 1 Corinthians 15,44b-49 and
Romans 8,9-13. TGr.T 14: 1996 ⇒12,6264. ^RCBQ 60 (1998) 147-
148 (*Harrington, Wilfrid J.*).

G5.9 Secunda epistula ad Corinthios

6153 **Barnett, Paul William** The second epistle to the Corinthians. 1997
⇒13,6519. ^RBib. 79 (1998) 132-134 (*Lambrecht, Jan*); RB 105
(1998) 630-631 (*Murphy-O'Connor, J.*); Pacifica 11 (1998) 329-330
(*Watson, Nigel*); LouvSt 23 (1998) 374-377 (*Koperski, Veronica*).

6154 *Barnett, P.W.* Second Corinthians: why Paul wrote it. ^FJUDGE E.
1998 ⇒47. 138-152.

6155 **Blazen, Ivan T.** A call to ministry: receiving the stamp of the cross:
Paul's second letter to the Corinthians. Nampa, Idaho 1998, Pacific
140 pp. 0-8163-1581-7 [NThAR 2000,123].

6156 *Brown, Alexandra R.* The gospel takes place: Paul's theology of
power-in-weakness in 2 Corinthians. Interp. 52 (1998) 271-285.

6157 *Hafemann, Scott* Paul's use of the Old Testament in 2 Corinthians.
Interp. 52 (1998) 246-257.

6158 **Harvey, Anthony Ernest** Renewal through suffering: a study of 2
Corinthians. 1996 ⇒12,6279; 13,6524. ^RJThS 49 (1998) 772-775
(*Hickling, C.J.A.*); ABR 46 (1998) 92-93 (*Watson, Nigel M.*); ThLZ
123 (1998) 146-149 (*Mitchell, Margaret M.*).

6159 **Orsatti, Mauro** Armonia e tensioni nella comunità: la seconda lettera ai Corinti. Lettura pastorale della Bibbia: Bibbia e spiritualità 4:
Bo 1998, EDB 144 pp. L18.000. 88-10-21102-2.

6160 **Savage, Timothy B.** Power through weakness: Paul's understanding
of the Christian ministry in 2 Corinthians. MSSNTS 86: 1996
⇒12,6281; 13,6527. ^RRBBras 15 (1998) 550-552.

6161 **Scott, James M.** 2 Corinthians. NIBC: Peabody 1998, Hendrickson
xiv; 289 pp. $10 [BiTod 37,263—Senior, Donald].

6162 **deSilva, David A.** The credentials of an apostle: Paul's gospel in 2
Corinthians 1-7. N. Richland Hills, TX 1998, Bibal xiv; 132 pp [JBL
118,561s—Welborn, Laurence L.].

6163 *Kügler, Joachim* Paulus und der Duft des triumphierenden Christus: zum kulturellen Basisbild von 2 Kor 2,14-16. [F]HOFFMANN, P., Von Jesus. BZNW 93: 1998 ⇒43. 155-173.

6164 *Schürmann, Heinz* Die apostolische Existenz im Bilde; Meditation über 2 Kor 2,14-16a. Im Knechtsdienst Christi. 1998 <1963> ⇒198. 271-279.

6165 **Gruber, M.** **Margareta** Herrlichkeit in Schwachheit: eine Auslegung der Apologie des zweiten Korintherbriefs 2 Kor 2,14-6,13. FzB 89: Wü 1998, Echter 493 pp. DM56. 3-429-02041-7. Bibl.

6166 **Schröter, Jens** Der versöhnte Versöhner: Paulus als unentbehrlicher Mittler im Heilsvorgang zwischen Gott und Gemeinde nach 2 Kor 2,14-7,4. TANZ 10: 1993, ⇒9,6151... 12,6287. [R]ThRv 94 (1998) 68-70 (*Backhaus, Knut*).

6167 *Schröter, Jens* Schriftauslegung und Hermeneutik in 2 Korinther 3: ein Beitrag zur Frage der Schriftbenutzung des Paulus. NT 40 (1998) 231-275.

6168 *Kelly, Douglas F.* Prêcher avec puissance la parole de Dieu...?: 2 Corinthiens 4:1-6. RRef 49/2 (1998) 1-13.

6169 *Allen, Ronald J.* 2 Corinthians 4:7-18. Interp. 52 (1998) 286-289.

6170 *Kelly, Douglas F.* La vie derrière le message: 2 Corinthiens 4:7-18. RRef 49/5 (1998) 1-10.

6171 *Vanoni, Gottfried* 'Geglaubt habe ich, deshalb habe ich geredet' (Ps 116,10 und 2 Kor 4,13): zur Verwendung von Bibelzitaten in der theologischen Argumentation—zugleich ein Versuch zusammenzudenken, was zusammengehört. [F]BSTEH, A. 1998 ⇒17. 511-535.

6172 *Kuyper, Abraham* When what is mortal is swallowed up by life: 2 Corinthians 5:4. Kerux 13/3 (1998) 3-7.

6173 *Byars, Ronald P.* 2 Corinthians 5:12-17. Interp. 52 (1998) 290-293.

6174 *Hubbard, Moyer* Was Paul out of his mind?: re-reading 2 Corinthians 5.13. JSNT 70 (1998) 39-64.

6175 *Särkiö, Riitta* Die Versöhnung mit Gott—und mit Paulus: zur Bedeutung der Gemeindesituation in Korinth für 2 Kor 5.14-21. StTh 52 (1998) 29-42.

6176 *Goulder, Michael* "So all died" (2 Cor 5.14). [F]POKORNÝ, P. 1998 ⇒90. 141-148.

6177 *Lampe, Peter* Die urchristliche Rede von der "Neuschöpfung des Menschen" im Lichte konstruktivistischer Wissenssoziologie. Exegese und Methodendiskussion. TANZ 23: 1998 ⇒208. 21-32 [5,17].

6178 *Bieringer, Reimund* Die Liebe des Paulus zur Gemeinde in Korinth: eine Interpretation von 2 Korinther 6,11. SNTU.A 23 (1998) 193-213.

6179 *Cyran, Włodzimierz* Wezwanie do wspólnoty z apostołem (2 Kor 6, 11-13; 7,2-4) [Die Aufforderung zur Gemeinschaft mit dem Apostel (2 Kor 6,11-13; 7,2-4)]. Roczniki Teologiczne 45/1 (1998) 123-134 Zsfg. 134. **P.**

6180 *Olley, John W.* A precursor of the NRSV?: 'sons and daughters' in 2 Cor 6.18. NTS 44 (1998) 204-212.

6181 **Angstenberger, Pius** Der reiche und der arme Christus: die Rezeptionsgeschichte von 2 Kor 8,9 zwischen dem zweiten und dem sechsten Jahrhundert. Hereditas 12: 1997 ⇒13,6548. [R]WieWei 61 (1998) 171-172 (*Grieser, Heike*); ThPh 73 (1998) 279-280 (*Sieben, H.J.*).

6182 *Lambrecht, Jan* Paul's boasting about the Corinthians: a study of 2 Cor. 8:24-9:5. NT 40 (1998) 352-368.

6183 *Peterson, Brian K.* Conquest, control, and the cross: Paul's self-portrayal in 2 Corinthians 10-13. Interp. 52 (1998) 258-270.
6184 **Peterson, Brian K.** Eloquence and the proclamation of the gospel in Corinth. SBL.DS 163: Atlanta 1998, Scholars xiii; 209 pp. 0-7885-0445-2 [10-13].
6185 **Walker, Donald Dale** Paul's offer of leniency (2 Cor 10:1): populist ideology and rhetoric in a Pauline letter fragment (2 Cor 10:1-13:10). ^DCh 1998, 555 pp.
6186 *Niederwimmer, Kurt* Ecclesia sponsa Christi: Erwägungen zu 2. Kor. 11,2f. und Eph. 5,31f. Gesammelte Aufsätze. BZNW 90: 1998 <1992> ⇒182. 217-225.
6187 *Langkammer, Hugolin* Tak zwana mowa błazna świętego Pawła (2 Kor 11,16-12,13 [The co-called Paul's boast (2 Cor 11,16-12,13]. Roczniki Teologiczne 45/1 (1998) 135-148 Sum. 148. **P.**
6188 *Walton, Jon M.* 2 Corinthians 12:1-10. Interp. 52 (1998) 293-296.

G6.1 Ad Galatas

6189 **Becker, Jürgen; Luz, Ulrich** Die Briefe an die Galater, Epheser und Kolosser. NTD 8,1: Gö 1998, Vandenhoeck & R 244 pp. DM48. 3-525-51340-2.
6190 **Esler, Philip Francis** Galatians. New Testament Readings: L 1998, Routledge xiv; 290 pp. £17. 0-415-11036-X. Bibl.
6191 ^T**Garzón Bosque, Isabel** Juan CRISÓSTOMO: comentario a la Carta a los Gálatas [In epistulam ad Galatas commentarius]. ^E*Zincone, Sergio.* Biblioteca de Patrística 34: 1996 ⇒12,6326. ^RRevAg 41 (1998) 1206-1208 (*Sánchez Navarro, L.A.*).
6192 **Luther, Martin** Galatians. Crossway Classic Commentaries: Wheaton, IL 1998, Crossway xxiii; 25-303 pp. 0-89107-994-7.
6193 **Martyn, J. Louis** Galatians: a new translation with introduction and commentary. AncB 33a: 1997 ⇒13,6561. ^RETR 73 (1998) 616-618 (*Cuvillier, Élian*); Interp. 52 (1998) 423-425 (*Cosgrove, Charles H.*).
6194 **Matera, Frank J.** Galatians. Sacra Pagina 9: 1992 ⇒8,6507... 12,6331. ^RRBBras 15 (1998) 552-554.
6195 **Pitta, Antonio** Lettera ai Galati. SOCr 9: 1996 ⇒12,6333. ^RRivBib 46 (1998) 364-366 (*Cipriani, Settimio*);
       Lettere ai Galati e ai Romani 1998 ⇒5935.
6196 **Vouga, François** An die Galater. HNT 10: Tü 1998, Mohr viii; 162 pp. DM68. 3-16-147002-8 [RB 106,480].
6197 **Witherington III, Ben** Grace in Galatia: a commentary on St. Paul's letter to the Galatians. E 1998, Clark xvii; 477 pp. £17.50. 0-567-08612-7. ^RIBSt 20 (1998) 141-144 (*McCullough, J.C.*).

6198 *Bachmann, Michael* 4QMMT und Galaterbrief, *m'śj htwrh* und ἔργα νόμου. ZNW 89 (1998) 91-113.
6199 *Barbaglio, Giuseppe* La legge mosaica nella Lettera ai Galati. ^FMARTINI, C. RivBib.S 33: 1998 ⇒75. 391-410.
6200 **Barlone, Sandro** Giustificazione e libertà nel primo Commento di LUTERO alla lettera ai Galati (Galaterbriefvorlesung 1516-1517). Contributi teologici: R 1998, Dehoniane 109 pp. 88-396-0760-9. Bibl.

6201 [TE]Beer, Theobald; Stockhausen, Alma von Erklärungen Martin
LUTHERS zum Brief des hl. Paulus an die Galater. Weilheim-
Bierbronnen 1998, Gustav-Siewerth-Akademie 375 pp. 3-928273-90-
6. Institut für Lutherforschung der Gustav-Siewerth-Akademie.

6202 *Brucker, Ralph* "Versuche ich denn jetzt, Menschen zu überreden
...?": Rhetorik und Exegese am Beispiel des Galaterbriefes. Exegese
und Methodendiskussion. TANZ 23: 1998 ⇒208. 211-236.

6203 Choi, Gab Jong Living by the Spirit: a study of the role of the Spirit
in Paul's letter to the Galatians. [D]Iliff 1998, 401 pp.

6204 *Jürgens, Burkhard* Der kranke Mann am Bosporus: Anamnese der
Verschriftlichung im Galaterbrief. [F]LÖNING, K. 1998 ⇒66. 131-141.

6205 Kern, Philip H. Rhetoric and Galatians: assessing an approach to
Paul's epistle. MSSNTS 101: C 1998, CUP xiv; 304 pp. $60. 0-521-
63117-3. Bibl.

6206 *Lategan, Bernard C.* Reading the letter to the Galatians from an
apartheid and a post-*apartheid* perspective. The personal voice.
1998 ⇒250. 128-141.

6207 Longenecker, Bruce W. The triumph of Abraham's God: the transformation of identity in Galatians. E 1998, Clark xiii; 236 pp. £15. 0-
567-08617-8.

6208 *Maschke, Timothy H.* The authority of scripture: LUTHER's approach
to allegory in Galatians. Luther Digest 6 (1998) 8-10 Sum. of Logia
4/2 (1995) 25-31.

6209 *Meynet, Roland* Solidarité humaine dans l'Épître aux Galates. StMiss
47 (1998) 1-20.

6210 Morland, Kjell Arne The rhetoric of curse in Galatians: Paul con-
fronts another gospel. 1995 ⇒11/1,5021. [R]ThLZ 123/4 (1998) 384-
387 (*Bachmann, Michael*).

6211 Scott, James M. Paul and the nations: the Old Testament and Jewish
background of Paul's mission to the nations with special reference to
the destination of Galatians. WUNT 2/84: 1995, ⇒11/1,5026...
13,6583. [R]RBBras 15 (1998) 544-546.

6212 Smiles, Vincent M. The gospel and the law in Galatia. Michael Glazier: ColMn 1998, Liturgical xii; 286 pp. $24. Diss. Fordham [BiTod
37,61—Senior, Donald].

6213 *Stanley, Christopher D.* Biblical quotations as rhetorical devices in
Paul's letter to the Galatians. SBL.SPS 37: 1998 ⇒402. 700-730.

6214 *Borgen, Peder* A response to FREDRIKSEN's 'Judaism, the circumcision of Gentiles, and apocalyptic hope: another look at Galatians 1
and 2'. Recruitment. 1998 ⇒320. 245-250.

6215 *Fredriksen, Paula* Judaism, the circumcision of Gentiles, and
apocalyptic hope: another look at Galatians 1 and 2. Recruitment.
1998 ⇒320. 209-244.

6216 Ciampa, Roy E. The presence and function of scripture in Galatians
1 and 2. WUNT 2/102: Tü 1998, Mohr xiii; 449 pp. DM128. 3-16-
146895-3. [D]Aberdeen 1996; Bibl.

6217 Okoronkwo, Uche Cyprian The 'other' gospel in Gal 1:6-9. Extr.
Diss. Urbaniana. [D]*Biguzzi, Giancarlo.* R 1998, v; 68 pp [NThAR
2000,64].

6218 *Becht, Michael* Die Autorität des Evangeliums: Galater 1,8-9 und das
Problem der Autorität der Schrift im Spiegel der spätmittelalterlichen
Theologie. [F]BOYLE L. 1998, III, 11-25.

6219 *Barnikol, Ernst* The non-Pauline origin of the parallelism of the apostles Peter and Paul: Galatians 2:7-8. JHiC 5 (1998) 285-300.

6220 *Cocchini, Francesca* La recezione della 'controversia' di Antiochia (Gal 2,11-14) nelle comunità christiane di ambiente orientale. V Simposio di Tarso. 1998 ⇒395. 225-235.

6221 *Holmberg, Bengt* Jewish versus Christian identity in the early church?. RB 105 (1998) 397-425 [2,11-21].

6222 **Eckstein, Hans-Joachim** Verheissung und Gesetz: eine exegetische Untersuchung zu Galater 2,15-4,7. WUNT 2/86: 1996 ⇒12,6356; 13,6592. ᴿATG 61 (1998) 291-292 (*Rodríguez Carmona, A.*); JBL 117 (1998) 153-155 (*Martyn, J. Louis*).

6223 *Merklein, Helmut* 'Nicht aus den Werken des Gesetzes...': eine Auslegung von Gal 2,15-21. Studien zu Jesus und Paulus II. WUNT 105: 1998 <1996> 303-315.

6224 *Korang, John Kwame* Paul's christocentric soteriology: a study of Paul's theological propositio [Gal 2,15-21]. Hekima Review 19 (1998) 58-68 Sum. 58.

6225 *Morland, Kjell Arne* Expansion and conflict: the rhetoric of Hebrew bible citations in Galatians 3. Recruitment. 1998 ⇒320. 251-271.

6226 **Tran, Martin Duc** The inclusive unity of the children of God: a biblico-rhetorical analysis of the letter of Paul to the Galatians 3,1-5,1. Excerpt Diss. Gregoriana. ᴰ*Meynet, Roland*. R 1998, 136 pp.

6227 *Merk, Otto* Der Beginn der Paränese im Galaterbrief. ᶠMERK O. BZNW 95: 1998 <1969> ⇒79. 238-259 [3,1-5,12].

6228 *O'Neill, J.C.* "Did you receive the spirit by the works of the law?" (Gal 3:2): the works of the law in Judaism and the Pauline corpus. ABR 46 (1998) 70-84.

6229 *Young, Norman H.* Who's cursed—and why? (Galatians 3:10-14). JBL 117 (1998) 79-92.

6230 *Penna, Romano* 'Il giusto per fede vivrà': la citazione di Ab 2,4 (TM e LXX) in Gal 3,11 e Rom 1,17. V Simposio di Tarso. 1998 ⇒395. 85-94.

6231 *Burchard, Christoph* Noch ein Versuch zu Galater 3,19 und 20. Studien NT. WUNT 107: 1998 <1993> ⇒140. 184-202.

6232 *Dobbeler, Axel von* Metaphernkonflikt und Missionsstrategie: Beobachtungen zur personifizierenden Rede vom Glauben in Gal 3,23-25. ThZ 54 (1998) 14-35.

6233 *Strus, Andrzej* 'Plenitudo temporis': cronologia della salvezza in Gal 4,4. ᶠHERIBAN J. 1998 ⇒41. 57-84.

6234 *Ibáñez, Javier; Mendoza, Fernando* El hijo de Dios, nacido de mujer: Gál 4,4 en la patrística griega de los siglos I y II. EstMar 64 (1998) 487-514.

6235 ᴱ**Vanhoye, Albert** La foi agissant par l'amour (Galates 4,12-6,16). SMBen.BE 13: 1996 ⇒12,277. ᴿBen. 45 (1998) 454-456 (*Ranzato, Agostino*).

6236 *Murphy-O'Connor, Jerome* Gal 4:13-14 and the recipients of Galatians. RB 105 (1998) 202-207.

6237 *Bachmann, Michael* Die andere Frau: synchrone und diachrone Beobachtungen zu Gal 4,21-5,1. Jud. 54 (1998) 144-164.

6238 *Grohmann, Marianne* Sara und Hagar: Anfragen an die Exegese von Gal 4,21-31 von der Wirkungsgeschichte her. PzB 7 (1998) 53-74.

6239 *Manns, Frédéric* Paul et sa lecture juive des Écritures. V Simposio di Tarso. 1998 ⇒395. 29-39 [4,21-31].

6240 *vonEhrenkrook, Jason Q.* Galatians 4:21-31: hermeneutical gymnastics or historical interpretation. CBTJ 14/1 (1998) 50-65.
6241 *Weder, Hans* Die Normativität der Freiheit: eine Überlegung zu Gal 5,1.13-25. [F]KLEIN, G. 1998 ⇒52. 129-145.
6242 *Lambrecht, Jan* The right things you want to do: a note on Galatians 5,17d. Bib. 79 (1998) 515-524.
6243 *Stoevesandt, Hinrich* Säen zum ewigen Leben. [F]KLEIN, G. 1998 ⇒52. 297-311 [6,8].
6244 **Faliyala, Joseph Musuyu** La *kainē ktisis* en St. Paul: (Gal 6,15 et 2 Co 5,17). [D]Urbaniana extr. 1998: [D]*Virgulin, Stefano.* R 1998, xxxix; 52 pp. [NThAR 2000,153].

G6.2 **Ad Ephesios**

Becker, J., *al.*, Die Briefe... Galater, Epheser... 1998 ⇒6189.
6245 **Best, Ernest** A critical and exegetical commentary on Ephesians. ICC: E 1998, Clark xxix; 686 pp. £40. 0-567-08565-1. Bibl. [R]RRT (1998/4) 103-104 (*Chaplin, Doug*).
6246 **Kreitzer, Larry Joseph** The epistle to the Ephesians. Epworth Commentaries: 1997 ⇒13,6621. [R]IThQ 63 (1998) 407-408 (*McConvery, Brendan*).

6247 **Cooper, Stephen Andrew** Metaphysics and morals in Marius VICTORINUS' commentary on the letter to the Ephesians: a contribution to the history of neoplatonism and christianity. AmUSt.P 155: 1995, ⇒11/1,5066; 13,6626. [R]JEarlyC 6 (1998) 678-679 (*Barnes, Michel René*).
6248 **Fieger, Michael** Im Schatten der Artemis: Glaube und Ungehorsam in Ephesus. Bern 1998, Lang 213 pp. 3-906760-58-8 [NThAR 1999,45].
6249 **Günther, Matthias** Die Frühgeschichte des Christentums in Ephesus. ARGU 1: Fra [2]1998, Lang xi; 249 pp. 3-631-33181-9 [NThAR 1999,5].
6250 **Hume, C.R.** Reading through Colossians and Ephesians. L 1998, SCM vii; 152 pp. 0-334-02720-9. Bibl.
6251 *Lemmer, Richard* ἡ οἰκονομία τοῦ μυστηρίου τοῦ ἀποκεκρυμμένου ἀπὸ τῶν αἰώνων ἐν τῷ θεῷ—understanding 'body of Christ' in the letter to the Ephesians. Neotest. 32 (1998) 459-495.
6252 **Lincoln, Andrew T.; Wedderburn, A.J.M.** The theology of the later Pauline letters. 1993 ⇒9,6248; 11/1,5068. [R]EvQ 70 (1998) 276-279 (*Turner, Max*)
6253 **Love, Richard Deane, II** Pauline contextualization at Ephesus: power and leadership issues with special reference to Sundanese folk Muslims. [D]Fuller 1998, 363 pp.
6254 *Maloney, Elliott C.* God's power in Christ Jesus. BiTod 36 (1998) 349-353.
6255 **Moritz, Thorsten** A profound mystery: the use of the Old Testament in Ephesians. NT.S 85: 1996 ⇒12,6402. [R]ThLZ 123 (1998) 382-384 (*Lindemann, Andreas*); EvQ 70 (1998) 359-361 (*Williams, H. Drake*); CBQ 60 (1998) 373-375 (*Fiore, Benjamin*).
6256 *Perkins, Pheme* Ephesians: an introduction. BiTod 36 (1998) 341-347.

6257 **Strelan, Rick** Paul, Artemis, and the Jews in Ephesus. BZNW 80: 1996 ⇒12,6408; 13,6632. ᴿCBQ 60 (1998) 589-591 (*Reid, Barbara E.*); JThS 49 (1998) 260-263 (*Barclay, John M.G.*).

6258 *Sellin, Gerhard* Adresse und Intention des Epheserbriefes. ᶠKLEIN, G. 1998 ⇒52. 171-186 [1,1].

6259 *Newman, Carey C.* Ephesians 1:3—a primer to Paul's grammar of God. RExp 95 (1998) 89-101.

6260 *Avril, Anne* La bénédiction d'Ephésiens 1,3-14 à la lumière de la tradition rabbinique. Cahiers Ratisbonne 3 (1997) 56-79. Rias./sum. 79.

6261 *Hübner, Hans* Erkenntnis Gottes und Wirklichkeit Gottes: theologisch-hermeneutische Gedanken zu Eph 3,14-19. ᶠPOKORNÝ, P. 1998 ⇒90. 176-184.

6262 **Harris, W. Hall** The descent of Christ: Ephesians 4:7-11 and traditional Hebrew imagery. AGJU 32: 1996 ⇒12,6418. ᴿBS 155 (1998) 497-499 (*Hoehner, Harold W.*).

6263 *Kreitzer, Larry J.* The Plutonium of Hierapolis and the descent of Christ into the 'lowermost parts of the earth' (Ephesians 4,9). Bib. 79 (1998) 381-393.

6264 *Sellin, G.* Imitatio Dei: traditions- und religionsgeschichtliche Hintergründe von Eph 5,1-2. ᶠPOKORNÝ, P. 1998 ⇒90. 298-313.

6265 *Kreitzer, Larry J.* 'Crude language' and 'shameful things done in secret' (Ephesians 5.4, 12): allusions to the cult of Demeter/Cybele in Hierapolis?. JSNT 71 (1998) 51-77.

6266 *Gamba, Giuseppe G.* 'Redimentes tempus' (Ef 5,16; Col 4,5). ᶠHERIBAN J. 1998 ⇒41. 113-130.

6267 *Osiek, Carolyn* The Ephesian household code. BiTod 36 (1998) 360-364 [5,21-6,9].

6268 **Dawes, Gregory W.** The body in question: metaphor and meaning in the interpretation of Ephesians 5:21-33. Bibl.Interp. 30: Lei 1998, Brill xiv; 264 pp. $85.50. 90-04-10959-5.

6269 *Whang, Y.C.* Cohabitation or conflict: Greek household management and christian *Haustafeln*. Religion & sexuality. 1998 ⇒302. 85-100 [5,21-33].

6270 *Wild, Robert A.* 'Put on the armor of God'. BiTod 36 (1998) 365-370 [6,10-20].

6271 *Gudorf, Michael E.* The use of πάλη in Ephesians 6:12. JBL 117 (1998) 331-335.

G6.3 **Ad Philippenses**

6272 **Fee, Gordon D.** Paul's letter to the Philippians. NIC.NT: 1995, ⇒11/1,5089; 13,6647. ᴿThZ 54 (1998) 177-178 (*Weber, Beat*); JThS 49 (1998) 775-777 (*Hooker, Morna D.*).

6273 **Floor, L.** Filippenzen: een gevangene over de stijl van Christus. Commentar op het Nieuwe Testament: Kampen 1998, Kok 213 pp. *f*50. 90-242-6218-6 [Interpretatie 7/2,31—Hoet, Hendrik].

6274 **Légasse, Simon** A carta aos Filipenses e a carta a Filémon. Cadernos Bíblicos 63: Lisboa 1998, Difusora Bíblica 56 pp [Bib(L) 7/7,189—Negreiros, Fernando de].

6275 **Walter, Nikolaus; Reinmuth, Eckart; Lampe, Peter** Die Briefe an die Philipper, Thessalonicher und an Philemon. NTD 8.2: Gö 1998, Vandenhoeck & R 232 pp. DM44. 3-525-51381-X.

6276 [E]**Bakirtzis, Charalambos; Koester, Helmut** Philippi at the time of Paul and after his death. Harrisburg 1998, Trinity xv; 87 pp. $16. 1-56338-263-6 [ThD 46,285—Heiser, W. Charles].

6277 *Bakirtzis, Charalambos* Paul and Philippi: the archaeological evidence. Philippi. 1998 ⇒460. 37-48.

6278 *Bateman, Herbert W.* Were the opponents at Philippi necessarily Jewish?. BS 155 (1998) 39-61.

6279 **Bormann, Lukas** Philippi: Stadt und Christengemeinde zur Zeit des Paulus. NT.S 78: 1995 ⇒11/1,5097; 12,6423. [R]EstAg 33 (1998) 162-163 (*Cineira, D.A.*); ThZ 54 (1998) 178-179 (*Rese, Martin*).

6280 *Briggs, Sheila* Der Brief an die Gemeinde in Philippi: die Aufrichtung der Gedemütigten. Kompendium Feministische Bibelauslegung. [E]**Schottroff, L.**: 1998 ⇒H8.9. 625-634.

6281 *Callahan, Allen Dwight* Dead Paul: the apostle as martyr in Philippi. Philippi. 1998 ⇒460. 67-84.

6282 *Holloway, Paul A.* The apocryphal epistle to the Laodiceans and the partitioning of Philippians. HThR 91 (1998) 321-325.

6283 **Holloway, Paul Andrew** 'Disce gaudere': Paul's consolation of the church at Philippi. [D]Ch 1998, 215 pp.

6284 *Koester, Helmut* Paul and Philippi: the evidence from early christian literature. Philippi. 1998 ⇒460. 49-65.

6285 *Koukouli-Chrysantaki, Chaido* Colonia Iulia Augusta Philippensis. Philippi. 1998 ⇒460. 5-35.

6286 *Murray, George W.* Paul's corporate witness in Philippians. BS 155 (1998) 316-326.

6287 **Peterlin, Davorin** Paul's letter to the Philippians in the light of disunity in the Church. NT.S 79: 1995 ⇒11/1,5104; 13,6653. [R]CrSt 19 (1998) 421-423 (*Stroumsa, Guy G.*)

6288 **Pilhofer, Peter** Die erste christliche Gemeinde Europas. Philippi, 1. WUNT 2/87: 1995 ⇒11/1,5106... 13,6650. [R]JEH 49 (1998) 501-502 (*Capper, Brian J.*).

6289 *Porter, Stanley E.; Reed, Jeffrey T.* Philippians as a macro-chiasm and its exegetical significance. NTS 44 (1998) 213-231.

6290 *Pretorius, Emil* Role models for a model church: typifying Paul's letter to the Philippians. Neotest. 32 (1998) 547-571.

6291 **Reed, Jeffrey T.** A discourse analysis of Philippians: method and rhetoric in the debate over literary integrity. JSNT.S 136: 1997 ⇒13,6654. [R]Bib 79 (1998) 293-297 (*Du Toit, Andrie*).

6292 *Sellew, Philip* Laodiceans and Philippians revisited: a response to Paul Holloway. HThR 91 (1998) 327-329.

6293 *Triacca, Achille M.* L'Epistola ad Philippenses nell'odierna liturgia 'eucaristica' romana: dal suo uso verso un'esegesi liturgica. [F]HERIBAN J. 1998 ⇒41. 373-426.

6294 *Vanni, Ugo* Verso la struttura letteraria della lettera ai Filippesi. V Simposio di Tarso. 1998 ⇒395. 61-83.

6295 *Mara, Maria Grazia* Utilizzazioni di Fil 1,15-18 nella chiesa antica. V Simposio di Tarso. 1998 ⇒395. 215-223.

6296 **Reimer, Raymond Hubert** 'Our citizenship is in heaven': Philippians 1:27-30 and 3:20-21 as part of the apostle Paul's political theology. [D]Princeton Theol. Sem. 1998, 326 pp.

6297 ^E**Dodd, Brian J.; Martin, Ralph Philip** Where christology began: essays on Philippians 2. LVL 1998, Westminster x; 169 pp. $25. 0-664-25619-8. Bibl.
6298 *Brown, Colin* Ernst Lohmeyer's *Kyrios Jesus*;
6299 *Dunn, James D.G.* Christ, Adam, and preexistence;
6300 *Fowl, Stephen* Christology and ethics in Philippians 2:5-11;
6301 *Hawthorne, Gerald F.* In the form of God and equal with God (Philippians 2:6);
6302 *Martin, Ralph P.* Carmen Christi revisited;
6303 *Morgan, Robert* Incarnation, myth, and theology: Ernst Käsemann's interpretation of Philippians 2:5-11. Where christology began. 1998 ⇒6297. 6-42/74-95/140-153/96-110/1-5/43-73.
6304 *Manzi, Franco* L'uso liturgico del paradosso di Filippesi 2,5-11 nel primo prefazio comune. EL 112 (1998) 3-17 Sum. 3.
6305 *Luongo, Gennaro* Paolo maestro e compagno dei martiri. V Simposio di Tarso. 1998 ⇒395. 253-267 [2,6-8].
6306 *Basevi, Claudio* Estudio literario y teológico del himno christológico de la epístola a los Filipenses (Phil 2,6-11). ScrTh 30 (1998) 439-472.
6307 *Lüdemann, Gerd; Janßen, Martina* Phil 2,6-11 und gnostische Christushymnen aus Nag Hammadi. ^FSTEGEMANN, H. BZNW 97: 1998 ⇒111. 488-511.
6308 **Brucker, Ralph** "Christushymnen" oder "epideiktische Passagen"?: Studien zum Stilwechsel im Neuen Testament und seiner Umwelt. FRLANT 176: 1997 ⇒13,6660. ^RBZ 42 (1998) 278-282 (*Vollenweider, Samuel*); ThLZ 123 (1998) 985-987 (*Schenk, Wolfgang*) [2,6-11].
6309 *Kim, Jean K.* An Asian interpretation of Philippians 2.6-11. Escaping Eden. BiSe 65: 1998 ⇒278. 104-122.
6310 *Grelot, Pierre* Ἐν μορφῇ θεοῦ ὑπάρχων: étude sur *Ph* 2,6-11. RThom 98 (1998) 631-638.
6311 *Wegener, Mark I.* Philippians 2:6-11—Paul's (revised) hymn to Jesus. CThMi 25 (1998) 507-517.
6312 *Gómez, Francisco* Un texto litúrgico paulino desvirtuado. Phase 38 (1998) 391-393 [2,8].
6313 *Bauckham, Richard J.* The worship of Jesus in Philippians 2:9-11;
6314 *Kreitzer, Larry J.* 'When he at last is first!': Philippians 2:9-11 and the exaltation of the Lord. Where christology began. 1998 ⇒6297. 128-139/111-127.
6315 *VanDrunen, David* In the apostle's absence: Philippians 2:19-30. Kerux 13/3 (1998) 8-15.
6316 *Dodd, Brian J.* The story of Christ and the imitation of Paul in Philippians 2-3. Where christology began. 1998 ⇒6297. 154-161.

6317 **Berz, Fabian** Unser Bürgerrecht ist im Himmel: Phil 3,2-21 als briefliche Mahnrede gegen eine falsche Selbstsicherheit. ^DLuzern 1998-1999: ^D*Kirchschläger*.
6318 **Koperski, Veronica** The knowledge of Christ Jesus my Lord: the high christology of Philippians 3:7-11. 1996 ⇒12,6169; 13,6666 ^RJBL 117 (1998) 155-156 (*Silva, Moisés*).
6319 *Fitzmyer, Joseph A.* 'To know him and the power of his resurrection' (Phil 3:10). To advance the gospel. 1998 <1970> ⇒150. 202-217.
6320 *Holloway, Paul A.* Bona Cogitare: an Epicurean consolation in Phil 4:8-9. HThR 91 (1998) 89-96.

6321 *Fee, Gordon D.* To what end exegesis?: reflections on exegesis and spirituality in Philippians 4:10-20. BBR 8 (1998) 75-88.
6322 **Peterman, Gerald W.** Paul's gift from Philippi: conventions of gift-exchange and christian giving. SBL.MS 92: 1997 ⇒13,6668. ᴿBib 79 (1998) 297-299 (*Fee, Gordon D.*) [4,10-20].

G6.4 Ad Colossenses

6323 *Aletti, Jean-Noël* Colossesi: una svolta nella cristologia neotestamentaria: difficoltà e proposte. ᶠHERIBAN J. 1998 ⇒41. 131-145.
6324 **Aletti, Jean-Noël** Lettera ai Colossesi. 1994 ⇒10,6123; 12,6447. ᴿAnton. 73 (1998) 159-160 (*Nobile, Marco*).
6325 **Arnold, Clinton E.** The Colossian syncretism: the interface between christianity and folk belief at Colossae. WUNT 2/77: 1995, ⇒11/1,5129; 12,6448. ᴿAUSS 36 (1998) 112-113 (*Yorke, Gosnell L.O.R.*); CBQ 60 (1998) 554-555 (*Wild, Robert A.*); EvQ 70 (1998) 154-155 (*Moritz, Thorsten*); JBL 117 (1998) 156-158 (*Hurtado, L.W.*).
      Becker, J., Die Briefe an die Galater... Kolosser 1998 ⇒6189.
6326 **Garland, David E.** Colossians and Philemon. NIV application commentary: GR 1998, Zondervan 389 pp. 0-310-48480-4.
6327 *Gildemeister, Thomas R.* Christology and the focus of faith: readings from Paul's letter to the Colossians in year C. QR 18/1 (1998) 89-110.
      Hume, C.R. Reading through Col. & Eph. 1998 ⇒6250.
6328 **Martin, Troy W.** By philosophy and empty deceit: Colossians as response to a Cynic critique. JSNT.S 118: 1996 ⇒12,6452; 13,6675. ᴿJBL 117 (1998) 542-544 (*Downing, F. Gerald*).
6329 *Roberts, J.H.* Jewish mystical experience in the early christian era as background to understanding Colossians. Neotest. 32 (1998) 161-189.
6330 *Schmithals, Walter* Literarkritische Analyse des Kolosserbriefs ᶠKLEIN, G. 1998 ⇒52. 149-170.
6331 **Wilson, Walter T.** The hope of glory: education in the epistle to the Colossians. NT.S 88: 1997 ⇒13,6677. ᴿJThS 49 (1998) 777-780 (*Moule, C.F.D.*).
6332 *Wilson, Walter T.* The "practical" achievement of Colossians: a theological assessment. HBT 20/1 (1998) 49-74.

6333 *Basevi, Claudio* Col 1,15-20: las posibles fuentes del "himno" cristológico y su importancia para la interpretación. ScrTh 30 (1998) 779-802.
6334 *Lamp, Jeffrey S.* Wisdom in Col 1:15-20: contribution and significance. JETS 41 (1998) 45-53.
6335 *Hölscher, Andreas* Christus als Bild Gottes: zum Hymnus des Kolosserbriefes. Religiöse Sprache. 1998 ⇒1144. 114-133 [1,15-20].
6336 *Merk, Otto* Erwägungen zu Kol 2,6f. ᶠMERK O. BZNW 95: 1998 <1989> ⇒79. 292-301.
6337 *Niederwimmer, Kurt* Vita abscondita: Erwägungen zu Kol. 3,1-4. Gesammelte Aufsätze. BZNW 90: 1998 <1989> ⇒182. 185-195.
6338 *Standhartinger, Angela* Singen wider die Hoffnungslosigkeit: sozialgeschichtliche Bibelauslegung zu Kolosser 3,12-17. JK 59 (1998) 222-225.

[*Ad Philemonem* Vid. G7.4]

G6.6 Ad Thessalonicenses

6339 **Gaventa, Beverly Roberts** First and Second Thessalonians. Interpretation Commentaries: LVL 1998, Westminster xiii; 138 pp. $22. 0-8042-3142-7.

6340 **Holmes, Michael W.** The NIV Application Commentary: 1 & 2 Thessalonians. GR 1998, Zondervan 303 pp. $22 [CTJ 34,210ss— Weima, Jeffrey A.D.].

6341 *Hurd, John C.* Thoughts preliminary to writing a commentary on 1 & 2 Thessalonians. Earlier letters of Paul... ARGU 8: 1998 <1977> ⇒163. 97-108.

6342 **Kapkin, David** 1 y 2 Tesalonicenses: ya viene el Señor. Escuela Bíblica: Medellín 1998, n.p. v; 284 pp.

6343 **Richard, Earl J.** First and Second Thessalonians. 1995, ⇒12,6463. ᴿNeotest. 32 (1998) 244-245 (*Cornelius, E.M.*).

6344 **Verhoef, Eduard** De brieven aan de Tessalonicenzen. Kampen 1998, Kok 310 pp. 90-242-6170-8 [NThAR 1998,368].
      Walter, N. Die Briefe... Thess. 1998 ⇒6275.

6345 **Weima, Jeffrey A.D.; Porter, Stanley E.** An annotated bibliography of 1 and 2 Thessalonians. NTTS 26: Lei 1998, Brill ix; 292 pp. ƒ180/$106. 90-04-10740-1.

6346 *Bickmann, Jutta* Der erste Brief an die Gemeinde in Thessalonich: Gemeinschaft bilden im Widerstand gegen den Tod. Kompendium Feministische Bibelauslegung. ᴱ**Schottroff, L.**: 1998 ⇒H8.9. 646-653.

6347 **Bickmann, Jutta** Kommunikation gegen den Tod: Studien zur paulinischen Briefpragmatik am Beispiel des Ersten Thessalonicherbriefes. ᴰMünster: ᴰ*Löning, K.*, FzB 86: Wü 1998, Echter xii; 365 pp. DM48. 3-429-01994-X.

6348 *Hurd, John C.* Concerning the structure of 1 Thessalonians. Earlier letters of Paul... ARGU 8: 1998 <1972> ⇒163. 47-83.

6349 *Merk, Otto* Miteinander: zur Sorge um den Menschen im ersten Thessalonicherbrief. ᶠMERK O. BZNW 95: 1998 <1993> ⇒79. 374-382;

6350 Zur Christologie im ersten Thessalonicherbrief. ᶠMERK O. BZNW 95: 1998 <1991> ⇒79. 360-373.

6351 *Simpson, John W.* Shaped by the stories: narrative in 1 Thessalonians. AsbTJ 53/2 (1998) 15-25.

6352 *Merk, Otto* 1 Thessalonicher 2,1-12: ein exegetisch-theologischer Überblick: paper for Studiorum Novi Testamenti Societas, 51th [!] General Meeting, Strasbourg, August 6-10, 1996. ᶠMERK O. BZNW 95: 1998 ⇒79. 383-403.

6353 *Hurd, John C.* Paul ahead of his time: 1 Thess. 2:13-16. Earlier letters of Paul... ARGU 8: 1998 <1980> ⇒163. 117-133.

6354 *Collins, Raymond F.* The function of paraenesis in 1 Thess 4,1-12; 5,12-22. EThL 74 (1998) 398-414.

6355 *Merk, Otto* 1 Thessalonicher 4,13-18 im Lichte des gegenwärtigen Forschungsstandes. ᶠMERK O. BZNW 95: 1998 <1997> ⇒79. 404-421.

6356 *Crüsemann, Marlene* Der zweite Brief an die Gemeinde in Thessalonich: Hoffen auf das gerechte Gericht Gottes. Kompendium Feministische Bibelauslegung. [E]**Schottroff, L.**: 1998 ⇒H8.9. 654-660.
6357 *Hurd, John C.* Concerning the authenticity of 2 Thessalonians. Earlier letters of Paul... ARGU 8: 1998 <1983> ⇒163. 135-161.
6358 *Merk, Otto* Überlegungen zu 2 Thess 2,13-17. [F]MERK O. BZNW 95:
1998 <1994> ⇒79. 422-431.

G7.0 Epistulae pastorales

6359 *Asake, Musa Nchock* An exposition of 1 Timothy 3:1-7 and Titus
1:5-9 with application to Bajju ECWA Churches in northern Nigeria.
[D]Dallas 1998, 271 pp.
6360 *Biguzzi, Giancarlo* L'autore delle Lettere Pastorali e Timoteo. Il
deposito della fede. RivBib.S 34: 1998 ⇒6363. 81-111.
6361 *Butzer, Evi* Die Witwen der Pastoralbriefe. TeKo 21/3 (1998) 25-52.
6362 *D'Ambrosio, Domenico* Istanze e prospettive teologico-pastorali delle lettere a Timoteo e Tito. Il deposito della fede. RivBib.S 34: 1998
⇒6363. 9-18.
6363 [E]**De Virgilio, Giuseppe** Il deposito della fede: Timoteo e Tito. Riv-
Bib.S 34: Bo 1998, EDB 278 pp. L32.000. 88-10-30222-2. [R]LASBF
48 (1998) 609-610 (*Bottini, Giovanni Claudio*).
6364 *(a) De Virgilio, Giuseppe* Aspetti e profili della solidarietà nelle Lettere Pastorali; *(b) Della Corte, Ernesto* Carisma e ministeri nelle Lettere Pastorali; *(c) Fabris, Rinaldo* La cristologia soteriologica nelle
Lettere Pastorali; *(d) Marcheselli-Casale, Cesare* Le Lettere Pastorali
a Timoteo e a Tito: analisi letteraria e strategia retorica: per un contributo allo status quaestionis dell'esegesi sulle Lettere Pastorali; *(e)
Marucci, Corrado* L'ecclesiologia delle Lettere Pastorali; *(f) Mosetto,
Francesco* La bibbia e il pastore: la sacra scrittura nelle Lettere
Pastorali; *(g) Pitta, Antonio* Paolo dopo e al di là di Paolo: il
paolinismo nelle Pastorali; *(h) Redalié, Yann* "Discernere i tempi"
nelle Lettere Pastorali; *(i) Tábet, Michelangelo* San Paolo e i suoi
collaboratori. Il deposito. 1998 ⇒6363. 195-221/177-193/131-141/
19-38/143-162/113-130/39-52/237-251/53-79.
6365 *Duff, Jeremy* P46 and the Pastorals: a misleading consensus?. NTS
44 (1998) 578-590.
6366 **Harding, Mark** Tradition and rhetoric in the Pastoral Epistles.
Studies in Biblical Literature 3: NY 1998, Lang xiii; 253 pp. 0-8204-
3767-0. Bibl.
6367 *Hinlicky, Paul R.* Theology of a martyr: proclaiming Christ from the
Pastoral Epistles today. Pro Ecclesia 7 (1998) 350-357.
6368 **Lau, Andrew Y.** Manifest in flesh: the epiphany christology of the
Pastoral Epistles. WUNT 2/86: 1996, ⇒12,6926. [R]BZ 42 (1998)
282-284 (*Oberlinner, Lorenz*); NT 40 (1998) 398-400 (*Towner,
Philip H.*).
6369 **Marcheselli Casale, Cesare** Le Lettere Pastorali: le due lettere di
Timoteo e la lettera a Tito. SOCr 15: 1995 ⇒11/1,5184. [R]EstAg 33
(1998) 163-164 (*Cineira, D.A.*); Hum(B) 53 (1998) 1053-1054
(*Montagnini, Felice*).
6370 *Merk, Otto* Glaube und Tat in den Pastoralbriefen. [F]MERK O. BZNW
95: 1998 <1975> ⇒79. 260-271.

6371 **Miller, James D.** The Pastoral Letters as composite documents. MSSNTS 93: 1997 ⇒13,6718. ᴿJThS 49 (1998) 780-781 (*Grayston, K.*); RStT 17/2 (1998) 92-93 (*Litke, Wayne*).
6372 **Reuter, Rainer** Synopse zu den Briefen des Neuen Testaments. Synopsis of the New Testament letters II: die Pastoralbriefe. ARGU 6: Fra 1998, Lang 592 pp. 3-63131-457-4 [NThAR 1998,368].
6373 **Richards, William Austin** Difference and distance in post-Pauline Christianity: an epistolary analysis of the Pastorals. ᴰEmmanuel Col. of Victoria U. in U. of Toronto 1998, 336 pp.
6374 **Stettler, Hanna** Die Christologie der Pastoralbriefe. WUNT 2 105: Tü 1998, Mohr Bibl. xiii; 397 pp. DM118. 3-16-147056-7.

G7.2 1-2 ad Timotheum

6375 *Gruenler, Royce G.* The mission-lifestyle setting of 1 Tim 2:8-15. JETS 41 (1998) 215-238.
6376 *Ghiberti, Giuseppe* "Rex regnantium et dominus dominantium" (1Tm 6,15). ᶠMARTINI, C. RivBib.S 33: 1998 ⇒75. 437-451.

6377 **Oberlinner, Lorenz** Kommentar zum zweiten Timotheusbrief. Die Pastoralbriefe, 2. HThK 11/2: 1995, ⇒11/1,5196; 12,6509. ᴿCoTh 68/1 (1998) 235-239 (*Załeski, Jan*).
6378 *Orselli, Alba Maria* San Paolo e i maghi d'Egitto. V Simposio di Tarso. 1998 ⇒395. 183-190 [2 Tim 3,8].

G7.3 Ad Titum

6379 **Cotrozzi, Stefano** Exegetischer Führer zum Titus- und Philemon-brief: ein Wort-für-Wort-Überblick über sämtliche Auslegungs- und Übersetzungsvarianten. Theologisches Lehr- und Studienmaterial 1; Biblia et Symbiotica 16: Bonn 1998, Verl. für Kultur und Wiss. 177 pp. 3-926105-95-X [NThAR 1998,368].
6380 **Oberlinner, Lorenz** Kommentar zum Titusbrief. Die Pastoralbriefe, 3. HThK 11/2-3: 1996 ⇒12,6512; 13,6738. ᴿOrdKor 39/1 (1998) 108-109 (*Giesen, Heinz*); CoTh 68/1 (1998) 239-244 (*Załeski, Jan*).

6381 *Hagner, Donald A.* Titus as a Pauline letter. SBL.SPS 37: 1998 ⇒402. 546-558.
6382 *Niederwimmer, Kurt* Zenas, der Jurist (Tit. 3,13). Gesammelte Aufsätze. BZNW 90: 1998 <1995> ⇒182. 267-279.
6383 *Söding, Thomas* Gottes Menschenfreundlichkeit: eine exegetische Meditation von Titus 3. GuL 71 (1998) 410-422.

G7.4 Ad Philemonem

6384 *Bieberstein, Sabine* Der Brief an Philemon: Brieflektüre unter den kritischen Augen Aphias. Kompendium Feministische Bibelausle-gung. ᴱSchottroff, L.: 1998 ⇒H8.9. 676-682.
6385 **Burtchaell, James Tunstead** Philemon's problem: a theology of grace. GR ²1998, Eerdmans xvi; 334 pp. $18 [BiTod 37,259—Senior, Donald].
6386 **Callahan, Allen Dwight** Embassy of Onesimus: the letter of Paul to Philemon. 1997 ⇒13,6685. ᴿTrin.Journal 19 (1998) 107-110 (*Wei-ma, Jeffrey A.D.*).

Cotrozzi, S. Exeget. Führer zum... Philemonbrief 1998 ⇒6379.
6387 *Dunham, Robert E.* Philemon 1:1-25. Interp. 52 (1998) 191-194.
Garland, D. Colossians and Philemon 1998 ⇒6326.
Walter, N., *al.*, Die Briefe an... Philemon 1998 ⇒6275.

G8 Epistula ad Hebraeos

6388 **Giavini, Giovanni** Lettera agli Ebrei: una grande omelia su Gesù
       sacerdote. La Bibbia nelle nostre mani 13: CinB 1998, San Paolo 56
       pp. 88-215-3780-3. Bibl.
6389 **Gräßer, Erich** An die Hebräer. 2. Teilbd: Hebr 7,1-10,18. Evang.-
       Kath. Kommentar zum Neuen Testament 17/2: 1993 ⇒10,6208;
       12,6518. [R]RBBras 15 (1998) 556-557;
6390 An die Hebräer, 3. Teilband: Hebr 10,19-13,25. 1997 ⇒13,6739.
       [R]LASBF 48 (1998) 179-266 (*Casalini, Nello*).
6391 **Long, Thomas G.** Hebrews. 1997 ⇒13,6741. [R]IBSt 20 (1998) 130-
       132 (*Campbell, Dennis*); CBQ 60 (1998) 576-577 (*Swetnam, James*).
6392 **MacLeod, David J.** The epistle to the Hebrews. Dubuque, IA 1998,
       Emmaus 190 pp. $4.50 [BS 156,115s—Zuck, Roy B.].
6393 **Paciorek, Antoni** List do Hebrajczyków: thumaczenie, wstęp i
       komentarz. Biblia Lubelska: Lublin 1998, KUL 165 pp. 83-228-
       0381-8/674-4 [NThAR 2000,218]. P.
6394 [E]**Parker, T.H.L.** Ioannis CALVINI: opera exegetica: commentarius in
       epistolam ad Hebraeos. 1996 ⇒12,6520; 13,6742. [R]BHR 60 (1998)
       554-558 (*Hagen, Kenneth*).

6395 **Anderson, David Russell** The royal and priestly contribution of
       Psalm 110 to the book of Hebrews. [D]Dallas 1998, 358 pp.
6396 **Backhaus, Knut** Der Neue Bund und das Werden der Kirche: die
       Diatheke-Deutung des Hebräerbriefs im Rahmen der frühchristlichen
       Theologiegeschichte. NTA 29: 1996, ⇒12,6523. [R]CBQ 60 (1998)
       140-142 (*Swetnam, James H.*); JThS 49 (1998) 792-795 (*Browne,
       Arnold S.*).
6397 **deSilva, David Arthur** Despising shame: the social function of the
       rhetoric of honor and dishonor in the epistle to the Hebrews. SBL.DS
       152: 1995 ⇒11/1,5225; 13,6750. [R]CBQ 60 (1998) 363-364 (*Davids,
       Peter H.*)
6398 **Dunill, John** Covenant and sacrifice in the letter to the Hebrews.
       MSSNTS 75: 1992 ⇒8,6737... 10,6219. [R]Pacifica 11 (1998) 331-
       332 (*Barry, Romuald J.*)
6399 **Garuti, Paolo** Alle origini dell'omiletica cristiana: la lettera agli
       Ebrei: note di analisi retorica. ASBF 38: 1995 ⇒11/1,5228; 13,6751.
       Introd. *Boismard, M.-E.* [R]CrSt 19 (1998) 655-658 (*Penna, Romano*);
       RivBib 46 (1998) 114-116 (*Pitta, Antonio*).
6400 *Gräßer, Erich* "An die Hebräer"—eine antijüdische Schrift?.
       [F]SCHRAGE, W. 1998 ⇒101. 305-317.
6401 *Grogan, G.W.* The Old Testament concept of solidarity in Hebrews.
       TynB 49 (1998) 159-173.
6402 **Johnson, Richard Warren** The sociological function of the critique
       of the levitical system in the epistle to the Hebrews. [D]New Orleans
       Baptist Theol. Sem. 1998, 274 pp.
6403 *Lane, William L.* Living a life of faith in the face of death: the witness
       of Hebrews. Life in the face of death. 1998 ⇒252. 247-269.

6404 **Leschert, Dale F.** Hermeneutical foundations of Hebrews: a study in the validity of the epistle's interpretation of some core citations from the psalms. NABPR.DS 10: 1994 ⇒10,6228; 13,6759. ^RAUSS 36 (1998) 141-143 (*Kuma, Hermann V.A.*).

6405 *Long, Thomas G.* Bold in the presence of God: atonement in Hebrews. Interp. 52 (1998) 53-69.

6406 *MacCullough, J.C.* Anti-semitism in Hebrews?. IBSt 20 (1998) 30-45.

6407 **Manzi, Franco** Melchisedek e l'angelologia nell'epistola agli Ebrei e a Qumran.AnBib 136: 1997 ⇒13,6761. ^RGr. 79 (1998) 181-182 (*Marconi, Gilberto*); CivCatt 149/1 (1998) 513-515 (*Prato, G.L.*).

6408 *März, Claus-Peter* Melchisedek: bibeltheologische Überlegungen zu den Melchisedek-Bezügen im Hebräerbrief. ^FBSTEH, A. 1998 ⇒17. 229-250.

6409 *Panimolle, Salvatore A.* La fede nell'epistola agli Ebrei. La fede nella bibbia. DSBP 21: 1998 ⇒224. 142-163.

6410 **Taut, Konrad** Anleitung zum Schriftverständnis?: die heiligen Schriften nach dem Hebräerbrief. THEOS 20: Ha 1998, Kovač vi; 163 pp. 3-86064-676-1. ^DLeipzig 1996 [NThAR 1998,302].

6411 *Thompson, James W.* The appropriate, the necessary, and the impossible: faith and reason in Hebrews. ^FFERGUSON, E. NT.S 90: 1998 ⇒25. 302-317.

6412 **Trotter, Andrew H.** Interpreting the epistle to the Hebrews. GNTE 6: 1997 ⇒13,6745. ^RBS 155 (1998) 249-50 (*Constable, Thomas L.*).

6413 *Vanhoye, Albert* Lettera agli Ebrei. Dizionario di omiletica. 1998 ⇒533. 768-771 [AcBib 10,516].

6414 **Wider, David** Theozentrik und Bekenntnis: Untersuchungen zur Theologie des Reden Gottes im Hebräerbrief. BZNW 87: 1997 ⇒13,6772. ^RJThS 49 (1998) 789-791 (*Swetnam, James*).

6415 **Wray, Judith Hoch** Rest as a theological metaphor in the epistle to the Hebrews and the gospel of Truth: early christian homiletics of rest. SBL.DS 166: Atlanta, GA 1998, Scholars xviii; 206 pp. $35. 0-7885-0511-4. Bibl.

6416 *Marconi, Gilberto* Gli angeli nella lettera agli ebrei (esegesi di Eb 1,5-14; 2,5-16). ED 51/2-3 (1998) 67-89. Sum. 67.

6417 *Scott, Brett R.* Jesus' superiority over Moses in Hebrews 3:1-6. BS 155 (1998) 201-210.

6418 *Gleason, Randall C.* The Old Testament background of the warning in Hebrews 6:4-8. BS 155 (1998) 62-91.

6419 *Casalini, Nello* Per un commento a Ebrei (II): Eb 10,19-13,25. SBFLA 48 (1998) 179-266.

6420 **Eisenbaum, Pamela Michelle** The Jewish heroes of christian history: Hebrews 11 in literary context. SBL.DS 156: 1997 ⇒13,6787. ^RCBQ 60 (1998) 561-562 (*Koester, Craig R.*); JBL 117 (1998) 754-756 (*Howard, George*).

6421 *Rhee, Victor* Chiasm and the concept of faith in Hebrews 11. BS 155 (1998) 327-345.

6422 *Heininger, Bernhard* Hebr 11.7 und das Henochorakel am Ende der Welt. NTS 44 (1998) 115-132.

6423 *Niederwimmer, Kurt* Vom Glauben der Pilger: Erwägungen zu Hebr. 11,8-10 und 13-16. Gesammelte Aufsätze. BZNW 90: 1998 <1992> ⇒182. 207-216.

6424 **Croy, Noah Clayton** Endurance in suffering: a study of Hebrews 12:1-13 in its rhetorical, religious, and philosophical context. MSSNTS 98: C 1998, CUP x; 250 pp. 0-521-59305-0.
6425 *Paciorek, Antoni* 'Jezus Chrystus wczoraj i dziś, ten sam także na wieki' (Hbr 13,8) ['Jesus Christ is the same yesterday, today, and forever' (Heb 13,8). Roczniki Teologiczne 45/1 (1998) 149-166. Sum. 148. **P.**

G9.1 1 Petri

6426 **Achtemeier, Paul J.** 1 Peter: a commentary on First Peter. Hermeneia: 1996, ⇒12,6577; 13,6795. [R]AUSS 36 (1998) 111-112 (*Coutsoumpos, Otis*); CBQ 60 (1998) 135-137 (*Bernas, Casimir*); JThS 49 (1998) 795-799 (*Horrell, David G.*); SJTh 51 (1998) 384-386 (*Stenschke, Christoph*); RBBras 15 (1998) 557-559; JBL 117 (1998) 163-166 (*Michaels, J. Ramsey*).
6427 **Davids, Peter H.** The first epistle of Peter. 1990, ⇒6,6729... 8,6772. [R]BTB 28 (1998) 84 (*Elliott, John H.*).
6428 **Horrell, David G.** The epistles of Peter and Jude. Epworth Commentaries: C 1998, Epworth xx; 187 pp. 0-7162-0523-8. Bib.
6429 **Knoch, Otto Bernhard** Le due lettere di Pietro: la lettera di Giuda. 1996, ⇒12,6567. [R]CivCatt 149/2 (1998) 204-205 (*Scaiola, D.*).
6430 **Schweizer, Eduard** Der erste Petrusbrief. ZBK.NT 15: Z [4]1998, Theol. Verl. 107 pp. 3-290-17189-2 [NThAR 1999,255].
6431 **Vries, E. de** 1 en 2 Petrus, Judas. Tekst en toelichting: Kampen 1998, Kok 226 pp. ƒ45. 90-242-9285-9 [ITBT 7/4,32—Verhoef, E.].

6432 [E]**Amphoux, Christian-Bernard; Bouhot, Jean-Paul** La lecture liturgique des épîtres catholiques dans l'Église ancienne. Histoire du texte biblique 1: 1996, ⇒12,6559; 13,6791. [R]EL 112/2 (1998) 189-190 (*Manzi, Franco*).
6433 **Bechtler, Steven Richard** Following in his steps: suffering, community, and christology in 1 Peter. SBL.DS 162: Atlanta, GA 1998, Scholars xiv; 239 pp. 0-7885-0485-1. Bibl.
6434 **Campbell, Barth L.** Honor, shame, and the rhetoric of 1 Peter. SBL.DS 160: Atlanta, GA 1998, Scholars x; 266 pp. 2-7885-0510-62. Bibl.
6435 *Colpe, Carsten* TATIAN "aus Assyrien", MARCION "aus Sinope" und die Gegner der "aus Rom" schreibenden Autoren der beiden Petrusbriefe und des 1. Clemensbriefes. [F]POKORNÝ, P. 1998 ⇒90. 42-54.
6436 **De Iaco, Cosimo** Condotta di vita e missione nella prima lettera di Pietro. Exc. [D]Gregoriana 1998: [D]*Rasco, Emilio*; 188 pp.
6437 *Foulkes, Irene* Der erste Brief des Petrus: Überlebensstrategien für bedrängte Gemeinden. Kompendium Feministische Bibelauslegung. [E]**Schottroff, L.**: 1998 ⇒H8.9. 701-707.
6438 *Herzer, Jens* Petrus oder Paulus?: Studien über das Verhältnis des ersten Petrusbriefes zur paulinischen Tradition. WUNT 103: Tü 1998, Mohr ix; 337 pp. DM168. 3-16-146848-1.
6439 **Martin, Troy W.** Metaphor and composition in 1 Peter. SBL.DS 131: 1992 ⇒8,6788; 9,6444. [R]BTB 28 (1998) 37-38 (*Elliott, John*).
6440 *Misset-Van de Weg, Magda* The Sarah imagery in 1 Peter. Use of sacred books. 1998 ⇒263. 111-126.

6441   *Noè, Virgilio* La tomba dell'apostolo Pietro, meta privilegiata del pellegrinaggio giubilare. Quaderni di Scienze Religiose 7 (1998) 9-21.

6442   **Thurén, Lauri Toumas** Argument and theology in 1 Peter: the origins of Christian paraenesis. JSNT.S 114: 1995, ⇒11/1,5286; 13,6809. ^RTJT 14/1 (1998) 107-109 (*Webb, Robert L.*); Bibl.Interp. 6 (1998) 455-457 (*Horrell, David*); JBL 117 (1998) 162-163 (*Boring, M. Eugene*).

6443   *Van Rensburg, Fika J.* Christians as 'resident and visiting aliens': implications of the exhortations to the πάροικοι and παρεπίδημοι in 1 Peter for the church in South Africa. Neotest. 32 (1998) 573-583.

6444   **Tite, Philip L.** Compositional transitions in 1 Peter: an analysis of the letter-opening. 1997, ⇒13,6811. ^RRStT 17/1 (1998) 111-113 (*Leske, Adrian M.*) [1,1-14].

6445   *Bosetti, Elena* La prima lettera di Pietro: il comportamento dei figli di Dio (1Pt 1,13-25); l'esortazione ai presbiteri e conclusione (1 Pt 5,1-11). Presbyteri 32 (1998) 49-60, 216-228 [part no. 5,7].

6446   *Krentz, Edgar* Order in the "House" of God: the Haustafel in 1 Peter 2:11-3:12. ^FSNYDER, G. 1998 ⇒104. 279-285.

6447   *Giesen, Heinz* Lebenszeugnis in der Fremde: zum Verhalten der Christen in der paganen Gesellschaft (1 Petr 2,11-17). SNTU.A 23 (1998) 113-152.

6448   *Alvarado, Rolando* 'Dad razón de vuestra esperanza'. SalTer 86 (1998) 721-732 [3,15].

6449   *Schmocker, Katharina* Elpis oder Hoffnung: eine zukunftsgerichtete Auseinandersetzung mit dem Anspruch in 1 Petr 3,15. ^DLuzern 1995/96: ^D*Kirchschläger, W.* Bern 1998, Lang 157 pp. [NThAR 1998, 302].

6450   *Engel, Werner* Christus Victor: eine Untersuchung zu Gattung und Struktur des vorliterarischen Christushymnus 1 Petr 3,18-22. PzB 7 (1998) 137-147.

6451   **Dubis, Kevin Mark** Messianic woes in First Peter: suffering and eschatology in 1 Peter 4:12-19. ^DUnion Theol. Sem. in Virginia 1998, 307 pp.

G9.2 2 Petri

6452   *Bauckham, Richard J.* 2 Peter and the apocalypse of Peter. The fate of the dead. NT.S 93: 1998 ⇒132. 290-303.

6453   *Foulkes, Irene* Der zweite Brief des Petrus: Wegweiser zu einem 'gottgefälligen Leben'. Kompendium Feministische Bibelauslegung ^E**Schottroff, L.**: 1998 ⇒H8.9. 708.

6454   *Hodges, Zane C.* Making your calling and election sure: an exposition of 2 Peter 1:5-11. Journal of the Grace Evangelical Society 11 (1998) 21-33.

6455   *Malan, Gert; Van Aarde, Andries G.* 'n kennissosilogiese benadering tot die dag van die Here in 2 Petrus. HTS 54 (1998) 529-543.

G9.4 **Epistula Jacobi**...data on both apostles James

6456 ^E**Aland, B.**, *al.*, Die katholischen Briefe: 1, Text: 1) Der Jakobus-brief; 2) Begleitende Materialien. NT graecum: editio maior critica, 4. 1997 ⇒13,6823. ^RNT 40 (1998) 195-203 (*Elliott, J.K.*)

6457 *Burchard, Christoph* A further glimpse at the Armenian version of the epistle of James <1997>;

6458 Zur altarmenischen Übersetzung des Jakobusbriefes <1994>. Studien NT. WUNT 107: 1998 ⇒140. 345-357/358-386.

6459 **Field, David** James. Crossway Bible Guide: Leicester 1998, Cross-way 184 pp. 1-85684-174-X.

6460 *Hahn, Ferdinand; Müller, Peter* Der Jakobusbrief. ThR 63 (1998) 1-73.

6461 ^E**Herbers, Klaus; Santos Noia, Manuel** Liber Sancti Jacobi: Codex Calixtinus. Santiago de Compostela 1998, Grafinova xxx; 337 pp. 84-453-2298-2. Transcripción a partir del Códice original; Jacobus Maior.

6462 **Johnson, Luke Timothy** The letter of James. AncB 37A: 1995 ⇒ 11/1,5303... 13,6828. ^RJR 78 (1998) 102-104 (*Jackson-McCabe, Matt A.*).

6463 **MacArthur, John** James. MacArthur NT Commentary: Ch 1998, Moody 308 pp. $22 [BS 156,498ss—Zuck, Roy B.].

6464 **Marconi, Gilberto** Lettere di Giacomo e di Giuda: primo esame di coscienza della chiesa. La Bibbia nelle nostre mani 10: CinB 1998, San Paolo 52 pp. 88-215-3720-X. Bibl.

6465 **Sleeper, Charles Freeman** James. Abingdon NT Commentaries: Nv 1998, Abingdon 152 pp. 0-687-05816-3. Bibl.

6466 **Ahrens, Matthias** Der Realitäten Widerschein oder Arm und Reich im Jakobusbrief: eine sozialgeschichtliche Untersuchung. Alektor-Hochschulschriften: B 1995, Alektor 160 pp. DM34.80. 3-88425-061-2. ^RThR 63 (1998) 69-70 (*Hahn, Ferdinand; Müller, Peter*).

6467 **Bernheim, Pierre-Antoine** James, brother of Jesus. 1997, ⇒13, 6825. ^RCIR 48/1 (1998) 98-99 (*Brent, Allen*);

6468 Jacques, frère de Jésus. 1996 ⇒12,6613; 13,6824. ^RRSR 86 (1998) 442-443 (*Guillet, Jacques*).

6469 *Chilton, Bruce* The brother of Jesus and the interpretation of scrip-ture. Use of sacred books. 1998 ⇒263. 29-48.

6470 *Dannemann, Irene* Der Brief des Jakobus: Streiten um den Weg der Gerechtigkeit. Kompendium Feministische Bibelauslegung. ^E**Schottroff, L.**: 1998 ⇒H8.9. 694-700.

6471 **Eisenman, Robert H.** James the brother of Jesus: recovering the true history of early christianity. 1997, ⇒13,6827. ^RDSD 5/1 (1998) 94-97 (*Brent, Allen*).

6472 **Hartin, Patrick J.** James and the Q sayings of Jesus. JSNT.S 47: 1991, ⇒7,5782... 10,6289. ^RThR 63 (1998) 55-57 (*Hahn, Ferdinand; Müller, Peter*).

6473 **Jackson-McCabe, Matt A.** Logos and law in the letter of James: the law of nature, the law of Moses, and the law of freedom. ^DCh 1998, 422 pp.

6474 *Kasiłowski, Piotr* How to be wealthy?: the letter of James and the problem of wealth. FolOr 34 (1998) 35-44.

6475 **Klein, Martin** "Ein vollkommenes Werk": Vollkommenheit, Gesetz und Gericht als theologische Themen des Jakobusbriefes. BWANT 139: 1995 ⇒11/1,5313; 12,6620. ^RThRv 94 (1998) 72-74 (*Luck, Ulrich*); JBL 117 (1998) 160-162 (*Penner, Todd C.*).

6476 **Konradt, Matthias** Christliche Existenz nach dem Jakobusbrief: eine Studie zu seiner soteriologischen und ethischen Konzeption. Diss. StUNT 22: Gö 1998, Vandenhoeck & R 406 pp. DM158. 3-525-53376-4.

6477 **León Azcárate, Juan Luis de** Santiago, el hermano del Señor. Asociación Bíblica Española 34: Estella (Navarra) 1998, Verbo Divino 261 pp. 84-8169-261-1. Bibl.

6478 **Martinez, Aquiles Ernesto** On labelling prominent and deviant behavior: James' portrayal of the poor and the wealthy under sociological scrutiny. ^DIliff 1998, 527 pp.

6479 *Niebuhr, Karl-Wilhelm* Der Jakobusbrief im Licht frühjüdischer Diasporabriefe. NTS 44 (1998) 420-443.

6480 **Penner, Todd C.** The epistle of James and eschatology: re-reading an ancient christian letter. JSNT.S 121: 1996 ⇒12,6622; 13,6849 ^RCBQ 60 (1998) 380-381 (*Lodge, John G.*); ThLZ 123 (1998) 256-258 (*Burchard, Christoph*).

6481 **Popkes, Wiard** Adressaten, Situation und Form des Jakobusbriefes. SBS 125/126: 1986 ⇒2,4999... 5,6459. ^RThR 63 (1998) 67-68 (*Hahn, Ferdinand; Müller, Peter*).

6482 *Rhoads, David* The letter of James: friend of God. CThMi 25 (1998) 473-486.

6483 *Tiller, Patrick A.* The rich and poor in James: an apocalyptic proclamation. SBL.SPS 37: 1998 ⇒402. 909-920.

6484 **Tsuji, Manabu** Glaube zwischen Vollkommenheit und Verweltlichung: eine Untersuchung zur literarischen Gestalt und zur inhaltlichen Kohärenz des Jakobusbriefes. WUNT 2/93: 1997 ⇒13,6853. ^RThR 63 (1998) 23-24, 27-29 (*Hahn, Ferdinand; Müller, Peter*).

6485 *Verseput, Donald J.* Wisdom, 4Q185, and the epistle of James. JBL 117 (1998) 691-707.

6486 *Simoens, Yves* 'Dieu ne tente personne' (Jacques 1,13): interprétation d'un texte de saint Jacques. Telema 96 (1998) 5-15.

6487 *Collins, Clifford John* Coherence in James 1:19-27. JOTT 10 (1998) 80-88.

6488 *Bauer, Karl-Adolf* "... durch Werke gerecht, nicht durch Glauben allein"?: Anmerkungen zur homiletischen Vergegenwärtigung von Jak 2,14-16. ^FSCHRAGE, W. 1998 ⇒101. 165-169.

6489 *Bauckham, Richard J.* The tongue set on fire by hell (James 3:6). The fate of the dead. NT.S 93: 1998 ⇒132. 119-131.

6490 *Pfligersdorffer, Georg* Demut und Gnade: zu Jakobus 4,6 bei AUGUSTINUS. ^FSPEYER, W. JAC.E 28: 1998 ⇒107. 244-252.

G9.6 Epistula Judae

6491 *Allen, Joel S.* A new possibility for the three-clause format of Jude 22-3. NTS 44 (1998) 133-143.

6492 *Cozijnsen, Bert* A critical contribution to the *Corpus Hellenisticum Novi Testamenti*: Jude and HESIOD. Use of sacred books. 1998 ⇒263. 79-109.

Horrell, D. The epistles of Peter and Jude 1998 ⇒6428.
6493 *Joubert, Stephan J*. Facing the past: transtextual relationships and historical understanding in the letter of Jude. BZ 42 (1998) 56-70.
6494 **Landon, Charles** A text-critical study of the epistle of Jude. JSNT.S 135: 1996, ⇒12,6628. [R]BiTr 49 (1998) 353-354 (*Omanson, Roger L*.); ThLZ 123 (1998) 255-256 (*Heiligenthal, Roman*); JThS 49 (1998) 289-291 (*Parker, D.C.*).
6495 **Lyle, Kenneth R**. Ethical admonition in the epistle of Jude. Studies in Biblical Literature 4: NY 1998, Lang xvii; 152 pp. £25/$41. 0-8204-3838-3 [JThS 51,292ss—Horrell, David G.].
Marconi, G. Lettere di Giacomo e di Giuda 1998 ⇒6464.
Vries, E. de 1 en 2 Petrus, Judas 1998 ⇒6431.
6496 *Whallon, William* On the text of Jude 12. Computers and the Humanities 32 (1998) 65-66 Sum. 65.

XIII. Theologia Biblica

H1.1 Biblical Theology [OT] God

6497 **Alkofer, Andreas-Pazificus** Der himmlische Figaro: biblische Gottesbilder, die aus dem Rahmen fallen. Wü 1998, Echter 137 pp. 3-429-02043-3 [NThAR 1999,71].
6498 *Alves, Herculano* Imagens de Deus no Antigo Testamento. Bib(L) 7/7[6?] 35-68.
6499 *Armellada, Bernardino de* ¿Reformable el Dios todopoderoso?. Evangelio y Vida 40 (1998) 159-161.
6500 **Armstrong, Karen** Storia di Dio: da Abramo a oggi: 4000 anni alla ricerca di Dio. [T]*Mosca, Aldo*: Venezia 1998, Tascabili Marsilio 492 pp. L19.000. [R]SapDom 51 (1998) 485-486 (*Di Tora, Marcello*).
6501 **Baudler, Georg** El Jahwe Abba: wie die Bibel Gott versteht. 1996 ⇒12,6636; 13,6868. [R]FrRu 4 (1998) 291-292 (*Renker, Alwin*).
6502 *Baudler, Georg* El-Jahwe-Abba: der biblische Gott und die Theodizeefrage. ThG 41 (1998) 242-251.
6503 *Blumenthal, David R*. Confronting the character of God: text and praxis. [F]BRUEGGEMANN, W. 1998 ⇒16. 38-51.
6504 *Botha, Willem J*. The love frame in the bible: a cognitive linguistic analysis. Faith and fiction. 1998 ⇒410. 56-83.
6505 **Bottero, Jean; Quaknin, Marc-Alain; Moingt, Joseph** La più bella storia di Dio—chi è il Dio della bibbia?. Mi 1998, Mondadori 154 pp. L27.000 [Presbyteri 33,76s—Scalia, Felice];
6506 A mais bela história de Deus: quem é o Deus da Bíblia?. Ponto de Encontro: Porto 1998, Asa 176 pp. [R]Igreja e Missão 50 (1998) 271-272 (*Couto, A.*).
6507 **Briend, Jacques** Dieu dans l'Écriture. LeDiv 150: 1992 ⇒8,7002... 11/2,2769. [R]Cahiers de l'Atelier 477 (1998) 80-85 (*Durand, Xavier*);
6508 Dios en la Escritura. 1995 ⇒13,6871. [R]San Juan de la Cruz 21 (1998) 133-134 (*Hidalgo Parejo, Juan*).
6509 *Chisholm, Robert B*. Does God deceive?. BS 155 (1998) 11-28.
6510 *Clines, David J.A.* Yahweh and the God of christian theology. OT essays, 2. JSOT.S 293: 1998 <1980> ⇒142. 498-507.

6511 *Crenshaw, James L.* The sojourner has come to play the judge: theodicy on trial. [F]BRUEGGEMANN, W. 1998 ⇒16. 83-92.

6512 *Ego, Beate* "Der Herr blickt herab von der Höhe seines Heiligtums": zur Vorstellung von Gottes himmlischen Thronen in exilisch-nachexilischer Zeit. ZAW 110 (1998) 556-569.

6513 *Fretheim, Terence E.* Some reflections on Brueggemann's God [F]BRUEGGEMANN, W. 1998 ⇒16. 24-37.

6514 **Gantt, Charles Anthony** Do not let your God deceive you: the idea of divine deception in the Hebrew Bible. [D]Harvard 1998, 268 pp.

6515 **Goodman, Lenn E.** God of Abraham. 1996, ⇒12,6641; 13,6876 [R]Thom. 62 (1998) 327-331 (*Burrell, David B.*); AJSR 23 (1998) 337-340 (*Bland, Kalman P.*).

6516 *Helm, Paul* God in dialogue. [F]WRIGHT D. 1998 ⇒126. 223-240.

6517 *Hurowitz, Victor* From storm God to abstract being: how the deity became more distant from Exodus to Deuteronomy. BiRe 14/5 (1998) 40-47.

6518 *Jakobs, Monika* Die Macht der Bilder: zur Bedeutung biblischer Gottesbilder für eine christliche feministische Theologie. JBTh 13 (1998) 237-259.

6519 *Janowski, Bernd* Der eine Gott der beiden Testamente: Grundfragen einer Biblischen Theologie. ZThK 95 (1998) 1-36.

6520 **Kaiser, Otto** Der Gott des Alten Testaments, 2: Wesen und Wirken: Jahwe, der Gott Israels, Schöpfer der Welt und des Menschen. UTB 1747; UTB für Wissenschaft: Gö 1998, Vandenhoeck & R 320 pp. 3-525-03279-X.

6521 **Latvus, Kari** God, anger and ideology: the anger of God in Joshua and Judges in relation to Deuteronomy and the priestly writings. JSOT.S <vol. 279>: Shf 1998, Academic 108 pp. £37.50/$60. 1-85075-922-7. Bibl.

6522 **Lightner, Robert P.** The God of the bible and other gods: is the christian God unique among world religions?. GR 1998, Kregel 216 pp. 0-8254-3154-9. Bibl.

6523 *Luke, K.* Yahweh's net. ITS 35 (1998) 18-31.

6524 *Mallau, Hans H.* Gott ist einer!": zentrale Aussagen des Jahweglaubens im Alten Testament. Zeitschrift für Theologie und Gemeinde 3 (1998) 256-265.

6525 **Martin-Achard, Robert** Dios de toda fidelidad: los grandes temas bíblicos a través de Israel. Barc 1998, Gayata 120 pp [Mayéutica 24,535—Tonatiuh, Javier].

6526 *Meagher, P.M.* The enigma of God. VJTR 62 (1998) 596-605.

6527 **Mills, Mary E.** Images of God in the Old Testament. ColMn 1998, Liturgical x; 159 pp. $20. 0-8146-5935-7. Bibl. [ThD 46,377—Heiser, Charles].

6528 *Moberly, R.W.L.* "God is not a human that he should repent" (Numbers 23:19 and 1 Samuel 15:29). [F]BRUEGGEMANN, W. 1998 ⇒16. 112-123.

6529 *Nemeck, Francis Kelly; Coombs, Marie Theresa* Imaging and addressing God in prayer: using female and male metaphors. EeT(O) 29/1 (1998) 91-113.

6530 *Passoni Dell'Acqua, Anna* Innovazioni lessicali e attributi divini: una caratteristica del giudaismo alessandrino?. [F]MARTINI, C. RivBib.S 33: 1998 ⇒75. 87-108.

6531 *Péter-Contesse, René* Dieu est-il jaloux?. CEv 106 (1998) 61-64.

6532 *Pigott, Susan M.* The kingdom of the warrior God: The Old Testament and the Kingdom of Yahweh. SWJT 40/2 (1998) 5-20.
6533 *Rebic, Adalbert* Wer sind die Starken im Alten Testament?: Widerstand gegen und Ergebung in Gott. IKaZ 27 (1998) 385-394.
6534 *Schwartz, G. David* God and the stranger. HBT 20/1 (1998) 33-48.
6535 *Smith, Mark S.* The death of "dying and rising Gods" in the biblical world: an update, with special reference to Baal in the Baal cycle. SJOT 12 (1998) 257-313.
6536 **Soulen, R. Kendall** The God of Israel and christian theology. 1996 ⇒12,6660; 13,6896. [R]JR 78 (1998) 454-456 (*Sonderegger, Katherine*).
6537 *Terrien, Samuel* The metaphor of the rock in biblical theology. [F]BRUEGGEMANN, W. 1998 ⇒16. 157-171.
6538 **Van der Ven, Johannes A.** God reinvented?: a theological search in texts and tables. Empirical Studies in Theology 1: Lei 1998, Brill 273 pp. 90-04-11330-4. Bibl.
6539 **Vincent, Jean M.** Das Auge hört: die Erfahrbarkeit Gottes im Alten Testament. BThSt 34: Neuk 1998, Neuk 136 pp. 3-7887-1664-9.
6540 *Vogels, Walter* The imminent transcendent creator of Gn 1. ScEs 50 (1998) 227-233.
6541 *Westermann, Claus* The complaint against God. [F]BRUEGGEMANN, W. 1998 ⇒16. 233-241.

H1.4 Femininum in Deo—**God as father and mother**

6542 **Alonso Schökel, Luis** Dio Padre: meditazioni bibliche. [T]*Pahk, Johan Yeong-Sik*: Bibbia e Preghiera 19: [n.p.] 1998, [Catholic Publishing House] 290 pp. 89-321-0311-9. **Korean**.
6543 **Amato, A.** El evangelio del Padre. S 1998, Secretariado Trinitario 154 pp [Comunidades 27/1,42—González, Manuel].
6544 *Bagnard, Guy* Le Père dans la révélation chrétienne. Com(F) 23-24/6-1 (1998-1999) 7-13.
6545 **Barbaso, Adérito Gomes** Jovens com Deus Pai às portas do terceiro milénio. Terceiro Milénio 3: Lisboa 1998, Paulinas 245 pp. [R]Bib(L) 7/7 (1998) 166-167 (*Frederico, Carlos*).
6546 *Batut, Jean-Pierre* 'Dieu le Père tout-puissant': réflexion à propos d'un mot litigieux. Com(F) 23-24/6-1 (1998-1999) 57-74.
6547 *Benzi, Guido* Paternità e maternità di Dio. Presenza Pastorale 68 (1998) 295-304.
6548 *Boespflug, François* Apophatisme théologique et abstinence figurative: sur l'"irreprésentabilité" de Dieu (le Père). RevSR 72 (1998) 446-468.
6549 *Chantraine, Georges* Dieu le Père. Com(F) 23-24/6-1 (1998-1999) 15-28.
6550 *D'Alessandro, Sandra* La paternità di Dio nell'esperienza di Israele. Presenza Pastorale 68 (1998) 305-314.
6551 Deus Pai; Penitência; Maria. Bíblica, Série científica 7.7: [Lisboa] 1998, [Bíblica] 191 pp. 972-652-156-4. Semana Bíblica Nacional (21: Lisboa).
6552 Deus Pai de misericórdia. Lisboa 1998, Paulinas Comissão Teológico-Histórica do grande jubileu do ano 2000 118 pp. [R]Bib(L) 7/7 (1998) 182-183 (*Morgado, Lopes*).

6553 *Domergue, Marcel* Dieu père?: oui, mais comment?;
6554 L'image et la parole. Croire aujourd'hui 59 (1998) 20-22/23-26.
6555 **Durrwell, François-Xavier** Le Père: Dieu en son mystère. 1987
      ⇒3,6436... 5,7079*. [R]AETSC 3 (1998) 211-213 (*Duffy, Kevin*).
6556 *Espezel, Alberto* Le Père et la rédemption. Com(F) 23-24/6-1 (1998-
      1999) 49-55.
6557 *Jacobone, Lello* L'iconografia di Dio Padre. Presenza Pastorale 68
      (1998) 347-354.
6558 **Marchel, W.** Dieu Père dans le Nouveau Testament. [T]*Cé, Madeleine*
      P 21998 <1966>, Cerf 144 pp [LV(L) 247,110—Sagne, J.-C.].
6559 **Muñoz Iglesias, S.** Padre de Jesús y padre nuestro (lo que dice la
      Sagrada Escritura). M 1998, Espiritualidad 236 pp. [REsp
      58,167—Brändle, Francisco].
6560 **Pikaza, Xabier** Para descubrir el camino del Padre: nueve itinerarios
      para el encuentro con Dios. Estella 1998, Verbo Divino 215 pp. 84-
      8169-275-1 [TeCa 73,133s—Barrado Fernández, P.].
6561 *Ramos, José A.M.* A paternidade de Deus no Próximo Oriente Anti-
      go. Bib(L) 7/7 (1998) 7-34.
6562 *Simoens, Yves* Le seigneur d'Israël et le père de Jesús-Christ. Com(F)
      23-24/6-1 (1998-1999) 33-47.
6563 *Soares, Fernando* Deus-Pai, 'rico em misericórdia'. Bib(L) 7/7
      (1998) 69-72.
6564 *Vasse, Denis; D'Orazio, Marie-José* Père selon la chair, et paternité
      de Dieu. Croire aujourd'hui 59 (1998) 27-30. Interview.
6565 *Ventura, Fernando* Deus Pai, revelado em Jesus Cristo. Bib(L) 7/7
      (1998) 73-83.
6566 A voz, Deus Pai. Lisboa 1998, Paulinas Comissão Pastoral e Mis-
      sionária do grande jubileu do ano 2000 187 pp. [R]Bib(L) 7/7 (1998)
      183-184 (*Morgado, Lopes*).

H1.7 Revelatio

6567 *Angelini, Giuseppe* Introduzione: la rivelazione attestata: la bibbia fra
      testo e teologia. [F]MARTINI C., Rivelazione. 1998 ⇒74 ix-xxiii.
6568 **Arnaldez, Roger** Révolte contre Jéhovah: essai sur l'originalité de la
      révélation chrétienne. P 1998, Cerf 143 pp. FF145 [EeV 109,156s—
      Jay, Pierre].
6569 **Biord Castillo, Raúl** La resurrección de Cristo como revelación:
      análisis del tema en la teología fundamental a partir de la *Dei Ver-
      bum*. TGr.T 38: R 1998, E.P.U.G. 308 pp. €16,52. 88-7652-788-5.
6570 *Collins, John J.* The tension between revelation and natural theology.
      [F]BETZ, H. 1998 ⇒10. 20-25.
6571 **Gunton, Colin E.** A brief theology of Revelation. E [2]1998, Clark x;
      134 pp. 0-567-29293-2. The 1993 Warfield Lectures; Bibl.
6572 *Jeanrond, Werner G.* The significance of revelation for biblical
      theology. Biblical Interpretation 6 (1998) 243-257.
6573 *Kangudi, Kabwatila* La révélation de Dieu comme polysémique.
      RAT 22 (1998) 165-178.
6574 **Knoch, Wendelin** Gott sucht den Menschen: Offenbarung, Schrift,
      Tradition.AMATECA 4: 1997 ⇒13,6912. [R]ZKTh 120 (1998) 331-
      332 (*Neufeld, Karl H.*).

6575 ^{TE}**Marquet, Jean-François; Courtine, Jean-François** F.W. SCHELLING: Philosophie de la révélation II: livre III. 1994 ⇒10, 7091. ^RRTL 29 (1998) 393-394 (*Brito, E.*).

6576 *Sæbo, Magne* Revelation in history and as history: observations on a topical theme from an Old Testament point of view. On the way to canon. 1998 <1981> ⇒194. 182-196.

6577 *Scheuer, Jacques* Révélation, parole, écriture: entre histoire des religions et théologies. NRTh 120 (1998) 444-463.

H1.8 Theologia fundamentalis

6578 *Bórmida, Jerónimo* Los materiales; revelación, inspiración, historia. Soleriana 10 (1998) 173-210.

6579 *Droge, Arthur J.* Conversion as a native category. ^FBETZ, H. 1998 ⇒10. 392-397.

6580 **González de Cardedal, Olegario** La entraña del cristianismo. S 1998, Secretario Trinitario 952 pp. ^RRelCult 44 (1998) 691-698 (*Torre, Rafael de la*).

6581 *Hübner, Hans* Fundamentaltheologie und biblische Theologie. ThLZ 123 (1998) 443-458.

6582 *Krentz, Edgar* Conversion in early Christianity. ^FBETZ, H. 1998 ⇒10. 49-58.

6583 *Marconcini, Benito* La fede nell'Antico Testamento. La fede nella bibbia. DSBP 21: 1998 ⇒224. 11-57.

6584 *McGrath, Alister E.* Biblical models for apologetics. BS 155 (1998) 3-10, 131-138, 259-265, 387-393.

6585 **Waldenfels, Hans** Einführung in die Theologie der Offenbarung. Die Theologie: 1996 ⇒12,6696; 13;6921. ^RED 51/2-3 (1998) 366-367 (*Muya, J. Ilunga*).

H2.1 Anthropologia theologica—VT & NT

6586 **Alonso Schökel, Luis** Símbolos matrimoniales en la biblia. 1997 ⇒13,6923. ^RCBQ 60 (1998) 515-516 (*Craghan, John F.*).

6587 *Anderson, Jeff S.* The social function of curses in the Hebrew Bible. ZAW 110 (1998) 223-237.

6588 *Asmis, Elizabeth* Inner and outer selves in harmony. ^FBETZ, H. 1998 ⇒10. 83-87.

6589 **Bacchiocchi, Samuele** Immortality or resurrection ?: a biblical study on human nature and destiny. Biblical Perspectives 13: Berrien Springs 1998, Biblical Perspectives 304 pp. Forew. *Clark Pinnock.*

6590 **Banting, Blayne Alexander** Proclaiming the Messiah's mirth: a rhetorico-contextual model for the interpretation and proclamation of humour in selected gospel sayings. ^DAcadia 1998, 341 pp.

6591 *Barasch, Moshe* Adam the panphysiognomist: a stage in modern physiognomics. Self, soul and body. SHR 78: 1998 ⇒286. 67-86.

6592 **Barsotti, Divo** L'uomo nel vangelo. Le spighe: R 1998, Borla 153 pp. 88-263-1257-5.

6593 *Barton, Stephen C.* 'Glorify God in your body' (1 Corinthians 6.20): thinking theologically about sexuality. Religion & sexuality. 1998 ⇒302. 366-379.

6594 *Bauer, Johannes B.* Zur Vorstellung des "Verrückt"-Seins. ^FSPEYER, W. JAC.E 28: 1998 ⇒107. 1-3.
6595 *Bowie, Angus* Exuvias effigiemque: Dido, Aeneas and the body as sign. Changing bodies. 1998 ⇒352. 57-79.
6596 *Böttrich, Christfried* Fasten im Neuen Testament. ZdZ 52/1 (1998) 11-15.
6597 *Burkert, Walter* Towards Plato and Paul: the "inner" human being ^FBETZ, H. 1998 ⇒10. 59-82.
6598 *Cacciari, Massimo* Il grande codice: bibbia, lingua e cultura. Bibbia, popoli e lingue. 1998 ⇒381. 63-77.
6599 *Cahill, Lisa Sowle; McEvenue, Sean* El significado general de la sexualidad en la biblia. RevBib 60 (1998) 195-204.
6600 *Castello, Gaetano* Inculturazione e studio della bibbia. La terra e il seme. BTNap 19: 1998 ⇒310. 39-52.
6601 *Chalendar, Xavier de* Le plaisir dans la bible. Alliance 120 (1998) 38-39.
6602 *Clark, Gillian* Bodies and blood: late antique debate on martyrdom, virginity and resurrection. Changing bodies. 1998 ⇒352. 99-115.
6603 **Destro, Adriana; Pesce, Mauro** Antropologia delle origini cristiane. Quadrante 78: 1997 <1995>, ⇒13,6936. ^RBTB 28 (1998) 120-122 (*Elliott, John H.*); RivBib 46 (1998) 93-97 (*Elliott, John H.*).
6604 *Destro, Adriana; Pesce, Mauro* Self, identity, and body in Paul and John. Self, soul and body. SHR 78: 1998 ⇒286. 184-197.
6605 *Dov Hercenberg, Bernard* La transcendance du regard et la mise en perspective du Tekhelet ("bleu" biblique). RHPhR 78 (1998) 387-411.
6606 *Dubied, Pierre-Luigi* Der Geruch: unser Verhältnis zur Realität, zum Mitmenschen und zu Gott im Zeitalter der Vernetzung: theologische Abhandlung gegen den Schöpferwahn der "Postmoderne". Ebenbild Gottes. BThSt 33: 1998 ⇒255. 170-180.
6607 *Elliott, John H.* The anthropology of christian origins. BTB 28 (1998) 120-125.
6608 *Fabian, Dapila N.* The socio-religious role of witchcraft in the Old Testament culture: an African insight. OTEs 11 (1998) 215-239.
6609 *Finamore, John F.* Iamblichean dream theory. Mediators of the divine. SFSHJ 163: 1998 ⇒287. 155-164.
6610 *Gilbert, Maurice* L'anthropologie biblique <1981>;
6611 Suivre le Seigneur <1993>. Il a parlé par les prophètes. 1998 ⇒155. 69-80/355-370.
6612 **Gilhus, Ingvild** Saelid Laughing gods, weeping virgins: laughter in the history of religion. 1997 ⇒13,6949. ^RStudies in World Christianity 4 (1998) 273-276 (*Wyatt, N.*).
6613 **Girard, René** La vittima e la folla: violenza del mito e cristianesimo. Treviso 1998, Santi Quaranta 171 pp. L22.000.
6614 *Gonzalez, Carlos Ignacio* Le souffle de Yahvé. LV.F 53/1 (1998) 35-46 Sum. 46; Rés. 2.
6615 **Griffin, Jeffery Dale** An investigation of idiomatic expressions in the Hebrew Bible with a case study of anatomical idioms. ^DMid-America Baptist Theol. Sem. 1998, 181 pp.
6616 *Hawley, Richard* The dynamics of beauty in classical Greece. Changing bodies. 1998 ⇒352. 37-54.
6617 *Häußling, Ansgar* Jenseits von Anfang und Ende: zur Frage nach der Freiheit. ^FLORETZ O.: AOAT 250: 1998 ⇒65. 325-347.

6618 *Hieke, Thomas* "Geh zur Ameise, du Fauler ..." (Spr 6,6): zur Beurteilung der menschlichen Arbeit in den Psalmen und der biblischen Weisheitsliteratur. LebZeug 53 (1998) 19-31;

6619 Staub vom Ackerboden oder wenig geringer als Gott?: Menschenbilder des Alten Testaments in spannungsvoller Beziehung. LebZeug 53 (1998) 245-261.

6620 *Koenen, Klaus* "Wem ist Weh? Wem ist Ach? ... Wer hat trübe Augen?": zur Funktion von Rätselfragen im Alten Testament. BN 94 (1998) 79-86.

6621 *Küng, Hans* Being a christian as discipleship of Jesus. Hans Küng: breaking through. 1998 ⇒58. 129-167.

6622 **Lindström, Fredrik** Det sårbara livet: livsföståelse och gudserfarenhet i Gamla testamentet. Projekt Nytt GT: Lund 1998, Arcus 264 pp. [TTK 70,155s—Stordalen, Terje].

6623 *Link, Christian* Gottesbild und Menschenrechte. Ebenbild Gottes. BThSt 33: 1998 ⇒255. 147-169.

6624 *Lobkowicz, Nikolaus* Der "christliche Sinn" der Arbeit: eine historische Skizze. IKaZ 27 (1998) 193-204.

6625 *Mathys, Hans-Peter* Einleitung zu *Ebenbild Gottes*. Ebenbild Gottes. BThSt 33: 1998 ⇒255. 1-8.

6626 [E]**McCarthy, John** The whole and divided self: the bible and theological anthropology. 1997 ⇒13,6965. [R]ThTo 55 (1998) 470, 472, 474 (*Capps, Donald*).

6627 *Mertes, Klaus* Zerreißt Eure Kleider!: Gedanken und Anregungen zu Klageriten. Entschluss 53/11 (1998) 10-11.

6628 *Meskell, Lynn* The irresistible body and the seduction of archaeology;
6629 *Montserrat, Dominic* Introduction;
6630 Unidentified human remains: mummies and the erotics of biography. Changing bodies. 1998 ⇒352. 139-161/1-9/162-197.

6631 **Moore, Stephen D.** God's gym: divine male bodies in the Bible. NY 1996, Routledge viii; 185 pp. 8-415-91756-5. [R]JBL 117 (1998) 736-738 (*Martin, Dale B.*).

6632 *Moule, C.F.D.* Reflections on so-called triumphalism. Forgiveness. 1998 <1987> ⇒180. 30-40.

6633 *Murray, Penelope* Bodies in flux: OVID's Metamorphoses. Changing bodies. 1998 ⇒352. 80-96.

6634 **Osiek, Carolyn; Balch, David** Families in the New Testament world: households and house churches. 1997, ⇒13,6973. [R]BiRe 14/1 (1998) 12, 14-15 (*Duling, Dennis C.*); BTB 28 (1998) 85-86 (*Poetker, Katrina*); TS 59 (1998) 323-324 (*Wire, Antoinette Clark*).

6635 **Overholt, Thomas W.** Cultural anthropology and the OT. 1996 ⇒13,6974. [R]JBL 117 (1998) 112-114 (*Simkins, Ronald A.*).

6636 *Paquette, Eve* La consommation du sang, de l'interdit biblique à l'avidité vampirique. Religiologiques 17 (1998) 37-52.

6637 **Pimentel, João Paulo** Maternidade e vida à luz do evangelho. Lisboa 1998, DIEL 198 pp. 972-8040-19-9 [Theologica 35,255s—Silva, Fernando].

6638 *Podella, Thomas* Fasten im Alten Testament—ein Akt kollektiver Trauer. Entschluss 53/2 (1998) 21-23.

6639 *Rashkow, Ilona N.* Daddy-dearest and the 'invisible spirit of wine'. Genesis. 1998 ⇒219. 82-107.

6640 **Rizzini, Ilaria** L'occhio parlante: per una semiotica dello sguardo nel mondo antico. Memorie, Cl. di scienze morali 77: Venezia 1998, Istituto Veneto di Scienze viii; 204 pp. 88-86166-62-1. Bibl.

6641 *Seitz, Christopher* Human sexuality viewed from the bible's understanding of the human condition. Word without end. 1998 <1995> ⇒200. 263-275.
6642 *Smith, Mark S.* The heart and innards in Israelite emotional expressions: notes from anthropology and psychobiology. JBL 117 (1998) 427-436.
6643 *Stein, André* Reflecting on biblical children: from Adam and Eve, Isaac and Jesus to the betrayal and sacrifice of our children. ᶠCARGAS H. 1998 ⇒19. 135-146.
6644 *Stevenson, Jane* Nacktleben. Changing bodies. 1998 ⇒352. 198-212.
6645 *Stowers, Stanley K.* On the comparison of blood in Greek and Israelite ritual. ᶠFRERICHS, E. BJSt 320: 1998 ⇒28. 179-194.
6646 *Stöhr, Martin* Die Sprache der Freiheit ist biblisch. JK 59/1 (1998) 9-12, 14-19.
6647 **Stümke, Volker** Den Seinen gibt der Herr—den Schlaf: eine exegetische und systematisch-theologische Studie zu einer Gabe Gottes. Wechselwirkungen 29: Waltrop 1998, Spenner 85 pp. 3-933688-03-5 [NThAR 1999,251].
6648 *Thijssen, Herman* Gods troon. ITBT 6/3 (1998) 28-30.
6649 *Tóth, Cvetka* The metaphysical reason for the will to guilt. Jerusalem studies. ÄAT 40: 1998 ⇒361. 371-378.
6650 *Van Staalduine-Sulman, E.* Mag God vergeleken worden met eens mens?. Interpretatie 6/4 (1998) 9-11.
6651 **Vidovic, P. Franjo** Homo patiens: Leid und Leidbewältigung im biblischen Schrifttum und seinem antiken Umfeld. ᴰGraz 1996-1997: ᴰ*Woschitz, K.M.* [ThRv 94,xi].
6652 *Vlahogiannis, Nicholas* Disabling bodies. Changing bodies. 1998 ⇒352. 13-36.
6653 *Vollenweider, Samuel* Der Menschgewordene als Ebenbild Gottes: zum frühchristlichen Verständnis der Imago Dei. Ebenbild Gottes. BThSt 33: 1998 ⇒255. 123-146.
6654 *Weber, Reinhard* Die Distanz im Verhältnis zur Welt bei Epiktet, Jesus und Paulus. ᶠSTEGEMANN, H. BZNW 97: 1998 ⇒111. 327-349.
6655 *Weippert, Helga* Altisraelitische Welterfahrung: die Erfahrung von Raum und Zeit nach dem Alten Testament. Ebenbild Gottes. BThSt 33: 1998 ⇒255. 9-34.
6656 *Weyermann, Maja* Die Typologie von Adam-Christus und Eva-Maria und ihr Verhältnis zueinander. IKZ 88 (1998) 204-224.
6657 *Wilfong, Terry* Reading the disjointed body in Coptic: from physical modification to textual fragmentation. Changing bodies. 1998 ⇒352. 116-136.
6658 **Wolff, Hans Walter** Antropologia del Antiguo Testamento. ²1997 ⇒13,6996. ᴿNatGrac 45 (1998) 399-400 (*Rey Escapa, Jaime*).
6659 **Zambo Mveng, Samuel Rémi** Le mystère du nom: indices bibliques et réalités africaines. Yaoundé 1998, CLE 125 pp. 2-7235-0360-8f [NThAR 1999,178].

H2.8 Œcologia VT & NT—saecularitas

6660 **Boersema, Jan J.** Thora en Stoa over mens en natuur: een bijdage aan het milieudebat over duurzaamheid en kwaliteit. 1997 ⇒13, 6998. ᴰGroningen. ᴿITBT 6/4 (1998) 18-19 (*Van Hoogstraten, H.D.*)

6661 *Bullmore, Michael A.* The four most important biblical passages for a christian environmentalism. Trinity Journal 19 (1998) 139-162.
6662 *Kuhlmann, Helga* Herrschaftsauftrag und Geschlechterdifferenz. BThZ 15 (1998) 56-76.
6663 **Primavesi, Anne** Del Apocalipsis al Génesis: ecología, feminismo, cristianismo. ^T*Martínez Riu, Antonio* 1995, ⇒12,6732; 13,7006. ^RRevAg 41 (1998) 845-848 (*López, Luisa*).
6664 **Winkler, Ulrich** Vom Wert der Welt: das Verständnis der Dinge in der Bibel und bei BONAVENTURA: ein Beitrag zu einer ökologischen Schöpfungstheologie. Salzburger theologische Studien 5: 1997 ⇒13,1619. ^RCFr 68 (1998) 690-694 (*Maranesi, Pietro*).

H3.1 *Foedus*—The Covenant; the Chosen People; Providence

6665 *Alexander, Ralph H.* A new covenant—an eternal people (Jeremiah 31). Israel. 1998 ⇒6675. 169-206.
6666 ^E**Avemarie, Friedrich; Lichtenberger, Hermann** Bund und Tora: zur theologischen Begriffsgeschichte in alttestamentlicher, frühjüdischer und urchristlicher-Tradition. WUNT 92: 1996 ⇒12,6736. ^ROrdKor 39 (1998) 364-365 (*Giesen, Heinz*).
6667 *Backhaus, Knut* Das Bundesmotiv in der frühkirchlichen Schwellenzeit: Hebräerbrief, Barnabasbrief, Dialogus cum Tryphone. Der ungekündigte Bund?. QD 172: 1998 ⇒240. 211-231.
6668 **Beaucamp, Paul-Évode** Le fait biblique: alliance ancienne et nouvelle. Bible et vie chrétienne: P 1998, Lethielleux 217 pp. FF106. 2-283-61024-9.
6669 **Deneken, Michel** Où donc est votre Dieu?: parler aujourd'hui de la providence. Petite encyclopédie moderne du christianisme: P 1998, Desclée de B 208 pp. FF130. 2-220-04237-5 [BCLF 606,503].
6670 *Frankemölle, Hubert* Vorwort. Der ungekündigte Bund?. QD 172: 1998 ⇒240. 7-16.
6671 *Gilbert, Maurice* Les alliances <1982>;
6672 Engagement et fidélité <1982>. Il a parlé par les prophètes. 1998 ⇒155. 99-118/371-386.
6673 *Gräbe, Petrus J.* The new convenant: perspectives from the Lord's supper traditions and from the Pauline letters. Scriptura 65 (1998) 153-167.
6674 **Groß, Walter** Zukunft für Israel: Alttestamentliche Bundeskonzepte und die aktuelle Debatte um den Neuen Bund. SBS 176: Stu 1998, Katholisches Bibelwerk 219 pp. DM59. 3-460-04761-5. Bibl.
6675 ^E**House, H. Wayne** Israel: the land and the people: an evangelical affirmation of God's promises. GR 1998, Kregel 348 pp. 0-8254-2879-3.
6676 *Jochum, Herbert* Ecclesia und Synagoga: Alter und Neuer Bund in der christlichen Kunst;
6677 *Kirchschläger, Walter* "Bund" in der Herrenmahltradition. Der ungekündigte Bund?. QD 172: 1998 ⇒240. 248-276/117-134.
6678 *Klappert, Bertold* Die Öffnung des Israelbundes für die Völker: Karl Barths Israeltheologie und die Bundestheologie der reformierten Reformation. ^FSCHRAGE, W. 1998 ⇒101. 331-348.
6679 *Lohfink, Norbert* Kinder Abrahams aus Steinen: wird nach dem Alten Testament Israel einst der "Bund" genommen werden?. Der ungekündigte Bund?. QD 172: 1998 ⇒240. 17-43.

6680 *Löning, Karl* Eschatologische Krise und (Neuer) Bund: zum Stellenwert des Bundes-Motivs im Zusammenhang neutestamentlicher Soteriologien. Der ungekündigte Bund?. QD 172: 1998 ⇒240. 78-116.
6681 *Otto, Eckart* Die Ursprünge der Bundestheologie im Alten Testament und im Alten Orient. ZAR 4 (1998) 1-84.
6682 *Pawlikowski, John T.* Single or double covenant?: contemporary perspectives. ᶠCARGAS H. 1998 ⇒19. 147-162.
6683 **Römer, Thomas** Le peuple élu et les autres: l'Ancien Testament entre exclusion et ouverture. Poliez-le-Grand 1997, Moulin.
6684 *Rüterswörden, Udo* Bundestheologie ohne ברית. ZAR 4 (1998) 85-99.
6685 *Safrai, Chana* Bund der Rishonim/der Ersten und der Bund für die Goyim. Der ungekündigte Bund?. QD 172: 1998 ⇒240. 64-77.
6686 *Schmidt, Werner H.* "Volk" Gottes: Einsichten des Alten Testaments. ᶠSCHRAGE, W. 1998 ⇒101. 211-222.
6687 **Simian-Yofre, Horacio** La "chiesa" dell'Antico Testamento: costituzione, crisi e speranza della comunità credente dell'Antico Testamento. 1997 ⇒13,7023. ᴿRivBib 46 (1998) 235-237 (*Boschi, Bernardo Gianluigi*); BeO 40 (1998) 247-248 (*Tábet, Michelangelo*).
6688 *Spillman, Joann* The image of covenant in christian understanding of Judaism. JES 35/1 (1998) 63-84.
6689 *Stefani, Piero* L'alleanza di pace e la comune pasqua messianica. Studi ecumenici 16 (1998) 301-313.
6690 **Vogel, Manuel** Das Heil des Bundes: Bundestheologie im Frühjudentum und im frühen Christentum. TANZ 18: 1996 ⇒12,6759; 13,7025. ᴿThLZ 123 (1998) 258-260 (*Levin, Christoph*).
6691 *Vorgrimler, Herbert* Der ungekündigte Bund: systematische Aspekte. Der ungekündigte Bund?. QD 172: 1998 ⇒240. 232-247.
6692 *Zehetbauer, Markus* Die Bedeutung des Zwölferkreises für die Botschaft Jesu: eine Skizze des Zusammenhangs von Bund, Gottesbild und Ethik im Alten Testament, Frühjudentum und Neuen Testament. MThZ 49 (1998) 373-397.

H3.5 *Liturgia, spiritualitas VT*—OT prayer

6693 *Autexier, Maria* śyḥ—de la méditation dans la bible. ᶠMARGAIN, J. 1998, 233-240.
6694 **Baker, David W.; Heath, Elaine A.** More light on the path: daily scripture readings in Hebrew and Greek. GR 1998, Baker 384 pp. $22. Collab. *Baker, Morven* [AUSS 37,288—Miller, James E.].
6695 *Ballhorn, Egbert* Die O-Antiphonen: Israelgebet der Kirche. JLH 37 (1998) 9-34.
6696 **Bermejo, Luis M.** Alone with God alone: a biblical 30-day retreat. 1997, ⇒13,7029. ᴿBIBh 24 (1998) 132-133 (*Arikat, Sebastian*).
6697 **Bianchi, Enzo** La lettura spirituale della bibbia. I triangoli 45: CasM 1998, Piemme 104 pp. 88-384-2809-3.
6698 *Blijlevens, Ad* Reflecties op het Romeinse lezingenboek. PrakTh 25 (1998) 515-525.
6699 **Bras, Kick** Zoeken, nooit verzadigd zijn: gedachten over de mystieke weg. Kampen 1998, Kok 107 pp. ƒ25. 90-242-8570-4 [Interpretatie 7/2,33—Meereboer, Bep].

6700 *Braulik, Georg* Die alttestamentlichen Lesungen der drei österlichen Tage: ein Beitrag zur Erneuerung des Römischen Meßlektionars. LJ 48 (1998) 3-41.

6701 **Cocagnac, Maurice** I simboli biblici: percorsi spirituali. Bo 1998, EDB 922 pp. 88-10-24101-0.

6702 *Davis, Kenneth G.* Petitionary prayer in scripture. BiTod 36 (1998) 377-381.

6703 *De Benedetti, Paolo* La preghiera di Israele. L'uomo davanti a Dio. 1998 ⇒300. 125-135.

6704 [E]**De Zan, Renato** Dove rinasce la parola: bibbia e liturgia, 3. 1993, ⇒13,7032. [R]Ben. 45 (1998) 453-454 (*Ranzato, Agostino*).

6705 *De Zan, Renato* Linguaggio liturgico e bibbia. RPLi 36/3 (1998) 3-10.

6706 *Dohmen, Christoph* Wozu, Gott?: biblische Klage gegen die Warum-Frage im Leid. BiLi 71 (1998) 314-320.

6707 [E]**Felicetti, Christa** Gebete aus der Bibel. Graz 1998, Styria 199 pp. DM24.80. 3-222-12666-6 [OrdKor 40,495—Heinemann, F.K.].

6708 *Gensch, Brigitte* Hat das 'Elohimwesen' Mensch ein Maß?: eine Andacht zu Psalm 8. [F]MARQUARDT, F.-W. 1998 ⇒72. 233-240.

6709 *Gilbert, Maurice* La prière des sages d'Israël. Il a parlé par les prophètes. 1998 <1980> ⇒155. 333-352.

6710 Un giorno, una parola: letture bibliche quotidiane per il 1998. 1997. Federazione delle chiese evangeliche in Italia ⇒13,7036. [R]PalCl 77 (1998) 950-951 (*Lavarda, Girolamo*).

6711 *Görg, Manfred* Erinnere Dich!: ein biblischer Weg zum Lernen und Leben des Glaubens. MThZ 49 (1998) 23-32.

6712 *Hieke, Thomas* Schweigen wäre gotteslästerlich: zur Phänomenologie und Theologie der Klage im Alten Testament. BiLi 71 (1998) 287-304.

6713 **Houseman, Michael; Severi, Carlo** Naven or the other self: a relational approach to ritual action. [T]*Fineberg, Michael.* SHR 79: Lei 1998, Brill xvi; 301 pp. 90-04-11220-0. 19 pl.

6714 *Janssen, Henk* Creatief omgaan met het RK-lectionarium. Interpretatie 6/4 (1998) 23-24.

6715 [E]**Kiley, Mark** Prayer from Alexander to Constantine: a critical anthology. 1997, ⇒13,7037. [R]SCI 17 (1998) 262-263 (*Cerra, Gabriela*).

6716 **Lafser, Christine O'Keefe** An empty cradle, a full heart. Ch 1998, Loyola Univ. Pr. 249 pp. $11 [BiTod 37,255—Bergant, Dianne].

6717 **Lameri, Angelo** L'anno liturgico come itinerario biblico. Interpretare la Bibbia oggi 4; Leggere la Bibia nella liturgia 5: [Brescia] 1998, Queriniana 117 pp. 88-399-2481-7. Bibl.

6718 **Leloup, J.-Y.** Deserto, desertos. [T]*Alves, Ephraim F.*: Petrópolis 1998, Vozes 104 pp.

6719 *Lohfink, Norbert* Antiguo Testamento y liturgia. [T]*Giménez, Josep*: SelTeol 37 (1998) 328-336;

6720 Die Wurzeln der Herz-Jesu-Verehrung im Alten Testament. Jetzt 3 (1998) 12-22.

6721 **Martini, Carlo Maria** Vivir con la biblia: meditar con los protagonistas de la biblia guiados por un experto. [T]*Urbina, Pedro A.*: Barc 1998, Planeta 306 pp. PTA2.600. 8408-02606-2 [Isidorianum 8,389].

6722 **Masini, Mario** La 'lectio divina': teologia, spiritualità, metodo. 1996, ⇒12,6773; 13,7044. [R]CDios 111/1 (1998) 338 (*Gutiérrez, J.*);

EstB 56 (1998) 564-565 (*Precedo, M.J.*); CivCatt 149/2 (1998) 419-420 (*Scaiola, Đ.*);

6723   Lectio divina: an ancient prayer that is ever new. ^T*Lane, E.*: NY 1998, Alba ix; 103 pp. $6. 0-8189-0813-0 [PIBA 21,121—Magennis, F.].

6724   *Matos, Henrique Cristiano José* Leitura orante da Bíblia: fonte de renovação espiritual. Convergência 33 (1998) 503-512.

6725   *Miller, Patrick D.* Prayer and divine action. ^FBRUEGGEMANN, W. 1998 ⇒16. 211-232.

6726   *Monshouwer, Dirk* Alttestamentliche Lektionare: eine ökumenische Ergänzung zu den Erörterungen von Hansjakob Becker, Georg Braulik und Norbert Lohfink. BiLi 71 (1998) 50-55;

6727   Heden, in uw oren!: die schrift lezen in de liturgie. ITBT 6/8 (1998) 22-24.

6728   **Morosi, Ezio** Intorno al fuoco di Dio: meditazioni. R 1998, Borla 219 pp. 88-263-1265-6.

6729   **Myers, Susan E.** Pronunciation guide for the Sunday lectionary. Ch 1998, Liturgy Training Publications 46 pp. $2 [BiTod 37,392—Bergant, Dianne].

6730   ^E**Neal, Connie** Spiritual renewal bible. GR 1998, Zondervan x; 1408 pp. $33 [BS 156,505—Betker, Pam].

6731   *Negruzzo, Simona* Proclamare la parola di Dio. RPLi 207 (1998) 54-59.

6732   *Nowell, Irene* Teach us how to pray. BiTod 36 (1998) 208-213.

6733   **Pacomio, Luciano** Guida alla lettura della bibbia per vivere la vita: percorso spirituale in 50 tappe. CasM 1998, Piemme 392 pp. 88-384-4144-8.

6734   **Pennington, Basil** Lectio divina: renewing the ancient practice of praying the scriptures. NY 1998, Crossroads xiv; 164 pp. $15. 0-8245-1736-9 [Month 32,409s—Kinsella, Nivard].

6735   **Rheinbay, Paul** Biblische Bilder für den inneren Weg: das Betrachtungsbuch des Ignatius-Gefährten Hieronymus NADAL (1507-1580). Deutsche Hochschulschriften 1080: Hänsel-Hohenhausen 1995, Fouqué 278 pp. FS62. 3-8267-1080-0. ^RGuL 71/3 (1998) 238-239 (*Wollbold, Andreas*).

6736   *Ris, Gerard* Het lectionarium van 1969. PrakTh 25 (1998) 497-514.

6737   **Rossi De Gasperis, Francesco** La roccia che ci ha generato: un pellegrinaggio nella Terra Santa come esercizio spirituale. [Seoul] 1998, [Catholic Publishing House] 250 pp. 89-321-0312-7. **Korean**.

6738   **Rossi de Gasperis, Francesco; Carfagna, Antonio** Dalla creazione alla terra promessa. Prendi il libro e mangia!. Bibbia e Spiritualità 3: Bo 1998, Dehoniane 1 388 pp. L44.000. 88-10-21101-4.

6739   *Schenker, Adrian* Altes Testament und Liturgie. ALW 40 (1998) 170-181.

6740   *Seitz, Christopher* The lectionary as theological construction. Word without end. 1998 <1995> ⇒200. 300-318.

6741   **Vezzoli, Ovidio** Domenica, giorno del Signore: percorsi di lettura biblico-liturgica. Interpretare la Bibbia oggi 4; Leggere la Bibia nella liturgia 2: [Brescia] 1998, Queriniana 158 pp. L21.000. 88-399-2478-7. Bibl.

6742   **Werline, Rodney Alan** Penitential prayer in Second Temple Judaism: the development of a religious institution. SBL Early Judaism and Its Literature 13: Atlanta, GA 1998, Scholars xi 238 pp. $40. 0-7885-0325-1. Bibl.

6743 **West, Fritz** Scripture and memory: the ecumenical hermeneutic of the three-year lectionaries. 1997, ⇒13,7060. [R]Worship 72/2 (1998) 186-189 (*Sloyan, Gerard S.*).

6744 **Witkam, Jeroen** De stilte van het woord: van bijbelwoord naar diepteinkeer. Tielt 1998, Lannoo 144 pp. FB495. 90-209-3333-7 [ITBT 7/3,34—Van der Woude, Bert L.].

H3.7 *Theologia moralis VT*—**OT moral theology**

6745 *Andrés, J.F.* La limosna. EvV 40/2 (1998) 58-61.

6746 *Assmann, Jan; Janowski, Bernd; Welker, Michael* Richten und rette: zur Aktualität der altorientalischen und biblischen Gerechtigkeitskonzeption. Gerechtigkeit. 1998 ⇒283. 9-35.

6747 **Barton, John** Ethics and the Old Testament. L 1998, SCM xii; 100 pp. £8 [R]RRT 1998/2, 51-2 (*Vinten, Gerald*)].

6748 *Cahill, Lisa Sowle; McEvenue, Sean* El significado general de la sexualidad en la biblia. RevBib 60 (1998) 195-204.

6749 *Chrostowski, Waldemar* Wolność i posłuszeństwo w Biblii [Liberté et obéissance dans la bible]. AtK 131 (1998) 177-190. **P.**

6750 *Clines, David J.A.* Sin and maturity <1976>;

6751 Ethics as deconstruction, and, the ethics of deconstruction <1995>. OT essays, 1. JSOT.S 292: 1998 ⇒142. 555-573/95-125.

6752 **Consoli, Massimo** Ecce homo: l'omosessualità nella bibbia. Mi 1998, Kaos 155 pp. 88-7953-076-3. Bibl.

6753 **Countryman, Louis William** Sesso e morale nella bibbia [T]*Girardet, Maria Sbaffi* PBT 45: T 1998, Claudiana 326 pp. L38.000. 88-7016-283-4. Bibl.

6754 **Dietrich, Walter; Link, Christian** Die dunklen Seiten Gottes: Willkür und Gewalt. 1997, ⇒13,7069. [R]FrRu 4 (1998) 300-301 (*Oberforcher, Robert*).

6755 **Dubay, Thomas** Authenticity: a biblical theology of discernment. Ft. Collins, Colo. 1998, Ignatius 279 pp. [R]HPR 98/11-12 (1998) 81-83 (*Grace, Madeleine*).

6756 *Gilbert, Maurice* L'universalité des normes morales. Il a parlé par les prophètes. 1998 <1986> ⇒155. 119-133.

6757 **Görg, Manfred** Der un-heile Gott: die Bibel im Bann der Gewalt. Dü 1995, Patmos 192 pp. [R]FrRu 5 (1998) 299-300 (*Oberforcher, Robert*).

6758 *Grabowski, John S.* Made not begotten: a theological analysis of human cloning. Ethics & Medicine 14 (1998) 69-72.

6759 *Grelot, Pierre* Le vocabulaire biblique de la compassion. VS 728 (1998) 421-432.

6760 **Guest, Gerald Bentley** Queens, kings, and clergy: figures of authority in the thirteenth-century moralized Bibles. [D]NY 1998, 517 pp.

6761 **Guetta Sadun, Silvia; Mannucci, Andrea** I tuoi seni son grappoli d'uva: la sessualità nella bibbia. [Tirrenia (Pisa)] 1998, Del Cerro 127 pp. 88-8216-018-1. Prefazione di *Leonardo Trisciuzzi*. Bibl.

6762 *Henry, Carl F.H.* Commentary: reflections on death and suicide. Ethics & Medicine 14 (1998) 66-69.

6763 *Houtman, Cornelis* Wer kann Sünden vergeben außer Gott allein?: über menschliche Vergebung im Alten Testament. BN 95 (1998) 33-44.

6764   *Jackson, Bernard S.* "Law" and "justice" in the bible. JJS 49 (1998) 218-229.
6765   *Koch, Klaus* Şädaq und Ma'at: konnektive Gerechtigkeit in Israel und Ägypten?. Gerechtigkeit. 1998 ⇒283. 37-64.
6766   **Maguire, Daniel C.** Il cuore etico della tradizione ebraico-cristiana: una lettura laica della bibbia. Orizzonti biblici: [Assisi] 1998, Cittadella 394 pp. 88-308-0642-0.
6767   *Masiá, Juan* Sexual anthropology and christian ethics. KaKe 67 (1998) 167-190 Sum. v. **Japanese.**
6768   *Mathys, Hans-Peter* "Und es wird im Hause des Herrn der Heerscharen kein Krämer mehr sein an jenem Tag" (Sach 14,21): Altes Testament und Volkswirtschaft. ThZ 54 (1998) 97-110.
6769   *Mayes, Preston L.* Cities of refuge. CBTJ 14/1 (1998) 1-25.
6770   **Monz, Heinz** Gerechtigkeit bei Karl MARX und in der Hebräischen Bibel: Übereinstimmung, Fortführung und zeitgenössische Identifikation. Baden-Baden 1995, Nomos. 3-7890-4083-5. ᴿARSP 84 (1998) 448-450 (*Steußloff, Hans*); FrRu NF 5 (1998) 217-219 (*Zademach, Wieland*).
6771   **Nissinen, Martti** Homoeroticism in the biblical world: a historical perspective. ᵀ*Stjerna, Kirsi:* Ph 1998, Fortress vii; 208 pp. $24. 0-8006-2985-X. Bibl.
6772   *Oberforcher, Robert* Gott als Vorkämpfer der Humanität: biblische Befreiungserfahrung und prophetische Sozialkritik. ThG 41 (1998) 92-104.
6773   *Patrick, Dale* God's commandment. ᶠBRUEGGEMANN, W. 1998 ⇒16. 93-111.
6774   *Pieris, Aloysius* Christ and our mission: in the light of the value-system revealed to Israel and to the church as against today's dominant system. Ignis 27/1 (1998) 3-33.
6775   *Pilch, John J.* The power of the curse. BiTod 36 (1998) 313-317.
6776   **Rae, Scott B.** Brave new families: biblical ethics and reproductive technologies. 1996, ⇒12,6817. ᴿEthics & Medicine 14 (1998) 90 (*Stetson, Brad*).
6777   *Rizzi, Armido* 'Ama lo straniero...': la paradossale identità biblica. FilTeo 12 (1998) 244-253 Sum. 244.
6778   *Sæbo, Magne* Reflections on Old Testament ethics: its dual character and its modern application. On the way to canon. 1998 <1992> ⇒194. 162-181.
6779   *Schenker, Adrian* Sollen oder dürfen?: zum Sinn alttestamentlicher Ethik. Jetzt 3 (1998) 3-5.
6780   *Schmitt, Hans-Christoph* Die Gegenwartsbedeutung der Ethik des Alten Testaments: Überlegungen zu Ernst Würthweins Studie "Verantwortung". ZThK 95 (1998) 295-312.
6781   **Schreiner, Josef** An deinen Geboten habe ich meine Freude: Beiträge zur Ethik des Alten Testaments. Wü 1998, Echter 96 pp. 3-429-01980-X.
6782   *Seifrid, Mark* Gottes Gerechtigkeit im Alten Testament und bei Paulus: eine Skizze. JETh 12 (1998) 25-36.
6783   ᴱ**Seow, Choon-Leong** Homosexuality and christian community. 1996, ⇒12,6820; 13,7094. ᴿPro Ecclesia 7 (1998) 498-499 (*Matzko, David McCarthy*).
6784   **Sheriffs, Deryck** The friendship of the Lord: an Old Testament spirituality. 1996, ⇒12,6821; 13,7095. ᴿThZ 54 (1998) 269-270 (*Weber, Beat*).

6785 **Verkindère, Gérard** La justice dans l'Ancien Testament. CEv 105: P 1998, Cerf 67 pp. FF35. 0222-9714.

6786 **Weinfeld, Moshe** Social justice in ancient Israel and in the ancient Near East. 1995 ⇒11/2,3266; 12,6827. [R]JQR 89 (1998) 185-190 (*Eichler, Barry L.*).

6787 *Wojciechowski, Michał* The unity of biblical ethics. FolOr 34 (1998) 59-64.

6788 **Wold, Donald J.** Out of order: homosexuality in the bible and the ancient Near East. GR 1998, Baker 238 pp. $18. 0-8010-2114-6 [ThD 46,295—Heiser, W. Charles].

6789 **Wright, Christopher J.H.** Walking in the ways of the Lord: the ethical authority of the Old Testament. 1995, ⇒11/2,3268; 13,7102 [R]JThS 49 (1998) 719-720 (*Rogerson, J.W.*).

6790 *Zulu, E.* Reconciliation from an African perspective: an alternative view. OTEs 11 (1998) 182-194.

H3.8 *Bellum et pax VT-NT*—War and peace in the whole bible

6791 [E]**Bianchi, Enzo** La violenza. PSV 37 (1998) 3-321.

6792 **Boyd, Gregory A.** God at war: the bible and spiritual conflict. 1997 ⇒13,7104. [R]BS 155 (1998) 234-236 (*Pyne, Robert A.*).

6793 **Duncan, Andrew; Opatowski, Michel** War in the Holy Land: from Meggido to the West Bank. [Gloucester] 1998, Sutton xii; 212 pp. 0-7509-1500-5. Foreword by *Robert O'Neill.*

6794 **Herzog, Chaim; Gichon, Mordechai** Battles of the Bible. [2]1997 ⇒13,7110. [R]VT 48 (1998) 570-571 (*Emerton, J.A.*).

6795 *Krašovec, Jože* Der Gott der Heerscharen (die Bibel und der Krieg). ThRv 94 (1998) 135-146.

6796 *Lohfink, N.* 'La guerra sancta' e la 'scomunica' nella bibbia. PSV 37 (1998) 83-94.

6797 **McCarthy, Patricia** Of passion and folly: a scriptural foundation for peace. ColMn 1998, Liturgical x; 128 pp. $12 [BiTod 36,323—Bergant, Dianne].

6798 *Mello, Alberto* L'eccesso della violenza e la doppia consolazione;

6799 *Peretto, Elio* Violenza e linguaggio biblico;

6800 *Prato, Gian Luigi* Tratti di violenza nel volto di Dio. PSV 37 (1998) 95-103/25-51/11-24.

6801 **Randall, Albert B.** Theologies of war and peace among Jews, Christians and Muslims. TST 77: Lewiston, NY 1998, Mellen (14) v, 476 pp. 0-7734-8254-7. Bibl.

6802 **Römer, Thomas** Dieu obscur: le sexe, la cruauté et la violence dans l'Ancien Testament. 1996, ⇒12,6841. [R]DBAT 29 (1998) 290-291 (*Diebner, B.J.*).

6803 **Schwartz, Regina M.** The curse of Cain: the violent legacy of monotheism. 1997, ⇒13,7112. [R]ThTo 54 (1998) 534, 536-537 (*Brueggemann, Walter*); BiRe 14/2 (1998) 10, 12 (*Ackerman, Susan*); JR 78 (1998) 614-616 (*Al-Azmeh, Aziz*).

6804 **Seevers, Boyd** The practice of ancient Near Eastern warfare with comparison to the biblical accounts of warfare from the conquest to the end of the united monarchy. [D]Trinity 1998, 399 pp.

6805 *Thoma, Clemens* Gerechtigkeit und Frieden in jüdisch-rabbinischer Optik. VSVD 39 (1998) 161-164.

6806 *Vanoni, Gottfried* 'Justice and peace embrace' (Ps 85:11): stimuli towards an SVD focus taken from the Old Testament. VSVD 39 (1998) 145-157.
6807 **Wénin, André** Pas seulement de pain...: violence et alliance dans la Bible: essai. LeDiv 171: P 1998, Cerf 303 pp. FF195. 2-204-05814-9. Bibl.
6808 **Wood, John A.** Perspectives on war in the bible. Macon, GA 1998, Mercer University Press viii; 184 pp. $18. 0-86554-564-2.

H4.1 Messianismus

6809 *Abegg, Martin G.; Evans, Craig A.; Oegema, Gerbern S.* Bibliography of messianism and the Dead Sea scrolls;
6810 *Abegg, Martin G.; Evans, Craig A.* Messianic passages in the Dead Sea scrolls. [F]BETZ O. & VAN DER WOUDE A. 1998 ⇒11. 204-214/ 191-203.
6811 *Alexander, Philip S.* The king Messiah in rabbinic Judaism. King and Messiah. JSOT.S 270: 1998 ⇒378. 456-473.
6812 *Alexander, Thomas D.* Royal expectations in Genesis to Kings: their importance for biblical theology. TynB 49 (1998) 191-212.
6813 **Banon, David** Le messianisme. Que sais-je? 3377: P 1998, PUF 127 pp. FF42. 2-13-049243-6. Bibl.; BCLF 603,2466.
6814 *Barton, John* The Messiah in Old Testament theology. King and Messiah. JSOT.S 270: 1998 ⇒378. 365-379.
6815 *Bergler, Siegfried* Jesus, Bar Kochba und das messianische Laubhüttenfest. JSJ 29 (1998) 143-191.
6816 *Bonaiuti, Renzo* Il messia sconfitto. Testimonianze 41/2 (1998) 29-35.
6817 *Boschi, Bernardo Gianluigi* Il messianismo nella bibbia. SacDo 43/6 (1998) 59-76.
6818 *Brooke, George J.* Kingship and Messianism in the Dead Sea scrolls. King and Messiah. JSOT.S 270: 1998 ⇒378. 434-455.
6819 *Buetubela, Balembo* Le messianisme et le Messie dans le Nouveau Testament. RAT 22 (1998) 149-162.
6820 *Charlesworth, James H.* Challenging the *consensus communis* regarding Qumran messianism (1QS, 4QS MSS);
6821 Introduction: messianic ideas in early Judaism;
6822 Messianology in the biblical pseudepigrapha. [F]BETZ O. & VAN DER WOUDE A. 1998 ⇒11. 120-134/1-8/21-52.
6823 *Chester, Andrew* Messianism, torah and early christian tradition. Tolerance. 1998 ⇒440. 318-341.
6824 **Cohn-Sherbok, Dan** The Jewish Messiah. 1997 ⇒13,7123. [R]Theol. 101 (1998) 145-146 (*Bayfield, Tony*).
6825 *Dan, Joseph* The two meanings of Hasidic messianism. [F]FRERICHS, E. BJSt 320: 1998 ⇒28. 391-407.
6826 *Dexinger, Ferdinand* Reflections on the relationship between Qumran and Samaritan messianology. [F]BETZ O. & VAN DER WOUDE A. 1998 ⇒11. 83-99.
6827 **Eastman, Mark; Smith, Chuck** The search for Messiah. Fountain Valley, CA [2]1996, Joy 276 pp. 0-936728-50-7 [NThAR 2000,186].
6828 *Evans, Craig A.* Are the 'son' texts at Qumran messianic?: reflections on 4Q369 and related scrolls. [F]BETZ O. & VAN DER WOUDE A. 1998 ⇒11. 135-153.

6829 *Green, Joel B.* The death of Jesus and the ways of God: Jesus and the gospels on messianic status and shameful suffering. Interp. 52 (1998) 24-37.

6830 *Hohnjec, Nikola* Isus Krist Sin Božji i Veliki svećenik: tumacenje Ps 2 i Hebr 1,5; 5,5. BoSm 68 (1998) 327-345. **Croatian.**

6831 **Horbury, William** Jewish messianism and the cult of Christ. L 1998, SCM vi; 234 pp. £18. 0-334-02713-6. Bibl.

6832 *Horbury, William* Messianism in the Old Testament Apocrypha and Pseudepigrapha. King and Messiah. JSOT.S 270: 1998 ⇒378. 402-433.

6833 **Idel, Moshe** Messianic mystics. NHv 1998, Yale University Press x; 451 pp. $40. 0-300-06840-9. Bibl.

6834 **Kaiser, Walter C.** The messiah in the Old Testament. 1995, ⇒11/2, 3327... 13,7134. ^{R}EvQ 70 (1998) 63-64 (*Osgood, Joy*).

6835 *Koch, Klaus* Heilandserwartungen im Judäa der Zeitenwende. Die Schriftrollen von Qumran. 1998 ⇒6858. 107-135.

6836 *Kundert, Lukas* Apokalypse und Erlösung—Juden im antiken Rom: ein Versuch der Deutung des leidenden Messias in bSanh 98a. Jud. 54 (1998) 247-255.

6837 **Laato, Antti J.** A star is rising: the historical development of the Old Testament royal ideology and the rise of the Jewish messianic expectations. University of South Florida, International Studies in Formative Christianity and Judaism 5: Atlanta, GA 1998, Scholars xii; 456 pp. $80. 0-7885-0420-7. Bibl.

6838 **Lenowitz, Harris** The Jewish messiahs: from the Galilee to Crown Heights. L 1998, OUP viii; 297 pp. $45. 0-19-511492-2 [SCJ 30,868s—Walton, Michael T.].

6839 *Lichtenberger, Hermann* Messianic expectations and messianic figures in the Second Temple period. ^{F}BETZ O. & VAN DER WOUDE A. 1998 ⇒11. 9-20.

6840 *Mason, Rex* The Messiah in the postexilic Old Testament literature. King and Messiah. JSOT.S 270: 1998 ⇒378. 338-364.

6841 **Mayer, Reinhold** War Jesus der Messias?: Geschichte der Messiasse Israels in drei Jahrtausenden. Tü 1998, Bilam 448 pp. DM38/28. 3-933373-01-8; -0-X.

6842 *Mendels, Doron* Pseudo-Philo's *Biblical antiquities*, the 'fourth philosophy', and the political messianism of the first century CE. Identity. JSPE.S 24: 1998 <1991> ⇒174. 294-313.

6843 *Merklein, Helmut* Ägyptische Einflüsse auf die messianische Sohn-Gottes-Aussage des Neuen Testaments. Studien zu Jesus und Paulus II. WUNT 105: 1998 <1996> ⇒176. 3-30.

6844 *Misiarczyk, Leszek* La tradizione sul Messia nascosto nelle antiche fonti giudaiche e cristiane [Ambrosius Mediolanensis]. Vox Patrum 34-35 (1998) 311-319 Riass. 318. **P.**

6845 *Nocke, Franz-Josef* Der kommende Messias und der gekommene Christus: zum Zusammenhang von Christologie und Eschatologie: zugleich ein Beitrag zum jüdisch-christlichen Dialog. ^{F}BSTEH, A. 1998 ⇒17. 310-328.

6846 *Oberhänsli-Widmer, Gabrielle* Der leidende Messias in der jüdischen Literatur. Jud. 54 (1998) 132-143.

6847 **Oegema, Gebern S.** The anointed and his people: messianic expectations from the Maccabees to Bar Kochba. JSEP.S 27: Shf 1998, Academic 356 pp. £50. 1-85075-848-4. Bibl.

6848   *Oegema, Gerbern S.* Messianic expectations in the Qumran writings: theses on their development. ^FBETZ O. & VAN DER WOUDE A. 1998 ⇒11. 53-82.
6849   *Pearson, Brook W.R.* Dry bones in the Judean Desert: the Messiah of Ephraim, Ezekiel 37, and the post-revolutionary followers of Bar Kokhba. JSJ 29 (1998) 192-201.
6850   *Pritz, Ray A.* The remnant of Israel and the Messiah. Israel. 1998, ⇒6675. 61-73.
6851   **Rachlevsky, Seffi** חמורו של משיח [Der Esel des Messias]. TA 1998, Yediot Ahronot 510 pp [FrRu 6,146s—Breslauer, Richard]. **H.**
6852   **Ravitzky, Aviezer** Messianism, Zionism, and Jewish religious radicalism. 1996, ⇒12,6873. ^RReligion 28 (1998) 417-419 (*Neusner, Jacob*); JR 78 (1998) 89-98 (*Gruenwald, Ithamar*).
6853   *Rochais, Gérard* L'influence de quelques idées-forces de l'apocalyptique sur certains mouvements messianiques et prophétiques populaires juifs du 1er siècle. Jésus de Nazareth. 1998 ⇒253. 177-208.
6854   *Rose, Wolter H.* Messianic expectations in the early post-exilic period. TynB 49 (1998) 373-376.
6855   *Sæbo, Magne* On the relationship between 'messianism' and 'eschatology' in the Old Testament: an attempt at a terminological and factual clarification. On the way to canon. 1998 <1993> ⇒194. 197-231.
6856   **Scardelai, Donizete** Movimentos messiânicos no tempo de Jesus: Jesus e os outros messias. Biblioteca de estudos bíblicos: São Paulo 1998, Paulus 377 pp. 85-349-1143-6 [PerTeol 31,146].
6857   *Seitz, Christopher* Royal promises in the canonical books of Isaiah and the Psalms. Word without end. 1998 ⇒200. 150-167.
6858   ^E**Talmon, Shemaryahu** Die Schriftrollen von Qumran: zur aufregenden Geschichte ihrer Erforschung und Deutung. Rg 1998, Pustet 158 pp. 3-7917-1592-5.
6859   *Thomas, Robert L.* The mission of Israel and of the Messiah in the plan of God. Israel. 1998 ⇒6675. 261-280.
6860   **Toaff, Elio; Elkann, Alain** Il Messia e gli ebrei. Mi 1998, Bompiani 121 pp. 88-452-3865-2.
6861   *VanderKam, James C.* Messianism and apocalypticism. Encyclopedia of apocalypticism I. 1998 ⇒507. 193-228.
6862   **Wise, Michael O.** The first Messiah: investigating the Savior before Christ. SF 1998, HarperCollins 342 pp. $25 [BiTod 38,122—Bergant, Dianne].
6863   *Wolverton, Robert E.* From Omega to Alpha: the creation of a hero-messiah. Memorial Ray SUMMERS. 1998 ⇒115. 257-264.
6864   **Zimmermann, Johannes** Messianische Texte aus Qumran: königliche, priesterliche und prophetische Messiasvorstellungen in den Schriftfunden von Qumran. ^DTü 1997: WUNT 2/104: Tü 1998, Mohr xvi; (2) 542 pp. DM138. 3-16-147057-5. Bibl.

H4.3 *Eschatologia VT*—OT hope of future life

6865   *Bieberstein, Klaus* Der lange Weg zur Auferstehung der Toten: eine Skizze zur Entstehung der Eschatologie im Alten Testament. ^FVENETZ, H. 1998 ⇒122. 3-16.
6866   *Hendel, Ronald S.* Getting back to the garden of Eden. BiRe 14/6 (1998) 17, 47.

6867 *Jonker, Louis C.* Hope beyond the pre-exilic period: the inter-relationship of the creation and temple/Zion traditions during the monarchical and exilic periods. Scriptura 66 (1998) 199-215.

6868 *Kaiser, Otto* Die ersten und die letzten Dinge. Gesammelte Aufsätze. BZAW 261: 1998 <1994> ⇒166. 1-17. Zsfg., sum. 17.

6869 *Uehlinger, Christoph* Totenerweckungen—zwischen volkstümlicher Bettgeschichte und théologischer Bekenntnisliteratur. [F]VENETZ, H. 1998 ⇒122. 17-28.

H4.5 *Theologia totius VT*—General Old Testament theology

6870 **Breukelman, Frans** Biblische Theologie II: Debharim: der biblische Wirklichkeitsbegriff. Kampen 1998, Kok 366 pp. *f*79.50. 90-242-6158-9. [R]Interpretatie 6/7 (1998) 33-34 (*Wöhle, Andreas*).

6871 **Brueggemann, Walter** Theology of the Old Testament: testimony, dispute, advocacy. 1997 ⇒13,7170. [R]ThTo 55 (1998) 266, 268-269 (*Gerstenberger, Erhard S.*).

6872 *Brueggemann, Walter* Theology of the Old Testament: a prompt retrospect. [F]BRUEGGEMANN, W. 1998 ⇒16. 307-320.

6873 *Clines, David J.A.* Predestination in the Old Testament. OT essays, 2. JSOT.S 293: 1998 <1975> ⇒142. 524-541.

6874 *Diebner, Bernd J.* Vom Alten Testament zur Biblischen Theologie: Karel A. Deurloo nachträglich zum 60. (62.) Geburtstag. DBAT 29 (1998) 9-14.

6875 *Gottwald, Norman K.* Rhetorical, historical, and ontological counterpoints in doing Old Testament theology. [F]BRUEGGEMANN, W. 1998 ⇒16. 11-23.

6876 **Helyer, Larry R.** Yesterday, today and forever: the continuing relevance of the Old Testament. 1996 ⇒12,6886. [R]BBR 8 (1998) 244-245 (*Martens, Elmer A.*).

6877 **House, Paul R.** Old Testament theology. DG 1998, InterVarsity 655 pp. 0-8308-1523-6. Bibl.

6878 **Janowski, Bernd** Stellvertretung: alttestamentliche Studien zu einem theologischen Grundbegriff. SBS 165: 1997 ⇒13,535. [R]BZ 42 (1998) 295-297 (*Schenker, Adrian*); JBL 117 (1998) 715-716 (*Williamson, H.G.M.*).

6879 *Knierim, Rolf P.* The task of Old Testament theology: substance, method and cases. RStR 24 (1998) 37-42.

6880 **Müller, Hans-Peter** Glauben, Denken und Hoffen: alttestamentliche Botschaften in den Auseinandersetzungen unserer Zeit. Altes Testament und Moderne 1: Müns 1998, Lit 319 pp. 3-8258-3331-3.

6881 **Ortlund, Raymond C.** Whoredom: God's unfaithful wife in biblical theology. 1996 ⇒12,462. [R]Trin.Journal 19 (1998) 103-107 (*Aucker, W. Brian*).

6882 **Perdue, Leo G.** The collapse of history: reconstructing Old Testament theology. Overtures to Biblical theology: 1994, ⇒10,7396; 12,6892. [R]CV 40/1 (1998) 74-85 (*Prudký, Martin*).

6883 **Preuss, Horst Dietrich** Old Testament theology, 1. [T]*Perdue, Leo G.* 1995 ⇒11/2,3390; 13,7185. [R]BS 155 (1998) 240-241 (*Merrill, Eugene H.*);

6884 Old Testament theology, 1-2. 1996 ⇒11/2,3390... 13,7186. [R]JSSt 43 (1998) 142-145 (*Tomes, Roger*) BiRe 14/2 (1998) 17 (*Anderson, Gary A.*); HeyJ 39 (1998) 325-328 (*McNamara, Martin*);

6885 Old Testament theology, 2. 1996 ⇒12,6894; 13,7186. ᴿNew Theology Review 11/1 (1998) 108-109 (*Lenchak, Timothy A.*); JThS 49 (1998) 170-172 (*Davidson, Robert*).
6886 *Reimer, David J.* Old Testament christology. King and Messiah. JSOT.S 270: 1998 ⇒378. 380-400.
6887 *Reumann, John* Profiles, problems, and possibilities in biblical theology today—Part I. KuD 44 (1998) 61-85.
6888 *Schmidt, Werner* Einsichten und Aufgaben alttestamentlicher Theologie und Hermeneutik. VF 43/2 (1998) 60-75.
6889 **Schmitt, Armin** Wende des Lebens: Untersuchungen zu einem Situations-Motiv der Bibel. BZAW 237: 1996 ⇒12,6899; 13,7190. ᴿOLZ 93 (1998) 664-666 (*Wächter, Ludwig*); CBQ 60 (1998) 345-347 (*Gladson, Jerry F.*).
6890 *Stuhlmann, Rainer* "Kreuzestheologie" in der jüdischen Bibel. ᶠSCHRAGE, W. 1998 ⇒101. 79-91.
6891 *Sweeney, Marvin A.* Reconceiving the paradigms of Old Testament theology in the post-Shoah period. Biblical Interpretation 6 (1998) 142-161.
6892 *Van der Kooij, A.* In het voorbijgaan: Godsontmoeting als onderbreking. Interpretatie 6/1 (1998) 25-28.
6893 **Van Groningen, Gerard** From creation to consummation. Sioux Center, IA 1996, Dordt College Press 604 pp. 0-932914-34-9. $37 [OTEs 12,378s—Van Tonder, C.A.P.].

H5.1 *Deus*—NT—God [as Father ⇒H1.4]

6894 **Duquesne, Jacques** Le Dieu de Jésus. 1997 ⇒13,7198. ᴿSR 27 (1998) 210-211 (*Béland, Jean-Pierre*).
6895 **Le Guillou, Marie-Joseph** El misterio del Padre: fe de los apóstoles; gnosis actuales. Ensayos 122: M 1998, Encuentro 275 pp. 84-7490-477-3.
6896 *Merklein, Helmut* Die Einzigkeit Gottes als die sachliche Grundlage der Botschaft Jesu. Studien zu Jesus und Paulus II. WUNT 105: 1998 <1987> ⇒175. 154-173.
6897 *Niederwimmer, Kurt* Zur praedicatio de Deo im Neuen Testament. Gesammelte Aufsätze. BZNW 90: 1998 <1983> ⇒182. 142-151.
6898 **Pacomio, Luciano** Il Padre: Dio di ogni consolazione (2 Corinzi 1,3). CasM 1998, Piemme 120 pp. 88-384-4181-2.
6899 *Savasta, Carmelo* Il nome divino nel Nuovo Testamento. RivBib 46 (1998) 89-92.
6900 *Schroeder, Christoph* "Standing in the breach": turning away the wrath of God. Interp. 52 (1998) 16-23.

H5.2 Christologia ipsius NT

6901 *Amato, Angelo* Gesù Cristo, centro del giubileo. Com(I) 160-161 (1998) 16-27.
6902 *Becker, Jürgen* Geisterfahrung und Christologie: ein Vergleich zwischen Paulus und Johannes. ᶠSTEGEMANN, H. BZNW 97: 1998 ⇒111. 428-442.
6903 *Betz, Hans Dieter* Heroenverehrung und Christusglaube. Gesammelte Aufsätze IV. 1998 <1996> ⇒134. 128-151.

6904 **Bloesch, Donald G.** Jesus Christ: savior & lord: christian foundations. Carlisle 1997, Paternoster 304 pp. 0-85364-594-9.

6905 *Bobadilla, David* Cristología bíblica y ética social cristiana. Voces 12 (1998) 61-92.

6906 *Borg, Marcus J.* A vision of the christian life. The meaning of Jesus. 1998 ⇒3857. 229-250. ·

6907 *Bormann, Paul* Jesus, der Wundertäter. Jesus Christus—Gottes Sohn. 1998 ⇒6914. 213-221.

6908 *Böhler, Dieter* Jesus als Davidssohn bei Lukas und Micha. Bib. 79 (1998) 532-538.

6909 **Brown, Raymond Edward** Jésus dans les quatre évangiles: introduction à la christologie du Nouveau Testament. [T]*Degorce, Jean-Bernard; Barrios-Delgado, Dominique*: LiBi 111: 1996, ⇒12,6912. [R]RB 105 (1998) 623-626 (*Devillers, Luc*); CEv 103 (1998) 72-73 (*Quesnel, M.*).

6910 **Casciaro, José María; Monforte, J.M.** Jesucristo, salvador de la humanidad. 1996 ⇒12,6914. [R]Carthaginensia 14 (1998) 223-224 (*Álvarez Barredo, M.*).

6911 **Cullmann, Oscar** Cristología del Nuevo Testamento. 1997 ⇒13, 7211. [R]Studium 38 (1998) 341-342 (*López, L.*); RET 58 (1998) 256-259 (*Barrado, P.*).

6912 **Dupuis, Jacques** Homme de Dieu, Dieu des hommmes: introduction à la christologie. P 1995, Cerf 288 pp. 2-204-05137-3. [R]LTP 54/2 (1998) 438-9 (*Nault, François*).

Ebert, D. Wisdom in NT christology. 1998 ⇒6945.

6913 [E]**Ernst, Josef** Jesus Christus—Gottes Sohn: Herausforderung 2000. Bonifatius Kontur 657: Pd 1998, Bonifatius 273 pp. DM29,80. 3-89710-065-7.

6914 *Frankemölle, Hubert* Wie können wir heute Jesus Christus verkündigen?. Jüdische Wurzeln. BBB 116: 1998 <1995> ⇒151. 457-464;

6915 Neutestamentliche Christologien vor dem Anspruch alttestamentlicher Theologie. Jüdische Wurzeln. 1998 <1974> ⇒151. 45-71.

6916 *Heriban, Jozef* Il Cristo "preesistente", o Gesù Cristo nella sua esistenza divino-umana?. [F]POKORNÝ, P. 1998 ⇒90. 149-162.

6917 **Karrer, Martin** Jesus Christus im Neuen Testament. GNT 11: Gö 1998, Vandenhoeck & R 380 pp. DM68. 3-525-51380-1. [R]StPat 45 (1998) 259-262 (*Segalla, Giuseppe*).

6918 *Kulisz, Józef; Baliszewska, Aleksandra Mostowska* Czy Jezus wiedsiał, że jest Bogiem? [Jésus savait-il qu'il était Dieu?]. Bobolanum 9 (1998) 281-305 Rés. 305. **P**.

6919 **Liderbach, Daniel** Christ in the early christian hymns. NY 1998, Paulist vii; 153 pp. $15. 0-8091-3809-3 [JEarlyC 7,463s—McDonald, William P.].

6920 **Luttenberger, Gerard H.** Who do you say that I am?: an introduction to christology in the gospels and early church. Mystic, CT 1998, Twenty-Third 382 pp. $25. 0-89622-924-6 [ThD 46,278—Heiser, W. Charles].

6921 **Macquarrie, John** Christology revisited. L 1998, SCM 123 pp. 0-334-02737-3.

6922 *Merklein, Helmut* Christus als Bild Gottes im Neuen Testament. JBTh 13 (1998) 53-75 [Col 1,15-20];

6923 Marana ("unser Herr") als Bezeichnung des nabatäischen Königs: eine Analogie zur neutestamentlichen Kyrios-Bezeichnung?. [F]HOFFMANN, P. Von Jesus. BZNW 93: 1998 ⇒43. 25-41.

6924 *Miguel González, José María de* Significado de Jesucristo para el hombre de hoy. Isidorianum 7 (1998) 403-430 Sum. 403.
6925 *Moral Palacio, José Ángel del* La revelación de Dios en Jesús. AnáMnesis 15 (1998) 57-75.
6926 *Muñoz León, Domingo* Encarnación de Cristo: estudio bíblico. Est Trin 32 (1998) 39-75.
6927 **Nouailhat, René** La genèse du christianisme: de Jérusalem à Chalcédoine. 1997 ⇒13,7230. ᴿSR 27 (1998) 83-84 (*Lamirande, Émilien*).
6928 **O'Collins, Gerald** Christology: a biblical, historical, and systematic study of Jesus. 1995 ⇒11/2,3545... 13,7231. ᴿAUSS 36 (1998) 303-305 (*Trieyer, Humberto R.*);
6929 Cristologia. BTCon 90: 1997 ⇒13,7232. ᴿRdT 39 (1998) 926-928 (*Gamberini, Paolo*).
6930 *Pagazzi, Giovanni Cesare* 'Unico Dio generato' (Gv 1,18): idee per una cristologia del 'Figlio'. Teol(Br) 23 (1998) 66-99 Sum. 99.
6931 **Penna, Romano** I ritratti originali di Gesù il Cristo: inizi e sviluppi della cristologia neotestamentaria. 1996 ⇒12,6932; 13,7236. ᴿRiv Bib 46 (1998) 492-496 (*Pitta, Antonio*); CBQ 60 (1998) 378-380 (*Pilch, John J.*).
6932 *Perroni, Marinella* L'essere-corpo di Gesù. Servitium 120 (1998) 43-53.
6933 *Rivas, Luis Heriberto* Cristo Salvador ùnico y universal en algunos himnos del Nuevo Testamento. Teol(BA) 71 (1998) 37-61.
6934 *Rowland, Christopher* Christ in the New Testament. King and Messiah. JSOT.S 270: 1998 ⇒378. 474-496.
6935 *Salas Martínez, Jesús* ¿Qué queremos decir cuando afirmamos que Jesús es 'el Hijo de Dios'?. SalTer 87 (1998) 387-406.
6936 **Sanz Valdivieso, Rafael** Biblia y cristología. 1992 ⇒9,7599. ᴿVyV 56 (1998) 309-311 (*Álvarez Barredo, Miguel*).
6937 **Schnackenburg, Rudolf** La persona de Jesucristo reflejada en los cuatro evangelios. Barc 1998, Herder 459 pp. Pta4.600. 84-254-2021-0. ᴿBib(L) 7/7 (1998) 156-157 (*Alves, Herculano*).
6938 *Seim, Jürgen; Geyer, Hans-Georg* Solus Christus—das eine Wort Gottes im Horizont der Heiligen Schrift. ᶠSᴄʜʀᴀɢᴇ, W. 1998 ⇒101. 3-23.
6939 **Sweeley, John W.** Jesus in the gospels: man, myth, or God. SF 1998, International Scholars xxiii; 205 pp. 1-57309-330-0. Bibl.
6940 **Tábet, Miguel Angel** Jesúcristo unico salvador del mundo: ayer, hoy y siempre: cristología y soteriolgía bíblicas. n.p. 1997, Centro Teológico Sacerdotal 159 pp. Jornadas de Estudio para Sacerdotes;
6941 **Tábet, Miguel Angel; Izquierdo, César** Jesúcristo, Salvador del Mundo. Colección Teológica 8: [Santafé de Bogotá] 1997, Ediciones Universidad de la Sabana 217 pp. 958-12-0130-0.
6942 **Witherington, Ben** The many faces of the Christ: the christologies of the New Testament and beyond. Companions to the New Testament: NY 1998, Crossroad vii; 264 pp. $20. 0-8245-1705-9 [BiTod 37,63—Senior, Donald].
6943 *Wright, N.T.* The divinity of Jesus;
6944 The truth of the gospel and christian living. The meaning of Jesus. 1998 ⇒3857. 157-168/207-228.
6945 **Ebert, Daniel J.** Wisdom in New Testament christology with special reference to Hebrews 1:1-4. ᴰTrinity 1998, 351 pp.

H5.3 *Christologia praemoderna*—Patristic to Reformation

6946 *Deneken, Michel* L'affirmation de Dieu en Jésus Christ: voie négative et christologie: du Nouveau Testament à Chalcédoine. RevSR 72 (1998) 485-501.

6947 **Fernández Lois, Abel H.A.** La cristología en los comentarios a Isaías de CIRILO de Alejandria y TEODORETO de Ciro. ᴰLateranum: R 1998, Pont. Univ. Lateranensis 429 pp.

6948 **Gieschen, Charles A.** Angelomorphic christology: antecedents and early evidence. AGJU 42: Lei 1998, Brill xvi; 403 pp. ƒ185/$109. 90-04-10840-8.

6949 **Grillmeier, A.** Cristo en la tradición cristiana: desde el tiempo apostólico hasta el Concilio de Calcedonia (451). VeIm 143: 1997 ⇒13,7260. ᴿEstTrin 32/1-2 (1998) 235-236 (*Bustinza, Pedro*); ActBib 35 (1998) 156-158 (*Vives, Josep*);

6950 Christ in christian tradition, 2/2: the church of Constantinople in the sixth century. 1995, ⇒11/2,3464... 13,7262. ᴿNew Theology Review 11/1 (1998) 115-116 (*Gros, Jeffrey*);

6951 Fragmente zur Christologie: Studien zum altkirchlichen Christusbild. ᴱ*Hainthaler, Theresia*. 1997 ⇒13,7261. ᴿThG 41/1 (1998) 70-71 (*Fuchs, Gotthard*);

6952 Le Christ dans la tradition chrétienne, 2/4: l'église d'Alexandrie, la Nubie et l'Ethiopie après 451. CFi 192: 1996, ⇒12,6947; 13,7264. Collab. *Hainthaler, Theresia*. ᴿContacts 182 (1998) 190-92 (*Larchet, Jean-Claude*).

6953 **Martínez Fraseda, Francisco** La gracia y la ciencia de Jesucristo: historia de la cuestión en ALEJANDRO de Hales, Odón RIGALDO, *Summa Halensis* y BUENAVENTURA. 1997 ⇒13,7269. ᴿSan Juan de la Cruz 21 (1998) 147-149 (*Baldeón, Alfonso*); CFr 68 (1998) 354-357 (*Armellada, Bernardino de*); Anton. 73 (1998) 372-377 (*Sileo, Leonardo*).

6954 **Pokorny, Petr** Jesus in the eyes of his followers: newly discovered manuscripts and old christian confessions. Dead Sea Scrolls & Christian Origins Library 4: North Richland Hills, Texas 1998, BIBAL x; 100 pp. 0-941037-65-7. Bibl.

6955 **Pons, Guillermo** Jesucristo en los Padres de la iglesia. 1997 ⇒13, 7273. ᴿSan Juan de la Cruz 21 (1998) 140-141 (*Maqueda Gil, Antonio*).

6956 ᵀ**Pons Pons, Guillermo** Juan DAMASCENO: homilías cristológicas y marianas. 1996 ⇒12,6955. ᴿRevAg 41 (1998) 835-836 (*Sánchez Navarro, L.A.*).

6957 *Thümmel, Hans Georg* Desideria für die Dogmengeschichtsschreibung der ersten vier Jahrhunderte. BThZ 15 (1998) 22-40.

H5.4 *(Commentationes de) Christologia* moderna

6958 **Amato, Angelo** Jesús el Señor. M 1998, BAC xx; 567 pp. 84-7914-349-5. ᴿVyV 56 (1998) 500-502 (*Fernández González, Demetrio*).

6959 *Backhaus, Knut* 'Das Göttliche an unserem Gott ist seine Menschlichkeit': Jesus von Nazaret und die Kirche heute. Jesus Christus—Gottes Sohn. 1998 ⇒6913. 191-212.

6960 **Balthasar, Hans Urs von** Gesù e il cristiano: il cristiano e l'angoscia: chi è il cristiano? Cordula: la verità è sinfonica: con occhi semplici: Gesù ci conosce?: noi conosciamo Gesù?. Già e non ancora 337: Mi 1998, Jaca 511 pp. 88-16-30337-9.

6961 **Beckford, Robert** Jesus is dread: black theology and black culture in Britain. L 1998, Darton, L & T xii; 194 pp. £11. [R]RRT (1998/4) 87-89 (*Lartey, Emmanuel*).

6962 *Bernhardt, Reinhold* Christologie im Kontext einer "Theologie der Religionen". MdKI 49 (1998) 83-87 .

6963 *Buggert, Donald W.* Saint Jesus or Jesus Savior?. New Theology Review 11/2 (1998) 20-31.

6964 *Colombo, Enrico* Sulla cristologia filosofica di Xavier TILLIETTE. RTLu 3/1 (1998) 115-132 Sum., Zsfs., som. 131s.

6965 **Cowdell, Scott** Is Jesus unique?: a study of recent christology. 1996 ⇒12,6974; 13,7294. [R]Pacifica 11 (1998) 225-230 (*Garrett, Graeme*); Horizons 25 (1998) 120-121 (*Knitter, Paul F.*); JR 78 (1998) 446-447 (*Healy, Nicholas M.*); VJTR 62 (1998) 361-362 (*Amaladoss, M.*).

6966 *Ernst, Josef* Das Jesusgebet;

6967 Moderne Jesusbücher christologisch durchleuchtet;

6968 An der Schwelle des 3.Jahrtausends: das Evangelium von Jesus Christus. Jesus Christus—Gottes Sohn. 1998 ⇒6913. 223-237/171-189/15-27.

6969 **Fédou, Michel** Regards asiatiques sur le Christ. CJJC 77: P 1998, Desclée 297 pp. FF180. 2-7189-0948-X [BCLF 607,733].

6970 *Francis, B. Joseph* Towards an ecumenical christology. ITS 35/1 (1998) 5-17.

6971 *Fuchs, Ottmar* Christologische Karriere als Kehre in der Theodizee: pastoraltheologische Aspekte. [F]HOFFMANN, P., Von Jesus. BZNW 93: 1998 ⇒43. 571-613.

6972 *Fuhs, Hans F.* Der Kreuzestod Jesu Christi im Licht der Opferung Isaaks. Jesus Christus—Gottes Sohn. 1998 ⇒6913. 97-111.

6973 **Garcia de Alba, Juan Manuel** Cristo Jesus: conhecê-lo, amá-lo, segui-lo. [T]*Figueiredo, Maria Antonia Pires de Carvalho*: Bauru 1998, Ed. Univ. do Sagrado Coração 211 pp. 85-86259-24-1 [PerTeol 86,118s—Vitório, Jaldemir].

6974 *Gispert-Sauch, George* Christ and the Indian mystical tradition—Swami Abhishiktananda. Jeevadhara 28 (1998) 193-206 Sum. 193.

6975 *Griffiths, Paul J.* One Jesus, many Christs. Pro Ecclesia 7/2 (1998) 152-171.

6976 **Grogan, Geoffrey** The Christ of the bible and the church's faith. Ross-shire 1998, Mentor 288 pp. 1-8579-2266-2 [Evangel 17,99s—Reid, Jim].

6977 *Harrison, Nonna Verna* The maleness of Christ. SVTQ 42 (1998) 111-151.

6978 **Heller, Jan** Bůh sestypující [Der herabsteigende Gott]. Praha 1994, Kalich 160 pp. [R]CV 40 (1998) 167-171 (*Kämmerer, Thomas*).

6979 **Hünermann, Peter** Cristología. 1997 ⇒13,7307. [R]Isidorianum 7 (1998) 281-283 (*Calero, Antonio M*[a]); ScrTh 30 (1998) 704-705 (*Mateo-Seco, L.F.*).

6980 *Iammarrone, Giovanni* Gesù 'servo' e il tema del suo 'servizio' nella cristologia sistematica cattolica contemporanea. Gesù Servo. 1998 ⇒210. 115-155.

6981 **Karlić, Ivan** Il Gesù della storia nella teologia di J. MOLTMANN. 1996 ⇒12,6997. ᴿBog.Smo. 68 (1998) 280-287 (*Dogan, Nikola*).
6982 **Kuitert, H.M.** Jezus: nalatenschap van het christendom: schets voor een christologie. Baarn 1998, Ten Have pp [ITBT 7/4,25—Hack, Christine].
6983 **MacLeod, Donald** The person of Christ. DG 1998, InterVarsity 303 pp. $16. 0-8308-1537-6 [ThD 46,279—Heiser, W. Charles].
6984 *Manus, Ukachukwu Chr.* African christologies: the centre-piece of African christian theology. ZMR 82 (1998) 3-23.
6985 **Marchesi, Giovanni** La cristologia trinitaria di Hans Urs VON BALTHASAR. 1997 ⇒13,7315. ᴿRSR 86 (1998) 326-328 (*Tilliette, Xavier*).
6986 *Marino, Antonio* Jesucristo, mediador ùnico y universal de salvación: la cristología del documento 'El cristianismo y las religiones'. Teol(BA) 71 (1998) 115-139.
6987 *Mathew, C.P.* Christ and human fellowship in secular culture—according to M.M. Thomas. Jeevadhara 28 (1998) 221-235 Sum. 221.
6988 **Mazzotta, Francesco** I titoli cristologici nella cristologia cattolica contemporanea: uno studio delle aree italiana, francofona, ispano-latino americana. Contributi teologici: R 1998, Dehoniane 397 pp. 88-396-0758-7. Pref. di *Gerald O'Collins, SJ.*
6989 **McGrath, Alister E.** The making of modern German christology 1750-1990. ²1994 ⇒10,7497. ᴿKeTh 49 (1998) 159-60 (*Jansen, H.*).
6990 *McGrath, James F.* Change in christology: New Testament models and the contemporary task. IThQ 63 (1998) 39-50.
6991 **Moltmann, Jürgen** Cristo para nosotros hoy. 1997 ⇒13,7321. ᴿThX 48 (1998) 362-365 (*Gutiérrez Jaramillo, Mario*).
6992 *Mußner, Franz* Die Schoa und der Jude Jesus: Versuch einer Christologie nach Auschwitz. FrRu 4 (1998) 272-278.
6993 *Nordhues, Paul* Jesus Christus—Gottes Sohn: zur Einführung. Jesus Christus—Gottes Sohn. 1998 ⇒6913. 9-14.
6994 **Pagazzi, Giovanni Cesare** La singolarità di Gesù come criterio di unità e differenza nella chiesa. 1997 ⇒13,7330. ᴿZKTh 120 (1998) 113-116 (*Neufeld, Karl H.*).
6995 ᴱ**Painadath, Sebastian** Christ in Asia. Jeevadhara 28 (1998) 157-252.
6996 *Parappally, Jacob* Sebastian Kappen's vision of a contextual christology. Jeevadhara 28 (1998) 236-252 Sum. 236.
6997 **Pikaza, X.** Éste es el hombre: manual de cristología. 1997 ⇒13, 7337. ᴿEstTrin 32/1-2 (1998) 230-231 (*Aurrecoechea, José Luis*); Cart. 14 (1998) 463-464 (*Martínez Fresneda, F.*).
6998 **Purdy, Vernon Lee** The christology of John MACQUARRIE. ᴰFuller 1998, 386 pp.
6999 *Schönborn, Christoph* Il cammino della cristologia moderna: tentativo di una diagnosi. Com(I) 158 (1998) 82-92.
7000 **Schwarz, Hans** Christology. GR 1998, Eerdmans xii; 352 pp. $25. 0-8028-4463-4.
7001 *Sequeri, Pierangelo* L'interesse teologico di una fenomenologia di Gesù: giustificazione e prospettive. Teol(Br) 23 (1998) 289-329.
7002 **Singh, Narendra** The particularity of Christ and the plurality of religions: a dialectical paradigm for developing a Christian theology of religions. ᴰAsbury 1998, 245 pp.
7003 **Thompson, William H.** The struggle for theology's soul: contesting scripture in christology. 1996 ⇒12,7031; 13,7357. ᴿNew Theology Review 11/4 (1998) 89-90 (*Viladesau, Richard*).

7004 **Tilliette, Xavier** Il Cristo della filosofia: prolegomeni a una cristologia filosofica. 1997 ⇒13,7359. ᴿCivCatt 149/3 (1998) 540-542 (*Lorizio, G.*).
7005 *Veliath, Dominic* Christ and religious pluralism—Raimundo Panikkar. Jeevadhara 28 (1998) 207-220 Sum. 207.

H5.5 *Spiritus Sanctus; pneumatologia*—The Holy Spirit

7006 **Alonso Schökel, Luis** Al aire del Espíritu: meditaciones bíblicas. El pozo de Siquem 91: Sdr 1998, Sal Terrae 126 pp. 84-293-1242-0.
7007 *Angelini, Giuseppe* Lo Spirito Santo e la nascita vera dell'uomo. Ambr. 74 (1998) 326-392.
7008 *Ardusso, Franco* Lo Spirito nella bibbia. FilTeo 12 (1998) 527-543.
7009 *Barcelón, Emilio* El Espíritu Santo, creador de unidad y fuente de pluralidad: el Espíritu Santo, 'alma y agente principal' de la comunión eclesial. TE 42 (1998) 151-197.
7010 **Borragán Mata, Vicente** Ríos de agua viva: el Espíritu Santo: amor, poder y vida. Mi 1998, San Pablo 238 pp [Augustinus 43,152—Oldfield, John J.].
7011 *Bottini, Claudio* Lo Spirito di Dio. TS(I) sett-ott (1998) 48-51.
7012 *Cormier, Philippe* 'Je vous enverrai un Défenseur'. Com(F) 23/1-2 (1998) 116-132.
7013 *Espeja, Jesús* 'Debes profetizar de nuevo...': lo que el Espíritu dice a las iglesias. MisEx(M) 163 (1998) 18-33.
7014 **Fanuli, Antonio** Colloqui biblici, 2: per una riscoperta intelligente e amorosa dello Spirito Santo nella storia di Dio con gli uomini. Bibbia, Proposte e metodi: T 1998, Elle Di Ci 123 pp. 88-01-01075-3.
7015 **Fernandez Lago, J.** El Espíritu Santo en el mundo de la biblia. Santiago de Compostela 1998, Inst. Teológico Compostelano 205 pp. PTA1.500 [Studium 38,523s—López, L.].
7016 *Ferraro, Giuseppe* Lo Spirito Santo e la proclamazione della parola di Dio. RPLi 206 (1998) 51-56.
7017 **González, Carlos Ignacio** El Espíritu del Señor que da la vida: teología del Espíritu santo. 1997, ⇒13,7375. ᴿRTLi 32/1-2 (1998) 227-228 (*Bambarén, Luis A.*).
7018 *Helewa, Giovanni* Un fiume di acqua viva dal trono di Dio e dell'agnello. RVS 52 (1998) 121-132.
7019 *Kavunkal, Jacob* Neo-Pentecostalism: a missionary reading. VJTR 62 (1998) 407-422.
7020 **Keener, Craig S.** The Spirit in the gospels and Acts. 1997 ⇒13,7380. ᴿTrinJ 19 (1998) 235-238 (*Bayer, Hans F.*).
7021 *Krieger, Klaus-Stefan* Der Heilige Geist bei Lukas und Johannes. AnzSS 107 (1998) 466-471.
7022 **Manns, Fr.** Là où est l'Esprit, là est la liberté. Vivre la parole: P 1998, Médiaspaul 223 pp. FF125.
7023 *Martínez, Daniel* El artesano: el Espíritu Santo en la biblia. Soleriana 10 (1998) 145-171.
7024 *Meagher, P.M.* The Easter Spirit;
7025 Pentecost Spirit: to witness;
7026 The Spirit, Lent and a new way of being Church. VJTR 62 (1998) 181-185/273-279/119-123.
7027 **Minguet Mico, José** El Espíritu Santo según San Pablo. 1997 ⇒13,6173. ᴿAnVal 24 (1998) 253-255 (*Arnau-García, Ramón*).

7028 *Moule, C.F.D.* The Holy Spirit and scripture <1981>;
7029 The Holy Spirit in the scriptures <1971>. Forgiveness. 1998 ⇒180. 211-224/119-131.
7030 **Naldini, Mario** Tempi dello spirito: voci dei padri. Letture patristiche 6: F 1998, Nardini 132 pp. 88-10-42038-1.
7031 *Peixoto, João da Silva* O Espírito Santo na oração da igreja. Theologica 33 (1998) 77-104.
7032 **Pons, Guillermo** El Espíritu Santo en los Padres de la iglesia. Textos Patrísticos: Mi 1998, Ciudad N 156 pp. 84-89651-37-X. Bibl.
7033 **Ravasi, Gianfranco** Leggere la bibbia nello Spirito: ciclo di conferenze tenute al Centro culturale S. Fedele di Milano. Conversazioni bibliche: Bo 1998, EDB Bibl. 119 pp. 88-10-70963-2;
7034 Lo Spirito Santo nelle scritture: ciclo di conferenze tenute al Centro Culturale S. Fedele di Milano. Conversazioni bibliche: Bo 1998, EDB 147 pp. 88-10-70964-0. Bibl.
7035 **Rivas, Luis Heriberto** El Espíritu Santo en las Sagradas Escrituras. BA 1998, Lumen 128 pp. [R]Revista de Teología 35 (1998) 57 (*Castiglioni, Mario*).
7036 *Rogelio Bustos, J.* La ley del Espíritu, experiencia de plenitud y consumación de la ley antigua: acercamiento ético-bíblico. RTLi 32/1-2 (1998) 23-42 Sum. 23.
7037 *Rota Scalabrini, Patrizio* Dal Giordano al Calvario, condotto dallo Spirito. RPLi 206 (1998) 3-11.
7038 **Schürmann, Heinz** Duch daje zycie: pomoc w medytacji i modlitwie [Der Geist macht lebendig]. Poznan 1998, Ksiegarnia Sw. Wojciecha 126 pp. 83-7015-433-6. P.
7039 **Solivan, Samuel** The spirit, pathos and liberation: toward an Hispanic pentecostal theology. Journal of Pentecostal Theology. Supplement series 14: Shf 1998, Academic 160 pp. 1-85075-942-1. Bibl.
7040 [E]**Tanzarella, Sergio** La personalità dello Spirito Santo: in dialogo con Bernard Sesboüé. RdT Library 4: CinB 1998, San Paolo 409 pp. 88-215-3897-4.
7041 *Tábet, Miguel Ángel* Lo Spirito Santo, testimone di Gesù. Annales theologici 12/1 (1998) 3-34.
7042 **Turner, Max** The Holy Spirit and spiritual gifts: then and now. 1996, ⇒12,7054; 13,7392. [R]EvQ 70 (1998) 287-288 (*Marshall, I. Howard*).
7043 **Wild-Wey, Thomas** Inspiration: biblische Skizzen zum Heiligen Geist: eine Einführung für Theologie und Gemeinde. Biblia et Symbiotica 17: Bonn 1998, Witterschlick 99 pp. DM25. 3-932829-02-6 [ThZ 56,282—Weber, Beat].
7044 *Woodcock, Eldon* The seal of the Holy Spirit. BS 155 (1998) 139-163.

H5.6 *Spiritus et Filius;* 'Spirit-Christology'

7045 *Bordoni, Marcello* Lo Spirito Santo nel mistero della croce. La Sapienza della Croce 13/1 (1998) 5-16.
7046 **Dunn, James D.G.** The Christ and the Spirit: 1. christology; 2. pneumatology. E 1998, Clark xix; 462; xvi; 382 pp. £20. 0-567-08631-3; -2-1.

7047 **Durrwell, François-Xavier** Jésus, Fils de Dieu dans l'Esprit-Saint. CJJC 71: 1997 ⇒13,7401. ᴿRThom 98 (1998) 471-473 (*Emery, Gilles*).
7048 *Forte, Bruno* El Espíritu Santo y Jesús de Nazaret. ScrTh 30 (1998) 813-829.
7049 *Gelabert, Martín* Cristo presente por el Espíritu en la comunidad de los discípulos (repercusiones para la vida consagrada). TE 42 (1998) 199-212.
7050 *Hahn, Eberhard* 'Il vous fera accéder à la vérité tout entière': sur la relation entre la christologie et la pneumatologie. Hokhma 69 (1998) 1-13.
7051 *Marchesi, Giovanni* Lo Spirito Santo e Gesù il Cristo. CivCatt 149/3 (1998) 351-364.
7052 *Moriconi, B.* Lo Spirito e il Cristo. RVS 52 (1998) 376-396.
7053 **Pixley, Jorge V.** Vida no Espírito: o projeto messiânico de Jesus depois da ressurreição. 1997 ⇒13,7403. ᴷPerTeol 30 (1998) 306-309 (*Konings, Johan*).

H5.7 *Ssma Trinitas—* **The Holy Trinity**

7054 *Bordoni, Marcello* Cristologia e pneumatologia nel contesto trinitario: approccio biblico-sistematico. MF 98 (1998) 559-602.
7055 *Viviano, Benedict Thomas* The Trinity in the Old Testament: from Daniel 7:13-14 to Matt 28:19. ThZ 54 (1998) 193-209.

H5.8 *Regnum messianicum, Filius hominis—* **Messianic kingdom, Son of Man**

7056 *Brooks, James A.* The Kingdom of God in the New Testament. SWJT 40/2 (1998) 21-37.
7057 *Buth, Randall* A more complete Semitic background for בר-אנשא, 'son of man'. The function of scripture. 1998 ⇒236. 176-189.
7058 *Clines, David J.A.* Ecce vir, or, gendering the son of man. Biblical studies. JSOT.S 266: 1998 ⇒380. 352-375.
7059 *Cunz, Martin* Il rispetto dell'altro, mistero dell'epoca messianica. Studi Fatti Ricerche 83 (1998) 3-5.
7060 *Galot, Jean* Il Figlio dell'uomo. CivCatt 149/3 (1998) 227-238.
7061 **Harvey, Andrew** Son of man: the mystical path to Christ. NY 1998, Tarcher xix; 299 pp. 0-87477-912-X. Photographs by *Eryk Hanut*.
7062 **Mateos, Juan; Camacho, Fernando** El hijo del hombre: hacia la plenitud humana. En los orígines del cristianismo 9: 1995, ⇒11/2,3662; 13,7418. ᴿCarthaginensia 14 (1998) 222-223 (*Sanz Valdivieso, R.*); Gr. 79 (1998) 182-183 (*Marconi, Gilberto*).
7063 *Moule, C.F.D.* 'The Son of Man': some of the facts. Forgiveness. 1998 <1995> ⇒180. 205-207.
7064 *Ramos, Felipe F.* La 'figura' del Hijo del hombre. NatGrac 45/1 (1998) 107-135;
7065 El Hijo del hombre y el reino. StLeg 39 (1998) 89-119.
7066 **Schenk, Wolfgang** Das biographische Ich-Idiom 'Menschensohn' in den frühen Jesus-Biographien. FRLANT 177: 1997 ⇒13,7421. ᴿBZ 42 (1998) 261-264 (*Dormeyer, Detlev*).

7067 **Schrupp, Ernst** Israel und der Messias: Versöhnung durch Jesus Christus in endzeitlicher Perspektive. 1997 ⇒13,7422. ᴿLM 37/8 (1998) 45 (*Bergler, Siegfried*).

7068 *Slater, Thomas B.* 'Comparisons and the son of man'. BiBh 24 (1998) 67-78.

7069 *Theobald, Christoph* Le messianisme chrétien: une manière de s'introduire dans le processus de mondialisation. RSR 86 (1998) 77-98.

H6.1 *Creatio, sabbatum NT*; The Creation [⇒E1.6]

7070 *Barr, James* Greek culture and the question of natural theology. ᶠBᴇᴛᴢ, H. 1998 ⇒10. 5-19.

7071 **Corina, Rocco Aldo** L'universale bellezza dell'anima creatrice: l'affascinante suggestivo misterioso viaggio dell'uomo nelle meraviglie dell'immenso bene metafisico. Foggia 1998, Bastogi 94 pp. 88-8185-112-1. Bibl.

7072 ᴱ**Delver, J.A.** Van zondag naar sabbat: een dagboek bij de Schrift in het perspectief van kerk en Israël. 1997 ⇒13,7428. ᴿITBT 6/3 (1998) 34 (*Stroes, Herman*).

7073 *Kaiser, Jürgen* Sabbat IV: Sabbat im Christentum / Sabbatianismus. TRE 29. 1998 ⇒501. 528-533.

7074 *Lieggi, Jean Paul* Dies Christi: la resurrezione. Presenza Pastorale 68 (1998) 227-244.

7075 **Minear, Paul S.** Christians and the new creation: Genesis motifs in the New Testament. 1994 ⇒10,1645... 12,1351. ᴿEvQ 70 (1998) 66-67 (*Vadala, J. Gregory*).

7076 *Oberforcher, Robert* Verheißung des Lebens: die biophile Grundhaltung der biblischen Offenbarung. Gott finden. 1998 ⇒304. 115-135.

7077 **Russell, David Michael** The "new heavens and new earth": hope for the creation in Jewish apocalyptic and the New Testament. 1996 ⇒12,7087. ᴿCBQ 60 (1998) 586-587 (*Okoye, James C.*); JThS 49 (1998) 273-275 (*Hubbard, Moyer*).

7078 *Schaller, Berndt* Sabbat III: Neues Testament. TRE 29. 1998 ⇒501. 525-527.

7079 *Schlosser, Jacques* La création dans la tradition des *Logia*. Jésus de Nazareth. 1998 ⇒253. 319-348.

7080 **So, Ky-Chun** The Sabbath controversy of Jesus: between Jewish Law and the Gentile mission. ᴰClaremont 1998, 209 pp.

7081 *Stefani, Piero* Il sabato ebraico e la domenica cristiana. Festa e bibbia. 1998 ⇒403. 71-91.

7082 **Talstra, Eep** Een roostervrije dag: vrije wandeling langs teksten en ervaringen. Kampen 1998, Kok 123 pp. ƒ30. 90-24209-396-0 [Str. 65,953—Beentjes, Panc].

H6.3 *Fides, veritas in NT*—Faith and truth

7083 **Ansaldi, Jean** Dire la foi aujourd'hui: petit traité de la vie chrétienne. Poliez-le-Grand 1995, Moulin 109 pp. ᴿEstB 56 (1998) 565-566 (*Asenjo, J.*).

7084 **Buber, Martin** Due tipi de fede: fede ebraica e fede cristiana. ᵀ*Sorrentino, S.* Classici del pensiero cristiano 11: CinB 1995, San Paolo

284 pp. L38.000. 88-215-2980-0. [R]Hum(B) 53 (1998) 574-575 (*Ragazzi, Cesare*); RSEc 15 (1997) 135-136 (*Morandini, Simone*).

7085 **Burchard, Christoph** Formen der Vermittlung christlichen Glaubens im Neuen Testament: Beobachtungen anhand von κήρυγμα, μαρτυρία und verwandten Wörtern. Studien NT. WUNT 107: 1998 <1978> ⇒140. 265-292.

7086 **Hernández Ruiz, Justo** La fe y sus tres etapas: bíblica-eclesiástica-racional. Soria n.d., author 200 + 14 pp. [R]StOv 26 (1998) 259-260 (*Recio Garcia, Tomás*).

7087 *Honecker, Martin* Das Problem des Fundamentalismus und das Fundament des Glaubens. [F]KLEIN, G. 1998 ⇒52. 273-284.

7088 *Marconi, Gilberto* La fede nelle lettere di Gc, 1-2 Pt e Gd. La fede nella bibbia. DSBP 21: 1998 ⇒224. 208-216.

7089 **Maris, J.W.** Geloof en schriftgezag. Apeldoornse Studies 36: Apeldoorn 1998, Theologische Universiteit 54 pp. ƒ17.50 [GThT 98,138].

7090 *Panimolle, Salvatore A.* Credo, Signore; aumenta la mia fede!. La fede nella bibbia. DSBP 21: 1998 ⇒224. 7-10.

7091 **Ranke-Heinemann, U.** No y amén: invitación a la duda. M 1998, Trotta 315 pp [EstAg 33,399—Marcos, T.].

7092 **Vögtle, Anton** Unnötige Glaubensbarrieren: neutestamentliche Texte und ihre Glaubensaussagen. [E]*Diebold-Scheurmann, Carola*. SBS 174: Stu 1998, Katholisches Bibelwerk 159 pp. DM41.80. 3-460-04741-0.

7093 **Wallis, Ian G.** The faith of Jesus Christ in early christian traditions. MSSNTS 84: 1995 ⇒11/2,2218... 13,7453. [R]EstB 56 (1998) 559-562 (*Rodríguez-Ruiz, M.*).

H7.0 **Soteriologia NT**

7094 *Bray, Gerald* Justification: the reformers and recent New Testament scholarship. Luther Digest 6 (1998) 102-107 Sum. of Churchman 109/2 (1995) 102-56.

7095 *Burchard, Christoph* Nicht aus Werken des Gesetzes gerecht, sondern aus Glauben an Jesus Christus—seit wann?. Studien NT. WUNT 107: 1998 <1996> ⇒140. 230-240.

7096 *Fitzmyer, Joseph A.* Alonso Schökel and δικαιοσύνη Θεοῦ. EstB 56 (1998) 107-109.

7097 **Heyer, C.J. den** Jesus and the doctrine of atonement: biblical notes on a controversial topic. L 1998, SCM xi; 144 pp. 0-334-02733-0.

7098 [E]**Jüngel, Eberhard** Zur Rechtfertigungslehre. ZThK.B 10: Tü 1998, Mohr (4) 279 pp. 3-16-147090-7.

7099 *Klein, Hans* Rechtfertigung aus Glauben als Ergänzung der Rechtfertigung durch das Gesetz. [F]SCHRAGE, W. 1998 ⇒101. 155-164.

7100 *Lange, Günter* Stellvertretende Sühne: ein Bild oder das Bild vom Tode Jesu?: Günter Lange im Gespräch mit Hermann-Josef Lauter und Franz-Josef Nocke. KatBl 123 (1998) 99-105.

7101 *Löser, Werner* Jetzt aber seid ihr Gottes Volk" (1 Petr 2,10): Rechtfertigung und sakramentale Kirche. ThPh 73 (1998) 321-333.

7102 *Merklein, Helmut* Der Sühnetod Jesu nach dem Zeugnis des Neuen Testaments. Studien zu Jesus und Paulus II. WUNT 105: 1998 <1990> ⇒176. 31-59.

7103 *Nocke, Franz-Josef* Jesus von Nazaret—erlöstes und erlösendes Leben. KatBl 123 (1998) 91-92.
7104 *O'Collins, Gerald* Jesus Christ the liberator: in the context of human progress. StMiss 47 (1998) 21-35.
7105 **Pasquariello, Ronald D.** Jesus and the message of love. St. Joseph, Mich. 1998, Cosmic Concepts ix; 177 pp. 0-9620507-7-6 [NThAR 2000,124].
7106 **Ray, Darby Kathleen** Deceiving the devil: atonement, abuse, and ransom. Cleveland 1998, Pilgrim x; 165 pp. $16.
7107 *Rüegger, Heinz* Ökumenische Erwägungen im Zusammenhang mit der "Gemeinsamen Erklärung zur Rechtfertigungslehre". US 53 (1998) 57-72.
7108 *Scheffczyk, Leo* Die "Gemeinsame Erklärung zur Rechtfertigungslehre" und die Norm des Glaubens, Teil II. Theologisches 28 (1998) 125-132.
7109 *Schürmann, Heinz* Jesu stellvertretender Sühnetod: ein Versuch, annähernd zu verstehen. KatBl 123 (1998) 82-83.
7110 *Stubenrauch, Bertram* Konsens ohne Einigkeit?: Versöhnungshilfen im neuentbrannten Streit um die Rechtfertigung. TThZ 107 (1998) 230-242.
7111 **Stuhlmacher, Peter** Was geschah auf Golgatha?: zur Heilsbedeutung von Kreuz, Tod und Auferweckung Jesu. Calwer Taschenbibliothek 71: Stu 1998, Calwer 94 pp. 3-7668-3563-7.
7112 *Theobald, Michael* Rechtfertigung und Ekklesiologie nach Paulus: Anmerkungen zur "Gemeinsamen Erklärung zur Rechtfertigungslehre". ZThK 95 (1998) 103-117.
7113 **Zahl, Paul Francis Matthew** Die Rechtfertigungslehre Ernst Käsemanns. CThM.ST 13: 1996 ⇒12,7123. [R]ThLZ 123 (1998) 155-157 (*Landmesser, Christof*).

H7.2 *Crux, sacrificium*; **The Cross, the nature of sacrifice** [⇒E3.4]

7114 *Anderwald, Andrzej* Krzyż jako znak wiarygodności chrześcijaństwa [La croix comme signe de la credibilité chrétienne]. AtK 131 (1998) 321-322.
7115 **Baudler, Georg** Das Kreuz: Geschichte und Bedeutung. 1997 ⇒13, 7483. [R]ThG 41/1 (1998) 67-69 (*Häring, Bernhard*).
7116 **Bestul, Thomas H.** Texts of the Passion: Latin devotional literature and medieval society. 1996, ⇒12,7129. [R]ChH 67/1 (1998) 137-138 (*Blastic, Michael W.*); Spec. 73 (1998) 1111-1113 (*Sticca, Sandro*).
7117 *Blenkinsopp, Joseph* Sacrifice, social maintenance and the non-ordination of women. NBl 79 (1998) 137-145.
7118 *Cobb, Donald* Les deux natures du Christ au Calvaire. Hokhma 67 (1998) 19-44 Sum., rés. 19.
7119 *Kiecker, James G.* 'Theologia crucis et theologia gloriae': the development of LUTHER's theology of the cross. Luther Digest 6 (1998) 114-16 Sum. of WLQ 92/3 (1995) 179-188.
7120 **Levenson, Jon D.** The death and resurrection of the beloved son: the transformation of sacrifice in Judaism and christianity. 1993 ⇒9,7998... 12,7138. [R]REJ 157 (1998) 409-411 (*Ciunci, Jennifer*).
7121 *Moule, C.F.D.* The sacrifice of Christ <1956> ;

7122 The scope of the death of Christ <1977>. Forgiveness. 1998 ⇒180. 135-176/3-18.
7123 *Murphy, George L.* The theology of the cross and God's work in the world. Zygon 33 (1998) 221-231 Sum. 221.
7124 *Niemand, Christoph* Jesus Tod—ein Opfertod?. ThPQ 146 (1998) 115-124.
7125 *Prieur, Jean-Marc* La dimension cosmique de la crucifixion du Christ et de la croix dans la littérature chrétienne ancienne. RHPhR 78/2 (1998) 39-56.
7126 *Schillebeeckx, Edward* Das historische Scheitern Jesu am Kreuz und Gottes "Trotzdem": Auferstehung und Sendung des Heiligen Geistes, der weht, wo er will. KatBl 123 (1998) 93-98.
7127 *Vouga, François* L'attrait du christianisme primitif dans le monde antique. RThPh 130 (1998) 257-268.

H7.4 *Sacramenta, gratia*

7128 **Booth, Robert R.** Children of the promise: the biblical case for infant baptism. Darlington, UK 1995, Evangelical 206 pp. $10. 0-87552-167-5. ᴿCTJ 32/1 (1997) 176-177 (*Van Dyk, Wilbert M.*).
7129 **Brito Guimarães, Pedro** Os sacramentos como atos eclesiais e proféticos: um contributo ao coneito dogmático de sacramento à luz da exegese contemporânea. TGr.T 46: R 1998, E.P.U.G. 448 pp. €23,24. 88-7652-808-3.
7130 *Cordeiro, José Leão* O sacramento da penitência, (re)conversão ao a-mor do Pai. Bib(L) 7/7 (1998) 85-97.
7131 **Frettlöh, Magdalene L.** Theologie des Segens: biblische und dog-matische Wahrnehmungen. Mü 1998, Kaiser 436 pp. 3-579-00394-1. Bibl.
7132 **Hartman, Lars** Auf den Namen des Herrn Jesus: die Taufe in den neutestamentlichen Schriften. SBS 148: 1992 ⇒9,8039. ᴿITS 35/1 (1998) 91-92 (*Legrand, L.*).
7133 **Kleinschmidt, Frank** Ehefragen im Neuen Testament: Ehe, Ehelosigkeit, Ehescheidung, Verheiratung Verwitweter und Geschie-dener im Neuen Testament. ARGU 7: Fra 1998, Lang 302 pp. DM89. 3-631-33001-4. Diss. Göttingen 1997.
7134 **Kranemann, Benedikt** Sakramentliche Liturgie im Bistum Münster: eine Untersuchung handschriftlicher und gedruckter Ritualien und der liturgischen Formulare vom 16. bis zum 20. Jahrhundert. LWQF 83: Müns 1998, Aschendorff xxx; 360 pp. 3-402-04061-1. Bibl.
7135 *Logan, Alastair H.B.* Post-baptismal chrismation in Syria: the evidence of IGNATIUS, the Didache and the Apostolic Constitutions. JThS 49 (1998) 92-108.
7136 **Lona, Horacio E.** Gracia y comunidad de salvación: el fundamento bíblico. Estudios Proyecto 21: BA 1998, Salesiano 188 pp. 950-858-020-8 [ActBib 71,32—O'Callaghan, J.].
7137 **Sorci, Pietro** La festa del perdono: la parola di Dio nel sacramento della riconciliazione. Interpretare la Bibbia oggi. 4. Leggere la Bibia nella liturgia 4: Brescia 1998, Queriniana 110 pp. 88-399-2480-9. Bibl.
7138 **Valle, Felipe del** Los siete sacramentos y su fundamento biblico. Santiago 1998, San Pablo 36 pp [Revista católica 100,84—Cortez C., Juan Carlos].

7139   **Vogel, Arthur A.** Radical christianity and the flesh of Jesus: the
       roots of eucharistic living. 1995, ⇒11/1,3208; 13,7526. ᴿVJTR 62
       (1998) 524-526 (*Gonsalves, Francis*).
7140   *Vollmer, Jochen* Ist die Taufe von Unmündigen schriftgemäß?. EvTh
       58 (1998) 332-350.

H7.6 *Ecclesiologia, Theologia missionis, laici*—The Church

7141   *Arens, Edmund* Zwischen biblischem Tun und postmodernem Text:
       zur Aktualität des Zeugnisses. NZM 54 (1998) 81-97.
7142   *Bertacchini, Roberto* Le liste di nomi nel NT: quale valore
       ecclesiologico?. RdT 39 (1998) 93-106.
7143   *Borgen, Peder* Proselytes, conquest, and mission. Recruitment. 1998
       ⇒320. 57-77.
7144   *Bowe, Barbara E.* Reading the bible through Filipino eyes. Miss. 26
       (1998) 345-360 Sum. 345.
7145   **Brownson, James V.** Speaking the truth in love: New Testament
       resources for a missional hermeneutic. Christian mission and modern
       culture: Harrisburg, PA 1998, Trinity viii; 86 pp. 1-56338-239-3.
7146   *Burchard, Christoph* Jesus für die Welt: über das Verhältnis von
       Reich Gottes und Mission. Studien NT. WUNT 107: 1998 <1980>
       ⇒140. 51-64.
7147   *Carvalho, José Ornelas de* A igreja brota do Pentecostes: perspectiva
       neotestamentária. Theologica 33 (1998) 41-75.
7148   *Corsani, Bruno* "La chiesa" nel dialogo cattolico-luterano. ᶠMARTINI,
       C. RivBib.S 33: 1998 ⇒75. 109-114.
7149   *Dal Covolo, Enrique* Laici e laicità nei primi secoli della chiesa.
       1995, ⇒12,7183. ᴿRSLR 34 (1998) 356-61 (*Mazzucco, Clementina*).
7150   *Franks, Martha* Election, pluralism, and the missiology of scripture
       in a postmodern age. Miss. 26 (1998) 329-343 Sum. 329.
7151   *Greinacher, Norbert* Ist die Kirche noch zu retten?: die Bedeutung
       von Religion und der Sitz im Leben der institutionalisierten Kirchen
       in der säkularisierten Gesellschaft von heute. ᶠVENETZ, H. 1998
       ⇒122. 205-220.
7152   **Grelot, Pierre** Regole e tradizioni del cristianesimo primitivo.
       Piemme. Religione: CasM 1998, Piemme 381 pp. 88-384-3040-3.
7153   **Haag, Herbert** ¿Qué iglesia quería Jesús?. Barc 1998, Herder 156
       pp. ᴿBib(L) 7/7 (1998) 157-158 (*Alves, Herculano*).
7154   *Hatcher, Mark J.* Contextualizing the Creed through structured bible
       study. Miss. 26 (1998) 315-328 Sum. 315.
7155   *Kertelge, K.* From the Jüngergemeinde of Jesus to the early Christian
       church. Neotest. 32 (1998) 425-432.
7156   **Klaiber, Walter** Call and response: biblical foundations of a theol-
       ogy of evangelism. 1997 ⇒13,7555. ᴿAUSS 36 (1998) 139-141
       (*Burrill, Russell*).
7157   *Klassen, William* Normative self-definitions of Christianity in the
       New Testament. ᶠSNYDER, G. 1998 ⇒104. 91-105.
7158   *Lap-yan, Kung* Priesthood of all believers and rights of all humans.
       Jian Dao 10 (1998) 59-80 Sum. 79.
7159   ᴱ**Larkin Jr., William J.; Williams, Joel F.** Mission in the New
       Testament: an evangelical approach. ASMS 27: Mkn 1998, Orbis
       Bibl. xix; 266 pp. 1-57075-169-2.

7160 *Leonardi, Giovanni* Gesù il servo modello del servizio nella chiesa: studio della prospettiva neotestamentaria. Gesù Servo. 1998 ⇒210. 29-113.

7161 *Lips, Hermann von* New Testament aspects of ecclesiology. ThD 45 (1998) 221-225 <BThZ 13,60-70. ⇒12,7202.

7162 **Lohfink, Gerhard** Braucht Gott die Kirche?: zur Theologie des Volkes Gottes. FrB 1998, Herder 432 pp. DM39.80. 3-451-26544-3;

7163 Gottes Volksbegehren: biblische Herausforderungen. Mü 1998, Neue Stadt 267 pp. 3-87996-392-4.

7164 *Luter, A. Boyd* Israel and the nations in God's redemptive plan. Israel. 1998 ⇒6675. 283-297.

7165 *Marucci, Corrado* Spunti ecclesiologici nella fonte Q. ^FMARTINI, C. RivBib.S 33: 1998 ⇒75. 155-170.

7166 **Mora Paz, César** Biblia y pastoral. Autores 17: Bogotá 1998, CELAM 490 pp.

7167 *Müller, Klaus W.* Das Alte Testament als Rahmenbedingung für die Verkündigung des Evangeliums. em 14 (1998) 127-133.

7168 *Niederwimmer, Kurt* Kirche als Diaspora. Gesammelte Aufsätze. BZNW 90: 1998 <1981> ⇒182. 102-112.

7169 **Nobile, Marco** Ecclesiologia biblica. CSB 30: 1996 ⇒12,7207; 13,7560. ^RRivBib 46 (1998) 487-489 (*De Virgilio, Giuseppe*).

7170 *Pfürtner, Stephan H.* Wie ich mir Kirche wünsche. ^FVENETZ, H. 1998 ⇒122. 239-248.

7171 *Pivot, Maurice* Témoins du Christ ressuscité dans une église en acte d'annonce de l'évangile. Spiritus 39 (1998) 413-424.

7172 **Ramachandra, Vinoth** Gods that fail: modern idolatry and christian mission. 1996 ⇒12,7209. ^RRTR 57 (1998) 92-93 (*Mascord, Keith*).

7173 *Rivera Carrera, Norberto* La sagrada escritura en la nueva evangelización. Voces 12 (1998) 133-144.

7174 *Rossing, Barbara* Modele der Koinonia im Neuen Testament und in der Alten Kirche. LWB.D 42 (1998) 61-74.

7175 *Sänger, Dieter* Heiden—Juden—Christen: Erwägungen zu einem Aspekt frühchristlicher Missionsgeschichte. ZNW 89 (1998) 145-172.

7176 *Schürmann, Heinz* Aufbau und Struktur der neutestamentlichen Verkündigung <1949>;

7177 Auf der Suche nach dem 'Evangelisch-Katholischen'; zum Thema 'Frühkatholizismus' <1981>;

7178 Frühkatholizismus im Neuen Testament: Präliminarien zur Problemstellung <1981>. Gesammelte Beiträge. 1998 ⇒197. 65-90/191-233/183-190;

7179 Kirche als offenes System. Im Knechtsdienst Christi. 1998 <1972> ⇒198. 161-179.

7180 **Sieben, Hermann Josef** Vom Apostelkonzil zum Ersten Vatikanum: Studien zur Geschichte der Konzilsidee. KonGe.U: 1996 ⇒12,7214; 13,7569. ^RCHR 84 (1998) 701 (*Izbicki, Thomas M.*).

7181 *Sordi, Marta* L'ambiente storico culturale greco-romano della missione cristiana nel primo secolo. RstB 10/1-2 (1998) 217-229.

7182 **Steyne, Philip M.** Schritt halten mit dem Gott der Völker: Weltmission im Alten und Neuen Testament. ^T*Kloser, Bruni; Klose, Dietmar; Weber, Stefan.* Theologisches Lehr- und Studienmaterial 3: Bonn 1998, Verl. für Kultur und Wiss. 293 pp. 3-932859-05-0. Bibl. 288-293 [NThAR 2000,91].

7183 **Sugden, Chris** Seeking the Asian face of Jesus: the practice and theology of christian social witness in Indonesia and India 1974-1996. 1997 ⇒13,7571. ᴿExchange 27/3 (1998) 275-277 (*Hoekema, Alle*).

7184 *Taylor, Justin* The community of Jesus' disciples. PIBA 21 (1998) 25-32.

7185 *Van Butselaar, Jan* The gospel and culture study. Exchange 27/3 (1998) 236-247.

7186 Volk Gottes, Gemeinde und Gesellschaft. JBTh 7. 1992. ᴿThR 63 (1998) 451-452 (*Gestrich, Christof*).

7187 *Vouga, François* Die religiöse Attraktivität des frühen Christentums. ThGl 88 (1998) 26-38.

7188 **Zorn, Raymond O.** Christ triumphant: biblical perspectives on his church and kingdom. E 1997 <1962>, Banner of Truth xvi; 244 pp. £13. 0-85151-696-3 [SBET 18,215—Cartwright, Hugh M.].

H7.7 *Œcumenismus*—The ecumenical movement

7189 **Ariarajah, Wesley** La biblia y las gentes de otras religiones. Pastoral 58: Sdr 1998, Sal Terrae 120 pp. PTA1.350. 84-293-1286-2 [EE 74,616—Izuzquiza, D.].

7190 *Frankemölle, Hubert* Biblische Grundlagen einer Ökumene der Weltreligionen?. Jüdische Wurzeln. BBB 116: 1998 <1994> ⇒151. 445-456.

7191 *Heinelt, Hubert* Ökumenische Bibelarbeit: der Stern über Bethlehem (Mt 2,1-12). Lebendige Katechese 20 (1998) 79-80.

7192 **Knitter, Paul F.** Una terra, molte religioni: dialogo interreligioso e responsabilità globale. Pref. *Küng, Hans*. Teologia/Saggi: Assisi 1998, Cittadella 330 pp. 88-308-0639-0. Bibl.

7193 *Moede, Gerald F.* Seven bible studies on the unity of the church. Mid-Stream 37 (1998) 333-347.

7194 *Segalla, Giuseppe* Primo simposio fra studiosi di NT ortodossi e non ortodossi, Neamts (Romania), 4-11 settembre 1998. StPat 45 (1998) 719-728.

H7.8 **Amt**—*Ministerium ecclesiasticum*

7195 *Brovelli, Franco* Presiedere l'Eucaristia: quattro immagini bibliche. RCI 79 (1998) 380-391.

7196 **Campbell, R. Alastair** The elders: seniority within earliest christianity. 1994 ⇒11/2,4342; 12,7235. ᴿSJTh 51 (1998) 514-516 (*Clarke, Andrew D.*).

7197 ᴱ**Cattaneo, Enrico** I ministeri nella Chiesa antica: testi patristici dei primi tre secoli. 1997 ⇒13,7589. ᴿEL 112 (1998) 409-410 (*Manzi, Franco*); ScC 126 (1998) 688-690 (*Manzi, Franco*); RSLR 34 (1998) 665-666 (*Lucca, Claudia*); RdT 39 (1998) 133-135 (*Marafioti, Domenico*); CivCatt 149/1 (1998) 619-620 (*Ferraro, G.*).

7198 *Eckert, Jost* 'Ministers of the new covenant': NT perspectives on church office. ThD 45 (1998) 239-247 <TThZ 106,60-78.

7199 **Eisen, Ute E.** Amtsträgerinnen im frühen Christentum: epigraphische und literarische Studien. FKDG 61: 1996 ⇒12,7240; 13,7594. ᴿRHE

93 (1998) 486-489 (*Zeegers, Nicole*); JThS 49 (1998) 340-342 (*Downing, F. Gerald*); BZ 42 (1998) 152-155 (*Kitzberger, Ingrid*).

7200 *Gonneaud, Didier* Dans le sacerdoce d'Israël, le ministère de Jésus. NRTh 120 (1998) 18-31.

7201 **Heid, Stefan** Zölibat in der frühen Kirche: die Anfänge einer Enthaltsamkeitspflicht für Kleriker in Ost und West. 1997 ⇒13,7599 ᴿCHR 84 (1998) 523-524 (*Kelly, Joseph F.*); ThPh 73 (1998) 585-587 (*Stieben, H.J.*).

7202 **Hermans, Theo** ORIGÈNE: théologie sacrificielle du sacerdoce des chrétiens. ThH 102: 1996 ⇒12,7248; 13,7600. ᴿLTP 54 (1998) 625-626 (*Guindon, Henri-M.*)

7203 **Kaufman, Peter Ivan** Church, book, and bishop: conflict and authority in early Latin christianity. 1996 ⇒12,7251. ᴿJThS 49 (1998) 348-353 (*Maier, H.O.*).

7204 *Kirchschläger, Walter* Leiten in der Kirche: biblische Bilder aus dem Neuen Testament. LS 49 (1998) 176-180.

7205 *Leonardi, Giovanni* Cristo il servo: modello dei ministeri-servizi nella chiesa: uno sguardo alle prime comunità cristiane per un rinnovamento nel Terzo Millenio. StPat 45 (1998) 577-595;

7206 I discepoli del Gesù terreno e i ministeri nelle prime comunità: rottura o normale evoluzione?. ᶠMARTINI, C. Riv Bib.S 33: 1998 ⇒75. 455-485.

7207 *Pikaza Ibarrondo, Xabier* Carisma de Jesús, institución cristiana: evangelio y ministerio eclesial. RET 58 (1998) 345-402, 437-482. Res., sum. 345.

7208 **Schöllgen, Georg** Die Anfänge der Professionalisierung des Klerus und das kirchliche Amt in der syrischen Didaskalie. JAC.E 26: Müns 1998, Aschendorff viii; 227 pp. 3-402-08110-5.

7209 *Schürmann, Heinz* ,... und Lehrer': die geistliche Eigenart des Lehrdienstes und sein Verhältnis zu anderen geistlichen Diensten im neutestamentlichen Zeitalter <1977>;

7210 Die zwei unterschiedlichen Berufungen, Dienste und Lebensweisen im einen Presbyterium <1977>;

7211 Weltpriestertum und Rätestand: quaestiones disputandae <1984>;

7212 Rückblick auf den Ursprung: die (innere) geistliche Gestalt <1985>. Im Knechtsdienst Christi. 1998 ⇒198. 58-103/189-205/248-255/ 185-188;

7213 Lehrende in den neutestamentlichen Schriften: ihre Angewiesenheit auf andere geistliche Gaben und ihre Verwiesenheit an andere geistliche Dienste. Gesammelte Beiträge. 1998 <1987> ⇒197. 136-162.

7214 *Terbuyken, Peri* Priesteramt und Opferkult bei Juden und Christen in der Spätantike. ᶠSPEYER, W. JAC.E 28: 1998 ⇒107. 271-284.

7215 *Tergel, Alf* The Christian churches and the social order in the modern age. StTh 52 (1998) 57-68.

7216 *Vanhoye, Albert* La novità del sacerdozio di Cristo. CivCatt 149/1 (1998) 16-27.

7217 *Van Zyl, Hermie C.* The evolution of church leadership in the New Testament—a new consensus?. Neotest. 32 (1998) 585-604.

H8.0 **Oratio**, *spiritualitas personalis et publica*, **liturgia**

7218 *Andia, Ysabel de* L'onction. Com(F) 23/1-2 (1998) 54-70.

7219 *Andrés, J.F.* La oración de Jesús. EvV 40 (1998) 164-166.

7220 **Basile, Djro Djro** Parle, (Seigneur), ton serviteur écoute (1 Sam 3, 10): approche exégetico-spirituelle de l'écoute de la parole de Dieu dans la vocation de Samuel, et dans les "autres textes" de vocation de l'Ancien et du Nouveau Testament. R 1998, Teresianum 112 pp. Extr. Diss.

7221 *Beuken, Wim* "Please give me some of your son's love-fruits" (Gen 30:14): apportioning or sharing God's election?. LouvSt 23 (1998) 203-220.

7222 **Bianchi, Enzo** La parole construit la communauté. ᵀ*Bourgine, Martin.* CCist 60 (1998) 323-332.

7223 La bibbia e il messale. Città del Vaticano 1997, Vaticana CD-ROM, versione 1.21 ⇒13,457. L225.000. ᴿAng. 75/2 (1998) 284-287 (*Stancati, T.*).

7224 *Bof, Giampiero* Preghiera cristiana e preghiera del Cristo. L'uomo davanti a Dio. 1998 ⇒300. 162-183.

7225 **Bouyer, Louis** Mysterion: dal mistero alla mistica. Collana di mistica: Città del Vaticano 1998, Vaticana 356 pp. 88-209-2556-7.

7226 **Brown, Raymond Edward** Christ in the gospels of the ordinary sundays: essays on the gospel readings of the ordinary sundays in the three-year liturgical cycle. ColMn 1998, Liturgical viii; 110 pp. 0-8146-2542-8.

7227 **Burton-Christie, Douglas** La parola nel deserto: scrittura e ricerca della santità. Magnano 1998, Qiqajon 488 pp. L60.000 [CuMon 34, 465—Alexander, Max].

7228 *Buscemi, Marcello* Commento biblico alle 'sette armi spirituali' di S. CATERINA da Bologna: quinta arma: *memento mori*. StFr 95 (1998) 363-382.

7229 **Butterweck, Christel** 'Martyriumssucht' in der Alten Kirche?: Studien zur Darstellung und Deutung frühchristlicher Martyrien. BHTh 87: 1995 ⇒12,9431. ᴿJAC 41 (1998) 241-242 (*Seeliger, Hans Reinhard*).

7230 *Buzetti, Carlo* Quando, come e dove i cristiani traducono la bibbia insieme. RivLi 85 (1998) 951-961.

7231 *Coda, Piero* La preghiera trinitaria e l'unità dei discepoli. L'uomo davanti a Dio. 1998 ⇒300. 139-161.

7232 *Costa, Eugenio* Tradurre la bibbia per la liturgia. RivLi 85 (1998) 943-950.

7233 **Cullmann, Oscar** Das Gebet im Neuen Testament: zugleich Versuch einer vom Neuen Testament aus zu erteilenden Antwort auf heutige Fragen. ²1997 <1994> ⇒13,7632. ᴿÖR 47/1 (1998) 152-153 (*Held, Heinz Joachim*);

7234 La preghiera nel Nuovo Testamento: una risposta alle domande odierne. PBT 39: 1995 ⇒11/2,4432... 13,7630. ᴿRStRel 12 (1998) 530-531 (*Lorusso, Giacomo*).

7235 *Cuva, Armando* Il lezionario paolino 'maggiore' della liturgia delle ore. ᶠHERIBAN J. 1998 ⇒41. 427-442.

7236 *Demoustier, Adrien* Ejercicios espirituales y culturas: ante la sagrada escritura. Manresa 70 (1998) 111-127 Som. 111.

7237 *Díaz Mateos, Manuel* 'No despreciar la profecía': Espíritu, profecía y vida religiosa. RTLi 32/1-2 (1998) 121-134 Sum. 121.

7238 *Eigenmann, Urs* Geist in Wirklichkeit: Aspekte einer Reich-Gottes-Spiritualität und -Mystik. ᶠVENETZ, H. 1998 ⇒122. 119-127.

7239 *Estévez, Elisa* 'No temas: yo estoy contigo'. SalTer 86 (1998) 699-709.

7240 **Fenske, Wolfgang** "Und wenn ihr betet..." (Mt. 6,5): Gebete in der zwischenmenschlichen Kommunikation der Antike als Ausdruck der Frömmigkeit. StUNT 21: 1997 ⇒13,7633. ᴿJThS 49 (1998) 802-804 (*Gelston, A.*); JAC 41 (1998) 236-238 (*Frenschkowski, Marco*); ThLZ 123 (1998) 59-60 (*Rebell, Walter*).

7241 *Festorazzi, Franco* La lettura personale e comunitaria della bibbia: il contributo della nuova traduzione. La traduzione. 1998 ⇒222. 175-180.

7242 **Finn, Thomas M.** From death to rebirth: ritual and conversion in antiquity. 1997 ⇒13,7634. ᴿChH 67/1 (1998) 114-116 (*Francis, James A.*).

7243 *Finotto, Albino* Una vita consegnata a Cristo e alla chiesa: pastori secondo il cuore di Dio. Presbyteri 32/3 (1998) 205-209.

7244 **Fischer, Georg; Hasitschka, Martin** Sulla tua parola: vocazione e sequela nella bibbia. Bibbia e preghiera 32: R 1998, AdP 158 pp. 88-7357-177-8.

7245 *Gerhards, Albert* Liturgie und Bild—Zumutung und Chancen einer wechselhaften Beziehung. JBTh 13 (1998) 281-291.

7246 **Habtemichael-Kidane** L'ufficio divino della Chiesa Etiopica: studio storico-critico con particolare riferimento alle ore cattedrali. OCA 257: R 1998, Pontificio Istituto Orientale 399 pp. 88-7210-320-7.

7247 *Hasitschka, Martin* "Um Mitternacht priesen sie Gott in Lobliedern" (Apg 16,25): Lobpreis Gottes in Leidenssituationen als ein Merkmal biblischer Spiritualität. Gott finden. 1998 ⇒304. 49-59.

7248 *Hermans, Jo* Das Martyrium: ein Vorbild christlicher Tapferkeit. IKaZ 27 (1998) 395-401.

7249 *Herzig, Anneliese* Vom dreifaltigen Gott in gleicher Weise angesprochen und berufen: Frauen und Männer im Neuen Testament. Jetzt 3 (1998) 23-26.

7250 *Horbury, William* The cult of Christ and the cult of the saints. NTS 44 (1998) 444-469.

7251 **Jeggle-Merz, Birgit** Erneuerung der Kirche aus dem Geist der Liturgie: der Pastoralliturgiker Athanasius WINTERSIG / Ludwig A. WINTERSWYL. LWQF 84: Müns 1998, Aschendorff 449 pp. 3-402-0406-3-8. Bibl.

7252 *Joest, Christoph* "Wenn Du vollkommen sein willst ..." (Mk 19,21): die Bibel—der Mutterboden des frühen Mönchtums. EuA 74 (1998) 357-372.

7253 **John, Frère di Taizé** L'avventura della santità: fondamenti biblici e prospettive attuali. Padova 1998, EMP 184 pp. L20.000 [PalCl 77, 949—Lavarda, Girolamo].

7254 *Kirchschläger, Walter* Begründung und Formen des liturgischen Leitungsdienstes in den Schriften des Neuen Testaments. Wie weit trägt?. 1998 ⇒305. 20-45;

7255 Die liturgische Versammlung: eine neutestamentliche Bestandsaufnahme. HlD 52 (1998) 11-24.

7256 **Koenig, John** Rediscovering New Testament prayer: boldness and blessing in the name of Jesus. Harrisburg, PA 1998 <1992>, Morehouse ix; 203 pp. $15 [AThR 81,483s—Smith, James V.].

7257 *Korherr, Edgar Josef* Die Bibel als Gebetsschule: Gebetserziehung: Thesen und Tips (6). Entschluss 53/6 (1998) 29.

7258   *Kourie, Celia* Mysticism: gift for the church. Neotest. 32 (1998) 433-457.
7259   *Kraft, Sigisbert* Die Versammlung der Gläubigen und der ökumenische Lernprozeß. US 53 (1998) 40-56.
7260   **Lang, Bernhard** Sacred games: a history of christian worship. 1997 ⇒13,7682. ᴿCHR 84 (1998) 702-703 (*Baldovin, John F.*); JThS 49 (1998) 498-500 (*Bradshaw, Paul F.*);
7261   Heiliges Spiel: eine Geschichte des christlichen Gottesdienstes. Mü 1998, Beck 575 pp. DM78. 3-406-44075-4. 60 ill. [ZKTh 121,339s—Meyer, Hans Bernhard].
7262   *Lorenzo Leal, N.J.* La palabra de Dios en la liturgia hispano-mozárabe. Actas... IX Jornadas Bíblicas. 1998 ⇒376. 145-154.
7263   *Löffler, Irene* "Auch die Mutter war überaus bewundernswert, und sie hat es verdient, daß man sich an sie mit Hochachtung erinnert:" Frauen in der Perikopenordnung—eine Stellungnahme aus der Sicht der Frauenseelsorge. BiLi 71 (1998) 245-251.
7264   *Maggioni, Bruno* Il discernimento nei vangeli. Servitium 32 (1998) 467-472.
7265   *Malipurathu, Thomas* Formation from a biblical perspective. VSVD 39 (1998) 339-356.
7266   *Martini, Carlo Maria* Lectio divina en de weg van een roeping ᵀ*Flohr, Huub.* Cardoner 17 (1998) 82-88.
7267   *Matos, Henrique C.J.* Lectura orante de la biblia: fuente de renovación espiritual. Alternativas 5/11-12 (1998) 113-128 [ThIK 21/1,71].
7268   *Niederwimmer, Kurt* Nachfolge Jesu nach dem Neuen Testament. Gesammelte Aufsätze. BZNW 90: 1998 <1987> ⇒182. 163-184.
7269   **Obermann, Andreas** An Gottes Segen ist allen gelegen: eine Untersuchung zum Segen im Neuen Testament: mit einem Ausblick auf kirchliches Segenshandeln heute. BThSt 37: Neuk 1998, Neuk 142 pp. 3-7887-1705-X. Bibl.
7270   **O'Donnell, Desmond; Mohen, Maureen** Praying the good news: a rich resource of psalmed prayers from the New Testament. L 1998, Fount xv; 200 pp. £10. ᴿDoLi 48 (1998) 255-256 (*Fagan, Seán*).
7271   **O'Hara, Tom** At home with Jesus: contemplation and scripture. Richmond 1998, Aurora 136 pp. AUS$17. 1-86355-061-5. ᴿACR 75 (1998) 498-499 (*Richardson, Donald*).
7272   **Old, Hughes O.** The reading and preaching of the scriptures in the worship of the christian church: 1, the biblical period. GR 1998, Eerdmans x; 383 pp. $35. 0-8028-4356-5;
7273   2, the patristic age. GR 1998, Eerdmans viii; 481 pp. $42. 0-8028-4357-3.
7274   *Overath, Joseph* Zölibat und Weizenkorn: eine biblische Besinnung. Theologisches 28 (1998) 293-300.
7275   *Paz, Miguel* El origen de las formas del culto cristiano según Odo CASEL. Alpha Omega 1 (1998) 474-495 Sum. 495.
7276   **Race, Marianne; Brink, Laurie** In this place: reflections on the land of the gospels for the liturgical cycles. ColMn 1998, Liturgical xviii; 219 pp. $20. 0-8146-2491-X [BiTod 37,60—Senior, Donald].
7277   **Radeck, Heike** Ignatianische Exerzitien und Bibliodrama: ein hermeneutischer Strukturvergleich. Praktische Theologie heute 35: Stu 1998, Kohlhammer 173 pp. DM39.80. 3-17-015277-7. Diss. Marburg [ThLZ 125,949s—Keßler, Hildrun].

7278 *Ribera-Mariné, Ramon* La pregària com a diàleg entre l'home i Déu, amb el rerefons de la Bíblia. Qüestions de Vida Cristiana 190 (1998) 94-100.

7279 *Rivera, Enrique* Sentido cristiano del tiempo. EvV 40/2 (1998) 56-57.

7280 *Robles, Constantino* El seguimento de Jesús. StLeg 39 (1998) 153-170.

7281 *Rouwhorst, Gerard* Liturgical time and space in early christianity in light of their Jewish background. Sanctity of time. 1998 ⇒303. 265-284.

7282 *Schäffer, Wilhelm* "Wort Gottes—heute für mich": Hinweise für die persönliche Schriftbetrachtung. Lebendige Katechese 20 (1998) 31-34.

7283 **Schlatter, Adolf** Die Gründe der christlichen Gewißheit: das Gebet. TVG: Orientierung: Wu 1998, Brockhaus 95 pp. 3-7655-9078-9.

7284 *Schürmann, Heinz* Ignatianische Exerzitien im Dienste weltpriesterlicher Spiritualität. LebZeug 53 (1998) 88-114.

7285 **Serna, Eduardo de la** Diálogo entre la biblia y TERESA de Lisieux: preguntas desde América Latina. R 1998, Pont. Fac. Teresianum xiv; 103 pp. Pars diss.; Bibl.

7286 *Sinoir, Michel* Das Beten auf den Knien im Licht der Heiligen Schrift. Una Voce-Korrespondenz 28 (1998) 147-166, 187-199.

7287 *Sodi, Manlio* Annunciare la parola di Dio nei 'tempi forti' dell'anno liturgico. ᶠHERIBAN J. 1998 ⇒41. 443-469.

7288 *Van der Horst, Pieter Sortes*: sacred books as instant oracles in late antiquity. Use of sacred books. 1998 ⇒263. 143-173.

7289 **Vanhoye, Albert** Pedro y Pablo. M 1998, PPC 245 pp. 84-288-1489-9.

7290 *Varickasseril, Jose* A woman who resembles Jesus in his public ministry. IMR 20/3 (1998) 53-61 [Theresa of Calcutta].

7291 **Velamparampil, Cyrus** The celebration of the liturgy of the word in the Syro-Malabar qurbana: a biblico-theological analysis. OIRSI 194: Kottayam 1997, Pont. Oriental Institute of Religious Studies 350 pp. [MD 223,151s—Dalmais, Irénée-Henri].

7292 *Vella, Alexander* The bible in the writings of St. THÉRÈSE of the Child Jesus. Carmel 37/1-2 (1998) 73-82.

7293 **Vian, Itamar; Colombo, Aldo** O evangelho no cotidiano. São Paulo 1998, Paulus 223 pp [REB 58,1008].

7294 **Weber, Hans-Ruedi** Vivre à l'image du Christ. ᵀMonsarat, Jean-Pierre. P 1998, Les Bergers 90 pp. FF59. 2-85304-134-4. Introd. de *Paul Keller* [RHPhR 80,311—Pfrimmer, Th.].

7295 **Williams, Bill** Naked before God: the return of a broken disciple. Harrisburg, PA 1998, Morehouse xiii; 327 pp. $20 [AThR 81,523s —Wallace, Catherine M.].

7296 **Wünsche, Peter** Kathedralliturgie zwischen Tradition und Wandel: zur mittelalterlichen Geschichte der Bamberger Domliturgie im Bereich des Triduum Sacrum. LWQF 80: Müns 1998, Aschendorff xxxii; 494 pp. 3-402-04059-X. Bibl.

7297 *Yamb, Gervais* Le devenir chrétien comme vocation: une réflexion théologique et spirituelle sur la liberté humaine face à Jésus-Christ. Telema 96 (1998) 17-26.

7298 *Young, Robin Darling* Ancient culture and the shape of early christian discipleship. Com(US) 25/1 (1998) 151-159.

H8.2 Theologia moralis NT

7299 **Anderson, J. Kerby** Moral dilemmas: biblical perspectives on contemporary ethical issues. Nv 1998, Word 263 pp [Faith & Mission 17/2,92s—Magnuson, Kenneth T.].

7300 *Bockmuehl, Markus* Jewish and christian public ethics in the early Roman empire. Tolerance. 1998 ⇒440. 342-355.

7301 *Carraud, Vincent* Vom Haß auf den Diebstahl und der Liebe zum Dieb. IKaZ 27 (1998) 15-24.

7302 **Countryman, Louis William** Sesso e morale nella bibbia. ^T*Girardet, Maria Sbaffi*. PBT 45: T 1998, Claudiana 326 pp. L38.000. 88-7016-283-4. Bibl.

7303 *Cranfield, C.E.B.* A response to Professor Richard B. Hays' *The moral vision of the New Testament. On Romans.* 1998 ⇒143. 167-175.

7304 *Davies, Meg* Is there a future for New Testament ethics?. Auguries. JSOT.S 269: 1998 ⇒225. 184-203.

7305 *Dopffel, Helmut* Du sollst dir kein Bildnis machen ...": Replik einer Replik. PTh 87 (1998) 168-174;

7306 Von Gottesleugnern, Knabenschändern und gleichgeschlechtlichen Partnerschaften: die Bibel im kirchlichen Streit um Homosexualität. PTh 87 (1998) 132-154.

7307 *Eibach, Ulrich* Gleichgeschlechtliche Liebe—Gleichwertigkeit der Lebensformen der Geschlechter?: zum Beitrag von Helmut Dopffel. PTh 87 (1998) 155-167.

7308 *Eid, Volker* "Gleichzeitigkeit" mit Jesus von Nazaret?: Überlegungen zum Zusammenhang von Glaube, Bibel und Moral. ^FHOFFMANN, P., Von Jesus. BZNW 93: 1998 ⇒43. 553-569.

7309 **Fernández, Aurelio** El mensaje moral de Jesús de Nazaret. Pelícano: M 1998, Palabra 395 pp. 84-8239-254-9. ^REphMar 48 (1998) 577-578 (*Vico Peinado, José*).

7310 *Finkbeiner, Scott* The commandments of Jesus Christ to his disciples. CBTJ 14/1 (1998) 35-49.

7311 **Fischer, Klaus P.** 'Heute, wenn ihr seine Stimme hört': Beiträge zu einer Theologie des Kairós. W 1998, Passagen 120 pp. DM28. 3-85-165-299-1 [ThG 41,234—Häring, Bernhard].

7312 **Francis, James A.** Subversive virtue: asceticism and authority in the second-century pagan world. 1995 ⇒11/2,8378. ^RSVTQ 42/1 (1998) 99-102 (*Choufrine, Arkadi*); HeyJ 39 (1998) 198-199 (*Sylwanowicz, M.*).

7313 **Gaziaux, Éric** L'autonomie en morale: au croisement de la philosophie et de la théologie. BEThL 138: Lv 1998, Univ. Pr. xvi; 760 pp. 90-6186-916-1. Bibl.

7314 *Hagemann, Ludwig* Die Menschenrechte im Verständnis der drei monotheistischen Religionen: Judentum—Christentum—Islam. JRTR 6 (1998) 88-99.

7315 *Hampe, Michael* Vertrag und Tugend: Bedingungen der Gerechtigkeit. Gerechtigkeit. 1998 ⇒283. 205-226.

7316 **Hart, Colin** The ethics of the gospels. GESt 111: C 1998, Grove 24 pp. 1-85174-386-3 [NThAR 1999,45].

7317 *Hasitschka, Martin* Homosexualität—eine Frage der Schöpfungsordnung. ZNT 2 (1998) 54-60 [Rom 1,26-27; 1 Cor 6,9; 1 Tim 1,10].

7318   **Hays, Richard B.** The moral vision of the New Testament. 1996,
       ⇒12,7334; 13,7724. ᴿMoTh 14 (1998) 455-7 (*Hütter, Reinhard*);
       Teol(Br) 23 (1998) 100-109 (*Segalla, Giuseppe*); ThTo 55/1 (1998)
       97-98 (*Bretzke, James T.*); Studies in World Christianity 4 (1998)
       277-279 (*McDonald, J.I.H.*); JBL 117 (1998) 358-360 (*Martin, Dale
       B.*). ⇒7303.
7319   ᴱ**Hoose, Bernard** Christian ethics: an introduction. L 1998, Cassell
       xiv; 338 pp. £55/20. 0-304-70264-1. ᴿNBl 79 (1998) 409-410 (*Bo-
       land, Vivian*).
7320   *Höffe, Otfried* Kontexte der Gerechtigkeitsfrage. Gerechtigkeit. 1998
       ⇒283. 227-243.
7321   **Johnson, Steven Robert** Seeking the imperishable treasure: wealth,
       wisdom and a saying of Jesus in the New Testament, the Gospel of
       Thomas and Q. ᴰClaremont 1998, 197 pp.
7322   **Kwon, Soon-Gu** Christ as example: the Imitatio Christi: motive in
       biblical and christian ethics. Uppsala Studies in Social Ethics 21: U
       1998, Univ. 231 pp. 91-554-4182-3. Bibl.
7323   **Matera, Frank J.** New Testament ethics: the legacies of Jesus and
       Paul. 1996 ⇒12,7341; 13,7734. ᴿLouvSt 23 (1998) 79-80 (*Verhey-
       den, Joseph*); Teol(Br) 23 (1998) 109-114 (*Segalla, Giuseppe*); CBQ
       60 (1998) 370-371 (*Pattee, Stephen*); Salm. 45 (1998) 340-342
       (*Flecha, J.-R.*).
7324   **Mcdonald, J. Ian H.** The crucible of christian morality. L 1998,
       Routledge viii; 247 pp. £15.
7325   **Meeks, Wayne A.** As origens da moralidade cristã: os dois primeiros
       séculos. 1997 ⇒13,7736. ᴿPerTeol 30 (1998) 459-461 (*Junges, J.
       Roque*).
7326   *Meeks, Wayne A.* The christian beginnings and christian ethics: the
       hermeneutical challenge. ET 9 (1998) 171-180.
7327   *Merk, Otto* Aspekte zur diakonischen Relevanz von 'Gerechtigkeit',
       'Barmherzigkeit' und 'Liebe'. ᶠMERK, O. BZNW 95: 1998 <1990>
       ⇒79. 337-349.
7328   *Mieth, Dietmar* Ehe und Ehelosigkeit im Zeichen der Auferstehung.
       ᶠVENETZ, H. 1998 ⇒122. 249-256.
7329   *Mitchell, Margaret M.* Reading to virtue. ᶠBETZ, H. 1998 ⇒10. 110-
       121.
7330   *Mongillo, Dalmazio* Le richieste morali nel primo annuncio del
       vangelo. Ad Gentes 2 (1998) 154-172 Sum., som. 172.
7331   *Moule, C.F.D.* Retribution or restoration?. Forgiveness. 1998
       <1992> ⇒180. 41-47.
7332   **Mueller, Joan** Is forgiveness possible?. ColMn 1998, Liturgical iv;
       (2) 114 pp. 0-8146-2470-7. Bibl.
7333   *Murchison, D. Cameron* Scripture, tradition, knowledge and
       experience: a review of some recent literature from the church's con-
       versation on homosexuality. ER 50 (1998) 48-53.
7334   *Noguez, Armando* Las tareas de la ética del Nuevo Testamento.
       Voces 12 (1998) 43-60.
7335   **Pinckaers, Servais** The sources of christian ethics. 1995 ⇒11/2,
       4672; 12,7348. ᴿPro Ecclesia 7/2 (1998) 249-250 (*Matzko, David
       McCarthy*) [1 Cor 1,18-31].
7336   *Piva, Pompeo* La dimora di Dio con gli uomini: radice di esigenze
       etiche. Studi ecumenici 16 (1998) 355-365.

7337 *Rogelio Bustos, J.* La ley del Espíritu, experiencia de plenitud y consumación de la ley antigua: acercamiento ético-bíblico. RTLi 32/1-2 (1998) 23-42 Sum. 23.

7338 *Ruch, Barbara* "Ehrfurcht gebührt allem Lebendigen und seinem Wachstum" (Ruth C. Cohn). FVENETZ, H. 1998 ⇒122. 287-296.

7339 *Ruston, Roger* Using the bible for christian morals. Month 31 (1998) 506-514.

7340 *Scheuermann, Georg* Il giubileo negli autori del Nuovo Testamento. Le origini degli anni giubilari. 1998 ⇒2236. 139-183.

7341 **Schirone, S.; Scognamiglio, R.** Ricchi per ogni generosità: economia e uso dei beni nel Nuovo Testamento. Monopoli 1998, Vivere In 326 pp. L16.000 [Asp. 46,301s—Silvano, Carlo].

7342 *Seitz, Christopher* Sexuality and scripture's plain sense: the christian community and the law of God. Word without end. 1998 ⇒200. 319-339.

7343 **Shaw, Teresa M.** The burden of the flesh: fasting and sexuality in early Christianity. Mp 1998, Fortress xi; 298 pp. $21. 0-8006-27652.

7344 **Siker, Jeffrey S.** Scripture and ethics: twentieth-century portraits. 1997 ⇒13,7749. RHorizons 25 (1998) 131-133 (*Cahill, Lisa Sowle*); CBQ 60 (1998) 173-174 (*Harrington, Daniel J.*); RRelRes 40 (1998) 87-88 (*Melendez, Rita M.*); JR 78 (1998) 467-469 (*Reames, Kent*).

7345 *Stegemann, Wolfgang* Homosexualität—ein modernes Konzept. ZNT 2 (1998) 61-68 [Rom 1,26-27; 1 Cor 6,9].

7346 *Süss, René* De wereld is maakbaar. Interpretatie 6/8 (1998) 9-13.

7347 *Tamarut, Anton* Solidarnost kao evandeoska vrijednost. BoSm 68 (1998) 257-276. **Croatian.**

7348 *Theobald, Michael* Biblische Weisungen zur Homosexualität?: Plädoyer für einen vernünftigen Umgang mit der Schrift. WuA(M) 39/2 (1998) 92-94.

7349 *Topel, John* The tarnished golden rule (Luke 6:31): the inescapable radicalness of christian ethics. TS 59 (1998) 475-485.

7350 *Vogler, Werner* Wertewandel im Neuen Testament. ZdZ 52/1 (1998) 27-32.

7351 *Walf, Knut* Gemeindeethos und aktuelles Kirchenrecht. FVENETZ, H. 1998 ⇒122. 231-238.

7352 *Weder, Hans* Gesetz und Gnade: zur Lebensgrundlage des ethischen Handelns nach dem Neuen Testament. FSCHRAGE, W. 1998 ⇒101. 171-182.

7353 *Wodka, Andrzej* L'oblativitá neotestamentaria e il discorso etico-morale. StMor 36 (1998) 203-238 Sum. res. 238.

H8.4 *NT de reformatione sociali*—Political action in Scripture

7354 *Cañaveral Orozco, Aníbal* Aportes para una lectura campesina de la biblia. Alternativas 5/11-12 (1998) 185-202 [ThIK 21/1,71].

7355 *Girardi, Giulio* El jubileo, denucia de la transición y rescate del proyecto revolucionario de Jesús. Alternativas 5/13 (1998) 81-109 [ThIK 21/1,72].

7356 *Holderegger, Adrian* Politik aus christlicher Inspiration: die schwierige Vermittlung christlicher Visionen—ein Essay. FVENETZ, H. 1998 ⇒122. 277-286.

7357 *Mendels, Doron* Jesus and the politics of his day. Identity. JSPE.S 24: 1998 <1994> ⇒174. 440-451.
7358 *Miguez, Néstor O.* Una mirada política. Alternativas 5/11-12 (1998) 61-74 [ThIK 21/1,71].
7359 **O'Donovan, Oliver** The desire of the nations: rediscovering the roots of political theology. 1996 ⇒12,7368; 13,7761. ᴿThTo 54/4 (1998) 552-553 (*Tinder, Glenn*).
7360 **Oschwald, Hanspeter** Bibel, Mystik und Politik: die Gemeinschaft Sant'Egidio. FrB 1998, Herder 141 pp. DM24.80. ᴿGuL 71/4 (1998) 312-3 (*Batlogg, Andreas*).
7361 *Paimoen, Eddy* The bible, politics, and democracy. Stulos theological journal 6/1-2 (1998) 33-49.

H8.5 Theologia liberationis latino-americana...

7362 *Croatto, J. Severino* The function of the non-fulfilled promises: reading the pentateuch from the perspective of the Latin-American oppressed people. The personal voice. 1998 ⇒250. 38-51.
7363 ᴱ**Fornet-Betancourt, Raúl** Befreiungstheologie: kritischer Rückblick und Perspektiven für die Zukunft. 1997 ⇒13,7762. 3 vols. ᴿREB 58 (1998) 751-755 (*Berkenbrock, Volney J.*).
7364 *Miller, Gabriele* Lateinamerika: Methoden des Umgangs mit der Schrift ins Deutsche übertragen. Lebendige Katechese 20 (1998) 68-71.
7365 ᴱ**Schrijver, G. de** Liberation theologies on shifting grounds: a clash of socio-economic and cultural paradigms. BEThL 135: Lv 1998 Peeters xi; 453 pp. 90-429-0302-3.
7366 **Schürger, Wolfgang** Theologie auf dem Weg der Befreiung: Geschichte und Methode des Zentrums für Bibelstudien in Brasilien. EMMÖ: 1995 ⇒13,7768. ᴿZMR 82/2 (1998) 138-139 (*Schoenborn, Paul Gerhard*).
7367 **Sobrino, Jon** Jesus the liberator. 1993 ⇒10,8550... 13,7770. ᴿVJTR 62 (1998) 363-364 (*Amaladoss, M.*).

7368 **Munga, Stephen I.** Beyond the controversy: a study of African theologies of interculturation and liberation. STL 55: Lund 1998, University Press 388 pp. 91-7966-532-2. Bibl.

H8.7 *Mariologia*—The mother of Jesus in the NT

7369 *Baudoz, Jean-François* 'Marie, de laquelle est né Jésus' (Mt 1,16): la virginité de Marie dans la tradition synoptique. EtMar (1998) 9-23.
7370 ᴱ**Beinert, Wolfgang; Petri, Heinrich** Handbuch der Marienkunde, 1: Theologische Grundlegung: geistliches Leben, 2: Gestaltetes Zeugnis: gläubiger Lobpreis. ²1996/97 ⇒12,7399. ᴿGuL 71 (1998) 151 (*Steinmetz, Franz-Josef*); EeT 29 (1998) 262-266 (*Laberge, Léo*); Mar. 60 (1998) 663-666 (*Gambero, Luigi*).
7371 *Blanchard, Yves-Marie* Né d'un vouloir de chair?: la conception virginale au regard du quatrième évangile. EtMar (1998) 25-34.
7372 **Borgeaud, Philippe** La mère des dieux: de Cybèle à la Vierge Marie. 1996 ⇒12,7403. ᴿAnCl 67 (1998) 402-403 (*Turcan, Robert*).

7373 **Buby, Bertrand** Mary of Galilee, 3: the Marian heritage of the early church. 1996 ⇒12,7407. [R]Pacifica 11/1 (1998) 117-118 (*Farrell, Marie*); ACR 75/1 (1998) 132 (*Farrell, Marie*).

7374 *Cardellino, Lodovico* La "Madre di Gesù" simbolo di Israele (Gv 1,47; 2,1-5.12; 7,5; 11,2.28.33; 12,1-8; 19,25-27; 20,17; Mt 1,2.11.18-25; 12,46,50 e 13,55 par; 26,6-13 par; Lc 1,26-38; 7,36-50; 10,38-42). BeO 40 (1998) 19-62.

7375 *Charlat, Régine du Marie.* Mission de l'Église 118 (1998) 15-16.

7376 **Connelly, Douglas** Mary: what the bible really says. DG 1998, Inter-Varsity 132 pp. $10 [BS 156,115—Zuck, Roy B.].

7377 *Cothenet, Édouard* La virginité de Marie dans les Apocryphes. EtMar (1998) 53-69.

7378 *Coyle, Kathleen* Mary, proto-disciple: a Lukan perspective. EAPR 35 (1998) 149-166.

7379 **Cunneen, Sally** A la recherche de Marie: la femme et le symbole [T]*Moret, Marie-Claude.* P 1996, Desclée de Brouwer 336 pp [SR 29,220s—Slattery, Maureen].

7380 *Dasnabédian, Thamar* Marie dans les évangiles apocryphes arméniens. ParOr 23 (1998) 79-87.

7381 **De Fiores, Stefano** Maria nella vita secondo lo spirito. Religione: CasM 1998, Piemme 294 pp. 88-384-4037-9. Bibl.

7382 *Domergue, Marcel* Marie en cinq tableaux. Croire aujourd'hui 61 (1998) 18-20.

7383 *Drews, Wolfram* 'Gerne wollen wir sie als unsere Lehrmeisterin annehmen': Überlegungen zur Stellung der Jungfrau Maria im theologischen Denken Johannes CALVINs. [F]MARQUARDT, F.-W. 1998 ⇒72. 77-102.

7384 *Fleming, Kathryn* Mary over Bethlehem. Holy Land 18 (1998) 182-187.

7385 **García Barriuso, P.** Días grandes de María. M 1998, Palabra 247 pp [Comunidades 28/1,43s—González, M.].

7386 **Haag, Herbert,** *al.*, Maria: Kunst, Brauchtum und Religion in Bild und Text. FrB 1997, Herder 272 pp. DM128.

7387 [T]**Hansbury, Mary** JACOB of Serug: on the mother of God. Crestwood, NY 1998, St. Vladimir's Seminary Press viii; 102 pp. 0-88141-184-1. Introd. *Sebastian Brock*; Bibl.

7388 *Harvey, Susan* Ashbrook Incense offerings in the Syriac Transitus Mariae: ritual and knowledge in ancient christianity. [F]FERGUSON, E. NT.S 90: 1998 ⇒25. 175-191.

7389 *Jeanjean, Benoît* La virginité de Marie selon saint JÉRÔME, polémiciste et exégète. EtMar (1998) 85-104.

7390 JUAN PABLO II La virgen María. M 1998, Palabra 266 pp [EstAg 33,443—Luis, P. de].

7391 *La Potterie, Ignace de* Mariologie et exégèse biblique depuis le IIe Concile du Vatican. De cultu mariano saeculo XX a Concilio Vatican II usque ad nostros dies. Città del Vaticano 1998, Acta congressus mariologici-mariani in civitate Onubensi (Huelva) anno 1992 celebrati. 119-148 [AcBib 10,514].

7392 *Laurentin, René* Singularité significative des textes sur la virginité de Marie et leur omniprésence dans le Nouveau Testament. EtMar (1998) 35-51.

7393 **Llamas, Enrique** María de Nazaret: imagen y mensaje para el siglo XXI. M 1998, Edicel 400 pp. [R]EstJos 52 (1998) 249-251 (*Jésus María, José de*); Ter. 49 (1998) 726-728 (*Pasquetto, Virgilio*).

7394	*Madec, Goulven* Marie, vierge et mère, selon saint AMBROISE et saint AUGUSTIN. EtMar (1998) 71-83.
7395	María en el designio de Dios y la comunión de los santos I: en la historia y la Escritura. Groupe des Dombes. DiáTeol 33 (1998) 69-137.
7396	Marie dans le dessein de Dieu et la communion des saints, 1: dans l'histoire et l'Écriture. 1997. Groupe des Dombes. ⇒13,7791. ᴿScEs 50 (1998) 389-390 (*Lison, Jacques*);
7397	2: controverse et conversion. P 1998, Bayard 99 pp. Groupe des Dombes. ᴿScEs 50 (1998) 406-408 (*Lison, Jacques*).
7398	**McHugh, John** Maryja w Nowym Testamencie. ᵀ*Czarnocki, A.* Niepokalanów 1998, Franciszkanów 526 pp [CoTh 69,203ss—Bartosik, Grzegorz M.]. **P**.
7399	*Outtier, Bernard* Dormition et assomption de Marie: à propos d'un livre récent. Apocrypha 9 (1998) 301-304.
7400	**Pelikan, Jaroslav** Mary through the centuries. 1996 ⇒12,7437; 13, 7815. ᴿWorship 72/1 (1998) 88-89 (*Carr, Anne*); CHR 84 (1998) 305-306 (*Galvin, John P.*); Japanese Mission Journal 52 (1998) 212-213 & Gr. 79 (1998) 589-591 (*Kroeger, James H.*).
7401	*Peretto, Elio* Apocrifi e pietà popolare Mariana. RivLi 85 (1998) 333-350.
7402	**Pikaza, Xabier** La amiga de Dios: el mensaje mariano del Nuevo Testamento. 1996 ⇒12,7439. ᴿPhilipSac 33 (1998) 371-373 (*Mina, Macario Ofilada*).
7403	**Rinaldi, Bonaventura** La Madonna della fede tra le donne moderne: per una rielaborazione della teologia femminile. Mi 1996, Massimo 239 pp. L29.000 [CBQ 62,157s—Kealy, Sean P.].
7404	*Riße, Günter* Sehnsucht der Seele: Maria, die Mutter Jesu, in der Begegnung der abrahamitischen Religionen. LebZeug 53 (1998) 139-145.
7405	*Romero Pose, Eugenio* El paralelismo Eva-María en la primera teología cristiana. EstMar 64 (1998) 157-176 [Rev 12].
7406	*Roten, Johann G.* L'état actuel de la question sur la virginité de Marie. EphMar 48 (1998) 163-219 Sum. 219.
7407	*Samaha, John* A New Testament gallery of Marian images. Holy Land 18 (1998) 190-194.
7408	*Terra, Pedro* Maria, escrínio de esperança, harpa de Deus segundo a bíblia. RCB 85/86 (1998) 123-126.
7409	*Thompson, Thomas A.* The Virgin Mary in art. EphMar 48 (1998) 319-322.
7410	*Toldy, Teresa Martinho* Maria, rosto filial do crente. Bib(L) 7/7 (1998) 137-148.
7411	**Toniolo, Ermanno Maria** Bibliografia mariana 9—1990-1993. SPFTM 53: R 1998, Marianum xvi; 635 pp. ᴿMar. 60 (1998) 643-645 (*Longère, Jean*).
7412	*Wackerbarth, Dieter* Maria nella liturgia luterana: la figura e la presenza liturgica di Maria in relazione alle scelte di fondo bibliche della Riforma. RivLi 85 (1998) 257-292.
7413	*Zelinskij, Vladimir* Maria, lo Spirito Santo e la santità: una riflessione ortodossa. Com(I) 158 (1998) 38-44.
7414	*Zundel, Maurice* Il mistero di Maria. Monastica 39/1 (1998) 39-47.

H8.8 *Feminae NT*—Women in the NT and church history

7415 TEAmonville Alegría, Nicole d' El amor de Magdalena. 1996 ⇒12, 7453; 13,7826. RQVC 189 (1998) 197-198 (*Höhensteiger, Petrus*).

7416 Arjava, Antti Women and law in late antiquity. 1996 ⇒12,7454; 13,7827. RClR 48 (1998) 360-361 (*Coke, Gillian*).

7417 *Balbi, Giovanna* Tradizione agiografica nella Spagna medievale: le vite di Maddalena e Marta. AISP 11 (1998) 97-144.

7418 Bernabé Ubieta, Carmen María Magdalena. 1994, ⇒10,8716... 12,7455. REstB 56 (1998) 267-281 (*Urbán, A.*).

7419 Carpenter, Christine The women around Jesus. Portland 1996, CMC xv; 254 pp. 1-887999-53-1. Bibl. [NThAR 2000,153].

7420 Clark, Gillian Women in late antiquity. 1994 ⇒9,9323... 12,7459. RGn. 70 (1998) 82-84 (*Felber, Anneliese*).

7421 *Corley, Kathleen E.* The egalitarian Jesus: a christian myth of origins;

7422 Women and the crucifixion and burial of Jesus: "He was buried: on the third day He was raised". Forum 1 n.s. (1998) 291-325/181-225.

7423 *French, Dorothea R.* Maintaining boundaries: the status of actresses in early christian society. VigChr 52 (1998) 293-318.

7424 Grelot, Pierre A condição da mulher segundo o Novo Testamento. TSilva, José Augusto da. Aparecida 1998, Santuário 175 pp. 2-220-03574-3 [PerTeol 31,148].

7425 Haldas, Georges Marie de Magdala. 1997 ⇒13,7837. RNV 73/2 (1998) 103-4 (*Morerod, Charles*).

7426 Hearon, Holly Elizabeth Witness and counter-witness: the function of the Mary Magdalene tradition in early Christian communities. DGraduate Theol. Union 1998, 283 pp.

7427 Heine, Susanne Women and early christianity: are the feminist scholars right?. 1987 ⇒4,9902... 7,8814. RSal. 60 (1998) 766-767 (*Fusco, Roberto*).

7428 Janssen, Claudia Elisabet und Hanna: zwei widerständige alte Frauen in neutestamentlicher Zeit: eine sozialgeschichtliche Untersuchung. Mainz 1998, Grünewald 246 pp. 3-7867-2071-1.

7429 *King, Karen L.* Canonization and marginalization: Mary of Magdala. Conc(GB) 3 (1998) 29-36 [Conc(I) 34,404-415; Conc(P) 276,334-343; Conc(D) 34,261-269].

7430 *Kowalski, Beate* Jesus und die Frauen im Johannesevangelium. Jesus Christus—Gottes Sohn. 1998 ⇒6913. 151-169.

7431 Letsch-Brunner, Silvia Marcella—discipula et magistra: auf den Spuren einer römischen Christin des 4. Jahrhunderts. BZNW 91: B 1998, de Gruyter xi; 272 pp. 3-11-015808-6.

7432 MacDonald, Margaret Y. Early christian women and pagan opinion: the power of hysterical women. 1996 ⇒12,7474; 13,7839. RBZ 42 (1998) 287-290 (*Melzer-Keller, Helga*); SR 27 (1998) 214-215 (*Richardson, Peter*); CBQ 60 (1998) 579-580 (*Osiek, Carolyn*); JR 78 (1998) 621-622 (*Calef, Susan*); JEarlyC 6 (1998) 150-151 (*McLeese, Constance E.*); JThS 49 (1998) 337-339 (*Trevett, Christine*).

7433 Maisch, Ingrid Mary Magdalene: the image of a woman through the centuries. TMaloney, Linda M. ColMn 1998, Liturgical ix; 185 pp. $20. 0-8146-2471-5 [ThD 46,279—Heiser, W. Charles].

7434 Marjanen, Atti The woman Jesus loved: Mary Magdalene in the Nag Hammadi library and related documents. NHS 40: 1996 ⇒12, 7475; 13,7840. RCBQ 60 (1998) 164-165 (*Timbie, Janet A.*).

7435   **Melzer-Keller, Helga** Jesus und die Frauen... nach der synoptischen Überlieferung. Herders Biblische Studien 14: 1997, ⇒13,7841. ^{R}STV 36/2 (1998) 193-198 (*Załęski, Jan*).

7436   *Navarro, Solange* 'Ne serait-il pas le Christ?': femmes missionnaires dans l'évangile. Mission de l'Église 118 (1998) 4-9.

7437   *Osiek, Carolyn* Women in house churches. ^{F}SNYDER, G. 1998 ⇒104. 300-315.

7438   *Oyeronke, Olajubu* Jesus' attitude towards women: a model for the church in Africa today. AfER 40 (1998) 183-188.

7439   *Quaglia, Rocco* Gli incontri de Gesù: le donne 'minori'. 1997 ⇒13, 7846. ^{R}Anime e Corpi 36 (1998) 526-527.

7440   **Quéré, F.** Las mujeres del evangelio. Bilbao 1998, Mensajero 240 pp [SalTer 86,262].

7441   **Ruckstuhl, Eugen** Jesus, Freund und Anwalt der Frauen: Frauenpräsenz und Frauenabwesenheit in der Geschichte Jesu. 1996 ⇒12,7481. ^{R}CoTh 68/2 (1998) 181-186 (*Załeski, Jan*).

7442   **Sawyer, Deborah F.** Women and religion in the first christian centuries. 1996 ⇒12,884; 13,7849. ^{R}Latomus 57 (1998) 702-703 (*Adkin, N.*); CBQ 60 (1998) 587-588 (*Love, Stuart L.*).

7443   **Synek, Eva Maria** Heilige Frauen der frühen Christenheit. ÖC 43: 1994 ⇒11/2,5248; 12,7485. ^{R}ThRv 94 (1998) 470-472 (*Jensen, Anne*).

7444   *Thimmes, Pamela* Memory and re-vision: Mary Magdalene research since 1975. CurResB 6 (1998) 193-226.

7445   **Thompson, Mary R.** Mary of Magdala, apostle and leader. 1995 ⇒11/2,5252; 13,7853. ^{R}EstB 56 (1998) 130-132 (*Navarro, M.*).

7446   **Thurston, Bonnie Bowman** Women in the New Testament: questions and commentary. Companions to the New Testament: NY 1998, Crossroad xiii; 170 pp. $15. 0-8243-1670-2.

7447   **Tunc, Suzanne** Des femmes aussi suivaient Jésus: essai d'interprétation de quelques versets des évangiles. P 1998, Desclé De B 184 pp. FF120. 2-220-04175-1 [Etudes 389/1-2,140—Guillet, Jacques].

7448   **Van Bremen, Riet** The limits of participation: women and civic life in the Greek east in the Hellenistic and Roman periods. 1996 ⇒12,7488. ^{R}AnCl 67 (1998) 517-519 (*D'Hautcourt, Alexis*).

H8.9 *Theologia feminae*—**Feminist theology**

7449   *Ackerman, Susan* We've come a long way, baby (but still hav a ways to go). BiRe 14/5 (1998) 19, 54.

7450   *Adam, Margaret B.* This is my story, this is my song ...: a feminist claim on scripture, ideology and interpretation. Escaping Eden. BiSe 65: 1998 ⇒278. 218-232.

7451   *Amador, J.D.* Feminist biblical hermeneutics: a failure of theoretical nerve. JAAR 66/1 (1998) 39-57.

7452   **Bail, Ulrich** Gegen das Schweigen klagen: eine intertextuelle Studie zu den Klagepsalmen Ps 6 und Ps 55 und der Erzählung von der Vergewaltigung Tamars. Gü 1998, Gü'er 246 pp. DM48. 3-579-00187-6 [ThLZ 124,896—Krispenz, Jutta].

7453   **Bird, Phyllis** Missing persons and mistaken identities: women and gender in ancient Israel. 1997 ⇒13,114. ^{R}HBT 20 (1998) 160-161 (*Bowen, Nancy R.*).

7454 *Bird, Phyllis A.* What makes a feminist reading feminist?: a qualified answer. Escaping Eden. BiSe 65: 1998 ⇒278. 124-131.

7455 **Brenner, Athalya** The intercourse of knowledge: on gendering desire and 'sexuality' in the Hebrew Bible. 1997 ⇒13,7861. ᴿThLZ 123 (1998) 845-846 (*Schroer, Silvia*); JThS 49 (1998) 205-207 (*Guest, P. Deryn*).

7456 *Butting, Klara* Freundin und Weggefährtin: neue Lebensgeschichten aus alten Texten. Evangelische Aspekte 8/3 (1998) 9-12.

7457 *Butzer, Evi* Die Schrift hinter dem Spiegel "weiblicher" Erfahrungen: Bibellektüre aus dekonstruktivistisch-feministischer Sicht. TeKo 21/3 (1998) 3-16.

7458 **Caron, Gérald** Des femmes aussi faisaient route avec Lui: perspectives féministes sur la bible. 1995 ⇒13,7865. ᴿScEs 50 (1998) 384-386 (*Archambault, Jean-Marie*).

7459 *Caron, Gérald* La bible déstabilisée: enjeu de la critique féministe radicale. EeT(O) 29 (1998) 199-220.

7460 **Cheney, Emily** She can read: feminist reading strategies for biblical narrative. 1996 ⇒12,7500: 13,7866. ᴿAThR 80/1 (1998) 129-130 (*Crammer, Corinne*).

7461 *Clark, Elizabeth A.* The lady vanishes: dilemmas of a feminist historian after the "linguistic turn". ChH 67 (1998) 1-31.

7462 *Conti, Cristina* Hermenéutica feminista. Alternativas 5/11-12 (1998) 93-112 [ThIK 21/1,71].

7463 *Dannemann, Irene* Die Akten der Xanthippe, Polyxena und Rebekka oder: drei Frauen und zwei Löwinnen. Kompendium Feministische Bibelauslegung. 1998 ⇒7511. 748-756.

7464 *De Benedetti, Paolo* E maschio e femmina li creò. Maschio. 1998 ⇒313. 117-120.

7465 *Dewey, Joanna* From oral stories to written text. Conc(GB) 3 (1998) 20-28 [Conc(I) 34,389-403; Conc(P) 276,322-333; Conc(D) 34, 250-260].

7466 *Dube Shomanah, Musa W.* Scripture, feminism and post-colonial contexts. Conc(GB) 3 (1998) 45-54 [Conc(I) 34,428-442; Conc(P) 276,355-367; Conc(D) 34,278-287].

7467 **Ellens, Deborah L.** A comparison of the conceptualization of women in the sex laws of Leviticus and in the sex laws of Deuteronomy. ᴰClaremont 1998, 573 pp.

7468 *Eltrop, Bettina; Janssen, Claudia* Das Protevangelium des Jakobus: die Geschichte Gottes geht weiter. Kompendium Feministische Bibelauslegung. 1998 ⇒7511. 795-800.

7469 *Fewell, Danna Nolan* Changing the subject: retelling the story of Hgar the Egyptian. Genesis. 1998 ⇒219. 182-194.

7470 *Fiorenza, Elisabeth Schüssler* In memoria di lei: una ricostruzione femminista delle origini cristiane. Sola Scriptura 14: T 1990, Claudiana iv; 397 pp. 88-7016-115-3. ᴿSal. 60 (1998) 780-781 (*Fusco, Roberto*);

7471 Gesù figlio di Miriam, profeta di Sophia. Sola Scriptura 17: 1996 ⇒12,7508; 13,7873. ᴿRivBib 46 (1998) 496-500 (*Penna, Romano*); RdT 39 (1998) 140-143 (*Ferretti, Cloe Taddei*);

7472 Jesus—Miriams Kind, Sophias Prophet: kritische Anfragen feministischer Christologie. 1997 ⇒13,7875. ᴿBZ 42 (1998) 284-287 (*Melzer-Keller, Helga*); ZNT 1/2 (1998) 78-80 (*Alkier, Stefan*); EK (1998/10) 613 (*Kreß, Harmut*);

7473   Sharing her word: feminist biblical interpretation in context. Boston 1998, Beacon xv; 222 pp. $23. 0-8070-1230-0;
7474   *Al.*, As sagradas escrituras das mulheres. Petrópolis 1998, Vozes 140 pp.
7475   *Fiorenza, Elisabeth Schüssler* Die heiligen Schriften der Frauen. Conc(D) 34 (1998) 233-236;
7476   Jesus—Miriams Kind, Sophias Prophet. ZNT 2 (1998) 78-80.
7477   *Fulkerson, Mary McClintock* 'Is there a (non-sexist) bible in this church?': a feminist case for the priority of interpretive communities. MoTh 14/2 (1998) 225-242. Theology and scriptural imagination 63-80 ⇒246.
7478   *Gebara, Ivone* Welche Schriften sind heilige Autorität?: die ambivalente Rolle der Bibel im Leben der lateinamerikanischen Frauen. Conc(D) 34 (1998) 237-249.
7479   **Gerstenberger, Erhard S.** Yahweh, the patriarch: ancient images of God and feminist theology. 1996 ⇒12,7510. ᴿThTo 55/1 (1998) 114, 116-117 (*O'Connor, Kathleen*).
7480   **Goldstein, Elyse** ReVisions: seeing Torah through a feminist lens. Woodstock, VT 1998, Jewish Lights 207 pp. 1-58023-047-4. Bibl.
7481   *Graham, Susan Lochrie* Patriarchy's middle managers: another handmaid's tale. Escaping Eden. BiSe 65: 1998 ⇒278. 244-265.
7482   *Green, Elisabeth* La teologia femminista: un'introduzione ed una proposta. Maschio. 1998 ⇒313. 121-134.
7483   *Grümbel, Ute* Im Blickpunkt: Abendmahl: "Ich kann mir nicht vorstellen, daß die Einstellung zwischen Mann und Frau im wesentlichen unterschiedlich ist ...". EvTh 58/1 (1998) 49-73.
7484   *Habermann, Bonna Devora* Praxis-Exegese: eine jüdische feministische Hermeneutik. Conc(D) 34 (1998) 323-334.
7485   **Isherwood, Lisa; Stuart, Elizabeth** Introducing body theology. Introductions in Feminist Theology 2: Shf 1998, Academic 164 pp. 1-85075-995-2. Bibl.
7486   **King, Nicholas** Whispers of liberation: feminist perspectives on the New Testament. Mahwah 1998, Paulist iv; 189 pp. $16. 0-8091-3816-6.
7487   *Kirk-Duggan, Cheryl A.* What difference does difference make in feminist hermeneutics?: a personal essay. Escaping Eden. BiSe 65: 1998 ⇒278. 266-278.
7488   **Klee, Deborah** Menstruation in the Hebrew Bible. ᴰBoston Univ. 1998, 136 pp.
7489   *Kwok, Pui-lan* Überlegungen zu den heiligen Schriften von Frauen. Conc(D) 34 (1998) 335-343.
7490   *Lieu, Judith M.* The 'attraction of women' in/to early Judaism and christianity: gender and the politics of conversion. JSNT 72 (1998) 5-22.
7491   *Martin, Joan M.* Die SklavInnenerzählungen und Womanistische Ethik. Conc(D) 34 (1998) 296-305.
7492   *Masenya, Madipoane* A Bosadi (Womanhood) reading of Genesis 16. OTEs 11 (1998) 271-287.
7493   *McKay, Heather A.* She said to him, he said to her: power talk in the bible or Foucault listens at the keyhole. BTB 28 (1998) 45-51.
7494   **McLeese, Constance Ellen** Augustine on Adam's rib and Eve's sin: an evaluation of theological sexism in Augustine's exegesis of Gen. 2:15-25 and Gen. 3. ᴰMontréal 1998, 463 pp.

7495 *Medina, Magdalena* Experiencia bíblica con mujeres de la 'ciénaga': leyendo la Biblia con ojos de mujer. TE 42 (1998) 261-266.

7496 ᴱ**Newsom, Carol A.** Da Genesi a Neemia. La Biblia delle donne: un commentario, 1. 1996 ⇒12,1232; 13,7894. ᴿRdT 39 (1998) 454-456 (*D'Alario, Vittoria*); RivBib 46 (1998) 104-06 (*Perroni, Marinella*).

7497 ᴱ**O'Grady, Kathleen; Gilroy, Ann L.; Gray, Janette** Bodies, lives, voices: gender in theology. Shf 1998, Academic 273 pp. 1-85075-854-9.

7498 *Parratt, Saroj N.A.* Frauen als Quellen einer "mündlichen heiligen Schrift": das Beispiel einer asiatischen Gesellschaft. Conc(D) 34 (1998) 305-312.

7499 **Pauwels, Anne** Women changing language. Real language: L 1998, Longman xvi; 267 pp. 0-582-09961-7. Bibl.

7500 *Pearson, Brook W.R.* Method, metaphor and mammaries: the ideology of feminist New Testament criticism. Religion & sexuality. 1998 ⇒302. 226-239.

7501 **Peppa, Constantina** Die Töchter der Kirche Christi und die Frohe Botschaft des Sohnes Gottes: eine Studie über die aktive Präsenz der Frauen und ihre besonderen Dienste im Frhchristentum und in Gemeinden der ungeteilten Alten Kirche. Katerini 1998, Epektasi 294 pp [OrthFor 13/1,78ss—Brun, Maria].

7502 *Pippin, Tina* Feminist theories and exegesis. Exegese und Methodendiskussion. TANZ 23: 1998 ⇒208. 271-280.

7503 *Raiser, Elisabeth* Kehrt um zu Gott—seid fröhlicher Hoffnung: einige Gedanken zum Thema der nächsten Vollversammlung des Ökumenischen Rates der Kirchen aus Frauensicht. ÖR 47/2 (1998) 165-176.

7504 **Rehmann, Luzia Sutter** Vom Mut, genau hinzusehen: feministisch-befreiungstheologische Interpretationen zur Apokalyptik. Luzern 1998, Exodus 160 pp. 3-905577-28-3.

7505 *Ringe, Sharon H.* Places at the table: feminist and postcolonial biblical interpretation. The postcolonial bible. 1998 ⇒695. 136-151.

7506 **Ruether, Rosemary Radford** Introducing redemption in christian feminism. Introductions in Feminist Theology 1: Shf 1998, Academic 134 pp. $20. 1-85075-888-3. Bibl.

7507 *Sampson, Emily Walter* "More than any man has ever done": Julia Smith's search for the meaning of God's word. BiRe 14/2 (1998) 40-45, 54-55.

7508 *Sattler, Dorothea* Gesammelte Nachdenklichkeit: neuere Beiträge zur theologischen Frauenforschung. ThRv 94 (1998) 603-614.

7509 ᴱ**Schmidt, Eva Renate; Korenhof, Mieke; Jost, Renate** Rilettture bibliche al femminile. 1994 ⇒10,8822; 12,7536. ᴿHenoch 20 (1998) 371-372 (*Berruto, Anna Maria*).

7510 **Schottroff, Luise** Lydia's impatient sisters. ᵀ*Rumscheidt, Martin & Barbara.* 1995 ⇒11/2,5240... 13,7908. ᴿNew Theology Review 11/1 (1998) 109-110 (*Reid, Barbara*); CBQ 60 (1998) 588-589 (*Gillman, Florence Morgan*); JR 78 (1998) 172-174 (*Castelli, Elizabeth A.*).

7511 ᴱ**Schottroff, Luise; Wacker, Marie-Theres** Kompendium Feministische Bibelauslegung. Gü 1998, Kaiser xx; 832 pp. DM125. 3-579-00391-7.

7512 **Schottroff, Luise; Schroer, Silvia; Wacker, Marie-Theres** Bijbel in vrouwelijk perspectief. Baarn 1998, Ten Have 276 pp. ƒ45. 90-259-4703-4 [Str. 66/1,86s—Beentjes, Panc];

7513   Feminist interpretation: the bible in woman's perspective. Ph 1998, Fortress 254 pp. £13/$19. 0-8006-2999-X [RRT 6,220s—Guest, D.].
7514   **Schrein, Shannon** The feminist christologies of Sallie McFague and Elizabeth A. Johnson. ColMn 1998, Liturgical 123 pp. $34. 0-814-65876-8 [Pacifica 12,103s—Hunt, Anne].
7515   *Schroer, Silvia* Frauengeschichte hat ein Recht auf Namen. ᶠVᴇɴᴇᴛᴢ, H. 1998 ⇒122. 129-135.
7516   *Smith, Carol* 'It's in the book': using the bible in discussions of human sexuality. Religion & sexuality. 1998 ⇒302. 125-134.
7517   *Strobel, Regula* Feministisch-theologische Kritik an Kreuzestheologien. KatBl 123 (1998) 84-90.
7518   *Tamez, Elsa* Das Leben der Frauen als heiliger Text. Conc(D) 34/3 (1998) 288-296.
7519   *Thimmes, Pamela* Marking boundaries inside and outside: the ongoing tasks of feminist hermeneutics;
7520   What makes a feminist reading feminist?: another perspective;
7521   *Throckmorton, Burton H.* Why the New Testament and Psalms: an inclusive version?. Escaping Eden. 1998 ⇒278. 279-282/132-140/177-181.
7522   **Thurston, Anne** Knowing her place: gender and the gospels. Dublin 1998, Gill and Macmillan 124 pp. IR£9. 0-7171-2679-X.
7523   **Torjesen, Karen Jo** Cuando las mujeres eran sacerdotes: el liderazgo de las mujeres en la iglesia primitiva y el escándalo de su subordinación con el auge del cristianismo. 1996 ⇒12,7547. ᴿBib(L) 7/7 (1998) 151-153 (*Alves, Herculano*).
7524   *Weisgerber, Gerhard* Das endlich ist Bein von meinem Bein ...": den Rang der Frau zurechtrücken—und das ausgerechnet mit Genesis 1-3?. rhs 41 (1998) 122-126.
7525   *Wolters, Al* Cross-gender imagery in the bible. BBR 8 (1998) 217-228.

H9.0 Eschatologia NT, *spes*, hope

7526   **Alison, James** Living in the end times: the last things re-imagined. L 1997, SPCK 203 pp. 0-281-05076-7.
7527   **Alonso Schökel, Luis** Nadzieja [Speranza]. Uwierzyc Milosci. Biblioteka Poslanca Serca Jezusowego 3: Kraków 1998, Wydawnictwo WAM 349 pp. 83-7097-524-0. **P.**
7528   **Arens, Eduardo F.** Biblia y fin del mundo: una visión integral y exegética. Lima 1998, Paulinas 159 pp. 9972-686-17-5.
7529   **Balabanski, Vicky** Eschatology in the making: Mark, Matthew and the Didache. MSSNTS 97: 1997 ⇒13,7919. ᴿJThS 49 (1998) 746-749 (*Wenham, David*).
7530   **Berger, Klaus** Is met de dood alles afgelopen?. Kampen 1998, Kok 234 pp. ƒ34.90. 90-242-9336-7 [KeTh 51,161s—Spijkerboer, A.A.].
7531   *Borg, Marcus J.* The second coming then and now. The meaning of Jesus. 1998 ⇒3857. 189-196.
7532   ᴱ**Brower, Kent; Elliott, Mark** Eschatology in bible and theology: evangelical essays at the dawn of a new millennium. DG 1997, InterVarsity 347 pp. $25 [BS 157,371s—Burns, J. Lanier].
7533   *Brueggemann, Walter* Suffering produces hope. BTB 28 (1998) 95-103.

7534 **Castellucci, Erio** *Le realtà future*: nella pienezza della gioia pasquale: la centralità dell'ermeneutica nell'escatologia cristiana. SacDo.MS 43,3-4: Bo 1998, Studio Domenicano 316 pp.

7535 **Collins, Adela Yarbro** Cosmology and eschatology in Jewish and Christian apocalypticism. JSJ.S 50: Lei 1996, Brill xii; 261 pp. 90-04-10587-5. ᴿThLZ 123/4 (1998) 372-373 (*Frenschkowski, Marco*); JSJ 29 (1998) 350-351 (*Tigchelaar, Eibert J.C.*).

7536 *Fabris, Rinaldo* Immagini di punizione eterna nel Nuovo Testamento. PSV 37 (1998) 199-211.

7537 *Khoo, Jeffrey* The reality and eternality of hell: Luke 16:19-31 as proof. Stulos theological journal 6/1-2 (1998) 67-76.

7538 *Le Grys, Alan* The wisdom of too much eschatology. ᶠASHTON J. JSNT.S 153: 1998 ⇒6. 129-136.

7539 *McGinn, Bernard* The last judgment in christian tradition. Encyclopedia of apocalypticism II. 1998 ⇒507. 361-401.

7540 *Merklein, Helmut* Eschatologie im Neuen Testament <1987>;
7541 Gericht und Heil: zur heilsamen Funktion des Gerichts bei Johannes dem Täufer, Jesus und Paulus <1990>. Studien zu Jesus und Paulus II. WUNT 105: 1998 ⇒176. 82-113/60-81.

7542 *Mitchell, Margaret M.* A tale of two apocalypses. CThMi 25 (1998) 200-209 [Mt 24-25; 2 Thess 1-2].

7543 *Moltmann, Jürgen* Im Ende—Gott. Conc(D) 34 (1998) 457-465.
7544 **Moltmann, Jürgen** L'avvento di Dio: escatologia cristiana. ᵀ*Pezzetta, D.* BTCon 100: Brescia 1998, Queriniana 385 pp. ᴿED 51/2-3 (1998) 363-364 (*Mondin, B.*).

7545 *Saldarini, Anthony J.* Counting time. BiRe 14/4 (1998) 22, 51.

7546 *Schreiner, Josef* Alttestamentliches Wort zur christlichen Jahrtausendwende. Edith-Stein-Jahrbuch 4 (1998) 135-153.

7547 *Van der Horst, Pieter* "The elements will be dissolved with fire": the idea of cosmic conflagration in Hellenism, ancient Judaism, and early Christianity. Hellenism—Judaism—Christianity. 1998 ⇒Q6.5. 271-292.

H9.5 *Theologia totius [VT-] NT*—General [OT-] NT theology

7548 **Balla, Peter** Challenges to New Testament theology: an attempt to justify the enterprise. WUNT 2/95: 1997, ⇒13,7955. ᴿTrin.Journal 19 (1998) 118-122 (*Yarbrough, Robert W.*).

7549 *Barth, Gerhard* Biblische Theologie: Versuch einer vorläufigen Bilanz. EvTh 58 (1998) 384-399.

7550 *Beauchamp, Paul* È possibile una teologia biblica?. ᶠMARTINI C., Rivelazione. 1998 ⇒74. 319-332.

7551 *Bockmuehl, Markus* Humpty Dumpty and New Testament theology. Theol. 101 (1998) 330-338.

7552 **Childs, Brevard S.** Die Theologie der einen Bibel, 2: Hauptthemen. 1996 ⇒12,7583; 13,7963. ᴿZKTh 120 (1998) 103-104 (*Oberforcher, Robert*);
7553 Teologia biblica: Antico e Nuovo Testamento. ᵀ*Gatti, Enzo.* Piemme. Theologica: CasM 1998, [Piemme] 800 pp. L90.000. 88-384-3098-5. ᴿStPat 45 (1998) 263-265 (*Segalla, Giuseppe*).

7554 **Díaz Mateos, Manuel** La hablaré al corazón. Lima 1998, CEP 208 pp [PerTeol 31,145].

7555   **Gnilka, Joachim** Theologie des Neuen Testaments. 1994 ⇒10,8929
       ... 13,7967. [R]JThS 49 (1998) 302-305 (*Morgan, Robert*).
7556   Teología del Nuevo Testamento. [T]*Díaz Rodeelas, Juan M.* Biblioteca
       de ciencias bíblicas y orientales 3: M 1998, Trotta 538 pp. 84-8164-
       240-1.
7557   **Grelot, Pierre** La tradition apostolique: règle de foi et de vie pour
       l'église. 1995 ⇒11/2,265; 12,126. [R]EstB 56 (1998) 562-564 (*Rodrí-
       guez-Ruiz, M.*).
7558   **Hübner, Hans** Biblische Theologie des Neuen Testaments. 1990-
       1995, ⇒9,9650... 13,7968. 3 vols. [R]ThZ 54 (1998) 172-177; 273-279
       (*Barth, Gerhard*);
7559   Teologia biblica del Nuovo Testamento, 1: prolegomeni. 1997 ⇒13,
       7970. [R]Protest. 53 (1998) 361-362 (*Ronchi, Sergio*); SdT 20 (1998)
       95-96 (*Ciniello, Nino*).
7560   **Ingraffia, Brian D.** Postmodern theory and biblical theology. 1995
       ⇒11/2,5663; 12,7592. [R]HeyJ 39 (1998) 330-331 (*McNamara, Mar-
       tin*); JR 78 (1998) 288-290 (*Jadlos, Jane E.*); JBL 117 (1998) 170-
       172 (*Aichele, George*).
7561   **Johnson, Luke Timothy** Religious experience in earliest christiani-
       ty. Mp 1998, Fortress viii; 199 pp. $20 [CThMi 25,396–Pickett, R.].
7562   *Merk, Otto* Theologie des Neuen Testaments und biblische Theolo-
       gie. [F]MERK O. BZNW 95: 1998 <1995> ⇒79. 98-129.
7563   *Niederwimmer, Kurt* Erwägungen zur Disziplin 'Theologie des Neu-
       en Testaments'. Gesammelte Aufsätze. BZNW 90: 1998 <1993>
       ⇒182. 226-233.
7564   *Olson, Dennis T.* Biblical theology as provisional monologization: a
       dialogue with Childs, Brueggemann and Bakhtin. BiblInterp. 6
       (1998) 162-180.
7565   *Reumann, John* Profiles, problems, and possibilities in biblical theol-
       ogy today—Part II: New Testament. KuD 44 (1998) 145-169.
7566   **Schmithals, Walter** The theology of the first christians. 1997 ⇒13,
       7986. [R]HBT 20 (1998) 168-169 (*Fekkes, Jan*).
7567   *Segalla, Giuseppe* Teologia biblica: necessaria e difficile... pos-
       sibile?: per una teoria olistica della rivelazione attestata nella bibbia.
       Annales theologici 12/2 (1998) 291-326.
7568   *Sequeri, PierAngelo* La struttura testimoniale delle scritture sacre:
       teologia del testo. [F]MARTINI C., Rivelazione. 1998 ⇒74. 3-27.
7569   **Strecker, Georg** Theologie des Neuen Testaments. [E]*Horn, Friedrich
       Wilhelm.* De-Gruyter-Lehrbuch: 1996 ⇒12,7608; 13,7987. [R]BZ 42
       (1998) 126-128 (*Söding, Thomas*).
7570   **Thüsing, Wilhelm** Die neutestamentlichen Theologien und Jesus
       Christus, 2: Programm einer Theologie des Neuen Testaments mit
       Perspektiven für eine biblische Theologie. Dü 1998, Patmos 362 pp.
       DM78. 3-402-03409-3.
7571   *Vogels, Walter* Trends in biblical theology. ThD 45 (1998) 123-128.
7572   **Watson, Francis** Text and truth: redefining biblical theology. 1997
       ⇒13,7993. [R]RRT (1998/1) 50-53 (*Goulder, Michael*); TS 59 (1998)
       324-326 (*Brueggemann, Walter*); HBT 20 (1998) 156-157 (*Ollen-
       burger, Ben*); Bib. 79 (1998) 586-590 (*Claudel, Gérard*); Theol. 101
       (1998) 211-213 (*Houlden, Leslie*).

XIV. Philologia biblica

J1.1 Hebraica *grammatica*

7573 *Andersen, Francis I.; Forbes, A. Dean* Towards clause-type concordances of the Tanakh. Bible et informatique. 1998 ⇒386. 41-70.

7574 *Azevedo, Joaquim* A note on verb-compound subject agreement in Biblical Hebrew. BN 94 (1998) 33-43.

7575 *Blau, Joshua* Remarks on the development of some pronominal suffixes in Hebrew. Topics. 1998 <1982> ⇒136. 138-145:

7576 Hebrew and North West Semitic: reflections on the classification of the Semitic languages <1978> 308-332;

7577 Hebrew stress shifts, pretonic lengthening, and segolization: possible cases of Aramaic interference in Hebrew syllable structure <1978> 104-119;

7578 On the history and structure of Hebrew 1998, 11-19;

7579 Marginalia semitica I-III <1971, 1972, 1977> 185-265;

7580 The monophthongization of diphthongs as reflected in the use of vowel letters in the pentateuch <1995> 21-25;

7581 Non-phonetic conditioning of sound change and Biblical Hebrew <1979> 26-35;

7582 The parallel development of the feminine ending -*at* in Semitic languages <1980> 126-137;

7583 On pausal lengthening, pausal stress shift, Philippi's Law and rule ordering in Biblical Hebrew <1981> 36-49;

7584 Redundant pronominal suffixes denoting intrinsic possession <1979> 146-154;

7585 Some difficulties in the reconstruction of 'Proto-Hebrew' and 'Proto-Canaanite' <1968> 266-282;

7586 Some remarks on the prehistory of stress in Biblical Hebrew <1979> 120-125;

7587 Some Ugaritic, Hebrew, and Arabic parallels <1982> 333-338;

7588 On some vestiges of universalization of the units and tens of the *cardinalia* 21-99 in Arabic and Hebrew <1978> 181-184;

7589 Studies in Hebrew verb formation <1971> 155-180;

7590 Weak' phonetic change and the Hebrew *śîn*: <1977> 50-68;

7591 Introduction: on the history and structure of Hebrew. Topics in Hebrew and Semitic linguistics. 1998 ⇒136. 11-19.

7592 **Bombeck, Stefan** Das althebräische Verbalsystem aus aramäischer Sicht: Masoretischer Text, Targume und Peschitta. EHS.T 591: 1997 ⇒13,8005. ᴿBiOr 55 (1998) 485-486 (*Verheij, Arian*).

7593 **Bornemann, Robert** A grammar of Biblical Hebrew, part 1: an introduction to Biblical Hebrew, part 2: continuing Biblical Hebrew. Lanham 1998, University Press of America 285 pp. $32.50. 0-7618-1185-0 [ThD 46,259—Heiser, W. Charles].

7594 **Chisholm, Robert B., Jr.** From exegesis to exposition: a practical guide to using Biblical Hebrew. GR 1998, Baker 304 pp. $20 [AUSS 37,294—Stefanovic, Zdravko].

7595 *Coetzee, A.W.* Syllabification and epenthesis in Tiberian Hebrew—perspectives from Optimality Theory. JSem 9 (1997) 87-128 Sum. 87.

7596 *Dahan, Gilbert* La connaissance des langues bibliques dans le monde chrétien d'Occident, XIIᵉ-XIVᵉ siècle. Les origines du Collège de France. ᴱ**Fumaroli, Marc**, P 1998, Collège de France. 327-355 [RBen 110,136—Bogaert, P.-M.].

7597 **Disse, Andreas** Informationsstruktur im Biblischen Hebräisch: sprachwissenschaftliche Grundlagen und exegetische Konsequenzen einer Korpusuntersuchung zu den Büchern Deuteronomium, Richter und 2 Könige. ATSAT 56/1-2: St. Ottilien 1998, EOS 2 vols; xi; 419; 83 pp. 3-88096-556-0; -462-9. Diss. Tübingen 1996; Bibl.

7598 **Driver, Samuel Rolles** A treatise on the use of the tenses in Hebrew and some other syntactical questions. Introd. *Garr, Randall*. Biblical Resource: GR ⁴1998 <1892 [3rd ed.]>, Eerdmans 306 pp. $30. 0-8028-4160-0 [BiTod 36,259—Bergant, Dianne].

7599 *Dyk, Janet* Valency patterns and translation proposals (abstract). Bible et informatique. 1998 ⇒386. 283.

7600 *Eldar, Ilan* Hebrew philology between the East and Spain: the concept of derivation as a case study. JSSt 43 (1998) 49-61.

7601 *Ernst, Alexander B.* Lehrbücher des Biblischen Hebräisch: einige deutschsprachige Neuerscheinung der 90er Jahre. VF 43/2 (1998) 2-13.

7602 *Fernández Tejero, Emilia; Fernández Marcos, Natalio* Benedicti Ariae MONTANI in librum de hebraicis idiotismis. RevAg 41 (1998) 997-1016.

7603 *Fox, Joshua* מכפל בע' הפעל במשקלי השמות בעברית ובשאר השפות השמיות [Gemination in C₂ of noun patterns in Hebrew and other Semitic languages]. Leš. 61 (1998) 19-30 Sum. II.

7604 *García-Jalón de la Lama, Santiago* La gramática hebrea de la Regiomontana. RevAg 41 (1998) 973-996.

7605 **García-Jalón de la Lama, Santiago** La gramática hebrea en Europa en el siglo XVI: guía de lectura de las obras impresas. BSal.E 204: S 1998, Universidad Pontificia 206 pp. 84-7299-437-6 [BAEO 35, 399s—Valle R., C. del].

7606 *Gianto, Agustinus* Mood and modality in classical Hebrew. ᶠRAINEY, A. IOS 18: 1998 ⇒96. 183-198.

7607 *Gordon, Constance W.* l"j collectives of the Qetûl formation. ᶠGORDON, C. JSOT.S 273: 1998 ⇒31. 64-68.

7608 *Gosling, F.A.* An interesting use of the waw consecutive. ZAW 110 (1998) 403-410.

7609 **Groß, Walter** Die Satzteilfolge im Verbalsatz alttestamentlicher Prosa: untersucht an den Büchern Dtn, Ri und 2Kön. FAT 17: 1996 ⇒12,7639. ᴿBiOr 55 (1998) 483-484 (*Verheij, Arian*).

7610 **Hadas-Lebel, Mireille** Histoire de la langue hébraique, des origines à l'époque de la mishna. REJ.Collection 21: ⁴1995 ⇒13,8019. ᴿJBL 117 (1998) 131-132 (*Hostetter, Edwin C.*).

7611 *Heide, Martin* Ein Lehrbuch für Könner. BN 95 (1998) 18-20.

7612 **Horsnell, Malcolm John Albert** A review and reference grammar for Biblical Hebrew. Hamilton, Ontario 1998, McMaster Univ. xi; 464 pp. 0-920603-48-3.

7613 *Jenni, Ernst* Vollverb und Hilfsverb mit Infinitiv—Ergänzung im Hebräischen. ZAH 11 (1998) 50-67.

7614 *Joosten, Jan* The functions of the Semitic D stem: Biblical Hebrew materials for a comparative-historical approach. Or. 67 (1998) 202-230.

7615 *Kedar-Kopfstein, Benjamin* Lexikalisches und grammatisches Material. ZÁH 11 (1998) 90-108.

7616 *Kemp, William; Desrosiers-Bonin, Diane* Marie d'Ennetières et la petite grammaire hébraïque de sa fille d'après la dédicace de l' *Epistre* à Marguerite de Navarre (1539). BHR 60/1 (1998) 117-134.

7617 *Khan, Geoffrey* The book of Hebrew grammar by the Karaite Joseph BEN NOAH1. JSSt 43 (1998) 265-286.

7618 *Krispenz, Jutta* Grammatik und Theologie in der Botenformel. ZAH 11 (1998) 133-139.

7619 **Kuriyagawa, Fukuko** Fundamentals of the Hebrew language. Tokyo 1998, Daigako-Shurin 464 pp [Leš. 62,vi—Rosenhouse, Judith; Kowner, Rotem]. **J**.

7620 **Martin, James** Hebräische Elementargrammatik. ^T*Hagedorn, A.C.* UTB.W 1945: Tü 1998, Mohr xii; 199 pp. DM19.80. 3-16-145536-9 [ThLZ 124,160s—Beyse, Karl-Martin].

7621 **Massey, Keith Andrew** The concord of collective nouns and verbs in Biblical Hebrew: a controlled study. ^DWisconsin—Madison 1998, 176 pp.

7622 **Miller, Cynthia Lynn** The representation of speech in Biblical Hebrew narrative: a linguistic analysis. HSM 55: 1996 ⇒12,7655; 13,8037. ^RBSOAS 61 (1998) 327-328 (*Williamson, H.G.M.*); BiOr 55 (1998) 481-483 (*Verheij, Arian*); CBQ 60 (1998) 126-127 (*Person, Raymond F.*); JQR 89 (1998) 230-235 (*Meier, Samuel*).

7623 *Naudé, J.A.* The syntactic status of the ethical dative in Biblical Hebrew. JSem 9 (1997) 129-165 Sum. 129.

7624 *Noegel, Scott B.* A slip of the reader and not the reed II. JBQ 26 (1998) 93-100.

7625 *Prato, Gian Luigi* Babilonia terra d'"esilio" e centro propulsore dell'ebraismo: un fenomeno di dissociazione valutativa. ^FMARTINI, C. RivBib.S 33: 1998 ⇒75. 57-76.

7626 **Putnam, Frederic Clarke** A cumulative index to the grammar and syntax of Biblical Hebrew. 1996 ⇒12,7660. ^RBS 155 (1998) 118-119 (*Taylor, Richard A.*).

7627 *Qimron, Elisha* הצעה חדשה לפירוש צורות העתיד בעברית הקדומה [A new approach toward interpreting the imperfect verbal forms in Early Hebrew]. Leš. 61 (1998) 31-43 Sum. III.

7628 La questione ebraica: rassegna di studi sulla morfologia dell'ebraismo, vol. 1. [Padova] 1998, Ar 134 pp.

7629 **Richter, Wolfgang** Materialien einer althebräischen Datenbank: Nominalformen. ATSAT 51; MUS.ATSAT 51: St. Ottilien 1998, EOS xii; 82 pp. 3-88096-551-X.

7630 ^M**RUBINSTEIN, Eliezer** Studies in Hebrew language. Teuda 9: 1995 ⇒11/2,161. ^RJJS 49 (1998) 373-374 (*Morgenstern, Matthew*); BiOr 55 (1998) 882-884 (*Muraoka, Takamitsu*).

7631 *Sadka, Isaac* זהר מאת |האפוזיציה—היחס השלישי?| למאמר תגובה :ההקבלה 70-57 'עמ ,[תשנ|ו], לשוננו נט |לבנת ומאיר סלע [Response to "Ap-position—the third relation?" (Leš. 59 [1995]: 57-70)]. Leš. 61 (1998) 233-250 Sum. IV. **H**.

7632 *Shatil, Nimrod* לתולדות היחסים בין כינויים אחדים [Historical relations between two pronominal elements]. Leš. 61 (1998) 7-17 Sum. I. **H**.

7633 *Siewert, Klaus* Sondersprachliche Hebraismen. ZAH 11 (1998) 82-4.

7634 *Syring, Wolf Dieter* QUEST 2—computergestützte Philologie und Exegese. ZAH 11 (1998) 85-89.

7635 *Tropper, Josef* Althebräisches und semitisches Aspektsystem. ZAH 11 (1998) 153-190.
7636 *Van der Heide, Albert* Hebraica veritas: hebreeuwse taal en jodendom. Interpretatie 6/8 (1998) 19-21.
7637 *Verheij, Arian J.C.* Quelques remarques sur la distribution des racines à n. Bible et informatique. 1998 ⇒386. 161-163.
7638 *Voigt, Rainer* Der Artikel im Semitischen. JSSt 43 (1998) 221-258.
7639 *Volgger, David* Die Pendenskonstruktion und ihre grammatische Diskussion. SBFLA 48 (1998) 105-124 Sum. 516.
7640 **Wesselius, J.W.** Korte grammatica van het Bijbels Hebreeuws. Bussum 1998, Coutinho 123 pp. ƒ39.50. Met CD [GThT 98,138].
7641 **Zevit, Ziony** The anterior construction in classical Hebrew. SBL.MS 50: Atlanta, GA 1998, Scholars xiii; 94 pp. $25. 0-7885-0443-6. Bibl.
7642 *Zewi, Tamar* The syntactical status of exceptive phrases in Biblical Hebrew. Bib. 79 (1998) 542-548.

J1.2 **Lexica et inscriptiones hebraicae;** *later Hebrew*

7643 **Alonso Schökel, Luis** Dicionário bíblico hebraico-português. 1997 ⇒13,8078. ᴿRBBras 15 (1998) 438-440.
7644 *Becking, Bob* Does a recently published Paleo-Hebrew inscription refer to the Solomonic temple?. BN 92 (1998) 5-11.
7645 *Berlejung, Angelika; Schüle, Andreas* Erwägungen zu den neuen Ostraka aus der Sammlung Moussaïeff. ZAH 11 (1998) 68-73.
7646 *Bons, Eberhard* Konnte eine Witwe die *naḥalah* ihres verstorbenen Mannes erben?: Überlegungen zum Ostrakon 2 aus der Sammlung Moussaïeff. ZAR 4 (1998) 197-208.
7647 *Bordreuil, P.; Israel, F.; Pardee, D.* King's command and widow's plea: two new Hebrew ostraca of the biblical period. NEA(BA) 61/1 (1998) 2-13.
7648 *Bräker, Antje, al.,* Lexikalisches und grammatisches Material. ZAH 11 (1998) 210-224.
7649 ᴱ**Clines, David J.A.** א. The dictionary of classical Hebrew, 1. 1993 ⇒9,9718... 13,8085. ᴿJNES 57 (1998) 41-42 (*Pardee, Dennis*);
7650 ב-ר. The dictionary of classical Hebrew, 2. 1995, ⇒12,7681; 13,8086. ᴿJAOS 118 (1998) 437-439 (*Fitzmyer, Joseph A.*); ThLZ 123 (1998) 128-129 (*Körner, Jutta*);
7651 ט-ר. The dictionary of classical Hebrew, 3. 1996 ⇒12,7682; 13,8086. ᴿThLZ 123 (1998) 846-847 (*Körner, Jutta*); JThS 49 (1998) 197-198 (*Gibson, J.C.L.*);
7652 Yodh-Lamedh. The dictionary of classical Hebrew, 4. Shf 1998, Academic 642 pp. £100/$150. 1-85075-681-3.
7653 *Clines, David J.A.* The Dictionary of Classical Hebrew. OT essays, 2. JSOT.S 293: 1998 <1990> ⇒142. 602-612.
7654 *Corre, Alan D.* The influence of Hebrew on Portuguese. ᶠGORDON, C. JSOT.S 273: 1998 ⇒31. 512-516.
7655 *Cross, Frank Moore; Eshel, Esther* The missing link: does a new inscription establish a connection between Qumran and the Dead Sea scrolls?. BArR 24/2 (1998) 48-53, 69.
7656 *Crown, A.D.* Codicography and codicology in Samaritan manuscripts. ᶠMARGAIN, J. 1998 ⇒71. 165-184.

7657 *Demichelis, Maria Sita* Il manoscritto II Collezione Firkovič, I. Ebr.-Ar. 1679. Henoch 20 (1998) 329-337.

7658 *Deutsch, Robert* First impression: what we learn from king Ahaz's seal. BArR 24/3 (1998) 54-56, 62.

7659 [E]**Donner, H.** ־י. W. Gesenius: Hebräisches und Aramäisches Handwörterbuch über das Alte Testament. 1995, Lief. 2. ⇒11/2,5762. [R]VT 48 (1998) 270-273 (*Emerton, J.A.*).

7660 *Dothan, Trude* Cultural crossroads: Deir el-Balah & the cosmopolitan culture of the Late Bronze Age. BArR 24/5 (1998) 24-37, 70, 72, 74.

7661 *Elizur, Binyamin, al.*, מן העבודה במילון ההיסטורי [The Historical Dictionary Project]. Leš. 61 (1998) 145-158 Sum. VIII.

7662 *Eph'al, Israel; Naveh, Joseph* Remarks on the recently published Moussaieff ostraca. IEJ 48 (1998) 269-273.

7663 *Garbini, Giovanni* Note di lessicografia ebraica. StBi 118: [Brescia] 1998, Paideia 198 pp. L33.000. 88-394-0557-7.

Gogel, S. A grammar of epigraphic Hebrew 1998 ⇒8090.

7664 **Hempel, Charlotte** The laws of the Damascus document: sources, tradition and redaction. StTDJ 29: Lei 1998, Brill xii; 217 pp. $78. 90-04-11150-6. Bibl.

7665 *Hess, Richard S.* Issues in the study of personal names in the Hebrew Bible. CurResB 6 (1998) 169-192.

7666 *Hurowitz, Victor* Notes on a recently published administrative document. IEJ 48 (1998) 132-135.

7667 **Hüttenmeister, Frowald-Gil** אוצר ראשי תיבות וקיצורים במצבות AHG: Abkürzungsverzeichnis hebräischer Grabinschriften. 1996 ⇒12,7695. [R]REJ 157 (1998) 418-419 (*Nahon, Gérard*).

7668 **Kaltner, John** The use of Arabic in Biblical Hebrew lexicography. CBQMS 28: 1996 ⇒12,7847; 13,8101. [R]JQR 89 (1998) 191-193 (*Fassberg, Steven E.*).

7669 [E]**Koehler, L.; Baumgartner, W.** ׳-ḥ; ṭ-ʿ; p-ś. The Hebrew and Aramaic lexicon of the Old Testament. [TE]*Richardson, Mervyn E.J.* 1994-1996, collab. *Jongeling-Vos, G.J.; Regt, L.J. de* ⇒12,7699; 13,8103. 3 vols. [R]VT 48/1 (1998) 118-120 (*Emerton, J.A.*);

7670 rʾh-tšʿ. Hebräisches und aramäisches Lexikon zum Alten Testament, 4. [3]1990 ⇒6,9200...9,9741. [R]VT 48 (1998) 111-116 (*Emerton, J.A.*);

7671 Hebräisches und aramäisches Lexikon zum AT. Lei [3]1995, Brill 2 vols. $603.50. [R]VT 48 (1998) 116-117 (*Emerton, J.A.*);

7672 A bilingual dictionary of the Hebrew and Aramaic Old Testament: English and German. Lexicon in Veteris Testamenti Libros, 1953-1985: Lei 1998, Brill. Suppl. to a bilingual dictionary of the Hebrew and Aramaic OT. lxx; 1138, (li-lii); [xl, 227] pp. 90-04-11278-2.

7673 *Lehmann, Reinhard G.* Typologie und Signatur: Studien zu einem Listenostrakon aus der Sammlung Moussaieff. UF 30 (1998) 397-459.

7674 *Lemaire, André* Les formules de datation en Palestine au premier millénaire avant J.-C. Temps vécu. 1998 ⇒445. 53-82.

7675 *Mendecki, Norbert* Epigraf z Tell Siran [De epigrapho e Tell Siran]. RBL 51 (1998) 35-38. P.

7676 **Muraoka, Takamitsu** Modern Hebrew for biblical scholars. Wsb [2]1998 <1982>, Harrassowitz xlv; 183 pp. DM48. 3-447-04082-3.

7677 *Mykytiuk, Lawrence J.* Is Hophni in the ʿIzbet Ṣarṭah ostracon?. AUSS 36/1 (1998) 69-80;

7678 **Mykytiuk, Lawrence James** Identifying Biblical persons in Hebrew inscriptions and two stelae from before the Persian era. ᴰWisconsin —Madison 1998, 334 pp.

7679 *Naveh, Joseph* Scripts and inscriptions in ancient Samaria. IEJ 48 (1998) 91-100.

7680 *Norin, Stig* The age of the Siloam inscription and Hezekiah's tunnel. VT 48 (1998) 37-48.

7681 *Noy, David* Letters out of Judaea: echoes of Israel in Jewish inscriptions from Europe. Jewish local patriotism. JSPE.S 31: 1998 ⇒414. 106-117.

7682 *Orazi, Stefano* Manoscritti salvati dal rogo: le pergamene ebraiche di Cagli. RasIsr 64/2 (1998) 29-68.

7683 ᴱ**Perani, Mauro; Campanini, Saverio** I frammenti ebraici di Bologna: Archivio di Stato e collezioni minori. 1997 ⇒13,8119. ᴿRivBib 46 (1998) 229-231 (*Fumagalli, Pier Francesco*);

7684 I frammenti ebraici di Modena: Archivio storico comunale. 1997 ⇒ 13,8120. ᴿRivBib 46 (1998) 229-231 (*Fumagalli, Pier Francesco*).

7685 **Pérez Fernàndez, Miguel** An introductory grammar of Rabbinic Hebrew. 1997 ⇒13,8118. ᴿLeš. 61 (1998) 159-166 [H.] (*Blau, Joshua*).

7686 *Podolsky, Baruch* Notes on Hebrew etymology. ᶠRAINEY, A. IOS 18: 1998 ⇒96. 199-205.

7687 *Qimron, Elisha* כתובות עבריות חדשות וייחודי לשונן [New Hebrew inscriptions: their linguistic contribution]. Leš. 61 (1998) 181-185 Sum. I.

7688 **Renz, Johannes** Schrift und Schreibertradition. ADPV 23: 1997 ⇒13,8125. ᴿBiOr 55 (1998) 486-487 (*Lemaire, A.*).

7689 **Reymond, Philippe** Dizionario di ebraico e aramaico biblici. 1995 ⇒11/2,5775; 13,8126. ᴿSal. 60 (1998) 574-575 (*Loss, Nicolò M.*).

7690 **Rosén, Haiim B.** Hebrew at the crossroads of cultures. 1995 ⇒11/2,5776. ᴿBiOr 55 (1998) 247-249 (*Van der Heide, Albert*).

7691 *Segert, Stanislav* Hebrew Essenes—Aramaic christians. ᴹKLAWEK A. 1998 ⇒51. 169-184.

7692 *Shehadeh, Haseeb* The influence of Arabic on modern Hebrew. ᶠMARGAIN, J. 1998 ⇒71. 149-161.

7693 *Sivan, Daniel* The Gezer Calendar and Northwest Semitic languages. IEJ 48 (1998) 101-105.

7694 **Testa, E.N.** Nomi personali semitici biblici angelici profani: studio filologico e comparativo. 1994 ⇒11/2,5780. ᴿCDios 111/1 (1998) 325-326 (*Gutiérrez, J.*).

7695 ᴱ**Van Bekkum, Wout Jac.** Hebrew poetry from late antiquity: liturgical poems of Yehudah. AGJU 43: Lei 1998, Brill xxx; (4) 183 pp. 90-04-11216-2.

7696 *Yardeni, Ada* Breaking the missing link: Cross and Eshel misread the Qumran ostracon relating the settlement to the Dead Sea scrolls. BArR 24/3 (1998) 44-47.

J1.3 **Voces** *ordine alphabetico consonantium* **hebraicarum**

Akkadian

7697 *ḥalbu: Loretz, Oswald* Akkadisch-ugaritisch ḥalbu/ḫlb-hebräisch ḥlb (Ps 81,17): ein Beitrag zur Sozialgeographie Altsyrien-Palästinas ᶠRömer, W. AOAT 253: 1998 ⇒97. 223-244.

7698   *na'āsu*: Tawil, Hayim Late Hebrew-Aramaic לעם, Akkadian *na'āsu*: a
       lexicographical note V. Beit Mikra 156 (1998) 96-94 sum. 94. **H**;
7699   *saklu*: Hebrew סכל-שׂכל, Akkadian *saklu*: a lexicographical note III.
       Beit Mikra 153 (1998) 216-203 sum. 202. **H**.
7700   *urpatu(m)*: Olmo Lete, G. del Le phén. *'rpt*, l'acc. *urpatu(m)* et le
       groupe lexical */g-r-b/p*. Transeuphratène 14 (1998) 167-174.

Aramaic

7701   גְּלְגַּל: Grelot, P. גַּלְגַּל (Ézéchiel 10, 2.6.13 et Daniel 7,9). Transeuphra-
       tène 15 (1998) 137-147.
7702   כף ;רגל; יד: Péter-Contesse, René Main, pied, paume?: les noms des
       extrémités des membres (יד, רגל, כ) en hébreu et en araméen biblique.
       RB 105 (1998) 481-491.
7703   כפא: Fitzmyer, Joseph A. Aramaic kepha' and Peter's name in the
       New Testament. To advance the gospel. 1998 <1979> ⇒150. 112-
       124.
       לעם: Tawil, H. Late Hebrew-Aramaic לעם 1998 ⇒7698.

Hebrew

7704   אבל: Clines, David J.A. Was there an *'bl* II 'be dry' in Classical
       Hebrew?. OT essays, 2. JSOT.S 293: 1998 <1992> ⇒142. 585-594.
7705   אָז: Raffeld, Meir לפרשנותה של התיבה 'אז'—במקרא על פי חיבור פולמוסי
       מהמאה ה-19 [Interpretations of the biblical word 'az' in light of a rare
       19th century work]. BetM 154-155 (1998) 306-313 Sum. 335.
7706   אמן: Seybold, Klaus Zur Vorgeschichte der liturgischen Formel
       'Amen'. Studien zur Psalmenauslegung. 1998 <1992> ⇒201. 260-
       269.
7707   בשׁ: Hamilton, Gordon J. New evidence for the authenticity of "bšt"
       in Hebrew personal names and for its use as a divine epithet in bibli-
       cal texts. CBQ 60 (1998) 228-250.
7708   בליעל: Autexier, Maria Bly'l: implications d'un champ sémantique
       clos. "Lasset uns Brücken bauen...". BEAT 42: 1998 ⇒401. 45-57.
7709   בְּרִיאָה: Bindi, Stefano בְּרִיאָה. Semantics. 1998 ⇒354. 3-10.
7710   גאל: Bojorge, Horacio Go'el: el Dios Pariente en la cultura bíblica.
       Strom. 54 (1998) 33-83.
7711   גלה: Gosling, F.A. An open question relating to the Hebrew root גלה.
       ZAH 11 (1998) 125-132.
7712   דֶּרֶךְ: Aitken, James K. דֶּרֶךְ. Semantics. 1998 ⇒354. 11-37.
7713   דרך: **Zender, Markus Philipp** Wegmetaphorik im Alten Testament:
       eine semantische Untersuchung der alttestamentlichen und altorienta-
       lischen Weg-Lexeme mit besonderer Berücksichtigung der metapho-
       rischen Verwendung. ᴰBasel 1996-1997: ᴰJenni, E. [ThRv 94,vii].
7714   הָדַם: Salvesen, Alison הָדַם. Semantics. 1998 ⇒354. 38-43.
7715   הָדָר: Rubinstein, Yakov האתרוג במשנה ובתלמוד [The etrog—is it 'Peri
       ets hadar']. Beit Mikra 153 (1998) 175-178 Sum. 196.
7716   היה: Isaksson, Bo "Aberrant" usages of introductory *wehaya* in the
       light of text linguistics. "Lasset uns Brücken bauen...". BEAT 42:
       1998 ⇒401. 9-25.
       חלב: Loretz, O. 1998 ⇒7697.

7717 חלה II: *Seybold, Klaus* Reverenz und Gebet: Erwägungen zu der Wendung *ḥillā panîm*. Studien zur Psalmenauslegung. 1998 <1976> ⇒201. 244-259.

7718 חֶסֶד; χάρις: *Goud, Johan* Genade. ITBT 6/1 (1998) 29-30.

7719 חֹסֶד: *Swetnam, James* Hesed w Starym Testamencie a *eleos* w Nowym [Old Testament *hesed* and New Testament *eleos*. RBL 51 (1998) 251-260 [AcBib 10,515]. P.

כַּף; רֶגֶל, יָד: *Péter-Contesse, R.* Main, pied, paume? 1998 ⇒7702.

7720 יָרַד; עָלָה: *Dorn, Louis O.* 'Going down' and 'going up'. BiTr 49 (1998) 239-245.

7721 כָּבוֹד: **Struppe, Ursula** Die Herrlichkeit Jahwes in der Priesterschrift. ÖBS 9: 1988 ⇒4,a270...7,9160. [R]ThR 63 (1998) 257-259 (*Schmidt, Ludwig*).

7722 כּוּשׁ: *Høyland, Marta* An African presence in the Old Testament?: David Tuesday Adamo's interpretation of the Old Testament Cush passages. OTEs 11 (1998) 50-58.

7723 כְּנַעַן: *Hess, Richard S.* Occurrences of "Canaan" in late Bronze Age archives of the west Semitic world. [F]*Rainey, A.* IOS 18: 1998 ⇒96. 365-372.

7724 כְּסָּא: *Salvesen, Alison* כְּסָּא. Semantics. 1998 ⇒354. 44-65.

7725 כתב: **Schaack, Thomas** Die Ungeduld des Papiers: Studien zum alttestamentlichen Verständnis des Schreibens anhand des Verbums *ktb* im Kontext administrativer Vorgänge. [D]Kiel 1996-97: [D]*Donner, H.* BZAW 262: B 1998, De Gruyter ix; 382 pp. DM198. 311-015907-4.

7726 כֶּתֶר: *Salvesen, Alison* כֶּתֶר. Semantics. 1998 ⇒354. 67-73.

7727 לְאֹם: *Malamat, Abraham* A recently discovered word for 'clan' in Mari and its Hebrew cognate. Mari and the bible. 1998 <1995> ⇒173. 165-167.

7728 לְמַעַן: *Chinitz, Jacob* L'Maan: the teleological cause in the pentateuch. JBQ 26 (1998) 189-192.

לעם: *Tawil, H.* Late Hebrew-Aramaic לעם. 1998 ⇒7698.

7729 מְאֵרָה: *Aitken, James K.* מְאֵרָה. Semantics. 1998 ⇒354. 74-78.

7730 מַעְגָּל II: *Aitken, James K.* מַעְגָּל II. Semantics. 1998 ⇒354. 79-85.

7731 מרזח: **McLaughlin, John Leo** The marzeah in the prophetic literature: an examination of the references and possible allusions in light of the extra-biblical evidence. [D]U. of St Michael's College 1998, 258 pp.

7732 מרזח: **Woo, Taek Joo** The marzeah institution and rites for the dead: a comparative and systemic study with special attention to the eighth-century prophets. [D]Graduate Theological Union 1998, 310 pp.

7733 מִשְׁעוֹל: *Aitken, James K.* מִשְׁעוֹל. Semantics. 1998 ⇒354. 86-88.

7734 נֵזֶת: *Salvesen, Alison* נֵזֶת. Semantics 1998 ⇒354. 89-100.

7735 נַעַר; נערה: **Leeb, Carolyn S.** Away from the father's house: the social location of the na'ar and na'arah in Ancient Israel. [D]Lutheran School of Theology 1998, 237 pp.

7736 נָקַב II: *Aitken, James K.* נָקַב II. Semantics. 1998 ⇒354. 101-105.

שׂכל; סכל...: *Tawil, H.* Hebrew שׂכל-סכל, Akkadian *saklu*. 1998 ⇒7698.

7737 עֵזֶר: *Ska, Jean Louis* 'Gli voglio fare un alleato che sia suo omologo' (Gen. 2,18): a proposito del termine 'ezer—'aiuto'. [T]*Cervigni, Lucilla*: Firmana 18 (1998) 61-68.

7738 עֲטָרָה: *Salvesen, Alison* עֲטָרָה. Semantics. 1998 ⇒354. 106-113.

7739 עם: *Zurro Rodríguez, Eduardo* Valor comparativo de la partícula 'im. EstB 56 (1998) 251-260.

7740 עשק: *Salm, Eva* 'ašaq = "unterdrücken"?: Überlegungen zur Bedeutung der Wurzel ʿšq anhand der vorexilischen Prophetentexte Am 3,9; 4,1; Hos 5,11; 12,8; Mi 2,2. ^FRUPPERT, L. FzB 88: 1998 ⇒99. 335-353.

7741 עת *Sznycer, Maurice* En guise de conclusion: note sur le terme désignant le 'temps' dans les langues ouest-sémitiques. Temps vécu. 1998 ⇒445. 235-238.

7742 פאה: *Samarrai, Alauddin* Notices on Pe'ah, Fay' and Feudum ^FGordon, C. JSOT.S 273: 1998 ⇒31. 243-250.

7743 פנימה: *Malamat, Abraham* Is there a word for the royal harem in the bible?: the *inside* story. Mari and the bible. 1998 <1995> ⇒173. 172-174.

7744 צֶדֶק: *Ish-Horowicz, Moshe* Righteousness (Tsedek) in the Bible and its rabbinic interpretations. Interpretation of the Bible. JSOT.S 289: 1998 ⇒389. 577-587.

7745 צדק: *Jackson, Bernard S.* Justice and righteousness in the bible: rule of law or royal paternalism?. ZAR 4 (1998) 218-262.

7746 צלם: *Clines, David J.A.* The etymology of Hebrew *ṣelem*. OT essays, 2. JSOT.S 293: 1998 <1974> ⇒142. 577-584.

7747 צרעה: *Kislev, Mordechai E.* זיהויי צֶרעה: בתנ״ך ובדברי חז״ל [Reidentification of צרעה in the bible and in rabbinic literature]. Leš. 61 (1998) 51-60 Sum. IV.

7748 קֶבֶב: *Aitken, James K.* Semantics. 1998 ⇒354. 114-121.

7749 רגל: *Voigt, Rainer* 'Fuß' (und 'Hand') im Äthiopischen, Syroarabischen und Hebräischen. ZAH 11 (1998) 191-199.

7750 רחוב: *Clines, David J.A.* Squares and streets: the distinction of רְחוֹב 'square' and רְחֹבוֹת 'streets'. OT essays, 2. JSOT.S 29: 1998 ⇒142. 631-636.

שכל: *Tawil, H.* Hebrew שכל-סכל, Akkadian *saklu*. 1998 ⇒7698.

7751 שֶׁבֶט: *Salvesen, Alison* שֵׁבֶט. Semantics. 1998 ⇒354. 122-136.

7752 שׁוּר: *Firth, David G.* A note on the meaning of שׁוּרר in the Psalms. OTEs 11 (1998) 40-49.

7753 שכב: *Hopkins, Simon* II Sam. 17:28—beds, sofas, and Hebrew lexicography. SCI 17 (1998) 1-9.

Phoenician

'rpt: *Olmo Lete, G. del* Le phén. *'rpt* 1998 ⇒7700.

Ugaritic

7754 ṯrry/t: *Olmo Lete, G. del* Notes on Semitic lexicography (I): the proto-Semitic cluster /ṯr(r:w:y)/ and Ug. *ṯrry/t*. AulOr 16 (1998) 187-192.

ḫlb: *Loretz, O.* Akkadisch-ugaritisch ḫalbu/ḫlb 1998 ⇒7697.

7755 ṯhm: *Watson, Wilfred G.E.* Delimiting Ugaritic *ṯhm*: a brief report. UF 30 (1998) 745-749.

J1.5 *Phoenicia, ugaritica*—**Northwest Semitic** [⇒T5.4]

7756 **Aartun, Kjell** Die minoische Schrift, Sprache und Texte, 2: Linear A-Inschriften. Wsb 1997, Harrassowitz 893 pp. DM310 [RBBras 16,506s].
7757 *Al-Ghul, Omar; El-Khouri, Lamia* Ein Graffito aus *Tell Abū Ḥaraz.* ZDPV 114 (1998) 155-161.
7758 *Arnaud, D.* Le dialecte d'Alalah: un examen préliminaire. AulOr 16 (1998) 143-186.
7759 **Beckman, Gary** Texts from the vicinity of Emar in the collection of Jonathan Rosen. 1996 ⇒12,7774. ᴿBSOAS 61 (1998) 326 (*Fleming, Daniel E.*); WO 29 (1998) 184-190 (*Tsukimoto, Akio*).
7760 *Blau, Joshua* Short philological notes on the Inscription of Meša`. Topics in Hebrew... linguistics. 1998 <1979-80> 344-359.
7761 *Colless, Brian E.* The Canaanite syllabary. Abr-n. 35 (1998) 28-46.
7762 *Cunchillos Ilarri, Jesús-Luis* Organisation et spécifications de la Banque de données "Banco de Datos Filológicos Semíticos Nordoccidentales". Bible et informatique. 1998 ⇒386. 345-356.
7763 **Dietrich, Manfried,** *al.*, The cuneiform alphabetic texts from Ugarit. ²1995 ⇒11/2,5891... 13,8203. ᴿRBBras 15 (1998) 461-463.
7764 *Dietrich, Manfried; Loretz, Oswald* Der Text der Krughenkelinschrift KTU 6.2. UF 30 (1998) 887-888.
7765 *Ford, J.N.* "Ninety-nine by the evil eye and one from natural causes": KTU2 1.96 in its Near Eastern context. UF 30 (1998) 201-278.
7766 *Fox, Joshua* The Ugaritic divine epithet *ybmt limm* and the biblical *'emîm.* UF 30 (1998) 279-288.
7767 *Gulde, Stefanie* KTU 1.23—die Beschwörung der *Agzrym bn ym.* UF 30 (1998) 289-334.
7768 *Heltzer, M.* Phoenician epigraphic miscellanea. AulOr 16 (1998) 77-84.
7769 **Hoftijzer, Jean; Jongeling, K.** Dictionary of the North-West Semitic inscriptions. 1995 ⇒11/2,5895... 13,8207. ᴿBiOr 55 (1998) 221-225 (*Segert, Stanislav*); JAOS 118 (1998) 96-97 (*Rendsburg, Gary A.*); JNES 57 (1998) 42-43 (*Pardee, Dennis*).
7770 *Holloway, Steven W.* KTU 1.162 and the offering of a shield. UF 30 (1998) 353-361.
7771 **Izre'el, Shlomo** Canaano-Akkadian. Languages of the world, Materials 82: Mü 1998, Lincom-Europa viii; 80 pp. 3-89586-126-4. Bibl.
7772 *Lemaire, André* La tablette ougaritique alphabétique UF 29, 826 replacée dans son contexte. UF 30 (1998) 461-466.
7773 *Lozachmeur, H.* Épigraphe sur jarre d'Éléphantine (collection Charles Clermont-Ganneau, n° 248) (Pl. VI). TEuph 15 (1998) 183-186.
7774 **Masami, Tanigawa** Ugarito no Shinwa: Baalu no Monogatari. Kokubunjishi (Japan) 1998, Shinp√sha 267 pp. 4-7974-0327-6. Bibl. **J.**
7775 *Page, Hugh R.* Divine anatomy and social reality in the Ugaritic Baal myth: an exploration into the use of the body as interpretive lens. UF 30 (1998) 603-613.
7776 *Pardee, D.* A brief reply to G. del Olmo Lete's reply. AulOr 16 (1998) 255-260;
7777 Remarks on J.T.'s [Josef Tropper] "Epigraphische Anmerkungen". AulOr 16 (1998) 85-102.

7778 **Rainey, Anson F.** Canaanite in the Amarna tablets: a linguistic analysis of the mixed dialect used by the scribes from Canaan. HO 1/25: 1996 ⇒12,10432. 4 vols. ^RJSSt 43 (1998) 134-137 (*Hess, Richard S.*); BiOr 55 (1998) 458-465 (*Fox, J.*); JAOS 118 (1998) 595-597 (*Van Soldt, W.H.*); AJSR 23 (1998) 245-247 (*Rendsburg, Gary A.*).

7779 *Rainey, Anson F.* Syntax, hermeneutics and history. IEJ 48 (1998) 239-251.

7780 *Rendsburg, Gary* On the potential significance of the Linear A inscriptions recently excavated in Israel. AulOr 16 (1998) 289-294.

7781 *Röllig, Wolfgang* Sinn und Form: formaler Aufbau und literarische Struktur der Karatepe-Inschrift. ^FÇAMBEL H. 1998 ⇒4. 675-680.

7782 *Sader, Hélène* Phoenician inscriptions from Beirut. ^MWARD W. 1998 ⇒123. 203-213.

7783 **Sivan, Daniel** A grammar of the Ugaritic language. HO 1/28: 1997 ⇒13,8213. ^ROr. 67 (1998) 539-542 (*Gianto, Agustinus*); SEL 15 (1998) 117-119 (*Watson, Wilfred G.E.*).

7784 *Streck, Michael P.* Das Kasussystem des Amurritischen. Annäherung. ZDMG.S 11: 1998 ⇒449. 113-118.

7785 *Sznycer, Maurice* Une inscription néopunique de la région de Maktar conservée au British Museum de Londres. Sem. 48 (1998) 41-59 Sum. 41.

7786 **Tropper, Josef** Die Inschriften von Zincirli. ALASP: 1993, ⇒9, 9833... 13,8218. ^RSyr. 75 (1998) 303-305 (*Schattner-Rieser, Ursula*).

7787 *Tropper, Josef* Corrigenda zu KTU2: Wirtschaftstexte. UF 30 (1998) 697-702;

7788 Epigraphische Anmerkungen zur Neuauflage von KTU (2). AulOr 16 (1998) 292-294;

7789 "Pleonastisches" und in posttopikaler Stellung im Ugaritischen und in anderen semitischen Sprachen. OLoP 29 (1998) 21-31;

7790 Untersuchungen zu ugaritischen Wirtschaftstexten. UF 30 (1998) 679-696.

7791 *Watson, Wilfred G.E.* Non-Semitic words in the Ugaritic lexicon (3). UF 30 (1998) 751-760.

7792 *Yamada, Masamichi* The family of Zu-Ba‘la the diviner and the Hittites. ^FRAINEY, A. IOS 18: 1998 ⇒96. 323-334.

7793 *Younger, K. Lawson Jr.* The Phoenician inscription of Azatiwada: an integrated reading. JSSt 43 (1998) 11-47.

J1.6 Aramaica

7794 *Amadasi Guzzo, Maria Giulia* L'Idumée entre la fin de l'époque perse et le début de la période hellénistique: nouveaux ostraca araméens. Or. 67 (1998) 532-538.

7795 *Ambros, Arne A.* Arabisch kontra Nabatäisch: Überlegungen zur Prähistorie des Prestige der 'Arabiya. Annäherung. ZDMG.S 11: 1998 ⇒449. 167-172.

7796 **Beyer, Klaus** Die aramäischen Inschriften aus Assur, Hatra und dem übrigen Ostmesopotamien (datiert 44 v.Chr. bis 238 n. Chr.). Gö 1998, Vandenhoeck & R 191 pp. 3-525-53645-3.

7797 *Biran, Avraham* Biblical Dan and the house of David inscription: from the late Bronze Age to the Iron Age. ^FDOTHAN, T. 1998 ⇒23. 479-481.

7798   *Blau, Joshua* Minutiae aramaicae. Topics in Hebrew... linguistics. 1998 <1987> ⇒136. 290-298.
7799   *Botha, P.J.* The textual strategy and intent of the Bar-Rakib inscription. JSem 8/1 (1996) 1-11 Sum. 1.
7800   *Contini, Riccardo* Considerazioni sul presunto "dativo etico" in Aramaico pre-cristiano. ^FMARGAIN, J. 1998 ⇒71. 83-94.
7801   *Dempsey, Deirdre A.* Ostracon from the 1995 season at Tell Numrîn, Jordan: (Tab. XLVIII). Or. 67 (1998) 507-508.
7802   *Díez Merino, L.* El trasfondo semítico del Nuevo Testamento y la lengua de Jesús de Nazaret. AulOr 16 (1998) 111-127.
7803   *Eksell, Kerstin* On some verbal modificators in Neo-Aramaic: with a short comparison to Arabic dialects. AcOr 59 (1998) 52-74.
7804   ^E**Eph'al, Israel; Naveh, Joseph** Aramaic ostraca of the fourth century BC from Idumaea. 1996 ⇒12,7813; 13,8233. ^RBiOr 55 (1998) 235-238 (*Lemaire, A.*).
7805   **Folmer, M.L.** The Aramaic language in the Achaemenid period. OLA 68: 1995 ⇒11/1,5935. ^RJAOS 118 (1998) 586-587 (*Lipiński, Edward*).
7806   *Geller, Mark J.* New documents from the Dead Sea: Babylonian science in Aramaic. ^FGORDON, C. JSOT.S 273: 1998 ⇒31. 224-229;
7807   The Aramaic incantation in cueiform script (AO 6489=TCL 6,58). JEOL 35-36 (1997-2000) 127-146.
7808   **Herranz Marco, Mariano** Huellas de arameo en los evangelios y en la catequesis cristiana primitiva. 1997 ⇒13,3983. ^REstAg 33 (1998) 385-386 (*Cineira, D.Á.*); LASBF 48 (1998) 602-604 (*Bissoli, Giovanni*).
7809   *Hillers, Delbert R.* Palmyrene Aramaic inscriptions and the bible. ZAH 11 (1998) 32-49.
7810   **Hillers, Delbert R.; Cussini, Eleonora** Palmyrene Aramaic texts. 1996 ⇒12,7819; 13,8240. ^RArOr 66 (1998) 170-172 (*Segert, Stanislav*); Syr. 75 (1998) 334-335 (*Lozachmeur, Hélène*).
7811   **Hvidberg-Hansen, Finn Ove** The Palmyrene Inscriptions Ny Carlsberg Glyptotek. K 1998, Carlsberg Glyptotek 109 pp. 87-7452-207-8. 133 phot.; Bibl.
7812   *Kaizer, T.* De Dea Syria et aliis diis deabusque: a study of the variety of appearances of Gad in Aramaic inscriptions and on sculptures from the Near East in the first three centuries AD (part 2). OLoP 29 (1998) 33-62.
7813   *Kottsieper, Ingo* Die Inschrift vom Tell Dan und die politischen Beziehungen zwischen Aram-Damaskus und Israel in der 1. Hälfte des 1. Jahrtausends vor Christus. ^FLORETZ O. AOAT 250: 1998 ⇒65. 475-500.
7814   *Lemaire, André* Les nouveaux fragments de la stèle araméenne de Tell Dan: philologie et histoire. ^FMARGAIN, J. 1998 ⇒71. 41-52;
7815   The Tel Dan stela as a piece of royal historiography. JSOT 81 (1998) 3-14.
7816   *Lipiński, Edouard* "Leadership": the roots *dbr* and *ngd* in Aramaic. ^FLORETZ O. AOAT 250: 1998 ⇒65. 501-514.
7817   *Lozachmeur, Hélène* Deux épigraphes sur jarre d'Éléphantine (Collection Charles Clermont-Ganneau, n° 272 et X5). ^FMARGAIN, J. 1998 ⇒71. 53-61;
7818   Un nouveau graffito araméen provenant de Saqqâra. Sem. 48 (1998) 147-149.

7819 *Malbran-Labat, Florence* La trilingue de Behistun et les singularités de la version babylonienne. Sem. 48 (1998) 61-74 Sum. 61.

7820 *Muraoka, T.; Rogland, M.* The waw consecutive in Old Aramaic?: a rejoinder to Victor Sasson. VT 48 (1998) 99-104.

7821 *Muraoka, Takamitsu* Again on the Tel Dan inscription and the Northwest Semitic verb tenses. ZAH 11 (1998) 74-81.

7822 **Muraoka, Takamitsu; Porten, Besalel** A grammar of Egyptian Aramaic. HO 1/32: Lei 1998, Brill xlix; 393 pp. *f*187; $110. 90-04-10499-2. [R]ArOr 66 (1998) 278-280 (*Segert, Stanislav*).

7823 *Müller-Kessler, Christa* Eine aramäische 'Visitenkarte': eine spätbabylonische Tontafel aus Babylon. MDOG 130 (1998) 189-195.

7824 **Naveh, Joseph; Shaked, Shaul** Magic spells and formulae: Aramaic incantations of late antiquity. 1993 ⇒9,9860... 11/2,5962. [R]OLZ 93 (1998) 500-501 (*Oelsner, Joachim*).

7825 *Nehmé, Laïla* Une inscription nabatéenne inédite de Boṣrà (Syrie) [F]MARGAIN, J. 1998 ⇒71. 63-73.

7826 *Noll, K.L.* The God who is among the Danites. JSOT 80 (1998) 3-23.

7827 *Pardee, Dennis* Deux brèves remarques épigraphiques à propos de l'inscription araméenne de Tell Fekheryé. Sem. 48 (1998) 145-147;

7828 Les documents d'Arslan Tash: authentiques ou faux?. Syr. 75/1 (1998) 15-54.

7829 *Pennacchietti, Fabrizio A.* Iscrizioni aramaiche Hatrene su un sostegno fittile. Mes. 33 (1998) 275-289.

7830 *Porten, Bezalel* The revised draft of the letter of Jedaniah to Bagavahya (TAD A4.8 = Cowley 31). [F]GORDON, C. JSOT.S 273: 1998 ⇒31. 230-242.

7831 *Puech, É.* Inscriptions araméennes du Golfe: Failaka, Qala'at al-Bahreïn et Mulayha (ÉAU). TEuph 16 (1998) 31-55.

7832 **Rodrigues Pereira, Alphons S.** Studies in Aramaic poetry (c. 100 B.C.E. - c. 600 C.E.). SSN 34: 1997 ⇒13,8256. [R]BiOr 55 (1998) 497-499 (*Lipiński, E.*); JJS 49 (1998) 368-371 (*Morgenstern, Matthew*); VigChr 52 (1998) 447-448 (*Rouwhorst, G.*).

7833 *Salvesen, Alison* The legacy of Babylon and Nineveh in Aramaic sources. Legacy of Mesopotamia. 1998 ⇒328. 139-161.

7834 *Schattner-Rieser, Ursula* Note sur *d et la (non-)dissimilation des pharyngales en araméen: à propos d'un chaînon manquant découvert à Qumrân. [F]MARGAIN, J. 1998 ⇒71. 95-100.

7835 *Sznycer, Maurice* Quelques observations sur le passage de l'araméen au pehlevi. [F]MARGAIN, J. 1998 ⇒71. 101-107

7836 *Tropper, Josef* Grammatische Probleme des Biblisch-Aramäischen. OLoP 29 (1998) 5-19.

7837 *Tsereteli, Konstantin* Les inscriptions araméennes de Géorgie. Sem. 48 (1998) 75-88 Sum. 75.

J1.7 Syriaca

7838 *Blau, Joshua* The origin of open and closed *e* in Proto-Syriac. Topics in Hebrew... linguistics. 1998 <1969> ⇒136. 299-307.

7839 *Bohas, Georges* Les "états du nom" en syriaque;

7840 *Briquel-Chatonnet, Françoise* Notes d'un érudit du siècle de Louis XIV ou le syriaque sans peine. [F]MARGAIN, J. 1998 ⇒71. 109-115/ 117-121.

7841 **Brock, Sebastian P.** A brief outline of Syriac literature. Moran Etho 9: Kottayam 1998, St. Ephrem Ecumenical Research Institute 312 pp. [ITS 37,340—Legrand, L.].

7842 *Hunter, Erica C.D.* Syriac ostraca from Mesopotamia. Symposium Syriacum VII. 1998 ⇒415. 617-639.

7843 *Muraoka, Takamitsu* On the classical Syriac particles for "between". ^FMARGAIN, J. 1998 ⇒71. 135-142.

7844 **Payne-Smith, Robert** A compendious Syriac dictionary: founded upon the Thesaurus Syriacus of R. Payne Smith. ^E*Payne Smith, Jessie* WL 1998 <1976>, Eisenbrauns 626 pp. 1-57506-032-9.

7845 *Pazzini, Massimo* Progetto di dizionario siriaco-italiano del Nuovo Testamento. SBFLA 48 (1998) 305-313 Sum. 518.

7846 *Teixidor, Javier* Autour de la conjonction syriaque. ^FMARGAIN, J. 1998 ⇒71. 143-148.

7847 *Voigt, Rainer* Das emphatische p des Syrischen. Symposium Syriacum VII. 1998 ⇒415. 527-537.

J1.8 Akkadica (sumerica)

7848 *Altman, Ammon* On some assertions in the "Historical Prologue" of the Šaušgamuwa vassal treaty and their assumed-legal meaning. Rencontre Assyriologique Internationale 34. 1998 ⇒452. 99-107.

7849 *André-Salvini, Béatrice; Salvini, Mirjo* Un nouveau vocabulaire trilingue sumérien-akkadien-hourrite de Ras Shamra. General studies... Nuzi 10/2. ^E**Owen, D.** 1998 ⇒T6.5. 3-40.

7850 *Assante, Julia* The *kar.kid / ḫarimtu*, prostitute or single woman?: a reconsideration of the evidence. UF 30 (1998) 5-96.

7851 *Balke, Thomas E.* Anmerkungen zum Terminus bar-ra(-)kar-ra in den neusumerischen Wirtschaftstexten. ^FRÖMER, W. AOAT 253: 1998 ⇒ 97. 1-16.

7852 *Bauer, Josef* Georgica Sumerica. Or. 67 (1998) 119-125.

7853 **Black, Jeremy A.** Reading Sumerian poetry. Athlone Publications in Egyptology and Ancient Near Eastern Studies: L 1998, Athlone xii; 205 pp. 0-485-93003-X. Bibl.

7854 **Borger, Rykele** Beiträge zum Inschriftenwerk Assurbanipals: die Prismenklassen A, B, C = K, D, E, F, G, H, J, T sowie andere Inschriften. Wsb 1996, Harrassowitz xviii; 388 pp. 3-447-03791-1. ^ROLZ 93 (1998) 169-174 (*Dalley, Stephanie*).

7855 *Borger, Rykle* Zum Emesal-Vokabular. ^FRÖMER, W. AOAT 253: 1998 ⇒97. 17-37.

7856 ^E**Brinkman, J.A. Š.** The Assyrian Dictionary of the Oriental Institute of the University of Chicago, 17. 1989-1994 ⇒65,758... 10,9146. ^RBiOr 55 (1998) 817-824 (*Borger, R.*).

7857 **Buccellati, Giorgio** A structural grammar of Babylonian. Wsb 1996, Harrassowitz xxxiv; 512 pp. 3-447-03612-5. ^RBiOr 55 (1998) 172-185 (*Kouwenberg, N.J.C.*).

7858 *Cavigneaux, Antoine; Ismail, Bahija Khalil* Eine zweisprachige Hymne aus dem Haus des Beschwörungspriesters. Acta Sumerologica (Hiroshima) 20 (1998) 1-12.

7859 *Charpin, Dominique* L'évocation du passé dans les lettres de Mari. Intellectual life. 1998 ⇒450. 91-110.

7860 *Civil, Miguel* Bilingual teaching. ^FBORGER R. 1998 ⇒12. 1-7.

7861 ᴱCole, Steven William; Machinist, Peter B. Letters from priests to the kings Esarhaddon and Assurbanipal. SAAS 13: Helsinki 1998, University Pr. Ill. ed. by *Julian Reade*: xxx; 221 pp. 951-570-437-5.

7862 *D'Agostino, Franco* Some considerations on humour in Mesopotamia. RSO 72 (1998) 273-278.'

7863 *Diakonoff, Igor M.* The earliest Semitic society: linguistic data. JSSt 43 (1998) 209-219.

7864 *Dietrich, Manfried* Bel-ibni, König von Babylon (703-700): die Rolle des Königs in den neubabylonischen Briefen. ᶠRÖMER, W. AOAT 253: 1998 ⇒97. 81-108.

7865 *Dietrich, Manfried bulut beli* "Lebe, mein König!": ein Krönungshymnus aus Emar und Ugarit und sein Verhältnis zu mesopotamischen und westlichen Inthronisationsliedern. UF 30 (1998) 155-200.

7866 **Durand, Jean-Marie** Les documents épistolaires du palais de Mari, 2. LAPO 17: P 1998, Cerf €28,20. 2-204-055961-7.

7867 *Frahm, Eckart* Humor in assyrischen Königsinschriften. Intellectual life. 1998 ⇒450. 147-162.

7868 **Frayne, Douglas Ralph** Ur III period (2112-2004 BC). 1997 ⇒13, 8271. ᴿRA 92 (1998) 93-94 (*Charpin, D.*).

7869 *Garelli, Paul* Réflexions sur la zitti ekallim d'époque médio-assyrienne. ᶠBORGER R. 1998 ⇒12. 123-125.

7870 **Gehlken, E.** Uruk: spätbabylonische Wirtschaftstexte. 1990 ⇒6, e442*... 10,13709. ᴿBiOr 55 (1998) 59-79 (*Van Driel, G.*).

7871 **Gelb, Ignace; Kienast, Burkhart** Die altakkadischen Königsinschriften des dritten Jahrtausends v. Chr. 1990 ⇒6,e443; 7,d712. ᴿBiOr 55 (1998) 44-59 (*Westenholz, Joan Goodnick*).

7872 *Geller, M.J.* Reflexives and antipassives in Sumerian verbs. Or. 67 (1998) 85-106.

7873 *Hirsch, Hans* Kommen und Gehen in Nippur. ᶠLORETZ O. AOAT 250: 1998 ⇒65. 369-382.

7874 **Huehnergard, John** A grammar of Akkadian. HSM 45: 1997 ⇒13, 8279. ᴿThLZ 123 (1998) 1191-1192 (*Müller, Hans-Peter*); CBQ 60 (1998) 531-532 (*Gianto, Agustinus*); BiOr 55 (1998) 814-816 (*Kouwenberg, N.J.C.*);

7875 Key to a grammar of Akkadian. HSS 46: Atlanta, Ga. 1998, Scholars viii; 137 pp. 0-7885-0427-4.

7876 *Hunger, Hermann* Zur Lesung sumerischer Zahlwörter. ᶠRÖMER, W. AOAT 253: 1998 ⇒97. 179-183.

7877 *Ikeda, Jun* The Akkadian language of Carchemish: evidence from Emar and its vicinities. Acta Sumerologica (Hiroshima) 20 (1998) 23-62;

7878 *Ikeda, Jun* The Akkadian language of Emar: texts related to a diviner's family. ᶠRAINEY, A. IOS 18: 1998 ⇒96. 33-61.

7879 **Kah-jin Kuan, Jeffrey** Neo-Assyrian historical inscriptions and Syria Palestine. Jian Dao Diss. 1: Shf 1995, Academic 281 pp. $80/30. 962-7997-09-9/10-2. ᴿZAW 110 (1998) 304-305 (*Köckert, M.*).

7880 ᴱKataja, L.; Whiting, R. Grants, decrees and gifts of the Neo-Assyrian period. 1995 ⇒11/2,b381. ᴿBiOr 55 (1998) 194-196 (*Pečirková, Jana*).

7881 **Kämmerer, Thomas R.; Schwiderski, Dirk** Deutsch-Akkadisches Wörterbuch. AOAT 255: Müns 1998, Ugarit-Verlag xiv; 589 pp. 3-927120-66-9.

7882 *Klein, Jacob* The sweet chant of the churn: a revised edition of
Išmedagan J. ^FRÖMER, W. AOAT 253: 1998 ⇒97. 205-222.

7883 *Koch, Johannes* Zur Bedeutung von *ina UGU tur-ri* ... in zwei
Astronomical Diaries. WO 29 (1998) 109-123.

7884 *Lion, Brigitte* La conception de la pauvreté dans les textes littéraires
akkadiens. Intellectual life. 1998 ⇒450. 199-214.

7885 *Mayer, Walter* Nabonids Herkunft. ^FRÖMER, W. AOAT 253: 1998 ⇒
97. 245-261.

7886 *Márquez Rowe, Ignacio* Notes on the Hurro-Akkadian of Alalaḫ in
the mid-second millennium B.C.E. ^FRAINEY, A. IOS 18: 1998 ⇒96.
63-78.

7887 **Millard, Alan** The eponyms of the Assyrian empire 910-612 B.C.
1994 ⇒10,11140*; 11/2,9468. ^ROr. 67 (1998) 280-284 (*Schramm,
Wolfgang*).

7888 *Mompeán, Juan Oliva* Neue Kollationen und Anmerkungen zu einigen Alalaḫ VII-Texten. UF 30 (1998) 587-601.

7889 *Müller, Gerfrid G.W.* Die sumerischen Texte aus dem Kapuzinerklos-
ter in Münster. ^FLORETZ O. AOAT 250: 1998 ⇒65. 557-568.

7890 *Pomponio, Francesco* Presagi ingannevoli. WO 29 (1998) 53-57.

7891 *Reiner, Erica* Apodoses and logia. ^FLORETZ O. AOAT 250: 1998 ⇒
65. 651-654.

7892 *Rogland, Max* hmtndbjm. Abr-n. 35 (1998) 65-73.

7893 *Römer, W.H.Ph.* Beiträge zum Lexikon des Sumerischen (6): zu Pfei-
len, Köchern und Bogen. ^FBORGER R. 1998 ⇒12. 303-312.

7894 **Römer, Willem H. Philibert** Die Sumerologie: Einführung in die
Forschung und Bibliographie in Auswahl. AOAT 262: Mü ²1999,
Ugarit-Verlag xii; 250 pp. 3-927120-72-3. Bibl. ^RUF 30 (1998) 929-
931 (*Zeeb, F.*).

7895 *Schramm, Wolfgang* Performative Verbalformen im Sumerischen
^FBORGER R. 1998 ⇒12. 313-322.

7896 *Selz, Gebhard J.* Die Etana-Erzählung: Ursprung und Tradition eines
der ältesten epischen Texte in einer semitischen Sprache. Acta
Sumerologica (Hiroshima) 20 (1998) 181-200.

7897 **Seminara, Stefano** L'accadico di Emar. Materiali per il vocabolario
sumerico 6: R 1998, "La Sapienza", Dipart. di St. Or. 644 pp. Bibl.

7898 ^E**Sjöberg, Åke W.** The Sumerian dictionary of the University Museum of the University of Pennsylvania, 1: A.—Pt. 3. Ph 1998, Babylonian Section of the Univ. Museum xlv; 217 pp. 0-934718-63-6.

7899 *Sjöberg, Åke W.* Sumerian texts and fragments in the University of
Pennsylvania Museum related to rulers of Isin. ^FRÖMER, W. AOAT
253: 1998 ⇒97. 345-378.

7900 *Skaist, Aaron* The chronology of the legal texts from Emar. ZA 88
(1998) 45-71.

7901 *Slanski, Kathryn E.* A note on the coordinating particle -ma in the
Old Akkadian letter greeting formula. ^FRAINEY, A. IOS 18: 1998
⇒96. 9-17.

7902 *Soden, Wolfgang von* "Eilig, schnell" und "langsam" in altorientalischen Sprachen. ^FBORGER R. 1998 ⇒12. 323-327.

7903 **Soden, Wolfram von** Grundriss der akkadischen Grammatik. ^E*Mayer, Werner R.* AnOr 33: ³1995 ⇒11/2,6044; 13,8302. ^RBSOAS 61
(1998) 126-127 (*Geller, M.J.*).

7904 *Steible, Horst* Die Erhöhung der Baba: zu einem Fall von 'Umwid-
mung' unter Gudea von Lagaš dargestellt an den Texten der Statuen E
und G. ^FRÖMER, W. AOAT 253: 1998 ⇒97. 379-395.

7905 *Steiner, Gerd* Der "Sohn eines Armen" und seine Fische (Uruinimgina 6 ii 10'-14' und iii 6'-9');
7906 *Stol, M.* Die altbabylonische Stadt Ḫalḫalla. ᶠRÖMER, W. AOAT 253: 1998 ⇒97. 397-413/415-445;
7907 Einige kurze Wortstudien. ᶠBORGER R. 1998 ⇒12. 343-352.
7908 *Streck, Michael P.* The tense systems in the Sumerian-Akkadian linguistic area. Acta Sumerologica (Hiroshima) 20 (1998) 181-200.
7909 *Streck, Michael P.* Zur Gemination beim akkadischen Verbum. Or. 67 (1998) 523-531.
7910 **Tadmor, Hayim** The inscriptions of Tiglath-pileser III, king of Assyria. 1994 ⇒10,11149... 13,8303. ᴿBiOr 55 (1998) 192-194 (*Jas, R.M.*); JAOS 118 (1998) 280-281 (*Grayson, A. Kirk*).
7911 *Tammuz, Oded* Do me a favor!: the art of negotiating according to Old Babylonian letters. Intellectual life. 1998 ⇒450. 379-388.
7912 *Tropper, Josef* Die infirmen Verben des Akkadischen. ZDMG 148 (1998) 7-34.
7913 **Ulshöfer, Andrea Maria** Die altassyrischen Privaturkunden. FAOS. B 4: FrB 1995, Steiner x; 503 pp. FS186. 3-515-06833-3. ᴿJAOS 118 (1998) 582-585 (*Veenhof, Klaas R.*).
7914 *Vaan, J.M.C.T. de* Idiom im Neubabylonischen (I): Erläuterungen zum Vokabular des Generals Bel-ibni. ᶠRÖMER, W. AOAT 253: 1998 ⇒97. 71-80.
7915 *Veldhuis, Niek* A late Old Babylonian proto-kagal/nigga text and the nature of the acrographic series. Acta Sumerologica (Hiroshima) 20 (1998) 201-216.
7916 *Zadok, Ran* Notes on Borsippean documentation of the eighth-fifth centuries B.C.E. ᶠRAINEY, A. IOS 18: 1998 ⇒96. 249-296.
7917 *Zadok, Tikva* The use of the subordinating particles inumi/inu/inuma "when" in Old Babylonian royal inscriptions. ᶠRAINEY, A. IOS 18: 1998 ⇒96. 19-32.

J2.7 Arabica

7918 **Cassarino, Mirella** Traduzioni e traduttori arabi dall'VIII all'XI secolo. Piccoli saggi 3: R 1998, Salerno 158 pp. 88-8402-257-6. Bibl.
7919 *Diem, Werner G.* Rex SMITH and Moshalleh AL-MORAEKHI: the Arabic papyri of the John Rylands University Library of Manchester;
7920 *Holes, Clive* Retention and loss of the passive verb in the Arabic dialects of northern Oman and eastern Arabia;
7921 *Kahl, Oliver* Quṣṭa ibn Luqa on sleeplessness;
7922 *Maraqten, Mohammed* Writing materials in pre-Islamic Arabia. JSSt 43 (1998) 89-111/347-362/311-326/287-310.
7923 *Muranyi, Miklos* Über ein Muwaṭṭa-Fragment in der Zawiya al-Naṣiriyya in Tamagrut (Marokko);
7924 *Sima, Alexander* Neuinterpretation einer jüngst entdeckten sabäischen Buß- und Sühneinschrift aus dem Wadi Šuẓayf. WO 29 (1998) 149-157/127-139.

J3.0 **Aegyptia**

7925 *Berger, Paul-Richard* Reconstructing and deciphering the inscription
      of Nahr el-Kelb by computer. Bible et informatique. 1998 ⇒386.
      369-373.
7926 *Bochi, Patricia A.* Gender and genrè in ancient Egyptian poetry: the
      rhetoric of performance in the Harpers' Songs. JARCE 35 (1998) 89-
      95.
7927 *Browne, Gerald M.* Miscellanea Nubiana III. Or. 67 (1998) 115-118;
7928 The Old Nubian stative. Or. 67 (1998) 237-238.
7929 **Browne, Gerald Michael** Old Nubian textual criticism. Beiträge zur
      Sudanforschung 8: W 1998, Institut f. Afrikanistik der Univ. 36 pp.
      Bibl.
7930 **Caluwe, Albert de** Un livre des morts sur bandelette de momie.
      1991 ⇒7,9335*. ᴿJNES 57 (1998) 303-309 (*Mosher, Malcolm*).
7931 ᴱᵀ**Cauville, Sylvie** Le temple de Dendara, les chapelles osiriennes.
      Bibliothèque d'études 117-119: Le Caire 1997, IFAO Et Dendara
      X/1-2 (compositions hiéroglyphiques par *J. Hallof* et *H. Van den
      Berg*, photographies par *A. Lecler* et dessins par *B. Lenthéric* 5 vols.
7932 **Collier, Mark; Manley, Bill** How to read Egyptian hieroglyphs: a
      step-by-step guide to teach yourself. Berkeley, CA 1998, Univ. of
      California xii; 179 pp. 0-520-21597-4. Ill. by *R. Parkinson*; Bibl.
7933 *Dayan, Galit* The term "p3-t2wf" in the Spiegelberg Papyrus;
7934 *Depuydt, Leo* The meaning of Old and Middle Egyptian Jw in light
      of the distinction between narration and discussion. Jerusalem
      studies. ÄAT 40: 1998 ⇒361. 133-135/19-36;
7935 Word-splitting forces in Egyptian. Or. 67 (1998) 231-236.
7936 *Dijkstra, Meindert* The element -hr in Egypto-Semitic names. BN 94
      (1998) 5-10.
7937 *Edel, Elmar* Die Ramseslisten Simons, ETL XXII c-d Standort der
      Ortsnamenlisten; Zitierweise und Umschriften. ᶠRAINEY, A. IOS 18:
      1998 ⇒96. 229-246.
7938 *Egberts, Arno* Hard times: the chronology of "The report of
      Wenamun" revised. ZÄS 125 (1998) 93-108.
7939 ᴱ**Fischer-Elfert, Hans-Werner** Lesefunde im literarischen Stein-
      bruch von Deir-el-Medineh. Kleine ägyptische Texte 12: 1997
      ⇒13,8320. ᴿBiOr 55 (1998) 741-747 (*Gasse, A.*).
7940 **Foster, John L.** Thought couplets in the Tale of Sinue. 1993 ⇒9,
      9953... 12,7861. ᴿRdE 49 (1998) 273-274 (*Gasse, Annie*).
7941 **Galán, José M.** Cuatro viajes en la literatura del antiguo Egipto.
      Banco de datos filológicos semíticos noroccidentales. Monografías 3:
      M 1998, Consejo Superior de Investigaciones Científicas xii; 245 pp.
      84-00-07719-9.
7942 *Goedicke, Hans* Comments concerning the "Story of the eloquent
      peasant". ZÄS 125 (1998) 109-125;
7943 The song of the princesses (*Sinuhe* B 269-279). BSÉG 22 (1998) 29-
      36.
7944 *Görg, Manfred* Die Hieroglyphen: kein Krypto-Hebräisch: J.G.L.
      KOSEGARTEN und die Anfänge der deutschsprachigen Ägyptologie.
      BN 91 (1998) 20-28.
7945 *Grimal, Nicolas* Le roi, les ennemis et la pyramide;
7946 *Haikal, Fayza* A gesture of thanksgiving in ancient Egypt. ᶠSTADEL-
      MANN R. 1998 ⇒109. 263-271/291-292.

7947 **Hannig, Rainer; Vomberg, Petra** Wortschatz der Pharaonen in Sachgruppen: Kulturhandbuch Ägyptens. Hannig-Lexica 2; Kulturgeschichte der antiken Welt 72: Mainz 1998, Von Zabern xii; 1029 pp. 3-8053-2543-6.

7948 *Haran, Adina* Nationalism and the sin of conquest in the texts of Kamose (K3-ms): Carnarvon Tablet No. 1, Stela No. I and Stela No. II;

7949 *Israeli, Shlomit* ₫w n ʿnḫ ("breath of life") in the Medinet Habu war texts. Jerusalem studies. ÄAT 40: 1998 ⇒361. 265-269/271-287.

7950 *Jansen-Winkeln, Karl* Beiträge zu den Privatinschriften der Spätzeit. ZÄS 125 (1998) 1-13;

7951 Drei Denkmäler mit archaisierender Orthographie. Or. 67 (1998) 155-172.

7952 *Kahl, Jochem* "Es ist vom Anfang bis zum Ende so gekommen, wie es in der Schrift gefunden worden war": zur Überlieferung der Erzählung des Sinuhe. ᶠLORETZ O. AOAT 250: 1998 ⇒65. 383-400.

7953 *Kákkosy, László; Takács, Gábor* Two observations on the etymology of Osiris. ArOr 66 (1998) 243-254.

7954 *Kühne, Cord* Meki, Megum und Mekum/Mekim. ᶠRAINEY, A. IOS 18: 1998 ⇒96. 311-322.

7955 *Lesko, Leonard H.* Women and priests in two Egyptian stories ᶠFRERICHS, E. BJSt 320: 1998 ⇒28. 217-224.

7956 **Lüddeckens, Erich** Demotische Urkunden aus Hawara, 1: Umschrift, Übersetzung und Kommentar. VOHD.S 28: Stu 1998, Steiner 298 pp. 3-515-05408-1. Mitarb. *R.W. Daniel; Rolf Wassermann*.

7957 *Martin, Geoffrey T.* Foreigners in the Memphite tombs of Ḥoremḥeb and Maya. Jerusalem studies. ÄAT 40: 1998 ⇒361. 207-209.

7958 *Menu, Bernadette* La désignation juridique des femmes, d'après les documents contractuels et judiciaires de l'Égypte ancienne. ᴹWARD W. 1998 ⇒123. 183-187.

7959 *Migahid, Abd-El-Gawad* Eine demotische Personenliste aus dem Serapeum. ZÄS 125 (1998) 125-137.

7960 *Morenz, Ludwig D.* Die schmähende Herausforderung des Thebaners D'rj an Hty. WO 29 (1998) 5-20;

7961 Söhne und Frauen. BN 91 (1998) 7-11.

7962 **Ockinga, Boyo G.** Mittelägyptische Grundgrammatik: Abriss der mittelägyptischen Grammatik. ᴱ*Brunner, Hellmut*. Mainz 1998, Von Zabern xi; 180 pp. 3-8053-2389-1.

7963 ᵀ**Parkinson, Richard B.** The tale of Sinuhe and other Egyptian poems 1940-1640 BC. 1997 ⇒13,8333. ᴿJEA 84 (1998) 241-243 (*Franke, Detlef*); BiOr 55 (1998) 738-741 (*Burkhard, Günter*).

7964 **Peden, A.J.** Egyptian historical inscriptions of the twentieth dynasty. 1994 ⇒10,11107. ᴿJNES 57 (1998) 157-158 (*Spalinger, Anthony*).

7965 *Reintges, C.H.* Ancient Egyptian in 3D: synchrony, diachrony and typology of a dead language. Or. 67 (1998) 447-476.

7966 *Richter, Sebastian Tonio* Leib oder Leber?: zum Wort *MOCE* im demotischen P: Magical XIII,12;

7967 *Schenkel, Wolfgang* Standardtheorie und invertierte Standardtheorie;

7968 *Schipper, Bernd Ulrich* Von der 'Lehre des Sehetep-jb-Re' zur 'Loyalistischen Lehre'. ZÄS 125 (1998) 137-139/140-160/161-179.

7969 **Shirun-Grumach, Irene** Offenbarung, Orakel und Königsnovelle. 1993 ⇒9,11990; 13,8336. ᴿRdE 49 (1998) 276-280 (*Gasse, Annie*).

7970 *Shisha-Halevy, A.* A first structural grammar of Demotic. BiOr 55 (1998) 587-600.

7971 **Spalinger, Anthony J.** The private feast lists of ancient Egypt. ÄA 57: 1996 ⇒12,7884. ^RDiscEg 41 (1998) 107-108 (*Strudwick, Nigel*).

7972 *Sweeney, Deborah* Letters of reconciliation from ancient Egypt. Jerusalem studies. ÄAT 40: 1998 ⇒361. 353-369.

7973 *Tower Hollis, Susan* Ancient Israel as the land of exile and the 'otherworld' in ancient Egyptian folktales and narratives. ^FGORDON, C. JSOT.S 273: 1998 ⇒31. 320-337.

7974 *Vittmann, Günter* Tradition und Neuerung in der demotischen Literatur. ZÄS 125 (1998) 62-77.

7975 *Zeidler, Jürgen* Beiträge zur Nominalbildung des Ägyptischen. WO 29 (1998) 21-32.

7976 *Zonhoven, Louis* Studies on the *sḏm.t=f* verb form in Classical Egyptian. ZÄS 125 (1998) 78-92.

J3.4 Coptica

7977 *Bosson, Nathalie* Amulette-palimpseste magique du musée du Louvre. Or. 67 (1998) 107-114.

7978 **Boud'Hors, Anne** Catalogue des fragments coptes de la Bibliothèque Nationale et Universitaire de Strasbourg, I: fragments bibliques. CSCO.Sub 99; CSCO 571: Lv 1998, Peeters Bibl. vii; 170 pp. €47. 90-429-0017-2.

7979 ^E**Krause, Martin** Ägypten in spätantik-christlicher Zeit: Einführung in die koptische Kultur. Sprachen und Kulturen des Christlichen Orients 4: Wsb 1998, Reichert viii; 393 pp. 3-89500-079-5.

7980 *Modras, Krzysztof* Sin and forgiveness in DEMETRIUS of Antioch, De Nativitate. Jerusalem studies. ÄAT 40: 1998 ⇒361. 323-329.

7981 **Myszor, Wincenty** Jezyk koptyjski: kurs podstawowy dialektu saidzkiego opracowanie studyjne. Wsz 1998, Wydawnictwo Akademii Teologii Katolickiej 166 pp. 83-7072-119-2. **P.**

7982 *Richter, Sebastian* ρμπου und ρμπϣιρε: zwei Komposita jüngerer Bildungsweise im koptischen Ostrakon Ägyptisches Museum der Universität Leipzig Inv.-Nr. 1611. ZÄS 125 (1998) 56-62.

7983 *Schulz, Regine; Kolta, Sabri* Schlangen, Skorpione und feindliche Mächte: ein koptisch-arabischer Schutzspruch. BN 93 (1998) 89-104.

7984 **Störk, Lothar** Die Handschriften der Staats- und Universitätsbibliothek Hamburg: die Handschriften aus Dair Anbā Maqār. Koptische Handschriften, 2, Teil 2. Stu 1995, Steiner 2 696 pp. ^ROLZ 93 (1998) 165-9 (*Schenke, Hans-Martin*); OCP 62 (1996) 453-4 (*Luisier, Ph.*);

7985 Die Handschriften der Staats- und Universitätsbibliothek Hamburg: Addenda und Corrigenda to Tl. 1. Koptische Handschriften, 3/3. VOHD 21, no. 3: Stu 1996, Steiner 128 pp. DM96. 3-515-02574-X. ^RBiOr 55 (1998) 435-438 (*MacCoull, L.S.B.*).

7986 *Van Esbroeck, Michel* La légende d'Apa Jeremias et Apa Johannes et les fragments Chester Beatty Copte 829. Or. 67 (1998) 1-63.

7987 *Young, Dwight W.* Pages from a copy of Shenute's eighth canon. Or. 67 (1998) 64-84;

7988 Two leaves from a copy of Shenute's ninth canon. WZKM 88 (1998) 281-301;

7989 Coptic manuscripts from the White Monastery: works of Shenute I-II. 1993 ⇒10,9249. ^RJNES 57 (1998) 155-157 (*Mirecki, Paul*).

7990 *Youssef, Youhanna Nessim* Two liturgical quotations from Coptic hagiographical texts. Abr-n. 35 (1998) 145-149.

J3.8 Aethiopica

7991 *Arbach, Mounir; Bâfaqîh, Muhlammad 'Abd al-Qâdir* Nouvelles données sur la chronologie des rois du Hadramawt;
7992 *Bron, François* Un fragment d'inscription qatabanite en bronze;
7993 *Drewes, A.J.* Noms propres dans les documents épigraphiques de l'Éthiopie. Sem. 48 (1998) 109-126/149-150/127-143.
7994 *Gajda, Iwona; Arbach, Mounir; Bron, François* Une nouvelle inscription sudarabique des Haṣbaḥides. Sem. 48 (1998) 101-108.
7995 **Hayajneh, Hani** Die Personennamen in den qatabänischen Inschriften: lexikalische und grammatische Analyse im Kontext der semitischen Anthropomastik. Texte und Studien zur Orientalistik 10: Hildesheim 1998, Olms 416 pp.
7996 *Weninger, Stefan* Die altsabäische Personenwidmung RES 4982: (zugleich ein Nachtrag zur sabäischen Onomastik);
7997 Zur Realisation des ḍ(< *ḏ) im Altäthiopischen. WO 29 (1998) 140-146/147-148.

J4.0 Anatolica

7998 *Fincke, Jeanette* Beiträge zum Lexikon des Hurritischen von Nuzi, 2;
7999 More joins among the texts from Arrapḫa (Kirkuk);
8000 *Giorgieri, Mauro* Die erste Beschwörung der 8. Tafel des šalašu-Rituals;
8001 *Giorgieri, Mauro; Röseler, Ingeborg* Hurritisch *kirman(i)*: ein Beitrag zu den hurritischen Numeralia. General studies... Nuzi 10/2. ᴱOwen, D. 1998 ⇒T6.5. 41-48/49-62/71-86/87-94.
8002 **Kosak, Silvin** Konkordanz der Keilschrifttafeln III/1: die Texte der Grabung 1933: 1/c - 1300/c. StBT 42: Wsb 1998, Harrassowitz xii, 281 pp. 3-447-04052-1.
8003 *Maidman, M.P.* JEN 775-780: the text editions. General studies... Nuzi 10/2. ᴱOwen, D. 1998 ⇒T6.5. 95-123.
8004 *Mellink, Machteld H.* Bilinguals and the alphabet in Cilicia, Tabal and Phrygia. ᶠÇAMBEL H. 1998 ⇒4. 495-498.
8005 *Richter, Thomas* Anmerkungen zu den hurritischen Personennamen des ḫapiru-Prismas aus Tigunanu;
8006 *Skaist, Aaron* A Hurrian term at Emar;
8007 *Wilhelm, Gernot* Hurr. šinussi "Scheuklappe"?;
8008 Zur Suffixaufnahme beim Instrumental [Hurritisch]. General studies ..Nuzi 10/2. ᴱOwen, D. 1998 ⇒T6.5. 125-34/169-71/173-6/177-180.

8009 **Jinbachian, Manuel M.** Les techniques de traduction dans la Genèse en arménien classique. 1998, Fundação C. Gulbenkian.

J5.1 Graeca *grammatica*

8010 *Baumert, Norbert* εἰς το mit Infinitiv. FgNT 11 (1998) 7-24.
8011 **Black, David Alan** It's still Greek to me: an easy-to-understand guide to intermediate Greek. GR 1998, Baker 192 pp. 0-8010-2181-2 [FgNT 11,132—Peláez, Jesús].

8012 ^E**Boned Colera, Pilar; Rodríguez Somolinos, Juan** Repertorio
bibliográfico de la lexicografía griega (RBLG). M 1998, Consejo
Superior de Investigaciones Científicas xix; 540 pp. Ptas4.808. Dicc.
Griego-Español, Anejo III [CÉg. 73,378—Nachtergael, Georges].

8013 ^E**Brixhe, Claude** La Koiné grecque antique III: les contacts. Études
anciennes 17: Nancy 1998, ADRA 161 pp. [REG 113,229ss—Lé-
toublon, Françoise].

8014 **Brixhe, Claude** Phonétique et phonologie du grec ancien I: quelques
grandes questions. BCILL 82: 1996 ⇒12,7892. ^RAnCl 67 (1998)
383-385 (*Bile, Monique*); BSLP 93 (1998) 163-165 (*Lamberterie,
Charles de*).

8015 *Burchard, Christoph* Fußnoten zum neutestamentlichen Griechisch.
Studien NT. WUNT 107: 1998 <1970; 1978> ⇒140. 315-329, 330-
344.

8016 **Buzzetti, Carlo** Nuovi studenti del Nuovo Testamento greco: proposte e strumenti per un corso-base. R 1995, LAS 109 pp. L20.000.
88-1213-0390-8. ^RAng. 73 (1996) 589-590 (*De Santis, Luca*).

8017 **Campbell, Malcolm** Classical Greek prose: a basic vocabulary: a
classified list of 1500 of the commonest words. L 1998, Bristol Classical vi; 112 pp. 1-85395-5592.

8018 *Ceglia, Luca* L'evoluzione della costruzione perifrastica verbale nel
Greco del Nuovo Testamento. AGI 83/1 (1998) 20-44.

8019 ^E**Cuzzolin, Pierluigi** Studi di linguistica greca. Materiali linguistici,
Univ. Pavia 16: Mi 1995, Angeli 208 pp. L30.000. ^RBSLP 93 (1998)
165-168 (*Hodot, René*).

8020 *Dahan, Gilbert* La connaissance du grec dans les correctoires de la
Bible du XIIIe siècle. Du copiste au collectionneur: mélanges
d'histoire des textes et des bibliothèques en l'honneur d'André
VERNET. ^E**Nebbiai-Dalla Guarda, Donatella; Genest, Jean-
François** Bibliologia 18: Turnhout 1998, Brepols [89-109 RBen
110,136—Bogaert, P.-M.].

8021 **Delebecque, E.** Études sur le grec du Nouveau Testament. 1995 ⇒
11/2,248. ^RCDios 211 (1998) 649-650 (*Gutiérrez, J.*).

8022 **Dickey, Eleanor** Greek forms of address: from Herodotus to Lucian.
1996 ⇒12,7898. ^RSCI 17 (1998) 235-238 (*Shalev, Donna*).

8023 **Duhoux, Yves** Le verbe grec ancien: éléments de morphologie et
syntaxe historiques. 1992 ⇒8,9827... 11/2,6282. ^RGn. 70 (1998) 97-
100 (*Plath, Robert*).

8024 **Ellul, Danielle; Flichy, Odile** Le grec du Nouveau Testament par les
textes: méthode d'initiation au grec de la koinè à l'aide de textes tirés
du Nouveau Testament. Instruments pour l'étude des langues de
l'Orient Ancien 1: Lausanne 1998, Du Zèbre 304 pp. 2-9700088-5-8.

8025 ^E**Fraser, P.M.; Matthews, E.** Lexicon of Greek personal names, 3A:
the Peloponnese, western Greece, Sicily and Magna Graecia. Oxf
1997, Clarendon xxxi; 519 pp. £80. 0-19-815229-9.

8026 ^E**Hansen, Dirk U.** Das attizistische Lexikon des Moeris: quel-
lenkritische Untersuchung und Edition. Sammlung griechischer und
lateinischer Grammatiker 9: B 1998, De Gruyter 181 pp. 3-11-
014836-6.

8027 **Ildefonse, F.** La naissance de la grammaire dans l'antiquité grecque.
Histoire des doctrines de l'antiquité classique 20: P 1997, Vrin 490
pp. FF250. 2-7116-1311-9 [ClR 50,609s—Blank, D.L.].

8028 **Klug, Wolfgang** Erzählstruktur als Kunstform: Studien zur künstlerischen Funktion der Erzähltempora im Lateinischen und im Griechischen. 1992 ⇒9,10107. ᴿGn. 70 (1998) 1-4 (*Hofmann, Heinz*).
8029 *Lee, John A.L.; Horsley, G.H.R.* A lexicon of the New Testament with documentary parallels: some interim entries, 2. FgNT 11 (1998) 57-84.
8030 *Lust, Johan* A lexicon of the Three and the transliterations in Ezekiel. Origen's Hexapla. TSAJ 58: 1998 ⇒399. 274-301.
8031 *Makujina, John* Modal possibilities for the elliptical verb in the imperative-comparative clause in NT Greek. FgNT 11 (1998) 43-55;
8032 Verbs meaning "command" in the New Testament: determining the factors involved in the choice of command-verbs. EstB 56 (1998) 357-369.
8033 **Martínez Hernández, Marcos** Semántica del griego antiguo. M 1997, Clasicas xx; 362 pp [BSL 95/2,165—Mawet, Francine].
8034 **Martorell, Enrique** El griego del Nuevo Testamento, 1: los escritos juaninos: análisis completo al texto griego del evangelio, las cartas y el Apocalipsis de Juan. Terrassa 1998, Clie 459 pp. 84-8267-013-1 [NThAR 2000,218].
8035 *Piñero, Antonio* New Testament philology bulletin: no. 21, 22. FgNT 11 (1998) 143-175; 177-205.
8036 **Ravarotto, E.** Grammatica elementare greca per lo studio del Nuovo Testamento: nozioni, esercizi, vocabolario. ᴱ*Pesce, Angelo*: R ²1998 <1984>, Antonianum 212 pp [RivBib 47,225s—Ognibeni, Bruno].
8037 **Rogers, Cleon L., Jr.; Rogers, Cleon L. III; Rienecker, Fritz** The new linguistic and exegetical key to the Greek New Testament. GR 1998, Zondervan xl; 652 pp. 0-310-20175-6. Rev. ed.; Bibl.
8038 **Rusconi, Carlo** Vocabolario del greco del Nuovo Testamento. 1996 ⇒12,7916. ᴿRivBib 46 (1998) 341-342 (*Biguzzi, Giancarlo*); Bib. 79 (1998) 444-445 (*Passoni Dell'Acqua, Anna*); CivCatt 149/1 (1998) 309-310 (*Scaiola, D.*).
8039 *Rydbeck, Lars* The language of the New Testament. TynB 49 (1998) 361-368.
8040 *Rydbeck, Lars* Die Sprache des N.T. SEÅ 63 (1998) 225-231.
8041 **Sollamo, Raija** Repetition of the possessive pronouns in the Septuagint. 1995 ⇒11/2,2600... 13,8374. ᴿVT 48 (1998) 132-133 (*Satterthwaite, P.E.*).
8042 **Swetnam, James** Morfologia. Il greco del Nuovo Testamento, Parte prima. 1995 ⇒11/2,6329... 13,8377. 2 vols. ᴿHum(B) 53 (1998) 735-738 (*Menestrina, Giovanni*).
8043 Vocabulario griego del Nuevo Testamento. Biblioteca de est. bíb. minor 5: S 1998, Sígueme 209 pp. 84-301-1351-7 [ActBib 71,38—O'Callaghan, J.].
8044 **Voelz, J.W.** Fundamental Greek grammar. St. Louis ²1993, Concordia $30. 0-570-04252-6. ᴿAJTh 12 (1998) 447-448 (*Muthuraj, J.G.*).
8045 *Voigt, Rainer* Griechischer Wortindex zu Anton Schalls 'Studien über griechische Fremdwörter im Syrischen'. Symposium Syriacum VII. 1998 ⇒415. 539-543.
8046 **Wenham, John W.** Inleiding tot het Grieks van het Nieuwe Testament. ᵀᴱ*Bieringer, Reimund; Vandecasteele-Vanneuville, Frederique*. Lv 1998, Peeters xiv; 298 pp. 90-6831-959-0.
8047 **West, M.L.** The east face of Helicon: west Asiatic elements in Greek poetry and myth. 1997 ⇒13,8380. ᴿAulOr 16 (1998) 261-268 (*Pòrtulas, Jaume*).

8048 **Wouters, Alfons** The Chester Beatty Codex Ac. 1499: a Graeco-Latin lexicon on the Pauline epistles and a Greek grammmar. 1988 ⇒4,2657... 7,9584*. ^RCÉg 73 (1998) 160-162 *(Lenaerts, Jean)*.

J5.2 Voces *ordine alphabetico consonantium* graecarum

8049 ἀγάπαω: *Gangemi, Attilio* Il senso di ἀγάπαω e φιλέω nei LXX, nel NT e nel vangelo di Giovanni. Synaxis 16/1 (1998) 7-114.

8050 ἁγιασμός: *Kucharski, Jacek* Pole semantyczne rzeczownikowej formy ἁγιασμός w kanonicznych księgach Septuaginty [The semantic field of the noun form ἁγιασμός in the canonical books of the Septuagint]. Roczniki Teologiczne 45/1 (1998) 55-89 Sum. 88 P.

8051 ἅγιος: *Maragno, Mary* L'espressione del sacro in S. Paolo ed in altri autori del Nuovo Testamento. ^FHERIBAN J. 1998 ⇒41. 341-347.

8052 δοῦλος: *Ellingworth, Paul* Servant, slave, or what?. BiTr 49 (1998) 123-126.

8053 ἐκκλησία: *Cattaneo, Arturo* Un contributo dell'esegesi biblica alla teologia della chiesa particolare: riflessioni sul termine *ekklesia*. RTLu 3 (1998) 557-567.

ἔλεος: *Swetnam, J. Hesed...eleos*. 1998 ⇒7719.

8054 ἐπισκέπτομαι: *Margot, Jean-Claude* Les 'visites' de Dieu. Cahiers de Traduction Biblique 30 (1998) 10-15.

8055 κεχαριτωμένη: *Buzzetti, Carlo* "Kecharitôménê" = "Full of grace"?: translating today under three influences: the Greek, the Vetus Latina, the Vulgate. Interpretation of the Bible. JSOT.S 289: 1998 ⇒389. 1329-1340.

8056 κοινωνία: *Calduch-Benages, Nuria* La koinonia nella vita religiosa. Consacrazione e Servizio 46/3 (1998) 9-22.

8057 κύριος: *Fitzmyer, Joseph A.* New Testament *Kyrios* and *Maranatha* and their Aramaic background. To advance the gospel. 1998 <1981> ⇒150. 218-235.

8058 ναζωραῖος: *Mimouni, Simon C.* Les nazoréens: recherche étymologique et historique. RB 105 (1998) 208-262.

8059 ναζωραῖος: *Nodet, Etienne* "Les nazoréens": discussion. RB 105 (1998) 263-265.

8060 νόμος: *Winger, Michael* Meaning and law. JBL 117 (1998) 105-110.

8061 ὀνοκένταυρος: *Piccinini, Elissa* ὀνοκενταυρος: demone o animale?: (dalla "nascita" biblica alla esegesi patristica). VetChr 35 (1998) 119-131.

8062 πίστις: *Cranfield, C.E.B.* On the πίστις Χριστοῦ question. On Romans. 1998 ⇒143. 81-97.

8063 σοφία: *Ellens, J. Harold* Sophia in Rabbinic hermeneutics and the curious Christian corollary. Interpretation of the Bible. JSOT.S 289: 1998 ⇒389. 521-548.

8064 σύνκρισις: *Sheerin, Daniel* Rhetorical and hermeneutic *synkrisis* in patristic typology. ^FHALTON T. 1998 ⇒36. 22-39.

8065 πληρωμα: *Otero Lazaro, Tomas* Reflexiones sobre el significado de πληρωμα en las cartas a los Colosenses y Efesios. Burg. 39/1 (1998) 9-30.

ὑψωθῆναι: *Kobayashi, H.* What did John... see? 1998 ⇒5483.

φιλέω: *Gangemi, A.* Il senso di.. nei LXX, nel NT 1998 ⇒8049.

8066 φοβούμενοι: *Stanton, G.N.* 'God-fearers': neglected evidence in Justin Martyr's *Dialogue with Trypho*. ^FJUDGE E. 1998 ⇒47. 43-52.

χάρις: *Goud, Johan* Genade ⇒7718.

J5.4 *Papyri et inscriptiones graecae*—Greek epigraphy

8067 *Balconi, Carla, al.*, Testi recentemente pubblicati. Aeg. 78 (1998) 133-200.
8068 *Betz, Hans Dieter* The changing self of the magician according to the Greek magical papyri;
8069 Jewish magic in the Greek magical papyri (PGM VII.260-71);
8070 Secrecy in the Greek magical papyri. Gesammelte Aufsätze IV. 1998 <1997> ⇒134. 175-205/187-205/152-174.
8071 **Boffo, Laura** Iscrizioni greche e latine per lo studio della bibbia. 1994 ⇒10,9379; 13,8419. ᴿGn. 70 (1998) 467-469 (*Klauck, Hans-Josef*).
8072 **Bommas, Martin** Die heidelberger Fragmente des magischen Papyrus Harris. Schriften der phil.-hist. Kl. der Heidelberger Akademie der Wissenschaften 4: Heid 1998, Winter vii; 55 pp. 3-8253-0585-6. Vorgelegt am 10. Mai 1997 von *Jan Assmann*.
8073 ᴱ**Capasso, Mario** Ricerche di papirologia letteraria e documentaria. Papyrologica Lupiensia 6: [Galatina (Lecce)] 1998, Congedo 173 pp. 88-8086-234-0.
8074 **Capasso, Mario** Papiri documentari greci. 1993 ⇒9,10203; 10,9384. ᴿBiOr 55 (1998) 161-164 (*Boyaval, Bernard*).
8075 *Carlini, Antonio* Papiri cristiani e tradizione dei testi biblici e patristici. Papyrologica florentina 30. 1998 ⇒427. 25-38.
8076 *Casanova, Gerardo* Incollare, arrotolare, maneggiare, restaurare papiri: note filologiche e bibliologiche. Aeg. 78 (1998) 117-122.
8077 **Coles, Revel A.** The Oxyrhynchus papyri 60 [4009-4092]. PEES.GR 80: 1994 ⇒10,9386. ᴿCEg 73 (1998) 162-168 (*Lenaerts, Jean*).
8078 *Cotton, Hannah M.* The law of succession in the documents from the Judaean Desert again. SCI 17 (1998) 115-123.
8079 *Damati, Emanuel* Three Greek inscriptions from eastern Galilee. ʿAtiqot 35 (1998) 151-155.
8080 **Dubois, Laurent** Les inscriptions grecques dialectales de Grande-Grèce, I: colonies eubéennes, colonies ioniennes, emporia. HEMGR 21: Genève 1995, Droz Ill. 204 pp. ᴿRAr (1998/2) 434-435 (*Bouffier, S. Collin*).
8081 *Duval, Noël; Saxer, Victor* Un nouveau reliquaire africain et l'évêché Midilensis (Études d'Archéologie chrétienne nord-africaine XXV). Syr. 75/1 (1998) 245-262.
8082 **El-Aguizy, Ola** A palaeographical study of Demotic papyri in the Cairo Museum from the reign of King Taharka to the end of the Ptolemaic period (684-30 B.C.). MIFAO 113: Le Caire 1998, Institut Français d'Archéologie Orientale xvi; 456 pp. 2-7247-0227-1. Bibl.
8083 ᴱ**Engels, Lodewijk J.: Hofmann, Heinz** Spätantike, mit einem Panorama der byzantinischen Literatur. Neues Handbuch der Literaturwissenschaft. Wsb 1997, Aula 4 xviii: 758 pp.
8084 *Fiema, Z.T.* Die Papyri von Petra. WUB 7 (1998) 48.
8085 **Finkelberg, Margalit** The birth of literary fiction in ancient Greece. Oxf 1998, Clarendon 222 pp. 0-19-815095-4. Diss. Hebr. Univ. 1985 [SCI 19,285ss—Rotstein, Andrea].

8086   *Franklin, Simon* A note on a pseudepigraphal allusion in Oxyrhyn-
       chus papyrus no. 4365. VT 48 (1998) 95-96.
8087   *Gatier, Pierre-Louis* Inscriptions grecques de Résafa. DaM 10
       (1998) 237-241.
8088   *Gauer, Heinz* Zur Silbentrennung griechischer Wörter in byzantini-
       schen Handschriften des neunten bis fünfzehnten Jahrhunderts. ByZ
       91 (1998) 321-326.
8089   *Gawlikowski, Michel* Deux publicains et leur tombeau. Syr. 75/1
       (1998) 145-151.
8090   **Gogel, Sandra Landis** A grammar of epigraphic Hebrew. SBL
       Resources for Biblical Study 23: Atlanta, GA 1998, Scholars xx; 522
       pp. $45. 1-55540-287-9. ᴰChicago; ᴰ*Pardee, D.* Bibl.
8091   **Gregg, Robert C.; Urman, Dan** Jews, pagans, and christians in the
       Golan Heights: Greek and other inscriptions of the Roman and By-
       zantine eras. SFSHJ 140: 1996 ⇒12,7963. ᴿREByz 56 (1998) 301-
       302 (*Feissel, Denis*); FgNT 11 (1998) 129-130 (*Porter, Stanley E.*).
8092   *Groll, Sarah I.* The Egyptian background of the Exodus and the
       crossing of the Reed Sea: a new reading of Papyrus Anastasi VIII.
       Jerusalem studies. ÄAT 40: 1998 ⇒361. 173-192.
8093   ᴱ**Handley, E.W.** The Oxyrhynchus papyri: 64. PEES.GR 84: 1997
       ⇒13,8432. ᴿCIR 48 (1998) 449-451 (*Ireland, Stanley*).
8094   *Harris, B.F.* The use of scripture in some unidentified theological
       papyri. ᶠJUDGE E. 1998 ⇒47. 228-232.
8095   **Haslam, M.W.,** *al.,* The Oxyrhynchus papyri: 65 [Nos. 4442-493].
       PEES.GR 85: L 1998, Egypt Exploration Soc. for the Brit. Acad. xii;
       212 pp.
8096   ᴱ**Hornblower, Simon; Spawforth, Antony** The Oxford Companion
       to Classical Civilization. Oxf 1998, OUP Bibl. xxv; 794 pp. 0-19-
       860165-4.
8097   *Horsley, G.H.R.* Epigraphy as an ancilla to the study of the Greek
       Bible: a propos of a recent anthology of inscriptions. Bib. 79 (1998)
       258-267.
8098   ᴱ**Jördens, Andrea** Griechische Papyri aus Soknopaiu Nesos (P.
       Louvre I). PTA 43: Bonn 1998, Habelt xxii; 325 pp. 3-7749-2838-X.
       Collab. *Zauzich, Karl-Theodor*; Bibl.
8099   *Kerkeslager, Allen* The apology of the potter: a translation of the pot-
       ter's oracle. Jerusalem studies. ÄAT 40: 1998 ⇒361. 67-79.
8100   ᴱ**Kramer, Bärbel** Akten des 21. Internationalen Papyrologenkon-
       gresses, Berlin 13.-19.8.1995. APF.B 3: 1997 ⇒13,367. 2 vols.
       ᴿAeg. 78 (1998) 224-226 (*Daris, Sergio*).
8101   ᴱ**Laks, A.; Most, G.W.** Studies on the Derveni papyrus. 1997
       ⇒13,8441. ᴿCIR 48 (1998) 451-452 (*Palmer, John A.*).
8102   **Llewelyn, S.R.** A review of Greek inscriptions and papyri published
       in 1982-83. New documents illustrating early christianity, 7. 1994 ⇒
       10,9401; 13,8444. ᴿGn. 70 (1998) 257-260 (*Wischmeyer, Wolfgang*);
8103   A review of the Greek inscriptions and papyri published in 1984-85.
       New documents illustrating early Christianity 8: North Rhyde, Aus-
       tralia 1998, Macquarie Univ. 198 pp. £24/$35. 0-8028-4518-5.
8104   *Loffreda, Stanislao* Lucerna bizantina con iscrizione bidirezionale.
       SBFLA 48 (1998) 489-494.
8105   *McBride, D.R.* Gnostic and traditional Egyptian religious affinities in
       the magical papyri. JSSEA 27 (1997) 43-59 Sum. 42.

8106 ᴱMerkelbach, Reinhold; Stauber, Josef Steinepigramme aus dem griechischen Osten: 1, die Westküste Kleinasiens von Knidos bis Ilion. Stu 1998, Teubner xv; 647 pp. 3-519-07446-X.

8107 Naldini, Mario Il cristianesimo in Egitto: lettere private nei papiri dei secoli II-IV. BPat 32: Fiesole ²1998, Nardini 464 pp. Bibl.

8108 O'Callaghan, José Papiros literarios griegos del fondo Palau-Ribes. 1993 ⇒9,10230; 11/2,6473. ᴿEstB 56 (1998) 134-137 (Urbán. A.).

8109 ᴱPestman, P.W.; Rupprecht, H.-A. Berichtigungsliste der griechischen Papyrusurkunden aus Ägypten 10. Lei 1998, Brill x; 351 pp. 90-04-11133-6.

8110 ᴱPleket, H.W.; Stroud, R.S. Supplementum epigraphicum graecum, 40-41. 1990-1994 ⇒11/2,6477. ᴿGn. 70 (1998) 322-327 (Ehrhardt, Norbert).

8111 Puglia, Enzo La cura del libro nel mondo antico: guasti e restauri del rotolo di papiro. N 1997, Liguori 166 pp. ᴿAeg. 78 (1998) 226-229 (Montevecchi, Orsolina).

8112 Rupprecht, Hans-Albert Sammelbuch griechischer Urkunden aus Ägypten 20 [Nr. 14069-15202]. 1997 ⇒13,8452. ᴿCÉg 73 (1998) 180-185 (Nachtergael, Georges).

8113 Rupprecht, Hans-Albert Marriage contract regulations and documentary practice in the Greek papyri. SCI 17 (1998) 60-76.

8114 Rutherford, Ian Canons of style in the Antonine age: idea—theory and its literary context. Oxford Classical Monographs: Oxf 1998, Clarendon viii; 168 pp. $55.

8115 Saïd, S.; Trédé, M.; Le Boulluec, A. Histoire de la littérature grecque. P 1997, PUF xvi; 720 pp. FF148 [RHPhR 80,292s—Gain, B.].

8116 ᴱᵀShelton, J.C.; Whitehorne, J.E.G. The Oxyrhynchus papyri: 62. PEES.GR 82: 1995 ⇒12,7971. ᴿCÉg. 73 (1998) 362-365 (Lenaerts, Jean).

8117 ᴱSheridan, Jennifer A. Columbia Papyri IX: the Vestis Militaris Codex. ASP 39: Atlanta, GA 1998, Scholars 174 pp. 0-7885-0446-0. Bibl.

8118 Teeter, Timothy M. Columbia papyri XI. ASP 38: Atlanta, GA 1998, Scholars xiv; 97 pp. 0-7885-0433-9. Bibl.

8119 Van Rossum-Steenbeeck, Monique Greek Reader's Digest?: studies on a selection of subliterary papyri. Mn.S 175: Lei 1998, Brill xix; 361 pp. 90-04-10953-6. Bibl.

8120 Vleeming, Sven P. Ostraka varia: tax receipts and legal documents... chiefly of the Early Ptolemaic Period. 1994 ⇒11/2,6480. ᴿBiOr 55 (1998) 372-387 (Devauchelle, Didier).

8121 Wardy, Robert The birth of rhetoric. 1996 ⇒12,7973. ᴿSCI 17 (1998) 238-240 (Winterbottom, Michael).

8122 Wolff, Hans Julius Vorlesungen über Juristische Papyruskunde: gehalten an der...Albert-Ludwigs-Universität Freiburg im Wintersemester 1967/68 und Sommersemester 1968. ᴱWolf, Joseph Georg. Freiburger Rechtsgeschichtliche Abhandlungen 30: B 1998, Duncker & H 138 pp. 3-428-09521-9.

8123 ᴱWorp, K.A. Greek papyri from Kellis, I. 1995, ⇒11/2,6484. ᴿJEA 84 (1998) 261-263 (Thomas, J. David).

8124 Yon, Jean-Baptiste Remarques sur une famille caravanière à Palmyre. Syr. 75/1 (1998) 153-160.

J6.5 **Latina**

8125   *Bonfante, Larissa* LIVY and the monuments. [F]GORDON, C. JSOT.S
       273: 1998 ⇒31. 480-492.
8126   *Cancik-Lindemaier, Hildegard* SENECA's collection of epistles: a
       medium of philosophical communication. [F]BETZ, H. 1998 ⇒10. 88-
       109.
8127   [E]**Dominik, William J.** Roman eloquence. 1997 ⇒13,8466. [R]SCI 17
       (1998) 240-241 (*Winterbottom, Michael*).
8128   **Filippi, Giorgio** Indice della raccolta epigrafica di San Paolo Fuori
       le Mura. Inscriptiones Sanctae Sedis 3: Città del Vaticano 1998,
       Monumenti, Musei e Gallerie Pontificie 209 pp. Bibl.
8129   *Greer, Rowan A.* CICERO's sketch and LACTANTIUS's plan.
       [F]FERGUSON, E. NT.S 90: 1998 ⇒25. 155-174.
8130   [E]**Grondeux, Anne; Merrilees, Brian; Monfrin, Jacques** Duo
       Glossaria: Glossarium Gallico-Latinum: anonymi montepessulanensis
       dictionarius: le glossaire latin-français du Ms. Montpellier H236: le
       Glossaire Français-Latin du Ms. Paris Lat. 7684. CChr.CM 2; Lexica
       Latina Medii Aevi. Nouveau recueil des lexiques latin-français du
       Moyen Age 2: Turnholti 1998, Brepols 271 pp. 2-503-50783-2.
8131   [E]**Hajdú, Kerstin** Pseudo Herodianus: De Figuris:
       Überlieferungsgeschichte und kritische Ausgabe. Sammlung griechi-
       scher und lateinischer Grammatiker 8: B 1998, De Gruyter 168 pp. 3-
       11-014836-6.
8132   **McGurk, Patrick** Gospel books and early Latin manuscripts. CStS
       606: Aldershot 1998, Variorum xii; 344 pp. £57.50. 0-86078-684-6.
8133   **Morwood, James** A dictionary of Latin words and phrases. Oxf
       1998, OUP xiv; (2) 224 pp. 0-19-860109-3.
8134   **Wardy, Robert** The birth of rhetoric. 1996 ⇒12,7973. [R]SCI 17
       (1998) 238-240 (*Winterbottom, Michael*).

J8 **Language, writing and the Bible**

8135   **Bennett, Patrick R.** Comparative Semitic linguistics: a manual. WL
       1998, Eisenbrauns xii; 269 pp. $29.50. 1-57506-021-3. Bibl.
8136   *Bordreuil, Pierre; Pardee, Dennis* La plus ancienne attestation épi-
       graphique de la lettre proto-sémitique {Ḍ}. [F]MARGAIN, J. 1998 ⇒71.
       37-40.
8137   *Branca, Vittore* Il linguaggio biblico nel mondo contemporaneo.
       Studium 94 (1998) 837-842.
8138   **Brown, Michelle P.** The British Library guide to writing and scripts:
       history and techniques. The British Library Guides: L 1998, British
       Library 96 pp. 0-7123-4583-3. Bibl.
8139   **Campbell, Lyle** Historical linguistics: an introduction. E 1998, Edin-
       burgh University Press xx; 396 pp. 0-7486-0775-7. Bibl.
8140   **Chomsky, Noam Avram** On language: CHOMSKY's classic works
       language and responsibility and reflections on language in one
       volume. NY 1998, New viii; 269 pp. 1-565-84475-0.
8141   *Clines, David J.A.* Philology and power. OT essays, 2. JSOT.S 293:
       1998 <1995> ⇒142. 613-630.
8142   **Edzard, Lutz** Polygenesis, convergence and entropy: an alternative
       model of linguistic evolution applied to Semitic linguistics. Wsb
       1998, Harrassowitz 207 pp. DM98. 3-447-04102-1. [D]Berkeley 1992.

8143   *Finkelberg, Margalit* Bronze Age writing: contacts between east and west. The Aegean. ᴱ**Cline, E.** 1998 ⇒T1.1. 265-272.

8144   *Fox, Joshua* Isolated nouns in the Semitic languages. ZAH 11 (1998) 1-31.

8145   **Goddard, Cliff** Semantic analysis: a practical introduction. Oxford Textbooks in Linguistics: Oxf 1998, OUP xv; 411 pp. 0-19-870016-4. Bibl.

8146   *Gubler, Marie-Louise* So vielerlei Arten von Sprachen gibt es in der Welt, und keine ist ohne sinnvollen Laut ... (1 Kor 14,10f): Sprache und Sprachen. Diak. 29 (1998) 75-86.

8147   **Horwich, Paul** Truth. Oxf 1998, Clarendon xviii; 157 pp. 0-19-875223-7. Bibl.

8148   The Indo-European languages. ᴱ*Giacalone Ramat, Anna; Ramat, Paolo.* Routledge language family descriptions: L 1998, Routledge xxiii; 526 pp. 0-415-06449-X.

8149   *Kieffer, René* From linguistic methodology to the discovery of a world of metaphors. Semeia 81 (1998) 77-93.

8150   *Knudsen, Ebbe Egede* Central Semitic **yaqtulum* reconsidered: a rejoinder to J. Tropper. JSSt 43 (1998) 1-9.

8151   *Koffi, Ettien* There is more to 'and' than just conjoining words. BiTr 49 (1998) 332-343.

8152   ᴱ**Lapointe, Steven G.; Brentari, Diane K.; Farrell, Patrick M.** Morphology and its relation to phonology and syntax. Stanford, CA 1998, CSLI Publications viii, 440 pp. 0-57586-112-7.

8153   **Larson, Richard K.; Segal, Gabriel** Knowledge of meaning: an introduction to semantic theory. CM 1997, MIT Press xvii (2) 639 pp. 0-262-62100-2. Bibl.

8154   **McCarter, P. Kyle** Ancient inscriptions: voices from the biblical world. Wsh 1996, Biblical Archaeology Society xii; 179 pp. $39.55. Accompanying 140 slides; $100. ᴿArOr 66 (1998) 75-77 *(Segert, Stanislav)*

8155   *Millard, A.R.* The knowledge of writing in Iron Age Palestine. "Lasset uns Brücken bauen...". BEAT 42: 1998 ⇒401. 33-39.

8156   *Müller, Hans-Peter* Zu den semitisch-hamitischen Konjugationssystemen. ZAH 11 (1998) 140-152.

8157   *Niemann, Hermann Michael* Kein Ende des Büchermachens in Israel und Juda (Koh 12,12)—wann begann es?. BiKi 53 (1998) 117-134.

8158   *Olmo Lete, G. del* The monoconsonantal lexical series in Semitic. AulOr 16 (1998) 37-75.

8159   ᴱ**Ostertag, Gary** Definite descriptions: a reader. CM 1998, MIT Press xii; 411 pp. 0-262-65049-5. Bibl.

8160   **Petrucci, Armando** Writing the dead: death and writing strategies in the western tradition. Stanford 1998, Stanford Univ. Press xviii; 163 pp. £25. 0-8047-2859-3 [CIR 51,136s—Scourfield, J.H.D.].

8161   **Pisani, Vittore** Glottologia indeuropea: manuale di grammatica comparata delle lingue indeuropee, con speciale riguardo del greco e del latino. T ⁴1998, Rosenberg & S xlvi; 325 pp. 88-7011-016-8. Bibl.

8162   ᴱ**Porter, Stanley E.** Handbook of classical rhetoric in the Hellenistic period 330 B.C.- A.D. 400. 1997 ⇒13,8494. ᴿFgNT 11 (1998) 135-136 *(Peláez, Jesús)*.

8163   ᴱ**Rapallo, Umberto; Garbugino, Giovanni** Grammatica e lessico delle lingue 'morte'. Collana del Dipartimento di Scienze Glottoetnologiche dell'Università degli studi di Genova 3: [Alessandria] 1998, Dell'Orso x; 286 pp. 88-7694-254-8.

8164 **Ratcliffe, Robert R.** The "broken" plural problem in Arabic and comparative Semitic: allomorphy and analogy in non-concatenative morphology. Amsterdam studies in the theory and history of linguistic science 4; Current issues in linguistic theory 168: Amst 1998, Benjamins xi; 261 pp. 90-272-3673-9. Bibl.

8165 *Ratcliffe, Robert R.* Defining morphological isoglosses: the 'broken' plural and Semitic subclassification. JNES 57/2 (1998) 81-123.

8166 **Raurell, Frederic** 'I Déu digué...': la paraula feta història. 1995 ⇒ 11/2,1129...13,8495. ᴿNatGrac 45 (1998) 165-66 (*Ramos, Felipe F.*).

8167 *Röllig, Wolfgang* Nordsemitisch-Südsemitisch?: zur Geschichte des Alphabets im 2. Jt. v. Chr. ᶠRАINEY, A. IOS 18: 1998 ⇒96. 79-88.

8168 **Schapiro, Meyer** Palabras, escritos e imágines: semiótica del lenguaje. M 1998, Encuentro 165 pp. ᴿSoleriana 10 (1998) 297-299 (*Delpiazzo, J.C.*).

8169 *Testen, David* The derivational role of the Semitic N-stem. ZA 88 (1998) 127-145;

8170 Semitic terms for "myrtle": a study in covert cognates. JNES 57 (1998) 281-290.

8171 **Testen, David D.** Parallels in Semitic linguistics: the development of Arabic la- and related Semitic particles. SStLL 26: Lei 1998, Brill xi; 235 pp. 90-04-10973-0. Bibl.

8172 **Yardeni, Ada** The book of Hebrew script. 1997 ⇒13,8507. ᴿBArR 24/5 (1998) 64, 66, 68 (*Vaughn, Andrew G.*).

8173 **Zewi, Tamar** A syntactical study of verbal forms affixed by -n(n) endings in classical Arabic, Biblical Hebrew, El-Amarna Akkadian and Ugarit. AOAT 260: Müns 1999, Ugarit-Verlag 211 pp. 3-9271-2071-5. Bibl. ᴿUF 30 (1998) 947-948 (*Tropper, Josef*).

8174 *Zinkuratire, Victor* Morphological and syntactical similarities between Hebrew and Bantu languages. NAOTS 4 (1998) 14-19.

XV. Postbiblica

κ1.1 Pseudepigrapha [=catholicis 'Apocrypha'] *VT generalis*

8175 *Aranda Pérez, Gonzalo* I giudei nella diaspora;

8176 L'esempio e la parola dei profeti;

8177 Nuove narrazioni della storia biblica;

8178 Nuove preghiere. Letteratura giudaica. 1998 ⇒8180. 347-366/329-338/290-310/339-346.

8179 **Aranda Pérez, G.; García Martínez, F.; Pérez Fernandez, M.** Literatura judía intertestamentaria. 1996 ⇒12,8021. ᴿCarthaginensia 14 (1998) 214-216 (*Marín Heredia, F.*);

8180 Letteratura giudaica intertestamentaria. Introduzione allo studio della Bibbia 9: [Brescia] 1998, Paideia 501 pp. L79.000. 88-394-0568-2.

8181 *Atkinson, Kenneth* Towards a redating of the Psalms of Solomon: implications for understanding the Sitz im Leben of an unknown Jewish sect. JSPE 17 (1998) 95-112.

8182 **Blackburn, Rollin James** Hebrew poetic devices in the Greek text of the Psalms of Solomon. ᴰTemple 1998, 221 pp.

8183 *Blessing, Kamila* Desolate Jerusalem and barren matriarch: two instinct figures in the pseudepigrapha. JSPE 18 (1998) 47-69.
8184 *Carey, Greg* The Ascension of Isaiah: an example of early christian narrative polemic. JSPE 17 (1998) 65-78.
8185 **Charlesworth, James H.** The Old Testament pseudepigrapha & the New Testament. Harrisburg ²1998 <1985>, Trinity xlii; 145 pp. $15. 1-56338-257-1 [ThD 46,262—Heiser, W. Charles].
8186 *Charlesworth, James H.* The fourteen literary collections for studying early Judaism and christian origins: the place of the Odes of Solomon. ᶠPOKORNÝ, P. 1998 ⇒90. 185-207;
8187 Introduction. Critical reflections on the Odes of Solomon;
8188 The original language of the Odes of Solomon;
8189 Selected and annotated bibliography with status quaestionis. Critical reflections on the Odes of Solomon. JSPE.S 22: 1998 ⇒8190. 14-20/78-136/261-285.
8190 **Charlesworth, James Hamilton** Critical reflections on the Odes of Solomon: literary setting, textual studies, gnosticism, the Dead Sea scrolls and the gospel of John. JSPE.S 22; Distinguished Scholars Collection: Shf 1998, Academic 302 pp. 1-85075-660-0. Bibl.
8191 *Drijvers, Hendrik J.W.* Salomo/Salomoschriften III: Sapientia Salomonis, Psalmen Salomos und Oden Salomos. TRE 29. 1998 ⇒501. 730-732.
8192 *Gruen, Erich S.* Jews, Greeks, and Romans in the third Sibylline Oracle. Jews in a Graeco-Roman world. 1998 ⇒337. 15-36.
8193 **Haelewyck, J.-C.** Clavis Apocryphorum Veteris Testamenti. CChr Clavis Apocryphorum Veteris Testamenti: Turnhout 1998, Brepols xxviii; 243 pp. 2-503-50702-6.
8194 *Joosten, Jan* Odes de Salomon 7,3a: observations sur un hellénisme dans le texte syriaque. ZNW 89 (1998) 134-135.
8195 *Knibb, Michael A.* Perspectives on the Apocrypha and Pseudepigrapha: the Levi traditions. ᶠVAN DER WOUDE, A. VT.S 73: 1998 ⇒121. 197-213.
8196 *Knights, Chris H.* The Abode of the Blessed: a source of the story of Zosimus?. JSPE 17 (1998) 79-93.
8197 *Lattke, M.* The *Odes of Solomon*: discoveries, editions, and the problem of dating. ᶠJUDGE E. 1998 ⇒47. 61-70;
8198 Forschungsgeschichtliche Bibliographie 1985-1997 mit Ergänzungen bis 1984. Die Oden Salomos. 1998 ⇒8199. 233-53 [BuBbgB 24,15].
8199 **Lattke, Michael** Die Oden Salomos in ihrer Bedeutung für Neues Testament und Gnosis: IV. OBO 25/4: FrS 1998, Universitätsverlag xii; 272 pp. FS83. 3-7278-1164-1.
8200 **Merkel, Helmut** Sibyllinen. Apokalypsen, Lfg. 8. Jüdische Schriften aus hellenistisch-römischer Zeit 5. Gü 1998, Mohn 103 pp. DM78. 3-579-03958-X.
8201 *Nickelsburg, George W.E.* Patriarchs who worry about their wives: a haggadic tendency in the Genesis Apocryphon. Biblical perspectives. StTDJ 28: 1998 ⇒441. 137-158.
8202 **Otzen, Benedikt** Kommentar til de Apokryfe Bøger. K 1998, Danske Bibelselskab 235 pp. 87-7523-410-6 [SEÅ 64,151—Block, P.].
8203 **Satran, David** Biblical prophets in Byzantine Palestine: reassessing the Lives of the Prophets. SVTP 11: 1995 ⇒11/2,6745; 13,8525. ᴿRTL 29 (1998) 523-525 (*Haelewyck, J.-Cl.*); Cathedra 87 (1998) 169-74 [H.] (*Limor, Ora*); JNES 57 (1998) 65-67 (*Collins, John J.*).

8204 *Schröter, Jens* Gerechtigkeit und Barmherzigkeit: das Gottesbild der Psalmen Salomos in seinem Verhältnis zu Qumran und Paulus. NTS 44 (1998) 557-577.

8205 [TE]**Schwemer, Anna Maria** Studien zu den frühjüdischen Prophetenlegenden: *Vitae prophetarum.* TSAJ 49-50: 1995-1996 ⇒12,8036; 13,8526. 2 vols. [R]JAC 41 (1998) 234-236 *(Maier, Johann).*

8206 [T]**Schwemer, Anna Maria** Vitae prophetarum: jüdische Schriften aus hellenistisch-römischer Zeit, 1/7. 1997 ⇒13,8528. [R]BiOr 55 (1998) 893-896 *(Van Henten, J.W.).*

8207 [E]**Stone, Michael Edward; Bergren, Theodore A.** Biblical figures outside the bible. Valley Forge, PA 1998, Trinity Bibl. xiii; 433 pp. $35. 1-56338-247-4.

8208 **Troiani, Lucio** Letteratura giudaica di lingua greca. Apocrifi dell'Antico Testamento, 5. 1997 ⇒13,8531. [R]Henoch 20 (1998) 120-121 *(Gabba, Emilio)*; PaVi 43/2 (1998) 57-58 *(Manzi, Franco).*

K1.2 Henoch

8209 *Alexander, Philip S.* From son of Adam to second god: transformations of the biblical Enoch. Biblical figures. 1998 ⇒8207. 87-122.

8210 **Argall, Randal A.** 1 Enoch and Sirach: a comparative literary and conceptual analysis of the themes of revelation, creation and judgment. 1995 ⇒11/2,6750. [R]RB 105 (1998) 139-141 *(Nápole, G.).*

8211 *Carey, Greg* 'How to do things with (apocalyptic) words: rhetorical dimensions of apocalyptic discourse. LexTQ 33 (1998) 85-101 [Bu BbgB 30,10].

8212 **Chialà, Sabino** Libro delle parabole di Enoc: testo e commento. St Bi 117: 1997 ⇒13,8536. [R]RivBib 46 (1998) 347-9 *(Manzi, Franco).*

8213 *Chialà, Sabino* Elementi storico-culturali in un testo "apocalittico" al volgere della nostra era: il libro delle parabole in Enoc. RstB 10/1-2 (1998) 153-177.

8214 *Kugel, James* 4Q369 "Prayer of Enosh" and ancient biblical interpretation. DSD 5 (1998) 119-148.

8215 *Morisi, Marzia* Per l'origine dell'Apocalittica: dall'ambivalenzà delle nozze miste greche all'ambiguità delle nozze miste giudaiche. Anton. 73 (1998) 483-504 Sum. 483.

8216 *Nickelsburg, George W.E.* The books of Enoch at Qumran: what we know and what we need to think about. [F]STEGEMANN, H. BZNW 97: 1998 ⇒111. 99-113;

8217 Enochic wisdom: an alternative to the Mosaic Torah?. [F]FRERICHS, E. BJSt 320: 1998 ⇒28. 123-132.

8218 *Olson, Daniel C.* Enoch and the Son of Man in the epilogue of the Parables. JSPE 18 (1998) 27-38.

8219 *Orlov, Andrei A.* Titles of Enoch—metatron in 2 Enoch. JSPE 18 (1998) 71-86.

8220 **VanderKam, James C.** Enoch: a man for all generations. 1996 ⇒12,8045; 13,8542. [R]Bib. 79 (1998) 438-444 *(Chialà, Sabino).*

K1.3 Testamenta

8221 *Aranda Pérez, Gonzalo* La via indicata dai padri: i testamenti. Letteratura giudaica. 1998 ⇒8180. 311-328.

8222 **Kugler, Robert A.** From patriarch to priest: the Levi-Priestly tradition from Aramaic Levi to Testament of Levi. SBL Early Judaism and its Literature 9: 1996 ⇒12,8047; 13,8545. [R]CBQ 60 (1998) 120-121 (*Day, Linda*); JBL 117 (1998) 353-355 (*Aschim, Anders*).
8223 **Munoa, Phillip B.** Four powers in heaven: the interpretation of Daniel 7 in the Testament of Abraham. JSPE.S 28: Shf 1998, Academic 170 pp. £31.50. 1-85075-885-9. Bibl.
8224 *Stone, Michael E.* Some further reading in the Hebrew Testament of Naphtali. JJS 49 (1998) 346-347.

K1.6 **Jubilaea, Adam, Asenet**

8225 *Berger, Klaus* Jubiläenbuch. RAC 146. 1998 ⇒495. 31-38.
8226 **Schubert, Friedemann** Tradition und Erneuerung: Studien zum Jubiläenbuch und seinem Trägerkreis. [D]Leipzig 1996: [D]*Seidel, H.* EHS. G 771: Fra 1998, Lang 282 pp. 3-631-32540-1 [NThAR 1998,301].
8227 *Van Ruiten, J.T.A.G.M.* Biblical interpretation in Jubilees 3:1-31. "Lasset uns Brücken bauen...". BEAT 42: 1998 ⇒401. 315-319.

8228 *Anderson, Gary A.* Adam and Eve in the "Life of Adam and Eve". Biblical figures. 1998 ⇒8207. 7-32.
8229 *Borgonovo, Gianantonio* La mediazione di Adamo: un conflitto interpretativo originario. ScC 126 (1998) 337-370.
8230 [T]**Monferrer Sala, Juan Pedro** Historia de Adán y Eva. Textos y Estudios de la Literatura Árabe Cristiana 1: Granada 1998, Sociedad de Estudios del Cristianismo Oriental 145 pp. 84-922847-8-1. [R]IslChr 24 (1998) 252-254 (*Epalza, Míkel de*).
8231 *Pettorelli, J.-P.* La vie latine d'Adam et Eve. ALMA 56 (1998) 5-104.
8232 [E]**Stone, Michael E.** Armenian apocrypha relating to Adam end Eve. SVTP 14: 1996 ⇒12,8058. [R]OrChr 82 (1998) 280-281 (*Van Esbroeck, Michel*); JThS 49 (1998) 450-451 (*Thomson, R.W.*).

8233 **Bohak, Gideon** Joseph and Aseneth and the Jewish temple in Heliopolis. SBL Early Judaism and Its Literature 10: 1996 ⇒13,1861. [R]CBQ 60 (1998) 555-557 (*Attridge, Harold W.*).
8234 **Burchard, Christoph** Gesammelte Studien zu Josef und Aseneth. SVTP 13: 1996 ⇒12,119. [R]ThLZ 123 (1998) 48-49 (*Herzer, Jens*).
8235 **Humphrey, Edith McEwan** The ladies and the cities: transformation and apocalyptic identity in Joseph and Aseneth, 4 Ezra, the Apocalypse and The Shepherd of Hermas. JSPE.S 17: 1995 ⇒11/2, 6798; 13,8570. [R]AsbTJ 53 (1998) 203-204 (*Longenecker, Bruce W.*); JBL 117 (1998) 375-377 (*Cook, Stephen L.*).
8236 *Kraemer, Ross S.* Aseneth as wisdom. Wisdom and psalms. 1998 ⇒221. 218-239.
8237 **Kraemer, Ross Shepard** When Aseneth met Joseph: a late antique tale of the biblical patriarch and his Egyptian wife, reconsidered. NY 1998, OUP xviii; 365 pp. $60. 0-19-511475-2. Bibl.
8238 *Piñero, Antonio* Literatura Judeo-Helenística intertestamentaria: José y Asenet: imagen de la mujer, nueva hipótesis interpretativa. EE 73 (1998) 129-134.

8239 **Standhartinger, Angela** Das Frauenbild im Judentum der hellenistischen Zeit: ein Beitrag anhand von 'Joseph und Aseneth'. 1995 ⇒ 11/2,6800; 13,1876. ᴿJQR 88 (1998) 362-365 (*Van Dam, Shanti S.*).

K1.7 Apocalypses, ascensiones

8240 *Albrile, Ezio* Il mistero di Seth: sincretismo gnostico in una perduta apocalisse. Laur. 39 (1998) 413-453.
8241 *Aranda Pérez, Gonzalo* Le apocalissi: origine del male e vittoria di Dio. Letteratura giudaica. 1998 ⇒8180. 232-289.
8242 *Bauckham, Richard* The conflict of justice and mercy: attitudes to the damned in apocalyptic literature <1990>;
8243 Early Jewish visions of hell <1990>;
8244 Descents to the underworld <1992>;
8245 A quotation from 4Q Second Ezekiel in the Apocalypse of Peter <1992>;
8246 The Apocalypse of the Seven Heavens: the Latin version <1993>;
8247 The Apocalypse of Peter: a Jewish christian apocalypse from the time of Bar Kokhba <1994>;
8248 Visiting the places of the dead in the extra-canonical apocalypses <1995>. Fate of the dead. NT.S 93: 1998 ⇒132. 132-148/49-80/9-48/259-268/304-331/160-258/81-96;
8249 Jews and Jewish christians in the land of Israel at the time of the Bar Kochba war, with special reference to the *Apocalypse of Peter*. Tolerance. 1998 ⇒440. 228-238;
8250 The Ascension of Isaiah: genre, unity and date;
8251 AUGUSTINE, 'the compassionate' christians, and the Apocalypse of Peter;
8252 The four apocalypses of the virgin Mary. The fate of the dead. NT.S 93: 1998 ⇒132. 363-390/149-159/332-362.
8253 **Carozzi, Claude** Eschatologie et au-delà: recherches sur l'*Apocalypse de Paul*. 1994 ⇒10,9639c. ᴿRHE 93 (1998) 490-492 (*Haelewyck, Jean-Claude*).
8254 *Frankfurter, David* Early christian apocalypticism: literature and social world. Encyclopedia of apocalypticism I. 1998 ⇒507. 415-453.
8255 **Harlow, Daniel C.** The Greek *Apocalypse of Baruch (3 Baruch)* in Hellenistic Judaism and early christianity. SVTP 12: 1996 ⇒12,8066; 13,8576. ᴿJEarlyC 6 (1998) 318-319 (*Spencer, John R.*); CBQ 60 (1998) 155-157 (*Bergren, Theodore A.*).
8256 *Havelaar, Henriette W.* The use of scripture in the Coptic Gnostic Apocalypse of Peter (*NHC* VII,3). Use of sacred books. 1998 ⇒263. 221-233.
8257 *Helmer, Robert C.* Art imitating life: suffering and redemption in an early Christian apocalypse. ᶠSNYDER, G. 1998 ⇒104. 316-323.
8258 **Helmer, Robert C.** 'That we may know and understand': gospel tradition in the Apocalypse of Peter. ᴰMarquette 1998, 173 pp.
8259 **Norelli, Enrico** L'Ascensione di Isaia: studi su un apocrifo al crocevia dei cristianesimi. 1994 ⇒13,8579. ᴿJThS 49 (1998) 323-324 (*Bauckham, Richard*).
8260 ᴱSilverstein, Theodore; Hilhorst, Anthony Apocalypse of Paul: a new critical edition of three long Latin versions. Cahiers d'orienta-

lisme 21: 1997 ⇒13,8582. ^RMAe 67/1 (1998) 123-4 (*Palmer, Nigel*); RHE 93 (1998) 492-493 (*Haelewyck, Jean-Claude*); JThS 49 (1998) 309-313 (*Elliott, J.K.*); VigChr 52 (1998) 213-217 (*Tromp, J.*).

8261   **Tardieu, Michel; Hadot, Pierre** Recherches sur la formation de l'Apocalypse de Zostrien et les sources de Marius VICTORINUS: "Porphyre et Victorinus": questions et hypothèses. 1996 ⇒12,8072. ^RJAC 41 (1998) 252-256 (*Schenke, Hans-Martin*).

8262   *Van Lent, Jos* Les apocalypses coptes de l'époque arabe: quelques réflexions. Études Coptes V. 1998 ⇒451. 181-195.

K2.1 Philo judaeus alexandrinus [⇒M5.2]

8263   *Berchman, Robert M.* Arcana mundi: magic and divination in the *De Somniis* of PHILO of Alexandria. Mediators of the divine. SFSHJ 163: 1998 ⇒287. 115-154.

8264   **Birnbaum, Ellen** The place of Judaism in PHILO's thought: Israel, Jews, and proselytes. BJSt 290; StPhilo.M 2: 1996 ⇒13,8585. ^RCBQ 60 (1998) 145-146 (*Murphy, Frederick J.*); AJSR 23 (1998) 250-253 (*Terian, Abraham*); JSJ 29 (1998) 101-103 (*Bekken, Per Jarle*); VigChr 52 (1998) 323-325 (*Geljon, A.C.*).

8265   **Borgen, Peder** PHILO of Alexandria: an exegete for his time. NT.S 86: 1997 ⇒13,8586. ^RJJS 49 (1998) 350-352 (*Mendelson, Alan*).

8266   *Borgen, Peder* The crossing of the Red Sea as interpreted by PHILO: biblical event—liturgical model—cultural application. ^FSNYDER, G. 1998 ⇒104. 77-90.

8267   *Bos, Abraham P.* PHILO of Alexandria: a Platonist in the image and likeness of Aristotle. Studia Philonica Annual 10 (1998) 66-86.

8268   *Burnette-Bletsch, Rhonda* At the hands of a woman: rewriting Jael in Pseudo-PHILO. JSPE 17 (1998) 53-64.

8269   **Calabi, Francesca** The language and the law of God: interpretation and politics in PHILO of Alexandria. SFSHJ 188: Atlanta, GA 1998, Scholars xi; 158 pp. $40. 0-7885-0498-3. Bibl.;

8270   Linguaggio e legge di Dio: interpretazione e politica in FILONE di Alessandria. Ferrare 1998, Corso 181 pp. Bibl.

8271   *Cohen, Naomi G.* The elucidation of Philo's *Spec.Leg. 4,137-8: 'Stamped too with genuine seals'*. Classical studies in honor of David SOHLBERG. ^E**Katzoff, Ranon; Petroff, Yaakov; Schaps, David.** Ramat Gan 1996, Bar Ilan Univ. Pr. 510 pp. 153-166.

8272   Études philoniennes. 1996 ⇒12,8094; 13,8603. ^RETR 73 (1998) 270-271 (*Léonard, Jeanne Marie*); ThLZ 123 (1998) 379-380 (*Siegert, Folker*); RSR 86 (1998) 604-606 (*Beaude, Pierre-Marie*).

8273   *Fisk, B.N.* Scripture shaping scripture: the interpretive role of biblical citations in Pseudo-PHILO's episode of the golden calf. JSPE 17 (1998) 3-23.

8274   *Hartman, Lars* The human desire to converse with the divine: DIO of Prusa and PHILO of Alexandria on images of God. ^FBERGMAN J. 1998 ⇒9. 163-171.

8275   *Hay, David M.* The veiled thoughts of the Therapeutae. Mediators of the divine. SFSHJ 163: 1998 ⇒287. 167-184.

8276   **Jacobson, Howard** A commentary on Pseudo-PHILO's *Liber antiquitatum biblicarum*. AGJU 31: 1996 ⇒12,8087; 13,8596. ^RCBQ 60

(1998) 160-161 (*Adler, William*); ThLZ 123 (1998) 48-51 (*Reinmuth, Eckart*).
8277 *Kamesar, Adam* PHILO, the presence of 'paideutic' myth in the pentateuch, and the 'principles' or Kephalaia of Mosaic discourse. Studia Philonica Annual 10 (1998) 34-65.
8278 *Kamsler, Harold M.* PHILO Judaeus: linking biblical Judaism and Hellenistic beliefs. JBQ 26 (1998) 111-115.
8279 **Laporte, J.** Teologia liturgica di FILONE d'Alessandria e ORIGENE. Mi 1998, Paoline 226 pp [RivLi 87,691—Calvano, Corrado].
     ^E**Lévy, C.** PHILON...et le langage de la philosophie 1998 ⇒433.
8280 *Niehoff, Maren R.* PHILO's views on paganism. Tolerance. 1998 ⇒ 440. 135-158.
8281 *Osborn, Eric* PHILO and CLEMENT: quiet conversion and noetic exegesis. Studia Philonica Annual 10 (1998) 108-124.
8282 *Pawlaczyk, Anna* PHILO in Poland since the Second World War. Studia Philonica Annual 10 (1998) 125-130.
8283 *Pearce, Sarah* Belonging and not belonging: local perspectives in PHILO of Alexandria. Jewish local patriotism. JSPE.S 31: 1998 ⇒ 414. 79-105.
8284 **Runia, David** PHILO & the church fathers. VigChr.S 32: 1995 ⇒12, 8098. ^RThLZ 123 (1998) 264-266 (*Burkhardt, Helmut*).
8285 *Runia, David T.* A new PHILO word index. Studia Philonica Annual 10 (1998) 131-134.
8286 *Runia, David T., al.*, PHILO of Alexandria: an annotated bibliography 1995. Studia Philonica Annual 10 (1998) 135-175.
8287 *Siegert, Folker* The Philonian fragment *De Deo*: first English translation. Studia Philonica Annual 10 (1998) 1-33.
8288 **Sly, Dorothy I.** PHILO's Alexandria. 1996 ⇒12,8101; 13,8610. ^RVig Chr 52 (1998) 117-118 (*Runia, D.T.*).
8289 *Szesnat, Holger* 'Mostly aged virgins': PHILO and the presence of the Therapeutrides at Lake Mareotis. Neotest. 32 (1998) 191-201;
8290 'Pretty boys' in PHILO's *De Vita Contemplativa*. Studia Philonica Annual 10 (1998) 87-107.
8291 *Taylor, Joan E.; Davies, Philip R.* The so-called Therapeutae of De Vita Contemplativa: identity and character. HThR 91 (1998) 3-24.
8292 **Torallas Tovar, S.** FILÓN de Alejandría: sobre los sueños; sobre José. 1997 ⇒13,8615. ^RCDios 211 (1998) 658-659 (*Gutiérrez, J.*).
8293 *Troiani, Lucio* L'ellenismo nel pensiero giudaico fino a FILONE. RstB 10/1-2 (1998) 69-80.
8294 *Vogel, Manuel* Geschichtstheologie bei Pseudo-PHILO, Liber Antiquitatum Biblicarum. Internationales Josephus-Kolloquium. 1998 ⇒490. 175-195.
8295 *Winston, David* PHILO and the rabbis on sex and the body. Poetics Today 19 (1998) 41-62 Sum. 41.

κ2.4 *Evangelia apocrypha*—Apocryphal gospels

8296 *Backus, Irena* Christoph SCHEURL and his anthology of "New Testament Apocrypha" (1506, 1513, 1515). Apocrypha 9 (1998) 133-156.
8297 *Berder, Michel* Was uns die Apokryphen lehren. WUB 10 (1998) 52-54.

8298 **Bernabé Pons, Luis F.** El texto morisco del Evangelio de San Bernabé. Estudios Historicos 57: Granada 1998, Universidad de Granada 313 pp. 84-338-2418-X.

8299 [E]**Bovon, François; Geoltrain, Pierre** Ecrits apocryphes chrétiens, 1. 1997 ⇒13,8641. [R]Etudes (April 1998) 551-552 (*Gibert, Pierre*); OCP 64/1 (1998) 232-235 (*Poggi, V.*); NT 40 (1998) 300-306 (*Elliott, J.K.*); ETR 73 (1998) 619-621 (*Cuvillier, Élian*); CEv 103 (1998) 74-75 (*Berder, M.*).

8300 *Canal, José M.* En torno al evangelio del Pseudo-Mateo. Mar. 60 (1998) 153-154, 197-237.

8301 **Charlesworth, James H.** Authentic apocrypha. North Richland Hills, TX 1998, BIBAL 68 pp. $9 [BiTod 36,325—Senior, Donald].

8302 **Crossan, John Dominic** The birth of christianity: discovering what happened in the years immediately after the execution of Jesus. SF 1998, Harper SF xxxiv; 653 pp. $32. 0-06-061659-8 [Gospel of Peter]. Bibl. [R]America 179/15 (1998) 23-24 (*Osiek, Carolyn*).

8303 *Crossan, John Dominic* The gospel of Peter and the canonical gospels: independence, dependence, or both?. FORUM 1/1 (1998) 7-51.

8304 **Cross, James E.** Two Old English apocrypha and their manuscript source: 'The gospel of Nicodemus' and 'The avenging of the Saviour'. CSASE 19: 1996 ⇒12,8110. [R]JEarlyC 6 (1998) 331-332 (*Smith, Clyde Curry*).

8305 *De Conick, April D.* Entering God's presence: sacramentalism in the gospel of Philip. SBL.SP part 1. SBL.SPS 37: 1998 ⇒402. 483-523.

8306 *Desreumaux, Alain* Jésus et ses apocryphes. Graphè 7 (1998) 31-43.

8307 *Dewey, Arthur J.* The passion narrative of the gospel of Peter: redaction and interpretation. FORUM 1/1 (1998) 53-69.

8308 *Dochhorn, Jan* Warum gab es kein Getreide im Paradies?: eine jüdische Ätiologie des Ackerbaus in Ev Phil 15. ZNW 89 (1998) 125-133.

8309 *Elliott, J. Keith* The influence of the New Testament apocrypha [F]POKORNÝ, P. 1998 ⇒90. 130-140.

8310 [E]**González Núñez, J.** El Protoevangelio de Santiago. 1997 ⇒13, 8649 [ved. infr. ⇒8340]. [R]Mayéutica 24 (1998) 286-287 (*Flores, Miguel*); Mar. 60 (1998) 650-652 (*Fernández, Domiciano*); ScrTh 30 (1998) 693-695 (*Chapa, J.*).

8311 *Graham Brock, Ann* What's in a name: the competition for authority in early christian texts. SBL.SPS 37: 1998 ⇒402. 106-124.

8312 *Hartenstein, Judith; Petersen, Silke* Das Evangelium nach Maria: Maria Magdalena als Lieblingsjüngerin und Stellvertreterin Jesu. Kompendium Feministische Bibelauslegung. 1998 ⇒7511. 757-767.

8313 [E]**Hedrick, C; Mirecki, P.** The gospel of the Savior. Santa Rosa 1995, Polebridge 165 pp. pl. 123-151.

8314 *Howard, George* Shem-Tob's Hebrew Matthew and early Jewish christianity. JSNT 70 (1998) 3-20.

8315 *Kaestli, Daniel* Apokryphe Überlieferungen und ihre Historizität. WUB 10 (1998) 55-57.

8316 [ET]**Leloup, Jean-Yves** O evangelho de Maria (Míriam de Mágdala). [T]*Alves de Lima, Lise Mary.* Petrópolis 1998, Vozes 188 pp. F89 [REB 58,999];

8317 El evangelio de María: Myriam de Magdala. Barc 1998, Herder 211 pp. PTA2.100. 84-254-2056-3 [Proyección 46,239].

8318 *Markschies, Christoph* "Neutestamentliche Apokryphen": Bemerkungen zu Geschichte und Zukunft einer von Edgar Hennecke im Jahr 1904 begründeten Quellensammlung. Apocrypha 9 (1998) 97-132.

8319 ᴱ**Miller, Robert J.** The complete gospels: annotated scholars version. 1994 ⇒10,4176. ᴿHeyJ 39 (1998) 71-73 (*McNamara, Martin*).

8320 *Petersen, William L.* The Vorlage of Shem-Tob's 'Hebrew Matthew'. NTS 44 (1998) 490-512.

8321 *Quarles, Charles L.* The Protevangelium of James as an alleged parallel to creative historiography in the synoptic birth narratives. BBR 8 (1998) 139-149.

8322 **Turner, Martha Lee** The gospel according to Philip. NHMS 38: 1996 ⇒12,8123; 13,8674. ᴿJEarlyC 6 (1998) 333-334 (*McGowan, Andrew*); CBQ 60 (1998) 175-177 (*Perkins, Pheme*).

K2.7 *Alia apocrypha NT*—Apocryphal Acts of apostles

8323 *Bolyki, János* 'Head downwards': the cross of Peter in the light of the apocryphal Acts, of the New Testament and of the society-transforming claim of early christianity. Apocryphal Acts of Peter. 1998 ⇒8324. 111-122 [BuBbgB 30,17].

8324 ᴱ**Bremmer, Jan M.** The Apocryphal Acts of Peter: magic, miracles and gnosticism. Studies on the Apocryphal Acts of the Apostles 3: Lv 1998, Peeters vii; 213 pp. 90-429-0019-9.

8325 *Bremmer, Jan N.* Aspects of the Acts of Peter: women, magic, place and date. Apocryphal Acts of Peter. 1998 ⇒8324. 1-20 [BuBbgB 30,17].

8326 *Czachesz, István* Who is deviant?: entering the story-world of the Acts of Peter. Apocryphal Acts of Peter. 1998 ⇒8324. 84-96 [Bu BbgB 30,17].

8327 *Herczeg, Pál Theios aner* traits in the apocryphal *Acts of Peter*. Apocryphal Acts of Peter. 1998 ⇒8324. 29-38 [BuBbgB 30,17].

8328 *Karasszon, István* Agrippa, king and prefect. Apocryphal Acts of Peter. 1998 ⇒8324. 21-28 [BuBbgB 30,17].

8329 *Lalleman, Pieter J.; Bremmer, Jan N.* Bibliography of the Acts of Peter. Apocr. Acts...Peter. 1998 ⇒8324. 200-202 [BuBbgB 30,18].

8330 *Luttikhuizen, Gerard P.* Simon Magus as a narrative figure in the Acts of Peter;

8331 *Misset-Van de Weg, Magda* 'For the Lord always takes care of his own': the purpose of the wondrous works and deeds in the Acts of Peter. Apocryphal Acts of Peter. 1998 ⇒8324. 39-51/97-110 [Bu BbgB 30,17].

8332 *Thomas, Christine M.* Revivifying resurrection accounts: techniques of composition and rewriting in the Acts of Peter cc.25-28. Apocryphal Acts of Peter. 1998 ⇒8324. 65-83 [BuBbgB 30,17].

8333 *Westra, Liuwe H.* Regulae fidei and other credal formulations in the Acts of Peter. Apocryphal Acts of Peter. 1998 ⇒8324. 134-147 [BuBbgB 30,17].

8334 ᴱ**Amsler, Frédéric** Actes de l'apôtre Philippe. Apocryphes 8: 1996 ⇒12,8149. ᴿCBQ 60 (1998) 553-554 (*Mangan, Céline*).

8335 *Artés Hernández, José Antonio* Evangelios canónicos y Acta Apostolorum Apocrypha: estudio de algunos lugares paralelos. FgNT 11 (1998) 25-42.

8336 *Aubin, Melissa* Reversing romance?: the Acts of Thecla and the ancient novel. Ancient fiction. 1998 ⇒1118. 257-272.

8337 [E]**Bremmer, Jan M.** The apocryphal Acts of John. Studies on the Apocryphal Acts of the Apostles 1: 1995 ⇒11/2,6886; 13,8683 [R]StPat 45/1 (1998) 158-160 (*Moda, Aldo*);

8338 The apocryphal Acts of Paul and Tecla. Studies on the Apocryphal Acts of the Apostles 2: 1996 ⇒12,8136. [R]StPat 45/1 (1998) 160-161 (*Moda, Aldo*); NT 40 (1998) 405-406 (*Elliott, J.K.*); JThS 49 (1998) 804-807 (*Wilson, R. McL.*).

8339 *Briquel-Chatonnet; Desreumaux, A.; Thekeparampil, J.* Découverte d'un manuscrit très important contenant des textes apocryphes dans la bibliothèque de la métropole de l'Église de l'Est à Trichur, Kérala, Inde. Symposium Syriacum VII. 1998 ⇒415. 587-597.

8340 *Dolbeau, François* Une liste d'apôtres et de disciples compilée en Italie du Nord. AnBoll 116 (1998) 5-24 [BuBbgB 24,14].

8341 *Dubois, Jean-Daniel* Sommos dans la version copte des Actes de Pilate (XVI,7). Apocrypha 9 (1998) 291-299.

8342 *Faerber, Robert* L'ermite de Thèbes et le diable. Apocrypha 9 (1998) 225-261.

8343 *Hilhorst, Anthony* The text of the Actus Vercellenses. Apocryphal Acts of Peter. 1998 ⇒8324. 148-160 [BuBbgB 30,17].

8344 **Hvalvik, Reidar** The struggle for scripture and covenant: the purpose of the epistle of Barnabas and Jewish-Christian competition in the second century. WUNT 2/82: 1996 ⇒12,10844; 13,8697. [R]JEarlyC 6 (1998) 325-327 (*Hull, Robert F.*); JThS 49 (1998) 807-811 (*Carleton Paget, James*); ThRv 94 (1998) 517-519 (*Backhaus, Knut*); JAC 41 (1998) 238-241 (*Vinzent, Markus*); ThLZ 123 (1998) 149-151 (*Schille, Gottfried*).

8345 **Jones, F. Stanley** An ancient Jewish christian source on the history of christianity: Pseudo-Clementine *Recognitions* 1.27-71. SBL.TT 27 CA 2: 1995 ⇒12,10833; 13,8698. [R]ThRv 94 (1998) 522-523 (*Winkler, Gabriele*); BiOr 55 (1998) 896-898 (*Van Amersfoort, J.*).

8346 *Kaestli, Jean-Daniel* Un témoin latin du Protévangile de Jacques: l'homélie Postulatis filiae Ierusalem en l'honneur de sainte Anne (BHL 483-485). Apocrypha 9 (1998) 179-223 [⇒K2.4].

8347 *Konstan, David* Acts of love: a narrative pattern in the apocryphal Acts. JEarlyC 6 (1998) 15-36.

8348 **Lalleman, Pieter J.** The Acts of John: a two-stage initiation into Johannine Gnosticism. [D]Groningen. Studies on the Apocryphal Acts of the Apostles 4: Lv 1998, Peeters vii; 309 pp. 90-429-0573-5. Bibl.

8349 *Lucchesi, Enzo* La légende de Simon et Théonoé: un nouveau témoin?. AnBoll 116 (1998) 354-354 [BuBbgB 30,19].

8350 *Norelli, Enrico* Le papyrus Egerton 2 et sa localisation dans la tradition sur Jésus: nouvel examen du fragment 1. Jésus de Nazareth. 1998 ⇒253. 397-435 [BuBbgB 24,16].

8351 *Obrycki, Kazimierz* Męczeństwo świętego Piotra apostoła, spisane przez Linusa biskupa [De martyrio beati Petri apostoli a Lino conscripto]. WST 10 (1998) 167-178 Sum. 178.

8352 *Poupon, Gérard* L'origine africaine des Actus Vercellenses. Apocryphal Acts of Peter. 1998 ⇒8324. 192-199 [BuBbgB 30,17].

8353 *Price, Robert M.* Docetic epiphanies: a structuralist analysis of the apocryphal Acts. JHiC 5/2 (1998) 163-187.

8354 ᴱᵀ**Prieur, Jean-Marc** Actes de l'apôtre André. 1995 ⇒13,8715.
ᴿNT 40 (1998) 298-299 (*Elliott, J.K.*).

8355 *Starowieyski, Marek* Éléments apologétiques dans les Apocryphes.
Apologistes chrétiens. 1998 ⇒421. 187-197.

8356 *Strus, Andrzej* Una *haggada* familiare sulla passione e morte di S.
Stefano protomartire. Sal. 60 (1998) 81-96;

8357 L'origine de l'apocryphe grec de la Passion de S. Étienne: à propos
d'un texte de deux manuscrits récemment publiés. EL 112 (1998) 18-
57 Summarium 18.

8358 *Synek, Eva M.* Die Apostolischen Konstitutionen—ein "christlicher
Talmud" aus dem 4. Jh. Bib. 79 (1998) 27-56.

8359 *Witakowski, Witold* Etiopskie apokryficzne Akta Apostołów [Ethio-
pic Apocryphal Acts of the Apostles]. WST 10 (1998) 153-166 Sum.
166.

K3.1 Qumran—*generalia*

8360 *Amar, Zohar* The ash and the red material from Qumran. DSD 5
(1998) 1-15.

8361 *Bar-Ilan, Meir* Die knifflige Arbeit der Schreiber;

8362 *Baur, Wolfgang* Die Veröffentlichung der Ergebnisse der Grabungen
von Qumran und En Feschcha;

8363 *Bélis, Mireille* Ein spannender Fortsetzungsroman. WUB 9 (1998)
52-53/7/40-41.

8364 *Broshi, Magen* Qumran—die archäologische Erforschung: ein
Überblick. Die Schriftrollen von Qumran. 1998 ⇒6858. 27-50;

8365 Was Qumran, indeed, a monastery?: the consensus and its chal-
lengers, an archaeologist's view. Caves of enlightenment. 1998 ⇒
467. 19-37.

8366 *Broshi, Magen; Eshel, Hanan* Wohnen in Kalk und Mergel. WUB 9
(1998) 14-15.

8367 *Callaway, Phillip R.* Future prospects of scrolls and Khirbet Qumran
research: a prophecy of concrete realism. Qumran Chronicle 8/1-2
(1998) 21-47.

8368 **Campbell, Jonathan G.** The Dead Sea scrolls: the complete story.
Berkeley 1998, Ulysses xv; 220 pp. $13. 1-56975-092-0. = 'Deci-
phering the Dead Sea scrolls' ⇒12,8164; Bibl. [NThAR 2000, 153].

8369 *Cansdale, L.* Qumran, its names past and present: a literary and
archaeological investigation. ᶠJUDGE E. 1998 ⇒47. 23-33.

8370 **Cansdale, Lena** Qumran and the Essenes: a re-evaluation of the
evidence. TSAJ 60: 1997 ⇒8733. ᴿDSD 5/1 (1998) 99-104 (*Magness, Jodi*); RB 105 (1998) 281-285 (*Puech, Émile*); RdQ 18 (1998)
437-441 (*Puech, Émile*).

8371 *Chmiel, Jerzy* Quelle herméneutique est utile pour interpréter les
textes du Désert de Juda?. ᴹKLAWEK A. 1998 ⇒51. 117-121.

8372 *Ciecieląg, Jerzy* Coins from the so-called Essene settlements on the
Dead Sea and chronology of archaeological strata at Qumran. Qumran Chronicle 8/1-2 (1998) 15-16 abstract.

8373 *Crawford, Sidnie White* How archaeology affects the study of texts:
reflections on the category 'rewritten bible' at Qumran. Caves of
enlightenment. 1998 ⇒467. 39-53.

8374 *Dombrowski, Bruno W.W.* Qumranologica VII. FolOr 34 (1998) 193-
202.

8375 *Fabry, Heinz-Josef* Was steht in den Schriften aus Qumran?. WUB 9 (1998) 34-35.

8376 ^E**Fabry, Heinz-Josef**, *al.*, Qumranstudien. 1996 ⇒12,307; 13,8743. ^RJSJ 29 (1998) 103-105 (*Martone, Corrado*).

8377 **Fitzmyer, Joseph A.** 101 pytan o Qumran [Responses to 101 questions on the Dead Sea scrolls]. ^T*Fizia, Teresa*. Biblioteka zwojów, NT 4: Krakow 1997, WAM xxiii; 254 pp. 83-7097-355-8. Ill.; Bibl. [QS 70,5335*]. P.

8378 *Fröhlich, Ida* "Narrative exegesis" in the Dead Sea scrolls. Biblical perspectives. StTDJ 28: 1998 ⇒441. 81-99.

8379 *García Martínez, F.* Los manuscritos del Mar Muerto: Qumrán entre el Antiguo y el Nuevo Testamento. Actas... IX Jornadas Bíblicas. 1998 ⇒376. 33-52;

8380 Der Glaubenskrieg um Qumran. WUB 9 (1998) 3-6, 8;

8381 New perspectives on the study of the Dead Sea scrolls. ^FVAN DER WOUDE, A. VT.S 73: 1998 ⇒121. 230-248.

8382 ^E**García Martínez, Florentino; Tigchelaar, Eibert J.C.** The Dead Sea Scrolls study edition, 2: 4Q274-11Q31. Lei 1998, Brill 628-1360 pp. 90-04-11059-3;

8383 The Dead Sea scrolls: study edition, 1: 1QI-4Q273. 1997 ⇒13,8750. ^RRdQ 18 (1998) 446-447 (*Puech, Émile*).

8384 **García Martínez, Florentino; Trebolle Barrera, Julio** The people of the Dead Sea Scrolls: their writings, beliefs and practices. 1995 ⇒ 11/2,7103...13,8751. ^RAJSR 23 (1998) 253-55 (*Bernstein, Moshe J.*);

8385 Os homens de Qumran: literatura, estrutura e concepções religiosas. ^T*Gonçalves Pereira, Fernando*. 1996 ⇒12,8182; 13,8752. ^RPerTeol 30 (1998) 302-306 (*Konings, Johan*);

8386 Gli uomini di Qumran: letteratura, struttura sociale e concezioni religiose. StBi 113: 1996 ⇒12,8183; 13,8753. ^RSal. 60 (1998) 571 (*Vicent, R.*).

8387 *García Martínez, Florentino; Tigchelaar, Eibert J.C.* Bibliography of the Dead Sea scrolls. RdQ 18 (1998) 459-490, 605-639.

8388 *Gleßmer, Uwe* Die "Sonnenuhr" aus Qumran. WUB 9 (1998) 26-27;

8389 Die Texte von Qumran—zum gegenwärtigen Stand ihrer Erforschung. ZNT 2 (1998) 2-17.

8390 **Golb, Norman** Wer schrieb die Schriftrollen vom Toten Meer? 1994 ⇒12,8184. ^RJud. 54/1-2 (1998) 115-117 (*Krupp, Michael*).

8391 **Harrington, Daniel J.** Wisdom texts from Qumran. Literature of the Dead Sea Scrolls: 1996 ⇒12,8186. ^RDSD 5 (1998) 237-245 (*Harding, James E.*); CBQ 60 (1998) 115-116 (*Murphy, Roland E.*); JAC 41 (1998) 227-230 (*Fabry, Heinz-Josef*); Or. 67 (1998) 143-146 (*Bianchi, Francesco*).

8392 *Hidiroglou, Patricia* Aquädukt, Becken und Zisternen: die Nutzung des Wassers. WUB 9 (1998) 28-29.

8393 *Hirschfeld, Yizhar* Early Roman manor houses in Judaea and the site of Khirbet Qumran. JNES 57/3 (1998) 161-189.

8394 *Humbert, Jean-Baptiste* Die verschiedenen Deutungen der Qumran-Siedlung. WUB 9 (1998) 18-24.

8395 *Ilan, Tal* How women differed. BArR 24/2 (1998) 38-39, 68.

8396 *Kapera, Zdzisław J.* Archaeological interpretations of the Qumran settlement: a brief review of hypotheses on the fiftieth anniversary of the Dead Sea discoveries. Qumran Chronicle 8/1-2 (1998) 18-19 abstract;

8397 Archaeological interpretations of the Qumran settlement: a rapid review of hypotheses fifty years after the discoveries at the Dead Sea. ^MKLAWEK A. 1998 ⇒51. 15-33;

8398 Current bibliography on the Dead Sea scrolls 1998 (Part I). Qumran Chronicle 8/1-2 (1998) 133-158;

8399 Recent research of the Qumran cemetery. ^MKLAWEK A. 1998 ⇒51. 77-86.

8400 *Konik, Jacek; Kisielewicz, Marcin* Computer analysis of the south esplanade in Khirbet Qumran. Qumran Chronicle 8/1-2 (1998) 97-104.

8401 ^E**Kronholm, Tryggve** Qumranlitteraturen: fynden och forskningsresultaten: föreläsningar vid ett symposium i Stockholm. 1996 ⇒12, 8192. ^RDSD 5/1 (1998) 104-107 (*Aschim, Anders*).

8402 *Krupp, Michael* 51 Jahre Entdeckung der Schriftrollen vom Toten Meer: eine literarische Nachlese. Jud. 54 (1998) 103-118.

8403 **Lange, Armin** Weisheit und Prädestination: weisheitliche Urordnung und Prädestination in den Textfunden von Qumran. StTDJ 18: 1995 ⇒11/2,7107; 13,8764. ^RVT 48 (1998) 126-127 (*Bockmuehl, Markus*); FolOr 34 (1998) 184-188 (*Dombrowski, Bruno W.W.*); JQR 88 (1998) 366-368 (*VanderKam, James C.*); JBL 117 (1998) 735-736 (*Kugler, Robert A.*).

8404 ^E**Laperrousaz, Ernest-Marie** Qoumrân et les manuscrits de la Mer Morte: un cinquantenaire. 1997 ⇒13,8766. ^RRevBib 60 (1998) 53-55 (*Croatto, J. Severino*); Henoch 20 (1998) 366-370 (*Milano, Maria Teresa*).

8405 *Levy, Abraham* Bad timing: time to get a new theory. BArR 24/4 (1998) 18-23.

8406 **Maaß, Hans** Qumran: Texte kontra Phantasien. 1994 ⇒10,9669; 11/2,6944. ^RDBAT 29 (1998) 302-304 (*Diebner, B.J.*).

8407 *Magness, Jodi* The archaeology of Qumran: a review. Qumran Chronicle 8/1-2 (1998) 49-62;

8408 The chronology of Qumran, Ein Feshkha and Ein el-Ghuweir. ^MKLAWEK A. 1998 ⇒51. 55-76;

8409 Two notes on the archaeology of Qumran. BASOR 312 (1998) 37-44.

8410 **Maier, Johann** Die Qumran-Essener: die Texte vom Toten Meer. 1995-1996 ⇒12,8196; 13,8769. 3 vols. ^RJud. 54/1-2 (1998) 107-108 (*Krupp, Michael*); ThLZ 123 (1998) 51-55 (*Maurer, Alexander*)· CBQ 60 (1998) 124-125 [of vols 1-2] (*Cook, Edward M.*).

8411 *Mébarki, Farah* Erinnerungen eines Entdeckers. WUB 9 (1998) 9-13.

8412 *Neusner, Jacob* What is 'a Judaism'?: seeing the Dead Sea library as the statement of a coherent Judaic religious system: a programmatic statement. Jewish law. 1998 ⇒181. 65-84.

8413 *Otzen, Benedikt* Nye Qumranskrifter i deres jødiske kontekst. DTT 61/1 (1998) 1-22.

8414 *Piovanelli, Pierluigi* Die geheimnisvollen Friedhöfe von Qumran. WUB 9 (1998) 31-33.

8415 **Price, Randall** Secrets of the Dead Sea Scrolls. 1996 ⇒12,8202 ^RDSD 5 (1998) 248-252 (*Trafton, Joseph L.*).

8416 *Puech, Émile* The necropolises of Khirbet Qumrân and 'Ain el-Ghuweir and the Essene belief in afterlife. BASOR 312 (1998) 21-36.

8417 *Rohrhirsch, Ferdinand* Zu der Nützlichkeit der Philosophie in der Archäologie: eine Paraphrasierung von 'Wissenschaftstheorie und Qumran'. FolOr 34 (1998) 71-94.

8418 **Roitman, Adolfo** A day at Qumran: the Dead Sea sect and its scrolls. 1997 ⇒13,8783. ^RJud. 54/1-2 (1998) 117-118 (*Krupp, Michael*).

8419 *Roitmann, Adolfo* Eine gravierte Kalksteinscheibe als astronomisches Meßinstrument. WUB 9 (1998) 26.

8420 *Rosengren Petersen, Allan* The archaeology of Khirbet Qumran. Qumran between OT and NT. JSOT.S 290: 1998 ⇒327. 249-260.

8421 *Saldarini, Anthony J.* Babatha's story: personal archive offers a glimpse of ancient Jewish life. BArR 24/2 (1998) 28-33, 36-37, 72-74.

8422 **Schiffman, Lawrence H.** Reclaiming the Dead Sea Scrolls. 1994 ⇒ 10,9676... 13,8784. ^RJud. 54 (1998) 114-115 (*Krupp, Michael*).

8423 *Segert, Stanislav* Access to the Dead Sea Scrolls—3. CV 40/1 (1998) 44-72.

8424 *Sen, Felipe* Addenda to the Spanish bibliography on the Dead Sea scrolls 1989-1997;

8425 Qumran and Nag Hammadi;

8426 Selected bibliography on Qumran, Gnosis, Judaism and New Testament. ^MKLAWEK A. 1998 ⇒51. 223-228/185-210/211-222.

8427 ^E**Shanks, Hershel** Los manuscritos del Mar Muerto: el principal descubirmiento contemporáneo sobre el judaísmo, el cristianismo y la biblia. Paidós origines 5: Barc 1998, Paidós 398 pp [EfMex 17, 274ss—Zesati Estrada, Carlos].

8428 *Shanks, Hershel* The enigma of Qumran: four archaeologists assess the site. BArR 24/1 (1998) 24-37, 78-84.

8429 **Shanks, Hershel** The mystery and meaning of the Dead Sea Scrolls. NY 1998, Random xxi; 246 pp. 0-679-45757-7. Bibl.

8430 *Smelik, K.A.D.* Recente ontwikkelingen in het onderzoek naar de Dode-Zeerollen. Bijdr. 59 (1998) 204-234.

8431 *Stegemann, Hartmut* Ein halbes Jahrhundert Qumranforschung. WUB 9 (1998) 36-38;

8432 Qumran, Qumran—und längst kein Ende. ThRv 94 (1998) 483-488;

8433 Die Schriftrollen von Qumran: Geschichte ihrer Entdeckung, Erforschung und Auslegung. Die Schriftrollen von Qumran. 1998 ⇒6858. 11-26.

8434 *Stendahl, Krister* Qumran and supersessionism—and the road not taken. PSB 19 (1998) 134-142.

8435 **Strugnell, John** Ein junger Wissenschaftszweig. WUB 9 (1998) 76-77.

^E**Talmon, S.** Die Schriftrollen von Qumran 1998 ⇒6858.

8436 *Talmon, Shemaryahu* Bilanz und Ausblick nach 50 Jahren Qumranforschung. Die Schriftrollen von Qumran. 1998 ⇒6858. 137-158.

8437 **Thordson, Thord & Maria** Qumran and the Samaritans. 1996 ⇒12, 8215. ^RCoTh 68/1 (1998) 226-229 (*Chrostowski, Waldemar*).

8438 *Tov, Emanuel* The dimensions of the Qumran scrolls. DSD 5 (1998) 69-91;

8439 Fünf Jahrzehnte Erforschung der Rollen vom Toten Meer. ThPQ 146 (1998) 52-63.

8440 *Tronina, Antoni* Półwiecze odkryć w Qumran przegląd polskich publikacji [50. anni delle scoperte a Qumran: una rassegna delle pubblicazioni polacche]. Roczniki Teologiczne 45/1 (1998) 91-100 Som. 100.

8441   [E]**Ulrich, Eugene; VanderKam, James** The community of the renewed covenant: the Notre Dame Symposium on the Dead Sea Scrolls. CJAn 10: 1994 ⇒11/2,538... 13,8792. [R]BiOr 55 (1998) 885-888 (*Van der Kooij, A.*).

8442   **Vanderkam, James C.** Manoscritti del Mar Morto: il dibattito recente oltre le polemiche. 1995 ⇒12,8225. [R]PaVi 43/2 (1998) 61-62 (*Rolla, Armando*);

8443   Einführung in die Qumranforschung: Geschichte und Bedeutung der Schriften vom Toten Meer. Uni-Taschenbücher 1998: Gö 1998, Vandenhoeck & R 232 pp. DM39.80. 3-525-03292-7.

8444   *Vanderkam, James C.* Authoritative literature in the Dead Sea scrolls. DSD 5 (1998) 382-402.

8445   *Van der Woude, Adam S.* Fakten contra Phantasien: die Bedeutung der Rollen vom Toten Meer für die Bibelwissenschaft und die Kunde des Frühjudentums. [F]VAN DER Woude, A. VT.S 73: 1998 ⇒121. 249-271.

8446   **Vermes, Geza** The complete Dead Sea Scrolls in English. 1997 ⇒13,8795. [R]JJS 49 (1998) 349-350 (*Brock, Sebastian*); JR 78 (1998) 602-604 (*Wise, Michael O.*).

8447   [T]**Wise, Michael Owen**, *al.*, The Dead Sea Scrolls: a new translation. 1996 ⇒12,8230; 13,8797. [R]Month 31 (1998) 158-159 (*King, Nicholas*); FolOr 34 (1998) 199-200 (*Dombrowski, Bruno W.W.*); JBL 117 (1998) 531-533 (*Brady, Monica L.W.*).

8448   [E]**Wise, Michael Owen**, *al.*, Methods of investigation of the Dead Sea Scrolls and the Khirbet Qumran site. 1994 ⇒11/2,540; 12,8229. [R]JNES 57 (1998) 67-71 (*Davies, Philip R.*).

K3.4 *Qumran,* libri biblici et parabiblici

8449   *Aschim, Anders* The genre of 11QMelchizedek. Qumran between OT and NT. JSOT.S 290: 1998 ⇒327. 17-31.

8450   *Barzilai, Gabriel* פולמוסי חיבור פי על במקרא—'אז' התיבה של לפרשנותה 19-ה מהמאה [The fate of the wicked of Sodom and Gomorrah in an ancient interpretation from Qumran (4Q252 Col 3)]. BetM 154-155 (1998) 323-331 Sum. 335.

8451   [E]**Brooke, George** Qumran Cave 4, XVII: parabiblical texts, part 3. DJD 22: 1996 ⇒12,8237. [R]JR 78 (1998) 427-428 (*Douglas, Michael*); JThS 49 (1998) 207-210 (*Lim, Timothy H.*).

8452   *Brooke, George J.* Some remarks on 4Q252 and the text of Genesis. Textus 19 (1998) 1-25.

8453   *Crawford, Sidnie White* A response to Elizabeth Owen's "4QDeutn: a pre-Samaritan text?". DSD 5 (1998) 92-94.

8454   *Cryer, Frederick H.* Genesis in Qumran. Qumran between OT and NT. JSOT.S 290: 1998 ⇒327. 98-112.

8455   **Douglas, Michael Charles** Power and praise in the Hodayot: a literary critical study of 1 QH 9:1-18:14. [D]Ch 1998, 433 pp.

8456   *Fabry, Heinz-Josef* Der Psalter in Qumran. [F]LOHFINK N. 1998 ⇒64. 137-163.

8457   *Flint, Peter; Ulrich, Eugene; Skehan, Patrick W.* The preliminary edition of 4QPs c (4Q85). RdQ 18 (1998) 343-357;

8458 A scroll containing "biblical" and "apocryphal" psalms: a preliminary edition of 4QPsf (4Q88). CBQ 60 (1998) 267-282;

8459 A preliminary edition of 4QPs j (4Q91). BBR 8 (1998) 89-96;

8460 A preliminary edition of 4QPsk (4Q92). JSSt 43 (1998) 259-263;

8461 Three psalms of praise from Qumran: the preliminary editions of 4QPsl and 4QPsn. JNSL 24/2 (1998) 35-44.

8462 *Flint, Peter W.* The contribution of the cave 4 psalms scrolls to the psalms debate. DSD 5 (1998) 320-333.

8463 *Flint, Peter W.; Alvarez, Andrea E.* Two biblical scrolls from Nahal Hever (XHev/SeNum b and XHev/SeDeut) (once claimed to be from "Wadi Seiyal"). RdQ 18 (1998) 531-540.

8464 ^E**García Martínez, Florentino** Testi di Qumran. Biblica: Studi e Testi 4: 1996 ⇒12,8252; 13,8814. ^RAsp. 45 (1998) 265-267 (*Di Palma, G.*); Sal. 60 (1998) 781-782 (*Vicent, R.*); Gr. 79 (1998) 565-571 (*Ferraro, Giuseppe*).

8465 *García Martínez, Florentino* Testi di Qumran: letteratura esegetica;

8466 Testi di Qumran: letteratura parabiblica. Letteratura giudaica. 1998 ⇒8180. 75-99/100-148.

8467 *Høgenhaven, Jesper* The Isaiah scroll and the composition of the book of Isaiah. Qumran between OT and NT. JSOT.S 290: 1998 ⇒327. 151-158.

8468 *Jastram, Nathan* A comparison of two "proto-Samaritan" texts from Qumran: 4QPaleoExod m and 4QNum b. DSD 5 (1998) 264-289.

8469 *Kister, Menahem* A common heritage: biblical interpretation at Qumran and its implications. Biblical perspectives. StTDJ 28: 1998 ⇒441. 101-111.

8470 *Lange, Armin* Die Endgestalt des protomasoretischen Psalters und die Toraweisheit: zur Bedeutung der nichtessenischen Weisheitstexte aus Qumran für die Auslegung des protomasoretischen Psalters. ^FLOHFINK N. 1998 ⇒64. 101-136.

8471 **Lim, Timothy H.** Holy Scripture in the Qumran commentaries and Pauline letters. 1997 ⇒13,6333. ^RDSD 5 (1998) 246-8 (*Murphy-O'-Connor, Jerome*); JThS 49 (1998) 781-4 (*Stanley, Christopher D.*).

8472 *Main, Emmanuelle* For King Jonathan or against?: the use of the bible in 4Q448. Biblical perspectives. StTDJ 28: 1998 ⇒441. 113-135.

8473 *Mébarki, Farah* Die Bibliothek von Qumran. WUB 9 (1998) 43-49.

8474 *Nitzan, Bilhah* Post-biblical *rib* pattern admonitions in 4Q302/302A and 4Q381 69, 76-77. Biblical perspectives. StTDJ 28: 1998 ⇒441. 159-174.

8475 *Olofsson, Staffan* Qumran and LXX. Qumran between OT and NT. JSOT.S 290: 1998 ⇒327. 232-248.

8476 *Rofé, Alexander* 4QMidrash Samuel?—observations concerning the character of 4QSam^a. Textus 19 (1998) 63-74.

8477 *Schiffman, Lawrence H.* The case of the day of atonement ritual. Biblical perspectives. StTDJ 28: 1998 ⇒441. 181-188.

8478 *Seybold, Klaus* Das Hymnusfragment 11QPs XXVII 9-15: Auslegung und Einordnung. Studien zur Psalmenauslegung. 1998 <1986> ⇒201. 199-207.

8479 *Steck, Odil Hannes* Bemerkungen zur Abschnittgliederung der ersten Jesajarolle von Qumran (1QIsa) im Vergleich mit redaktionsgeschichtlichen Beobachtungen im Jesajabuch. ^FSTEGEMANN, H. BZNW 97: 1998 ⇒111. 12-28.

8480   *Steudel, Annette* Auf der Suche nach dem verlorenen Text. WUB 9 (1998) 50-51.

8481   *Talmon, Shemaryahu* Fragments of Hebrew writings without identifying sigla of provenance from the literary legacy of Yigael YADIN. DSD 5 (1998) 149-157.

8482   *Thompson, Thomas L.* 4QTestimonia and bible composition: a Copenhagen lego hypothesis. Qumran between OT and NT. JSOT.S 290: 1998 ⇒327. 261-276.

8483   *Tov, Emanuel* The rewritten book of Joshua as found at Qumran and Masada. Biblical perspectives. StTDJ 28: 1998 ⇒441. 233-256.

8484   ᴱ**Ulrich, Eugene** Qumran Cave 4 IX: Deuteronomy, Joshua, Judges, Kings. DJD 12: 1995 ⇒11/2,6967; 13,8833. ᴿDSD 5/1 (1998) 111-117 *(Eshel, Esther)*;

8485   Qumran Cave 4, X: the Prophets. DJD 15: 1997 ⇒13,8835. ᴿZAW 110 (1998) 481-482 *(Lange, A.)*; JSSt 43 (1998) 377-379 *(Herbert, Edward D.)*.

8486   ᴱ**Ulrich, Eugene; Cross, Frank Moore** Qumran Cave 4 VII: Genesis to Numbers. DJD 12: 1994 ⇒11/2,6966a...13,8836. ᴿJSSt 43 (1998) 169-172 *(Stuckenbruck, Loren T.)*.

8487   *Ulrich, Eugene; Metso, Sarianna* A preliminary edition of 4QJobᵃ. ᶠSTEGEMANN, H. BZNW 97: 1998 ⇒111. 29-38.

8488   *Waard, Jan de* 4QProv and textual criticism. Textus 19 (1998) 87-96.

K3.5 *Qumran*—varii rotuli et fragmenta

8489   **Alexander, Philip S.; Vermes, Geza** Qumran Cave 4 XIX: Serekh ha-Yahad and two related texts. DJD 26: Oxf 1998, Clarendon xvii; 253 pp. £65. 0-19-826981-1.

8490   ᴱ**Baumgarten, Joseph** Qumran Cave 4 XIII: the Damascus Document (4Q266-273). DJD 18: 1996 ⇒8283; 13,8842. ᴿBAR 24/2 (1998) 66, 68 *(Shanks, Hershel)*; DSD 5 (1998) 233-237 *(Schiffman, Lawrence)*; JR 78 (1998) 604-605 *(Levine, Baruch A.)*.

8491   *Baumgarten, Joseph M.* Scripture and law in 4Q265. Biblical perspectives. StTDJ 28: 1998 ⇒441. 25-33.

8492   *Bockmuehl, Markus* Redaction and ideology in the rule of the community (1QS/4QS). RdQ 18 (1998) 541-560.

8493   *Broshi, Magen* Ptolas and the Archelaus massacre (4Q468g=4Qhistorical text B). JJS 49 (1998) 341-345.

8494   *Caquot, André* Les testaments qoumrâniens des pères du sacerdoce. RHPhR 78/2 (1998) 3-26.

8495   ᴱ**Charlesworth, James H.** The Rule of the Community and related documents. The Dead Sea Scrolls: Hebrew, Aramaic, and Greek texts with English translations, 1. 1994 ⇒10,9698... 12,8285. ᴿRdQ 18 (1998) 441-445 *(Puech, Émile)*; FrRu 5 NF (1998) 45-46 *(Rapp, Hans A.)*;

8496   Damascus Document, War Scroll, and related documents. The Dead Sea Scrolls: Hebrew, Aramaic, and Greek texts with English translations, 2. 1994 ⇒12,8286; 13,8852. ᴿJAC 41 (1998) 226-227 *(Maier, Johann)*; BAEO 33 (1997) 440-441 *(Sen, Felipe)*.

8497   **Chyutin, Michael** The new Jerusalem scroll from Qumran [1QJNar]: a comprehensive reconstruction. JSPE.S 25: 1997 ⇒13,8853. ᴿRdQ 18 (1998) 453-457 *(Tigchelaar, Eibert)*.

8498 *Collins, John J.; Green, Deborah A.* The tales from the Persian court (4Q550a-e). [F]STEGEMANN, H. BZNW 97: 1998 ⇒111. 39-50.
8499 *Conley, Michael* Understanding the intent of 1Q Serek. [M]KLAWEK A. 1998 ⇒51. 137-149.
8500 *Davies, John A.* The 'Temple Scroll' from Qumran and the ultimate temple. RTR 57/1 (1998) 1-217.
8501 *Dimant, Devorah* 4Q386 ii-iii: a prophecy on Hellenistic kingdoms?. RdQ 18 (1998) 511-529.
8502 *Elgvin, Torleif* The mystery to come: early Essene theology of revelation. Qumran between OT and NT. JSOT.S 290: 1998 ⇒327. 113-150.
8503 **Eshel, Esther**, *al.*, Poetical and liturgical texts, 1. Qumran Cave 4, VI. DJD 11: Oxf 1998, Clarendon ix; 473 pp. £70. 0-19-826380-5 [JThS 50,206s—Lim, T.H.].
8504 *Fabry, Heinz-Josef* Das "Jachad"-Ostrakon aus Chirbet Qumran. WUB 9 (1998) 16.
8505 [E]**Garcia Martinez, Florentino** Qumran Cave 11, 2: 11Q2-18, 11Q20-31. DJD <vol. 23>: Oxf 1998, Clarendon xv; 487 pp. $90. 0-19-826959-5.
8506 *García Martínez, Florentino* Testi di Qumran: letteratura di contenuto escatologico;
8507 Testi di Qumran: Rotolo de Rame (3Q15);
8508 Testi di Qumran: testi astronomici, calendari e oroscopi;
8509 Testi di Qumran: testi halakici e regole;
8510 Testi di Qumran: testi liturgici. Letteratura giudaica;
8511 Testi di Qumran: testi poetici. Letteratura giudaica. 1998 ⇒8180. 57-74/204-206/187-203/20-56/160-186/149-168.
8512 *Gmirkin, Russell* Historical allusions in the War Scroll. DSD 5 (1998) 172-214.
8513 [E]**Ibba, Giovanni** Il 'rotolo della guerra'. Quaderni di Henoch 10: T 1998, Zamorani 305 pp. 88-7158-069-9 [NThAR 1999,45].
8514 *Jacobson, Howard* 11Q30, Fgs 8-10 (1). RdQ 18 (1998) 595.
8515 *Kuhn, Heinz-Wolfgang* Konkordanzen und Indizes zu den nicht-biblischen Qumrantexten auf Papier und Microfiche-aus dem Münchener Projekt: Qumran und das Neue Testament (2., völlig neu bearbeitete Fassung). [F]STEGEMANN, H. BZNW 97: 1998 ⇒111. 197-209.
8516 *Kvalvaag, Robert W.* The spirit in human beings in some Qumran non-biblical texts. Qumran between OT and NT. JSOT.S 290: 1998 ⇒327. 159-180.
8517 *Laperrousaz, Ernest-Marie* Das Geheimnis der Kupferrolle. WUB 9 (1998) 63.
8518 *Laubscher, Frans du T.* The Zadokite element in the Qumran documents in the light of CD 4:3. JNSL 24/1 (1998) 165-175.
8519 *Luccassen, Birgit* Josua, Richter und CD. RdQ 18 (1998) 373-396.
8520 *Maier, Johann* Die Tempelrolle. WUB 9 (1998) 71-72.
8521 *Mendels, Doron* 'On kingship' in the Temple Scroll and the ideological *Vorlage* of the seven banquets in the 'Letter of Aristeas to Philocrates'. Identity. JSPE.S 24: 1998 <1979> ⇒174. 324-333.
8522 **Metso, Sarianna** The textual development of the Qumran Community Rule. 1997 ⇒13,8872. [R]ThLZ 123 (1998) 144-146 (*Frey, Jörg*).
8523 *Metso, Sarianna* The use of Old Testament quotations in the Qumran community Rule. Qumran between OT and NT. JSOT.S 290: 1998 ⇒327. 217-231.

8524 *Naveh, Joseph* Fragments of an Aramaic magic book from Qumran. IEJ 48 (1998) 252-261.
8525 *Nebe, G. Wilhelm* Qumranica III—zu unveröffentlichten Handschriften vom Toten Meer: Vertrag über den Kauf eines Eselsfohlen aus dem Jahr 122 nach Chr. (5/6Hev 8). ZAH 11 (1998) 205-209;
8526 4Q174, 1-2, I, 6f im Lichte von Sektenschrift und Jub 2,22. RdQ 18 (1998) 581-587.
8527 *Niebuhr, Karl-Wilhelm* 4Q 521,2 II—ein eschatologischer Psalm ᴹKLAWEK A. 1998 ⇒51. 151-168.
8528 *Oegema, Gerbern S.* Tradition-historical studies on 4Q252. ᶠBETZ O. & VAN DER WOUDE A. 1998 ⇒11. 154-174.
8529 *Puech, Émile* L'alphabet cryptique A en 4QSe (4Q259). RdQ 18 (1998) 429-435.
8530 **Puech, Émile** Qumrân Grotte 4.XVIII: textes hébreux (4Q521-4Q 528, 4Q576-4Q579). DJD 25: Oxf 1998, Clarendon xviii; 229 pp. $105. 019826948X. 15 pl. 2 fascim. [DSD 6,352s—Collins, John J.].
8531 *Puech, Émile; Lacoudre, Noel; Mébarki, Farah* Die Kupferrolle—Konservierung und neue Erkenntnisse. WUB 9 (1998) 64-66.
8532 *Sacchi, Paolo* Su un passo di difficile comprensione della 'Regola della Comunità' (1QS 1,5). ᶠSIERRA J. 1998 ⇒102. 475-483.
8533 *Satlow, Michael L.* 4Q502 a New Year festival?. DSD 5 (1998) 57-68.
8534 *Schiffman, Lawrence H. Ir ha-miqdash* and its meaning in the Temple Scroll and other Qumran texts. Sanctity of time. 1998 ⇒303. 95-109.
8535 *Schmidt, Francis* Ancient Jewish astrology: an attempt to interpret 4Qcryptic (4Q186);
8536 *Schuller, Eileen M.* The use of biblical terms as designations for non-biblical hymnic and prayer compositions. Biblical perspectives. StTDJ 28: 1998 ⇒441. 189-205/207-22.
8537 *Segal, Michael* Biblical exegesis in 4Q158: techniques and genre. Textus 19 (1998) 45-62.
8538 *Shemesh, Aharon* 4Q271.3: a key to sectarian matrimonial law. JJS 49 (1998) 244-263.
8539 *Stegemann, Hartmut* More identified fragments of 4QDd (4Q269). RdQ 18 (1998) 497-509.
8540 *Stone, Michael E.* Warum Naphtali?: eine Diskussion im Internet. Jud. 54 (1998) 188-191.
8541 *Strugnell, John; Schuller, Eileen* Further Hodayot manuscripts from Qumran?. ᶠSTEGEMANN, H. BZNW 97: 1998 ⇒111. 51-72.
8542 *Tigchelaar, Eibert J.C.* הבא ביחד 4QInstruction (4Q418 64+199+66 par 4Q417 1 i 17-19) and the height of the columns of 4Q418. RdQ 18 (1998) 589-593.
8543 *Wenthe, Dean O.* The use of the Hebrew scriptures in 1QM. DSD 5 (1998) 290-319.
8544 **Wolters, Albert M.** The Copper Scroll: overview, text and translation. 1996 ⇒12,8317. ᴿCBQ 60 (1998) 352-353 (*Dempsey, Deirdre Ann*).
8545 *Zimmermann, Johannes* Observations on 4Q246—the 'Son of God'. ᶠBETZ O. & VAN DER WOUDE A. 1998 ⇒11. 175-190.

K3.6 Qumran et Novum Testamentum

8546   **Annandale-Potgieter, Joan** Qumran in and around the bible: a new look at the Dead Sea scrolls. Pretoria 1998, Van Schaik 106 pp. 0-627-02352-5 [NThAR 2000,123].

8547   *Arens K., Eduardo* Qumrán y el cristianismo. Paginas 149 (1998) 82-94.

8548   **Berger, Klaus** Qumran und Jesus. 1994 ⇒10,9710. [R]DBAT 29 (1998) 304-305 *(Diebner, B.J.)*.

8549   **Betz, O.; Riesner, R.** Jesús, Qumrán y el Vaticano. 1994 ⇒11/2, 7055. [R]EE 73 (1998) 511-513 *(Piñero, Antonio)*.

8550   *Brooke, George J.* Shared intertextual interpretations in the Dead Sea scrolls and the New Testament. Biblical perspectives. StTDJ 28: 1998 ⇒441. 35-57.

8551   *Charlesworth, James H.* John the Baptizer, Jesus, and the Essenes. Caves of enlightenment. 1998 ⇒467. 75-103.

8552   [E]**Charlesworth, James H.; Weaver, Walter P.** The Dead Sea scrolls and the christian faith: in celebration of the jubilee year of the discovery of Qumran Cave I. Faith and Scholarship Colloquies: Harrisburg 1998, Trinity xviii; 76 pp. $12. 1-56338-232-6.

8553   *Collins, John J.* Jesus, messianism and the Dead Sea scrolls. [F]BETZ O. & VAN DER WOUDE A. 1998 ⇒11. 100-119.

8554   *Dunn, James D.G.* Paul and the Dead Sea scrolls. Caves of enlightenment. 1998 ⇒467. 105-127.

8555   *Fabry, Heinz-Josef* Qumran und das frühe Christentum. Die Schriftrollen von Qumran. 1998 ⇒6858. 71-105.

8556   *Holmén, Tom* Divorce in CD 4:20-5:2 and 11QT 57:17-18: some remarks on the pertinence of the question. RdQ 18 (1998) 397-408.

8557   *Knohl, Israel* יוסף בן ומשיח ,ארמילוס האל' בן 'על [On 'the son of God', Armilus and Messiah son of Joseph]. Tarb. 68 (1998) 13-37 Sum. vii.

8558   **Mayer, Bernhard** Christen und Christliches in Qumran?. 1992 ⇒8, a391...11/2,7069. [R]Augustinus 43 (1998) 160-1 *(Eguiarte, Enrique)*.

8559   *Puech, Émile* Christliche Schriften in Qumran?. WUB 9 (1998) 62;

8560   Die Kreuzigung und die altjüdische Tradition. WUB 9 (1998) 73-75.

8561   **Schick, Alexander** Faszination Qumran: Wissenschaftskrimi, Forscherstreit und wahre Bedeutung der Schriftrollen vom Toten Meer. Bielefeld 1998, Christl. Literaturverbreitung 159 pp. 3-89397-382-6; 3-85666-397-5. Num. ill.

8562   **Silberman, Neil Asher** The hidden scrolls: christianity, Judaism, and the war for the Dead Sea Scrolls. 1994, 1995 ⇒10,9724. [R]DSD 5/1 (1998) 107-111 *(Crawford, Sidnie White)*.

8563   **Stegemann, Hartmut** Los esenios, Qumrán, Juan Bautista y Jesús. 1996 ⇒12,8332; 13,8902. [R]Teol. 34 (1998) 191-192 *(Hubeňák, F.)*;

8564   Gli Esseni, Qumran, Giovanni Battista e Gesù. 1996 ⇒12,8333; 13,8903. [R]FilTeo 12/1 (1998) 183-185 *(Pedrazzoli, Mauro)*;

8565   The Library of Qumran: on the Essenes, Qumran, John the Baptist, and Jesus. GR 1998, Eerdmans ix; 290 pp. £16. 0-8028-6167-9. Bibl.

8566   *Ulfgard, Håkan* "Realistik bibelutläggning" efter Qumranfynden: telningen i den yttersta tiden-det nya förbundet före och efter Jesus. SEÅ 63 (1998) 147-166.

8567   *Vázquez Allegue, Jaime* Abba Padre! (4Q372 1, 16): Dios como Padre en Qumrán. EstTrin 32 (1998) 167-186.

8568   *Wright, N.T.* Paul and Qumran. BiRe 14/5 (1998) 18, 54.

K3.8 Historia et doctrinae Qumran

8569 **Berger, Klaus** Qumran: Funde—Texte—Geschichte. Universal-Bibliothek 9668: Stu 1998, Reclam 145 pp. 3-15-009668-5.

8570 *Beyerle, Stefan* Der Gott der Qumraniten: Anmerkungen zum Gottesbild der Qumran-Texte aus der Sicht der Mischna, der Talmudim, frühen Midraschim und des JOSEPHUS. Henoch 20 (1998) 271-289.

8571 *Brewer, David I.* Nomological exegesis in Qumran 'divorce' texts. RdQ 18 (1998) 561-579.

8572 *Brooke, G.J.* From 'assembly of supreme holiness for Aaron' to 'sanctuary of Adam': the laicization of temple ideology in the Qumran scrolls and its wider implications. JSem 8 (1996) 119-145 Sum. 119.

8573 *Christiansen, Ellen Juhl* The consciousness of belonging to God's covenant and what it entails according to the Damascus document and the Community Rule. Qumran between OT and NT. JSOT.S 290: 1998 ⇒327. 69-97.

8574 *Crawford, Sidnie White* Lady wisdom and dame folly at Qumran. DSD 5 (1998) 355-366;

8575 Lady Wisdom and dame Folly at Qumran. Wisdom and psalms. 1998 ⇒221. 205-217.

8576 *Davies, P.R.* The Judaism(s) of the Dead Sea scrolls: the Qumran scrolls: one Judaism?: whose Judaism?. JSem 8 (1996) 146-169 Sum. 146.

8577 *Dimant, Devorah* Dualism at Qumran: new perspectives. Caves of enlightenment. 1998 ⇒467. 55-73.

8578 *Eshel, H.* A history of the Qumran sect and historical details in the scrolls. JSem 8 (1996) 170-209 Sum. 170.

8579 **Flusser, David** Das essenische Abenteuer—die jüdische Gemeinde vom Toten Meer, Auffälligkeiten bei Jesus, Paulus, Didache und Martin BUBER. 1994 ⇒11/2,7065. ᴿJud. 54/1-2 (1998) 110-111 (*Krupp, Michael*);

8580 La setta di Qumran: alla scoperta degli esseni. CasM 1998, Piemme 125 pp. 88-384-2838-7.

8581 *Fröhlich, Ida* 4Q510-11 (Songs of the Sage) and Qumran demonology. Qumran Chronicle 8/1-2 (1998) 16-17 abstract.

8582 *García Martínez, Florentino* Apocalypticism: in the Dead Sea scrolls. Encyclopedia of apocalypticism I. 1998 ⇒507. 162-192;

8583 The history of the Qumran community in the light of recently available texts. Qumran between OT and NT. JSOT.S 290: 1998 ⇒327 194-216.

8584 *Golb, Norman* The present status of the theory of Jerusalem origin of the Dead Sea scrolls. Qumran Chronicle 8/1-2 (1998) 13-14 abstract.

8585 **Golb, Norman** Qui a écrit les manuscrits de la mer Morte?: enquête sur les rouleaux du désert de Juda et sur leur interprétation contemporaine. ᵀ*Kronlund, Sonia; Champromis, Lorraine.* P 1998, Plon 476 pp. FF169. 2-259-18388-3. Bibl. [BCLF 602,2265].

8586 ᴱ**Kampen, John; Bernstein, Moshe J.** Reading 4QMMT: new perspectives on Qumran law and history. 1996 ⇒12,8353; 13,8924. ᴿCBQ 60 (1998) 396-397 (*Crawford, Sidnie White*).

8587 *Leonardi, Giovanni* I documenti extra-biblici di Qumrân e le origini della comunità essenica (secondo gli studi di F. García Martínez e collaboratori). StPat 45/1 (1998) 127-136.

8588 *Lichtenberger, Hermann* Die qumran-essenischen Reinigungsriten und die Johannestaufe. WUB 9 (1998) 30.

8589 *Lübbe, J.C.* The significance of the tribal divisions in the Dead Sea scrolls. JSem 8 (1996) 210-222 Sum. 210.

8590 *Lyons, W.J.; Reimer, A.M.* The demonic virus and Qumran studies: some preventative measures. DSD 5 (1998) 16-32.

8591 *Mach, Michael* Conservative revolution?: the intolerant innovations of Qumran. Tolerance. 1998 ⇒440. 61-79.

8592 *Maier, Johann* Die Qumrangemeinde im Rahmen des frühen Judentums. Die Schriftrollen von Qumran. 1998 ⇒6858. 51-69.

8593 *Manzi, Franco* Il peccato, la sua universalità e le sue origini negli scritti qumranici. ScC 126 (1998) 371-405.

8594 *Martone, Corrado* Calendari e turni sacerdotali a Qumran. ^FSIERRA J. 1998 ⇒102. 325-356.

8595 *Morray-Jones, C.R.A.* The temple within: the embodied divine image and its worship in the Dead Sea scrolls and other early Jewish and Christian sources. SBL.SPS 37: 1998 ⇒402. 400-431.

8596 **Paul, André** Les manuscrits de la mer Morte. 1997 ⇒13,8931. ^RHenoch 20 (1998) 116-120 (*Sacchi, Paolo*).

8597 *Regev, Eyal* The sectarian controversies about the cereal offerings. DSD 5 (1998) 33-56.

8598 *Stachowiak, Lech Remigiusz* The ethics of the Qumran community and Pauline ethics. ^T*Pasicki, Adam.* Qumran Chronicle 8/1-2 (1998) 63-82.

8599 *Taylor, Joan; Higham, Thomas* Problems of Qumran's chronology and the radiocarbon dating of palm log samples in locus 86. Qumran Chronicle 8/1-2 (1998) 83-95.

8600 *Tigchelaar, Eibert J.C.* Sabbath halakha and worship in 4QWays of righteousness: 4Q421 11 and 13+2+8 par 4Q264a 1-2. RdQ 18 (1998) 359-372.

8601 *Ulfgard, Håkan* The Teacher of Righteousness, the history of the Qumran community, and our understanding of the Jesus movement: texts, theories and trajectories. Qumran between OT and NT. JSOT.S 290: 1998 ⇒327. 310-346.

8602 *VanderKam, James C.* The Judean desert and the community of the Dead Sea scrolls. ^FSTEGEMANN, H. BZNW 97: 1998 ⇒111. 159-71;

8603 The people of the Dead Sea scrolls. SEÅ 63 (1998) 129-146.

8604 *Wacholder, Ben Zion*: Historiography of Qumran: the sons of Zadok and their enemies. Qumran between OT and NT. JSOT.S 290: 1998 ⇒327. 347-377.

8605 **Widengren, Geo; Hultgard, Anders; Philonenko, Marc** Apocalyptique iranienne et dualisme qoumrânien. 1995 ⇒11/2,7127; 12,8368. ^RCBQ 60 (1998) 408-409 (*Berquist, Jon L.*).

K4.1 Sectae iam extra Qumran notae: Esseni, Zelotae

8606 *Bilde, Per* The Essenes in PHILO and JOSEPHUS. Qumran between OT and NT. JSOT.S 290: 1998 ⇒327. 32-68.

8607 **Boccaccini, Gabriele** Beyond the Essene hypothesis: the parting of the ways between Qumran and Enochic Judaism. GR 1998, Eerdmans xxi; 230 pp. 0-8028-4360-3.

8608   *Broshi, Magen* Hatred—an Essene religious principle and its chris-
       tian consequences. ᶠSTEGEMANN, H.. BZNW 97: 1998 ⇒111. 245-
       252.
8609   *Dombrowski, Bruno W.W.* Golb's hypothesis: analysis and conclu-
       sions. ᴹKLAWEK A. 1998 ⇒51. 35-54.
          Flusser, D. La setta di Qumran... esseni 1998 ⇒8580.
8610   **Hengel, Martin** Gli zeloti: ricerche sul movimento di liberazione
       giudaico dai tempi di Erode I al 70 d.C. 1996 ⇒12,8374; 13,8948.
       ᴿRivBib 46 (1998) 240-244 (*Jossa, Giorgio*); Gr. 79 (1998) 759-762
       (*Prato, Gian Luigi*); Anton. 73 (1998) 365-366 (*Nobile, Marco*).
8611   *Hirschfeld, Y.* Ein Essener-Dorf in der Oase von En-Gedi?. WUB 9
       (1998) 92-94.
8612   *Longenecker, Bruce W.* The wilderness and revolutionary ferment in
       first-century Palestine: a response to D.R. Schwartz and J. Marcus.
       JSJ 29 (1998) 322-336.
8613   *Mendels, Doron* Hellenistic utopia and the Essenes. Identity. JSPE.S
       24: 1998 <1979> ⇒174. 420-439.
8614   **Riesner, Rainer** Essener und Urgemeinde in Jerusalem: neue Funde
       und Quellen. Studien zur biblischen Archäologie und Zeitgeschichte
       6: Wu ²1998, Brockhaus xi; 215 pp. 3-7655-9806-2.
8615   **Stegemann, Hartmut** The Library of Qumran: on the Essenes, Qum-
       ran, John the Baptist, and Jesus. GR 1998, Eerdmans ix; 290 pp. £16.
       0-8028-6167-9. Bibl.
8616   *Stemberger, Günter* Qumran, die Essener und andere jüdische Grup-
       pen der Zeit. WUB 9 (1998) 67-70.
8617   *Wenning, Robert* Essener auf dem Zion?. WUB 9 (1998) 78-79.
8618   *Zissu, Boaz* "Qumran type" graves in Jerusalem: archaeological
       evidence of an Essene community?. DSD 5 (1998) 158-171.

K4.3 Samaritani

8619   *Coggins, Richard* Jewish local patriotism: the Samaritan problem.
       Jewish local patriotism. JSPE.S 31: 1998 ⇒414. 66-78.
8620   *Crown, Alan D.* Qumran, Samaritan halakha and theology and pre-
       tannaitic Judaism. ᶠGORDON, C. JSOT.S 273: 1998 ⇒31. 420-441.
8621   *Daise, Michael* Samaritans, Seleucids, and the epic of Theodotus.
       JSPE 17 (1998) 25-51.
8622   *Dexinger, Ferdinand* Samaritaner. TRE 29. 1998 ⇒501. 750-756;
8623   Samarytanie w nauce i historii [Die Samaritaner in Forschung und
       Geschichte]. ACra 30-31 (1998-1999) 435-451 Zsfg. 451. **P**.
8624   *Di Segni, Leah* The Samaritans in Roman-Byzantine Palestine: some
       misapprehensions. Religious... communities. 1998 ⇒347. 51-66.
8625   *Morabito, Vittorio* Les samaritains de Sicile;
8626   *Pummer, Reinhard* The Samaritans in Egypt. ᶠMARGAIN, J. 1998 ⇒
       71. 195-201/213-232.
8627   **Rabello, Alfredo Mordechai** Giustiniano, ebrei e samaritani. 1987-
       1988 ⇒4,b89...8,a437. ᴿLTP 54/1 (1998) 178-180 (*Hermon, Ella*).
8628   *Robert, Philippe de* Le monothéisme samaritain et l'islam. ᶠMAR-
       GAIN, J. 1998 ⇒71. 185-194.
8629   **Thordson, Thord & Maria** Qumran and the Samaritans. 1996 ⇒12,
       8215. ᴿCoTh 68/1 (1998) 226-229 (*Chrostowski, Waldemar*).

8630 *Vardaman, E. Jerry* Were the Samaritan military leaders, Rufus and Gratus, at the time of Herod's death, the later Roman Judean governors who preceded Pontius Pilate?. ᴹSUMMERS R. 1998 ⇒115. 191-202.

K4.5 *Sadoqitae, Qaraitae*—**Cairo Genizah; Zadokites, Karaites**

8631 *Bochman, Victor* Hidden treasures: 100 years since the discovery of the Cairo *Genizah*. Ariel 106 (1998) 7-14.
8632 *Geller, M.J.; Levene, Dan* Magical texts from the Genizah (with a new duplicate). JJS 49 (1998) 334-340.
8633 **Lange, Nicholas de** Greek Jewish texts from the Cairo Genizah. TSAJ 51: 1996 ⇒12,7959. ᴿByZ 91 (1998) 110-12 (*Jacoby, David*); JQR 89 (1998) 182-184 (*Cohen, Shaye J.D.*); FrRu NF 5 (1998) 213-214 (*Decker, Thomas*); JJS 49 (1998) 377-379 (*Bowman, Stephen*).
8634 **Schur, Nathan** The Karaite encyclopedia. BEAT 38: 1995 ⇒13, 8965. ᴿJSSt 43 (1998) 384-385 (*Khan, Geoffrey*).
8635 *Wacholder, Ben Zion* The preamble to the Damascus Document: a composite edition of 4Q266-4Q268. HUCA 69 (1998) 31-47.

K5 **Judaismus prior vel totus**

8636 *Adelman, Howard* Italian Jewish women. Jewish women. 1998 ⇒ 1076. 150-168.
8637 *Ameling, Walter* Die jüdischen Gemeinden im antiken Kleinasien. Jüdische Gemeinden. 1998 ⇒8688. 29-55.
8638 **Avemarie, Friedrich** Tora und Leben: Untersuchungen zur Heilsbedeutung der Tora in der frühen rabbinischen Literatur. TSAJ 55: 1996 ⇒12,8398; 13,8969. ᴿSal. 60 (1998) 158-159 (*Vicent, R.*).
8639 ᴱ**Avery-Peck, Alan J.; Green, William S.; Neusner, Jacob** The Annual of Rabbinic Judaism: ancient, medieval, and modern. Lei 1998, Brill vi; 181 pp. $73.50. 90-04-11217-0.
8640 *Avidov, A.* Peer solidarity and communal loyalty in Roman Judaea. JJS 49 (1998) 264-279.
8641 *Baltrusch, Ernst* Bewunderung, Duldung, Ablehnung: das Urteil über die Juden in der griechisch-römischen Literatur [dazu: Corrigendum in Klio 81, 1999, S.218]. Klio 80 (1998) 403-421.
8642 *Barclay, John M.G.* Who was considered an apostate in the Jewish diaspora?. Tolerance. 1998 ⇒440. 80-98.
8643 *Baskin, Judith R.* Introduction;
8644 Jewish women in the Middle Ages. Jewish women. ²1998 ⇒1076. 15-24/101-127;
8645 Rabbinic-patristic exegetical contacts: some new perspectives. RStR 24 (1998) 171-173.
8646 *Bauckham, Richard* Life, death, and the afterlife in second temple Judaism. Life in the face of death. 1998 ⇒252. 80-95.
8647 *Baumgarten, Albert* Graeco-Roman voluntary associations and ancient Jewish sects. Jews in a Graeco-Roman world. 1998 ⇒337. 93-111;
8648 Finding oneself in a sectarian context: a sectarian's food and its implications. Self, soul and body. SHR 78: 1998 ⇒286. 125-147.

8649   *Beaude, Pierre-Marie* Bulletin du Judaïsme ancien. RSR 86 (1998) 589-618.
8650   **Benovitz, Moshe** Kol Nidre: studies in the development of rabbinic votive institutions. BJSt 315: Atlanta, GA 1998, Scholars x; 203 pp. 0-7885-0476-2. Bibl.
8651   **Berger, Michael S.** Rabbinic authority. NY 1998, OUP xii; 226 pp. 0-19-512269-0. Bibl.
8652   *Blecker, Iris Maria* Rituelle Reinheit vor und nach der Zerstörung des Zweiten Tempels: essenische, pharisäische und jesuanische Reinheitsvorstellungen im Vergleich. [F]LÖNING, K. 1998 ⇒66. 25-40.
8653   *Boccaccini, Gabriele* Il banchetto escatologico nei documenti del giudaismo medio. L'eucaristia nella bibbia. DSBP 19: 1998 ⇒218. 72-81.
8654   *Boer, Martinus C. de* The Nazoreans: living at the boundary of Judaism and christianity. Tolerance. 1998 ⇒440. 239-262.
8655   *Braun, Thomas* The Jews in the late Roman empire. SCI 17 (1998) 142-171.
8656   *Brenner, Michael* Jüdische Geschichte an deutschen Universitäten— Bilanz und Perspektive. HZ 266 (1998) 1-21.
8657   *Cohen, Shaye J.D.* On murdering or injuring a proselyte. [F]FRERICHS, E. BJSt 320: 1998 ⇒28. 95-108.
8658   *Collins, John J.* Natural theology and biblical tradition: the case of Hellenistic Judaism. CBQ 60 (1998) 1-15.
8659   **Colombo, R.,** *al.,* Quattro porte per conoscere l'ebraismo: midrash, mishna, talmud, targum. T 1998, Amicizia Ebraico-Cristiana 78 pp [SIDIC 32/3,26—Capuano, Daniele].
8660   *Cook, Johann* Towards the dating of the tradition "the Torah as surrounding fence". JNSL 24/2 (1998) 25-34.
8661   **Deines, Roland** Die Pharisäer im Spiegel christlicher und jüdischer Forschung seit WELLHAUSEN und GRAETZ. WUNT 101: 1997 ⇒13, 8982. [R]EstAg 33 (1998) 605 (*Cineira, D.A.*).
8662   **Draï, Raphaël** La pensée juive et l'interrogation divine: exégèse et épistémologie. 1996 ⇒12,8414. [R]RHPhR 78 (1998) 468-469 (*Pfrimmer, T.*).
8663   *Ego, Beate* "Maß gegen Maß": Reziprozität als Deutungskategorie im rabbinischen Judentum. Gerechtigkeit. 1998 ⇒283. 163-182.
8664   *Fine, Stephen* This is the Thora that Moses set before the children of Israel: scripture and authority in rabbinic Judaism. RExp 95 (1998) 523-532.
8665   *Fishbane, Michael* The Hebrew Bible and exegetical tradition. Intertextuality. OTS 40: 1998 ⇒394. 15-30 [Num 15].
8666   **Fishbane, Michael A.** The exegetical imagination: on Jewish thought and theology. CM 1998, Harvard University Press xi; 235 pp. $19. 0-6742-7461-X.
8667   *Fontana, Raniero* La voix du Sinaï. [T]*Attinger, Daniel.* Cahiers Ratisbonne 3 (1997) 49-55.
8668   *Goldenberg, Robert* Sabbat II: Judentum. TRE 29. 1998 ⇒501. 521-525.
8669   *Goodman, Martin* Jews, Greeks, and Romans. Jews in a Graeco-Roman world. 1998 ⇒337. 3-14.
8670   **Graetz, Heinrich** Geschichte der Juden: von den ältesten Zeiten bis auf die Gegenwart, 2: Geschichte der Israeliten vom Tode des Königs Salomo (um 977 vorchristlicher Zeit) bis zum Tode des Juda Mak-

K5 Judaism from its origins

kabi (160): *(a)* 1, Vom Tode des König Salomo bis zum babylonischen Exile (586). B ²1998, Arani xii; 467 pp. 3-7605-8673-2;

8671 *(b)* 2, babylonischen Exile (586) bis zum Tode des Juda Makkabi (160). B ³1998, Arani xi; 429 pp. 3-7605-8673-2;

8672 Geschichte der Juden: von den ältesten Zeiten bis auf die Gegenwart, *(a)* 3: Geschichte der Judäer von dem Tode Juda Makkabis bis zum Untergang des judäischen Staates—1-2. B ⁵1998, Arani xii; 363 + vii + 370-856 pp. 3-7605-8673-2;

8673 *(b)* 4: Geschichte der Juden vom Untergang des jüdischen Staates bis zum Abschluß des Talmud. B ⁴1998, Arani xii; 483 pp. 3760586732.

8674 *Greenspoon, Leonard J.* Between Alexandria and Antioch: Jews and Judaism in the Hellenistic period. The Oxford history. 1998 ⇒326. 421-465.

8675 **Hachlili, Rachel** Ancient Jewish art and archaeology in the diaspora. HO 1 35: Lei 1998, Brill xxxiii; 499, ca. 70 pp. 90-04-10878-5.

8676 *Hahn, Ferdinand* "Der die Toten lebendig macht": Auferstehung der Toten im Frühjudentum. Entschluss 53/6 (1998) 8-9.

8677 *Hahn, Johannes* Die jüdische Gemeinde im spätantiken Antiochia: Leben im Spannungsfeld von sozialer Einbindung, religiösem Wettbewerb und gewaltsamem Konflikt. Jüdische Gemeinden. 1998 ⇒ 8688. 57-89.

8678 **Hammer, Reuven** Entering the High Holy Days: a guide to the origins, themes, and prayers. Ph 1998, [Jewish Publication Society of America] xix; 252 pp. 0-8276-0609-5. Bibl.

8679 *Harvey, Graham* Synagogues of the Hebrews: "Good Jews" in the Diaspora. Jewish local patriotism. JSPE.S 31: 1998 ⇒414. 132-147.

8680 **Hayes, John Haralson; Mandell, Sara** The Jewish people in classical antiquity: from Alexander to Bar Kochba. LVL 1998, Westminster xiii; 246 pp. $28. 0-664-25727-5. Bibl.

8681 **Heilman, Samuel C.** Synagogue life: a study in symbolic interaction. New Brunswick, NJ 1998, Transaction xxvii; 321 pp. 0-7658-0433-6. With a new introduction and afterword by the author; Bibl.

8682 *Horbury, William* Early christians on synagogue prayer and imprecation. Tolerance. 1998 ⇒440. 296-317.

8683 **Hruby, Kurt** Aufsätze zum nachbiblischen Judentum und zum jüdischen Erbe der frühen Kirche. ᴱ*Osten-Sacken, Peter von der.* ANTZ 5: 1996 ⇒12,8428; 13,8995. ᴿRSR 86 (1998) 614-615 (*Beaude, Pierre-Marie*); FrRu 5 NF (1998) 49-50 (*Reichrath, Hans L.*).

8684 *Hurtado, L.W.* First-century Jewish monotheism. JSNT 71 (1998) 3-26.

8685 ᴱ**Isaac, B.; Oppenheimer, A.** Studies on the Jewish diaspora in the Hellenistic and Roman periods. Teʻuda 12: 1996 ⇒12,8434. ᴿSCI 17 (1998) 255-257 (*Price, Jonathan*).

8686 Italia judaica: gli ebrei nello Stato pontificio fino al Ghetto (1555): atti del VI Convegno internazionale Tel Aviv, 18-22 giugno 1995. Pubblicazioni degli Archivi di Stato. Saggi 47: R 1998, Ministero per i Beni Culturali e Ambientali 307 pp. 88-7125-148-2.

8687 *Jones, Siân* Identities in practice: towards an archaeological perspective on Jewish identity in antiquity. Jewish local patriotism. JSPE.S 31: 1998 ⇒414. 29-49.

8688 ᴱ**Jütte, Robert; Kustermann, Abraham P.** Jüdische Gemeinden und Organisationsformen von der Antike bis zur Gegenwart. Wsb 1998, Albus 280 pp. 3-928127-53-5.

8689 *Klawans, Jonathan* Idolatry, incest, and impurity: moral defilement in ancient Judaism. JSJ 29 (1998) 391-415.
8690 *Koch, Klaus; Gleßmer, Uwe* Neumonds-Neujahr oder Vollmonds-Neujahr?: zu spätisraelitischen Kalender-Theologien. ᶠSTEGEMANN, H. BZNW 97: 1998 ⇒111. 114-136.
8691 *Kraemer, Ross S.* Jewish women in the diaspora world of late antiquity. Jewish women. ²1998 ⇒1076. 46-72.
8692 **La Maisonneuve, Dominique de** Le judaïsme. Tout simplement: P 1998, L'Atelier 176 pp [SIDIC 32/3,25s—Cuche, Jacqueline].
8693 **Lamm, Norman** The Shema: spirituality and law in Judaism as exemplified in the Shema, the most important passage in the Torah. Ph 1998, Jewish Publication Soc. of America xv; 222 pp. 0-8276-06559.
8694 *Langer, Ruth* From study of scripture to a reenactment of Sinai: the emergence of the synagogue Torah service. Worship 72/1 (1998) 43-67.
8695 *Leith, Mary Joan Winn* Israel among the nations: the Persian period. The Oxford history. 1998 ⇒326. 367-419.
8696 *Lenhardt, Pierre* Le renouvellement (hiddush) de l'alliance dans le judaïsme rabbinique. Cahiers Ratisbonne 3 (1997) 126-175 Riass., sum. 175.
8697 *Levine, Lee* Synagogue leadership: the case of the archisynagogue. Jews in a Graeco-Roman world. 1998 ⇒337. 195-213.
8698 **Levine, Lee I.** Judaism and Hellenism in antiquity: conflict or confluence?. Stroum Lectures in Jewish Studies: Seattle 1998, Univ. of Washington Pr. xiii; 227 pp. $20. 0-295-97682-9. Bibl.
8699 **Levison, John R.** The Spirit in first-century Judaism. 1997 ⇒13, 9005. ᴿJJS 49 (1998) 356-357 (*O'Brien, David P.*); EE 73 (1998) 669-671 (*Piñero, Antonio*).
8700 *Lichtenberger, Hermann* Organisationsformen und Ämter in den jüdischen Gemeinden im antiken Griechenland und Italien. Jüdische Gemeinden. 1998 ⇒8688. 11-27.
8701 *Lieber, Andrea Beth* Where is sacrifice in the heavenly temple?: reflections on the role of violence in Hekhalot traditions. SBL.SP part 1. SBL.SPS 37: 1998 ⇒402. 432-446.
8702 *Magen, Yitzhak* Ancient Israel's Stone Age: purity in second temple times. BArR 24/5 (1998) 46-52.
8703 **Magonet, Jonathan** Mit der Bibel durch das jüdische Jahr. GTBS 1443: Gü 1998, Gü'er 128 pp. 3-579-01443-9.
8704 *Maier, Johann* Zu den Anfängen der rabbinischen Theologie. Internationales Josephus-Kolloquium. 1998 ⇒490. 159-174.
8705 *Martone, Corrado* Credere in Dio negli antichi scritti giudaici. La fede nella bibbia. DSBP 21: 1998 ⇒224. 58-68.
8706 **Merkel, H.** Sibyllinen. Jüdische Schriften aus hellenistisch-römischer Zeit 5/8: Gü 1998, Gü'er 1043-1140 pp [Henoch 21,369— Ubigli, Liliana Rosso].
8707 *Neusner, Jacob* After the advent of criticism, what happens?: seven recent books on formative Judaism: its history, literature, and religion. JHiC 5/2 (1998) 238-284;
8708 The shape of Judaism. Jewish law. 1998 ⇒181. 3-19.
8709 **Neusner, Jacob** From scripture to 70: the pre-rabbinic beginnings of the halakah. SFSHJ 192: Atlanta, Ga. 1998, Scholars xxxii; 253 pp. 0-7885-0517-3.

8710 ^E**Neusner, Jacob; Avery-Peck, Alan J.** Judaism in late antiquity: III: where we stand: issues and debates in ancient Judaism. HÖ 40: Lei 1998, Brill xiv; 250 pp. 90-04-11186-7.

8711 **Noethlichs, Karl Leo** Das Judentum und der römische Staat: Minderheitenpolitik im antiken Rom. 1996 ⇒12,8452. ^RHZ 266 (1998) 470-473 (*Baltrusch, Ernst*); TRG 54 (1998) 404-405 (*Sirks, A.J.B.*); ZSSR.R 115 (1998) 516-523 (*Botermann, Helga*).

8712 **Ognibeni, Bruno** La seconda parte del Sefer 'oklah we'oklah. 1995 ⇒11/2,7225; 12,8453. ^RRB 105 (1998) 271-272 (*Schenker, Adrian*).

8713 ^E*Ombrosi, Orietta* Emmanuel LÈVINAS: la laicità e il pensiero d'Israele. FilTeo 12 (1998 <1960>) 335-349.

8714 *Pearce, Sarah; Jones, Siân* Introduction: Jewish local identities and patriotism in the Graeco-Roman period. Jewish local patriotism. JSPE.S 31: 1998 ⇒414. 13-28.

8715 **Pearl, Chaim** Theology in rabbinic stories. Peabody 1997, Hendriksen 180 pp [Faith & Mission 17/1,83ss—Harris, Greg].

8716 *Perrot, Charles* La pluralité théologique du judaïsme au 1er siècle de notre ère. Jésus de Nazareth. 1998 ⇒253. 156-176.

8717 *Piattelli, Abramo Alberto* Lo Spirito di Dio nell'Ebraismo. Lat. 64 (1998) 435-437.

8718 *Remaud, Michel* Mérite des pères. Cahiers Ratisbonne 3 (1997) 18-48 Riass., sum. 48.

8719 **Rutgers, Leonard Victor** The hidden heritage of diaspora Judaism. Contributions to Biblical Exegesis and Theology 20: Lv 1998, Peeters 320 pp. FB290. 90-429-0666-9. Bibl.

8720 *Satlow, Michael L.* Rhetoric and assumptions: Romans and rabbis on sex. Jews in a Graeco-Roman world. 1998 ⇒337. 135-144.

8721 *Schaller, Berndt* 4000 Essener—6000 Pharisäer: zum Hintergrund und Wert antiker Zahlenangaben. ^FSTEGEMANN, H. BZNW 97: 1998 ⇒111. 172-182.

8722 *Schams, Christine* The status and functions of Jewish scribes in the second-temple period. TynB 49 (1998) 377-380.

8723 **Schäfer, Peter** Judeophobia: attitudes towards the Jews in the ancient world. 1997 ⇒13,9023. ^RChH 67 (1998) 556-558 (*Fredriksen, Paula*); Zion 63 (1998) 461-464 H (*Niehoff, Maren R.*).

8724 ^E**Schoeps, Julius H.** Neues Lexikon des Judentums. Gü 1998, Bertelsmann 896 pp. 3-577-10604-2. Überarb. Neuausg.

8725 **Scholem, Gershom Gerhard** Conceptos básicos del judaísmo: Dios, creación, revelación, tradición, salvación. ^T*Barbero, José Luis.* Paradigmas 21: M 1998, Trotta 139 pp. 84-8164-237-1.

8726 **Schwartz, Howard** Reimagining the Bible: the storytelling of the rabbis. NY 1998, OUP xiv; 289 pp. 0-19-511511-2. Bibl.

8727 *Schwartz, Joshua* Gambling in ancient Jewish society and in the Graeco-Roman world. Jews in a Graeco-Roman world. 1998 ⇒337. 145-165;

8728 The patriotic Rabbi: Babylonian scholars in Roman period Palestine. Jewish local patriotism. JSPE.S 31: 1998 ⇒414. 118-131.

8729 ^E**Sierra, Sergio J.** La lettura ebraica delle Scritture. La Bibbia nella Storia 18: 1995 ⇒11/2,388...13,9028. ^RCrSt 19 (1998) 419-421 (*Cova, Gian Domenico*).

8730 **Slingerland, H. Dixon** Claudian policymaking and the early imperial repression of Judaism at Rome. SFSHJ 160: 1997 ⇒13,9030.

^{R}RHPhR 78 (1998) 337-338 (*Blanchetière, F.*); JJS 49 (1998) 358-360 (*Noy, David*).
8731 *Stefani, Piero* La fede negli scritti rabbinici. La fede nella bibbia. DSBP 21: 1998 ⇒224. 69-82.
8732 *Stemberger, Günter* Qumran, die Pharisäer und das Rabbinat. ^{F}STE-GEMANN, H. BZNW 97: 1998 ⇒111. 210-224;
8733 Salomo/Salomoschriften II: Judentum. TRE 29. 1998 ⇒501. 727-30.
8734 **Stern, Sacha** Jewish identity in early rabbinic writings. 1994 ⇒10, 9821; 13,9033. ^{R}Religion 28 (1998) 303-305 (*Neusner, Jacob*).
8735 *Stern, Sacha* Dissonance and misunderstanding in Jewish-Roman relations. Jews in a Graeco-Roman world. 1998 ⇒337. 241-250.
8736 **Tsairi, Anat; Shama, Galit** Catalogue of the recordings in the tape archives of the Hebrew University language traditions project, 3. Hebrew University language traditions projects 21: J 1998, Magnes 135 pp. 964-350-062-7. H.
8737 *Van der Horst, Pieter W.* Neglected Greek evidence for early Jewish liturgical prayer. JSJ 29 (1998) 278-296;
8738 Papyrus Egerton 5: Christian or Jewish?. ZPE 121 (1998) 173-182.
8739 **Vidal-Naquet, Pierre** The Jews: history, memory, and the present. 1996 ⇒12,8479. ^{R}Jdm 47/1 (1998) 120-122 & Religion 28 (1998) 424-426 (*Neusner, Jacob*).
8740 **Wander, Bernd** Gottesfürchtige und Sympathisanten: Studien zum heidnischen Umfeld von Diasporasynagogen. WUNT 104: Tü 1998, Mohr xiii; 276 pp. DM178. 3-16-146865-1. Diss.-Habil. Heidelberg.
8741 *Wegner, Judith Romney* The image and status of women in classical rabbinic Judaism. Jewish women. ^{2}1998 ⇒1076. 73-100.
8742 **Weinberger, Leon J.** Jewish hymnography: a literary history. L 1998, The Littman Library of Jewish Civilization xxiii; 492 pp. 1-874774-30-7. bibl.
8743 *Weiß, Hans-Friedrich* Sadduzäer. TRE 29. 1998 ⇒501. 589-594.
8744 ^{E}**Werblowsky, R.J. Zwi; Wigoder, Geoffrey** The Oxford dictionary of the Jewish religion. 1997 ⇒13,9041. ^{R}ChH 67 (1998) 631-632 (*Cohen, Shaye J.D.*).
8745 **Williams, Margaret H.** The Jews among the Greeks and Romans: a diasporan sourcebook. L 1998, Duckworth xiii; 236 pp. £40/£15. 0-7156-2811-9/2-7 [JThS 50,748ss—Barclay, John M.G.].
8746 **Wise, Michael Owen** Thunder in Gemini and other essays on the history, language and literature of second temple Palestine. JSPE.S 15: 1994 ⇒10,231...13,9042. ^{R}JSSt 43 (1998) 379-381 (*Swanson, Dwight*).
8747 *Yavetz, Zvi* Latin authors on Jews and Dacians. Hist. 47 (1998) 77-107.

K6.0 **Mišna**, tosepta; Tannaim

8748 **Bornhäuser, Hans; Mayer, Gunter** Die Tosefta, Seder II: Moëd, 3: Sukka—Jom tob—Rosch ha-Schana. 1993, ⇒11/2,7248. ^{R}JAOS 118 (1998) 227-232 (*Goldberg, Abraham*).
8749 *Goldberg, Abraham* A Kohlhammer translation (with commentary) of Tosefta tractates in Moed. JAOS 118 (1998) 227-232.
8750 *Halbertal, Moshe* Coexisting with the enemy: Jews and pagans in the Mishnah. Tolerance. 1998 ⇒440. 159-172.

8751 *Kalmin, Richard* Relationships between rabbis and non-rabbis in rabbinic literature of late antiquity. JSQ 5 (1998) 156-170.

8752 **Lapin, Hayim** Early rabbinic civil law and the social history of Roman Galilee: a study of the Mishnah tractate Baba' Mesi'a'. BJSt 307: 1996 ⇒12,8491; 13,9048. [R]JQR 89 (1998) 199-204 (*Hayes, Christine*); JBL 117 (1998) 132-134 (*Satlow, Michael L.*).

8753 [T]**Mayer, Günter; Lisowsky, Gerhard** Die Tosefta: Seder I: Zeraim. 3: Kilajim - Maaser rischon. Rabbinische Texte. Erste Reihe I.1,3: Stu 1998, Kohlhammer vii; 187 pp. DM368. 3-17-015407-9. Bibl.

8754 *Neusner, Jacob* Comparing sources: mishnah/tosefta and gospel;
8755 Religious belief and economic behavior: how religions renew the social order;
8756 The theological anthropology of classical Judaism;
8757 Who owns Eden?: and from the bible to the torah. Jewish law. 1998 ⇒181. 119-135/85-101/103-118/43-61.

8758 **Neusner, Jacob** The place of the Tosefta in the Halakhah of formative Judaism: what Alberdina Houtman didn't notice. SFSHJ 156: Atlanta, GA 1998, Scholars ix; 221 pp. 0-7885-0454-1.

8759 *Pérez Fernández, Miguel* La Mishna. Letteratura giudaica. 1998 ⇒8180. 375-411.

8760 **Reichman, Ronen** Mishna und Sifra: ein literarkritischer Vergleich paralleler Überlieferungen. TSAJ 68: Tü 1998, Mohr xiii; 279 pp. DM168. 3-16-146897-X. Bibl.

8761 **Strassburger, Bert W.** Midor el dor (from generation to generation): additional chapters of שנות דורו רשימות. Kefar Saba 1998, הוצאת חוג ידידי המדרשיה בישראל 122 pp. 965-469-009-8 [NThAR 1999,4].

8762 [E]**Valle, C. del** La Misná. [2]1997 ⇒13,9059. [R]RevAg 41 (1998) 1205-1206 (*Sabugal, Santos*).

K6.5 Talmud; midraš

8763 **Akenson, Donald Harman** Surpassing wonder: the invention of the bible and the talmuds. NY 1998, Harcourt, Brace xi; 658 pp. $40. 0-15-100418-8.

8764 *Alexander, Philip S.* 'Homer the prophet of all' and 'Moses our teacher': late antique exegesis of the Homeric epics and of the Torah of Moses. Use of sacred books. 1998 ⇒263. 127-142.

8765 *Blumenthal, David R.* Reading creation. Bibel und Midrasch. FAT 22: 1998 ⇒8766. 117-166.

8766 [E]**Bodendorfer, Gerhard; Millard, Matthias** Bibel und Midrasch: zur Bedeutung der rabbinischen Exegese für die Bibelwissenschaft. FAT 22: Tü 1998, Mohr xiii; 307 pp. DM168. 3-16-146857-0.

8767 *Bodendorfer, Gerhard* Hermeneutik und rabbinische Literatur: Einführung zum ersten Teil. Bibel und Midrasch. FAT 22: 1998 ⇒8766. 11-12;

8768 Zur Historisierung des Psalters in der rabbinischen Literatur. [F]LOHFINK, N. 1998 ⇒64. 215-234.

8769 *Böhl, Felix* Demut und Prophetie: Eldad und Medad nach der frühen rabbinischen Überlieferung. [F]RUPPERT, L. FzB 88: 1998 ⇒99. 15-30.

8770 **Brody, Robert** A hand-list of rabbinic manuscripts in the Cambridge Genizah collections. Cambridge University Library. Genizah Series 5: C 1998, CUP xiii; 353 pp. 0-521-58400-0. 24 pl.

8771 *Büchner, D.* Midrash: a bibliographical essay. JSem 8/1 (1996) 49-78 Sum. 49.
8772 *Chevelen, Eric M.* Discovering the talmud. First Things 85 (1998) 40-44.
8773 *Edrei, Arye* "To fulfill the wishes of the deceased": on the validity of wills in rabbinic literature. HUCA 69 (1998) *105-*141. H.
8774 **Evers, R.** De echte tora: de geschiedenis van de talmoed. Kampen 1998, Kok 136 pp. *f*25. 90-242-6197-X [ITBT 7/2,31—Groeneveld, A.K.].
8775 **Fisch, Menachem** Rational rabbis: science and talmudic culture. 1997 ⇒13,9068. [R]Religion 28 (1998) 422-424 (*Neusner, Jacob*).
8776 *Fishbane, Michael* Midrash and the meaning of scripture. Interpretation of the Bible. JSOT.S 289: 1998 ⇒389. 549-563.
8777 *Fraade, Steven D.* Looking for legal Midrash at Qumran. Biblical perspectives. StTDJ 28: 1998 ⇒441. 59-79.
8778 **Gerhardsson, Birger** Memory and manuscript, 1: oral tradition and written transmission in rabbinic Judaism and early Christianity; 2: Tradition & transmission in early christianity. Biblical resource: GR 1998 <1961, 1964>, Eerdmans xlvi; 379, 47 pp. 0-8028-4366-2. Foreword *Jacob Neusner* [Alpha Omega 2,544s—Furlong, Jude].
8779 **Ginzberg, Louis** Abraham, Jacob. Les légendes des juifs, 2. Patrimoines: Judaïsme: P 1998, Cerf 2 296 pp. FF185. 2-204-06136-0 [BCLF 604,30s];
8780 Dalla creazione al diluvio. Le leggende degli ebrei. 1998 Adelphi 454 pp. L38.000 [Presbyteri 32,400].
8781 **Girón Blanc, Luis F.** Textos escogidos del talmud. En torno al Talmud: Barc 1998, Ríopiedras 205 pp. 84-7213-144-0 [EstB 56,569].
8782 *Gradwohl, Roland* Auf den Spuren jüdischer Bibelexegese: am Beispiel von Ex 2,1-10. EvErz 50 (1998) 282-289.
8783 **Hansel, Georges** Explorations talmudiques. P 1998, Jacob 298 pp. FF150. 2-7381-0578-5. collab. *Méchoulan, Éric*; Bibl. [BCLF 602,2267].
8784 **Hauptman, Judith** Rereading the rabbis: a woman's voice. [Boulder, CO] 1998, WestviewPress xv; 285 pp. 0-8133-3400-4. Bibl.
8785 *Hayes, Christine E.* Displaced self-perceptions: the deployment of *Mînîm* and Romans in *B. Sanhedrin* 90b-91a. Studies... in Jewish history. 1998 ⇒347. 249-289.
8786 **Hayes, Christine Elizabeth** Between the Babylonian and Palestinian Talmuds: accounting for Halakhic difference in selected Sugyot from Tractate Avodah Zarah. 1997 ⇒13,9075. [R]JJS 49 (1998) 366-368 (*Schwartz, Joshua*).
8787 **Hezser, Catherine** The social structure of the rabbinic movement in Roman Palestine. TSAJ 66: 1997 ⇒13,9076. [R]JJS 49 (1998) 362-365 (*Schwartz, Joshua*).
8788 **Hoffman, Lawrence** Covenant of blood: circumcision and gender in rabbinic Judaism. 1996 ⇒12,8511. [R]JAOS 118 (1998) 600-601; (*Steinberg, Naomi*); AJSR 23 (1998) 256-258 (*Zeidman, Reena*).
8789 [T]**Hüttenmeister, Frowald Gil** Sota: die des Ehebruchs verdächtige Frau. Übersetzung des Talmud Yerushalmi 3/2: Tü 1998, Mohr xxix; 283 pp. DM198. 3-16-147045-1. Hinzuziehung eines Manuskriptes von *Leo Prijs*; Bibl.
8790 **Jacobs, Irving** The midrashic process: tradition and interpretation in rabbinic Judaism. 1995 ⇒11/2,7292...13,9078. [R]JSSt 43 (1998) 177-178 (*Niehoff, Maren*).

8791 **Lenhard, Doris** Die rabbinische Homilie: ein formanalytischer Index. FJS 10: Fra 1998, Gesellschaft zur Förderung Judaistischer Studien (10) 541 pp. 3-922056-07-5. Bibl.

8792 *Lenhardt, Pierre* L'exégèse (midrash) de la tradition d'Israël: sa grandeur et ses limites. Cahiers Ratisbonne 5 (1998) 9-43 Riass., sum. 43.

8793 *Linafelt, Tod* "Mad midrash" and the negative dialectics of post-holocaust biblical interpretation. Bibel und Midrasch. FAT 22: 1998 ⇒ 8766. 263-274.

8794 *Lyke, Larry L.* What does Ruth have to do with Rahab?: midrash *Ruth Rabbah* and the Matthean genealogy of Jesus. The function of scripture. 1998 ⇒236. 262-284.

8795 *Millard, Matthias* Bibelinterpretation am Beispiel Genesis und Exodus: Einführung zum zweiten Teil. Bibel und Midrasch. FAT 22: 1998 ⇒8766. 115-116.

8796 *Morfino, Mauro M.* 'Siepe alla sapienza è il silenzio': la sobrietà come caratteristica esistenziale dell'ascolatatore della parola di Dio nel trattato *Pirqé Abot* e nel *Midrash Abot de Rabbi Natan.* [F]ALBERTI, O. 1998 ⇒3192. 477-544.

8797 *Muñoz León, Domingo* Principios basicos de la exégesis rabínica. RevBib 60 (1998) 117-121.

8798 *Mutius, Hans-Georg von* Pirke Abot V,2 als Beleg für eine bisher unbekannte Fassung von Abrahams Stammbaum in Genesis 11,10-26. BN 91 (1998) 16-19.

8799 **Navè Levinson, Pnina** Introduzione alla teologia ebraica. [E]*De Benedetti, Paolo.* CinB 1996, San Paolo 245 pp. 88-215-3121-X [R]FilTeo 12 (1998) 431-432 (*Ferraris, Luisa*).

8800 *Neudecker, Reinhard* 'Io sono il Signore, tuo Dio...': interpretazioni rabbiniche su Es 20,2 (Dt 5,6). CivCatt 149/2 (1998) 249-260 [⇒12, 1938];

8801 Midrash. Dizionario di omiletica. 1998 ⇒533. 934-938.

8802 *Neusner, Jacob* In the view of Rabbinic Judaism, what, exactly, ended with prophecy?. Mediators of the divine. SFSHJ 163: 1998 ⇒287. 45-60.

8803 **Oberhänsli-Widmer, Gabrielle** Biblische Figuren in der rabbinischen Literatur: Gleichnisse und Bilder zu Adam, Noah und Abraham im Midrasch Bereschit Rabba. Judaica et Christiana 17: Fra 1998, Lang 395 pp. DM94. 3-906759-66-0. Bibl.

8804 *Pérez Fernández, Miguel* Il midrash. Letteratura giudaica. 1998 ⇒8180. 412-466.

8805 *Poorthuis, Marcel* Moses' rod in Zipporah's garden. Sanctity of time. 1998 ⇒303. 231-264.

8806 *Poorthuis, M.J.H.M.* Rebekah as a virgin on her way to marriage: a study in midrash. JSJ 29 (1998) 438-462.

8807 **Quarles, Charles L.** Midrash criticism: introduction and appraisal. Lanham 1998, Univ. Press of America 145 pp. $60.

8808 *Remaud, Michel* De Moïse à Josué. Cahiers Ratisbonne 4 (1998) 98-119 Riass., sum. 119;

8809 Le 'chef de la foi': Abraham et Jésus. Cahiers Ratisbonne 5 (1998) 44-57 Riass., sum. 57 [Heb 12,2].

8810 *Sarason, Richard S.* Interpreting rabbinic biblical interpretation: the problem of midrash, again. [F]FRERICHS, E. BJSt 320: 1998 ⇒28. 133-154.

8811 ESchäfer, Peter The Talmud Yerushalmi and Graeco-Roman culture. TSAJ 71: Tü 1998, Mohr viii; 690 pp. 3-16-146951-8.

8812 Sperber, Daniel Magic and folklore in rabbinic literature. 1994 ⇒11/2,328. RRSR 86 (1998) 599-601 (Beaude, Pierre-Marie).

8813 Stern, David Midrash and theory: ancient Jewish exegesis and contemporary literary studies. Rethinking theory: Evanston 1996, Northwestern Univ. Press viii; 118 pp. $50. RJR 78 (1998) 310-311 (Hirshman, Marc).

8814 Teugels, Lieve Concern for the unity of Tenakh in the formation of Aggadat Bereshit. Use of sacred books. 1998 ⇒263. 187-202;

8815 Midrash in the bible or midrash on the bible?: critical remarks about the uncritical use of a term;

8816 Thoma, Clemens Theologische Tendenzen in rabbinischen Gleichnissen. Bibel und Midrasch. FAT 22: 1998 ⇒8766. 43-63/65-73.

8817 TTownsend, John T. Exodus and Leviticus. Midrash Tanḥuma. 1997 ⇒13,9100. RAThR 80 (1998) 422-423 (Culberton, Philip).

8818 Werman, Golda MILTON and midrash. Wsh 1995, Catholic Univ. of America Pr. 266 pp. $55. 0-8132-0821-1. RJdm 47/1 (1998) 115-120 (Kolbrener, William).

8819 Wright, Terry R. Midrash and the genesis of modern fiction—Wiesel, Steinbeck and the remarkable Cain. Bibel und Midrasch. FAT 22: 1998 ⇒8766. 235-262.

8820 Zakovitch, Yair David's birth and childhood in the bible and the Midrashim on Psalms. FLOHFINK, N. 1998 ⇒64. 185-198 [1 Sam 16].

K7.1 Judaismus mediaevalis, generalia

8821 Bareket, Elionar Books of records of the Jerusalemite court from Cairo Geniza in the first half of the eleventh century. HUCA 69 (1998) *1-*55. H.

8822 Brody, Robert The Geonim of Babylonia and the shaping of medieval Jewish culture. NHv 1998, Yale Univ. Pr. xxii; 382 pp. £27.50. 0-300-07047-0. Bibl.

8823 Cohen, Mark R. Under crescent and cross: the Jews in the Middle Ages. 1994 ⇒10,9886; 11/2,7345. RJR 77 (1997) (1998) 449-454 (Kraemer, Joel L.).

8824 Gaimani, Aharon Rabbinic emissaries and their contacts with Yemenite Jewry. HUCA 69 (1998) 101-125.

8825 Graetz, Heinrich Geschichte der Juden: von den ältesten Zeiten bis auf die Gegenwart, 5: Geschichte der Juden vom Abschluß des Talmuds (500) bis zum Aufblühen der jüdisch-spanischen Kultur (1027); 6: Geschichte der Juden vom Aufblühen der jüdisch-spanischen Kultur (1027) bis Maimunis Tod. B ⁴1998, Arani xix; 572 + xi; 406 pp. 3-7605-8673-2 [⇒8670-8673].

8826 Marcus, Ivan G. The foundation legend of Ashkenazic Judaism. FFRERICHS, E. BJSt 320: 1998 ⇒28. 409-418.

8827 Melammed, Renée Levine Sephardi women in the medieval and early modern periods. Jewish women. ²1998 ⇒1076. 128-149.

8828 ESonnino, Giovanni Carlo IBN GABIROL, Shelomoh: sorgente di vita: traduzione della versione ebraica negli estratti di SHEM TOV ibn Falaquera. Judaica: Ancona 1998, Transeuropa 127 pp. 88-7828-116-6.

8829 **Veltri, Giuseppe** Magie und Halakha: Ansätze zu einem empirischen Wissenschaftsbegriff im spätantiken und frühmittelalterlichen Judentum. TSAJ 62: 1997 ⇒13,9118. [R]JR 78 (1998) 655-656 (*Betz, Hans Dieter*).
8830 *Yuval, Israel Jacob* Heilige Städte, heilige Gemeinden—Mainz als das Jerusalem Deutschlands. Jüdische Gemeinden. 1998 ⇒8688. 91-101.

K7.2 Maimonides

8831 **Bouganim, Ami** Maïmonide: le rabbin philosophe. L'Essentiel: P 1998, Alliance israélite universelle 100 pp. FF68. 2-902969-18-X [BCLF 611-612,1728].
8832 *Brague, Rémi* Maïmonide en français: quelques ouvrages récents (1979-1996). RMM 4 (1998) 585-603.
8833 *Kasher, Hannah* "Why is the land in ruins?" (Jeremiah 9:11): religious transgression versus natural historical process in the writing of Maimonides and his disciples. HUCA 69 (1998) *143-*156. **H.**
8834 **Laras, Giuseppe** Mosè Maimonide: il pensiero filosofico. Maestri del pensiero 11: Brescia 1998, Morcelliana 251 pp. 88-372-1686-6.
8835 *Sokol, Moshe* Maimonides on freedom of the will and moral responsibility. HThR 91 (1998) 25-39.
8836 **Stern, Josef** Problems and parables of law: Maimonides and NAHMANIDES on reasons for the commandments (Ta'amei Ha-Mitzvot). SUNY Series in Judaica: Hermeneutics, Mysticism and Religion: Albany 1998, State Univ. of NY Pr. xiv; 201 pp. 0-7914-3823-6. Bibl.

K7.3 Alteri magistri Judaismi mediaevalis

8837 *Alborghetti, Patrizio* RASHI di Troyes: appunti per uno studio. RTLu 3 (1998) 463-475.
8838 **Eisen, Robert** GERSONIDES on providence, covenant, and the chosen people: a study in medieval Jewish philosophy and biblical commentary. SUNY Series in Jewish Philosophy: NY 1995, SUNY Press 257 pp. $57.50/19. 0-7914-2314-X/3-1. [R]AJSR 23 (1998) 258-263 (*Kaplan, Lawrence*); JQR 88 (1998) 332-336 (*Manekin, Charles H.*).
8839 *Graf, Friedrich Wilhelm* SAADJA ben Josef al-Fayyumi Gaon (822-942). TRE 29. 1998 ⇒501. 512-514.
8840 **Idel, Moshe; Perani, Mauro** NAHAMANIDE esegeta e cabbalista. Studi e Testi: F 1998, Giuntina 409 pp. 88-8057-059-5. Bibl. [R]Amicizia Ebraica-Cristiana 33 (1998) 46-47 (*Lelli, Fabrizio*).
8841 [T]**Korobkin, N. Daniel** [JUDAH HALEVI:] The Kuzari: in defense of the despised faith. Northvale, NJ 1998, Jason Aronson xxxiii; 507 pp. 0-7657-9970-7.
8842 *Rottzoll, Dirk U.* "Der Verständige wird es verstehen..."—zu den redaktionsgeschichtlichen Ansätzen bei Abraham IBN ESRA und ihrer Interpretationsgeschichte. Bibel und Midrasch. FAT 22: 1998 ⇒ 8766. 75-95.
        Stern, J. Problems...of law... NAHMANIDES 1998 ⇒8836.
8843 *Van der Heide, Albert* Salomo ben Isaak (RASCHI) (1040?-1105). TRE 29. 1998 ⇒501. 736-740.

K7.4 *Qabbalâ, Zohar, Merkabā*—Jewish mysticism

8844 **Busi, Giulio** La Qabbalah. Biblioteca Essenziale Laterza 12: R 1998, Laterza 158 pp. 88-420-5620-0. Bibl.
8845 **Cooper, David A.** God is a verb: kabbalah and the practice of mystical Judaism. NY 1998, Riverhead xviii; 333 pp. 1-57322-055-8.
8846 *Davila, James R.* 4QMess ar (4Q534) and Merkavah mysticism. DSD 5 (1998) 367-381.
8847 **Drosnin, Michael** O código da Bíblia. 1997 ⇒13,9131. ᴿDid(L) 28/1 (1998) 219-225 (*Vaz, Armindo Dos Santos*).
8848 *Fletcher-Louis, Crispin H.T.* Heavenly ascent or incarnational presence?: a revisionist reading of the *Songs of the Sabbath Sacrifice.* SBL.SP part 1. SBL.SPS 37: 1998 ⇒402. 367-399.
8849 **Hanson, Kenneth** Kabbalah: three thousand years of mystic tradition. Tulsa, OK 1998, Council Oak 270 pp. 1-5717-8072-6. Bibl.
8850 **Idel, Moshe** La cabale, nouvelles perspectives. ᵀ*Mopsik, Charles.* P 1998, Cerf 550 pp. FF290. 2-204-05946-3 [MoBi 117,70—Bouretz, Pierre].
8851 **Laenen, J.H.** Joodse mystiek: een inleiding. Kampen 1998, Kok 302 pp. ƒ45. 90-242-9397-9 [Interpretatie 7/2,33—Meereboer, Bep].
8852 **Leon-Jones, Karen Silvia de** Giordano Bʀᴜɴᴏ and the kabbalah: prophets, magicians and rabbis. 1997 ⇒13,9130. ᴿSCJ 29 (1998) 939-940 (*Burnett, Stephen G.*).
8853 *Mach, Michael* From apocalypticism to early Jewish mysticism?. Encyclopedia of apocalypticism I. 1998 ⇒507. 229-264.
8854 **Maier, Johann** Die Kabbalah. 1995 ⇒11/2,7447. ᴿOLZ 93 (1998) 195-197 (*Wächter, Ludwig*);
8855 La cabbala: introduzione. 1997 ⇒13,9138. ᴿRivBib 46 (1998) 500-503 (*Ibba, Giovanni*).
8856 *Pedaya, Haviva* The divinity as place and time and the holy place in Jewish mysticism. ᴹPRAWER J. 1998 ⇒93. 73-83.
8857 *Schäfer, Peter* Tochter, Schwester, Braut und Mutter: Bilder der Weiblichkeit Gottes in der frühen Kabbala. Saec. 49 (1998) 259-279.
8858 **Scholem, Gershom** La kabbale: une introduction, origines, thèmes et biographies. Patrimoines, Judaïsme: P 1998, Cerf 703 pp. FF290. 2-204-05297-3. Préf. de *Joseph Dan*; BCLF 606,506;
8859 Las grandes tendencias de la mística judía. Árbol del Paraíso 6: 1996 ⇒12,8604. ᴿCDios 111/1 (1998) 336-337 (*Gutiérrez, J.*).
8860 *Teugels, Lieve* Holiness and mysticism at Sinai according to the Mekhilta de Rabbi Iꜱʜᴍᴀᴇʟ. Sanctity of time. 1998 ⇒303. 113-133.
8861 **Troisi, Luigi** Dizionario della kabbalah. Foggia 1998, Bastogi 279 pp. 88-8185-125-3. Bibl.
8862 *Viterbi, Benedetto Carucci* 'Colui che forma la luce e crea le tenebre, fa la pace e crea il male; sono Io, Dio, che faccio tutto questo' (Is 45,7): l'altro lato: Dio e il male nella mistica ebraica. PSV 37 (1998) 105-113.

K7.5 **Judaismus saec. 14-18**

8863 **Chamla, Mino** Sᴘɪɴᴏᴢᴀ e il concetto della tradizione ebraica. 1996 ⇒12,8612. ᴿFilosofia Politica 12 (1998) 310-312 (*Visentin, S.*).

8864 **Graetz, Heinrich** Geschichte der Juden: von den ältesten Zeiten bis auf die Gegenwart, *(a)* 7: Geschichte der Juden von Maimunis Tod (1205) bis zur Verbannung der Juden aus Spanien und Portugal—1-2; *(b)* 9: Geschichte der Juden von der Verbannung der Juden aus Spanien und Portugal (1494) bis zur dauernden Ansiedlung der Marranen in Holland (1618). B ^{4}1998, Arani xv; 463 + xv; 505 + xiv; 573 pp. 3-7605-8673-2;

8865 *(c)* 10: Geschichte der Juden von der dauernden Ansiedelung der Marranen in Holland (1618) bis zum Beginne der Mendelssohnschen Zeit (1750). B ^{3}1998, Arani xi; 532 pp. 3-7605-8665-1;

8866 *(d)* 11: Geschichte der Juden vom Beginn der Mendelssohnschen Zeit (1750) bis in die neueste Zeit (1848). B ^{2}1998, Arani xiv; 612 pp. 3-7605-8673-2 [⇒8670-8673; 8825].

8867 *Krochmalnik, Daniel* Die Psalmen in Moses MENDELSSOHNs Utopie des Judentums. ^{F}LOHFINK, N. 1998 ⇒64. 235-267.

8868 *Novinsky, Anita* Political Zionism in the Portuguese Renaissance (Damiao de Gois). ^{F}FRERICHS, E. BJSt 320: 1998 ⇒28. 419-429.

K7.7 Hasidismus et Judaismus saeculi XIX

8869 **Bechtoldt, Hans-Joachim** Die jüdische Bibelkritik im 19. Jahrhundert. 1995 ⇒11/2,k288b... 13,9147. ^{R}REJ 157/1-2 (1998) 249-250 (*Laplanche, François*).

8870 **Krassen, Miles** Uniter of heaven and earth: Rabbi Meshullam Feibush HELLER of Zbarazh and the rise of Hasidism in eastern Galicia. SUNY Series in Judaica: Hermeneutics, Mysticism and Religion: Albany, NY 1998, SUNY Pr. 309 pp. 0-7914-3818-X. Bibl.

8871 ^{E}**Leoni, Daniela** Maestri del chassidismo: JAKOV JOSEF di Polonnoje; ELIMELECH di Lizensk. R 1997, Città N 300 pp. L38.000. ^{R}CivCatt 149/3 (1998) 315-317 (*Prato, G.L.*).

8872 **Merkley, Paul Charles** The politics of Christian Zionism, 1891-1948. L 1998, Cass x; 223 pp. 0-7146-48507. Bibl.

8873 *Sarna, Jonathan D.* A forgotten 19th-century prayer for the United States government: its meaning, significance, and surprising author. ^{F}FRERICHS, E. BJSt 320: 1998 ⇒28. 431-440.

8874 **Wiskind-Elper, Ora** Tradition and fantasy in the tales of Reb NAHMAN of Bratslav. SUNY Series in Judaica: Hermeneutics, Mysticism and Religion: Albany 1998, SUNY Pr. ix; 310 pp. 0-7914-3813-9. Bibl.

K7.8 Judaismus contemporaneus

8875 **Adler, Rachel** Engendering Judaism: an inclusive theology and ethics. Ph 1998, Jewish xxviii; 269 pp. $35. 0-8276-0584-6 [ThD 46, 255—Heiser, W. Charles].

8876 **Avînerî, Selomo** Profile des Zionismus: die geistigen Ursprünge des Staates Israel: 17 Porträts. Gü 1998, Mohn 256 pp. 3-579-02092-7.

8877 *Bernstein, Deborah S.* Daughters of the nation: between the public and private spheres in pre-state Israel. Jewish women. 1998 ⇒1076. 287-311.

8878   *Boccaccini, Gabriele* Middle Judaism and its contemporary interpreters (1993-1997): what makes any Judaism a Judaism?. Henoch 20 (1998) 349-356.

8879   *Bodenheimer, Alfred* Offenbarung und Moderne: zu den Schriften von Rabbiner Leo ADLER. Jud. 54 (1998) 180-187.

8881   **Breslauer, S. Daniel** Toward a Jewish (m)orality: speaking of a postmodern Jewish ethics. CSRel 53: Westport, CONN 1998, Greenwood xi (2) 167 pp. 0-313-30603-6. Bibl.

8881   *Friedman, R.Z.* FREUD's religion: Oedipus and Moses. RelSt 34 (1998) 135-149.

8882   *Galchinsky, Michael* Engendering liberal Jews: Jewish women in Victorian England. Jewish women. 1998 ⇒1076. 208-226.

8883   *Garber, Zev* Know Sodom, know Shoah. ᶠCARGAS H. 1998 ⇒19. 83-98.

8884   **Halivni, David Weiss** Revelation restored: divine writ and critical responses. Boulder 1997, Westview 144 pp. $20/£12.50.

8885   *Hertz, Deborah* Emancipation through intermarriage?: wealthy Jewish salon women in old Berlin;

8886   *Hyman, Paula E.* East European Jewish women in an age of transition, 1880-1930;

8887   Gender and the immigrant: Jewish experience in the United States;

8888   *Kaplan, Marion A.* Tradition and transition: Jewish women in imperial Germany. Jewish women. 1998 ⇒1076. 193-207/270-286/312-336/227-247.

8889   **Klein, Michele** A time to be born: customs and folklore of Jewish birth. Ph 1998, Jewish Publication Society of America xxxi; 336 pp. 0-8276-0608-7. Bibl.

8890   *Kreß, Hartmut* Bildung und Menschenbild im neuzeitlichen Judentum am Beispiel von Moses MENDELSSOHN und Martin BUBER. Ev Erz 50 (1998) 311-320.

8891   *Levinson, Pnina Navè* Lehrerinnen der Tradition. EvErz 50 (1998) 272-282.

8892   *Liron, Hannah* Im Spannungsfeld zwischen westlichem und orientalischem Judentum: drei Werke israelischer Autoren. Jud. 54 (1998) 56-65.

8893   *Malino, Frances* The women teachers of the Alliance Israélite Universelle, 1872-1940. Jewish women. 1998 ⇒1076. 248-269.

8894   ᴱ**Manekin, Charles H.** Freedom and moral responsibility: general and Jewish perspectives. Studies and texts in Jewish history and culture 2: [Bethesda, MD] 1997, Univ. Press of Maryland viii; 273 pp. 1-883053-293.

8895   *Millard, Matthias* Bibelinterpretation nach der Shoa: Einführung zum dritten Teil. Bibel und Midrasch. FAT 22: 1998 ⇒8766. 231-233.

8896   *Morgenstern, Matthias* Die Heimkehr des Enkels: Isaac BREUER und sein umstrittenes Erbe. Jud. 54 (1998) 165-179.

8897   *Moses, A.D.* Structure and agency in the Holocaust: Daniel J. GOLDHAGEN and his critics. HTh 37 (1998) 194-219.

8898   *Oberhänsli-Widmer, Gabrielle* Die Optik der Übersetzerin ein Gespräch mit Ruth Achlama;

8899   Gottesbilder in säkularer Holocaust-Literatur: Theologien der Schoa und Aharon APPELFELDs Die Eismine. Jud. 54 (1998) 66-76/231-46.

8900   **Petuchowski, Jakob J.** Wie Juden beten. GTBS 718: Gü 1998, Gü'er 124 pp. 3-579-00718-1.

8901 *Schröder, Bernd* Elieser SCHWEID: Judentum als Kultur: eine moderne israelische Selbstdefinition und ihre (religions-) pädagogischen Implikationen: eine Skizze. Jud. 54 (1998) 201-213;
8902 Jüdisches lernen und jüdisches Lernen—ein Beispiel aus dem gegenwärtigen Israel. EvErz 50 (1998) 290-297.
8903 *Schulte, Christoph* Erpresste Vergebung: Absolution für den Kommandanten von Auschwitz?. Jud. 54 (1998) 261-267.
8904 **Seidler, Meir** Schma Jisrael: Einheit—die jüdische Sicht. Eichenau 1998, Kovar 142 pp.
8905 *Shaked, Gershon* Die konservative Revolution der jungen israelischen Dichter: Tendenzen der achtziger und neunziger Jahre. Jud. 54 (1998) 36-55.
8906 [T]**Sierra, Sergio Josef; Bekhor, Shlomo** Siyach Yitzchàk: libro di preghiere di rito sefardita completo. Mi 1998, DLI 940 pp. 88-86674-06-6.
8907 *Tophoven, Irmgard* Israel in der Zerreißprobe?: Staat und Gesellschaft unter dem Druck der Orthodoxie. rhs 41 (1998) 163-172.
8908 *Umansky, Ellen M.* Spiritual expressions: Jewish women's religious lives in the United States in the nineteenth and twentieth centuries. Jewish women. 1998 ⇒1076. 337-363.
8909 *Weissler, Chava* Prayers in Yiddish and the religious world of Ashkenazic women. 1998 ⇒1076. 169-192.
8910 *Zimmermann, Heidy* Gedichte von Yehuda Amichai: Hebräisch in deutscher Erstübersetzung. Jud. 54 (1998) 21-35;
8911 Lieder über Krieg und Frieden: zur Lyrik von Yehuda Amichai. Jud. 54 (1998) 5-20.

K8 *Philosemitismus*—Jewish Christian relations

8912 **Abrams, Judith Z.** Judaism and disability: portrayals in ancient texts from the Tanach through the Bavli. Wsh 1998, Gallaudet University Press xi; 236 pp. $50. 1-56368-068-8.
8913 **Abulafia, Anna Sapir** Christians and Jews in dispute: disputational literature and the rise of anti-Judaism in the West (c. 1000-1150). CStS 621: Aldershot 1998, Variorum xvi; 310 pp. $90. 086078-6617.
8914 *Anderson, Bernhard W.* Einleitung. Christentum aus jüdischer Sicht. VIKJ 25: 1998 ⇒9026. 245-249.
8915 *Avril, Anne; Lenhardt, Pierre* Trois chemins: Emmaüs, Gaza et Damas. Cahiers Ratisbonne 5 (1998) 11-56 Riass., sum. 56.
8916 *Baeck, Leo* Geheimnis und Gebot (1921/22);
8917 HARNACKs Vorlesungen über das Wesen des Christentums (1901);
8918 Judentum in der Kirche (1925);
8919 Romantische Religion (1922, 1938). Christentum aus jüdischer Sicht. VIKJ 25: 1998 ⇒9026. 59-68/55-58/104-120/69-103.
8920 *Baltrusch, Ernst* Die Christianisierung des Römischen Reiches: eine Zäsur in der Geschichte des Judentums?. HZ 266 (1998) 23-46.
8921 [E]**Baumann, Arnulf H.** Auf dem Wege zum christlich-jüdischen Gespräch: 125 Jahre Evangelisch-lutherischer Zentralverein für Zeugnis und Dienst unter Juden und Christen. Münsteraner Judaistische Studien 1: Müns 1998, LIT 231 pp. 3-8258-3688-6.
8922 *Baumann, Arnulf H.* Der Zentralverein heute: zur heutigen Position des Ev.-Luth. Zentralvereins für Zeugnis und Dienst unter Juden und

Christen e. V. Internationales Josephus-Kolloquium. 1998 ⇒490. 218-220.
8923 *Becker, Thorsten* 'Das ist doch ein sehr westliches Thema': Antijuda-ismus in der Christenlehre in der DDR. [F]MARQUARDT, F.-W. 1998 ⇒72. 125-139.
8924 **Beck, Norman A.** Mündiges Christentum im 21. Jahrhundert: die antijüdische Polemik des Neuen Testaments und ihre Überwindung. VIKJ 26: B 1998, [Institut Kirche und Judentum] xiv; 448 pp. 3-923095-28-7. Bibl.
8925 *Berger, Joel* Für unser Selbstverständnis benötigen wir die Christen und ihre Kirche nicht. FrRu 4 (1998) 263-265.
8926 *Bethmann, Andreas* 'Der jud ist unseres hergots als wol als ich': Jo-hannes REUCHLINs Einstellung zu den Juden im 'Gutachten über das jüdische Schrifttum' (1511). [F]MARQUARDT, F.-W. 1998 ⇒72. 53-76.
8927 **Blanchetière, François** Aux sources de l'anti-judaïsme chrétien: IIe-IIIe siècles. 1995 ⇒11/2,7584. [R]RSR 86 (1998) 612-613 (*Beaude, Pierre-Marie*).
8928 *Blanchetière, François* The threefold christian anti-Judaism. Tolerance. 1998 ⇒440. 185-210.
8929 *Bodendorfer, Gerhard* Die Schuld der Christen am Holocaust: zu den Dokumenten der katholischen Kirche nach dem Zweiten Vatikanum;
8930 Wie kam es zur Judenvernichtung in Deutschland und Österreich?: ein Bericht über drei Neuerscheinungen;
8931 *Bodendorfer-Langer, Gerhard* "Ent-Schuldigung" statt Schuldbe-kenntnis: eine Stellungnahme zum vatikanischen Dokument "Wir ge-denken: eine Reflexion über die Shoa". BiLi 71 (1998) 10-24/25-29/146-151.
8932 *Borowski, Irwin J.* Introduction: removing the anti-Judaism from the New Testament. Removing the anti-Judaism. 1998 ⇒249. 9-20.
8933 [E]**Bosco, Nynfa** Ebraismo, cristianesimo e antisemitismo in Russia. Biblioteca di filosofia e teologia, Testi 3: N 1998, Scientifiche Italiane 124 pp. 88-8114-595-2.
8934 *Boys, Mary C.* Beyond 'removing' anti-Judaism: the theological and educational task of reframing christian identity. Removing the anti-Judaism. 1998 ⇒249. 88-102.
8935 *Braun, Thomas* The Jews in the late Roman empire. SCI 17 (1998) 142-171.
8936 *Buber, Martin* Die Brennpunkte der jüdischen Seele (1930): (Rede auf einer von den vier Judenmissionsgesellschaften deutscher Zunge einberufenen Studientagung in Stuttgart im März 1930);
8937 Kirche, Staat, Volk, Judentum (1933): aus einem Zwiegespräch mit Karl Ludwig Schmidt im Jüdischen Lehrhaus in Stuttgart (14. Januar 1933);
8938 Zum Abschluß (1961);
8939 Zwei Glaubensweisen (1950). Christentum aus jüdischer Sicht. VIKJ 25: 1998 ⇒9026. 134-142/143-153/165-166/154-164.
8940 [ET]**Bunte, Wolfgang** Anonymus: tractatus adversus Judaeum (1122). 1993 ⇒9,10961; 11/2,7591. [R]CCMéd 41 (1998) 184-185 (*Schrek-kenberg, Heinz*).
8941 *Burke, David G.* Translating 'the Jews' (*hoi Ioudaioi*) in the New Testament: comparing the pertinent passages in recent English ver-sions. Removing the anti-Judaism. 1998 ⇒249. 63-87.

8942 *Cabanel, Patrick* Procès de Jésus: procès des juifs au XIXe siècle: quelques réflexions d'un historien. Procès de Jésus. 1998 ⇒392. 179-191.

8943 *Capelli, Piero* Ebrei e cristiani dall'epoca di Gesù al 1000. Sette e Religioni 8/1 (1998) 5-51.

8944 **Carmichael, Joel** The satanizing of the Jews: origin and development of mystical anti-Semitism. 1992 ⇒9,10963. ^{R}Jdm 47 (1998) 376-377 (*Nicholls, William*).

8945 *Casper, Bernhard* Einleitung. Christentum aus jüdischer Sicht. VIKJ 25: 1998 ⇒9026. 169-177.

8946 **Comeau, Geneviève** Catholicisme et judaïsme dans la modernité: une comparaison. Cogitatio fidei 210: P 1998, Cerf 350 pp. 2-204-06058-5. Bibl.

8947 *Cunningham, Philip A.* Jews and Judaism in Catholic religious textbooks: progress, problems, and recommendations. Removing the anti-Judaism. 1998 ⇒249. 134-142.

8948 **Dahan, Gilbert** La polémique chrétienne contre le judaïsme au moyen âge. 1991 ⇒8,a723; 9,10973. ^{R}CCMéd 41 (1998) 190-191 (*Schreckenberg, Heinz*);

8949 The christian polemic against the Jews in the Middle Ages. ^{T}*Gladding, Jody*. ND 1998, Univ. of Notre Dame xii; 130 pp. $8 [TS 60, 579s—McMichael, Steven J.].

8950 *Doetzel, Audrey* Law and love in Judaism and christianity: the teaching ministries and christian conversion. Removing the anti-Judaism. 1998 ⇒249. 103-133.

8951 *Dutheil, Jacques* Procès de Jésus, procès des juifs. Procès de Jésus. 1998 ⇒392. 203-210.

8952 *Ehrlich, Ernst Ludwig* Stellungnahme zur Ansprache Johannes Paul II vor der Vollversammlung der Päpstlichen Bibelkommission. FrRu NF 5 (1998) 70-71.

8953 *Etchegaray, Roger* Est-ce que le christianisme a besoin du judaïsme?. Cahiers Ratisbonne 3 (1997) 9-17 Riass., sum. 17.

8954 ^{T}**Formentín Ibáñez, J.** Jaime PÉREZ de Valencia: tratado contra los judíos. Polémica judeocristiana: M 1998, Aben Ezra xliv; 352 pp. [BAEO 35,382—Sen, Felipe].

8955 *Frankemölle, Hubert* Jüdisch-christlicher Dialog: interreligiöse und innerchristliche Aspekte <1992>;

8956 Die 'Kirche Gottes in Christus': zum Verhältnis von Christentum und Judentum als Anfrage an christliches Selbstverständnis <1995>;

8957 Die Entstehung des Christentums aus dem Judentum: historische, theologische und hermeneutische Aspekte <1992>. Jüdische Wurzeln. BBB 116: 1998 ⇒151. 407-430/431-444/11-43.

8958 *Gargano, Innocenzo* Le relazioni ebraico-cristiane come compito fondamentale *nel* e *per* l'ecumenismo. VM 52 (1998) 7-14.

8959 *Geller, Barbara* Transitions and trajectories: Jews and christians in the Roman Empire. The Oxford history. 1998 ⇒326. 561-596.

8960 *Goldberg, Louis* Historical and political factors in the twentieth century affecting the identity of Israel. Israel. 1998 ⇒6675. 113-141.

8961 **Goldmann, Manuel** 'Die große ökumenische Frage...': zur Strukturverschiedenheit christlicher und jüdischer Tradition und ihrer Relevanz für die Begegnung der Kirche mit Israel. 1997 ⇒13,9218. ^{R}FrRu 4 (1998) 297-298 (*Mayer, Reinhold*).

8962 **Gow, Andrew Colin** The red Jews: antisemitism in an apocalyptic age 1200-1600. SMRT 55: Lei 1995, Brill 420 pp. $134.50. 90-04-10255-8. [R]HZ 266/2 (1998) 488-489 *(Schmieder, Felicitas)*.

8963 *Graetz, Michael* Les lectures juives de Jésus au 19e siècle. Jésus de Nazareth. 1998 ⇒253. 489-499.

8964 *Groppe, Lothar* Pinchas E. LAPIDE, Rom und die Juden. Theologisches 28 (1998) 94-99.

8965 *Harrington, Daniel J.* Is the New Testament anti-Jewish?: the need to develop a sense of history. IThQ 63 (1998) 123-132.

8966 **Harvey, Graham** The true Israel: uses of the names Jew, Hebrew and Israel in ancient Jewish and early Christian literature. AGJU 35: 1996 ⇒12,8659; 13,9219. [R]CBQ 60 (1998) 331-332 *(Bernas, Casimir)*; JBL 117 (1998) 529-531 *(Barclay, John M.G.)*.

8967 *Haverkamp, Alfred* "Concivilitas" von Christen und Juden in Aschkenas im Mittelalter. Jüdische Gemeinden. 1998 ⇒8688. 103-136.

8968 *Herberg, Will* Ein Jude sieht auf Jesus <1966>;

8969 Judentum und Christentum—ihre Einheit und Verschiedenheit <1952>;

8970 *Heschel, Abraham Joshua* Erneuerung des Protestantismus: eine jüdische Stimme <1963>;

8971 Eine hebräische Würdigung Reinhold NIEBUHRs <1956>;

8972 Jüdischer Gottesbegriff und die Erneuerung des Christentums <1967>;

8973 Keine Religion ist ein Eiland <1965>;

8974 Mehr als Innerlichkeit <1955>. Christentum aus jüdischer Sicht. VIKJ 25: 1998 ⇒9026. 268-275/250-267/315-323/296-314/342-358/324-341/291-295.

8975 *Heschel, Susannah* Redemptive anti-Semitism: the de-Judaization of the New Testament in the Third Reich. [F]TYSON J. 1998 ⇒120. 235-263.

8976 *Hoehner, Harold W.* Israel in Romans 9-11. Israel. 1998 ⇒6675. 145-167.

8977 *Hoffmann-Axthelm, Dagmar* Die Judenchöre in Bachs Johannes-Passion: der Thomaskantor als Gestalter lutherischer Judenpolemik. FrRu NF 5 (1998) 103-111.

8978 **Horbury, William** Jews and christians: in contact and controversy. E 1998, Clark viii; 342 pp. £28. 0-567-08590-2. Bibl. [R]JJS 49 (1998) 357-358 *(Edwards, M.J.)*.

8979 *House, H. Wayne* The church's appropriation of Israel's blessings. Israel. 1998 ⇒6675. 77-110.

8980 [T]**Iritano, Massimo** JOACHIM de Flore: agli ebrei. Soveria Mannelli (Catanzaro) 1998, Rubbettino 245 pp. 88-7284-600-5. Traduzione, introduzione e note; Testo latino a fronte; Pres. di *Bruno Forte*.

8981 *Jansen, Reiner* "Wünscht Jerusalem Frieden": christliche Einstellungen zu Juden und Judentum am Beispiel von Jerusalem. Jud. 54 (1998) 214-230.

8982 JOHANNES PAUL II Ansprache 31.10.1997. FrRu 5 NF (1998) 85-87. Tagung Vatikan 30.10-1.11.1997: Die Wurzeln des Antijudaismus im christlichen Bereich.

8983 *Kampling, Rainer* Zur Polemik der Bilder: Motive des kirchlichen Antijudaismus und ihre Rezeption in der bildenden Kunst des Mittelalters. Religiöse Sprache. 1998 ⇒1144. 225-243.

8984 *Kee, Howard Clark* The issue: historical setting and contemporary methods for dealing with anti-Judaism in christianity. Removing the anti-Judaism. 1998 ⇒249. 21-29.

8985 **Keith, Graham** Hated without cause: a survey of anti-semitism. 1997 ⇒13,9224. [R]Studies in World Christianity 4/1 (1998) 114-117 (*Hayman, A.P.*); CTJ 33 (1998) 541-544 (*Madany, Bassam M.*).

8986 *Koelle, Lydia* "...die Wurzel trägt dich": systematische Theologie in Israels Gegenwart. Fundamentaltheologie: Fluchtlinien und gegenwärtige. [E]Müller, Klaus. Rg 1998, Pustet. 3-7917-1589-5. 369-387.

8987 **Krauss, Samuel** History. The Jewish-Christian controversy from the earliest times to 1789, 1. TSAJ 56: 1996 ⇒12,8668; 13,9230. [R]Pacifica 11/2 (1998) 217-218 (*Sim, David C.*); FJB 25 (1998) 174-175 (*Trautner-Kromann, Hanne*).

8988 [E]**Kraus, Wolfgang** Christen und Juden: Perspektiven einer Annäherung. 1997 ⇒13,212. [R]GuL 71 (1998) 237-238 (*Frammelsberger, Karin*).

8989 *Kriener, Katja* Sola scriptura im Horizont eines jüdisch-christlichen Gesprächs. [F]SCHRAGE, W. 1998 ⇒101. 33-42.

8990 **Laato, Anni Maria** Jews and christians in De duobus montibus Sina et Sion: an approach to early Latin Adversus Iudaeos literature. Abo 1998, Akademi Univ. Pr. 232 pp. [D]Abo [JEarlyC 7,621s—Kraus, J.].

8991 *Larsen, David L.* A celebration of the Lord our God's role in the future of Israel. Israel. 1998 ⇒6675. 301-323.

8992 **Lieu, Judith M.** Image and reality: the Jews in the world of the christians in the second century. 1996 ⇒12,8673. [R]JEarlyC 6 (1998) 681-682 (*Efroymson, David P.*); Theol. 101 (1998) 59 (*Gould, Graham*).

8993 [E]**Limor, Ora; Stroumsa, Guy G.** Contra Iudaeos: ancient and medieval polemics between christians and Jews. TSMJ 10: 1996 ⇒12, 8676. [R]DA 54 (1998) 417-418 (*Steiner, Hannes*).

8994 Lire l'Ancien Testament (contribution à une lecture catholique de l'Ancien Testament pour permettre le dialogue entre Juifs et chrétiens). FV 97/1 (1998) 87-102. Comité Épiscopale Français pour les Relations avec le Judaïsme.

8995 *Lustiger, J.-M.* Juifs et chrétiens, demain?. NRTh 120 (1998) 529-543.

8996 **Maccoby, Hyam** A pariah people: the anthropology of antisemitism. 1996 ⇒12,8679. [R]Jdm 47 (1998) 373-376 (*Nicholls, William*).

8997 **Manns, Frédéric** Une approche juive du Nouveau Testament. Initiations bibliques: P 1998, Cerf 298 pp. FF195. 2-204-05811-4. [R]LASBF 48 (1998) 610-611 (*Chrupcała, Lesław Daniel*).

8998 [E]**Marguerat, Daniel** Le déchirement: Juifs et chrétiens au premier siècle. MoBi 32: 1996 ⇒12,192; 13,9236. [R]RSR 86 (1998) 608-612 (*Beaude, Pierre-Marie*).

8999 *Martyn, J. Louis* Einleitung. Christentum aus jüdischer Sicht. VIKJ 25: 1998 ⇒9026. 33-54.

9000 *Masset, Pierre* Judaïsme et christianisme: "l'étoile de la rédemption" de Franz ROSENZWEIG. NRTh 120 (1998) 384-403.

9001 *Merkle, John C.* Einleitung. Christentum aus jüdischer Sicht. VIKJ 25: 1998 ⇒9026. 279-290.

9002 **Mimouni, Simon Claude** Le judéo-christianisme ancien: essais historiques. Préf. *A. Caquot.* Patrimoines: P 1998, Cerf (6) ii; 547 pp. FF300. 2-2040-59374. Bibl. [R]POC 48 (1998) 440-442 (*Attinger, D.*).

9003   **Montefiore, Hugh W.** On being a Jewish christian: its blessings and its problems. L 1998, Hodder & S x; 195 pp. 0-340-71377-1. Bibl.
9004   *Murray, Robert* Hebrew Bible, Jewish Scriptures, Christian Old Testament. Month 31 (1998) 468-474.
9005   *Mußner, Franz* Die Schoa und der Jude Jesus: Versuch einer Christologie nach Auschwitz. FrRu 4 (1998) 272-278.
9006   *Neusner, Jacob* Judaism and christianity in the beginning: time for a category-reformation?. BBR 8 (1998) 229-237.
9007   **Neusner, Jacob; Chilton, Bruce** The intellectual foundations of christian and Jewish discourse; the philosophy of religious argument. 1997 ⇒13,9250. ^{R}RelSt 34 (1998) 354-356 (*Leaman, Oliver*);
9008   Jewish-Christian debates: God, kingdom, Messiah. Ph 1998, Fortress xiv; 240 pp. £16. 0-8006-3109-9.
9009   *Paszta, Zbigniew* Chrzéscijaństwo i judaizm: porozumienie i jego trudności. CoTh 68/2 (1998) 41-57. **P.**
9010 ^{E}**Pohl, Walter** Strategies of distinction: the construction of ethnic communities, 300-800. Collab. *Reimitz, Helmut.* Transformation of the Roman World 2: Lei 1998, Brill vii; 347 pp. 90-04-10846-7. Bibl.
9011   *Poli, Eliseo* Ebrei e cristiani dalle crociate al primo novecento;
9012   Le radici cristiane dell'antigiudaismo;
9013   *Ragazzi, Cesare* Ebrei e cristiani negli anni della svolta. Sette e Religioni 8/1 (1998) 52-117/162-171/118-161.
9014   *Rampin, Gianpietro; Remondi, Giordano* Il dialogo ebraico-cristiano a Camaldoli (1890-1992): caratteristiche e prospettive. VM 52 (1998) 61-177.
9015   *Rapse, Lucia* MANETHO on the Exodus: a reappraisal. JSQ 5 (1998) 124-155.
9016   *Remondi, Giordano* Indice dei numeri riguardanti il 'Colloquio ebraico-cristiano' di Camaldoli. VM 52 (1998) 53-60.
9017   **Rendtorff, Rolf** Christen und Juden heute: neue Einsichten und neue Aufgaben. Neuk 1998, Neuk 154 pp [FrRu 7,306].
9018   *Rogers, Eugene F.* Supplementing BARTH on Jews and gender: identifying God by anagogy and the spirit. MoTh 14 (1998) 43-81.
9019   *Romig, Friedrich* Kirche und Shoah. Theologisches 28 (1998) 256-258.
9020   *Rosenzweig, Franz* Eine Anmerkung zum Anthropomorphismus <1928>;
9021   Auswahl aus den Briefen;
9022   Der Stern der Erlösung <1921>;
9023   Weltgeschichtliche Bedeutung der Bibel <1929>. Christentum aus jüdischer Sicht. VIKJ 25: 1998 ⇒9026. 237-238/179-195/196-236/ 239-242.
9024   **Rossi De Gasperis, Francesco** Cominciando da Gerusalemme (Lc 24,47): la sorgente della fede e dell'esistenza cristiana. 1997 ⇒13, 7449. ^{R}Studi Fatti Ricerche 84 (1998) 11-12 (*Geroldi, Cesare*); ZKTh 120 (1998) 203-205 (*Fischer, Georg*).
9025 ^{E}**Rothschild, Fritz A.** Jewish perspectives on christianity. 1996 ⇒12,8696. ^{R}RRT (1998/2) 36-38 (*Wollaston, Isabel*);
9026   Christentum aus jüdischer Sicht: fünf jüdische Denker des 20. Jahrhunderts über das Christentum und sein Verhältnis zum Judentum. VIKJ 25: B 1998, Inst. Kirche und Judentum 380 pp. 3-923095-27-9.
9027   *Rothschild, Fritz A.* Einführung ⇒9026. 11-29.

9028 *Rutgers, Leonard V.* The importance of scripture in the conflict between Jews and christians: the example of Antioch. Use of sacred books. 1998 ⇒263. 287-303.

9029 *Saldarini, Anthony J.* How do we understand early Jews and christians?: the changing paradigm. Removing the anti-Judaism. 1998 ⇒249. 30-42;

9030 The social world of christian Jews and Jewish christians. Studies... in Jewish history. 1998 ⇒347. 115-154.

9031 **Sanders, Jack T.** Schismatics, sectarians, dissidents, deviants: the first one hundred years of Jewish-Christian relations. 1993 ⇒9,11073 ...12,8697. ^RBBR 8 (1998) 229-232 (*Neusner, Jacob*).

9032 *Sanders, James A.* The hermeneutics of translation. Removing the anti-Judaism. 1998 ⇒249. 43-62.

9033 *Sauter, Gerhard* Hoffen mit Israel?. ^FSCHRAGE W. 1998 ⇒101. 349-360.

9034 *Savage, Dorothy* Jews and Judaism in Protestant/christian curriculum. Removing the anti-Judaism. 1998 ⇒249. 157-162.

9035 **Schoon, Simon** Onopgeefbaar verbonden: op weg naar vernieuwing in de verhouding tussen de kerk en het volk Israël. Kampen 1998, Kok 270 pp. ƒ40. 90-242-9402-9 [ITBT 7/4,33—Evers, L.].

9036 **Schreckenberg, Heinz** Die christlichen Adversus-Judaeos-Texte und ihr literarisches und historisches Umfeld. EHS.T 172: 1991-1995 ⇒ 7,a221... 13,9268. ^RCrSt 19 (1998) 658-660 (*Todeschini, Giacomo*);

9037 Die Juden in der Kunst Europas: ein historischer und theologischer Bildatlas. 1996 ⇒12,8701; 13,9270. ^RCrSt 19 (1998) 558-560 (*Todeschini, Giacomo*); FrRu NF 5 (1998) 131-133 (*Trutwin, Werner*).

9038 *Schubert, Kurt* Drei Tage im Vatikan—ein Anlaß zum Nachdenken;

9039 Judenhaß—Schuld der Christen?!;

9040 Pastorales Schreiben, nicht umfassende historische Darstellung";

9041 Stellungnahme zu kritischen Stellungnahmen zur Shoah-Erklärung des Vatikans. BiLi 71 (1998) 30-32/2-9/144-146/152-153.

9042 **Shain, Milton** Antisemitism. L 1998, Bowerdean. ^RJdm 47 (1998) 377-378 (*Nicholls, William*).

9043 *Soulen, R. Kendall* Removing anti-Judaism. Removing the anti-Judaism. 1998 ⇒249. 149-156.

9044 *Stegemann, Ekkehard* Einleitung. Christentum aus jüdischer Sicht. VIKJ 25: 1998 ⇒9026. 123-133.

9045 **Steiman, Lionel Bradley** Paths to genocide: antisemitism in Western history. L 1998, Macmillan xv; 284 pp. 0-333-71667-1. Bibl.

9046 Stellungnahmen zu "Wir gedenken". BiLi 71 (1998) 268-270.

9047 *Stemberger, Günter* Jewish-christian contacts in Galilee (fifth to seventh centuries). Sharing the sacred. 1998 ⇒306. 131-146.

9048 *Steymans, Hans Ulrich* Zu den jüdischen Wurzeln des Christentums. Edith Stein Jahrbuch 4 (1998) 121-133.

9049 *Thoma, Clemens* Das Einrenken des Ausgerenkten: Beurteilung der jüdisch-christlichen Dialog-Geschichte seit dem Ende des Zweiten Weltkrieges. Bulletin der Schweizerischen Gesellschaft für Judaistische Forschung 7 (1998) 2-16;

9050 Jésus dans la polémique juive de l'antiquité tardive et du Moyen-Âge. Jésus de Nazareth. 1998 ⇒253. 477-487;

9051 Der Jude Jesus im Deutschen Reichstag 1904. FrRu 4 (1998) 241-245;

9052 Überlegungen zur Papstrede. FrRu 5 NF (1998) 81-84. Tagung Vatikan 30.10-1.11.1997: Die Wurzeln des Antijudaismus im christlichen Bereich ⇒8982.

9053 **Tomson, Peter J.** Als dit uit de hemel is...Jezus en de schrijvers van het Niuwe Testament in hun verhouding tot het jodendom. 1997 ⇒ 13,9284. ^RColl. 28/1 (1998) 107-108 (*Hoet, Hendrik*); JSJ 29 (1998) 114-116 (*Oegema, G.S.*).

9054 ^E**Van Loopik, M.** Tweespalt en verbondenheid: joden en christenen in historisch perspectief: joodse reacties op christelijke theologie. Sleutelteksten in godsdienst en theologie 23: Zoetermeer 1998, Meinema 202 pp. ƒ35. 90-211-6123-0 [GThT 98,137].

9055 **Walsh, George** The role of religion in history. New Brunswick, NJ 1998, Transaction viii; 196 pp. 1-5600-368-5.

9056 *Weber, Bernd* Übernahm und verbreitete die Kirche den Rassismus?: kritische Anmerkungen zu D.J. GOLDHAGEN. rhs 41 (1998) 186-201.

9057 *Wiese, Christian* "Nicht einschlafen lassen die Blitze der Trauer" (Nelly Sachs): die Bedeutung der jüdischen Theologie nach Auschwitz für christliches Gedenken an die Schoah. EvErz 50 (1998) 297-310.

9058 **Wilson, Stephen G.** Related strangers: Jews and christians 70-170 CE. 1995 ⇒11/2,7752... 13,9292. ^RLTP 54 (1998) 423-7 (*Poirier, Paul-Hubert*); BBR 8 (1998) 232-237 (*Neusner, Jacob*).

9059 **Wistrich, Robert S.** Antisemitism: the longest hatred. 1991 ⇒8, a798... 11/2,7753. ^RJdm 47 (1998) 371-373 (*Nicholls, William*).

9060 **Wohlmuth, Josef** Im Geheimnis einander nahe: theologische Aufsätze zum Verhältnis von Judentum und Christentum. 1996 ⇒12, 8715. ^RIst. 43 (1998) 350-352 (*Dupuy, B.*); FrRu 5 NF (1998) 38-41 (*Strolz, Walter*).

9061 *Wojciechowski, Michal1* More about the anti-Jewish bias in the New Testament translations. CoTh 68A (1998) 83-88.

XVI. Religiones parabiblicae

M1.1 Gnosticismus classicus

9062 *Attridge, Harold W.* What gnostics knew. ^FFERGUSON, E. NT.S 90: 1998 ⇒25. 1-21.

9063 *Baum, Wolfgang* Forschungsprojekt des Instituts für katholische Theologie an der TU Dresden: "Die Institutionalisierung christlicher Überlieferung in Auseinandersetzung mit der Gnosis". MThZ 49 (1998) 155-157.

9064 *Cannuyer, Christian* Une introduction à la sotériologie des gnostiques. MSR 55/2 (1998) 7-31 Rés., sum. 7.

9065 *Garcia Cordero, Maximiliano* Interpretaciones "gnósticas" de la persona y mensaje de Jesús. CTom 125 (1998) 421-471.

9066 *Godwin, Joscelyn* STOCKHAUSEN's Donnerstag aus Licht and gnosticism;

9067 *Hanegraaff, Wouter J.* The New Age movement and the esoteric tradition;

9068 Romanticism and the esoteric connection. Gnosis and hermeticism. 1998 ⇒422. 347-358/359-382/237-268.

9069 *Lettieri, Gaetano* Lo gnosticismo: la sua essenza e le sue origini. Lat. 64 (1998) 629-648.
9070 **Logan, Alastair H.B.** Gnostic truth and christian heresy: a study in the history of Gnosticism. 1996 ⇒12,8720. ᴿCBQ 60 (1998) 574-576 (*Sheridan, Mark*); JBL 117 (1998) 166-168 (*King, Karen L.*).
9071 **Lüdemann, Gerd; Janssen, Martina** Suppressed prayers: Gnostic spirituality in early christianity. L 1998, SCM 174 pp. £15. 0-334-02716-0. Bibl.
9072 *Mahé, Jean-Pierre* Gnostic and hermetic ethics. Gnosis and hermeticism. 1998 ⇒422. 21-36.
9073 *Markschies, Christoph* KERINTH: wer war er und was lehrte er?. JAC 41 (1998) 48-76.
9074 **Roukema, Riemer** Gnosis & geloof in het vroege christendom: een inleiding tot de gnostiek. Zoetermeer 1998, Meinema 215 pp. *f*35. 90-211-3708-9 [ITBT 7/4,32—Parmentier, Martien].
9075 **Rudolph, Kurt** Gnosis und spätantike Religionsgeschichte: gesammelte Aufsätze. 1996 ⇒12,147. ᴿThLZ 123 (1998) 341-344 (*Lattke, Michael*); BiOr 55 (1998) 502-504 (*Helderman, J.*).
9076 *Scholer, David M.* Bibliographia gnostica: Supplementum II/1. NT 40 (1998) 73-100.
9077 *Stroumsa, Gedaliahu G.* Gnostische Gerechtigkeit und Antinomismus: Epiphanes' "Über die Gerechtigkeit" im Kontext. Gerechtigkeit. 1998 ⇒283. 149-161.
9078 *Turner, John D.* To see the light: a Gnostic appropriation of Jewish priestly practice and sapiential and apocalyptic visionary lore. Mediators of the divine. SFSHJ 163: 1998 ⇒287. 63-113.
9079 *Van den Broeck, Roelof* The Cathars: medieval gnostics?;
9080 Gnosticism and hermeticism in antiquity: two roads to salvation. Gnosis and hermeticism. 1998 ⇒422. 87-108/1-20.
9081 **Van den Broek, Roelof** Studies in Gnosticism and Alexandrian christianity. NHMS 39: 1996 ⇒12,8752. ᴿVigChr 52 (1998) 221-224 (*Van den Hoek, Annewies*).
9082 *Van Egmond, Daniel* Western esoteric schools in the late nineteenth and early twentieth centuries;
9083 *Voss, Karen-Claire* Spiritual alchemy: interpreting representative texts and images. Gnosis and hermeticism. 1998 ⇒422. 311-346/147-181.
9084 **Williams, Michael Allen** Rethinking 'Gnosticism': an argument for dismantling a dubious category. 1996 ⇒12,8754. ᴿJEarlyC 6 (1998) 684-685 (*Smith, Carl B.*).
9085 *Zyla, Roy T.* Divine providence in Sethian Gnosticism. SBL.SP part 1. SBL.SPS 37: 1998 ⇒402. 125-147.

M1.3 Valentinus; Corpus hermeticum; Orphismus

9086 **Bermejo Rubio, Fernando** La escisión imposible: Lectura del gnosticismo valentiniano. Plenitudo Temporis. Estudios sobre los orígenes y la antigüedad cristiana 5: S 1998, Publicaciones Universidad Pontificia 416 pp. PTA3.200. 84-7299-426-0. Bibl.
9087 *Betz, Hans Dieter* `Der Erde Kind bin ich und des gestirnten Himmels': zur Lehre vom Menschen in den orphischen Goldplättchen;

9088   Hermetism and Gnosticism: the question of the Poimandres. Gesammelte Aufsätze IV. 1998 ⇒134. 222-243/206-221.
9089   ᵀᴱColpe, Carsten; Holzhausen, Jens Das Corpus Hermeticum deutsch, 1: die griechischen Traktate und der lateinische 'Asclepius', 2: Exzerpte, Nag-Hammadi-Texte, Testimonien.˙ Clavis Pansophiae 7: Stu 1997, xiii; 316 + viii; 317-665 pp. 3-7728-1530-8/1-6. Frommann Übersetzung, Darstellung, Kommentierung in drei Teilen; im Auftrag der Heidelberger Akademie der Wissenschaften. ᴿThLZ 123 (1998) 134-136 (Schenke, Hans-Martin).
9090   Edighoffer, Roland Hermeticism in early Rosicrucianism;
9091   Faivre, Antoine Renaissance hermeticism and the concept of western esotericism;
9092   Godwin, Joscelyn Music and the hermetic tradition. Gnosis and hermeticism. 1998 ⇒422. 197-215/109-123/183-196.
9093   Griffiths, J. Gwyn 'Eternal torment' in the Hermetic Asclepius. Jerusalem studies. ÄAT 40: 1998 ⇒361. 45-55.
9094   Hanegraaff, Wouter J. Romanticism and the esoteric connection;
9095   Leijenhorst, Cees Francesco PATRIZI's hermetic philosophy. Gnosis and hermeticism. 1998 ⇒422. 237-268/125-146.
9096   Löhr, Gebhard Verherrlichung Gottes durch Philosophie: der hermetische Traktat II im Rahmen der antiken Philosophie- und Religionsgeschichte. WUNT 2/97: 1997 ⇒13,9312. ᴿJAC 41 (1998) 224-226 (Wilson, R. McL.).
9097   Mazzanti, Angela Maria Gli uomini dèi mortali: una rilettura del Corpus Hermeticum. Origini n.s. 2: Bo 1998, EDB 122 pp. 88-10-20702-5. Bibl.
9098   Quispel, Gilles The Asclepius: from the hermetic lodge in Alexandria to the Greek eucharist and the Roman mass;
9099   Van Meurs, Jos William BLAKE and his gnostic myths;
9100   Versluis, Arthur Christian theosophic literature of the seventeenth and eighteenth centuries. Gnosis and hermeticism. 1998 ⇒422. 69-77/269-309/217-236.

M1.5 **Mani**, *dualismus*; **Mandaei**

9101   Cinal, Stanisław Les anges-prêtres dans les Šîrôt ʾôlat haš-šabbat de Qumrân (4Q400-407) et les 'utria dans le Dîwān Nahrawāṭa des Mandéens. ᴹKLAWEK A. 1998 ⇒51. 123-136.
9102   ᵀDemaria, Serena I capitoli LXIX e LXX dei Kephalaia copti manichei: traduzione e commento. Archeologia e storia della civiltà egiziana e del vicino Oriente antico. Materiali e studi 3: Imola (Bo) 1998, La mandragora xi; 118 pp. 88-86123-47-7. Bibl.
9103   Deutsch, Nathaniel The Gnostic imagination: Gnosticism, Mandaeism, and Merkabah mysticism. 1995 ⇒11/2,7814. ᴿJR 78 (1998) 307-308 (Spinner, Gregory).
9104   Heuser, Manfred The manichaean myth according to the Coptic sources. Studies in manichaean literature. NHMS 46: 1998 ⇒339. 1-108.
9105   Lieu, Samuel N.C. Manichaeism in Mesopotamia and the Roman east. Religions in the Graeco-Roman World 118: 1994, ⇒10,10190... 13,9340. ᴿVigChr 52 (1998) 112-113 (Van Oort, J.);
9106   Manichaeism in Central Asia and China. NHMS 45: Lei 1998, Brill xiii; 258 pp. 90-04-10405-4.

9107 *Philonenko, Marc* Jeux de signes hiéroglyphiques et spéculations tri-
nitaires dans le Psautier manichéen copte. ^FBERGMAN, J. 1998 ⇒9.
303-306.

9108 **Reeves, John C.** Jewish lore in Manichaean cosmogony: studies in
the book of Giants traditions. 1992 ⇒8,a842... 11/2,7826. ^RJNES 57
(1998) 50-51 (*Wasserstrom, Steven M.*).

9109 **Richter, Siegfried G.** Die Aufstiegspsalmen des Herakleides: Untersuchungen zum Seelenaufstieg und zur Seelenmesse bei den Ma-
nichäern. Sprachen und Kulturen des Christlichen Orients 1: Wsb
1997, Reichert 212 pp. 3-89500-056-6. Bibl.

9110 *Ries, Julien* Économie du salut et rôle des sauveurs selon les textes
manichéens occidentaux. MSR 55/2 (1998) 49-65 Rés., sum. 49.

9111 *Van Oort, Johannes* Manichaeism: its sources and influences on
western christianity. Gnosis and hermeticism. 1998 ⇒422. 37-51.

9112 *Van Tongerloo, Alois* Le salut et les sauveurs dans les documents manichéens orientaux. MSR 55/2 (1998) 69-79 Rés., sum. 69.

9113 ^E**Welburn, Andrew** Mani, the Angel and the Column of Glory: an
anthology of Manichaean texts. E 1998, Floris 296 pp. 0-86315-274-
0. Bibl.

9114 **Wurst, Gregor** Die Bêma-Psalmen. 1996 ⇒12,8782; 13,9351.
^ROLZ 93 (1998) 450-453 (*Plisch, Uwe-Karsten*); BiOr 55 (1998)
796-799 (*Oerter, Wolf B.*); JThS 49 (1998) 371-373 (*Kuhn, K.H.*);
VigChr 52 (1998) 109-111 (*Reck, Christiane*).

M2.1 Nag Hammadi, *generalia*

9115 **Franzmann, Majella M.** Jesus in the Nag Hammadi writings. 1996
⇒12,8784. ^RBiOr 55 (1998) 249-251 (*Myszor, Wincenty*); JR 78
(1998) 431-432 (*Williams, Michael A.*); OLZ 93 (1998) 666-674
(*Schröter, Jens*); CBQ 60 (1998) 564-565 (*Schoedel, William R.*);
JEarlyC 6 (1998) 151-152 (*Voelker, John*); JThS 49 (1998) 313-317
(*Wilson, R. McL.*); JBL 117 (1998) 544-546 (*Hedrick, Charles W.*).

9116 **Funk, Wolf-Peter** Concordance des textes de Nag Hammadi, les
codices VIII et IX. Bibliothèque copte de Nag Hammadi, Concordances 5: Lv 1997, Peeters xxxi; 607 pp. FB2.500. 90-6831-980-9.

9117 *García Bazán, Francisco* Dios Padre como Uno y Ser en los escritos
gnósticos de Nag Hammadi: en torno a la metafísica del Exodo, 3,14;

9118 *Moreno Garrido, Jaime* La metáfora de la cámara nupcial en los
escritos de Nag Hammadi. TyV 39 (1998) 325-344/364-376.

9119 *Myszor, Wincenty* Nag-Hammadi-Schriften nach literarischen Gattungen. Vox Patrum 34-35 (1998) 321-334 Zsfg. 334 **P**.

9120 ^E**Pearson, Birger A.** Nag Hammadi Codex VII. NHMS 30: 1996 ⇒
12,8786; 13,9363. ^RCBQ 60 (1998) 377-378 (*Wilfong, Terry G.*);
JAOS 118 (1998) 589-590 (*Denzey, Nicola*).

9121 ^E**Piñero, Antonio** Textos gnósticos. Paradigmas 14: 1997 ⇒13,
9365. ^RCDios 211 (1998) 659-660 (*Gutiérrez, J.*); StMon 40/1
(1998) 159-161 (*López García, A.*); Diadokhē 1 (1998) 159-168
(*Moreno, Jaime*).

9122 *Plisch, Uwe-Karsten* Textverständnis und Übersetzung: Bermerkun-
gen zur Gesamtübersetzung der Texte des Nag-Hammadi-Fundes
durch den Berliner Arbeitskreis für Koptisch-Gnostische Schriften.
HBO 26 (1998) 73-87.

9123 **Reeves, John C.** Heralds of the good realm: Syro-Mesopotamian Gnosis and Jewish traditions. NHMS 41: 1996 ⇒12,8787. [R]CBQ 60 (1998) 128-129 (*Basser, Herbert*); JEarlyC 6 (1998) 142-143 (*Bingham, D. Jeffrey*); JThS 49 (1998) 320-322 (*Stroumsa, Guy G.*).

9124 **Richter, Siegfried** Exegetisch-literarkritische Untersuchungen von Herakleidespsalmen des koptisch-manichäischen Psalmenbuches. 1994, ⇒10,10193...13,9367. [R]BiOr 55 (1998) 504-506 (*Smagina, Eugenia*)

9125 *Robinson, James M.* Nag Hammadi: the first fifty years. The fifth gospel. 1998 ⇒9140. 77-110.

9126 *Siegert, F.* Le vocabulaire grec des documents de Nag Hammadi. Études Coptes V. 1998 ⇒451. 175-180.

9127 [E]**Turner, John D.; McGuire, Anne** The Nag Hammadi library after fifty years. NHMS 44: 1997, Proceedings of the 1995 Society of Biblical Literature Commemoration ⇒13,341. [R]JEH 49 (1998) 705-707 (*Frend, W.H.C.*); ThLZ 123 (1998) 975-980 (*Schröter, Jens*).

M2.2 *Evangelium etc. Thomae*—**The Gospel of Thomas**

9128 **Patterson, Stephen J.; Robinson, James McConkey,** *al.*, The fifth gospel: the gospel of Thomas comes of age. Harrisburg, Pennsylvania 1998, Trinity 119 pp. $15. 1-5633-8249-0. Bibl.

9129 *Asgeirsson, Jon Ma.* Arguments and audience(s) in the Gospel of Thomas (Part II). SBL.SP part 1. SBL.SPS 37: 1998 ⇒402. 325-342.

9130 **Asgeirsson, Jon Ma.** Doublets and strata: towards a rhetorical approach to the Gospel of Thomas. [D]Claremont 1998, 236 pp.

9131 *Bethge, Hans-Gebhard, al.*, English translation [Thomasevangelium]. The fifth gospel. 1998 ⇒9128. 7-32;

9132 *Bethge, Hans-Gebhard* "Werdet Vorübergehende": zur Neubearbeitung des Thomasevangeliums für die Synopsis Quattuor Evangeliorum. Bericht der Hermann Kunst-Stiftung. 1998 ⇒1230. 42-52.

9133 *Bosson, Nathalie L'évangile selon Thomas*: le sacré et la question de la gnose d'après les logia utilisant explicitement les termes 'vie' et 'mort'. [E]**Marconot, Jean-Marie; Aufrère, Sydney H.** Montpellier 1998, Univ. Paul Valéry. Actes du Colloque Montpellier, le 20 mars 1998. 141-161 [BuBbgB 30,96].

9134 **De Conick, April D.** Seek to see him: ascent and vision mysticism in the gospel of Thomas. SVigChr 33: 1996 ⇒12,8792; 13,9376. [R]JBL 117 (1998) 758-760 (*Meyer, Marvin*).

9135 *Dunderberg, Ismo Thomas* and the beloved disciple;

9136 *Thomas'* I-sayings and the gospel of John. Thomas at the crossroads. 1998 ⇒273. 65-88/33-64 [BuBbgB 30,96].

9137 *Hartenstein, Judith; Petersen, Silke* Das Evangelium nach Thomas: frühchristliche Überlieferungen von Jüngerinnen Jesu oder: Maria Magdalena wird männlich. Kompendium Feministische Bibelauslegung. 1998 ⇒7511. 768-777.

9138 *Kaestli, Jean-Daniel* L'utilisation de l'*Évangile de Thomas* dans la recherche actuelle sur les paroles de Jésus. Jésus de Nazareth. 1998 ⇒253. 373-395 [BuBbgB 24,90].

9139 *Kuntzmann, Raymond* La conception gnostique du salut dans *Le livre de Thomas* (NH II,7). MSR 55/2 (1998) 33-46 Rés., sum. 33.

9140 *Luttikhuizen, Gerard* Vroege tradities over Jezus in een niet-canonieke bron: het Evangelie naar Tomas. TTh 38 (1998) 120-143.
9141 *Marjanen, Antti* Is *Thomas* a gnostic gospel?;
9142 *Thomas* and Jewish religious practices;
9143 Women disciples in the *Gospel of Thomas*. Thomas at the crossroads. 1998 ⇒273. 107-139/163-182/89-106 [BuBbgB 30,96].
9144 **Martin, Gerhard Marcel** Das Thomas-Evangelium: ein spiritueller Kommentar. Stu 1998, Radius 319 pp. 3-87173-160-9.
9145 *Meyer, Marvin* Seeing or coming to the child of the living one?: more on gospel of Thomas saying 37. HThR 91 (1998) 413-416.
9146 *Patterson, Stephen J.* Understanding the gospel of Thomas today. The fifth gospel. 1998 ⇒9128. 33-75.
9147 *Poirier, Paul-Hubert* Les Actes de Thomas et le Manichéisme. Apocrypha 9 (1998) 263-289.
9148 *Robbins, Vernon K.* Enthymemic texture in the Gospel of Thomas. SBL.SP part 2. SBL.SPS 37: 1998 ⇒402. 343-366.
9149 *Schenke, Hans-Martin* Das sogenannte "Unbekannte Berliner Evangelium" (UBE). ZAC 2 (1998) 199-213.
9150 *Sen, Felipe* El evangelio de Tomás. BAEO 34 (1998) 339-345.
9151 **Trevijano Etchevarria, R.** Estudios sobre el evangelio de Tomás. 1997 ⇒13,9389. ᴿEstAg 33 (1998) 174-176 (*Luis, P. de*); StPat 45 (1998) 527-528 (*Corsato, Celestino*).
9152 *Tuckett, Christopher M.* The gospel of Thomas: evidence for Jesus?. NedThT 52/1 (1998) 17-32.
9153 *Uro, Risto* Is *Thomas* an Encratite gospel? [BuBbgB 30,96];
9154 *Thomas* and oral gospel tradition. Thomas at the crossroads. 1998 ⇒273. 140-162/8-32 [BuBbgB 30,97].
9155 **Valantasis, Richard** The gospel of Thomas. 1997 ⇒13,9393. ᴿSVTQ 42 (1998) 412-416 (*Behr, John*).

M2.3 *Singula scripta*—**Various titles [⇒K3.4]**

9156 ᴱᵀ**Bethge, Hans-Gebhard** Der Brief des Petrus an Philippus: ein neutestamentliches Apokryphhon aus dem Fund von Nag Hammadi. TU 141: 1997 ⇒13,9397. ᴿJThS 49 (1998) 318-320 (*Wilson, R. McL.*)
9157 *Heldermann, Jan* A Christian gnostic text: the Gospel of Truth. Gnosis and hermeticism. 1998 ⇒422. 53-68.
9158 **King, Karen L.** Revelation of the unknowable God: a gnostic text from the Nag Hammadi library. Santa Rosa, CA 1995, Polebridge 224 pp. $30. 0-944344-44-5. ᴿJBL 117 (1998) 172-173 (*Wisse, Frederik*).
9159 *Mahé, Jean-Pierre* A reading of the Discourse on the Ogdoad and the Ennead (Nag Hammadi codex VI.6). Gnosis and hermeticism. 1998 ⇒422. 79-85.
9160 ᵀ**Nagel, Peter** Der Tractatus Tripartitus aus Nag Hammadi Codex I (Codex Jung). Studien und Texte zu Antike und Christentum 1: Tü 1998, Mohr vi; 120 pp. 3-16-147033-8.

M3.5 **Religiones mundi cum christianismo comparatae**

9161   *Bloom, Maureen* The legacy of 'sacred' and 'profane' in ancient Israel: interpretations of DURKHEIM's classifications. JSQ 5 (1998) 103-123.
9162   **Bonanate, Ugo** Il Dio degli altri: il difficile universalismo di Bibbia e Corano. Nuova cultura 56: 1997 ⇒13,9410. ᴿIslChr 24 (1998) 228-229 (*Borrmans, Maurice*).
9163   **Dalai Lama** The good heart: a Buddhist perspective on the teachings of Jesus. 1996 ⇒12,8804. ᴿBuddhist-Christian Studies 18 (1998) 240-241 (*Steele, Springs*).
9164   **Ganeri, Anita** Unter dem weiten Regenbogen: biblische Geschichten und Mythen aus den Religionen der Welt. 1997 ⇒13,9415. ᴿDiak. 29 (1998) 357-358 (*Bee-Schroedter, Heike*).
9165   *Grenholm, Carl-Henric* Introduction;
9166   *Hjelde, Sigurd* Religionswissenschaft und Theologie: die Frage ihrer gegenseitigen Abgrenzung in historischer Perspektive. StTh 52 (1998) 83-84/85-102.
9167   ᴱ**Idinopulos, Thomas A.; Wilson, Brian C.** What is religion?: origins, definitions, and explanations. SHR 81: Lei 1998, Brill ix; 180 pp. 90-04-11022-4. Bibl.
9168   *Karrer, Martin* Zuwendung zu den Völkern—lohnt eine religionstheologische Entdeckung des Neuen Testaments?. ᶠBSTEH, A. 1998 ⇒ 17. 152-178.
9169   ᴱ**Loya, Joseph A.; Ho, Wan-Li; Jih, Chang-Shin** The Tao of Jesus: an experiment in inter-traditional understanding. Mahwah 1998, Paulist xiii; 185 pp. $15. 0-8091-3764-X [ThD 46,278—Heiser, W.C.].
9170   ᴱ**Molendijk, Arie L.; Pels, Peter** Religion in the making: the emergence of the sciences of religion. SHR 80: Lei 1998, Brill xii; 318 pp. 90-04-11239-1.
9171   *Nielsen, Kirsten* Theology and the study of religion: schizophrenia or dialogue?. StTh 52 (1998) 103-115.
9172   **Pace, Fabio Maria** Per una storia delle religioni: temi e concetti della ricerca storico-religiosa. Saggi 5: Mi 1998, Terziaria xvii; 364 pp. 88-86818-29-7.
9173   *Painadath, Sebastian* Christ, church and the diversity of religions. Jeevadhara 28 (1998) 161-192 Sum. 161.
9174   *Python, Vincent* Jésus et le Dalaï-lama: convergences et divergences entre bouddhisme et christianisme. Sources 24 (1998) 226-237.
9175   *Räisänen, Heikki* Comparative religion, theology, and New Testament exegesis. StTh 52 (1998) 116-129.
9176   **Smart, Ninian** The world's religions. C ²1998, CUP 608 pp. 0-521-63748-1. Bibl.
9177   *Van Bragt, Jan* Apocalyptic thought in christianity and Buddhism. Japanese Mission Journal 52 (1998) 161-170.
9178   *Wikström, Owe* Depression and the absence of God: religious studies and/or theology in clinical research. StTh 52 (1998) 130-146.

M3.6 *Sectae*—**Cults**

9179   **Boring, M. Eugene** Disciples and the bible: a history of Disciples biblical interpretation in North America. 1997 ⇒13,9438. ᴿHR 37 (1998) 475-477 (*Baird, William*).

9180 **Dane, J.** 'De vrucht van bijbelsche opvoeding': populaire leescultuur en opvoeding in protestants-christelijke gezinnen, circa 1880-1940. 1996 ⇒12,8812. ^RBMGN 113 (1998) 577-579 (*Sturm, Johan*).

9181 **James, William** Le varie forme dell'esperienza religiosa: uno studio sulla natura umana. Scienze delle religioni: [Brescia] 1998, Morcelliana 455 pp. 88-372-1677-7. Introd. di *Giovanni Filoramo*.

9182 **Jannot, Jean-René** Devins, dieux et démons: regards sur la religion de l'Étrurie antique. Antiqua: P 1998, Picard 207 pp. 2-7084-0523-3. Bibl.

9183 *Mantovani, Ennio* Challenges of the bible to christian life in PNG today. Catalyst 28 (1998) 102-116.

9184 *Moripe, S.* Holiness and taboo in the Zion christian church. Acta Theologica 18/1 (1998) 1-9.

9185 **Newport, John P.** The New Age movement and the biblical worldview: conflict and dialogue. GR 1998, Eerdmans xv; 614 pp. $35. 0-8028-4430-8.

9186 **Odasso, Giovanni** Bibbia e religioni: prospettive bibliche per la teologia della religione. R 1998, Urbaniana Univ. Pr. 416 pp. L45.000.

9187 **Panaino, Antonio** Tessere il cielo: considerazioni sulle tavole astronomiche, gli oroscopi e la dottrina dei legamenti tra Induismo, Zoroastrismo, Manicheismo e Mandeismo. Serie orientale Roma 79: R 1998, Istituto Italiano per l'Africa e l'Oriente 214 pp. Bibl.

9188 **Peyrot, Bruna** Dalla Scrittura alle scritture. Soggetti e genere: T 1998, Rosenberg & S 125 pp [Cultura valdese] ^RBSBS 96 (1998) 753-755 (*Fratini, Marco*).

9189 *Sepulveda, Juan* Lectura pentecostal de la biblia en Chile. Alternativas 5/11-12 (1998) 231-240 [ThIK 21/1,71].

9190 *Templeton, D.A.* 'Scottish presbyterianism'. ^FPOKORNÝ, P. 1998 ⇒ 90. 321-327.

9191 **Tilley, Maureen A.** The bible in christian north Africa: the Donatist world. 1997 ⇒13,9442. ^RChH 67 (1998) 748-751 (*Tabbernee, William*).

M3.8 Mythologia

9192 **Allen, Douglas** Myth and religion in Mircea ELIADE. Levittown 1998, Taylor and F. 375 pp.

9193 ^E**Alon, Ilai; Gruenwald, Ithamar; Singer, Itamar** Concepts of the other in Near Eastern religions. IOS 14: 1994 ⇒11/2,392. ^RJAOS 118 (1998) 275-276 (*Smith, Mark Stratton*).

9194 *Beyhl, Friedrich Ernst* Anmerkungen zum Drachenblut und zu den Namen der Insel Soqotra. ZDMG 148 (1998) 35-82.

9195 **Bottéro, Jean,** *al.,* L'Orient ancien et nous. 1996 ⇒12,8830; 13,9444. ^RRB 105 (1998) 466-467 (*Tarragon, J.-M. de*).

9196 **Brisson, L.** Introduction à la philosophie du mythe, 1: sauver les mythes. Essais d'art et de philosophie: P 1996, Vrin 243 pp. FF125. 2-7116-127-6 [CIR 50,614s—Dowden, Ken].

9197 *Bron, François* Notes sur le culte d'Athirat en Arabie du Sud préislamique. ^FMARGAIN, J. 1998 ⇒71. 75-79.

9198 *Fabre-Serris, Jacqueline* Mythologie et littérature à Rome: la réécriture des mythes aux 1ers siècles avant et après J.-C. Sciences humaines: Lausanne 1998, Payot 272 pp [ASSR 108,72—Le Mer, R.].

9199 **Ferrari, Anna** Il tempo e il labirinto: immagini del mito classico. L'avventura letteraria: T 1998, Tirrenia Stampatori 147 pp. 88-7763-337-9. Bibl.

9200 [E]**Goodison, Lucy; Morris, Christine** Ancient goddesses: the myths and the evidence. L 1998, British Museum Press 224 pp. 0-7141-1761-7 [Kernos 12,301—Pirenne-Delforge, Vinciane].

9201 *Lucci, Laila* La biblica e la mitica "madre dei viventi". BeO 40 (1998) 193-218.

9202 **Lyons, Deborah** Gender and immortality: heroines in ancient Greek myth and cult. Princeton 1997, Princeton Univ. Press xvii; 267 pp. $39.50. 0-691-01100-1. [R]Prudentia 30/1 (1998) 52-54 (*Mitchell, Lynette G.*).

9203 *Merk, Otto* Das Problem des Mythos zwischen Neologie und 'religionsgeschichtlicher Schule' in der neutestamentlichen Wissenschaft [F]MERK O. BZNW 95: 1998 <1988> ⇒79. 24-46.

9204 **Rohl, David M.** Legend: the genesis of civilisation. A test of time 2: L 1998, Century (10) 454 pp. 0-7126-7747-X. Bibl.

9205 **Shlain, Leonard** The alphabet versus the goddess: the conflict between word and image. NY 1998, Viking xiv; 463 pp. 0-670-87883-9. Bibl.

M4.0 Religio romana

9206 **Baudy, Dorothea** Römische Umgangsriten: eine ethologische Untersuchung der Funktion von Wiederholung für religiöses Verhalten. RVV 43: B 1998, de Gruyter xi; 299 pp. 3-11-016077-3.

9207 **Beard, Mary; North, John; Price, Simon R.F.** Religions of Rome, v.1: a history; v.2: a sourcebook. C 1998, CUP 2 vols; xxiv + 454; xiv + 416 pp. £16+£16. 0-521-31682-0/45646-0.

9208 *Becker, Hans-Jürgen* Earthquakes, insects, miracles, and the order of nature. Talmud Yersushalmi, 1. 1998 ⇒8811. 387-396 [BuBbgB 30,110].

9209 *Bolt, Peter G.* Life, death, and the afterlife in the Greco-Roman world. Life in the face of death. 1998 ⇒252. 51-79.

9210 *Buchheit, Vinzenz* Einheit durch Religion in Antike und Christentum. [F]SPEYER, W. JAC.E 28: 1998 ⇒107. 35-43.

9211 *Cancik, Hubert* The end of the world, of history, and of the individual in Greek and Roman antiquity. Encyclopedia of apocalypticism I. 1998 ⇒507. 84-125.

9212 *Fauth, Wolfgang* Magie und Mysterium in den Metamorphosen des Apuleius. [F]Speyer, W.. 1998 ⇒107. 131-144 [BuBbgB 30,110].

9213 *Feeney, Denis* Literature and religion at Rome: cultures, contexts, and beliefs. Roman literature and its contexts: C 1998, CUP xii; 161 pp. £12. 0-521-55921-9. Bibl. [R]Prudentia 30/2 (1998) 50-55 (*Stevenson, Tom*).

9214 *Gatier, Pierre-Louis* Monuments du culte "dolichénien" en Cyrrhestique. Syr. 75/1 (1998) 161-169.

9215 *Guimier-Sorbets, Anne-Marie* Une forme originale de syncrétisme religieux. MoBi 111 (1998) 34-37 [BuBbgB 30,110].

9216 *Habicht, Christian* Messianic elements in the prechristian Greco-Roman world. Toward the millennium. 1998 ⇒264. 47-55 [BuBbgB 30,110].

9217 ^E**Hinard, F.; Lambert, M.-F.** La mort au quotidien dans le monde romain. De l'archéologie à l'histoire: P 1995, De Boccard Colloque, Paris 1993 257 pp. 2-7018-0096-X. ^RClR 48/1 (1998) 226-227 (*Percival, John*).

9218 *Hoheisel, Karl* Römische Religion. TRE 29. 1998 ⇒501. 311-319.

9219 **Janes, Dominic** God and gold in late antiquity. C 1998, CUP xii; 211 pp. 0-521-59403-0. Bibl.

9220 *Löhr, Gebhard* Religionskritik in der griechischen und römischen Antike: methodologische und inhaltliche Vorüberlegungen zu einer religionswissenschaftlichen Darstellung. Saec. 49 (1998) 1-21.

9221 **Marco Simn, Francisco** Flamen dialis: el sacerdote de Júpiter en la religión romana. 1996 ⇒12,8847. ^REM 66 (1998) 420-422 (*Delgado Delgado, José A.*).

9222 *Mayak, I.L.* The Roman gods according to Aulus Gellius. VDI 224 (1998) 263-272 Sum. 271. R.

9223 **Muth, Robert** Einführung in die griechische und römische Religion. Da:Wiss ²1998, xi; 423 pp. 3-534-13654-3.

9224 **Staples, Ariadne** From good goddess to vestal virgins: sex and category in Roman religion. L 1998, Routledge x; 207 pp. 0-415-13233-9. Bibl.

9225 **Turcan, Robert** Rome et ses dieux. La vie quotidienne: P 1998, Hachette 272 pp. 8 pl. 18 phot. [CRAI 1999,932s—Turcan, Robert].

9226 *Ward, Roy Bowen* The public priestesses of Pompeii. ^FFERGUSON, E. NT.S 90: 1998 ⇒25. 318-334.

M4.5 Mithraismus

9227 *Aune, D.E.* Expansion and recruitment among Hellenistic religions: the case of Mithraism. Recruitment. 1998 ⇒320. 39-56.

9228 *Beck, Roger* The mysteries of Mithras: a new account of their genesis. JRS 88 (1998) 115-128.

9229 **Mastrocinque, Attilio** Studi sul mitraismo: (il mitraismo e la magia). Historica 4: R 1998, Bretschneider Bibl. x; 168 pp. 88-7689-000-0.

9230 **Ulansey, David** Die Ursprünge des Mithraskults: Kosmologie und Erlösung in der Antike. Da:Wiss 1998, 134 pp.

M5.1 *Divinitates Graeciae*—Greek gods and goddesses

9231 *Bach, Alice* Whatever happened to Dionysus?. Biblical studies. JSOT.S 266: 1998 ⇒380. 91-116;

9232 Whitewashing Athena: gaining perspective on Bernal and the bible. JSOT 77 (1998) 3-19.

9233 **Baumgarten, R.** Heiliges Wort und heilige Schrift bei den Griechen: Hieroi Logoi und verwandte Erscheinungen. ScriptOralia 110; Reihe A, Altertumswissenschaftliche Reihe 26: Tü 1998, Narr 250 pp. DM 96. 3-8233-5420-5.

9234 **Bermejo Barrera, J.C.,** *al.*, Los orígenes de la mitología griega. 1996 ⇒12,8860. ^RRHR 215 (1998) 511-14 (*Bruit Zaidman, Louise*).

9235 ^E**Blundell, Sue; Williamson, Margaret** The sacred and the feminine in Ancient Greece. L 1998, Routledge x; 192 pp. 0415-126630. Bibl.

9236   **Bremmer, Jan N.** Greek religion. 1994 ⇒11/2,8461. ᴿHR 38 (1998) 95-98 (*Grottanelli, Cristiano*);

9237   Götter, Mythen und Heiligtümer im antiken Griechenland. 1996 ⇒ 12,8861. ᴷAnCl 67 (1998) 394-395 (*Pirenne-Delforge, Vinciane*).

9238   *Brenk, Frederick* Artemis of Ephesos: an avant garde goddess. Actes du VIᵉ colloque international du Centre International d'Etude de la Religion grecque antique. ᴱ**Motte, A.; Pirenne-Delforge, V.** Liège 1998. 157-171 [AcBib 10,511].

9239   *Brown, Michael L.* Was there a west Semitic Asklepios?. UF 30 (1998) 133-154.

9240   **Burkert, Walter** Sauvages origines: mythes et rites sacrificiels en Grèce ancienne. ᵀ*Lenfant, Dominique.* Vérité des mythes: P 1998, Les Belles Lettres 189 pp. 2-251-32427-5.

9241   **Burnett, Anne Pippin** Revenge in Attic and later tragedy. Sather Classical Lectures 62: Berkeley, CA 1998, University of California xviii; 306 pp. 0-520-21096-4.

9242   **Calame, Claude** Mythe et histoire dans l'antiquité grecque: la création symbolique d'une colonie. 1996 ⇒12,8863; 13,9468. ᴿAnCl 67 (1998) 450-451 (*Constancio, Patrick*);

9243   Thésée et l'imaginaire athénien: légende et culte en Grèce. ²1996 ⇒12,8862. ᴿClR 48 (1998) 342-343 (*Harrison, Thomas*).

9244   **Cavanagh, William; Mee, Christopher** A private place: death in prehistoric Greece. Studies in Mediterranean Archaeology 125: Jonsered 1998, Astroms xiv; 258 pp. 90-7081-178-4. Bibl.

9245   **Diez de Velasco, Francisco** Lenguajes de la religión: mitos, símbolos e imágenes de la Grecia Antigua. Paradigmas 20: M 1998, Trotta 188 pp. 84-8164-230-4. Bibl.

9246   **Dillon, Matthew** Pilgrims and pilgrimage in ancient Greece. L 1997, Routledge xix; 308 pp. $70 [JR 80,543ss—Hanges, J.C.].

9247   **Georgoudi, Stella; Vernant, Jean-Pierre** Mythes grecs au figuré: de l'antiquité au baroque. 1996 ⇒12,8868. ᴿAJA 102 (1998) 457-458 (*Lyons, Deborah*).

9248   *Goodison, Lucy; Morris, Christine* Beyond the Great Mother: the sacred world of the Minoans. Ancient goddesses. 1998 ⇒298. 113-132.

9249   *Holladay, Carl R.* Pseudo-Orpheus: tracking a tradition. ᶠFERGUSON, E. NT.S 90: 1998 ⇒25. 192-220.

9250   **Mikalson, Jon D.** Religion in Hellenistic Athens. Hellenistic Culture and Society 29: Berkeley 1998, Univ. of California Pr. xii; 364 pp. $48. 0520210239. ᴿPrudentia 30/2 (1998) 63-7 (*Ehrhardt, C.T.H.R.*).

9251   ᴱ**Motte, André; Pirenne-Delforge, Vinciane; Wathelet, Paul** Mentor 2 (1986-1990): guide bibliographique de la religion grecque / Bibliographical survey of Greek religion. Kernos Suppl. 6: Liège 1998, Univ. de Liège 531 pp [RSFen 26,143—Ribichini, Sergio].

9252   **Parker, Robert** Athenian religion: a history. 1996 ⇒12,8878. ᴿPrudentia 30/2 (1998) 73-77 (*Stevenson, Tom*); JR 78 (1998) 161-162 (*Johnston, Sarah Iles*); AJP 119 (1998) 293-295 (*Cole, Susan G.*).

9253   **Penglase, Charles** Greek myths and Mesopotamia. 1994 ⇒10, 10614; 12,8879. ᴿBiOr 55 (1998) 852-855 (*Limet, Henri*).

9254   *Schunack, Gerd* Glaube in griechischer Religiosität. ᶠSTEGEMANN, H. BZNW 97: 1998 ⇒111. 296-326.

9255   *Voyatzis, Mary E.* From Athena to Zeus: an A-Z guide to the origins of Greek goddesses. Ancient goddesses. 1998 ⇒298. 133-147.

M5.2 *Philosophorum critica religionis*—Greek philosopher religion

9256 *Andreev, Yu. V.* Apologia of paganism or on religiosity of ancient
Greeks. VDI 224 (1998) 125-134 Sum. 134. **R.**

9257 *Bechtle, Gerald* La problématique de l'âme et du cosmos chez PHI-
LON et les médio-platoniciens [BuBbgB 30,106];

9258 *Bouffartigue, Jean* La structure de l'âme chez PHILON: terminologie
scolastique et métaphores [BuBbgB 30,106];

9259 *Desbordes, Bernadette A.* Un exemple d'utilisation de la philosophie:
la stratégie du recours à la thèse des lieux naturels [BuBbgB 30,107];

9260 *Guignard, Vincent* Le rapport de PHILON d'Alexandrie à la philosophie grecque dans le portrait des empereurs [BuBbgB 30,104];

9261 *Lévy, Carlos* Éthique de l'immanence, éthique de la transcendance: le
problème de l'*oikeiôsis* chez PHILON [BuBbgB 30,107];

9262 *Martín, José Pablo* La configuration semántica ἀρχή—νοῦς—θεός
en FILÓN: una temprana combinación de Platón y Aristóteles [Bu-
BbgB 30,106];

9263 *Michel, Alain* PHILON d'Alexandrie et l'Académie [BuBbgB 30,106].
Philon d'Alexandrie. 1998 ⇒433. 377-392/59-75/393-448/459-
469/153-164/165-182/493-502.

9264 *Müller, Hans-Peter* Anfänge der Religionskritik bei den Vorsokrati-
kern. 'Geglaubt habe ich, deshalb habe ich geredet'. FBSTEH, A.
Religionswissenschaftliche Studien 47: 1998 ⇒17. 281-295.

9265 *Perrot, Charles* La conscience selon saint Paul. Une parole pour la
vie: hommage à Xavier THÉVENOT. EMédevielle, Geneviève; Doré,
Joseph. P 1998, Cerf. 145-153 [BuBbgB 30,107].

9266 *Petit, Alain* PHILON et le pythagorisme: un usage problématique
[BuBbgB 30,106];

9267 *Radice, Roberto* Le judaïsme alexandrin et la philosophie grecque:
influences probables et points de contact [BuBbgB 30,104]. Philon
d'Alexandrie. 1998 ⇒433. 471-482/483-492.

9268 **Stead, C.** Philosophy in christian antiquity. 1994 ⇒10,13943:
11/2,g478. RCIR 48 (1998) 358-360 (*O'Daly, G.J.P.*).

M5.3 *Mysteria eleusinia; Hellenistica*—Mysteries; Hellenistic cults

9269 *Brenk, Frederick* Caesar and the evil eye or what to do with και συ
τεκνον. FMACKENDRICK P. 1998 ⇒68. 31-50 [AcBib 10,389].

9270 **Brisson, Luc** Orphée et l'orphisme dans l'antiquité gréco-romaine.
Collected Studies 476: Aldershot 1995, Variorum viii; 301 pp. $87.
50. 0-860-78453-3. RNumen 45 (1998) 321-324 (*McClintock, Giuliana Scalera*).

9271 **Graf, Fritz** La magie dans l'antiquité gréco-romaine. 1994 ⇒10,
10671; 11/2,8596. RASSR 43/2 (1998) 63-64 (*Le Mer, Régis*).

9272 **Pakkanen, Petra** Interpreting early Hellenistic religion: a study
based on the mystery cult of Demeter and the cult of Isis. 1996 ⇒12,
8906. RAnCl 67 (1998) 403-405 (*Pirenne-Delforge, Vinciane*).

9273 **Pettazzoni, Raffaele** I misteri: saggio di una teoria storico-religiosa.
1997 ⇒13,9499. RSMSR 64 (1998) 223-229 (*Lanzi, Silvia*).

9274 *Stowers, Stanley K.* A cult from Philadelphia: oikos religion or cultic
association?. FFERGUSON, E. NT.S 90: 1998 ⇒25. 287-301.

9275 **Stroumsa, Guy G.** Hidden wisdom: esoteric traditions and the roots of christian mysticism. 1996 ⇒13,9500. ᴿNumen 45 (1998) 222-223 (*Martin, Luther H.*); JR 78 (1998) 268-69 (*Kannengiesser, Charles*).

M5.5 **Religiones anatolicae**

9276 *Fauth, Wolfgang* Hethitische Beschwörungspriesterinnen—israelitische Propheten: differente Phänotypen magischer Religiosität in Vorderasien. ᶠLORETZ O. AOAT 250: 1998 ⇒65. 289-318.
9277 *Gordon, Cyrus H.* The Near East background of the Rigveda. ᴹWARD W. 1998 ⇒123. 117-120.
9278 *Gütenbrock, Hans G.* To drink a god;
9279 *Hutter, Manfred* Magie und Religion im Tunnawiya-Ritual KBo XXI1-KUB IX 34-KBo XXI 6. Rencontre Assyriologique Internationale 34. 1998 ⇒452. 121-129/79-92.
9280 **Neu, Erich** Das hurritische Epos der Freilassung I: Untersuchungen zu einem hurritisch-hethitschen Textensemble aus Ḫattuša. StBT 32: 1996 ⇒12,8920. ᴿZAR 4 (1998) 290-295 (*Otto, Eckart*).
9281 *Richter, Thomas* Die Lesung des Götternamens AN.AN.MAR.TU. General studies... Nuzi 10/2. ᴱ**Owen, D.** 1998 ⇒T6.5. 135-137.
9282 **Singer, Itamar** Muwatalli's prayer to the assembly of gods through the storm-god of lightning (CTH 381). 1996 ⇒12,8921. ᴿBiOr 55 (1998) 215-217 (*Hutter, Manfred*); OLZ 93 (1998) 460-464 (*Popko, Maciej*); Or. 67 (1998) 135-139 (*Haas, Volkert*).
9283 *Torri, Giulia* Ittita: "Bove, madre del brulicare di formiche": alcune osservazioni sul rituale di maštigga (KUB LVIII 79). SEL 15 (1998) 69-76.
9284 **Van Gessel, B.H.L.** Onomasticon of the Hittite pantheon, 1-2. HO 1 33: Lei 1998, Brill xxiii; xv; 1069 pp. ƒ434.50; $256. 90-04-10809-2. ᴿBiOr 55 (1998) 855-858 (*Popko, Maciej*).
9285 **Yoshida, Daisuke** Untersuchungen zu den Sonnengottheiten bei den Hethitern. 1996 ⇒12,8923. ᴿBiOr 55 (1998) 475-478 (*Hutter, Manfred*).

M6.0 **Religio canaanaea, syra**

9286 **Albertz, Rainer** A history of Israelite religion in the Old Testament period, 1: from the beginnings to the end of the monarchy. 1994 ⇒ 10,10690...13,9504. ᴿJNES 57 (1998) 224-27 (*Holloway, Steven W.*).
9287 *Albertz, Rainer* Biblische oder Nicht-Biblische Religionsgeschichte Israels?: ein Gespräch mit Oswald LORETZ. ᶠLORETZ O. AOAT 250: 1998 ⇒65. 27-41.
9288 ᴱ**Becking, B.; Dijkstra, M.** Eén God alleen...?: over monotheïsme in Oud-Israël en de verering van de godin Asjera. Kampen 1998, Kok 181 pp. ƒ35. 90-242-9225-5 [GThT 98,137].
9289 **Binger, Tilde** Asherah: goddesses in Ugarit, Israel and the Old Testament. JSOT.S 232: 1997 ⇒13,9509. ᴿCBQ 60 (1998) 320-322 (*Smith, Mark S.*); SEL 15 (1998) 119-121 (*Watson, Wilfred G.E.*).
9290 **Blazquez, José Maria,** *al.,* Historia de las religiones antiguas: Oriente, Grecia y Roma. 1993 ⇒9,11619; 11/2,8643. ᴿSyr. 75 (1998) 305-308 (*Contenson, Henri de*).

9291 *Bordreuil, Pierre* Astarté, la dame de Byblos. CRAI (1998/4) 1153-1164.

9292 **Brody, Aaron Jed** "Each man cried out to his God": the specialized religion of Canaanite and Phoenician seafarers. HSM 58; Harvard Semitic Museum Publications: Atlanta 1998, Scholars x; 177 pp. 0-7885-0466-5.

9293 *Cardellini, Innocenzo* La ricerca attuale sullo sviluppo storico della religione dell'antico Israele. Lat. 64 (1998) 621-627.

9294 *Carstens, Pernille* Why does the god have a cup in his hand?: an examination of the Ahiram sarcophagus and the drinking vessels at the table of display in the Hebrew Bible from a ritualistic point of view. SJOT 12 (1998) 214-232.

9295 **Cornelius, Izak** The iconography of the Canaanite gods Reshef and Ba'al. OBO 140: 1994 ᴿAulOr 16 (1998) 135-136 (*Olmo Lete, G. del*).

9296 *Demsky, Aaron* Discovering a goddess. BArR 24/5 (1998) 53-58 [Ekron].

9297 *Dirven, Lucinda* The arrival of the goddess Allat in Palmyra. Mes. 33 (1998) 297-307.

9298 *Doldán, Felipe L.* Monoteísmo de Israel y religiones en el Antiguo Testamento. Teol(BA) 71 (1998) 11-36 Res. 36.

9299 ᴱ**Fine, Steven** Sacred realm: the emergence of the synagogue in the ancient world. 1996 ⇒12,8937; 13,9530. ᴿAJA 102 (1998) 445-446 (*Branham, Joan R.*).

9300 **Görg, Manfred** Ein Haus im Totenreich: Jenseitsvorstellungen in Israel und Ägypten. Düsseldorf 1998, Patmos 200 pp. 3-491-72398-1 [NThAR 1999,44].

9301 **Grätz, Sebastian** Der strafende Wettergott: Erwägungen zur Traditionsgeschichte des Abad-Fluchs im Alten Orient und im Alten Testament. BBB 114: Bodenheim 1998, Philo (8) 328 pp. 3-8257-0078-X.

9302 *Kottsieper, Ingo* El—ein aramäischer Gott?:—eine Antwort. BN 94 (1998) 87-98.

9303 *Köckert, Matthias* Von einem zum einzigen Gott: zur Diskussion der Religionsgeschichte Israels. BThZ 15 (1998) 137-175.

9304 *Liwak, Rüdiger* Bibel und Babel: wider die theologische und religionsgeschichtliche Naivität. BThZ 15 (1998) 206-233.

9305 *Loretz, Oswald* Religionsgeschichte(n) Altsyrien-Kanaans und Israel-Judas—Sammelbesprechung. UF 30 (1998) 889-907.

9306 **Lundager Jensen, Hans J.** Gammeltestamentlig religion: en indføring. Frederiksberg 1998, ANIS 292 pp. 87-7457-222-9 [NThAR 1999,253].

9307 *Maier, Christl; Tropper, Josef* El—ein aramäischer Gott?. BN 93 (1998) 77-88.

9308 *Merklein, Helmut; Wenning, Robert* Die Götter der Nabatäer. WUB 7 (1998) 60-61.

9309 **Merlo, Paolo** La dea Asratum—Atiratu—Asera: un contributo alla storia della religione semitica del nord. ᴰPont. Univ. Lateranense; ᴰ*Gelio, Roberto*. Corona Lateranensis: R 1998, Pont. Università Lateranense 285 pp. L25.000. 88-465-0031-8.

9310 *Merlo, Paolo* Le religioni semitiche dell'ambiente dell'Antico Testamento (1992-1997). Lat. 64 (1998) 611-620.

9311 *Milgrom, Jacob* The nature and extent of idolatry in eighth-seventh century Judah. HUCA 69 (1998) 1-13.

9312   **Niditch, Susan** Ancient Israelite religion. 1997 ⇒13,9558. ᴿBTB
       28/1 (1998) 39-40 (*Burns, John Barclay*); RRelRes 40 (1998) 92-93
       (*Schneider, Mareleyn*); JR 78 (1998) 479-480 (*Olyan, Saul M.*).
9313   *Niehr, Herbert* Aspekte des Totengedenkens im Juda der Königszeit:
       eine Problemskizze. ThQ 178 (1998) 1-13;
9314   Herkunft, Geschichte und Wirkungsgeschichte eines Unterweltsgot-
       tes in Ugarit, Phönizien und Israel. UF 30 (1998) 569-585.
9315   **Niehr, Herbert** Religionen in Israels Umwelt: Einführung in die
       nordwestsemitischen Religionen Syrien-Palästinas. NEB Ergänzungs-
       band zum AT 5: Wü 1998, Echter 255 pp. DM48. 3-429-01981-8.
       ᴿEstTrin 32 (1998) 437-438 (*Vázquez Allegue, Jaime*).
9316   *O'Connell, James* The God of Israel: from Abraham to Mary. Month
       31/2 (1998) 50-57.
9317   *Olmo Lete, G. del* La ofrenda *dġt* y la 'venganza de la sangre'. AulOr
       16 (1998) 129-131.
9318   ᵀᴱ**Olmo Lete, Gregorio del** Mitos, leyendas y rituales de los semitas
       occidentales. Pliegos de Oriente: Barcelona 1998, Trotta 315 pp. 84-
       8164-284-3. Bibl.
9319   **Olmo Lete, Gregorio del** La religión cananea según la liturgia de U-
       garit. 1992 ⇒9,11918...11/2,8704. ᴿSef. 58 (1998) 439-440 (*Vita,
       J.P.*).
9320   *Page, Hugh R.* The three zone theory and Ugaritic conceptions of the
       divine. UF 30 (1998) 615-631.
9321   **Petersen, Allan Rosengren** The royal God: enthronement festivals
       in Ancient Israel and Ugarit?. JSOT.S 259; Copenhagen International
       Seminar 5: Shf 1998, Academic 121 pp. 1-85075-864-6. Bibl.
9322   **Podella, Thomas** Das Lichtkleid JHWHs: Untersuchungen zur Ge-
       stalthaftigkeit Gottes im Alten Testament und seiner altorientalischen
       Umwelt. FAT 15: 1996 ⇒12,1946. ᴿOLZ 93 (1998) 495-497
       (*Schunck, Klaus-Dietrich*).
9323   *Proop, William H.C.* Santa and his Asherah. BiRe 14/6 (1998) 44-46.
9324   **Rabinowitz, Jacob J.** The faces of God: Canaanite mythology as
       Hebrew theology. [Woodstock, CT] 1998, [Spring] 116 pp. 0-88214-
       117-1. Bibl.
9325   *Schäfer-Lichtenberger, Christa* פתגיה—Göttin und Herrin von Ekron.
       BN 91 (1998) 64-76.
9326   **Trémouille, Marie-Claude** ᵈḤebat: une divinité syro-anatolienne.
       1997 ⇒13,9564. ᴿMes. 33 (1998) 377-379 (*Jasink, A.M.*).
9327   *Van der Toorn, Karel* Goddesses in early Israelite religion. Ancient
       goddesses. 1998 ⇒298. 83-97;
9328   Currents in the study of Israelite religion. CurResB 6 (1998) 9-30.
9329   *Wiggins, Steve A.* What's in a name?: Yariḫ at Ugarit. UF 30 (1998)
       761-779.
9330   *Wyatt, N.* Arms and the king: the earliest allusions to the Chaoskampf
       motif and their implications for the interpretation of the Ugaritic and
       biblical traditions. ᶠLORETZ O. AOAT 250: 1998 ⇒65. 833-882 [Ex
       14,16; Ps 74,13-15].

                    M6.5 **Religio aegyptia**

9331   **Abitz, Friedrich** Pharao als Gott in den Unterweltsbüchern des Neu-
       en Reiches. OBO 146: 1995 ⇒11/2,8735; 13,9572. ᴿJAOS 118
       (1998) 597-598 (*Troy, Lana*).

9332 **Andrews, Carol A.R.** Egyptian mummies. L ²1998, British Museum 96 pp. 0-7141-2139-8.

9333 *Assmann, Jan* A dialogue between self and soul: Papyrus Berlin 3024. Self, soul and body. SHR 78: 1998 ⇒286. 384-403;

9334 Mono-, pan-, and cosmotheism: thinking the 'one' in Egyptian theology. Orient 33 (1998) 130-149.

9335 *Aufrère, Sydney H.* Flore pharaonique et croyances égyptiennes. BSÉG 22 (1998) 5-16.

9336 *Beinlich, Horst* Datenbank der Ritualszenen. Feste im Tempel, 4. ÄAT 33,2: 1998 ⇒479. 1.

9337 *Betro, Marilina* Il Libro della Notte e le guide dell'aldilà. Or. 67 (1998) 509-522.

9338 *Bickel, Susanne* Changes in the image of the creator God during the Middle and New Kingdoms. Proceedings 7th Cong. of Egyptologists. 1998 ⇒475. 165-172.

9339 *Bolshakov, Andrey O.* Man and his double in Egyptian ideology of the Old Kingdom. ÄAT 37: 1997 ⇒13,9578. ᴿOLZ 93 (1998) 619-627 (*Jánosi, Peter*).

9340 **Bradshaw, Joseph** The night sky in Egyptian mythology. 1997 ⇒ 13,9581. ᴿBiOr 55 (1998) 400-404 (*Tobin, Vincent Arieh*).

9341 *Campagno, Marcelo* God-kings and king-gods in ancient Egypt. Proceedings 7th Cong. of Egyptologists. 1998 ⇒475. 237-243.

9342 *Chevalier, Nathalie* Mumien warten auf Rettung. WUB 8 (1998) 53.

9343 *Dakin, Alec Naylor* Of the untranslatability of maat and some questions about the *Tale of the eloquent peasant*. Proceedings 7th Cong. of Egyptologists. 1998 ⇒475. 237-243.

9344 **David, Rosalie** The ancient Egyptians: beliefs and practices. The Sussex library of religious beliefs and practices: Brighton ²1998, Sussex Academic xvii; 262 pp. 1-898723-72-9. Bibl.

9345 *Deaton, John Charles* The religious significance of the Egyptian lion headed water spout. Discussions in Egyptology 41 (1998) 29-32.

9346 *Dunand, Françoise* 'Mort avant l'heure...': sur l'espérance de vie en Egypte tardive. ᶠQUAEGEBEUR J. 1998 ⇒94. 961-974.

9347 **Dunand, Françoise; Lichtenberg, Roger** Les momies et la mort en Égypte. P 1998, Errance 255 pp. 2-87772-162-0. Préf. *Jean Yoyotte*; Bibl.

9348 **Duquesne, Terence** Black and gold god: colour symbolism of the god Anubis with observations on the phenomenology of colour in Egyptian and comparative religion. 1996 ⇒12,8997. ᴿDiscussions in Egyptology 40 (1998) 169-172 (*Kákosy, László*).

9349 *DuQuesne, Terence* Observations on the Book of Night: with reference to Gilles ROULIN *Le livre de la nuit (1996)*. Discussions in Egyptology 40 (1998) 81-92.

9350 **Egberts, A.** In quest of meaning: a study of the Ancient Egyptian rites of consecrating the meret-chests and driving the calves. 1995 ⇒ 11/2,8757. 2 vols. ᴿJAOS 118 (1998) 447-449 (*Graefe, Erhard*).

9351 *Ellis, Normandi* Kheperi, Ra, Atum: the light forms of birth, death, and rebirth. Parabola 23/4 (1998) 6-18.

9352 *Favard-Meeks, Christine* Behbeit el-Hagara: le "temple de la fête" et la famille osirienne;

9353 *Feder, Frank* Das Ritual sʿḥʿḳ šn.t als Tempelfest des Gottes Min. Feste im Tempel, 4. ÄAT 33,2: 1998 ⇒479. 123-133/31-54.

9354   *Feucht, Erika* Fisch- und Vogelfang im w3 d-w r des Jenseits. Jerusa-
       lem studies. ÄAT 40: 1998 ⇒361. 37-44.
9355   **Forman, Werner; Quirke, Stephen** Hieroglyphs and the afterlife in
       ancient Egypt. 1996 ⇒12,9000; 13,9595. [R]JARCE 35 (1998) 205-
       206 (*Delia, Robert D.*).
9356   **Franco, Isabelle** Rites et croyances d'éternité. Bibliothèque de l'E-
       gypte ancienne: P 1993, Pygmalion 308 pp. €18,29. 2-85704-386-4.
       [R]CÉg 73 (1998) 78-79 (*Labrique, Françoise*).
9357   **Frankfort, Henry** La religión del Antiguo Egipto: una interpretaci-
       ón. Barc 1998, Laertes 256 pp [RF 239,444].
9358   **Frankfurter, David T.M.** Religion in Roman Egypt: assimilation
       and resistance. Princeton, NJ 1998, Princeton University Press xvi;
       314 pp. $49.50. 0-691-02685-8. 23 pl.; bibl.
9359   *Gal, Orly* Uncleanliness and sin, cleanliness and purity. Jerusalem
       studies. ÄAT 40: 1998 ⇒361. 243-245.
9360   *Gnirs, Andra Maria* Die levantische Herkunft des Schlangengottes.
       [F]STADELMANN R. 1998 ⇒109. 197-209.
9361   **Goyon, Jean-Claude** Rê, Maât et Pharaon ou le destin de l'Egypte
       antique. Lyon 1998, A.C.V. 204 pp. FF149. 2-913033-01-6.
9362   *Grieshammer, Reinhard* Zum Fortwirken ägyptischer und israeli-
       tisch-jüdischer Unschuldserklärungen in frühchristlichen Texten Ä-
       gyptens. Jerusalem studies. ÄAT 40: 1998 ⇒361. 247-264.
9363   *Gundlach, Rolf* Tempelfeste und Etappen der Königsherrschaft in der
       18. Dynastie. Feste im Tempel, 4. ÄAT 33,2: 1998 ⇒479. 55-75.
9364   **Gülden, Svenja A.; Munro, Irmtraut** Bibliographie zum Altägypti-
       schen Totenbuch. Wsb 1998, Harrassowitz x; 189 pp. DM98. 3-447-
       04077-7. collab. *Regner, Christina; Sütsch, Oliver* [DiscEg
       44,95s—DuQuesne, Terence].
9365   *Hassan, Fekri A.* The earliest goddesses of Egypt. Ancient god-
       desses. 1998 ⇒298. 98-112.
9366   **Herbin, François René** Le livre de parcourir l'éternité. OLA 58:
       1994 ⇒10,12675...13,9602. [R]Or. 67 (1998) 266-68 (*Meyer, Robert*).
9367   *Hollis, Susan* Otiose deities and the ancient Egyptian pantheon.
       JARCE 35 (1998) 61-72.
9368   **Hornung, Erik** Altägyptische Jenseitsbücher: ein einführender Über-
       blick. 1997 ⇒13,9604. [R]BiOr 55 (1998) 404-406 (*Guilhou, N.*);
9369   Akhenaton: la religione della luce nell'antico Egitto. [T]*Salone, Clau-
       dio*. Piccoli saggi 1: R 1998, Salerno 143 pp. 88-8402-255-X. Pres.
       di *Christian Sturtewagen*.
9370   **Ikram, Salima; Dodson, Aidan** The mummy in ancient Egypt: e-
       quipping the dead for eternity. L 1998, Thames & H 351 pp. £30. 0-
       500-05088-0. 485 pl. & ill.; Bibl. [Antiquity 72,936—Sinclair, A.].
9371   *Jansen-Winkeln, Karl* Die Inschrift der Porträtstatue des Hor.
       MDAI.K 54 (1998) 227-235;
9372   Zur Datierung und Stellung des "Vorlesepriesters" Petamenophis.
       WZKM 88 (1998) 165-175.
9373   *Kákkosy, László; Takács, Gábor* Two observations on the etymology
       of Osiris. ArOr 66 (1998) 243-254.
9374   *Koemoth, P.* Isis, les arbres et la mandragore d'après un manuscrit il-
       lustré du XVe siècle. OLoP 29 (1998) 145-162.
9375   *Koester, Helmut* The cult of the Egyptian deities in Asia minor. Per-
       gamon. [E]**Koester, H.** HThS 46: 1998 ⇒T8.4. 111-135.

9376 **Krauss, Rolf** Astronomische Konzepte und Jenseitsvorstellungen in den Pyramidentexten. ÄA 59: Wsb 1998, Harrassowitz xvi; 297 pp. DM128. 3-447-03979-5.
9377 [T]**Kurth, Dieter** Treffpunkt der Götter: Inschriften aus dem Tempel des Horus von Edfu. Dü [2]1998 <1994>, Artemis & W ⇒11/2,8785. 419 pp. 3-7608-1203-1.
9378 **Lessing, Erich; Vernus, Pascal** Dieux de l'Égypte. P 1998, Imprimerie Nationale 202 pp. 2-7433-0293-3. Bibl.
9379 **Lichtheim, Miriam** Moral values in ancient Egypt. OBO 155: 1997 ⇒13,9611. [R]AcOr 59 (1998) 237-240 (*Naguib, Saphinaz-Amal*).
9380 *Lohmann, Katherina* Das Gespräch eines Mannes mit seinem Ba. SAÄK 25 (1998) 207-236 Zsfg. 207.
9381 *Loprieno, Antonio* Le Pharaon reconstruit: la figure du roi dans la littérature égyptienne au 1er millénaire avant J.C. BSFE 142 (1998) 4-24.
9382 **Lüscher, Barbara** Untersuchungen zu Totenbuch Spruch 151. Studien zum Altägyptischen Totenbuch: Wsb 1998, Harrassowitz xxvii; 342 pp. DM120. 3-447-03968-X. 26 pl.; 84 fig. [DiscEg 44, 91ss—DuQuesne, Terence].
9383 *Meltzer, Edmund S.* Religious experience and the Egyptian underworld. JSSEA 27 (1997) 60-61 Sum. 60.
9384 *Meyer, Robert* Zwischen göttlicher Intervention und Offenbarung: Bemerkungen zur Wiederaufnahme einer ägyptologischen Diskussion. OLZ 93 (1998) 277-288.
9385 *Meyer, Sibylle* Festlieder zum Auszug Gottes. Feste im Tempel, 4. ÄAT 33,2: 1998 ⇒479. 135-142.
9386 *Miosi, Frank T.* Prolegomena to the future study of Egyptian ethics. SSEA Journal 26 (1996) 67-80 Sum. 67.
9387 *Ogdon, Jorge R.* Studies in ancient Egyptian magical thought, VI: on certain probable Egyptian archetypes of the classical (western) witch. Discussions in Egyptology 41 (1998) 49-53.
9388 **Perpillou-Thomas, Françoise** Fêtes d'Égypte ptolémaïque et romaine. StHell 31: 1993 ⇒10,10771; 11/2,8797. [R]Gn. 70 (1998) 331-334 (*Huß, Werner*).
9389 **Pinch, Geraldine** Votive offerings to Hathor. 1993 ⇒9,11980; 12,9019. [R]JAOS 118 (1998) 569-570 (*Bleiberg, Edward*).
9390 **Poo, Mu-Chou** Wine and wine offering in the religion of ancient Egypt. 1995 ⇒11/2,8799; 13,9620. [R]BiOr 55 (1998) 114-119 (*Meeks, Dimitri*); Or. 67 (1998) 126-127 (*Scandone Matthiae, Gabriella*).
9391 *Quack, Joachim Friedrich* Kontinuität und Wandel in der spätägyptischen Magie. SEL 15 (1998) 77-94.
9392 [E]**Quirke, Stephen G.J.** The temple in ancient Egypt: new discoveries and recent research. 1997 ⇒13,300. [R]Antiquity 72 (1998) 710-712 (*Thomas, Susanna*).
9393 *Radwan, Ali* Thutmosis III. als Gott. [F]STADELMANN R. 1998 ⇒109. 329-340.
9394 *Roth, Ann Macy* Buried pyramids and layered thoughts: the organisation of multiple approaches in Egyptian religion. Proceedings 7th Cong. of Egyptologists. 1998 ⇒475. 991-1003.
9395 **Roulin, Gilles** Le livre de la nuit: une composition égyptienne de l'au-delà. OBO 147/1-2: 1996 ⇒12,9022; 13,9627. [R]BiOr 55 (1998) 96-99 (*Koemoth, Pierre P.*); Or. 67 (1998) 509-522 (*Betrò, Marilina*); AuOr 16 (1998) 138-140 (*Quevedo Alvarez, A.J.*).

9396 *Roulin, Gilles* The book of the Night: a royal composition documenting the conceptions of the hereafter at the beginning of the nineteenth
dynasty. Proc. 7th Cong. of Egyptologists. 1998 ⇒475. 1005-1013.
9397 **Smith, M.** The liturgy of opening the mouth for breathing. 1993 ⇒
10,10780... 12,9024. ᴿCÉg 73 (1998) 75-77 (*Chauveau, Michel*).
9398 *Smith, Mark* A new Egyptian cosmology. Proc. 7th Cong. of Egyptologists. 1998 ⇒475. 1075-1079.
9399 *Spalinger, Anthony* The limitations of formal ancient Egyptian
religion. JNES 57/4 (1998) 241-260;
9400 Praise God and pay the priests. Ä&L 7 (1998) 43-57.
9401 **Stricker, B.H.** Zijn en worden, I. 1997 ⇒13,9633. ᴿDiscussions in
Egyptology 41 (1998) 81-82 (*DuQuesne, Terence*).
9402 *Waitkus, Wolfgang* Zur Deutung von zwei Besuchsfesten der Göttlichen Stätte (*j³ t-nṯrjt*) von Edfu. Feste im Tempel, 4. ÄAT 33,2: 1998
⇒479. 155-174.
9403 *Wiebach-Koepke, Silvia* Motive des Sonnenlaufes in den Totenbuch-
Sprüchen des Neuen Reiches. SAÄK 25 (1998) 353-375 Zsfg. 353.
9404 **Wilkinson, Alix** The garden in ancient Egypt. L 1998, Rubicon xvii;
206 pp. 0-948695-48-X. Bibl.
9405 *Yamauchi, Edwin* Life, death, and the afterlife in the ancient Near
East. Life in the face of death. 1998 ⇒252. 21-50.
9406 **Zecchi, Marco** A study of the Egyptian god Osiris Hemag. 1996 ⇒
12,9032. ᴿBiOr 55 (1998) 755-758 (*Koemoth, Pierre P.*).

M7.0 Religio mesopotamica

9407 *Abusch, Tzvi* The internalization of suffering and illness in Mesopotamia: a development in Mesopotamian witchcraft literature. SEL 15
(1998) 49-58;
9408 Ghost and god: some observations on a Babylonian understanding of
human nature. Self, soul and body. SHR 78: 1998 ⇒286. 363-383.
9409 **Adinolfi, M.** Miti e riti religiosi dell'antica Mesopotamia. Montella,
AV 1998, Dragonetti 101 pp [RivBib 48,83—Rolla, Armando].
9410 *Beckman, Gary* Ištar of Nineveh reconsidered. JCS 50 (1998) 1-10.
9411 **Behrens, Hermann** Die Ninegalla-Hymne: die Wohnungnahme I-
nannas in Nippur in altbabylonischer Zeit. FAOS 21: Stu 1998,
Steiner 164 pp. DM64. 3-515-06478-8. 11 pl.
9412 *Berlejung, Angelika* Kultische Küsse: zu den Begegnungsformen
zwischen Göttern und Menschen. WO 29 (1998) 80-97.
9413 **Bottéro, Jean** La plus vieille religion: en Mésopotamie. Folio
Histoire 82: P 1998, Gallimard 448 pp pp. 2-07-032863-5 [RB 106,
452—Tournay, R.J.].
9414 **Butler, Sally A.L.** Mesopotamian conceptions of dreams and dream
rituals. AOAT 258: Müns 1998, Ugarit-Verlag xxxix; 475 pp. 3-
927120-65-0. 20 pl.
9415 **Chiodi, Silvia Maria** Offerte "funebri" nella Lagas presargonica.
Materiali per il vocabolario sumerico 5,1-2: 1997 ⇒13,2026. ᴿUF 30
(1998) 912-917 (*Balke, Thomas E.*).
9416 **Cunningham, Graham** 'Deliver me from evil': Mesopotamian incantations 2500-1500 BC. StP.SM 17: 1997 ⇒13,9647. ᴿBiOr 55
(1998) 850-852 (*Veldhuis, N.*).
9417 *Cunningham, Graham* Summoning the sacred in Sumerian incantations. SEL 15 (1998) 41-48.

9418 *Dandamayeva, M.M.* When did Chaldeans become soothsayers?. VDI 224 (1998) 56-60 Sum. 60. **R.**

9419 *Dick, Michael B.* The relationship between the cult image and the deity in Mesopotamia. Intellectual life. 1998 ⇒450. 111-116.

9420 *Farber, Walter* mara/at Anim oder : des Anu Töchterlein (in Singular und Plural, Text und Bild). ᶠBORGER R. 1998 ⇒12. 59-69.

9421 ᴱ**Finkel, I.L.; Geller, M.J.** Sumerian gods and their representations. 1997 ⇒13,9653. ᴿSEL 15 (1998) 124-125 (*Xella, Paolo*).

9422 *Finkel, Irving L.* A study in scarlet: incantations against Samana;

9423 *Geller, Markham J.* An incantation against curses. ᶠBORGER R. 1998 ⇒12. 71-106/127-140.

9424 **Groneberg, Brigitte R.M.** Lob der Ištar: Gebet und Ritual an die altbabylonische Venusgöttin: Tanatti Ištar. Cuneiform Monographs 8: 1997 ⇒13,9659. ᴿOLZ 93 (1998) 453-455 (*Reynolds, Frances*).

9425 *Hallo, William W.* Two letter-prayers to Amurru. ᶠGORDON, C. JSOT.S 273: 1998 ⇒31. 397-410.

9426 *Heimpel, Wolfgang* Anthropomorphic and bovine Lahmus. ᶠRÖMER, W. AOAT 253: 1998 ⇒97. 129-149;

9427 A circumambulation rite. Acta Sumerologica (Hiroshima) 20 (1998) 13-16.

9428 **Hutter, Manfred** Religionen in der Umwelt des Alten Testaments, 1: Babylonier, Syrer, Perser. 1996 ⇒12,9050; 13,9663. ᴿThLZ 123 (1998) 350-354 (*Dietrich, Manfried L.G.*); Bib. 79 (1998) 141-143 (*Bonnet, Corinne*).

9429 **Jonker, Gerdien** The topography of remembrance: the dead, tradition and collective memory in Mesopotamia. SHR 68: 1995 ⇒11/2, 8841... 13,9665. ᴿJNES 57 (1998) 74-75 (*Biggs, Robert D.*).

9430 *Lambert, W.G.* The qualifications of Babylonian diviners. ᶠBORGER R. 1998 ⇒12. 141-158.

9431 **Leick, Gwendolyn** The challenge of chance: an anthropological view of Mesopotamian mental strategies for the dealing with the unpredictable. Intellectual life. 1998 ⇒450. 195-198.

9432 **Litke, Richard L.** A reconstruction of the Assyro-Babylonian god-lists: AN: da-nu-um and AN: Anu sa ameli. Texts from the Babylonian collection 3: NHv 1998, The Yale Babylonian Collection xv; 283 pp. 47 pl.

9433 *Livingstone, Alasdair* The use of magic in the Assyrian and Babylonian hemerologies and menologies. SEL 15 (1998) 59-67.

9434 *Macgregor, Sherry* Two Neo-Assyrian examples of Lahmus. ᶠRÖMER, W. AOAT 253: 1998 ⇒97. 150-156.

9435 *Matsushima, Eiko* On the Lubuštu-ceremony of Bel in the seventh century B.C. Acta Sumerologica (Hiroshima) 20 (1998) 111-120.

9436 *Maul, Stefan M.* Der assyrische König—Hüter der Weltordnung. Gerechtigkeit. Kulte, Kulturen: 1998 ⇒283. 65-77;

9437 *Marduk, Nabû und der assyrische Enlil: die Geschichte eines sumerischen Šuꞌilas. ᶠBORGER R. 1998 ⇒12. 159-197.

9438 *Michalowski, Piotr* The unbearable lightness of Enlil. Intellectual life. 1998 ⇒450. 237-247.

9439 *Michel, Cécile* Les mites dꞌAssyrie: myths in the Assyrian texts of the second millennium B.C. JAOS 118 (1998) 325-331.

9440 *Pettinato, G.* Lipit-Eštar e la dea Nanaja. ᶠRÖMER, W. AOAT 253: 1998 ⇒97. 267-279.

9441 **Pettinato, Giovanni** La scrittura celeste: la nascita dell'astrologia in Mesopotamia. Saggi: Mi 1998, Mondadori 418 pp. L36.000. 88-04-40800-6. Bibl. ᴿBeO 40 (1998) 248-254 (*Sardini, Davide*).

9442 *Radner, Karen* Der Gott Salmanu ("Sulmanu") und seine Beziehung zur Stadt Dur-Katlimmu. WO 29 (1998) 33-51.

9443 **Reiner, Erica** Astral magic in Babylonia. TAPhS 85/4: 1995 ⇒11/2, 8847; 13,9680. ᴿOLZ 93 (1998) 455-458 (*Geller, Mark J.*);

9444 Babylonian planetary omens, 3. Cuneiform monographs: Groningen 1998, Styx viii; 290 pp. ƒ185. 90-5693-0117. Collab. *David Pingree*.

9445 *Ribichini, Sergio* La magia nel Vicino Oriente antico: introduzione tematica e bibliografica. SEL 15 (1998) 3-16.

9446 **Rochberg, Francesca R.** Babylonian horoscopes. TAPhS 88,1: Ph 1998, The American Philosophical Society xi; 164 pp. $20. 0-87169-881-1. Bibl.

9447 *Römer, W.H.Ph.* Eine Schicksalsentscheidung Enlils für König Lipi-teštar von Isin: Teil eines šir-nam-gala Ninisinas: Sumerische Hymnen IV. ᶠLORETZ O. AOAT 250: 1998 ⇒65. 669-683.

9448 *Spycket, A.* Une femme porteuse de chevreau (Pl. VII). Transeuphratène 16 (1998) 121-126.

9449 **Tinney, Steve** The Nippur lament: royal rhetoric and divine legitimation in the reign of Isme-Dagon of Isin (1953-1935 B.C.). 1996 ⇒12, 9062. ᴿBiOr 55 (1998) 809-813 (*Katz, D.*).

9450 *Torti, Rita* Ninurta, un dio misericordioso. RivBib 46 (1998) 3-17.

9451 *Van Dijk, J.J.A.* Inanna raubt den "großen Himmel": ein Mythos. ᶠBORGER R. 1998 ⇒12. 9-38.

9452 **Vanstiphout, Herman** Helden en goden van Sumer. Nijmegen 1998, SUN 253 pp. ƒ39.50. 90-6168-434-X.

9453 *Völling, Elisabeth* Bemerkungen zu einem Onyxfund aus Babylon. MDOG 130 (1998) 197-221.

9454 *Watanabe, Chikako Esther* Symbolism of the royal lion hunt in Assyria. Intellectual life. 1998 ⇒450. 439-450.

9455 *Westenholz, Joan* Goodnick Goddesses of the ancient Near East 3000-1000 BC. Ancient goddesses. 1998 ⇒298. 63-82.

9456 **Wiggermann, F.A.M.** Mesopotamian protective spirits: the ritual texts. 1992 ⇒9,12033. ᴿOLZ 93 (1998) 636-639 (*Böck, Barbara; Coruña, A.*).

M7.5 Religio persiana

9457 *Ahn, Gregor* Schöpfergott und Monotheismus: systematische Implikationen der neueren Gatha-Exegese. ᶠLORETZ O. AOAT 250: 1998 ⇒65. 15-26.

9458 *Arjomand, Saïd Amir* Artaxerxes, Ardašir, and Bahman. JAOS 118 (1998) 245-248.

9459 **Caner, Ertugrul** Bronzene Votivbleche von Giyimli. Archäologie in Iran und Turan 2: Rahden/Westf. 1998, Marie Leidorf viii; 205 pp. 3-89646-702-6. 147 pl.; Bibl.; Deutsches Archäologisches Institut, Eurasien-Abt. Aussenstelle Teheran.

9460 **Krasnowolska, Anna** Some key figures of Iranian calender mythology: (winter and spring). Kraków 1998, [The Grant of Jagiellonian University. The Faculty of Philology] 261 pp. 83-7052-445-1. Bibl.

9461 **Stausberg, Michael** Faszination Zarathustra: Zoroaster und die europäische Religionsgeschichte der frühen Neuzeit: 1-2. RVV 42: B 1998, de Gruyter xl; 1084 pp. 3-11-014959-1.
9462 **Widengren, Geo; Hultgard, Anders; Philonenko, Marc** Apocalyptique iranienne et dualisme qoumrânien. 1995 ⇒11/2,7127; 12,8368. ᴿCBQ 60 (1998) 408-409 (*Berquist, Jon L.*).

M8.2 *Muhammad et asseclae*—Qur'an and early diffusion of Islam

9463 *Borrmans, Maurice* Le livre et ses lectures [le Coran]. MoBi 115 (1998) 12-13.
9464 *Casciaro, José María* Jesús en el Corán. ScrTh 30 (1998) 13-38.
9465 *Déclais, Jean-Louis* La bible racontée par les premiers musulmans. NRTh 120 (1998) 216-232;
9466 Les histoires des prophètes: une relecture musulmane de la bible. MoBi 115 (1998) 48-50;
9467 Un livre qui confirme et qui contrôle. MoBi 115 (1998) 43-46.
9468 *Déclais, Jean-Louis; Platti, Emilio; Borrmans, Maurice* Les grandes figures bibliques dans le Coran. MoBi 115 (1998) 57-65.
9469 **Gil, Moshe** A history of Palestine, 634-1099. 1997 ⇒13,9691. ᴿStIsl 87 (1998) 159-162 (*Mouton, Jean-Michel*).
9470 ᴱ**Mébarki, Farah** Le Coran et la Bible. MoBi 115 (1998) 90 pp. 0154-9049.
9471 *Mohsen, Ismaïl* L'exégèse coranique à travers l'histoire. MoBi 115 (1998) 38-41.
9472 *Reeber, Michel* La pédagogie des signes: une approche thématique du Coran. MoBi 115 (1998) 51-54.
9473 **Sfar, Mondher** Le Coran, la Bible et l'Orient ancien. P ²1998, SFAR 447 pp. 2-9511936-1-0. Bibl.
9474 *Troll, Christian W.* Jesus Christ and christianity in Abdullah Yusuf Ali's English interpretation of the Qur'an. IslChr 24 (1998) 77-101.
9475 *Wadud, Amina* Auf der Suche nach der Stimme der Frau in einer Hermeneutik des Korans. Conc(D) 34 (1998) 269-277.
9476 *Wheeler, Brannon* Moses or Alexander?: Qur'an 18:60-65 in early islamic exegesis. JNES 57/3 (1998) 191-215.

M8.4 Islamic-christian relations

9477 **Adang, Camilla** Muslim writers on Judaism and the Hebrew Bible: from Ibn RABBAN to Ibn HAZM. IPTS 22: 1996 ⇒12,9074; 13,9690. ᴿBiOr 55 (1998) 287-293 (*Günther, Sebastian*).
9478 ᵀ**Bottini, Laura** Al-Kindí: Apologia del cristianesimo. Di fronte e attraverso 457; Patrimonio Culturale Arabo Cristiano 4: Mi 1998, Jaca 316 pp. 88-16-40457-4. Bibl.
9479 *Cate, Patrick O.* Islamic values and the gospel. BS 155 (1998) 355-370.
9480 *Farahian, Edmond* The Koran and the Bible: the figure of Abraham;
9481 *Farahian, Edmond; Van Nispen tot Sevenaer, Christiaan* Approches biblico-théologiques de l'Islam. Understanding and discussion. 1998 ⇒281. 13-29/31-57.

9482 *Gobillot, Geneviève* Jésus selon les mystiques musulmans. Graphè 17 (1998) 69-135.
9483 *Khoury, Adel Theodor* Christen und Muslime für eine "Miteinander-Identität". JRTR 6 (1998) 31-39.
9484 **Lazarus-Yafeh, Hava** Intertwined worlds: medieval Islam and bible criticism. 1992 ⇒8,b702; 9,12179. ᴿJNES 57 (1998) 292-293 (*Firestone, Reuven*).
9485 **Moucarry, Chawkat Georges** Pardon, repentir, conversion: études de ces concepts en Islam et de leurs équivalents bibliques. 1997 ⇒ 13,9695. ᴿIslChr 24 (1998) 254-255 (*Gabus, Jean-Paul*).
9486 **Moussali, Antoine** La croix et le croissant, le christianisme face à l'islam. P 1997, De Paris 117 pp. ᴿSedes Sapientiae 65 (1998) 77-80 (*Laurent, Annie*).
9487 **Pulcini, Theodore** Exegesis as polemical discourse: Ibn HAZM on Jewish and christian scriptures. AAR, the religions 2: Atlanta 1998, Scholars 216 pp. $45/$20. 0-7885-0396-02/-95-2. ᴿIslam and Christian-Muslim Relations 9 (1998) 382-383 (*Thomas, David*).
9488 **Räisänen, Heikki** Marcion, Muhammad and the Mahatma: exegetical perspectives on the encounter of cultures and faiths. 1997 ⇒13, 9698. ᴿIslam and Christian-Muslim Relations 9/1 (1998) 123-124 (*Leirvik, Oddbjørn*); Exchange 27 (1998) 186-187 (*Steenbrink, Karel*); Studies in World Christianity 4/1 (1998) 112-114 (*Jack, Alison*); ThLZ 123 (1998) 959-960 (*Elsas, Christoph*); Theol. 101 (1998) 56-57 (*Nineham, Dennis*).
9489 **Schimmel, Annemarie** Jesus und Maria in der islamischen Mystik. 1996 ⇒12,9087. ᴿOCP 64/1 (1998) 226-227 (*Troll, Chr.W.*).

M8.5 **Religiones Indiae** et Extremi Orientis

9490 *Chemparathy, George* A fundamental difference in the nature of bible and Veda as 'sacred scriptures'. ᶠBSTEH, A. 1998 ⇒17. 63-80.
9491 **Dalaï-Lama XIV** Le Dalaï-Lama parle de Jésus: une perspective bouddhiste sur les enseignements de Jésus. 1996 ⇒12,9089. ᴿSources 24 (1998) 226-237 (*Python, Vincent*).
9492 *Friedli, Richard* Reinkarnation und Auferstehung: Hindu-christliche Differenz oder Äquivalenz?. ᶠVENETZ, H. 1998 ⇒122. 109-116.
9493 **Holdrege, Barbara** Veda and torah: transcending the textuality of scripture. Albany 1996, State University of New York Press xiii; 765 pp. $20. ᴿHR 37 (1998) 404-405 (*Gold, Daniel*).
9494 **Senécal, Bernard** Jésus le Christ à la rencontre de Gautama le Bouddha: identité chrétienne et bouddhisme. Préf. *Gira, D.* Théologies: P 1998, Cerf 252 pp. FF145. ᴿSources 24 (1998) 270-271 (*Python, Vincent*).

XVII. Historia Medii Orientis Biblici

Q1 *Syria prae-islamica, Canaan* Israel Veteris Testamenti

9495 ^E**Levy, Thomas E.** The archaeology of society in the Holy Land. 1995, Pb. 1998 ⇒11/2,a054; 12,9477. ^RPEQ 130 (1998) 172-173 (*Philip, Graham*); CBQ 60 (1998) 397-399 (*Bloch-Smith, Elizabeth*).

9496 **Ahlström, Gösta W.** The history of ancient Palestine. JSOT.S 146: 1993 ⇒9,12326... 13,9709. ^RBZ 42 (1998) 103-106 (*Engel, Helmut*).

9497 *Anbar, Moshé* L'expédition d'Ešnunna et les relations entre Mari et Andarig durant les années ZL 3x1 et ZL 4x1: problèmes chronologiques. ^FRAINEY, A. IOS 18: 1998 ⇒96. 297-309.

9498 **Ash, Paul Stephen** The relationship between Egypt and Palestine during the time of David and Solomon: a reexamination of the evidence. ^DEmory 1998, 198 pp.

9499 **Barstad, Hans** The myth of the empty land: a study in the history and archaeology of Judah during the 'exilic' period. SO.S 28: 1996 ⇒12,9095; 13,9714. ^RPEQ 130 (1998) 68-69 (*Bartlett, John R.*); BiOr 55 (1998) 904-906 (*Geus, C.H.J. de*); RivBib 46 (1998) 102-103 (*Boschi, Bernardo Gianluigi*).

9500 *Bartl, Karin* Das Ende der Spätbronzezeit und das 'dunkle Zeitalter' im westlichen Vorderasien. Zwischen Euphrat und Indus. 1998 ⇒318. 193-208.

9501 *Beckerath, Jürgen von* Über chronologische Berührungspunkte der altägyptischen und der israelitischen Geschichte. ^FLORETZ O. AOAT 250: 1998 ⇒65. 91-99.

9502 *Bietak, Manfred* Gedanken zur Ursache der ägyptisierenden Einflüsse in Nordsyrien in der Zweiten Zwischenzeit. ^FSTADELMANN R. 1998 ⇒109. 165-176.

9503 **Bietenhard, Sophia Katharina** Des Königs General: die Heerführertraditionen in der vorstaatlichen und frühen staatlichen Zeit und die Joabgestalt in 2 Sam 2-20; 1 Kön 1-2. OBO 163: Gö 1998, Vandenhoeck & R xiv; 363 pp. DM130. 3-525-53799-9. ^DBerne 1996/97; Bibl.

9504 **Bock, Sebastian** Kleine Geschichte Israels: von den Anfängen bis zur neutestamentlichen Zeit. FrB ²1998, Herder 192 pp. 3-451-265-36-2 [NThAR 1998,334].

9505 *Bunimovitz, Shlomo* On the edge of empires—Late Bronze Age (1500-1200 BCE). Archaeology of society. 1998 ⇒9495. 320-331.

9506 *Campbell, Edward F.* A land divided: Judah and Israel from the death of Solomon to the fall of Samaria. The Oxford history. 1998 ⇒326. 273-319.

9507 *Caramelo, Francisco José Gomes* War motivations of the Hebrew people in face of the Neo-Babylonic offensive. Rencontre Assyriologique Internationale 34. 1998 ⇒452. 499-506.

9508 *Cazelles, H.* Archéologie, histoire et institutions en Israël. Transeuphratène 14 (1998) 133-152.

9509 *Charpin, Dominique* Toponymie amorrite et toponymie biblique: la ville de Ṣîbat/Ṣobah. RA 92/1 (1998) 79-92.

9510 *Cogan, Mordechai* Into exile: from the Assyrian conquest of Israel to the fall of Babylon. The Oxford history. 1998 ⇒326. 321-365.

9511 *Coldstream, Nicolas* The first exchanges between Euboeans and Phoenicians: who took the initiative?. ^FDOTHAN, T. 1998 ⇒23. 353-360.

9512 *Coogan, Michael David* In the beginning: the earliest history. The Oxford history. 1998 ⇒326. 3-31.

9513 *Davies, Philip R.* The future of "biblical history". Auguries. JSOT.S 269: 1998 ⇒225. 126-141.

9514 *Day, John* The Canaanite inheritance of the Israelite monarchy. King and Messiah. JSOT.S 270: 1998 ⇒378. 72-90.

9515 *Dever, William G.* Archaeology, ideology, and the quest for an "ancient" or "biblical" Israel. NEA(BA) 61/1 (1998) 39-52;

9516 Hurrian incursions and the end of the Middle Bronze Age in Syria-Palestine: a rejoinder to Nadav Na'aman. ^MWARD W. 1998 ⇒123. 91-110;

9517 Israelite origins and the "nomadic ideal": can archaeology separate fact from fiction?. ^FDOTHAN, T. 1998 ⇒23. 220-237;

9518 What did the biblical writers know, and when did they know it?. ^FFRERICHS, E. BJSt 320: 1998 ⇒28. 241-257.

9519 **Dion, Paul Eugène** Les araméens à l'Âge du fer: histoire politique et structures sociales. ÉtB 34: 1997 ⇒13,9736. ^RBiOr 55 (1998) 232-235 (*Lipiński, E.*); WO 29 (1998) 202-206 (*Sader, Hélène*).

9520 *Dothan, Trude* Initial Philistine settlement: from migration to coexistence. ^FDOTHAN, T. 1998 ⇒23. 148-161.

9521 *Drews, Robert* Canaanites and Philistines. JSOT 81 (1998) 39-61.

9522 *Durand, J.-M.* Réalités amorrites et traditions bibliques. RA 92/1 (1998) 3-40.

9523 **Ehrlich, Carl S.** The Philistines in transition: a history from ca. 1000-730 B.C.E. Studies in the History and Culture of the Ancient Near East 10: 1996 ⇒12,9117. ^RCBQ 60 (1998) 524-525 (*Hauer, Christian*); JBL 117 (1998) 720-721 (*Meyers, Carol*).

9524 **Elgavish, David** השירות הדיפלומטי במקרא ובתעודות מן המזרח הקדום [The diplomatic service in the bible and ancient Near Eastern sources]. J 1998, 298 pp [Zion 64,379ss—Tammuz, Oded]. **H**.

9525 *Eph'al, Israel* Changes in Palestine during the Persian period in light of epigraphic sources. IEJ 48 (1998) 106-119.

9526 *Faulstich, E.W.* Studies in O.T. and N.T. chronology. ^MSummers, R. 1998 ⇒115. 97-117.

9527 *Finkelstein, Israel* The great transformation: the 'conquest' of the highlands frontiers and the rise of the territorial states. Archaeology of society. 1998 ⇒9495. 349-365;

9528 Philistine chronology: high, middle or low?. ^FDOTHAN, T. 1998 ⇒ 23. 140-147.

9529 *Fortin, Michael* New horizons in ancient Syria: the view from 'Atij. Near Eastern archaeology 61 (1998) 15-24 [ZID 24,360].

9530 ^E**Fritz, Volkmar O.; Davies, Philip R.** The origins of the ancient Israelite states. JSOT.S 228: 1996 ⇒12,9122. ^RCBQ 60 (1998) 183-185 (*Murray, Pius*).

9531 *Gangloff, Frederic* In search of 'ancient Israel' / 'Palestine'?: new prospects (1970s to the present), (Part 2). ThRev 19 (1998) 3-28.

9532 *Gitin, Seymour* Philistia in transition: the tenth century BCE and beyond. ^FDOTHAN, T. 1998 ⇒23. 162-183.

9533 *Goodblatt, David* From Judeans to Israel: names of Jewish states in antiquity. JSJ 29 (1998) 1-36.

9534 *Gunn, David M.* Colonialism and the vagaries of scripture: Te Kooti in Canaan (a story of bible and dispossession in Aotearoa/New Zealand). [F]BRUEGGEMANN, W. 1998 ⇒16. 127-142.

9535 **Habib, Ascer David** Storia del popolo ebraico: il periodo biblico. Percorsi storici: R 1998, EdUP 94 pp. 88-86268-53-X. Bibl.

9536 *Hacohen, David ben-Gad* גבולה הדרומי של ארץ־ישראל בספרות התנאית ובמקרא [The southern boundary of the land of Israel in tannaitic literature and the bible]. Cathedra 88 (1998) 15-38 Sum. 181. **H.**

9537 *Hamilton, Mark W.* The past as destiny: historical visions in Sam'al and Judah under Assyrian hegemony. HThR 91 (1998) 215-250.

9538 **Herzog, Roman** Staaten der Frühzeit: Ursprünge und Herrschaftsformen. Mü [2]1998, Beck 329 pp. DM48. 3-406-42922-X [BiOr 57,135].

9539 *Holladay, John S.* The kingdoms of Israel and Judah: political and economic centralization in the Iron IIA-B (ca. 1000-750 BCE). Archaeology of society. 1998 ⇒9495. 368-398.

9540 *Hübner, Ulrich* Early Arabs in pre-Hellenistic Palestine in the context of the Old Testament. [F]LINDNER, M. BBB 118: 1998 ⇒62. 34-48.

9541 *Iacovou, Maria* Philistia and Cyprus in the eleventh century: from a similar prehistory to a diverse protohistory. [F]DOTHAN, T. 1998 ⇒23. 332-344.

9542 **Kaiser, Walter C.** A history of Israel: from the Bronze Age through the Jewish wars. Nv 1998, Broadman xx; 540 pp. $35. 08054-62848.

9543 *Kaswalder, Peter* 'Prince of Ekron' I. [T]*Heinsch, James.* Holy Land 18 (1998) 201-207.

9544 **Keel, Othmar; Uehlinger, Christoph** Göttinnen, Götter und Gottessymbole: neue Erkenntnisse zur Religionsgeschichte Kanaans und Israels aufgrund bislang unerschlossener ikonographischer Quellen. QD 134: FrB [4]1998, Herder xiv; 562 pp. 3-451-02134-X [NThAR 1999,3].

9545 **Kofoed, Jens Bruun** Israels historie som teologisk disciplin. K 1998, Dansk Bibel-Institut 94 pp [SEÅ 64,149s—Skott, Siv].

9546 **Kuhrt, Amélie** The ancient Near East c.3000-330 BC. 1995 ⇒11/2, 9457; 13,9762. 2 vols. [R]JNSL 24/2 (1998) 204-205 (*Cornelius, Izak*);

9547 The ancient Near East, 1-2. L 1998, Routledge xxviii; 381 + xix; 385-782 pp. 0-415-01353-4/16763-9/12872-2/16764-7.

9548 *LaBianca, Øystein S.; Younker, Randall W.* The kingdoms of Ammon, Moab and Edom: the archaeology of society in Late Bronze/Iron Age Transjordan (ca. 1400-500 BCE). Archaeology of society. 1998 ⇒9495. 399-415.

9549 **Langston, Scott M.** Cultic sites in the tribe of Benjamin: Benjamite prominence in the religion of Israel. AmUSt.TR 200: NY 1998, Lang 275 pp. 0-8204-3818-9 [NThAR 1999,3].

9550 **Lemche, Niels Peter** The Israelites in history and tradition. Library of Ancient Israel: L 1998, SPCK ix; 246 pp. $26. 0-664-22075-4. Bibl.

9551 *Lemche, Niels Peter* New perspectives on the history of Israel. [F]VAN DER WOUDE, A. VT.S 73: 1998 ⇒121. 42-60;

9552 The origin of the Israelite state: a Copenhagen perspective on the emergence of critical historical studies of ancient Israel in recent times. SJOT 12 (1998) 44-63.

9553 *Liverani, Mario* L'immagine dei fenici nella storiografia occidentale. StStor 39/1 (1998) 5-22.

9554 **Maier, Johann** Entre los dos testamentos: historia y religión en la época del segundo templo. BEB 89: 1996 ⇒12,9140; 13,9769. ^RRevAg 41 (1998) 827 (*Sabugal, Santos*).

9555 *Malamat, Abraham* Introductory essay: Mari and the bible: a comparative perspective. Mari and the bible. 1998 ⇒173. 1-10.

9556 *Mendels, Doron* Hecataeus of Abdera and a Jewish *Patrios politeia* of the Persian period (Diodorus Siculus 40.3). Identity. JSPE.S 24: 1998 <1983> ⇒174. 334-351.

9557 *Millard, Alan* Books in the late Bronze Age in the Levant. ^FRAINEY, A. IOS 18: 1998 ⇒96. 171-181.

9558 **Miller, Robert Donald** A social history of highland Israel in the 12th and 11th centuries B.C.E. AA 1998, 499 pp. ^DMichigan; microfiche [NThAR 1999,179].

9559 *Mojola, Aloo Osotsi* The 'tribes' of Israel?: a bible translator's dilemma. JSOT 81 (1998) 15-29.

9560 *Na'aman, Nadav* מסע שישק לארץ ישראל בראי כתובות המצריות, המקרא והממצא הארכיאולוגי [Shishak's campaign to Palestine as reflected by the epigraphic, biblical and archaeological evidence]. Zion 63 (1998) 247-276 Sum. XXI. H;

9561 Two notes on the history of Ashkelon and Ekron in the late eighth-seventh centuries B.C.E. TelAv 25 (1998) 219-227.

9562 *Oredsson, Dag* Jezreel—its contribution to Iron Age chronology. SJOT 12 (1998) 86-101.

9563 *Pitard, Wayne T.* Before Israel: Syria-Palestine in the Bronze Age. The Oxford history. 1998 ⇒326. 33-77.

9564 **Pixley, Jorge** Heilsgeschichte von unten: eine Geschichte des Volkes Israel aus der Sicht der Armen (1220 v.Chr.-135 n.Chr.). Nürnberg 1997, Athmann 146 pp. DM29,80.

9565 *Redmount, Carol A.* Bitter lives: Israel in and out of Egypt. The Oxford history. 1998 ⇒326. 79-121.

9566 **Ricciotti, Giuseppe** Storia d'Israele. 1997 <1932-1933> ⇒13,9786. ^RRSLR 34 (1998) 353-356 (*Bolgiani, Franco*).

9567 **Sacchi, Paolo** Storia del secondo tempio: Israele tra il IV secolo a.C. ed il I d.C. 1994 ⇒112,9237... 13,9787. ^RHenoch 20 (1998) 110-115 (*Mazzinghi, Luca*).

9568 *Sasson, Jack M.* The king and I: a Mari king in changing perceptions. JAOS 118 (1998) 453-470;

9569 About "Mari and the bible". RA 92/2 (1998) 97-124.

9570 **Schams, Christine** Jewish scribes in the Second-Temple period. JSOT.S 291: Shf 1998, Academic 363 pp. 1-85075-940-5. Bibl.

9571 *Scheffler, Eben* Debating the late-dating of the Old Testament. OTEs 11 (1998) 522-533.

9572 **Schoors, Antoon** Die Königreiche Israel und Juda im 8. und 7. Jahrhundert v. Chr.: die assyrische Krise. Biblische Enzyklopädie 5: Stu 1998, Kohlhammer 235 pp. DM42. 3-17-012334-3.

9573 *Shaheen, Alaael-din* Syro-Palestinian-Egyptian relations in the Early Bronze II period: reassessment. GöMisz 163 (1998) 95-100.

9574 *Silberman, Neil Asher* The sea peoples, the Victorians, and us: modern social ideology and changing archaeological interpretations of the late Bronze Age collapse. ^FDOTHAN, T. 1998 ⇒23. 268-275.

9575 *Simonetti, Cristina* Gli editti di remissione in Mesopotamia e nell'antica Siria. Le origini degli anni giubilari. 1998 ⇒2236. 11-73.

9576 **Snell, Daniel C.** Life in the ancient Near East, 3100-332 B.C.E. 1997 ⇒13,9793. ^RJAOS 118 (1998) 601-602 (*Sack, Ronald H.*); JBL 117 (1998) 718-720 (*Fleming, Daniel E.*).

9577 **Soggin, J.A.** Nueva historia de Israel: de los orígenes a Bar Kochbá. 1997 ⇒13,9794. ^REstAg 33 (1998) 159-160 (*Mielgo, C.*); St Juan de la Cruz 14 (1998) 282-284 (*Noguera, Juan Luis*).

9578 *Stager, Lawrence E.* The impact of the Sea peoples in Canaan (1185-1050 BCE). Archaeology of society. 1998 ⇒9495. 332-348.

9579 *Stern, Ephraim* The relations between the sea peoples and the Phoenicians in the twelfth and eleventh centuries BCE. ^FDOTHAN, T. 1998 ⇒23. 345-352.

9580 *Stieglitz, Robert R.* The Phoenician-Punic menology. ^FGORDON, C. JSOT.S 273: 1998 ⇒31. 211-221.

9581 **Sturm, Josef** La guerre de Ramsès II contre les hittites. ^T*Vandersleyen, Claude.* Connaissance de l'Égypte Ancienne 6: 1996 ⇒12,9165; 13, 9796. ^ROLZ 93 (1998) 448-450 (*Kitchen, Kenneth A.*).

9582 *Tsirkin, Ju.B.* The Tyrian power and her disintegration. RSFen 26 (1998) 175-189.

9583 **Tubb, Jonathan N.** Peoples of the past: Canaanites. L 1998, British Museum 160 pp. $33. 0-7141-2089-8. Bibl.

9584 *Van Zyl, Danie C.* From survival to domination: hope in the pre-monarchical until the early monarchical period of Israel. Scriptura 66 (1998) 189-197.

9585 **Whitelam, Keith W.** The invention of ancient Israel: the silencing of Palestinian history. 1996 ⇒12,9172; 13,9801. ^RPEQ 130 (1998) 162-165 (*Frendo, Anthony*); HeyJ 39 (1998) 189-193 (*Prior, Michael*); JBL 117 (1998) 117-119 (*Holloway, Steven W.*).

9586 *Younger, K. Lawson* The deportation of the Israelites. JBL 117 (1998) 201-227.

Q2 Historiographia—*theologia historiae*

9587 **Bagnall, Roger S.** Reading papyri, writing ancient history. 1995 ⇒ 11/2,9268; 12,9178. ^RBiOr 55 (1998) 787-792 (*Hauben, Hans*).

9588 *Barc, Bernard* Bible et mathématiques à la période hellenistique. ^FMARGAIN, J. 1998 ⇒71. 269-279.

9589 *Braun, Lucien* Historiographie et iconographie philosophiques. RHPhR 78/1 (1998) 3-14.

9590 **Brettler, Marc Zvi** The creation of history in ancient Israel. L ²1998 <1995>, Routledge ⇒11/2,9276. xv; 254 pp.
   ^E**Coogan, M.** The Oxford history... biblical world 1998 ⇒326.

9591 ^{TE}**Cordiano, Giuseppe; Zorat, Marta** DIODORO Siculo: biblioteca storica: libri I-VIII: mitologia e protostoria dei popoli orientali, dei Greci e dei Romani. I classici di storia, sez. greco romana 8,1: Mi 1998, Rusconi 736 pp. 88-18-16012-5. Bibl.

9592 *Cornelius, Izak* Introducing the history of the Ancient Near East. JNSL 24/2 (1998) 201-206.

9593 *DiTommaso, Lorenzo* A note on DEMETRIUS the chronographer, Fr. 2.11 (= Eusebius, PrEv 9.21.11). JSJ 29 (1998) 81-91.

9594 *Eslinger, Lyle* Ezekiel 20 and the metaphor of historical teleology: concepts of biblical history. JSOT 81 (1998) 93-125.

9595 **Finegan, Jack** Handbook of biblical chronology: principles of time reckoning in the ancient world and problems of chronology in the bible. Princeton 1998, Princeton University Press xxxvii; 426 pp. $35. 1-56563-143-9. [R]CV 40 (1998) 163-167 (*Segert, Stanislav*).

9596 **Finley, Moses I.** Problemi e metodi di storia antica. Pref. *Arnaldo Momigliano*. Biblioteca Universale Laterza 487: R 1998, Laterza xii; 204 pp. 88-420-5579-4.

9597 *Freund, Yossef* Characteristics of biblical historiography. JBQ 26 (1998) 177-183.

9598 **Green, Peter** Classical bearings: interpreting ancient history and culture. Berkeley, CA 1998, University of California 328 pp. 0-520-20811-0.

9599 *Hallo, William W.* New directions in historiography (Mesopotamia and Israel). [F]RÖMER, W. AOAT 253: 1998 ⇒97. 109-128.

9600 *Kallai, Zecharia* Joshua and Judges 1 in biblical historiography;
9601 Aspects of literary composition in biblical historiography. Biblical historiography. 1998 ⇒167. 243-260/261-283.

9602 *Lehmkühler, Karsten* "Geschichte durch Geschichte überwinden": zur Verwendung eines Zitates. JETh 12 (1998) 115-137.

9603 *Lux, Rüdiger* Erinnerungskultur und Zensur im alten Israel. BThZ 15 (1998) 190-205.

9604 *Mendels, Doron* 'Creative history' in the Hellenistic Near East in the third and second centuries BCE: the Jewish case. Identity. JSPE.S 24: 1998 <1988> ⇒174. 357-393.

9605 **Mortley, Raoul** The idea of universal history from Hellenistic philosophy to early christian historiography. TSR 67: 1996, ⇒13,9835. [R]JThS 49 (1998) 324-328 (*Burgess, R.W.*).

9606 *Pasto, James* When the end is the beginning?: or when the biblical past is the political present: some thoughts on ancient Israel, "postexilic Judaism," and the politics of biblical scholarship. SJOT 12 (1998) 157-202.

9607 *Reid, Garnett H.* Minimalism and biblical history. BS 155 (1998) 394-410.

9608 *Roux, Jurie le* Israel's past and the feeling of loss (or: deconstructing the 'minimum' of the 'minimalists' even further). OTEs 11 (1998) 477-486.

9609 **Shrimpton, G.S.** History and memory in ancient Greece. Montreal 1997, McGill-Queen's Univ. Press xvii; 318 pp. £28. 0-7735-1021-4 [CIR 50,434s—Lewis, Sian].

9610 *Winter, B.W. Christentum und Antike*: Acts and Paul's *Corpus* as ancient history. [F]JUDGE E. 1998 ⇒47. 121-130.

Q3 *Historia Ægypti*—Egypt

9611 *Ahituv, Shmuel* Egypt that Isaiah knew. Jerusalem studies. ÄAT 40: 1998 ⇒361. 3-7.

9612 **Aldred, Cyril** The Egyptians. [E]Dodson, Aidan. Ancient Peoples and Places 18: L [3]1998, Thames and H. 224 pp. 0-500-28036-3. Bibl.

9613 **Alston, R.** Soldier and society in Roman Egypt: a social history. L 1998 <1995>, Routledge viii; 263 pp. 0-415-18606-4 [DiscEg 43, 57ss—La'da, Csaba A.].

9614 **Arnold, Dieter** Building in Egypt. 1991 ⇒7,b651...12,9548. [R]Disc Eg 41 (1998) 89-92 (*Matthews, Valerie*).

9615 *Aston, David A.; Bader, Bettina* Einige Bemerkungen zum späten Neuen Reich in Matmar. MDAI.K 54 (1998) 19-48.

9616 *Baines, John* Ancient Egyptian kingship: official forms, rhetoric, context. King and Messiah. JSOT.S 270: 1998 ⇒378. 16-53.

9617 **Beckerath, Jürgen von** Chronologie des ägyptischen Neuen Reiches. HÄB 39: 1994 ⇒10,11078... 13,9857. ᴿJNES 57 (1998) 309-311 *(Wente, Edward F.)*.

9618 *Ben-Tor, Daphna* The relations betwen Egypt and Palestine during the Middle Kingdom as reflected by contemporary Canaanite scarabs. Proceedings 7th Cong. of Egyptologists. 1998 ⇒475. 149-163.

9619 **Bernand, André** Leçon de civilisation. P 1994, Fayard 492 pp. ᴿAulOr 16 (1998) 295-297 *(Pòrtulas, Jaume)*.

9620 **Bleiberg, Edward** The official gift in ancient Egypt. Norman 1996, Univ. of Oklahoma Press xv; 173 pp. $28.

9621 *Blumenthal, Elke* Sinuhes persönliche Frömmigkeit. Jerusalem studies. ÄAT 40: 1998 ⇒361. 213-231.

9622 *Bolshakov, Andrey O.; Soushchevski, Andrey G.* Hero and society in ancient Egypt (I-II). GöMisz 163 (1998) 7-25; 164 (1998) 21-31.

9623 *Botta, Félix Alejandro* Sin and forgiveness in the Demotic story of Setne I. Jerusalem studies. ÄAT 40: 1998 ⇒361. 233-241.

9624 **Bowring, John** Report on Egypt 1823-1838: under the reign of Mohamed Ali. Triade exploration's Major Reprint Series 1: L 1998, Triade Exploration (22), 550 pp. 0-9527827-1-5. Notes, index, bibl.

9625 ᴱ**Bresciani, Edda** L'Antico Egitto. [Novara] 1998, De Agostini 351 pp. 88-415-5259-X.

9626 **Callender, Gae** Egypt in the Old Kingdom: an introduction. L 1998, Longman 208 pp. £24. 0-582-81226-7. Many fig. [DiscEg 44, 118ss—Matthews, Valerie].

9627 ᴱ**Camplani, Alberto** L'Egitto cristiano: aspetti e problemi in età tardo-antica. SEAug. 56: 1997 ⇒13,9862. ᴿJThS 49 (1998) 365-368 *(Frend, W.H.C.)*.

9628 *Castel Ronda, Elisa* Algunos aspectos generales del clero en el Antiguo Egipto: estudio prelminar II. BAEO 33 (1997) 277-291.

9629 **Cervellò Autuori, Josep** Egipto y África: origen de la civilización y la monarquía faraónicas en su contexto africano. AulOr.S 13: 1996 ⇒12,9210. ᴿDiscEg 41 (1998) 75-80 *(DuQuesne, Terence)*.

9630 **Clagett, Marshall** Calendars, clocks, and astronomy. Ancient Egyptian science, 2. 1995 ⇒11/2,b496. ᴿJAOS 118 (1998) 75-76 *(Depuydt, Leo)*.

9631 **Cribiore, Raffaella** Writing, teachers, and students in Graeco-Roman Egypt. ASP 36: 1996 ⇒12,9214. ᴿByZ 91 (1998) 515-516 *(Harrauer, Hermann)*; Aeg. 78 (1998) 221-222 *(Daris, Sergio)*.

9632 **Currid, John D.** Ancient Egypt and the Old Testament. 1997 ⇒13,9864. ᴿAUSS 36 (1998) 117-119 *(Drey, Philip)*.

9633 **David, Ann Rosalie** Handbook to life in ancient Egypt. NY 1998, Facts on File xvi; (2) 382 pp. 0-8160-3312-9. Bibl.

9634 ᴱ**Davies, W. Vivian; Schofield, Louise** Egypt, the Aegean and the Levant. 1995 ⇒11/2,461; 13,274. ᴿArOr 66 (1998) 172-173. *(Smoláriková, Květa)*; BiOr 55 (1998) 387-394 *(Phillips, J.)*.

9635 *Depuydt, Leo* Ancient Egyptian star clocks and their theory. BiOr 55/1-2 (1998) 6-44.

9636 *Devauchelle, Didier* Un problème de chronologie sous Cambyse. Transeuphratène 15 (1998) 9-17.

9637 *Di Nóbile Carlucci, Laura* Apuntes sobre Nefertari, esposa y reina. BAEO 34 (1998) 47-64.

9638 **Doxey, Denise M.** Egyptian non-royal epithets in the Middle Kingdom: a social and historical analysis. PÄ 12: Lei 1998, Brill 435 pp. ᴰPennsylvania 1995. ᴿJSSEA 27 (1997) 101-103 (*Sagrillo, Troy L.*).

9639 ᴱ**Eide, T.**, *al.*, Fontes historiae nubiorum: textual sources for the history of the Middle Nile Region, 2: from the mid-fifth to the first century BC. 1996 ⇒12,9219. ᴿOr. 67 (1998) 127-9 (*Hofmann, Inge*).

9640 *El-Saady, Hassan* Considerations on bribery in Ancient Egypt. SAÄK 25 (1998) 295-304 Sum. 295.

9641 **Feucht, Erika** Das Kind im Alten Ägypten. 1995 ⇒13,9875. ᴿJESHO 41 (1998) 118-121 (*Roth, Ann Macy*).

9642 *Fikhman, I.F.* On onomastics of Greek and Roman Egypt. ᶠSOHL-BERG, D. 1996. ⇒8271. 403-414.

9643 **Gabolde, Marc** D'Akhenaton à Toutänkhamon. Collection de l'Institut d'Archéologie et d'Histoire de l'Antiquité 3: P 1998, De Boccard (6), lxx; 315 pp. 2-911971-02-7. Bibl.

9644 **Gallo, Carlo** L'astronomia egizia: dalle scoperte archeologiche alla misurazione del tempo. Muzzio scienza: [Padova] 1998, Muzzio xviii; 196 pp. 88-7021-874-0. Pres. *Walter Ferreri*; Bibl.

9645 *Goedicke, Hans* Khu-u-Sobek's fight in 'Asia'. Ä&L 7 (1998) 33-37.

9646 *Goelet, Ogden Jr; Levine, Baruch A.* Making peace in heaven and on earth: religious and legal aspects of the treaty between Ramesses II and Hattušili III. ᶠGORDON, C. JSOT.S 273: 1998 ⇒31. 252-299.

9647 **Görg, Manfred** Die Beziehungen zwischen dem alten Israel und Ägypten: von den Anfängen bis zum Exil. EdF 290: 1997 ⇒13,9878. ᴿOLZ 93 (1998) 663-664 (*Pfeifer, Gerhard*).

9648 ᴱ**Grimal, Nicolas-Christophe** Les critères de datation stylistiques à l'Ancien Empire. BEt 120: [Le Caire] 1998, Institut Français d'Archéologie Orientale x; 419 pp. 2-7247-0206-9.

9649 **Gundlach, Rolf** Der Pharao und sein Staat: die Grundlegung der ägyptischen Königsideologie im 4. und 3. Jahrtausend. Da:Wiss 1998, xv; 320 pp. DM78. 3-534-12343-3. ᴿJEA 84 (1998) 237-238 (*Malek, Jaromir*).

9650 **Gurrid, John** Ancient Egypt and the Old Testament. GR 1997, Baker 269 pp. £13.50. Foreword by *Kenneth A. Kitchen*.

9651 **Hasel, Michael G.** Domination and resistance: Egyptian military activity in the southern Levant, ca. 1300-1185 B.C. PÄ 11: Lei 1998, Brill xxiii; 372 pp. ƒ212/$124.50. 90-04-10984-6. Bibl.

9652 *Higginbotham, Carolyn R.* The Egyptianizing of Canaan: how iron-fisted was Pharaonic rule in the city-states of Syria-Palestine?. BArR 24/3 (1998) 37-43, 69.

9653 **Hölbl, Günther** Geschichte des Ptolemäerreiches. 1994 ⇒10,11245. ᴿBiOr 55 (1998) 156-159 (*Anagnostou-Canas, Barbara*).

9654 **Jacq, Christian** Die Ägypterinnen: eine Kulturgeschichte. ᵀ*Schmidt, Thorsten*. Z 1998, Artemis & W. 336 pp. 3-538-07074-1. Bibl.

9655 ᴱ**Johnson, Janet H.** Life in...Egypt. 1992 ⇒8,719. ᴿOLZ 93 (1998) 157-165 (*Kákosy, Lászlo*); CÉg 73 (1998) 69-70 (*Meulenaere, Herman de*).

9656 *Kahn, Dan-El* Divine intervention and the surrender of Nimrod in the Pi(ankh)y Stela (lines 34-58). Jerusalem studies. ÄAT 40: 1998 ⇒361. 285-294.

9657 **Kamil, J.** The ancient Egyptians—life in the Old Kingdom. 1996 ⇒ 12,9229. ᴿBiOr 55 (1998) 395-397 (*El-Metwally, Emad*).

9658 *Kloth, Nicole* Beobachtungen zu den biographischen Inschriften des Alten Reiches. SAÄK 25 (1998) 189-205 Zsfg. 189.

9659 **Lacovara, Peter** The New Kingdom royal city. 1997 ⇒13,9891. ᴿDiscussions in Egyptology 41 (1998) 67-70 *(Aston, D.A.)*.

9660 **Lampela, Anssi** Rome and the Ptolemies of Egypt: the development of their political relations, 273-80 B.C. Commentationes Humanarum Litterarum 111: [Helsinki] 1998, Societas Scientiarum Fennica (7); 301 pp. 951-653-295-0. Bibl.

9661 **Martín Valentín, Francisco J.** Amen-hotep III: el esplendor de Egipto. El legado de la historia 1: M 1998, Alderabá 366 pp. 84-88676-34-4.

9662 **Menu, Bernadette** Recherches sur l'histoire juridique, économique et sociale de l'ancienne Égypte II. BEt 122: [Le Caire] 1998, Institut Français d'Archéologie Orientale viii; 423 pp. 2-7247-0217-4.

9663 *Meurer, Georg* "Wer etwas Schlechtes sagen wird, indem er ihre Majestät lästert, der wird sterben": wie verwundbar waren das äyptische Königtum bzw. der einzelne Herrscher?. Jerusalem studies. ÄAT 40: 1998 ⇒361. 307-321.

9664 **Montserrat, Dominic** Sex and society in Graeco-Roman Egypt. 1996 ⇒12,9237; 13,9901. ᴿDiscEg 41 (1998) 83-87 *(La'da, Csaba)*; ClR 48 (1998) 419-420 *(Rathbone, D.W.)*; JEA 84 (1998) 256-258 *(Robins, Gay)*.

9665 **Mordrzejewski, Joseph Mélèze** The Jews of Egypt: from Rameses II to Emperor Hadrian. 1995 ⇒11/2,7212; 13,9900. ᴿJSSt 43 (1998) 363-365 *(Bohak, Gideon)*;

9666 Les juifs d'Égypte de Ramsès II à Hadrien. 1997 ⇒13,9899. ᴿRSO 72 (1998) 313-319 *(Ciampini, Emanuele)*.

9667 *Moreno Garcia, Juan Carlos* La population *mrt*: une approche du problème de la servitude dans l'Egypte du IIIᵉ millénaire (I). JEA 84 (1998) 71-83.

9668 *Morenz, Ludwig D.* Fremde als potentielle Feinde: die prophylaktische Szene der Erschlagung der Fremden in Altägypten. Annäherung. ZDMG.S 11: 1998 ⇒449. 93-103.

9669 **Mysliwiec, Karol** Herr beider Länder: Ägypten im 1. Jahrtausend v. Chr. ᵀ*Kachlak, Tadeusz*. Kulturgeschichte der antiken Welt 69: Mainz 1998, von Zabern 288 pp. 3-8053-1966-5.

9670 ᴱ**O'Connor, David; Silverman, David P.** Ancient Egyptian kingship. 1995 ⇒11/2,9409; 13,9904. ᴿJARCE 35 (1998) 200-201 *(Goedicke, Hans)*; JAOS 118 (1998) 286-287 *(Bleiberg, Edward)*.

9671 *Onasch, Angela* Der Titel "Schreiber des Königs"—Ursprung und Funktion. Jerusalem studies. ÄAT 40: 1998 ⇒361. 331-343.

9672 **Peden, A.J.** The reign of Ramesses IV. 1994 ⇒10,11107... 13,9907. ᴿJNES 57 (1998) 158-159 *(Spalinger, Anthony)*.

9673 *Polz, Daniel* Theben und Avaris: zur 'Vertreibung' der Hyksos. ᶠSTADELMANN R. 1998 ⇒109. 219-231;

9674 The Ramsesnakht dynasty and the fall of the New Kingdom: a new monument in Thebes. SAÄK 25 (1998) 257-293 Sum. 257.

9675 *Poo, Mu-Chou* Encountering the strangers: a comparative study of cultural consciousness in ancient Egypt, Mesopotamia, and China. Proceedings 7th Cong. of Egyptologists. 1998 ⇒475. 885-892.

9676 **Pressl, Diana Alexandra** Beamte und Soldaten: die Verwaltung in der 26. Dynastie in Ägypten (664-525 v.Chr.). EHS 779: Fra 1998, Lang 338 pp [OLZ 94,647ss—Gnirs, Andrea Maria].

9677 *Rabehl, Silvia* Der Königssohn von Kusch, Mrj-msw, in München. Jerusalem studies. ÄAT 40: 1998 ⇒361. 81-85.
9678 ᴱ**Rowlandson, Jane** Women and society in Greek and Roman Egypt: a sourcebook. C 1998, CUP xxi; 406 pp. $A45. 0-5215-8815-4 [Prudentia 31,163ss—McKechnie, Paul].
9679 *Ryholt, Kim* King Qareḥ, a Canaanite king of Egypt during the Second Intermediate Period. IEJ 48 (1998) 194-200;
9680 Hotepibre, a supposed Asiatic king in Egypt with relations to Ebla. BASOR 311 (1998) 1-6.
9681 *Sabbahy, Lisa K.* The king's mother in the Old Kingdom with special reference to the title *sꜣt-nṯr*. SAÄK 25 (1998) 305-310 Sum. 305.
9682 **Schneider, Thomas** Ausländer in Ägypten während des Mittleren Reiches und der Hyksoszeit, 1: die ausländischen Könige. ÄAT 42/1: Wsb 1998, Harrassowitz 208 pp. 3-447-04049-1.
9683 ᴱ**Shirun-Grumach, Irene** Jerusalem studies in egyptology. ÄAT 40: Wsb 1998, Harrassowitz ix; 406 pp. 3-447-04085-8.
9684 **Smith, Stuart Tyson** Askut in Nubia: the economics and ideology of Egyptian imperialism in the second millennium BC. L 1995, Kegan P 242 pp. £75/$127.50. 0-7103-0500-1. Num. ill. ᴿJESHO 41 (1998) 503-505 (*Snape, Steven*); CÉg 73 (1998) 89-94 (*Gratien, Brigitte*); JEA 84 (1998) 243-246 (*Aston, D.A.*).
9685 ᴱ**Spencer, Jeffrey** Aspects of early Egypt. 1996 ⇒12,243; 13,9915. ᴿJARCE 35 (1998) 197-198 (*Houlihan, Patrick F.*).
9686 *Stadnikow, Sergei* Himmelsrichtungen und Bogenvölker als Herrschaftsbereiche des ägyptischen Königs in den Pyramidentexten. Proceedings 7th Cong. of Egyptologists. 1998 ⇒475. 1095-1102.
9687 *Strauß-Seeber, Christine* Amenophis III. in Medinet Habu. Feste im Tempel, 4. ÄAT 33,2: 1998 ⇒479. 143-153.
9688 **Strouhal, Eugen** Ägypten zur Pharaonenzeit: alltag und gesellschaftliches Leben. Tü 1994, Wasmuth 280 pp. DM98. 3-8030-1043-8. 289 ill.; phot. *Werner Forman.* ᴿWO 29 (1998) 171-173 (*Feucht, Erika*).
9689 **Tyldesley, Joyce** Nefertiti: Egypt's sun queen. L 1998, Viking xvii; 232 pp. £17. 0-670-86998-8. 39 fig.; 19 pl. [Antiquity 72,937—Sinclair, Anthony].
9690 **Vandersleyen, Claude** De la fin de l'Ancien Empire à la fin du Nouvel Empire. L'Égypte et la vallée du Nil, 2. 1995 ⇒11/2,9427... 13,9919. ᴿJNES 57 (1998) 294-298 (*Murnane, William J.*).
9691 *Vandersleyen, Claude* Les guerres de Mérenptah et de Ramsès III contre les peuples de l'ouest, et leurs rapports avec le Delta. Proceedings 7th Cong. of Egyptologists. 1998 ⇒475. 1197-1203.
9692 *Van Dijk, Jacobus* Elite en goddelijk koningschap in Egypte aan het eind van de achttiende dynastie. Phoenix 44/1 (1998) 7-20.
9693 **Vinson, Steve** The Nile boatman at work. MÄSt 48: Mainz 1998, Von Zabern xi; 210 pp. 3-8053-2454-5. Bibl.
9694 *Vivas Sáinz, Inmaculada* Los contactos entre Egipto y el Egeo durante el II período intermedio y los comienzos de la XVIII dinastía: nuevas perspectivas. BAEO 34 (1998) 65-78.
9695 *Wachsmann, Shelley* Were the Sea Peoples Mycenaeans?: the evidence of ship iconography. Res maritimae. 1998 ⇒491. 339-356.
9696 **Warburton, David A.** State and economy in ancient Egypt: fiscal vocabulary of the New Kingdom. OBO 151: 1997 ⇒13,9923. ᴿETR 73 (1998) 267-269 (*Smyth, Françoise*); WO 29 (1998) 174-177

(*Quack, Joachim Friedrich*); AcOr 59 (1998) 235-237 (*Pierce, Richard Holton*).

9697 *Watrin, Luc* The relationship betwen the Nile delta and Palestine during the fourth millennium: from early exchange (naqada I-II) to the colonisation of southern Palestine (Naqada III). Proceedings 7th Cong. of Egyptologists. 1998 ⇒475. 1215-1226.

9698 **Watterson, Barbara** Ancient Egypt. Sutton Pocket histories: [Gloucester] 1998, Sutton xix; 108 pp. 0-7509-1913-2. Bibl.

9699 **Way, Thomas von der** Untersuchungen zur Spätvor- und Frühgeschichte Unterägyptens. 1993 ⇒11/2,9431; 13,9926. [R]BiOr 55 (1998) 109-113 (*Wilkinson, Toby A.H.*).

9700 *Weinstein, James M.* Egyptian relations with the eastern Mediterranean world at the end of the second millennium BCE. [F]DOTHAN, T. 1998 ⇒23. 188-196.

9701 *Wiener, Malcolm H.; Allen, James P.* Separate lives: the Ahmose stela and the Theran eruption. JNES 57/1 (1998) 1-28.

9702 **Wilkinson, Toby A.H.** State formation in Egypt: chronology and society. 1996 ⇒12,9250; 13,9927. [R]BiOr 55 (1998) 105-109 (*Trigger, Bruce G.*); DiscEg 40 (1998) 159-164 (*Ciałowicz, Krzystof M.*).

Q4.0 Historia Mesopotamiae

9703 *André-Salvini, Béatrice* La conscience du temps en Mésopotamie. Temps vécu. 1998 ⇒445. 29-37.

9704 *Azize, Joseph* Who was responsible for the Assyrian King List?. Abr-n. 35 (1998) 1-27.

9705 *Battini, Laura* Les portes urbaines de la capitale de Sargon II: étude sur la propagande royale à travers les données archéologiques et textuelles. Intellectual life. 1998 ⇒450. 41-55.

9706 **Bauer, Josef; Englund, Robert K.; Krebernik, Manfred** Mesopotamien: Späturuk-Zeit und frühdynastische Zeit. OBO 160,1: FrS 1998, Universitätsverlag 627 pp. FS175. 3-7278-1166-8.

9707 *Beaulieu, Paul-Alain* Bax'u-asitu and Kaššaya, daughters of Nebuchadnezzar II. Or. 67 (1998) 173-201.

9708 **Brack-Bernsen, Lis** Zur Entstehung der babylonischen Mondtheorie: Beobachtung und theoretische Berechnung von Mondphasen. Boethius 40: 1997 ⇒13,9934. [R]ZA 88 (1998) 287-291 (*Koch, J.*).

9709 *Canby, Jeanny Vorys* The stela of Ur-Nammu reconsidered. Rencontre Assyriologique Internationale 34. 1998 ⇒452. 211-219.

9710 **Charvát, Petr** On people, signs and states: spotlights on Sumerian society, c.3500-2500 B.C. Prague 1998, Oriental Institute 117 pp. 80-85425-28-9. Bibl.

9711 *Crüsemann, Nicola; Feller, Barbara; Heinz, Marlies* Prestigegüter und Politik: Aspekte internationaler beziehungen im 2. Jt. v. Chr. Zwischen Euphrat und Indus. 1998 ⇒318. 175-192.

9712 *Dalley, Stephanie* The influence of Mesopotamia upon Israel and the bible. Legacy of Mesopotamia. 1998 ⇒328. 57-83;

9713 Yabâ, Atalyā and the foreign policy of late Assyrian kings. SAA Bulletin 12 (1998) 83-98.

9714 *Dalley, Stephanie; Reyes, A.T.* Mesopotamian contact and influence in the Greek world, 1: to the Persian conquest; 2: Persia, Alexander, and Rome. Legacy of Mesopotamia. 1998 ⇒328. 85-106; 107-124.

9715 **De Meis, Salvo; Hunger, Hermann** Astronomical dating of Assyrian and Babylonian reports. SOR 81: R 1998, Istituto Italiano per
l'Africa e l'Oriente 95 pp. 18 fig.
9716 **Dunstan, William E.** The ancient Near East. Ancient civilizations:
Fort Worth 1998, Harcourt, B & W xvi; 332 pp. 0-03035-2991. Bibl.
9717 *Ehrenberg, Erica* Archaism and individualism in the late Babylonian
period. Intellectual life. 1998 ⇒450. 125-140.
9718 **Elayi, Josette; Sapin, Jean** Beyond the river: new perspectives on
Transeuphratene. JSOT.S 250: Shf 1998, Academic 191 pp. £35/$58.
1-85075-678-3.
9719 **Forest, Jean-Daniel** Mésopotamie: l'apparition de l'état VIIe-IIIe
millénaires. 1996 ⇒12,9261. ^RNEA(BA) 61 (1998) 69-70 (*Schwartz,
Glenn M.*); Paléorient 24/2 (1998) 122-124 (*Frangipane, Marcella*).
9720 *Frahm, Eckart* Sanherib und die Tempel von Kuyunjik. ^FBORGER R.
1998 ⇒12. 107-121.
9721 **Frame, Grant** Babylonia 689-627 B.C.: a political history. 1992
⇒8,b992... 11/2,9446. ^RAt. 86 (1998) 605-606 (*Mora, Clelia*);
ZDMG 148 (1998) 204-206 (*Schramm, Wolfgang*);
9722 Rulers of Babylonia from the second dynasty of Isin to the end of
Assyrian domination (1157-612 B.C.). 1995 ⇒11/2,9447; 12,9262
^RBiOr 55 (1998) 843-849 (*Borger, R.*).
9723 *Garelli, Paul* Les dames de l'empire assyrien. Intellectual life. 1998
⇒450. 175-181.
9724 **Gasche, Hermann**, *al.*, Dating the fall of Babylon: a reappraisal of
second-millennium chronology (a joint Ghent-Chicago-Harvard project). Mesopotamian History and Environment 2; Memoirs 4: Ghent
1998, University of Ghent vi; (2) 104 pp. Bibl. ^RRA 92 (1998) 187-
188 (*Amiet, Pierre*).
9725 *Gasche, H.*, *al.*, A correction to: Dating the fall of Babylon: a reappraisal of second-millennium chronology (= MHEM 4), Ghent and
Chicago, 1998. Akkadica 108 (1998) 1-4.
9726 *Gerber, Manuel* Die Inschrift H(arran)1.A/B und die neubabyloni-
sche Chronologie. ZA 88 (1998) 72-93.
9727 *Grayson, A. Kirk* Assyrian expansion into Anatolia in the Sargonid
age (c. 744-650 BC). Rencontre Assyriologique Internationale 34.
1998 ⇒452. 131-135.
9728 **Grayson, Albert Kirk** Assyrian rulers of the early first millennium
BC II (858-745 BC). 1996 ⇒12,9266; 13,9947. ^RBiOr 55 (1998)
189-192 (*Fuchs, Andreas*); ZA 88 (1998) 286-287 (*Streck, M.P.*).
9729 *Heinz, Marlies* Migration und Assimilation im 2.Jt. v. Chr.: die Kas-
siten. Zwischen Euphrat und Indus. 1998 ⇒318. 165-174.
9730 *Lafont, Sophie* Fief et féodalité dans le Proche-Orient ancien. Les
féodalités. 1998 ⇒321. 517-630.
9731 *Lambert, W.G.* Kingship in ancient Mesopotamia. King and Messiah.
JSOT.S 270: 1998 ⇒378. 54-70.
9732 **Lamprichs, Roland** Die Westexpansion des neuassyrischen Reiches:
eine Strukturanalyse. AOAT 239: 1995 ⇒11/2,9460. ^RThLZ 123
(1998) 354-358 (*Niemann, Hermann Michael*).
9733 *Lamprichs, Roland* Der Expansionsprozeß des neuassyrischen Reiches: Versuch einer Neubewertung. Zwischen Euphrat und Indus.
1998 ⇒318. 209-221.
9734 *Lanfranchi, Giovanni B.* Esarhaddon, Assyria and Media. SAA Bulletin 12 (1998) 99-109.

9735 **Larsen, Mogens Trolle** The conquest of Assyria: excavations in an antique land 1840-1860. 1996 ⇒12,9272. RJAOS 118 (1998) 573-574 (*Bahrani, Zainab*); BiOr 55 (1998) 799-804 (*Frahm, E.*).

9736 **Mayer, Walter** Politik und Kriegskunst der Assyrer. 1995 ⇒11/2, 9466; 13,9953. ROLZ 93 (1998) 458-460 (*Freydank, Helmut*); WO 29 (1998) 98-108 (*Bagg, Ariel M.*); JAOS 118 (1998) 445-446 (*Liverani, Mario*).

9737 *Mayer, Walter* Der Weg auf den Thron Assurs: Sukzession und Usurpation im assyrischen Königshaus. FLORETZ O. AOAT 250: 1998 ⇒65. 533-555.

9738 *Michel, Cécile; Rocher, Patrick* La chronologie du IIe millénaire revue à l'ombre d'une éclipse de soleil. JEOL 35-36 (1997-2000) 111-126.

9739 **Morrison, Eric David** A form-critical study of Assyrian royal inscriptions containing building texts. DClaremont 1998, 282 pp.

9740 *Murphy, Susana B.* The notion of moral economy in the study of the ancient Near East. Intellectual life. 1998 ⇒450. 269-281.

9741 *Na'aman, Nadav* Sargon II and the rebellion of the Cypriote kings against Shilṭa of Tyre. Or. 67 (1998) 239-247.

9742 **Nemet-Nejat, Karen Rhea** Cuneiform mathematical texts as a reflection of everyday life in Mesopotamia. AOS 75: 1993 ⇒11/2, 6385; 12,9275. RZDMG 148 (1998) 199-200 (*Schramm, Wolfgang*).

9743 *Nigro, Lorenzo* Legittimazione e consenso: iconologia, religione e politica nelle stele di Sargon di Akkad. MFRANKFORT H. 1998 ⇒26. 351-392.

9744 *Oded, B.* History vis-à-vis propaganda in the Assyrian royal inscriptions. VT 48 (1998) 423-425.

9745 **Oded, Bustenay** War, peace, and empire: justifications for war in Assyrian royal inscriptions. 1992 ⇒8,7398... 12,9276. RJAOS 118 (1998) 89-91 (*Galter, Hannes D.*).

9746 *Pardo Mata, Pilar* El Neolítico y los inicios de la complejidad social: el caso de las tierras altas de Mesopotamia (norte de Iraq), 1. BAEO 34 (1998) 285-296 Res., sum. 285.

9747 *Patrón de Smith, Ana Fund* Something must change to avoid any change: ideology against social history in the ancient Near East. Intellectual life. 1998 ⇒450. 163-174.

9748 *Pfälzner, Peter* Eine Modifikation der Periodisierung Nordmesopotamiens im 3. Jtsd. v. Chr.. MDOG 130 (1998) 69-71.

9749 *Pingree, David* Legacies in astronomy and celestial omens. Legacy of Mesopotamia. 1998 ⇒328. 125-137.

9750 **Porter, Barbara Nevling** Images, power and politics: figurative aspects of Esarhaddon's Babylonian policy. 1993 ⇒11/2,9472; 12, 9278. RWO 29 (1998) 190-196 (*Bagg, Ariel M.*).

9751 *Reade, J.E.* Assyrian eponyms, kings and pretenders, 648-605 BC. Or. 67 (1998) 255-265.

9752 *Reade, J.E.; Finkel, I.L.* Assyrian eponyms, 873-649 BC. Or. 67 (1998) 248-254.

9753 **Rollinger, Robert** HERODOTs babylonischer Logos. 1993 ⇒10, 11146; 12,9280. RAt. 86 (1998) 561-563 (*Mora, Clelia*).

9754 *Rollinger, Robert* Überlegungen zu HERODOT, XERXES und dessen angeblicher Zerstörung Babylons. AltOrF 25 (1998) 339-373.

9755 **Saggs, H.W.F.** Babylonians. 1995 ⇒11/2,9476; 13,9959. ROLZ 93 (1998) 640-641 (*Feller, Barbara*); JNES 57 (1998) 228-230 (*Sack, Ronald H.*).

9756   Salvini, Mirjo The earliest evidences of the Hurrians before the formation of the reign of Mittanni. ᶠCOTSEN L. 1998 ⇒21. 99-115.
9757   Saporetti, Claudio; Chiera, Giovanna L'eroe nel canestro: tre storie parallele di fondatori di imperi. Mesopotamika 1: [Viareggio (LU)] 1998, Lunaris 79 pp.
9758   Schippmann, Klaus Geschichte der alt-südarabischen Reiche. Da:Wiss 1998, x; 141 pp. 3-534-11623-2.
9759   ᴱSefati, Yitschak Love songs in Sumerian literature: critical edition of the Dumuzi-Inanna songs. Bar-Ilan Studies in Near Eastern Languages and Culture: [Ramat-Gan] 1998, Bar-Ilan University Press 445 pp. 965-226-203-X. Bibl.
9760   Selz, Gebhard J. Über Mesopotamische Herrschaftskonzepte: zu den Ursprüngen mesopotamischer Herrscherideologie im 3. Jahrtausend. ᶠRÖMER, W. AOAT 253: 1998 ⇒97. 281-344.
9761   Steinkeller, Piotr The historical background of Urkesh and the Hurrian beginnings in northern Mesopotamia. ᶠCOTSEN L. 1998 ⇒21. 75-98.
9762   Swerdlow, Noel M. The Babylonian theory of the planets. Princeton, NJ 1998, Princeton Univ. Pr. xv; 246 pp. $39.50/£27.50. 0-691-01196-6. Bibl.
9763   Tadmor, Hayim Nabopalassar and Sin-shum-lishir in a literary perspective. ᶠBORGER R. 1998 ⇒12. 353-357.
9764   Tuman, Vladimir S. Astrological omens from lunar eclipses as a source for Babylonian chronology. Rencontre Assyriologique Internationale 34. 1998 ⇒452. 609-628.
9765   Van Driel, G. Eighth century Nippur. BiOr 55 (1998) 333-345.
9766   Westenholz, Joan Goodnick Objects with messages: reading Old Akkadian royal inscriptions. BiOr 55 (1998) 44-59;
9767   The theological foundation of the city: the capital city and Babylon. Capital cities. 1998 ⇒492. 43-54.
9768   Yamada, Shigeo The conquest of Til-barsip by Shalmaneser III: history and historiography. Acta Sumerologica (Hiroshima) 20 (1998) 217-225;
9769   The manipulative counting of the Euphrates crossings in the later inscriptions of Shalmaneser III. JCS 50 (1998) 87-94.
9770   Yuhong, Wu Kings of Kazallu and Marad in the early OB period. Rencontre Assyriologique Internationale 34. 1998 ⇒452. 221-227.

Q4.5 Historia Persiae—Iran

9771   Briant, Pierre Histoire de l'empire perse: de Cyrus à Alexandre. 1996 ⇒12,9291; 13,9971. ᴿOr. 67 (1998) 285-287 (Koch, Heidemarie); AnCl 67 (1998) 458-460 (Duplouy, Alain); JEA 84 (1998) 253-256 (Brosius, Maria); Mediterraneo Antico 1/1 (1998) 1-13 (Corsaro, Mauro).
9772   Carter, Elizabeth An interpretation of the Middle Elamite remains from Anshan, Tall-i Malyan, Iran. Rencontre Assyriologique Internationale 34. 1998 ⇒452. 681-688.
9773   Dandamayev, M.A. Official ideology and private life in the Achaemenid empire. VDI 224 (1998) 48-56 Sum. 56. R.
9774   Derakhshani, Jahanshah Die Arier in den nahöstlichen Quellen des 3. und 2. Jahrtausends v. Chr. Grundzüge der Vor- und Frühgeschich-

te Irans, Geschichte und Kultur des Alten Ostiran 1,2: Teheran 1998, International Publications of Iranian Studies (4) vii; 300 pp. 964-90368-1-4. Bibl.

9775 **Frei, Peter; Koch, Klaus** Reichsidee und Reichsorganisation im Perserreich. OBO 55: [2]1996 ⇒12,9293. [R]ThLZ 123 (1998) 1188-1190 (*Hartenstein, Friedhelm*).

9776 **Jacobs, Bruno** Die Satrapienverwaltung im Perserreich zur Zeit Darius' III. BTAVO.B 87: 1994 ⇒10,11152. [R]AMI 30 (1998) 341-344 (*Rollinger, Robert*).

9777 *Lincoln, Bruce* Apocalyptic temporality and politics in the ancient world. Encyclopedia of apocalypticism I. 1998 ⇒507. 457-475.

9778 **Tuplin, Christopher** Achaemenid studies. Historia Einzelschriften 99: Stu 1996, Steiner 226 pp. DM78.

Q5 *Historia Anatoliae*–Asia Minor, Hittites [⇒T8.2]

9779 *Akurgal, Ekrem* Classification and chronology of the Hattian and Hittite periods in Anatolian history. [F]ÇAMBEL H. 1998 ⇒4. 25-33.

9780 *Alp, Sedat* Zur Datierung des Ulmitešup-Vertrags. AltOrF 25 (1998) 54-60.

9781 **Beckman, Gary** Hittite diplomatic texts. SBL Writings from the Ancient World 7: 1996 ⇒12,9302; 13,9983. [R]BiOr 55 (1998) 217-219 (*Archi, A.*); BArR 24/6 (1998) 54, 58 (*Rainey, Anson*).

9782 **Bryce, Trevor R.** The kingdom of the Hittites. Oxf 1998, OUP xvii; 464 pp. £45. 0-19-814095-9. Bibl. [R]RBBras 15 (1998) 467-468.

9783 *Esin, Ufuk* Einige Hinweise zur Entstehung der frühbronzezeitlichen Fürstentümer in Anatolien. [F]Çambel H. 1998 ⇒4. 339-344.

9784 *Giorgadze, G.* Zum Kauf und Verkauf von Grund und Boden in der hethitischen Gesellschaft. AltOrF 25 (1998) 95-103.

9785 *González Salazar, Juan Manuel* El reino Anatolio de Ḫatti (segunda mitad del II° milenio a.C.) y su preocupación por los aspectos fronterizos. BAEO 33 (1997) 227-240;

9786 Los inicios de la organización administrativo-periférica de las regiones septentronales de Anatolia (fases finales) del s. XV y los inicios del s. XIV a.C.): los últimos soberanos del *Reino Medio* hittita. BAEO 34 (1998) 379-397.

9787 **Gurney, O.R.** Los hititas. [T]*Herranz, Augusto.* Barc 1995, Laertes 237 pp. 84-7584-247-7. [R]BAEO 34 (1998) 426-428 (*González Salazar, Juan Manuel*).

9788 **Hoffner, Harry Angier** Hittite Myths. [E]*Beckman, Gary M.* SBL Writings from the Ancient World 2: Atlanta, GA [2]1998, Scholars xi; 121 pp. $15. 0-7885-0488-6. Bibl.

9789 *Houwink ten Cate, Philo H.J.* The scribes of the Masat letters and the GAL DUB.SAR(.MEŠ) of the Hittite capital during the final phase of the early empire period. [F]RÖMER, W. AOAT 253: 1998 ⇒97. 157-178.

9790 **Klock-Fontanille, Isabelle** Les Hittites. QSJ 3349: P 1998, PUF 127 pp. 2-13-048966-4. Bibl.

9791 *Lebrun, R.* Hittites et Hourrites en Palestine-Canaan. Transeuphratène 15 (1998) 153-163.

9792 **Lehmann, Gustav Adolf** "Römischer Tod" in Kolophon/Klaros: neue Quellen zum Status der "freien" Polisstaaten an der Westküste

Kleinasiens im späten zweiten Jahrhundert v. Chr. NAWG Phil.-hist. Kl. 1998,3: Gö 1998, Vandenhoeck & R 70 pp.

9793 *Niemeier, Wolf-Dietrich* The Mycenaeans in western Anatolia and the problem of the origins of the sea peoples. [F]DOTHAN, T. 1998 ⇒23. 17-65.

9794 *Oliva, Juan C.* Én torno a los Hurritas y su papel en el Próximo Oriente Antiguo. BAEO 33 (1997) 241-254.

9795 *Popko, Maciej* Zum Wettergott von Ḫalab. AltOrF 25 (1998) 119-125.

9796 **Schuler, Chr.** Ländliche Siedlungen und Gemeinden im hellenistischen und römischen Kleinasien. Vestigia 50: Mü 1998, Beck xiii; 386 pp [At. 89,265s—Boffo, Laura].

9797 **Schwemer, Daniel** Akkadische Rituale aus Hattusa: die Sammeltafel KBo XXXVI 29 und verwandte Fragmente. Texte der Hethiter 23: Heid 1998, Winter xxiii; 193 pp. DM98. 3-8253-0815-4.

9798 *Singer, Itamar* A city of many temples: Ḫattuša, capital of the Hittites. [M]PRAWER J. 1998 ⇒93. 32-44.

9799 *Soysal, Oğuz* Beiträge zur althethitischen Geschichte (II): zur Textwiederherstellung und Datierung von KUB XXXI 64+ (CTH 12). AltOrF 1998, 25 5-33

9800 **Strobel, Karl** Die Galater: Geschichte und Eigenart der keltischen Staatenbildung auf dem Boden des hellenistischen Kleinasien. 1996 ⇒12,9310. [R]HZ 267 (1998) 447-448 (*Zimmermann, Martin*).

9801 *Tavares, António Augusto* Institutions of the "Children of Het" in Hebron into the context of Middle East;

9802 *Trokay, Madeleine* Relations artistiques entre Hittites et Kassites. Rencontre Assyr. Internationale 34. 1998 ⇒452. 321-329/253-261.

9803 Turchia antica: antik Türkiye. R 1998, Logart 207 pp.

9804 [E]**Van den Hout, Theo P.J.** The purity of kingship: an edition of CHT 569 and related Hittite oracle inquiries of Tuthaliya IV. DMOA 25: Lei 1998, Brill xxi; 371 pp. $86/ƒ146. 90-04-10986-2.

9805 *Vanhaverbeke, H.; Vermeersch, P.M.; Waelkens, M.* What's in a name?: the epipalaeolithic, the aceramic and the early neolithic on the territory of Sagalassos (Pisidia, Turkey). NEA(BA) 61/3 (1998) 175-176.

9806 **Zimansky, Paul E.** Ancient Ararat: a handbook of Urartian studies. Anatolian and Caucasian studies: Delmar 1998, Caravan Books x; 332 pp. 0-88206-091-0.

Q6.1 Historia Graeciae classicae

9807 *Ameling, Walter* Landwirtschaft und Sklaverei im klassischen Attika. HZ 266 (1998) 281-315.

9808 **Baurain, Claude** Les grecs et la méditerranée orientale: des 'siècles obscurs' à la fin de l'époque archaïque. Nouvelle Clio, l'histoire et ses problèmes: P 1997, PUF lxxxiv; 632 pp. FF198 [Gn. 73,66ss—Haider, Peter W.].

9809 **Blum, Hartmut** Purpur als Statussymbol in der griechischen Welt. Ant. 1. Abhandlungen zur Alten Geschichte 47: Bonn 1998, Habelt xiv; 319 pp. 3-7749-2875-4. Bibl.

9810 **Burckhardt, Jacob** The Greeks and Greek civilization. [T]*Stern, Sheila;* [E]*Murray, Oswyn.* NY 1998, St. Martin's xliv; 449 pp. 0-312-19276-2. Bibl.

9811 **Coulet, C.** Communiquer en Grèce ancienne: écrits, discours, information, voyages. 1996 ⇒12,9314. [R]JHS 118 (1998) 243 (*Greenwood, Emily*).

9812 **Davidson, James N.** Courtesans & fishcakes: the consuming passions of classical Athens. NY 1998, St. Martin's xxvi; 372 pp. 0-312-18559-6. Bibl.

9813 *Deger-Jalkotzy, Sigrid* 'The last Mycenaeans and their successors' updated. [F]DOTHAN, T. 1998 ⇒23. 114-128.

9814 **Demand, N.** History of ancient Greece. 1996 ⇒12,9315. [R]ClR 48 (1998) 371-372 (*Bowden, Hugh*).

9815 *Dihle, Albrecht* Die Krise der Legitimation "gerechter" Ordnung im Griechenland des fünften Jahrhunderts v. Chr. Gerechtigkeit. 1998 ⇒283. 141-147.

9816 **Doblhofer, Georg** Vergewaltigung in der Antike. 1994 ⇒12,9316. [R]Gn. 70 (1998) 4-7 (*Fantham, Elaine*).

9817 *Doumas, Christos G.* Aegeans in the Levant: myth and reality [F]DOTHAN, T. 1998 ⇒23. 129-137.

9818 **Eder, Birgitta** Argolis, Lakonien, Messenien: vom Ende der mykenischen Palastzeit bis zur Einwanderung der Dorier. DÖAW Phil.-Hist. Kl. Mykenische Studien 17: W 1998, Verlag der ÖAW 236 pp. 3-70-01-2736-7. Bibl.

9819 *Faraguna, Michele* Aspetti amministrativi e finanziari della monarchia macedone fra IV et III secolo a.C. At. 86 (1998) 349-395.

9820 *Flaig, Egon* Ehre gegen Gerechtigkeit: Adelsethos und Gemeinschaftsdenken in Hellas. Gerechtigkeit. 1998 ⇒283. 97-140.

9821 **Garland, Robert** Daily Life of the ancient Greeks. Greenwood Press "Daily life through history": Westport, CONN 1998, Greenwood xxiii; 234 pp. 0-313-30383-5. Bibl.

9822 *Gordon, Cyrus H.* The common background of Greek and Hebrew civilizations. Hellenic and Jewish arts. 1998 ⇒439. 1-6.

9823 **Hamel, Debra** Athenian generals: military authority in the classical period. Mn.S 182: Lei 1998, Brill xvii; 250 pp. 90-04-10900-5. Bibl.

9824 *Hidalgo de la Vega, María José; Sayas Abengochea, Juan José; Roldán Hervás, José Manuel* Historia de la Grecia Antigua. Historia Salamanca de la Antigüedad, manuales universitarios 58: S 1998, Universidad 485 pp. 84-7481-8893. 18 ill. [Kernos 12,326—Krings, V.].

9825 **Krings, Véronique** Carthage et les Grecs c. 580-480 av. J.-C.: textes et histoire. [D]Liège 1996. [D]*Bonnet, Corinne & Lancel, Serge*. Studies in the history and culture of the ancient Near East 13: Lei 1998, Brill xiii; 427 pp. 90-04-10881-5.

9826 [E]**Langdon, Susan** New light on a dark age: exploring the culture of Geometric Greece. 1997 ⇒13,9992. [R]AJA 102 (1998) 630-631 (*Antonaccio, Carla M.*).

9827 **Lefèvre, François** L'amphictionie pyléo-delphique: histoire et institutions. BEFAR 298: Athènes 1998, École Française 350 pp. Bibl. [CRAI 1999,731s—Amandry, Pierre].

9828 *Maeir, Aren M.* Philistines in Sardinia?: a critical reappraisal. UF 30 (1998) 497-510.

9829 **Miller, Margaret Christina** Athens and Persia in the fifth century BC: a study in cultural receptivity. 1997 ⇒13,9995. [R]Prudentia 30/1 (1998) 55-57 (*McKechnie, Paul*).

9830 **Mitchell, L.G.** Greeks bearing gifts: the public use of private relationships in the Greek world, 435-323 BC. C 1997, CUP xiv; 248 pp. £40/$60. 0-52155-435-7 [JHS 120,185—Van Wees, Hans].

9831   **Osborne, Robin** Greece in the making, 1200-490 B.C. 1996 ⇒12, 9323. ᴿAJA 102 (1998) 629-630 (*Thomas, Carol G.*).

9832   **Patterson, Cynthia B.** The family in Greek history. CM 1998, Harvard University Press (12); 286 pp. 0-674-29270-7.

9833   **Polacco, Luigi** Kyklos: la fenomenologia del cerchio nel pensiero e nell'arte dei greci. Memorie, Classe di scienze morali lettere ed arti 76: Venezia 1998, Istituto veneto di scienze lettere ed arti ix; 136 pp. 88-86166-60-5.

9834   **Santosusso, Antonio** Soldiers, citizens, and the symbols of war: from classical Greece to republican Rome, 500-167 BC. 1997 ⇒13, 9997. ᴿIHR 20 (1998) 944-946 (*Hodgkinson, Michael*).

9835   *Small, David B.* Surviving the collapse: the oikos and structural continuity between late Bronze Age and later Greece. ᶠDOTHAN, T. 1998 ⇒23. 283-291.

9836   ᵀ**Waterfield, Robin** HERODOTUS: Historiae: the histories. Oxford world's classics: Oxf 1998, OUP li; 773 pp. 0-19-282425-2. With an introduction and notes by *Carolyn Dewald*; Bibl.

Q6.5 Alexander, Seleucidae; historia Hellenismi

9837   *Agouridis, S.* Aristeas' letter: problems of the Hellenistic kingship as discussed by Jews and Greeks in Alexandria. Hellenic and Jewish arts. 1998 ⇒439. 33-40.

9838   **Barclay, John M.G.** Jews in the Mediterranean diaspora from Alexander to Trajan (323 BCE-117 CE). 1996 ⇒12,9326; 13,10000. ᴿBib. 79 (1998) 138-141 (*Sievers, Joseph*); JThS 49 (1998) 724-727 (*Kraabel, A.T.*); AJSR 23 (1998) 247-250 (*Himmelfarb, Martha*); HeyJ 39 (1998) 193-194 (*Winter, Michael M.*).

9839   **Baslez, Marie-Françoise** Bible et histoire: judaïsme, hellénisme, christianisme. P 1998, Fayard 450 pp. FF150. 2-213-60202-6 [MoBi 116,77—Gibert, Pierre].

9840   **Baynham, Elizabeth** Alexander the Great: the unique history of Quintus Curtius. AA 1998, University of Michigan Press xiv; 237 pp. 0-472-10858-1. Bibl.

9841   **Bergmann, Marianne** Die Strahlen der Herrscher: theomorphes Herrscherbild und politische Symbolik im Hellenismus und in der römischen Kaiserzeit. Mainz 1998, Von Zabern xvi; 338 pp. DM184. 3-8053-1916-9. 55 pl. [AJA 103,572ss—Brilliant, Richard].

9842   *Betz, Hans Dieter* Antiquity and christianity;
9843   The birth of christianity as a Hellenistic religion: three theories of origin <1994>. Gesammelte Aufsätze IV. 1998 ⇒134. 267-90/100-27.

9844   **Bock, Emil** Caesars and apostles: Hellenism, Rome and Judaism. E 1998, Floris 368 pp. 0-86315-273-2. Bibl.

9845   *Brague, Rémi* Athens, Jerusalem, Mecca: Leo STRAUSS's 'Muslim' understanding of Greek philosophy. PoeT 19 (1998) 235-259 Sum. 235.

9846   **Brown, John Pairman** Israel and Hellas. BZAW 231: 1995 ⇒11/2, 9197... 13,10007. ᴿCarthaginensia 14 (1998) 220-221 (*Sanz Valdivieso, R.*); ASEs 15/1 (1998) 298-299 (*Tampellini, Stefano*); ThLZ 123 (1998) 36-38 (*Kratz, Reinhard Gregor*).

9847   *Cagni, Luigi* Elementi storico-culturali in Mesopotamia nei periodi persiano ed ellenistico. RstB 10/1-2 (1998) 25-58.

9848 ^E**Cartledge, P.; Garnsey, P.; Gruen, E.** Hellenistic constructs: essays in culture, history and historiography. Hellenistic Culture and Society 26: 1997 ⇒13,10008. ^RClR 48 (1998) 380-383 (*Davidson, James*).

9849 Dreams and suicides: the Greek novel from antiquity to the Byzantine Empire. L 1996, Routledge 248 pp. £40/$65. 0-415-07005-8.

9850 **Droysen, Johann Gustav** Geschichte des Hellenismus: 1, Geschichte Alexanders des Großen; 2, Geschichte der Diadochen; 3, Geschichte der Epigonen. Da 1998, Primus xv; 467; 443 + xxiii; 563 pp.

9851 *Engberg-Pedersen, Troels* The Hellenistic *Öffentlichkeit*: philosophy as a social force in the Greco-Roman world. Recruitment. 1998 ⇒ 320. 15-37.

9852 **Freyne, Seán** Galilee: from Alexander the Great to Hadrian: 323 BCE to 135 CE: a study of Second Temple Judaism. E 1998, Clark xvii; 491 pp. 0-567-08627-5.

9853 ^E**Funck, Bernd** Hellenismus: Beiträge zur Erforschung von Akkulturation und politischer Ordnung in den Staaten des hellenistischen Zeitalters. 1997, Akten des Internationalen Hellenismus-Kolloquium 1994, Berlin ⇒13,10014. ^RMes. 33 (1998) 404-410 (*Lippolis, C.*).

9854 *Gabriel, A.* Crisis and hope in Graeco-Roman period. BiBh 24 (1998) 284-295.

9855 *Garbini, Giovanni* Eupolemo storico giudeo. RANL 9 (1998) 613-634 Sum. 613.

9856 ^E**Gauger, Jörg-Dieter** Sibyllinische Weissagungen. Sammlung Tusculum: Mü 1998, Artemis Griechisch/deutsch = Oracula Sibyllina. Auf der Grundlage der Ausg. von Alfons Kurfeß neu übers. und hrsg. 564 pp. 3-7608-1701-7.

9857 **Gera, Dov** Judaea and Mediterranean politics, 219 to 161 B.C.E. Brill's Series in Jewish Studies 8: Lei 1998, Brill xii; 362 pp. $114.50. 90-04-09441-5. Bibl.

9858 **Gigante, Marcello** Altre ricerche filodemee. Biblioteca della parola del passato 18: N 1998, Macchiaroli 189 pp. 88-85823-23-8. Presentazione di *Fulvio Tessitore*.

9859 *Görgemanns, Herwig* Woher kommt das Übel in der Welt?: ein Vergleich einiger antiker und moderner Konzepte. Internationales Josephus-Kolloquium. 1998 ⇒490. 196-209.

9860 **Green, Peter** Alexander to Actium: the Hellenistic age. 1990 ⇒6, 653...11/2,9631. ^RJNES 57 (1998) 52-54 (*Manning, J.G.*).

9861 **Gruen, Erich S.** Heritage and Hellenism: the reinvention of Jewish tradition. Berkeley, CA 1998, University of California at Berkeley xx; 335 pp. $38/£27.50. 0-520-21052-2. Bibl.

9862 **Gullini, Giorgio** L'ellenismo. Un enciclopedia del Mediterraneo EDM. Sezione storia 12: Mi 1998, Jaca 152 pp. 88-16-43612-3. Bibl.

9863 **Gutzwiller, Kathryn J.** Poetic garlands: Hellenistic epigrams in context. Hellenistic Culture and Society 28: Berkeley 1998, University of California Press xiii; 358 pp. 0-520-20857-9. Bibl.

9864 **Habicht, C.** Athens from Alexander to Antony. 1997 ⇒13,10017. ^RClR 48 (1998) 385-386 (*Ogden, Daniel*).

9865 **Hammond, N.G.L.** The genius of Alexander the Great. 1997 ⇒13, 10019. ^RClR 48 (1998) 378-379 (*Devine, A.M.*).

9866 **Hayes, John Haralson; Mandell, Sara** The Jewish people in classical antiquity: from Alexander to Bar Kochba. LVL 1998, Westminster xiii; 246 pp. $28. 0-664-25727-5. Bibl.

9867   *Horowitz, Brian* The demolition of reason in Lev Shestov's Athens and Jerusalem. Poetics Today 19 (1998) 221-233 Sum. 221.

9868   *Keel, Othmar* Die kultischen Maßnahmen Antiochus' IV. in Jerusalem: Religionsverfolgung und/oder Reformversuch?: eine Skizze. Interpretation of the Bible. JSOT.S 289: 1998 ⇒389. 217-244.

9869   ᴱᵀ**Konstan, David**, *al.*, PHILODEMUS: on frank criticism. SBL.TT 13; GRRS 43: Atlanta 1998, Scholars xi; 191 pp. $35. 0-7885-0434-7.

9870   *Longxi, Zhang* Cultural differences and cultural constructs: reflections on Jewish and Chinese literalism. PoeT 19 (1998) 305-328 Sum. 305.

9871   *Mendels, Doron* On identity: an essay on Hellenism, Judaism and christianity in Palestine in the Hellenistic era. Identity. JSPE.S 24: 1998 ⇒174. 13-34.
          Mendels, D. Identity..studies in Hellenistic history 1998 ⇒174.

9872   **Moreschini, Claudio** PLUTARCO: l'E di Delfi: introduzione, testo critico, traduzione e commento. Corpus Plutarchi Moralium 27: N 1997, D'Auria 157 pp. 88-7092-136-0. Dipart. di Fil. e Politica dell'IUO [FgNT 12,173—Brenk, F.E.].

9873   **Morgan, Teresa** Literate education in the Hellenistic and Roman worlds. Cambridge Classical Studies: C 1998, CUP xv; 364 pp. £40. 0-521-58466-3 [CÉg 74,379—Straus, Jean A.].

9874   *New, Elisa* Bible leaves! Bible leaves! Hellenism and Hebraism in MELVILLE's *Moby-Dick*. PoeT 19 (1998) 281-303 Sum. 281.

9875   *Noel, Daniel* Femmes au vin à Athènes. ASSR 43 (1998) 147-185.

9876   *Pelletier-Hornby, Paulette* La ville—miroir de l'héllenisme. MoBi 111 (1998) 12-17.

9877   **Rescigno, Andrea** PLUTARCO: l'eclissi degli oracoli: introduzione, testo critico, traduzione e commento. Corpus Plutarchi Moralium 19: N 1995, D'Auria 157 pp. 88-7092-107-7. Dipart. di Fil. e Politica dell'IUO [FgNT 12,174—Brenk, F.E.].

9878   **Rostovcev, Michael I.** Gesellschafts- und Wirtschaftsgeschichte der hellenistischen Welt, 1-3. Da 1998, Primus Num. ill. xix; 476; lxviii + viii; 478-1062; lxix-cxii + 1064-1600 pp.

9879   *Siegert, Folker* Die hellenistisch-jüdische Theologie als Forschungsaufgabe. Internationales Josephus-Kolloquium. 1998 ⇒490. 9-30.

9880   *Stern, David* The captive woman: Hellenization, Greco-Roman erotic narrative and rabbinic literature. PoeT 19 (1998) 91-127 Sum. 91.

9881   *Stone, Donald D.* Matthew ARNOLD and the pragmatics of Hebraism and Hellenism. PoeT 19 (1998) 179-198 Sum. 179.

9882   **Stoneman, R.** Alexander the Great. 1997 ⇒13,10030. ᴿCIR 48 (1998) 525-526 (*Ogden, Daniel*).

9883   **Striker, Gisela** Essays on Hellenistic epistemology and ethics. 1996 ⇒12,9349. ᴿCIR 48 (1998) 355-356 (*Barnes, Jonathan*).

9884   **Swain, Simon** Hellenism and empire: language, classicism, and power in the Greek world AD 50-250. 1996 ⇒12,9350. ᴿIJCT 4 (1998) 477-480 (*Bowersock, G.W.*); AJP 119 (1998) 307-309 (*Gleason, Maud W.*).

9885   **Van der Horst, Pieter Willem** Hellenism—Judaism—Christianity: essays on their interaction. Contributions to Biblical Exegesis and Theology 8: Lv ²1998 <1994>, Peeters 342 pp. 90-429-578-6. ᴿJThS 49 (1998) 284-285 [of 1st ed.] (*Sawyer, Deborah F.*).

9886   *Veltri, Giuseppe* The rabbis and PLINY the Elder; Jewish and Greco-Roman attitudes toward magic and empirical knowledge. PoeT 19 (1998) 63-89 Sum. 63.

Will, Édouard Historica graeca-hellenistica 1998 ⇒207.
9887   *Wolosky, Shira* An 'other' negative theology: on DERRIDA's 'How to avoid speaking: denials'. PoeT 19 (1998) 261-280 Sum. 261.

9888   **Constantelos, Demetrios J.** Christian Hellenism: essays and studies in continuity and change. Hellenism 13; Studies in the Social & Religious History of the Mediaeval Greek World: New Rochelle, New York 1998, Caratzas xii; 302 pp. 0-89241-523-1.

Q7 Josephus Flavius

9889   ^E**Mason, Steve** Understanding Josephus: seven perspectives. JSEP.S 32: Shf 1998, [Academic] 260 pp. £43.25. 1-85075-878-6.

9890   *Barclay, John M.G.* Josephus v. Apion: analysis of an argument. Understanding Josephus. 1998 ⇒9889. 194-221 [BuBbgB 30,51].
9891   *Begg, Christopher* David and Mephibosheth according to Josephus. AUSS 36/2 (1998) 165-182 [2 Sam 9];
9892   David's capture of Jebus and its sequels according to Josephus. EThL 74 (1998) 93-108 [2 Sam 5; 1 Chr 11];
9893   Josephus' account of the Benjaminite war. SBFLA 48 (1998) 273-304 Sum. 518 [Judg 20-21].
9894   David's dismissal by the Philistines according to Josephus. ThZ 54 (1998) 111-119 [1 Sam 29];
9895   The end of King Jehoiakim: the afterlife of a problem. JSem 8/1 (1996) 12-20 Sum. 12 [2 Kgs 24,6];
9896   David's double victory according to Josephus. EM 66 (1998) 27-48 Sum. 27 [2 Sam 10];
9897   David's first sparing of Saul according to Josephus. Laur. 39 (1998) 455-471 [1 Sam 24];
9898   The revolt of Sheba according to Josephus. Jian Dao 9 (1998) 1-26 Sum. 26 [2 Sam 20,1-22];
9899   The return of the ark according to Josephus. BBR 8 (1998) 15-37 [1 Sam 6-7];
9900   The assassination of Ishbosheth according to Josephus. Anton. 73 (1998) 241-251 Sum. 241 [2 Sam 4];
9901   **Begg, Christopher** Josephus' account of the early divided monarchy (AJ 8,212-420): rewriting the bible. BEThL 108: 1993 ⇒9,12640... 11/2,9659. ^RAnton. 73 (1998) 160-162 (*Nobile, Marco*).
9902   **Ben Zeev, Marina Pucci** Jewish rights in the Roman world: the Greek and Roman documents quoted by Josephus Flavius. TSAJ 74: Tü 1998, Mohr xvi; 520 pp. DM198. 3-16-147043-5 [ThD 46,382— Heiser, Charles].
9903   *Ben-Zeev, Miriam Pucci* Ant. 14.186-267: a problem of authenticity. ^FSOHLBERG, D. 1996 ⇒8271. 193-216.
9904   *Beyer, David W.* Josephus reexamined: unraveling the twenty-second year of Tiberius. ^MSummers. 1998 ⇒115. 85-96.
9905   *Bilde, Per* Josephus and Jewish apocalypticism. Understanding Josephus. 1998 ⇒9889. 35-61 [BuBbgB 30,51].
9906   *Bohrmann, Monette* Die Beziehungen zwischen Johannes aus Giskala und Josephus in der Frage des Ölhandels. Internationales Josephus-Kolloquium. 1998 ⇒490. 136-143.

510   Elenchus of Biblica 14, 1998   [XVII. Historia

9907 **Bohrmann, Monette** Flavius Josèphe: les Zélotes et Yavneh. 1989
      ⇒5,b628... 7,6302. ᴿLTP 54/1 (1998) 175-178 (*Hermon, Ella*).
9908 **Feldman, Louis H.** Studies in Josephus' rewritten Bible. JSJ.S 58:
      Lei 1998, Brill xxi; 663 pp. 90-04-10839-4. Bibl.;
9909 Josephus's interpretation of the bible. Hellenistic Culture and Society
      27: Berkeley 1998, Univ. of California xvi; 837 pp. 0-520-20853-6.
      Bibl.
9910 *Feldman, Louis H.* Josephus' portrait of Aaron. ᶠSOHLBERG, D. 1996
      ⇒8271. 167-192.
9911 ᴱ**Feldman, Louis H; Levinson, John R.** Josephus' *Contra Apionem*.
      AGJU 34: 1996, ⇒12,9384; 13,10064. ᴿThLZ 123 (1998) 138-139
      (*Wiefel, Wolfgang*).
9912 *Feuchtwanger, Lion* Der jüdische Krieg. BiKi 53 (1998) 89-91.
9913 **Gerber, Christine** Ein Bild des Judentums für Nichtjuden von Flavi-
      us Josephus: Untersuchungen zu seiner Schrift *Contra Apionem*.
      AGJU 40: 1997 ⇒13,10065. ᴿThLZ 123 (1998) 971-973 (*Schröder,
      Bernd*).
9914 **Gnuse, Robert Karl** Dreams and dream reports in the writings of Jo-
      sephus: a traditio-historical analysis. AGJU 36: 1996 ⇒12,9385.
      ᴿCBQ 60 (1998) 152-154 (*Feldman, Louis H.*)
9915 *Hadas-Lebel, Mireille* La prise de Jérusalem selon Flavius Josèphe:
      l'évènement et son interprétation juive, romaine et chrétienne. Procès
      de Jésus. 1998 ⇒392. 155-164.
9916 *Hansen, Günther Christian* Textkritisches zu Josephus. Internationa-
      les Josephus-Kolloquium. 1998 ⇒490. 144-158.
9917 *Harding, Mark* Making old things new: prayer texts in Josephus' *An-
      tiquities*, 1-11: a study in the transmission of tradition. ᶠJUDGE E.
      1998 ⇒47. 1-14.
9918 *Höffken, Peter* Hiskija und Jesaja bei Josephus. JSJ 29 (1998) 37-48.
9919 *Kalms, Jürgen U.* Project-presentation: a bilingual edition of Jose-
      phus with commentary: Vita, Contra Apionem and Antiquitates.
      Bible et informatique 1998 ⇒386. 377-379.
9920 **Krieger, Klaus-Stefan** Geschichtsschreibung als Apologetik bei Fla-
      vius Josephus. 1994 ⇒11/2,9694; 13,10068. ᴿRSR 86 (1998) 603-
      604 (*Beaude, Pierre-Marie*).
9921 *Krieger, Klaus-Stefan* Josephus—ein Anhänger des Aufstandsführers
      El`azar ben Hananja: Überlegungen zur religiös-politischen
      Orientierung des späteren Historiographen zu Beginn des Jüdischen
      Krieges. Internationales Josephus-Kolloquium. 1998 ⇒490. 93-105;
9922 Priester, Bandenchef, Geschichtsschreiber: Leben und Werk des
      Flavius Josephus. BiKi 53 (1998) 50-54.
9923 *Leonhardt, Jutta* Vergleich der Vita des Josephus mit PHILOs Legatio
      ad Gaium. Internationales Josephus-Kolloquium. 1998 ⇒490. 106-
      135.
9924 *Lichtenberger, Hermann* Josephus über Johannes den Täufer, Jesus
      und Jakobus. BiKi 53 (1998) 67-71.
9925 *Maier, Johann* Die biblische Geschichte des Flavius Josephus. BiKi
      53 (1998) 55-58.
9926 *Mason, Steve* An essay in character: the aim and audience of Jo-
      sephus's Vita. Internat. Josephus-Kolloquium. 1998 ⇒490. 31-77;
9927 Should any wish to enquire further (Ant. 1.25): the aim and audience
      of Josephus's *Antiquities/Life*. Understanding Josephus. 1998 ⇒
      9889. 64-103 [BuBbgB 30,51].

9928 *Mayer-Schärtel, Bärbel* Das Frauenbild des Josephus. BiKi 53 (1998) 84-86.

9929 **Mayer-Schärtel, Bärbel** Das Frauenbild des Josephus: eine sozial-geschichtliche und kultanthropologische Untersuchung. 1995 ⇒11/2, 9699; 13,10070. ᴿThLZ 123 (1998) 139-144 (*Wischmeyer, Oda*).

9930 **McLaren, James S.** Turbulent times?: Josephus and scholarship on Judaea in the first century CE. Shf 1998, Academic 283 pp. £50. 1-85075-891-3 [RRT 6,154s—Rodgers, Zuleika].

9931 *Mulzer, Martin* Josephus und der Text des Alten Testaments. BiKi 53 (1998) 59-60.

9932 *Rajak, Tessa* The *Against Apion* and the continuities in Josephus's political thought. Understanding Josephus. 1998 ⇒9889. 222-246 [BuBbgB 30,51].

9933 *Schmidt, Francis* Histoire du judaïsme à l'époque hellénistique et romaine: destin et providence (suite). AEPHE.R 106 (1998) 217-220 [BuBbgB 30,51].

9934 *Schwartz, Daniel R.* Josephus' Tobiads: back to the second century?. Jews in a Graeco-Roman world. 1998 ⇒337. 47-61.

9935 *Siegert, Folker* Édition grecque-allemande de Flavius Josèphe sur base informatique. Bible et informatique. 1998 ⇒386. 375-376;

9936 Das Münsteraner Josephus-Projekt. BiKi 53 (1998) 87-88.

9937 *Sievers, Joseph* Aussagen des Josephus zu Unsterblichkeit und Leben nach dem Tod. Internationales Josephus-Kolloquium. 1998 ⇒490. 78-92;

9938 Josephus und die Zeit "zwischen den Testamenten". BiKi 53 (1998) 61-66;

9939 Josephus and the afterlife. Understanding Josephus. 1998 ⇒9889. 20-34 [BuBbgB 30,51].

9940 ᶠSᴍɪᴛʜ, **Morton** Josephus and the history of the Greco-Roman period. ᴱ*Parente, Fausto; Sievers, Joseph* 1994 ⇒10,123. ᴿJAOS 118 (1998) 137-138 (*Attridge, Harold W.*); RSR 86 (1998) 602-603 (*Beaude, Pierre-Marie*).

9941 **Spilsbury, Paul** The image of the Jew in Flavius Josephus' Para-phrase of the Bible. TSAJ 69: Tü 1998, Mohr xiv; 286 pp. DM148. 3-16-146869-4. Bibl.

9942 *Spilsbury, Paul* God and Israel in Josephus: a patron-client relation-ship. Understanding Josephus. 1998 ⇒9889. 172-191 [BuBbgB 30, 51].

9943 *Sterling, Gregory E.* The invisible presence: Josephus's retelling of Ruth. Understanding Josephus. 1998 ⇒9889. 104-171 [BuBbgB 30, 52].

9944 *Thatcher, Tom* Literacy, textual communities, and Josephus' Jewish War. JSJ 29 (1998) 123-142.

9945 *Van Segbroeck, Frans* Flavius Josephus opnieuw vertaald. Inter-pretatie 6/3 (1998) 10-12.

9946 *Vogel, Manuel* Josephus' Contra Apionem und der antike Antijudaismus. BiKi 53 (1998) 79-83.

9947 *Weiss, Herold* The sabbath in the writings of Josephus. JSJ 29 (1998) 363-390.

Q8.1 *Roma Pompeii et Caesaris*—**Hyrcanus to Herod**

9948 **Fenn, Richard** The death of Herod: an essay in the sociology of religion. 1992 ⇒8,d179... 11/2,9679. ᴿJR 78 (1998) 305-307 (*Mach, Michael*).
9949 **Kokkinos, Nikos** The Herodian dynasty: origins, role in society and eclipse. ᴰ*Millar, Fergus*: JSP.S 30: Shf 1998, Academic 518 pp. £55/$85. 1-85075-690-2. Bibl.
9950 *Levine, Amy-Jill* Visions of kingdoms: from Pompey to the first Jewish revolt. The Oxford history. 1998 ⇒326. 467-514.
9951 *Puech, Émile* Le grand prêtre Simon (III) fils d'Onias III, le maître de justice?. ᶠSTEGEMANN, H. BZNW 97: 1998 ⇒111. 137-158.
9952 **Roller, Duane W.** The building program of Herod the Great. Berkeley, CA 1998, Univ. of California Pr. xvii; 351 pp. $50. 0-520-20934-6. Bibl.; 49 ill.; 15 maps & plans; 14 charts. ᴿBAR 24/4 (1998) 59-61 (*Burrell, Barbara*).

Q8.4 **Zeitalter Jesu Christi:** *particular/general*

9953 **Alston, Richard** Aspects of Roman history, AD 14-117. L 1998, Routledge xix; 342 pp. 0-415-13237-1. Bibl.
9954 **Bleicken, Jochen** Augustus: eine Biographie. B 1998, Fest 799 pp. €39,88 [HZ 270,165ss—Dahlheim, Werner].
9955 *Brändle, Rudolf; Stegemann, Ekkehard W.* The formation of the first "Christian congregations" in Rome in the context of the Jewish congregations. Judaism and Christianity. 1998 ⇒230. 117-127.
9956 **Brehm, H. Alan** Reconstructing New Testament history: RITSCHL reconsidered. ᴹSUMMERS R. 1998 ⇒115. 141-167.
9957 **Dabrowa, Edward** The governors of Roman Syria from Augustus to Septimius Severus. Ant., Abh. zur Alten Geschichte 45: Bonn 1998, Habelt 276 pp. 3-7749-2828-2. Bibl.
9958 **Eck, Werner** AUGUSTUS und seine Zeit. Beck'sche 2084; Wissen: Mü 1998, Beck 128 pp. 3-406-41884-8.
9959 *Faulstich, E.W.* Studies in O.T. and N.T. chronology. ᴹSUMMERS R. 1998 ⇒115. 97-117.
9960 **Fedalto, Giorgio** Quando festeggiare il 2000?: problemi di cronologia cristiana. CinB 1998, San Paolo 100 pp. €7,23.
9961 **Galinsky, Karl** Augustan culture: an interpretive introduction. 1996 ⇒12,9413; 13,10083. ᴿCIR 48 (1998) 396-398 (*Booth, Joan*).
9962 **Horsley, Richard A.** Galilee: history, politics, people. 1995 ⇒11/2,b077; 13,10085. ᴿJAOS 118 (1998) 87 (*Meyers, Eric M.*); AUSS 36 (1998) 133-134 (*Drey, Philip R.*); TJT 14/1 (1998) 98-100 (*Arnal, William E.*); CBQ 60 (1998) 569-571 (*Hanson, K.C.*).
9963 **Hurlet, F.** Les collègues du prince sous Auguste et Tibère. Ecole française de Rome 227: R 1997, Ecole française de Rome 692 pp. 2-7283-0372-X [CIR 51,119s—Hall, Lindsay G.H.].
9964 *Millar, Fergus* The Roman city-state under the emperors 29 BC-AD 69. Sidere. Prudentia.S: 1998 ⇒353. 113-134. Todd Memorial Lecture 1997.
9965 *Rabello, Alfredo Mordechai* Civil justice in Palestine from 63 BCE to 70 CE. ᶠSOHLBERG D. 1996 ⇒8271. 293-306.

9966 **Schäfer, Thomas** Spolia et signa: Baupolitik und Reichskultur nach dem Parthererfolg des Augustus. NAWG Phil.-hist. Kl. 1998,2: Gö 1998, Vandenhoeck & R 81 pp.

9967 **Schürer, Emil** Storia del popolo giudaico al tempo di Gesù Cristo (175 a.C.-135 d.C.), 3/1 . ^E*Vermes, Geza*: BSSTB 12: 1997 ⇒13,10092. ^RRdT 39 (1998) 923-924 (*Prato, Gian Luigi*); Anton. 73 (1998) 366-367 (*Nobile, Marco*).

9968 **Schwartz, Daniel** Agrippas ha-rishon, melekh Yehudah ha-aharon. 1987, ⇒6,b773; 8,d259. ^RREJ 157/1-2 (1998) 252-254 (*Woog, Agnès*). **H.**

9969 *Smith, Robert W.* New evidence regarding early Christian chronology: a reconsideration. ^MSUMMERS R. 1998 ⇒115. 133-139.

9970 **Southern, Pat** AUGUSTUS. L 1998, Routledge xv; 271 pp. 0-415-16-631-4. Bibl.

9971 *Vardaman, E. Jerry* A provisional chronology of the New Testament: Jesus through Paul's early years. ^MSUMMERS R. 1998 ⇒115. 313-20.

9972 **Vouga, François** Geschichte des frühen Christentums. 1996 <1994> ⇒10,11335; 12,9419. ^RHZ 266/1 (1998) 167-168 (*Molthagen, Joachim*).

9973 **Ziethen, Gabriele** Gesandte vor Kaiser und Senat: Studien zum römischen Gesandtschaftswesen zwischen 30 v.Chr. und 117 n.Chr. Scripta Mercaturae: Kampen 1994, Pharos 339 pp. €29,65. 3-92813-468-X. ^RGn. 70 (1998) 720-722 (*Ziegler, Karl-Heinz*).

Q8.7 *Roma et Oriens*, prima decennia post Christum

9974 ^E**Arbore Popescu, Grigore** TRAIANO: ai confini dell'impero. Mi 1998, Electa 348 pp. 88-435-6676-8. Bibl.

9975 **Birley, Anthony R.** HADRIAN: the restless emperor. Roman imperial biographies: L 1998, Routledge xviii; 399 pp. 0-415-16544-X. Bibl.

9976 **Botermann, Helga** Das Judenedikt des Kaisers CLAUDIUS: römischer Staat und Christiani im 1. Jahrhundert. Hermes.E 71: 1996 ⇒12,9421; 13,10095. ^RJAC 41 (1998) 230-233 (*Schwartz, Daniel R.*); ZSSR.R 115 (1998) 510-515 (*Scherberich, Klaus*); ZKG 109 (1998) 107-109 (*Klein, Richard*).

9977 *Gray-Fow, Michael J.G.* Why the christians?: NERO and the great fire. Latomus 57 (1998) 595-616.

9978 *Grzybek, Erhard; Sordi, Marta* L'''Edit de Nazareth' et la politique de NÉRON à l'égard des chrétiens. ZPE 120 (1998) 279-291.

9979 *Jocelyn, H.D.* Poetry and philosophy in first-century B.C. Rome: LUCRETIUS and the nature of the universe. Sidere. Prudentia.S: 1998 ⇒353. 85-111.

9980 *McLaren, J.S.* Christians and the Jewish revolt, 66-70 C.E. ^FJUDGE E. 1998 ⇒47. 53-60.

9981 **Shotter, David** NERO. 1997 ⇒13,10103. ^RAnCl 67 (1998) 494-496 (*Benoist, Stéphane*); Latomus 57 (1998) 932-934 (*Bradley, K.R.*).

9982 **Strocka, Volker Michael** Die Regierungszeit des Kaisers CLAUDIUS (41-54 n. Chr.). 1994 ⇒11/2,9829. ^RAnCl 67 (1998) 490-492 (*Galsterer, Hartmut*).

Q9.1 *Historia Romae generalis et* **post-christiana**

9983 *Anderson, James D.* The impact of Rome on the periphery: the case
of Palestina—Roman period (63 BCE-324 CE). Archaeology of
society. 1998 ⇒9495. 446-468.
9984 **Ausbüttel, Frank** Die Verwaltung des römischen Kaiserreiches: von
der Herrschaft des AUGUSTUS bis zum Niedergang des Römischen
Reiches. Da:Wiss 1998, viii; 222 pp. 3-534-12272-0.
9985 **Barker, G.; Rasmussen, T.** The Etruscans. Oxf 1998, Blackwell xii;
379 pp. £25. 0-631-17715-9. 117 ill. ᴿAntiquity 72 (1998) 966-967
(Izzet, Vedia).
9986 ᴱ**Barzano, A.** Il cristianesimo nelle leggi di Roma imperiale. Letture
cristiane del primo millennio 24: 1996 ⇒12,9428. ᴿAsp. 45 (1998)
429-431 *(Longobardo, Luigi).*
9987 **Bauman, Richard A.** Crime and punishment in ancient Rome. 1996
⇒12,4929. ᴿZSRG.R 115 (1998) 605-615 *(Klingenberg, Georg).*
9988 **Bellen, Heinz** Grundzüge der römischen Geschichte, 2: die Kaiserzeit von AUGUSTUS bis DIOCLETIAN. Da 1998, Primus 344 pp [At.
89,286—Marcone, Arnaldo].
9989 *Bernand, André* Le rêve d'une métropole universelle. MoBi 111
(1998) 40-45.
9990 ᴱ**Clauss, Manfred** Die römischen Kaiser: 55 historische Portraits
von CAESAR bis IUSTINIAN. 1997 ⇒13,10108. ᴿZSSR.R 115 (1998)
729-730 *(Jakab, Éva).*
9991 **Duncan-Jones, Richard** Money and government in the Roman
Empire. 1994 ⇒11/2,c806; 12,10737. ᴿGn. 70 (1998) 216-219
(Herz, Peter).
9992 **Erdkamp, Paul** Hunger and the sword: warfare and food supply in
Roman Republican wars (264-30 B.C.). Dutch Monographs on
Ancient History and Archaeology 20: Amst 1998, Gieben 324 pp.
90-5063-608-X.
9993 ᴱ**Finn, James K.; Groten, Frank J. Jr.** Res publica conquassata:
readings on the fall of the Roman Republic. Classical studies pedagogy series: Detroit, MICH 1998, Wayne State University Press 242
pp. 0-8143-2678-1. Bibl.
9994 **Flower, Harriet I.** Ancestor masks and aristocratic power in Roman
culture. 1996, ⇒12,9443. ᴿAJA 102 (1998) 448-49 *(Saller, Richard).*
9995 **Forbis, Elizabeth** Municipal virtues in the Roman empire: the evidence of Italian honorary inscriptions. Beiträge zur Altertumskunde
79: 1996 ⇒12,9444. ᴿHZ 267 (1998) 736-738 *(Andermahr, Anna
Maria).*
9996 **Gardner, Jane F.** Family and familia in Roman law and life. Oxf
1998, Clarendon x; 305 pp. £45 [Gn. 73,229ss—Linke, Bernhard].
9997 ᴱ**Hawley, R.; Levick, B.** Women in antiquity: new assessments.
1995 ⇒13,10114. ᴿAnCl 67 (1998) 411-413 *(Hemelrijk, Emily A.).*
9998 *Hezser, Catherine* 'Privat' und 'öffentlich' im Talmud Yerushalmi
und in der griechisch-römischen Antike. Talmud Yerushalmi, 1. 1998
⇒8811. 423-579 [BuBbgB 30,104].
9999 **Inglebert, Hervé** Les romains chrétiens face à l'histoire de Rome:
histoire, christianisme et romanités en Occident dans l'Antiquité tardive (IIIᵉ-Vᵉ siècles). 1996 ⇒13,9448. ᴿAnCl 67 (1998) 508-510
(Wankenne, Jules).

10000 **Isaac, Benjamin** The Near East under Roman rule: selected papers. Mn.S 177: Lei 1998, Brill xix; 481 pp. €117,98. 90-04-10736-3.

10001 **EJones, P.; Sidwell, K.** The world of Rome: an introduction to Roman culture. 1997 ⇒13,10116. RClR 48 (1998) 417-419 (*Barker, Peter*).

10002 **Krause, Jens-Uwe** Gefängnisse im Römischen Reich. 1996 ⇒12, 9449. RZSSR.R 115 (1998) 615-623 (*Klingenberg, Georg*).

10003 **Le Gall, J.; Le Glay, M.** El imperio romano, 1: el alto imperiale, desde la batalla de Actium (31 a.C.) hasta la muerte de Severo Alejandro (235 d.C.). M 1995, Akal 569 pp. RCDios 211 (1998) 654-656 (*Gutiérrez, J.*).

10004 **Le Glay, Marcel,** *al.,* A history of Rome. 1996 ⇒12,9450. RHZ 267 (1998) 449-451 (*Schulz, Raimund*) Prudentia 30/2 (1998) 55-59 (*Sharp, Michael*)

10005 **Lendon, J.E.** Empire of honour: the art of government in the Roman world. 1997 ⇒13,10119. RHZ 267 (1998) 728-730 (*Schulz, Raimund*).

10006 *Mendels, Doron* A note on the speeches of Nabis and T. Quinctius Flamininus (195 BCE). Identity. JSPE.S 24: 1998 ⇒174. 261-268.

10007 **Mommsen, Theodor** A history of Rome under the emperors TKrotjzl, Clare; EDemandt, Barbara; Demandt, Alexandre L 1996, Routledge ix; 642 pp. £20. 0-415-20647-2 [AnCl 69,492ss—Benoist, Stéphane].

10008 **Morley, Neville** Metropolis and hinterland: the city of Rome and the Italian economy 200 B.C. - A.D. 200. 1996 ⇒12,9453. RAJA 102 (1998) 451-452 (*Peña, J. Theodore*).

10009 **Nippel, Wilfried** Public order in ancient Rome. 1995, ⇒11/2,9918; 12,9454. RPrudentia 30/1 (1998) 59-63 (*Stevenson, Tom*); Gn. 70 (1998) 566-568 (*Gruen, Erich S.*).

10010 *Oppenheimer, Aharon* Jewish penal authority in Roman Judaea. Jews in a Graeco-Roman world. 1998 ⇒337. 181-191.

10011 **Peachin, Michael** *Iudex vice Caesaris*: deputy emperors and the administration of justice during the principate. Heidelberger althistorische Beiträge und epigraphische Studien 21: Stu 1996, Steiner x; 267 pp.

10012 **Philip, T.V.** East of Euphrates: early christianity in Asia. Delhi 1998, ISPCK 192 pp. $9. 81-721441-5.

10013 **Ratti, Stéphane** Les empereurs romains d'AUGUSTE à DIOCLÉTIEN dans le Bréviaire d'Europe: les livres 7 à 9: introduction, traduction et commentaire. 1996 ⇒12,9455. RAnCl 67 (1998) 357-358 (*Chausson, François*).

10014 **Rutgers, L.V.** The Jews in late ancient Rome. 1995 ⇒11/2,a014; 13,10127. RJAC 41 (1998) 233-234 (*Finney, Paul Corby*).

10015 **Sandgren, Leo Dupree** We have no king but Caesar: Jewish legitimation of Roman rule from Judas Maccabeus to Judah Ha-Nasi (164 BCE-235 CE). DNorth Carolina, Chapel Hill 1998, 346 pp.

10016 **Santalucia, B.** Diritto e processo penale nell'antica Roma. Mi ²1998 <1989>, Giuffrè xx; 330 pp [At. 88,321ss—Laffi, Umberto].

10017 **Schwartz, Robert N.** The Roman Empire: a concise history of the first two centuries. Lanham MD 1998, University Press of America xii; 170 pp. $49/29.50. 0-7618-1172-9/3-98. 32 fig. [Antiquity 73,928—James, N.].

10018 *Vössing, Konrad* Schreiben lernen, ohne lesen zu können?: zur Methode des antiken Elementarunterrichts. ZPE 123 (1998) 121-125.

10019 **Woolf, Greg** Becoming Roman: the origins of provincial civilization in Gaul. C 1998, CUP xv (3); 296 pp. 0-521-41445-8. Bibl.

Q9.5 Byzantine Empire

10020 *Bowersock, Glen W.* The Greek Moses: confusion of ethnic and cultural components in later Roman and early Byzantine Palestine. Religious... communities. 1998 ⇒347. 31-48.

10021 *Geiger, Joseph* Aspects of Palestinian paganism in late antiquity. Sharing the sacred. 1998 ⇒306. 3-17.

10022 *Gibson, Shimon; Vitto, Fanny; Di Segni, Leah* An unknown church with inscriptions from the Byzantine period at Khirbet Makkûs near Julis. SBFLA 48 (1998) 315-334.

10023 **Grant, Michael** From Rome to Byzantium: the fifth century AD. L 1998, Routledge xiii; 203 pp. 0-415-14753-0. Bibl.

10024 *Isaac, Benjamin* Jews, christians and others in Palestine: the evidence from EUSEBIUS. Jews in a Graeco-Roman world. 1998 ⇒337. 65-74.

10025 **Liebeschuetz, John Hugo W.G.** Barbarians and bishops: army, church, and state in the age of ARCADIUS and CHRYSOSTOM. Oxf 1998, Clarendon xiv; 312 pp. 0-19-814073-8. Bibl.

10026 *Pena, Ignacio* Chinán o el paso del paganismo al cristianismo en Siria. SBFLA 48 (1998) 483-488.

10027 *Rubin, Zeev* PORPHYRIUS of Gaza and the conflict between christianity and paganism in southern Palestine. Sharing the sacred. 1998 ⇒306. 31-66.

10028 **Safrai, Ze'ev** The missing century: Palestine in the fifth century: growth and decline. Palaestina Antiqua 9: Lv 1998, Peeters 220 pp. 90-6831-985-X. Bibl.

10029 *Taha, Hamdan* A Byzantine tomb at the village of Rammun. SBFLA 48 (1998) 335-344.

XVIII. Archaeologia terrae biblicae

T1.1 General biblical-area archeologies

10030 [E]**Alcina Franch, J.** Diccionario de Arqueología. M 1998, Alianza 955 pp. [BAEO 35,376—Sen, Felipe].

10031 [E]**Cline, Eric H.; Harris-Cline, Diane** The Aegean and the Orient in the second millennium: proceedings of the 50th anniversary symposium, Cincinnati, 1997. Liège 1998, Univ. de Liège xxvii; 363 pp.

10032 **Durusau, Patrick** High places in cyberspace: a guide to biblical and religious studies, classics, and archaeological resources on the internet. Scholars Handbook: Atlanta 1998, Scholars xiii; 302 pp. $30. 0-7885-0492-4.

10033   *Finkelstein, David* Bible archaeology or archaeology of Palestine in the Iron Age?: a rejoinder. Levant 30 (1998) 167-174.
10034   **Frend, William H.C.** The archaeology of early christianity. 1996 ⇒12,9476; 13,11073. ^REHR 113 (1998) 130-131 *(Henig, Martin)*; New Theology Review 11/4 (1998) 83-84 *(Hoppe, Leslie, J.)*.
10035   **Hoerth, Alfred J.** Archaeology and the Old Testament. GR 1998, Baker 447 pp. $45. 0-8010-1129-9. Bibl.
10036   **Kitchen, K.A.** Traces d'un monde: bible et archéologie. P 1997, PBU. ^RApoll. 71 (1998) 774-777 *(Molino, Stefano)*.
10037   *Lehmann, Gunnar* Zum Stand der Archäologie in Palästina. Zwischen Euphrat und Indus. 1998 ⇒318. 241-250.
10038   **Leuthäusser, Werner** Die Entwicklung staatlich organisierter Herrschaft in frühen Hochkulturen am Beispiel der Vorderen Orients. EHS 22: Fra 1997, Lang 317 pp. 3-631-33426-5.
10039   ^E**Levy, Thomas E.** The archaeology of society in the Holy Land. 1995, Pb. 1998, ⇒11/2,a054; 12,9477. ^RPEQ 130 (1998) 172-173 *(Philip, Graham)*; CBQ 60 (1998) 397-399 *(Bloch-Smith, Elizabeth M.)*.
10040   ^E**Meyers, Eric M.** The Oxford encyclopedia of archaeology in the Near East. 1997, 5 vols. ^RBAR Jan-Feb 1998, 70, 72 *(Shanks, Hershel)*; JSP 17 (1998) 123-124 *(Vanderkam, James C.)*; AJA 102 (1998) 607-610 *(Yoffee, Norman)*.
10041   **Moorey, Peter Roger Stuart** Un secolo di archeologia biblica ^T*Nigro, Lorenzo*: Saggi di archeologia 4: Mi 1998, Electa 165 pp. 88-435-6516-8. Bibl.
10042   **Pedersén, Olof** Archives and libraries in the ancient Near East 1500-300 B.C. Bethesda 1998, CDL xxii; 291 pp. 1-883053-39-0.
10043   **Piccirillo, M.** Vangelo e archeologia: tracce cristiane in Palestina. La Bibbia nelle nostre mani 9: CinB 1998, S. Paolo 5-75 pp [SMSR 64,386—Acconci, Alessandra].
10044   *Schick, Robert* The archaeology of Palestine/Jordan in the early Ottoman period. Aram 9-10 (1997-1998) 563-575.
10045   *Shanks, Hershel* San Francisco tremors: not earthquakes, just academic rumbles. BArR 24/2 (1998) 54-56 , 60-61.
10046   **Sichtermann, Hellmut** Kulturgeschichte der klassischen Archäologie. 1996 ⇒12,9483. ^RAJA 102 (1998) 429-430 *(Hauser, Stefan)*.
10047   *Wolff, Samuel* Travel guide to Israel: a handbook of current excavations. Arch. 51/3 (1998) 56-59.

T1.2 Musea, organismi, exploratores

10048   Along the routes of the Phoenicians; Sur les routes de Phéniciens. R 1998, Argos 109 pp. 88-85897-50-9. Mostra a cura della Associazione Civita; Carthage, Musée National 10.9-25.10.1998.
10049   **Berlev, Oleg D.; Hodjash, Svetlana** Catalogue of the monuments of ancient Egypt: from the museums of the Russian Federation, Ukraine, Bielorussia, Caucasus, Middle Asia and the Baltic States. OBO.A 17: Gö 1998, Vandenhoeck & R xiii; 329 pp. DM144. 3-525-53898-7. 208 pl.; Bibl.
10050   ^E**Bonilauri, Franco; Maugeri, Vincenza** Musei ebraici in Europa: Jewish museums in Europe: orientamenti e prospettive: trends and perspectives. Mi 1998, Electa 137 pp. 88-435-6625-3.

10051   *Ciampini, Emanuele M.; Di Paolo, Silvana* La collezione Egizia Giamberardini in un museo dell'Aquilano. SBFLA 48 (1998) 495-512.

10052   ᴱ**Donadoni Roveri, Anna Maria; Tiradritti, Francesco** Kemet: alle sorgenti del tempo. Mi 1998, Electa Catalogo della mostra tenuta a Ravenna, Museo Nazionale 1 marzo - 28 giugno 1998; Bibl. 317 pp. 88-435-6042-5.

10053   *La gloire d'Alexandrie, 7 mai - 26 juillet 1998.* P 1998, [Musées] 335 pp. 2-87900-398-9. Musée du Petit Palais; Bibl.

10054   ᴱ**Harper, Prudence O.**, *al.*, Discoveries at Ashur on the Tigris: Assyrian origins. 1995 ⇒11/2,a098. ᴿSyr. 75 (1998) 323-324 *(Garelli, Paul).*

10055   **Jørgensen, Mogens** Catalogue Egypt I (3000-1550 B.C.). 1996 ⇒12,9495. ᴿArOr 66 (1998) 176-177 *(Bárta, Miroslav).*

10056   ᴱ**La Regina, Adriano** Palazzo Massimo alle Terme. R 1998, Electa Museo Nazionale Romano (Roma); Bibl. 291 pp. 88-435-6609-1.

10057   *Liphschitz, Nili* Timber identification of wooden Egyptian objects in museum collections in Israel. TelAv 25 (1998) 255-276.

10058   **Nielsen, Anne Marie; Østergaard, Jan Stubbe** The eastern Mediterranean in the Hellenistic period: Ny Carlsberg Glyptotek. 1997 ⇒13,10164. ᴿMes. 33 (1998) 396-397 *(Invernizzi, A.).*

10059   *Piccirillo, Michele* Il museo dei Francescani. TS(I) (sett.-ott. 1998) 38-40.

10060   *Reiner, E.* Celestial omen tablets and fragments in the British Museum. ᶠBORGER R. 1998 ⇒12. 215-302.

10061   **Sacchi, Livio** Daniel LIBESKIND: museo ebraico, Berlino. Universale di architettura 47: T 1998, Testo & I 90 pp. 88-86498-56-X. Bibl.

10062   **Schär, Heinrich** Mehr also ein Buch—die Bibel: Entstehung, Geschichte, Aktualität. Fellbach 1998, 41 pp. Ausstellung Fellbacher Bank,...vom 29. April bis 5. Juni 1998; ill. [NThAR 1998,299].

10063   **Schmidt, Stefan** Katalog der ptolemäischen und kaiserzeitlichen Objekte aus Ägypten im Akademischen Kunstmuseum Bonn. 1997 ⇒13,10166. ᴿCÉg 73 (1998) 191-193 *(Nachtergael, Georges).*

10064   *Seger, Joe D.* ASOR policy on preservation and protection of archaeological resources. BASOR 309 (1998) 1-2.

10065   ᴱ**Silverman, David P.** Searching for ancient Egypt. Ithaca 1997, Cornell Univ. Press Catalogue of travelling exhibition; 342 pp. £47. 0-8014-3482-3 [BiOr 57,305ss—Tooley, Angela M.J.].

10066   ᴱ**Tiradritti, Francesco** Egyptian treasures: from the Egyptian Museum in Cairo. [Vercelli] 1998, White star 416 pp. 88-8095-324-9. Photographs by Araldo De Luca; Bibl. 413-416.

10067   **Van Haarlem, Willem M.** Corpus antiquitatum aegyptiacarum: loose-leaf-catalogue of Egyptian antiquities. Corpus antiquitatum aegyptiacarum 3: Amst 1995, Allard Pierson Museum 90-71211-24-X. ᴿBiOr 55 (1998) 142-144 *(Teeter, Emily).*

10068   ᴱ**Wildung, Dietrich** Sudan: ancient kingdoms of the Nile. ᵀ*Manuelian, Peter der; Guillaume, Kathleen*: P 1997, Flammarion 400 fig. xii; 428 pp. $85.

T1.3 *Methodi*—Science in archaeology

10069   **Barbanera, Marcello** L'archeologia degli italiani: storia, metodi e orientamenti dell'archeologia classica in Italia. Nuova biblioteca di cultura: R 1998, Riuniti xxii; 255 pp. 88-359-4485-6. Contributo di Nicola Terrenato; Bibl.

10070   *Buccellati, Giorgio* Archaeology's publication problems. NEA(BA) 61/2 (1998) 118-120.

10071   **Buck, C.E.; Cavanagh, W.G.; Litton, C.D.** Bayesian approach to interpreting archaeological data. 1996 ⇒12,9506. ^RAJA 102 (1998) 187-188 *(Orton, Clive)*.

10072   ^E**Eggert, Manfred K.H.; Veit, Ulrich** Theorie in der Archäologie: zur englischsprachigen Diskussion. Tübinger Archäologische Taschenbücher 1: Müns 1998, Waxmann 400 pp. €19,43. 3-89325-594-X [ThLZ 124,1203—Conrad, Diethelm].

10073   **Elliott, Mark** Archaeology, Bible and interpretation: 1900-1930. ^DArizona 1998, 392 pp.

10074   **Gran-Aymerich, Ève** Naissance de l'archéologie moderne, 1798-1945. Préf. *Leclant, Jean;* Foreword *Laronde, André*: P 1998, CNRS 536 pp. 2-271-05570-9. 151 phot.

10075   *Halpern, Baruch* Research design in archaeology: the interdisciplinary perspective. NEA(BA) 61/1 (1998) 53-65.

10076   **Hodder, Ian** Interpreting archaeology: finding meaning in the past. 1997 ⇒13,10174. ^RJNES 57 (1998) 231-232 *(Joffe, Alexander H.)*.

10077   *Krannich, Torsten* Arbeitshilfen zur Archäologie im Internet. ZAC 2 (1998) 299-303.

10078   ^E**Moscati, Paola; Tagliamonte, Gianluca** Methodological trends and future perspectives in the application of GIS in archaeology. Archeologia e calcolatori 9: F 1998, All'insegna del giglio 379 pp. 88-7814-134-8. Bibl.

10079   *Pilhofer, Peter; Witulski, Thomas* Archäologie und Neues Testament: von der Palästinawissenschaft zur lokalgeschichtlichen Methode. Exegese und Methodendiskussion. TANZ 23: 1998 ⇒208. 237-255.

10080   *Richter, Arnd Immo* Von der Unnötigkeit des Zweifels in der kritischen Forschung. DBAT 29 (1998) 244-258.

10081   *Silberman, Neil Asher* Whose game is it anyway?: the political and social transformations of American biblical archaeology. Archaeology under fire. 1998 ⇒349. 175-188.

10082   **Thomas, Julian** Time, culture and identity: an interpretive archaeology. Material Cultures: L 1998, Routledge viii; 267 pp. $80/28. 0-415-11861-1/19787-2 [AJA 105,330s—Hitchcock, Louise A.].

10083   *Trigger, Bruce G.* Archaeology and epistemology: dialoguing across the Darwinian chasm. AJA 102 (1998) 1-34 Sum. 1.

T1.4 *Exploratores*—Excavators, pioneers

10084   *Cesarini, Giovanna* Processi e modelli: l'archeologia di Colin RENFREW. ASNSP 4/2,2 (1997) 363-410.

10085   **Long, Burke O.** Planting and reaping ALBRIGHT: politics, ideology, and interpreting the Bible. 1997 ⇒13,10178. ^RVT 48 (1998) 127-129 *(Emerton, J.A.)*; ThTo 54 (1998) 565-566, 568-569

(*Brueggemann, Walter*); CBQ 60 (1998) 333-335 (*Fitzmyer, Joseph A.*).
10086 **Raymond, André** Égyptiens et Français au Caire 1798-1801. Bibliothèque générale 18: Le Caire 1998, Institut Français d'Archéologie Orientale (4) 391 pp. 2-7247-0215-8.

T1.5 *Materiae primae*—metals, glass; stone

10087 **Dercksen, Jan Gerrit** The Old Assyrian copper trade in Anatolia. 1996 ⇒12,9529. [R]Or. 67 (1998) 271-277 (*Michel, Cécile*).
10088 **Dussart, Odile** Le verre en Jordanie et en Syrie du Nord. BAH 152: Beyrouth 1998, Institut français d'Archéologie du Proche-Orient 336 pp. 2-7053-0570-X. 76 pl. 29 fig. Rés. arabe [CRAI 1999/4,1179—La Genière, Juliette de].
10089 *Kletter, Raz; Brand, Etty* A new look at the Iron Age silver hoard from Eshtemoa. ZDPV 114 (1998) 139-154.
10090 *Muhly, James D.* Copper, tin, silver and iron: the search for metallic ores as an incentive for foreign expansion. [F]DOTHAN, T. 1998 ⇒23. 314-329.
10091 *Muhly, J.D.; Stech, Tamara; Maddin, Robert* Çayönü and the beginnings of metallurgy in Anatolia and Mesopotamia. Rencontre Assyriologique Internationale 34. 1998 ⇒452. 533-545.
10092 *Pilch, John J.* Mirrors and glass. BiTod 36 (1998) 382-386.
10093 *Rossoni, Gabriele* I tridenti metallici nel Vicino Oriente antico tra uso pratico e simbologia: proposte di interpretazione di una particolare classe di materiali. [M]FRANKFORT H. 1998 ⇒26. 561-590.
10094 *Winter, Tamar* (1990-1988) כלי הזכוכית מחורבת חרמשית [The glass vessels from Ḥorvat Ḥermeshit (1988-1990)]. ʿAtiqot 34 (1998) 173-177 Sum. 10*. H.

T1.7 Technologia antiqua; architectura

10095 **Barber, Elizabeth Wayland** Women's work: the first 20,000 years: women, cloth and society in early times. 1994 ⇒10,11764 [R]Gn. 70 (1998) 411-415 (*Wagner-Hasel, Beate*).
10096 **Schiaparelli, Giovanni** Scritti sulla storia dell'astronomia antica. Mi 1998, Mimesis 462 + 397+ 338 pp.
10097 *Stech, Tamara* Thoughts on ancient craft and craftsmanship in southwest Asia. [F]ÇAMBEL H. 1998 ⇒4. 729-733.

10098 **Arnold, Dieter** Building in Egypt. 1991, ⇒7,b651... 12,9548 [R]DiscEg 41 (1998) 89-92 (*Matthews, Valerie*).
10099 *Arnold, Felix* Die Priesterhäuser der Chentkaues in Giza: staatlicher Wohnungsbau als Interpretation der Wohnvorstellungen für einen "Idealmenschen". MDAI.K 54 (1998) 1-18.
10100 *Banning, E.B.* The neolithic period: triumphs of architecture, agriculture, and art. NEA (BA) 61/4 (1998) 188-237.
10101 *Brands, Gunnar* Der sogenannte Audienzsaal des al-Mundir in Resafa. DaM 10 (1998) 211-235.
10102 **DeVries, LaMoine F.** Cities of the biblical world. 1997 ⇒13, 10204. [R]Bibl.Interp. 6 (1998) 440-442 (*Moran, Maureen*); Neotest. 32 (1998) 241-242 (*Botha, Pieter J.J.*).

10103 **Donderer, Michael** Die Architekten der späten römischen Republik und der Kaiserzeit: epigraphische Zeugnisse. ErF 69: 1996 ⇒ 12,9556. [R]AnCl 67 (1998) 435-436 (*Tarpin, Michel*).

10104 *Enea, Alessandra* Trasformazioni architettoniche in Palestina tra la fine del Calcolitico e il Bronzo Antico I. [M]FRANKFORT H. 1998 ⇒26. 163-176.

10105 *Fourdrin, Jean-Pascal* L'association de la niche et de l'archère dans les fortifications élevées en Syrie entre le VIe et le XIIe siècle. Syr. 75/1 (1998) 279-294.

10106 **Ginouvès, René; Martin, Roland** Espaces architecturaux, bâtiments et ensembles. Dictionnaire méthodique de l'architecture grecque et romaine, 3. CEFR 84: R 1998, École Française de Rome. 2-7283-0529-3.

10107 **Gros, Pierre** Les monuments publics. L'architecture romaine du début du IIIe siècle av. J.-C. à la fin du haut-empire. 1996 ⇒12, 9563. [R]AJA 102 (1998) 614-615 (*MacDonald, William*).

10108 *Grossmann, Peter; Hafiz, Mohammed* Results of the 1995/96 excavations in the north-west church of Pelusium (Farama-West). MDAI.K 54 (1998) 177-182.

10109 **Hirschfeld, Y.** The Palestinian dwelling in the Roman-Byzantine period. 1995 ⇒11/2,a257. [R]BiOr 55 (1998) 267-270 (*Wright, G.R. H.*); PEQ 130 (1998) 170-171 (*Dauphin, Claudine M.*); Syr. 75 (1998) 329-330 (*Braemer, Frank*).

10110 *Humbert, Jean-Baptiste* Qumrân, esséniens et architecture. [F]STEGEMANN, H. BZNW 97: 1998 ⇒111. 183-196.

10111 **Kahn, L.C.** King Herod's temple to Roma and Augustus at Caesarea Maritima. Hellenic and Jewish arts. 1998 ⇒439. 123-142.

10112 *Kochavi, Moshe* The eleventh century BCE tripartite pillar building at Tel Hadar. [F]DOTHAN, T. 1998 ⇒23. 468-478.

10113 **Kubba, S.A.A.** Architecture and linear measurement during the Ubaid period in Mesopotamia. BAR internat. ser. 707: Oxf 1998, Archaeopress x; 366 pp. 0-86054-944-5. Bibl.

10114 *Lauffray, Jean* Contribution à l'histoire de la charpenterie: une représentation de ferme à poinçon suspendu en Syrie du Nord au VIe siècle. Syr. 75/1 (1998) 225-230.

10115 *Lembke, Katja* Die Sphingenallee von Saqqara und ihre Werkstatt. MDAI.K 54 (1998) 267-273.

10116 *Lilliu, Giovanni* Aspetti e problemi dell'ipogeismo mediterraneo. AANL.M 9/10,2: R 1998, Accademia Nazionale dei Lincei 123-202. 45 pl.

10117 **Loader, N. Claire** Building in Cyclopean masonry: with special reference to the Mycenaean fortifications on mainland Greece. Studies in Mediterranean Archaeology and Literature, Pocket-book 148: [Göteborg] 1998, Astroms x; 225 pp. 91-7081-1407. Bibl.

10118 **Murray, Peter; Murray, Linda** The Oxford companion to christian art and architecture. 1996 ⇒12,9575. [R]JEarlyC 6 (1998) 686-688 (*Jensen, Robin*).

10119 **Negev, Avraham** The architecture of Oboda: final report. Qedem 36: 1997 ⇒13,10217. [R]BArR 24/6 (1998) 56 (*Meyers, Eric*); NEA (BA) 61 (1998) 182 (*Oleson, John Peter*).

10120 *Özgüç, Tahsin* The palaces of the Old Assyrian colonial age. Rencontre Assyriologique Internationale 34. 1998 ⇒452. 467-472.

10121   *Parapetti, Roberto* Capitelli nabatei a Gerasa. Mes. 33 (1998) 309-319.

10122   **Pilgrim, Cornelius von** Elephantine XVIII: Untersuchungen in der Stadt des Mittleren Reiches und der Zweiten Zwischenzeit. 1996 ⇒ 12,9581. [R]BiOr 55 (1998) 411-415 (*Aston, D.A.*).

10123   *Richardson, Peter* Architectural transitions from synagogues and house churches to purpose-built churches. [F]SNYDER, G. 1998 ⇒ 104. 373-389.

10124   **Ristow, Sebastian** Frühchristliche Baptisterien. JAC.E 27: Mü 1998, Aschendorff iv; 384 pp. 37 ill.
        Roller, D. The building program of Herod. 1998 ⇒9952.

10125   *Rusconi, Franco* Architettura e bibbia nella chiesa di Santa Maria Goretti a Cesenatico. ACr 86 (1998) 301-309.

10126   *Safrai, Zeev* מבני השדה הקדומים—הכפר בארץ־ישראל בתקופה הרומית [Ancient field structures—the village in Eretz Israel during the Roman period]. Cathedra 89 (1998) 7-40 Sum. 197. **H**.

10127   **Sauvage, Martin** La brique et sa mise en oeuvre en Mésopotamie: des origines à l'époque achéménide. P 1998, Recherches sur les Civilisations 467 pp. €44,21. 2-86538-272-9 [BiOr 57,695s—Wright, G.R.H.].

10128   **Schreiber, Jürgen** Die Siedlungsarchitektur auf der Halbinsel O-man vom 3. bis zur Mitte des 1. Jahrtausends v.Chr. Altertumskunde des Vorderen Orients 9: Müns 1998, Ugarit-Verlag xii; 253 pp. 3-927120-61-8. Bibl.

10129   **Sear, Frank** Roman architecture. L [3]1998 <1982>, Routledge 288 pp. £17. 0-415-20093-8 [Latomus 59,702s—Gros, Pierre].

10130   *Stern, Eliezer* Der architektonische Komplex des Johanniterordens. WUB 8 (1998) 50-52.

10131   *Turnheim, Y.* Hellenistic elements in Herodian architecture and decoration. Hellenic and Jewish arts. 1998 ⇒439. 143-170.

10132   *Viviani R., María Teresa* La fuerza de lo vernáculo en la arquitectura cristiana del Medio Oriente (S. IV-V). TyV 39 (1998) 398-415.

10133   *Webber, Alan* A consideration of the dimensions of walls contained in Mishnah Bava Batra 1:1. JSJ 29 (1998) 92-100.

10134   *Weiss, Zeev* Greco-Roman influences on the art and architecture of the Jewish city in Roman Palestine. Religious... communities. 1998 ⇒347. 219-246.

10135   **White, Michael L.** Social origins of christian architecture. HThS 42: 1997 ⇒13,10224. [R]BZ 42 (1998) 157-158 (*Klauck, Hans-Josef*).

T1.9 *Supellex*—**Artifacts**

10136   **Herrmann, Georgina** The small collections from Fort Shalmaneser. Ivories from Nimrud 5. 1992 ⇒8,e931; 10,12619. [R]JNES 57 (1998) 150-153 (*Winter, Irene J.*).

10137   [E]**Herrmann, Georgina** The furniture of western Asia, ancient and traditional. 1996 Papers...at the Institute of Archaeology, University College London, 1993 ⇒12,313. [R]AJA 102 (1998) 642-643 (*Lapatin, Kenneth D.S.*); Mes. 33 (1998) 355-359 (*Negro, F.*); JAOS 118 (1998) 451-452 (*Muscarella, Oscar White*).

10138 *Maxwell-Hyslop, K.R.* A note on the purpose and use of copper-bronze axeheads. Rencontre Assyriologique Internationale 34. 1998 ⇒452. 33-37.

10139 **Svarth, Dan** Egyptisk møbelkunst fra Faraotiden/ Egyptian furniture making in the age of the Pharaohs. Aarhus 1998, Aarhus Univ. Press 151 pp. DKR248. 87-89224-39-6 [BiOr 57,340s—Sliwa, J.].

T2.1 *Res militaris*—military matters

10140 Goedicke, Hans The rules of conduct for Egyptian military. WZKM 88 (1998) 109-142.

10141 *Hays, J. Daniel* From the land of the bow: black soldiers in the ancient Near East. BiRe 14/4 (1998) 28-33, 50-51.

10142 *Lemaire, A.* Chars et cavaliers dans l'ancien Israël. Transeuphratène 15 (1998) 165-182.

10143 **Sage, M.M.** Warfare in ancient Greece: a source book. L 1996, Routledge xxvii; 252 pp. 0-415-14354-3 [SCI 19,181ss—Shatzman, Israel].

10144 *Van Lerberghe, Karel* Old-Babylonian soldiers at Sabum. [F]RÖMER, W. AOAT 253: 1998 ⇒97. 447-455.

10145 **Vita, Juan-Pablo** El ejército de Ugarit. 1995 ⇒11/2,a349; 13, 10849. [R]Or. 67 (1998) 139-143 (*Heltzer, Michael*).

10146 *Ziermann, Martin* Bemerkungen zu den Befestigungen des Alten Reiches in Ayn Asil und in Elephantine. MDAI.K 54 (1998) 341-359.

T2.2 *Vehicula, nautica*—transport, navigation

10147 *Artzy, Michal* Routes, trade, boats and "nomads of the sea". [F]DOTHAN, T. 1998 ⇒23. 439-448.

10148 *Georgiou, Hara* Seafaring, trade routes, and the emergence of the Bronze Age: urban centers in the eastern Mediterranean. Res maritimae. 1998 ⇒491. 117-124.

10149 **Patai, Raphael** The children of Noah—Jewish seafaring in ancient times. Princeton 1998, Princeton Univ. Pr. viii; 227 pp. 0-691-01580-5. Collab. Hornell, James; Lundquist, John M. [Jud. 55, 197s—Schreiner, Stefan].

10150 *Raban, Avner* Some remarks on shipbuilding heritage and ancient peoples. [F]GORDON, C. JSOT.S 273: 1998 ⇒31. 40-61.

10151 **Wachsmann, Shelley** Seagoing ships & seamanship in the Bronze Age Levant. Foreword *Bass, George F.*: College Station, Tex 1998, Texas A & M University Press xii; 417 pp. 0-89096-709-1. Bibl.

T2.4 *Athletica*—sport, games

10152 *Bouet, Alain* Complexes sportifs et centres monumentaux en occident romain: les exemples d'Orange et Vienne. RAr 1 (1998) 33-105.

10153 **Decker, Wolfgang** Sport in der griechischen Antike. 1995 ⇒13, 10236. [R]QUCC n.s. 59/2 (1998) 169-172 (*Bernardini, Paola A.*).

10154 **Decker, Wolfgang; Herb, Michael** Bildatlas zum Sport im Alten Ägypten. 1994 ⇒9,13235; 13,10237. 2 vols. ᴿBiOr 55 (1998) 144-145 (*Meulenaere, H.J.A. de*).
10155 **Golden, Mark** Sport and society in ancient Greece. Key Themes in Ancient History: C 1998, CUP xiii; 216 pp. £14. 0-521-49790-6 [CIR 50,213ss—Van Wees, Hans].
10156 **Kyle, D.G.** Spectacles of death in ancient Rome. L 1998, Routledge xii; 288 pp. £45. 0-415-09678-2 [JRS 89,236—Plass, Paul].
10157 *Pilch, John J.* Games, amusements, and sports. BiTod 36 (1998) 250-255.

T2.5 *Musica, drama, saltatio*—music, drama, dance

10158 *Bar-Asher, Moshe* Notes sur le vocabulaire musical dans le sharḥ biblique marocain. JA 286 (1998) 55-83 Sum. rés. 55.
10159 ᴱ**Bélis, Annie** De la pierre au son: musiques de l'antiquité grecque. 1996, Productions K617; Ensemble Kérylos disque compact DDD; 47'29" [RB 103,471s—Devillers, Luc].
10160 **Bordier, Jean-Pierre** Le Jeu de la Passion: le message chrétien et le théâtre français (XIIIe-XVIe s.). BQS 58: P 1998, Champion 864 pp. €114,34. 2-85203-646-0 [MAe 68,337s—Runnalls, G.A.].
10161 **Ceccarelli, Paola** La pirrica nell'antichità greco romana: studi sulla danza armata. Pisa 1998, Istituti editoriali e poligrafici internazionali 274 pp. 88-8147-140-X. 24 pl. [Kernos 13,282s—Goulaki-Voutira, A.].
10162 **Dumbrill, Richard J.** Musicology and organology of the ancient Near East. L 1998, Tadema xl; 638 pp. 0-9533633-0-9. Bibl.
10163 *Fictoor, Chris* De bijbel komt tot klinken: over de relatie tussen bijbel en muziek. Interpretatie 6/8 (1998) 17-18.
10164 **Fischer, Kurt von** Die Passion: Musik zwischen Kunst und Kirche. 1997 ⇒13,4934. ᴿEK (1998/4) 238 (*Mörchen, Roland*); LM 37/8 (1998) 42 (*Merten, Werner*).
10165 **Foley, Edward** Foundations of christian music: the music of pre-Constantinian christianity. 1996 ⇒12,9615. ᴿPro Ecclesia 7 (1998) 501-503 (*Joncas, Jan·Michael*).
10166 *Gurney, O.R.; West, M.L.* Mesopotamian tonal systems: a reply. Iraq 60 (1998) 223-227.
10167 *Keel, Othmar* Musikalische Meditation zu "König David" von René Morax und Arthur Honegger. ᶠVENETZ, H. 1998 ⇒122. 265-275.
10168 *Koitabashi, Matahisa* Music in the texts from Ugarit. UF 30 (1998) 363-396.
10169 *Lawergren, Bo* Distinctions among the Canaanite, Philistine, and Israelite lyres, and their global lyrical contexts. BASOR 309 (1998) 41-68.
10170 *Loader, J.A.* Johannes BRAHMS, agnosticism and some other wisdom. SeK 19 (1998) 616-627 Sum. 616.
10171 **Marissen, Michael** Lutheranism, anti-Judaism, and Bach's `St. John Passion' with an annotated translation of the libretto. NY 1998, OUP xii; 109 pp. $17 [JR 81,120s—Westermeyer, Paul].
10172 **McKinnon, James** The temple, the church fathers and early western chant. VCS: Brookfield, VT 1998, Ashgate xii; 300 pp. $90. 0-86078-688-9 [ThD 46,375—Heiser, Charles].

10173 *Schinke, Gerhard* Halleluja—preist Gott mit Pauken und Tanz: Psalm 150 beim Wort genommen. Choreae 5/2 (1998) 117-124.

10174 *Spero, Shubert* King David, the temple, and the Halleluyah chorus. Jdm 47 (1998) 411-423.

10175 *Wilson, Stephen G.* Early christian music. ^FSNYDER, G. 1998 ⇒104. 390-401.

10176 **Younger, John G.** Music in the Aegean Bronze Age. Jonsered 1998, Åström xi; 108 pp. SEK200. 91-7081-124-5. 25 pl. [Antiquity 72,934—Sinclair, Anthony].

10177 *Yuasa, Yuko* Performing sacred texts. Conc(GB) 3 (1998) 81-90.

T2.6 *Vestis*, **clothing**; *ornamenta*, **jewellry**

10178 *Scheyhing, Hans* Das Haar in Ritualen des alten Mesopotamien: der Umgang mit Haar im Bereich von Religion und Kult. WO 29 (1998) 58-79.

10179 *Schneider-Ludorff, Helga* Filz in Nuzi?. General studies... Nuzi 10/2. 1998 ⇒T6.5. 163-168.

10180 *Strobel, August* Zum Problem der Aufbewahrung der heiligen Gewänder. ZNW 89 (1998) 114-117.

10181 *Brosch, Na'ama* Two jewelry hoards from Tiberias. 'Atiqot 36 (1998) 1-9.

10182 *Golani, Amir; Sass, Benjamin* Three seventh-century B.C.E. hoards of silver jewelry from Tel Miqne-Ekron. BASOR 311 (1998) 57-81.

T2.8 **Utensilia**; *pondera et mensurae*—**weights and measures**

10183 **Lilyquist, Christine** Egyptian stone vessels. 1995 ⇒13,10258. ^RBiOr 55 (1998) 136-139 (*Günther, Peter*).

10184 *Liphschitz, Nili* Timber analysis of household objects in Israel: a comparative study. IEJ 48 (1998) 77-90.

10185 **Müller-Karpe, Michael** Prähistorische Bronzefunde Abt. II: Metallgefäße in Iraq I/14. 1993 ⇒11/2,a511; 13,10259. ^RJNES 57 (1998) 153-155 (*McMahon, Augusta*).

10186 *Buzzetti, Carlo* Come tradurre i termini di misura nel NT?: analisi di testi e notazioni di traduttologia. ^FHERIBAN J. 1998 ⇒41. 259-281.

10187 *Caquot, André; Sérandour, Arnaud* La périodisation: de la bible à l'apocalyptique. Temps vécu. 1998 ⇒445. 83-98.

10188 **Hitzl, Konrad** Die Gewichte griechischer Zeit aus Olympia: eine Studie zu den vorhellenistischen Gewichtssystemen in Griechenland. 1996 ⇒12,9648. ^RAJA 102 (1998) 632-633 (*Kroll, John H.*).

10189 *Horowitz, Wayne; Tammuz, Oded* A multiplication table for 40 in the Israel Museum. IEJ 48 (1998) 262-264.

10190 **Kletter, Raz** Economic keystones: the weight system of the Kingdom of Judah. JSOT.S 276: Shf 1998, Academic 299 pp. £46/$70. 1-85075-920-0. Bibl.

10191   *Muroi, Kazuo* Expressions of a unit in Babylonian mathematics.
Acta Sumerologica (Hiroshima) 20 (1998) 121-126.
10192   *Ribichini, Sergio* Quelques remarques sur le 'temps' phénicien.
Temps vécu. 1998 ⇒445. 99-119.
10193   *Seger, Joe D.* Stone scale weights of the Judean standard from Tell
Halif. ᶠFRERICHS, E. BJSt 320: 1998 ⇒28. 357-372.
10194   **Vanderkam, James C.** Calendars in the Dead Sea scrolls: measuring time. The Literature of the Dead Sea Scrolls: L 1998, Routledge
136 pp.

T3.0 **Ars antiqua,** *motiva, picturae* [icones T3.1 infra]

10195   **Albenda, Pauline** Monumental art of the Assyrian empire:
dynamics of composition styles. Monographs on the Ancient Near
East 3/1: Malibu 1998, Undena iv; 72 pp. 0-890003-500-6. Bibl.
10196   **Altenmüller, Hartwig** Die Wanddarstellungen im Grab des Mehu
in Saqqara. Archäologische Veröffentlichungen 42: Mainz 1998,
Von Zabern 287 pp. €152,36. 3-8053-0504-4. Phot. Dieter
Johannes; 104 pl. [OLZ 95,17ss—Baud, M.].
10197   **Bazant, Jan** Roman portraiture: a history of its history. Praha
1995, Koniasch 188 pp. 21 ill. ᴿGn. 70 (1998) 153-156 (*Giuliani,
Luca*).
10198   *Beck, Pirhiya* סוגיות באמנות של ארץ־ישראל: על דמות המושל ובעיות נלוות
באמנות של תקופת הברונזה התיכונה [The figure of the ruler and related
problems in Middle Bronze Age art (first half of the second millennium BCE)]. Cathedra 87 (1998) 7-36 Sum. 189. **H.**
10199   **Belting, Hans** Image et culte: une histoire de l'art avant l'époque
de l'art. P 1998, Cerf 790 pp. €68,6. 2-204-05829-7. 305 ill. [ETR
74,136s—Reymond, Bernard].
10200   *Berlejung, Angelika* Geheimnis und Ereignis: zur Funktion und
Aufgabe der Kultbilder in Mesopotamien. JBTh 13 (1998) 109-
143.
10201   **Berlejung, Angelika** Die Theologie der Bilder: Herstellung und
Einweihung von Kultbildern in Mesopotamien und die alttestamentliche Bilderpolemik. ᴰHeidelberg 1997: OBO 162: Gö 1998,
Vandenhoeck & R xii; 547 pp. 3-525-53308-X.
10202   **Borg, Barbara** 'Der zierlichste Anblick der Welt...': ägyptische
Porträtmummien. Mainz 1998, Von Zabern 107 pp. €34,77. 3-
8053-2263-1. 123 ill. [OLZ 95,143ss—Parlasca, Klaus].
10203   *Brown, John Pairman* Images and their names in classical Israel
and Hellas. Hellenic and Jewish arts. 1998 ⇒439. 7-32.
10204   **Celani, Alessandro** Opere d'arte greche nella Roma di AUGUSTO.
Aucnus 8: N 1998, Scientifiche Italiane 379 pp. 88-8114-632-0.
10205   **Clarke, John R.** Looking at lovemaking: constructions of sexuality
in Roman art 100 B.C.-A.D. 250. Berkeley 1998, California UP
xvii; 372 pp. $40.
10206   *Cornelius, Izak* The iconography of the Canaanite gods Reshef and
Baal: a rejoinder. JNSL 24/2 (1998) 167-177.
10207   **Eder, Christian** Die ägyptischen Motive in der Glyptik des östlichen Mittelmeerraumes zu Anfang des 2. Jts. v. Chr.. OLA 71:
1995 ⇒11/2,a697. ᴿOr. 67 (1998) 292-294 (*Collon, Dominique*);
CÉg 73 (1998) 94-96 (*Clerc, Gisèle*); DiscEg 42 (1998) 147-149
(*Phillips, Jacke*).

10208 **Eschweiler, Peter** Bildzauber im alten Ägypten: die Verwendung von Bildern und Gegenständen in magischen Handlungen nach den Texten des Mittleren und Neuen Reiches. OBO 137: 1994 ⇒12, 9671; 13,10275. [R]AcOr 59 (1998) 229-232 (*Pierce, Richard H.*).

10209 *Frankel, Rafael; Ventura, Raphael* The Miṣpe Yamim bronzes. BASOR 311 (1998) 39-55.

10210 *Freyberger, K.S.* Zwei Männerporträts aus der Sammlung des Max Freiherrn von Oppenheim in Köln. DaM 10 (1998) 155-170.

10211 *Hammond, Philip C.; Mellott-Khan, Teresa* Nabataean faces from Petra. ADAJ 42 (1998) 319-330.

10212 **Holtzmann, Bernard; Pasquier, Alain** Histoire de l'art antique: l' art grec. P 1998, Ecole du Louvre 363 pp [REG 113,689s—Maffre, Jean-Jacques].

10213 *Hunter, Erica C.D.* Who are the demons?: the iconography of incantation bowls. SEL 15 (1998) 95-115.

10214 [E]**Kahil, Lily** Lexicon iconographicum mythologiae classicae, 8: Thespiades-Zodiacus et Supplementum, Abila-Thersites. Z 1997, Artemis 139 fig.; 824 pl.; 2 vols; xxxiv; 1209 + 918 pp. FS1.940. 3-7608-8758-9 [AJA 105,105—Ridgway, Brunilde S.].

10215 *Kákosy, László* A new source of Egyptian mythology and iconography. Proc. 7th Cong. of Egyptologists. 1998 ⇒475. 619-624.

10216 **Keel, Othmar** Die Welt der altorientalischen Bildsymbolik und das Alte Testament: am Beispiel der Psalmen. 1996 ⇒12,2753. [R]OLZ 93 (1998) 499-500 (*Zwickel, Wolfgang*);

10217 Goddesses and trees, new moon and Yahweh: ancient Near Eastern art and the Hebrew Bible. JSOT.S 261: Shf 1998, Academic 207 pp. 1-85075-915-4. Bibl.

10218 **Koch, Nadia** De picturae initiis: die Anfänge der griechischen Malerei im 7. Jahrhundert v. Chr. 1996 ⇒12,9684; 13,10285. [R]JHS 118 (1998) 249-250 (*Arafat, K.W.*).

10219 *Langdon, Susan* Significant others: the male-female pair in Greek geometric art. AJA 102 (1998) 251-270 Sum. 251.

10220 *Lilyquist, Christine* The use of ivories as interpreters of political history. BASOR 310 (1998) 25-33.

10221 *Marciniak, Marek L.* Trompe l'oeil in Ramesside painting: accident or purpose?. MDAI.K 54 (1998) 275-278.

10222 *Mazzoni, Stefania* L'arte siro-ittita nel suo contesto archeologico. [M]FRANKFORT H. 1998 ⇒26. 287-327.

10223 *Morgan, Lyvia* Power of the beast: human-animal symbolism in Egyptian and Aegean art. Ä&L 7 (1998) 17-31.

10224 *Nigro, Lorenzo* The two steles of Sargon: iconology and visual propaganda at the beginning of royal Akkadian relief. Iraq 60 (1998) 85-102.

10225 *Pardo Mata, Pilar* Descubiertas las pinturas antropomorfas más antiguas de época neolítica (Siria). BAEO 34 (1998) 407-408.

10226 *Rey-Coquais, Jean-Paul* Deux stèles inscrites de Syrie du Nord. Syr. 75/1 (1998) 193-200.

10227 *Robins, Gay* Piles of offerings: paradigms of limitation and creativity in ancient Egyptian art. Proceedings 7th Cong. of Egyptologists. 1998 ⇒475. 957-963.

10228 *Russell, John Malcolm* The program of the palace of Assurnasirpal II at Nimrud: issues in the research and presentation of Assyrian art. AJA 102 (1998) 655-715.

10229 *Schreiner, Stefan* Die Ambivalenz des Bildes: jüdische Kunst und bibliches Bilderverbot. Orien. 62 (1998) 9-10, 102-104, 112-115.

10230 **Snodgrass, Anthony** Homer and the artists: text and picture in early Greek art. C 1998, CUP xii; 186 pp. 0-521-62022-8. Bibl.

10231 *Sourouzian, Hourig* Raccords Ramessides. MDAI.K 54 (1998) 279-292.

10232 **Spivey, N.** Greek art. 1997 ⇒13,10300. ^RPrudentia 30/1 (1998) 68-71 (*Stevenson, Tom*).

10233 **Steinhart, Matthias** Das Motiv des Auges in der griechischen Bildkunst. Mainz 1995, Von Zabern xiv; 144 pp. 3-8053-1792-1. Num. ill. ^RAnCl 67 (1998) 542-543 (*Martens, Didier*).

10234 **Stewart, Andrew** Art, desire, and the body in ancient Greece. 1997 ⇒13,10301. ^RAJA 102 (1998) 438-39 (*Kampen, Natalie B.*).

10235 **Tassignon, Isabelle** Iconographie et religion dionysiaques en Gaule belgique et dans les deux Germanies. 1996 ⇒12,9700. ^RAnCl 67 (1998) 584-586 (*Raepsaet-Charlier, Marie-Thérèse*).

10236 ^E**Tefnin, Roland** La peinture égyptienne ancienne: un monde de signes à préserver: actes du Colloque international de Bruxelles, avril 1994. MonAeg 7: Bru 1997, Fondation Égyptologique Reine Élisabeth 24 pl.; 50 fig.; 175 pp. ^RAeg. 78 (1998) 205-207 (*Pernigotti, Sergio*).

10237 **Tsiafakis, Despoina** Η Θράκη στην αττική εικονογραφία του 5ου Αιώνα π.χ. Παράτημα θρακικής επετηρίδας 4: Komotini 1998, Center for Thracian Studies 80 pl.; 8 fig.; 403 pp. 1106-3823 [AJA 104,138—Shapiro, H.A.] G.

10238 *Van Lepp, Jonathan* Spatial relationship and arrangement in Egyptian art. SSEA Journal 26 (1996) 93-120 Sum. 93.

10239 **Walker, Susan; Bierbrier, Morris L.** Ancient faces: mummy portraits from Roman Egypt. 1997 ⇒13,10304. ^RAJA 102 (1998) 210-211 (*Montserrat, Dominic*).

10240 *Weber, Thomas* Ein verkanntes Kriegerköpfchen in Amman. ^FLIND-NER, M. BBB 118: 1998 ⇒62. 102-109.

10241 *Wildung, Dietrich* Chef-d'oeuvre et produit de masse: l'original et la copie en Égypte ancienne. Diog(F) 183 (1998) 3-7.

10242 *Zbikowski, Dörte* Altägypten in der europäischen Kunst: das Beispiel Paul KLEE. Annäherung. ZDMG.S 11: 1998 ⇒449. 621-628.

10243 *Ziffer, Irit* The portrait of a king. Capital cities. 1998 ⇒492. 187-212.

T3.1 *Icones*—ars postbiblica

10244 ^E**Adams, Ann Jensen** REMBRANDT's "Bathsheba reading King David's letter". Masterpieces of western painting: C 1998, CUP 35 ill. xiv; 214 pp. $55/16. 0-521453-91-7/9-86-9.

10245 **Amar, Ariella; Jacoby, Ruth** Ingathering of the nations: treasures of Jewish art: documenting an endangered legacy. J 1998, The Center for Jewish Art 133 pp. 965-395-008-6. Introd. *Bezalel Narkiss*; Bibl.

10246 *Angheben, Marcel* Apocalypse XXI-XXII et l'iconographie du portail central de la nef de Vézelay. CCMéd 41 (1998) 209-240. Sum., rés. 209.

10247 **Bacci, Michele** Il penello dell'evangelista: storia delle immagini sacre attribuite a san Luca. Piccola biblioteca GISEM 14: Pisa 1998, GISEM 440 pp. 88-467--123-2. Bibl. [NThAR 1999,253].

10248 *Baert, Barbara* Le sacramentaire de Gellone (750-790) et l'invention de la croix: l'image entre le symbole et l'histoire. ACr 86 (1998) 449-460.

10249 *Balicka-Witakowska, Ewa* The crucified thieves in Ethiopian art: literary and iconographical sources. OrChr 82 (1998) 204-256;

10250 Remarks on the decoration and iconography of the Syriac gospels, British Library, Add. 7174. Symposium Syriacum VII. 1998 ⇒415. 641-659.

10251 **Balicka-Witakowska, Ewa** La crucifixion sans crucifié dans l'art éthiopien: recherches sur la survie de l'iconographie chrétienne de l'antiquité tardive. Bibliotheca nubica et aethiopica 4: 1997 ⇒13,10309. ᴿByZ 91 (1998) 503-504 (*Elbern, Victor H.*); POC 48 (1998) 215-217 (*Attinger, D.*); LASBF 48 (1998) 616-617 (*Paczkowski, Mieczysław Celestyn*).

10252 **Barbet, Alix; Vibert-Guigue, Claude** Les peintures des nécropoles romaines d'Abila et du nord de la Jordanie I-II. 1994 ⇒10, 12362; 12,9915. RGn. 70 (1998) 378-380 (*Weber, Thomas*).

10253 **Ben-Arieh, Yehoshua** Painting the Holy Land in the nineteenth century. J 1997, 320 pp. Num. ill.

10254 **Bigham, Stéphane** L'icône dans la tradition orthodoxe. P 1995, Médiaspaul 270 pp. ᴿContacts 50/1 (1998) 93-94 (*Minet, Jacques*).

10255 *Bœspflug, François; Heck, Christian* L'incarnation et le génie des images en occident du VIIIᵉ au XVᵉ siècle. MoBi 114 (1998) 40-75.

10256 *Calcagnini, Daniela* Considerazioni sull'apparato figurativo delle iscrizioni: il tema di Lazzaro. ᶠNESTORI A. 1998 ⇒86. 113-125.

10257 *Cartlidge, David R.* Which path at the crossroads?: early Christian art as a hermeneutical and theological challenge. ᶠSNYDER, G. 1998 ⇒104. 357-372.

10258 **Castiñeiras Gonzáles, Manuel Antonio** Introducción al método iconográfico. Barc ¹⁰1998, Ariel 251 pp. 108 fig. [AIA 59,203s— Manso Porto, Carmen].

10259 *Čičinaze, Izolda* Das Evangelium von Mokvi und die georgische Miniatur an der Wende vom 13. zum 14. Jahrhundert. Georgica 21 (1998) 137-143.

10260 *Cifani, Arabella; Monetti, Franco* Due inediti dipinti di soggetto biblico di Gerolamo Cenatempo, pittore napoletano. ACr 86 (1998) 380-382.

10261 *Clément, Olivier* Petite introduction à la théologie de l'icône;

10262 Pour une théologie de la beauté. Contacts 50/1 (1998) 25-32; 51-6.

10263 *Coirault-Neuburger, Sylvie* Le menzogne dell'icona. ReSo 13 (1998) 6-18 Sum. 6.

10264 **Corcoran, Lorelei H.** Portrait mummies from Roman Egypt. 1995 ⇒11/2,a826a; 13,10510. ᴿJEA 84 (1998) 258-260 (*Kurth, Dieter*).

10265 **Crippa, Maria Antonietta; Zibawi, Mahmoud** L'art paléochrétien. Les grandes saisons de l'art chrétien: P 1998, Zodiaque 500 pp. €97,57. 200 col. pl.; 400 ill. [MoBi 116,78—Spieser, Jean-Michel];

10266 L'arte paleocristiana: visione e spazio dalle origini a Bizanzio. Mi 1998, Jaca 496 pp. 88-16-60210-4. Introd. di *Julien Ries*; Bibl.

10267 *Dassmann, Ernst* Der eine Christus und die vielen Christusbilder. LS 49 (1998) 367-368.

10268 **Elsner, J.** Imperial Rome and christian triumph: the art of the Roman Empire AD 100-450. Oxford History of Art: Oxf 1998, OUP xvi; 297 pp. £9. 0-19-284201-3. 163 ill.; 16 plans; 3 maps [ClR 50,241ss—Davies, Glenys];

10269 Art and the Roman viewer: the transformation of art from the pagan world to christianity. 1995 ⇒12,9720; 13,10323. ᴿAnCl 67 (1998) 592-593 (*Balty, Janine*); HeyJ 39 (1998) 78-79 (*Louth, Andrew*).

10270 **Engemann, Josef** Deutung und Bedeutung frühchristlicher Bild-werke. 1997 ⇒13,10324. ᴿRQ 93 (1998) 137-140 (*Heid, Stefan*); JBTh 13 (1998) 293-299 (*Jeremias-Büttner, Gisela*).

10271 *Exum, J. Cheryl* Lovis Corinth's Blinded Samson. Biblical Inter-pretation 6 (1998) 410-425.

10272 *Ferreiro, Alberto* Simon Magus and Simon Peter in a Baroque altar relief in the cathedral of Oviedo, Spain. Hagiographica 5 (1998) 141-158.

10273 *Finney, Paul Corby* A late-antique tunic fragment in St. Louis ᶠFERGUSON, E. NT.S 90: 1998 ⇒25. 114-119.

10274 **Finney, Paul Corby** The invisible God: the earliest christians on art. 1994 ⇒11/2,a574... 13,10326. ᴿRHE 93 (1998) 481-486 (*Zee-gers, Nicole*).

10275 **Folda, Jaroslav** The art of the crusaders in the Holy Land. C 1995, CUP 704 pp $100/£60. 0-521-45383-6. Ill. ᴿChH 67 (1998) 361-362 (*McGinn, Bernard*).

10276 *Fornberg, Tord* The cross, the snake, and the lotus: some notes on the role of images for inter-religious understanding. ᶠBERGMAN J. 1998 ⇒9. 115-136.

10277 **Friedman, John B.; Wegmann, Jessica M.** Medieval iconogra-phy: a research guide. Garland Medieval Bibliographies 20; Gar-land Reference Library of the Humanities 1870: NY 1998, Garland xxiv; 437 pp. $95. 0-8153-1753-0 [JEH 51,133—Backhouse, J.].

10278 *Gambino, Rosanna* L'icona del volto di Cristo: ovvero la ierofania di *un* dio. Schede Medievali 34-35 (1998) 167-173.

10279 **Gisolfi, Diana; Sindling-Larsen, Staale** The rule, the bible, and the council: the library of the Benedictine Abbey at Praglia. Col-lege Art Association Monograph of the Fine Arts 4: Seattle 1998, Univ. of Washington Pr. xiii; 201 pp. $55. 0-295-97661-6. ᴿCHR 84 (1998) 555-556 (*O'Gorman, James F.*).

10280 *Grant, Robert M.* Lions in early christian literature. ᶠFERGUSON, E. NT.S 90: 1998 ⇒25. 147-154.

10281 ᵀᴱGriffith, **Sidney Harrison** A treatise on the veneration of the holy icons written in Arabic by Theodore Abu Qurrah, Bishop of Harran. Eastern Christian Texts in Translation 1: 1997 ⇒13,10335. ᴿATT 4/1 (1998) 246-249 (*Gramaglia, Pier Angelo*).

10282 **Guerrier, Francesca** Peintures bibliques. P 1997, Cerf 110 pp. 2-204-05890-4. 50 pl. [ETR 76,304—Cottin, Jérôme].

10283 **Hranitzky, Katharina** Die schönsten Bilder aus der Wenzelsbibel. Graz 1998, Akademische 72 pp. 3-201-01700-0. 24 pl. [Biblos 47, 328—Diethart, Johannes].

10284 *Hultgård, Anders* The Magi and the star—the Persian background in texts and iconography. ᶠBERGMAN J. 1998 ⇒9. 215-225.

10285 ᴱ**Iñiguez y Ruiz de Clavijo, M.** El Hijo del Hombre: el rostro de Cristo en el arte. M 1998, Conferencia Episcopal Española 261 pp. [EstAg 34,400—Sierra de la Calle, B.].

10286 *Jacobone, Lello* L'iconografia di Dio Padre. Presenza Pastorale 68 (1998) 347-354.

10287 *Jasper, David* J.M.W. TURNER: interpreter of the bible. Biblical studies. JSOT.S 266: 1998 ⇒380. 299-314.

10288 *Jensen, Robin A.* Dining in heaven: the earliest christian visions of paradise. BiRe 14/5 (1998) 32-39, 48-49.

10289 *Kessler, Herbert L.* "Thou shalt paint the likeness of Christ himself": the Mosaic prohibition as provocation for christian images ᶠNARKISS, B. 1998 ⇒85. 124-139.

10290 **Knipp, Philip David Ezra** 'Christus Medicus' in der frühchristlichen Sarkophagskulptur: ikonographische Studien zur Sepulkralkunst des späten vierten Jahrhunderts. SVigChr 37: Lei 1998, Brill xv; 213 pp. 90-04-10862-9. Bibl.

10291 ᴱ**Kohlschein, Franz; Wünsche, Peter** Heiliger Raum: Architektur, Kunst und Liturgie in mittelalterlichen Kathedralen und Stiftskirchen. LWQF 82: Müns 1998, Aschendorff xxvii; 394 pp. 3-402-04-062-X. Bibl.

10292 *Kramer, Phyllis Silverman* The dismissal of Hagar in five art works of the sixteenth and seventeenth centuries. Genesis. 1998 ⇒219. 195-217.

10293 *Lange, Günter* Auf Abrahams Schoß: zum Paradiesbild des Landgrafenpsalters. KatBl 123 (1998) 127-130.

10294 *Lazar, M.* Making darkness visible: Orpheus, David and Christ in CHAGALL's 'Harrowing of the innerworld'. Hellenic and Jewish arts. 1998 ⇒439. 267-292.

10295 **Lazarev, Viktor Nikitich** The Russian icon: from its origins to the sixteenth century. ᵀ*Joly Dees, C.*: ColMn 1997, Liturgical 404 pp. $100.

10296 *Leisch-Kiesl, Monika* Wie kam die Schlange ins Bild?: einige Beobachtungen zur Darstellung des "Sündenfalls". BiKi 53 (1998) 27-30.

10297 *Maguire, Henry* Davidic virtue: the crown of Constantine Monomachos and its images. ᶠNARKISS, B. 1998 ⇒85. 117-123.

10298 *Marsh, Clive* REMBRANDT the etcher: mission and commission as factors in New Testament interpretation. BiblInterp 6 (1998) 381-409.

10299 **Mathews, Thomas F.** The art of Byzantium: between antiquity and the Renaissance. The Everyman Art Library: L 1998, Weidenfeld and N 176 pp. 0-297-82398-1. Bibl.

10300 **Murray, Peter & Linda** The Oxford companion to christian art and architecture. 1996 ⇒12,9575. ᴿJEarlyC 6 (1998) 686-688 (*Jensen, Robin*).

10301 *Neipp, Bernadette* Images du Christ dans le bouillonnement du 19ᵉ siècle: un renouveau de l'art religieux?. Jésus de Nazareth. 1998 ⇒253. 89-106.

10302 **Onasch, Konrad; Schnieper, Annemarie** Ikonen: Faszination und Wirklichkeit. 1995 ⇒12,9743. ᴿOrthFor 12 (1998) 132-134 (*Ivanov, Vladimir*).

10303 **Parry, Kenneth** Depicting the Word: Byzantine iconophile thought of the eighth and ninth centuries. The Medieval Mediterranean 12: 1996 ⇒12,9744. ᴿCTJ 33 (1998) 515-517 (*Payton, James R.*)

10304 **Partridge, Loren** MICHELANGELO: *The Last Judgment*: a glorious restoration. 1997 ⇒13,10360. ᴿSCJ 29 (1998) 503-507 (*Shrimplin, Valerie*).

10305 **Passarelli, Gaetano** Icone delle dodici grandi feste bizantine. Corpus bizantino slavo: Mi 1998, Jaca 272 pp. 88-1660201-5. Bibl.

10306 *Pearson, Birger A.* Gnostic iconography. ᶠBERGMAN J. 1998 ⇒9. 289-301.

10307 **Pelikan, Jaroslav** Gesù: l'immagine attraverso i secoli. Mi 1998, Mondadori 254 pp [RTLu 4,345ss—Amadò, Michele].

10308 *Perraymond, Myla* Il ciclo di Sansone (Gd. 14, 15, 16): genesi e diffusione di un tema iconografico. ᶠNESTORI A. 1998 ⇒86. 643-667.

10309 *Pillinger, Renate* Anthropomorphe Darstellungen Gott-Vaters in alttestamentlichen Szenen der frühchristlichen Kunst. JBTh 13 (1998) 171-194.

10310 *Piltz, Elisabeth* Byzantine illuminations in the Kongelige bibliothek in Copenhagen. Byzantium and Islam. 1998 ⇒488. 123-135.

10311 *Piovano, Adalberto* Immagine, liturgia e parola: alcuni orientamenti per una lettura dell'icona II. RCI 79 (1998) 574-587.

10312 *Ranucci Rossi, Cristina* Gesti ed atteggiamenti nella plastica paleocristiana: note sul sarcofago di civita Castellana. RivAC 74 (1998) 297-310.

10313 **Rigon, Fernando** Le tre grazie: iconografie dall'antichità a oggi, dal classicismo al marketing. [Cittadella (Padova)] 1998, Biblos 191 pp. 88-86214-79-0.

10314 ᴱ**Roberts, Helene E.** Encyclopedia of comparative iconography: themes depicted in works of art, v.1, A-L; v.2, M-Z.. Chicago 1998, Dearborn 2 Vols. 1-57958-009-2.

10315 **Rombold, Günter** Ästhetik und Spiritualität: Bilder, Rituale, Theorien. Stu 1998, Katholisches Bibelwerk 261 pp [ThPh 75, 306ss—Splett, J.].

10316 *Rosenberg, Joel* What the bible and old movies have in common. Biblical Interpretation 6 (1998) 266-291.

10317 *Ruoß, Anja* Christliche chinesische Kunst. China Heute 17 (1998) 73-75.

10318 **Schade, Herbert** Lamm Gottes und Zeichen des Widders: zur kosmologisch-psychologischen Hermeneutik der Ikonographie des 'Lammes Gottes'. FrB 1998, Herder 263 pp. €45. 3-451-26543-5. 110 pl. ᴿGuL 71 (1998) 473-474 (*Sudbrack, Josef*).

10319 **Schefold, Karl** Der religiöse Gehalt der antiken Kunst und die Offenbarung. Kulturgeschichte der antiken Welt 78: Mainz 1998, Von Zabern 580 pp. 3-8053-2351-4. Collab. *Jenny, Mirjam T.*

10320 *Schiffer, Walter* Marc CHAGALLs Bilder der biblischen Botschaft—ein 'Bildmidrasch'. KatBl 123 (1998) 345-351.

10321 *Schlegelberger, Bruno* Der Dialog der Bilder: Rezeption und Interpretation von christlichen Bildern in indianischen Kulturen. Religiöse Sprache. 1998 ⇒1144. 244-281.

10322 **Schrenk, Sabine** Typos und Antitypos in der frühchristlichen Kunst. JAC.E 21: 1995 ⇒11/2,a611... 13,10371. ᴿJThS 49 (1998) 344-346 (*Finney, Paul Corby*).

10323 *Seidel, Linda* Apocalypse and apocalypticism in western medieval art. Encyclopedia of apocalypticism II. 1998 ⇒507. 467-506.

10324 *Sheen, Erica* 'The light of God's law': violence and methaphysics in the '50s widescreen biblical epic. BiblInterp 6 (1998) 292-312.
10325 *Spieser, Jean-Michel* De l'anonymat à la gloire des images: de Rome à Byzance du IIIe au XVe siècle. MoBi 114 (1998) 8-39.
10326 **Steinberg, Leo** The sexuality of Christ in Renaissance art and in modern oblivion. ²1997 ⇒13,10376. ^RBiblInterp. 6 (1998) 426-436 (*Jasper, David*).
10327 *Stichel, Rainer* Scenes from the life of king David in Dura Europos and in Byzantine art. ^FNARKISS, B. 1998 ⇒85. 100-116.
10328 *Taschner, Johannes* Mit wem ringt Jakob in der Nacht?: oder: der Versuch, mit REMBRANDT eine Leerstelle auszuleuchten. BiblInterp 6 (1998) 367-380.
10329 *Thümmel, Hans Georg* Die theologische Auseinandersetzung um die Ikone. JBTh 13 (1998) 197-208.
10330 **Thümmel, Hans Georg** Die Frühgeschichte der östkirchlichen Bilderlehre: Texte und Untersuchungen zur Zeit vor dem Bilderstreit. 1992 ⇒8,e35...11/2,a618. ^RJThS 49 (1998) 346-348 (*Louth, Andrew*).
10331 **Van der Coulen, Peter** De Schrift verbeeld: oudtestamentische prenten uit renaissance en barok. Nimègues 1998, Nijmegen Univ. Pr. 352 pp. 178 ill. [BHR 61,737—Engammare, Max].
10332 ^EVan der Horst, Koert; Noel, William; Wüstefeld, Wilhelmina C.M.** The Utrecht psalter in medieval art: picturing the psalms of David. 1996 ⇒12,9758. ^RJEH 49 (1998) 524-6 (*Marner, Dominic*).
10333 *Van Moorsel, Paul* A different Melchisedech?: some iconographical remarks. ^FGrossmann P. 1998 ⇒33. 329-342.
10334 *Verson, Timothy* 'Omnes de Saba': l'Epifania nell'arte fiorentina del quattrocento. Festa e bibbia. 1998 ⇒403. 105-125.
10335 *Wackernagel, Wolfgang* In der Verborgenheit liegt das Bild: über das Entbildetwerden und die Bedeutung von Andachtsbildern bei Meister ECKHART mit Hinweis auf eine Buchmalerei der HILDEGARD von Bingen und eine Lithographie von Otto DIX. JBTh 13 (1998) 209-234.
10336 *Wagoner, Robert E.* Presence and absence in early christian art ^FSNYDER, G. 1998 ⇒104. 327-343.
10337 *Weber, Franz* Von macht-vollen Bildern—und macht-losen Armen: zur Ambivalenz religiöser Symbole in der lateinamerikanischen Volksfrömmigkeit. JBTh 13 (1998) 261-278.
10338 *Welker, Michael* Sozio-metaphysische Theologie und Biblische Theologie: zu Eilert Herms: "Was haben wir an der Bibel?". JBTh 13 (1998) 309-322.
10339 *Werbick, Jürgen* Trugbilder oder Suchbilder?: ein Versuch über die Schwierigkeit, das biblische Bilderverbot theologisch zu befolgen. JBTh 13 (1998) 3-27.
10340 **Williams, John** The illustrated Beatus: a corpus of the illustrations of the commentary on the Apocalypse: vol. 1: introduction; vol. 2: the 9th and 10th centuries; vol. 3: the 10th and 11th centuries. L 1994-1998, Harvey M 3 vols; 216+318+386 pp.
10341 *Wolf, Gerhard* Laetare filia Sion: ecce ego venio et habitabo in medio tui: images of Christ transferred to Rome from Jerusalem. ^FNARKISS, B. 1998 ⇒85. 418-429.
10342 *Yuasa, Yuko* Über die künstlerische Darstellung heiliger Texte. Conc(D) 34 (1998) 312-322.

10343   *Zimmermann, Barbara* Die Codexillustration als neuer Kunst-
        zweig—Spiegel einer geänderten Funktion des Buches in der Spät-
        antike. Use of sacred books. 1998 ⇒263. 263-285.

T3.2 Sculptura

10344   *Al-Salihi, Wathiq I.* The camel-rider's stele and related sculpture
        from Hatra. Iraq 60 (1998) 103-108.
10345   **Andreae, Bernard** Schönheit des Realismus: Auftraggeber, Schöp-
        fer, Betrachter hellenistischer Plastik. Kulturgeschichte der antiken
        Welt 77: Mainz 1998, Von Zabern 336 pp. €34,77. 3-8053-2348-4.
        353 fig. [AJA 103,716s—Fullerton, Mark D.].
10346   **Baumer, Lorenz E.** Vorbilder und Vorlagen: Studien zu klassi-
        schen Frauenstatuen und ihrer Verwendung für Reliefs und Statuet-
        ten des 5. und 4. Jahrhunderts vor Christus. Acta Bernensia 12:
        1997 ⇒13,10384. [R]AJA 102 (1998) 634-635 (*Lawton, Carol L.*).
10347   **Belli Pasqua, Roberta** Scultura di età romana in 'basalto'. 1995,
        ⇒13,10400. [R]AnCl 67 (1998) 563-564 (*Evers, Cécile*).
10348   [E]**Borbein, Heinrich** Antike Plastik, 24. Mü 1995, Hirmer 58 pl.
        138 pp. €122,71. 3-7774-6950-5. [R]AnCl 67 (1998) 530-533 (*Her-
        mary, Antoine*); Gn. 70 (1998) 697-702 (*Hoff, Ralf von den*).
10349   *Briquel-Chatonnet, Françoise; Lozachmeur, Hélène* Un nouveau
        bas-relief palmyrénien. Syr. 75/1 (1998) 137-143.
10350   *Burns, John Barclay* Female pillar figurines of the Iron Age: a
        study in text and artifact. AUSS 36 (1998) 23-49.
10351   *De Cree, F.* Egyptian influence on chalcolithic Palestinian sculp-
        ture?—some stylistic elements of the Beersheva figurines reconsid-
        ered. GöMisz 165 (1998) 23-38.
10352   *Gersht, Rivka* Roman copies discovered in the land of Israel.
        [F]SOHLBERG, D. 1996 ⇒8271. 433-450.
10353   *Hagemann, Ludwig* "Die den Leib des Gottes genährt hat": Anmer-
        kungen zu einem neuentdeckten Grabrelief der Amme Tutancha-
        muns. JRTR 6 (1998) 7-12.
10354   **Hamiaux, Marianne** Les sculptures grecques, 2: la période hellé-
        nistique (IIIe-1er siècles avant J.-C.). Musée du Louvre, Dépt. des
        antiquités grecques: P 1998, Réunion des musées nationaux 336 pp.
        €68,6. 2-7118-3603-7. 510 fig. [AJA 103,158s—Ridgway, B.S.].
10355   *Humbert, Jean-Baptiste* Die byzantinischen Figurinen vom Fried-
        hof von Samra. WUB 7 (1998) 53.
10356   **Josephson, Jack A.** Egyptian royal sculpture of the Late Period
        400-246 B.C. 1997 ⇒13,10394. [R]BiOr 55 (1998) 123-124 (*Meule-
        naere, H.J.A. de*).
10357   **Laboury, Dimitri** La statuaire de Thoutmosis III: essai d'interpré-
        tation d'un portrait royal dans son contexte historique. Aegyptiaca
        Leodiensia 5: Liège 1998, Univ. de Liège, Centre Informatique de
        Philosophie et Lettres 723 pp. Bibl.
10358   **Lawton, Carol L.** Attic document reliefs: art and politics in an-
        cient Athens. 1995 ⇒11/2,a652. [R]At. 86 (1998) 563-567 (*Slavazzi,
        Fabrizio*).
10359   *Nigro, Lorenzo* Visual role and ideological meaning of the enemies
        in the royal Akkadian relief. Intellectual life. 1998 ⇒450. 283-297.
        [E]**Palagia, O.** Regional schools in Hellenistic sculpture 1998 ⇒
        487.

10360 ᴱ**Pollitt, J.J.; Palagia, O.** Personal styles in Greek sculpture. 1996 ⇒12,9775. ᴿCIR 48 (1998) 426-428 (*Arafat, K.W.*).

10361 *Rehak, Paul; Younger, John G.* International styles in ivory carving in the Bronze Age. The Aegean. 1998 ⇒10031. 229-256.

10362 **Riis, Poul Jorgen** Vulcientia Vetustiora: a study of archaic Vulcian bronzes. Det Kongelige Danske Videnskabernes Selskab. Historisk-filosofiske Skrifter 19: K 1998, Munksgaard 137 pp. 87-73042897.

10363 **Rolley, Claude** La sculpture grecque, 1: des origines au milieu du Vᵉ siècle. 1994 ⇒10,11943*. ᴿGn. 70 (1998) 231-234 (*Junker, Klaus*).

10364 **Russell, John Malcolm** From Nineveh to New York: the strange story of the Assyrian reliefs in the Metropolitan Museum and the hidden masterpiece at Canford School. NHv 1997, Yale Univ. Pr. 232 pp. 0-300-06459-4. Contrib. by *Judith McKenzie* and *Stephanie Dalley*; Bibl.

10365 *Schmandt-Besserat, Denise* 'Ain Ghazal "monumental" figures. BASOR 310 (1998) 1-17;

10366 A stone metaphor of creation. NEA(BA) 61/2 (1998) 109-117 ['En Gazal].

10367 **Schröder, Stephan F.** Die Porträts. Katalog der antiken Skulpturen des Museo del Prado in Madrid. 1993 ⇒9,13527. ᴿAnCl 67 (1998) 564-566 (*Balty, Jean Ch.*).

10368 **Spivey, Nigel** Understanding Greek sculpture: ancient meanings, modern readings. 1996 ⇒12,9779. ᴿJHS 118 (1998) 245-247 (*Palagia, Olga*).

10369 *Sweeney, Deborah* The man on the folding chair: an Egyptian relief from Beth Shean. IEJ 48 (1998) 38-53.

10370 *Uehlinger, Christoph* "...und wo sind die Götter von Samarien?": die Wegführung syrisch-palästinischer Kultstatuen auf einem Relief Sargons II. in Ḫorṣabad/Dur-Šarrukin. ᶠLORETZ O. AOAT 250: 1998 ⇒65. 739-776 [Ḫorṣabad/Dur-Šarrukin].

10371 **Webb, Pamela A.** Hellenistic architectural sculpture: figural motifs in western Anatolia and the Aegean islands. 1996 ⇒12,9781. ᴿAJA 102 (1998) 446-447 (*Roccos, Linda Jones*).

T3.3 *Glyptica*; **stamp and cylinder seals**, scarabs, amulets

10372 *Aufrecht, Walter E.* Two iron age seals: Hebrew and Aramaic ᶠFRERICHS, E. BJSt 320: 1998 ⇒28. 233-239.

10373 **Avigad, Nahman** Corpus of West Semitic stamp seals. ᴱSass, Benjamin: 1997 ⇒13,10411. ᴿBAR (Jan-Feb 1998) 68, 70 (*Lemaire, André*).

10374 *Beck, Pirhiya* Middle Bronze Age cylinder seal and cylinder seal impression from Lachish. TelAv 25 (1998) 174-183.

10375 **Davis, Eli; Frenkel, David A.** The Hebrew amulet: biblical-medical-general. 1995 ⇒11/2,c432. ᴿAJSR 23 (1998) 122-124 (*Stillman, Yedida K.*). H.

10376 **Deutsch, Robert; Heltzer, Michael** Windows to the past. 1997 ⇒13,10415. ᴿBAR 24/4 (1998) 58-59 (*Shanks, Hershel*).

10377 **Feghali-Gorton, Andrée** Egyptian and Egyptianizing scarabs: a typology of steatite, faience and paste scarabs from Punic and other Mediterranean sites. Oxf. Univ. Committee for Archaeology, Mon. 44: Oxf 1996, OUP vii; 191 pp. £25. 0-947816-43-7.

10378 *Gonnet, Hatice* Remarques sur les sceaux de Muwatalli II. Rencontre Assyriologique Internationale 34. 1998 ⇒452. 263-267.
10379 *Görg, Manfred* Ein weiterer Skarabäus mit dem Hyksosnamen Hy3n aus Palästina/Israel. BN 91 (1998) 5-6.
10380 *Györy, Hedvig* Remarks on Amarna amulets. Proceedings 7th Cong. of Egyptologists. 1998 ⇒475. 497-507.
10381 ᴱ**Gyselen, Rika** Sceaux d'Orient et leur emploi. Res Orientales 10: 1997 ⇒13,10421. ᴿMes. 33 (1998) 388-390 (*Bollati, A.*).
10382 *Hartung, Ulrich* Prädynastische Siegelabrollungen aus dem Friedhof U in Abydos (Umm el-Qaab). MDAI.K 54 (1998) 187-217.
10383 *Herr, Larry G.* The palaeography of West Semitic stamp seals. BASOR 312 (1998) 45-77.
10384 **Keel, Othmar** Corpus der Stempelsiegel-Amulette aus Palästina/Israel: von den Anfängen bis zur Perserzeit: *(a)* Einleitung. OBO. A 10: 1995 ⇒11/2,a706... 13,10428a. ᴿSyr. 75 (1998) 333-334 (*Amiet, Pierre*);
10385 *(b)* Band I: Von Tell Abu Farag bis 'Atlit: Katalog. OBO.A 13: 1997 ⇒13,10429. ᴿBArR 24/5 (1998) 62, 64 (*Lemaire, André*); AcOr 59 (1998) 242-243 (*Groth, Bente*).
10386 *Keel, Othmar; Schroer, Silvia* Darstellungen des Sonnenlaufs und Totenbuchvignetten auf Skarabäen. ZÄS 125 (1998) 13-29.
10387 ᴱ**Klengel-Brandt, Evelyn** Mit sieben Siegeln versehen: das Siegel in Wirtschaft und Kunst des Alten Orients. 1997 ⇒13,10430. ᴿWO 29 (1998) 200-202 (*Röllig, Wolfgang*).
10388 *Krauss, Rolf* An examination of Khyan's place in W.A. WARD's seriation of Hyksos royal scarabs. Ä&L 7 (1998) 39-42.
10389 **Marcus, Michelle I.** Emblems of identity and prestige: the seals and sealings from Hasanlu, Iran. 1996 ⇒12,9815. ᴿAJA 102 (1998) 623-624 (*Aruz, Joan*).
10390 *Matoušová-Rajmová, Marie* Über das Zeichnen der Siegel. ArOr 66 (1998) 270-272.
10391 **Matthews, Donald M.** The early glyptic of Tell Brak: cylinder seals of third millennium Syria. OBO.A 15: 1997 ⇒13,10436. ᴿMes. 33 (1998) 350-352 (*Mollo, P.*).
10392 *Müller-Kessler, Christa* A Mandaic gold amulet in the British Museum. BASOR 311 (1998) 83-88.
10393 *Nauerth, Claudia* Fortuna Christiana: spätantike Glücksbringer aus Ägypten. DBAT 29 (1998) 235-243.
10394 *Otto, Adelheid* A Middle Bronze Age cylinder seal from the jar burial F167 at Tell Ahmar. Abr-n. 35 (1998) 120-134 [Til-Barsip].
10395 *Teissier, Beatrice* Sealing and seals: seal-impressions from the reign of Hammurabi on tablets from Sippar in the British Museum. Iraq 60 (1998) 109-186.
10396 *Uehlinger, Christoph* Westsemitisch beschriftete Stempelsiegel: ein Corpus und neue Fragen. Bib. 79 (1998) 103-119.
10397 **Van Wyk, Koot** Squatters in Moab: a study in iconography, history, epigraphy, orthography, ethnography, religion and linguistics of the ANE. 1996 ⇒12,9832. ᴿCBQ 60 (1998) 132-134 (*Aufrecht, Walter E.*).
10398 **Wallenfels, Ronald** Seleucid archival texts in the Harvard Semitic Museum: text editions and catalogue raisonné of the seal impressions. Cuneiform Monographs 12: Groningen 1998, STYX xx; 179 pp. 90-5693-012-5. Bibl. 149-154.

T3.4 **Mosaica**

10399 **Balty, Janine** Mosaïques antiques du Proche-Orient, chronologie, iconographie, interprétation. Centre de Recherches d'Histoire ancienne 140: Besançon 1995, Université 392 pp. 52 pl. [R]RAr (1998/2) 438-439 (*Guimiers-Sorbets, Anne-Marie*).

10400 *Guimier-Sorbets, Anne-Marie* Alexandrie: les mosaïques hellénistiques découvertes sur le terrain de la nouvelle *Bibliotheca Alexandrina*. RAr 2 (1998) 263-290 Sum. 263.

10401 *Hachlili, Rachel* Iconographic elements of Nilotic scenes on Byzantine mosaic pavements in Israel. PEQ 130 (1998) 106-120.

10402 *Kühnel, Gustav* Between Jerusalem and Bethlehem: the dating of a newly recovered tessera of crusader mosaic decoration. [F]NARKISS, B. 1998 ⇒85. 151-157.

10403 **Ling, Roger** Ancient mosaics. L 1998, British Museum Pr. 144 pp. $20. 0-691-00404-8. Num. pl.

10404 *Mack, Hananel* ייחודו של גלגל המזלות מבית הכנסת בזיפורי ומדרשים מארץ־ישראל [The unique character of the Zippori synagogue mosaic and Eretz Israel midrashim]. Cathedra 88 (1998) 39-56 Sum. 181. **H**.

10405 *Merrony, Mark W.* The reconciliation of paganism and christianity in the early Byzantine mosaic pavements of Arabia and Palestine. SBFLA 48 (1998) 441-482 Sum. 521.

10406 *Monfrin, Francoise* Mosaiken erzählen die Bibel. WUB 8 (1998) 42-49.

10407 **Odišeli, Manana Džumberovna** Spätantike und frühchristliche Mosaike in Georgien. DÖAW: W 1995, ÖAW 70 pp. €20,96. 3-70-01-2187-3. Ill. [R]JAC 41 (1998) 275-9 (*Khroushkova, Ludmila G.*).

Osborne, J. Mosaics... in Roman churches 1998 ⇒10415.

10408 **Pfrommer, Michael** Untersuchungen zur Chronologie und Komposition des Alexandermosaiks auf antiquarischer Grundlage. Aegyptiaca Treverensia 8: Mainz 1998, Von Zabern ix; 241 pp. 3-8053-2028-0. Bibl.

10409 *Piccirillo, Michele* Les mosaïques d'époque omeyyade des églises de la Jordanie. Syr. 75/1 (1998) 263-278.

10410 **Pisapia, Maria** Stella Mosaici antichi in Italia. Mosaici antichi in Italia: ℞ 1989, Istituto Poligrafico dello Stato 90 pp. €41,32. [R]Gn. 70 (1998) 148-153 (*Donderer, Michael*).

10411 *Stemberger, Günter* Biblische Darstellungen auf Mosaikfußböden spätantiker Synagogen. JBTh 13 (1998) 145-170.

10412 *Talgam, R.* פסיפסי ארץ־ישראל לאור תגליות השנים האחרונות [Mosaics in Israel in the light of recent discoveries]. Qad. 31 (1998) 74-89.

10413 *Vriezen, Karel J.H.* Inscriptions in mosaic pavements in Byzantine *Palaestina/Arabia* quoting texts from the Old Testament. Use of sacred books. 1998 ⇒263. 247-261.

10414 *Wisskirchen, Rotraut* Zum Gerichtsaspekt im Apsismosaik von S. Pudenziana/Rom. JAC 41 (1998) 178-192.

10415 **Osborne, J.; Claridge, A.** Mosaics and wallpaintings in Roman churches, 1. 1996 ⇒12,9837. [R]RivAC 74 (1998) 616-621 (*Minasi, Mara*).

T3.5 *Ceramica*, **pottery**

[E]**Arcelin, P.** La quantification des céramiques. 1998 ⇒457.

10416 **Aston, David A.**, *al.*, Die Keramik des Grabungsplatzes Q I, Teil 1: corpus of fabrics, wares and shapes. Forschungen in der Ramses-Stadt: die Grabungen des Pelizaeus-Museums Hildesheim in Qantir - Pi- Ramesse 1: Mainz 1998, Von Zabern xxvi; (2) 743 pp. 3-8053-1918-5. Bibl.

10417 *Åström, Paul* Ceramics: influences east and west. The Aegean. 1998 ⇒10031. 257-263.

10418 [E]**Ballet, Pascale** Cahiers de la céramique égyptienne 2. Le Caire 1991, Publ. de l'Institut français d'archéologie orientale 304 fig.; 29 pl. 219 pp. 2-7247-0106-2. [R]BiOr 55 (1998) 129-133 (*López Grande, María J.*);

10419 Cahiers... 3. Le Caire 1993, Publ. de l'Institut... 210 fig.; 4 pl. xix; 201 pp. 2-7247-0130-5. [R]BiOr 55 (1998) 133-136 (*López Grande, María J.*).

10420 *Benedettucci, Francesco* La produzione ceramica della regione moabita nell'età del Ferro. [M]FRANKFORT H. 1998 ⇒26 57-81.

10421 **Berlin, Andrea; Slane, Kathleen Warner** Tel Anafa II.1: the Hellenistic and Roman pottery: the plain wares and the fine wares. 1997 ⇒13,10449. [R]AJA 102 (1998) 444-445 (*Downey, Susan B.*).

10422 **Boleslaw, Ginter; Kammerer-Grothaus, Helke** Frühe Keramik und Kleinfunde aus El-Târif. Archäologische Veröffentlichungen 40: Mainz 1998, Von Zabern x; 101 pp. 3-8053-0502-8. Deutsches Archäologisches Institut. Abteilung Kairo; Bibl.

10423 *Cohen-Weinberger, Anat* Petrographic analysis of the Egyptian forms from Stratum VI at Tel Beth-Shean. [F]DOTHAN, T. 1998 ⇒23. 406-412.

10424 **Faltings, Dina** Die Keramik der Lebensmittelproduktion im Alten Reich: Ikonographie und Archäologie eines Gebrauchsartikels. Studien zur Archäologie und Geschichte Altägyptens 14: Heid 1998, Orientverlag xi; 317 pp. 3-927552-32-1. Bibl.

10425 *Finkielsztejn, G.* Timbre amphoriques du Levant d'époque hellénistique (Pl. V). Transeuphratène 15 (1998) 83-121.

10426 *Fuscaldo, Perla* A preliminary report on the pottery from the late Hyksos period settlement at 'Ezbet Helmi (area H/III, strata D/3 and D/2). Ä&L 7 (1998) 59-69.

10427 *Gal, Zvi* כבול בארץ וישראלים פניקים [Phoenicians and Israelites in the 'land of Cabul']. Cathedra 88 (1998) 7-14 Sum. 181 [Rosh Zayit, Hurvat].

10428 *Gilboa, Ayelet* Iron I-IIa pottery evolution at Dor—regional contexts and the Cypriot connection. [F]DOTHAN T. 1998 ⇒23. 413-425.

10429 *Gudovitch, Shlomo; Pipano, Shlomo* חרס כלי קבוצת — רבדים מחצבת הכלקוליתית התקופה משלחי [A late chalcolithic pottery assemblage from the Revadim quarry]. 'Atiqot 35 (1998) 1*-5* Sum. 159.

10430 [E]**Hallager, Erik & Birgitta P.** Late Minoan III pottery: chronology and terminology. 1997 ⇒13,10454. [R]AJA 102 (1998) 435-436 (*Rutter, Jeremy B.*).

10431 **Heesen, P.** The J.L. Theodor collection of Attic black-figure vases. 1996 ⇒12,9864. [R]JHS 118 (1998) 250-251 (*Sparkes, Brian A.*).

10432   **Hoffmann, Herbert** Sotades: symbols of immortality on Greek
        vases. 1997 ⇒13,10459. [R]Antiquity 72 (1998) 967-968 (*Spivey,
        Nigel*).
10433   *Killebrew, Ann* Ceramic typology and technology of late Bronze II
        and Iron I assemblages from Tel Miqne-Ekron: the transition from
        Canaanite to Philistine culture. [F]DOTHAN, T. 1998 ⇒23. 379-405.
10434   *Klinger, Sonia* Two Attic lekythoi in the Israel Museum depicting
        animals. IEJ 48 (1998) 201-222.
10435   **Köhler, E. Christiana** Tell el-Fara în: Buto III: die Keramik von
        der späten Naqada-Kultur bis zum frühen Alten Reich (Schichten
        III bis VI). Archäologische Veröffentlichungen 94: Mainz 1998,
        Von Zabern xix; 149 pp. 3-8053-1859-6. Deutsches Archäologi-
        sches Institut. Abteilung Kairo.
10436   *Lehmann, Gunnar* Trends in the local pottery development of the
        late Iron Age and Persian period in Syria and Lebanon, ca. 700 to
        300 B.C. BASOR 311 (1998) 7-37.
10437   *Le Mière, M.; Picon, M.* Les débuts de la céramique au Proche-
        Orient. Paléorient 24/2 (1998) 5-26 Rés. sum. 5.
10438   **Leonard, Albert** An index to the Late Bronze Age Aegean pottery
        from Syria-Palestine. 1994 ⇒10,12041. [R]JNES 57 (1998) 145-146
        (*Cline, Eric H.*).
10439   *Liebowitz, Harold; Dehnisch, Anne M.* A mould-made seated terra-
        cotta cat from Beth Gan. IEJ 48 (1998) 174-182.
10440   *Lipinski, E.* Le corail dans les textes sémitiques. OLoP 29 (1998)
        75-87.
10441   *Marchetti, Nicolò* Chronologia relativa e significato delle culture
        del Bronzo Antico I in alta Mesopotamia, Siria e Anatolia.
        [M]FRANKFORT H. 1998 ⇒26. 237-285.
10442   *Marzahn, Joachim* Farbe in Assur: frühe Farbdiapositive in der
        Archäologie (1909-1910). MDOG 130 (1998) 223-239.
10443   *Mazar, Amihai* On the appearance of red slip in the Iron Age I
        period in Israel. [F]DOTHAN, T. 1998 ⇒23. 368-378.
10444   *Mazzoni, Stefania* The Syro-Anatolian common glyptic styles:
        some remarks. Rencontre Assyriologique Internationale 34. 1998
        ⇒452. 513-522.
10445   *Meyers, Carol* Fumes, flames or fluids?: reframing the cup-and-
        bowl question. [F]GORDON, C. JSOT.S 273: 1998 ⇒31. 30-39.
10446   [E]**Meyza, Henryk; Mlynarczyk, Jolanta** Hellenistic and Roman
        pottery in the eastern Mediteranean—advances in scientific studies.
        Wsz 1995, Centre d'Archéologie Méd. de l'Acad. Pol. des Sciences
        Acts of the II Nieborów Pottery Workshop, Nieborów 18-
        20.12.1993; many ill. x; 498 pp. 83-901809-0-1. [R]Latomus 57
        (1998) 703-704 (*Demarolle, J.-M.*).
10447   **Moignard, E.** Corpus vasorum antiquorum, Great Britain, Fasc.
        18. 1997 ⇒13,10462. [R]ClR 48 (1998) 430-31 (*Stafford, Emma J.*).
10448   [E]**Moore, Mary B.** Corpus vasorum antiquorum: USA 33. Getty
        Museum, Malibu 8: Malibu 1998, xii; 174 pp. $100. 0-89236-134-
        4. 44 fig.; 76 pl.; 4 tables [AJA 104,136—Ferrari, Gloria].
10449   **Munsterberg, Hugo & Marjorie** World ceramics: from prehis-
        toric to modern times. NY 1998, Penguin 191 pp. 0-670-86741-1.
10450   *Müller-Karpe, Andreas* Zum Töpferhandwerk bei den Hethitern.
        Rencontre Assyriologique Internationale 34. 1998 ⇒452. 361-364.

10451   **Sallaberger, Walther** Der babylonische Töpfer und seine Gefässe nach Urkunden altsumerischer bis altbabylonischer Zeit sowie lexikalischen und literarischen Zeugnissen. Mesopotamian History and Environment, H, Memoirs 3: Ghent 1996, Univ. of Ghent viii; 163 pp. FS90/65. 9 pl.

10452   *Sapin, J.* "Mortaria": un lot inédit de Tell Keisan: essai d'interprétation fonctionnelle. Transeuphratène 16 (1998) 87-120.

10453   **Schiering, Wolfgang** Minoische Töpferkunst: die bemalten Tongefässe der Insel des Minos. Kulturgeschichte der antiken Welt 73: Mainz 1998, Von Zabern viii; 253 pp. 3-8053-2334-4. 73 fig., 8 col. pl., 80 pl. [AJA 103,705s—Walberg, Gisela].

10454   *Sørensen, Lone Wriedt* Traveling pottery connections between Cyprus, the Levant, and the Greek world in the Iron Age. Res maritimae. 1998 ⇒491. 285-299.

10455   **Stiehler, G.; Delgado, Alegria** Die kassitische Glyptik. 1996 ⇒12,9886. ᴿMes. 33 (1998) 352-354 (*Negro, F.*).

10456   *Szafranlski, Zbigniew E.* Seriation and aperture index 2 of the beer bottles from Tell el-Dabʻa. Ä&L 7 (1998) 95-119.

10457   *Vagnetti, Lucia* Variety and function of the Aegean derivative pottery in the central Mediterranean in the late Bronze Age. ᶠDOTHAN, T. 1998 ⇒23. 66-77.

T3.6 **Lampas**

10458   **Bailey, Donald M.** A catalogue of the lamps in the British Museum IV: lamps of metal and stone, and lampstands. 1996 ⇒12,9892. ᴿAnCl 67 (1998) 575-576 (*Baratte, François*); RAr (1998/2) 433 (*Hellmann, Marie-Christine*).

10459   *Donceel, Robert* Poursuite des travaux de publication du matériel archéologique de Khirbet Qumrān: les lampes en terre-cuite. ᴹKLAWEK A. 1998 ⇒51. 87-104.

10460   *Magness, Jodi* Illuminating Byzantine Jerusalem: oil lamps shed light on early christian worship. BArR 24/2 (1998) 40-43, 46 -47, 70-71.

10461   **Młynarczyk, Jolanta** Alexandrian and Alexandria-influenced mould-made lamps of the Hellenistic period. 1997 ⇒13,10481. ᴿCÉg 73 (1998) 194-195 (*Nachtergael, Georges*).

10462   *Sussman, Varda* The binding of Isaac as depicted on a Samaritan lamp. IEJ 48 (1998) 183-189.

T3.7 *Cultica*—**cultic remains**

10463   *Aggoula, Basile* L'Esagil de Shamash ou le grand temple de Hatra (Pls: I-VII). Transeuphratène 14 (1998) 33-77.

10464   *Alpi, Frédéric; Kowalski, Slawomir; Waliszewski, Tomasz* Une église byzantine découverte à Anâne (Liban Sud). Syr. 75/1 (1998) 231-243.

10465   *Breton, Jean-François* Les temples de Maʻin et du Jawf (Yémen): état de la question. Syr. 75/1 (1998) 61-80.

10466   **Cook, J.M.; Nicholls, R.V.** Old Smyrna excavations: the temples of Athena. BSA.S 30: L 1998, British School at Athens xxviii; 248

pp. £50. 0-904887-28-6. 42 fig.; 30 pl. [AJA 104,801—Pfaff, Christopher A.].

10467 *Dentzer-Feydy, Jacqueline* Remarques sur le temple de Rîmet Hâzem (Syrie du Sud). Syr. 75/1 (1998) 201-211.

10468 **Freyberger, Klaus Stefan** Die frühkaiserzeitlichen Heiligtümer der Karawanenstationen im hellenisierten Osten: Zeugnisse eines kulturellen Konflikts im Spannungsfeld zweier politischer Formationen. Damaszener Forschungen 6: Mainz 1998, Von Zabern xvi; 138 pp. €101,24. 3-8053-2268-2. 72 pl.; 39 app. [ZDPV 116,79ss—Lichtenberger, Achim].

10469 **George, A.R.** House most high: the temples of ancient Mesopotamia. 1993 ⇒9,14178; 11/2,b377. ᴿJAOS 118 (1998) 81-82 (*Robertson, John F.*).

10470 **Mark, Ira S.** The sanctuary of Athena Nike in Athens: architectural stages and chronology. Hesp.S 26: Princeton, NJ 1993, American School of Classical Studies at Athens xv; 160 pp. $50. 0-87661-526-4. ᴿGn. 70 (1998) 235-240 (*Wesenberg, Burkhardt*).

10471 *McKay, Heather A.* Ancient synagogues: the continuing dealectic between two major views. CurResB 6 (1998) 103-142.

10472 **Pfeifer, Michael** Der Weihrauch: Geschichte, Bedeutung, Verwendung. 1997 ⇒13,10491. ᴿEL 112 (1998) 414-416 (*Raffa, Vincenzo*); BiLi 71 (1998) 383-384 (*Forsthuber, Franz*).

10473 *Piccirillo, Michele* Die Kirchen von Madaba. WUB 7 (1998) 44-6.

10474 *Porter, R.M.* An Egyptian temple at Beth Shean and Ramesses IV. Proc. 7th Cong. of Egyptologists. 1998 ⇒475. 903-910.

10475 *Pummer, Reinhard* How to tell a Samaritan synagogue from a Jewish synagogue. BArR 24/3 (1998) 24-35.

10476 *Sauvage, Martin* La construction des ziggurats sous la troisième dynastie d'Ur. Iraq 60 (1998) 45-63.

10477 *Schmidt, Klaus* Frühneolithische Tempel: ein Forschungsbericht zum präkeramischen Neolithikum Obermesopotamiens. MDOG 130 (1998) 17-49.

10478 *Taylor, Joan E.* A second temple in Egypt: the evidence for the Zadokite temple of Onias. JSJ 29 (1998) 297-321.

10479 *Tholbecq, Laurent* Der nabatäische Tempel im Wadi Ram. WUB 8 (1998) 53.

10480 **Thüngen, Susanne von** Die frei stehende griechische Exedra. Mainz 1994, Von Zabern ix; 183 pp. FS244. 3-8053-1471-X. Num. ill. ᴿRAr (1998/1) 125-126 (*Hellmann, Marie-Christine*).

10481 *Tsafrir, Yoram* The fate of pagan cult places in Palestine: the archaeological evidence with emphasis on Bet Shean. Religious... communities. 1998 ⇒347. 197-218.

10482 ᴱ**Urman, Dan; Flesher, Paul V.M.** Ancient synagogues: historical analysis and archaeological discovery. StPB 47/1: 1995 ⇒11/2,a812... 13,10496. ᴿRSR 86 (1998) 589-591 (*Beaude, Pierre-Marie*); JBL 117 (1998) 355-357 (*Strange, James F.*).

10483 *Van Haarlem, Willem M.* Archaic shrine models from Tell Ibrahim Awad. MDAI.K 54 (1998) 183-185.

10484 *Vörös, Gyozo; Pudleiner, Rezso* Preliminary report of the excavations at Thoth Hill, Thebes: the pre-11th dynasty temple and the western building (season 1996-1997). MDAI.K 54 (1998) 335-340.

10485 *Weippert, Helga* Kultstätten als Orte der Begegnung am Beispiel des chalkolithischen Heiligtums von Gīlat. ZDPV 114 (1998) 106-136.

10486   *Wimmer, Stefan* (No) more Egyptian temples in Canaan and Sinai. Jerusalem studies. ÄAT 40: 1998 ⇒361. 87-123 [Serabit el-Ḥadim; Timna].

T3.8 Funeraria; *Sindon*, the Shroud

10487   *Assman, Jan* Der Ort der Toten: Bemerkungen zu einem verbreiteten Totenopferspruch. ꟻSTADELMANN R. 1998 ⇒109. 235-245.
10488   **Aubert, Liliane** Les statuettes funéraires de la deuxième Cachette à Deir el-Bahari. P 1998, Cybele 128 pp. 2-9512092-0-7. Contrib. de Jacques-F. Aubert, Jeanne Bulté, Jean Yoyotte; Bibl. 113-118.
10489   *Bács, Tamás A.* First preliminary report on the work of the Hungarian mission in Thebes in Theban Tomb No 65 (Nebamun/Imiseba). MDAI.K 54 (1998) 49-64.
10490   *Bárta, Miroslav* Serdab and statue placement in the private tombs down to the fourth dynasty. MDAI.K 54 (1998) 65-75.
10491   *Beauchamp, Paul* Grabkunst mit biblischer Botschaft. WUB 8 (1998) 36-41.
10492   ᴱ**Branigan, Keith** Cemetery and society in the Aegean Bronze Age. Sheffield Studies in Aegean Archaeology 1: Shf 1998, Academic 173 pp. 1-85075-822-0.
10493   **Brier, Bob** The encyclopedia of mummies. [New York] 1998, Facts on File vii; 248 pp. 0-8160-3108-8. Bibl.
10494   *Brito Galindo, Andrés; Rodríguez Almenar, Jorge Manuel* La Iglesia, la Síndone y la fe. BiFe 24 (1998) 123-140.
10495   *Cancik-Lindemaier, Hildegard* Corpus: some philological and anthropological remarks upon Roman funerary customs. Self, soul and body. SHR 78: 1998 ⇒286. 417-429.
10496   *Carreira, Manuel M.* Materia y resurrección: epílogo. BiFe 24 (1998) 196-210;
10497   La Sábana Santa: desde el punto de vista de la física. BiFe 24 (1998) 141-172.
10498   *Chappaz, Jean-Luc* Répertoire annuel des figurines funéraires, 11. BSEG 22 (1998) 93-106.
10499   *Chéhadeh, Kamel; Griesheimer, Marc* Les reliefs funéraires du tombeau du prêtre Rapsônès (Babulin, Syrie du Nord). Syr. 75/1 (1998) 171-192.
10500   **Chioffi, Laura** Mummificazione e imbalsamazione a Roma ed in altri luoghi del mondo romano. Opuscula epigraphica, Università degli studi di Roma La Sapienza, Dipart. di scienze storiche... 8: R 1998, Quasar 95 pp. 88-7140-131-X. Bibl.
10501   *Chmiel, Jerzy* Całun Turyński Anno Domini 1998 [De Sindone Taurinensi Anno Domini 1998]. RBL 51 (1998) 47-50. **P.**
10502   **Comparelli, G.** L'Uomo della Croce: meditazioni davanti alla Sindone. CasM 1998, Piemme 64 pp. €4,13 [La Sapienza della Croce 13,401—Renzi, Stanislao].
10503   *DaSilva, Aldina* Offrandes alimentaires aux morts en Mésopotamie. Religiologiques 17 (1998) 9-17.
10504   *Domínguez, José Javier* La Síndone: estudio médico. BiFe 24 (1998) 85-121.
10505   *Dreyer, Günter, al.*, Umm el-Qaab: Nachuntersuchungen im frühzeitlichen Königsfriedhof, 9/10: Vorbericht. MDAI.K 54 (1998) 77-167 [Abydos].

10506 **Dubarle, A.-M.; Leynen, Hilda** Histoire ancienne du linceul de Turin, 2: 944-1356. P 1998, Guilbert 146 pp [REByz 58,289—Flusin, Bernard].

10507 **Eaton-Krauss, M.** The sarcophagus in the tomb of Tutankhamun. 1993 ⇒9,14362*... 13,10962. ᴿJNES 57 (1998) 159-160 (*Teeter, Emily*).

10508 *Eaton-Krauss, M.* The sarcophagus in the tomb of Tutankhamun: a clarification. JEA 84 (1998) 210-212.

10509 **El-Saady, Hassan** The tomb of Amenemhab, no. 44 at Gurnah: the tomb-chapel of a priest carrying the shrine of Amun. Wmr 1996, Aris & P 50 pp. ᴿAeg. 78 (1998) 201-203 (*Pernigotti, Sergio*).

10510 *Fischer, Peter M.* A Late Bronze to Early Iron Age tomb at Sahem, Jordan. NEA BA) 61/4 (1998) 255.

10511 **Gamer-Wallert, Ingrid** Von Giza bis Tübingen: die bewegte Geschichte der Mastaba G 5170. Tü 1998, Klöpfer & M 79 pp. 3-931402-33-9.

10512 *García García, Luis* La Síndone y Sudario: presentes en la sepultura de Jesús. BiFe 24 (1998) 61-84.

10513 *Getzov, Nimrod; Avshalom-Gorni, Dina; Muqari, Abdullah* [מגדל העמק] מיתקנים וקברים בשולי אל־מג'ידל] [Installations and tombs near El-Mujeidil (Migdal HaʻEmeq)]. ʻAtiqot 34 (1998) 195-207 Sum. 12*.

10514 ᴱ**Ghiberti, G.; Casale, U.** Dossier sulla Sindone. Brescia 1998, Queriniana 252 pp. €14,46 [ATT 5,248ss—Tuninetti, Giuseppe].

10515 *Ghiberti, Giuseppe* Pastorale della Sindone. RCI 79 (1998) 668-679.

10516 *Gnemmi, Dario* Da un archetipo di Daniele CRESPI: la sindone nel culto privato. BSPNov 89 (1998) 295-297.

10517 *Görsdorf, Jochen; Dreyer, Günter; Hartung, Ulrich* 14C dating results of the archaic royal necropolis Umm el-Qaab at Abydos. MDAI.K 54 (1998) 169-175.

10518 *Guglielminetti, Marziano* Due testimonianze del pellegrinaggio di San Carlo alla Sindone (1578): Filiberto Pingone e Francesco Adorno. Studia Borromaica 12 (1998) 253-260.

10519 **Guscin, Mark** The Oviedo cloth. C 1998, Lutterworth 128 pp. £10. 0-7188-2985-9. 15 ill.

10520 *Hachmann, Rolf* Die Gräber der Könige aus dem Hause David in Jerusalem und ihr Totenritual. ᶠÇAMBEL H. 1998 ⇒4. 375-394.

10521 **Haerinck, E.; Overlaet, B.** Chamahzi Mumah: an Iron Age III graveyard. Acta Iranica. 3. Textes et mémoires 19; Luristan Excavation Documents 2: [Lovanii] 1998, [Peeters] (6) 218 pp. 90-429-0027-X. Bibl.

10522 *Hamilakis, Yannis* Eating the dead: mortuary feasting and the politics of memory in the Aegean Bronze Age societies. Cemetery and society. 1998 ⇒322. 115-132.

10523 **Herdejürgen, Helga** Die antiken Sarkophagreliefs VI: die dekorativen Sarkophage 2:1: stadtrömische und italische Girlandensarkophage 1: die Sarkophage des ersten und zweiten Jahrhunderts. 1996 ⇒12,9943. ᴿRAr (1998/1) 141-142 (*Turcan, Robert*); AnCl 67 (1998) 567-569 (*Gaggadis-Robin, Vassiliki*).

10524 **Hoare, Rodney** The Turin Shroud is genuine. L 1998, Souvenir 192 pp. £8. 0-285-63471-2 [Month 33,160s—Nicholson, Paul].

10525 *Jackson, John P.* La Sábana Santa: ¿nos muestra la resurrección?. BiFe 24 (1998) 173-195.

10526 *Jackson, Rebecca* La Síndone y los ritos funerarios judíos: consideraciones. BiFe 24 (1998) 450-475.

10527 **Kanawati, Naguib; McFarlane, Ann** Deshasha: the tombs of Inti, Shedu and others. 1993 ⇒12,9948. [R]CÉg 73 (1998) 82-85 (*Meeks, Dimitri*).

10528 **Kockel, Valentin** Porträtreliefs stadtrömischer Grabbauten. 1993 ⇒11/2,a838. [R]RAr (1998/2) 435-438 (*Balty, Jean Charles*).

10529 *Kogan-Zehavi, Elena* The tomb and memorial of a chain-wearing anchorite at Kh. Tabaliya, near Jerusalem. 'Atiqot 35 (1998) 135-149.

10530 **Koortbojian, Michael** Myth, meaning and memory on Roman sarcophagi. 1995 ⇒11/2,a839; 12,9954. [R]AnCl 67 (1998) 566-567 (*Baratte, François*).

10531 *Lipinski, E.* Unpublished funerary relief busts from Palmyra. OLoP 29 (1998) 63-73.

10532 *Magness, Jodi* The Mausolea of Augustus, Alexander, and Herod the Great. [F]FRERICHS, E. BJSt 320: 1998 ⇒28. 313-329.

10533 *Magness, Jodi; Avni, Gideon* Jews and christians in a late Roman cemetery at Beth Guvrin. Religious... communities. 1998 ⇒347. 87-114.

10534 **Marinelli, Emanuela** O Sudário: uma imagem 'impossível'. [T]*Lemos, Benôni*: São Paulo 1998, Paulus 158 pp. 85-349-1277-7 [PerTeol 31,146].

10535 *Menu, B.* La "voie de Dieu" dans les inscriptions du tombeau de Pétosiris. Transeuphratène 16 (1998) 21-30.

10536 **Mrogenda, Ute** Die Terrakottafiguren von Myrina: eine Untersuchung ihrer möglichen Bedeutung und Funktion im Grabzusammenhang. EHS.A 63: 1996 ⇒12,9966. [R]Mes. 33 (1998) 394-396 (*Menegazzi, R.*).

10537 **Munro, Peter** Der Unas-Friedhof Nord-West 1. 1993 ⇒11/2,b598. [R]ArOr 66 (1998) 174-176 (*Bárta, Miroslav*).

10538 *Noy, David* Where were the Jews of the Diaspora buried?. Jews in a Graeco-Roman world. 1998 ⇒337. 75-89.

10539 *Petrosillo, Orazio* Il volto di Cristo sulla Sindone. Il Volto dei Volti 1/1 (1998) 78-89 Som. Sum. 89.

10540 **Pumpenmeier, Frauke** Eine Gunstgabe von seiten des Königs: ein extrasepulkrales Schabtidepot Qen-Amuns in Abydos. Studien zur Archäologie und Geschichte Altägyptens 19: Heid 1998, Orientverlag ix; 97 pp. 3-927552-31-3. Bibl.

10541 *Rodante, Sebastiano* Il linguaggio evangelico 'visivo' della sindone. Anime e Corpi 36 (1998) 351-360.

10542 *Rodríguez Almenar, Jorge Manuel* La Síndone de Turín: introducción y estudio histórico. BiFe 24 (1998) 9-60.

10543 *Roobaert, Arlette* The middle bronze age jar burial F167 from Tell Ahmar (Syria). Abr-n. 35 (1998) 97-105 [Ahmar].

10544 **Roth, Ann Macy** A cemetery of palace attendants including G 2084-2099, G 2230+2231, and G 2240. Giza Mastabas 6: Boston 1995, Museum of Fine Arts xxvi; 175 pp. $100. 210 pl.; 91 fig. [JNES 59,143s—Polz, Daniel].

10545 *Sagiv, Nahum; Zissu, Boaz; Avni, Gideon* מערות קבורה מימי הבית השני בתל גודד, שפלת יהודה [Tombs of the Second Temple period at Tel Goded, Judean foothills]. 'Atiqot 35 (1998) 7*-21* Sum. 159.

10546   **Säve-Söderbergh, Torgny** The Old Kingdom cemetery at Hamra Dom (El-Qasr wa es-Saiyad). 1994 ⇒10,12831; 12,10475. ᴿJNES 57 (1998) 302-303 (*Williams, Bruce*).

10547   **Schick, Tamar**, *al.*, The cave of the warrior: a fourth millennium burial in the Judean Desert. IAA Reports 5: J 1998, The Israel Antiquities Authority 137 pp. 965-406-035-3.

10548   **Schneider, Hans Diederik** The Memphite tomb of Horemheb II: a catalogue of the finds: sixtieth excavation memoir. 1996 ⇒12, 9975. ᴿBiOr 55 (1998) 415-418 (*Chappaz, Jean-Luc*).

10549   **Siliato, Maria Grazia** Contre-enquête sur le saint suaire. ᵀ*Liffran, Françoise*: P 1998, Plon 284 pp. €18,14. 2-259-18860-5 [BCLF 611-612,1718].

10550   *Smith, Patricia* A human skull from Tel Te'enim. TelAv 25 (1998) 104.

10551   *Smith, Patricia; Horwitz, Liora Kolska* Human and animal remains from the burial cave at Shaʿar Ephraim central. TelAv 25 (1998) 110-115.

10552   Speciale Sindone. Rivista diocesana di Roma 5/6 (1998) 1-167.

10553   *Stadelmann, Rainer; Alexanian, Nicole* Die Friedhöfe des Alten und Mittleren Reiches in Dahschur: Bericht über die im Frühjahr 1997 durch das Deutsche Archäologische Institut Kairo durchgeführte Felderkundung in Dahschur. MDAI.K 54 (1998) 293-317.

10554   **Strommenger, Eva; Kohlmeyer, Kay** Ausgrabungen in Tall Bi'a, Tuttul, 1: die altorientalischen Bestattungen. WVDOG 96: Saarbrücken 1998, SDV x; 167, 221 pp. 3-930843-34-X.

10555   **Strudwick, N. & H.M.** The tombs of Amenhotep, Khnumose, and Amenmose at Thebes. 1996 ⇒12,9981. ᴿBiOr 55 (1998) 119-121 (*Dziobek, Eberhard*); RdE 49 (1998) 280-285 (*Gasse, Annie*).

10556   **Teitelbaum, Dina** The relationship between ossuary burial and the belief in resurrection during late second temple period Judaism. M.A. ᴰCarleton University, Canada 1997, 199 pp. $34.50. UMI, Ann Arbor MI.

10557   *Thompson, Stephen E.* The significance of anointing in ancient Egyptian funerary beliefs. ᴹWARD W. 1998 ⇒123. 229-243.

10558   *Vasiljević, Vera* Über die relative Größe der Darstellungen des Grabherrn im Alten Reich. SAÄK 25 (1998) 341-351 Zsfg. 341.

10559   *Weksler-Bdolah, Shlomit* מצרות קבורה ומתקנים ממי הבית השני במצפור הר הצופים, ירושלים [Burial caves and installations of the second temple period at the Har Hazofim observatory (Mt. Scopus, Jerusalem)]. ʿAtiqot 34 (1998) 23*-54* Sum. 161. H.

10560   ᴱ**Wilkinson, Richard H.** Valley of the sun kings: new explorations in the tombs of the pharaohs. Tucson 1995, Univ. of Arizona Egyptian Expedition Papers from the Univ. of Arizona International Conf. on the Valley of the Kings 164 pp. 0-964-99580-8. ᴿOLZ 93 (1998) 443-448 (*Eaton-Krauss, Marianne*).

10561   **Willems, Harco** The coffin of Heqata (Cairo JdE 36418): a case study of Egyptian funerary culture of the Early Middle Kingdom. OLA 70: 1996 ⇒12,9987. ᴿOLZ 93 (1998) 438-443 (*Grajetzki, Wolfram*); BiOr 55 (1998) 772-775 (*Berlev, O.D.*).

T3.9 *Numismatica*, **coins**

10562   *Auge, Christian* Silbermünzen aus Tyros. WUB 9 (1998) 17.
10563   ^E**Balbi de Caro, Silvana; Benocci, Carla** La collezione sfragisti-
ca, v.1: la collezione Corvisieri romana. Bollettino di numismatica,
monografia 7/1: R 1998, Ministero per i Beni Culturali e Ambientali 296 pp. 88-240-3663-5.
10564   **Bartolini, P.; Perra, C.** Monete puniche della collezione Pispisa:
la serie II (264-241 A.C.). RSFen.S 26: R 1998, Consiglio
Nazionale delle ricerche 7-43 pp; 73 pl.
10565   *Bijovsky, Gabriela* The Gush Ḥalav hoard reconsidered. ʿAtiqot 35
(1998) 77-106. *Meyers, Eric M.*: Postscript to the Gush Ḥalav
hoard [107-8].
10566   **Bopearachchi, Osmund** Sylloge nummorum graecorum: the collection of the American Numismatic Society, part 9: Graeco-
Bactrian and Indo-Greek coins. NY 1998, American Numismatic
Society 174 pp.
10567   *Callot, Olivier* Notes de numismatique hellénistique. Syr. 75/1
(1998) 81-87.
10568   *Ciecielạg, Jerzy* Coins from the so-called Essene settlements on the
Dead Sea shores. ^MKLAWEK A. 1998 ⇒51. 105-115.
10569   **Elayi, Josette; Lemaire, André** Graffiti et contremarques ouest-
sémitiques sur les monnaies grecques et proche-orientales. Gaux
13: Mi 1998, Ennerre 228 pp. 17 fig. 39 pl. [SEL 16,121—Amadasi Guzzo, Maria Giulia].
10570   ^E**Gorini, Giovanni** Forme di contatto tra moneta locale e moneta
straniera nel mondo antico. Atti del Convegno internazionale,
Aosta 13-14 ottobre 1995. [Padova] 1998, Esedra 153 pp. 88-
86413-28-9.
10571   *Haerinck, E.* The shifting pattern of overland and seaborne trade in
SE-Arabia: foreign pre-islamic coins from Mleiha (Emirate of Shar-
jah, U.A.E.). Akkadica 106 (1998) 22-40.
10572   **Harl, Kenneth W.** Coinage in the Roman economy: 300 B.C. to
A.D. 700. 1996 ⇒12,10001; 13,10552. ^RCIR 48 (1998) 454-456
(*Williams, J.H.C.*); REByz 56 (1998) 305-306 (*Morrisson, Cécile*);
BZ 42 (1998) 139-142 (*Johnson, Leah*).
10573   ^E**King, Cathy E.; Wigg, David G.** Coin finds and coin use in the
Roman world. 1996 ⇒12,10004. ^RLatomus 57 (1998) 705-706
(*Zehnacker, H.*).
10574   **Kreitzer, Larry J.** Striking new images: Roman imperial coinage
and New Testament world. JSNT.S 134: 1996 ⇒12,10005. ^RJBL
117 (1998) 738-740 (*LiDonnici, Lynn R.*).
10575   *Leonard, Robert D.* A view of the current state of research on
Jewish coins. Qumran Chronicle 8/1-2 (1998) 129-131.
10576   *Le Rider, Georges* Le début du monnayage achéménide: continua-
tion ou innovation?. ^FÇAMBEL H. 1998 ⇒4. 663-673;
10577   Un trésor hellénistique de monnaies d'argent trouvé en Syrie en
1971 (CH II, 81). Syr. 75/1 (1998) 89-96.
10578   **Marot, Teresa** Las monedas del *Macellum* de *Gerasa* (Yaraš, Jor-
dania): approximación a la circulación monetaria en la provincia de
Arabia. M 1998, Casa de la Moneda 522 pp. 84-89157-11-1. 16 pl.
[RB 106,638].

10579 **Mildenberg, Leo** Vestigia leonis: Studien zur antiken Numismatik Israels, Palästinas und der östlichen Mittelmeerwelt. ᴱ*Hübner, Ulrich; Knauf, Ernst Axel*: NTOA 36: FrS 1998, Universitätsverlag xxii; 400 pp. FS140. 3-7278-1155-2.

10580 **Rebuffat, François** La monnaie dans l'Antiquité. 1996 ⇒12, 10010. ᴿAnCl 67 (1998) 440-441 (*Kayser, François*).

10581 *Ronen, Yigal* The weight standards of the Judean coinage in the late Persian and early Ptolemaic period. NEA(BA) 61/2 (1998) 122-126.

10582 *Rosenthal, Franz* Die Lidzbarski-Goldmedaille. ZDMG 148 (1998) 361-366.

10583 **Sear, David R.** The history and coinage of the Roman imperators 49-27 BC. L 1998, Spink xxxii; 360 pp. 0-907605-98-2. Bibl.

10584 **Troxell, H.A.** Studies in the Macedonian coinage of Alexander the Great. 1997 ⇒13,10561. ᴿCIR 48 (1998) 452-4 (*Ireland, Stanley*).

10585 *Wasserstein, David J.* The coins in the golden hoard from Tiberias;
10586 The silver coins in the mixed hoard from Tiberias. 'Atiqot 36 (1998) 10-14/15-22.

10587 *Weiser, Wolfram* Namen römischer Statthalter auf Münzen Kleinasiens: Corrigenda und Addenda zu Gerd Stumpfs Münzcorpus. ZPE 123 (1998) 275-290.

T4.2 *Situs effossi*, bulletins; **syntheses**

10588 A guide to '98 digs: the volunteer's view. BArR 24/1 (1998) 38-53.

10589 **Joffe, Alexander H.** Settlement and society in the Early Bronze Age I and II, southern Levant. 1993 ⇒11/2,a935; 13,10562. ᴿJNES 57 (1998) 316-320 (*Levy, Thomas E.*); JAOS 118 (1998) 281-282 (*Schaub, R. Thomas*).

10590 ᴱ*Wolff, Samuel* Travel guide to Israel: a handbook of current excavations. Arch. 51/3 (1998) 56-59;
10591 Archaeology in Israel. AJA 102 (1998) 757-807.

T4.3 **Jerusalem**, *archaeologia* et historia

10592 *Akerman, Luis Mariano* The evocative character of Louis Kahn's Hurva synagogue project, 1967-1974;

10593 *Alexander, Jonathan J.G.* "Jerusalem the Golden": image and myth in the Middle Ages in Western Europe;

10594 *Amishai-Maisels, Ziva* CHAGALL in the Holy Land: the real and the ideal;

10595 *Ankori, Gannit* Behind the walls: the real and ideal Jerusalem in contemporary Palestinian art. ᶠNARKISS, B. 1998 ⇒85. 245-253/254-264/513-542/575-585.

10596 *Arieli, Rotem* Human remains from the Har Haẓofim observatory tombs (Mt. Scopus, Jerusalem). 'Atiqot 35 (1998) 37-42.

10597 *Arnould, Caroline* Remarques sur la place et la fonction de la porte de Damas (porte romaine) dans la cité d'Aelia Capitolina. ZDPV 114 (1998) 179-183.

10598 **Auld, A. Graeme; Steiner, Margreet** Jerusalem, 1: from the Bronze Age to the Maccabees. Cities of the Biblical World: 1996

⇒12,10020. ^RPEQ 130 (1998) 68 (*Axe, Tony*); RB 105 (1998) 299-301 (*Murphy-O'Connor, J.*); BAR 24/4 (1998) 56-57 (*Taylor, Joan E.*).

10599   *Auld, Sylvia* The jewelled surface: architectural decoration of Jerusalem in the age of Süleyman-Qanuni;

10600   *Baer, Eva* Visual representations of Jerusalem's holy Islamic sites. ^FNARKISS, B. 1998 ⇒85. 467-479/384-392.

10601   *Bahat, Dan* Two recent studies of the archaeology of Jerusalem: review article;

10602   *Bar, Doron* Aelia Capitolina and the location of the camp of the tenth legion. PEQ 130 (1998) 51-62/8-19.

10603   *Baruch, Eyal* העורף הכלכלי של ירושלים בתקופה ההרודיינית [The economic hinterland of Jerusalem in the Herodian period]. Cathedra 89 (1998) 41-62 Sum. 197.

10604   **Biddle, Martin** Das Grab Christi: neutestamentliche Quellen—historische und archäologische Forschungen—überraschende Erkenntnisse. ^T*Pitt-Killet, Heike*: Biblische Archäologie und Zeitgeschichte 5: Gießen 1998, Brunnen 192 pp. 3-7655-9804-6 [NThAR 1999,45].

10605   *Bux, Nicola* Il pellegrinaggio a Gerusalemme all'origine del giubileo cristiano. Com(I) 160-161 (1998) 38-46.

10606   *Cahill, Jane* David's Jerusalem: fiction or reality?: it's there: the archaeological evidence proves it. BArR 24/4 (1998) 34-41.

10607   *Chrostowski, Waldemar* Jerozolima—Miasto Świete Chrześcijan: perspektywa katolicka. CoTh 68/2 (1998) 21-40. **P**.

10608   *Delsman, Wilhelmus C.* Jerusalem, eine heilige Stadt für drei Religionen. ^FRÖMER, W. AOAT 253: 1998 ⇒97. 63-70.

10609   *Deluga, Waldemar* Gravures et vues de Jérusalem dans les proskynetarions grecs et leurs copies serbes et russes du XVIIIème siècle. ^FNARKISS, B. 1998 ⇒85. 370-377.

10610   *Demsky, Aaron* Holy City and Holy Land as viewed by Jews and christians in the Byzantine period: a conceptual approach to sacred space. Sanctity of time. 1998 ⇒303. 285-296.

10611   *Dequeker, Luc* The holiness of Jerusalem and the origin of Qumran. "Lasset uns Brücken bauen...". BEAT 42: 1998 ⇒401. 27-31.

10612   *Díez, Florentino* El Gólgota y el Sepulcro: aportaciones de la arqueología. BiFe 24 (1998) 424-437.

10613   *Doukhan, Igor* Beyond the Holy City: symbolic intentions in the avant-garde urban utopia. ^FNARKISS, B. 1998 ⇒85. 565-574.

10614   **Döpp, Heinz-Martin** Die Deutung der Zerstörung Jerusalems und des Zweiten Tempels in Jahre 70 in den ersten drei Jahrhunderten n. Chr. Diss. TANZ 24: Tü 1998, Francke xvi; 364 pp. €49,8. 3-77-20-1875-0.

10615   *Fleck, Cathleen A.* Linking Jerusalem and Rome in the fourteenth century: the Italian bible of Anti-Pope Clement VII;

10616   *Folda, Jaroslav* Jerusalem and the holy sepulchre through the eyes of crusader pilgrims;

10617   *Friedman, Mira* CHAGALL's Jerusalem. ^FNARKISS, B. 1998 ⇒85. 430-452/158-164/543-564.

10618   *Geva, Hillel; Bahat, Dan* Architectural and chronological aspects of the ancient Damascus Gate area. IEJ 48 (1998) 223-235.

10619   ^E**Geva, Hillel** Ancient Jerusalem revealed. 1994 ⇒10,12217*; 11/2,970. ^RJNES 57 (1998) 221-223 (*Tappy, Ron*); Syr. 75 (1998) 308-310 (*Miroschedji, Pierre de*).

10620 *Gibson, Shimon; Avni, Gideon* The "Jewish-Christian" tomb from the Mount of Offence (Batn al-Hawa') in Jerusalem reconsidered. RB 105 (1998) 161-175.

10621 **Gibson, Shimon; Jacobson, David M.** Below the Temple Mount in Jerusalem. 1996 ⇒12,2496. ᴿRB 105 (1998) 301-303 (*Murphy-O'Connor, J.*).

10622 *Goethert, Rolf* Neues aus der Davidsstadt. WUB 10 (1998) 74-75.

10623 *Goldman-Ida, Batsheva* Black on white—a remembrance of Jerusalem. ᶠNARKISS, B. 1998 ⇒85. 203-209.

10624 **Grabar, Oleg** The shape of the holy: early Islamic Jerusalem. 1996 ⇒12,10051. ᴿRB 105 (1998) 266-271 (*Murphy-O'Connor, J.*) Islam 75 (1998) 94-103 (*Busse, Heribert*).

10625 *Granda, Ángel* El Gólgota y el Sepulcro: aplicación de la técnica geofísica del georadar. BiFe 24 (1998) 438-449.

10626 *Heyd, Milly* George SEGAL: the multifaceted sacrifice;

10627 Jerusalem: anti-myth. ᶠNARKISS, B. 1998 ⇒85. 617-627/586-599.

10628 *Houtman, Alberdina* 'They direct their heart to Jerusalem': references to Jerusalem and temple in Mishnah and Tosefta Berakhot. Sanctity of time. 1998 ⇒303. 153-166.

10629 *Jacoby, Ruth* The decoration and plan of Queen Helena's tomb in Jerusalem. ᶠNARKISS, B. 1998 ⇒85. 460-462.

10630 *Karski, Karol* Jerozolima—Miejscem dialogu i ekumenizmu?. CoTh 68/2 (1998) 65-73. **P.**

10631 *Kleinbauer, W. Eugene* The anastasis rotunda and christian architectural invention. ᶠNARKISS, B. 1998 ⇒85. 140-146.

10632 *Krochmalnik, Dnaiel* Der Nabel der Welt: die Sonderstellung Jerusalems in der jüdischen Tradition. FrRu NF 5 (1998) 187-195.

10633 *Krüger, Jürgen* WILLIAM II's perception of sacrality. Baalbek ᴱ**Hakimian, S.** 1998 ⇒T5.1. 89-95.

10634 *Kühnel, Bianca* The use and abuse of Jerusalem. ᶠNARKISS, B. 1998 ⇒85. XIX-XXXVIII.

10635 **Lafon, Jacques** Jérusalem. Clefs Politique: P 1998, Montchrestien 158 pp [IslChr 25,279ss—Rocalve, Pierre].

10636 *Laperrousaz, Ernest-Marie* La troisième muraille antique de la 'Colline occidentale' de Jérusalem. Syr. 75/1 (1998) 97-105.

10637 *Lidov, Alexei* Heavenly Jerusalem: the Byzantine approach;

10638 *Limor, Ora* The place of the end of days: eschatological geography in Jerusalem;

10639 *Linder, Amnon* The loss of christian Jerusalem in late medieval liturgy. ᶠNARKISS, B. 1998 ⇒85. 340-353/13-22/165-178.

10640 *Lipschits, Oded* Nebuchadrezzar's policy in 'Ḥattu-land' and the fate of the kingdom of Judah. UF 30 (1998) 467-487.

10641 *Livne-Kafri, Ofer* ירושלים במסורות המוסלמיות של אחרית הימים ויום הדין [Jerusalem in Muslim traditions of the 'end of days']. Cathedra 86 (1998) 23-56 Sum. 181. **H.**

10642 *Low, Peter* The city refigured: a Pentecostal Jerusalem in the San Paolo bible. ᶠNARKISS, B. 1998 ⇒85. 265-274.

10643 *Malamat, Abraham* Jerusalem on the eve of its destruction. Capital cities. 1998 ⇒492. 225-229.

10644 *Malinowski, Jerzy* Jerusalem in modern Jewish art in Poland and central-eastern Europe. ᶠNARKISS, B. 1998 ⇒85. 504-512.

10645 *Manzano, Braulio* El Gólgota y el Santo Sepulcro: ubicación. BiFe 24 (1998) 403-435.

10646 *Mazar, Benjamin; Eshel, Hanan* Who built the first wall of Jerusalem?. IEJ 48 (1998) 265-268.
10647 *Na'aman, Nadav* David's Jerusalem: fiction or reality?: it is there: ancient texts prove it. BArR 24/4 (1998) 42-44.
       ᶠNARKISS, B. The real and ideal Jerusalem 1998 ⇒85.
10648 **Neher-Bernheim, Renée** Jérusalem trois millénaires d'histoire: du roi David à nos jours. 1997 ⇒13,10614. ᴿREJ 157 (1998) 388-392 (*Couteau, Élisabeth*).
10649 *Nowogórski, Przemyslław* 3000 lat Jerozolimy w kontekście źródel historycznych i archeologicznych. CoTh 68/2 (1998) 9-16. **P.**
10650 *Ousterhout, Robert* Flexible geography and transportable topography. ᶠNARKISS, B. 1998 ⇒85. 393-404.
10651 *Parmentier, Martien* The lasting sanctity of Bethesda. Sanctity of time. 1998 ⇒303. 73-93.
10652 *Paszkiewicz, Piotr* In the shadow of the black eagle: Russia's imperial policy and its impact on the architecture of Jerusalem ᶠNARKISS, B. 1998 ⇒85. 480-491.
10653 **Pieraccini, Paolo** Gerusalemme, luoghi santi e comunità religiose nella politica internazionale. 1997 ⇒13,10618. ᴿCarthaginensia 14 (1998) 239-240 (*Cuenca Molina, J.F.*); RivBib 46 (1998) 343-345 (*Boschi, Bernardo Gianluigi*); POC 48 (1998) 442-3 (*Attinger, D.*).
10654 *Planas i Marcé, Sílvia; Boadas i Raset, Joan* Jerusalem from Girona: a sixteenth-century representation of the Holy City. ᶠNARKISS, B. 1998 ⇒85. 286-293.
10655 **Poorthuis, Marcel** Centrality of Jerusalem: introduction and overview: the centrality of Jerusalem. 1996 ⇒12,236; 13,10619. ᴿLouv St 23 (1998) 282-283 (*Eynikel, Erik*).
10656 *Posèq, Avigdor W.G.* The "New Jerusalem", the Star of Zion and the Mandala;
10657 *Pullan, Wendy* Jerusalem from Alpha to Omega in the Santa Prudenziana mosaic;
10658 *Revel-Neher, Elisheva* Antiquus populus, novus populus: Jerusalem and the people of God in the Germigny-des-prés Carolingian mosaic;
10659 *Rosen-Ayalon, Myriam* Jewish substratum, christian history and Muslim symbolism: an archaeological episode in Jerusalem. ᶠNARKISS, B. 1998 ⇒85. 325-339/405-417/54-66/463-466.
10660 *Rosenberg, Stephen* The Siloam tunnel revisited. TelAv 25 (1998) 116-130.
10661 *Sabar, Shalom* Messianic aspirations and Renaissance urban ideals: the image of Jerusalem in the Venice Haggadah, 1609. ᶠNARKISS, B. 1998 ⇒85. 294-312.
10662 *Safrai, Shmuel* Jerusalem and the temple in the Tannaitic literature of the first generation after the destruction of the temple. Sanctity of time. 1998 ⇒303. 135-152.
10663 *Saminsky, Alexander* A reference to Jerusalem in a Georgian gospel book;
10664 *Schlink, Wilhelm* The Gothic cathedral as Heavenly Jerusalem: a fiction in German art history. ᶠNARKISS, B. 1998 ⇒85. 354-369/ 275-285.
10665 *Schudrich, Michael* Jerozolima—Miasto Świete Zydów. CoTh 68/2 (1998) 17-20. **P.**

10666 *Schütz, Chana C.* Karl Friedrich SCHINKEL's design for the church of the Holy Sepulchre and the Prussian involvement in Jerusalem during the nineteenth century. [F]NARKISS, B. 1998 ⇒85. 492-503.

10667 *Schwartz, Seth* The Hellenization of Jerusalem and Shechem. Jews in a Graeco-Roman world. 1998 ⇒337. 37-45.

10668 *Segal, George* Reflections on my work while in Jerusalem;

10669 *Silver, Larry* Mapped and marginalized: early printed images of Jerusalem;

10670 *Smith, Kathryn A.* The destruction of Jerusalem miniatures in the Neville of Hornby Hours and their visual, literary and devotional contexts;

10671 *Starodoub, Tatiana Kh.* The idea of the Holy City in medieval Muslim painting. [F]NARKISS, B. 1998 ⇒85. 600-616/313-324/179-202/378-383.

10672 *Steiner, Margreet* The archaeology of ancient Jerusalem. CurResB 6 (1998) 143-168;

10673 David's Jerusalem: fiction or reality?: it's not there: archaeology proves a negative. BArR 24/4 (1998) 26-33.

10674 **Stoltmann, Dagmar** Jerusalem—Mutter—Stadt: zur Theologiegeschichte der Heiligen Stadt. MThA 57: Oros 1998, Altenberge 359 pp. €36,81. 3-89375-173-4.

10675 *Talmon, Shemaryahu* The signification of Jerusalem in biblical thought;

10676 *Taragan, Hanna* The image of the Dome of the Rock in Cairene Mamluk architecture. [F]NARKISS, B. 1998 ⇒85. 1-12/453-459.

10677 *Taylor, Joan E.* Golgotha: a reconsideration of the evidence for the sites of Jesus' crucifixion and burial. NTS 44 (1998) 180-203.

10678 **Walker, Peter W.L.** Jesus and the Holy City: New Testament perspectives on Jerusalem. 1996 ⇒12,10091; 13,10634. [R]Pacifica 11/2 (1998) 218-220 (*Pfitzner, Vic*); NEA(BA) 61 (1998) 68-69 (*Avalos, Hector*).

10679 *Weinfeld, Moshe* Jerusalem—a political and spiritual capital. Capital cities. 1998 ⇒492. 15-40.

10680 *Weksler-Bdolah, Shlomit* מיתקנים וחציבות בגלה שבירושלים [Installations and rock-cuttings at Giloh, Jerusalem]. 'Atiqot 34 (1998) 179-193 Sum. 11*. **H.**

10681 *Zuk, Mahmud Taha* Jerozolima—Miasto Święte Muzułmanów. CoTh 68/2 (1998) 59-63. **P.**

T4.4 Judaea, Negeb; *situs alphabetice*

10682 *Avner, Uzi; Magness, Jodi* Early Islamic settlement in the southern Negev. BASOR 310 (1998) 39-57.

10683 **Eshel, Hanan; Amit, David** מערות המפלת מתקפת מרד בר-כוכבה [Refuge caves of the Bar Kokhba revolt]. TA 1998, Eretz 241 pp. NIS60/45. 965-90215-0-X. Num. ill. [IEJ 50,149—Katzenstein, Hannah].

10684 **Finkelstein, Israel** Living on the fringe: the archaeology and history of the Negev, Sinai and neighbouring regions in the bronze and iron ages. 1995 ⇒13,10138. [R]ThZ 54 (1998) 168-169 (*Weber, Beat*); JAOS 118 (1998) 567-568 (*Dever, William G.*).

10685 *Shanks, Hershel* Where is the tenth century?. BArR 24/2 (1998) 56-60 [Megiddo; Gezer; Hazor].

10686 **Shereshevski, Joseph** Byzantine urban settlements in the Negev desert. 1991 ⇒7,d361... 10,12275. ᴿZDPV 114 (1998) 97-98 (*Hübner, Ulrich*).

10687 *Van den Brink, Edwin C.M.* Late protodynastic-early first dynasty Egyptian finds in late Early Bronze Age I Canaan: an update. Proc. 7th Cong. of Egyptologists. 1998 ⇒475. 215-225.

10688 *Wagner-Lux, Ute* Iudaea. RAC 146. 1998 ⇒495. 63-130.

10689 *Abu Salem*: *Gopher, Avi; Goring-Morris, A. Nigel* Abu Salem: a pre-pottery neolithic B camp in the central Negev highlands, Israel. BASOR 312 (1998) 1-20.

10690 *Arad*: ᴱ**Amiran, Ruth** Sixth to eighteenth seasons of excavation, 1971-1978, 1980-1984. Early Arad, 2. 1996 ⇒12,10105. ᴿOr. 67 (1998) 546-551 (*Nigro, Lorenzo*).

10691 *Ekron*: *Dothan, Trude* An early Phoenician cache from Ekron ᶠFRERICHS, E. BJSt 320: 1998 ⇒28. 259-272.

10692 *Görg, Manfred* Die Göttin der Ekron-Inschrift. BN 93 (1998) 9-10.

10693 *Naveh, Joseph* Achish-Ikausu in the light of the Ekron dedication. BASOR 310 (1998) 35-37.

10694 *En Boqeq*: **Gichon, Mordechai** 'En Boqeq, 1: Geographie und Geschichte der Oase. 1993, ⇒9,13828... 13,10644. ᴿPEQ 130 (1998) 77-78 (*Frendo, Anthony J.*).

10695 *Gath*: *Schniedewind, William M.* The geopolitical history of Philistine Gath. BASOR 309 (1998) 69-77.

10696 *Gezer*: **Dever, William G.** Gezer: a crossroad in ancient Israel. TA 1998, Hakibbutz Hameuchad 203 pp. NIS72. Num. ill. [IEJ 50,147s—Katzenstein, Hannah]. **H.**

10697 *Goded*: *Sagiv, Nahum; Zissu, Boaz; Avni, Gideon* מערות קבורה מימי יהודה, שפלת בתל גודד, הבית השני בתל [Tombs of the Second Temple period at Tel Goded, Judean foothills]. 'Atiqot 35 (1998) 7*-21* Sum. 159. **H.**

10698 *Hebron*: *Busse, Heribert* Die Patriarchengräber in Hebron und der Islam. ZDPV 114 (1998) 71-94.

10699 *Jericho*: *Nigro, Lorenzo* Gerico: le origini della città in Palestina: caratteri originali, sviluppo e crisi della prima urbanizzazione palestinese nel III millennio a.C.: il caso di Tell es-Sultan, antica Gerico. RPARA 69 (1996-1997) 187-214.

10700 *Marchetti, Nicolò; Nigro, Lorenzo; Sarie, Issa* Preliminary report on the first season of excavations of the Italian-Palestinian expedition at Tell es Sultan/Jericho, April-May 1997. PEQ 130 (1998) 121-144.

10701 ᴱ**Marchetti, Nicola; Nigro, Lorenzo** Scavi a Gerico, 1997: relazione preliminare sulla prima campagna di scavi e prospezioni archeologiche a Tell es-Sultan, Palestina. Quaderni di Gerico 1: R 1998, Università di Roma "La Sapienza" iii; 254 pp.

10702 *Masada*: ᴱ**Aviram, J.** Masada IV. 1994 ⇒10,12272; 12,10124 ᴿOLZ 93 (1998) 47-49 (*Japp, Sarah*).

10703 **Foerster, Gideon** Masada V: The Yigael Yadin excavations 1963-1965: final report: art and architecture. 1995 ⇒11/2,b047... 13,10656. ᴿOLZ 93 (1998) 50-52 (*Japp, Sarah*); BiOr 55 (1998) 520-525 & PEQ 130 (1998) 168-170 (*Wright, G.R.H.*).

10704 *Ziv, Yehuda* הדצמ תא שיבכל' :'הדצמ תא שיבכל' ראשוני המעפילים אל ההר ['To conquer Masada']. Cathedra 90 (1998) 115-144 Sum. 195. **H**.

10705 *Megiddo*: **Ussishkin, David** The destruction of Megiddo at the end of the late Bronze Age and its historical significance. [F]DOTHAN, T. 1998 ⇒23. 197-219.

10706 *Leonard, Albert; Cline, Eric H.* The Aegean pottery at Megiddo: an appraisal and reanalysis. BASOR 309 (1998) 3-39.

10707 *Mizpa*: **Katz, Hayah** A note on the date of the 'great wall' of Tell en-Naṣbeh. TelAv 25 (1998) 131-133.

10708 *Qitmit*: **Beit-Arieh, Itzhaq** Horvat Qitmit: an Edomite shrine in the biblical Negev. [E]*Beck, Pirhiya*. 1995 ⇒11/2,b054. [R]PEQ 130 (1998) 69-70 (*Bienkowski, Piotr*).

10709 *Revadim*: **Gudovitch, Shlomo; Pipano, Shlomo** — מחצבת רבדים קבוצת חרם כלי משלחי התקופה הכלקוליתית [A late chalcolithic pottery assemblage from the Revadim quarry]. 'Atiqot 35 (1998) 1*-5* Sum. 159. **H**.

10710 *Rimmon*: **Horwitz, Liora Kolska** Animal bones from Ḥorbat Rimmon: Hellenistic to Byzantine periods. 'Atiqot 35 (1998) 65-76.

10711 *Tabaliya*: **Kogan-Zehavi, Elena** The tomb and memorial of a chain-wearing anchorite at Kh. Tabaliya, near Jerusalem. 'Atiqot 35 (1998) 135-149.

10712 *Timnah*: **Kelm, George L.; Mazar, Amihai** Timnah, a biblical city in the Sorek valley. 1995 ⇒11/2,b055... 13,10663. [R]JAOS 118 (1998) 440 (*Seger, Joe D.*); JBL 117 (1998) 339-341 (*Hallote, Rachel S.*).

T4.5 Samaria, Sharon

10713 [E]**Raban, Avner; Holum, Kenneth G.** Caesarea Maritima: a retrospective after two millennia. DMOA 21: 1996 ⇒12,10146. [R]PEQ 130 (1998) 84-85 (*Jacobson, David M.*) OLZ 93 (1998) 504-513 (*Japp, Sarah*).

10714 **Tappy, Ron E.** The archaeology of Israelite Samaria: Early Iron Age through the ninth century BCE. HSS 44: 1992 ⇒8,e500... 13,10681. [R]Or. 67 (1998) 294-299 (*Frendo, Anthony J.*).

10715 *Zadok, Ran* A prosopography of Samaria and Edom/Idumea. UF 30 (1998) 781-828.

10716 *Zertal, Adam* The Iron Age I culture in the hill-country of Canaan—a Manassite perspective. [F]DOTHAN, T. 1998 ⇒23. 238-250.

10717 *Bethel*: **Scibona, Rocco** Betel e le tradizioni cananaiche e orientali dell'Antico Testamento anteriore. BeO 40/2 (1998) 65-98.

10718 *Caesarea Maritima*: **Carvalho, José Carlos** A marca de Cesareia Marítima na história do Novo Testamento e na missão paolina [The mark of Maritime Caesarea in New Testament history and Paul's mission]. HumTeo 19 (1998) 279-292 Sum. 359.

10719 *Holum, Kenneth G.* Identity and the late antique city: the case of Caesarea. Religious... communities. 1998 ⇒347. 157-177.

10720 *Hillard, T.W.; Beness, J.L.* Postclassical effects on classical shoreline sites: Straton's Tower/Caesarea Maritima, Israel and Torone, Chalkidike, Greece. Res maritimae. 1998 ⇒491. 125-151.

10721   Ḍahret et-Tawile: Finkelstein, Israel Two notes on northern Samaria: the "Einun pottery" and the date of the "Bull site". PEQ 130 (1998) 94-98.
10722   Dor: Stern, Ephraim New Phoenician elements in the architecture of Tel Dor, Israel. ᶠFRERICHS, E. BJSt 320: 1998 ⇒28. 373-388.
10723   Stern, Ephraim Buried treasure: the silver hoard from Dor. BArR 24/4 (1998) 46-51.
10724   ʿEn Ḥagit: Wolff, Samuel An Iron Age I site at ʿEn Ḥagit (northern Ramat Menashe). ᶠDOTHAN, T. 1998 ⇒23. 449-454.
10725   Khirbet Ibreiktas: Kletter, Raz; Rapuano, Yehudah A Roman well at Khirbet Ibreiktas. ʿAtiqot 35 (1998) 43-64.
10726   Maḥoza D-Yamnin: Vitto, Fanny Maḥoza D-Yamnin: a mosaic floor from the time of Eudocia?. ʿAtiqot 35 (1998) 109-134.
10727   Michmetat: Liverani, Mario Amarna Mikmate—biblical Michmethath. ZDPV 114 (1998) 137-138.
10728   Mizpa: Zorn, Jeffrey R. Indiana Zorn and the web site of Tell en-Naṣbeh. NEA(BA) 61/4 (1998) 257.
10729   Saʿar Efraim: Barkai, Ran Shaʿar Ephraim south: a late Natufian campsite. TelAv 25 (1998) 94-103.
10730   Oren, Ronit; Scheftelowitz, Naʾama The Tel Teʾenim and Shaʿar Ephraim project. TelAv 25 (1998) 52-93.
10731   Samaria: Köckert, Matthias Samaria. TRE 29. 1998 ⇒501. 744-750.
10732   Shechem: Mallet, Joel La prétendue fortification de Tell el-Fârʿah à l'époque du Fer. UF 30 (1998) 511-514.
10733   Sumaqa: ᴱDar, Shimon Sumaqa: a Jewish village on the Carmel. TA 1998, Eretz 408 pp. $24/18. Num. ill. [IEJ 50,147—Katzenstein, Hannah].
10734   Tell el Farʿah: Amiet, Pierre; Briend, Jacques; Courtois, Liliane Tell el Farʿah: histoire, glyptique et céramologie. OBO.A 14: 1996 ⇒12,10152. ᴿCBQ 60 (1998) 594-595 (Jacobs, Paul F.).
10735   Tell el-Hesi: Bennett, W.J.; Blakely, J.A. Tell el-Hesi 3: Tell el-Hesi: the Persian period. 1989 ⇒8,e451. ᴿPEQ 130 (1998) 166-168 (Bourke, Stephen).

T4.6 Galilaea; Golan

10736   Aune, David E. Jesus and the Romans in Galilee: Jews and gentiles in the Decapolis. ᶠBETZ, H. 1998 ⇒10. 230-251.
10737   Frankel, Rafael Some notes on the work of the survey of Western Palestine in Western Galilee. PEQ 130 (1998) 99-105.
10738   Gal, Zvi Israel in exile: deserted Galilee testifies to Assyrian conquest of the northern kingdom. BArR 24/3 (1998) 49-53.
10739   González Echegaray, J.; Guijarro Oporto, S. La arqueología de Galilea y el Jesús historico. Actas... IX Jornadas Bíblicas. 1998 ⇒376. 87-107.
10740   Herbert, Sharon C. Tel Anafa I.1-2: Final report. 1997 ⇒13, 10693. ᴿAJA 102 (1998) 444-445 (Downey, Susan B.).
10741   Horsley, Richard A. Archaeology, history, and society in Galilee. 1996 ⇒12,10170; 13,10689. ᴿCBQ 60 (1998) 568-569 (Oakman, Douglas E.); JSJ 29 (1998) 106-109 (Reed, Jonathan L.).
10742   Horsley, Richard Conquest and social conflict in Galilee. Recruitment. 1998 ⇒320. 129-168.

10743 *Marucci, Corrado* L'ambiente culturale della Galilea al tempo di Gesù. RstB 10/1/2 (1998) 231-249.

10744 *Rosenfeld, Ben-Zion* **H**. Places of rabbinic settlement in the Galilee, 70-400 C.E.: periphery versus center. HUCA 69 (1998) *57-*103.

10745 *Syon, Danny* בית גיתות' 'דומי באכזיב [A winepress at Akhziv]. ʿAtiqot 34 (1998) 85-99 Sum. 7* **H**.

10746 **Banias**: *Wilson, John F.; Tzaferis, Vassilios* Banias dig reveals king's palace. BArR 24/1 (1998) 54-61, 85.

10747 **Beth Shan**: **Asher, Ovadiah; Yehudit, Turnheim** 'Peopled' scrolls in Roman architectural decoration in Israel: the Roman theatre at Beth Shean/Scythopolis. Rivista di Archeologia S.12: R 1994, Bretschneider 186 pp. Num. ill. [R]RAr (1997) 419-420 (*Dentzer-Feydy, Jacqueline*).

10748 **James, Frances W.; McGovern, Patrick E.** The Late Bronze Egyptian garrison at Beth Shan: a study of levels VII and VIII. 1993 ⇒11/2,b086... 13,10699. 2 vols. [R]PEQ 130 (1998) 79-80 (*Chapman, Rupert*).

10749 **Bethsaida**: **Bernett, Monika; Keel, Othmar** Mond, Stier und Kult am Stadttor: die Stele von Betsaida (et-Tell). OBO 161: Gö 1998, Vandenhoeck & R viii; 175 pp. €34,26. 3-525-53798-0. collab. *Münger, Stefan*; Bibl.

10750 *Kuhn, Heinz-Wolfgang* Der neueste Stand der Grabungen auf et-Tell (Betsaida/Julias). WUB 10 (1998) 78-80.

10751 **Strickert, Fred** Bethsaida: home of the apostles. Michael Glazier: ColMn 1998, Liturgical x; 187 pp. $20. 0-8146-5519-X [BiTod 37, 61—Senior, Donald].

10752 *Villeneuve, Estelle* Betsaida, Dorf der Apostel: eine neue Entdeck-ung?. WUB 8 (1998) 54.

10753 **Dan**: *Biran, Avraham* Sacred spaces of standing stones, high places and cult objects at Tel Dan. BArR 24/5 (1998) 38-45, 70.

10754 *Geus, C.H.J. de* Dertig jaar opgravingen op Tel Dan, Israël II. Phoenix 44/1 (1998) 21-38.

10755 **Golan**: **Epstein, Claire** The chalcolithic culture of the Golan. IAA Reports 4: J 1998, Israel Antiquities Authority 352 pp. 965-406-032-9. contrib. by *Tamar Noy*; Bibl.

10756 **Hazor**: *Arnaud, D*. Hazor à la fin de l'âge du Bronze d'après un document méconnu: RS 20.225. AulOr 16 (1998) 27-35.

10757 *Ben-Tor, Amnon; Ben-Ami, Doron* Hazor and the archaeology of the tenth century B.C.E.. IEJ 48 (1998) 1-37.

10758 *Ben-Tor, Amnon* The fall of Canaanite Hazor—the "who" and "when" questions. [F]DOTHAN, T. 1998 ⇒23. 456-467.

10759 *Malamat, Abraham* Mari and Hazor: the implication for the Middle Bronze Age chronology <1992>;

10760 Hazor once again in new Mari documents <1989>;

10761 Mari and Hazor: trade relations in the Old Babylonian period <1993>. Mari and the bible. 1998 ⇒173. 51-55/41-44/45-50.

10762 **Jezreel**: *Woodhead, John* Royal cities in the Kingdom of Israel. Capital cities. 1998 ⇒492. 111-116.

10763 **Khirbet et-Tuwal**: *Eisenberg, Emanuel* Khirbet et-Tuwal: salvage excavations at an EB IB settlement in the Bet Sheʾan valley. ʿAtiqot 35 (1998) 1-7.

10764 *Qana*: *Herrojo, Julián* Nuevas aportaciones para el estudio de Khirbet Qana. SBFLA 48 (1998) 345-356 Sum. 520.

10765 *Sepphoris*: *Meyers, Carol* Sepphoris and 'Ein Zippori: earliest times through the Persian period;

10766 *Meyers, Eric M.* The early Roman period at Sepphoris: chronological, archaeological, literary, and social considerations. [F]FRERICHS, E. BJSt 320: 1998 ⇒28. 331-342/343-355.

10767 *Rutgers, Leonard V.* Some reflections on the archaeological finds from the domestic quarter on the acropolis of Sepphoris. Religious ... communities. 1998 ⇒347. 179-195.

10768 *Zangenberg, Jürgen* Die "Perle Galiläas": jüngste Ausgrabungen im neutestamentliche Sepphoris. WUB 10 (1998) 76-77.

10769 *Taanach*: *Finkelstein, Israel* Notes on the stratigraphy and chronology of Iron Age Ta'anach. TelAv 25 (1998) 208-218.

10770 *Tel Na'ama*: *Greenberg, Raphael, al.,* A sounding at Tel Na'ama in the Hula valley. 'Atiqot 35 (1998) 9-35.

T4.8 *Transjordania*: (East-) Jordan

10771 *Bordreuil, Pierre* Eine lange gemeinsame Geschichte mit Israel. WUB 7 (1998) 19-23, 25.

10772 *Egan, Virginia; Bikai, Patricia M.* Archaeology in Jordan. AJA 102 (1998) 571-606.

10773 *Finkelstein, Israel* From sherds to history: review article. IEJ 48 (1998) 120-131.

10774 *Görg, Manfred* Namenkundliches zum nördlichen Ostjordanland. BN 92 (1998) 12-15.

10775 [E]**Henry, Donald O.** The prehistoric archaeology of Jordan. BAR internat. series 705: Oxf 1998, Archaeopress v; 207 pp. 0-86054-888-0.

10776 **Henry, Donald O.** Prehistorical cultural ecology and evolution: insights from southern Jordan. 1995 ⇒12,10230. [R]AJA 102 (1998) 188-189 (*Levy, Thomas E.*).

10777 *Ibrahim, Moawiyah M.; Mittmann, Siegfried* Eine chalkolithische Stierskulptur aus Nordjordanien. ZDPV 114 (1998) 101-105.

10778 *Khouri, Rami G.* Von den Nomaden zu den ersten Städten;

10779 *Knauf, Ernst Axel* Jordanien in der Bibel;

10780 *Lindner, Manfred* Die Edomiter in Südjordanien. WUB 7 (1998) 12-13, 15, 17/26-30/57-58.

10781 *Negbi, Ora* "Were there sea peoples in the central Jordan valley at the transition from the Bronze Age to the Iron Age?": once again. TelAv 25 (1998) 184-207.

10782 [E]*Piccirillo, Michele* Ricerca storico-archeologica in Giordania XVIII—1998. SBFLA 48 (1998) 525-560.

10783 *Pouzet, Louis* Von der arabischen Eroberung bis zu LAWRENCE von Arabien;

10784 *Villeneuve, François* Die wechselvolle Geschichte eines goldenen Zeitalters;

10785 Jordanien;

10786 *Zayadine, Fawzi* Biblische Traditionen und archäologische Entdeckungen. WUB 7 (1998) 62-64/37-38, 43, 47-49/2-11/31-35.

10787 *Zeitler, John P.* Früheisenzeitliche Keramik aus Südjordanien. [F]LINDNER, M., BBB 118: 1998 ⇒62. 22-33.

10788 **Abu Ḥamed**: *Dollfus, Geneviève; Kafafi, Zeidan* Abu Hamid am Ufer des Jordan. WUB 7 (1998) 14-15.

10789 **ʿArʿaq ʾel-ʾAmir**: *Netzer, E.* ארמונו הקסום של הורקנוס לבית טוביה בעבר־הירדן [The enchanted palace built by Hyrcanus the Tobiad in Transjordan]. Qad. 31 (1998) 117-122.

10790 **Ashtaroth**: *Galil, Gershon* Ashtaroth in the Amarna period. ᶠRAINEY, A. IOS 18: 1998 ⇒96. 373-385.

10791 **Braq, Ḥirbet**: *Farajat, Suleiman; Marahla, Mohammad; Falahat, Hani* The excavations at Khirbat Braq. ᶠLINDNER, M. BBB 118: 1998 ⇒62. 120-131.

10792 **el-Handadua**: *Chesson, Meredith S.* Preliminary results of excavations at Tell el-Handaduq South (1993-96). PEQ 130 (1998) 20-34.

10793 **el-ʿUmayri**: *Herr, Larry G.* Tell el-ʿUmayri and the Madaba plains region during the late Bronze-Iron Age I transition. ᶠDOTHAN, T. 1998 ⇒23. 251-264.

10794 **Es-Samra**: ᴱ**Humbert, Jean-Baptiste; Desreumaux, Alain** Fouilles de Khirbet es-Samra en Jordanie, v.1: la voie romaine, le cimetière, les documents épigraphiques. Bibliothèque de l'Antiquité tardive: [Turnhout] 1998, Brepols xv; 674 pp. 2-503-50909-X. Bibl. 627-659.

10795 **Eṣ-Ṣifiya**: *Bienert, Hans-Dieter; Mahasneh, Hamzeh M.* Eṣ-Ṣifiya—eine Siedlung des frühen Neolithikums in Südjordanien. ᶠLINDNER, M. BBB 118: 1998 ⇒62. 9-21.

10796 **Gerasa**: *Gatier, Pierre-Louis* Dscherasch, das antike Gerasa. WUB 7 (1998) 49-52.

10797 *Kennedy, David* The identity of Roman Gerasa: an archaeological approach. Identities. 1998 ⇒469. 39-69.

10798 *Seigne, Jacques; Agusta-Boularot, Sandrine* Milliaires anciens et nouveaux de Gerasa. MEFRA 110/1 (1998) 261-295.

10799 **Ḥamid**: *Tal, Oren; Blockman, Noga A* salvage excavation at Tel Ḥamid (the lower terrace). TelAv 25 (1998) 142-173.

10800 **Ḥarra**: ᴱ**Betts, A.V.G.** The Harra and the Hamad: excavations and explorations in Eastern Jordan, 1. Sheffield archaeological monographs 9: Shf 1998, Academic al. xx; 252 pp. 1-85075-614-7.

10801 **Heshbon**: *LaBianca, Ölystein Sakala; Ray, Paul J.* Preliminary report of the 1997 excavations and restoration work at Tall Hisban (June 18 to July 11, 1997). AUSS 36/2 (1998) 245-257.

10802 **ʿIraq al-Amir**: *Ji, Chang-Ho C.* A new look at the Tobiads in ʿIraq al-Amir. SBFLA 48 (1998) 417-440 Sum. 520.

10803 **Jabesch-Gilead**: *Fischer, Peter M.* Tell Abu al-Charaz—das biblische Jabesch?. WUB 7 (1998) 23-24.

10804 **Mukhayyat**: *Michel, Anne* Trois campagnes de fouilles à Saint-Georges de Khirbat al-Mukhayyat (1995-1997): rapport final. SBFLA 48 (1998) 357-416 Sum. 520.

10805 **Nebo**: **Piccirillo, Michele; Alliata, Eugenio** Mount Nebo: new archaeological excavations 1967-1997. SBF.CMa 27: J 1998, Studium Biblicum Franciscanum 2 vols. Bibl. ᴿRivAC 74 (1998) 643-646 (*Severini, Francesca*):

10806 Objects from Mount Nebo: colour plates. 543-549;

10807 *Acconci, Alessandra* Elements of the liturgical furniture. 468-542.

10808 *Alliata, Eugenio; Bianchi, Susanna* The architectural phasing of the memorial of Moses. 151-191;

10809   *Benedettucci, Francesco; Sabelli, Roberto* The edifice at Rujm al-
        Mukhayyat. 128-131;
10810   The iron age. 110-127;
10811   *Cortese, Enzo; Niccacci, Alviero* Nebo in biblical tradition. 53-64;
10812   *Di Segni, Leah* The Greek inscriptions. 425-467;
10813   *Gitler, Haim* The coins. 550-567;
10814   *Marino, Luigi* New architectural surveys at Siyagha: observations
        on certain materials, structures and their state of conservation. 568-
        603;
10815   *Michel, Anne* The liturgical installations. 390-412;
10816   *Mortensen, Peder; Thuesen, Ingolf* The prehistoric periods. 85-99;
10817   *Ognibene, Susanna* The iconophobic dossier. 373-389;
10818   *Palumbo, Gaetano* The bronze age. 100-109;
10819   *Piccirillo, Michele* Pilgrims' texts. 71-83;
10820   The mosaics. 265-371;
10821   The churches on Mount Nebo: new discoveries. 221-263;
10822   The monastic presence. 193-219;
10823   The Roman Esbus-Livias road. 133-149;
10824   *Sabelli, Roberto; Dinelli, Ombretta* The region of Nebo: an area to
        be protected. 604-608;
10825   *Sanmorì, Chiara* The funerary practices. 413-424;
10826   *Piccirillo Michele; Alliata, Eugenio; Bianchi, Susanna* Analisi
        delle stratigrafie murarie del memoriale di Mosè sul Monte Nebo.
        ᴹFRANKFORT H. 1998 ⇒26. 437-462.

10827   **Pella**: *Hennessy, B.* Pella, eine reiche und befestigte Stadt. WUB 7
        (1998) 16-17.
10828   *Kieweler, H.-V.* Pella—die Geschichte einer Stadt. JSem 9 (1997)
        1-38 Sum. 1.
10829   **Petra**: **Amadasi Guzzo, Maria Giulia; Equini Schneider,
        Eugenia** Petra. Mü 1998, Hirmer 203 pp. €65,45. 3-7774-7880-6.
        Num. ill. [ZDPV 115,99ss—Wenning, Robert].
10830   *Bienert, Hans-Dieter; Lamprichs, Roland* Der archäologische
        Fundplatz Baʾja I: Keramik der Oberfläche: eine Auswahl. UF 30
        (1998) 97-131.
10831   **Bignasca, A.** Petra—Ez. Zantur I: Ergebnisse der Schweizerisch-
        Liechtensteinischen Ausgrabungen 1988-1992. Terra Achaeologica
        2: 1996 ⇒12,10258. ᴿMes. 33 (1998) 384-387 (*Messina, V.*).
10832   *Donner, Herbert* Die Klause, die der Schlucht den Namen gab
        (BRÜNNOW—DOMASZEWSKI Nr.460; DALMAN Nr.424).
        ᶠLINDNER, M. BBB 118: 1998 ⇒62. 110-119.
10833   *Gebel, Hans Georg K.* Die Petra-Region im 7. Jt. v. Chr.: Betrach-
        tungen zu Ausbildung und Auflösung einer frühneolithischen Sied-
        lungskammer. ᶠLINDNER, M. BBB 118: 1998 ⇒62. 1-8.
10834   *Joukowsky, Martha Sharp* Brown University 1997 excavations at
        the Petra Great Temple. ADAJ 42 (1998) 293-318;
10835   The Petra great temple project, 1993-1995: a three year assessment.
        ᶠFRERICHS, E. BJSt 320: 1998 ⇒28. 291-312.
10836   *Knauf, Ernst-Axel* Götter nach Petra tragen. ᶠLINDNER, M. BBB
        118: 1998 ⇒62. 92-101.
10837   *Kolb, Bernhard* Swiss-Liechtenstein excavations at Az-Zanṭūr in
        Petra 1997. ADAJ 42 (1998) 259-277.
10838   *McKenzie, J.S.; Reyes, A.T.; Schmidt-Colinet, A.* Faces in the rock
        at Petra and Median Saleh. PEQ 130 (1998) 35-50.

10839 *Merklein, Helmut; Wenning, Robert* Ein Verehrungsplatz der Isis in Petra neu untersucht. ZDPV 114 (1998) 162-178;

10840 Ein neuentdeckter Augenbetyl in der Ḥremiye-Schlucht nebst einer Übersicht über die bekannten nabatäischen Augenbetyle. ^FLINDNER, M. BBB 118: 1998 ⇒62. 71-91.

10841 *Nehmé, Laila* Petra, die Hauptstadt der Nabatäer. WUB 7 (1998) 39-42.

10842 *Parlasca, Klaus* Bemerkungen zum Isiskult in Petra. ^FLINDNER, M. BBB 118: 1998 ⇒62. 64-70.

10843 *Wright, George R.H.* The Khazne at Petra: its nature in the light of its name. DaM 10 (1998) 131-134.

10844 **Quṣer ʿAmra:** *Bisheh, Ghazi; Vibert-Guigue, Claude* Die omaijadischen Badeanlagen von Qusair Amra. WUB 7 (1998) 65-67.

10845 **Umm el-Jimal:** *De Vries, Bert, al.,* Umm el-Jimal: a frontier town and its landscape in northern Jordan. Journal of Roman archaeology, Suppl. 26: Portsmouth 1998, [Journal of Roman Archaeology] 248 pp. 1-887829-26-1. Bibl.

T5.1 Phoenicia—*Libanus*, Lebanon

10846 ^E**Sader, Hélène S.; Scheffler, Thomas; Neuwirth, Angelika** Baalbek: image and monument 1898-1998. Beiruter Texte und Studien 69: Stu 1998, Steiner xiv; 350 pp.

10847 **Briquel-Chatonnet, Françoise** Les relations entre les cités de la côte phénicienne et les royaumes d'Israël et de Juda. 1992 ⇒8, e636...11/2,b207. ^RAbr-n. 35 (1998) 150-152 (*Bunnens, Guy*).

10848 **Davie, May** Beyrouth au temps de la visite de Guillaume II en 1898. Baalbek. 1998 ⇒10846. 97-114.

10849 **Elayi, Josette; Sayegh, H.** Un quartier du port phénicien de Beyrouth au fer III / Perse: les objets. TEuph.S 6: P 1998, Gabalda 365 pp. 2-85021-111-7. Bibl.

10850 *Gaube, Heinz* Islamic Baalbek: the Qalʿah, the mosques and other buildings. Baalbek. 1998, 305-332.

10851 A German archaeologist in Baalbek: sketches by Walter Andrae (1898/99). Baalbek. 1998 ⇒10846. 173-182.

10852 ^E**Hakimian, Suzy; Rifaï, Toufic** Baalbek: 50 ans d'activité archéologique libanaise. Baalbek. 1998 ⇒10846. 341-347.

10853 *Hanssen, Jens* Imperial Discourses and an Ottoman excavation in Lebanon. Baalbek. 1998 ⇒10846. 157-172.

10854 *Hoffmann, Adolf* Terrace and temple: remarks on the architectural history of the temple of Jupiter in Baalbek;

10855 *Knauf, Ernst Axel* The Ituraeans: another Bedouin state. Baalbek. 1998 ⇒10846. 279-304/269-277.

10856 *Krumeich, Ralf* Darstellungen syrischer Priester an den kaiserzeitlichen Tempeln von Niha und Chehim im Libanon. DaM 10 (1998) 171-200.

10857 *Lankes, Hans Christian* The tablets of Baalbek. Baalbek. 1998 ⇒10846. 235-244.

10858 *Lembke, Katja* Die phönizischen anthropoiden Sarkophage aus den Nekropolen der Insel Arados. DaM 10 (1998) 97-130.

10859 *Lemke, Wolf-Dieter* The Kaiser in Lebanon: a collage;
10860 *Makdisi, Ussama* The "rediscovery" of Baalbek: a metaphor for empire in the nineteenth-century;
10861 *Nippa, Annegret* Curious self-representations: Baalbek and its visitors;
10862 *Reinstrom, Hinrich R.* Baalbek: the visitor's book of the Hotel Palmyra and German visitors 1888-1918;
10863 *Ruprechtsberger, Erwin M.* Archaeological and geodetical research in Baalbek;
10864 *Sader, Hélène; Scheffler, Thomas* Baalbek: an imperial visit and its consequences;
10865 *Sader, Hélène; Van Ess, Margarete* Looking for Pre-Hellenistic Baalbek;
10866 *Scheffler, Thomas* The Kaiser in Baalbek: tourism, archaeology, and the politics of imagination;
10867 *Sinno, Abdel-Raouf* The Emperor's visit to the east as reflected in contemporary Arabic journalism. Baalbek. 51-88/137-156/183-198/199-219/333-339/1-9/247-268/13-49/115-133.
10868 *Thalmann, Jean-Paul* In den Trümmern des Tell Arka. WUB 8 (1998) 54.
10869 *Tohme, Annie* Le Festival de Baalbek au carrefour des paradoxes libanais d'avant guerre. Baalbek. 1998 ⇒10846. 221-234.

T5.2 *Situs mediterranei* phoenicei et punici

10870 *Elayi, J.* Une nouvelle grotte cultuelle à Ibiza?. Transeuphratène 15 (1998) 55-67.
10871 **Vidal González, Pablo** La isla de Malta en época fenicia y punica. 1996 ⇒12,10286. ᴿAJA 102 (1998) 437 (*Gomez Bellard, Carlos*).

T5.4 Ugarit—*Ras Šamra*

10872 *Aboud, J.* Abschnitte vom Aqhat-Epos neu übersetzt und analysiert;
10873 *Astour, Michael C.* RDMN / RHADAMANTHYS and the motif of selective immortality. ᶠLORETZ O. AOAT 250: 1998 ⇒65. 1-13/ 55-89.
10874 **Baldacci, Massimo** Il libro dei morti dell'antica Ugarit. CasM 1998, Piemme 222 pp. 88-384-2992-8.
10875 *Blau, Joshua* On problems of polyphony and archaism in Ugaritic spelling. Topics in Hebrew... linguistics. 1998 <1968> ⇒136. 339-343.
10876 *Bonnet, Corinne* Les lettres de René DUSSAUD à Franz CUMONT conservées à l'Academia Belgica de Rome;
10877 *Bordreuil, Pierre* Le premier mot de l'herminette inscrite découverte à Ras Shamra en 1929: outil ou personnage?. ᶠLORETZ O. AOAT 250: 1998 ⇒65. 109-125/127-132.
10878 **Callot, Olivier** Ras-Shamra-Ougarit, X: la tranchée 'ville Sud': études d'architecture domestique. 1994 ⇒10,12480... 12,10291 ᴿRAr (1998/1) 145-147 (*Huot, Jean-Louis*); ᴿJAOS 118 (1998) 599-600 (*Dunham, Sally*) Syr. 75 (1998) 316-319 (*Vallet, Régis*).

10879 *Clines, David J.A.* Krt 111-114 (I iii 7-10): gatherers of wood and drawers of water. OT essays, 2. JSOT.S 293: 1998 <1976> 595-601.

10880 *Contenson, H. de* Ras Shamra et Mersin: état de la question. Paléorient 24/2 (1998) 111-113 Rés. sum. 111.

10881 *Cunchillos Ilarri, Jesús-Luis* Cadenas Quebradas. ^FLORETZ O. AOAT 250: 1998 ⇒65. 151-174.

10882 *Dalix, Anne-Sophie* Šuppiluliuma (II?) dans un texte alphabétique d'Ugarit et la date d'apparition de l'alphabet cunéiforme: nouvelle proposition de datation des 'Archives Ouest'. Sem. 48 (1998) 5-15 Sum. 5.

10883 *Dietrich, M.; Loretz, O.* Amurru, Yaman und die ägäischen Inseln nach den ugaritischen Texten. ^FRAINEY, A. IOS 18: 1998 ⇒96. 335-363;

10884 'Siehe da war er (wieder) munter!': die mythologische Begründung für eine medikamentöse Behandlung in KTU 1.114 (RS 24.258). ^FGORDON, C. JSOT.S 273: 1998 ⇒31. 174-198.

10885 *Dijkstra, Meindert* Astral myth of the birth of Shahar and Shalim (KTU 1.23). ^FLORETZ O. AOAT 250: 1998 ⇒65. 265-287.

10886 *Freu, Jacques* La fin d'Ugarit et de l'empire hittite: données nouvelles et chronologie. Sem. 48 (1998) 17-39 Sum. 17.

10887 *Gordon, Cyrus H.* Father's sons and mother's daughters in Ugaritic, in the ancient Near East and in Mandaic magic texts. ^FLORETZ O. AOAT 250: 1998 ⇒65. 319-324.

10888 *Greenstein, Edward L.* New readings in the Kirta Epic. ^FRAINEY, A. IOS 18: 1998 ⇒96. 105-123.

10889 *Healey, John F.* The kindly and merciful god: on some Semitic divine epithets. ^FLORETZ O. AOAT 250: 1998 ⇒65. 349-356.

10890 *Khoury, Adel Theodor* Eine koranische Predigt über Mose 20,1-76. ^FLORETZ O. AOAT 250: 1998 ⇒65. 427-435.

10891 *Korpel, Marjo C.A.* Exegesis in the work of Ilimilku of Ugarit. Intertextuality. OTS 40: 1998 ⇒394. 86-111.

10892 *Olmo Lete, G. del* A ritual for the country's salvation, KTU 1.162: a reappraisal. ^FGORDON, C. JSOT.S 273: 1998 ⇒31. 164-173.

10893 *Olmo Lete, G. del; Sanmartín, J.* Kultisches in den keilalphabetischen Verwaltungs- und Wirtschaftstexten aus Ugarit. ^FLORETZ O. AOAT 250: 1998 ⇒65. 175-197.

10894 *Pitard, Wayne T.* The binding of *yamm*: a new edition of the Ugaritic text KTU 1.83. JNES 57 (1998) 261-280.

10895 *Pope, Marvin A.* Adam, Edom and Holocaust. ^FGORDON, C. JSOT.S 273: 1998 ⇒31. 199-210.

10896 *Sivan, Daniel* The use of QTL and YQTL forms in the Ugaritic verbal system. ^FRAINEY, A. IOS 18: 1998 ⇒96. 89-103.

10897 **Smith, Mark S.** The Ugaritic Baal cycle, vol. 1: introduction with text, translation and commentary of KTU 1.1-1.2. VT.S 55: 1994 ⇒10,9107... 12,7801. ^RRB 105 (1998) 613-614 (*Tarragon, J.-M. de*); JNES 57 (1998) 46-48 (*Pardee, Dennis*).

10898 *Smith, Mark S.* Terms of endearment: Dog (klbt) and calf ('gl) in KTU 1.3 III 44-45. ^FLORETZ O. AOAT 250: 1998 ⇒65. 713-716.

10899 *Spronk, Klaas* Down with Hêlel!: the assumed mythological background of Isa. 14:12. ^FLORETZ O. AOAT 250: 1998 ⇒65. 717-26.

10900 *Tarragon, Jean-Michel de* Le rituel ugaritique KTU 1.40: quelques réflexions. ^FLoretz O. AOAT 250: 1998, 727-732

10901   *Tropper, Josef* Zur Sprache der Kurzalphabettexte aus Ugarit. [F]LO-
        RETZ O. AOAT 250: 1998 ⇒65. 733-738.
10902   *Van Soldt, Wilfred* Studies in the topography of Ugarit (3): groups
        of towns and their locations. UF 30 (1998) 703-744.
10903   **Vita, Juan-Pablo** El ejército de Ugarit. 1995 ⇒11/2,a349; 13,
        10849. [R]Or. 67 (1998) 139-143 (*Heltzer, Michael*).
10904   *Vita, Juan-Pablo* Datation et genres littéraires à Ougarit. Temps
        vécu. 1998 ⇒445. 39-52.
10905   **Wyatt, Nick** Religious texts from Ugarit: the words of Ilimilku and
        his colleagues. BiSe 53: Shf 1998, Academic 500 pp. £23. 1-
        85075-847-6. Bibl.
10906   *Yon, Marguerite* Ougarit et le port de Mahadou/Minet el-Beida.
        Res maritimae. 1998 ⇒491. 357-369.

T5.5 **Ebla**

10907   *Archi, Alfonso* The high priestess, dam-dingir, at Ebla. [F]LORETZ O.
        AOAT 250: 1998 ⇒65. 43-53;
10908   Two heads for the king of Ebla. [F]GORDON, C. JSOT.S 273: 1998
        ⇒31. 386-396.
10909   *Catagnoti, Amalia; Bonechi, Marco* Magic and divination at IIIrd
        millenium Ebla, 1: textual typologies and preliminary lexical
        approach. SEL 15 (1998) 17-39.
10910   [E]**Fronzaroli, Pelio** Miscellanea eblaitica, 4. QuSem 19: 1997 ⇒13,
        10866. [R]ArOr 66 (1998) 169-170 (*Segert, Stanislav*).
10911   **Fronzaroli, Pelio** Testi rituali della regalità (archivio L.2769).
        1993 ⇒10,12487*. [R]JAOS 118 (1998) 82-84 (*Biga, Maria G.*).
10912   *Gordon, Cyrus H.* Personal names of the "verb+deity" type from
        Ebla. Rencontre Assyriologique 34. 1998 ⇒452. 341-344.
10913   *Loretz, Oswald* Eblaitisch *Larugatu* = ugaritisch *lrgt*: Traditionen
        der Yariḫ-Verehrung in Ugarit. UF 30 (1998) 489-496.
10914   **Pagan, Joseph Martin** A morphological and lexical study of per-
        sonal names in the Ebla texts. ARET 3; ARES 3: R 1998, Missione
        Archeologica Italiana in Siria xix; 422 pp.
10915   *Pomponio, Francesco* The exchange ratio between silver and gold
        in the administrative texts of Ebla. Acta Sumerologica (Hiroshima)
        20 (1998) 127-134.
10916   *Xella, Paolo* The Eblaite god NIdabal. [F]LORETZ O. AOAT 250:
        1998 ⇒65. 883-895.

T5.8 **Situs effossi Syriae in ordine alphabetico**

10917   *Aurenche, Olivier* L'apport français au développement de la préhis-
        toire du Levant (1960-1997). Syr. 75/1 (1998) 9-14.
10918   *Falsone, Gioacchino* Tell Shiyukh Tahtani on the Euphrates: the
        University of Palermo salvage excavations in North Syria (1993-
        94). Akkadica 109-110 (1998) 22-64.
10919   *Martin, Lutz* Deutsche archäologische Feldforschungen zu vorhelle-
        nistischen Perioden in Syrien. AltOrF 25 (1998) 265-284.

10920   *Afis*: *Mazzoni, S.* Une nouvelle stèle d'époque araméenne de Tell
        Afis (Syrie) (Pls. I-VI). Transeuphratène 16 (1998) 9-19.

10921 *Aleppo*: *Khayyata, Wahid; Kohlmeyer, Kay* Die Zitadelle von Aleppo—vorläufiger Bericht über die Untersuchungen 1996 und 1997. DaM 10 (1998) 69-96

10922 *Amarna*: *Abu Assaf, Ali* Zur Datierung einer Statuette aus Tall Amarna in Syrien. DaM 10 (1998) 65-68.

10923 *Antioch Orontes*: *Patitucci, Stella* I castelli del principato d'Antiochia in rapporto alla viabilità: il settore settentrionale;

10924 *Uggeri, Giovanni* Antiochia sull'Oronte: profilo storico-urbanistico. V Simposio di Tarso. 1998 ⇒395. 331-356/301-329.

10925 *Apamea*: *Balty, Jean-Charles* "Hellenistische Überraschung" in Apameia. WUB 8 (1998) 53.

10926 *Atif*: *Fortin, Michel* Les fouilles canadiennes à Tell Atif (IIIe Mill.) sur le Moyen Khabour, en Syrie du Nord. Rencontre Assyriologique Internationale 34. 1998 ⇒452. 407-412;

10927 *'Atiǧ*: New Horizons in ancient Syria: the view from 'Atij. NEA (BA) 61/1 (1998) 15-24.

10928 *Banat*: *Porter, Anne; McClellan, Thomas* The third millennium settlement complex at Tell Banat: results of the 1994 excavations. DaM 10 (1998) 11-63.

10929 *Carchemish*: *Özyar, Aslı* The use and abuse of re-use at Karkamish. [F]ÇAMBEL H. 1998 ⇒4. 633-640.

10930 *Dura-Europos*: *Downey, Susan* Cult reliefs at Dura-Europos: problems of interpretation and placement. DaM 10 (1998) 201-210.

10931 *Halawa*: *Lüth, Friedrich* Von der befestigten Siedlung zur Tempelzitadelle: der vor- und frühdynastische Hügel B von Halawa, Nordsyrien. Rencontre Assyriologique 34. 1998 ⇒452. 23-31.

10932 *Hammam et-Turkman*: *Van Loon, Maurtis* The 1986 Excavation at Hammam et-Turkman. Rencontre Assyriologique 34. 1998 ⇒452. 677-680.

10933 *Hauran*: *Sartre-Fauriat, Annie* Culture et société dans le Hauran (Syrie du Sud) d'après les épigrammes funéraires (IIIe-Ve siècles ap: J.-C.). Syr. 75/1 (1998) 213-224.

10934 *Hazna*: *Munchaev, Rauf M.; Merpert, N.Ya.* Tell Hazna I—the most ancient cult centre in north-east Syria. [F]ÇAMBEL H. 1998 ⇒4. 499-514.

10935 *Kamid el-Loz*: *Weippert, Helga* Kumidi: die Ergebnisse der Ausgrabungen auf dem Tell Kamid el-Loz in den Jahren 1963 bis 1981. ZDPV 114 (1998) 1-38.

10936 *Mari*: *Finet, André* Mari et le Nord. Rencontre Assyriologique Internationale 34. 1998 ⇒452. 315-320.

10937 *Fleming, Daniel E.* Mari and the possibilities of biblical memory. RA 92 (1998) 41-78.

10938 *Heintz, Jean-Georges; Bodi, Daniel; Millot, Lison* Bibliographie de Mari: Supplément VII [1996-1997—Addenda & corrigenda—édition du 31 Déc. 1997]. Akkadica 109-110 (1998) 1-21.

10939 *Malamat, Abraham* Mari and its relations with the eastern Mediterranean. Mari and the bible. 1998 ⇒173. 33-40;

10940 Mari and its relations with the eastern mediterranean. [F]GORDON, C. JSOT.S 273: 1998 ⇒31. 411-418.

10941 **Ras Ibn Hani**: **Bounni, Adnan; Lagarce, Elisabeth; Lagarce, Jacques** Ras Ibn Hani, 1: le palais nord du Bronze Récent: fouilles 1979-1995, synthèse préliminaire. BAH 151: Beirut 1998, Institut

Français d'Archéologie du Proche-Orient 211 pp. 168 fig.; Préf.
Jean Leclant [RSFen 27,208s—Bartolini, Piero].
10942 *Til-Barsip*: *Jamieson, Andrew S.* Ceramic vessels from the Middle
Bronze Age jar burial F167 at Tell Ahmar. Abr-n. 35 (1998) 106-
119.

T6.1 Mesopotamia, *generalia*

10943 *Hauser, Stefan R.* Siehst du die Zeichen an der Wand?: zum Ende
altorientalischer Kultur. Zwischen Euphrat und Indus. 1998 ⇒318.
251-268.
10944 **Huot, Jean-Louis** Les premiers villageois de Mésopotamie. 1994
⇒11/2,b379. ᴿAJA 102 (1998) 624-625 (*Goring-Morris, Nigel*).
10945 **Kuklick, Bruce** Puritans in Babylon: the ancient Near East and
American intellectual life, 1880-1930. 1996 ⇒10,364. ᴿIJMES 30
(1998) 584-586 (*Maidman, Maynard P.*); JR 78 (1998) 122-123
(*Pals, Daniel L.*).
10946 *Merluzzi, Emanauela* Archeologia e luoghi di produzione artigiana-
le in Mesopotamia dal periodo protodinastico al paleobabilonese:
limiti e prospettive. ᴹFRANKFORT H. 1998 ⇒26. 329-349.
10947 **Potts, Daniel T.** Mesopotamian civilization: the material foundations. 1997 ⇒13,10919. ᴿAJA 102 (1998) 621-22 (*Roaf, Michael*).
10948 **Wilkinson, T.J.; Tucker, D.J.** Settlement development in the
north Jazira, Iraq. 1995 ⇒11/2,b395; 13,10367. ᴿOr. 67 (1998)
134-135 (*Kessler, Karlheinz*).

10949 **Parpola, Simo** Letters from Assyrian and Babylonian scholars.
SAAS 10: Helsinki 1993, University Press xxxix; 421 pp. FM396.
ᴿJAOS 118 (1998) 447 (*Jas, R.M.*).
10950 **Pedersén, Olof** Katalog der beschrifteten Objekte aus Assur.
ADOG 23: Saarbrücken 1997, SDV xxxvii; 345 pp.

T6.5 Situs effossi Iraq *in ordine alphabetico*

10951 *Curtis, John Briggs* British Museum excavations in the Saddam
Dam Salvage Project. Rencontre Assyr. 34. 1998 ⇒452. 393-398.

10952 *al-Rimah*: *Howard-Carter, Theresa* Shreds of Anatolian evidence
at Tell al-Rimah. Rencontre Assyr. 34. 1998 ⇒452. 109-119.
10953 **Postgate, Carolyn; Oates, David & Joan** The excavation at Tell
al-Rimah: the pottery. Wiltshire 1998, Aris & Phillips 275 pp.
£35/$75. 0-85668-700-6.
10954 *Assur*: *Mébarki, Farah* Die Hauptstadt Assur. WUB 10 (1998) 66-
71.
10955 **Miglus, Peter A.** Das Wohngebiet von Assur: Stratigraphie und
Architektur. WVDOG 93: 1996 ⇒12,10368. 2 vols. ᴿMes. 33
(1998) 364-366 (*Fiorina, P.*).
10956 *Babylon*: *Marzahn, Joachim* Babylon in der Geschichte. WUB 8
(1998) 62-67.
10957 **Schmid, Hansjörg** Der Tempelturm Etemenanki in Babylon. 1995
⇒11/2,6403; 13,10924. ᴿJAOS 118 (1998) 284-286 (*Dunham,
Sally*).

10958 **Dur-Kurigalzu**: *Mayer-Opificius, Ruth* Einige Funde aus Dur-Kuri-galzu. [F]RÖMER, W. AOAT 253: 1998 ⇒97. 263-266.
10959 *Gadara*: *Weber, Thomas* "Attika im Assyrerland". WUB 7 (1998) 54-56.
10960 **Khatuniyeh**: **Curtis, J.; Green, A.** Excavations at Khirbet Khatuniyeh: Saddam Dam report II. 1997 ⇒13,10927. [R]JRAS 8 (1998) 439-440 *(Collins, Paul)*.
10961 *Nineveh*: *Collon, Dominique* Ninive, die furchterregende assyrische Eroberin. WUB 9 (1998) 82-87.
10962 *Lanfranchi, Giovanni B.* The library at Nineveh. Capital cities. 1998 ⇒492. 147-156.
10963 **Matthiae, Paolo** Ninive. Centri e monumenti dell'antichità: Mi 1998, Electa 217 pp. 88-435-6208-8. Bibl.
10964 *Reade, Julian* LAYARD's *Nineveh and its remains*. Antiquity 72 (1998) 913-916.
10965 *Reader, J.E.* Greco-Parthian Nineveh. Iraq 60 (1998) 65-83.
10966 **Russell, John Malcolm** The final sack of Nineveh: the discovery, documentation, and destruction of King Sennacherib's throne room at Nineveh, Iraq. NHv 1998, Yale University Press 248 pp. £40/ $60. 0-300-07418-2. Bibl.
10967 *Nippur*: **Cole, Steven William** Nippur IV: the early Neo-Babylonian governor's archive from Nippur. 1996 ⇒12,10398. [R]JAOS 118 (1998) 443-444 *(Dandamayev, M.)*;
10968 Nippur in late Assyrian Times, c. 755-612 BC. SAAS 4: 1996 ⇒ 12,10397; 13,10934. [R]JAOS 118 (1998) 444-5 *(Dandamayev, M.)*.
10969 *Nuzi*: *Carnahan, J.W., al.,* Nuzi notes, 36-53;
10970 *Fincke, Jeanette* Appendix to EN 10/2: transliterations of selected EN 10/2 texts joined to previously published texts;
10971 Excavations at Nuzi 10/2, 66-174;
10972 Nuzi fragments from the estate of R.F.S. Starr. General studies... Nuzi 10/2. 1998 ⇒10975. 189-215/375-384/219-373/63-70.
10973 **Lacheman, E.R.; Morrison, M.A.; Owen, D.I.** The eastern archives of Nuzi; Studies on the civilization and culture of Nuzi and the Hurrians 4. Excavations at Nuzi 9/2: WL 1993, Eisenbrauns xii: 420 pp. $65. [R]ZA 88 (1998) 157-159 *(Müller, G.G.W.)*.
10974 **Müller, Gerfrid G.W.** Londoner Nuzi-Texte. SANTAG 4: Wsb 1998, Harrassowitz 285 pp. 3-447-04040-8.
10975 [E]**Owen, David I.; Wilhelm, Gernot** General studies and excavations at Nuzi 10/2. Studies on the civilization and culture of Nuzi and the Hurrians 9: Bethesda, MD 1998, CDL viii; 396 pp. 1-8830-53-26-9.
10976 *Scafa, Paola Negri* "ana pani abulli šat1ir": gates in the texts of the city of Nuzi. General studies... Nuzi 10/2. ⇒10975. 139-162.
10977 *Sippar*: *Al-Jadir, Walid* Decouverte d'une bibliothèque dans le temple de la ville de Sippar (Abu Habbah). Rencontre Assyriologique Internationale 34. 1998 ⇒452. 707-715.
10978 *Ur*: *Maekawa, Kazuya* Ur III Girsu records of labor forces in the British Museum. Acta Sumerologica (Hiroshima) 20 (1998) 63-110.
10979 *Sigrist, Marcel* The social landscape of the capital city: Ur. Capital cities. 1998 ⇒492. 157-167.
10980 *Uruk*: *Holloway, Steven W.* Sargon II and his redactors repair Eanna of Uruk. BR 43 (1998) 22-49.

10981   **Liverani, Mario** Uruk: la prima città. Biblioteca Essenziale
        Laterza 16: R 1998, Laterza viii, 138 pp. 88-420-5622-7. Bibl.
10982   *Pomponio, Francesco; Rositani, Annunziata* Rim-Anum di Uruk.
        ᶠLORETZ O. AOAT 250: 1998 ⇒65. 635-649.
10983   *Scholz, Bernhard* Korruption im seleukidischen Uruk?. Rencontre
        Assyriologique Internationale 34. 1998 ⇒452. 641-649.
10984   **Weiher, Egbert von** Teil 5: spätbabylonische Texte aus dem Plan-
        quadrat U 18. Uruk. Ausgrabungen in Uruk-Warka Endberichte 13:
        Mainz 1998, Von Zabern vii; (2) 199 pp. 3-8053-1850-2.
        Deutsches Archäol. Inst. Orient-Abt.

T6.7 Arabia

10985   **Breton, Jean-François** L'Arabie heureuse au temps de la reine de
        Saba': VIIIᵉ-Iᵉʳ siècle av. J.-C. La vie quotidienne: P 1998,
        Hachette 250 pp. 2-01-235373-8.
10986   **Crawford, Harriet E.W.** Dilmun and its Gulf neighbours. C 1998,
        CUP xiii; 170 pp. 0-521-58679-8. Bibl.

T6.9 Iran, *Persia*, Asia centralis

10987   **Archäologische Mitteilungen aus Iran** B 1995/1996, Reimer 88
        pl. 28 viii; 440 pp. €89,48. 0066-6033. ᴿMes. 33 (1998) 327-331
        (*Lippolis, C.*).
10988   *Hauben, H.* An American architect in Iran and Afghanistan: the
        John B. McCool correspondence (August-December 1937), part 2:
        the documents. OLoP 29 (1998) 241-269.
10989   *Perrot, Jean* Birth of a city: Susa. Capital cities. 1998 ⇒492. 83-
        97.
10990   ᴱ**Sarkhosh Curtis, Vesta; Hillenbrand, Robert; Rogers, J.M.**
        The art and archaeology of ancient Persia: new light on the Parthian
        and Sasanian empires. L 1998, Tauris xvi; 192 pp. 1-8606-4045-1.

T7.1 Ægyptus, *generalia*

10991   **Andreu, Guillemette** Egypt in the age of the pyramids. ᵀ*Lorton,*
        David: L 1997, Murray £20. 0-7195-5419-5 [Egyptian Archaeol-
        ogy 12,26—Hart, George].
10992   **Arnaudiès, Alain; Boutros, Wadie** Lexique pratique des chantiers
        de fouilles et de restauration. Bibliothèque générale 15: 1996
        ⇒12,10409. ᴿCÉg 73 (1998) 96-97 (*Mekhitarian, A.*).
10993   *Braun, Eliot; Van den Brink, Edwin C.M.* Some comments on the
        late EB I sequence of Canaan and the relative dating of tomb Uj at
        Umm el Gaʿab and graves 313 and 787 from Minshat Abu Omar
        with imported ware: views from Egypt and Canaan. Ä&L 7 (1998)
        71-94.
10994   **Buhl, Marie-Louise** Les dessins archéologiques et topographiques
        de l'Égypte ancienne faits par F.L. Norden 1737-1738. 1993
        ⇒11/2,b494. ᴿCÉg 73 (1998) 66-67 (*Meulenaere, Herman de*).
10995   **Davies, W. Vivian; Friedman, Renée** Egypt. L 1998, British Mus-
        eum 224 pp. 0-7141-1911-3. Bibl.;

10996 Unbekanntes Ägypten: mit neuen Methoden alten Geheimnissen auf der Spur. ^T*Busse, Friederike*: Da:Wiss 1998, 224 pp. Bibl.

10997 **Dominicus, Brigitte** Gesten und Gebärden in Darstellungen des Alten und Mittleren Reiches. 1994 ⇒11/2,a528. ^RBiOr 55 (1998) 125-129 (*Van Walsem, René*).

10998 ^E**Falck, Martin von; Lichtwark, Friedericke** Ägypten: Schätze aus dem Wüstensand: Kunst und Kultur der Christen am Nil. 1996 ⇒12,10412; 13,10950. ^ROrChr 82 (1998) 276-280 (*Scholz, Piotr*).

10999 **Gamer-Wallert, Ingrid** Vermerk: Fundort unbekannt: ägyptologische Entdeckungen bei Privatsammlern in und um Stuttgart. 1997 ⇒13,10951. ^RBiOr 55 (1998) 418-423 (*Haslauer, Elfriede*).

11000 **Ginter, Boleslaw; Kozlowski, Janusz K.** Predynastic settlement near Armant. 1994 ⇒11/2,b662. ^RBiOr 55 (1998) 406-409 (*Williams, Bruce*).

11001 **Jordan, Paul** Riddles of the Sphinx. Gloucester 1998, Sutton xxiv; 222 pp. 0-7509-15536. photographs by John Ross; Bibl.

11002 *Kirby, Christopher* Predynastic Egypt in the Ashmolean Museum, Oxford. Egyptian Archaeology 12 (1998) 23-25.

11003 *Leclant, Jean; Clerc, Gisèle* Fouilles et travaux en Égypte et au Soudan, 1996-1997 (Tab. XII-XLVII). Or. 67 (1998) 315-444.

11004 **Nibbi, Alessandra** Some geographical notes on ancient Egypt: a selection of published papers, 1975-1997. 1997 ⇒13,10953. ^RDisc-Eg 42 (1998) 151-153 (*Vandersleyen, Claude*).

11005 **Rodenbeck, Max** Cairo: the city victorious. L 1998, Picador xviii; 395 pp. 0-330-33709-2. Bibl.

11006 *Shih, Shang-Ying* Death in Deir el-Medina: a psychological assessment. JSSEA 27 (1997) 62-78 Sum. 62.

11007 **Vercoutter, Jean** A la recherche de l'Égypte oubliée. Découvertes Gallimard 1: [Paris] 1998, [Gallimard] 176 pp. 2-07-053090-6.

T7.2 Karnak

11008 **Azim, Michel, *al.*,** Karnak et sa topographie, 1: les relevés modernes du temple d'Amon-Re 1967-1984. P 1998, CNRS; ill. 186 pp. 2-271-05540-7.

11009 **Gabolde, Luc** Le "Grand Château d'Amon" de Sésostris Ier à Karnak: la décoration du temple d'Amon-Rê au Moyen Empire. MAIBL 17: P 1998, De Boccard 205 pp.

11010 *Labrique, Françoise* L'escorte de la lune sur la porte d'Évergète à Karnak. Feste im Tempel, 4. ÄAT 33,2: 1998 ⇒479. 91-121.

T7.3 Amarna

11011 *Artzi, Pinhas* Amarna Document 16. Rencontre Assyriologique Internationale 34. 1998 ⇒452. 507-511.

11012 *Cochavi-Rainey, Zipora* Some grammatical notes on EA 14. ^FRAINEY, A. IOS 18: 1998 ⇒96. 207-228.

11013 *Cruells, W.* The Halaf levels of Tel Amarna (Syria): first preliminary report. Akkadica 106 (1998) 1-21.

11014 *Hess, Richard S.* The Mayarzana correspondence: rhetoric and conquest accounts. UF 30 (1998) 335-351.

11015 *Huehnergard, John* A grammar of Amarna Canaanite. BASOR 310 (1998) 59-77.
11016 *Lemche, Niels Peter* Greater Canaan: the implications of a correct reading of EA 151:49-67. BASOR 310 (1998) 19-24.
11017 *Liverani, Mario* How to kill Abdi-Ashirta: EA 101, once again. ᶠRAINEY, A. IOS 18: 1998 ⇒96. 387-394.
11018 **Liverani, Mario** Le lettere dei "piccoli re". Le Lettere di el-Amarna. Testi del Vicino Oriente antico 2; Letterature mesopotamiche 3: [Brescia] 1998, Paideia 1 302 pp. 88-394-0565-8.
11019 **Reiche, Christina** Ein hymnischer Text in den Gräbern des Hwy, 'I'h-ms und Mry-R' in El-'Amarna: Text und Textsorte, Textanalyse und Textinterpretation: ein "sozio-kommunikativer" Ansatz. Göttinger Orientforschungen 4; Ägypten 35: Wsb 1998, Harrassowitz xi; 457 pp. 3-447-04009-2. bibl.
11020 *Shaw, Ian* Building a sacred capital: Akhenaten, El-Amarna and the 'House of the king's statue'. Capital cities. 1998 ⇒492. 55-64.
11021 *Smith, Scobie P.* The inflectional morphology of the YVQTVL-verb in the Šuwardata Amarna letters (EA 278-284, 366). ᶠRAINEY, A. IOS 18: 1998 ⇒96. 125-170.
11022 *Tropper, Josef* Das Verbalsystem der Amarnabriefe aus Jerusalem: Untersuchungen zur Verwendung der Präfixkonjugation. UF 30 (1998) 665-678.
11023 *Wilhelm, Gernot; Giorgieri, Mauro* Notes on the Mittani letter. General studies... Nuzi 10/2. 1998 ⇒10975. 181-186.

т7.4 **Memphis**, *Saqqara*—**Pyramides**, *Giza* (Cairo)

11024 *Aly, Mohamed Ibrahim* Unpublished blocks from Saqqara. MDAI.K 54 (1998) 219-226.
11025 **Butler, Hadyn R.** Egyptian pyramid geometry: architectural and mathematical pattening in Dynasty IV Egyptian pyramid complexes. Mississauga 1998, Benben 242 pp. 125 fig. ᴿJSSEA 27 (1997) 104-105 (*Hirsch, Antoine*).
11026 *Cannuyer, Christian* La description des pyramides par Diego de Mérida (1510). Jerusalem studies. ÄAT 40: 1998 ⇒361. 9-18.
11027 **David, Rosalie** The pyramid builders of ancient Egypt: a modern investigation of Pharaoh's workforce. London ²1996 <1986>, Routledge x; 264 pp. $20. 12 ill. 32 pl. [JAOS 119,692s—Leprohon, Ronald J.].
11028 **Giacobbo, Roberto; Luna, Riccardo** Il segreto di Cheope: alla ricerca del tesoro perduto delle piramidi. I volti della storia 26: Roma 1998, Newton Compton 250 pp. 88-8183-990-3. Bibl.
11029 **Hastings, Elizabeth Anne** The sculpture from the sacred animal necropolis at north Saqqara 1964-76. 1997 ⇒13,10981. ᴿBiOr 55 (1998) 122-123 (*Meulenaere, H.J.A. de*).
11030 **Janosi, Peter** Österreich vor den Pyramiden. ÖAW.PHK 648, Bd. VÄK 3: W 1997, Austrian Academy of Sciences Pr. 101 pp. €29,7. 3-7001-2664-6.
11031 *Krauss, Rolf* Zur Berechnung der Bauzeit an Snofrus Roter Pyramide. ZÄS 125 (1998) 29-37.
11032 *Martin, Geoffrey T., al.,* Preliminary report on the Saqqara excavations, season 1997. OMRM 78 (1998) 31-32.

11033 *Priskin, Gyula* The dimensions of the Great Pyramid. DiscEg 41 (1998) 55-66.

11034 *Raven, Maarten J., al.,* The date of the secondary burials in the tomb of Iurudef at Saqqara. OMRM 78 (1998) 7-30.

11035 [E]**Schmitz, Bettina** Untersuchungen zu Idu II: Giza: ein interdisziplinäres Projekt. Hildesheimer Ägyptologische Beiträge 38: 1996 ⇒12,10448. [R]BiOr 55 (1998) 409-411 (*Bolshakov, Andrey O.*).

11036 *Swelim, Nabil; Dodson, Aidan* On the pyramid of Ameny-Qemau and its canopic equipment. MDAI.K 54 (1998) 319-334.

11037 **Vörös, Gyözö** The temple on the pyramid of Thebes. Budapest 1998, 80 pp. fig. pl. [R]Aeg. 78 (1998) 208-209 (*Curto, Silvio*).

T7.5 Delta Nili; *Alexandria* [⇒T7.6]

11038 **Abd El-Maksoud, Mohamed** Tell Heboua (1981-1991): enquête archéologique sur la deuxième période intermédiaire et le Nouvel Empire à l'extrémité oriental du Delta. P 1998, Recherche sur les Civilisations 313 pp. 2-86538-270-2. Bibl.

11039 **Grimm, Günter** Alexandria: die erste Königsstadt der hellenistischen Welt: Bilder aus der Nilmetropole von Alexander dem Großen bis Kleopatra VII. Zaberns Bildbände zur Archäologie, Sonderhefte der antiken Welt: Mainz 1998, Von Zabern 168 pp. €34, 77. 3-8053-2337-9. Zeichnungen Denis, Ulrike; Pfrommer, Michael [ArOr 67,405s—Smoláriková, Květa].

11040 **Haas, Christopher** Alexandria in late antiquity: topography and social conflict. Ancient History and Society: Baltimore, MD 1997, Johns Hopkins Univ. Pr. xxviii; 494 pp. £37. 0-8018-5377-X. [R]ClR 48/1 (1998) 221 (*Alston, Richard*); AJA 102 (1998) 454-455 (*Venit, Marjorie Susan*); BiOr 55 (1998) 432-435 (*Heinen, Heinz*); JThS 49 (1998) 363-365 (*Barnes, T.D.*); VigChr 52 (1998) 115-117 (*Runia, D.T.*).

11041 *Herold, Anja* Piramesses—the northern capital: chariots, horses and foreign gods. Capital cities. 1998 ⇒492. 129-146.

11042 *Wilson, Penny* Sais: surveying the royal city. Egyptian Archaeology 12 (1998) 3-6.

T7.6 *Alii situs Ægypti* alphabetice

11043 *Abu Mina*: *Engemann, Josef* Ein Tischfuß mit Dionysos-Satyr-Darstellung aus Abu Mina/Ägypten. JAC 41 (1998) 169-177.

11044 *Alexandria*: **Empereur, Jean-Yves** Alexandria rediscovered. [T]*Maehler, M.*: L 1998, British Museum Press 255 pp. 0-7141-1921-0. Photographs by *Stéphane Compoint* / Sygma;

11045 Alexandrie redécouverte. P 1998, Fayard Phot. *Stéphane Compoint* / Sygma [CRAI (2000/3) 1039—Leclant, Jean].

11046 *Amara* [E]**Spencer, Patricia** Amara West I: the architectural report. 1997 ⇒13,10999. [R]JEA 84 (1998) 249-251 (*Alexander, John*).

11047 *'Ayn Asil*: **Midant-Reynes, Béatrix** Le silex de 'Ayn Asil: Oasis de Dakhla - Balat. DFIFAO 34: [Le Caire] 1998, Institut Français d'Archéologie Orientale vii (2) 68 pp. 2-7247-0230-1. Dessins *Marc Jarry, Michèle Reduron-Ballinger, Khaled Zaza.*

11048   *Bakchias*: ᴱ**Pernigotti, Sergio; Capasso, Mario** Bakchias IV: rap-
        porto preliminare della campagna di scavo del 1996. 1997 ⇒13,
        11000. ᴿCÉg 73 (1998) 190-191 (*Nachtergael, Georges*).
11049   *Berenike*: ᴱ**Sidebotham, Steven E.; Wendrich, Willemina Z.** Be-
        renike 1996: report of the 1996 excavations at Berenike (Egyptian
        Red Sea Coast) and the survey of the Eastern Desert. CNWS
        publications, special series 3: Lei 1998, Research School CNWS
        vii; 477 pp. 90-5789-001-1.
11050   *Deir el-Bahari*: *Pawlicki, Franciszek* Deir el-Bahari: restoring Hat-
        shepsut's temple. Egyptian Archaeology 12 (1998) 15-17.
11051   *Deir el-Medina*: **Leospo, Enrica; Tosi, Mario** Vivere nell'antico
        Egitto: Deir el-Medina, il villaggio degli artefici delle tombe dei re.
        Saggi: F 1998, Giunti 143 pp. 88-09-21289-4. 24 fig.; Bibl. ᴿAeg.
        78 (1998) 210-212 (*Curto, Silvio*).
11052   **Van Heel, Donker; Haring, Ben** The Deir el-Medina database.
        http://www.leidenuniv.nl/nino/dmd/dmd.html [OLZ 96,25-
        29—Burkard, Günter (*Burkard, G.*)].
11053   *Edfu*: *Egberts, Arno* Mythos und Fest: Überlegungen zur Dekora-
        tion der westlichen Innenseite der Umfassungsmauer im Tempel
        von Edfu. Feste im Tempel, 4. ÄAT 33,2: 1998 ⇒479. 17-29.
11054   **Kurth, Dieter** Edfou VIII: die Inschriften des Tempels von Edfu
        Abteilung I. Übersetzungen 1: Wsb 1998, Harrassowitz xvii; 409
        pp. 3-447-03862-4. Collab. *Behrmann, Almuth*.
11055   *El-Ashmunein*: **Bailey, D.M.** British Museum Expedition to
        Middle Egypt: excavations at El-Ashmunein: pottery, lamps and
        glass of the late Roman and early Arab periods. L 1998, British
        Museum 5 xv; 182 pp. 0-7141-09835.
11056   *el-Balamun*: **Spencer, A.J.** Excavations at Tell el-Balamun 1991-
        1994. 1996 ⇒12,10459. ᴿArOr 66 (1998) 173-174 (*Smoláriková,
        Kvĕta*).
11057   *Elephantine*: **Jenni, Hanna** Die Dekoration des Chnumtempels aus
        Elephantine durch Nektanebos II. Elephantine 17; Archäologische
        Veröffentlichungen 90: Mainz 1998, Von Zabern 161 pp. 3-8053-
        1984-3. Beitrag von *Susanne Bickel* über die Dekoration des Tem-
        pelhaustores unter Alexander IV. und der Südwand unter Augustus.
11058   *Esna*: *Derchain-Urtel, Maria-Theresia* Die Festbesucher in Esna.
        Feste im Tempel, 4. ÄAT 33,2: 1998 ⇒479. 3-15.
11059   *Fayyum*: **Davoli, Paola** L'archeologia urbana nel Fayyum di età el-
        lenistica e romana. Missione Congiunta delle Università di Bologna
        e di Lecce in Egitto, Monografie vol. 1: N 1998, Procaccini 382 pp.
        Bibl. ᴿAeg. 78 (1998) 209-210 (*Curto, Silvio*).
11060   *Gempaton*: *Kormyscheva, Eleonora* Festkalender im Kawa-Tempel
        (Versuch einer Rekonstruktion). Feste im Tempel, 4. ÄAT 33,2:
        1998 ⇒479. 77-89.
11061   *Narmouthis*: **Gallo, Paolo** Ostraca demotici e ieratici dall'archivio
        bilingue di Narmouthis: II (nn. 34-99). Quaderni di Medinet Madi
        3: Pisa 1998, ETS lxxi; 166 pp. 88-467-0073-2. Bibl. xi-xvi; 36 pl.
11062   *Qurnah*: **Negm, Maged** The tomb of Simut called Kyky: Theban
        tomb 409 at Qurnah. 1997 ⇒13,11013. ᴿAeg. 78 (1998) 203-204
        (*Pernigotti, Sergio*).
11063   *Saqqara*: *Harpur, Yvonne* Evolution of an expedition. Egyptian Ar-
        chaeology 12 (1998) 18-22.
11064   *Van Dijk, Jacobus* Restoring the burial chambers of Maya and Me-
        ryt. Egyptian Archaeology 12 (1998) 7-9.

11065   *Tanis*: ᴱ**Brissaud, Philippe; Zivie-Coche, Christiane M.** Tanis, travaux récents sur le Tell Sän El-Hagar: Mission française de fouilles de Tanis 1987-1997. P 1998, Noêsis 564 pp. 2-911606248.

11066   **Montet, Pierre Marie** Lettres de Tanis 1939-1940: la découverte des trésors royaux. ᴱ*Montet-Beaucour, Camille; Yoyotte, Jean*: Champollion, les hauts lieux sacrés de l'Égypte: Monaco 1998, Rocher 278 pp. 2-268-02884-4.

11067   *Tell el-Dab'a*: **Bietak, M.** Avaris: the capital of the Hyksos. 1996 ⇒12,10460; 13,11003. ᴿPEQ 130 (1998) 70-72 (*Uphill, E.P.*); JEA 84 (1998) 238-241 (*Phillips, Jacke*); ArOr 66 (1998) 80-82 (*Bárta, Miroslav*).

11068   *Tell el-Fara'în*: **Way, Thomas von der** Tell el-Fara'în: Buto I: Ergebnisse zum frühen Kontext: Kampagnen der Jahre 1983-1989. 1997 ⇒13,11006. ᴿBiOr 55 (1998) 764-68 (*Wilkinson, Toby A.H.*).

11069   *Tuna el-Gebel*: **Kessler, Dieter** Tuna el-Gebel II: die Paviankultkammer G-C-C-2. HÄB 43: Hildesheim 1998, Gerstenberg xii; 187 pp. 3-8067-8137-0. Beitrag von *Hans-Ulrich Onasch*; 84 pl.

11070   *Umm el-Qaab*: **Dreyer, Günter** Umm el-Qaab I: das prädynastische Königsgrab U-j und seine frühen Schriftzeugnisse. Archäologische Veröffentlichungen 86: Mainz 1998, Von Zabern ix; 197 pp. €101,24. 3-8053-2486-3. Beiträge von *Ulrich Hartung; Frauke Pumpenmeier*; Anhang von *Friedel Feindt; Margaret Fischer*; Deutsches Archäologisches Institut, Abt. Kairo.

T7.7 *Antiquitates Nubiae et alibi*: Egypt outside Egypt

11071   **Ciappa, Armando** The Sudan in the bible. Khartoum 1996, St Paul's Major Seminary 139 pp [NThAR 2000,216].

11072   **Gohary, Jocelyn** Guide to the Nubian monuments on Lake Nasser. [Cairo] 1998, The American University in Cairo Press vii; 145 pp. 977-424-462-1. Bibl.

11073   **O'Connor, David B.** Ancient Nubia. 1993 ⇒10,12839; 12,1047. ᴿCÉg 73 (1998) 85-89 (*Troy, Lana*).

11074   **Shinnie, Peter L.** Ancient Nubia. 1996 ⇒12,10473; 13,11020 ᴿBiOr 55 (1998) 145-147 (*Pierce, R.H.*).

11075   **Welsby, Derek A.** The kingdom of Kush, the Napatan and Meroitic empires. 1996 ⇒12,10474. ᴿArOr 66 (1998) 78-80 (*Krumphanzlová, Barbora*); BiOr 55 (1998) 147-154 (*Zach, Michael H.*).

T7.9 Sinai

11076   **Blum, Howard** The gold of Exodus: the discovery of the true Mount Sinai. NY 1998, Simon & S. 364 pp. $25. Also Video (Monument, CO; Reel, 1998, $25) [BArR 25/4,54—Hendel, R.].

11077   **El-Din, Morsi Saad** Sinai: the site & the history. Phot. *Taher, Ayman; Romano, Luciano*: NY 1998, NY Univ. Pr. 142 pp. $40. 0-8147-2203-2 [ThD 45,189—Heiser, W. Charles].

11078   *Görg, Manfred* Sirbal. BN 93 (1998) 5-8.

11079   *Grossmann, Peter; Jones, Michael; Meimaris, Yiannis* Report on the season in Firan-Sinai (February-March 1995). ByZ 91 (1998) 345-358.

11080   **Schultz, Joseph P.; Spatz, Lois** Sinai and Olympus: a comparative study. 1995 ⇒11/2,6736; 13,11023. ᴿAJSR 23 (1998) 119-122 (*Brown, John Pairman*).

T8.1 **Anatolia** *generalia*

11081   *Bartl, Karin* Mitteleisenzeitliche Kulturen im kleinasiatisch-nordsyrischen Raum. Zwischen Euphrat und Indus. 1998 ⇒318. 222-240.

11082   *Berns, Christof* Zur Datierung der Tempel in Seleukeia am Kalykadnos und in Elaiussa-Sebaste (Kilikien). DaM 10 (1998) 135-154.

11083   *Bietak, Manfred* Zur Chronologie der Mittleren Bronzezeit in der Levante. Rencontre Assyriologique 34. 1998 ⇒452. 345-360.

11084   *Bilgiç, Emin* Anatolisch-Assyrische politische Beziehungen und Eidprozedur bei einheimischer Verwaltung im Lichte der neuen Kültepe Texte. Rencontre Assyriologique 34. 1998 ⇒452. 473-78.

11085   *Bisi, Anna Maria* Souche anatolienne et influences exterieures dans les petits bronzes hittites. Rencontre Assyriologique 34. 1998 ⇒452. 275-280.

11086   *Burney, Charles* The kingdom of Urartu (Van): investigations into the archaeology of the early first millennium BC within eastern Anatolia (1956-1965). Ancient Anatolia. 1998 ⇒348. 143-162.

11087   *Efe, Turan* New concepts on Tarsus-Troy relations at the beginning of the EB3 Period;

11088   *Fiema, Ewa* New look at the sacral architecture of Anatolia during Late Chalcolithic and Early Bronze Age period;

11089   *Greenfield, Jonas C.* Arameans and Aramaic in Anatolia;

11090   *Harrak, Amir* Sources épigraphiques concernant les rapports entre assyriens et Hittites à l'Âge du Bronze Recent. Rencontre Assyriologique 34. 1998 ⇒452. 297-302/523-531/199-207/239-252.

11091   **Ivantchik, Askold I.** Les cimmériens au Proche-Orient. OBO 127: 1993 ⇒10,12862; 13,11024. ᴿSyr. 75 (1998) 302 (*Amiet, Pierre*).

11092   *Klengel-Brandt, Evelyn, al.,* Vorläufiger Bericht über die Ausgrabungen des Vorderasiatischen Museums auf Tall Knediğ / NO-Syrien: Zusammenfassung der Ergebnisse 1993-1997. MDOG 130 (1998) 73-82.

11093   *Lipiński, Edouard* Gyges et Lygdamis d'après les sources neo-assyriennes et hébraïques;

11094   *Michel, Cécile* Les suites de la mort d'un Tamkaru en Anatolie. Rencontre Assyriologique 34. 1998 ⇒452. 159-165/457-465.

11095   ᴱ**Mikasa, Prince Takahito** Essays on ancient Anatolia in the second millennium B.C. Bull... Mid. East. Culture Center in Japan 10: Wsb 1998, Harrassowitz vii; 307 pp [AfO 46s,424ss—Gerber, C.].

11096   *Mountjoy, P.A.* The East Aegean-West Anatolian interface in the late Bronze Age: Mycenaeans and the kingdom of Ahhiyawa. AnSt 48 (1998) 33-67.

11097   *Muscarella, Oscar White* Relations between Phrygia and Assyria in the 8th century B.C. Rencontre Assyr. 34. 1998 ⇒452. 149-157.

11098   *Taracha, Piotr* Neues zu Sprache und Kultur der Hattier. OLZ 93 (1998) 7-18.

11099   *Westenholz, Joan Goodnick* Relations Between Mesopotamia and Anatolia in the age of the Sargonic Kings. Rencontre Assyriologique Internationale 34. 1998 ⇒452. 5-22.

11100 *Yakar, Jak* Environmental factors affecting urbanization in Bronze Age Anåtolia. Capital cities. 1998 ⇒492. 99-109.

T8.2 Boğazköy—*Hethaei*, the Hittites

11101 *Czichon, Rainer M.* Studien zur Regionalgeschichte von Ḫattuša/Boğazköy 1997. MDOG 130 (1998) 83-92.
11102 *Hawkins, J. David* Hattusa: home to the thousand gods of Hatti. Capital cities. 1998 ⇒492. 65-82.
11103 **Hawkins, J. David** The hieroglyphic inscription of the sacred pool complex at Hattusa. 1995 ⇒11/2,b767. ᴿOLZ 93 (1998) 174-184 (*Giorgieri, Mauro*).
11104 *Müller-Karpe, Andreas, al.*, Untersuchungen in Kusakli 1997. MDOG 130 (1998) 93-174.
11105 *Neve, Peter* Restaurierungen in Boğazköy-Ḫattuša. ᶠÇAMBEL H. 1998 ⇒4. 515-530.
11106 *Van den Hout, Theo* A tale of two cities: twee nieuwe hettitische provinciale centra. Phoenix 44/1 (1998) 39-48.
11107 *Wouters, Werner* Boğazköy: royal correspondence between Assur and Hatti. Rencontre Assyriologique 34. 1998 ⇒452. 269-273.

T8.3 Ephesus; Pergamon

11108 *Hanig, Roman* Smyrna und Ephesus: einige Beobachtungen zum Verhältnis der beiden christlichen Gemeinden. BN 91 (1998) 29-46.
11109 *Thür, Hilke* Ephesos—Wohnen in einer antiken Großstadt: die Hanghäuser am Embolos. BiKi 53 (1998) 195-196.

11110 **Börker, Christoph; Burow, Johannes** Die hellenistischen Amphorenstempel aus Pergamon: der Pergamon-Komplex [Börker]; die übrigen Stempel aus Pergamon [Burow]. DAI, Pergamenische Forschungen 11: B 1998, De Gruyter xii; 160 pp. Ill.
11111 ᴱ**Koester, Helmut** Pergamon, citadel of the gods: archaeological record, literary description, and religious development. HThS 46: Harrisburg, Pa. 1998, Trinity xx; 443 pp. 75 pl. fig. 1-56338-261-X. Bibl.:
11112 *Collins, Adela Yarbro* Pergamon in early Christian literature 163-184;
11113 *Hoffmann, Adolf* The Roman remodeling of the Asklepieion 41-61;
11114 *Jones, Christopher* Aelius Aristides and the Asklepieion 63-76;
11115 *Kampmann, Ursula* Homonoia politics in Asia Minor: the example of Pergamon 373-393;
11116 *Kästner, Volker* The architecture of the great altar of Pergamon 137-161;
11117 *Nagy, Gregory* The library of Pergamon as a classical model 185-232;
11118 *Nohlen, Klaus* The "Red Hall" (Kizil Avlu) in Pergamon 77-110;
11119 *Palmer Bonz, Marianne* Beneath the gaze of the gods: the Pergamon evidence for a developing theology of empire 251-275;

11120 *Radt, Wolfgang* Recent research in and about Pergamon: a survey (ca. 1987-1997) 1-40;
11121 *Rheidt, Klaus* In the shadow of antiquity: Pergamon and the Byzantine millennium 395-423;
11122 *Schowalter, Daniel N.* The Zeus Philios and Trajan temple: a context for imperial honors 233-249;
11123 *Thomas, Christine M.* The sanctuary of Demeter at Pergamon: cultic space for women and its eclipse 277-298;
11124 *White, L. Michael* Counting the costs of nobility: the social economy of Roman Pergamon 331-371;
11125 *Wulf-Rheidt, Ulrike* The Hellenistic and Roman houses of Pergamon 299-330 ⇒11111.

T8.6 *Situs Anatoliae*—**Turkey sites; Urartu**

11126 ᴱ**Dever, William G.** Preliminary excavations reports: Sardis, Idalion, and Tell el-Handaquq North. AASOR 53: 1996 ⇒12, 10492 ᴿOLZ 93 (1998) 465-467 (*Bartl, Karin*); CBQ 60 (1998) 393-394 (*West, James E.*).
11127 *Doonan, O.* Survey of the hinterland of Sinop, Turkey. NEA(BA) 61/3 (1998) 178-179.
11128 **Milner, Nicholas P.** An epigraphical survey in the Kibyra-Olbasa Region conducted by *A.S. Hall*. British Institute of Archaeology at Ankara, Monograph 24; Regional Epigraphic Catalogue of Asia Minor 3: L 1998, British Institute of Archaeology at Ankara xi; x, 127 pp. 1-898249-10-5. Bibl.
11129 *Ruggieri, Vincenzo; Giordano, Franco* La pensiola di Alicarnasso in età bizzantina: le chiese di Tavsan Adasi e Monastir Dag: eredità monofisita?. OCP 64 (1998) 39-74, 265-303.

11130 *Aperlae*: *Hohlfelder, Robert L.; Vann, Robert L.* Uncovering the maritime secrets of Aperlae, a coastal settlement of ancient Lycia. NEA(BA) 61/1 (1998) 26-37.
11131 *Arslantepe*: **Di Nocera, Gian Maria** Die Siedlung der Mittelbronzezeit von Arslantepe: eine Zentralsiedlung von Beginn des zweiten Jahrtausends v. Chr. in der Ebene von Malatya (Türkei). R 1998, Visceglia xv; 191 pp. 88-87320-00-4. Bibl.
11132 *Bolkardağ*: *Aksoy, Behin* Prehistoric and early historic pottery of the Bolkardağ mining district;
11133 *Değimetepe*: *Esin, Ufuk* Die Tempel von Değimetepe während der Chalkolithischen Obedperiode;
11134 *Demircihüyük*: *Kull, Brigitte* Middle Bronze Age occupation at Demircihüyük. Rencontre Assyriologique 34. 1998 ⇒452. 565-572/659-676/699-705.
11135 *Elmah Karataş*: **Warner, Jayne L.** Elmah Karataş II: the Early Bronze Age village of Karataş. 1994 ⇒11/2,6843. ᴿJAOS 118 (1998) 80-81 (*Steadman, Sharon R.*).
11136 *Gordion*: *Simpson, Elizabeth* Symbols on the Gordion screens;
11137 *Gritille*: *Ellis, Richard S.* Excavations at Gritille;
11138 *Hahhum*: *Garelli, Paul* Hahhum un relais assyrien sur la route commerciale de la Cappadoce;
11139 *Harran*: *Yardimici, Nurettın* Harran;

11140   *Kanish*: *Veenhof, Klaas R.* The chronology of *Kārum* Kanish: some new observations. Rencontre Assyriologique 34. 1998 ⇒452. 629-639/651-658/451-456/167-169/421-450.

11141   *Karatepe*: *Güterbock, Hans G.* A visit to Karatepe. ᶠÇAMBEL H. 1998 ⇒4. 365-370.

11142   *Maşat*: *Alp, Sedat* Akkadian names of some scribes in the Maşat-Letters;

11143   *Melid*: *Hawkins, John D.* Hittites and Assyrians at Melid (Malatya). Rencontre Assyriologique 34. 1998 ⇒452. 47-61/63-77.

11144   *Nevali-Chori*: *Antonova, Ye.V.; Litvinsky, B.A.* At the sources of ancient culture of the Near East (excavations of Nevali-Chori). VDI 224 (1998) 36-48 Sum. 48. **R**.

11145   *Pisidian Antioch*: **Mitchell, S.; Waelkens, M.,** *al.,* Pisidian Antioch: the site and its monuments. L 1998, Duckworth xvii; 249 pp. 43 fig.; 146 ill. [REG 113,672—Hinard, François].

11146   *Sultantepe*; *Harran*: *Gurney, Oliver* Sultantepe and Harran. Ancient Anatolia. 1998 ⇒348. 163-176.

11147   *Tille Höyük*: *Summers, Geoffrey G.* Tille Höyük: control of an Euphrates crossing;

11148   *Yazılıkaya*: *Opfermann, Rudolf* War für die Hethiter Yazılıkaya ein "Hékur"?. Rencontre Assyr. 34. 1998 ⇒452. 399-406/229-237.

T9.1 Cyprus

11149   *Åström, Paul* Continuity or discontinuity: indigenous and foreign elements in Cyprus around 1200 BCE. ᶠDOTHAN, T. 1998 ⇒23. 80-86.

11150   *Buchholz, Hans-Günter* Ein syrisches Dreifußbecken in Zypern ᶠLORETZ O. AOAT 250: 1998 ⇒65. 133-150.

11151   *Bunimovitz, Shlomo* Sea peoples in Cyprus and Israel: a comparative study of immigration processes;

11152   *Cadogan, Gerald* The thirteenth-century changes in Cyprus in their East Mediterranean context. ᶠDOTHAN T. 1998 ⇒23. 103-13/6-16.

11153   *Herscher, Ellen* Archaeology in Cyprus. AJA 102 (1998) 309-354.

11154   *Karageorghis, Vassos* Hearths and bathtubs in Cyprus: a "sea peoples'" innovation?. ᶠDOTHAN T. 1998 ⇒23. 276-282.

11155   ᴱ**Karageorghis, Vassos; Michaelides, Demetrios** The development of the Cypriot economy from the prehistoric period to the present day. 1996 ⇒12,10499. ᴿAJA 102 (1998) 193-194 (*Webb, Jennifer M.*).

11156   ᴱ**Knapp, A.B.** Near Eastern and Aegean texts from the third to the first millennia BC, 2. 1996 ⇒12,10500; 13,11052. ᴿJAOS 118 (1998) 144 (*Cline, Eric H.*).

11157   **Knapp, A. Bernard** The archaeology of Late Bronze Age Cypriot society: the study of settlement, survey and landscape. 1997 ⇒13,11051. ᴿBiOr 55 (1998) 529-533 (*Wright, G.R.H.*).

11158   *Kopcke, Guenter* Cypriot figural bronzes: questions about Mycenaean civilization and sea people. ᶠDOTHAN T. 1998 ⇒23. 94-102.

11159   **Mee, Christopher; Steel, Louise** Corpus of Cypriote antiquities 17: the Cypriote collections in the University of Liverpool and the Williamson Art Gallery and Museum. Studies in Mediterr. archaeology 20,17: Göteborg 1998, 70 pp. SEK300. 91-7081-038-9. ill.

11160   *Negbi, Ora* Reflections on the ethnicity of Cyprus in the eleventh century BCE. ^FDOTHAN T. 1998 ⇒23. 87-93.
11161   Report of the Department of Antiquities Cyprus, 1996. Nicosia 1996, Department of Antiquities vi; 371 pp. 0070-2374. ill.
11162   *Rowe, Andrea H.* A current late Roman site in Nea Paphos, Cyprus;
11163   *Serwint, Nancy* Results of the CAARI International Conference, March 1998. NEA(BA) 61/3 (1998) 179/176.
11164   *Steel, Louise* Archaeology in Cyprus 1987-1997. ArRep 44 (1998) 137-149.
11165   **Vandenabeele, Frieda** Figurines on Cypriote jugs holding an oinochoe. Studies in Mediterranean archaeology 120: Jonsered 1998, Alström cxxxiii; 233 pp.

T9.3 *Graecia*, **Greece**

11166   **Rizakis, A.D.** Achaïe 2: la cité de Patras: épigraphie et histoire. Meletêmata 25: Athens 1998, Research Centre for Greek and Roman Antiquity viii; 487 pp. 960-7905-02-4. 59 pl.; 364 phot. [RB 103,479].
11167   **Styrenius, Carl-Gustaf** Asine: en svensk utgrävningsplats i Grekland. Studies in Mediterranean Archaeology and Literature, Pocketbook 151: Sto 1998, Merdelhavsmuseet 80 pp. 91-89242-00-9. Bibl.

11168   **Driessen, Jan; MacDonald, Colin F.** The troubled island: Minoan Crete before and after the Santorini eruption. Aegaeum 17: Liège 1997, Université 284 pp. €69,41. D-1997-0480-45. Num. ill. [AnCl 69,524ss—Schoep, Ilse].
11169   **MacGillivray, J.A.** Knossos: pottery groups of the old palace period. British School at Athens studies 5: L 1998, British School at Athens 195 pp. 0-904887-32-4. 156 pl.; bibl.
11170   *Rehak, Paul; Younger, John G.* Review of Aegean prehistory VII: neopalatial, final palatial, and postpalatial Crete. AJA 102 (1998) 91-173.
11171   ^E**Tsipopoulou, M.; Vagnetti, L.** Achladia: scavi e ricerche della Missione Greco-Italiana in Creta orientale (1991-1993). CNR Istituto per gli Studi Micenei ed Egeo-Anatolici, Incunabula Graeca 97: R 1995, Gruppo Editoriale Internazionale Maps, fig.; 218 pp. €139,44. 88-8011-071-3 [ClR 50,549—Warren, Peter].

11172   **Dickinson, Oliver** The Aegean Bronze Age. 1994, ⇒10,13128... 12,10517. ^RGn. 70 (1998) 338-345 (*Schiering, Wolfgang*).
11173   *French, Elizabeth B.* The ups and downs of Mycenae: 1250-1150 BCE. ^FDOTHAN, T. 1998 ⇒23. 2-5.
11174   **Manning, Sturt W.** The absolute chronology of the Aegean Early Bronze Age. 1995 ⇒11/2,a768; 12,10523. ^RJAOS 118 (1998) 440-442 (*Dever, William G.*).
11175   **Pilafidis-Williams, Korinna** The sanctuary of Aphaia on Aigina in the Bronze Age. Mü 1998, Hirmer ix; 194 pp. €16,45. 3-7774-8010-X. 2 fig;, 74 pl., 7 charts [AJA 103,706s—French, E.].
11176   **Sakellarakis, Yannis** Digging for the past. 1996 ⇒12,10524. ^RAJA 102 (1998) 430-431 (*Shanks, Michael*).

T9.6 Urbs Roma

11177 *Caillet, Jean-Pierre* Die Entstehung der christlichen Stadt. WUB 8 (1998) 16-25.

11178 ^E**Calci, Carmelo** Roma oltre le mura: lineamenti storico topografici del territorio della V circoscrizione. R 1998, Associazione culturale Roma oltre le mura 238 pp.

11179 *Caragounis, Chrys C.* From obscurity to prominence: the development of the Roman church between Romans and 1 Clement. Judaism and Christianity. 1998 ⇒230. 245-279.

11180 **Castriota, David** The ara pacis augustae and the imagery of abundance in later Greek and early Roman imperial art. 1995 ⇒11/2,c011; 12,10527. ^RGn. 70 (1998) 350-354 (*Sauron, Gilles*).

11181 **Claridge, Amanda** Rome: an Oxford archaeological guide. Oxford Archaeological Guides: Oxf 1998, OUP xv; 464 pp. 0-19-288003-9. Contrib. *Judith Toms* and *Tony Cubberley*.

11182 **Colini, Antonio Maria**, *al.*, Appunti degli scavi di Roma. ^{EBuzzetti,} ^{Carlo}: R 1998, Quasar 285 pp. 88-7140-136-0. v.1, Quaderni I bis-II bis-III-IV.

11183 *Donfried, Karl P.* In the first century: the nature and scope of the question. Judaism and Christianity. 1998 ⇒230. 1-13.

11184 **Favro, Diane** The urban image of Augustan Rome. 1996 ⇒12, 10529. ^RAJA 102 (1998) 208-209 (*Dyson, Stephen L.*).

11185 *Jeffers, James S.* Jewish and Christian families in first-century Rome. Judaism and Christianity. 1998 ⇒230. 128-150.

11186 *Klauck, Hans-Josef* Rom in der Bibel. WUB 8 (1998) 13-14.

Kolb, F. Rom: die Geschichte... in der Antike 1998 ⇒11470.

11187 *Lane, William L.* Social perspectives on Roman Christianity during the formative years from Nero to Nerva: Romans, Hebrews, 1 Clement;

11188 *Richardson, Peter* Augustan-era synagogues in Rome;

11189 *Rutgers, Leonard Victor* Roman policy toward the Jews: expulsions from the city of Rome during the first century C.E. Judaism and Christianity. 1998 ⇒230. 196-244/17-29/93-116.

11190 *Rüpke, Jörg* Kommensalität und Gesellschaftsstruktur: Tafelfreu(n)de im alten Rom. Saec. 49 (1998) 193-215.

11191 *Saint-Roch, Patrick* Das Petrusgrab. WUB 8 (1998) 26-29.

11192 **Scullard, Howard Hayes** The Etruscan cities and Rome. Baltimore 1998, Johns Hopkins University Pr. 320 pp. 0-8018-6072-5.

11193 *Snyder, Graydon F.* The interaction of Jews with non-Jews in Rome. Judaism and Christianity. 1998 ⇒230. 69-90.

11194 *Toit, A.B. du* 'God's beloved in Rome' (Rm 1:7): the genesis and socio-economic situation of the first generation christian community in Rome. Neotest. 32 (1998) 367-388.

11195 *Turcan, Robert* Die Christianisierung Roms und die Kunst. WUB 8 (1998) 5-12.

11196 *Walters, James C.* Romans, Jews, and Christians: the impact of the Romans on Jewish/Christian relations in first-century Rome;

11197 *White, L. Michael* Synagogue and society in imperial Ostia: archaeological and epigraphic evidence. Judaism and Christianity. 1998 ⇒230. 175-195/30-68.

11198 *Williams, Margaret* The structure of the Jewish community in Rome. Jews in a Graeco-Roman world. 1998 ⇒337. 215-228.

T9.7 **Catacumbae**

11199 **Bosio, Antonio** Roma sotteraneo. R 1998, Quasar 656 + 32 pp. €619,75. 200 ill. [CHR 86,305ss—Ditchfield, Simon].
11200 *Guyon, Jean* Die Heilsbotschaft in der frühchristlichen Kunst. WUB 8 (1998) 31-35.
11201 **Korte, Rainer** Voci dal profondo: meditazioni sulle catacombe cristiane di Roma. Città del Vaticano 1998, Libreria Editrice Vaticana 93 pp. 88-209-2573-7.
11202 **Nicolai, Vincenzo Fiocchi; Bisconti, Fabrizio; Mazzoleni, Danilo** Le catacombe cristiane di Roma: origini, sviluppo, apparati decorativi, documentazione epigrafica. Rg 1998, Schnell & S 207 pp. 3-7954-1192-0. 178 fig. Bibl.;
11203 Roms christliche Katakomben: Geschichte—Bilderwelt—Inschriften. [TDörr, Franziska]: Rg 1998, Schnell & S 208 pp. €29,65. 3-7954-1191-2. 178 pl. [JEH 51,368s—Frend, W.H.C.].
11204 **Pergola, Philippe** Le catacombe romane: storia e topografia. 1997 ⇒13,11075. [R]Asp. 45 (1998) 309-310 (*Parente, Ulderico*).

T9.8 *Archaeologia paleochristiana*—**early Christian archaeology**

11205 **Álvarez, Jesús** Arqueología cristiana. M 1998, BAC 200 pp. [Est Trin 33,476s—Arbizu, José M.ª].
11206 [E]**Cambi, Nenad; Marin, Emilio** Acta XIII congressus internationalis archaeologiae christianae. R 1998, Pont.Ist. di archeologia christiana Split 21 sept.-1 oct. 1994. 2500 pp.
11207 *Liverani, Paolo* Neue Entdeckungen der christlichen Archäologie in Rom. WUB 8 (1998) 25.
11208 *Parker, S. Thomas* An early church, perhaps the oldest in the world, found at Aqaba. NEA(BA) 61/4 (1998) 254.
11209 *Warland, Rainer* Von der christlichen Archäologie zur spätantiken Archäologie: Forschungen und Perspektiven eines Faches. ZAC 2 (1998) 3-15.

T9.9 *Roma: imperium occidentale*

11210 **De Kind, Richard E.L.B.** Houses in Herculaneum: a new view on the town planning and the building of Insulae III and IV. Circumvesuviana 1: Amst 1998, Gieben 332 pp. 90-5063-517-2. Bibl.
11211 **Köhler, Jens** Pompai: Untersuchungen zur hellenistischen Festkultur. 1996 ⇒12,10539. [R]Mes. 33 (1998) 402-404 (*Conti, M.C.*).

XIX. Geographia biblica

U1.0 **Geographica**

11212 [T]**Charvet, Pascal** STRABO: Geographica 17: le voyage en Egypte: un regard romain. P 1998, NiL 313 pp. 2-84111-068-0. Commentaires de *J. Yoyotte* et *P. Charvet*.

11213 *Fisch, Joana* "Crossing borders: Ancient Egypt, Canaan and Israel" Symposium. NEA(BA) 61/3 (1998) 177.
11214 *Geyer, B.* Géographie et peuplement des steppes arides de la Syrie du nord. Espace naturel. 1998 ⇒476. 1-8 Sum. rés. 1.
11215 **Horowitz, Wayne** Mesopotamian cosmic geography. Mesopotamian Civilizations 8: WL 1998, Eisenbrauns xiv; 410 pp. $52. 0-931464-99-4.
11216 [T]**Humbach, Helmut; Ziegler, Susanne** Ptolemaeus: geography, book 6: Middle East, Central and North Asia, China. Wsb 1998, Reichert x; 260 pp. 3-89500-061-2.
11217 [E]**Liverani, Mario** Neo-Assyrian geography. 1995 ⇒11/2,c081; 13, 11087. [R]BiOr 55 (1998) 252-257 (*Bonacossi, Daniele Morandi*).
11218 *Moreno García, Juan Carlos* Administration territoriale et organisation de l'espace en Egypte au troisième millénaire avant J.-C. (III-IV): *nwt m'wt et ḥwt-ᵓt.* ZÄS 125 (1998) 38-55.

U1.2 Historia geographiae

11219 *Ben-Arieh, Yehoshua* Biblical landscapes through western eyes: nineteenth-century painters envision the Holy Land. Land and community. 1998 ⇒466. 9-16.
11220 **Dohmen, Christoph** Orte der Bibel: Geschichten, Entdeckungen, Deutungen. Stu 1998, Kath. Bibelwerk 92 pp. 3-460-32793-6. Bibl. [NThAR 1999,1].
11221 *Kallai, Zecharia* Biblical historiography and biblical research 13-22;
11222 The boundaries of Canaan and the land of Israel in the bible: territorial patterns in biblical historiography <1975> 111-129;
11223 The campaign of Chedorlaomer and biblical historiography <1986-1989> 218-242;
11224 Conquest and settlement of Trans-Jordan: a historiographical study <1983> 175-185;
11225 Judah and Israel—a study in Israelite historiography <1978> 145-156;
11226 Judah and the boundaries of Jewish settlement under Persian rule 63-91;
11227 Organizational and administrative frameworks in the kingdom of David and Solomon <1977> 130-136;
11228 The settlement traditions of Ephraim: a historiographical study <1986> 202-210;
11229 The southern border of the land of Israel—pattern and application <1987> 211-217;
11230 Territorial patterns, biblical historiography and scribal tradition—a programmatic survey <1981> 157-164;
11231 The united monarchy of Israel—a focal point in Israelite historiography <1977> 137-144;
11232 The wandering-traditions from Kadesh-Barnea to Canaan: a study in biblical historiography <1982>. Biblical historiography. 1998 ⇒167. 165-174.
11233 *Mussner, Franz* Die Bedeutung des Studienjahres in Jerusalem für das Studium des Neuen Testaments. TThZ 107 (1998) 312-316.

11234   *Rainey, Anson F.* Notes on historical geography. UF 30 (1998) 633-644.
11235   *Schick, Robert* Palestine in the early Islamic period: luxuriant legacy. NEA(BA) 61/2 (1998) 74-108.
11236   *Van Soldt, W.* PRU 6 no. 78 (RS 19.41): towns in the land of Siyannu or in the land of Ugarit?. ᶠLORETZ O. AOAT 250: 1998 ⇒65. 777-784.
11237   *Wright, Henry E.* Origin of the climate and vegetation in the Mediterranean area. ᶠÇAMBEL H. 1998 ⇒4. 764-774.

U1.4 Atlas—maps

11238   *Cornelius, Izak* How maps "lie"—some remarks on the ideology of ancient Near Eastern and "scriptural" maps. JNSL 24/1 (1998) 217-230.
11239   ᴱ**Dowley, Tim** Atlas of the bible and christianity. 1997 ⇒13, 11110. ᴿRBBras 15 (1998) 452.
11240   **Due, Andrea; Laboa, Juan María** Atlas histórico del cristianismo. M 1998, San Pablo 322 pp. ᴿMCom 56 (1998) 540-542 (*Amor Pan, José Ramón*).
11241   Der große Bibelatlas. Augsburg 1998, Pattloch 144 pp. 3-629-00838-0 [[NThAR 1999,178].
11242   ᴱ**Kopp, Horst; Röllig, Wolfgang** TAVO: Register/General Index. 1994 ⇒10,13272*; 11/2,c127. 3 vols. ᴿJAOS 118 (1998) 87-89 (*Fuchs, Andreas*).
11243   **Lacroix, W.F.G.** Africa in antiquity: a linguistic and toponymic analysis of Ptolemy's map of Africa, together with a discussion of Ophir, Punt and Hanno's voyage. Nijmegen Studies in Development and Cultural Change 28: Saarbrücken 1998, Verlag für Entwicklungspolitik xi; 416 pp. €32,72. 3-88156-708-9. 21 maps [JAfH 40,477s—Phillips, Jacke].
11244   **Manley, Bill** Atlas historique de l'Égypte ancienne: de Thèbes à Alexandrie: la tumultueuse épopée des pharaons. ᵀ*Martinez, Philippe*: Atlas/Mémoires: n.p. 1998, Autrement 144 pp. 2-86260-751-7. Bibl.
11245   **Perego, Giacomo** Atlante Biblico interdisciplinare: scrittura, storia, geografia, archeologia e teologia a confronto. CinB 1998, San Paolo 124 pp. €14,98. 88-215-3827-3.
11246   ᴱ**Pritchard, James B.; Keel, Othmar; Küchler, Max** Herders großer Bibelatlas. FrB ³1996, Herder 255 pp. €25,46. 3-451-26138-3. ᴿRivBib 46 (1998) 99-102 (*Prato, Gian Luigi*).
11247   ᴱ**Renouard, Jean-Philippe** Le grand atlas de l'Égypte ancienne. P 1998, Atlas 399 pp. 2-7312-2314-6.
11248   **Strange, John** Stuttgarter Bibelatlas: historische Karten der biblischen Welt. Stu ³1998, Dt. Bibelges. 64 pp. 3-438-06030-2 [NThAR 1999,2].
11249   *Wajntraub, Eva; Wajntraub, Gimpel* Hebrew map showing the dispersion of the sons of Noah: by Jacob Auspitz, printed 1817. Land and community. 1998 ⇒466. 31-35.

U1.5 *Photographiae*; **Guide-books**, *Führer*

11250   **Howe, Kathleen Stewart** Revealing the Holy Land: the photo-
graphic exploration of Palestine. 1997 ⇒13,11118. [R]BAR 24/3
(1998) 58-9, 61 (*Feldman, Steven*).

11251   *Kennedy, David* Aerial archaeology in Jordan. Levant 30 (1998)
91-96.

11252   [E]**Acquistapace, Paolo; Turri, Ernani** Guida biblica e turistica della Terra Santa. Mi [3]1997, IPL 563 pp. €20,66. [E]*Ernani Turri*. [R]Civ
Catt 149/2 (1998) 197-198 (*Marchesi, G.*).

11253   **Elliger, Winfried** Mit Paulus unterwegs in Griechenland: Philippi,
Thessaloniki, Athen, Korinth. Stu 1998, Kath. Bibelwerk 119 pp.
3-460-32542-9 [NThAR 1998,336].

11254   **Gatz, Erwin** Roma christiana: ein kunst- und kulturgeschichtlicher
Führer über den Vatikan und die Stadt Rom>. Rg 1998, Schnell &
S 384 pp. €22,50. num. photos. [R]GuL 71 (1998) 474-475 (*Stein-
metz, Franz-Josef*).

11255   **Hurault, Louis** Guide de Terre Sainte routes bibliques: les chemins de la parole. P 1998, Fayard 512 pp. 2-213-60065-1. Collab.
Suzanne Tesseraud; cartes *Marcel Tesseraud*; phot. *Louis Hurault*.

11256   **Kilgallen, John J.** A New Testament guide to the Holy Land. Ch
[2]1998, Loyola Univ. Pr. xiv; 298 pp. $15. 0-8294-1041-4. Bibl.

11257   **Murphy-O'Connor, Jerome** The Holy Land: an Oxford archaeological guide from earliest times to 1700. Oxford Archaeological
Guides: Oxf [4]1998, OUP xxiv; 489 pp. 0-19-288013-6.

11258   **Raheb, Mitri; Strickert, Fred** Bethlehem 2000: past and present.
Waverly 1998, Wartburg 157 pp. $35 [BiTod 37,257—Bergant,
Dianne].

11259   **Ravasi, Gianfranco; Santucci, Luigi** Pellegrini in Terrasanta. Pellegrini 1: CinB [2]1993, San Paolo 238 pp. €12,91. 88-215-1348-3.
[R]Protest. 53 (1998) 372-373 (*Soggin, J.A.*).

11260   [E]**Trummer, Peter; Pichler, Josef** Heiliges Land—beiderseits des
Jordan: ein biblischer Reisebegleiter. Innsbruck 1998, Tyrolia 261
pp. 3-7022-2177-8/217-7.

U1.7 *Onomastica*—**Ancient sources of place names**

11261   **Falivene, Maria Rosaria** The Herakleopolite Nome: a catalogue
of the toponyms, with introduction and commentary. ASP 37:
Atlanta, GA 1998, Scholars xvii; 324 pp. 0-7885-0412-6.

11262   **Frayne, Douglas R.** The early dynastic list of geographical names.
AOS 74: 1992 ⇒8,g789... 12,10568. [R]WO 29 (1998) 196-197
(*Röllig, Wolfgang*).

11263   **George, A.R.** Babylonian topographical texts. OLA 40: 1992 ⇒8,
g790; 9,14940. [R]ZDMG 148 (1998) 201-204 (*Schramm, Wolfgang*).

11264   *Niedorf, Christian* Die Toponyme der Texte aus Alalaḫ IV. UF 30
(1998) 515-568.

11265   *Zeeb, Frank* Die Ortsnamen und geographischen Bezeichnungen
der Texte aus Alalaḫ VII. UF 30 (1998) 829-886.

U2.1 Geologia; Clima

11266   *Amar, Zohar* The production of salt and sulphur from the Dead Sea region in the tenth century according to at-Tamimi. PEQ 130 (1998) 3-7.

11267   **Bernbaum, Edwin** Sacred mountains of the world. Berkeley 1998, Univ. of California Press xxv; 291 pp. 0-520-21422-6. Bibl.

11268   *Court, Marie-Agnès* The soil record of an exceptional event at 4000 B.P. in the Middle East. Natural catastrophes. 1998 ⇒356. 93-108.

11269   **Higgins, Michael & Reynold** A geological companion to Greece and the Aegean. L 1996, Duckworth 256 pp. 0-7156-2722-8. 16 pl.; 10 fig.; 133 maps. [R]ClR 48 (1998) 392-393 (*Blundell, D.J.*).

11270   *Masse, W. Bruce* Earth, air, fire, and water: the archaeology of Bronze Age cosmic catastrophes;

11271   *Nur, Amos* The end of the Bronze Age by large earthquakes?. Natural catastrophes. 1998 ⇒356. 53-92/140-147.

11272   *Pilch, John J.* Caves. BiTod 36 (1998) 47-53.

11273   **Stephenson, F. Richard** Historical eclipses and earth's rotation. C 1997, CUP xvi; 557 pp. $160. 0-521-46194-4. [R]IBSt 20 (1998) 92-96 (*MacAdam, Henry Innes*).

11274   **Waldherr, Gerhard H.** Erdbeben: das aussergewöhnliche Normale: zur Rezeption seismischer Aktivitäten in literarischen Quellen vom 4. Jahrhundert v. Chr. bis zum 4. Jahrhundert n. Chr. Geographica Historica 9: Stu 1997, Steiner 272 pp. €49.8. 3-515-07070-2 [Latomus 59,720—Burnand, Yves].

   Uval, Beth The dew of heaven (Gen 27:28) 1998 ⇒11279.
   Wright, H. Climate... in the Mediterranean area 1998 ⇒11237.

U2.2 *Hydrographia*; rivers, seas, salt

11275   **Grewe, Klaus** Licht am Ende des Tunnels: Planung und Trassierung im antiken Tunnelbau. Mainz 1998, Von Zabern 218 pp. €39, 88. 3-8053-2492-8. 299 fig. [AJA 104,130—Aicher, Peter J.].

11276   **Menu, Bernadette** Les problèmes institutionnels de l'eau en É-gypte a\ncienne et dans l'antiquité méditerranéenne. 1994 ⇒10, 452. [R]JESHO 41 (1998) 505-508 (*Vleeming, S.P.*).

11277   *Raban, A.* מעגנים ונמלים בחופי הארץ בתקופת־הברונזה [Anchorages and harbors on the coast of Israel during the Bronze Age]. Qad. 31 (1998) 90-108.

11278   *Stieglitz, Robert R.* Hydraulic and fishing installations at Tel Tanninim. NEA(BA) 61/4 (1998) 256.

11279   *Uval, Beth* The dew of heaven (Gen 27:28). JBQ 26 (1998) 117-118.

11280   *Zangenberg, Jürgen* Das Tote Meer in neutestamentlicher Zeit. [F]LINDNER, M. BBB 118: 1998 ⇒62. 49-59.

U2.5 *Fauna*, animalia

11281   **Borowski, Oded** Every living thing: daily use of animals in Ancient Israel. L 1998, Altamira 296 pp. 0-7619-8919-6/8-8.

11282 *Briend, Jacques* Die Viehzucht in biblischen Zeiten. WUB 8 (1998) 55-56.

11283 *Brüning, Christian* "Lobet den Herrn, ihr Seeungeheuer und all ihr Tiefen!": Seeungeheuer in der Bibel. ZAW 110 (1998) 250-255 [Ps 148,7].

11284 [E]**Cassin, B.; Labarrière, J.-L.** L'animal dans l'antiquité. Bibliothèque de l'histoire de la philosophie: P 1997, Vrin xiv; 618 pp. €41,16. 2-7116-1323-2 [JHS 120,177s—Clark, Gillian].

11285 *Castel Ronda, Elisa* Propuesta para la reidentificación de algunas pieles de uso sacerdotal en el Antiguo Egipto. BAEO 34 (1998) 19-36.

11286 **Hamoto, Azad** Der Affe in der altorientalischen Kunst. FARG 28: Müns 1995, Ugarit Verlag xii; 176 pp. [R]JAOS 118 (1998) 581-582 (*Collon, Dominique*).

11287 *Heltzer, M.* On the Vth Century B.C.E. dogs from Ashkelon. Transeuphratène 15 (1998) 149-152.

11288 *Horwitz, Liora Kolska* Faunal remains from Middle Bronze Age Tel Te'enim. TelAv 25 (1998) 105-109.

11289 **Houston, Walter** Purity and monotheism: clean and unclean animals in biblical law. JSOT.S 140: 1993 ⇒9,2455... 12,2092. [R]JNES 57 (1998) 44-46 (*Pardee, Dennis*).

11290 *Leone, Aurora* Animali da trasporto nell'antico Egitto: una rassegna papirologica dalla dinastia dei Lagidi ai Bizantini. N 1998, Athena 215 pp. Bibl.

11291 **Linzey, Andrew; Cohn-Sherbok, Dan** After Noah: animals and the liberation of theology. 1997 ⇒13,11142. [R]IBSt 20 (1998) 137-41 (*Williams, Stephen N.*); RRT (1998/4) 28-31 (*Harvey, Graham*).

11292 **Osborn, Dale J.; Osbornová, Jana** The mammals of ancient Egypt. The Natural History of Egypt 4: Wmr 1998, Aris & P x; 213 pp. £45/35. 0-85668-522-4/10-9. Bibl. [R]DiscEg 42 (1998) 143-146 (*Houlihan, Patrick F.*).

11293 *Parlasca, Ingemarie* Neues zu den nabatäischen Kamelterrakotten. [F]LINDNER, M. BBB 118: 1998 ⇒62. 60-63.

11294 **Rice, Michael** The power of the bull. L 1998, Routledge xi; 316 pp. 0-415-09032-6. Bibl.

11295 *Vogel, Dan* Ambiguities of the eagle. JBQ 26 (1998) 85-92.

11296 *Wescott, Roger Williams* Consonantal apophony in Indo-European animal names. [F]GORDON, C. JSOT.S 273: 1998 ⇒31. 464-477.

U2.6 *Flora*; **plantae biblicae et antiquae**

11297 [E]**Amouretti, Marie-Claire; Brun, Jean-Pierre** La production du vin et de l'huile en méditerranée. Actes du symposium international, Centre C. Julian..., 20-22 nov. 1991. BCH.S 26: P 1993, Ecole française d'Athènes 626 pp. 2-86958-060-6. [R]Gn. 70 (1998) 124-127 (*Herz, Peter*).

11298 *Briend, Jacques; Quesnel, Michel* Die Rebe und der Wein. WUB 9 (1998) 89-91.

11299 **Bruzzone, Giovanni Battista** Piante e aromi della bibbia. Montella (Avellino) 1998, Dragonetti 114 pp [LASBF 48,589s—Bottini, Giovanni Claudio].

11300 **Farrar, Linda** Ancient Roman gardens. [Gloucester] 1998, Sutton xviii; 237 pp. 0-7509-1725-3. Bibl.
11301 *Heinsch, James* Francincense and myrrh. Holy Land 18 (1998) 208-214.
11302 **Manzi, Luigi** La viticoltura e l'enologia presso i romani. R 1998, Quasar 225 pp. 88-7140-110-2.
11303 *Rubinstein, Yakov* ובתלמוד במשנה האתרוג [The etrog—is it 'Peri ets hadar'?]. Beit Mikra 153 (1998) 175-178 Sum. 196. **H.**
11304 *Walsh, Carey; Zorn, Jeffrey R.* New insights from old wine presses. PEQ 130 (1998) 154-161 [Mizpa].
11305 *Warnock, Peter* From plant domestication to phytolith interpretation: the history of paleoethnobotany in the Near East. NEA(BA) 61/4 (1998) 238-252.
11306 ᴱ**Westenholz, Joan Goodnick** Sacred bounty sacred land: the seven species of the land of Israel. J 1998, Bible Lands Museum 220 pp. $48 [BArR 25/2,58—Hopkins, David C.].

U2.8 Agricultura, alimentatio

11307 **Bonacossi, Daniele Morandi** Tra il fiume e la steppa: insediamento e uso del territorio nella bassa valle del fiume Habur in epoca neo-assira I-II. 1996 ⇒12,10615. 2 vols. ᴿZA 88 (1998) 152-157 (*Hausleiter, A.*).
11308 **Born, Wina** Culinaire bijbel: eten en drinken in de bijbel. Kampen 1998, Kok 175 pp. €13,61. 90-242-9420-7 [Str. 66,762—Beentjes, Panc].
11309 ᴱ**Eitam, David; Heltzer, Michael** Olive oil in antiquity: Israel and neighbouring countries from the neolithic to the early Arab period. 1996, ⇒12,10618. ᴿBiOr 55 (1998) 902-903 (*Geus, C.H.J. de*).
11310 *Feliks, Yehuda* Jewish farmers and the sabbatical year. The jubilee challenge. 1997 ⇒13,2178. 165-170.
11311 **Frankel, Rafael**, *al.*, History and technology of olive oil in the Holy Land. 1994 ⇒11/2,c351; 12,10619. ᴿZDPV 114 (1998) 95-96 (*Genz, Hermann*).
11312 **Ikram, Salima** Choice cuts: meat production in ancient Egypt. OLA 69: 1995 ⇒11/2,c369. ᴿJARCE 35 (1998) 198-200 (*Houlihan, Patrick F.*).
11313 **Jursa, Michael** Die Landwirtschaft in Sippar in neubabylonischer Zeit. 1995 ⇒11/2,c370. ᴿBiOr 55 (1998) 468-473 (*Vargyas, Péter*); JESHO 41 (1998) 496-503 (*Stolper, Matthew W.*); OLZ 93 (1998) 641-647 (*Zawadzki, Stefan*).
11314 *Kaplony-Heckel, Ursula* Zur Landwirtschaft in Oberägypten: demotische Akten und Urkunden aus Gebelein (II. Jht. v. Chr.) und der arabische Leitfaden des Maḥzumi (+ 1189 n. Chr.). Jerusalem studies. ÄAT 40: 1998 ⇒361. 57-66.
11315 *Milano, Lucio* Aspects of meat consumption in Mesopotamia and the food paradigm of the Poor Man of Nippur. SAA Bulletin 12 (1998) 111-127.
11316 **Sahrhage, Dietrich** Fischfang und Fischkult im alten Ägypten. Kulturgeschichte der antiken Welt 70: Mainz 1998, Von Zabern 174 pp. 3-8053-1757-3. Bibl.
11317 *Sapin, Jean* À l'est de Gérasa: aménagement rural et réseau de communications. Syr. 75/1 (1998) 107-136.

11318 **Stepien, Marek** Animal husbandry in the ancient Near East: a pro-sopographic study of third-millennium Umma. [Bethesda, MD] 1996, CDL xii; 263 pp. 1-883053-25-0. Bibl.
11319 *Van der Spek, R.J.* Land tenure in Hellenistic Anatolia and Meso-potamia. Rencontre Assyriologique 34. 1998 ⇒452. 137-147.
11320 *Walsh, Carey Ellen* God's vineyard: Isaiah's prophecy as vintner's textbook. BiRe 14/4 (1998) 42-49, 52-53 [Isa 5,1-7].

U2.9 **Medicina** biblica et antiqua

11321 **Avalos, Hector I.** Illness and health care in the ancient Near East: the role of the temple in Greece, Mesopotamia, and Israel. HSM 54: 1995 ⇒11/2,c408... 13,11178. ᴿJSSt 43 (1998) 131-134 (*Geller, Mark*); CBQ 60 (1998) 105-106 (*Simkins, Ronald A.*).
11322 **Bardinet, Thierry** Les papyrus médicaux de l'Égypte pharaonique: traduction intégrale et commentaire. 1995 ⇒12,10632. ᴿBiOr 55 (1998) 735-738 (*Verhoeven, Ursula*).
11323 **Filer, Joyce** Disease. 1995 ⇒11/2,c441; 12,10635. ᴿArOr 66 (1998) 391-392 (*Hudec, Jozef*).
11324 ᴱ**Ginouvès, R.** L'eau, la santé et la maladie dans le monde grec. 1994 ⇒11/2,c447. ᴿRAr (1998/2) 426-429 (*Bouffier, Sophie C.*).
       ᶠ**KOLLESCH J.** Text & tradition... medicine 1998 ⇒56.
11325 ᴱ**Lucas, Ernest** Christian healing: what can we believe?. 1997 ⇒13,11184. ᴿEthics & Medicine 14 (1998) 92-93 (*Short, David*).
11326 **Marganne, Marie-Hélène** La chirurgie dans l'Égypte gréco-ro-maine d'après les papyrus littéraires grecs. Studies in ancient medicine 17: Lei 1998, Brill xxxii; 192 pp. 26 fig.; Bibl.
11327 *McConvery, Brendan* Ancient physicians and their art. BiTod 36 (1998) 306-312.
11328 **Nordheim, Mich von** "Ich bin der Herr, dein Arzt": der Arzt in der Kultur des alten Israel?. Würzburger medizinhistorische Forschun-gen 63: Wü 1998, Königshausen & N vii; 102 pp. 3-8260-1637-8.
11329 *Petrini, Massimo* Healing themes in the bible. Camillianum 9 (1998) 209-226.
11330 ᴱ**Rimon, Ofra** Illness and healing in ancient times. Haifa 1996, Hecht Museum, Univ. 46 pl.; 31 fig. 71 (Eng.) 65 (Heb.) pp. ᴿPEQ 130 (1998) 63-67 (*Dauphin, Claudine M.*).
11331 **Rosner, Fred** Medicine in the bible and the talmud: selections from classical Jewish sources. NY ²1995 <1977> ᴿEthics & Medi-cine 14 (1998) 91-92 (*Rutecki, Gregory W.*).
11332 ᴱ**Serbat, Guy** CELSE: de la médecine, I . 1995 ⇒11/2,c495. ᴿAnCl 67 (1998) 352-354 (*Marganne, Marie-Hélène*).
11333 ᴱ**Van der Eijk, Ph.J.; Horstmanshoff, H.F.J.; Schrijvers, P.H.** Ancient medicine in socio-cultural context. 1995 ⇒11/2,c438. 2 vols. ᴿLatomus 57 (1998) 744-745 (*Mazzini, I.*).
11334 **Wilkinson, John** The bible and healing: a medical and theological commentary. GR 1998, Eerdmans vii; 350 pp. 08028-3826-X. Bibl.

U3 *Duodecim tribus*; **Israel tribes**; *land ideology*

11335 *Allen, Ronald B.* The land of Israel. Israel. 1998 ⇒369. 17-33.

11336   *Dohmen, Christoph* Gelobtes, verheißenes oder heiliges Land?: ein christlicher Blick ins Zentrum der Bibel. rhs 41 (1998) 139-149.

11337   [E]**Grabbe, Lester L.** Leading captivity captive: 'the exile' as history and ideology. JSOT.S 278: Shf 1998, Academic 161 pp. £35/$57. 50. 1-85075-907-3.

11338   *Grossman, David* Communal land in biblical and talmudic traditions. Land and community. 1998 ⇒466. 59-66.

11339   *Jelinek, John A.* The dispersion and restoration of Israel to the land;
11340   *Kaiser, Walter C.* The land of Israel and the future return (Zechariah 10:6-12). Israel. 1998 ⇒369. 231-258/209-227.

11341   *Kallai, Zecharia* The reality of the land and the bible. Biblical historiography. 1998 <1983> ⇒167. 186-201.

11342   *Momigliano, Giuseppe* Le dodici tribù in ordine alterno: richiami e simboli della storia ebraica. [F]SIERRA J. 1998 ⇒102. 379-392.

11343   **Nieswandt, Reiner** Abrahams umkämpftes Erbe: eine kontextuelle Studie zum modernen Konflikt von Juden, Christen und Muslimen um Israel/Palästina. SBB 41: Stu 1998, Katholisches Bibelwerk xiv; 432 pp. 3-460-00411-8. Bibl.

11344   [E]**Pifko, Raphael; Zwickel, Wolfgang** Biblische Landverheißung und politische Realität: die Entstehung des Staates Israel aus theologischer und talmudischer Sicht. Hofgeismarer Vorträge 12: Hofgeismar 1998, Evang. Akad. 35 pp.

11345   **Weinfeld, Moshe** The promise of the land: the inheritance of the land of Canaan by the Israelites. 1993 ⇒9,15229... 13,11201. [R]JSSt 43 (1998) 146-148 (*Curtis, Adrian H.W.*); AJSR 23 (1998) 105-108 (*Brown, John Pairman*).

11346   **Willi, Thomas** Juda—Jehud—Israel: Studien zum Selbstverständnis des Judentums in persischer Zeit. FAT 12: 1995 ⇒11/2,c522 [R]JSSt 43 (1998) 375-377 (*Grabbe, Lester L.*); JBL 117 (1998) 726-728 (*Berquist, Jon L.*).

11347   *Zaretsky, Tuvya* Israel the people. Israel. 1998 ⇒369. 35-59.

U4 *Viae*, roads, routes

11348   **Esch, Arnold** Römische Straßen in ihrer Landschaft: das Nachleben antiker Straßen um Rom. Zaberns Bildbände zur Archäologie: Mainz 1997, Von Zabern 161 pp. €34,77. 3-8053-2010-8. 235 fig. [AnCl 69,551s—Corbiau, Marie Hélène].

11349   **Fischer, Moshe; Isaac, Benjamin; Roll, Israel** The Jaffa-Jerusalem roads. Roman roads in Judaea II. 1996 ⇒12,10646. [R]RB 105 (1998) 303-304 (*Murphy-O'Connor, J.*).

11350   *Jelonek, Tomasz* O wędrowaniu w Biblii [Wandering in the Bible]. Życie Duchowe 14/5 (1998) 53-68 Sum. 5.

11351   **Tazzi, Aldo Mario** Le strade dell'antica Roma: dal IV secolo a.C. al V secolo d.C. in Europa, Asia e Africa. R 1998, Dedalo 231 pp. 88-86599-16-1. Bibl.

11352   *Zayadine, Fawzi* Die Königsstraße. WUB 7 (1998) 35.

U5.0 *Ethnographia*, **sociologia**; *servitus*

11353   **Adamo, David Tuesday** Africa and the Africans in the Old Testament. Bethesda 1998, Christian University Press 208 pp. $55. 1-57309-204-5 [Interp. 53,86—Waters, John W.].

11354   **Aguirre, Rafael** Del movimiento de Jesús a la iglesia cristiana: ensayo de exégesis sociológica del cristianismo primitivo. Agora 4: Estella 1998, Verbo Divino 225 pp. 84-8169-156-9 [ThLZ 124, 1234—Barbaglio, Giuseppe].

11355   *Alonso Schökel, Luis* 'Ho fatto festa davanti al Signore'. Festa e bibbia. 1998 ⇒403. 93-104.

11356   **Arens, Eduardo F.** Asia Menor nos tempos de Paulo, Lucas e João: aspectos sociais e econômicos para a compreensao do Novo Testamento. Biblioteca de estudos bíblicos: São Paulo 1998, Paulus 212 pp. 85-349-0977-6. Bibl.

11357   **Assmann, Jan** Das kulturelle Gedächtnis: Schrift, Erinnerung und politische Identität in frühen Hochkulturen. [2]1997 ⇒13,11212. [R]ThLZ 123 (1998) 938-939 (*Pöttner, Martin*)

11358   [E]**Bail, Ulrike; Jost, Renate** Gott an den Rändern: sozialgeschichtliche Perspektiven auf die Bibel. 1996 ⇒12,10654. [R]FrRu 4 (1998) 289-290 (*Schwendemann, Wilhelm*).

11359   *Balch, David L.* Attitudes toward foreigners in 2 Maccabees, Eupolemus, Esther, Aristeas, and Luke-Acts. [F]FERGUSON, E. NT.S 90: 1998 ⇒25. 22-47.

11360   *Barton, Stephen C.* Living as families in the light of the New Testament. Interp. 52 (1998) 130-144.

11361   *Bauckham, Richard* Egalitarianism and hierarchy in the biblical traditions. [F]WRIGHT D. 1998 ⇒126. 259-273.

11362   **Berten, Ignace** Figures bibliques et sens du travail: 'que nous faut-il faire pour travailler aux œuvres de Dieu?'. ConBib 6: Bru 1998, Lumen Vitae 64 pp [NRTh 120,636].

11363   *Boshoff, Willem* Demografie, omgewing en oorlewing: die sentrale hoogland van Palestin as leefwêreld. OTEs 11 (1998) 375-385.

11364   *Botha, Pieter J.J.* Houses in the world. Neotest. 32 (1998) 37-74.

11365   *Burchard, Christoph* Erfahrungen multikulturellen Zusammenlebens im Neuen Testament. Studien NT. WUNT 107: 1998 <1983> ⇒140. 293-311 [Rom 3,27-31; Gal 3,10-12].

11366   *Carroll, Robert P.* Lower case bibles: commodity culture and the bible. Biblical studies. JSOT.S 266: 1998 ⇒380. 46-69.

11367   **Casson, Lionel** Everyday life in ancient Rome. Baltimore [2]1998, Johns Hopkins Univ. Pr. xi (2) 170 pp. 0-8018-5992-1.

11368   [E]**Chalcraft, D.J.** Social-scientific Old Testament criticism: a Sheffield reader. BiSe 47: 1997 ⇒13,11221. [R]RRT (1998/2) 79 (*Taylor, David*).

11369   **Combes, I.A.H.** The metaphor of slavery in the writings of the early church: from the New Testament to the beginning of the fifth century. JSNT.S 156: Shf 1998, Academic 210 pp. £35/$57.50. 1-85075-846-8. Diss. Cambridge 1991; Bibl.

11370   *Corpas de Posada, Isabel* El matrimonio y la familia en la Sagrada Escritura. Medellin 24 (1998) 5-41.

11371   *Cox, Harvey* L'ambivalenza della festa nella fede biblica;

11372   The ambiguous feast: festivity in biblical faith. Festa e bibbia. 1998 ⇒403. 127-135/135-143.

11373   *Crüsemann, Frank* Menschheit und Volk: Israels Selbstdefinition im genealogischen System der Genesis. EvTh 58/3 (1998) 180-195.

11374   **Dalby, A.** Siren feasts: a history of food and gastronomy in Greece. NY 1995, Routledge 336 pp. $25. 0-415-15657-2. ᴿCIR 48 (1998) 387-388 (*Wilkins, John*).

11375   *Dangl, Oskar* Vom Überleben zum Erleben: der Weg durch die Wüste. PzB 7 (1998) 29-42.

11376   *Davis, Derek H.* Thoughts on a civil religion: solution to religion clause jurisprudence. ᴹSummers R. 1998 ⇒115. 219-241.

11377   *Dever, William G.* Social structure in the early Bronze IV period in Palestine;

11378   Social structure in Palestine in the Iron II period on the eve of destruction. Archaeology of society. 1998 ⇒9495. 282-296/416-431.

11379   *Ebach, Jürgen* Die biblische Rede vom Volk Gottes angesichts der aktuellen deutschen Diskussion um nationale Identität. EvTh 58 (1998) 196-212.

11380   *Elliott, John H.* Phases in the social formation of early christianity: from faction to sect—a social scientific perspective. Recruitment. 1998 ⇒320. 273-313.

11381   *Exum, J. Cheryl; Moore, Stephen D.* Biblical studies / cultural studies. Biblical studies. JSOT.S 266: 1998 ⇒380. 19-45.

11382   *Fabris, Rinaldo* Bibbia e identità culturale. Bibbia, popoli e lingue. 1998 ⇒381. 31-46.

11383   **Fechter, Friedrich** Die Familie in der Nachexilszeit: Untersuchungen zur Bedeutung der Verwandtschaft in ausgewählten Texten des Alten Testaments. ᴰ*Wanker, G.*: BZAW 264: B 1998, De Gruyter ix; 377 pp. €98,17. 3-11-016205-9. Diss.-Habil. Erlangen 1997.

11384   ᴱ**Feinman, Gary M.; Marcus, Joyce** Archaic states. School of American Research advanced seminar: Santa Fe, New Mexico 1998, School of American Research Press Bibl. xiv; 427 pp. 0-933452-98-5.

11385   *Filoramo, Giovanni* La festa nella storia delle religioni. Festa e bibbia. 1998 ⇒403. 33-54.

11386   ᴱ**Fitzgerald, John T.** Greco-Roman perspectives on friendship. SBL Resources for Biblical Study 34: 1997 ⇒13,11230. ᴿAnCl 67 (1998) 341-343 (*Wankenne, Jules*); JR 78 (1998) 649-650 (*Crawford, Matthew B.*).

11387   **Fusco, Vittorio** Le prime comunità cristiane: tradizioni e tendenze nel cristianesimo delle origini. 1997 ⇒13,3980. ᴿRSR 86 (1998) 434-36 (*Guillet, Jacques*); CivCatt 149/3 (1998) 92-4 (*Scaiolà, D.*).

11388   Garnsey, Peter Ideas of slavery from Aristotle to Augustine. 1996, ⇒12,10680. ᴿJThS 49 (1998) 335-337 (*Noy, David*)

11389   *Glancy, Jennifer A.* House readings and field readings: the discourse of slavery and biblical / cultural studies. Biblical studies. JSOT.S 266: 1998 ⇒380. 460-477.

11390   **Grabbe, Lester L.** Priests, prophets, diviners, sages: a socio-historical study of religious specialists in Ancient Israel. 1995 ⇒11/2,c643. ᴿJAOS 118 (1998) 139-140 (*Hurowitz, Victor*); BBR 8 (1998) 240-242 (*Hess, Richard S.*).

11391   **Greifenhagen, Franz Volker** Egypt in the symbolic geography of the pentateuch: constructing biblical Israel's identity. ᴰDuke 1998, 522 pp.

11392 **Grimm, Veronika E.** From feasting to fasting, the evolution of a sin: attitudes to food in late antiquity. 1996 ⇒12,10684; 13,11231. [R]SCI 17 (1998) 263-265 (*Elm, Susanna*); AJP 119 (1998) 655-657 (*Donahue, John F.*).

11393 **Hanson, Kenneth C.; Oakman, Douglas E.** Palestine in the time of Jesus: social structures and social conflicts. Mp 1998, Fortress xx; 235 pp. £15. 0-8006-2808-X. Bibl.

11394 **Harrill, J. Albert** The manumission of slaves in early christianity. HUTh 32: 1995 ⇒11/1,4889... 13,11233. [R]ThG 41 (1998) 151-153 (*Giesen, Heinz*) [1 Cor 7,21].

11395 *Hartman, Lars* Inte sörja som de andra: reflektioner kring familjeriter i tidig kristen tid, särskilt sådana dödsfall. SEÅ 63 (1998) 249-260.

11396 **Hellerman, Joseph Harold** The church as a family: early christian communities as surrogate kin groups. [D]LA 1998, 356 pp.

11397 *Heltzer, Michael* The head (commandant) of the city (śar hā'īr) in Ancient Israel and Judah (compared with Neo-Assyrian functionaries). ASJ 20 (1998) 17-22.

11398 **Henderson, John B.** The construction of orthodoxy and heresy: neo-Confucian, Islamic, Jewish, and early Christian patterns. [Albany, NY] 1998, State University of New York Press vii; 265 pp. 0-7914-3759-0. Bibl.

11399 [E]**Herz, Peter; Kobes, Jörn** Ethnische und religiöse Minderheiten in Kleinasien: von der hellenistischen Antike bis in das byzantinische Mittelalter. Mainzer Veröffentlichungen zur Byzantinistik 2: Wsb 1998, Harrassowitz xx; 190 pp [REByz 58,300—Failler, A.].

11400 *Ilan, David* The dawn of internationalism—the Middle Bronze Age. Archaeology of society. 1998 ⇒9495. 297-319.

11401 **Ilan, Tal** Jewish women in Greco-Roman Palestine: an inquiry into images and status. 1996 ⇒12,10693; 13,11238. [R]JAOS 118 (1998) 570-573 (*Kraemer, Ross S.*).

11402 [E]**Joshel, Sandra R. Murnaghan, Sheila** Women and slaves in Greco-Roman culture: differential equations. L 1998, Routledge Bibl. xii; 287 pp. 0-415-16229-7.

11403 *King, Philip J.* Commensality in the biblical world. [F]FRERICHS, E. BJSt 320: 1998 ⇒28. 53-62.

11404 [E]**Kloppenborg, John S.; Wilson, Stephen G.** Voluntary associations in the Graeco-Roman world. 1996 ⇒12,10700. [R]JEarlyC 6 (1998) 152-154 (*Miller, Patricia Cox*).

11405 **Krause, Jens-Uwe** Witwen und Waisen im römischen Reich I-IV. 1994-1995 ⇒10,13621... 13,11244. [R]Gn. 70 (1998) 615-623 (*Weiler, Ingomar*); CIR 48 (1998) 414-417 (*Noy, David*).

11406 *Lafont, Sophie* Le roi, le juge et l'étranger à Mari et dans la bible. RA 92/2 (1998) 161-181.

11407 [E]**Laurence, Ray; Berry, Joanne** Cultural identity in the Roman Empire. L 1998, Routledge xi; 205 pp. £40. 0-415-13594-X.

11408 *Lemche, Niels Peter* The understanding of community in the Old Testament and in the Dead Sea scrolls. Qumran between OT and NT. JSOT.S 290: 1998 ⇒327. 181-193.

11409 **Maggioni, Bruno** Difensore delle vedove: la vedovanza nella bibbia. Mi 1998, OR 68 pp. €6,2. 88-8053-061-5.

11410 *Malipurathu, Thomas* Contrast community: its meaning and relevance for our times. VJTR 62 (1998) 606-623.

11411   ^E**Moxnes, Halvor** Constructing early christian families: family as
        social reality and metaphor. 1997 ⇒13,295. ^RJRH 22 (1998) 339-
        341 (*Horrell, David*); VigChr 52 (1998) 442-444 (*Reinhartz, A-
        dele*); INTAMS.R 4 (1998) 215-217 (*Kock, Claudia*).

11412   **Mödritzer, Helmut** Stigma und Charisma im Neuen Testament
        und seiner Umwelt. NTOA 28: 1994 ⇒10,13643... 12,10710.
        ^REstB 56 (1998) 132-134 (*González García, F.*).

11413   ^E**Nielsen, I. & H. Sigismund** Meals in a social context: aspects of
        the communal meal in the Hellenistic and Roman world. Aarhus
        Studies in Mediterranean Antiquity 1: Aarhus 1998, Aarhus U.P.
        245 pp. 56 fig. [REG 112,749—Hinard, François].

11414   *Norderval, Øyvind* Family-like care and solidarity as a pattern of
        social control in the ancient church. Recruitment. 1998 ⇒320. 347-
        356.

11415   ^E**Pilch, John J.; Malina, Bruce J.** Handbook of biblical social
        values. Peabody ²1998, Hendrickson xl; 223 pp. 1-565-63355-5
        [NThAR 2000,91].

11416   *Randellini, Lino* La minorità nel Nuovo Testamento. BeO 40/3
        (1998) 129-167.

11417   *Ravasi, Gianfranco* Perché la festa?: riflessioni bibliche. Festa e
        bibbia. 1998 ⇒403. 55-70.

11418   ^E**Rohrbaugh, Richard L.** The social sciences and New Testament
        interpretation. 1996 ⇒12,10715. ^RRevBib 60 (1998) 57-59 (*Levo-
        ratti, A.J.*).

11419   *Rosenfeld, Ben-Zion* Innkeeping in Jewish society in Roman Pales-
        tine. JESHO 41 (1998) 133-158 Sum. 133.

11420   **Ruffini, Ernesto, Card.** Fe cristiana y sociedad. ^E*Flecha, José-Román*:
        Cátedra Cardenal Ernesto Ruffini 1: S 1998, Cátedra Cardenal Er-
        nesto Ruffini; Universidad Pontificia 197 pp. 84-7299-433-3.

11421   *Sandnes, Karl Olav* The role of the congregation as a family within
        the context of recuitment and conflict in the early church. Recruit-
        ment. 1998 ⇒320. 333-346.

11422   **Scafi, Mario** La prostituzione nell'antichità: dai fenici ai babilone-
        si, dai persiani agli ebrei, dai greci alla Roma pagana: un panorama
        rigoroso ed esauriente su un argomento di universale interesse. Nu-
        ovepagine: R 1998, Serarcangeli 152 pp.

11423   *Schowalter, Daniel N.* Churches in context: the Jesus movement in
        the Roman world. The Oxford history. 1998 ⇒326. 517-559.

11424   *Scippa, Vincenzo* L'Antico Testamento e le culture del tempo. La
        terra e il seme. BTNap 19: 1998 ⇒310. 39-52.

11425   *Scott, William T.* The Bible John murders and media discourse,
        1969-1996. Biblical studies. JSOT.S 266: 1998 ⇒380. 478-497.

11426   *Seeman, Don* "Where is Sarah your wife?": cultural poetics of gen-
        der and nationhood in the Hebrew Bible. HThR 91 (1998) 103-125.

11427   *Seitz, Christopher* The city in christian scripture. Word without
        end. 1998 ⇒200. 276-291.

11428   *Sherratt, Susan* "Sea peoples" and the economic structure of the
        late second millennium in the eastern Mediterranean. ^FDOTHAN, T.
        1998 ⇒23. 292-313.

11429   *Sicre, José Luis* La solidaridad en el Antiguo Testamento. Proyec-
        ción 45 (1998) 273-284 Sum. 257.

11430   *Snyder, Graydon F.* Jesus before culture. Recruitment. 1998 ⇒320.
        113-128.

11431 **Solin, Heikki** Die stadtrömischen Sklavennamen: ein Namenbuch I, Lateinische Namen, II, Griechische Namen, III, Barbarische Namen. Forschungen zur antiken Sklaverei 2: 1996 ⇒12,10723 ^RHZ 266 (1998) 469-470 (*Grünewald, Thomas*); BSLP 93 (1998) 180-182 (*Dubois, Laurent*).

11432 **Sparks, Kenton Lane** Ethnicity and identity in Ancient Israel: prolegomena to the study of ethnic sentiments and their expression in the Hebrew Bible. ^DNorth Carolina 1996, ^{DVan Seters, J.}: WL 1998, Eisenbrauns xiv; 344 pp. $37.50. 1-57506-033-7.

11433 **Stegemann, Ekkehard W. & Wolfgang** Storia sociale del cristianesimo primitivo: gli inizi nel giudaismo e le comunità cristiane nel mondo mediterraneo. Studi religiosi: Bo 1998, EDB 775 pp. €40,8. 88-1040-797-0. Bibl. ^RLaós 5/2 (1998) 99-101 (*Calambrogio, Leone*).

11434 **Theissen, G.** De Jezusbeweging: een sociologische bijdrage tot de ontstaansgeschiedenis van het vroege christendom. Baarn 1998, Ten Have 127 pp [Coll. 29,329—Van Soom, Willy];

11435 Histoire sociale du christianisme primitif: Jésus—Paul—Jean. MoBi 33: 1996 ⇒12,10728; 13,11273. ^RSR 27 (1998) 355-357 (*Létourneau, Pierre*).

11436 **Thiel, Winfried** A sociedade de Israel no época pré-estatal. São Paulo 1993, Paulinas 158 pp. ^RThX 48 (1998) 475-476 (*Arrango, José Roberto*).

11437 **Verbruggen, Jan L.** Filial duties in the ancient Near East. ^DJohns Hopkins 1998, 294 pp.

11438 *Wengst, Klaus* Christliche Identitätsbildung im Gegenüber und im Gegensatz zum Judentum zwischen 70-135 d.Zt. KuI 13 (1998) 99-105.

11439 *Westbrook, Raymond* The female slave. Gender and law. JSOT.S 262: 1998 ⇒256. 214-238.

11440 **Yafé, F.C.** Profetas, reyes y hacendados en la época bíblica: estudio teológica-sociológico y crítico del Israel preclásico. BA 1998, Lumen 352 pp [Strom. 54,315].

U5.3 Commercium, oeconomica

11441 *Bresciani, E.* L'Egitto achemenide: Dario I e il canale del mar Rosso. Transeuphratène 14 (1998) 103-111.

11442 *Briend, Jaques; Quesnel, Michel* Die Handwerker. WUB 10 (1998) 64-65.

11443 *Brisch, Nicole* Die altassyrischen Handelskolonien in Anatolien. Zwischen Euphrat und Indus. 1998 ⇒318. 134-147 Mitarbeit von *Karin Bartl*.

11444 *Elat, Moshe* Die wirtschaftlichen Beziehungen der Assyrer mit den Arabern. ^FBORGER R. 1998 ⇒12. 39-57.

11445 **Fischer, Moshe L.** Marble studies: Roman Palestine and the marble trade. Xenia 40: Konstanz 1998, Universitätsverlag 323 pp. €80,78. 3-87940-547-6. Contrib. *Pearl, Z.; Grossmark, Tzional*; [ZDPV 115,91ss—Lichtenberger, Achim].

11446 ^E**Grimal, Nicolas-Christophe; Menu, Bernadette** Le commerce en Égypte ancienne. [Le Caire] 1998, Institut Français d'Archéologie Orientale ix; 297 pp. 2-7247-0216-6.

11447   **Jursa, Michael** Der Tempelzehnt in Babylonien vom siebenten bis
        zum dritten Jahrhundert v.Chr. AOAT 254: Müns 1998, Ugarit-
        Verlag viii; 145 pp. €41,93. 3-927120-59-6. ^RUF 29 (1997) 831-
        834 (*Müller, G.G.W.*).

11448   *Knapp, A. Bernard* Mediterranean Bronze Age trade: distance,
        power and place. Res maritimae. 1998 ⇒491. 193-205.

11449   *Lipiński, Edward* Aramaean economic thought. AltOrF 25 (1998)
        289-302.

11450   *Olivier, Hannes* Restitution as economic redress: the fine print of
        the Old Babylonian mešarum edict of Ammiṣaduqa. JNSL 24/1
        (1998) 83-99.

11451   **Pastor, Jack** Land and economy in ancient Palestine. 1997 ⇒13,
        11290. ^RCathedra 87 (1998) 163-168 **H**. (*Safrai, Zeev*).

11452   ^E**Price, B.B.** Ancient economic thought, 1. L 1997, Routledge x;
        271 pp. £47.50. 0-415-14930-4 [CIR 50,654s—Wilson, John-Paul].

11453   *Raban, Avner* Near Eastern harbors: thirteenth-seventh centuries
        BCE. ^FDOTHAN, T. 1998 ⇒23. 428-438.

11454   **Slotsky, Alice Louise** The bourse of Babylon: market quotations in
        the astronomical diaries of Babylonia. Bethesda 1997, CDL xiv;
        192 pp. 1-883053-42-0 [OLZ 95,409ss—Geller, Mark J.].

11455   *Stern, Ephraim* Between Persia and Greece: trade, administration
        and warfare in the Persian and Hellenistic periods (539-63 BCE).
        Archaeology of society. 1998 ⇒9495. 432-445.

11456   **Wattenmaker, Patricia** Household and state in upper Mesopota-
        mia: specialized economy and the social uses of goods in an early
        complex society. Smithsonian Series in Archaeological Inquiry:
        Wsh 1998, Smithsonian Institution Pr. xvi; 248 pp. 1-56098-782-0.
        Bibl.

11457   *Yener, K. Aslihan, al.,* Anatolian metal trade and lead isotope
        analysis. Rencontre Assyriologique 34. 1998 ⇒452. 547-564.

                    U5.7 **Nomadismus,** *ecology*

11458   *Fernandez-Tresquerres, Juan* Die Bauern vom Dschebel al-Mutaw-
        wak. WUB 8 (1998) 53.

11459   *Phillips, James L.; Belfer-Cohen, Anna; Saca, Iman N.* A collec-
        tion of natufian bone artefacts from old excavations at Kebara and
        El-Wad. PEQ 130 (1998) 145-153.

11460   **Saidel, Benjamin Adam** Arid zone pastoralists in the Early Bronze
        Age in the southern Levant. ^DHarvard 1998, 504 pp.

11461   *Sasson, Aharon* The pastoral component in the economy of hill
        country sites in the intermediate Bronze and Iron Ages: archaeo-
        ethnographic case studies. TelAv 25 (1998) 3-51.

11462   *Smith, John Masson* Nomads on ponies vs. slaves on horses. JAOS
        118 (1998) 54-62.

11463   *Van Driel, G.* The role of nomadism in a model of ancient Mesopo-
        tamian society and economy. JEOL 35-36 (1997-2000) 85-101.

U5.8 **Urbanismus**; *demographia*

11464 *Battini, Laura* Opposition entre acropole et ville basse comme critère de définition de la ville mésopotamienne. Akkadica 108 (1998) 5-29.

11465 *Böhme, Sabine; Kulemann, Sabina* Das frühbronzezeitliche Nordmesopotamien: nur provinzielles Hinterland?. Zwischen Euphrat und Indus. 1998 ⇒318. 91-99.

11466 **Castel, Corinne** Habitat urbain néo-assyrien et néo-babylonien: de l'espace bâti à l'espace vécu. 1992 ⇒10,12073. 2 vols. [R]Syr. 75 (1998) 198-300 (*Breniquet, Catherine*).

11467 **Endruweit, Albrecht** Städtischer Wohnbau in Ägypten: klimagerechte Lehmarchitektur in Amarna. 1994 ⇒10,12730... 12,9558. [R]JEA 84 (1998) 247-249 (*Shaw, Ian*).

11468 *Gophna, Ram* Early Bronze Age Canaan: some spatial and demographic observations. Archaeology of society. 1998 ⇒9495. 269-280.

11469 *Kirsch, Elisabeth; Larsen, Paul* Das Verhältnis zwischen Seßhaften und Nichtseßhaften in Mesopotamien am Ende des 3. und zu Beginn des 2. Jt. v. Chr. Zwischen Euphrat und Indus. 1998 ⇒318. 148-164.

11470 **Kolb, Frank** Rom: die Geschichte der Stadt in der Antike. Mü 1995, Beck 783 pp. FS71. 3-406-39666-6. 101 ill. [R]GGA 250/1-2 (1998) 2-27 (*Kienast, Dietmar*).

11471 *Machule, Dittmar* Ein neuer Forschungsansatz der Vorderasiatischen Archäologie?. OLZ 93 (1998) 413-438.

11472 *Margueron, J.-C.* Aménagement du territoire et organisation de l' espace en Syrie du Nord à l'âge du Bronze: limites et possibilités d' une recherche. Espace naturel. 1998 ⇒476. 167-178 Sum. rés. 167.

11473 *Segal, Arthur* Public plazas in the cities of Roman Palestine and Provincia Arabia. [F]SOHLBERG, D. 1996 ⇒8271. 451-487.

11474 *Sievertsen, Uwe* Äußere Gestalt und innere Organisation der frühen Stadtstaaten: neuere Forschungen zur frühdynastischen Zeit in Zentral- und Südmesopotamien. Zwischen Euphrat und Indus. 1998 ⇒318. 80-90.

11475 **Sperber, Daniel** The city in Roman Palestine. Oxf 1998, OUP viii; 200 pp. 0-19-509882-X.

11476 **Van de Mieroop, Marc** The ancient Mesopotamian city. 1997 ⇒ 13,11335. [R]BiOr 55 (1998) 806-808 (*Snell, Daniel C.*).

11477 [E]**Wilhelm, Gernot** Die orientalische Stadt. 1997 ⇒13,406. [R]OLZ 93 (1998) 639-640 (*Werner, Peter*).

11478 *Wasserstein, Abraham* The number and provenance of Jews in Graeco-Roman antiquity: a note on population statistics. [F]SOHLBERG D. 1996 ⇒8271. 307-317.

U6 **Narrationes peregrinorum et exploratorum**; *Loca sancta*

11479 *Albert, Bat-Sheva* עור על העלייה לרגל לארץ-ישראל בימי הביניים המוקדמים [On the importance of Frankish pilgrimage to the Holy Land (7th and 8th centuries)]. Cathedra 90 (1998) 33-52 Sum. 197 **H**.

11480 **Birch, Debra Julie** Pilgrimage to Rome in the Middle Ages: continuity and change. SHMR 13: [Woodbridge] 1998, Boydell x; 238 pp. 0-85115-636-3. Bibl.

11481 **Cunz, Martin** Die Fahrt des Rabbi NACHMAN von Brazlaw ins Land Israel (1798-1799). TSMJ 11: 1997 ⇒13,11340. [R]FJB 25 (1998) 178-186 (*Becker, Hans-Jürgen*).

11482 *Drobner, Hubertus R.* Die Palästina-Itinerarien der Alten Kirche als literarische, historische und archäologische Quellen. Aug. 38/2 (1998) 293-354.

11483 **García Martín, Pedro** La cruzada pacífica: la peregrinación a Jerusalén de Don Fadrique Enríquez de RIBERA. 1997 ⇒13,11344. [R]Hispania 58 (1998) 1194-1195 (*Bunes Ibarra, Miguel Angel de*).

11484 *Garzaniti, Marcello* Les apocryphes dans la littérature slave ecclésiastique de pèlerinage en Palestine (XIIe-XVe s.). Apocrypha 9 (1998) 157-177.

11485 **Grabois, Aryeh** Le pèlerin occidental en Terre Sainte au Moyen-Âge. Bibliothèque du Moyen Age 13: P 1998, De Boeck Univ. x; 11-266 pp. 2-8041-2799-0. Bibl.

11486 [E]**Guillaume, Jean; Pichois, Claude** Gérard de NERVAL: voyage en Orient. Folio classique 3060: P 1998, Gallimard 948 pp. 2-07-040-387-4. Préface d'*André Miquel*, texte établi et annoté par *Jean Guillaume* et *Claude Pichois* et présenté par *Claude Pichois*; Bibl.

11487 [ET]**Kappler, René** RICCOLD de Monte Croce: pérégrinations en Terre Sainte at au Proche Orient; lettres sur la chute de Saint-Jean d'Arc. Textes et Traductions des Classiques Français du Moyen Age 4: P 1997, Champion 272 pp. €21,34. 2-85203-632-0.

11488 **Lavarini, R.** Il pellegrinaggio cristiano: dalle sue origini al turismo religioso del XX secolo. Saggistica 71: Genova 1997, Marietti 732 pp. €29,95. 88-211-6008-2 [RivLi 87,691s—Troía, Pasquale].

11489 [T]**Maraval, Pierre** Récits des premiers pèlerins chrétiens au Proche Orient (IVe-VIIe siècle). 1996 ⇒12,10783; 13,11347. [R]NRS 82/1 (1998) 213-4 (*Racine, Pierre*).

11490 *Olivier, H.* The relationship between landscape resources and human occupation in Jordan in the nineteenth century. JSem 8/1 (1996) 96-110 Sum. 96.

11491 *Perrone, Lorenzo* Christian holy places and pilgrimage in an age of dogmatic conflicts: popular religon and confessional affiliation in Byzantine Palestine (fifth to seventh centuries). POC 48 (1998) 5-37.

11492 **Rees, Joan** Amelia EDWARDS: traveller, novelist & egyptologist. L 1998, Rubicon ix; 112 pp. 0-948695-61-7. Bibl.

11493 *Reiner, Elchanan* From Joshua to Jesus: the transformation of a biblical story to a local myth: a chapter in the religious life of the Galilean Jew. Sharing the sacred. 1998 ⇒306. 223-271.

11494 *Rostagno, Lucia* Pellegrini italiani a Gerusalemme in età ottomana: percorsi, esperienze, momenti d'incontro. OM 17/1 (1998) 63-157.

11495 *Schein, Sylvia* The 'female-men of God' and 'men who were women': female saints and Holy Land pilgrimage during the Byzantine period. Hagiographica 5 (1998) 1-36.

U7 *Crucigeri*—**The Crusades**; *Communitates Terrae Sanctae*

11496 *Boas, Adrian J.* The Frankish period: a unique medieval society emerges. NEA(BA) 61/3 (1998) 138-173.
11497 *Chazan, Robert* The First Crusade as reflected in the earliest Hebrew narrative. Viator 29 (1998) 25-38 Sum. vii.
11498 *Constable, Giles* The place of the crusader in medieval society. Viator 29 (1998) 377-403 Sum. vii.
11499 **Flori, Jean** La première croisade: l'occident chrétien contre l'Islam. 1996 ⇒12,10789. ᴿStMed 39 (1998) 477-478 (*Montesano, Marina*).
11500 **Grousset, René** Les Croisades. Quadrige 16: P 1994, PUF 128 pp. €7,47. 2-13-045810-6. ᶠSyr. 75 (1998) 322-323 (*Balard, Michel*).
. . ᶠHAMILTON, B. The Crusades and their sources 1998 ⇒37.
11501 ᴱᵀHousley, Norman Documents on the later crusades, 1274-1580. 1996 ⇒12,10790. ᴿIHR 20 (1998) 151-153 (*Cole, Penny J.*).
11502 *Ligato, Giuseppe* La prima crociata nel mosaico di Bobbio. TS(I) (sett-ott 1998) 10-12.
11503 **Maier, Christoph T.** Preaching the crusades: mendicant friars and the cross in the thirteenth century. 1994 ⇒11/2,c977; 12,10793 ᴿBECh 156/1 (1998) 254-255 (*Richard, Jean*).
11504 ᴱ**Phillips, Jonathan** The first crusade: origins and impact. 1997 ⇒13,11353. ᴿIHR 20 (1998) 149-151 (*Cowdrey, H.E.J.*).
11505 **Pringle, Denys** The churches of the Crusader Kingdom of Jerusalem: a corpus: II, L-Z [Churches outside Tyre]. C 1998, CUP xxiv; 456 pp. Drawings by *Leach, Peter E.* 0-521-39037-0 [RB 106,309s —Murphy-O'Connor, J.].
11506 *Reiner, Elchanan* השקר הגלוי והאמת הנסתרת: נוצרים, יהודים ומקומות קדושים בארץ ישראל במאה היב [Overt falsehood and covert truth: Christians, Jews, and holy places in twelfth-century Palestine]. Zion 63 (1998) 157-188 Sum. XIII.
11507 **Richard, Jean** Histoire des Croisades. 1996 ⇒12,10796. ᴿByZ 91 (1998) 575-577 (*Jaspert, Nikolas*).

11508 ᴱ**Butzkamm, Aloys** Wer glaubt was?: Religionsgemeinschaften im Heiligen Land. Pd 1998, Bonifatius 232 pp. €15,24 [BiKi 55,161].
11509 *Israele: da Mosè agli accordi di Oslo. Storia e civiltà* 46: Bari 1998, Dedalo 526 (4) pp. 88-220-0546-5. Introd. di *Franco Cardini*.
11510 **Schick, Robert** The christian communities of Palestine from Byzantine to Islamic rule: a historical and archaeological study. 1995 ⇒12,10800. ᴿBSOAS 61 (1998) 329-330 (*Hoyland, Robert*).
11511 *Walk, Joseph* Fünfzig Jahre Staat Israel: Interview mit Prof. Dr. Joseph Walk. rhs 41 (1998) 156-162.

XX. Historia scientiae biblicae

Y1.0 History of exegesis: General

11512 *André, Gunnel* Gamla testamentets exegetik och trons illusoriska vetande. SEÅ 63 (1998) 101-110.

11513 *Bardski, Krzysztof* Patristic interpretation of the scripture and modern biblical studies: methodological suggestions. FolOr 34 (1998) 23-29.
11514 **Brock, Sebastian P.** The bible in the Syriac tradition. Seeri Correspondence Course 1: Kottayam 1998, St. Ephrem Ecumenical Research Institute v; 99 pp [ITS 37,340—Legrand, L.].
11515 **Chadwick, Henry** Antike Schriftauslegung: pagane und christliche Allegorese: Activa und Passiva im antiken Umgang mit der Bibel. ᴱ*Markschies, Christoph*: Hans-Lietzmann-Vorlesungen 3: B 1998, De Gruyter xix; 87 pp. 3-11-016168-0.
11516 *Chadwick, Henry* Pagane und christliche Allegorese;
11517 Activa und Passiva im antiken Umgang mit der Bibel. Antike Schriftauslegung. 1998 ⇒11515. 1-23/25-87.
11518 ᴱ**Cipriani, Nello** Gcsú, il figlio: testi dei Padri della Chiesa. 1997 ⇒13,11367. ᴿHŭm(B) 53 (1998) 896-897 (*Arabito, Annalisa*).
11519 *Cox, Claude E.* The reading of the personal letter as the background for the reading of the scriptures in the early church. ᶠFERGUSON, E. NT.S 90: 1998 ⇒25. 74-91.
11520 **Drobner, Hubertus R.** Patrologia. CasM 1998, Piemme 742 pp. 88-384-4563-X. Presentazione di *Angelo Di Berardino.*
11521 ᴱ**FELICI, Sergio** Esegesi e catechesi nei Padri (secc. IV-VII). 1994 ⇒9,448*...12,10807. ᴾBen. 45 (1998) 456-457 (*Valli, Annamaria*).
11522 **Fiedrowicz, Michael** Prinzipien der Schriftauslegung in der Alten Kirche. Traditio christiana 10: Bern 1998, Lang xli; 202 pp. 3-906-760-70-7.
11523 **Gamble, Harry Y.** Books and readers in the early Church: a history of early christian texts. 1995 ⇒11/2,g094... 13,11371. ᴿLibrary Quarterly 68/1 (1998) 90-91, 93-94 (*Lynch, Beverly P.*); Latomus 57 (1998) 700-702 (*Charlet, J.-L.*); JAOS 118 (1998) 587-588 (*Holmes, Michael W.*).
11524 *Gerhardsson, Birger* Hur Svenskt Bibliskt Uppslagsverk kom till. SEÅ 63 (1998) 7-18.
11525 *Grech, Prosper S.* The Regula Fidei as a hermeneutical principle in patristic exegesis. Interpretation of the Bible. JSOT.S 289: 1998 ⇒389. 589-601.
11526 *Herzberg, Walter* Traditional commentators anticipating a modern literary approach. ᶠGORDON, C. JSOT.S 273: 1998 ⇒31. 517-532.
11527 **Hinson, E. Glenn** The early church: origins to the dawn of the Middle Ages. 1996 ⇒12,3879. ᴿJEarlyC 6 (1998) 327-329 (*Gustafson, Mark*); HR 37 (1998) 486-488 (*Ashanin, Charles B.*).
11528 **Ladner, Gerhart B.** God, cosmos and humankind: the world of early christian symbolism. 1995 ⇒11/2,g112; 13,11376. ᴿHeyJ 39 (1998) 345-346 (*Laird, Martin*).
11529 **Laporte, Jean** La Bible et les origines chrétiennes. 1996 ⇒12, 10814; 13,11377. ᴿOrChr 82 (1998) 258-259 (*Gahbauer, Ferdinand R.*).
11530 ᴱ**Le Boulluec, Alain** La controverse religieuse et ses formes. Patrimoines: P 1995, Cerf 432 pp. ᴿASEs 15 (1998) 521-523 (*Lusini, Gianfrancesco*).
11531 **Liébaert, Jacques; Spanneut, Michel; Zani, Antonio** Introduzione generale allo studio dei Padri della Chiesa. Brescia 1998, Queriniana 551 pp. 88-399-0101-9. Bibl.
11532 *Lombardi, Paolo* Critica della bibbia e critica delle religioni: alcune linee di sviluppo storico. Hum(B) 53 (1998) 672-688.

11533 **Lubac, Henri de** The four senses of scripture. Medieval exegesis, 1. ^T*Sebanc, Mark*: Ressourcement: GR 1998, Eerdmans xxiv; 466 pp. $45. Forew. *Robert L. Wilken* [AThR 82,205—Cameron, M.].

11534 *Luz, Ulrich* Die Bedeutung der Kirchenväter für die Auslegung der Bibel. DBM 17/2 (1998) 7-35 G.

11535 **Margerie, Bertrand de** Les Pères de l'Église commentent le Credo. Initiations aux Pères de l'Église: P 1998, Cerf 187 pp. 2-204-05706-1.

11536 *Marin, Marcello* Note patristiche. VetChr 35 (1998) 361-369.

11537 *McVey, Kathleen* The Chreia in the desert: rhetoric and the bible in the Apophthegmata Patrum. ^FFERGUSON, E. NT.S 90: 1998 ⇒25. 245-255.

11538 *Mihoc, Vasile* L'actualité de l'exégesè biblique des pères de l'Église. DBM 17/2 (1998) 36-46 G.

11539 *O'Loughlin, Thomas* Christ and the scriptures: the chasm between modern and pre-modern exegesis. Month 31 (1998) 475-485.

11540 **Raurell, Frederic** I Cappucini e lo studio della Bibbia. 1997 ⇒13, 11387. ^RLaur. 39 (1998) 533-537 (*Spinetoli, Ortensio da*); VyV 56 (1998) 307-309 (*Alvarez Barredo, Miguel*); CFr 68 (1998) 349-350 (*Armellada, Bernardino de*).

11541 **Reventlow, Henning Graf** Epochen der Bibelauslegung I-III. 1990-1997 ⇒6,k10... 13,11388. ^RSMSR 64 (1998) 230-234 (*Pani, Giancarlo*);

11542 Epochen der Bibelauslegung III: Renaissance, Reformation, Humanismus. Mü 1997, Beck 271 pp. 3-406-34987-0.

11543 *Ringgren, Helmer* Femtio år med Dödahavsrullarna. SEÅ 63 (1998) 125-128.

11544 *Rosendal, Bent* En rationalist og hans Bibel: Christian BASTHOLM og det Gamle Testamente. DTT 61/1 (1998) 23-32.

11545 ^E**Sæbø, Magne** Hebrew Bible/Old Testament: the history of its interpretation, 1: From the beginnings to the Middle Ages, 1: antiquity. 1996 ⇒12,10821; 13,11392. ^REeT(O) 29/1 (1998) 145-151 (*Laberge, Léo*); BiLi 71 (1998) 275-277 (*Oeming, Manfred*).

11546 **Tilley, Maureen A.** The bible in christian north Africa. Ph 1998, Fortress 232 pp. 0-8006-2880-2 [JEH 51,122s—Frend, W.H.C.].

11547 ^E**Van Oort, J.; Wickert, U.** Christliche Exegese zwischen Nicaea und Chalcedon. 1992 ⇒8,484*. ^RStPat 45/1 (1998) 205-206 (*Moda, Aldo*).

11548 ^E**Van Oort, Johannes; Wyrwa, Dietmar** Heiden und Christen im 5. Jahrhundert. Studien der Patristischen Arbeitsgemeinschaft (SPA) 5: Lv 1998, Peeters viii; 193 pp. 90-429-0711-8.

Y1.4 *Patres apostolici et saeculi II*—First two centuries

11549 *Alexandre, Monique* Apologétique judéo-hellénistique et premières apologies chrétiennes. Apologistes chrétiens. 1998 ⇒421. 1-40.

11550 *Bondavalli, Giovanna; Gianotti, Daniele* La 'violenza di Dio' nell' esegesi patristica fra II e III secolo. PSV 37 (1998) 215-229.

11551 **Campenhausen, Hans Freiherr von** The Fathers of the Church: combined edition of the Fathers of the Greek Church and the Fathers of the Latin Church. [Peabody, MASS] 1998, Hendrickson (12) 328 pp. 1-56563-095-5. Bibl.

11552 *Dal Covolo, Enrico* Conoscenza 'razionale' di Dio, contemplazione ed esperienza 'mistica': Ignazio di Antiochia, Clemente e Origene. V Simposio di Tarso. 1998 ⇒395. 237-251.

11553 **Jefford, Clayton, N.; Harder, Kenneth J.; Amezaga, Louis D.** Reading the Apostolic Fathers: an introduction. 1996 ⇒12,10832. ᴿOCP 64/1 (1998) 238-239 (*Farrugia, E.G.*).

11554 *Pouderon, Bernard* Réflexions sur la formation d'une élite intellectuelle chrétienne au IIᵉ siècle: les 'Écoles' d'Athènes, de Rome et d'Alexandrie. Apologistes chrétiens. 1998 ⇒421. 237-269.

11555 *Van der Horst, Pieter* PLATO's fear as a topic in early christian apologetics. Hellenism—Judaism—Christianity. 1998 ⇒9885. 257-68.

11556 CLEMENS A.: ᴱ**Le Boulluec, Alain** Clemens Alexandrinus: Stromata: les Stromates: Stromate VII. SC 428: 1997 ⇒13,11417. ᴿScEs 50 (1998) 250-251 (*Barry, Catherine*). [⇒11650].

11557 CLEMENS R.: *Amato, Angelo* Una lettura cristologica della *Secunda Clementis*: esistenza di influssi paolini?. ꟳHERIBAN J. 1998 ⇒41. 307-315.

11558 **Cote, Dominique** Le thème de l'opposition entre Pierre et Simon dans les 'Pseudo-Clementines'. ᴰLaval 1998, 331 pp.

11559 *Erlemann, Kurt* Die Datierung des ersten Klemensbriefes—Anfragen an eine communis opinio. NTS 44 (1998) 591-607.

11560 *Himuro, Misako* The phoenix in *The first epistle of Clement to the Corinthians*. Renaissance Studies 12 (1998) 523-544.

11561 *Jones, Stanley F.* Origines du christianisme: the Pseudo-Clementine basic writing and its sources. AEPHE.R 106 (1998) 321-323 [Bu BbgB 30,20].

11562 **Lindemann, A.** Die Clemensbriefe. HNT 17: 1992 ⇒8,k616; 11/2, g194. ᴿStPat 45/1 (1998) 207-209 (*Moda, Aldo*).

11563 ᵀ**Lona, Horacio E.** Der erste Clemensbrief. Kommentar zu den apostolischen Vätern 2: Gö 1998, Vandenhoeck & R 677 pp. €121, 24. 3-525-51682-7. ᴿRBBras 15 (1998) 564-565.

11564 DIDACHE: *Draper, Jonathan A.* WEBER, THEISSEN, and "wandering charismatics" in the Didache. JEarlyC 6 (1998) 541-576.

11565 ᴱ**Jefford, Clayton N.** The Didache in context: essays on its text, history and transmission. NT.S 77: 1995 ⇒10,248... 13,11424. ᴿThRv 94 (1998) 388-390 (*Rordorf, Willy*).

11566 *Niederwimmer, Kurt* Zur Entwicklungsgeschichte des Wanderradikalismus im Traditionsbereich der Didache <1977>;
11567 Doctrina apostolorum (cod. Mellic. 597) <1979>;
11568 Textprobleme der Didache <1982>;
11569 Der Didachist und seine Quellen <1995>. Gesammelte Aufsätze. BZNW 90: 1998 ⇒182. 70-87/88-94/128-141/243-266.

11570 **Niederwimmer, Kurt** The Didache: a commentary. Hermeneia: Mp 1998, Fortress xxvii; 288 pp. $52. 0-80066-027-7.

11571 ᴱᵀ**Rordorf, Willy; Tuilier, André** La doctrine des douze apôtres (Didachè): introduction, texte critique, traduction, notes. SC 248bis: P ²1998 <1978>, Cerf 266 pp.

11572 *Saxer, Victor* La Didachè: miroir de communautés chrétiennes du Iᵉʳ siècle. ꟳNESTORI A. 1998 ⇒86. 771-798.

11573 HERMAS: *Bryant, Joseph M.* Wavering saints, mass religiosity, and the crisis of post-baptismal sin in early christianity: a Weberian reading of 'The Shepherd of Hermas'. AES 39/1 (1998) 49-77 Sum. rés. Zsfg. 209.

11574 **Carlini, Antonio** Papyrus Bodmer XXXVIII: Erma: Il Pastore (Ia-IIIa visione). 1991 ⇒7,g47. [R]CÉg 73 (1998) 159-160 (*Lenaerts, Jean*).

11575 *Ernst, Ulrike* Der Hirt des Hermas: Ver-führung zum Umdenken in der erotischen Sophiakirche. Kompendium Feministische Bibelauslegung. 1998 ⇒7511. 778-788.

11576 [ET]**Körtner, Ulrich H.J.; Leutzsch, Martin** Patres Apostolici: Papiasfragmente; Hirt des Hermas. Schriften des Urchristentums 3: Da:Wiss 1998, viii; 510 pp. 3-534-14068-0. Bibl.

11577 *Osiek, Carolyn* The oral world of early Christianity in Rome: the case of Hermas. Judaism and Christianity. 1998 ⇒230. 151-172.

11578 *Stewart-Sykes, Alistair* Hermas the prophet and Hippolytus the preacher: the Roman homily and its social context. Preacher and audience. 1998 ⇒226. 33-63.

11579 IGNATIUS: *Edwards, Mark J.* Ignatius and the second century: an answer to R. Hübner. ZAC 2 (1998) 214-226.

11580 *Schöllgen, Georg* Die Ignatianen als pseudepigraphisches Briefcorpus: Anmerkung zu den Thesen von Reinhard M. HÜBNER. ZAC 2 (1998) 16-25.

11581 IRENAEUS: **Bingham, D. Jeffrey** Irenaeus' use of Matthew's gospel in Adversus haereses. [D]Dallas Theol. Sem. 1995: [D]*Blaising, Craig A.*: Traditio exegetica graeca 7: Lv 1998, Peeters xv; 357 pp. 90-6831-964-7. [R]Salm. 45 (1998) 483-486 (*Trevijano, R.*).

11582 *Grant, Robert McQueen* Irenaeus of Lyons. 1997 ⇒13,11441. [R]AThR 80 (1998) 273-274 (*Williams, A.N.*).

11583 [T]**Romero Pose, Eugenio** San Ireneo: demostración de la predicación apostólica. 1992 ⇒8,k658; 9,15732. [R]HumTeo 19 (1998) 373-375 (*Ribeiro, João*).

11584 JUSTINUS: [T]**Barnard, Leslie William** Justin Martyr: the first and second Apologies. ACW 56: 1997 ⇒13,11455. [R]NT 40 (1998) 299-300 (*Elliott, J.K.*); SVTQ 42/1 (1998) 85-97 (*Kesich, Veselin*).

11585 *Bidart, Rodrigo* Inostroza El Logos en Heráclito y San Justino. TyV 39 (1998) 345-352.

11586 *Fédou, Michel* La figure de Socrate selon Justin. Apologistes chrétiens. 1998 ⇒421. 51-66.

11587 *Hamman, Adalbert G.* Dialogue entre le christianisme et la culture grecque, des origines chrétiennes à Justin: genèse et étapes. Apologistes chrétiens. 1998 ⇒421. 41-50.

11588 *Lieu, Judith M.* Accusations of Jewish persecution in early christian sources, with particular reference to Justin Martyr and the *Martyrdom of Polycarp*. Tolerance. 1998 ⇒440. 279-295.

11589 *Stanton, Graham N.* Justin Martyr's *Dialogue with Trypho*: group boundaries, 'proselytes' and 'God-fearers'. Tolerance. 1998 ⇒440. 263-278.

11590 *Valenti, Giuseppina* Alcune osservazioni su Giustino martire, i Samaritani e la città di Neapolis. SMLR 64 (1998) 245-273.

11591 POLYCARPUS: ᵀ**Burini, Clara** Policarpo di Smirne: lettera ai filippesi, martirio. SOCr 26: Bo 1998, Dehoniane 178 pp. €13,43. 88-10-20617-7.

11592 ᵀ**Buschmann, Gerd** Das Martyrium des Polykarp: übersetzt und erklärt. KAV 6: Gö 1998, Vandenhoeck & R 453 pp. €76,69. 3-525-51681-9. Bibl. ᴿEstAg 33 (1998) 391-392 (*Luis, P. de*); BZ 42 (1998) 290-291 (*Klauck, Hans-Josef*).

11593 *Pani, Giancarlo* Il paolinismo di Policarpo di Smirne. V Simposio di Tarso. 1998 ⇒395. 191-213.

Y1.6 Origenes

11594 **Bendinelli, Guido** Il commentario a Matteo di Origene: l'ambito della metodologia scolastica dell'antichità. SEAug 60: R 1997, Inst. Patristicum Augustinianum 268 pp. 88-7961-037-6.

11595 *Castagno, Adele* Monaci Origen the scholar and pastor. Preacher and audience. 1998 ⇒226. 65-87.

11596 **Castellano, Antonio** La exegesis de Orígenes y de Heracleon a los testimonios del Bautista. Anales de la facultad de teología 49/1: Santiago 1998, Pont. Univ. Catolica de Chile 209 pp [NThAR 1998,367].

11597 *Castellano F., Antonio* El perfume del esposo: la dimensión sacramental en el "Comentario al Cantar de los Cantares", de Orígenes. TyV 39 (1998) 197-211.

11598 *Clements, Ruth Anne* τέλειος ἄμωμος: the influence of Palestinian Jewish exegesis on the interpretation of Exodus 12.5 in Origen's *Peri Pascha*. The function of scripture. 1998 ⇒236. 285-311.

11599 **Crouzel, Henri** Orígenes: un teólogo controvertido. BAC 586: M 1998, BAC 378 pp [EstAg 34,622—Luis, P. de].

11600 **Daley, Brian E.** Origen's *De Principiis*: a guide to the principles of christian scriptural interpretation. ᶠHALTON T. 1998 ⇒36. 3-21.

11601 **Daly, Robert** Origen: Treatise on the Passover. 1992 ⇒8,k673 ᴿEeT 29 (1998) 238 (*Coyle, John Kevi*).

11602 *Danieli, Maria Ignazia* La sete e la fama della parola: le *Omelie X e XVI sulla Genesi* di Origene. Sal. 60 (1998) 397-416.

11603 *Deriev, Denis* Origen: early christian writer I. Holy Land 18 (1998) 195-200.

11604 ᴱ**Dorival, Gilles; Le Boulluec, Alain** Origeniana Sexta: Origène et la Bible / Origen and the Bible. BEThL 118: 1995, Actes du Colloquium Origenianum Sextum Chantilly, 30 août - 3 septembre 1993 ⇒11/2,571... 13,11468. ᴿRTL 29 (1998) 97-102 (*Auwers, J.-M.*); FZPhTh 45 (1998) 313-314 (*Altendorf, Hans-Dietrich*); CrSt 19 (1998) 667-674 (*Pazzini, Domenico*).

11605 ᵀᴱ**Égron, Sr. Agnès** Origenes: Les écritures, océan de mystères: Genèse. Foi vivante: P 1998, Cerf 251 pp. €8,38. 2-204-05990-0. Bibl. [BCLF 602,2270].

11606 **Fédou, Michel** Christianisme et religions païennes dans le *Contre Celse* d'Origène. 1988 ⇒5,g708... 8,k677. ᴿEeT 29 (1998) 338-242 (*Coyle, John Kevin*).

11607 **Gasparro, Giulia Sfameni** Origene e la tradizione origeniana in occidente: letture storico-religiose. BSRel 142: R 1998, LAS 426 pp. €28,41. 88-213-0396-9. Bibl.

11608 ^E**Lies, Lothar** Origeniana Quarta. 1987 ⇒3,6646... 5,g712. ^REeT
29 (1998) 235-238 (*Coyle, John Kevin*).

11609 *Lluch Baixauli, Miguel* La interpretación de Orígenes al Decálogo.
ScrTh 30 (1998) 87-109.

11610 *Lubac, Henri de* Origen: 'On first principles' <1950>;

11611 Origen: The incarnation of Christ <1973>. Com(US) 25 (1998) 340
-356/357-365.

11612 *Lupi, João* Orígenes: concepção do saber, plano e método. Veritas
43 (1998) 475-482.

11613 **Neri, Umberto** Origene: testi ermeneutici. 1996 ⇒12,10900
^RRivBib 46 (1998) 251-254 (*Pazzini, Domenico*).

11614 *Perelli, Carlo* Eusebio e la critica di Porfirio a Origene: l'esegesi
cristiana dell'Antico Testamento come μεταληπτικὸς πρόπος.
AnScR 3 (1998) 233-261.

11615 *Perrone, Lorenzo* 'Mosè ci viene letto nella chiesa': introduzione
alle *Omelie sulla Genesis* di Origene. Sal. 60 (1998) 251-272.

11616 *Rickenmann, Agnell* La gloria humilis, espressione di amore del
Cristo incarnato in Origene. RTLu 3 (1998) 737-743.

11617 *Simonetti, Manlio* La sacra scrittura nel *Contro Celso*. Discorsi di
verità. 1998 ⇒420. 97-114.

11618 ^T**Smith, John Clark** Origen: homilies on Jeremiah and 1 Kings 28.
FaCh 97: Wsh 1998, Catholic Univ. of America Pr. xxi; 358 pp.
$37. 0-8132-0097-0 [AThR 81,484s—Greer, Rowan A.].

11619 **Trigg, Joseph W.** Origen. The Early Church Fathers: L 1998,
Routledge xiii; 292 pp. £15. 0-415-11836-0.

11620 *Vaccaro, Jody L.* Digging for treasure: Origen's spiritual interpretation of scripture. Com(US) 25 (1998) 757-775.

11621 *Williams, Rowan D.* Origenes—ein Kirchenvater zwischen
Orthodoxie und Häresie. ZAC 2 (1998) 49-64.

Y1.8 **Tertullianus**

11622 ^T**Aulisa, I.** Tertulliano: polemica contro i giudei <Italian>. R 1998,
Città N 170 pp. L20.000. Hum(B) 55,162

11623 ^E**Braun, René** Tertullien: contre Marcion. SC 368, 399: 1991-1994
⇒6,k122... 13,11479. 2 vols. ^RAnCl 67 (1998) 374-375 (*Savon,
Hervé*); RTL 29/1 (1998) 94-96 (*Auwers, J.-M.*).

11624 *Dal Covolo, Enrico* La cristologia di Tertulliano: lo 'status
quaestionis'. ^FHERIBAN J. 1998 ⇒41. 317-323.

11625 *Dunn, Geoffrey D.* Tertullian and Rebekah: a re-reading of an
"anti-Jewish" argument in early christian Literature. VigChr 52
(1998) 119-145.

11626 *Fredouille, Jean-Claude* Tertullien dans l'histoire de l'apologétique. Apologistes chrétiens. 1998 ⇒421. 271-281.

11627 *Michaels, J. Ramsey* Almsgiving and the kingdom within: Tertullian on Luke 17:21. CBQ 60 (1998) 475-483.

11628 **Osborn, Eric Francis** Tertullian, first theologian of the West. 1997
⇒13,11483. ^RJThS 49 (1998) 820-822 (*Rist, J.M.*); AnnTh 12
(1998) 537-542 (*Leal, Jerónimo*); VigChr 52 (1998) 327-328 (*Van
Winden, J.C.M.*).

11629 *Stroumsa, Guy G.* Tertullian on idolatry and the limits of tolerance.
Tolerance. 1998 ⇒440. 173-184.

11630   *Van der Lof, L. Johan* Uso que de la tipología bíblica hace Tertuli-
        ano, en consideración a la historia de la iglesia. Augustinus 43
        (1998) 133-144.

Y2.0 *Patres graeci*—The Greek Fathers

11631   *Capizzi, Nunzio* Fil 2,7 nella cristologia antiapollinarista dei padri
        cappadoci: un suggerimento per la cristologia contemporanea. ᶠHE-
        RIBAN J. 1998 ⇒41. 325-340.
11632   *Dorival, Gilles* L'apologétique chrétienne et la culture grecque.
        Apologistes chrétiens. 1998 ⇒421. 423-465.
11633   ᴱ**Geerard, Maurice; Noret, Jacques** Clavis Patrum Graecorum:
        Supplementum. CChr: Turnhout 1998, Brepols xviii; 516 pp. 2-
        503-05061-1; adiuvantibus F. Gloire et J. Desmet.
11634   ᵀ**Grant, Robert M.; Menzies, Glen W.** Joseph's bible notes
        (Hypomnestikon). SBL.TT 41/9> 1996 ⇒12,10908; 13,11488.
        ᴿJEarlyC 6 (1998) 314-315 (*Kealy, Seán P.*).
11635   *Sesboué, Bernard; Fédou, Michel* Bulletin de théologie patristique
        grecque. RSR 86 (1998) 221-248.

11636   ARISTIDE: *Chapot, Frédéric* Les Apologistes grecs et la création du
        monde: à propos d'Aristide, *Apologie*, 4,1 et 15,1. Apologistes
        chrétiens. 1998 ⇒421. 199-218.
11637   ATHANASIUS: *Abramowski, Luise* Biblische Lesarten und
        athanasianische Chronologie. ZKG 109 (1998) 237-241.
11638   **Anatolios, Khaled** Athanasius: the coherence of his thought. L
        1998, Routledge viii; 258 pp. 0-415-18637-4. Bibl.
11639   *Kannengiesser, Charles* The Athanasian understanding of scripture.
        ᶠFERGUSON, E. NT.S 90: 1998 ⇒25. 221-229.
11640   *Meyer, John R.* Athanasius' use of Paul in his doctrine of salvation.
        VigChr 52 (1998) 146-171.
11641   **Wojciechowski, Michal** Atanazy z Aleksandrii: o wcieleniu Slo-
        wa. Pisma Starochrzescijanskich Pisarzy 61: Wsz 1998, Akademia
        Teologii Katolickiej 91 pp. 83-7072-105-2. **P.**

11642   BASILIUS: **Girardi, Mario** Basilio di Cesarea interprete della Scrit-
        tura: lessico, principi ermeneutici, prassi. QVetChr 26: Bari 1998,
        Edipuglia 338 pp. €25,82. 88-7228-219-5. Bibl.
11643   CHRYSOSTOMOS: **Belezos, Konstantinos I.** Χρυσόστομος καί
        σύγχρονη βιβλική έρευνα: ή χρονολογική ταξινόηση τῶν
        ἐπιστολοῶν τοῦ ᾽Απ. Παύλου. Athen 1998, Diigisi 196 pp. 960-
        7951-02-6 [OrthFor 13/1,76ss—Nikolakopoulos, Konstantin].
11644   ᴱᵀ**Brottier, Laurence** Chrysostomus: homiliae in Genesim: ser-
        mons sur la Genèse. SC 433: P 1998, Cerf 410 pp. 2-204-05996-X.
        Bibl. ᴿPOC 48 (1998) 210-212 (*Leduc, F.*).
11645   *Gignac, Francis T.* Evidence for deliberate scribal revision in
        Chrysostom's *Homilies on the Acts of the Apostles.* ᶠHALTON T.
        1998 ⇒36. 209-225.
11646   *Hill, Robert C.* Chrysostom, interpreter of the psalms. EstB 56
        (1998) 61-74;
11647   A Pelagian commentator on the Psalms?. IThQ 63 (1998) 263-271.
11648   *Van Willigen, M.A.* The rhetorical use of the text of the Old Testa-
        ment by John Chrysostom. Bible..informatique. 1998 ⇒386. 381-8.

11649 ^E**Zincone, Sergio** Giovanni Crisostomo: omelie sull'oscurità delle profezie. Verba Seniorum. NS 12: R 1998, Studium 255 pp. 88-382-3798-0. Bibl. ^RAug. 38 (1998) 501-503 (*Grossi, Vittorino*).

11650 CLEMENS A.: ^T**Merino Rodríguez, Marcelo** Clemente de Alejandría: Stromata I, II-III: cultura y religión: conoscimiento religioso y continencia auténtica. Fuentes Patrísticas 7, 10: M 1996-1998, Ciudad Nueva 2 vols. 88-89651-. Introd., notas [⇒11556].

11651 CYRIL A.: ^E**Burns, W.H.** Cyrillus Alexandrinus: epistulae paschales: lettres festales: XII-XVII Tome III. SC 434: P 1998, Cerf 315 pp. 2-204-06079-8. Texte grec par W.H. Burns. Traduction et annotation par Marie-Odile Boulnois et Bernard Meunier.

11652 *McGuckin, J.A.* Moses und das Geheimnis Christi in der Exegese des Cyrill von Alexandrien. ThQ 178 (1998) 272-286.

11653 DIONYSIUS A.: *Cavallero, Pablo A.* Las escrituras y el LOGOS en LOS NOMBRES DIVINOS del Pseudo-Dionisio. EstB 56 (1998) 97-105.

11654 **Rorem, Paul; Lamoreaux, John C.** John of Scythopolis and the Dionysian corpus: annotating the Areopagite. Oxford Early Christian Studies: Oxf 1998, Clarendon x; 294 pp. 0-19-826970-6. Bibl.

11655 ^{TE}**Witakowski, Witold** Dionysius (Telmahrensis): Chronicle (known also as the Chronicle of Zuqnin), 3: Pseudo-Dionysius of Tel-Mahre. Translated Texts for Historians 22: 1996 ⇒12,10919. ^RBiOr 55 (1998) 499-502 (*Van Ginkel, J.J.*).

11656 EVAGRIUS P.: ^{ET}**Géhin, Paul; Guillaumont, Antoine & Claire** Evagrius Ponticus: kephalaia gnostica: sur les pensées. SC 438: P 1998, Cerf 349 pp. 2-204-06081-X. Bibl.

11657 GREGORIUS Naz.: ^E**Metreveli, Helene; Tchelidze, Edisher** Gregorius Nazianzenus: Opera: versio iberica I: orationes, I, XLV, XLIV, XLI. CChr.SG 36; Corpus Nazianzenum 5: Turnhout 1998, Brepols xl; 297 pp. 2-503-40361-1. Bibl.

11658 *Noble, T.A.* Gregory Nazianzen's biblical christology. ^FWRIGHT D. 1998, 1-28.

11659 GREGORIUS Nys.: *Spataro, Roberto* 'Beati i puri di cuore perché vedranno Dio' nel *De Beatitudinibus* di Gregorio di Nissa. Sal. 60 (1998) 417-457.

11660 GREGORIUS Thaum.: ^T**Slusser, Michael** Gregorius Thaumaturgus: life and works. FaCh 98: Wsh 1998, The Catholic University of America Pr. xxi; 199 pp. $30. 0-8132-0098-9. Bibl.

11661 JOHANNES Damasc.: ^T**Migliarini, Margherita** Johannes Damascenus: disputatio christiani et saraceni: controversia tra un saraceno e un cristiano <Italian>. ^E*Rizzi, Giovanni*: Ecumenismo e dialogo: Mi 1998, Centro Ambrosiano 76 pp. 88-8025-108-2.

11662 LUCIAN Samosata: *Cancik, Hubert* Lucian on conversion: remarks on Lucian's dialogue Nigrinos. ^FBETZ, H. 1998 ⇒10. 26-48.

11663 MAXIMUS Conf.: *Boudignon, Christian* Silence ou exégèse de Maxime le Confesseur. ASEs 15 (1998) 353-363.

11664   **Louth, Andrew** Maximus el Confesor: tratados espirituales. 1997
⇒13,4669. [R]Ang. 75 (1998) 173-274 (*Degórski, Bazyli*);
11665   Maximus the confessor. 1996 ⇒12,10930. [R]AThR 80 (1998) 275,
277 (*Constas, Nicholas*); SVTQ 42/1 (1998) 102-104 (*Behr, John*);
JR 78 (1998) 432-433 (*Theodoropoulos, Helen Creticos*).
11666   *Louth, Andrew* Recent research on St Maximus the Confessor: a
survey. SVTQ 42/1 (1998) 67-84.
11667   [T]**Ponsoye, Emmanuel** Saint Maxime le Confesseur: lettres. Introd.
Larchet, Jean-Claude. Sagesses Chrétiennes: P 1998, Cerf 241 pp.
[R]Contacts 50 (1998) 283-284 (*Minet, Jacques*);
11668   Maxime le Confesseur: opuscules théologiques et polémiques. Introd. *Larchet, Jean-Claude.* Sagesses Chrétiennes: P 1998, Cerf
281 pp. [R]Contacts 50 (1998) 284-285 (*Minet,Jacques*).

11669   MELITO Sardes: *Cohick, Lynn* Melito of Sardis's Περὶ Πασχά and
its "Israel". HThR 91 (1998) 351-372.
11670   METHODIUS O.: **Patterson, Lloyd George** Methodius of Olympus:
divine sovereignty, human freedom, and life in Christ. 1997
⇒13,11506b. [R]TS 59 (1998) 326-328 (*Bright, Pamela*).
11671   OECUMENIUS: *Lamoreaux, John C.* The provenance of Ecumenius'
commentary on the Apocalypse. VigChr 52 (1998) 88-108.
11672   PTOLEMAEUS: [E]**Hübner, Wolfgang** (post F. Boll et Ae. Boer) Ptolemaeus, Claudius: opera exstant omnia: v.III 1, Apoteles-
matica. BSGRT: Stu [2]1998, Teubneri lxxv; 439 pp. 3-519-01746-6.
11673   THEODORET Cyros: **Guinot, Jean-Noël** L'exégèse de Théodoret de
Cyr. ThH 100: 1995 ⇒11/2,g403... 13,11508. [R]RSR 86 (1998)
232-236 (*Sesboüé, Bernard*).
11674   **Ha, Sung Soo** Das Hoheliedkommentar Theodorets von Kyros als
Beitrag zum Verständnis der antiochenischen Theologie. [D]Frei-
burg/B 1996-1997, [D]*Frank, K.S.* [ThRv 94,xi].

Y2.4 Augustinus

11675   *Barbàra, Maria Antonietta* I frammenti attribuiti ad Ambrogio e
Agostino nella tradizione catenaria bizantina. ASEs 15/1 (1998)
275-280.
11676   *Bochet, Isabelle* L'écriture et le maître intérieur selon Augustin.
RevSR 72 (1998) 20-37.
11677   *Bogaert, Pierre-Maurice* La bible d'Augustin: état des questions et
application aux sermons Dolbeau. Augustin prédicateur: Actes du
Colloque international de Chantilly, 5-7 sept. 1996. [E]**Madec, G.**
EAug, Antiquité 159: P 1998, Institut d'Etudes Augustiniennes 547
pp. 33-47 [REAug 44,346].
11678   *Bright, Pamela* En-spirited waters: baptism in the Confessions of
Augustine. [F]FERGUSON, E. NT.S 90: 1998 ⇒25. 48-58.
11679   *Cassidy, Eoin Per Christum Hominem ad Christum Deum*: Augustine's homilies on John's gospel. Studies in patristic christology.
1998 ⇒412. 122-143.
11680   *Cazier, Pierre* Le *De consensu euangelistarum* d'Augustin et
l'historicité des évangiles. Graphè 17 (1998) 45-68.
11681   *Cipriani, Nello* Agostino lettore dei commentari paolini di Mario
Vittorino. Aug. 38 (1998) 413-428.

11682 ^{TE}Dyson, R.W. Aurelius Augustinus: de civitate dei: the city of God against the pagans. Cambridge Texts in the History of Political Thought: C 1998, CUP xxxiii; 1243 pp. 0-521-46843-4.

11683 *Feldmann, Erich* Psalmenauslegung der Alten Kirche: Augustinus. ^FLOHFINK N. 1998 ⇒64. 297-322.

11684 **Ferraro, Giuseppe** Lo spirito e Cristo: nel commento al quarto vangelo e nel trattato trinitario di Sant'Agostino. 1997 ⇒13,11517. ^RCivCatt 149/1 (1998) 300-301 *(Cattaneo, E.)*.

11685 **Fiedrowicz, Michael** Könnte ich dich je vergessen, Jerusalem?: der Gottesstaat im Spiegel der Psalmendeutung Augustins. 1997 ⇒ 13,11518. ^RMayéutica 24 (1998) 232-233 *(Eguiarte, Enrique)*.

11686 *Gori, Franco* La tradizione manoscritta delle Enarrationes in Psalmos 141-150 di Agostino: studio preliminare per l'edizione critica. Aug. 38 (1998) 455-489.

11687 *Langa Aguilar, Pedro* Jesucristo, en la vida de san Agustín. Augustinus 43 (1998) 79-105.

11688 **Lössl, Josef** Intellectus gratiae: die erkenntnistheoretische und hermeneutische Dimension der Gnadenlehre Augustinus von Hippo. 1997 ⇒13,11526. ^RRelSt 34/2 (1998) 224-227 *(Stone, Martin)*.

11689 *Marin, Marcello* Historia e derivati in Agostino: note retoriche ed esegetiche. VetChr 35 (1998) 97-118.

11690 **Rist, John M.** Augustine. 1994 ⇒11/2,g473; 13,11529. ^REvQ 70 (1998) 92-93 *(Wright, David F.)*; Gn. 70 (1998) 117-120 *(Bastiaensen, A.A.R.)*.

11691 **Studer, Basil** The grace of Christ and grace of God in Augustine of Hippo: christocentrism or theocentrism?. 1997 ⇒13,11533. £23 ^RDoLi 48 (1998) 510-511 *(McCarthy, Thomas)*.

11692 ^T**Tarulli, Vincenzo** Sant'Agostino: il consenso degli evangelisti, 10/1. R 1996, Città N cxxxv; 545 pp. €51,65. ^RCivCatt 149/4 (1998) 444-445 *(Cremascoli, G.)*.

11693 *TeSelle, Eugene* Exploring the inner conflict: Augustine's sermons on Romans 7 and 8. SBL.SP/2. SBL.SPS 37: 1998 ⇒402. 968-990.

Y2.5 Hieronymus

11694 *Béné, Charles* Érasme de Rotterdam et Marc Marule de Split, biographes de saint Jérôme. ^FLANCEL S. 1998 ⇒59. 197-212 [REAug 44,350].

11695 ^E**Cola, Silvano** San Girolamo: le lettere, 1: lettere I-LII. R 1996, Città N 470 pp. €30,99. ^RCivCatt 149/4 (1998) 100-102 *(Cremascoli, G.)*

11696 *Fürst, Alfons* Hieronymus über die heilsame Täuschung. ZAC 2 (1998) 97-112.

11697 *Gilbert, Maurice* Saint Jérôme, traducteur de la bible. Il a parlé par les prophètes. 1998 <1986> ⇒155. 9-28.

11698 **Jay, Pierre** Jérôme lecteur de l'écriture. CEv.S 104: P 1998, Cerf 75 pp. €6,1. 0222-9706:

11699 La Bible dans la vie de Jérôme 13-17;
11700 Comment recevoir l'écriture 33-38;
11701 De la traduction à l'exégèse 26-32;
11702 Jérôme traducteur: révisions et traductions du texte biblique 19-25;
11703 L'héritage de Jérôme 71-72;

11704   Pages d'évangiles 61-69;
11705   Prophètes et psaumes 39-59 ⇒11698.
11706   Jerónimo (San): Obras completas, 1: obras homiléticas. BAC 293:
        M 1998, BAC 1035 pp. 84-7914-403-3. Lat.-Sp. [ATG 62,287—
        Peña, E.].
11707   **Krumeich, Christa** Hieronymus und die christlichen feminae cla-
        rissimae. 1993 ⇒11/2,g512. ᴿGn. 70 (1998) 79-81 (*Clark, Eliza-
        beth A.*).
11708   *Laurence, Patrick* Jérôme, la culture grecque et les femmes. Apolo-
        gistes chrétiens. 1998 ⇒421. 315-331.
11709   *Newman, Hillel Isaac* Between Jerusalem and Bethlehem: Jerome
        and the Holy Places of Palestine. Sanctity of time. 1998 ⇒303.
        215-227.
11710   **Scourfield, J.H.D.** Consoling Heliodorus: a commentary on Je-
        rome Letter 60. 1993 ⇒9,16043... 11/2,g523. ᴿIThQ 63 (1998) 95-
        96 (*Brown, Dennis*).

        Y2.6 **Patres Latini** *in ordine alphabetico*

11711   *Daley, Brian E.* Apocalypticism in early christian theology. Ency-
        clopedia of apocalypticism II. 1998 ⇒507. 3-47.
11712   *Ramelli, Ilaria* Alcune osservazioni sulle origini del cristianesimo
        in Spagna: la tradizione patristica. VetChr 35 (1998) 245-256.
11713   *Van der Lof, Laurens J.* IRENAEUS' and AUGUSTINE's use of typol-
        ogy. Aug(L) 48/1-2 (1998) 107-129.

11714   AMBROSIUS: *Barbàra, Maria Antonietta* I frammenti attribuiti ad
        Ambrogio e Agostino nella tradizione catenaria bizantina. ASEs 15
        (1998) 275-280.
11715   *Cattaneo, Enrico* Il 'Cantico dei Cantici' nelle catechesi mistagogi-
        che di Sant'Ambrogio di Milano. CivCatt 149/3 (1998) 29-41.
11716   *Feldmann, Erich* Christologische Ansätze des Ambrosius von
        Mailand und ihre Voraussetzungen. ᶠHOFFMANN, P., Von Jesus.
        BZNW 93: 1998 ⇒43. 529-549.
11717   *Paciorek, Antoni* Ambrosianische Anregungen in der Bibelausle-
        gung. Vox Patrum 34-35 (1998) 95-105 Zsfg. 104. **P.**
11718   **Ramsey, Boniface** Ambrose. 1997 ⇒13,11561. ᴿRRT 1998/2, 43-
        44 (*Carleton Paget, James*).
11719   *Turek, Waldemar* Paolo maestro di vita spirituale nelle *Lettere* di
        Ambrogio. V Simposio di Tarso. 1998 ⇒395. 269-279.

11720   CASSIODORUS: ᵀᴱ**Santiago Amar, Pío B.** Casiodoro: iniciación a
        las sagradas escrituras. M 1998, Ciudad N 235 pp. Introd. y notas
        [Eccl(R) 13,247s—Izquierdo, A.].
11721   **Troncarelli, Fabio** Vivarium: i libri, il destino. IP 33: Steenbrugis
        1998, Abbatia Sancti Petri 108 pp. 2-503-50676-3. 44 pl.
11722   *Walsh, P.G.* Cassiodorus teaches logic through the Psalms. ᶠHAL-
        TON T. 1998 ⇒36. 226-234.
11723   CYPRIANUS: *Burns, J. Patout* Cyprian's eschatology: explaining
        divine purpose. ᶠFERGUSON, E. NT.S 90: 1998 ⇒25. 59-73.
11724   EUSEBIUS Caesar.: *Fitzgerald, John T.* Eusebius and the little
        labyrinth. ᶠFERGUSON, E. NT.S 90: 1998 ⇒25. 120-146.

11725 ·*Gallagher, Eugene V.* Prophecy and patriarchs in Eusebius' apologetic. Mediators of the divine. SFSHJ 163: 1998 ⇒287. 203-223.

11726 [T]**Migliore, Franzo** Eusebius Caesariensis: de ecclesiastica theologia: teologia ecclesiastica. CTePa 144: R 1998, Città N 259 pp. 88-311-3144-3. Introduzione, traduzione e note.

11727 [TE]**Velasco-Delgado, Argimiro** Eusebio de Cesarea: historia eclesiástica. 1997 ⇒13,11572. 2 vols. [R]EsVe 28 (1998) 499-500 (*Gómez, Vito T.*).

11728 GREGORIUS Elvira: [ET]**Pascual Torró, J.** Gregorio de Elvira: tratados sobre los libros de las santas escrituras. Fuentes Patrísticas 9: 1997 ⇒13,11575. [R]StPat 45 (1998) 283-284 (*Corsato, Celestino*); EfMex 16 (1998) 250-251 (*López García, Francisco Manuel*);

11729 Gregorius Illiberitanus: De fide: La fe. Fuentes Patrísticas 11: M 1998, Ciudad N 198 pp. 84-89651-52-3. Introd., notas J. Pascual; texto lat., apar. crit. de Manlio Simonetti.

11730 GREGORIUS Magnus: *Clark, Francis* Authorship of the commentary In 1 Regum: implications of A. de Vogüé's discovery. RBen 108 (1998) 61-79.

11731 **Motta, Carlo** La 'lectio divina' in San Gregorio Magno: presupposti, pratica e apporti esistenziali. Exc. [D]Gregoriana: [D]*Padovese, Luigi*: R 1998, 86 pp.

11732 *Vogüé, Adalbert de* La glossa ordinaria et le commentaire des Rois attribué à Grégoire le Grand. RBen 108 (1998) 58-60.

11733 HIPPOLYTUS: *Ayán, Juan José* María y Cristo en la exégesis de Hipólito al Antiguo Testamento. EstMar 64 (1998) 177-202.

11734 *Colpe, Carsten* Die "eklesaitische Unternehmung" in Rom, ihre Hintergründe und ihre mögliche Einwirkung auf das Häresienbild des Bischofs Hippolyt. [F]SPEYER, W. JAC.E 28: 1998 ⇒107. 57-69.

11735 IRENAEUS [⇒11581-3]: *Brox, Norbert* Die biblische Hermeneutik des Irenäus. ZAC 2 (1998) 26-48.

11736 *Fantino, J.* Le passage du premier Adam au second Adam comme expression du salut chez Irénée de Lyon. VigChr 52 (1998) 418-29.

11737 *Kannengiesser, Charles* The "speaking God" and Irenaeus's interpretative pattern: the reception of Genesis. ASEs 15 (1998) 337-52.

11738 *Singles, Donna* L'homme aux prises avec la gloire. LV(L) 239 (1998) 53-62.

11739 JUVENCUS: *Braun, Ludwig; Engel, Andreas* 'Quellenwechsel' im Bibelepos des Iuvencus. ZAC 2 (1998) 123-138.

11740 LUCIFERO Cagliari: *Marin, Marcello* Retorica ed esegesi in Lucifero di Cagliari. VetChr 35 (1998) 227-244.

11741 MAXIMUS: *Maritano, Mario* La sacra scrittura nei *Sermoni* e nel ministero episcopale di Massimo di Torino. ATT 4/2 (1998) 116-166.

11742 NOVATIAN: **Papandrea, James Leonard** 'Between two thieves': the christology of Novatian as 'dynamic subordination,' influenced by his historical context, and his New Testament interpretation. [D]Northwestern 1998, 620 pp.

11743 POTAMIUS: **Conti, Marco** The life and works of Potamius of Lisbon: a biographical and literary study with English translation and a

complete commentary on the extant works of Potamius: Epistula ad
Athanasium, De Lazaro, De Martyrio Isaiae Prophetae, Epistula de
Substantia, Epistula Potami. IP 32: Steenbrugis 1998, Abbatia S.
Petri xviii; 190 pp. 2-503-50688-7. Bibl.

11744   PRISCILLIAN: *Ferreiro, Alberto* Priscillian and Nicolaitism. VigChr
52 (1998) 382-392.

11745   PROSPER Aquitanus: [T]**Barbàra, Maria Antonietta** Prosper Aquitanus: la vocazione dei popoli. CTePa 143: R 1998, Città N 195 pp.
88-311-3143-5. Introduzione, traduzione e note.

11746   TYCHONIUS: [E]**Leoni, Luisa; Leoni, Daniela** Ticonio: sette regole
per la scrittura. 1997 ⇒13,11588. [R]LASBF 48 (1998) 614-615
(*Paczkowski, Mieczysław Celestyn*).

11747   **Browne, Gerald Michael** The Old Nubian martyrdom of Saint
George. CSCO.Sub 101: Lv 1998, Peeters viii; 47 pp. 90-429-
0676-6. Bibl.

Y3.0 Medium aevum, *generalia*

11748   **Brown, Catherine** Contrary things: exegesis, dialectic, and the
poetics of didacticism. Figurae: Stanford 1998, Stanford Univ.
Press xviii; 209 pp. $45 [ChH 69,418ss—Levy, Ian Christopher].

11749   *Herren, Michael W.* Irish biblical commentaries before 800.
[F]BOYLE L., I, 1998 ⇒13. 391-407.

11750   [E]**Lerner, Robert E.** Neue Richtungen in der hoch- und spätmittelalterlichen Bibelexegese. Schriften des Historischen Kollegs, Kol-
loquien 32: Mü 1996, Oldenbourg 191 pp. [R]ThR 63 (1998) 230-
232 (*Ohst, Martin*).

Y3.4 Exegetae mediaevales [Hebraei ⇒K7]

11751   AQUINAS: [E]**Philippe, M.-D.** Thomas d'Aquin: commentaire sur l'é-
vangile de saint Jean, 1: le prologue; la vie apostolique du Christ. P
1998, Cerf 685 pp. €74,7.

11752   BEDA: [E]**Bayless, Martha; Lapidge, Michael** Collectanea Pseudo-
Bedae. Scriptores Latini Hiberniae 14: Dublin 1998, Dublin Inst.
for Advanced Studies xiii; 329 pp [PIBA 22,126—McNamara, M.].

11753   BERNARD Clairvaux: *Brigitte, Soeur* Gesù e Gesù crocifisso in San
Bernardo. La Sapienza della Croce 12-13/4-1 (1997-1998) 339-
351; 17-24 sum. 339.

11754   [E]**Hendrix, Guido** Index biblicus in opera omnia S. Bernardi. Sancti
Bernardi opera 9: Brepols 1998, Turnhout xvi; 816 pp. 2-503-507-
44-1 [RBen 108,396.].

11755   [TE]**Tell, Isidoro** Bernardus Claraevallensis: sermoni sul Salmo 90.
ScrMon 20: Bresseo di Teolo (PD) 1998, Scritti Monastici lxxvii;
172 pp. 88-85931-25-1. Introduzione, traduzione e note.

11756   GIOACCHINO da Fiore: *Dutra Rossatto, Noeli* Hermenêutica e leitura da história em Joaquim de Fiore. Veritas 43 (1998) 513-523.

11757   **Grundmann, Herbert** Gioacchino da Fiore: vita e opere. Centro
internaz. di Studi Gioachimiti... testi e strumenti 8: R 1997, Viella
xxxiii; 261 pp.

11758 ISIDORUS Seville: *O'Loughlin, Thomas* Christ as the focus of Genesis exegesis in Isidore of Seville. Studies in patristic christology. 1998 ⇒412. 144-162.

11759 ISIDORUS Pelusiota: [TE]Évieux, Pierre Isidore de Péluse: Lettres I...1214-1413. SC 422: 1997 ⇒13,11604. [R]ScEs 50 (1998) 248-249 (*Barry, Catherine*).

11760 LULLUS Raimundus: [E]Euler, Walter Opera Latina 106-113: Ianuae et in Monte Pessulano anno 1303 composita. CChr.CM 115; Raimundi Lulli, opera latina 23: Turnholti 1998, Brepols xxv; 291 pp. 2-503-04151-5.

11761 [E]Madre, Aloisius Lullus, Raimundus: Opera Latina 130-133: In Monte Pessulano et Pisis anno 1308 composita. CChr.CM 114: Turnholti 1998, Brepols xxiv; 364 pp. 2-503-04141-8.

11762 OLIVI P.: [E]Flood, D.; Gál, G. Peter of John Olivi on the bible: principia quinque in sacram scripturam: postilla in Isaiam et in 1 ad Corinthios. Text 18: 1997 ⇒13,11605. [R]CFr 68 (1998) 695-697 (*Armellada, Bernardino de*).

11763 *Vian, Paolo* L'opera esegetica di Pietro di Giovanni Olivi: uno status quaestionis. AFH 91 (1998) 395-454.

11764 PETER de Blois: [E]Wollin, C. Carmina. CChr.CM 128: Turnholti 1998, Brepols 714 pp. 2-503-03281-8. Bibl.

11765 PIETRO Galatino: *Leftley, Sharon A.* Beyond Joachim of Fiore: Pietro Galatino's Commentaria in Apocalypsim. FrS 55 (1998) 137-67.

11766 RABAN Maur: *Fransen, Paul-Irénée* La fin inédite du commentaire de Raban Maur sur le Deutéronome. RBen 108 (1998) 80-103.

11767 RAIMUNDUS Sabunde: *Reinhardt, Klaus* Die Bedeutung der Heiligen Schrift in der Theologia naturalis des Raimundus von Sabunde (+1436). TThZ 107 (1998) 111-122.

11768 SALIMBENE de Adam: [E]Scalia, Giuseppe Salimbene di Adamo: Cronica. CChr.CM 125: Turnholti 1998, Brepols lxiv; 507 pp. 2-503-04251-1.

11769 THEOPHYLAKTOS Achrida: *Podskalsky, Gerhard* Theophylaktos von Achrida als Exeget in der slavischen Orthodoxie. Studi sull' Oriente Cristiano 2/1 (1998) 75-84.

11770 ŠUBHALMARAN: *Lane, David J.* The well of life: Šubḥalmaran's use of scripture. Symposium Syriacum VII. 1998 ⇒415. 49-59.

Y4.1 Luther

11771 *Asendorf, Ulrich* Luther und Hegel: Untersuchungen zur Grundlegung einer neuen systematischen Theologie. Luther Digest 6 (1998) 72-97. Sum. of *Luther und Hegel* (1982) 1-163.

11772 **Barlone, Sandro** Giustificazione e libertà nel primo Commento di Lutero alla Lettera ai Galati (Galaterbriefvorlesung 1516-1517). Contributi teologici: R 1998, Dehoniane 109 pp. 88-396-0760-9. Bibl.

11773 *Baue, Frederic W.* Luther on preaching as explanation and exclamation. Luther Digest 6 (1998) 38-41. Sum. of LuthQ 9 (1995) 405-418.

11774 *Begrich, Gerhard* Wirkmächtiges Wort: Sprache als Theologie in Luthers Bibelübersetzung. Diak. 29 (1998) 87-94.

11775   *Bourgine, Martin B.* Crux sola: la christologie de Luther à la lumière de sa theologia crucis. Irén. 71/1 (1998) 62-83.
11776   *Brecht, Martin* Römerbriefauslegungen Martin Luthers. [F]KLEIN, G. 1998 ⇒52. 207-225.
11777   **Burandt, Christian Bogislav** Der eine Glaube zu allen Zeiten— Luthers Sicht der Geschichte auf Grund der Operationes in psalmos 1519-1521. [D]Hamburg 1995: [D]*Lohse*: Hamburger Theologische Studien 14: Ha 1997, LIT xi; 287 pp. 3-8258-3007-1 [ZKG 112, 113ss—Basse, Michael].
11778   [T]*Büttgen, Philippe* De la liberté du chrétien: préfaces à la Bible. 1996 ⇒12,10992. [R]RThom 98 (1998) 512-514 (*Bavaud, Georges*).
11779   **Forde, Gerhard O.** On being a theologian of the cross: reflections on Luther's Heidelberg disputation, 1518. 1997 ⇒13,11608. [R]TrinJ 19 (1998) 238-241 (*Gramm, Kent*).
11780   [E]**Junghans, H.** Lutherjahrbuch, 65. Gö 1998, Vandenhoeck & R 268 pp. €36,81. 3-525-87430-8 [ThLZ 125,537s—Koch, Ernst].
11781   **Lienhard, Marc** Martim Lutero, tempo, vida e mensagem. [T]*Altmann, Walter; Hofmeister, Roberto Pich*: São Leopoldo 1998, Sinodal 410 pp [REB 241,242s—Lepargneur, Hubert].
11782   *Pasierbek, Wit* Duchowa spuścizna Marcina Lutra [Martin Luther's spiritual bequest]. Życie Duchowe 14/5 (1998) 107-124 Sum. 6.
11783   *Sander-Gaiser, M.H.* Het woord van God als weg om te leren: Luthers visie op leren en speelse leervormen. Luther Digest 6 (1998) 58-60. Sum. of Luther-Bulletin 4 (1995) 65-76.
11784   **Schwarz, Reinhard** Luther. Gö 1998, Vandenhoeck & R 271 pp. [SCJ 30,226s—Corpis, Duane].
11785   *Sherman, Franklin* Luther and the Jews: an American perspective. Internationales Josephus-Kolloquium. 1998 ⇒490. 210-217.
11786   **Wöhle, Andreas H.** Luthers Freude an Gottes Gesetz: eine historische Quellenstudie zur Oszillation des Gesetzesbegriffes Martin Luthers im Licht seiner alttestamentlichen Predigten. Fra 1998, Haag & H 334 pp. 3-8613-76601 [ITBT 6/7,34—Monshouwer,D.].

Y4.3 Exegesis et controversia saeculi XVI

11787   *Murdock, Graeme* The importance of being Josiah: an image of Calvinist identity. SCJ 29 (1998) 1043-1059 Sum. 1043.
11788   **Reventlow, Henning Graf** Renaissance, Reformation, Humanismus. Epochen der Bibelauslegung, 3. Mü 1997, Beck 271 pp. €34, 77. 3-4-6-34987-0 [OrdKor 40,367s—Heinemann, Franz Karl].
11789   **Wengert, Timothy J.** Human freedom, christian righteousness: Philip MELANCHTHON's exegetical dispute with ERASMUS of Rotterdam. Oxford studies in historical theology: NY 1998, OUP xiii; 239 pp. $45. 0-19-511529-5. Bibl.

Y4.4 Periti aetatis reformatoriae

11790   ALPHONSO Zamora: *Pérez Fernández, M.* Los estudios de hebreo en el siglo de oro español: Alfonso de Zamora. Actas... IX Jornadas Bíblicas. 1998 ⇒376. 17-31.
11791   ARIAS Montano: Benito Arias Montano (1527-1598). CDios 111/1 (1998) 5-6.

11792   *Lazcano, Rafael* Benito Arias Montano (1527-1598). RevAg 41 (1998) 923-928;
11793   Benito Arias Montano: bibliografía. RevAg 41 (1998) 1157-1195.
11794   *Morocho Gayo, Gaspar* Avance de datos para un inventario de las obras y escritos de Arias Montano. CDios 111/1 (1998) 179-275.
11795   ARMINIUS: *Clarke, F. Stuart* Arminius's use of Ramism in his interpretation of Romans 7 and 9. [F]WRIGHT D. 1998 ⇒126. 131-146.

11796   CALVIN: **Battles, Ford Lewis** Interpreting John Calvin. 1996 ⇒12, 11000. [R]ThTo 55/1 (1998) 108, 110-111 (*Leith, John H.*).
11797   *Elliott, Mark W.* Calvin the hebraiser?: influence and independence in Calvin's Old Testament lectures, with special reference to the 'commentary' on Jeremiah. [F]WRIGHT D. 1998 ⇒126. 99-112.
11798   *Greene-McCreight, Kathryn* "We are companions of the patriarchs" or scripture absorbs Calvin's world. MoTh 14 (1998) 213-224.
11799   **Hansen, Gary Neal** John Calvin and the non-literal interpretation of Scripture. [D]Princeton Theol. Sem. 1998, 421 pp.
11800   *Kearsley, Roy* Calvin and the power of the elder: a case of the rogue hermeneutic?;
11801   *Lane, Anthony N.S.* The sources of Calvin's citations in his Genesis commentary. [F]WRIGHT D. 1998 ⇒126. 113-129/47-97.

11802   ERASMUS: *Lienhard, Marc* Les radicaux du XVIe siècle et Érasme. RHPhR 78 (1998) 261-279.
11803   FLACIO Illirico: [T]**Neri, Umberto** Flacio Illirico: comprendere le scritture. Epifania della parola 10; Testi ermeneutici 5: Bo 1998, Dehoniane 80 pp. €9,3. 88-10-40233-2.
11804   GASPAR de Grajal: **Domínguez Reboiras, Fernando** Gaspar de Grajal (1530-1575): frühneuzeitliche Bibelwissenschaft im Streit mit Universität und Inquisition. [D]Freiburg/B: [D]*Smolinsky, H.* RGST 140: Mü 1998, Aschendorff liv; 744 pp. €99,19. 3-402-03804-8.

11805   MARCUS Lombardus: **Knoch-Mund, Gaby** Disputationsliteratur als Instrument antijüdischer Polemik... Marcus Lombardus. 1997 ⇒13,11632. [R]FrRu 4 (1998) 287-289 (*Niewöhner, Friedrich*).
11806   MARTÍNEZ de Cantalapiedra: **Alonso Artero, José Antonio** 'Liber septimus Hypotyposeon Theologicarum': los sentidos bíblicos. R 1998, Pont. Univ. Sanctae Crucis vi; 390 pp.
11807   MELANCHTHON: **Classen, Carl Joachim** Die Bedeutung der Rhetorik für Melanchthons Interpretation profaner und biblischer Texte. NAWG Ph.-hist. Kl. 1998,5: Gö 1998, Vandenhoeck & R 40 pp.

11808   ZWINGLI: **Hoburg, Ralf** Seligkeit und Heilsgewißheit: Hermeneutik und Schriftauslegung bei Huldrych Zwingli bis 1522. CThM.ST 11: 1994 ⇒12,11012. [R]Zwing. 25 (1998) 184-188 (*Schindler, Alfred*).
11809   *Reventlow, Henning Graf* Zwinglis Jesaja-Kommentar: eine methodologische Studie. [F]RUPPERT, L. FzB 88: 1998 ⇒99. 311-334.

Y4.5 *Exegesis post-reformatoria*—Historical criticism to 1800

11810   *Bedon, Vincent* SIMON, BOSSUET et la bible. NRTh 120 (1998) 60-74.

11811   ^E**Force, James E.; Popkin, Richard H.** The books of nature and
scripture: recent essays on...biblical criticism in the Netherlands of
SPINOZA's time and the British Isles of NEWTON's time. 1994 ⇒10,
14579*; 11/2,k176. ^RHeyJ 39 (1998) 206-207 (*Hamilton, Alastair*).

11812   **Harrisville, Roy A.; Sundberg, Walter** The bible in modern culture: theology and historical-critical method from SPINOZA to KÄ-
SEMANN. 1995 ⇒11/1,k460... 13,11641. ^RRStT 17/1 (1998) 107-
109 (*Badley, Jo-Ann*).

11813   **Laplanche, F.** La bible en France entre mythe et critique: XVIe-
XIXe siècle. 1994 ⇒10,14588; 11/2,k193. ^RCrSt 19/1 (1998) 225-
227 (*Pitassi, Maria-Cristina*).

11814   *Merk, Otto* Anfänge neutestamentlicher Wissenschaft im 18. Jahrhundert <1980>;

11815   Von Jean-Alphonse TURRETINI zu Johann Jakob WETTSTEIN
<1988>. ^FMERK O. BZNW 95: 1998 ⇒79. 1-23/47-70.

11816   *Preus, J. Samuel* The bible and religion in the century of genius, 1:
religon on the margins: conversos and collegiants; 2: the rise and
fall of the bible; 3: the hidden dialogue in SPINOZA's Tractatus; 4:
prophecy, knowledge and study of religion. Religion 28 (1998) 3-
14, 15-27, 111-124, 125-138.

Y4.7 Auctores 1600-1800 alphabetice

11817   BONJOUR: *Aufrere, Sydney; Bosson, Nathalie* Le Père Guillaume
Bonjour (1670-1714): un orientaliste méconnu porté sur l'étude du
copte et le déchiffrement de l'égyptien. Or. 67 (1998) 497-506.

11818   BUXTORF: **Burnett, Stephen G.** From christian Hebraism to Jewish
studies: Johannes Buxtorf... and Hebrew learning in the seventeenth
century. SHCT 68: 1996 ⇒12,11016. ^RSCJ 29/1 (1998) 100-101
(*Po-chia Hsia, R.*); Zion 63 (1998) 351-353 **H.** (*Carlebach, Elisheva*); JJS 49 (1998) 387-388 (*Goldish, Matt*).

11819   EDWARDS: ^E**Stein, Stephen J.** Jonathan Edwards: notes on scripture. NHv 1998, Yale Univ. Press xiv; 674 pp. $80. 0-300-07189-1.
[ThD 45,364—Heiser, W. Charles].

11820   GABLER: *Sæbo, Magne* Johann Philipp Gabler at the end of the
eighteenth century: history and theology. On the way to canon.
1998 <1987> ⇒194. 310-326.

11821   JONES: **Murray, Alexander** Sir William Jones, 1746-1794: a commemoration. Introd. *Gombrich, Richard*: Oxf 1998, OUP xvi; 169
pp. 0-19-920190-0.

11822   KANT: *Colombo, Enrico* Kant e l'esegesi biblica. RTLu 3 (1998)
601-610.

11823   LINDGREN: *Hidal, Sten* Henrik Gerhard Lindgren som översättare
av Gamla testamentet. SEÅ 63 (1998) 93-99.

11824   OWEN: *Trueman, Carl* Faith seeking understanding: some neglected aspects of John Owen's understanding of scriptural interpretation. ^FWRIGHT D. 1998 ⇒126. 147-162.

11825   RITSCHL: *Schäfer, Rolf* Ritschl, Albrecht (1822-1889)/Ritschlsche
Schule. TRE 29. 1998 ⇒501. 220-238.

11826   ROSMINI: *Valle, Alfeo* Rosmini e la sacra scrittura. RRFC 91/1
(1998) 45-96.

11827   SCHLEIERMACHER: *Dembowski, Hermann* Schleiermacher und die
Juden. ^FSCHRAGE, W. 1998 ⇒101. 319-329.

11828 SMITH: *Sæbo, Magne* William Robertson Smith at the end of the nineteenth century: theology and history and sociology of religion. On the way to canon. 1998 <1995> ⇒194. 327-335.

11829 SPINOZA: **Cassuto, Philippe** Spinoza et les commentateurs juifs: commentaire biblique au premier chapitre du Tractatus Theologico-Politicus de Spinoza. Aix-en-Provence 1998, Publications de l'Université de Provence 238 pp. €22,87. 2-85399-424-4 [FV 98/5,114 —Robert, Philippe de].

11830 TYNDALE: *Barnett, Mary Jane* From the allegorical to the literal (and back again): Tyndale and the allure of allegory;

11831 *Cummings, Brian* The theology of translation: Tyndale's grammar;

11832 *Decoursey, Matthew* The semiotics of narrative in *The Obedience of a christian man*;

11833 *Hammond, Gerald* Tyndale's knowledge of Hebrew: from the Old Testament to the New;

11834 *Parker, Douglas H.* Tyndale's biblical hermeneutics. Word, Church, and State. 1998 ⇒229. 63-73/36-59/74-86/26-35/87-101.

Y5.0 *Saeculum XIX*—Exegesis—19th century

11835 **Bediako, Gillian M.** Primal religion and the bible: William Robertson SMITH and his heritage. JSOT.S 246: 1997 ⇒13,11671 [R]Exchange 27/3 (1998) 285-7 (*Mey, Marc de*); JThS 49 (1998) 696-699 (*Johnstone, William*); Missionalia 26 (1998) 450-451 (*Van Niekerk, Attie*).

11836 [TE]**Bowie, Andrew** Friedrich SCHLEIERMACHER: hermeneutics and criticism and other writings. Cambridge Texts in the History of Philosophy: C 1998, CUP xl; 284 pp. $60/19. 0-521-59149-X/8-6. Bibl.

11837 **Crites, Stephen** Dialectic and gospel in the development of HEGEL's thinking. University Park 1998, Pennsylvania State Univ. Pr. xvii; 572 pp. $65 [JHP 37,540s—Stepelvich, Lawrence S.].

11838 **DiPuccio, William** The interior sense of scripture: the sacred hermeneutics of John W. NEVIN. Studies in American Biblical Hermeneutics 14: Macon 1998, Mercer Univ. Press xii; 228 pp. $19 [ChH 68,732s—Griffioen, Arie].

11839 *Graf, Friedrich Wilhelm* La théologie critique au service de l'émancipation bourgeoise: David Friedrich STRAUẞ (1808-1874). RThPh 130 (1998) 151-172.

11840 **Hauzenberger, Hans** Basel und die Bibel: die Bibel als Quelle ökumenischer, missionarischer... Impulse in der ersten Hälfte des 19. Jahrhunderts. 1996 ⇒12,11022. [R]ThZ 54 (1998) 84-85 (*Kuhn, Thomas K.*); Zwing. 25 (1998) 201-203 (*Blaser, Klauspeter*).

11841 *Knuth, Hans Christian* Ferdinand Christian BAURS "Paulus" und sein Verhältnis zu HEGEL in der Spätzeit. [F]KLEIN, G. 1998 ⇒52. 227-244.

11842 *Kratz, Reinhard Gregor* Die Entstehung des Judentums: zur Kontroverse zwischen E. MEYER und J. WELLHAUSEN. ZThK 95 (1998) 167-184.

11843 **Niccoli, Elena; Salvarani, Brunetto** In difesa di "Giobbe e Salomon": LEOPARDI e la bibbia. Pref. *Raimondi, Ezio*: Il castello di Atlante 14: Reggio Emilia 1998, Diabasis 179 pp. 88810-30519. Bibl.

Sæbo, M. William Robertson SMITH 1998 <1995> ⇒11828.

11844   **Treloar, Geoffrey R.** LIGHTFOOT the historian: the nature and role of history in the life and thought of J.B. Lightfoot (1828-1889) as churchman and scholar. WUNT 2/103: Tü 1998, Mohr xiii; 465 pp. €65,45. 3-16-146866-X. Bibl.

11845   ᴱ**Walter, Wolfgang** Hermann Samuel REIMARUS 1694-1768: Beiträge zur Reimarus-Renaissance in der Gegenwart. Veröffentlichungen der Joachim-Jungius-Gesellschaft der Wissenschaften Hamburg 85: Gö 1998, Vandenhoeck & R 52 pp. 3-525-86276-8.

11846   **Waubke, Hans-Günther** Die Pharisäer in der protestantischen Bibelwissenschaft des 19. Jahrhunderts. BHTh 107: Tü 1998, Mohr xiv; 379 pp. €91,01. 3-16-146971-2 [RB 106,480].

Y6.0 *Saeculum XX*—20th Century Exegesis

11847   *Alonso Schökel, Luis* Dos glosas a dos comentarios. EstB 56 (1998) 237-249 [G.J. Wenham, *Genesis* 1987-1994 ⇒10,1635... 13,1534 (Gen 4,1-5; Ps 39); W. Brueggemann, *Genesis* 1982 ⇒63,1995... 1,1945 (Gen 50,15-21)].

11848   **Fitzmyer, Joseph A.** The Biblical Commission's document *The interpretation of the Bible in the church*: text and commentary. SubBi 18: 1995, ⇒11/2,1424... 13,11676. ᴿAlpha Omega 1 (1998) 316-317 (*Izquierdo, Antonio*).

11849   **Koenen, Klaus** Unter dem Dröhnen der Kanonen: Arbeiten zum Alten Testament aus der Zeit des Zweiten Weltkriegs. Neuk 1998, Neuk 118 pp. €15,24. 3-7887-1656-8. ᴿJud. 54 (1998) 268-270 (*Bauer, Uwe F.W.*); KZG 11 (1998) 392-395 (*Lüder, Andreas*).

11850   ᴱ**Kolocotroni, Vassiliki; Goldman, Jane; Taxidou, Olga** Modernism: an anthology of sources and documents. E 1998, Univ. Pr. xx; 632 pp. 0-7486-0974-1.

11851   **Léon-Dufour, Xavier** Dios se deja buscar: diálogo de un biblista con Jean-Maurice de Montremy. Nueva alianza 144: S 1998, Sígueme 165 pp. 84-301-1332-0 [BiFe 25,156—Sáenz Galache, M.].

11852   **Naber, Hildegard** Die Bedeutung des Alten Testaments für die christliche Theologie: Positionen deutschsprachiger katholischer Alttestamentler des 20.Jhs. ᴰMünster: ᴰ*Zenger, E.* 1998-1999.

11853   *Rydlo, Jozef M.* La sacra scrittura presso i cattolici slovachi. ᶠHERIBAN J. 1998 ⇒41. 283-304.

11854   **Seidel, Hans Werner** Die Erforschung des Alten Testaments in der katholischen Theologie seit der Jahrhundertwende. BBB 86: 1993, ⇒9,16766; 11/2,k466. ᴿThR 63 (1998) 134-135 (*Perlitt, Lothar*).

11855   ALONSO SCHÖKEL: *Busto Sáiz, José Ramón* Luis Alonso Schökel, S.J. en la muerte de un maestro. MCom 56 (1998) 285-296.

11856   BAECK: *Merk, Otto* Judentum und Christentum bei Leo Baeck. ᶠMERK O. BZNW 95: 1998 <1976> ⇒79. 143-158.

11857   BALDENSPERGER: *Merk, Otto* Wilhelm (Guillaume) Baldensperger (1856-1936). ᶠMERK O. BZNW 95: 1998 <1982> ⇒79. 175-186.

11858   BARCLAY: **Rawlins, Clive** William Barclay—the authorized biography. L 1998, Fount 312 pp. £9. 0-00-628097-8.

11859   BARNABAS: **Kollmann, Bernd** Joseph Barnabas: Leben und Wirkungsgeschichte. SBS 175: Stu 1998, Katholisches Bibelwerk 109 pp. 3-460-04751-8. Bibl.

11860 BARTH: *Beckmann, Klaus* Christus, "nicht von jedem her": Karl Barths Entdeckung der biblischen Offenbarungskontinuität und seine Kritik an SCHLEIERMACHER. EvTh 58/2 (1998) 119-140.

11861 *Colwell, John E.* Perspectives on Judas: Barth's implicit hermeneutic. ^FWright D. 1998 ⇒126. 163-179.

11862 *Davie, Martin* The resurrection of Jesus Christ in the theology of Karl Barth. Proclaiming..resurrection. 1998 ⇒384. 107-130.

11863 *Merk, Otto* Karl Barths Beitrag zur Erforschung des Neuen Testaments. ^FMERK O. BZNW 95: 1998 <1989> ⇒79. 187-211.

11864 *Trowitzsch, Michael* Die Klärung der Lichtverhältnisse: zu Karl Barths Schriftauslegung. ZDT 14 (1998) 153-167.

11865 BEA: **Schmidt, Stjepan** Agostino Bea: il cardinale dell'unità. R 1998, Città N 950 pp [Obnovljeni Život 54,286s—Tomić, C.].

11866 BONHOEFFER: *Cipriani, Settimio* Bonhoeffer di fronte alla bibbia: una lettura attualizzante in rapporto a Cristo e alla chiesa. Asp. 45/1 (1998) 53-66.

11867 BOUSSET: *Merk, Otto* Wilhelm Bousset (1865-1920)/Theologe ^FMERK O. BZNW 95: 1998 <1982> ⇒79. 159-174.

11868 BRICHTO: *Wolf, Arnold Jacob* Brichto's bible. Jdm 47 (1998) 480-486.

11869 BROWN: *Duffy, Kevin* The ecclesial hermeneutic of Raymond E. Brown. HeyJ 39 (1998) 37-56.

11870 BUBER: *Gonsalves, Francis* A theological epilogue to Buber's dialogue. VJTR 62 (1998) 580-595.

11871 BULTMANN: *Merk, Otto* Aus (unveröffentlichten) Aufzeichnungen Rudolf Bultmanns zur Synoptikerforschung <1989>;

11872 Zu Rudolf Bultmanns Auslegung des 1. Thessalonicherbriefes <1985>. ^FMERK O. BZNW 95: 1998 ⇒79. 130-142/350-359.

11873 CLAUDEL: **Claudel, Paul** Le poëte et la bible. P 1998, Gallimard 1900 pp. €59,46. 2-07-074292-X. ^RVS 727 (1998) 373-375 (*Verdin, Philippe*).

11874 CULLMANN: *Merk, Otto* Zum 90. Geburtstag von Oscar Cullmann. ^FMERK O. BZNW 95: 1998 <1992> ⇒79. 231-234.

11875 DEIST: *Botha, Pieter J.J.* History, scripture and revelation: a conversation with Ferdinand Deist. OTEs 11 (1998) 386-414.

11876 *Venter, P.M.* Kanon en teks by Deist. OTEs 11 (1998) 582-599.

11877 DUHM: *Smend, Rudolf* Wissende Prophetendeutung: zum 150. Geburtstag Bernhard Duhms: Vortrag in der Dorfkirche St. Matthäi zu Bingum am 10. Oktober 1997. ThZ 54 (1998) 289-299.

11878 DUMÉZIL: *Coutau-Bégarie, Hervé* L'oeuvre de Georges Dumézil: catalogue raisonné suivi de textes de Georges Dumézil. P 1998, Économica 211 pp. 2-7178-3548-2. Bibliographie de G. Dumézil.

11879 DUPONT: **Standaert, Benoît** "Au carrefour des écritures": le père Jacques Dupont moine exégète. Cahiers de Clerlande 6: [Ottignies] 1998, Publications de Saint-André] 109 pp. Bibl.

11880 FLORENSKIJ: *Žák, L'ubomir* L'interpretazionre di Fil 2,6-8 e la concezione della *kenosis* nell'opera di P.A. Florenskij. ^FHERIBAN J. 1998 ⇒41. 349-371.

11881 GOULDER: **Goodacre, Mark S.** Goulder and the gospels: an examination of a new paradigm. JSOT.S 133: 1996 ⇒12,11058. ^RJThS 49 (1998) 233-237 (*Tuckett, C.M.*). ScrB 28 (1998) 46-48 (*Greenhalgh, Stephen*); JBL 117 (1998) 742-744 (*Gundry, Robert H.*).

11882   HABERMAS: *Urrea Carrillo, Mauricio* Jürgen Habermas: hermené-
         utica y mundo de la vida. Qol 17 (1998) 71-79 [BuBbgB 27,8].
11883   HERIBAN: *Blatnický, Rudolf* Profilo biografico e produzione lettera-
         ria del Prof. Jozef Heriban. [F]HERIBAN J. 1998 ⇒41. 473-493.
11884   HESCHEL: **Kaplan, Edward K.; Dresner, Samuel H.** Abraham Jo-
         shua Heschel: prophetic witness. NHv 1998, Yale Univ. Press x;
         402 pp. $35. 0-300-07186-8. 34 ill. [ThD 47,176—W.C. Heiser].
11885   KAUFMANN: **Krapf, Thomas** Yehezkel Kaufmann: ein Lebens-
         und Erkenntnisweg zur Theologie der hebräischen Bibel. 1990
         ⇒6,m31... 10,14804. [R]REJ 157/1-2 (1998) 250-252 (*Rothschild,
         Jean-Pierre*).
11886   KÄSEMANN: *Klostergaard Petersen, Anders* I korsets tegn: Ernst
         Käsemanns teologi. DTT 61/2 (1998) 133-156.
11887   *Zahl, Paul F.* A tribute to Ernst Käsemann and a theological testa-
         ment. AThR 80 (1998) 382-394.
11888   KLAWEK: *Kapera, Zdzisław J.* The Rev. Aleksy Klawek (1890-
         1969)—the university scholar. [M]KLAWEK A. 1998 ⇒51. 229-246.
         Bibl. 247-248.
11889   KÜMMEL: *Merk, Otto* Werner Georg Kümmel als Paulusforscher:
         einige Aspekte. [F]KLEIN, G. 1998 ⇒52. 245-256.
11890   LAGRANGE: [E]**Couturier, Guy** Les patriarches et l'histoire: autour
         d'un article inédit du père M.-J. Lagrange. LeDiv: P 1998, Cerf 337
         pp. €25,92. 2-204-06173-5. Préf. *Gourgues, Michel* [RB 106,475].
11891   **Montagnes, Bernard** Padre Lagrange 1855-1938: all'origine del
         movimento biblico nella Chiesa cattolica. CinB 1998, San Paolo
         190 pp. 88-215-3881-8.
11892   LÉVINAS: *Dennes, Maryse* Les sources russes de la philosophie d'
         Emmanuel Lévinas. BLE 99 (1998) 325-346.
11893   *Maldame, Jean-Michel* Emmanuel Lévinas face au sacré: de la tour
         de Babel à l'échelle de Jacob. BLE 99 (1998) 399-418.
11894   LUBAC: **Lubac, Henri de** Meine Schriften im Rückblick. Theologi-
         a Romanica 21: 1996 ⇒12,11063. [R]ThRv 94 (1998) 627-628 (*Mül-
         ler, Gerhard L.*); ZKTh 120 (1998) 413-419 (*Neufeld, Karl H.*).
11895   **Voderholzer, Rudolf** Die Einheit der Schrift und ihr geistiger
         Sinn: der Beitrag Henri de Lubacs zur Erforschung von Geschichte
         und Systematik christlicher Bibelhermeneutik. [D]München 1997:
         [D]*Müller, G.L.*: SlgHor 31: Einsiedeln 1998, Johannes 564 pp.
         €33,23. 3-89411-344-8 [NThAR 1998,365].
11896   **Wood, Susan K.** Spiritual exegesis and the church in the theology
         of Henri de Lubac. GR 1998, Eerdmans ix; 182 pp. 0-8028-4486-3.
         Bibl.
11897   MARTINI: *Fabris, Rinaldo* Carlo Maria Martini al servizio della
         Parola. [F]MARTINI, C. RivBib.S 33: 1998 ⇒75. 9-29 Bibl.
11898   **METZGER, Bruce Manning** Reminiscences of an octogenarian.
         1997 ⇒13,11716. [R]IThQ 63 (1998) 410-2 (*McConvery, Brendan*).
11899   **MOLTMANN-WENDEL, Elisabeth** Autobiography. 1997 ⇒13,
         11717. [R]RRT (1998/4) 81-83 (*Slee, Nicola*).
11900   MOWINCKEL: *Sæbø, Magne* Sigmund Mowinckel in his relation to
         the literary critical school. On the way to canon. 1998 <1988> ⇒
         194. 336-348.
11901   MUILENBURG: *Anderson, Bernhard W.* A teacher like Elijah. BiRe
         14/1 (1998) 16, 47.
11902   NORDEN: *Betz, Hans Dieter* Eduard Norden und die frühchristliche
         Literatur. Gesammelte Aufsätze IV. 1998 <1994> ⇒10. 78-99.

11903   PEDERSEN: *Frerichs, Ernest S.* The social setting of the peoples of the ancient Near East: an assessment of Johannes Pedersen (1883-1977). [M]WARD W. 1998 ⇒123. 111-115.
11904   PERDUE: *Odell, Margaret S.* History or metaphor: contributions to Old Testament theology in the works of Leo G. Perdue. RStR 24 (1998) 241-245.
11905   PIXLEY: **Fricke, Michael** Bibelauslegung in Nicaragua: Jorge Pixley im Spannungsfeld von Befreiungstheologie, historisch-kritischer Exegese und baptistischer Tradition. 1997 ⇒13,11719. [R]ThLZ 123 (1998) 1200-1201 (*Erbele, Dorothea*).
11906   POPE: *Smith, Mark S.* A potpourri of popery: marginalia from the life and notes of Marvin H. Pope. UF 30 (1998) 645-664.
11907   PRINSLOO: *Cloete, T.T.* Prof W S Prinsloo en die omdigting van die Psalms. SeK 19 (1998) 500-512.
11908   RAD, G. von: *Seitz, Christopher* The historical-critical endeavor as theology: the legacy of Gerhard von Rad. Word without end. 1998 ⇒200. 28-40.
11909   RICŒUR: *Askani, Hans-Christoph* Paul Ricœur, lecteur de la bible. BLE.S 2 (1998) 47-60.
11910   RIENECKER: *Eber, Jochen* Zum Gedenken an Fritz Rienecker (27.5.1897-15.8.1965). ThBeitr 29/4 (1998) 209-226.
11911   ROSENZWEIG: [T]**Evard, Jean-Luc** Franz Rosenzweig: L'écriture, le verbe et autres essais. P 1998, PUF iv; 176 pp. €22,71.
11912   *Marquet, Jean-François* Unité et totalité chez F. Rosenzweig: étude sur l'architecture de L'Étoile de la Rédemption. ArPh 61/3 (1998) 427-446.
11913   *Zak, Adam* Rosenzweig, Franz (1886-1929). TRE 29. 1998 ⇒501. 418-424.
11914   ROWLEY: *Coxon, Peter W.* Rowley, Harold Henry (1890-1969). TRE 29. 1998 ⇒501. 446-448.
11915   SCHÜRMANN: [E]*Ehrhardt, Theresia* Bibliographie Heinz Schürmann: Veröffentlichungen 1949-1998. Gesammelte Beiträge. 1998 ⇒197. 293-323.
11916   SCHWEITZER: *Nakonieczny, Rafał* Współczesny geniusz apostołem Biblii: sylwetka Alberta Schweitzera [Albert Schweitzer: genius et Bibliorum apostolus]. RBL 51 (1998) 138-141.
11917   **Schweitzer, Albert** Gespräche über das Neue Testament. [E]*Döbertin, Winfried* [2]1994 ⇒10,14819. [R]OrthFor 12 (1998) 265-266 (*Nikolakopoulos, Konstantin*).
11918   STEIN: **Rastoin, C.** Édith Stein et le mystère d'Israël. Genève 1998, Ad Solem 168 pp [NRTh 122,285s—Hausman, N.].
11919   SUMMERS: *Dilday, Russell* Eulogy for Ray Summers;
11920   *Garrett, James Leo* The writings of Ray Summers;
11921   *Hilburn, Glenn O.* Published and unpublished works by Ray Summers. Memorial Ray Summers. 1998 ⇒115. 2-6/21-42/43-58.
11922   TEEPLE: *Aune, David E.* The contribution of Howard Merle Teeple to New Testament scholarship. BR 43 (1998) 70-81.
11923   VICTORINUS: **Raspanti, Giacomo** Mario Vittorino exegeta di S. Paolo. Bibliotheca Philologica 1: 1996 ⇒12,11082. [R]CBQ 60 (1998) 169-170 (*Madigan, Kevin*).
11924   VISCHER: **Felber, Stefan** Wilhelm Vischer als Ausleger der Heiligen Schrift: eine Untersuchung zum Christuszeugnis des Alten Tes-

taments. ^DErlangen 1997: ^D*Slenzka, R.*: FSÖTh 89: Gö 1998, Vandenhoeck & R 414 pp. 3-525-56296-9 [RTL 29,575].

11925   VÖGTLE: *Merk, Otto* Begegnen und erkennen: das Matthäusevangelium im Werk Anton Vögtles. ^FMERK O. BZNW 95: 1998 <1991>
⇒79. 212-230.

11926   WESTERMANN: *Klemm, Peter* "Gedenket an eure Lehrer": Rezensi-
on zu den jüngsten Veröffentlichungen von Claus Westermann.
BThZ 15 (1998) 279-282.

Y6.3 *Influxus Scripturae saeculo XX*—Survey of current outlooks

11927   *Theron, J.* Wat is charismatiese teologie?: 'n oorsig oor resente ver-
wikkelinge. Acta Theologica 18/1 (1998) 29-49.

11928   *Van Rensburg, J. Janse; Cilliers, J.H.J.* 'N poimenetiese ondersoek
na 'n basisteorie vir die pastoraat aan okkultgekweldes. Acta Theologica 18/2 (1998) 33-57.

11929   *Wojciechowski, Michał* Bible and biblical studies in Poland. FolOr
34 (1998) 17-22.

Y7.2 *Congressus biblici*: nuntii, *rapports, Berichte*

11930   *Clines, David J.A.* From Copenhagen to Oslo: what has (and has
not) happened at congresses of the IOSOT;

11931   From Salamanca to Cracow: what has (and has not) happened at
SBL international meetings. OT essays, 1. JSOT.S 292: 1998
⇒142. 194-221/158-193;

11932   *Crocetti, Giuseppe* L'incontro del cristiano con Cristo nell'
eucaristia: memoriale della sua morte de della sua risurrezione: VI
Settimana biblica, Pragelato 25-29 agosto 1997. RivLi 85/1 (1998)
155-157.

11933   L'esegesi biblica cristiana nel II secolo (Trani, 20-24 aprile 1998).
VetChr 35 (1998) 371-379.

11934   *Focant, Camille* L'unité Luc-Actes: Colloquium biblicum Lovaniense XLVII. RTL 29 (1998) 563-567.

11935   *Hoppe, Rudolf* 52. General Meeting der Studiorum Novi Testamenti Societas vom 4.-8. August 1997 in Birmingham. BZ 42 (1998)
159-160.

11936   *Kapera, Zdzisław J.* SBL in Cracow. The Sixteenth International
Meeting of the Society of Biblical Literature Cracow, July 18-22,
1998. FolOr 34 (1998) 9-16.

11937   *Lust, J.* Sixteenth IOSOT Congress. 2-7.8.1998 Oslo. EThL 74
(1998) 538-539.

11938   *Maffei, Anna; d'Auria, Marta; Gajewski, Pavel.* Corano e Bibbia:
Convegno internazionale di Biblia (24-26 ottobre 1997). Amicizia
Ebraica-Cristiana 33 (1998) 56-60.

11939   *Minissale, Antonino* [Il X congresso della *International Organisation for Septuagint and Cognate Studies* Oslo, 31.7-1.8, 1998]. Synaxis 16 (1998) 706-707;

11940   Il XVI congresso dell'*IOSOT* ad Oslo>: 2-7.8, 1998. Synaxis 16
(1998) 701-706.

11941 *Nowak, Władysław* VII Międzynarodwe Sympozjum Józefologiczne na Malcie (1997) [De VII Internationali Symposio de S. Joseph in insula Melita (1997)]. RBL 51 (1998) 141-146.

11942 *Pisarek, Stanisław* General Meeting SNTS po raz trzeci w Birmingham (Anglia) [General Meeting SNTS for the third time in Birmingham]. AtK 130 (1998) 119-24.

11943 *Poon, Ronnie S.; Tong, Lancelot S.* Society of Biblical Literature 1997 meeting. Jian Dao 9 (1998) 233-234. C.

11944 *Segalla, Giuseppe* LIII congresso annuale della Studiorum N.T. Societas: Copenhagen 4-7 agosto 1998. StPat 45 (1998) 713-717.

11945 *Snyman, S.D.* Indrukke van die XVIth Congress of the International Organisation for the Study of the Old Testament (IOSOT), Oslo, Noorweë 2-7 Augustus 1998. Acta Theologica 18/2 (1998) 108-112.

11946 *Toniolo, Chiara Ferrari, al.,* Quinto seminario di specializzazione in 'Storia dell'esegesi cristiana e giudaica antica' (Trani, 7-12 aprile 1997. ASEs 15/1 (1998) 281-283.

11947 *Van Belle, G.* Studiorum Novi Testamenti Societas: 53rd General Meeting: 4-7.8.1998 Copenhagen. EThL 74 (1998) 535-536.

11948 *Verheyden, J.* The unity Luke-Acts: Colloquium biblicum Lovaniense XLVII (1998). EThL 74 (1998) 516-526.

11949 XXI Semana Bíblica Nacional: conclusões: Fátima 23-28.8.1998. Bib(L) 7/7 (1998) 149-150.

Y7.4 *Congressus theologici*: **nuntii**

11950 *Bühler, Pierre* Dal testo all'immagine—dall'immagine al testo. Fil-Teo 12 (1998) 439-451. Un colloquio de ermeneutica nel quadro della convenzione tra le università della Svizzera romanda e dell'est francese (Neuchâtel, 11-12 settembre 1997).

11951 Cuarto congreso internacional sobre la Sagrada Familia. EstJos 52 (1998) 243-245.

11952 *Pagazzi, Giovanni Cesare* La fenomenologia di Gesù. RdT 39 (1998) 777-781. Milano 16-17 giugno 1998.

11953 *Pignataro, M. Agnese* XI simposio internazionale mariologico (Roma, 7-10 oct. 1997). Mar. 59 (1998) 664-679.

11954 *Ponce Cuéllar, Miguel* Semana de *Estudios Marianos* de la Sociedad Mariológica Española. Mar. 59 (1998) 659-663 (Córdoba, 10-13 sept. 1997).

11955 *Tong, Lancelot S.* American Academy of Religion 1997 meeting. Jian Dao 9 (1998) 235-236. **C.**

Y7.8 *Congressus philologici, archaeologici*: **nuntii**

11956 Acta de la XXXIV asamblea general [de la Asociación Española de Orientalistas] celebrada en Santa María de Huerta (Soria), el día 4 de Mayo de 1997. BAEO 33 (1997) 414-415.

11957 *Geva, H.* קונגרס בינלאומי לציון חמישים שנה לגילוי מגילות מדבר יהודה [International congress: 50 years after the discovery of the Dead Sea scrolls]. Qad. 31 (1998) 135-136. **H.**

11958 *Homès-Fredericq, D.; Degraeve, A.* XLVe Rencontre assyriolo-
       gique internationale / XLVe Internationale assyriologische ontmoe-
       ting: coopération internationale 1998. Akkadica 107 (1998) 1-43,
       65-67.
11959 ᴱ*Kapera, Zdzisław J.* Abstracts of the Qumran papers from the SBL
       in Cracow, 1998. Qumran Chronicle 8/1-2 (1998) 13-19;
11960 The fifth international colloquium on the Dead Sea scrolls Kraków-
       Zakrzówek 1995: general remarks. ᴹKLAWEK A. 1998 ⇒51. 7-12;
11961 Qumran at the SBL in Cracow. Qumran Chronicle 8/1-2 (1998) 9-
       12.
11962 *Llagostera, Esteban* XXXV asamblea general de la Asociación
       Española de Orientalistas. BAEO 34 (1998) 410-416.
11963 *Rapp, Hans A.* Der zwölfte 'World Congress of Jewish Studies'.
       FrRu NF 5 (1998) 72-74. Jerusalem 25.7-5.8.1997.

                  Y8.0 *Periti*: **Scholars, personalia, organizations**

11964 *Amphoux, Christian-Bernard; Frey, Albert; Schattner-Rieser,
       Ursula* Jean Margain, un ami et un maître. ᶠMARGAIN, J. 1998
       ⇒71. 9-13.
11965 Bibliographie R. Borger. ᶠBORGER R. 1998 ⇒12. 359-368.
11966 *Bieberstein, Sabine; Kosch, Daniel* Bibliographie Hermann-Josef
       Venetz (Auswahl). ᶠVENETZ, H. 1998 ⇒122. 305-308.
11967 *Caquot, André* Rapport sur l'état et l'activité de l'École biblique et
       archéologique française de Jérusalem, 1997-1998. CRAI 3 (1998)
       937-940.
11968 *Citrini, Tullio; Vergottini, Marco* Bibliografia del biblista Carlo M.
       Martini (1951-1980). ᶠMARTINI C., Rivelazione, 1998 ⇒74. 337-
       356.
11969 *Clines, David J.A.* Research, teaching and learning in Sheffield: the
       material conditions of their production;
11970 The Sheffield department of biblical studies: an intellectual bio-
       graphy. Auguries. JSOT.S 269: 1998 ⇒225. 294-302/14-89.
11971 *Cole, Graham A.* Professor Peter SINGER on christianity: charac-
       terised or caricatured?. RTR 57 (1998) 80-90.
11972 *Dlugosz, Darius* In praise of Josef Tadeusz MILIK. RdQ 18 (1998)
       495-496.
11973 **Grootaers, Jan** Actes et acteurs à Vatican II. BEThL 139: Lv
       1998, Peeters xxiv; 602 pp. 90-429-0706-1. Bibl. 566-586.
11974 *Haarbeck, Ako* Dank an Siegfried Meurer. ᶠMEURER, S. 1998 ⇒
       81. 7-10.
11975 *Heil, Christoph; Reichardt, M.* Publikationen von Paul Hoffmann.
       ᶠHOFFMANN, P., Von Jesus. BZNW 93: 1998 ⇒43. 631-640.
11976 *Holter, Knut* The institutional context of Old Testament scholarship
       in Africa. OTEs 11 (1998) 452-461.
11977 *Hulet, Clayton H.* Walter Brueggemann: a selected bibliography,
       1961-1998. ᶠBRUEGGEMANN, W. 1998 ⇒16. 321-340.
11978 *JOANNES PAULUS II* Lettera al Rev. Don Francesco Mosetto, Presi-
       dente dell'Associazione Biblica Italiana, in occasione del 50o della
       sua fondazione. RivBib 46 (1998) 413-415.
11979 *Kapera, Zdzisław J.* Decoration of the Champollion of Scrolls
       Józef Tadeusz MILIK. Qumran Chronicle 8/1-2 (1998) 1-6.

11980 *Kaufhold, Hubert* Anton BAUMSTARKs wissenschaftliches Testament: zu seinem 50. Todestag am 31. Mai 1998. OrChr 82 (1998) 1-52.

11981 *Kosch, Daniel* Dem Leben auf der Spur: zum Werk von Hermann-Josef Venetz. [F]VENETZ, H. 1998 ⇒122. 299-304.

11982 *Laurentin, René* Hommage au père Aristide M. SERRA, OSM, 5è laureat du 'Prix Laurentin—Pro Ancilla Domini'. Mar. 59 (1998) 690-698.

11983 *Lemaire, André* Témoignage en faveur de Josef Tadeusz MILIK. Qumran Chronicle 8/1-2 (1998) 7-8.

11984 **Martin, Paul-Aimé** Le mouvement biblique au Canada: l'association catholique des études bibliques au Canada dans les années 1940 et 1950. 1996 ⇒12,11127. [R]Études d'histoire religieuse 64 (1998) 82-83 (*Lacroix, Benoît*).

11985 *Maurer, Alexander* Bibliographie von Prof. Dr. Dr. Hartmut Stegemann 1956-1998. [F]STEGEMANN, H. BZNW 97: 1998 ⇒111. 519-526.

11986 *McCready, Wayne O.* Shields of bronze polished like mirrors—biblical studies and the academy. BCSBS 57 (1998) 19-38. CSBS Annual Meeting 1997: Presidential Address.

11987 *Miller, Donald E.* Graydon F. Snyder as ethicist and educator in the Anabaptist tradition. [F]SNYDER, G. 1998 ⇒104. 3-25.

11988 **Mirsky, Jeannette** Sir Aurel STEIN: archaeological explorer. Ch 1998, University Press xiii; 585 pp. 0-226-53177-5.

11989 *Mosetto, Francesco* Cinquant'anni della Associazione Biblica Italiana: breve cronistoria. RivBib 46 (1998) 385-412.

11990 *Renker, Alwin* Prof. Dr. Clemens THOMA zum 65. Geburtstag. FrRu NF 5 (1998) 150-153.

11991 *Ruini, Card. Camillo* Lettera a Don Francesco Mosetto, Presidente dell'Associazione Biblica Italiana. RivBib 46 (1998) 415-418.

11992 **Scharfenecker, Uwe** Die katholisch-theologische Fakultät Gießen 1830-1859: Ereignisse, Strukturen, Personen. Diss. St. Georgen 1995/96. [D]*Wolf, Hubert*: VKZG.F 81: Pd 1998, Schöningh 747 pp. 3-506-79986-X.

11993 *Scroggs, Robin* "By their fruits you will recognize them": trenches into the theological and exegetical directions of Graydon F. Snyder. [F]SNYDER, G. 1998 ⇒104. 39-54.

11994 *Seitz, Christopher* `We are not prophets or apostles': the *Biblical Theology* of B.S. CHILDS. Word without end. 1998 <1994> ⇒200. 102-109.

11995 *Spangenberg, Izak* Op pad na 2000—oftewel, oor al die dinge wat gebeur het. OTEs 11 (1998) 534-566.

11996 *VanderKam, James C.* A tribute to Eugene ULRICH on the occasion of his sixtieth birthday. DSD 5 (1998) 262-263.

11997 **Vermes, Geza** Providential accidents: an autobiography. L 1998, SCM xi; 258 pp. £20. 0-334-02722-5. [R]DSD 5 (1998) 252-255 (*Brooke, George J.*); JJS 49 (1998) 348-349 (*De Lange, Nicholas*); ET 109 (1997-98) 320 (*Rodd, C.S.*).

11998 *Wiles, Virginia* Analogies for our common life: reflections on Graydon F. Snyder as teaching theologian. [F]SNYDER, G. 1998 ⇒104. 26-38.

11999 [E]**Wilhelm, Gernot** Zwischen Tigris und Nil: 100 Jahre Ausgrabungen der Deutschen Orient-Gesellschaft in Vorderasien und Ägypten. Zaberns Bildbände zur Archäologie: Mainz 1998, Von Zabern/ Deutsche Orient-Gesellschaft (ADOG) 144 pp. 3-8053-2490-1.

Y8.5 *Periti*: in memoriam

12000   Alonso Schökel, Luis 15.2.1920-10.7.1998. ᴿBib. 79 (1998) 446-447; Il Regno 43 (1998) 569-570 (*Filippi, Alfio*); MCom 56 (1998) 285-296 (*Busto Saiz, José Ramón*); AcBib 10/5 (1998-1999) 570-571 (*Bovati, Pietro*) & 571-574 (*Egaña, Francisco Javier*).

12001   Amyx, Darrell Arlynn 2.4.1911-10.1.1997. ᴿAJA 102 (1998) 179-180 (*Bell, Evelyn E.; Forbes, Barbara A.*).

12002   Asensio, Felix 21.2.1909-10.7.1998. ᴿAcBib 10/5 (1998-99) 576.

12003   Baillet, Maurice 1923-1998. ᴿRdQ 18 (1998) 339-341 (*Puech, É-mile*).

12004   Beck, Pirhiya 1931-1998. ᴿTelAv 25 (1998) 139-141 (*Ziffer, Irit*). H.

12005   Beebe, H. Keith ob. 13.7.1997. ᴿEThL 75,265.

12006   Bertrangs, Albert 22.2.1925-9.10.1997. ᴿEThL 74 (1998) 241 (*Van Belle, G.*).

12007   Brown, Raymond Edward 22.5.1928-8.8.1998. ᴿTablet (1998) 1107 (*Wansbrough, Henry; Stanton, Graham*); America 179/5 (1998) 5-6 (*Harrington, Daniel J.*); EThL 74 (1998) 506-511 (*Neirynck, F.*); CBQ 60 (1998) 514; BiTod 36 (1998) 340 (*Senior, Donald*).

12008   Cagni, Luigi Giovanni 4.3.1929-27.1.1998. ᴿOr. 67 (1998) 303-305 (*Pomponio, Francesco*); Henoch 20 (1998) 107-109 (*Pettina-to, Giovanni*); Barnabiti Studi 15 (1998) 337-385 [bibl. 374ss] (*Cagni, Giuseppe M.*); AION 56 (1996) 433-436 (*Graziani, Simo-netta*).

12009   Cargas, Harry James 18.6.1932-18.8.1998. ꟳCARGAS J.

12010   Deist, Ferdinand Etienne 9.8.1944-13.7.1997. ᴿOTEs 11/3 (1998) ii-x (incl. bibl.); JNSL 24/1 (1998) v-xi (incl. bibl.).

12011   Dekkers, Eligius 20.6.1915-15.12.1998. ᴿEThL 75,251-254—Lamberigts, M.

12012   Dupont, Jacques 19.12.1915-10.9.1998. ᴿAcBib 10/5 (1998-1999) 575.

12013   Edel, Elmar 12.3.1914-25.4.1997. ᴿZÄS 125 (1998) I-III (*Görg, Manfred*).

12014   Feuillet, André 1909-26.11.1998. ᴿRICP 73,215-217—Cothenet, Édouard.

12015   Frede, Hermann Josef 12.9.1922-29.5.1998. ᴿRTL 29 (1998) 558-563 (*Gryson, Roger*).

12016   Garofalo, Salvatore 17.4.1911-25.10.1998 ᴿAcBib 10/5 (1998-1999) 576.

12017   Grzybek, Stanisław 1915-1998. ᴿRBL 52,70-75 (Bibl. III, 83-84)—Matras, Tadeusz.

12018   Hug, Herbert 1907-1998. ᴿJud. 54 (1998) 256-60 (*Jansen, Reiner*).

12019   Jacob, Edmond 1.11.1909-17.1.1998. ᴿRHPhR 78 (1998) 259-260 (*Collange, J.-F.*); ZAW 110 (1998) 485-488 (*Heintz, Jean-Georges*).

12020   Jaspers, Willibrord Hermann 20.10.1926-21.3.1998. ᴿBVLI 42 (1998) 14.

12021   Kammenhuber, Annelies 19.3.1922-24.12.1995 ⇒13,11786. ᴿZA 88 (1998) 161-163 (*Frantz-Szabó, Gabriella*).
12022   Käsemann, Ernst 1906-1998. ᴿABR 46 (1998) 85 (*Osborn, E.F.*).
12023   La Bonnardière, Anne-Marie 1906-1998. ᴿREAug 44 (1998) 153-158 (*Paoli, Elisabeth*).
12024   Lapide, Pinchas 1922-23.10.1997. ᴿFrRu NF 1 (1998) 153-155 (*Renker, Alwin*).
12025   Malatesta, Edward J. 31.5.1932-27.1.1998. ᴿNZM 54/3 (1998) 217-218 (*Malek, Roman*).
12026   Merendino, Pio ob. nov. 1998, aet. 66. ᴿAcBib 10 (1997-98) 459.
12027   Miller, Donald G. ob. 22.2.1997, aet. 87. ᴿInterp. 52 (1998) 228.
12028   Mitton, C. Leslie 1907-3.1998. ᴿET 109 (1997-98) 257 (*Rodd, C.S.*)
12029   Moscati, Sabatino 24.11.1922-8.9.1997. ᴿOr. 67 (1998) 306-310 (*Amadasi Guzzo, Maria Giulia*); RANL 9 (1998) 771-774/775-779/781-785 (*Falzea, Angelo; Garbini, Giovanni; Gnoli, Gherardo*); RPARA 70 (1997-1998) 327-328 (*Susini, Gian Carlo*); AcBib 10/4 (1997-1998) 460-463 (Cf. L'Osservatore Romano, 10 sett. 1998—D. Mazzoleni).
12030   Olivier, Johannes Petrus Jacobus (Hannes) 31.1.1945-25.3.1998. ᴿOTEs 11/1 (1998) 5.
12031   Pope, Marvin Hoyle 1916-1997. ᴿZAW 110 (1998) 325-26 (*Cross, Frank Moore*).
12032   Prausnitz, Moshe 1922-1998. ᴿQad. 32/1,59-60—Tadmor, M. **H**.
12033   Prinsloo, Willem Sterrenberg 19.8.1944-5.10.1997. ᴿOTEs 12/3,ii-viii (incl. bibl.).
12034   Pritchard, James Bennet 4.10.1909-1.1.1997. ᴿAJA 102 (1998) 175-177 (*Dyson, Robert H.*).
12035   Roemer, Hans Robert 18.2.1915-15.7.1997. ᴿZDMG 148 (1998) 1-6 (*Glassen, Erika*).
12036   Rzeszutek, Zdzisław 1918-1998. ᴿRBL 52,84-87—Marecki, Józef.
12037   Saadé, Gabriel 29.11 1922-15.5.1997. ᴿSyr. 75 (1998) 295-296 (*Contenson, Henri de; Al-Maqdissi, Michel*).
12038   Scharbert, Josef 1919-1998. RBL 51 (1998) 148-9 (*Chmiel, Jerzy*); IZBG 44 (1997-1998) vi (*Feld, Geburgis*).
12039   Skilton, John H. 17.9.1906-22.7.1998. ᴿWThJ 60 (1998) 183-184.
12040   Soden, Wolfram von 19.6.1908-6.10.1996. ᴿOr. 67 (1998) 311-314 (*Hunger, Hermann*).
12041   Storme, Albert 1917-1997. ᴿSBLFA 48 (1998) 629-636 (*Bottini, Giovanni Claudio*).
12042   Summers, Ray 1910-1992. ᴹSUMMERS R. 1998 ⇒115. 2-6 (*Dilday, Russell*); xi-xiii (*Finegan, Jack*); 12-19 (*Flanders, Henry Jackson*); The writings of Ray Summers 21-42 (*Garrett, James Leo*); 10-11 (*Hamblin, Robert L.*); Bibl. 43-58 (*Hilburn, Glenn O.*); xv-xvi (*Reynolds, Herbert H.*); 7-9 (*Vardaman, E. Jerry*).
12043   Swaim, J. Carter ob. 7.8.1997, aet. 93. ᴿEThL 74 (1998) 245 (*Collins, R.F.*).
12044   Thüsing, Wilhelm 18.5.1921-24.5.1998. ᴿBiKi 53 (1998) 225-226 (*Kertelge, Karl*).
12045   Van Buren, Paul M. ob. 1998. ᴿEThL 75,266.
12046   Virgulin, Stefano 26.12.1918-6.8.1997. ᴿAcBib 10/4 (1997-1998) 463-464.

12047   Ward, William A. 1928-1996. [RM]WARD W. 1998 ⇒123. ix-x (bibl.
        xi-xx) *(Lesko, Leonard H. & Barbara S.)*.
12048   Weitzman, Michael Perry 1946-21.3.1998. [R]BAIAS 16 (1998) 117-
        119 *(Jacobson, David)*.
12049   Wessetzky, Vilmos 2.2 1909-6.2.1997. [R]ZÄS 125 (1998) V-VII
        (Luft, Ulrich).
12050   Wiefel, Wolfgang ob. 23.10.1998. ThLZ 124,241.
12051   Wikgren, Allen P. 3.12.1906-7.5.1998. [R]BASPap 35 (1998) 123-
        124 *(Wilfong, Terry G.)*.
12052   Will, Ernest 25.4.1913-24.9.1997. [R]RAr (1998/1) 119-124 *(Tate,
        Georges)*; ADAJ 42 (1998) 11-13 *(Zayadine, F.)*; Syr. 75/1 (1998)
        1-8 (bibl.).

Index Alphabeticus

Auctorum

[D]dir. dissertationis [E]editor [F]Festschrift [M]mentio [R]recensio [T]translator/vertens

Aadhil A 2122
Aartun K 7756
Abadie P 2569 2596
Abaiev W [F]1
Abbamonte G [R]3821
Abbà G [R]1121
Abd El-Maksoud M 11038
Abdullah Yusuf Ali [M]9474
Abegg M 6809s
Abella J 1595
Abhishiktananda S [M]6974
Abitz F 9331
Abma H 4520
Aboud J 10872
Abraham W 988
Abrahamsen W 3834
Abramovitch H [M]1125
Abrams J 8912
Abrego J 3736 de Lacy J 3269
Abulafia A 128 8913
Abusch T 9407s
Acconci A 10807
Acheson S 1103
Achlama R [M]8898
Achtemeier E 925s 3617 P 6426 [R]5206
Ackerman S 1071 7449 [R]6803
Ackermann S 595

Acquistapace P [E]11252
Adair J 1237
Adam A 1176 2371 M 7450
Adamo D 11353
Adams A [E]10244 J 4921
Adang C 9477
Adelman H 8636
Adeso P 5475
Adinolfi M 5866 6131 9409
Adkin N [R]7442
Adler L [M]8879 R 8875 W 5660 [R]8276
Adorno F [M]10518 T [M]2953
Adriaanse H 989
Aegidius Rom. 3021
Aejmelaeus L [R]6064
Afzal C 5673
Agan C [R]4893
Ages A 1938
Aggoula B 10463
Agouridis S 9837
Agrippa d'Aubigné [M]1701
Aguirre R 4787 11354 Monasterio R 3765 3835
Agurides S 692 4414
Agusta-Boularot S 10798
Aḥituv S 1957 [E]369

2314
Ahlström G 9496
Ahn G 9457
Ahrens M 6466
Aichele G 4105 4679s [E]260 [R]7560
Aitken J 7712 7729s 7733 7736 7748 M [E]364
Akenson D 596 8763
Akerboom T 5571
Akerman L 10592
Akslen L [R]2783
Aksoy B 11132
Akurgal E 9779
Aland B 1274s [E]6456 K 1277 [E]1276 4657
Al-Azmeh A 990 [R]6803
Aláez O 1681
Albanis E [R]538
Albenda P 10195
Alberigo G [F]2
Albert B 11479
Albertus M [M]5325
Albertz R 9286s [R]2022
Alborghetti P 6136 8837
Albrecht R 3426
Albrektson B 3027
Albright W [M]10085
Albrile E 8240
Alcalá M 893
Alcáin J 981
Alcina Franch J [E]10030

Anzulewicz P 210
Aparicio A 4347 **Rodrí-**
guez Á 2809 4948
Aphrahat ^{M}5919
Apicella A 2271
Apollinaris L ^{M}5700
   5707
Apollodorus ^{M}1784
Apollonius T ^{M}4404
Appelfeld A ^{M}8899
Applegate J 3475 4985
   ^{R}3466
Aquinas ^{M}4375 5499
   5973 6028 6043 11751
Arabito A ^{R}11518
Arafat K ^{R}10218 10360
Arambarri J ^{R}1631
Arana A 2015
Arand C 4366
Aranda G ^{R}370 1013 **Pé-**
   rez G 3575 8175-80
   8221 8241 ^{R}1015
Ararat N 2895
Arbach M 7991 7994
Arbore Popescu G ^{E}9974
Arcelin P ^{E}457
Arcella L ^{E}282
Archambault J ^{R}7458
Archi A 10907s ^{R}9781
Ardovino A 5748
Ardusso F 597 7008
Arendse R 3839
Arens E 5523 7141 7528
   11356 **K** ^{E}8547
Argall R 8210
Argemi A 1358
Argoud G ^{E}458
Ariarajah W 7189
Arias Montano B
   ^{M}11791-4
Arieli R 10596
Aries W 1818
Arikat S ^{R}6696
Aristide ^{M}11636
Arjava A 7416
Arjomand S 9458
Arkadas D 5296
Arlandson J 4820
Armellada B de 653 6499
   ^{R}6953 11540 11762
Armellini F 4659
Arminius ^{M}11795
Arminjon B 5258

Armistead D 3603
Armogathe J 5572
Armstrong C 1073 **D**
   ^{E}211 ^{E}3840 **K** 6500
Arnal W ^{E}3841 ^{R}9962
Arnaldez R 6568
Arnaoutoglou I 2125
Arnaud D 7758 10756
Arnaudiès A 10992
Arnau-García R ^{R}5832
   7027
Arnéra G 3842
Arnold B 1606 ^{R}1970
   C 6325 **D** 9614
   10098 **F** 10099 **M**
   ^{M}9881
Arnould C 10597 **J**
   1697
Arntz K 929
Arrango J ^{R}11436
Arslan E 316
Artés Hernández J 8336
Artola A 5993
Artus O 1542 1558
   2258
Artzi P 2440 11011
Artzy M 10147
Arumí i Blancafort E
   4069
Aruz J ^{R}10389
Arzt S 2637s
Asake M 6359
Aschim A 8449
   ^{R}8222 8401
Aschkenasy N 1074
Ascione A ^{R}632
Ascough R 5217 5890
   ^{R}358
Asendorf U 1607
   11771
Asenjo J ^{R}7083
Asensio F 12002
Asgeirsson J 9129s
Ash P 2323 9498
Ashanin C ^{R}11527
Ashby G 1959
Asher O 10747
Asheri D ^{R}366s
Ashton J ^{E}5282 J ^{F}6 **M**
   4976
Askani H 1479 11909
   ^{R}1479
Aslanoff C 3538

Aslanov C ^{R}83
Asmis E 6588
Asper M ^{E}432
Asperti S 1359
Assante J 7850
Assmann J 1990s 6746
   9333 9334 10487
   11357 ^{E}283 286 **J**
   ^{M}8072
Astigarraga J ^{E}579
Aston D 9615 10416
   ^{R}9659 9684 10122
Astour M 10873
Asurmendi J 3266
   ^{R}3547
Athanasius ^{M}11637-41
Athenagoras A ^{M}4645
Atkins P ^{R}4699
Atkinson K 8181
Atra B 5160
Attinger D ^{R}2544 9002
   10251 10653 ^{T}8667
Attridge H 9062 ^{R}8233
   9940
Atwan R ^{E}4070
Aubert L 10488
Aubin M 8337
Aucker W ^{R}6881
Audet J 3767
Auffret P 2800 2820
   2860 2877 2906
Aufrecht W 10372
   ^{R}10397
Aufrère S 9335 11817
Auge C 10562
Augustin M ^{E}401
Augustinus H 5301
   11682 11692 ^{M}705
   2842 4314 5703 5910
   7394 8251 11675-
   11714
Auld A 2329 2341 10598
   S 10599
Aulisa I ^{T}11622
Aulus Gellius ^{M}9222
Aumann J ^{T}3873
Aune D 5549-51 9227
   10736 11922 ^{M}5629
Aurenche G ^{R}1055 **O**
   10917 ^{E}476
Aurrecoechea J ^{R}4170
   6997
Aus R 5462

Barbaso A 6545
Barbàra M 11675 11714 ^{T}11745
Barber E 10095
Barberá C 599
Barbet A 10252
Barbi A 5004 5078 5175 5191
Barbieri E 1362s 5100 ^{R}983
Barc B 9588
Barcelón E 7009
Barclay J 5983 8642 9838 9890 ^{E}285 ^{R}6257 8966 **W** ^{M}11858
Barcley W 5788
Bardinet T 11322
Bardski K 697 3138 11513
Bareket E 8821
Bar-Ilan M 1075 8361
Barkai R 10729
Barker G 9985 **K** 3714 **M** 2507 3576 **P** 2306 ^{R}10001
Bar-Kochva B 2655
Barksdale E 1682
Barlone S 6200 11772
Barnabas J ^{M}11859
Barnard L ^{T}11584
Barnes J ^{R}9883 **M** ^{R}6247 **P** 5519 **R** ^{R}3316 **T** ^{R}11040
Barnett M 11830 **P** 6153s
Barnikol E 6219
Bar-On S 2143
Barr D 5552 **G** 5101 6047 J 1642-4 7070
Barrado P ^{R}2274 3810 6911
Barreiro Á 5032
Barrelet M ^{F}8
Barrett C 131 5082 ^{R}5731
Barré M 2838
Barrios-Delgado D ^{T}6909
Barry C ^{R}3025 11556 11759 **R** ^{R}6398 **W** 3845
Barsotti D 6592

Barstad H 3388 9499
Bartelmus R 3355
Bartelt A 3353
Barth G 4538 7549 ^{R}7558 **K** 5924 ^{M}6136 6678 9018 11860-4
Barthel J 2257
Bartholomew C 698 3139
Bartl K 9500 11081 ^{E}318 ^{E}444 ^{R}11126
Bartlett J 2656 ^{E}319 ^{R}9499
Bartolini P 10564
Bartolomé J 5723 5867
Barton J 991s 1178s 6747 6814 ^{E}699 **S** 3818 5853 6593 11360
Baruch E 10603
Barzano A ^{E}9986
Barzilai G 1853 8450
Bascom R 3115
Basevi C 5789 6306 6333 ^{R}5798
Bash A 5912 ^{R}3798
Basile D 7220
Basilius C ^{M}11642
Baskin J 8643-5 ^{E}1076
Baslez M 9839
Basser H 4766 ^{E}2237 ^{R}9123
Basset L 5030
Bast R 2070
Bastholm C ^{M}11544
Bastiaensen A ^{R}11690
Bateman H 6278
Batlogg A ^{R}7360
Bats M ^{E}462
Battaglia O 3768 **W** 4539
Batten A 4977
Battini L 9705
Battles F 11796
Batut J 6546
Bauckham R 132 1180 3819 4682 5050 5715 6313 6452 6489 8242

8243-8252 8646 11361 ^{E}213 5083 ^{R}8259
Baudler G 4367 6501s 7115
Baudoz J 4465 7369 ^{E}214
Baudry G ^{E}529
Baue F 11773
Bauer A 3476s **D** 3593 ^{R}5334 **J** 6594 7852 9706 **K** 6488 **U** 2403 5062 ^{R}1179 11849
Baugh L 4072
Bauks M 1560 1645
Baum A 993 **W** 9063
Bauman R 9987
Baumann A 8922 ^{E}8921 **G** 3110 3113 3732
Baumer L 10346
Baumert N 5750 6137 8010 ^{R}5555
Baumgart N 1762
Baumgarten A 5692 8647s ^{E}286 **J** 8491 ^{E}8490 **R** 9233
Baumgartner J ^{D}5475 ^{T}1962 **W** ^{E}7669-2
Baumstark R 11980
Baur F ^{M}11841 **W** 4783 8362
Baurain C 9808
Bavaud G ^{R}11778
Baxter L 1413
Bayer H ^{R}7020 **O** 2077
Bayfield T ^{R}6824
Bayless M ^{E}11752
Baynham E 9840
Bayun L 2276
Bazak J 2824
Bazant J 10197
Bazelaire T de ^{R}4575
Bâfaqîh M 7991
Bács T 10489
Báez S 5298
Bárta M 10490 ^{R}10055 10537 11067
Bea A ^{M}11865
Beal T 3140 ^{E}215
Beale G 5575 ^{R}5599
Beam K 1400
Beard M 9207

Bernabé Pons L 8298
Ubieta C 7418
Bernand A 9619 9989
Bernardini P [R]10153
Bernardus C [M]11753ss
Bernard-Marie 4073
Bernas C [R]6426 8966
Bernbaum E 11267
Bernbeck R [E]318
Bernett M 10749
Bernhardt R 6962
Bernheim P 6467s
Berns C 11082
Bernstein D 8877 **M**
 [E]8586 [R]8384 **R** 1992
Berquist J [R]8605 9462
 11346
Berrigan D 3597
Berrouard M [T]5301
Berruto A 5693 [R]7509
Berry J [E]11407
Bertacchini R 7142
Bertalot R 1819 5719
 W 894
Bertazzoli R 5577
Berten I 11362
Bertrangs A 12006
Bertuletti A 1182
Berz F 6317
Besserman L 1158
Best E 6245
Bestul T 7116
Bethge H 9131s [E]9156
Bethmann A 8926
Betori G 5103
Betro M 9337 [R]9395
Bettoni A [R]5262
Betts A [E]10800
Betz D 582 **H** 134 703
 3851 4043 4306s
 4777 5870 6903
 8068ss 9087s 9842-
 9843 11902 [R]8829
 [F]10 **O** 135 3852 8549
 [F]11
Beuken W 2903 3382
 7221 [R]3340
Beutler J 5226s 5302
 5524 [D]4762 [R]4211
 5337
Beyer D 9904 **K** 7796
 M [R]1420

Beyerle S 2310s
 3577 8570
Beyhl F 9194
Beza T [M]5573
Béland J [R]6894
Bélis A [E]10159 **M**
 8363
Béné C 11694
Bénétreau S 3853
Bérubé C [R]5647
Bianca M 4369
Bianchi E 1608 2144
 6697 7222 [E]6791 **F**
 2208 3209 [R]3160
 8391 **S** 10808
 10826 [R]3033 **U**
 [E]409
Bianquis T [E]536
Bickel S 9338
Bickmann J 6346s
Bidart R 11585
Bidaut B 1993 4884
Biddle M 2342 3715
 4595 10604 [R]1959
 2172 3510
Bieberstein K 6865 **S**
 4885 5019 6384
 11966
Biebuyck B [E]410
Bielecki T 4534
Bienert H 10795
 10830
B i e n k o w s k i P
 [R]10708
Bierbrier M 10239
 [E]1519
Bieringer R 6178
 [E]6051 [T]8046
B i e t a k M 9 5 0 2
 11067 11083 [E]463
Bietenhard S 2492
 3716 9503
Biezunski G 1254
Biga M [R]10911
Biger G 3419
Biggs R [R]474 9429
Bigham S 10254
Bignasca A 10831
B i g u z z i G 5 1 0 4
 5578-5580 5666
 5668 6360 [R]5550
 8038

Bijovsky G 10565
Bikai P 10772
Bilde P 8606 9905
Bile M [R]8014
Bilgiç E 11084
Bindella F 2016
Bindi S 7709
Binger T 9289
B i n g h a m D 4 2 0 4
 11581 [R]9123
Biord Castillo R 6569
Biran A 7797 10753
Birch B 3618 **D** 11480
Bird P 7453s
B i r d s a l l J 1 4 4 5
 [R]5259
Birkner R 655
Birley A 9975
B i r n b a u m E 8264 **G**
 [R]137
Bisconti F 11202s
Bisheh G 10844
Bisi A 11085
Bissoli C 1367 **G** 1260
 [R]7808
Bivar A [R]444
Bizetti P 5105
Bizjak J [R]2954
Black C 5106 [R]5272 **D**
 8011 **F** 706 3029 **J**
 7853
Blackburn B 4684 **R**
 8182
Blacketer R 2277
B l a i s i n g C [D]4204
 11581
B l a k e G [R]3830 **W**
 [M]9099
Blakely J 10735
B l a n c h a r d Y 5 3 0 3
 7371
Blanchetière F 8927s
 [R]8730
B l a n c o Pacheco S
 5107
Bland D 3090 **K** [R]6515
Blaschke A 1861
Blaser K [R]11840
Blasi F [R]3801
Blastic M [R]7116
Blatnický R 11883
Blattenberger D 6112

Borgman P 1820
Borgonovo G 711 1626 2934 8229
Bori P ^E5448
Boriaud J ^E1159
Boring M 9179 ^R4307 6442
Bormann L 6279 **P** 6907
Born W 11308
Bornemann R 7593
Bornhäuser H 8748
Bornkamm G 5724
Borowski I 8932 ^E249 **O** 11281
Borragán Mata W 7010
Borrell A 4808 ^E465
Borrmans M 4074 9463 9468 ^R9162
Borromeo C ^M10518
Borse U ^R5198
Bortolini J 657 4175
Bortone G 1160 ^E375
Borucki J ^R2109
Borzumato F 3030
Bos A 8267
Bosch J ^R5698 **Navarro J** 1517
Boschi B 2657 6817 ^R6687 9499 10653
Bosco N ^E8933
Boscolo G 4750
Bosetti E 1077 6445 **M** 4887
Boshoff W 11363
Bosio A 11199
Bosshard-Nepustil E ^R3755
Bossman D ^R1175
Bosson N 7977 9133 11817
Bossuyt P 5109s
Bostock G ^R4903
Botermann H 9976 ^R8711
Botha J 712s **P** 2724 2898 5871 7799 11364 11875 ^R5876 10102 **W** 6504
Botta F 9623
Bottari G ^M1374
Bottero J 6505s 9195

9413
Botterweck G ^E499
Bottigheimer R 633
Bottini C 7011 **G** ^R6363 12041 **L** 2209 ^T9478
Bottino A 5111
Boud'Hors A 7978
Boudignon C 11663
Bouffartigue J 9258
Bouffier S ^R8080 11324
Bouganim A 8831
Bouhot J 1354 ^E1344 6432
Boulanger Limonchy C 2535
Boulnois M ^T11651
Bounni A 10941
Bourgeois A ^R317 **H** ^E214 ^R4103
Bourgine M 11775 ^T7222
Bourguet D 4371
Bourke S ^R10735
Bournazel E ^E321
Bourquin Y 875s
Bousset W ^M11867
Boutros W 10992
Bouttier M 3863 ^R5159
Bouyer L 7225
Bouzon E 2126
Bovati P 2104 3671s ^R12000
Bovon F 3772 4864s ^E8299
Bowden H ^R9814
Bowe B 4205 6065 7144 ^R6075
Bowen N ^R7453
Bowersock G 10020 ^R9884
Bowie A 6595 ^T11836
Bowman S ^R8633
Bowring J 9624
Boyarin D ^R1990
Boyaval B ^R8074
Boyd G 3864 6792
Boyer F 5581
Boyle L ^F13
Boynton S 4262

Boys M 8934
Böcher O 5582s ^R4402 5555
Böck B ^R9456
Böckler A 3560
Böhl F 8769
Böhlemann P ^R4819
Böhler D 6908
Böhm T 5416
Böhme S 11465
Böhmisch F ^R3015
Böll H ^M1172
Börker C 11110
Bösen W 4545
Böttrich C 6596
Bórmida J 6578
Brack-Bernsen L 9708
Bradley K ^R9981
Bradshaw J 9340 **P** ^R7260
Brady C ^R78 **M** ^R8447
Braemer F ^R10109
Brague R 8832 9845
Brahms J ^M10170
Brakke D 714
Brambilla F 4598 5038
Branca W 8137
Brand E 10089 **M** ^E1416
Brandenburger E 139 **S** ^E4128
Brands G 10101
Brandscheidt R 1563
Brandt P 1280
Braner B ^E1609
Branham J ^R9299
Branick V ^R3807 **W** 3773
Branigan K ^E322 10492
Brant J 5306
Brantschen J 4599
Bras K 6699
Brasher B 5694
Braulik G 2272 2278 6700 ^M6726
Braun C von ^R1064 **E** 10993 **L** 9589 11739 **R** ^E11623 **T** 8655 8935 **W** 5022 ^R4111 5401
Bravo Aragón J 693 **Lazcano C** 4600

Buckley J 5491 ^E246
Buckwalter H 4888
Budd P 2170 2238
Buetubela B 4687
   6819
Bugg C 2380
Buggert D 6963
Buhl M 10994
Buis P ^R429
Bull K ^R5543
Bullmore M 6661
Bultmann R 1686
   ^M796 3835 11871s
Bunes Ibarra M de
   ^R11483
Bunimovitz S 9505
   11151
Bunnens G ^R10847
Bunte W ^E8940
Burandt C 11777
Burchard C 140 4308
   4372 4502 4796
   5049 5988 5999
   6016 6040 6151
   6231 6457s 7085
   7095 7146 8015
   8234 11365 ^R6480
Burckhardt J 9810
Burdon C 5584
Bureau B 2878
Burgess J 718s R
   ^R9605
Burgos M de ^R5924
Burigana R 895
Burini C ^T11591
Burke D 8941 T 6001
Burkert W 6597 9240
Burkes S ^R3128
Burkhard G ^R7963
Burkhardt H ^R8284
Burl A ^F18
Burne-Jones ^M3029
Burnett A 9241 G
   5984 S 11818 ^R8852
Burnette-Bletsch R
   2105 8268
Burney C 11086
Burns C ^R3077 J
   10350 11723 ^R3811
   9312 W ^E11651
Burow J 11110
Burr D 5553
Burrell B ^R9952 D

^R6515
Burridge R 3820
   ^R4056
Burrill R ^R7156
Burskog S ^E4196
Burtchaell J 6385
Burton-Christie D
   7227 ^R5612
Buscemi A 5725
   ^R5740 M 5792
   7228
Busch P 5684 ^R3985
Buschmann G
   ^T11592
Busey R 5070
Bush F 2410 2639
Busi G 8844
Busse F ^T10996 H
   2508 10698
   ^R10624 U 5063
   5430
Bustinza P ^R6949
Busto Saiz J 2572
   11855 ^R12000
Buth R 7057
Butler B 5585 H
   11025 S 9414 T
   2344
Butterweck C 7229
Butterworth M 4601
Butting K 2640 7456
Butzer E 6361 7457
Butzkamm A ^E11508
Bux N 10605
Buxtorf J ^M11818
Buzzard A 4044
Buzzetti C 636 720
   1371-3 7230 8016
   8055 10186 ^E222
   1369s 11182
Bücher O ^R5638
Büchner D 8771 F
   658
Bühler C 659 P 4602
   11950 ^E425
Bürkle H ^R5215
Büsing G 1649
Büttgen P ^T11778
Byargeon R 3189
   4373
Byars R 6173
Byl J 2531
Bynum C 6138

Byrne B 5926 ^R5932 J
   ^R4577 P ^R621
Byron B 5431

Caba J ^D5475
Cabanel P 8942
Cabra P 4263
Cacciari M 6598
Cadogan G 11152
Cagnasso F 5209
Cagni G ^R12008 L
   9847 12008 ^E3273
Cahill J 10606 L 6599
   6748 ^R7344 M 3866
   4661 ^E4662 T 637
Cahn W ^R1909
Caillet J 11177
Caird G 1134
Calabi F 8269s
Calabrese W 1374
Calambrogio L
   ^R11433
Calame C 9242s
Calaway B 5586
Calcagnini D 10256
Calci C ^E323 11178
Calderini S 1716
Calderone S ^E324
Calduch-Benages N
   3236 8056
Calef S ^R7432
Calero A 3867 ^R4559
   6979
Callahan A 6281 6386
Callaway P 8367
Callender D 3540 G
   9626
Callot O 10567 10878
Calloud J 1763 4176
Callow K 721
Caluwe A 7930
Calvin J 5520 6057
   ^M2277 2947 7383
   11796-01
Camacho F 4671s
   7062
Camarero M 5456
Cambi N ^E11206
Cammarota G ^R625
Campagno M 9341
Campanini S ^E7683-
   7684

Ceja L 5574
Celan P ^{M}1169
Celani A 10204
Cenatempo G ^{M}10260
Cerbelaud D 1717
1764s
Ceresko A ^{R}1874 3344
Cereti G 4360
Cerra G ^{R}6715
Ceruti-Cendrier M
3831
Cervellò Autuori J
9629
Cervigni L ^{T}2226 7737
Cesarano N ^{E}1545
Cesarini G 10084 **R**
1135
Cé M ^{T}6565
Cha J 3717
Chacko M 1963
Chadwick H 11515-7
Chagall M ^{M}10294
10320 10594 10617
Chakoian K 4965
Chalcraft D ^{E}11368
Chalendar X 6601
Chalier C 2079
Chamard-Bois P 4803
4810
Chamla M 8863
Chance J 5113 ^{E}1118
Chantraine G 6549
Chapa J ^{R}8310
Chapalain C 2936
Chaplin D ^{R}6245
Chapman R ^{R}10748 **S**
996
Chapot F 11636
Chappaz J 585 10498
^{R}10548
Chappin M ^{R}4472
Charlat R 7375
Charlesworth J 4045s
5588 6820ss 8185-90
8301 8495 8551
^{E}325 467 8496 8552
Charlet J ^{R}11523
Charpentier F ^{E}1161
Charpin D 7859 9509
^{R}7868
Charvát P 9710
Charvet P ^{T}11212
Chatelion Counet P
660

Chattaway P 4076
Chaucer W ^{M}1158
Chausson F ^{R}10013
Chauveau M ^{R}9397
Chazan R 11497
Chazelle C 2684
Chazon E ^{E}441
Châtillon J ^{E}3093
Chávarry F ^{R}5723
Chemparathy G 9490
Cheney E 7460 **M**
2937
Chennattu R 5472
Cheon S 3215
Chesnutt R ^{R}5793
Chesson M 10792
Chester A 6823
Chevalier N 9342
Chevelen E 8772
Chew K 860
Chéhadeh K 10499
Chialà S 8212s
^{R}8220
Chiappo M ^{R}5667
Chiarinelli L ^{E}897
Chiera G 9757
Chiesa B 1238 1281
^{R}2708
Childs B 7552s
^{M}7564 11994
Chilton B 1261 3872
4295 4807 5726
6469 9007s ^{R}1546
Chinitz J 7728
Chiodi S 2050 9415
Chioffi L 10500
Chirassi I ^{E}428
Chisholm R 6509
7594 ^{R}2410 3409
Chittister J 2771
Chmiel J 724 8371
10501 ^{R}12038
Cho Y 2725
Choi G 6203
Cholin M 5417
Chomarat J ^{E}3122
Chomsky N 8140
Chopineau J 725
Choufrine A ^{R}7312
Chouraqui A 1995
Christensen D 997
Christian D ^{E}468
Christiansen E 5793
8573

Christianson E 3142s
3205
Christie Y 5589
Chrostowski W 2564
6749 10607 ^{R}2326
8437 8629
Chrupcała L 4826
4889 ^{R}4737 4849
4872 8997
Chrysostomos ^{M}4359
4516 5770 11644-9
Chyutin M 8497
Ciałowicz K ^{R}9702
Ciampa R 6216
Ciampini E 10051
^{R}9666
Ciappa A 11071
Ciccarese M ^{E}661
Čičinaze I 10259
Ciecieląg J 8372
10568
Ciezkowski A ^{M}4380
Cifani A 10260
Cilliers J 11928
Cimosa M 1296s 1917
4523
Cinal S 9101
Cineira D ^{R}4402 5337
5490 6279 6369
7808 8661
Ciniello N ^{R}7559
Cipriani N 11681
^{E}11518 **S** 224 5794
11866 ^{R}6195
Citrini T 11968
Ciunci J ^{R}7120
Civil M 7860
Clackson S 1887
^{R}1337
Clagett M 9630
Claret B 1718
Claridge A 10415
11181
Clark D 3759 **E** 7461
^{R}11707 **F** 11730 **G**
6602 7420
Clarke A 5891 ^{R}6112
7196 **E** ^{T}2273 **F**
11795 **G** ^{E}469 **J**
10205 **K** 1282
Clarysse W 552
Classen C 11807
Claudel G ^{R}7572 **P**
11873

Corsato C ^{R}4467 9151 11728
Cortes E ^{T}2274
Cortese E 2150 10811 ^{R}1601 2697 4109
Cortesi A 2460 3699
Coruña A ^{R}9456
Corwin C 2729
Cory C ^{R}5281
Cosgrove C 5946 ^{R}6193
Costa E 1376 7232 **G** ^{R}138
Costacurta B 2452
Cote D 11558
Cothenet É 7377
Cotrozzi S 6379
Cotsen L ^{F}21
Cottam S ^{E}472
Cotter J 2685
Cotterell P 3677
Cotton H 8078
Couffignal R 2448 2455
Coulet C 9811
Coulson W ^{E}487
Countryman L 962 5312 6753 7302
Couroyer B 22
Court J 3777 4158 **M** 11268
Courtine J ^{T}6575
Courtois L 10734
Cousar C 5795 ^{R}6122
Cousin H 3778
Coutau-Bégarie H 11878
Couteau É ^{R}10648
Couto A 1964 5114 ^{R}498 1850s 3125 6506
Coutsoumpos O ^{R}6426
Couturier G ^{E}11890
Cova G ^{R}632 5749 8729
Cowdell S 6965
Cowdrey H ^{R}11504
Cox C 1299s 11519 ^{R}3595 **H** 11371s
Coxon P 11914
Coyle J ^{R}4594 11601 11606 11608 **K** 7378
Cozijnsen B 6492

Craffert P 1185 5892
Craghan J ^{R}2022 2907 6586
Craig K 2400 2643 **W** 3874s
Crammer C ^{R}7460
Cranfield C 143 4264 4521 4603 5796 5927 5947-52 5995 5998 7303 8062
Cravotta G ^{R}562
Crawford B 2435 **H** 10986 ^{R}471 **M** ^{R}11386 **S** 8373 8453 8574s ^{R}1145 8562 8586 **T** 1245 4891
Creach J 2709 2730s
Creagh-Fuller T ^{R}45
Creason S ^{R}2964
Cremascoli G ^{E}983 ^{R}3005 11692 11695
Crenshaw J 3064s 3145 3667 6511 ^{R}3250
Crespi D ^{M}10516
Cribiore R 9631
Crippa M 10265s
Crites S 11837
Croatto J 732 1650 3454 7362 ^{R}1619 8404
Croce V ^{R}1732
Crocetti G 11932
Cromwell O ^{M}978
Cross F 1000 2669 7655 ^{E}1518 8486 ^{R}12031 **J** 8302 **L** ^{E}408
Crossan J 8303s
Crotty R 3876
Crouch J ^{T}3847
Crouzel H 11599 ^{T}2828
Crown A 2331 7656 8620
Croy N 6424
Cruells W. 11013
Crüsemann F 1078 2106 11373 ^{E}292 ^{R}1048 **M** 6356 **N** 9711

Cryer F 327 8454 ^{R}2283
Crystal D 5171
Cuccu R ^{T}1377
Cuenca Molina J ^{R}10653
Culberton P ^{R}8817
Culley R ^{R}1149 2713
Cullmann O 6911 7233s ^{M}11874
Culpepper R 733 5229 ^{R}4111
Cummings B 11831
Cumont F ^{M}10876
Cunchillos Ilarri J 7762 10881
Cunneen S 7379
Cunningham G 9416s **L** ^{R}4581 **M** ^{E}226 **P** 8947
Cunz M 7059 11481
Cuomo L 3007
Curci G ^{R}377
Currid J 9632
Curti C 5697
Curtis A ^{E}3462 ^{R}2083 11345 **B** 3620 **J** 10951 10960
Curto S ^{R}11037 11051 11059
Curtoni M 4963
Cussini E 7810
Cuva A 7235
Cuvillier E 3877 4341 ^{R}5142 5800 6193 8299
Cuzzolin P ^{E}8019
Cyprian ^{M}11723
Cyran W 6179
Cyrillus A 11651 ^{M}5031 11652
Cywinski E 4925
Czachesz I 8327
Czajkowski M ^{R}241
Czichon R 11101
Çambel H ^{F}4

D'Agostino B ^{E}462 **F** 7862 ^{R}1802 2136
D'Alario V ^{R}7496
D'Alessandro S 6550
D'Ambrosio D 6362

Delaney C 1822s
Delcorno C 1381
Delebecque É. 8021
Delgado A 10455 **Delgado J** [R]9221
Delia R [R]9355
Delicostopoulos A 1449
Dell K 3066 [R]24 [R]1081
Della Rocca 602
Dell'Era A 3568
Delmaire J 4078
Delobel J 5115 [R]80 1290
Deloche P 2046
Delorme J 738 4757
Delpiazzo J [R]8168
Delsman W 10608
Deluga W 10609
Delver J [E]7072
Demand N 9814
D e m a n d t B & A [E]10007
Demaria S [T]9102
Demarolle J [R]10446
Dembowski H 11827
Demetrius A [M]7980
Demichelis M 7657
Demke C 3880 [R]4626
Demoustier A 7236
Dempsey C 3562 [R]119 3900 **D** 2592 7801 [R]8544
Demsky A 9296 10610
Demy T 3294
Den Dulk M 1597
den Hollander A 1450
Deneken M 6669 6946
Dennes M 11892
Dennison J 3665
Dentzer-Feydy J 10467 [R]10747
Denzey N [R]9120
Depuydt L 7934s 9635 [R]9630
Dequeker L 10611
Derakhshani J 9774
Derbes A 4550
Derby J 1598
Derchain-Urtel M 11058
Dercksen J 10087
Derickson G 5913

Deriev D 11603
Dermience A [R]299 3889
D e r r e n b a c k e r R [R]4060 4145 4733
Derrett J 4421 4778 4954 5467 5513
Derrida J [M]9887
Desbordes B 9259
Desclais J 1768
Deselaers P 2942 3008
DeSilva D 2667 5688 6162 6397
Desjardins M 1108 [E]3841
DeSmet R [R]5779
Desreumaux A 8306 8326 [E]10794
Desrosiers-Bonin D 7616
Dessel J [R]319
Destro A 5210 6603s
Dettwiler A 4463 5478
Deurloo K 1952 [M]6874
Deutsch N 9103 **R** 7658 10376
Devauchelle D 9636 [R]8120
Dever W 9515s 9518 10696 11377s [E]11126 [R]10684 11174
Devijver J 603
Devillers L 5313 [R]5417 6909
Devine A [R]9865
DeVries L 10102 **S** 3281
D e w e y A 8307 **J** 7465
Dexinger F 6826 8622s
Déclais J 9465-8
Dénouée C [R]4292
Di Berardino A [E]294 **P** 639
Di Lagopesole C 3033
Di Lella A [R]1411 1544 3227

Di Nocera G 11131
Di Nóbile Carlucci L 9637
Di Palma G [R]5809 8464
Di Paolo S 10051
Di Porto B 1824 4551
Di Sante C 739 4376
Di Segni L 8624 10022 10812
Di Tora M [R]6500
Diakonoff I 7863
D i a n i c h S 4 5 5 1 [E]5595
Dias M 1953
DiCicco M 4788
Dick M 3417 9419 **P** [M]1108
Dickerson P 6066
Dickey E 8022
Dickinson O 11172
Didier-Weill A 1996 5728
D i e b n e r B 1 0 0 3 s 1880s 1890s 1919 2019 3455 3700 4474 6874 [R]40 92 878 1097 1937 2087 3850 3937 3961 4018 4991 6802 8406 8548
Diederen A 6147
Diedrich F 3662
Diefenbach M 5314
D i e g o de M é r i d a [M]11026
Dieleman J 3067
Diem W 7919
Dienst K 4746 4748
Dieterlé C 2373
Dieterman J 863
Dietrich M 2436 7763s 7864s 10883s [R]2506 9428 **W** 6754 [E]2078 [R]3624 3673
Dietzfelbinger C 5479
D i e z de V e l a s c o F 9245
Dihle A 9815
Dijkstra M 3692 7936 10885 [E]9288
Dilday R 11919
Dillmann R 662 1079

Duling D 4482 ^R6634
Dumais M 4309s
Dumbrill R 10162
Dumézil G 11878
Dumontier M ^E3093
Dumoulin P 1080
Dunand F 9346s
Duncan A 6793 -**Jones R** 9991
Dunderberg I 9135s
Dunham R 6387 **S** ^R10878 10957
Dunill J 6398
Dunn G 11625 **J** 148 1187 5116 5800 5854 5953 6299 7046 8554 ^E5872 ^M5949 ^R4035 5800 **T** 6046
Dunstan W 9716
Dupertuis R ^R4111
Duplouy A ^R9771
Dupont J 4979 12012 ^M11879 -**Roc R** 1485
Dupuis J 6912
Dupuy B ^R396 3817 9060
Duquesne J 3883s 6894 9348 **T** 9349 ^R9401 9629
Duquoc C 4695 ^E1997
Duraisingh C ^E411
Durand J 7866 9522 ^E474 **X** ^R6507
Durken D 5509
Durkheim E ^M1596 9161
Durrwell F 6564 7047
Durusau P 10032
Dussart O 10088
Dussaud R ^M10876
Dutheil J 8951
DuToit D 5318
Dutra Rossatto N 11756
Duval F ^E590 **N** 8081
Duvelot W 4047
Dvorak J 5319
Dwyer T 4696
Dyck J 2570
Dyer K 4791
Dyk J 7599

Dyson R ^R12034 ^T11682·**S** ^R11184
Dziedzic A 1701
Dziobek E ^R10555

E
astman M 6827
Eaton J 3284 - **Krauss M** 10507s ^R10560
Ebach J 2943 11379 ^R741
Eber J 11910
Ebert D 6945
Ebner F 6118 **M** 4159 4764 5511 ^R404 5318
Echlin E 4062
Eck W 9958
Eckert J 5801 7198 ^R6064 **L** ^R1229
Eckey W 4664
Eckhart M ^M5326 10335
Eckstein H 6222
Edel E 1863 7937 12013
Edelman D 2051 ^E232
Eden K 744
Edenburg C 2457
Eder B 9818 **C** 10207
Edighoffer R 9090
Edin M 4213
Edrei A 8773
Edwards D 864 **D** ^E330 **J** 1163 **M** 11579 11819 ^R8978 **R** ^R5340
Edzard D ^R318 **L** 8142
Efe T 11087
Efroymson D ^R8992
Egan W 10772
Egaña F ^R12000
Egberts A 7938 9350 11053
Eggen W 5465
Egger P 4552
Eggert M ^E331 10072

Egger-Wenzel R 2984 R 3259 ^E3229
Ego B 588 6512 8663 ^T2645
Egron A 615
Eguiarte E ^R8558 11685
Ehman J 5075
Ehrenberg E 9717
Ehrhardt C ^R9250 **N** ^R8110 **T** ^E11915
Ehrlich C 2347 9523 **E** 8952
Ehrman B ^E80
Eibach U 7307
Eichler B ^R6786
Eid W 7308
Eide T ^E9639
Eidevall G 3634
Eigenmann U 7238
Eisen A 2281 **R** 8838 **U** 4697 7199
Eisenbaum P 6420
Eisenberg E 10763
Eisenman R 6471
Eisinger W ^D955
Eitam D ^E11309
Ekenberg A 2052
Eksell K 7803
El-Aguizy O 8082
Elat M 11444
Elayi J 9718 10849 10870
Elazar D 1864ss
Elbern V ^R10251
Eldar I 7600
El-Din M 11077
Elgavish D 9524
Elgvin T 8502
Eliade M ^M9192
Elizur B 7661
Elkann A 6860
El-Khouri L 7757
Ellens D 7467 **J** 8063
Elliger W 11253
Ellingworth P 1419 1486 6067 8052 ^R1233 1282 5771
Elliott J 6607 8309 11380 ^R1277 1282 1285 1287 3433 5763 5874 6058

Farajat S 10791
Farber W 9420
Farfán Navarro E 3418
Farina M 4894
Farkasfalvy D 1189
4131
Farkaš P 5681
Farmer C 5322 **M**
R7373 **R** **R**5618 **W**
1006 3432 3848
4132 **E**262 1535
3430
Farnell F 269 1224
Farrar L 11300
Farrell M **R**7373 **P**
E8152
Farris S 934s
Farrugia E **R**11553
Farthing G 556
Fassberg S **R**7668
Fassetta R **T**3052
Faucher A **R**231 1568
3520
Faulstich E 9526 9959
Fausti S 4179
Fauth W 2186 9212
Favard-Meeks C 9352
Favaro G **R**4241 4713
4905
Favro D 11184
Faye J 2349
Fechter F 11383
Fedalto G 9960
Feder F 1327 9353
Federici T 4608
Fee G 5804 6272 6321
R6322
Feeney D 9213
Feghali-Gorton A
10377
Fehribach A 5323
Feigenson E **E**237
Feinman G **E**11384
Feissel D **R**8091
Fekkes J 5599 **R**7566
Felber A **R**7420 **S**
11924
Feld G 2187 **R**12038 **H**
E5262
Feldman L 9908ss
E9911 **R**9914 **S**
R11250 **Y** 1892
Feldmann E 11683

11716
Feldmeier R 4312
E4311 **R**4018
Felicetti C **E**6707
Felici S **E**11521
Feliks Y 11310
Feller B 9711 **R**9755
Felten G 2892 2902
Fenn R 9948
Fenske W 5434 7240
Fenz A 2775
Ferguson E **F**25 **T**
2686
Fergusson D 1652
Ferlo R 640
Fernandez Lago J
7015 -**Tresquerres**
J 11458
Fernando A 5085 **G**
5428
Fernández A 7309 **B**
R465 4170 **D** **R**8310
Eyzaguirre S 6025
González D R6958
L 6947 **Marcos N**
1113 1301s 2572
7602 **R**1550 2333
Ramos F 4429
Tejero E 1113
7602
Feron M **M**2791
Ferrada Moreira A
R5729
Ferrari A 9199 **P**
5117
Ferraris L **R**8799
Ferraro G 5324ss
7016 11684 **R**5340
7197 8464
Ferreira J 5327
Ferreiro A 936
10272 11744
Ferrer J **E**3129
Ferretti C **R**7471
Ferry J 3514
Festorazzi F 7241
Feucht E 9354 9641
R9688
Feuchtwanger L
9912
Feuerstein R 3392
Feuillet A 5231
Fewell D 7469

Feyerick A **E**1613
Fédou M 6969 11586
11606 11635
Fictoor C 10163
Fiedler P 1190
Fiedrowicz M 747
2711 11522 11685
Fieger M 6248
Field D 6459 **F** **M**3024
Fiema E 11088 **Z** 8084
Fijnvandraat J 3745
Fikhman I 9642
Filer J 11323
Filho C 4417
Filippi A **R**12000 **G**
8128
Filoramo G 6120
11385 **E**3784
Finamore J 6609
Finan T **E**412
Fincke J 7998s
10970ss
Findeis H 5328
Fine S 8664 **E**9299
Finegan J 9595
Finet A 10936
Finkbeiner S 7310
Finkel I 9422 9752
E9421
Finkelberg M 8085
8143
Finkelstein D 10033 **I**
9527s 10684 10721
10769 10773
Finkielsztejn G 10425
Finley J 3424 **M** 9596
Finn J **E**9993 **T** 7242
Finney P 10273s
R10014 10322
Finotto A 7243
Finsterbusch K 5183
5882
Fiore B **R**6255 **G da**
M11756s
Fiorenza E 5600 7470-
6
Fiorina P **R**448 456
10955
Firestone R **R**9484
Firth D 7752
Fisch J 11213 **M** 8775
Fischer A 3147 3194
G 3519 7244

Fredriksen P 6215 ^{R}8723
Freedman D 152s 2669 ^{E}1241 ^{F}27
Freeman T 1771
Fregni G 2628
Frei H ^{M}931 **P** 9775
Freiman E ^{E}1609
French D 7423 **E** 11173
Frend W 10034 ^{R}473 9127 9627
Frendo A ^{R}9585 10694 10714
Frenkel D 10375
Frenschkowski M 4217 ^{R}7240 7535
Frerichs E 11903 ^{F}28
Fretheim T 965 1568 6513 ^{R}1630
Frettlöh M 7131
Freu J 10886
Freud S ^{M}1992 8881
Freund R 2071 **Y** 9597
Frevel C ^{R}1987
Frey A 11964 **J** 5329s ^{R}5336 8522
Freyberger K 10210 10468
Freydank H ^{R}9736
Freyne S 3891 9852
Fricke M 11905
Frickenschmidt D 1192
Friedli R 9492
Friedman J 10277 **M** 10617 **R** 1569 8881 10995s ^{R}152 **S** 2646
Fries J 2593
Friesen A 4655
Frings C 4773
Fritz W 2315 2552 ^{E}9530
Froehlich K 965
Frogneux N ^{E}413
Frolov S 3058
Fronzaroli P 10911 ^{E}10910
Frost N 1826
Fröhlich I 8378 8581
Frühwald-König J 5331
Fry E 1622 3120
Frymer-Kensky T 1083

1684 2111 ^{E}256
Fuchs A 4136s ^{R}9728 11242 **G** 2917 3478 ^{R}5934 6951 **O** 905 6971
Fuellenbach J 4487
Fuente A 753 5332 ^{E}465
Fuhs H 6972
Fujita N 2733
Fulkerson M 7477
Fulton R 3035
Fumagalli P ^{R}7683s
Funck B ^{E}9853
Funk R 3892s **W** 9116
Furlong J ^{R}1718
Furnish W 6069
Fuscaldo P 10426
Fusco R ^{R}7427 7470 **W** 3894s 11387
Fuster S 5698
Futato M 1653
Fürst A 5753 11696
Füssel K 4738

Gabba E ^{R}8208
Gabler J ^{M}11820
Gabolde L 11009 **M** 9643
Gabriel A 9854
Gabriella del Signore 2632
Gabrion H 557
Gabus J ^{R}9485
Gadamer H 754
Gaffin R 5807
Gager J 5808
Gaggadis-Robin V ^{R}10523
Gagnon R 5048
Gagos T 1400
Gahbauer F ^{R}11529
Gahler S 2827
Gaimani A 8824
Gajda I 7994
Gajewski P 11938
Gal O 9359 **Z** 10427 10738
Galambush J ^{R}3697
Galand de R 3093
Galán J 7941

Galchinsky M 8882
Galeotti G 1725
Galil G 2493 10790
Galinsky K 9961
Gallagher E 11725 **M** 641 **R** 4830
Gallazzi S 755 2211
Gallo C 9644 **I** 3821 **P** 11061
Galot J 4508 7060
Galsterer H ^{R}9982
Galter H ^{R}9745
Galvin J ^{R}7400
Gamba G 4183 4740 5017 5914 6266
Gamberini P ^{R}6929
Gambero L ^{R}7370
Gambino R 10278
Gamble H 11523
Gamer-Wallert I 10511 10999
Gameson R 1348
Gandara A 1654
Gane R 2154
Ganeri A 9164
Gangemi A 8049
Gangloff F 3666 9531 ^{R}619
Gantt C 6514
Garavaglia G 1382s
Garber Z 8883 ^{R}2245 2389
Garbini G 2602 7663 9855 ^{R}12029
Garbowski C 1726
Garbugino G ^{E}8163
García Barriuso P 7385 **Bazán F** 9117 **Cordero M** 9065 **de Alba J** 6973 **Domene J** ^{R}4719 **García L** 10512 **J** 2776 **-Jalón de la Lama S** 7604s **Martín P** 11483 **Martínez F** 1790 8179s 8379-81 8384-7 8465s 8506-11 8582s ^{E}242 8382s ^{E}8464 8505 **Moreno A** 1570 5232 5263 5284 5333 ^{R}178 3994 5456 5485

6671s 6709 6756 11697

Gilboa A 10428 **R** 1632

Gildemeister T 6327

Giles T 1084

Gilhus I 6612

Gillespie T 6122

Gilles-Sabaoun É 643

Gilliéron B 4556

Gillingham S 605 2735 R27 2419

Gillman F R7510

Gillmayr-Bucher S 1115 1902 2404

Gilman S E538

Gilmont J R903

Gilroy A E7497

Giménez J T6719

Ginouvès R 10106 E11324

Ginter B 11000

Ginzberg L 8779s

Giombi S R1171

Giordani G 4267

Giordano C F29 **F** 11129

Giorgadze G 9784

Giorgieri M 8000s 11023 R11103

Giorgini F 4557

Giraldo R 5717

Girard M 2713 4867 **R** 6613

Girardet M T6753 7302

Girardi G 7355 **M** 11642 E393

Girón Blanc L 8781

Girzone J 3896

Gisolfi D 10279

Gispen W E509

Gispert-Sauch G 6974

Gitin S 3288 9532 E477s

Gitler H 10813

Giuliani L R10197

Giurisato G 4895 5528

Give B de R4103

Given M 5883

Giversen S E374

Glad C 5855

Gladding J T8949

Gladigow B E525

Gladson J R610 6889

Glancy J 757 6070 11389

Glassen E R12035

Gleason M R9884 **R** 6418

Glessmer U 1546 8388s 8690

Gmirkin R 8512 ,

Gnadt M 4219

Gnemmi D 10516

Gneuss H 2688

Gnidovec F 5507

Gnilka J 1143 3897 4430 5729s 7555s

Gnirs A 9360

Gnoli G R12029

Gnuse R 2022 2491 4941 9914 R2334

Gobillot G 9482

Goddard C 8145

Godding R R544

Godwin J 9066 9092

Goedicke H 7942s 9645 10140 R9670

Goelet O 9646

Goethert R 10622

Gogel S 8090

Gohary J 11072

Golani A 10182

Golb N 8390 8584s M8609

Gold D R9493

Goldberg A 8749 R8748 L 8960

Golden M 10155

Goldenberg G 156 F30 **R** 8668

Goldfajn T 865

Goldhill S R5592

Goldingay J 758 966 1194 3351 3422

Goldish M R11818

Goldman J E11850 **S** 1941 -**Ida B** 10623

Goldmann M 8961

Goldstein E 7480

Goldsworthy G 4613

Golitzin A E531

Gollinger H 666

Golomb D 1263 R2432

Gomes P 606

Gomez Bellard C· R10871

Gonneaud D 7200

Gonnet H 10378

Gonsalves F 5810 11870 R7139

González Blanco A E288 336 **Buelta B** 4993 **C** 6614 7017 **Caballero A** 4868 **de Cardedal O** 1116 3898 6580 **Echega-ray J** 10739 **Fernán-dez R** E288 **Fraile A** R4429 4940 **García F** R11412 **J** 2837 2840 5285 **Núñez J** E8310 **R** R5484 **Salazar J** 9785s R9787

Gooch P 4558

Goodacre M 2437 4137 11881 R4872 4901 5282

Goodblatt D 9533

Goodhart S 2053

Goodison L 9248 E298 9200

Goodman L 6515 **M** 8669 E337

Goody J 1007

Gopher A 10689

Gophna R 11468

Gorday P R217

Gordon C 7607 9277 9822 10887 10912 F31 **R** 1329 2473 E2573 R2389

Gori F 11686 R4871

Goring-Morris A 10689 N R10944

Gorini G E10570

Gorman F 1571 2172 R2170

Gosling F 2986 7608 7711

Gosse B 1195 1867s 2054 2489 2849 3330 3479 3509

Gottlieb C 3370 **G** F32

Gottwald N 2212 6875 M710

Grousset R 11500
Gruber M 1889 2946
3648 6165 [T]2715
Gruen E 8192 9861
[E]9848 [R]10009
Gruenler R 6375
Gruenwald I 3584
[E]9193 [R]6852
Grundmann H 11757
Gruson P [R]3778
Grümbel U 7483
Grün A 4980
Grünbeck E 2833
Grünewald T [R]11431
Gryson R [E]3331 3433s
[R]12015
Grzybek E 9978 S
2796
Gu Cheng [M]4080
Guardini R 2779
Gubler M 4615 5530
8146 [R]5862
Gudorf M 6271
Gudovitch S 10429
10709
Guenther A 3622
Guerra Gomez M 4522
5506
Guerrier F 10282
Guerriero E [E]300
Guest G 6760 [E]1385 P
2383 [R]512 7455
Guetta Sadun S 6761
Guérard M [E]3010
Guggenberger W [R]918
Guglielminetti M
10518
Guignard W 9260
Guijarro Oporto S
3904 4160 10739
Guilhou N [R]9368
Guillaud M 1999
[R]4074
Guillaume J 3787
[E]11486 P 2370 2391
Guillaumin J [E]458
Guillaumont A [E]11656
C [E]11656
Guillemette Y [R]5308
Guillet J 559 5856
5894ss 6072 [R]271
3772 3854 4066
4465 4667 4670

4865 5128 5142
5159 6468 11387
Guimier-Sorbets A
9215 10400
[R]10399
Guindon H [R]615
7202
Guinot J 5700 11673
Gulde S 7767
Gullini G 9862
Gundlach R 9363
9649 [E]479 [F]34
Gundry R [R]4670
11881
Gunkel H 1615 2696
Gunn D 9534 [E]215
Gunton C 3905 6571
Gurney O 9787
10166 11146
Gurrid J 9650
Guscin M 10519
Gustafson M [R]11527
Guth A 1702
Guthrie D [E]1536
Gutiérrez J [R]2 49 223
1113 5295 5340
5397 5576 5594
5668 5725 5774
6722 7694 8021
8292 8859 9121
10003 **Jaramillo**
M [R]6991 M [R]2326
Guttenberg A 2780
Gutzwiller K 9863
Guyon J 11200
Guyot P [T]3788
Guzman E 1053
Gülden S 9364
Günther M 5201
6249 P [R]10183 S
[R]9477
Güntner D 2873
Gütenbrock H 9278
Güterbock H 11141
Güting E 5754
Györy H 10380
Gyselen R [E]338
[E]10381

Ha S 11674
Haacker K 6019
Haag E 3395 3760
7153 7386 [R]3600

Haak R 3292 3740
[R]232
Haarbeck A 11974
Haarmann H 967
Haas A 1117 C 11040
V [R]9282
Haase R 2128ss [R]2132
W [E]243s
Habel N 1828
Habermann B 7484 R
5335
Habermas J [M]845
11882
Habib A 9535
Habicht C 9216 9864
Habtemichael-Kidane
7246
Hachlili R 8675 10401
Hachmann R 10520
Hack C 3906
Hackett J 2384
Hacohen D 9536
Hadas-Lebel M 7610
9915
Hadey J 3480
Hadfield A 5701
Hadot P 8261
Hadrianus [M]9975
Haelewyck J 8193
[R]8203 8253 8260
Haerinck E 10521
10571
Hafemann S 6157
Hafiz M 10108
Hagedorn A 4811
Hagemann L 7314
10353
Hagen K [R]6394
Hagene S 5218
Hagner D 4161 4186
4221 6381
Hahn E 7050 F 158
3585 5811 6115
6460 8676 [F]35 [R]6466
6472 6481 6484 J
8677
Hahne B 4984
Haight R 3907
Haikal F 7946
Hajdú K [E]8131
Hakimian S [E]10852
Hakkenberg M
[R]1450

Healy N ^{R}6965
Hearon H 7426
Heath E 6694
Hecataeus A ^{M}9556
Hecht A 667
Heck C 1909 10255
Heckel U ^{E}385
Hedrick C 4703
  ^{E}8313 ^{R}9115
Heer J 5557 5606
Heesen P 10431
Hegel F ^{M}11771
  11837
Hegele G 764
Heid S 5543 7201
  ^{R}10270
Heide M 7611
Heidegger M ^{M}5748
Heidemanns K ^{R}301
Heil C 2803 4140
  4345 11975 ^{E}4139
  4157 J 4519 5757
Heiligenthal R 3909s
  ^{R}6494
Heilman S 8681
Heim K 2853 ^{R}3108
Heimpel W 9426s
Heine S 7427
Heinelt H 7191
Heinen C ^{T}1413 H
  ^{R}11040
Heininger B 3531
  5857 6422
Heinsch J 11301
Heinsch J ^{T}9543
Heinsohn G 2056
Heintz F 5188 J 10938
  ^{R}12019 M 9711
  9729 ^{E}318
Heinze A 5607 R 4616
Heinzerling R 1772
Held H ^{R}7233
Helderman J ^{R}9075
Heldermann J 9157
Helewa G 7018
Heller D 4617 J 2190
  2822 6978 ^{F}40 K
  1727 5179 R 867
Hellerman J 11396
Hellholm D 4352 6050
Hellmann M ^{R}10458
  10480
Helm P 6516

Helmer R 8257s
Heltzer M 1912 2405
  2615 7768 10376
  11287 11397
  ^{E}11309 ^{R}10145
  10903
Helyer L 6876
Hemelrijk E ^{R}9997
Hempel C 7664
  ^{R}3063 3580
Hempelmann H ^{E}765
Hendel R 1242 1618
  4316 6866 ^{R}1630
  1990
Henderson J 11398
Hendricks W 4268
Hendrickx H 4873s
Hendrix G ^{E}11754 S
  968
Hengel M 159s 1488
  5233 5731s 8610
  ^{E}»385 1304
Hengstl J ^{R}2123
Henig M ^{R}10034
Henne P 1331
Hennecke E ^{M}8318
Hennessy B 10827
Henry C 6762 D
  10776 ^{E}10775 E
  ^{R}2106 M ^{R}1518
  1523 ^{T}5520
Hensell E ^{R}6012
Hens-Piazza G 2559
  4106
Hentschel G 2462
  2479
Heracleon ^{M}11596
Heras G 3832 3911s
Herb M 10154
Herberg W 8968s
Herbers K ^{E}6461
Herbert E 2473
  ^{R}8485 S 10740
Herbin F 9366
Herczeg P 8328
Herdejürgen H
  10523
Hergenröder C 5337
Heriban J 6916 ^{F}41
  ^{M}11883
Hermans J 7248 T
  7202
Hermanson E 3679

Hermary A ^{R}10348
Hermisson H 161 2948
  2989 3070 3345s
  3396-9 3436-8 3481s
  3506 ^{R}3404
Hermon E ^{R}8627 9907
Hermosilla Molina A
  4559
Hernández Ruiz J 7086
  Urigüen R ^{R}4059
Herodotos ^{M}9754
Herold A 11041
Herr B 1914 D 2412 L
  10383 10793
Herranz Marco M
  7808
Herren M 11749
Herrera Sánchez C
  6073
Herrmann D 4269 G
  ^{10136}^{E}10137 S 3495
Herrojo J 10764
Herscher E 11153
Hertig P 4225s ^{R}4836
Hertog C 2372
Hertz D 8885
Herz P ^{E}11399 ^{R}9991
  11297
Herzberg W 11526
Herzer J 3532 6438
  ^{R}8234
Herzig A 7249
Herzman R ^{E}5593
Herzog C 6794 R 9538
Heschel A 8970-4
  ^{M}11884 S 4050 8975
Hesiod ^{M}1689
Hess R 2376 7665
  7723 11014 ^{E}668
  ^{R}610 7778 11390
Hesse G 4081
Hester J 5758
Hettema T 1008
  ^{R}1949
Heuser M 339 9104
Heyd M 10626s
Heyer C 3913 5733
  7097
Hezser C 8787 9998
Hibbard A 2817
Hickling C ^{R}6158
Hidal S 11823
Hidalgo de la Vega M

Horowitz B 9867 **W** 10189 11215
Horrell D 6075 6428 ^R6051 6426 6442 11411
Horsley G 8029 8097 ^R5409 **R** 769 4162 6059 9962 10741-10742
Horsnell M 7612
Horstmanshoff H ^E11333
Horwich P 8147
Horwitz L 10551 10710 11288
Hossfeld F 1572 2739s
Hostetter E 2316 ^R7610
Hotze G 5814
Houk C 3702
Houlden L ^R4301 7572
Houlihan P ^R9685 11312 11292
House H 8979 ^E6675 **P** 2494 3623 6877
Houseman M 6713
Housley N ^E11501
Houston J 4400 **W** 11289
Houtman A 10628 ^E303 **C** 1548 2097 6763
Houwink ten Cate P 9789
Howard D 1119 2366 2369 2858 **G** 8314 ^R6420 **K** 2156 - **Brook W** 5339 - **Carter T** 10952
Howe K 11250
Hoyland R ^R11510
Hoyle F 1704
Hoyt T ^E1403
Höffe O 7320
Höffken P 2536 3387 3400 9918 ^R3388 3404
Höhensteiger P ^R7415
Höhn H ^R2085
Höhne-Sparborth J 1728
Hölbl G 9653
Hölscher A 6335

^E1144
Hörner W ^E1685
Höslinger N 938 1424
Høgenhaven J 8467
Høyland M 7722
Hranitzky K 10283
Hrovat J 1454
Hruby K 8683
Huarte J ^R5152
Hubaut M 3918
Hubbard M 6174 ^R7077
Hubble R 2994
Hubeňák F ^R8563
Huber K 3703
Hudec J ^R11323
Hudson D ^R3668
Huehnergard J 7874s 11015
Hug H 12018 **J** ^R1743
Hugenberger G 3762
Hughes T 4899
Huizing K ^R4084 4088
Hulet C 11977
Hull R ^R8344
Hultgård A 3586 8605 10284
Hultgren A 4227
Human D 2832
Humbach H ^T11216
Humbert J 8394 10110 10355 ^E10794
Hume C 6250
Humphrey E 8235
Humphreys C 2253 **W** 2648 ^R1156 2626 2643s 2652
Hunger H 7876 9715 ^R12040
Hungs F 6049
Hunt A 6076
Hunter E 7842 10213 **J** 2741
Huot J 10944 ^R10878
Hupper W ^E560
Hurault L 11255
Hurd J 163 1199 4704 5760ss 6077 6341 6348 6353

6357
Hurlet F 9963
Hurowitz V ^R3322 3635 11390 **W** 2510 6517 7666
Hurtado L 6108 8684 ^R6325
Hurwitz M 1659
Huscava E 670
Huß W ^R9388
Hutchens K 3542
Hutter M 9279 9428 ^R9282 9285
Huwyler B 3483
Huyzer R ^R650
Hübner H 3222 5763 6261 6581 7558s ^R1309 **U** 9540 ^E10579 ^R10686 **W** ^E11672
Hünermann P 4468 6979
Hüttenmeister F 7667 ^T8789
Hütter R ^R7318
Hvalvik R 8344
Hvidberg-Hansen F 7811
Hvidt N 6123
Hyland S 1120
Hyman G ^R4068 **P** 8886s
Hymes D 2259 3670

Iacovou M 9541
Iamblichus ^M3318 6609
Iammarrone G 6980
Ibba G ^E8513 ^R8855
Ibn Ezra A ^M8842
Ibrahim M 10777
Ice T 3294
Idel M 6833 8840 8850
Idinopulos T ^E9167
Ignatius A ^M11552 11579s
Ikeda J 7877s
Ikram S 9370 11312
Ilan D 11400 **T** 4353 8395 11401
Ildefonse F 8027

Jewett R 5957 6041
Jésus María J de
  R7393
Ji C 10802
Jih C E9169
Jiménez Hernández E
  2464
Jinbachian M 8009
Jinkins M 2744
JOANNES PAULUS II
  7390 8982 11978
Jobes K 2649s
Jobling D 2427 M710
Jobsen A 2951
Jocelyn H 9979
Jochum H 2952 6676
Jodock D R633
Joerg U E1427
Joest C 7252
Joffe A 10589 R477
  10076
Johannsen F 671
John F 7253
Johner M 4317
Johns L 5609s
Johnson E 4755 J 3790
  E9655 L 773 5202
  5930 6462 7561
  M3954 R3888 3892
  10572 R 6402 R873
  S 7321
Johnston M 774 S
  R9252
Johnstone C 1200 W
  1973 2574 R11835
Jomier J 2023 R1835
Joncas J R103 10165
Jones B R3618 C
  11113 F 8345 G
  E284 I 4435 L 5341
  E246 M 11079 N
  6078 P E10001 S
  11561 8687 8714
  E414 W M11821
Jonge M 1936 3922
Jongeling K 7769
Jonker G 9429 L 1201
  3704 6867
Joosten J 1549 2192ss
  3636 4187 7614
  8194
Jordan P 11001
Josaitis N 3791

Josephson J 10356
Josephus Flavius
  M2120 2513 8570
  8606 9889-9947
Joshel S E342 11402
Jospe R 2213
Jossa G 909 3923
  R8610
Jossua J 4082
Jost R E7509 11358
Joubert S 6493
Joukowsky M
  10834s
Joyce P 3543
Joynes C 4705 R2542
Jördens A E8098
Jørgensen M 10055
Juckel A 1332
Judah HaLevi M8841
Judge E F47
Julien P R1996 5728
Jull T 2394
Jung R 4618
Junges J R7325
Junghans H E11780
Junker K R10363
Jursa M 11313
  11447
Justinus M 11584
  M5705 M11585-90
Juvencus M11739
Jüngel E 6094 E7098
Jürgens B 6204
Jütte R E8688

Kabasele Mukenge
  A 3526
Kaestli D 8315 J
  8346 9138
Kafafi Z 10788
Kahana H R2650
Kahil L E10214
Kah-jin Kuan J 7879
Kahl J 7952 O 7921
  W 775 869 4401
  4741
Kahn D 9656 L
  10111 M10592
Kaimakis D 1306
Kaiprampatt G 4117
Kaiser G 4083 J
  7073 O 166 609

644 1687 2133 2158
  2805 2830 3073
  3153-6 3240s 3258
  3261 6520 6868
  R3072 3079 3177 W
  6834 9542 11340
Kaizer T 7812
Kakule Vyakuno J
  3457
Kalimi I 1893 2575s
Kalin E 5958
Kallai Z 167 1974
  2378 2529 9600s
  11221-32 11341
Kalluveettil P 776
Kalmin R 8751
Kalms J 9919 E490
Kaltner J 2821 7668
Kamano N 3186
Kamčatnov A 1455
Kamesar A 8277
Kamil J 9657
Kaminsky J R2964
Kamlah J 588
Kammenhuber A
  12021
Kammerer G 2953 -
  Grothaus H 10422
Kampen J 4229 E8586
  N R10234
Kamphaus F F48
Kampling R 8983
  E1144
Kampmann S R4087 U
  11114
Kamsler H 8278
Kanagaraj J 5342 5816
Kanawati N 10527
Kangudi K 6573
Kannengiesser C
  11639 11737 R9275
Kant I M11822
Kanzian C E304
Kaper O E483
Kapera Z 8396-9
  11888 11936 11960s
  11979 E11959
Kapkin D 6342
Kaplan E 11884 L
  R8838 M 8888
Kaplony-Heckel U
  11314
Kappen S M6996

Klappert B 6678
Klassen W 4562 6037
7157
Klauck H 1202 4734
5123 5236 5764
11186 ^{R}4178 8071
10135 11592
Klawans J 8689
Klawek A ^{F}51 ^{M}11888
Klee D 7488 **P** ^{M}10242
Klein C 3157 **G** 2332
^{F}52 **H** 4928 7099 **J**
7882 **M** 1264 6475
8889 **R** 2591 ^{E}3788
^{R}32 9976 **W** 5959
Kleinbauer W 10631
Kleiner M 2459
Kleinschmidt F 4362
7133
K l e m m P 1 1 9 2 6
^{R}206 892
K l e n g e l - B r a n d t E
11092 ^{E}10387
Klenicki L 2214
Kletter R 10089 10190
10725
Klijn A ^{F}53
Klimek P 779
Klimkeit H 339
Kline M 969 ^{R}3125 .
Klingbeil G 2195
Klingenberg G ^{R}9987
10002
K l i n g e r E ^{F}2862 **S**
10434
Klinghardt M ^{R}1037
K l o c k - F o n t a n i l l e I
9790
Klopfenstein M 169
1661 2955 ^{E}2078
Kloppenberg J 4143
Kloppenborg J 5885
^{E}11404 ^{R}4252 4679
4733
Klopper F 780
Klostergaard Petersen
A 11886
Kloth N 9658
Klöckener M ^{E}305
Klug W 8028
Klusmann C 3925
Klutz T ^{R}3811
Kmiecik U 4708

K n a p p A 1 1 1 5 7
11448 ^{E}11156
Knauer B ^{E}1123
Knauf E 1573 10779
1 0 8 3 6 1 0 8 5 5
^{E}10579
Knibb M 8195
Knierim R 6879 ^{F}54
Knight J 4901
Knights C 8196
Knipp P 10290
Knipping B 1574
Knitter P 7192 ^{R}6965
K n o c h O 6 4 2 9 **W**
6 5 7 4 -**M u n d G**
11805
Knohl I 1056 8557
^{M}5680
Knoll G 4460
Knoppers G 2477
2495 2577 ^{R}2579
Knowles M ^{R}6122
Knudsen E 8150
Knuth H 11841
Kobayashi H 5483
Kobes J ^{E}11399
K o c h D 6 0 7 9 **H**
^{R}9 7 7 1 **J** 7 8 8 3
^{R}9 7 0 8 **K** 2 0 2 4
3600 6765 6835
8 6 9 0 9 7 7 5 **N**
10218
Kochanek P 1 6 3 4
1797
Kochavi M 10112
Kock C ^{R}11411
Kockel W 10528
Koehler L ^{E}7669-2
Koelle L 8986
K o e m o t h P 9 3 7 4
^{R}9395 9406
Koenen K 3297 3616
6620 11849
Koenig J 4526 7256
Koerrenz R 672
K o e s t e r C ^{R}5 2 7 2
6420 **H** 4620 6284
9375 ^{E}460 6276
11116 ^{F}55
Koet B 4955
Koffi E 1490 8151
Kofoed J 9545
Kofsky A 1830 ^{E}306

Kogan-Zehavi E 10529
10711
Kohl K ^{E}525
Kohlenberger J 1404
Kohlmeyer K 10554
10921
Kohlschein F ^{E}10291
Koitabashi M 10168
Kokkinos N 9949
Kolarcik M ^{R}2183
Kolb B 10837 **F** 11470
Kolbrener W ^{R}8818
Kollesch J ^{F}56
K o l l m a n n B 4 4 0 2
11859
Kolocotroni W ^{E}11850
K o l o s k i - O s t r o w A
^{E}344
Kolta S 7983
Koltun-Fromm N 2814
Konik J 8400
Konings J ^{R}5032 5245
5270 7053 8385
Konkel M 3574
Konrad W 781
Konradt M 6476
Konstan D 870 8347
^{E}9869
Koole J 3403s
Koops R 2553
Koorevaar H 2080
Koortbojian M 10530
Kopciowski E 1575
Kopcke G 11158
K o p e r s k i V ^{R}5 7 3 1
6153 **W** 6318
Kopp H ^{E}11242
Korang J 6224
Korenhof M ^{E}7509
Korherr E 7257
Kormyscheva E 11060
Korobkin N ^{T}8841
Korpel M 2672 3405s
3442 10891
Korsak M 1729
Korte R 11201
Kosak S 8002
Kosch D 3926 4621
11966 11981
Koskenniemi E 4403s
Kossow R ^{T}1139 3780
Kostka U 5060
Kosztolnyik Z ^{R}4472

Lémonon J 3778 4567
Léonard J R3087 8272
Léon-Dufour X 4189s
5269s 5484s M11851
Létourneau P 3932
R11435
Lévinas E M11892s
Lévy C 9261 E433
Licharz W R1417
Licht J 2241
Lichtenberg R 9347
Lichtenberger H 6839
8588 8700 9924
E6666
Lichtheim M 9379
Lichtwark F E10998
Liderbach D 6919
LiDonnici L R10574
Lidov A 10637
Lieb M 3557
Lieber A 8701
Liebers R 4118
Liebeschuetz J 10025
Liebowitz H 10439
Lieggi J 7074
Lienhard J R2247
T4903 M 11781
11802
Lies L E11608
Lieu J 5350 7490 8992
11588 R285 3798
5272 S 9105s
Liébaert J 11531
Lifschitz D 2718
Ligato G 11502
Lightfoot J M11844
Lightner R 6522
Likeng P 3098
Lilliu G 10116
Lilyquist C 10183
10220
Lim T 2060 5765 8471
R8451 Y 5193
Lima M 3663
Limbeck M 5821
Limet H R9253
Limor O 10638 E8993
R8203
Lin B 5208
Linafelt T 3522 8793
R4572
Lincoln A 5351 6252
B 9777

Lindemann A 5150
6146 11562 E3776
R6255
Linden N 1579 4126
Linder A 10639
Lindgren H M11823
Lindner M 10780 F62
Lindström F 6622
Ling R 10403
Link C 6623 6754
Linnemann E 1205
Linss W 5916
Linville J 2496
Linzey A 11291
Lion B 7884 R91 110
Liong H 4438
Liperi B 4163
Liphschitz N 3419
10057 10184
Lipiński E 7816
10440 10531
11093 11449
R7805 7832 9519
Lippe W 2883
Lippolis C R444
9853 10987
Lips H 5766 7161
Lipschits O 10640
Lipton D R2007
Liron H 8892
Liscia Bemporad D
E434
Lison J R7396s
Lisowsky G T8753
Liss H 2049
Litfin D 940
Litke R 9432 W
R6371
Little E 5438
Litton C 10071
Litvinsky B 11144
Litwak K 5822
Liverani M 9553
10727 10981
11017s E11217
R9736 P 11207
Livingstone A 9433
Livne-Kafri O 10641
Livshits W F63
Liwak R 9304
Llagostera E 11962
Llamas E 7393
Llewelyn S 5767

8102s
Lloyd-Jones D 6017
Lluch Baixauli M
11609
Loader J 1580 1951
3099 10170 N 10117
W 3933s
Lobkowicz N 6624
Lobrichon G 1350
Lodge J 6012 R6480
Loewenthal E 1896
Loffreda S 8104
Logan A 7135 9070
Loh J 1735
Lohfink G 171 1206
7162s N 172 1581
2284 2292 3161-5
3184 3187 3195
3198s 3203 3211s
6679 6719s 6796 F64
M6726 R630 1548
Lohmann K 9380
Lohmeyer E M6298
Lohse E 4439s 4978
5974 D11777 R116
205 4552 4503 5934
Lomas K R426
Lombaard C 2745 R54
1186 1201
Lombard H 5352
Lombardi A R592 M
4938 P 11532
Lona H 7136 T11563
Long B 10085 R2463 T
4191 6391 6405
E248 W 3207
Longacre R 5960
Longenecker B 6207
8612 R 4624 6141
E252 391 3796 R5845
5932 8235
Longère J R7411
Longman T 3125 E521
Longobardo L R393
9986
Longxi Z 9870
Loprieno A 9381
Lorber J 4274
Lorenzen T 4625
Lorenzin T R2705
2730
Lorenzini E 5353
Lorenzo Leal N 7262

Magnani G 3938
Magnante A 4972 5079
Magne J 4569
Magness J 8407ss 10460 10532s 10682 R8370
Magonet J 2004 8703
Maguire D 6766 **H** 10297
Mahasneh H 10795
Maher M 1265
Mahé J 9072 9159
Maidman M 8003 R10945
Maier C 2961 3112 3496 9307 11503 **G** 3536 **H** R3811 7203 **J** 2300 8410 8520 8592 8704 8854 8855 9554 9925 R8205 8496 **P** 4294 R4035
Mailer N 4088
Maimonides M2267 8833 8835s
Main E 8472
Mainville O E231
Maisch I 7433
Makdisi U 10860
Makujina J 8031s
Malamat A 173 1774 1872 1975 2160s 2266 2438ss 2450s 2478 3301-6 3550 7727 7743 9555 10643 10759ss 10939s F69
Malan F 5898 **G** 6455
Malatesta E 12025
Malbran-Labat F 7819
Maldamé J 613 11893
Małecki Z 3408
Malek J R9649 **R** R12025
Malherbe A 5875
Malina B 3798 5271 5619 5690 5859 E11415 M1222 R881
Malino F 8893
Malinowski J 10644
Malipurathu T 7265 11410

Mallau H 6524
Mallet J 10732
Maloney E 6254 R4509 **G** 5899
Maltese E E346
Maltz M 1125
Maluf L 2196
Malzoni C 4799
Mandelbrote S 1106
Mandell S 8680 9866
Manekin C E8894 R8838
Maness S 5900
Manetho M9015
Mangan C R8335
Mangatt G 4570
Mango C F70
Mangoni B 5105
Manicardi E 4840 5077
Manjaly T 4841
Mankowski P 1492
Manley B 7932 11244
Manning J R9860 **S** 11174 R364
Manns F 2005 3799 4711 5151s 5354 5516 6239 7022 8997
Mannucci A 6761
Manser M E522
Mantels H 4981 5007
Mantovani E 9183
Manus U 6984
Manzano B 10645
Manzi F
Manzi F 4629 5069 5961 6304 6407 8593 R6432 7197 7197 8208 8212 **L** 11302
Maqueda Gil A R3019 6955
Mara M 5703 6295
Marafioti D 3513 R7197
Maragno M 8051
Marahla M 10791
Marais J 874
Maranesi P 1664 R1427 6664

Maraqten M 7922
Maraval P T11489
Marc Marule de Split M11694
Marcabru M1775
Marchadour A E392 4571
Marchel W 6565
Marcheselli-Casale C 3939 6369
Marchesi G 6985 7051 R11252
Marchetti N 10441 10700 E10701
Marciniak M 10221
Marcion M6435
Marco Simn F 9221
Marconcini B 4127 6583 R3269 3339 3671
Marconi G 5469 6416 6464 7088 R5668 6056 6407 7062
Marcos I 788
Marcus D 2605 R2548 **I** 8826 **J** 4572 4779 5460 E11384 R4724 **L** M11805 **M** 10389
Margain J E209 F71
Margalit B 3307
Marganne M 11326 R11332
Margerie B 11535
Margolis M M1303 2338
Margot J 8054
Marguerat D 875s 3940-3 4441 4505 5125 E253 8998
Marguerite de Navarre M7616
Margueron J 11472
Marie d'Ennetières M7616
Mařik T 1800
Marin M 11536 11689 11740 E393 11206
Marinelli E 10534
Marino A 6986 **L** 10814
Mariottini C 3763
Maris J 7089
Marissen M 10171

4276
Mazar A 10443 10712
^E478 **B** 10646
Mazarakis Ainian A
^E486
Mazza E 4527 **F** 589
Mazzanti A 9097
Mazzeo M 5621s 6032
Mazzinghi L 1977
3218s 3225 4240
^R9567
Mazzini I ^R11333
Mazzocchi L 4241
4713 4905
Mazzola R 673
Mazzoleni D 11202s
Mazzoni S 10222
10444 10920
Mazzotta F 6988
Mazzucco C ^R7149
März C 3945 4630
6408 ^R5479 5817
Márquez Rowe I 7886
^R474
Mbuwayesango D
3386
McAuliffe J ^R4095
McBride D 8105
McCarter P 8154
McCarthy C ^R1333 **J**
^E6626 **P** 6797 **T**
^R11691
McCaughey T ^R1061
McClellan T 10928
McClintock G ^R9270
McCollough C ^E330
McComiskey T 3627
McConvery B 3264
11327 ^R247 2580
3464 4186 4487
6246 11898
McConville J 2285
^R3471
McCready W 11986
McCullough J ^R6197
McDade J 3946
McDaniel J ^R932
McDermott J 2320
Mcdonald J 7324
^R7318 **L** 1013 ^R279
P ^R873 3807 6076
McDonnell K 4300
4303

McEvenue S 6599
6748
McFarlane A 10527
McGaughty L 3947
McGinn B 7539
˙ ^R10275
McGovern B 2498 **P**
10748
McGowan A ^R8322
McGrath A 6584
6989 **J** 5452 6990
McGraw L ^R5804
5873
McGuckin J 11652
McGuire A ^E9127
McGurk P 8132
McHugh J 7398
McIlwain T 646
McIver R 4242
McKane W 3466
3713
McKay H 7493
10471
McKechnie P ^R5660
9829
McKenna M 1924
McKenzie A 4192 **J**
10838 **L** 4631 **S**
2324 ^E257 ^R77
2328 2565
McKevitt D 4091
McKim D ^E517 ^R112
913
McKinlay J 3077
McKinnon J 10172
McKnight S 3948
^R3841
McLaren J 9930
9980
McLaughlin J 7731
^R2949 3298
McLay T 1307 3594s
McLean B 5827
McLeese C 7494
^R7432
McMahon A ^R10185
McNamara M 2690
2748 ^F78 ^R805
1633 2389 2683
4171 4661 5083
6054 6884 7560
8319
McNeil B 4528

McNicol A 4509
^E4145
McQueen L 3668
McVey K 11537
Meadors E ^R4129 5455
Meadowcroft T 3596
Meadows J 2267
Meagher P 4243 4876
6526 7024ss
Mealand D 5754
Mędali S ^E241
Medina M 7495
Mee C 9244 11159
Meeks D ^R9390 10527
W 7325s
Megged M ^M1125
Meggitt J 5486 5734
^R1742 3786 3798
Mehramooz M 3124
Meier C ^R1663 **H** 5902
J 3949 4053-4054
^M4051 **L** 2006 **S**
^R884 7622
Meimaris Y 11079
Meinhold A 2414 3117
Meirovich H 1600
Meiser M 4164 ^R3248
Meisinger H 4503
Meißner S 5769
Mekhitarian A ^R10992
Melaerts H ^E436
Melammed R 8827
Melanchthon P
^M11807
Melbourne B ^R3796
Melchert C 674 3078
Meldau W 5559
Melendez R ^R7344
Melito S ^M11669
Mell U 4745 ^R2542
Mellink M 8004 **O**
^R3797
Mello A 2697 3467
4193 6798
Mellott-Khan T 10211
Meltzer E 9383
Melugin R 3445 3675
^E3333
Melville H ^M9874
Melzer-Keller H 4092
7435 ^R7432 7472
Mendecki N 3638
7675

Millard A 7887 8155
9557 ᴿ1149 **M** 1636
2749 8795 8895
ᴱ8766
Miller C 7622 **D** 3168
11987 12027 **G** 2399
7364 **J** 1015 6371
ᴿ1619 **K** 5689 **M**
9829 **P** 2750 6725
ᴿ2290 11404 **R** 3954
4202 4988 9558
ᴱ8319 ᴿ744 **S** 6042
Millot L 10938
Mills D 5532 **M** 6527
W 1524 ᴱ563 1582
Milner N 11128
Mimouni S 8058 9002
Mina M ᴿ4524 4719
7402
Minasi M ᴿ10415
Minear P 7075
Minet J ᴿ10254 11667s
Minette de Tillesse C
877s
Minguet Mico J 5832
7027
Minissale A 3230 3244
11939s ᴿ379 1637
3226 3248
Minkoff H ᴱ259
Minois G 1737
Minotta D ᴱ2540
Miosi F 9386
Miquel P 615
Miranda A 5735
Mirecki P ᴱ418 ᴱ8313
ᴿ7989
Miroschedji P de
ᴿ10619
Mirsky J 11988
Mishor M ᴿ30
Misiarczyk L 6844
Misiurek J 5238
Miskotte K 944
Misset-Van de Weg M
6440 8332
Mistrorigo A 519
Misztal W 5833
Mitchell L 9830 ᴿ9202
M 5547 5770 7329
7542 ᴿ5720 5859
6158 **S** 11145 **T**
ᴿ2493 **W** 1493

Mitri T 1836
Mittmann S 10777 -
Richert U 4277
Mitton C 12028
Miyake L 1837
Mínguez N ᵀ1562
Mirete Pina A 5625
Mlinar A ᴿ4437
Młynarczyk J 10461
ᴱ10446
Moatti-Fine J 2354
ᵀ2333
Moberly R 1838
6528 **W**ᴿ614
Moda A ᴿ385 4684
5207 8338 8339
11547 11562
Modras K 7980
Moede G 7193
Moeris ᴹ8026
Moeser M 4763
Moessner D 4990
Mohen M 7269
Mohsen I 9471
Moignard E 10447
Moingt J 6505s
Mojola A 1494 9559
Molendijk A ᴱ9170
Molinero E ᵀ3907
Molino S ᴿ969
10036
Mollo P ᴿ10391
Moloney F 5272s
5359s 5487s 5497
ᴿ5295 5367 5405
5926 **R** ᴿ4528
Molthagen J ᴿ9972
Moltmann J 6991
7543s ᴹ5651 5790
-**Wendel E** 11899
Moltz H 3684
Molyneaux B 351
Momigliano G 11342
Mommer P ᴿ2987
Mommsen T 10007
Mompeán J 7888
Mondin B ᴿ7544
Monetti F 10260
Monferrer Sala J
ᴿ1014 1562 ᵀ8230
Monforte J 616 6910
Monfrin F 10406 **J**
ᴱ8130

Mongillo D 6043 7330
Monheim M 1095
Monshouwer D 4407
5435 6726s ᴿ4126
Montagnes B 11891
Montagnini F 4789
ᴿ6369
Montague G ᴿ4858
Montano Benito A
ᴹ1252 7602
Monteagudo Á ᴿ4596
Montefiore H 9003
Montero D 2325
Montesano M ᴿ11499
Montet P 11066
Montevecchi O ᴿ8111
Montserrat D 6629s
9664 ᴱ352 ᴿ10239
Monz H 6770
Moo D 5932
Moor J de 1148 1667
2029 2672 3405s
4780 ᴱ394
Moore J 1883 **M** 2268
2416 ᴱ10448 ᴿ2417
S 792 2668 3955
5361 5626 5861
6631 11381 ᴱ225
380 ᴿ5401
Moorey P 10041
Moorhead J ᴿ4408
Mora C 675 ᴿ9721
9753 **Paz C** 7166 **V**
ᴿ3770
Morabito W 8625
Morag S 3655 ᶠ83
Moraglia F ᴱ308
Moral Palacio J 6925
Moran M ᴿ10102
Morandini S 5627
ᴿ7084
Morata A ᴿ4904
Morax R ᴹ10167
Mordrzejewski J 9665s
Moreau A ᴱ459 **L** 1738
Moreland J ᴱ279
Moreno García A ᴱ178
J 9667 11218 ᴱ4383
ᴿ9121 **Garrido J**
9118
Morenz L 7960s 9668
Morerod C ᴿ4416 5739
7425

Muth R 9223
Muthuraj J R850 8044
Mutius H 1911 3119
8798
Muya J R6585
Müller B 5009 **C** 2532
R4838 **G** 7889 10974
R10973 11894 11447
H 796 1169 1690
2751 3056 6880
8156 9264 R7874 **K**
7167 R646 4836 **M**
1309 5771 5772 **P**
3959 4744 4790
6460 R6466 6472
6481 6484 **U** 4633
5691 R4560 **W** 2585
-**Fahrenholz G**
2219-**Karpe A**
10450 11104 -**Karpe**
M 10185 -**Kessler C**
1339 7823 10392
Müllner I 1093 1127
2482
Münch-Labacher G
5031
Myers C 797 **D** 1059 **S**
6729
Mykytiuk L 7677s
Mynatt D 1245
Myriam Sr 2788
Mysliwiec K 9669
Myszor W 7981 9119
R9115

N a'aman N 2486
2560s 2561 9560s
9741 10647
Naber H 11852
Nachtergael G 2857
R8112 10063 10461
11048
Naden R 5630
Nagel E R1937 **P**
T9160
Naguib S R9379
Nagy G 11117
Nahman Bratslav
11481
Nahmanides M8836
8840
Nahon G R7667

Nakonieczny R
11916
Naldini M 7030 8107
Nanos M 5963 R2295
5926
Nardi C̃2355
Nardoni E 1739
Naredi-Rainer P
2515
Narkiss B F85
Naro M E419
Narrowe M 1740
Nash K 2199 **R** 1411
Naudé J 7623
Nauerth C 10393
Nault F R6912
Naumann T 1839
Nautin P 3960
Navarro Lecanda A
985 **M** R7445
Puerto M E4896 **S**
7436 R4636
Naveh J 7662 7679
7824 8524 10693
E7804 R2118
Navè Levinson P
8799
Navia Velasco C 798
Nazor A 1462
Nápole G 2621
R8210
Neal C E6730
Nebe G 8525s
Need S R4820 5347
Neef H 1897s
Negbi O 10781
11160
Negev A 10119
Negm M 11062
Negro F R10137
10455
Negruzzo S 6731
Neher-Bernheim R
10648
Nehmé L 7825
10841
Neils J E355
Neipp B 10301
Neira F R4600
Neirynck F 5055
5274 E564 R4139
5455 12007
Nel P 2752 3081

R2669
Nelson J 2356 **R** 2334s
R2280 2500
Nemeck F 6529
Nemet-Nejat K 9742
Nemo P 2962
Nereparampil L 4167
Neri U 4322 11613
T799 11803
Nesselrath H R3122
Nestori A F86
Netzer E 10789
Neu E 9280
Neubrand M 677 5989
Neudecker R 2200
8800s
Neudorfer H 2554
5184
Neuenschwander B
5364
Neufeld D R5481 **K**
R913 6574 6994
11894
Neumann B 973 **J**
3961
Neuner J 4288 5035
Neusner J 181 1741
5223 8412 8707ss
8754-8 8802 9006ss
E309 974 8639 8710
R6852 8734 8739
8775 9031 9058
Neuwirth A E10846
Neve P 11105
Neves J 4168
Nevin J M11838
New E 9874
Newby G R4111
Newman C 6259 **H**
11709 **J** 1858 2617
Newport J 9185 **K**
R5584
Newsom C 1539 E7496
Newsome J 1978
Newton D 6082
Neyrand L T3025s
Neyrey J 4244 4714
4811 5365 5859
Niang A R5804 5873
Nibbi A 11004
Niccacci A 3118 3371
10811 R84 152 2669
3079 3230

O'Loughlin F 4530 **T**
  11539 11758 **T** 5129
O'Neill J 3963 5153
  R262
Oates D 10953 **J**
  10953
O'Toole R 4845 R5144
Obbink D R1276
Oberforcher R 4323
  6772 7076 R1605
  5653 6754 6757
  7552
Oberhänsli-Widmer G
  6846 8803 8898s
Oberlinner L 6377
  6380 R6368
Obermann A 5367
  7271
Oberthür R 678
Oberweis M 4771
Obrycki K 8351
Occhipinti G E530
Ochs P 1208
Ockinga B 5002 7962
Odasso G 9186
Odeberg H M5452
Oded B 9744s
Odell M 3551 3559
  3565 11904 R2937
Oden T E4673
Odin K 4497 4501
Odišeli M 10407
O'Donovan O 4324
  7359
Oecumenius M11671
Oegema G 1017 6809
  6847s 8528 R9053
Oelmüller W 2084
  2965
Oelsner J R7824
Oeming M 802 1878
  R1605 11545
Oerter W R9114
Oesch J 1130
Oestreich B 3664
Ofer A 2377
Ofulue Y 1501
Ogden D 3804 R9864
  9882 **G** 3356
Ogdon J 9387
Ognibene S 10817
Ognibeni B 2786 2891
  8712

Ohhara M 5369
Ohler A 1209 2787
Ohly F E3018
Ohme H 1018
Ohst M R11750
Okland J 6096
Okorie A 4908
Okoronkwo U 6217
Okoye J R7077
Okure T 3588
Olbricht T E397
Old H 7272s
Olędzka-Frybesowa
  A 2698
Oleson J R10119
Olinger D 2008
Oliva J 9794
Olivar A 948
Oliveira A de R5911
  E R98
Oliveira L 4951
Oliver A 3685
Olivi P M3030 3049
  5553 11762s
Olivier H 11450
  11490 **J** 12030
Ollenburger B R7572
Oller G R127
Olley J 1247 2541
  6180
Olmo Lete G del
  7700 7754 8158
  9317 9319 10892s
  R2087 9295 T9318
Olofsson S 8475
Olshausen E F87
Olson D 2248 7564
  8218
Olsson B E4196
Olyan S 2163 2474
  3491 R9312
Omanson R 1288s
  6048 R2500 6494
Ombrosi O E8713
O'Meara R 5044
Onasch A 9671 **K**
  10302
Onuki T 4110
Oñate Ojeda J 5370
Oosterhoff B E509
Oosting B 2201
Opatowski M 6793
Opfermann R 11148

Opgen-Rhein H R3652
Oppel K 4325
Oppenheimer A 10010
  E8685
Orazi S 7682
Orchard H 5371
Orecchia C 803
Oredsson D 9562
Orel W 2434
Oren E E369 2314 **N**
  2484 **R** 10730
Organ B 2202
Origenes 1612 4198
  5923 M3044 5695
  6025 11552 11594-
  621
Orji C 2471
Orlov A 8219
Ornelas de Carvalho J
  4387
Oropeza B 6109
Orsatti M 2221 5182
  5464 5632s 6159
  E5130
Orselli A 6378
Orth G 4994
Ortkemper F 5546
Ortlund R 6881
Orton C R10071 **D**
  E4107
Osborn D 11292 **E**
  8281 11628 R12022
Osborne J 10415 **K**
  4634 **R** 9831 R355
Osbornová J 11292
Oschwald H 7360
Osculati R 5496
Osgood J R6834
Osiek C 5288 6267
  6634 7437 11577
  R7432 8303
Osman A 3805
Osten-Sacken P von
  der R4548
Oster R 5903
Ostermayer W 4326
Ostertag G E8159
Oswald W 2069
Oswalt J 3409
Oßwald E R1594
Otero L 8065
Otto A 10394 **E** 2117
  2134s 2288s 6681

Paulien J 5636
Paulsen H 184
Paulson G 3170 S 5133
Pauw D 4245
Pauwels A 7499
Pawlaczyk A 8282
Pawlicki F 11050
Pawlikowski J 6682
Pawlowski Z [R]852
Payne P 6134 -**Smith R** 7844
Payton J [R]982 10303
Paz M 7275
Pazdan M 5374
Pazzini D [R]11604 11613 **M** 7845
Peabody D 4147
Peachin M 10011
Pearce S 8283 8714 [E]414
Pearl C 8715
Pearson B 1859 6849 7500 10306 [E]9120 [R]786 5409 5859
Pečirková J 1463 [R]7880
Pedaya H 8856
Peden A 7964 9672
Pedersen **J** [M]11903 **K** 2753 **O** 10042 10950
Pedrazzoli M [R]8564
Pedrini A 4064
Pedro de Valencia 4383
Peiser B [E]356
Peixoto J 7031
Peklaj M 1464
Peláez J [R]8162
Pelikan J 914 4094 7400 10307 [R]6138
Pelland G 3044
Pelletier A 1776 - **Hornby P** 9876 S [R]1134 5560
Pels P [E]9170
Pelser G 5836 5997
Peltonen K 2579
Pena I 10026
Penchansky D [R]3111
Pender S [R]744
Penglase C 9253

Penicaud A 808 1804
Penkower J 1248
Penna R 3743 5738 5775 5877 6230 6931 [R]6399 7471
Pennacchietti F 3614s 7829
Penner T 6480 [R]6475
Pennington B 6734
Peña J [R]10008
Peppa C 7501
Perani M 1249 8840 [E]7683s
Percival J [R]9217
Perdue L 1060 6882 [M]11904
Perego G 11245
Pereira N 4355
Perelli C 11614
Peres I 4515
Peretto E 6799 7401
Pergola P 11204
Peri W 1388
Perini G 4717
Perkins J [E]1118 **P** 6256 [R]8322 **R** [R]3888
Perlitt L [R]11854
Pernigotti S [E]11048 [R]10236 10509 11062
Perpillou-Thomas F 9388
Perra C 10564
Perraymond M 10308
Perriman A 5776
Perron L [R]1665
Perrone L 11491 11615 [E]420
Perroni M 6932 [R]7496
Perrot C 3968 6013 8716 9265 **J** 10989
Perry T 3171
Person R 1250 3753 [R]7622
Pertini M 5466
Perugini A 4388
Pervo R 879 [R]4819
Pesce M 809 5210 6603s

Pesch R 4462 4471 **W** 2966
Pestman P [E]8109 [F]88
Peter de B [M]11764
Peterlin D 6084 6287
Peterman G 6322
Petersen A 5996 9321 **D** 3764 [E]248 [R]3687 **S** 8312 9137 **W** 8320
Peterson B 6183s **D** 4847 [E]5126 **E** 5637 5934 **G** [R]1707 **M** 2804 [E]531
Petit A 9266 **M** 1842
Petri H [E]7370
Petrini M 11329
Petrosillo O 10539
Petrucci A 8160
Petruzzi P [R]3784
Petry R 185
Pettazzoni R 9273
Pettinato G 9440s [R]12008
Pettinger M 1884
Pettorelli J 8231
Petuchowski J 8900
Peyron A [F]89
Peyrot B 9188
Pezza L [R]1686
Pezzini D 5209
Pezzoli-Olgiati D 2622 5638
Pérez Fernández M 1267 7685 8179s 8759 8804 11790 **Herrero F** 4718 - **Soba Díez del Corral J** 4409 **T** [R]4127
Péter-Contesse R 6531 7702
Pfälzner P 9748
Pfeifer G 3676 [R]9647 **M** 10472
Pfitzner V [R]10678
Pfligersdorffer G 6490
Pfrimmer T [R]5030 8662
Pfrommer M 10408
Pfüller W 3969
Pfürtner S 7170
Philip G [R]9495 10039 **T** 10012

Ruini C 11991
Ruiz de Galarreta J
  1623 de Gopegui J
  ᴿ1927 de la Peña J
  ᶠ98 Pérez M 4721
Rumianek R 2119
  3553 3567
Runge E 1432
Runia D 8284ss ᴿ8288
  11040
Runions E 3720
Ruoß A 10317
Rupert Deutz ᴹ5325
Ruppel H 826
Ruppert L ᶠ99 ᴿ1674
Rupprecht H 8112s
  ᴱ8109 ᴿ430
Ruprecht E 2847
Ruprechtsberger E
  10863   ʲ
Rusconi C 8038 F
  10125 R 5534 5647
  ᴱ3316
Ruspi W 4960
Russell D 7077 J 4641
  10228 10364 10966
Russo G ᴱ4642
Russotto M 2362 2388
Ruston R 7339
Ruszowski L 3458
Ruß R ᴱ1429
Rutecki G ᴿ11331
Rutgers L 8719 9028
  10014 10767 11189
  ᴱ263
Rutherford I 8114
Rutledge F 1131
Rutter J ᴿ10430
Ruyter B 5251
Rüegger H 7107
Rüpke J 11190
Rüterswörden U 917
  1748 6684
Rydbeck L 8039s
Rydlo J 11853
Ryen J 5383
Ryholt K 9679s
Ryken L ᴱ521
Ryou D 3729

Saadé G 12037
Saarisalo A ᶠ100

Sabar S 10661
Sabbahy L 9681
Sabelli R 10809
  10824
Sabin M 4798
Sabugal S ᴿ4170
  5256 8762 9554
Saca I 11459
Sacchi A 4761 6062
  L 10061 P 1585
  3590 8532 9567
  ᴿ8596
Sachot M 4066
Sachs N ᴹ2404
Sack R ᴿ9576 9755
Sacks R 2995
Sadananda D 5384
Sader H 7782 10864s
  ᴱ10846 ᴿ9519
Sa'diyah ᴹ1446 1543
  3020 3427 8839
Sadka I 7631
Safrai C 6685 S
  10662 Z 10028
  10126 ᴿ11451
Sage M 10143
Saggs H 9755
Saginala P 4786
Sagiv N 10545
  10697
Sagrillo T ᴿ9638
Sahrhage D 11316
Saidel B 11460
Saint-Roch P 11191
Saïd S 8115
Sakellarakis Y 11176
Sala M ᵀ4468
Salas Martínez J
  6935
Saldarini A 3084
  4996 5385 7545
  8421 9029s ᴿ4588
  5946
Sale G ᴿ1531
Saley R 2428
Salibi K 619 2429
Salimbene de A
  ᴹ11768
Sallaberger W 10451
Saller R ᴿ9994
Salm E 7740
Salmon ben Yeruham
  2708 ᴹ3427

Salowski M 1467
Salters R 3127 3524
Salvarani B 3174
  11843
Salvatore E 885
Salvesen A 1336 1554
  2430 2443 7714
  7724 7726 7734
  7738 7751 7833
  ᴱ399
Salvini M 7849 9756
  ᴱ489
Salzmann J ᴿ3157
Samaha J 7407
Samarrai A 7742
Saminsky A 10663
Samir S 1527
Sampathkumar A 1211
Sampson E 1409 7507
Sand A 4753
Sander-Gaiser M
  11783
Sanders E 3985 4055
  5743 ᴹ4001 J 1020
  1251 3986 4852
  9031s ᴱ236 1241 P
  2308
Sandgren L 10015
Sandnes K 5176 11421
Sanford J 5277
Sanmartín J 10893
Sanmorì C 10825
Sansoni U 2503
Sant K ᵀ1459
Santalucia B 10016
Sante C 4392
Santiago Amar P
  ᵀ11720
Santos B 5386 Noia M
  ᴱ6461
Santosusso A 9834
Santucci L 11259
Sanz Giménez-Rico E
  1673 Valdivieso R
  6936 ᴿ223 604 5740
  7062 9846
Sao C 823
Sapin J 9718 10452
  11317
Saporetti C 2139 9757
Sapp D 3448 4448
Saramago J 4097
Sarason R 8810

Schilling K 2545
Schimmel A 9489
Schindler A ^{R}2949
  11808
Schinke G 10173
Schipper B 2563 7968
Schippmann K 9758
Schirone S 7341
Schlageter J 3049
Schlatter A 5938 7283
  T 4793
Schlegelberger B
  10321
Schleiermacher F
  11836 ^{M}955 11827
  11836 11860
Schlette H 3990
Schlink W 10664
Schlor I 2173
Schlosser J 3991 4150
  5074 7079 ^{E}400
Schmandt-Besserat D
  10365s
Schmeling G 886 ^{E}358
Schmid H 10957 K
  2623 3510 M 5252
Schmidl M 5441
Schmidt D 3992 4579
  5157 E ^{E}7509 F
  2518 8535 9933 I
  826 K 10477 L 195
  1587-90 1903 1905
  1910 1929 2040
  2256 2270 ^{R}1571
  2063 2238ss 2242s
  2246 2248 2260
  2265 2268s 7721 S
  10063 11865 W
  2075 3317 6686
  6888 -Colinet A
  10838 -Lauber G
  5939
Schmieder F ^{R}8962
Schmithals W 3993
  4449 6330 7566
Schmitt A 1779 6889
  H 1954 3661 6780
Schmitz B ^{E}11035
Schmocker K 6449
Schmolinsky S ^{R}5553
Schnabel E 6125
  ^{R}5665 6121
Schnackenburg R

3994ss 6937
Schneider A 196 G
  ^{E}504s 1516 H
  10548 L ^{E}1417 M
  ^{R}9312 T 1507 9682
  ^{E}265 ^{R}1360 -Flume
  G 2758 -Ludorff
  H 10179
Schneiders S 5388
Schnelle U 3809
  5279 5389 ^{E}5653
Schnepf E 2546
Schnider F 5436
Schniedewind W
  10695 ^{R}2579 2736
Schnieper A 10302
Schober T 4346 4454
  4456 4481 4512
  5047
Schoberth I 4331 W
  4332
Schoedel W ^{R}9115
Schoenborn P ^{R}7366
Schoeps J ^{E}541 8724
Schofield L ^{E}9634
Scholem G 8725
  8858s
Scholer D 4151 9076
Scholl N 918 4197
Scholtissek K 5291
  5390 ^{E}5222 ^{R}5329
  5337 5479 5771
Scholz B 10983 P
  ^{R}10998 S 1933s
Schoon S 9035
Schoors A 3175s
  9572 ^{E}266
Schottroff L 5391
  5445 6086 7510
  7512s ^{E}7511
Schowalter D 11122
  11423
Schöllgen G 7208
  11580
Schönborn C 6999
Schöttler H 3997
Schrader L 1808
  3233 3249s
Schrage W 6132
  ^{F}101
Schramm W 7895
  ^{R}7887 9721 9742
  11263

Schreckenberg H
  9036s ^{R}8940 8948
Schreiber B 2090 J
  10128 S 5206 5434
Schrein S 7514
Schreiner J 3411 4949
  6781 7546 ^{R}3227
  3248 S 10229 T
  5940 5968 ^{R}5920
Schremer A 4365
Schrenk S 10322
Schreurs N 3998
Schrijver G ^{E}7365
Schrijvers P ^{E}11333
Schroeder C 6900
Schroer S 1064 2086
  2759 2961 3085
  7512s 7515 ^{R}7455
Schröder B 8901s
  ^{R}9913 R 4492 S
  10367
Schröer H 2760
Schröter J 3999 6166s
  8204 ^{R}9115 9127
Schrupp E 7067
Schubert F 8226 K
  9038-41
Schudrich M 10665
Schuil A 2064
Schuler C 9796
Schuller E 8536 8541
  ^{R}333
Schult H 1899
Schulte C 8903 H
  1097
Schultz J 11080
Schulz E ^{D}664 H 919
  5292 R 7983
  ^{R}10004s
Schulze L 827
Schulz-Rauch M 3639
Schunack G 9254
Schunck K 2606 ^{E}401
  ^{R}3725 9322
Schur N 8634
Schussman A 3554
Schüle A 7645
Schüngel-Straumann H
  1098 1751s
Schürer E 9967
Schürger W 7366
Schürmann H 197s
  1214-17 4000 4879

4939 4987 5222
5505 5905 6126
6164 7038 7109
7176-9 7209-13
7284 ᴹ11915
Schüssler K 1338
ᴱ1337 [vid. Fiorenza]
Schütz C 10666
Schwab H 4099
Schwager R 1753 4100
ᴱ311
Schwank B 4785 5500
Schwankl O 5253
Schwantes M ᴱ569
Schwartz B 3354 D
2661 2666 9934
9968 ᴿ9976 G 6534
ᴱ471 ᴿ9719 H 8726 J
2166 8727s ᴱ303
ᴿ330 8786s R 1153
6803 10017 ᴿ4412 S
10667
Schwarz H 7000 R
11784
Schweid E ᴹ8901
Schweitzer A 199 5841
11917 ᴹ796 3992
11916s
Schweizer E 828 6430
H 1945s
Schwemer A 4812
5731s 5744 ᴱ1304
ᵀ8205s D 9797
Schwendemann W
ᴿ11358
Schwiderski D 7881
Schwienhorst-Schön-
berger L 3177s 3201
ᴿ3126 3136 3147
3157s
Scibona R 10717
Scippa W 11424
Scognamiglio E ᴿ4405
R 7341 ᵀ4198
Scopello M 1780
Scott B 4001 6417 J
6161 6211 W 11425
Scourfield J 11710
Scriba A 2041
Scroggs R 11993
Scullard H 11192
Sear D 10583 F 10129
Sedlmeier F 2907 3723

Sed-Rajna G 2167
Seebass H 1674 2243
2250 2262
Seeliger H ᴿ7229
Seeman D 11426
Seevers B 6804
Sefati Y ᴱ9759
Segal A 5879 6143
11473 G 8153
10668 ᴹ10626 M
8537
Segalla G 829 920
4002 4250 5392
5422 7194 7567
11944 ᴿ5367 5397
5409 6917 7318
7323 7553
Seger J 10064 10193
ᴿ10712
Segert S 2309 7691
8423 ᴿ345 471
3956 7769 7810
7822 8154 9595
10910
Segovia F 830s 5394
5502 ᴱ267 684
5254 5393 ᴿ4105
Seibold J 685
Seidel H 11854 L
10323
Seidl T 620 2861 U
1809
Seidler M 8904
Seifert B 3640
Seifrid M 5969 6782
Seigne J 10798
Seijas de los Ríos G
3348
Seiler S 2469
Seim J 6938 T ᴿ511
Seitz C 200 686 832
976 1508 2042s
3335-8 3412 4003s
4120 4121s 6641
6740 6857 7342
11427 11908
11994
Seland T 4912 5181
Sellew P 6292
Sellin G 6258 6264
Selman M ᴱ522
Selvatico P 4643
Selz G 7896 9760

Seminara S 7897
Semler J ᴹ5860
Sen F 8424ss 9150
ᴿ8496
Seneca ᴹ5914 8126
Senécal B 9494
Senior D 4199 4251
4580 5395 ᴿ12007
Sensing T 6034
Seow C 3128 ᴱ6783
Sepmeijer F 3406
ᴱ3469
Seppilli T ᴱ428
Sepulveda J 9189
Sequeri P 7001 7568
Serbat G ᴱ11332
Serna E 7285
Serra A 4961 5039
Serwint N 11163
Sesboüé B 4005s
11635 ᴿ2833 3010
11673
Severi C 6713
Severini F ᴿ10805
Sevrin J 5396
Seybold K 201 2700s
2719 2761s 2810
2823 2841 2843
2850 2856 2869
2888 2896 2904
2970 3742 7706
7717 8478
Sérandour A 2607
10187
Sfar M 9473
Sfienti C ᴿ2934
Sgargi G ᴱ3632
Shafer B ᴱ359
Shaheen A 9573
Shain M 9042
Shaked G 8905 S 7824
Shalev D ᴿ8022 -
Khalifa N 2519
Shama G 8736
Shanks H 8428s 10045
10685 ᴱ360 8427
ᴿ8490 10040 10376
M ᴿ11176
Shantz C ᴿ4297
Sharon D 1754
Sharp D 1099 M
ᴿ10004
Sharpe J ᴱ1235

Shatil N 7632
Shatzmiller J ^{R}168
Shaw G 3318 **I** 11020
  ^{R}11467 **T** 7343
Shea C 887
Sheeley S 1025 1411
Sheen E 10324
Sheerin D 8064
S h e h a d e h H 7 6 9 2
  ^{R}2407
Shelley B 950
Shelton J ^{E}8116
Shemesh A 2307 8538
Shepherd D 1270
Shereshevski J 10686
Sheridan J ^{E}8117 ^{T}951
  M ^{R}9070
Sheriffs D 6784
Sherman F 11785
Sherratt S 11428
S h e r w o o d Y 3 3 1 9
  3649 3707
Shestov L ^{M}9867
Shields M 3564
Shih S 11006
Shillington W 6098
Shiner W 4724s
Shinnie P 11074
Shipp R 3368
Shire M ^{E}2065
S h i r u n - G r u m a c h I
  7969 ^{E}361 9683
Shisha-Halevy A 7970
Shlain L 9205
Shoemaker H 648
Shore P 4067
S h o r t D ^{R}1 1 3 2 5 **I**
  ^{R}1128
Shotter D 9981
Shrimplin V ^{R}10304
Shrimpton G 9609
Shuler P 4931
Shuster M 4007
Sibinga J 6110
Sichtermann H 10046
Sicre J 3810 11429
Sidebotham S ^{E}11049
Sidwell K ^{E}10001
Sieben H 7180 ^{R}2711
  6181
S i e b e r t - H o m m e s J
  2011 ^{E}268 ^{E}1100
Sieg F 4853

Siegelová J ^{E}592
Siegert F 4008s 4152
  8287 9126 9879
  9935s ^{E}490 ^{R}130
  8272
Sierra Bravo R 1529
  S ^{T}8 9 0 6 ^{E}8 7 2 9
  ^{F}102
S i e v e r s J 9 9 3 7 s s
  ^{R}9838
Sievertsen U 11474
Şiewert K 7633
Signore F ^{R}4850
Sigrist M 10979
Siker J 7344
Sikora R 5669
S i l b e r m a n N 8 5 6 2
  9574 10081 ^{E}362
Sileo L ^{R}6953
Siliato M 10549
S i l v a A d e 2 8 0 2
  ^{R}3775 **Castillo J**
  ^{T}1810 **D** 6087 **M**
  ^{R}6318 **Retamales S**
  3641
Silver L 10669
Silverman D ^{E}9670
  10065
Silverstein T ^{E}8260
Sim D 4252s 4337
  ^{R}8988
Sima A 7924
Simard N ^{R}1698
Simian-Yofre H 1218
  2547 2923 3179
  3339 3642 3643
  6687 ^{R}3626
S i m k i n s R 1 6 9 5
  ^{R}6635 11321
Simms G 621
S i m o e n s Y 5 3 9 7
  6486 6560
Simojoki A 5648
Simon R ^{M}1281
Simone M ^{R}1521
Simonetti C 9575 **M**
  5709 11617 ^{T}3050
Simotas P 1314
Simpson E 11136 **J**
  6351
S i m s - W i l l i a m s N
  ^{E}454
Sindling-Larsen S

10279
Singer C 5028 **I** 9282
  9 7 9 8 ^{E}9 1 9 3 **P**
  ^{M}11971
Singh N 7002
Singles D 4393 5710
  . 11738
Sinoir M 7286
Sipilä S 2338 2363
Sirat C 1254
Sirks A ^{R}8711
Sivan D 2674 7693
  7783 10896
Sixdenier G 2797
Sjöberg Å 7899 ^{E}7898
Ska J 1591 1811 2226
  7737 ^{R}1624 1630
Skaist A 7900 8006
Skehan P 8457-61
Skilton J 12039
Skinner A 3804
Skousen R 1406
Skulj E 2909
Slane K 10421
Slanski K 7901
Slater T 5649 7068
Slavazzi F ^{R}10358
Slee N ^{R}11899
Sleeper C 6465
Slingerland H 8730
Sloan R 4973
Slotsky A 11454
Sloyan G 4581 ^{F}103
  ^{R}294 5477 6743
S l u s s e r M ^{R}4 5 8 1
  ^{T}11660
Sly D 8288
Smagina E ^{R}9124
Small D 9835 ^{E}362
Smalley S 5255
Smart N 9176
Smelik K 2520 2562
  3188 3711 8430 **W**
  1271 2389
Smend R 202 11877
Smidt J 833 1219
Smiles W 6212
Smit J 3500
Smith C 1101 6827
  7516 ^{R}8302 9084 **D**
  5398 ^{F}5293 **G** 6004 **J**
  1026 3592 11462
  ^{M}7507 ^{T}11618 **K**

Stark R 3811s
Starnitzke D 5970
Starodoub T 10671
Starowieyski M 4411 8355
Starr R ^{F}110
Stauber J ^{E}8106
Staubli T 1064
Stausberg M 1028 9461
Stead C 9268
Steadman S ^{R}11135
Stec D ^{R}2918
Stech T 10091 10097
Steck O 1221 3321 3527 8479 ^{T}2653
Steel L 11159 11164
Steele S ^{R}9163
Steenbrink K ^{R}9488
Stefani P 1675 5652 6689 7081 8731 ^{E}403
Steffen U 3708
Stegemann E 11433 9044 9955 H 8431ss 8539 8563ss 8615 ^{F}111 ^{M}11985 W 4582s 7345 11433
Stegner W 4254
Steible H 7904
Steiman L 9045
Stein A 6643 E ^{M}11918 F ^{T}1181 H 2012 ^{E}449 S ^{E}11819
Steinbeck J ^{M}8819
Steinberg J 1948 L 10326
Steiner G 7905 J 687 M 10598 10672s R 2583
Steinhart M 10233
Steinkeller P 9761
Steinmetz D ^{F}112
Steins G 2608ss
Steitz W 5196
Stek J ^{F}113
Stemberger G 741 2763 5158 8616 8732s 9047 10411
Stendahl K 8434
Stendebach F 622
Stephenson F 11273
Stepien M 11318

Stepp P 4855
Sterling G 9943
Stern D 8813 9880 ^{E}312 E 9579 10130 10722s 11455 ^{E}478 ··J 8836 S 8734s ^{T}9810
Stettler H 6374
Steudel A 8480
Stevens J 5843
Stevenson J 6644 K 3573
Stewart A 10234 - Sykes A 4532 11578
Steymans H 2854 9048
Steyne P 7182
Stichel R 10327
Stieglitz R 9580 11278
Stiehler G 10455
Stipp H 2327 3470 3487
Stiver D ^{E}2339
Stocker M 2635
Stockhausen A ^{T}6201
Stoebe H 2431
Stoevesandt H 6243
Stojčevska-Antić W 1470
Stol M 7906s ^{E}1066
Stolp H 4102
Stoltmann D 10674
Stolyarov A 1471
Stolze J 3204
Stone B ^{M}723 D 9881 K 2328 M 8224 8540 ^{E}441 8207 8232
Stoneman R 9882
Storme A 12041
Storniolo I 2415
Stott J 5521 T 6088
Stottele C 4423
Stowell J 953
Stowers S 6014 6645 9274
Stöhr M 6646
Störk L 7984s
Strabeli M 6063
Strabo 11212
Stramare T 4282

4293 4461
Strange J 11248
Strassburger B 8761
Strauss H 2971 L ^{M}9845 M 1509
Strauß D ^{M}11839
Seeber C 9687
Streck M 1876 7784 7908s
Strecker G 7569 ^{E}5653
Strelan R 6257
Stricher J 4967 4970 ^{E}5167
Stricker B 9401
Strickert F 10751 11258
Strijdom J 4304
Striker G 9883
Strobel A 10180 K 9800 L 4014 R 4644 7517
Strocka W 9982
Strommenger E 10554
Stroud R ^{E}8110
Strouhal E 9688
Stroumsa G 838 9077 9275 11629 ^{E}286 306 440 8993
Strömberg A ^{E}485
Strudwick H 10555 N 10555
Strugnell J 8435 8541
Struppe U 623 7721
Strus A 6233 8356s
Strübind A 6033 K 4814
Stuart D 3627 E 7485
Stubenrauch B 7110
Stuckenbruck L 5654
Studer B 11691 ^{E}294
Stuhlmacher P 5941 7111 ^{E}3441 ^{F}114
Stuhlmann R 6890
Stulman L 3488
Stumpf G ^{M}10587
Sturm J 9581
Stümke W 6647
Styrenius C 11167
Sudo I 4499
Sugawara Y 4728
Sugden C 7183
Sugirtharajah R 839ss
Suhl A 4584

5972 11434s
Thekeparampil J 8326
Thelle R 3505
Theobald C 7069
  E3921 **M** 5508 5535
  7112 7348 R4726
  5249 5253
Theodoret C M2363
  5700 11673s
Theodoropoulos H
  R11665
Theophylaktos A
  M11769
Thérèse L M5298 7292
Theron J 11927
Théodoridès A F118
Thériault J 1032
Thiede C 203 1223
  3833 4200s 4535
Thiel W 3489 11436
  R3462 3487
Thiele W E3235
Thielman F R5851
Thiering B 5294
Thijssen H 6648
Thimmes P 7444
  7519s E278
Thiselton A R749 6121
Thoams J 5536
Tholbecq L 10479
Thoma C 5015 6805
  8816 9049-52 M4048
  11990
Thomas A 4856 **C** 889
  8333 11123 R9831 **D**
  R9487 **J** 1067 10082
  R8123 **M** M6987 **R**
  269 1224 5657 6859
  S R359 9392
Thompson H 3471 **J**
  6411 **L** 5568 R5615
  M 843 3826 5403
  7445 R4035 4911
  6011 **R** 5169 **S**
  10557 **T** 327 7409
  8482 R2495 **W** 7003
  R5202
Thomson F 1472 **R**
  R8232
Thordson M 8437
  8629 **T** 8437 8629
Thorton C 5207
Thoumieu M 1531

Thraede K 1133
Throckmorton B
  4021 7521
Thuesen I 10816
Thurén L 5864 6442
Thurston A 7522 **B**
  7446
Thümmel H 6957
  10329s
Thüngen S 10480
Thür H 11109
Thüsing W 7570
  12044
Ticonius M5706
Tiedemann H 5844
  5889
Tiffany F 1984
Tigchelaar E 3755
  8387 8542 8600
  E8382s R7535 8497
Tiller P 6483
Tilley M 9191 11546
Tilliette X de 4022
  7004 M6964 R6985
Tillmann N 2845
Timbie J R7434
Timm S R2078
Tinder G R7359
Tinney S 9449
Tiradritti F E10052
  10066
Tite P 6444
Titelmans F M5573
Toaff E 6860
Tobin V R1990 9340
Todeschini G R9036s
Toensing H 5463
Tohme A 10869
Toit A du 11194
  E3781 R6291 **C du**
  E270
Toland J 5862
Tolbert M 1033 E267
  684
Toldy T 7410
Tollington J 2390
Tolmie D 890 5404
  5490
Toloni G 2567 2589
  3267
Tomasetto D E4045
  T5927
Tombs D E302

Tomes R R6884
Tomson P 1034 2522
  9053
Tong L 11943 11955
Toniolo C 11946 **E**
  7411
Topel J 7349
Tophoven I 8907
Torallas Tovar S 8292
Torjesen K 7523
Tornos A 4610
Torrance T 844 R1652
Torre R de la R6580
Torres A R165 **Millan**
  F 688
Torri G 9283
Torti R 9450
Tosi M 11051
Touati C R1609
Tournay R 2875 4394
Tov E 1255-8 1556
  8438s 8483 E3468
  R2918
Tovey D 5405
Tower H 7973
Towner P R6368
Townsend J 5192
  T8817
Törnkvist R 3650
Tóth C 6649
Trafton J R8415
Tragan P 4533
Traianus M9974
Trainor M R3796
Tran M 6226
Trapp J 1540
Trautner-Kromann H
  R8988
Treanor O 4586
Treat J 3024
Trebolle Barrera J
  1035s 8384ss
Treiber M 955
Treiyer H R2494
Treloar G 11844
Tremblay J 4359
Tremolada P 4857
  5071s
Trevett C R7432
Trevijano Etchevarria
  R 9151 **R** R4204
  11581
Trexler R 4292

Van Amersfoort J
^{R}8345
Van Asseldonk O
^{R}1664
Van Beeck F ^{R}4581
Van Bekkum W 1812
^{E}7695
Van Belle G 5449
5515 11947 ^{R}12006
Van Bragt J 5712 9177
Van Bremen R 7448
Van Bruggen J 1226
4024
Van Butselaar J 7185
Van Cangh J 4801
Van Dam C 3322 **S**
^{R}8239
Van de Beek A 1038
Van de Mieroop M
11476
Van den Brink E
10687 10993
Van den Broeck R
9079ss ^{E}422
Van den Heever G
5407
Van den Hoek A 2851
^{R}9081
Van den Hout T 11106
^{E}9804
Van der Coulen P
10331
Van der Eijk P ^{E}11333
Van der Heide A 7636
8843 ^{R}7690
Van der Hoeven T
1756
Van der Horst K
^{E}10332 **P** 5008 7288
7547 8737s 9885
11555 ^{E}523 ^{T}3814
Van der Kooij A 1039s
1317 2595 3375
3378 6892 ^{E}407
1326 ^{R}333 8441
Van der Lof L 11630
11713
Van der Merwe C
1511 **D** ^{R}5304
Van der Ploeg J ^{R}1272
Van der Spek R 11319
Van der Steen E ^{R}477

Van der Toorn K
1069 3323 3609
9327s ^{E}407 523
2087
Van der Velden F
2872
Van der Ven J 6538
Van der Wal A 3213
Van der Watt J 5408
5538
Van der Woude A
8442 ^{F}11 121
^{R}3814
Van Deventer H 846
3607
Van Dijk J 9451
9690 11064
Van Donzel E 543
Van Driel G 9765
11463 ^{R}7870
Van Dyk W ^{R}7128
Van Egmond D 9082
Van Esbroeck M
1340 7986 ^{R}8232
Van Ess M 10865
Van Gent A 573
Van Gessel B 9284
Van Ginkel J ^{R}11655
Van Grol H 2616
Van Groningen G
6893
Van Haarlem W
10067 10483
Van Henten J 1940
5661 ^{R}8206
Van Hoogstraten H
^{R}6660
Van Iersel B 4676
Van Inwagen P ^{E}274
Van Kampen K
^{E}1235
Van Keulen P 2526
2565 ^{R}2534
Van Leeuwen T 1041
2232
Van Lent J 8262
Van Lepp J 10238
Van Lerberghe K
10144
Van Liere L ^{E}275
Van Loon M 10932
Van Loopik M ^{E}276

9054
Van Meenen B 5168
Van Meurs J 9099
Van Moorsel P 10333
Van Niekerk A ^{R}11835
Van Nispen C 9481
Van Oord J 1849
Van Oorschot J 3105
Van Oort J 9111
^{E}11547s ^{R}9105
Van Pelt B 650
Van Rensburg F 6443
11928 **J** 2677
Van Rhijn A 1901
Van Rooy H 2765
2910 2912
Van Rossum-
Steenbeeck M 8119
Van Ruiten J 1813
8227
Van Segbroeck F 9945
^{E}277 4025
Van Seters J 1604
1908 2103 ^{R}1149
Van Soldt W 10902
11236 ^{R}7778
Van Spanje T 847
Van Staalduine-Sul-
man E 6650 ^{E}2432
Van Tilborg S 5409
Van Tongerloo A 9112
^{E}446
Van Veldhuizen P
2557
Van Walsem R ^{R}10997
Van Wieringen A 1532
3357 ^{R}3410
Van Wijk-Bos J 2611
Van Wijmen L ^{E}593
Van Willigen M 11648
Van Winden J ^{R}11628
Van Wolde E 1678
2419
Van Wyk K 10397 **W**
1227 2613
Van Zyl A 2472 **D**
9584 **H** 7217
VanBuren P 626
Vance D 2678
Vandecasteele-Van-
neuville F ^{T}8046
Vandenabeele F 11165

Viviano B 4473 5423s
7055 ^{R}4239 4476 **P**
^{R}3466
Viviers H 2899
Vílchez J 2636 **Líndez
J** 2420
Vlahogiannis N 6652
Vledder E 4257
V l e e m i n g S 8 1 2 0
^{E}1066 ^{R}11276
Vllauri E 4029
Vocke H 1294
Voderholzer R 11895
Voelker J ^{R}9115
Voelz J 850 6038 8044
Vogel A 7139 **D** 11295
M 6690 8294 9946
Vogels W 980 1758
1850s 2013 2976
3324 6540 7571
^{R}842 2110 3617
Vogler W 7350
Vogüé A de 11732
^{M}11730 ^{T}2499
Voicu S 4284
V o i g t R 7638 7749
7847 8045 **S** ^{R}5386
Volgger D 2304 2523
2662 3451 7639
Vollenweider S 6653
^{R}6308
Vollmer J 7140
Voloshin M ^{M}4555
Vomberg P 7947
Vonach A 3191 3193
^{R}3563
vonEhrenkrook J 6240
Voorwinde S 5664
Vorgrimler H 6691
Vos C 2794 **H** 1044 **J**
4172
Voss K 9083
Vouga F 4689 5142
6196 7127 7187
9972
Voyatzis M 9255
Vögtle A 7092 ^{M}11925
Völling E 9453
Vörös G 10484 11037
Vössing K 10018
Vregille B ^{T}3025s
Vries A 1473 1514 **E**
6431 **L** 1515

Vriezen K 10413
Vroman A 2169

W aard J de 2421
8488
Wacholder B 8604
8635
Wachsmann S 9695
10151
Wachter R 2679
W a c k e r M 3 6 5 2
7512s ^{E}7511
Wackerbarth D 7412
W a c k e r n a g e l W
10335
Wadud A 9475
Waelkens M 9805
11145
Wagenaar J 3722
^{R}3717
Wagner H ^{E}3 1 5 **J**
5971 6093 **-Hasel
B** ^{R}10095 **-Lux U**
10688
Wagoner R 10336
Wahl H 3517 **O** 3252
3380 ^{D}2984 **T** 2795
Wahlde U von ^{R}5393
Wainwright E 4258s
5 4 1 0 ^{R}4 4 1 5 **G**
^{R}1518
Waitkus W 9402
Wajntraub E 11249
G 11249
Walaskay P 5096
Walborn R 3747
Waldenfels H 6585
Waldherr G 11274
Walf K 7351
W a l i s z e w s k i T
10464
Walk J 11511
Walkenhorst K 3253
Walker B ^{M}3834 **D**
6185 **P** 10678 **S**
10239 **W** 4916
6128
Wallace R 5745
Wallenfels R 10398
Wallis E 4730 **I** 7093
W 5960
Walls N ^{R}1692

Walsh C 3053 11304
11320 **G** 9055 **J**
2500 **P** 11722
Walter N 205 6144
6275 **W** ^{E}11845
Walters J 11196
Waltke B 956
Walton J 1557 6188
Walvoord J 3325
Wander B 8740
Wankenne J ^{R}244 9999
11386
Wannenmacher E 5676
Wansbrough H ^{R}12007
Wansink C 5746
Warburton D 9696
Ward G 4030 **J** ^{R}4111
R 9226 **W** 12047
^{M}123 10388
Wardy R 8121 8134
Wargnies P ^{R}2921
Warland R 11209
Warner J 11135
Warnock P 11305
Warren A 2305
Waschke E 3367
Washburn D 851
Washington H 2301
3106 ^{E}278 ^{R}1060
Wasserberg G 4917
6015
Wasserstein A 11478
D 1318 10585s
Wasserstrom S ^{R}9108
Watanabe C 9454
Waterfield R ^{T}9836
Waters L 2993
Wathelet P ^{E}9251
Watrin L 9697
Watson A 4031 4588 **F**
852s 3828 7572 **N**
^{R}6075 6153 6158 **W**
2680 3054 7755
7791 ^{R}7783 9289
Watt J 4860
Wattenmaker P 11456
Watterson B 9698
W a t t s J 891 2014
^{F}3326 **R** 4731 4772
Waubke H 11846
Way T von der 9699
11068
Wächter L ^{R}6889 8854

Situs

Taanach 10769
Tabaliya 10529 10711
Tanis 11065s
Te'enim 10550 10730
  11288
Thebes 10484 10489
  11037
Tiberias 10181 10585s

Tigunanu 8005
Til-Barsip 9768
  10394 10942
Timna 10486 10712
Torone 10720
Tuna el-Gebel 11069
Tuttul 10554
Tyre 9741 1056

Umm el-Jimal 10845
  el-Qaab 11070
Ur 10978s
Uruk 10980-4
Yazılıkaya 11148
Ziklag 10193
Zobah 9509

Voces

Akkadicae

urpatu(m) 7700
na'āsu 7698
saklu 7699

Aramaicae

גְּלְגָּל 7701
דבר 7816
יד 7702
כיפא 7703
כף 7702
לעם 7816
נגד 7816
רגל 7702

Graecae

ἀγάπαω 8049
ἁγιασμός 8050
ἅγιος 8051
Αιείῳ 5189
Ἀρνίον 5677
ἀχρεῖος 5054
δικαιοσύνη 8204
δοῦλος 8052
ἐκκλησία 6067
  8053
ἔλεος 7719
ἐπισκέπτομαι
  8054
ἐπιστηριζειν
  5103
εὐαγγελιζεσθαι
  4831
ἡμέρα 5355
κένωσις 11880
κεφαλή 6113

κεχαριτωμένη
  8055
κήρυγμα 7085
κοινωνία 8056
κρίσις 5809
κύριος 5116
  8057
λόγος 11585
μαρανα θα
  8057
μαρτυρία 7085
ναζωραῖος
  8058s
νόμος 6074
  8060
ξύλον 5840
ὀνοκενταυρος
  8061
πειρασμός
  4389
πίστις 8062
πλήρωμα 8065
πνευματικῶς
  5195
πορνεία 6097
σκόλοψ 5840
σπέρμα 5545
σταυρός 5840
σύνκρισις
  8064
σῶμα 5843
σωφία 8063
ὑπόκρισις
  5010
ὑψωθῆναι
  5483
φιλέω 8049
φοβούμενοι
  8066

χάρις 7718
ὥρα 5302

Hebraicae

אבל 7704
אז 7705
אמן 7706
אשר 3206
בוש 7707
בליעל 7708
בְּרִיאָה 7709
גאל 7710
גְּלְגָּל 7701
גלה 7711
דרך 7712s
הבל 3138 3165
  3168
הָדָם 7714
ה, ד, ר 7715
  11303
היה 7716
חלב 7697
חלה 7717
חנם 2955
חנן 10889
חסד 7718s
טוב 3175
יד 7702
יכל 3503
ירד 7720
כבוד 7721
כוש 7722
כנען 7723
כְּפָא 7724
כף 7702
כְּפֵר 2183
כרם 3056
כתב 7725

כְּתֶר 7726
לאם 7727
למען 7728
לעם 7698
מְאֵרָה 7729
מַעְגָּל 7730
מרזח 7731s
מְשָׁעוֹל 7733
נֵזֶת 7734
נער 7735
נערה 7735
נָקָב 7736
סכל 7699
סמך 557
עֵזֶר 7737
עֲטָרָה 7738
עלה 7720
עם 7739
ענו 8769
עשק 7740
עֵת 7741
פאה 7742
פנימה 7743
פקד 2251
פתה 3503
צבע 1656
צדק 6765 7744s
צלם 7746
צרעה 7747
קָבָב 7748
רגל 7702 7749
רחוב 7750
רחם 10889
שִׁיח 6693
שֹׂכל 7699
שָׁבֶט 7751
שׁורר 7752
שכב 2487 7753
שמר 2889

3-4 2040
3,1-4,17 2042
3,1-17 185
3,7 1867
3,13-15 2038
3,14 2015 2031s
  2036s 9117
4,10 2032
4,10-17 4473
4,24-26 2019
5 2504
6,2-9 2033
7-14 2049
7,14-11,10 2048
8,12-28 2047
12,5 11598
13,17-15,21
  8266
14-15 2051 2067
14 2504
14,13-14 3383
14,16 9330
14,28 3383
15 2670
15,8 2066
15,21 7503
16 2068
17 2060
17,8-16 2064
17,9 8168
17,13 8168
18,21 2120
19-24 2069
19,4 2759
19,18 2054
20-23 2124
20,1-3 2074
20,2 8800
20,2-7 2084
20,3 2078
20,4-5 2081
20,4-6 10229
20,12 2092
20,13 2093-6
20,23 2080
21-23 2099
21,2-11 2098
21,2-6 2100
21,12-17 2489
22,28-29 2103
22,30 2102
23,6-8 2120
23,10-11 2101

23,14-19 2143
23,20-33 1559
24 2142
24,4-7 2357
25-31 2150
29 2152
31,12-17 2155
32-34 2165
32 2504
32,10 8273
34,6 10889
34,7 2863
34,10-28 2141
34,18-26 2143
40,36-37 1567

Leviticus

2,4 2179
8 2152 2195
11 2184 2198
13,28-30 2206
15 2178
15,13-15 2206
16 2183 2186
  2203 2207
16,8-26 2190
17-26 2191s
  2194
17,15 2102
18 2188
18-20 2182
19,18 2200
22,8 2102
23 2197 2203
25 2209 2215
  2217s 2222
  2235
25,2-12 2101
25,10 2232
25,35-55 2100
26,39-45 2155

Numeri

1 2253
1-20 2240
1-4 2251
5,11-31 2114
6,24-26 2254
9,15-23 1567
10,11-36,13
  2255

10,11-12 1567
11-12 2256
11,4-34 2257s
11,26 8769
12 2259
12,1-2 2249
13-14 2260
15 8665
19,1-22 2261
20 2060
20,14-21 2262
22-24 2265
  2268ss
23,9 2266
23,19 6528
24,14-19 2267
24,17 2264
26 2253
27,1-11 2263
36 2263

Deuteronom.

1-3 2292
1,2 8842
3,23-29 2293
4 2284
4,47 2901
5 1172
5,8-10 10229
5,12-18 2073
6,4-9 1725
  2294s 2297
9-10 2284
10,17-18 2120
12 7597
12-26 2114
13 2298
14,1-17,13
  2299
14,21 2102
16,19 2120
17,17 2300
20-22 2301
22,6-7 2302
24,1-4 2303ss
24,19 2489
25,5-10 2489
27 2306
27,5-7 2357
28,68 2300
29,7 2901
29,28 2307

30,1-14 2284
31,14-16 8808
32 2309 2670
  6109
32,11 2759
32,12-14 6007
33 2310s
33,7 1955
33,17-34,6 2312
34,6-7 2313

Josue

1-3 2366
1,1-9 2360
1,8 2367
2,1-14 2369
2,10 2901
3-4 2370
3,14-4,7 2371
5,4-6 2372
7,26 2373
8,30-35 2357
9,10 2901
10 2374 11014
10,1-8 2375
10,4 2376
10,13 997
11,19 2375
15,61-62 2377
21 2378
23 2360
24 2360 2379
24,14-18 2380

Judices

1 2391
1,1-2,5 2392
2,6-3,6 2393
3 2394
3,7-4,24 2395
3,12-30 2385
4 7597
4-5 2396
5 2398
5,1-31 2397
  2399
7,7 2875
8,28 2875
11 2401
11,4-11 2400
11,30-40 2402

19 2811 2738
19,5 2532
20 2812
21 2813
22 188 817 2786
  2814-20
22,17 2821
22,30 2822
23 2738 2786
27,11 7752
29 2823s
29,7 2825
31 2826
32 2712
33 2827
35 3262
36-38 2828
36,2 2829
36,18-23 2829
37 2742
37,29 1871
38 2712
39 2830 11847
42 2786
43 2786
44 2831s
45 2833
46 2834s
48 2790
49 2742
50 2761 2790
51-72 2739
53 2790
54 2837
54,7 7752
55 2838s 7452
56 2840
56,3 7752
57 3262
58 2841
59,11 7752
61 2842
62 2790 2843
67 2844
68,32 7722
69 2845
72 3367
72,8 2846
72,10 2847
73 2742
73-83 2761
73,17 2848
74,13-15 9330

75 2849
76 2849s
81,17 7697
82 2851
85,11 849 6805s
85,11-12 2852
88,20-21 5213
89 2853s 3367
89,26 2846
89,41-42 1269
90 2786 2855s 11755
91 2786
91,13-16 2857
93-100 2858
94 2859s
95,7-11 2861
99 2863
100 2864s
100,1 2866
102 2712 2867
103 2868
104 2738 2869s
105 2745
105-106 1868
106,30-31 1936
107-145 2750 2768
109 2871s
110 2873ss 6395
110,3 2876
110,4 1859
112 2877
113,1-6 2878
114 2879
116,10 6171
118 2880s 3605
118,22-23 2882
118,24 2883
119 2786 2884ss
119,89-91 2887
120-134 2888
121 2889s
122 2786 2891ss

124 2738
126 2786 2894s
127 2786
127,1 2896
130 2712 2786
131 2897ss
132 2895
133 2900
135 2901
136,20 2901
137 2786
139 2786
141-150 11686
141 2904
143 2712
143,3-4 7608
145 2905s
147 2907
147,9 2908
148,7 11283
150 2909 10173

151-154 2912
151 2910s

Job

1-2 2978
2,10 2979
3 2670
4,13 2980
4,20-21 2981
5 2982
5,1-8 2983
9-10 2984
19,23-27 2985
19,25 2986
21-27 2987s
22 2989
24 2990s
32-37 2992ss
32-38 2995
35,15 2996
38-39 2997
38-41 2998
38,2 2999
38,41 2908

Canticum, **Song**

1,6 3056
3,6-11 3055
5,8 3057
7,1 3058

Proverbia

1-9 3111ss
1,1-19 3114
1,20-33 3115
7 3116
8,1-9,6 3115
14,28-35 3117
21,12 7699
23,26-24,22 3118
23,29-35 6620
24,16 3119
26,1-12 956
26,4-5 3120
26,20-28 3262
30,4 3121

Eces, **Qohelet**

1,1-11 3183
1,2 3184s
1,3-3,9 3186
1,4-11 3185 3187
2,12 3188
2,24-26 3189
3,1-9 3190
3,14 3191
3,15-16 3192
3,16-20 3193
3,16-21 3194
4,1-4 3193
4,17 3195
4,17-5,6 3196s
5,12-16 3198
5,17-19 3199
7,1-4 3200
7,15-18 3201
7,23-8,1 3202s
7,23-29 3204
7,25-29 3205
7,26 3206
7,27 4882
7,28 3207
8,1-15 3208

7,13-14 7055
9,24-25 3611
11 3608 3612
12,5-13 3613
13 3614ss

Hosea

1 3647 3653
1-2 3648
1-3 3649-52
2 3654
2,4-17 3655
2,4-25 3656
3 3653
4,1-10 3657
5,11 7740
6,2 3658
6,6 4213
9,7-9 3659
12 3660
12,3-5 3661
12,7 3662
12,8 7740
14,2-9 3663s
14,4-8 3665
14,9 3666

Joel

2,4-9 3669 9334
3,1-5 3670 5149

Amos

1,5 3690
2,6-16 3691
2,8 7810
3,9 7740
4,1 7740
4,13 3692
7-8 3693
7,2 7716
7,7-09 3694
9,7 7722

Abdias **Obadiah**

7 3726

Jonas

2 3711

3,10-4,11 3712

M i c h e a s
Micah

1,2-16 3721
2-5 3722
2,2 7740
4,1-5 3723s
5,1 6908

Nahum

1,1-3 3733
1,3-7 3733
1,10 2675
1,12 3733
1,15 3734

Habakkuk

2,3-4 3741
2 , 4 1 2 9 6
    3742ss 6230

Soph. **Zephan.**

1 3731
1,2 7624

Aggaeus
Haggai

1,2-4 3746

Zechariah

2,1-3,8 3729
9-10 3751
9,9 6851
9,10 2846
10,6-12 11340
12,10 3749
    3752
14 3750 6815

Malachi

2 3760
2,10-16 3759
3,20 2759

Matthaeus

1-4 4246
1 , 1 - 1 7 8 3 4
    4286
1,5 8794
1,19 4287
1,23 4288
2,1 4289
2,1-12 4290-3
    7191
2,16 4294
3,13-17 4303s
4,15-16 3364
4,23-5,2
5 4319
5-7 1421 4325
    4333s
5,3 4357
5,3-7,27 4307
5,3-12 4351
5,3-10 4358
5,13-14 4335
5,17 4207
5,17-20 4336
5,19 4337
5,21-48 4216
    4338ss 4341
5,31-32 4361
5,43-48 4342
6,1-18 4343
6,5 7240
6,9-13 4373
    4375 4383
6,11 4367
6 , 1 3 4 3 7 8
    4389 4394
6,24 4344
6,28 4345
7,12 4336
7,24-27 4346
8,5-13 4372
    4396
8,22 4397
9,13 4207
9,35-10,5 4305
10 1883
10,1-42 4414s
10,3 4416s
10,34 4207s
11,5 4418
11,12-16 4495
11,16-19 4419

12,18-21 4420
12,36 4421
12,39-42 3703
12,40 4422
12,43-45 4423
12,46-50 1433
13 4452s
13,1-9 4454
13,18-23 4454
13,24-30 4455s
13,31-32 4457
13,35 4458
13,36-43 4456
13,44-46 4459
13,47-50 4460
13,55 4461
14,13-21 4462
14,22-33 4463s
    5455
15,21-28 4465s
    7493
16,13-20 4473
16,17 4474
16,18 4475
17,1-9 4476
18 4334 4477
18,11 4478
18,12-14 4479ss
18,15-17 4482
18,21-35 4483
18,23-35 4484
19,28 4485
20,1-15 4491
20,1-16 4492s
20,20-23 4771
20,28 4207
2 1 , 1 - 9 4 1 3 6
    4494
21,12-22 4495
21,28-32 4496s
21,33-46 4498
    4782
21,43 4499
22,1-10 4500
22,1-14 4501
22,34-40 4502
22,35-40 4503
22,37-40 4319
22,38 4787
23 4504-7
24 4508s 7529
24-25 7542
24,1-26,2 4510

15,3-7 4479s
15,8-10 5036
15,11-32 3978
　5037-46
16 4895
16,1-9 5047s
16,16 5049
16,19-31 5050-3
　7537
17,10 5054
17,21 11627
17,33 5055
18,1-8 5056
18,9-14 5057ss
18,10-14 3978
　5046
18,18-30 4910
18,35-43 5060s
19,4 5062
19,11-27 5063s
19,11-28 5065
19,28-38 4136
　4494
20,9-18 5066
21,29-33 5067
22-23 5069
22,7-23 5070
22,15-20 4801
22,19-20 4536
22,28-30 4485
22,37 5071s
22,47-52 4805
22,54-23,25
　5073
23,1-49 5075
23,1-25 5074
23,33-43 5076
23,46 4812 5077
23,47-49 5076
24 5078s
24,10 4882
24,13-35 5080

Joannes

1 5419
1,1-5 5425
1,1-14 5418
1,1-18 5416
　5420 5423s
1,1-19 5422
1,14 5426s
1,16-19 11596

1,17 5428
1,18 5429
　6930
1,19-34 5430
1,28 5431
1,29 5432
1,35 5305
1,36 5432
1,39 5433
1,43-51 5434
2,1 5435
2,1-11 5402
2,1-11 5436ss
2,3-5 5439
2,13-22 5331
2,13-25 5440
2,23-3,21 5357
3 5441s
3,9 5345
3,22-30 5413
4 5443-6
4,1-26 5331
4,1-43 5413
4,1-44 5447
4,7-42 5402
4,23-24 5448
4,44 5449
5,1-6 5450
5,1-18 5331
　5451
5,14 5450
5,18 5452
6 5295
6,1-13 4462
6,1-15 5438
6,15 5454
6,16-21 5455
7 5331 6815
7-8 5456
7,1-51 5457
7,8-10 5458
7,37-39 5459
7,38 5460s
7,53-8,11
　5462s
8,1-11 5464s
8,25 5466
8,48 5413
9 5467s
9,1-41 5469s
10 5471s
10,16 5413
11 5446

11,54 5413
12,12-19 4494
12,13 5473
12,20-26 5474
12,20-36 5357
12,32 5475
12,37-50 5476
13 5491
13-17 5481
　5488
13,1-17,26
　5490
13,1-20 5492s
13,10 5494s
13,23-25 5412
13,31-16,33
　5478
14,9 5496
14,16 5497
14,23-29 5498
15 5499
15,1 5500
15,1-17 4785
15,27 5501
17 5327 5502
18-21 5484
18,1-14 5503
18,2-12 4805
18,15-16 5412
18,36 5504
19,9 5366
19,26-27 5412
　5505
19,28 4812
19,30 4522
　5506
20 5508
20,1-9 5509
20,1-18 5510s
20,2-10 5412
20,19-29 5512
20,20-23 5513
20,24-29 5514
20,30-31 5515
21 5305 5412
　5516
21,1-14 5455
21,11 5517
21,15-22 5518

Actus Apost.

1-7 5169

1,1-11 5170
2 5149 5171
2,1-41 5167
2,14-41 5172
2,36 5878
2,42-47 5150
　5173
3 5412
3,1-26 5174
4 5412
4,1-31 5175
4,12 5176
4,25 10183
4,27 5177
4,32-5,16 5091
4,32-35 4971
4,32-37 5150
5,1-11 5178
5,12-16 5150
5,17-42 5179
5,33-42 5180
6-7 5181
6,1 5137
6,1-7 5182
6,8-8,3 5183
7 5184s
7,58-8,1 5077
8 3440 5186
　7072
8,4-12,25 5187
8,5-25 5188
8,14-17 5412
8,26-40 5112
　5190
8,27 5189
9 5191
9,1-19 5735
9,1-29 5192
9,29 5137
9,30 5857
10 5193
10,1-11,18 5194
10,38 5177
11,8 5195
11,20 5137
11,25-26 5857
11,26 4835
12,1-24 5196
12,25 5197
13 5212
13-14 5208ss
13-28 5211
13,16-38 5213

3,10-14 6229
3,11 6230
3,19-20 6231
3,23-25 6232
4,4 6233s
4,12-6,16 6235
4,13-14 6236
4,21-5,1 6237
4,21-31 1079
  6238ss
5,1 4323 6241
5,13-15 6040s
5,17 6242
6,2 6040
6,8 6243
6,15 5834 6244

Ad Ephesios

1,1 6258
1,3 6259
1,3-14 6260
2,14-16 3792
3,14-19 6261
4,7-11 6262
4,9 6263
5,1-2 6264
5,4 6265
5,16 6266
5,21-6,9 6267
5,21-33 6268s
5,31-32 6186
6,10-20 6270
6,12 6271

Ad Philippenses

1,15-18 6295
1,27-30 6296
2 6297
2-3 6316
2,5-11 3792
  6298-04
2,6-11 6306-11
2,6-8 6305
  11880
2,7 11631
2,8 6312
2,9-11 6313s
2,19-30 6315
3,2-4,13 5783
3,2-21 6317
3,5-6 6148

3,7-11 6318
3,10 6319
3,20-21 6296
4,3 5141
4,8-9 6320
4,10-20 6321s

Colossenses

1,15-20 3792
  6333ss 6922
2,6-7 6336
3,1-4 6337
3,12-17 6338
4,5 6266

1 Thess.

2,1-12 6352
2,13-16 6353
4,1-12 6354
4,13-18 6355
5,12-22 6354

2 Thess.

1-2 7542
2,1-17 960
2,13-17 6358

1 ad Timoth.

1,10 7317
1,12-13 6148
2,8-15 6375
2,13-14 1723
3,1-7 6359
3,16 3792
4,1-5 1661
6,15 6376

2 ad Timoth.

2,11-13 3792
3,8 6378
3,16 972

Ad Titum

1,5-9 6359
3 6383
3,4-7 3792
3,13 6382

Ad Philemon.

1-25 6387

Ad Hebraeos

1,1-4 6945
1,5 6830
1,5-14 6416
2,5-16 6416
3,1-6 6417
5-7 1859
5,5 6830
6,4-8 6418
7,1-10,18 6389
10,19-13,25
  6419
11 6420s
11,7 6422
11,8-10 6423
11,13-16 6423
12,1-13 6424
12,2 8809
13,8 6425

Jacobi, **James**

1,13 6486
1,19-27 6487
2,14-26 6488
3,6 6489
4,6 6490

1 Petri

1,1-14 6444
1,13-25 6445
2,11-3,12 6446
2,11-17 6447
3,15 6448s
3,18-22 3792
  6450
4,12-19 6451
5,1-11 6445

2 Petri

1,5-11 6454

1 Joannis

2,18 5543
2,19 5544

3,4 5234
3,9 5545
3,18-20 5546

3 Joannis

9-10 5547

Jude

12 6496
22-23 6491

Apocalypsis
Revelation

1-3 5667s
2,4 5669
2,7 5670
2,9-10 5671
2,17 5672
4 5673
4,5-6 5674
4,6-7 5675
5 5676
5,6 5677
6,1-8,6 5678
6,1-2 5679
8,1 5680
11,3-13 4771
12 5681-4 7405
12-13 5685
12,14 5686
13,1-18 5687
14,6-13 5688
19-22 5689
19,7-9 5690
19,13 5691
20,13 5715
21-22 10246
21,1-7 5716
21,5 5717
21,6 5718s

END

Finito di stampare
nel mese di maggio 2002

presso la tipografia
"Giovanni Olivieri" di E. Montefoschi
00187 Roma - Via dell'Archetto, 10,11,12